KU-064-754

NELSON'S BIOGRAPHICAL DICTIONARY

NELSON'S BIOGRAPHICAL DICTIONARY

WITH A SHORT DICTIONARY OF MYTHOLOGY

Edited by

JOHN GUNN, M.A., D.Sc.

THOMAS NELSON AND SONS, LTD.

LONDON, EDINBURGH, PARIS, MELBOURNE

TORONTO, AND NEW YORK

PREFACE

DESPITE Charles Lamb's pleasant raillery against books of reference as " books which are no books—*biblia a-biblia,*" there is no doubt that such books have in modern times become practically indispensable. Among reference books a Biographical Dictionary must rank of major importance ; there can be few books of greater assistance to the student, the teacher, the scholar, and the intelligent reader generally.

NELSON'S BIOGRAPHICAL DICTIONARY eminently fulfils its purpose as a book of handy reference. It has been brought out in a form which will ensure its frequent use ; it is convenient in size ; it gives the information which is most commonly sought for, and gives it in the most concise form possible.

All persons of outstanding importance, from the earliest times to the present day, and from every country, are included if their names are at all likely to occur in the course of ordinary reading or study. They may be distinguished in literature, science, art, sport, statesmanship, or military affairs—all the activities of mankind receive attention.

With every notice the date and place of birth and death are given, if these are known, as well as the pronunciation of the name where this seems necessary. The brief account of each person's career is sufficient to indicate the importance of what he or she has done.

The book makes no claim to give a long monograph on each person, or an elaborate critical estimate of his work ; for these the reader must consult larger and more specialized volumes. In a word, it is not a book for the expert in any branch of study, but it will be a valuable aid to the ordinary student or reader. It will settle in a moment the facts of a man's life, when and where he lived, and what he did to make his name memorable.

The *Dictionary of Mythology* at the end continues the biographical plan of the book. It will be of value in explaining allusions, in solving many a difficulty, and in clearing up points regarding which the average reader may feel uncertain, telling him much that he would like to know, or that he once knew but has forgotten.

KEY TO PRONUNCIATION

ä as in mar (*mär*), psalm (*säm*), hurrah (*hurä'*).
a, ă ,, cat (*căt*), battle (*bătl*), abbot (*ăb'ot*).
ā ,, mate (*māt*), pain (*pān*), weight (*wāt*).
au, aw as in call (*cawl*), appal (*apawl'*), brought (*brawt*).
e as in sell (*sel*), ferry (*fer'i*).
ĕ ,, her (*hĕr*), fur (*fĕr*), gird (*gĕrd*).
ē ,, meet (*mēt*), leaf (*lēf*), mere (*mēr*).
i, ĭ ,, knit (*nit*), silly (*sil'i*), busy (*biz'i*).
ī, ȳ ,, white (*whīt*), arise (*arīz'*), might (*mīt*).
o ,, pot (*pot*), watch (*woch*), lorry (*lor'i*).
ō ,, grow (*grō*), know (*nō*), loaf (*lōf*).
ö ,, lord (*lörd*), resort (*rezört'*).
oo ,, room (*room*), glue (*gloo*), shoe (*shoo*).
u ,, full (*ful*), book (*buk*), could (*cud*).
ŭ ,, shun (*shŭn*), mud (*mŭd*), above (*abŭv'*).
ū ,, mute (*mūt*), few (*fū*), pure (*pūr*).
ou, ow as in doubt (*dout*), knout (*nowt*), aloud (*aloud'*).
oi as in coin (*koin*), buoy (*boi*), royal (*roi'al*).
ch ,, chime (*chīm*), catch (*kăch*).
ch ,, loch (*lo*ch), pibroch (*pē'bro*ch).
g ,, good (*gud*), linger (*ling'ger*).
j ,, jam (*jăm*), gem (*jem*), judge (*jŭj*).
n (nasal) as in entente (*äntänt'*), savant (*sävän*).
sh as in shove (*shŭv*), tension (*ten'shon*), action (*ăk'shon*).
zh ,, leisure (*lezh'ūr*), vision (*vizh'on*).
th ,, think (*think*), theme (*thēm*), health (*helth*).
th ,, thine (th*īn*), wreathe (*rē*th), though (th*ō*).
wh ,, while (*whīl*), somewhere (*sŭm'whār*).

When the accent is placed immediately after a vowel, that vowel is long; when the accent is placed after a consonant, the vowel of that syllable is short, as

ca'ble	cab'in	o'ral	or'ange
se'cret	sec'ond	pu'ny	pun'ish
pi'lot	pil'lar	ty'rant	tyr'anny

ABBREVIATIONS

Amer., American.
anc., ancient.
A.V., Authorized Version (Bible).

b., born.
B.B.C., British Broadcasting Corporation.
Brit., British.

c., *circa* (about).
Can., Canadian.
cent., century.
C.H., Companion of Honour.
chem., chemistry.
Chin., Chinese.
class., classical.
coll., college.

d., died.
Dan., Danish.

eccles., ecclesiastical.
ed., edited.
educ., educated.
Eng., English.
esp., especially.

fl., *floruit* (flourished).
Flem., Flemish.
Fr., French.

Ger., German.
gov.-gen., governor-general.
Gr., Greek.

Ind., Indian.
Ital., Italian.

Jap., Japanese.

Norweg., Norwegian.
N.T., New Testament.

O.E., Old English.
O.M., Order of Merit.
O.T., Old Testament.

parl., parliament.
P.C., Privy Council.
Pers., Persian.
Port., Portuguese.
pres., president.
Prot., Protestant.

Rom., Roman.
Russ., Russian.

Scot., Scottish.
soc., society.
Span., Spanish.
Swed., Swedish.

trans., translated.
Turk., Turkish.

univ., university.

BIOGRAPHICAL DICTIONARY

A

Aali Pasha, MEHEMET (1815–71), Turk. statesman, ambassador to Great Britain, 1841–4; was five times grand vizier; strongly urged reforms in Turk. government.

Aarestrup (*aw're-stroop*), CARL LUDWIG EMIL (1800–56), Dan. poet; *b.* Copenhagen; author of many charming love lyrics.

Aaron, brother of Moses; consecrated to the high priesthood (Exod. 28, 29; Lev. 8); is regarded as ancestor of all priests in Israel; *d.*, aged 123, on Mount Hor, in Edom.

Aasen (*aw'sen*), IVAR ANDREAS (1813–96), Norweg. philologist; of peasant origin, and self-educated; invented Landsmaal, a Norse literary language, free from Danish and other foreign contamination; wrote a Grammar, and a Dictionary of the Norweg. dialects.

Abauzit (*ä-bō-zē*), FIRMIN (1679–1767), Fr. scholar; *b.* Uzès, Languedoc; helped to translate N.T. into French, 1726.

Abbadie, (1) ANTOINE-THOMPSON D' (1810–97), and (2) ARNAUD MICHEL D' (1815–93), two brothers of French-Irish parentage; *b.* Dublin; famous for their travels in Abyssinia, 1837–48.

Abbas I., 'the Great' (1557–1628), Pers. monarch; extended his kingdom from the Tigris to the Indus; an enlightened ruler but tyrannical and cruel.

Abbas I. (1813–54), Egyptian pasha, assisted Turkey in Crimean War; was assassinated.

Abbas II. (1874–1923), last Khedive of Egypt (1892–1914); became strongly anti-British and sided with Turkey in the Great War; was deposed, and a Brit. protectorate established. Sudan reconquered and Aswan Dam constructed in his reign.

Abbasides (*ab-as'īdz*), caliphs of Baghdad, 750–1258.

Abbas Mirza (1783–1833), an able and enlightened shah of Persia; fought against Russia, 1811–13 and 1826–8.

Abbe (*ab'i*), CLEVELAND (1838–1916), U.S.A. meteorologist and astronomer; *b.* New York; director of Cincinnati Observatory, 1869–73; introduced 'standard' time to U.S.A., and system of daily weather forecasts.

Abbe, ERNST (1840–1905), Ger. physicist; *b.* Eisenach; owner of Zeiss optical works; improved lenses and invented several optical instruments.

Abbey, EDWIN AUSTIN (1852–1911), Amer. painter and illustrator; *b.* Philadelphia; mainly self-taught; R.A., 1898. Paintings include *Richard III. and Lady Anne*, *Crusaders sighting Jerusalem*, *Coronation of King Edward VII.*; numerous frescoes.

Abbot, GEORGE (1562–1633), Archbishop of Canterbury; *b.* Guildford; son of a cloth-worker;

one of the translators of the Bible, 1604; suspended by Charles I., 1627.

Abd-el-Kader (1807-83), Amir of Mascara, Algeria; hero of struggle against French in Algeria; honourable captive, 1847–52; lived later as Fr. pensioner in Damascus.

Abdel Krim, Moroccan chieftain; led the Rifs in opposition to Span. occupation, 1921 and 1925; surrendered to France, 1926; exiled to island of Réunion.

Abdul-Aziz (1830–76), 32nd Sultan of Turkey; risings in Crete and the Balkans, Bulgarian atrocities, and a conspiracy forced him to abdicate; assassinated some days later.

Abdul-Aziz Ibn Sa'ud. See IBN SA'UD.

Abdul-Hamid I. (1725–89), Turk. sultan from 1774; original 'Sick Man of Europe'; waged disastrous wars with Russia and Austria; ceded Crimea to Russia, 1784.

Abdul-Hamid II. (1842–1918), Sultan of Turkey, 1876–1909; Armenian atrocities earned for him the titles 'Abdul the Damned' and 'Great Assassin'; fought Russo-Turkish and Greek wars; deposed after 'Young Turk' revolution of 1908.

Abdul-Kadir. See ABD-EL-KADER.

Abdul-Medjid (1823–61), Sultan of Turkey, carried out reforms; accepted European aid against Mehemet Ali; refused to give up the Hungarian patriot Kossuth to Austria.

Abdur-Rahman Khan (1843–1901), Amir of Afghanistan from 1880; revolted against uncle, Shere Ali, 1863; was defeated, 1868, and exiled to Samarkand; on death of Shere Ali was installed amir by British; steadily pro-British during reign.

Abel ('breath'), second son of Adam and Eve; slain by brother Cain (Gen. 4).

Abel, SIR FREDERICK AUGUSTUS (1827–1902), Eng. chemist; *b.* London; chemist to War Office, 1854–88; part inventor of process of manufacturing guncotton and cordite; with Capt. Noble made important researches on explosion of gunpowder; invented apparatus for determining flash point of petroleum; first director of Imperial Institute, 1887; knighted, 1891; baronet, 1893.

Abel, NIELS HENRIK (1802–29), Norwegian mathematician; educated at Oslo; 'left the world's mathematicians with work for a century.' Distinguished for development of elliptical functions.

Abélard (*ä-bā-lär'*), PIERRE (1079–1142), Fr. scholar and theologian; *b.* near Nantes; in 1115 became canon of Notre-Dame, Paris, and achieved great success as teacher and lecturer; became tutor to Héloïse, niece of Canon Fulbert, and an affection sprang up between them. They were afterwards separated, and an act of violence was committed upon Abélard at the instance of Fulbert. Subsequently Abélard became a monk, and Héloïse took the veil. In his later years Abélard resumed teaching at the Paraclete hermitage, where he was buried, and Héloïse was afterwards laid in the same tomb. The remains of the lovers were, in 1817, removed to the cemetery of Père Lachaise, Paris.

Abencerrages (*a-ben'ser-āj-ēz*), powerful Moorish family in Granada in 15th cent.

Abercorn, JAMES ALBERT EDWARD HAMILTON, 3RD DUKE OF (1869–); treasurer to H.M. Household, 1903–5; senator of N. Ireland, 1921; gov.-gen. of N. Ireland since 1922.

Abercrombie, LASCELLES (1881–), Eng. poet and critic; *b.* Ashton-on-Mersey, Cheshire; prof. of Eng. literature, Leeds Univ.,

1922, and London Univ., 1929. Writings include *Interludes and Poems* (1908), *Emblems of Love* (1912), *Theory of Poetry* (1924), *Idea of Great Poetry* (1925), *Romanticism* (1926).

Abercromby, SIR RALPH (1734–1801), Brit. soldier; *b.* Menstrie, Clackmannanshire; commander-in-chief in W. Indies, 1795; commanded in Low Countries, 1799; was fatally wounded at Alexandria, March 21, 1801; monument in St. Paul's.

Aberdeen, GEORGE HAMILTON GORDON, 4TH EARL OF (1784–1860), Brit. statesman, successively colonial secretary, war secretary, foreign secretary, and prime minister, 1852–5; resigned owing to revelations of mismanagement of Crimean War; supported Peel in the repeal of the Corn Laws.

Aberdeen and Temair, JOHN CAMPBELL GORDON (1847–1934), 1ST MARQUESS OF, and 7TH EARL OF ABERDEEN; lord-lieutenant of Ireland, 1886 and 1905–15; gov.-gen. of Canada, 1893–8.

Abernethy, JOHN (1764–1831), Eng. physician; *b.* London; pupil of John Hunter; assistant-surgeon at St. Bartholomew's Hospital, London; emphasized connection of local diseases with digestive disorders.

Abigail, wife of Nabal, succoured King David (1 Sam. 25). Name used colloquially for a 'waiting maid.'

Abney, SIR WILLIAM DE WIVELESLIE (1844–1921), Eng. chemist and physicist; *b.* Derby; made valuable researches in photography.

About (*a-boo'*), EDMOND FRANÇOIS VALENTIN (1828–85), Fr. novelist; *b.* Dieuze, Lorraine; war correspondent during Franco-German War, 1870; was a strong republican; edited the *XIXe Siècle*; member Fr. Academy.

Abraham, the patriarch revered by the Hebrews as their progenitor and the founder of their religion. His covenant with Jehovah is frequently referred to in the O.T., and his faith eulogized in the N.T. Reverenced by Jews, Christians, and Moslems. See Gen. 11–25.

Abruzzi (*ä-broot'si*), PRINCE LUIGI AMADEO, DUKE OF THE (1873–1933), Ital. royal prince, explorer and scientist; *b.* Madrid; explored mts. in Alaska, Central Africa, Asia, and North Polar Regions. During Great War commanded Ital. navy, 1915–17.

Absalom, third and favourite son of King David; noted for personal beauty and length of his hair; during revolt against father was slain by Joab (2 Sam. 13–18).

Absalon, AXEL (1128–1201), Dan. churchman, statesman, sailor, and soldier; founded town now Copenhagen.

Abt, FRANZ (1819–85), Ger. composer; *b.* Eilenburg, Saxony; wrote many songs.

Abu-Bekr ('father of the maiden') (573–634), father-in-law of Mohammed; *b.* Mecca; first caliph of Islam; directed the compilation of the Koran.

Achard (*ä-shär'*), FRANZ KARL (1753–1821), Prussian chemist; *b.* Berlin; pioneer in beet-sugar production.

Achenbach, ANDREAS (1815–1910), Ger. painter; *b.* Cassel; pioneer of realistic style of painting landscape; among his pictures are *Hardanger Fjord* (1843), *Pontine Marshes* (1846), *Fish Market at Ostend* (1866).

Acheson (*äch'e-son*), EDWARD GOODRICH (1856–), U.S.A. chemist; *b.* Washington; introduced electric lighting to Holland, Italy, and Belgium; discovered carborundum, 1886; invented a method of making graphite, and various lubricants.

Ackermann, RUDOLPH (1764–

1834), Anglo-Ger. publisher; *b.* Schneeberg, Saxony; settled in England, and became pioneer of lithography and of popular annuals.

Ackté-Jalander, AÏNO (1876–), famous Finnish soprano and operatic singer; *b.* Helsinki; founded the Finnish opera in Helsinki.

Acland, SIR HENRY WENTWORTH (1815–1900), Eng. physician; *b.* near Exeter; prof. of medicine at Oxford; revived Oxford as medical school, and assisted in founding Oxford Univ. museum.

Acosta, JOSÉ DE (*c.* 1539–1600), Span. author; *b.* Medina del Campo; became Jesuit missionary to Peru, 1571; rector of Jesuit Coll., Salamanca, 1598; pub. famous *Historia Natural y Moral de las Indias* (1590).

Acton, JOHN EMERICH EDWARD D'ALBERG, 1ST BARON (1834–1902), Eng. historian; *b.* Naples; as a R.C. was denied admission to an Eng. univ. Opposed the doctrine of papal infallibility; was regius prof. of modern history at Cambridge, 1895; planned *Cambridge Modern History.*

Ad'albert (*c.* 1000–72), Ger. ecclesiastic; Archbishop of Hamburg-Bremen, 1043; papal legate for the north, 1052; made Bremen a city of great importance.

Adalbert, ST. (*c.* 700), early Eng. saint; founded church at Egmont, near Aalkmaar, in N. Holland; said to have been grandson of Oswald, King of Deira.

Adalbert, ST. (*c.* 950–97), 'the apostle of the Prussians,' created Bishop of Prague, 982; later preached in N. Germany and Poland; martyred.

Adam ('man'), the first created man, according to Genesis. Several Babylonian legends offer some, but none a very complete, parallel to the story of Adam.

Adam, ALEXANDER (1741–1809), Scot. headmaster and classical scholar; *b.* near Forres; rector of Royal High School, Edinburgh; Scott, Brougham, Jeffrey, and Horner were his pupils.

Adam (*a-dän'*), JULIETTE (1836–), Fr. journalist, memoirist, and novelist; *b.* Verberie, Oise; known as *La Grande Française,* a voluminous writer; founder and ed. of *La Nouvelle Revue.*

Adam (*a-dän'*), PAUL (1862–1920), Fr. novelist; *b.* Paris. Works include *Le Thé chez Miranda* (1886), *L'Enfant d'Austerlitz* (1901), *Le Trust* (1910), *Stéphanie* (1913), and during the Great War *Reims dévastée* and *Le Lion d'Arras.*

Adam, ROBERT (1728–92), Scot. architect; *b.* Kirkcaldy; designed the Adelphi, London; Admiralty gateway; Register House and Univ., Edinburgh, also many public buildings and private mansions; appointed architect to the king and the Board of Works, 1862; buried in Westminster Abbey.

[*Architecture of Robert and James Adam,* by Bolton (1922).]

Adam de la Halle (*c.* 1240–*c.* 1288), 'the hunchback of Arras,' Fr. lyric poet and dramatist; *b.* Arras; author of *Le Jeu de Robin et de Marion.*

Adam of Bremen, Ger. geographer and historian; *b.* Meissen, Saxony, in 11th cent.; *d. c.* 1076; canon of Bremen Cathedral; wrote a history of Hamburg and Bremen and the ecclesiastical history of the north.

Ad'amnan, biographer of St. Columba; *b.* in Donegal; became ninth abbot of Iona, 679.

Adams, JOHN (1735–1826), 2nd president U.S.A.; *b.* Quincy, Mass.; had large legal practice in Boston; entered Congress, 1774; in second Continental Congress secured appointment of Washington as commander-in-chief; in 1776 carried a resolution that the colonies should declare themselves independent; commissioner to France, 1778; ambassador to London, 1785; twice vice-president, U.S.A.; president, 1797.

Adams, John (*c.* 1760–1829), Eng. seaman; took leading part in mutiny of *Bounty*.

Adams, John Couch (1819–92), Eng. astronomer and mathematician; *b.* near Launceston; Lowndean prof. of astronomy at Cambridge, 1860; director of the observatory, 1861; simultaneously with Leverrier discovered planet Neptune, 1846.

Adams, John Quincy (1767–1848), 6th president of U.S.A. and eldest son of 2nd president; *b.* Quincy, Mass.; called to bar, 1790; ambassador to various European countries between 1794 and 1815; member of U.S.A. Senate, 1803–7; prof. of rhetoric at Harvard, 1806–9; secretary of state, 1817; president, 1825–9.

Adams, Sarah Flower (1805–48), Eng. hymn-writer; *b.* Great Harlow; author of 'Nearer, my God, to Thee' (1840), etc.

Adamson, Patrick (1537–92), Scot. prelate and scholar; *b.* Perth; Archbishop of St. Andrews from 1576; had long struggle with Presbyterians, but was supported by the king; excommunicated by General Assembly, 1588.

Adamson, Robert (1852–1902), Scot. philosopher; *b.* Edinburgh; prof. of philosophy and political economy at Manchester, 1876; prof. of logic at Aberdeen, 1893, and at Glasgow from 1895. Most important work, *Development of Modern Philosophy*.

Adamson, Rt. Hon. William (1863–1936), Scot. politician; began life as a miner; Labour M.P. for West Fife, 1910–31; chairman of parl. Labour party, 1917–21; secretary of state for Scotland, 1924 and 1929–31.

Adanson (*ä-dän-son'*), Michel (1727–1806), Fr. botanist; *b.* Aix-en-Provence; spent five years in Senegal studying natural history; pub. *Histoire Naturelle du Sénégal* (1757), *Familles naturelles des plantes* (1763).

Addison, Rt. Hon. Christopher (1869–), Eng. anatomist and statesman; *b.* Hogsthorpe, Lincs; prof. of anatomy at Cambridge and London, 1901; M.P. for Shoreditch, 1910–22, for Swindon, 1929–31, and 1934–5; first minister of health, 1919–21.

Addison, Joseph (1672–1719), Eng. essayist and poet; *b.* Milston, Wilts; educated Charterhouse and Oxford. His early verses and translations attracted the interest of Dryden, and Jacob Tonson, the publisher, who introduced him to men of rank and fashion, through whose patronage he was awarded a pension of £300, to allow him 'to travel and qualify himself to serve his majesty,' King William. From 1699 to 1703 he lived on the Continent, and wrote his *Letter to Lord Halifax*, *Dialogues on Medals*, and four acts of *Cato*, a classical play. Returning home, he was commissioned by Lord Halifax to celebrate the victory of Blenheim in verse, which resulted in *The Campaign* (1704), and Addison received a commissionership of appeal in excise. In 1706 he was made under-secretary of state; produced his opera, *Rosamond*. From 1708 was M.P. for Malmesbury. Having contributed to Steele's *Tatler* from 1709 to 1711, Addison started the *Spectator* in March 1711, and issued it daily till Dec. 1712. In 1717 he was appointed secretary of state, retiring in 1718. Addison's fame rests securely on the charming essays which he contributed to the *Spectator*.

[*Life*, by Courthope (1884).]

Adelaide, Queen (1792–1849), wife of William IV.; unpopular during Reform agitation; did much to purify Eng. court.

Adeler, MAX, pseudonym of CHARLES HEBER CLARK (1841–1915), Amer. humorist; author of *Out of the Hurly Burly, Elbow Room*, etc.

Ad'ler, HERMANN (1839–1911), chief rabbi of Brit. Hebrews; *b.* Hanover; principal of Jews' Coll., London, 1863. Wrote *Ibn Gabirol*, etc. Prominent social worker in London.

Admirable Crichton. See CRICHTON, JAMES.

Adonijah, fourth son of David, rebelling against Solomon, was executed (1 Kings 2).

Adrian. See HADRIAN.

Adrian, the name of six Popes. Adrian IV. (NICHOLAS BREAKSPEAR, *c.* 1100–59), the only Englishman ever elected Pope; *b.* Langley; abbot of St. Rufus, near Arles, 1137; cardinal-bishop of Albans, 1146; Pope, 1154.

Aehrenthal (*e-ren-täl'*), ALOIS, COUNT LEXA VON (1854–1912); *b.* Gross-Skal, Bohemia; Austro-Hungarian statesman, ambassador to various capitals, 1888–1906; foreign minister to Dual Monarchy, 1906–12. Powerful and obstinate, he annexed Bosnia and Hercegovina, 1908, and created diplomatic situation which was a factor in bringing about the Great War.

Ælfred (*äl'fred*) **the Ætheling** (*d.* 1036), younger brother of Edward the Confessor; asserted right to Eng. throne, 1036, but was defeated and blinded by Earl Godwin; died at Ely.

Ælfric (*äl'fric*) (*c.* 955–*c.* 1020), 'the grammarian'; great writer of O.E. prose; abbot of Eynsham, near Oxford; wrote famous *Homilies, Lives of the Saints*, and *Grammar and Glossary*. His scriptural paraphrases influenced the pioneer translations of the Bible.

Ælla, or ELLA (*d.* 588), first King of Deira, 559; immortalized by Gregory's famous pun, 'Alleluia shall be sung in Ælla's land.'

Æpi'nus, FRANZ ULRICH THEODOR (1724–1802), Ger. physicist; *b.* Rostock, Saxony; made researches in electricity; discovered properties of tourmaline.

Aertszen (*ärt'sen*), PIETER (1508–75), Dutch painter ('Long Peter'); *b.* Amsterdam; father of three painter sons. Best known work, *Crucifixion*, in Antwerp Museum; executed interiors and homely scenes.

Æschines (*es'ki-nēz*) (389–314 B.C.), Athenian orator; rival of Demosthenes and friend of Socrates; opposed proposal to reward Demosthenes, who replied with *De Corona*, and brought about his exile to Rhodes.

Æschylus (*es'ki-lus*) (525–456 B.C.), father of Gr. tragedy; *b.* Eleusis; fought against Persia at battles of Marathon, Salamis, Artemisium, and Platæa; produced about seventy dramas, of which only seven survive: *The Suppliants, Persæ, Seven against Thebes, Prometheus, Agamemnon, Choephoræ*, and *Eumenides*. He was the greatest of Gr. tragic poets; his plays, dealing with the larger issues of fate, show grandeur of conception.

Æsop (*ē'sop*) (*fl. c.* 550 B.C.), Gr. author of fables; traditionally a freed slave; sent on embassy to Crœsus at Delphi; excited ire by sarcastic tongue, and was hurled from a precipice. His fables handed down orally; collection known as *Æsop's Fables* derived from Gr. compilation (*c.* A.D. 230).

Afze'lius, ARVID AUGUST (1785–1871), Swed. poet and folklorist; trans. the 'Elder' *Edda*, and ed. *Svenske Folkvisor* (1814–16).

Agag, king of Amalekites; conquered by Saul and hewn in pieces by Samuel (1 Sam. 15).

Aga Khan. (1) HASAN ALI SHAH (1800–81), spiritual head of sect of Mohammedans; descended from Mohammed and royal house of Persia; fled from Persia to India; helpful to Napier and to Brit. Government, from whom he received large pension. (2) AGA SULTAN SIR MOHAMMED SHAH (1875–), grandson of above. Granted status of first-class chief in recognition of loyal services in Great War; took important part in Round Table Conference on India, 1930–1. Is a noted patron of the turf.

Agardh (*ä'gärd*), KARL ADOLF (1785–1859), distinguished Swed. scientist; *b.* Badstad; prof. of botany at Lund, 1812; bishop of Karlstad, 1834; noted for his work on the classification of algæ.

Agassiz (*ä-gä-sē'*), JEAN LOUIS RODOLPHE (1807–73), celebrated Swiss naturalist; *b.* Motier, Fribourg; earned world-wide reputation by his studies of fossil fish, 1833–44 and of the Alpine glaciers, 1838–40; went to U.S.A., 1846, became prof. of natural history at Harvard, 1848, where he founded museum of comparative zoology, 1858. Made an important expedition to Brazil, 1865. He profoundly influenced the whole course of natural history study in America.

Ag'atha, ST. (*d.* 251), Sicilian maiden who rejected the suit of Prefect Quintilianus, and was condemned to death at the stake. As she was being taken to her doom an earthquake occurred, and she subsequently died in prison. Her feast day is Feb. 5.

Agathocles (*ä-gath'ō-klēz*) (361–289 B.C.), a famous Tyrant of Syracuse; son of a potter. With an army of mercenaries he overthrew Syracusan oligarchy and assumed Tyrantship; made war against Carthage and won several brilliant victories, but was compelled to make peace, 306. His rule was generally popular.

Agesilaus II. (*a-je-si-lā'us*) (445–360 B.C.), King of Sparta; defeated Persians in Asia, and allied Athenians and Thebans at Coronea, 394; was defeated by Epaminondas at Mantinea, 362, but saved Sparta.

Agnes, ST. (*d.* 304), Christian maiden of Roman birth; refused to marry heathen son of Prefect Sempronius; ordered to be outraged and brought to the stake. Her honour was miraculously vindicated; but when the fagots round the stake would not burn, the executioner cut off her head with his sword. She is the patron saint of virgins; festival, Jan. 21.

Agnesi (*ä-nyā'sē*), MARIA GAETANA (1718–99), Ital. linguist, mathematician, and philosopher; *b.* Milan; succeeded her father as prof. of mathematics at Bologna, 1752; directress of a nunnery at Milan from 1754.

Agoult (*ä-goo'*), MARIE CATHERINE, COMTESSE D' (1805–76), Fr. authoress (pseudonym DANIEL STERN); *b.* Frankfurt-on-Main; friend of Chopin, Meyerbeer, Sainte-Beuve, Alfred de Vigny, George Sand, Heine, etc. After separation from her husband, became mistress of Franz Liszt; a daughter of this *liaison*, Cosima, became wife of Richard Wagner.

Agricola (or BAUER), GEORG (1490–1555), Ger. doctor; *b.* Glauchau, Saxony; the 'father of mineralogy,' who was the first to systematize it in his *De Re Metallica* (1556).

Agricola, GNÆUS JULIUS (A.D. 37–93), Roman general and statesman; governor of Britain, 78–85; subdued large part of Britain; established line of forts between Forth and Clyde; implanted Roman civilization and customs; discovered Britain to be an island; his successes aroused the jealousy of Domitian, and his later years were spent in retirement; life written by his son-in-law, Tacitus.

Agricola, Johann, originally Schnitter (1492–1566), Ger. Prot. reformer; *b.* Eisleben; formed intimacy with Luther, but promulgated doctrines which Luther pronounced to be antinomian. Dispute became bitter, and Agricola went to Berlin.

Agrippa, King. See under Herod.

Agrippa, Marcus Vipsanius (63–12 b.c.), commanded the Rom. fleet at battle of Actium, 31 b.c.; thrice consul; greatly improved Rome.

Agrippina. (1) The Elder (*d.* a.d. 33), daughter of Agrippa; married Germanicus, whom she accompanied on his campaigns. After husband's death was exiled and starved to death. (2) The Younger (a.d. 16–59), daughter of above, and mother of Nero; poisoned her third husband, Claudius, to secure throne for Nero, who eventually had her murdered.

Aguilera (*ä-gē-lā'rä*), Ventura Ruiz (1820–81), Span. lyric poet; *b.* Salamanca; influenced by Béranger and Lamartine.

Ahab (*c.* 875–*c.* 852 b.c.), King of Israel; married Jezebel, and by her influence introduced worship of Baal; killed in war with Syria at Ramoth Gilead (1 Kings 16 and 22).

Ahasuerus, King of Persia, husband of Esther, has been identified with Xerxes.

Ahaz (*c.* 740–724 b.c.), King of Judah, against the advice of Isaiah called in the aid of the King of Assyria against Israel, and so became his vassal (2 Kings 16 and 23).

Ahimelech, high priest of Israel, slain by Saul for his kindness to David (1 Sam. 22).

Ahithophel, O.T. character, renowned for sagacity, who espoused cause of Absalom (2 Sam. 15).

Ahmad (1898–), Shah of Persia, succeeded on father's abdication, 1909, country being under regency until coronation, 1914. During Great War maintained strict neutrality. In 1919 concluded Anglo-Persian agreement with this country. Deposed 1925.

Ahmed Fuad. See Fuad i.

Aicard (*ā-kär'*), Jean François Victor (1848–1921), Fr. poet, novelist, and dramatist; *b.* Toulon; member of Fr. Academy; wrote *Poèmes de Provence* and *La Chanson de l'Enfant*, both crowned by the Academy, and several novels; most successful play is *Le Père Lebounard* (1890).

Aidan, St. (*d.* 651), monk of Iona; converted Northumbria to Christianity; founded monastery of Lindisfarne; his piety is warmly praised by Bede.

Aikin, John (1747–1822), Eng. physician and writer; *b.* Kibworth-Harcourt, Leicestershire; a friend of Howard the philanthropist; wrote, with his sister Mrs. Barbauld, *Evenings at Home*; author of numerous biographical works. His daughter, Lucy Aikin (1781–1864), *b.* Warrington, wrote on history and biography.

Aimard (*ā-mär'*), Gustave (pen-name of Olivier Gloux) (1818–83), Fr. novelist; *b.* Paris; travelled extensively; organized Francs-tireurs against Germans, 1870–1; wrote adventure stories of the Fenimore Cooper stamp.

Ainger, Alfred, Canon (1837–1904), Eng. churchman and writer; *b.* London; Master of the Temple Church from 1894. Noted for biography and critical appreciation of Charles Lamb.

[*Life*, by Edith Sichel (1906).]

Ainley, Henry Hinchliffe (1879–), Eng. actor-manager; *b.* Leeds; toured in America, 1903; served in Great War; joint manager of St. James's Theatre, London.

Ainmüller (*īn'mil-er*), Max Emmanuel (1807–70), Ger. painter;

b. Munich; revived art of glass staining. Much of his glasswork is in Cologne, Ratisbon, Glasgow, and St. Paul's Cathedral, London.

Ainsworth, WILLIAM FRANCIS (1807–96), Eng. surgeon and geographer; *b.* Exeter; a founder of W. London Hospital; wrote works on his Asiatic travels.

Ainsworth, WILLIAM HARRISON (1805–82), Eng. novelist; *b.* Manchester; author of about forty novels (historical and antiquarian), remarkable for vigour of description and the construction of striking situations; best known are *Tower of London, Old St. Paul's,* and *Windsor Castle.*

Aird, SIR JOHN (1833–1911), Brit. contractor; *b.* London; with father erected Crystal Palace at Sydenham, 1851; constructed railways, docks, etc., all over world. Greatest work, construction of great dams at Aswan and Asyut on Nile, 1898–1902; M.P. for N. Paddington, 1887–1905.

Airy, SIR GEORGE BIDDELL (1801–92), Eng. astronomer; *b.* Alnwick; senior wrangler, Cambridge, 1823; prof. of mathematics and astronomy, Cambridge; organized the observatory; astronomer-royal, 1835–81; conducted numerous astronomical and meteorological researches, and brought the Royal Observatory, Greenwich, up to an unrivalled standard of usefulness; sent expeditions to observe the transits of Venus in 1874 and 1882, and was prominent in solar eclipse observations.

Aitken, WILLIAM MAXWELL. See BEAVERBROOK, BARON.

Aiton, WILLIAM (1731–93), Scot. botanist; *b.* near Hamilton; first director of the botanical gardens at Kew.

Akbar (THE GREAT), JELLALADIN MOHAMMED (1542–1605), Mogul emperor of India from 1556; a great conqueror and enlightened ruler; extended dominion over N. India; generous patron of literature; tolerated all religions; reduced excessive taxation, and created a system of roads and waterways.

A Kempis, THOMAS. See KEMPIS.

Akenside, MARK (1721–70), Eng. poet and physician; *b.* Newcastle-on-Tyne; son of a butcher; caricatured by Smollett in *Peregrine Pickle*; principal physician to Christ's Hospital, 1759; wrote *Pleasures of Imagination,* etc.

Alacoque (*ä-lä-kōk'*), MARGUERITE MARIE (1647–90), Fr. nun; *b.* Lauthecour, Saône-et-Loire; foundress of the worship of the Sacred Heart; canonized, 1920.

Alamanni, LUIGI (1495–1556), Ital. poet; *b.* Florence; driven from Florence by the Medici, he served Francis I. and Henry II. of France as ambassador.

Alarcon (*ä-lär-kōn'*), HERNANDO DE, Span. navigator of the 16th cent., ascended Colorado R.; surveyed coast of California.

Alarcón, JUAN RUIZ DE (1581–1639), Span. dramatist; *b.* Tlacho, Mexico; wrote many plays, including *La Verdad Sospechosa* (imitated in Corneille's *Le Menteur*); regarded as one of greatest Span. dramatists.

Alarcón, PEDRO ANTONIO DE (1833–91), Span. novelist; *b.* Guadix, Granada; served with Span. army in Morocco, and chronicled his experiences; wrote many novels.

Al'aric I. (*d.* 410), 'the Goth'; *b.* isl. of Peuce at mouth of Danube; revolted from Roman Empire and became King of Visigoths, 395; invaded Greece, 395–6, and forced Athens to pay ransom; in 402 invaded Upper Italy, but was defeated by Stilicho at Verona; captured and pillaged Rome, 410.

Alaric II. (484–507), King of Visigoths; slain in battle by Clovis, King of the Franks, near Poitiers.

Alban, St. (3rd cent.), first Brit. martyr; born at Verulam (now St. Albans); put to death during persecution of Christians, *c.* 304; church built on scene of his martyrdom by Offa of Mercia.

Alban'i, Dame (*née* Marie Louise Emma Cecilia Lajeunesse) (1852–1930), famous Canadian vocalist of Fr. descent; *b.* near Montreal; operatic and oratorio soprano.

Albany, Louise Maximilienne Caroline, Countess of (1753–1824), daughter of Gustavus Adolphus of Stolberg-Gedern; *b.* Mons; married Charles Edward Stuart, the Young Pretender, 1774, but obtained a separation, 1784. She became the mistress of Alfieri, the poet, who immortalized her.

Al-Battani, Mohammed Ben Jabir Ben Sinan, Abu Abdullah (*c.* 850–929), better known by his latinized name of *Albategnius*; *b.* Batan, Iraq; was the most illustrious of the Arabian astronomers.

Albemarle, 1st Duke of. See Monck.

Albert, Francis Charles Augustus Emanuel (1819–61), Prince Consort of Queen Victoria; *b.* Rosenau; younger son of Ernest, Duke of Saxe-Coburg-Gotha. Married Queen Victoria, 1840; received title of Prince Consort, 1857; suggested idea of Great Exhibition, 1851; bought Balmoral Castle as Scot. royal residence; died of typhoid at Windsor; did much to increase prosperity of Britain.

Albert Frederick Arthur George, Prince (1895–), second son of King George v. and Queen Mary; present at battle of Jutland; joined Air Force, 1917; promoted captain in 1919; subsequently entered Trinity Coll., Cambridge. Duke of York, 1920. Married Lady E. Bowes-Lyon, 1923. Carried through successful Australian tour, 1927; high commissioner of General Assembly Church of Scotland, 1929.

Albert (1875–1934), King of the Belgians; *b.* Brussels; succeeded his uncle Leopold ii., 1909. When Germany (1914) demanded that Belgium should grant free passage to the Ger. armies, the king and his ministers refused. Throughout the war the king was in the field with his army. He was of scientific turn of mind, interested in art and literature. Killed in mountaineering accident.

Albertus Magnus (1193 or 1206–80), scholastic philosopher; *b.* Swabia, Germany; known as 'the Universal Doctor'; a celebrated lecturer in science, theology, and philosophy; archbishop of Ratisbon; teacher of Thomas Aquinas; wrote scholarly expositions of Aristotle.

Albuquerque (*äl-boo-kĕr-ki*), Alphonso d' (1453–1515), Port. explorer and conqueror, often called 'the Great'; *b.* near Lisbon; in 1503 sailed for the East, captured Goa, Malacca, and isl. of Ormuz; established Port. power in India; led first European fleet into Red Sea. Died at sea.

Alcæus (*äl-sē'us*) (600 b.c.) of Lesbos, one of the greatest Gr. lyric poets; composed songs of war, hymns, and lyrics of love and wine; only fragments of his works remain. The Alcaic strophe, named after him, was a favourite metre of Horace.

Alcibiades (*äl-si-bī'ä-dēz*) (*c.* 450–404 b.c.), Athenian general and politician; was brought up by his uncle, Pericles; was accused of an outrage against the statues of Hermes, fled to Sparta, and became a dangerous enemy of Athens. Having made love to the wife of Agis ii. of Sparta, he was forced to take refuge in Asia Minor. Later he joined the Athenian fleet in the Ægean, and gained victories at Abydos, 411, and Cyzicus, 410, and captured Chalcedon and Byzantium for his native land. Permitted to return to Athens, 407, he became commander-in-chief, but was again exiled. He was murdered in Phrygia. He had probably the quickest intelligence of his time in Athens, but was wholly self-centred and without scruple.

Alcman, or ALCMÆON (7th cent. B.C.), Gr. poet; a Lydian of Sardis, and an emancipated slave; regarded as the inventor of love poetry. Few fragments of his work survive.

Alcock, SIR JOHN WILLIAM (1892–1919), Brit. airman; *b.* Manchester; served with distinction in the Great War; was, along with Sir Whitten Brown, the first airman to make a direct transatlantic flight from St. John's, Newfoundland, to Ireland, June 1919. Knighted for this feat. Killed while flying to Paris.

Alcock, SIR RUTHERFORD (1809–97), surgeon, diplomatist, and author; *b.* London; surgeon during Carlist War, 1836; held important consular appointments in China and Japan.

Alcott, LOUISA MAY (1832–88), Amer. writer for the young; *b.* Philadelphia; to begin with had hard life as dolls' dressmaker, teacher, and servant; best known book, *Little Women.*

Alcuin (*al'kwin*) (735–804), Eng. ecclesiastic and scholar; *b.* York; head of York cathedral school, 766; settled at court of Charlemagne, where he did much to spread civilization and learning; became head of St. Martin's Abbey, Tours, 796.

Alden, JOHN (1599–1687), one of the Pilgrim Fathers; settled at Duxbury, Mass.; his wife, Priscilla Mullens, is celebrated in Longfellow's *Miles Standish.*

Aldhelm. See EALDHELM.

Aldred (*d.* 1069), Archbishop of York, 1060; crowned William the Conqueror, 1066; first Eng. bishop to make a pilgrimage to Jerusalem.

Aldrich, THOMAS BAILEY (1836–1907), Amer. poet and novelist; *b.* Portsmouth, U.S.A.; ed. *Atlantic Monthly* (1881–90); prolific prose and verse writer; author of *The Ballad of Babie Bell, Story of a Bad Boy,* etc.

Aldrovan'di, ULISSI (1522–1605), Ital. naturalist; *b.* Bologna; prof. of botany at Bologna; made a large collection of specimens and founded botanic garden; wrote *Natural History* (1599–1602).

Aleander (*äl-ā-an'der*), HIERONYMUS (1480–1542), Ital. cardinal; *b.* near Venice; was Luther's leading opponent at Diet of Worms, 1521, and a zealous persecutor of the Reformers.

Aleardi (*ä-lā-ar'dē*), ALEARDO, COUNT (1812–78), Ital. poet; *b.* Verona; took part in revolutionary movement of 1848; author of many patriotic verses.

Alecsandri, VASILE (1821–90), Romanian poet and statesman; *b.* Bacau; collected Romanian songs and ballads; minister of foreign affairs, 1850; ambassador to France, 1885.

Alekhine, ALEXANDER (1892–), Russian chess player; *b.* Moscow; became naturalized Frenchman after Russian Revolution; defeated Capablanca, 1927.

Alembert (*ä-lon-bār'*), JEAN LE ROND D' (1717–83), Fr. philosopher and mathematician; a foundling; *b.* Paris; studied theology, law, and medicine, then finally mathematics; pub. researches on the integral calculus, on the nutation of the axis of the earth, and other physical problems; was associated with Diderot in the compilation of the *Dictionnaire Encyclopédique.*

Alesius (*ä-lē'shi-us*), ALEXANDER (1500–65), Scot. reformer; *b.* Edinburgh; convert of Patrick Hamilton; escaped to Germany 1532, became friend of Melanchthon and Luther; prof. of theology at Frankfurt-on-Oder and at Leipzig.

Alexander, name of eight Popes. ALEXANDER I. (Pope 106–115), believed to have died a martyr. ALEXANDER II. (Anselmo Baggio) (Pope 1061–73); *b.* Milan; reformed the Church. ALEXANDER III. (Orlando Bandinelli) (Pope 1159–81); *b.* Siena; antagonist of Frederick Barbarossa; presided at Lateran Council, 1179, which decreed a two-thirds majority of cardinals requisite for papal elections; in 1181 excommunicated William the Lion of Scotland. ALEXANDER IV. (Rinaldo) (Pope 1254–61), tried to reconcile Eastern and Western Churches. ALEXANDER V. (Peter Philargès) (Pope 1409–10); *b.* in Crete. ALEXANDER VI. (Rodrigo Borgia) (Pope 1492–1503), nephew of Calixtus III.; *b.* Xativa, Spain; early promoted in the Church, won his election by bribery, and during his pontificate aimed at providing handsomely for his natural children, the best known of whom were Cesare and Lucrezia Borgia; though a patron of art, has a worse reputation than any other Pope. ALEXANDER VII. (Fabio Chigi) (Pope 1655–67); *b.* Siena; a patron of learning, did much for the improvement of Rome. ALEXANDER VIII. (Pietro Ottoboni) (Pope 1689–91).

Alexander I. (1078–1124), King of Scotland, 1107; surnamed 'the Fierce'; son of Malcolm Canmore and Margaret; founded abbeys at Scone and Inchcolm.

Alexander II. (1198–1249), King of Scotland, 1214; son of William the Lion; subdued Argyll and Moray; died on the eve of an expedition against the Norsemen of the Western Islands.

Alexander III. (1241–85), King of Scotland, 1249; son of above; defeated King Haakon at Largs, after which the Hebrides and Isle of Man were ceded to the Scot. crown. Killed by fall over cliffs at Kinghorn. The period of Alexander II. and III. is known as 'the golden age of Scottish history.'

Alexander the Great (356–323 B.C.), King of Macedon; son of Philip II. of Macedon, and Olympias, sister of Alexander I. of Epirus. Educ. under Aristotle, 343–342. In 336 he succeeded his father. Suppressed the risings of the Illyrians and Triballians. Marched on the Thebans, who had taken up arms, and razed their city, sparing only the house of the poet Pindar. Alexander next prepared for a war against Persia; crossed the Hellespont, 334, with 35,000 men, and won a brilliant victory at the R. Granicus; during this campaign Alexander severed the 'Gordian Knot,' which, it was fabled, could only be untied by the conqueror of Asia. He next marched against Darius, whom he overthrew at Issus, 333. He then subdued Syria, Palestine, and Egypt, and founded the city of Alexandria, 331. He again marched against Darius, whom he routed at Arbela; Darius escaped, but Babylon and Susa surrendered to the conqueror, who then marched triumphantly into Persepolis, the Persian capital. He next invaded India, 326, but, after conquering the Punjab, he was compelled to return to Persia owing to revolt among his troops. Upon his return to Babylon he was suddenly smitten with fever, and died after eleven days, aged 32. He was buried in a golden coffin at Alexandria, and received divine honours.

[*Alexander's Empire*, by Mahaffy (1887); *Life*, by Wheeler (1900).]

Alexander (1893–1920), King of Greece; second son of King Constantine; succeeded 1917; boundaries of Greece extended during his reign.

Alexander I., PAULOVITCH (1777–1825), Tsar of Russia, 1801. He took part in various campaigns against Napoleon, but was obliged to conclude the Peace of Tilsit, 1807. After the disastrous Fr. campaign in Russia Alexander took a prominent part in the great struggle of 1813–14. During his reign Finland and Georgia were annexed. He abolished torture and the transference of peasants as mere chattels, founded schools, and fostered trade, but many of his ideals were unfulfilled.

Alexander II., NICOLAEVITCH (1818–81), Tsar of Russia, succeeded to the throne during the Crimean War, 1855. In 1877 he declared war on Turkey. The emancipation of the serfs was the chief event of his reign. The latter part of his reign was taken up with efforts to suppress the Nihilists, by whom he was assassinated.

Alexander III., ALEXANDROVITCH (1845–94), Tsar of Russia, 1881; broke away from Triple Alliance with Germany and Austria; ruled as an autocrat, and avoided wars.

Alexander I., OBRENOVITCH (1876–1903), King of Serbia; succeeded his father Milan, 1889; unpopular owing to his reactionary legislation and his marriage with Draga Mashin; both king and queen were assassinated.

Alexander I., King of Yugoslavia (1888–1934), second son of King Peter of Serbia; *b.* Cetinje; distinguished himself in Balkan Wars; commander-in-chief of Serbian armies during the Great War. Succeeded his father, 1921. In 1929 abolished the constitution and reigned as a dictator. Assassinated at Marseilles.

Alexander I. (of Battenberg) (1857–93), elected, 1879, Prince of Bulgaria; annexed Eastern Rumelia; forced to abdicate by Russia; restored to throne by a counter-revolution, but shortly afterwards abdicated, 1886.

Alexander OF HALES (*c.* 1175–1245), Eng. mediæval theologian; *b.* in Gloucestershire; member of Franciscan order; wrote *Summa Universa Theologiæ.*

Alexander, BOYD (1873–1910), Brit. explorer and naturalist; *b.* Cranbrook, Kent; crossed Africa from Niger to Nile, 1904–7; killed by natives on borders of Sudan.

Alexander, SIR GEORGE (1858–1918), Eng. actor and manager; *b.* Reading; called the Beau Brummell of the stage. Produced, among other plays, *The Prisoner of Zenda*, *If I were King*, and *His House in Order.*

Alexander, SIR WILLIAM (1567–1640), Earl of Stirling, Scot. courtier poet; was granted Nova Scotia by James I., 1621, and from 1626 was secretary of state for Scotland.

Alexander, WILLIAM (1824–1911), Prot. Archbishop of Armagh, and primate of all Ireland; *b.* Londonderry; a well-known theological writer and poet. His wife, CECIL FRANCES ALEXANDER, was a noted hymn writer.

Alexander Severus, MARCUS AURELIUS (208–35), Roman emperor, 222; proclaimed by Prætorians after murder of Heliogabalus; introduced many useful reforms; put to death by Prætorians at Mainz for offering peace to Germans.

Alexanderson, ERNST F. W. (1878–), inventor and engineer; *b.* Uppsala; emigrated to U.S.A., 1901; developed a high frequency alternator; has worked at television.

Alexandra, QUEEN (1844–1925) (ALEXANDRA CAROLINE MARIE CHARLOTTE LOUISE JULIE), daughter of Christian IX. of Denmark, wife of Edward VII., 1863; *b.* Copenhagen; took a deep interest in the welfare of her people; reorganized the army nursing service; during Great War worked devotedly on behalf of organizations for the relief and comfort of Brit. soldiers. Alexandra Day was instituted in 1912 to raise funds for hospitals, children's holiday funds, etc.

Alexei (*ä-lek'sī*), MICHAILOVICH (1629–76), Tsar of Russia, father of Peter the Great; introduced western ideas of civilization to Russia.

Alexei, PETROVITCH (1690–1718), eldest son of Peter the Great; *b.* Moscow; opposed his father's reforms, and resisted the 'westernizing' of the country.

Alex'ius I., COMNENUS (1048–1118), Byzantine emperor; *b.* Constantinople; succeeded 1081; by seeking help of West against Turks brought about First Crusade; recovered Asia Minor, aided by Godfrey of Bouillon; afterwards reformed administration.

Alfan'o, FRANCO (1877–), Ital. musician; *b.* near Naples; completed Puccini's unfinished *Turandot.*

Alfieri (*äl-fē-ā'rē*), COUNT VITTORIO (1749–1803), Ital. poet and dramatist; *b.* Asti; inherited an immense fortune. He formed an attachment with the Countess of Albany, and lived with her in Paris and in Florence. His great reputation rests on 19 tragedies—*e.g. Abele* and *Cleopatra*; besides lyrics and satires he wrote *Memoirs* (Eng. trans. 1810).

Alfon'so XIII. (1886–), posthumous son of Alfonso XII.; *b.* Madrid; King of Spain from birth till 1931; married, 1906, Princess Ena of Battenberg, niece of Edward VII. In 1923 power was seized by the military under General Primo de Rivera, who governed as dictator till 1930, being succeeded by General Berenguer as premier. On April 14, 1931, Republican successes at the municipal elections led Alfonso and his family to leave Spain. In Nov. 1931 the Cortes found him guilty of high treason, confiscated his property, and outlawed him.

Alford, HENRY (1810–71), Eng. divine, poet, and Biblical scholar; *b.* London; Dean of Canterbury, 1857–71; first ed. of *Contemporary Review*; wrote hymns, poems, and ed. the N.T. in Greek.

Alfred the Great (849–901), King of the W. Saxons; *b.* Wantage; fought against the Danes in Æthelred's reign; succeeded 871, and soon afterwards made peace. Danes of E. Anglia, under Guthrum, again invaded Wessex, 878, and Alfred had to withdraw to Athelney; raised army and defeated Guthrum at Ethandun, after which, by Peace of Wedmore, Danes retired east of Watling Street, and recognized Alfred as overlord. Struggle renewed, 893, by Danes from overseas, but ended in favour of Alfred. During peace which followed he enlarged navy, founded schools, codified and enforced the laws, trans. into Anglo-Saxon works by Orosius, Bede, Boethius, Gregory, etc., and encouraged the compilation of the Saxon *Chronicle.*

Algarot'ti, FRANCESCO, COUNT (1712–64), Ital. philosopher, poet, and art critic; *b.* Venice; travelled through Europe; in Paris became intimate with Voltaire; in Prussia became friend and chamberlain of Frederick the Great. Works include essays on art, etc.

Alhaz'en, IBN-AL-HAZAN (965–1039), Arab. astronomer and optician; *b.* Basra. His book on optics discussed refraction; said to have been the first to suggest the use of spectacles.

Ali Bey (1766–1818), name assumed by Domingo Badia y Leblich, Span. traveller who in eastern costume visited Morocco, Tripoli, Egypt, Arabia, Syria; entered Mecca as pilgrim; wrote *Travels in Asia and Africa*; *d.* Aleppo.

Alin, OSKAR JOSEF (1846–1900),

Swed. economist and historian; *b.* Falun; rector of Uppsala Univ.; many works on history of Sweden.

Al'ington, CYRIL ARGENTINE (1872–), Brit. educationist and writer; *b.* Ipswich; headmaster of Eton, 1916–33; chaplain to the King, 1921; Dean of Durham since 1933. Author of *A Schoolmaster's Apology* (1914), *Eton Fables* (1921), etc.

Ali Pasha (1741–1822), Albanian chief, surnamed 'the Lion'; served Turkey in war with Austria and Russia, 1787; created Pasha of Janina, 1788. In 1797 he secured for himself the Venetian coast line of Albania, and thereafter sided with France or Britain as advantage prompted. Sultan Mahmoud II. deposed and afterwards murdered him. Lord Byron introduces him in *Childe Harold's Pilgrimage*.

Al'ison, SIR ARCHIBALD (1792–1867), distinguished historian and legal writer; *b.* Shropshire; wrote *History of Europe*, *Lives* of Marlborough, Castlereagh, and others; *Principles of Population*, *Principles of the Criminal Law of Scotland*, etc.

Al-Khwarizmi (*-ku-war-iz'mē*), Arab. mathematician of 9th cent.; *b.* in Khorasan; his important treatise on Algebra gave its name to the science.

Al-Kindi, ABU YUSUF, Arab. philosopher (*fl.* 9th cent.); *b.* Basra; writer on logic and mathematics; commentator on Aristotle; regarded as father of Arab. philosophy.

Allan, DAVID (1744–96), Scot. artist; *b.* Alloa; called the 'Scottish Hogarth'; illustrated Ramsay's *Gentle Shepherd*.

Allan, SIR HUGH (1810–82), Can. financier; *b.* Saltcoats; organized Allan Line of steamships.

Allan, SIR WILLIAM, A.R.A. (1782–1850), Scottish historical painter; *b.* Edinburgh; painted *John Knox admonishing Mary Queen of Scots*, *Death of the Regent Murray*, and Russian subjects.

Allbutt, SIR THOMAS CLIFFORD (1836–1925), physician; *b.* Dewsbury; regius prof. of physic at Cambridge, 1892; inventor of short clinical thermometer.

Alleg'ri, GREGORIO (1582–1652), Ital. composer; *b.* Rome; chief work a *Miserere* sung yearly in Sistine Chapel.

Allen, CHARLES GRANT BLAIRFINDIE (1848–99), Can. scientist and man of letters, known as GRANT ALLEN; *b.* near Kingston, Ontario; wrote works on evolution, *The Woman Who Did* (1895), and numerous other novels.

Allen, SIR HUGH PERCY (1869–), Brit. musician; *b.* Reading; organist of New Coll., Oxford, 1901–18; director, Royal Coll. of Music, London, and prof. of music at Oxford since 1918; noted conductor of Bach choirs.

Allen, JAMES LANE (1849–1925), U.S.A. novelist; best-known work *The Choir Invisible* (1897).

Allen, WILLIAM (1532–94), Eng. cardinal; *b.* Rossall, Lancs; canon of York during Mary's reign; established coll. at Douai, 1568, for training priests; assisted in preparing Douai Bible; strongly encouraged Philip II. to invade England; made cardinal by Sixtus V., 1587.

Allenby, EDMUND HENRY HYNMAN, VISCOUNT (1861–), Eng. soldier; served in Bechuanaland, Zululand, and S. Africa; in Great War did valuable work with cavalry in retreat from Mons, 1914; commander of 5th Army Corps, 1915; commanded 3rd Army, 1915–17; commander-in-chief of Egyptian Expeditionary Force, 1917–19; captured Jerusalem, 1917, Damascus and Aleppo, 1918; this campaign eliminated Turkey from the War; field-marshal, 1919; viscounty and grant of £50,000, 1919; high commissioner for Egypt, 1919–25; captain of Deal Castle, 1925–6.

Alleyn (*al'en*), EDWARD (1566–1626), Eng. actor; *b.* London; chief actor of his time; owned theatres; founded and endowed Dulwich Coll.

All'ingham, WILLIAM (1824–89), poet and journalist; *b.* Ballyshannon, N. Ireland; noted for his lyrics, including *Up the Airy Mountain*; ed. *Fraser's Magazine*.

Allori (*äl-lō'rē*), CHRISTOFANO (1577–1621), Florentine portrait and altar painter; fine *Judith with Head of Holofernes*.

Almag'ro, DIEGO DE (1464–1538), Span. adventurer; associated with Pizarro in conquest of Peru; first European to enter Chile; rebelled against Pizarro, was defeated and put to death.

Al-Mansur (*c.* 707–75), second caliph of the Abbasid dynasty; cruel and perfidious, but a firm and energetic ruler and a patron of learning; founded Baghdad, 764.

Al'ma-Tad'ema, SIR LAWRENCE (1836–1912), historical and archæological painter; *b.* Dronryp, Holland; became a naturalized Englishman; excelled as painter of scenes from Gr. and Rom. life; painted *Sappho*, *Spring*, *Gold-fish*, *The Pyrrhic Dance*, *The Wine Shop*, etc.

Almeida (*äl-mā-ē'dä*), FRANCESCO DE (*c.* 1450–1510), Port. soldier; *b.* Lisbon; served with distinction under Ferdinand of Aragon against Moors; first viceroy of E. Indian possessions; superseded by Albuquerque; killed by natives at Table Bay.

Al'mon, JOHN (1737–1805), Eng. political pamphleteer and publisher; *b.* Liverpool; advocated freedom of the press; inspired one of the Letters of Junius; ed. correspondence of John Wilkes.

Almqvist (*älm'kvist*), KARL JONAS LUDWIG (1793–1866), Swed. miscellaneous writer; *b.* Stockholm; wrote novels, poems, plays, and historical sketches.

Alness, LORD, ROBERT MUNRO (1868–), Scot. politician and lawyer; *b.* Ross-shire; lord advocate, 1913; secretary for Scotland, 1916–22; lord justice clerk, 1922–33; baron, 1934.

A.L.O.E. See TUCKER, CHARLOTTE MARIA.

Aloysius (*ä-lō-is'i-us*), ST. See under GONZAGA.

Alpini (*äl-pē'nē*), PROSPERO (1553–1617), Ital. botanist; *b.* near Venice; prof. of botany at Padua from 1593; studied the flora of Egypt and discovered the bi-sexual nature of date palms and other plants; pub. first European account of coffee plant.

Alströmer (*äl'stre-mer*), JONAS (1685–1761), Swed. reformer; *b.* in Vestergötland; lived for a time in England, and on return to Sweden introduced Eng. industrial methods; imported sheep from England, Spain, and Angora.

Alt'dorfer, ALBRECHT (*c.* 1480–1538), Ger. painter and engraver; *b.* Regensburg, Bavaria; pupil of Dürer; most important picture is *The Battle of Arbela*.

Al'va (or ALBA), FERDINAND ALVAREZ DE TOLEDO, DUKE OF (1508–83), Span. statesman and soldier; fought at Pavia, and in Hungary, Algiers, and Italy, against Pope and French; notorious for his Netherlands administration, 1567–73, about 18,000 persons, including Counts Egmont and Horn, being executed.

Alvarad'o, PIETRO DE (1495–1541), Span. adventurer; *b.* Badajoz; lieutenant of Cortes in conquest of Mexico; conqueror and governor of Guatemala, 1523–4, and governor of Honduras, 1537.

Alvarez (*äl'vä-reth*), DON JOSÉ (1768–1827), leading Span. sculptor; *b.* Priego, Cordova; his fine statue of Ganymede in Prado; court sculptor to Ferdinand VII.

Alverstone, Lord (1842–1915), formerly Sir Richard Everard Webster; *b.* Cranleigh, Surrey; thrice attorney-general under Lord Salisbury. Served on Parnell Commission, 1888–9; Bering Sea question, 1893; Alaska Boundary Commission, 1903, etc.; master of the rolls, 1900; Lord Chief-Justice of England, 1900–13; pub. *Recollections of Bar and Bench* (1914).

Amadeo (*ä-mä-dā'o*), Giovanni Antonio (1447–1522), Ital. sculptor and architect of Renaissance period; *b.* Pavia; noted for his statues in Colleoni Chapel, Bergamo, and sculpture work, Milan Cathedral.

Amade'us VIII. (1383–1451), Duke of Savoy; extended his dominions, but retired, 1434, to hermitage of Ripaille; elected Pope, 1439, as Felix v., but was not recognized by the Church; returned to his hermitage.

Amanul'lah Khan (1892–), Amir of Afghanistan; succeeded Nasrullah Khan in 1919; adopted title of King, 1926; toured Europe with his queen, 1927–8, studying western civilization; returning, introduced reforms which caused revolt, 1928; abdicated, 1929.

Amar'i, Michele (1806–89), Ital. historian, Orientalist, and patriot; *b.* Palermo; wrote on the Sicilian Vespers, which caused his flight to Paris; joined Garibaldi, 1859; prof. of Arabic at Florence.

Ama'sis I. (16th cent. B.C.), King of Egypt, founder of 18th dynasty; successful warrior against the Hyksos. Amasis II. (570–526 B.C.), last king of anc. Egypt; an able ruler; his son was dethroned by the Persians.

Amat'i, Ital. family of Cremona, famed as violin makers. Andrea (*c.* 1525–1611) founded the industry; his brother Nicolo, and his own sons, Antonio (*d.* 1648) and Geronimo (*d.* 1630), were also distinguished makers. The most famous craftsman was Nicolo (*d.* 1684), son of Geronimo, who in 1625 produced the 'Grand Amati' violins; Antonio Stradivari was his pupil.

Ambrose, St. (*c.* 340–97), patron saint and bishop of Milan, 374; *b.* Trèves; one of the greatest figures of the Western Church; president of synod of Aquileia, 381, to consider Arian heresy; excommunicated Theodosius; great writer of hymns and author of saying, 'When in Rome do as Rome does.' *Ambrosian Chant,* choral music introduced from Eastern Church by him.

Amedeo (*ä-mā'dā-ō*), Ferdinando Maria di Savoia, Duke of Aosta (1845–90); *b.* Turin; third son of Victor Emmanuel II., King of Italy; vice-admiral of Ital. navy, 1868; ascended Span. throne, 1870; abdicated, 1873.

Amelot de la Houssaye (*äm-lō deläoo-sā*), Abraham Nicholas (1634–1706); Fr. historian; *b.* Orleans; wrote *Histoire du Gouvernement de Venise* (1676), exposing corruption of state, which led to his imprisonment; trans. Machiavelli's *Prince.*

Amerigo Vespucci. See Vespucci, Amerigo.

A'mery, Leopold Charles Maurice Stennet (1873–), Eng. politician; *b.* Gorakhpur, India; first lord of Admiralty, 1922–4; secretary for colonies and dominion affairs, 1924–9; has travelled much; strong advocate of tariffs; writer of many books on political questions.

Ames, Joseph (1689–1759), Eng. antiquary; *b.* Yarmouth; wrote invaluable *Typographical Antiquities*, dealing with Eng. printing from 1471–1600.

Am'herst, Baron Jeffrey (1717–97), Brit. field-marshal; *b.* Riverhead, Kent; commander-in-chief in America; captured Fort Duquesne, and Ticonderoga and Montreal, 1760; gov.-gen. of Brit. N. America, 1760–3.

Am'herst, William Pitt, Earl (1773–1857), nephew of above, diplomatist and statesman; mission to China failed, as he refused to 'kowtow' to emperor, 1816; gov.-gen. of India, 1823–8.

Amici (*ä-mē'-chē*), Giovanni Battista (1786–1863), Ital. astronomer; *b.* Modena; director of Florence Observatory; invented improvements in microscope and telescope.

Amicis (*ä-mē'chēz*), Edmondo de (1846–1908), Ital. soldier and author; *b.* Oneglia, Liguria; fought against Austrians, 1866; pub., 1868, *La Vita Militare*; retired from army, 1871. Wrote works of travel, poetry, and fiction, including *Il Cuore* (Eng. trans. *An Italian Schoolboy's Journal*).

Amiel (*ä-mē-el'*), Henri Frédéric (1821–81), Swiss philosopher; *b.* Geneva; prof. of philosophy, Geneva, 1854; his *Journal intime* trans. into Eng. by Mrs. Humphry Ward.

Am'man, Johann Conrad (1669–1730), Swiss physician; *b.* Schaffhausen; lived in Amsterdam; invented method of instructing deaf and dumb. Wrote *Surdus Loquens* (1692).

Ammanat'i, Bartolomeo (1511–92), Ital. sculptor and architect; masterpiece, Ponte della Trinita, over R. Arno; made additions to Pitti Palace.

Ammian'us Marcellinus (*c.* A.D. 330–400), last Lat. historian of the Rom. Empire; *b.* Antioch; continued history of Tacitus in thirty-one books (A.D. 96–378).

A'mos (*fl. c.* 760 B.C.), minor prophet; *b.* Tekoa, S. Judah; a shepherd. See Book of Amos.

Ampère, André Marie (1775–1836), Fr. physicist, *b.* near Lyons; prof. physics, Coll. of France, 1824; discovered relations between magnetism and electricity, and developed the science of electro-magnetism; name perpetuated in the ampère.

Amulree, William Warrender Mackenzie, 1st Lord (1860–), Scot. lawyer and politician; has frequently acted as arbitrator in industrial disputes; secretary of state for air, 1930–1; numerous publications on legal matters.

Am'undsen, Roald (1872–1928), Norweg. explorer; *b.* near Sarpsborg; was first to sail through N.W. Passage, 1906; leader of Norweg. Antarctic Expedition, 1910–12, reaching S. Pole, Dec. 14, 1911; *Maud* Expedition N.E. Passage, 1918–21; Transpolar Flight from Spitsbergen over N. Pole, 1926. Lost his life in attempt to rescue General Nobile near the N. Pole, 1928. Author of books dealing with his expeditions.

Amurath, name of five sultans of Turkey, beginning with Amurath I. (1319–89), first to make great headway in Europe, and concluding with Amurath V. (1840–1904), deposed 1876.

Amyot (*ä-mē-ō'*), Jacques (1513–94), Fr. humanist and translator; *b.* Melun; prof. of classics at Bourges; Bishop of Auxerre; earned title of 'prince of translators' for his version of Plutarch's *Lives* (1572).

Anacreon (*ä-năk'rē-on*) (*c.* 563–478 B.C.), Gr. lyric poet; *b.* Teos, Asia Minor; friend of Simonides; patronized by Hipparchus; wrote poems of love and wine, largely imitated in subsequent ages and known as *Anacreontics*.

Anasta'sius, four Popes: I. (398–401), opposed doctrines of Origen; II. (496–98); III. (911–13); IV. (1153–4).

Anasta'sius, two Byzantine emperors; I. (*c.* 430–518), married Zeno's widow, and thus became emperor; engaged in Isaurian (492–6) and Persian wars (502–5); active and prudent ruler. II. (*d.* 721), secretary to Emperor Philippicus, whom he succeeded; deposed by Theodosius; became a monk, 716; subsequently revolted, besieged Constantinople, was captured and put to death.

Anaxag'oras OF CLAZOMENÆ (*c.* 500–428 B.C.), Gr. philosopher, first to live in Athens; a friend of Pericles; when Pericles became unpopular, Anaxagoras had to leave the city; his ideas of matter anticipated the atomic theory; introduced doctrine that Mind or Reason orders the world.

Anaxarchus (*än-äks-ärk'us*) (4th cent. B.C.), Gr. philosopher, disciple of Democritus, favourite of Alexander the Great. Said to have been pounded to death in a mortar by Nicocreon of Cyprus.

Anaximan'der OF MILETUS (611–547 B.C.), second of the Ionic physicists; student of astronomy and geography; introduced the gnomon; taught obliquity of ecliptic; first map-maker amongst Greeks.

Ancus Marcius (*c.* 640–616 B.C.), fourth legendary king of Rome, grandson of Numa; bridged Tiber, founded Ostia, and established salt works.

Andersen, HANS CHRISTIAN (1805–75), Dan. poet and writer of fairy tales; *b.* Odense; son of a poor shoemaker; at age of fourteen went to seek his fortune in Copenhagen; ugly in appearance, clumsy in manners, and with little education, he failed in his search for employment, first in the theatres, and later as an operatic singer. After severe struggles he made friends who helped him, amongst others being King Frederick VI. The first series of the famous *Fairy Tales* appeared in 1835, and further instalments appeared at intervals during the remainder of his life. He also wrote travel books and an interesting *Autobiography.*

[*Life*, by Bain (1895).]

Anderson, ALEXANDER (1845–1909), 'Surfaceman,' Scot. minor poet; *b.* Kirkconnel; worked on railway; wrote *Songs of Labour, Songs of the Rail,* etc.; librarian of Edinburgh Univ., 1905–9.

Anderson, ELIZABETH GARRETT (1836–1917), physician; *b.* London; first woman licensed to practise in England; M.D. Paris; first Englishwoman mayor (Aldeburgh, 1908); dean and lecturer London School of Medicine for Women.

Anderson, JAMES (1739–1808), Scot. agriculturist and economist; *b.* near Edinburgh; wrote *Inquiry into the Nature of the Corn Laws* (1777); invented the 'Scotch plough'; ed. *The Bee* (1790–4).

Anderson, JOHN (1726–96), Scot. natural philosopher; *b.* Roseneath; prof. of Oriental languages, 1756, and of natural philosophy, 1760, at Glasgow Univ.; furthered application of science to industry; bequeathed his property for founding of Anderson's Coll., now Glasgow and West of Scotland Technical Coll.

Anderson, JOSEPH (1832–1916), Scot. antiquary; *b.* Arbroath; Rhind lecturer, 1879–82; ed. *The Orkneyinga Saga* (1873) and Drummond's *Ancient Scottish Weapons* (1881); pub. *Early Christian Monuments in Scotland* (1881–86). Keeper of National Museum of Antiquities, 1870–1913.

Anderson, MARY (1859–), U.S.A. actress; *b.* Sacramento, California; noted for beauty and fine voice; retired 1889; married 1890 Antonio de Navarro.

Anderson, SIR ROBERT (1841–1918), criminologist and lawyer; *b.* Dublin; adviser to Home Office, 1868; head of Criminal Investigation Dep., 1888–1901; author of *Times* articles 'Parnellism and Crime' (1887), and *Criminals and Crime,* etc.

Anderson, SIR ROBERT ROWAND (1834–1921), Scot. architect; *b.* Forres; designed Edinburgh Medical School, Edinburgh Conservative Club, dome of Edinburgh

Univ. (1886), and Scot. National Portrait Gallery.

Andersson, KARL JOHAN (1827–67), Swed. African explorer; *b.* Wermland; made first systematic exploration of Bechuanaland. Died during expedition to Kunene R.

Andrad'a e Sylva, BONIFACIO JOZÉ D' (1765–1838), Brazilian statesman and scientist; *b.* near Rio de Janeiro; prof. of metallurgy at Coimbra, Portugal, 1800; prominent in movement for Brazilian independence; exiled to France, 1823; returned 1829.

Andrassy (*on'drä-shē*). (1) GYULA, COUNT (1823–90), Hungarian statesman; *b.* Kosice; keen patriot and reformer; became vice-president of Hungarian Diet, 1865; first premier of Hungary, 1867; and in 1871 foreign minister for Austria. The 'Andrassy Note' (Dec. 1875) proposed concerted action by powers to secure reforms in Balkans. Helped to secure protectorate over Bosnia and Hercegovina for Austria. Concluded Austro-German treaty of alliance. (2) JULIUS, COUNT (1860–1929), Hungarian statesman; son of above; minister of interior, 1906–10; for foreign affairs, 1918. Tried to make a separate peace. Imprisoned in 1921 for supporting Emperor Charles in attempt to regain crown.

André (*an'drā*), JOHN (1751–80), Brit. soldier; *b.* London; fought in America during revolutionary war; selected to negotiate with Benedict Arnold for surrender of West Point; captured, tried, hanged, Oct. 2, 1780. Remains removed to Westminster Abbey, 1821.

Andrea del Sarto. See SARTO.

Andrée (*an'drā*), SALOMON AUGUST (1854–97), Swed. engineer; *b.* Grenna, on L. Vetter; undertook balloon voyage to N. Pole. Started from Danes Isl., N.W. Spitsbergen, July 11, 1897, and nothing further was known of him till Aug. 1930, when a Norweg. expedition discovered the bodies of the explorer and his companions on White Isl. in Spitsbergen group.

Andrew, ST., brother of Peter; a fisherman; first of Christ's disciples; said to have been crucified on an X-shaped cross at Patras in Achæa; patron saint of Scotland and of Russia. His day is Nov. 30.

Andrewes, LANCELOT (1555–1626), Eng. scholar and divine; *b.* London; successively Bishop of Chichester, Ely, and Winchester; a most learned divine, and unrivalled as a pulpit orator. Wrote *Manual of Private Devotions.*

Andrews, THOMAS (1813–85), Irish chemist; *b.* Belfast; president of the Northern Coll., Belfast; made researches on liquefaction of gases, and wrote on that and kindred topics.

And'réyev, LEONID NIKOLÁYEVICH (1871–1919), Russian short-story writer; *b.* Orel; a realist, delighting in the horrible. Among his stories are *The Tocsin, In the Mist, The Red Laugh,* and *S.O.S.* His symbolical plays include *The Life of Man.*

Androcles (*an'dro-klēz*) or ANDROCLUS, runaway Rom. slave. When recaptured and sent into the arena was fawned upon by a fierce lion, from whose foot he had formerly removed a thorn.

Androni'cus, four Byzantine emperors. I., COMNENUS (*c.* 1110–85); imprisoned for share in conspiracy against Emperor Manuel, 1153; escaped, 1165; subsequently became emperor, 1183; assassinated. Talented but licentious; great general and able statesman. II., PALÆOLOGUS THE ELDER (1260–1332); succeeded his father, 1282; very superstitious; during his time empire was devastated by Turks. III., PALÆOLOGUS THE YOUNGER (*c.*

1296–41), grandson of above, succeeded 1328. During his reign Turks conquered up to Bosporus; he also lost Bulgaria and greater part of Macedonia. IV. (1377–9), dethroned his father, John V., until latter was reinstated with the help of the Turks.

An'eurin, 6th-cent. Welsh poet known by poem *Gododin* (13th cent. MS.), describing Cymric wars with Saxons. Eng. trans. in Skene's *Four Ancient Books of Wales* (1866). Aneurin does not mention King Arthur.

Angeli, HEINRICH VON (1840–1925), noted Hungarian portrait painter; painted the Emperor Francis Joseph, Queen Victoria, etc., also historical pictures.

Angelico (*än-jel'ē-kō*), FRA (1387–1455), Ital. religious painter; real name Guido; *b.* Vicchio, Tuscany; became Dominican, 1408. Masterpiece of his central period frescoes at convent of San Marco, Florence. In 1445 invited to Rome; decorated chapel in Vatican, roof of Cappella Nuovo, cathedral of Orvieto; man of saintly life; great colourist.

[*Fra Angelico*, by R. L. Douglas (1902).]

Angell, SIR NORMAN (RALPH NORMAN ANGELL LANE) (1874–), journalist; *b.* Holbeach; author of *The Great Illusion* (1910), showing futility of war and consequent impoverishment, even of victors; numerous other works.

Angelo, MICHAEL. See MICHELANGELO.

Anglesey, HENRY WILLIAM PAGET, 1ST MARQUESS OF (1768–1854), soldier and politician; served with distinction in Peninsular War; commanded cavalry at Quatre Bras and Waterloo; lost a leg; lord-lieut. of Ireland (twice); established Irish Board of Education; field-marshal, 1846.

Angoulême (*on-goo-lām'*), CHARLES DE VALOIS, DUC D' (1573–1650), illegitimate son of Charles IX., intrigued against Henry IV.; prisoner in Bastille, 1605–16; restored to rank in army; created duke, 1619; commanded at La Rochelle, 1627, etc. Left *Memoirs*.

Angoulême, LOUIS ANTOINE DE BOURBON, DUC D' (1775–1844), son of Charles X. of France; *b.* Versailles; last dauphin of France; fled with father at outbreak of Revolution, 1789; resided in Poland and England; returned to France at Restoration; in 1830 abandoned claim to throne.

Ang'strom, ANDERS JONAS (1814–74), Swed. physicist; prof. of physics at Uppsala, 1858–74; researches in terrestrial magnetism and spectroscopy; made map of solar spectrum, 1868.

Animuccia (*ä-nē-moo'chä*), GIOVANNI (*c.* 1500–71), Ital. composer; chapel master at St. Peter's, 1555; wrote *Laudi Spirituali*, possible forerunners of oratorios.

Anna Comne'na (1083–1148), Byzantine princess and historian; daughter of Alexius I.; retired to a convent, and wrote her *Alexiad*, treating of her father's reign.

Anne (1665–1714), Queen of Great Britain and Ireland; second daughter of James II. by Anne Hyde; married Prince George of Denmark, 1683; succeeded 1702. Marlborough and his wife managed the queen. Marlborough continued war begun by William III., gaining his four great victories; Gibraltar was captured. In 1707 Treaty of Union with Scotland was signed. Abigail Masham supplanted the Duchess of Marlborough in Anne's favour. Impeachment of Sacheverell, 1710, was followed by fall of Whigs, the formation of Harley cabinet, and the disgrace of Marlborough, 1711. Peace of Utrecht signed, 1713. None of Anne's many children survived to succeed her, and the Elector of Hanover succeeded as George I. Anne's reign witnessed a great spiritual revival and much political and intellectual activity. Dull, obstinate, but homely and good-natured, she was deeply religious and 'entirely English' at heart.

[*Queen Anne*, by Paul (1907).]

Anne OF BRITTANY (1476–1514), daughter of Francis II., Duke of Brittany, whom she succeeded, 1488; forced to marry Charles VIII., and on his death became wife of Louis XII., thus adding Brittany to France.

Anne OF CLEVES (1515–57), fourth wife of Henry VIII. of England, daughter of John, Duke of Cleves; *b.* Cleves, Germany; her lack of charm disgusted Henry, and the marriage was annulled.

Anne OF DENMARK (1574–1619), queen of James VI. of Scotland, daughter of Frederick II. of Denmark; crowned queen of England, 1603; extravagant, but intelligent and well-meaning.

Anne Boleyn. See BOLEYN.

Anning, MARY (1799–1847), Eng. palæontologist; *b.* Lyme Regis; daughter of a carpenter; discovered the first Ichthyosaurus, 1811, the first Plesiosaurus, 1821, and the first Pterodactyl, 1828.

Annunzio. See D'ANNUNZIO.

Anquetil-Duperron (*onk-tĕl'doo-per-on'*), ABRAHAM HYACINTHE (1731–1805), Fr. Oriental scholar; *b.* Paris; pub. first European trans. of *Zend-Avesta* (1771), also Lat. trans. of Persian version of *Upanishads.*

Ansdell, RICHARD (1815–85), Eng. animal painter; *b.* Liverpool; shows influence of Landseer. *Stag at Bay*, *The Combat*, and *A Galloway Farm* are among his works. R.A., 1870.

An'selm, ST. (1033–1109); *b.* Aosta, Italy; distinguished mediæval churchman and statesman; entered monastery of Bec, 1060; abbot, 1078; came to England, 1092; appointed by William II. Archbishop of Canterbury, 1093; had long quarrel with William and Henry II. over question of investiture. Famous scholastic theologian; greatest work, *Cur Deus Homo*. Canonized 1494.

An'son, GEORGE, BARON (1697–1762), Brit. admiral; *b.* Shugborough, Staffs; circumnavigated globe, 1740–4; commanded Channel fleet in action off Finisterre, 1747; created baron same year; admiral of fleet, 1761. His *Voyage Round the World* (written by Richard Walter, his chaplain, 1748) still popular.

Anson, SIR WILLIAM REYNELL (1843–1914), Eng. jurist and scholar; *b.* Walberton, Sussex; formed school of law at Oxford; M.P. Oxford Univ., 1899; parl. secretary Board of Education, 1902–5; wrote *English Law of Contract* (1879), and *Law and Custom of the Constitution* (1881).

Anstey, F. (1856–1934), pseudonym of THOMAS ANSTEY GUTHRIE; Eng. humorist; *b.* Kensington; wrote *Vice Versa* (1882), which made a great hit, and *The Brass Bottle* (1900) (both dramatized), contributions to *Punch*, etc.

Antal'cidas, Spartan statesman and soldier; ambassador to Persians, with whom he concluded treaty, 387 B.C., by which all the Gr. cities of Asia Minor were annexed to Persian empire; again sent to Persia, 367 B.C.; committed suicide.

Anthony (or ANTONY), ST. (251–356), first Christian monk; *b.* Koma, Upper Egypt; lived many years in solitude near Arsinoë; early in 4th cent. organized monastic life; suffered strange temptations which have been favourite literary subject.

Antig'onus. (1) (382–301 B.C.), Macedonian general of Alexander the Great, known as Cyclops (one-eyed); made great conquests in Asia Minor and took title of king, 306 B.C.; slain at Ipsus, 301 B.C. (2) GON'ATAS (*c.* 319–239 B.C.), grandson of above, King of

Macedon, 283 B.C.; driven out by Pyrrhus, 273 B.C., but recovered kingdom. (3) DOSON (*d.* 220 B.C.), usurped kingdom of Macedonia, 229 B.C.; conquered Sparta, 220 B.C. (4) King of Judea (*c.* 80–37 B.C.), last of Maccabees to reign. Killed by Mark Antony.

Antim'achus (*fl.* 400 B.C.), Gr. epic and elegiac poet; chief works, *Thebais* (epic) and *Lydē* (elegy).

Antiochus (*an-tī'ō-kus*), name of thirteen kings of Syria (Seleucid dynasty). (1) I. (*r.* 281–252 B.C.), known as 'Soter' (saviour) for repelling invasion of Gauls. (2) II. (*d.* 246 B.C.), liberated Milesians from a tyrant; poisoned by his divorced wife. (3) III., THE GREAT (*r.* 223–187 B.C.), conquered Palestine and Cœle-Syria; protected Hannibal; involved in war with Romans; defeated at Thermopylæ (191 B.C.) and at Magnesia (190); compelled to yield all territory west of Mt. Taurus and pay heavy tribute; murdered by people for his extortions. (4) ANTIOCHUS EPIPHANES, son of above (King of Syria 175–164 B.C.); conquered large part of Egypt; twice took Jerusalem; bitterly oppressed Jews and caused Maccabean rebellion.

Antip'ater (*c.* 398–319 B.C.); Macedonian general, lieutenant of Philip and Alexander; became regent of Macedonia; defeated Spartans and overcame rebellious Gr. states, 322 B.C.

Antiphon (*an'ti-fon*) (480–411 B.C.), celebrated Attic orator; played important part in overthrow of the democracy; fifteen extant speeches.

Antomarchi (*än-to-mär'kē*), FRANCESCO (1780–1838), physician; *b.* Corsica; entered service of Napoleon at St. Helena, 1818, and pub. famous, but untrustworthy, *Derniers Moments de Napoléon* (1823).

Antonel'li, GIACOMO (1806–76), Ital. cardinal (cr. 1847); *b.* Sonnino; son of a woodcutter; had considerable influence over Pius IX. on anti-liberal and anti-national side; unscrupulous in finance and diplomacy.

Antoninus (*än-tō-nī'nus*) **Pius** (A.D. 86–161), Rom. emperor; *b.* near Lanuvium; adopted son of Hadrian, whom he succeeded, 138; simple and just ruler; in his reign Antonine's Wall was built from Forth to Clyde; adopted Marcus Aurelius.

Anto'nius, MARCUS, or MARK ANTONY (86–30 B.C.), distinguished soldier and supporter of Cæsar; appointed consul, 44 B.C. After Cæsar's murder, became one of the triumvirate, taking the eastern half of the empire, but his infatuation for Cleopatra led to his downfall. Defeated at Actium, he afterwards committed suicide.

Anville (*on-vēl'*), JEAN BAPTISTE BOURGUIGNON D' (1697–1782), Fr. geographer; *b.* Paris; his memoirs and maps on anc. geography are still considered indispensable.

Anwar'i, AUHAD UDDIN, Pers. 12th cent. poet and astrologer; his longest poem, *The Tears of Khorassan,* was rendered into Eng. verse by Fitzpatrick.

Apell'es, the greatest painter of antiquity, son of Pytheas, flourished latter part of 4th cent.; worked in Macedonia; none of his works extant.

Apol, LODEWYK FRANCISCUS HENDRIK (1850–), Dutch landscape painter; joined Barents's Arctic expedition, 1880, in order to study snow effects, and afterwards exhibited panoramic view, *Novaya Zemlya.*

Apollina'ris (*c.* A.D. 390), Bishop of Laodicea, founder of the Apollinarian heresy, denying the real humanity of Christ.

Apollodo'rus. (1) Gr. painter (*fl.* 400 B.C.), was the first to succeed in blending tones and in handling light and shade. (2)

Gr. dramatist (300–260 B.C.); wrote forty-seven comedies, from which Terence adapted his *Phormio* and *Hecyra*. (3) Gr. grammarian (*fl.* 140 B.C.); wrote many works, all lost except the *Bibliotheca*, a valuable collection of Gr. myths. (4) OF DAMASCUS, architect in Rome during reigns of Trajan and Hadrian; erected the Forum Trajani, and built a bridge across the Danube.

Apollo'nius. (1) OF PERGA (3rd cent. B.C.), Gr. geometrician and astronomer; lived at Alexandria, and ranks with Euclid and Archimedes among the founders of mathematical science. Was first to introduce terms *ellipse, parabola, hyperbola*. (2) RHODIUS (222–181 B.C.), Gr. poet and scholar; pupil of Callimachus; author of epic poem on the voyage of the Argonauts, to which Virgil owes much.

Apoll'os, an Alexandrian Jew, associated with St. Paul at Ephesus and Corinth; held by Luther to be author of Epistle to the Hebrews.

Ap'perley, CHARLES JAMES (1779–1843), Eng. sportsman and writer on sport—' Nimrod '; pub. *Hunting Reminiscences*, etc.

Appert (*ä-per'*), FRANÇOIS (1797–1840), Fr. technologist, discovered process of preserving food in hermetically sealed cans.

Appian'i, ANDREA (1754–1817), Ital. painter; *b.* Milan; disciple of Fr. painter David; known as ' the painter of the Graces ' from his frescoes at Monza and Milan.

Appo'nyi, ALBERT, COUNT (1846–1933), Hungarian statesman; *b.* Budapest; minister of education, 1906–10; in August 1916 approved of appointment of Hindenburg to command the Austro-Hungarian army; represented Hungary at the Assemblies of the League of Nations, 1924–5.

Aprax'in, FEODOR MATOYEVICH, COUNT (1671–1728), Russian soldier and naval constructor; lifelong friend of Peter the Great. As chief of the Admiralty, 1700–6, built fleets and constructed fortresses and harbours.

Apuleius (*ä-pū-lē'-us*), LUCIUS (2nd cent.), Lat. philosopher and satirist; *b.* Madaura, in Africa; studied at Carthage and Athens. His fame rests on his *Golden Ass*, a romance satirizing the vices of the age and of the priesthood in particular.

Aquinas (*ä-kwī'nas*), THOMAS—*i.e.* of Aquino—(*c.* 1227–74), theologian and saint; the *Angelic Doctor*; studied at Naples; became Dominican when seventeen; lectured at Rome and Bologna; canonized, 1323; greatest theologian of Western Church since St. Augustine, and greatest of the schoolmen; best work, *Summa Theologiæ*, maintaining that reason and revelation are the two sources of knowledge and cannot be contradictory.

Arab'i Pasha (*c.* 1839–1911), Egyptian soldier, revolutionary leader, and war minister; *b.* Lower Egypt; started national Egyptian party; defeated by Wolseley at Tel-el-Kebir, 1882; exiled to Ceylon; pensioned and returned to Egypt, 1901.

Ar'ago, DOMINIQUE FRANÇOIS JEAN (1786–1853), Fr. physicist; *b.* near Perpignan; became Biot's assistant for meridional measurements. In the Balearic Is. was imprisoned as a spy; escaped, and, after adventures in N. Africa, returned to France, 1809; became prof. of analytical geometry and astronomer of the Paris Observatory at age of twenty-three; director of the observatory, 1830. With Gay-Lussac he founded the *Annales de Chimie et de Physique*; conducted researches on rotary magnetism; investigated polarization of light, and made numerous discoveries in optics and magnetism. Was minister of war and marine in Provisional Government, 1848.

A'ram, Eugene (1704–59), Eng. schoolmaster and philologist; *b.* Ramsgill, Yorks; self-educated; kept school at Knaresborough, 1734–45. After the mysterious disappearance of his friend, Daniel Clark, he led roving life. Was first scholar to recognize affinity between Celtic and other European tongues. Arrested for murder of Clark, 1758; confessed guilt, and was executed. Aram is hero of a novel by Lytton and a poem by Hood.

Aran'da, Pedro Pablo Abarca de Boleo, Count of (1719–98), Span. statesman and general; *b.* near Huesca, Aragon; minister to Charles III. and Charles IV. of Spain; introduced Prussian drill system into Span. army; reorganized the Span. navy; expelled Jesuits from Spain, 1767.

Aran'y, Janos (1817–82), Hungarian poet; *b.* Nagy-Szalonta; one of the most illustrious of the literary men of Hungary; author of *Toldi* (1847), *Toldi Esteje* (Toldi's Evening), *Buda Halala* (The Death of Buda), *The Gypsies of Eida*, etc.

[*Life*, by Gaal (1898).]

Arber, Edward (1836–1912), Eng. man of letters; *b.* London; pub. reprints of rare books—*e.g.* *English Reprints* (30 vols. 1868–80). He reprinted Tyndale's N.T.

Arblay, Madame d'. See D'Arblay.

Arbois de Jubainville (*är-bwa' de zhu-ban'vēl*), Marie Henri d' (1827–1910), Fr. philologist and historian; *b.* Nancy; prof. of Celtic at Coll. de France; wrote *Cours de Littérature Celtique* (12 vols. 1883–1903), etc.

Arbuth'not, John (1667–1735), Scot. physician, wit, and author; *b.* Arbuthnott, Kincardineshire; settled in London; friend of Pope, Swift, and Gay; physician to Queen Anne; wrote *The History of John Bull* and *The Memoirs of Martinus Scriblerus.*

Arc, Jeanne d'. See Joan of Arc.

Arca'dius (A.D. 378–408), Rom. emperor of the East and Illyricum while his brother Honorius was emperor of the West. Their reigns saw the last struggles between Rome and the barbarians.

Arcesilaus (*är-ses-i-lā'us*) (316–241 B.C.), Gr. philosopher, founder of the New Academy, who, in opposition to the Stoics, held that we have no criterion of truth, and denounced dogmatism.

Arch, Joseph (1826–1919), Brit. Labour leader; *b.* Barford, Warwickshire; founded National Agricultural Labourers' Union, 1872; M.P. N.W. Norfolk, 1892–95.

[*Biography*, ed. by Lady Warwick (1898).]

Archelaus (*ar-ki-lā'us*). (1) King of Macedon (413–399 B.C.), succeeded to throne through series of murders. Befriended Euripides and Agathon. (2) General under Mithridates; tried to conquer Greece, 87 B.C., but was twice defeated; went over to Romans, 81 B.C. (3) His son became King of Egypt, 56 B.C., by marrying Berenice. (4) Son of Herod the Great, referred to in St. Matt. 2, 22. His rule was unpopular among the Jews; banished by Romans to Gaul, A.D. 7.

Archer, Frederick (1857–86), Eng. jockey; *b.* Cheltenham; had nine years of triumph, culminating in 1885 with five classic events—the Two Thousand Guineas, the Oaks, Derby, St. Leger, and Grand Prix. Steered 2,748 mounts to victory.

Archer, James (1824–1904), Scot. artist; *b.* Edinburgh; painted romantic subjects, figures, and portraits, including Prof. Blackie and Andrew Carnegie.

Archer, William (1856–1924), Brit. dramatic critic; *b.* Perth; trans. and popularized Ibsen; had profound knowledge of contemporary European drama, wrote numerous works and a play, *The Green Goddess.*

Archidamus (*ar-kid-ā'mus*), name of five Spartan kings. Archidamus III. (360–338 B.C.) defended Sparta against Thebans.

Archilochus (*är-kil'ō-kus*) (7th cent. B.C.), Gr. poet; *b.* Paro, Cyclades Is.; inventor of iambic verse; wrote elegiacs, lyrics, drinking songs, hymns, besides numerous satires.

Archimedes (*är-ki-mē'dēz*) (*c.* 287–212 B.C.), Gr. mathematician; *b.* Syracuse; studied in Alexandria; returned to native city; accidentally killed after its capture by Romans under Marcellus. Was most eminent mathematician of antiquity, and founded the science of hydrostatics; invented engines of war, the water-screw, and numerous other mechanical contrivances. Discovered the 'Principle of Archimedes' when taking a bath.

Archytas (*är-kī'tas*) OF TARENTUM (*c.* 347 B.C.), Gr. philosopher and mathematician, friend of Plato; invented a flying machine; enriched geometry with several original theorems.

Arco, GEORG VON, COUNT (1869–), Ger. engineer; inventor (with Prof. Slaby) of Telefunken system of wireless telegraphy, and deviser of improvements in high frequency machines for wireless telephony.

Arditi (*är-dē'tē*), LUIGI (1822–1903), Ital. composer and conductor; *b.* in Piedmont; first produced Wagner operas in London; chiefly remembered for his *Il Bacio* (vocal waltz).

Aren'sky, ANTON STEPANOVICH (1861–1906), Russian composer; *b.* Novgorod; prof. of music at Moscow, 1882; best known by his chamber music.

Aretino, PIETRO (1492–1556), Ital. dramatist and letter writer; *b.* Arezzo, Tuscany; his letters, satires, lampoons, and verses give a lively picture of a profligate age.

Argall, SIR SAMUEL (*c.* 1580–1626), Eng. adventurer; *b.* Bristol; deputy governor of Virginia, 1617; the captor of the Indian girl Pocahontas, daughter of the chief Powhatan, whom he took as a hostage for Brit. prisoners.

Argelander (*är-ge-län'der*), FRIEDRICH WILHELM AUGUST (1799–1875), Ger. astronomer; *b.* Memel; pupil of Bessel; chief astronomer successively at Abo, Helsinki, and Bonn; compiled a great catalogue and atlas of over 300,000 stars.

Argenson (*ar-zhon-son'*), D', Fr. family intimately connected with national affairs from time of Louis VIII. to end of 19th cent. (1) RENÉ DE VOYER, SEIGNEUR D' (1596–1651); Cardinal Richelieu gave him various state appointments, and Mazarin made him ambassador to Venice. (2) MARC RENÉ DE VOYER, MARQUIS D' (1652–1721); chief of police in Paris, 1697–1718, president of the Council of Finance, 1718–20; involved in the disastrous financial schemes of John Law. (3) RENÉ LOUIS DE VOYER, MARQUIS D' (1694–1757), son of (2); secretary for foreign affairs, 1744–7; chiefly remembered by his *Mémoires.* (4) MARC PIERRE DE VOYER, COUNT D' (1696–1764), brother of (3); war minister, 1742–57; friend of Diderot and Voltaire; disliked by Madame de Pompadour, through whom he was exiled; returned to Paris after her death. (5) MARC RENÉ DE VOYER, MARQUIS D' (1771–1842); for some time aide-de-camp to Lafayette during the Revolution.

Argyll. (1) ARCHIBALD CAMPBELL, 8TH EARL (1607–61); 1ST MARQUESS, 1641; took side of Covenanters, raised an army, and was defeated by Montrose, 1644; opposed the execution of Charles I.; supported the cause of Charles II., but subsequently made his submission to Cromwell, for which he was called to account at the Restoration, condemned, and beheaded in Edinburgh. See Scott's *Legend of Montrose.* (2) ARCHIBALD CAMPBELL, 9TH EARL (1629–85); executed for participation in Monmouth's rebellion. (3) ARCHIBALD CAMPBELL, 10TH EARL (1651–1703), 1ST DUKE, 1701, actively promoted Revolution, 1688; notorious for his association with massacre of Glencoe. (4) JOHN, 2ND DUKE (1678–1743), had distinguished service under Marlborough; led Royalist troops against Jacobites at Sheriffmuir, 1715. See Scott's *Heart of Midlothian.* (5) GEORGE, 8TH DUKE (1823–1900); lord privy seal, 1852; postmaster-general, 1855; Indian secretary, 1868; author of *Poems* (1894), *Primeval Man, The Unity of Nature,* etc. (6) JOHN (1845–1914), 9TH DUKE, son of (5), married, 1871, Princess Louise; gov.-gen. of Canada, 1878–83; author of *Canadian Pictures, Life of Queen Victoria,* etc.

Ari, THORGILSSON (1067–1148), 'the Learned'; Icelandic historian and genealogist; put traditional Norse tales into writing.

Arios'to, LUDOVICO (1474–1533), Ital. poet; *b.* Reggio, in Lombardy; studied law for five years; subsequently devoted himself to literary composition; early work attracted attention of Cardinal d'Este, who befriended him. Later he served the cardinal's brother, the Duke of Ferrara, and became governor of Garfagnana for three years; afterwards returned to Ferrara. Ariosto wrote comedies, but is chiefly remembered for his immortal epic, *Orlando Furioso* (1516), dealing with the wars of Charlemagne with the Saracens, and more intimately with the loves of Ruggero and Bradamante. Best Eng. trans. is by W. S. Rose (1823).

Aristarchus (*är-is-tar'kus*) OF SAMOS (*fl. c.* 270 B.C.), Gr. astronomer; first to assert that the earth moves round the sun; all works lost except *On the Sizes and Distances of the Sun and Moon.*

Aristarchus OF SAMOTHRACE (*c.* 150 B.C.), famous Gr. grammarian and founder of textual criticism; keeper of library at Alexandria; famous for his exhaustive labours in purifying the text of Homer.

Aristeides (*ar-is-tī'dēz*) (*c.* 530–468 B.C.), 'the Just,' Athenian statesman; commanded with distinction at Marathon, 490; became chief archon next year; banished for opposing naval policy of Themistocles; completed victory at Salamis, and commanded Athenians at Platæa, 479.

Aristip'pus OF CYRENE (430–356 B.C.), Gr. philosopher, founder of Cyrenaic school; pupil of Socrates; asserted that what gives the maximum of pleasure is good.

Aristophanes (*ar-is-tof'anēz*) (*c.* 450–375 B.C.), greatest comic poet of Greece; *b.* Athens. Fifty-four comedies are ascribed to him, but only eleven are extant: *The Acharnians* (425), *The Knights* (424), *The Clouds* (423), *The Wasps* (422), *The Peace* (421), *The Birds* (414), *The Lysistrata* (411), *The Thesmophoriazusæ* (411), *The Frogs* (405), *The Ecclesiazusæ* (393), and *The Plutus* (388). His plays, which are often the medium of his political opinions, show brilliant powers of wit, humour, and invective, and are further distinguished by originality of plot, cleverly planned situations, and graceful and vigorous dialogue. Probably the poet achieved his highest success in the exquisite lyrics which are interspersed through them. Aristophanes ranks with Shakespeare and Molière as one of the great comic dramatists of the world. Eng. trans. by W. J. Hickie, J. H. Frere, and B. B. Rogers.

[*Aristophanes*, by L. E. Lord (1925).]

Aristotle (*är'is-totl*) (384–322 B.C.), one of the greatest thinkers of history; *b.* Stagira, Macedonia; known as the *Stagirite.* Came to Athens, where he joined Plato's school, 367; on death of Plato, migrated to Assus in Mysia, where he opened a school; here he married Pytheas, the adopted daughter of Prince Hermias. In 344 B.C. moved to the isl. of Lesbos, and in 342, on settling in Macedonia, became tutor to Alexander the Great. Returning, in 335 B.C., to Athens, he taught philosophy in the walks of the Lyceum (the name Peripatetics given to his followers); in 323 he withdrew to Chalcis in Eubœa, where he died.

The writings of Aristotle, which are almost wholly the MSS. of lectures, deal with almost all the branches of knowledge known to his age. These are classed as theoretical (logic, metaphysics, and physics), practical (ethics, economics, politics), and productive (rhetoric and poetry).

Logic is regarded by Aristotle as not properly a branch of philosophy, but as a study of method. His logical treatises were called the *Organon*, or *Instrument*, by the Peripatetics.

The *metaphysics*, or 'first philosophy' of Aristotle, deals with being, as being; with the ultimate conditions of existence.

The *theology* completes the metaphysics. God is the one perfect Being in which all possibility is at the same time actuality.

Physics is called by Aristotle 'second philosophy,' and considers existence, so far as in motion, actual, sensible reality.

Aristotle's moral philosophy is included in the *Ethics* and *Politics*, which are to be taken as complementary works. In the *Ethics* is discussed the formation of individual character, taking the individual as a social and political being. The knowledge thus acquired, however, is mere theory; it is through the State that the best and happiest life is possible (*Politics*). Ethics investigates the supreme good at which the individual aims in all his actions. This is Happiness, which consists in an active life in conformity with reason. Such a life is possible through the attaining of virtue. The production through the state of the virtuous life of the citizen is discussed in the *Politics*.

In his *Rhetoric* Aristotle handles the art of persuasion; while in his fragment of the *Poetics*, dealing with the subject of tragedy, his pronouncements — *e.g.* on the 'Unities'—have largely influenced all later literary criticism.

[*Aristotle*, by W. D. Ross (1923).]

A'rius (*d.* 336), famous theologian; presbyter of Alexandria; from him Arian controversy took its name. According to Arius, the Son was a created being, hence not in orthodox sense 'perfect God.' Arius was excommunicated, 325, at Council of Nicæa; his heresy lived on till 7th cent.

Ark'wright, SIR RICHARD (1732–92), Eng. inventor; *b.* Preston; apprenticed to barber; took great interest in machinery used in manufacture of cotton; invented the spinning-frame, and made other improvements in processes of carding and spinning; established mills at Nottingham, and at Cromford (Derbyshire).

Ar'lington, HENRY BENNET, EARL OF (1618–85), Eng. statesman; *b.* Arlington, Middlesex; served on Royalist side in Civil War; at Restoration became keeper of privy purse, 1661;

secretary of state, 1662; created Earl of Arlington, 1672. On fall of Clarendon, 1667, he became a member of Cabal; impeached, 1674; resigned and became lord chamberlain. Arlington's personal character was selfish, and his public conduct that of an intriguer.

Ar'liss, GEORGE (1868–), Eng. actor and film actor; *b.* London; specializes in historical parts, as in Disraeli, Duke of Wellington, etc.

Arm'felt, GUSTAF MAURITZ (1757-1814), Swed. statesman and soldier; *b.* Åbo, Finland; fought with distinction against Russia, 1790; became a Russian subject after deposition of Gustavus IV.; was first gov.-gen. of Finland, 1812–13.

Armin, FRIEDRICH, SIXT VON (1851–1919), Ger. general; fought in Franco-German War; during Great War received surrender of Brussels, Aug. 1914; commanded an army in Somme battles, 1916; strongly opposed Allies at Passchendaele, 1918, and in offensive on Lys R., 1918; murdered at Asch by mob after Armistice.

Armin'ius, HERMANN (17 B.C.–A.D. 21), Ger. national hero; annihilated three legions of Romans under Quintilius Varus in the Teutoburger Wald; eventually defeated by Germanicus; exploits much used in Ger. literature.

Arminius, JACOBUS (1560–1609), Dutch religious leader; *b.* Oudewater, Holland; founder of Arminian school of theology, representing a revolt against the strict ideas of Calvin. He maintained that every man could be regenerated and saved if he would.

[*Life*, by Brandt (Eng. trans., 1854).]

Ar'mitage, EDWARD (1817–96), Eng. historical and mural painter; *b.* London; painted frescoes for the House of Lords, 1845 and 1847; A.R.A., 1867; R.A., 1872. Among his many pictures are *The Guards at Inkermann, The Battle of Meeanee,* and *The Spirit of Religion.*

Armour, PHILIP DANFORTH (1832–1901), U.S.A. merchant; *b.* Stockbridge, N.Y.; head of great pork-packing firm of Chicago. Noted philanthropist.

Armstrong, WILLIAM GEORGE, 1ST BARON (1810–1900), Eng. inventor, manufacturer, and philanthropist; *b.* Newcastle-on-Tyne; founded the Elswick Works, 1847; was engineer of rifled ordnance at Woolwich, 1859–63; made a free gift to nation of valuable patents; obtained water supply for his native town (Newcastle), and was lavish in charity. Created baron, 1887.

Arnauld (*är-nō'*), ANTOINE (1612–94), 'le grand Arnauld,' Fr. philosopher; connected with the convent of Port Royal; identified himself with religious doctrines of Jansen; author of *Port Royal Logic.*

Arnault (*är-nō'*), ANTOINE VINCENT (1766–1834), Fr. playwright and fabulist; *b.* Paris; for Napoleon he wrote a drama, *Scipion Consul* (1804), but recanted in *Germanicus* (1816). Best known for short poems, *Fables et Poésies* (1826).

Arndt (*ärnt*), ERNST MORITZ (1769–1860), Ger. poet and patriot; *b.* Schoritz, isl. of Rügen; was instrumental in abolition of serfdom, 1806. Prof. of modern history at Bonn, 1818; rector of univ., 1841. Was poet-laureate of War of Liberation; his patriotic songs include *Was ist des deutschen Vaterland?* Also wrote *Der Geist der Zeit.*

Arne, THOMAS AUGUSTINE (1710–78), Eng. composer; *b.* London; son of an upholsterer; leader in the revival of the glee. Wrote music for the *Masque of Alfred,* which contains 'Rule Britannia,' for *As you Like It,* and some oratorios.

Arneth (*är'net*), Alfred, Count (1819–97), Austrian historian; *b.* Vienna; keeper of Austrian State Archives, 1868; wrote *Prince Eugene of Savoy* (1858–9), *History of Maria Theresa* (1863–79), etc.

Ar'nim, Elizabeth Mary. See Russell, Countess.

Ar'nim, Harry Karl Kurt Eduard, Count von (1824–81), Prussian diplomat; *b.* in Pomerania; ambassador to Vatican, 1867; conducted negotiations for Treaty of Frankfort, 1871; ambassador to Paris, 1872; sentenced to imprisonment for stealing correspondence from Paris embassy, but escaped.

Arnold of Brescia (1100–55), Ital. monk; probably pupil of Abelard; accused of heresy by St. Bernard; denounced the worldliness and wealth of higher clergy; finally condemned and executed.

Arnold of Winkelried. See Winkelried.

Arnold, Benedict (1741–1801), Amer. general; *b.* Norwich, Connecticut, U.S.A.; originally a merchant, joined patriotic party on outbreak of War of Independence; distinguished himself greatly in many engagements; appointed governor of Philadelphia, 1778; reprimanded for alleged misconduct, 1780; subsequently detected in attempt to surrender West Point; escaped, and became a Brit. brigadier-general.

[*Life*, by I. N. Arnold (1880).]

Arnold, Sir Edwin (1832–1904), Eng. poet and journalist; won Newdigate Prize with poem, *The Feast of Belshazzar* (1852); principal of Sanskrit Coll. at Poona, 1856–61; afterwards on editorial staff of *Daily Telegraph*; best known by his *Light of Asia* (1879), an epic poem dealing with life of Buddha.

Arnold, Matthew (1822–88), Eng. poet and critic; *b.* Laleham, near Staines; son of Dr. Arnold of Rugby; educated at Rugby, Winchester, and Oxford; won Newdigate Prize with *Cromwell* (1843); prof. of poetry, Oxford, 1857–67; inspector of schools, 1851–86. His poetical works are: *The Strayed Reveller* (1849), and *Empedocles on Etna* (1852); *Poems* (1853); *Poems*, 2nd Series (1855); *Merope* (1858); *New Poems* (1867). Among his prose works are: *On Translating Homer, Essays in Criticism, Culture and Anarchy, Literature and Dogma, God and the Bible.* His poetry is more remarkable for its finished workmanship than for inspiration. At the same time it is distinguished by a haunting and exquisite harmony, great clarity of thought and expression, and a sense of restfulness. As critic, Arnold is scarcely less eminent than as a poet, and his opinions, expressed in lucid and excellent prose, undoubtedly exercised a most stimulating influence on his time. His work represents very well one phase of the Victorian controversy between science and religion.

[Monographs by G. Saintsbury (1899) and H. W. Paul (1902); *Letters*, ed. by G. W. E. Russell (1895).]

Arnold, Thomas (1795–1842), public school reformer, and one of the greatest of Eng. schoolmasters; *b.* W. Cowes, Isle of Wight; headmaster of Rugby, 1828–41; appointed prof. of modern history at Oxford, 1841. His remarkable influence over his pupils is well depicted by T. Hughes in *Tom Brown's School Days.*

[*Life*, by Dean Stanley (1845).]

Arnott, Neil (1788–1874), Scot. physician, scientist, and philanthropist; *b.* Arbroath; inventor of the water-bed and other appliances; Scottish universities benefited largely by his generous gifts.

Ar'pad (*c.* 870–907), national

hero of Hungary; founder of the dynasty that ruled Hungary from 889 to 1301.

Arran, EARLS OF. (1) JAMES HAMILTON (1475–1529), son of James, Lord Hamilton, and Mary, daughter of James II. of Scotland, created Earl of Arran, 1503. (2) JAMES HAMILTON, 2ND EARL (1515–75), son of above; Regent of Scotland, 1542–54; in 1549 created Duc de Châtelherault by King of France; after supporting in turn Prot. England and Catholic France, he finally espoused Mary's cause. (3) JAMES HAMILTON (1537–1609), son of preceding, became a strong Prot.; in 1561 became insane.

Ar'rebo, ANDERS KRISTENSEN (1587–1637), famous Dan. poet; Bishop of Trondhjem; wrote the *Hexaëmeron*, a poem on the Six Days of Creation, which inaugurated a new era in Dan. poetry.

Arrhenius (*ar-ē'ni-us*), SVANTE AUGUST (1859–1927), Swed. scientist; *b.* near Uppsala; prof. of physics of Stockholm Univ., 1895, and rector, 1897–1902; director of Nobel Institute from 1905; awarded Nobel prize, 1903; one of the originators of the science of physical chemistry. Author of several works on chemistry and physics.

Arriag'a, MANOEL JOSÉ DE (1839–1917), Port. politician; *b.* Horta, Azores; first president of Port. republic, 1911–15.

Ar'rian, FLAVIUS (*c.* A.D. 96–180), Gr. historian and philosopher; consul under Antoninus; wrote famous history of Alexander the Great.

Ar'rol, SIR WILLIAM (1839–1913), Scot. engineer; *b.* Houston, Renfrewshire; worked as a smith in Paisley; builder of Tay and Forth Bridges, Tower Bridge, London, and Nile Bridge, Cairo.

Arrowsmith. (1) AARON (1750–1823), Eng. map-maker; his most noted maps were those of the world, N. America, Scotland, and S. India. (2) JOHN (1790–1873), geographer; nephew of above; a founder of the Royal Geographical Society, 1830; well-known *London Atlas* pub. 1834.

Arse'nius. (1) Surnamed the SAINT (*d.* 450), a noble and scholarly Roman, tutor to sons of Theodosius the Great; retired into the Egyptian desert as an anchorite. (2) Surnamed AUTORIANUS, patriarch of Constantinople, 1255, and guardian of John IV.; excommunicated the emperor for ordering John to be blinded.

Artaxer'xes, name borne by four anc. Pers. monarchs. (1) Surnamed LONGIMANUS (464–425 B.C.), famous in Jewish history; warred with Greeks of Asia Minor. (2) Surnamed MEMNON (405–362 B.C.); his younger brother Cyrus, assisted by Greeks, rebelled against him, but was killed at Cunaxa, 401; story of Gr. retreat narrated by Xenophon. (3) Surnamed OCHUS (362–339 B.C.); reconquered Cyprus, Egypt, and Phœnicia by means of Gr. troops. (4) Founder of Sassanid dynasty (A.D. 226–40); waged war against Emperor Severus.

Artemido'rus. (1) Of Ephesus (*c.* 100 B.C.); geographer who compiled a work on general geography (now lost) drawn upon by Strabo. (2) Rom. soothsayer, time of Hadrian; wrote book on dreams.

Artemis'ia. (1) Queen of Halicarnassus (*fl.* 480 B.C.); fought in sea fight of Salamis. (2) Queen (*fl.* 353–350 B.C.), wife of Mausolus, King of Caria, built the mausoleum at Halicarnassus, one of Seven Wonders of the World.

Art'emus Ward. See BROWNE, C. F.

Artevelde (*är'te-vel-de*). (1) JACOB VAN (*c.* 1290–1345), Flem. patriot; *b.* Ghent; a brewer; tried to bring about union of provinces which afterwards became Belgium; killed in a street brawl. (2) PHILIP VAN (1340–82), son of above, military leader; killed at Roosebeke, 1382.

Arthur, KING (6th cent.), Brit. king, the actual facts of whose life are almost lost in legend. He is said to have been the son of Uther Pendragon. He was probably half-Roman, and chosen by the Christian Britons as general (*c.* A.D. 520) against the Saxons, whom he defeated; afterwards he fought the heathen Britons, and was betrayed and slain. After his death Arthur became a hero of Celtic legend in Cornwall, Wales, Cumberland, and Scotland, and in later centuries France and Germany added elements to the growing romance. Sir Thomas Malory collected the Arthurian cycle into his *Morte d'Arthur* (1470).

Arthur, DUKE OF CONNAUGHT. See CONNAUGHT.

Arthur, CHESTER ALAN (1830–86), 21st president (Republican) of U.S.A.; *b.* Fairfield, Vermont; successful lawyer; took part in Civil War; succeeded Garfield, 1881; term of office marked by tariff legislation, prohibition of polygamy in the territories, railway enterprise, and exposure of postal frauds.

Arthur, SIR GEORGE COMPTON ARCHIBALD (1860–), English soldier; served in Egyptian and S. African campaigns; private secretary to Lord Kitchener, 1914–16. Author of biographies of Kitchener, Wolseley, and Haig.

Artsybashev, MIKHAIL (1878–1927), Russian novelist and short story writer. *Sanin*, *The Breaking Point*, *Jealousy*, and a play, *War*, are among his works.

Ar'undel, THOMAS (1353–1414), Eng. churchman and politician; Bishop of Ely, 1374; Archbishop of York, 1388; Archbishop of Canterbury, 1396; five times Lord Chancellor of England. A great opponent of the Lollards.

A'sa, King of Judah (*c.* 918–877 B.C.); opposed to idolatry (1 Kings 15; 1 Chron. 14–16).

Asbjörnsen (*äs-byern'sen*), PETER CHRISTIAN (1812–85), Norweg. folklorist; *b.* Oslo; professionally a zoologist; was commissioner of woods and forests, 1856–76. His fame rests on his *Norwegian Popular Stories*.

Asbury, FRANCIS (1745–1816), Methodist churchman; *b.* Handsworth, Staffs; sent by Wesley as missionary to America; first Methodist bishop in U.S.A., 1784; did much to extend Methodism. Wrote a *Journal*.

[*Life*, by Asbury (1927).]

Ascham (*as'kam*), ROGER (1515–68), scholar, educator, and prose writer; *b.* Kirkby Wiske, Yorkshire; prof. of Greek at St. John's, Cambridge, 1540; wrote *Toxophilus* (1545), treating of archery; presented it to Henry VIII., who made him tutor to Princess Elizabeth; Latin secretary to Edward VI., Mary, and Elizabeth. Chief work, *The Scholemaster* (1570), treatise on education, commending gentleness rather than severity.

Asclepiades (*äs-kle-pī'a-dēz*). (1) Native of Bithynia; successful physician at Rome (beginning of Christian era); regarded as founder of Methodical School of Medicine. (2) Of Samos; lyric poet (*fl. c.* 270 B.C.); wrote epigrams; Asclepiadean metre possibly named after him.

Ashbourne (*ash'burn*), EDWARD GIBSON, 1ST BARON (1837–1913), Irish lawyer; *b.* Dublin; attorney-general for Ireland, 1877–80; three times lord chancellor of Ireland; associated with Land Purchase Act of 1885.

Ash'burnham, JOHN (1603–71), confidential agent of Charles I.; treasurer and paymaster of Royalist army; was with the king in the Isle of Wight, 1647; unjustly suspected of betraying the king's whereabouts; groom of the chamber after the Restoration.

Ashbur'ton, ALEXANDER BARING, 1ST BARON (second creation) (1774–1848), Eng. financier and politician; head of Baring Brothers' bank, 1810; M.P. for nearly thirty years; president of Board of Trade, 1834; peer, 1835; negotiated Ashburton Treaty for settling boundary between Canada and Maine, suppressing slave trade, etc.

Ashburton, JOHN DUNNING, 1ST BARON (1731–83), Eng. lawyer and politician; *b.* Ashburton, Devonshire; famous for defence of John Wilkes; solicitor-general, 1767–70; peer, 1782.

Ashley, SIR WILLIAM JAMES (1860–1927), Eng. economist; *b.* London; prof. of commerce, Birmingham Univ., 1901–25, and vice-principal, 1918–25. Member of numerous committees and Royal Commissions on industrial affairs, 1915–24. Author of many studies in economics.

Ashmead-Bartlett, ELLIS (1881–1931), war correspondent in Gallipoli campaign; wrote *Dispatches from Dardanelles* (1915) and *Tragedy of Central Europe* (1925).

Ash'mole, ELIAS (1617–92), Eng. antiquary; *b.* Lichfield; son of a saddler; educated at Oxford; founder of the Ashmolean Museum, Oxford; studied astrology; pub. *Theatrum Chymicum Britannicum*, *The Way to Bliss* (dealing with the 'philosopher's stone'), and a *History of the Order of the Garter*.

Aske, ROBERT (*d.* 1537), Eng. lawyer, leader of 'Pilgrimage of Grace,' 1536; disbanded his troops under fair promises; imprisoned and executed.

Askew (*as'kū*), ANNE (1521–46), Eng. Prot. martyr; *b.* Stallingborough, Lincoln; arrested for heresy, tried, racked, burnt at the stake.

Askew, CLAUDE ARTHUR CARY and ALICE, Eng. joint authors. Wrote many novels, including *The Shulamite*. Both drowned in Mediterranean when returning from Serbia, 1917, through submarine attack.

Askwith, GEORGE RANKEN, 1ST BARON (1861–), Eng. arbitrator; became chief industrial commissioner of the Board of Trade, 1911–19; acted as conciliator in numerous trade disputes; K.C.B., 1911; chairman of numerous arbitration and other committees; peerage, 1919.

Aso'ka, great Indian emperor of 'Peacock' dynasty (reigned *c.* 270 to 230 B.C.); adopted Buddhism and spread its doctrines by missionaries; carved edicts on stone pillars and rocks still extant.

Aspa'sia (*fl.* 5th cent. B.C.), most famous of Gr. courtesans; *b.* Miletus; woman of great charm; became mistress of Pericles, whom she instructed in oratory; their son legitimized. Charged with impiety and immorality, but acquitted by pleading of Pericles.

Asquith. See OXFORD AND ASQUITH.

Asseman'i. (1) JOSEPH SIMON (1687–1768), Syrian Orientalist; ed. and pub. many of the choicest MSS. in the Vatican Library, of which he was librarian. (2) SIMON (1752–1820), grandnephew of above; prof. of Oriental languages, Padua; detected spurious nature of Vella's history of the Saracens.

Asser (*d.* 909), Bishop of Exeter, and of Sherborne; friend, helper, and biographer of Alfred the Great. His *Life of Alfred* first printed in 1572.

Assisi, ST. FRANCIS OF. See FRANCIS.

Assollant (*äs-sō-lon'*), JEAN BAPTISTE ALFRED (1827–86), Fr. author; *b.* Aubusson; wrote lively and humorous novels. His *Aventures Merveilleuses du Capitaine Corcoran* (1867), and his *Histoire Fantastique du Célèbre Pierrot*, are well known.

As'sur-bani-pal (Gr. *Sardanapalus*), Assyrian king; grandson of Sennacherib; he subdued revolted provinces, but lost Egypt, 660. His brother (Babylonian king) declared war, but Babylon was starved into surrender, 648 B.C. When Assur-bani-pal died, *c.* 626, his empire was already decaying.

Aston, FRANCIS WILLIAM (1877–), Brit. chemist; *b.* Birmingham; research worker in physics and chemistry; Nobel prize (chemistry), 1922. In addition to numerous scientific papers wrote *Isotopes* (1922).

As'tor, famous Amer. family of Ger. origin, founded by (1) JOHN JACOB (1763–1848); *b.* Heidelberg; son of a butcher; fur trader; made fortune in real estate in New York, estimated at £6,000,000. (2) WILLIAM BACKHOUSE (1792–1875), eldest son of above, known as 'landlord of New York.' (3) JOHN JACOB (1822–90), son of (2). (4) JOHN JACOB (1864–1912), great-grandson of the founder of the family; served in the Philippines; drowned in the *Titanic* disaster. (5) WILLIAM WALDORF, 1ST VISCOUNT (1848–1919), only son of (3); *b.* New York; settled in England; bought the *Pall Mall Gazette* and *Pall Mall Magazine*; during Great War gave munificently to war funds; created baron, 1916; left £50,000,000. (6) WALDORF ASTOR, 2ND VISCOUNT (1879–), eldest son of (5); *b.* New York; educated Eton and Oxford; Parliament, 1910–17; under secretary to Local Government Board and to Ministry of Health, 1919–21; owner of *Observer*. (7) NANCY WITCHER, VISCOUNTESS (1879–), wife of (6); *b.* Mirador, Virginia; won her husband's former seat (Plymouth), 1919; first woman to sit in Brit. Parliament.

Astor'ga, EMANUELE, BARON D' (1681–1736), Ital. composer *b.* Naples; chiefly known for his *Stabat Mater* and for his chamber cantatas.

Atahualpa (*ä-tä-wäl'pä*) (*c.* 1502–33), last Inca of Peru; inherited Quito from father; wrested remainder of kingdom from his half-brother Huascar, 1532; treacherously captured by the Spaniards; strangled by order of Pizarro.

Athan'aric (*d.* 381), Prince of Visigoths; driven from mountains of Dacia by the Huns; took service with Theodosius, 381, at Constantinople.

Athana'sius, ST. (*c.* 296–373), Bishop of Alexandria, 328; sided actively against Arius in Arian controversy; was banished for refusing to readmit Arius to communion, 335; returned, 337, but was deposed on religious and political grounds, 339. Although pronounced guiltless by the Great Council or Synod at Rome, 340, he was not restored till 349. On three further occasions he suffered exile, but from 366 he continued his episcopal labours uninterruptedly. He left several writings. A zealous defender of the Nicene faith, of heroic if imperious character and great intellectual powers, his title, 'Father of Greek Orthodoxy,' is deservedly conferred.

[*Life*, by Bush (1888).]

Ath'elstan (895–940), Eng. king, 924; son of Edward the Elder, grandson of Alfred; won battle of Brunanburh, 937; gave England prestige on the Continent by marrying his sisters to European princes.

Athenæ'us, Gr. rhetorician (2nd cent.), wrote *Deipnosophistæ*, a dialogue dealing with a great variety of subjects connected with social life.

Athenag'oras (*fl.* 2nd cent. A.D.), Gr. apologist for Christianity; *b.* Athens; wrote *Legatio pro*

Christianis (177), defending Christians and attacking paganism.

Atherstone, William Guybon (1813–98), S. African geologist and medical practitioner. He discovered the diamond-bearing formations near Vaal R. and Kimberley.

Atherton, Gertrude Franklin (1859–), Amer. novelist; *b.* San Francisco; most recent of many works: *The Immortal Marriage* (1927), *Vengeful Gods* (1928), *The Sophisticates* (1931), *Adventures of a Novelist* (1932).

Athlone, Rt. Hon. Earl of, Alexander Augustus Frederick William Alfred George Cambridge (1874–); *b.* Kensington Palace; brother of Queen Mary; formerly Prince Alexander of Teck; relinquished this title, 1917; served in S. African and Great Wars; gov.-gen. of Union of S. Africa, 1923–31; governor of Windsor Castle, 1931.

Ath'oll, John George Stewart Murray, 8th Duke of (1871–), raised and commanded Scot. Horse in S. African War; commanded the regiment during the Great War. Only Brit. subject allowed to maintain a private regiment, the Atholl Highlanders. Katharine Marjory, wife of above; daughter of Sir J. H. Ramsay; m.p. for Kinross and West Perth since 1923; secretary to Board of Education, 1924–29.

Atos'sa (*fl.* 6th–5th cent. b.c.), Queen of Persia, daughter of Cyrus the Great, and wife successively of Cambyses (her brother), Smerdis, and Darius Hystaspis. Said to have been murdered by her son Xerxes.

At'talus, three kings of Pergamum, all allies of the Romans. (1) Soter (*r.* 241–197 b.c.) fought against Philip v. of Macedon. (2) Philadelphus (*r.* 159–138 b.c.) overthrew Prusias of Bithynia. (3) Philometor (*r.* 138–133 b.c.) left his kingdom to the Romans (prov. of Asia).

At'terbom, Peter Daniel Amadeus (1790–1855), great poet of Swed. romantic school; *b.* Asbo, E. Gothland; prof. of philosophy at Uppsala, 1828, and of literature, 1835. His dramatic poem, *The Fortunate Island*, contains some of the lyrics for which he was specially renowned.

At'terbury, Francis (1662–1732), Eng. politician and writer; *b.* Milton, Bucks; royal chaplain, 1691; supported High Church party; prominent in trial of Sacheverell, whose defence is attributed to him, 1710; Bishop of Rochester, 1713. After accession of George i. plotted in favour of Pretender; imprisoned, 1723, and finally exiled; *d.* Paris; buried, privately, in Westminster Abbey.

At'tila (*c.* 406–53), King of the Huns, known as the 'Scourge of God'; son of Mundzuk; put his brother Bleda to death, 444, and reigned alone; greatly extended his original kingdom (modern Hungary and Transylvania); overran Greece, Thrace, and Macedon, and made himself supreme from the Rhine to the Caspian; invaded Gaul, 451; defeated with great slaughter near site of Châlons-sur-Marne by Romans under Aëtius, and Visigoths under Theodoric. In 452 devastated northern Italy and threatened Rome, which was only saved by the appeal of Pope Leo i.; died on the night of his marriage.

[*Attila and the Huns*, by Hutton (1915).]

Attwood, Thomas (1765–1838), Eng. composer; organist of St. Paul's Cathedral, 1796; anthems, songs, glees, and coronation odes.

Atwood, George (1746–1807), Eng. mathematician; *b.* London; invented machine for demonstrating laws of falling bodies.

Auber (*o-bār'*), Daniel François Esprit (1782–1871), Fr. composer; *b.* Caen; his sparkling operas achieved world-wide popularity; best are: *Le Maçon* (1825), *Masaniello* (1828), *La Fiancée* (1829), *Fra Diavolo* (1830), *Le Domino Noir* (1837), *Les Diamants de la Couronne* (1841); over forty others.

Aubignac (*ō-bē-nyac'*), FRANÇOIS HÉDELIN, ABBÉ D' (1604–76), Fr. dramatist; *b.* Paris; was some time tutor to a nephew of Cardinal Richelieu. Wrote four tragedies and a treatise, *Pratique du Théâtre* (1657), laying down the 'Unities.'

Aubigné (*ō-bē-nyā'*), THÉODORE AGRIPPA D' (1550–1630), Fr. poet and historian; a militant Huguenot; friend of Henry of Navarre; famous for his *Mémoires*, his great epic, *Les Tragiques*, and his *Histoire Universelle.*

Au'brey, JOHN (1626–97), Eng. antiquary; *b.* near Malmesbury, Wilts; supplied Anthony à Wood with much quaint antiquarian information for the latter's *Athenæ Oxonienses.*

Aubusson (*ō-bu-son'*), PIERRE D' (1423–1503), Fr. soldier of fortune; served under Emperor Sigismund; joined Knights Hospitallers of St. John of Jerusalem; grand master, 1476; defended Rhodes against Turks, 1479; cardinal, 1489.

Audouin (*ō-doo-an'*), JEAN VICTOR (1797–1841), Fr. naturalist; *b.* Paris; prof. of entomology, Paris, 1833; wrote (with Milne-Edwards) *Histoire des Insectes nuisibles à la Vigne.*

Audran (*ō-dran'*), EDMOND (1842–1901), Fr. composer; *b.* Lyons; his light comic operas are well known, and include *La Cigale* and *La Poupée.*

Audubon (*äu'dū-bon*), JOHN JAMES (1780–1851), Amer. naturalist; *b.* Haiti; son of Fr. naval officer; founded Audubon Park in New York, and pub. *Birds* of *America.*

Auenbrugger von Auenbrugg (*ow-en-broog'er*), LEOPOLD (1722–1809), Austrian physician; *b* Graz; introduced method o diagnosing chest and abdomina diseases by percussion.

Auerbach (*ow'er-bach*), BERTHOLD (1812–82), Ger. novelist *b.* Nordstetten, Black Forest; o Jewish parentage; widely know for stories dealing with Blac Forest; was an authority o Spinoza.

Aufrecht (*owf'recht*), THEODO (1822–1907), Ger. philologist; *b* Leschnitz, Upper Silesia; catalogued Sanskrit MSS. in Bodleia Library; prof. of Sanskrit, Edinburgh, 1862–75, and Ind. languag and literature, Bonn, 1875–89; ed several Sanskrit classics.

Augereau (*ōzh-rō'*), PIERR FRANÇOIS CHARLES, DUC DE CASTIGLIONE (1757–1816), Fr. marshal *b.* Paris; distinguished himsel under Napoleon; made submission to Bourbons.

Augier (*ō-zhē-ā'*), GUILLAUM VICTOR EMILE (1820–89), Fr dramatist; *b.* Valence, Drôme writer of comedies distinguishe for their wholesome didacticism—*e.g. Gabrielle, La Ciguë, Le gendr de M. Poirier.*

Au'gustine, ST. (*d.* 612–14) first Archbishop of Canterbury apostle of Christianity to England sent by Pope Gregory I.; lande at Thanet, 597; converted Æthelbert of Kent; archbishop, 601 ranks high for monastic rathe than for missionary zeal.

Augustine, ST., OF HIPPO (354–430), one of the greatest Christian saints; *b.* in Numidia; son of a Christian mother, Monica, but himself a pagan till 387. His conversion to Christianity was the result of a gradual process of passing through not only intellectual and spiritual but moral conflicts. In 387 he was baptized; in 396 became Bishop of Hippo in N. Africa. His works are very voluminous—his *Confessions*, wherein he recounts his own experience; *De Civitate Dei*, in which he repels the attacks on Christianity made by paganism; his *De Trinitate* and commentary on St. John. His work has probably had a larger influence on the Church than that of any other single saint or theologian.

[*The Confessions of Augustine*, by Gibb and Montgomery (1899), and *The Letters of St. Augustine*, by Sparrow-Simpson (1919).]

Augustulus, ROMULUS, last emperor to rule in Rome; deposed and exiled, A.D. 476, when Odoacer conquered Italy.

Augus'tus Cæsar, GAIUS JULIUS CÆSAR OCTAVIANUS (63 B.C.–A.D. 14); *b.* Rome; son of Gaius Octavius and Atia, niece of Julius Cæsar, who adopted him, and subsequently declared him his heir; sent to Apollonia to be educated under Apollodorus, where the news reached him of Cæsar's murder, 44 B.C.; went to Rome and professed republican principles; subsequently threw in his lot with Antony and Lepidus, and formed the triumvirate, 43 B.C. With Antony he defeated Brutus and Cassius at Philippi, 42 B.C. Differences subsequently arising between the triumvirs, the empire was divided, Augustus taking the west, Antony the east, and Lepidus receiving Africa. Augustus deposed Lepidus, and making war on Antony, who had repudiated his wife, Octavia (sister of Augustus), defeated him at Actium, 31 B.C. He now became supreme ruler of the entire Rom. Empire, but restored the form of the republic, and achieved marked popularity by his reform of abuses, and of the administration of the provinces; cognomen Augustus conferred, 27 B.C. His later years were marked by brilliant victories in Asia, Spain, Gaul, and other places, but his army suffered a crushing defeat under Varus, in Germany, A.D. 9. Besides being one of the greatest statesmen the world has seen, Augustus did much to improve and beautify Rome. It was said that he found the city brick and left it marble. Amongst the great authors who adorned his reign were Virgil, Horace, Ovid, Tibullus, and Livy.

[*Augustus Cæsar* ('Heroes of the Nations' Series), by Firth (1903); *The Architect of the Roman Empire*, by Rice-Holmes (1928).]

Aulnoy (*ō-nwŏ'*), MARIE CATHERINE, COMTESSE D' (1650–1705), Fr. writer of novels, memoirs, and fairy stories; *b.* near Bourg-Achard, Eure; served France as secret agent; chiefly remembered for *Contes des Fées.*

Aulus Gellius. See GELLIUS, AULUS.

Aumale (*ō-mäl'*), HENRI EUGÈNE PHILIPPE LOUIS D'ORLÉANS, DUC D' (1822–97), Fr. administrator; fourth son of King Louis Philippe; *b.* Paris; served with distinction in Algeria, becoming governor in 1847; inspector-general of army in 1879.

Aurangzeb. See AURUNGZEBE.

Aure'lian, L. DOMITIUS AURELIANUS (*c.* 214–275), Rom. Emperor; *b.* Sirmium, Pannonia, of humble parents; general of Emperor Claudius II.; succeeded him as emperor, 270; ended Gothic War, resigning Dacia to Goths; secured the Rhine and Danube frontiers; destroyed Zenobia's monarchy; restored unity of empire, and began the rebuilding and enlargement of the walls of Rome; assassinated.

Aurelius, MARCUS (121–180), Rom. emperor and Stoic; *b.* Rome; original name, Marcus Annius Verus; adopted by his uncle, Antoninus Pius, emperor; educated by Stoic teachers; consul, 140; emperor, 161, with Verus as colleague; reign marked by various disasters—flood, famine, earthquakes, plagues, insurrections;

Parthian War concluded, 165; war against Marcomanni tribe, 168, 169; defeated Quadi, 174, and other Ger. tribes; put down insurrections in various provinces; pacified Syria; returned to Rome via Athens, 176; had 'triumph' for Ger. victories; again warred against Ger. tribes, 178, but died during campaign; has been blamed for share in persecution of Christians, 177. Although opposed to Christianity, his reign was distinguished by his care for the public morals, his humanitarian legislation regarding slaves, orphans, and gladiatorial shows, and his effective administration generally; wrote celebrated *Meditations*.

Auris'pa, GIOVANNI (*c.* 1369–1459), Ital. scholar; *b.* Noto, Sicily; brought many valuable Gr. MSS. from Constantinople, which are now preserved in Florence; did much to promote study of Greek.

Aurungzebe (*au'rung-zēb'*) (1618–1707), last great Mogul emperor; third son of Shah Jehan; deposed and imprisoned his father, 1658, and assassinated his two brothers; moved seat of government to Delhi; annexed Golconda and Bijapur; reign marked zenith of Mogul power, but internal decay and growing power of Mahrattas, led by Sivaji, brought about disintegration of the great empire.

Auso'nius, called DECIMUS MAGNUS (*c.* A.D. 310–395), poet of Rom. Gaul; *b.* Bordeaux; most interesting extant work is *Mosella.*

Au'sten, JANE (1775–1817), Eng. novelist; *b.* Steventon, Hants. Of her six novels, four were pub. anonymously: *Sense and Sensibility* (1811), *Pride and Prejudice* (1813), *Mansfield Park* (1814), *Emma* (1816); *Persuasion* and *Northanger Abbey* appeared posthumously (1818), with memoir and author's name. General recognition of her genius has come only in more recent years, though Scott, Tennyson, Coleridge, and Macaulay were enthusiastic admirers. Her characters are drawn from upper-class Eng. life. She shows remarkable gifts of humour and satire, and exquisite discernment of the workings of the feminine mind.

[*Life* ('English Men of Letters' Series), by Cornish (1913).]

Au'stin, ALFRED (1835–1913), Eng. poet; *b.* Headingley, Yorks; educated for the bar, but became leader-writer for the *Standard.* First successful work, *The Season: a Satire* (1861). Created poet-laureate, 1896. His most enduring work is contained in such prose volumes as *The Garden that I Love* (1894), and *In Veronica's Garden* (1895).

Austin, SIR HERBERT (1866–), Brit. manufacturer; *b.* Little Missenden, Bucks; a pioneer in the manufacture of light motor cars.

Austin, JOHN (1790–1859), Eng. jurist; *b.* Ipswich; served first in the army; was afterwards called to the bar, 1818; prof. of jurisprudence, Univ. Coll., London, 1826; greatest Eng. writer on science of law; founded modern school of analytical jurisprudence. Works: *The Province of Jurisprudence Determined* and *Lectures on Jurisprudence.*

Austin, SARAH (1793–1867), translator, wife of above, trans. Ranke's *History of the Popes* (1840); wrote *Germany from 1760 to 1814*; ed. her husband's *Lectures on Jurisprudence,* her daughter's (Lady Duff Gordon) *Letters from Egypt,* and *Memoirs of Sydney Smith.*

Autol'ycus OF PITANE (*c.* 300 B.C.), Gr. astronomer and mathematician, two of whose works are in Bodleian Library, Oxford.

Auwers (*ow'verz*), ARTHUR (1838–1915), Ger. astronomer; *b.* Göttingen; director of observatory at Potsdam.

Avebury (*ā'ber-i*), JOHN LUBBOCK,

1st Baron (1834–1913), Eng. banker, politician, and scientist; sat in Parliament for Maidstone and for London Univ.; vice-chancellor of latter; author of *Ants, Bees, and Wasps*; *Pleasures of Life*, etc. Among other measures was mainly instrumental in passing Bank Holidays Act, 1871.

Avellaneda (*ä-vä-lyä-nä'thä*), Gertrudis Gomez de (1816–73), Span. poetess, novelist, and dramatist; *b.* in Cuba; pen-name La Peregrina. Works: *Poesias Liricas*, *Dolores*, Biblical dramas, etc.

Averes'cu, Alexander (1859–), Romanian soldier; *b.* Ismail; fought against Turkey, 1877–8; military attaché at Berlin, 1895–8; minister of war, 1907; during war with Bulgaria, 1913, acted as chief of the general staff. Soon after Romania's entry into the Great War, 1916, he took supreme command of Romanian forces. Prime minister, 1918 and 1920; resigned, 1921. President and founder of the People's party, 1918.

Averroes (*a-ver'ō-ez*) (1126–98), Arab. philosopher; *b.* Cordova; lived in Spain and Morocco. Chief work, *Commentaries on Aristotle*.

Avicen'na (980–1037), noted Arab. philosopher; *b.* in Bukhara; studied medicine and philosophy, especially Aristotle's *Metaphysics*; became vizier; his pleasure-loving life hastened his death. Best-known works: *Canon of Medicine* and *Al Shifa* (the Book of Recovery).

Avila (*ä'vē-lä*), Juan de (1502–69), Span. priest and mystical writer; the Apostle of Andalusia; associated with monastic reforms of St. Teresa; beatified, 1893.

Avogad'ro, Amadeo, Conte di Quaregna (1776–1856), Ital. physicist; *b.* Turin; prof. of physics, Turin Univ.; discovered *Avogadro's Law*, that equal volumes of different gases, at same pressure and temperature, contain the same number of molecules.

Ayal'a, Pedro Lopez de (1332–1407), Span. soldier, chronicler, and poet; *b.* Vittoria; captured by Black Prince at Najera, 1367; wrote *Chronicle* of the four Castilian kings under whom he lived.

Ayala, Ramón Pérez de (1881–), Span. author and diplomatist; *b.* Oviedo; noted poet, novelist, and critic. Ambassador to Great Britain, 1931. Among works are *La Paz del Sendero* (1903), *Belarmino y Apolonio* (1921), *Luna de Miel* (1923), and *El Ombligo del Mundo* (1924).

Ayala y Herre'ra, Adelardo Lopez de (1828–79), Span. politician and dramatist; *b.* Guadalcanal; took part in revolution of 1868, but later joined Alfonso xii.'s cabinet; wrote many plays and some lyrical poetry.

Aye'sha (*c.* 610–77), favourite wife of Mohammed; *b.* Medina; after the Prophet's death, 632, secured the succession of her father Abu Bekr; revered by all faithful Mohammedans.

Aylesford (*ālz'ford*), Heneage Finch, 1st Earl of (1649–1719), Eng. lawyer; solicitor-gen.; was counsel for King James in trial of Titus Oates for libel.

Ayres, John (*fl.* 1680–1700), Eng. calligraphist; introduced Ital. script; dedicated book, *The Writing-Master*, to William iii.

Ayrton, William Edward (1847–1908), Eng. physicist; *b.* London; invented electrical measuring instruments. Hertha (1854–1923), wife of above, also a scientist; author of numerous scientific papers; discoverer of causes of sand-ripples on seashore; inventor of anti-gas fan used during Great War; only woman member of Institution of Electrical Engineers.

Ayscough (*ask'ew*), Samuel (1745–1804), Eng. librarian; *b.* Nottingham; called 'The Prince of Indexers'; was assistant librarian in Brit. Museum, 1785; had a large share in the 1787 Catalogue; indexed anc. rolls and charters; prepared Shakespeare Concordance.

Aytoun (*ā'ton*), WILLIAM EDMONDSTOUNE (1813–65), Scot. poet; *b.* Edinburgh; wrote *Lays of the Scottish Cavaliers*; part author of *Bon Gaultier Ballads* with Sir Theodore Martin; prof. of rhetoric at Edinburgh Univ., 1845; sheriff of Orkney, 1852; wrote many political articles for *Blackwood's Magazine.*

Azeglio (*äd-zāl'yō*), MASSIMO TAPARELLI, MARQUIS D' (1798–1866), Ital. statesman, landscape painter, and author; *b.* Turin; pub. two historical novels; was premier under Victor Emmanuel II.; urged the unification of Italy.

Azuni (*äd-zu'nē*), DOMENICO ALBERTO (1749–1827), Ital. jurist; *b.* in Sardinia; director of Univ. library, Cagliari; wrote book on European maritime law.

B

Bab'bage, CHARLES (1791–1871), Eng. mathematician; designed calculating machine which was never finished; prof. of mathematics at Cambridge; with Herschel and Peacock gave impulse to Eng. mathematical revival.

Baber ('the Tiger'), surname of ZAHIR UD-DIN MOHAMMED (1483–1530), famous Asiatic soldier; a descendant of Timur; conquered northern India, and founded Mogul dynasty.

Babeuf (*bä-boof'*), FRANÇOIS NOEL (1760–97), journalist and agitator during Fr. Revolution; engaged in plot to overthrow the Directory, and was guillotined.

Bab'ington, ANTHONY (1561–86), a Derbyshire gentleman who had been page to Mary Queen of Scots; headed R.C. plot to assassinate Elizabeth, and was executed.

Babrius (*bā'brē-us*) (*fl.* 3rd cent. A.D.), author of collection of fables written in Greek discovered in 1842 on Mt. Athos; MS. in Brit. Museum; source of our *Æsop's Fables.*

Bacchylides (*bä-kil'i-dēz*) (*fl.* 467 B.C.), Gr. lyric poet; nephew of Simonides; wrote many odes, elegies, and drinking songs.

Baccio d'Agnolo (*bä'cho d'an-yō'lo*) (1460–1543), Ital. wood carver, architect, and sculptor; did much carving for church of Santa Maria Novella and Palazzo Vecchio, Florence; architect of Bartolini Palace, Villa Borghese, and campanile of Santo Spirito.

Bach (*bäch*), JOHANN SEBASTIAN (1685–1750), Ger. composer; *b.* Eisenach, where his father was court and town musician. One of the greatest masters of music of all time. He had a thorough training as a musician at Lüneburg, and at eighteen became court musician at Weimar, and later was organist and concert director there, after holding appointments in Arnstadt and Mühlhausen. Before he was thirty he was considered the first organist of his time, and visited Ger. towns giving exhibitions of his wonderful skill on the organ. In 1723 Bach was made cantor at the Thomasschule in Leipzig, where he superintended the music in that church and in St. Nicholas. In later life he suffered from blindness. Bach composed a huge mass of music for secular and sacred purposes.

As a composer he did not come into his own until Mendelssohn abroad, and Dr. Samuel Wesley in England, made him known. His compositions for organ have seldom been equalled, never excelled. Fugues, toccatas, preludes, fantasias, and sonatas testify to his creative genius. His choral works include the *Christmas Oratorio*, the great *Mass in B Minor*, two Magnificats, five Passions, and five complete sets of cantatas. Bach summed up all that went before him and left no musical form as he found it.

Back, SIR GEORGE (1798–1878), Brit. admiral and Arctic explorer; *b.* Stockport; accompanied Franklin on his expeditions, 1819 and 1824; during the Ross Search Expedition discovered Back's or Great Fish R., 1834.

Back'haus, WILHELM (1884–), Ger. pianist, made a concert tour of the Continent and England, 1902–5, and America, 1912, as soloist with New York Symphony Orchestra; prof. of piano, Royal Coll. of Music, Manchester, since 1905.

Backhuysen (*bäk'hoi-zen*), LUDOLF (1631–1708), Dutch painter of sea-pieces, examples of whose works are in Berlin, Munich, Vienna, Paris, and in England.

Bacon, FRANCIS, BARON VERULAM AND VISCOUNT ST. ALBANS (1561–1626), Eng. lawyer, statesman, and philosopher; *b.* London; nephew of Lord Burghley. At twelve he entered Trinity Coll., Cambridge, and from 1576 practised law in Gray's Inn. As parliamentarian from 1584 he ranked high, alike for his judgment and his commanding charm of speech. In 1593 he offended the queen and her ministers by opposing them on important points of parliamentary procedure. From 1591 he was personal adviser of the young Earl of Essex, Burghley's rival at court, and from him received many favours. Burghley was not unfriendly to his nephew, and the queen gave him the reversion of the clerkship of the Star Chamber. On the trial of Essex for treason, Bacon as a queen's counsel had to assist in his prosecution.

In the reign of James I. he began to rise in public life. To James he dedicated his *Advancement of Learning* (1605). He became solicitor-general, 1607, attorney-general, 1613, lord keeper, 1617, lord chancellor and Baron Verulam, 1618. His greatest work, *Novum Organum* (*New Instrument*) (1620), powerfully advocates the free and ordered use of the mind. He became Viscount St. Albans in 1621, and in the same year charges of corruption were made against him by the Commons. He was found guilty, fined £40,000, and imprisoned in the Tower. After four days' imprisonment he was released; the fine was remitted; later he received a pardon and was granted a pension.

He devoted the remaining five years of his life to his *History of Henry VII.*, *Essays*, and *Apophthegms*. As a statesman he was extremely sagacious, and as a judge the most assiduous and faithful of his age. His work in philosophy and inductive science left a permanent mark on future study.

[*The Life and Letters of Lord Bacon*, by Spedding (1861–74); *Bacon* ('English Men of Letters'), by Dean Church (1884).]

Bacon, JOHN (1740–99), Eng. sculptor; chief works, the statues of Dr. Johnson and John Howard in St. Paul's, and of Lord Chatham in Westminster Abbey.

Bacon, SIR REGINALD HUGH SPENCER (1863–), Brit. admiral, a pioneer organizer of the naval torpedo service; in command of Dover patrol during the Great War.

Bacon, ROGER (1214–94), Eng. scientist and philosopher; *b.* near Ilchester; was a Franciscan friar; held that observation and experiment are first essentials of scientific discovery; is said to have invented gunpowder, and to have made a telescopic camera-obscura; constructed a magnifying glass and devised a rectified calendar; wrote *Opus Majus* (1265); bold ideas made him a suspect among eccles. authorities, and he was imprisoned, 1277–92.

Bacsanyi (*bŏ'chăn-yē*), JANOS (1763–1845), Hungarian poet and patriot, was embroiled in conspiracies, and was exiled; wrote *The Valour of the Magyars.*

Baden-Powell (*bā'den-poul*), ROBERT STEPHENSON, 1ST BARON (1857–), Brit. general; *b.* London; served in India and S. Africa; held Mafeking until its relief, 1900, and assisted in capture of Pretoria; established Boy Scouts, 1908, and Girl Guides, 1910; has written several books, chiefly on scouting.

Badham, CHARLES (1813–84), Eng. classical scholar; *b.* Ludlow; prof. of classics and logic at Sydney Univ., Australia; annotated editions of Plato and Euripides.

Badia y Lablich (*ba-dē'a ē lā-blēch*). See ALI BEY.

Baed'eker, KARL (1801–59), Ger. publisher; *b.* Essen; issued in 1839 the first of series of guide-books printed in German, French, and English, along lines of Murray's 'Handbooks'; these now deal with countries of the world most visited by tourists.

Baer, KARL ERNST VON (1792–1876), Russ. zoologist; *b.* Estonia; studied in Germany; held appointments in Königsberg and St. Petersburg (Leningrad); founder of science of comparative embryology.

Baeyer (*bā'yĕr*), JOHANN FRIEDRICH WILHELM ADOLPH VON (1835–1917), Ger. chemist; prof. of chemistry, Munich; researches in organic chemistry, especially on indigo; invented aspirin; Nobel prize in chemistry, 1905.

Baffin, WILLIAM (1584–1622), Eng. navigator; served as pilot in a Greenland voyage, 1612; spent two years in Spitsbergen whale fishing, 1613–14; pilot of *Discovery* in search of the N.W. Passage, 1615, when he surveyed Hudson's Strait; in following year discovered the bay which bears his name. He was killed at siege of Ormuz, 1622, helping the Persians against the Portuguese. Baffin was the first to attempt calculation of longitude by lunar observations. [*Voyages*, ed. by Sir C. R. Markham (1880).]

Bagehot (*baj'ot*), WALTER (1826–77), Eng. economist, journalist, critic, and banker; *b.* Langport, Somerset; called to bar, 1852, but entered his father's bank; ed. *The Economist* from 1860 until his death; notable works: *Physics and Politics* (1869), *The English Constitution* (1867), *Lombard Street* (1873), *Literary and Biographical Studies* (2 vols. 1879), and *Economic Studies* (1880). Distinguished for psychological insight and power of critical analysis.

Bag'gesen, JENS (1764–1826), Dan. lyrical poet; obtained education under adverse circumstances; attained great popularity with *Comical Tales* in verse when twenty-one; spent roving life; wrote with equal fluency in Danish and German; other works include *Labyrinthen* (1791), and pastoral poem, *Parthenais* (1803).

Bagration (*bă-gră-tē-ōn'*), PETER IVANOVITCH, PRINCE (1765–1812), Russ. general; distinguished himself at Austerlitz, 1805, Eylau and Friedland, 1807; captured the Åland Is. by march over ice, 1808; mortally wounded at Borodino.

Bahr, Hermann (1863–1934), Austrian playwright; *b.* Linz; one of leaders against naturalism in Ger. literature.

Baif (*ba-ēf'*), Jean Antoine de (1532–89), Fr. poet; *b.* Venice; friend of Ronsard; member of Pléiade; paraphrased Gr. and Lat. lyric poets; introduced classical forms into Fr. verse.

Baikie (*bā'ki*), William Balfour (1824–64), Scot. traveller and philologist; *b.* Kirkwall; surgeon and naturalist on Niger Expedition, 1854, and again in 1857, when he remained to explore, evangelize, and teach; trans. parts of Bible and Prayer Book into Hausa language.

Bailey (*bā'li*), Lieut.-Colonel Frederick Marshman (1882–), Scot. political officer and explorer; *b.* Edinburgh; took part in Tibet and Abor Expeditions; explored course of Brahmaputra in S. Tibet, 1913; minister plenipotentiary in Nepal since 1935.

Bailey, Nathan (*d.* 1742), Eng. lexicographer; a Seventh-Day Baptist; kept a boarding-house in Stepney; his *Universal Etymological English Dictionary* (1721) served as foundation for Johnson's later work.

Bailey, Philip James (1816–1902), Eng. poet; *b.* Nottingham; known as 'Festus Bailey' from his one long poem *Festus* (1839), a reconstruction of the Faust legend.

Bailey, Samuel (1791–1870), Eng. economic and philosophical writer; originally a cutler of Sheffield; wrote *Theory of Reasoning* (1851), and *Letters on the Philosophy of the Human Mind* (1856–63).

Bailey, Solon Irving (1854–1931), Amer. astronomer, prof. Harvard; founded observatory of Arequipa, Peru, 1889, and of El Misti, 1893, the highest in the world.

Baillet (*bä-yā'*), Adrien (1649–1706), Fr. scholar and critic; *b.* Neuville, in Picardy; wrote historical and antiquarian works.

Baillie, Lady Grizel (1665–1746), Covenanting heroine and song-writer; *b.* Berwickshire; daughter of Sir Patrick Hume, whom she secretly supplied with food in his hiding-place in the vault of Polwarth church; married a son of Scot. patriot Baillie of Jerviswoode; best-known song: 'Werena my heart licht I wad dee.'

Baillie, Joanna (1762–1851), Scot. dramatist and poet; *b.* Bothwell, Lanarkshire; life spent in London; chiefly remembered for her *Plays on the Passions* (1798), and Scot. songs.

Baillot (*bä-yō*), Pierre Marie François de Sales (1771–1842), Fr. violinist; *b.* and *d.* Paris; prof. in Conservatoire; his *Art du Violon* (1834) is a standard work.

Bailly (*bä-yē'*), Jean Sylvain (1736–93), Fr. astronomer and republican politician; *b.* Paris; pub. *Histoire de l'Astronomie* (1787); president of National Assembly, 1789; lost favour after 'Massacre of the Champ de Mars'; arrested and executed.

Baily, Edward Hodges (1788–1867), Eng. sculptor; *b.* Bristol; R.A., 1821; best works include statues of Wellington, Nelson (Trafalgar Square), etc., and sculptures on Marble Arch and in front of Buckingham Palace.

Baily, Francis (1774–1844), Eng. astronomer; *b.* Newbury; a founder of Royal Astronomical Soc., 1820; reformed *Nautical Almanac*; pioneer of modern solar eclipse expeditions; during eclipse, 1836, first noticed phenomenon known as 'Baily's Beads.'

Bain, Alexander (1818–1903), Scot. educationist and psychologist; *b.* Aberdeen; a weaver in early life, entered Marischal Coll., and became prof. of logic and English at Aberdeen, 1860; pub. *The Senses and the Intellect*, *The Emotions and the Will*, etc.

Baines, EDWARD (1774–1848), Leeds journalist; *b.* Walton-le-dale; as proprietor of *Leeds Mercury* established power of provincial press; advocated parl. reform and factory legislation.

Baird, SIR DAVID (1757–1829), Brit. general; *b.* E. Lothian; prisoner of Hyder Ali, 1780–4; stormed Seringapatam, 1799; commanded at capture of Cape Colony, 1806; was at siege of Copenhagen, 1807, and with Moore at Corunna, 1809.

Baird, JAMES (1802–76), Scot. coalowner and ironmaster at Gartsherrie, Lanarkshire; founded 'Baird Lectures' on theology, also 'Baird Trust for Church of Scotland.'

Baird, JOHN L. (1889–), Scot. inventor; *b.* Helensburgh; invented the Televisor by which scenes or objects may be transmitted by wire or wireless, and the Noctovisor, an apparatus for seeing in the dark.

Baird, SPENCER FULLERTON (1823–87), famous Amer. naturalist; secretary of Smithsonian Institution at Washington; commissioner of fisheries; author of *Birds of America*, etc.

Bairnsfather, BRUCE (1887–), humorist and war artist; *b.* in India; attained great popularity with *Fragments from France* (1915), humorous sketches of life in the trenches; also wrote popular play, *The Better 'Ole.*

Bajza (*boi'zo*), JOSEPH (1804–58), Hungarian poet and notable dramatic critic; director of National Theatre, Budapest.

Baker, SIR BENJAMIN (1840–1907), Eng. civil engineer; *b.* Frome, Somerset; was associated with Sir John Fowler in designing underground railways, the Forth Bridge, and other engineering enterprises; assisted in construction of Aswan barrage on R. Nile.

Baker, HENRY (1698–1774), Eng. naturalist and teacher of deaf mutes; *b.* London; assisted Defoe, his father-in-law, in the *Universal Spectator*; helped to found the Soc. of Arts; founder of Bakerian Lecture of the Royal Society.

Baker, SIR HERBERT (1862–), Eng. architect; *b.* Cobham, Kent; did much work in S. Africa, including Groote Schuur for Cecil Rhodes and Union Buildings at Pretoria; designed Legislative Buildings at New Delhi.

Baker, NEWTON DIEHL (1871–), U.S.A. lawyer and politician; *b.* Martinsburg, W. Virginia; war secretary in President Wilson's cabinet; organized Amer. forces during the Great War.

Baker. (1) SIR SAMUEL WHITE (1821–93), Eng. explorer; *b.* London; explored R. Atbara, traced course of White Nile, and discovered L. Albert; wrote *The Albert Nyanza* (1866), *Ismailia* (1874), etc. (2) VALENTINE (1827–87), known as BAKER PASHA; brother of (1); entered the Turk. service, and fought in Balkans, 1877; organized the Egyptian gendarmerie after the occupation of 1882; disastrously routed at El Teb, 1884, by the tribesmen of Osman Digna.

Bakewell, ROBERT (1725–95), Eng. agriculturist and breeder; best known for improving the Leicestershire breed of sheep, Dishley cattle, and farm-horses.

Bakst, LEON (1868–1924), Russ. painter; spent early life in St. Petersburg (Leningrad); famous as scene painter in Paris; designed settings for plays of D'Annunzio and Verhaeren.

Bakunin (*ba-koon'yēn*), MIKHAIL (1814–76), Russ. revolutionary; *b.* near Moscow; organized anarchical movements all over Europe; frequently extradited.

Balaguer (*bä-lä-gär'*), VICTOR

(1824–1901), Span. poet, historian, and politician; *b.* Barcelona; 'crowned,' 1843, for his *Don Enrique el Dadivoso*; Liberal leader, 1843–68; his writings stirred up Catalonian patriotism; held public offices, and became a senator.

Balakirev (*bä-lä'kēr-yef*), MILI ALEXEIEVITCH (1837–1910), Russ. musical composer; *b.* Nijni-Novgorod; with Lomakin he founded the Free School of Music in the interests of Russ. music; works include music to *King Lear* and *Islamey*; wrote many overtures.

Balard (*bä-lär'*), ANTOINE JÉRÔME (1802–76), Fr. chemist; *b.* Montpelier; discoverer of bromine, 1826; prof. of chemistry, Coll. de France, 1851.

Bal'bo, CESARE, COUNT (1789–1853), Ital. statesman and writer; *b.* Turin; employed by Napoleon in Paris and Rome; chief work, *Speranze d'Italia* (1843), advocating Ital. unity; prime minister, 1848.

Balbo, ITALO (1896–), Ital. politician; noted Fascist; as minister of aviation, 1929–33, brought Ital. aviation to front rank; gov.-gen. of Libia since 1933.

Balbo'a, VASCO NUÑEZ DE (1475–1517), Span. explorer; captain-general of Darien; crossed the isthmus, 1513, and was the first European to see the Pacific; appointed Admiral of the Pacific, but owing to the jealousy of the new governor of Darien, was tried for treason and executed. As a pioneer ranks second only to Columbus.

Bal'bus, L. CORNELIUS, Rom. statesman; *b.* Gades (Cadiz); made a Rom. citizen; accompanied Julius Cæsar as engineering officer to Spain and Gaul; consul, 40 B.C.—the first of foreign birth to be so honoured.

Baldwin I. (1058–1118), first Lat. King of Jerusalem; brother of Godfrey de Bouillon; joined in the First Crusade, 1096. BALDWIN II., King of Jerusalem, 1118–31, was almost constantly at war with the Moslems. BALDWIN III., King of Jerusalem, 1143–62; *b.* in Palestine; took part in second crusade, 1147; failed in attack on Damascus; popular ruler. BALDWIN IV., King of Jerusalem, 1173–83, a leper, resigned in favour of BALDWIN V., a child of six, poisoned, 1187, by his mother.

Baldwin I. (*d.* 1205), first Lat. Emperor of Constantinople, 1204; a leader in Fourth Crusade.

Baldwin, JAMES MARK (1861–1934), Amer. psychologist; *b.* Columbia, S. Carolina; has held professorships in U.S.A., Toronto (Canada), Mexico, and Paris; Herbert Spencer lecturer, Oxford, 1915–16; his *History of Psychology* (1913) is a standard work.

Baldwin, STANLEY, RT. HON. (1867–), Eng. statesman and leader of Conservative party; *b.* Bewdley, Worcs; president Board of Trade, 1921–2; chancellor of exchequer, 1922–3; prime minister, 1923–4, 1924–9, and 1935; lord president of the Council in National Government, 1931; pub. in 1926 *On England*, a volume of non-political addresses.

Bale, JOHN (1495–1563), Bishop of Ossory, dramatist, historian; *b.* Cove, Suffolk; zealously promoted the Reformation in Ireland; wrote the first literary history of England.

Balestier (*bal-es-tēr'*), CHARLES WOLCOTT (1861–91), Amer. novelist; *b.* Rochester, New York; collaborated with his brother-in-law, Rudyard Kipling, in *The Naulahka* (1892).

Balfe (*balf*), MICHAEL WILLIAM (1808–70), Irish musical composer; *b.* Dublin; most famous work, *The Bohemian Girl* (1843); wrote music for 'Come into the garden, Maud,' 'Killarney,' etc.

Balfour (*bal'foor*), Arthur James (1848–1930), 1st Earl, created 1922, Brit. statesman; *b.* Whittingehame, E. Lothian; Conservative member for Hertford, 1874; secretary for Scotland, 1886–7; as chief secretary for Ireland, 1887–91, carried Crimes Act through Parliament and set up Congested District Boards; first lord of Treasury and leader of House of Commons, 1891–1902; as prime minister, 1902–6, he instituted the Army Council and Imperial Defence Committee, and cemented the *Entente Cordiale*. Was the most brilliant parl. dialectician of his time. On outbreak of Great War, 1914, was a foremost supporter of all necessary measures, and in 1915 joined Mr. Asquith's Coalition government as first lord of the Admiralty. Was foreign secretary in Mr. Lloyd George's ministry. After the U.S.A. entered the war he conducted a most important mission to that country. In 1919 he was second Brit. representative at the Peace Conference in Paris; in 1921 took a large part in the International Conference at Washington, U.S.A., on subject of limitation of armaments. The Balfour Declaration advocating a national home for the Jewish people in Palestine was incorporated in the mandate for that country, 1922. In the Balfour note of 1922 he defined the attitude of the Brit. government to war debts and reparations. At Imperial Conference, 1926, was chairman of committee which determined status of Brit. Dominions. In philosophy he was equally famous. He was Gifford lecturer, Glasgow Univ., 1913–14 and 1922–3, and wrote *A Defence of Philosophic Doubt* (1879) and *The Foundations of Belief* (1895). Chancellor of Cambridge Univ., 1919.

[*Chapters of Autobiography*, (1930), by Arthur James, first Earl of Balfour; *Lord Balfour: A Memory* (1930), by Sir Ian Malcolm.]

Balfour, Francis Maitland (1851–82), Scot. biologist; *b.* Edinburgh; younger brother of A. J. Balfour; author of widely recognized treatise on *Comparative Embryology*; killed in Alpine accident.

Balfour, Gerald William, 2nd Earl (1853–), Brit. public official; *b.* Edinburgh; brother of 1st Earl. Chief Secretary for Ireland, 1895–1900; president of Board of Trade, 1900, of Local Government Board, 1906.

Balfour, Isaac Bayley (1853–1922), famous Scot. botanist; *b.* Edinburgh; successively prof. of botany at Glasgow, Oxford, and Edinburgh Universities; amongst other works, translated Goebel's *Organography of Plants*.

Balfour of Burleigh, Lord, Alexander Hugh Bruce (1849–1921), Scot. politician; *b.* Alloa; became sixth lord in 1869 by the removal of attainder of 1715; parl. secretary to Board of Trade, 1889–92, and secretary for Scotland, 1895–1903; acted as chairman of numerous commissions; established Congested Districts Boards, 1898; in 1916 was appointed chairman of government committee on commercial and industrial policy after the war; noted leader in Church of Scotland.

Ba'liol, John de (1249–1315), King of Scotland; son of Baliol of Barnard Castle, Durham, who founded Baliol Coll., Oxford, and Devorguilla of Galloway; raised to Scot. throne by Edward i., 1291; known as 'Toom Tabard' (empty coat), because of subservience to England; broke fealty to Edward i., defeated at Dunbar; *d.* at Bailleul, France, original home of family.

Ball, Albert (1897–1917), flight-commander, R.F.C., began his meteoric career in Feb. 1916. During Great War was described as 'the most daring, skilful, and successful pilot the R.F.C. has ever had'; killed in action; posthumous V.C.

Ball, JOHN (*d.* 1381), a leader of Peasants' Revolt, 1381, called by Froissart 'the mad priest of Kent'; remembered for his socialistic teaching; executed in presence of Richard II.

Ball, SIR ROBERT STAWELL (1840–1913), Irish astronomer; *b.* Dublin; prof. of astronomy, Dublin, and astronomer-royal of Ireland, 1874; Lowndean prof. of astronomy, Cambridge, 1892; best-known work, *The Story of the Heavens*.

Ballance, JOHN (1839–93), New Zealand statesman, of Irish birth; premier, 1891; instituted small holdings, with government aid; introduced progressive land and income taxes.

Ballantine, JAMES (1808–77), Scot. poet and artist; *b.* Edinburgh; did much for art of glass staining; specimens in House of Lords; wrote *The Gaberlunzie's Wallet*, and popular songs.

Ballantyne, JAMES (1772–1833), Scot. publisher; *b.* Kelso; schoolfellow of Sir Walter Scott, whose *Border Minstrelsy* he printed (1802); with his brother JOHN (1774–1821) established the firm of Ballantyne and Co., in which Scott was a secret partner; final bankruptcy of firm in 1826.

Ballantyne, ROBERT MICHAEL (1825–94), Scot. writer for boys; *b.* Edinburgh; six years in service of Hudson's Bay Co.; pub. about eighty stories, including *The Young Fur-Traders*, *The Coral Island*, and *The Dog Crusoe*.

Ballin, ALBERT (1857–1918), Ger. commercial magnate; *b.* Hamburg; founded the Hamburg-Amerika line; reorganized Germany's mercantile marine.

Balmat (*bäl-mä'*), JACQUES (1762–1834), Alpine guide; first to make ascent of Mont Blanc, 1786.

Balzac', HONORÉ DE (1799–1850), Fr. novelist; *b.* Tours; intended for the law but went to Paris, 1819, to seek his fortune as an author; struggled unsuccessfully for ten years; at age of thirty made a reputation with *Les Derniers Chouans*, *La Peau de Chagrin*, and other novels; conceived the idea of presenting, under the general title of the *Comédie Humaine*, a large series of novels which should give a complete panorama of modern life. Wrote some eighty novels in twenty years, working sometimes eighteen hours daily, yet was involved in debt to the end of his days. A genuine, if not subtle, sense of humour is shown by the *Contes Drôlatiques*. He is at his best in sketching tragedies of common people like *Le Père Goriot*; sought force rather than felicity of wording.

[Critical preface to *La Peau de Chagrin* (1895), by Saintsbury; *Honoré de Balzac* (1906), by Brunetière; *Aspects of Balzac* (1905), by Helm; *Life* (1910), by Lawton.]

Balzac, JEAN LOUIS GUEZ DE (1594–1654), Fr. author; *b.* Angoulême; patronized by Cardinal Richelieu; had much influence on purification of Fr. language; chiefly known for his *Lettres* and *Lettres Inédites*.

Bamberger (*bäm'berg-er*), LUDWIG (1823–99), Ger. politician and economist; republican leader in revolution, 1848; helped to found Ger. Imperial Bank; opposed Bismarck's policy of protection and colonial schemes.

Bampton, JOHN (1689–1751), Eng. theologian; founder of Bampton Lectures in Oxford, defending Christianity.

Bancroft, GEORGE (1800–91), Amer. historian and statesman; *b.* Worcester, Mass.; U.S.A.

minister at St. James's, London, 1846, at Berlin, 1867; best known for his famous *History of the United States*.

Bancroft, RICHARD (1544–1610), Archbishop of Canterbury, supported the royal power against the civil courts; took part in Hampton Court Conference, 1604, and in preparation of A.V. of Bible.

Bancrofts, THE, Eng. actors; SIR SQUIRE BANCROFT (1841–1926), and his wife, EFFIE WILTON (*d.* 1921), inaugurated the natural school of acting by their productions of the Robertson comedies, *Society*, *Ours*, *Caste*, etc.; retired 1885.

Bandel'lo, MATTEO (*c.* 1480–1562), Ital. novelist; *b.* near Tortona; famous for his collection of 200 *Novelle*; treasure-house for Elizabethan dramatists; finest, *Romeo and Juliet*, utilized by Shakespeare.

Banér, JOHAN (1596–1641), Swed. general; *b.* near Stockholm; ablest lieutenant of Gustavus Adolphus, after whose death he won victories at Wittstock, 1636, and Chemnitz, 1639.

Bang, HERMANN JOACHIM (1858–1912), Dan. author; *b.* in Zealand; one of best Dan. writers of fiction; his *Tine* (1889) won him the friendship of Ibsen.

Ban'im, JOHN (1798–1842), Irish novelist; *b.* Kilkenny; wrote *Tales of the O'Hara Family* (1825–26), and numerous other Irish melodramas and novels, assisted by his brother MICHAEL (1796–1874).

Banks, SIR JOSEPH (1743–1820), Brit. botanist; *b.* London; accompanied Captain Cook on his first voyage; known as 'the father of Australia' from share in first colonization at Botany Bay; president of Royal Soc. for forty-one years.

Banks, NATHANIEL PRENTISS (1816–94), Amer. politician and soldier; governor of Massachusetts, 1858; defended Washington from 'Stonewall' Jackson's army, 1862; took Port Hudson, 1863.

Banks, THOMAS (1735–1805), Eng. sculptor; *b.* London; works include *Achilles Enraged*, and group, *Shakespeare attended by Painting and Poetry*, at Stratford.

Ban'natyne, GEORGE (?1545–1608), collector of anc. Scot. poems; *b.* in Angus; *Bannatyne Club* was founded in his honour in Edinburgh, 1823, for publication of Scot. historical and literary MSS.

Ban'ting, SIR FREDERICK GRANT (1891–), Can. physician; joint discoverer of insulin, 1922, with Prof. Macleod and C. H. Best; awarded Nobel prize (jointly with Macleod); prof. of medical research, Toronto Univ., since 1923. Knighted 1934.

Ban'tock, SIR GRANVILLE (1868–), Brit. composer; *b.* London; succeeded Elgar as prof. of music at Birmingham Univ., 1908; numerous compositions include *Omar Khayyam*, *Atalanta in Calydon*, and *Hebridean Symphony*. Knighted 1930.

Banville (*bän-vēl'*), THÉODORE FAULLAIN DE (1823–91), Fr. poet; eulogized by Victor Hugo for his *Odes Funambulesques*; wrote plays, including *Gringoire* (1866), trans. by Sir Walter Besant and W. H. Pollock as *The Ballad-monger*.

Barab'bas, a robber whose release was demanded from Pilate in preference to that of Jesus.

Barbara, ST. (*fl.* 3rd cent.), Christian martyr; her legendary connection with thunderstorms has made her the patron of artillery; feast, Dec. 4.

Barbarossa. See FREDERICK I.

Bar'bauld, ANNA LETITIA (1743–1825), Eng. poetess, sister of Dr. John Aikin; *b.* in Leicestershire; wrote *Hymns in Prose for Children*; ed. the Eng. novelists in 50 vols.

Barbé (*bär-bā'*), Louis (1845–1926), historian; *b.* Cherbourg; schoolmaster in Dunkirk and Glasgow; historical works include the only biography of *Kirkaldy of Grange* (1897), and *In Byways of Scottish History* (1912).

Barbellion. See Cummings, Bruce.

Barberini, Ital. family of note in 17th cent.; Maffeo Barberini became Pope as Urban viii. (1623), and several relatives were cardinals; the rapacity with which they pillaged objects of art gave rise to saying, '*Quod non fecerunt barbari, fecerunt Barberini.*'

Bar'bour, John (1316–95), Scot. poet; regarded as father of Scot. poetry; archdeacon of Aberdeen; wrote a narrative poem, *The Brus,* in upwards of 13,000 lines, for which he received from King Robert ii., in 1377, a gift of £10, and in following year a life annuity of twenty shillings. *The Brus* was first printed at Edinburgh in 1571.

Barbusse (*bär-boos'*), Henri (1874–1935), Fr. author; *b.* Asnières (Seine); in Great War joined the ranks, and twice won the Croix de Guerre; wrote a remarkable war book, *Le Feu* (1916), a crushing indictment of war; other works include *Clarté* (1919), and *Manifeste aux Intellectuels* (1927).

Barclay, Alexander (1476–1552), Scot. poet; his eclogues were among first pastorals in English; chiefly remembered as author of free trans. of Sebastian Brandt's 'Ship of Fools.'

Barclay, Florence (1862–1921), Eng. novelist; *b.* in Surrey; wrote many sentimental and popular novels, including *The Rosary.*

Barclay, John (1758–1826), Scot. anatomist; *b.* in Perthshire; was largely instrumental in founding the Dick Veterinary Coll., Edinburgh.

Barclay, Robert (1648–90), Scot. Quaker; *b.* near Elgin; suffered persecution; travelled throughout Europe; author of the *Apology* (1678), an exposition of Quakerism.

Barclay de Tolly, Michael, Prince (1761–1818), Russ. field-marshal of Scot. extraction; *b.* in Livonia; served with distinction against Napoleon, 1806–7; made famous march over frozen Gulf of Bothnia against Swedes, 1809; commanded Russ. army during invasion of France, 1814.

Bar'ents, Willem (*d.* 1597), Dutch navigator; conducted three unsuccessful expeditions in search of N.E. Passage, 1594–7. On the third voyage he discovered Spitsbergen, rounded Novaya Zemlya, and there died. In 1871 his camp and relics were discovered, and in 1875 his Journal was found.

[*Voyages,* trans. and pub. by Hakluyt Soc. (1876).]

Barère de Vieuzac (*ba-rer' de vyoo-zäk'*), Bertrand (1755–1841), Fr. revolutionary; *b.* Tarbes; deputy to States-general, 1789; delegate to National Convention, 1792. He joined Robespierre after having attacked him; took employment under Napoleon; went over to Bourbons, 1814; banished as a regicide, 1815; accepted pension from Louis Philippe.

Baret'ti, Giuseppe Marc' Antonio (1719–89), Ital. critic; *b.* Turin; settled in London; associated with Dr. Johnson (Boswell's *Life*); secretary to Royal Academy; killed a man who attacked him in London, but acquitted after evidence by Johnson and his circle; compiled a *Dictionary and Grammar of the Italian Language.*

Barham (*bär'am*), Richard Harris, pen-name 'Thomas Ingoldsby' (1788–1845), Eng. humorist; *b.* Canterbury; priest-in-ordinary to Chapel Royal, 1824; famous for his *Ingoldsby Legends.*

Baring, family of Eng. financiers; Baring Brothers (1770–

1890), first banking house in Europe; members of the family have been prominent statesmen—*e.g.* Lords Ashburton, Northbrook, Revelstoke, Cromer.

Ba'ring, Hon. Maurice (1874–), Eng. author and journalist; son of 1st Lord Revelstoke; *b.* London; in diplomatic service, 1898–1904; war correspondent in Manchuria, Russia, and Turkey; served in R.F.C. during Great War; has written much on Russ. literature and Russ. people, besides plays and poems.

Baring-Gould, Rev. Sabine (1834–1924), Eng. author and clergyman; *b.* Exeter; writer of numerous novels, hymns, religious and antiquarian works.

Barker, Harley Granville. See Granville-Barker, Harley.

Barker, Sir Herbert A. (1869–), specialist in manipulative surgery; *b.* Southport; treated successfully over 40,000 cases of deranged knee cartilages, flat-foot, etc., and published articles on bloodless operations, and *Leaves from My Life* (1927).

Bark'la, Charles Glover (1877–), prof. of Natural Philosophy at Univ. of Edinburgh since 1913; Nobel prizeman in physics, 1917; has written on electric waves, X-rays, and secondary rays.

Barlow, Jane (1860–1917), Irish novelist; *b.* Clontarf; noted for her sympathetic sketches of Irish peasant life; authoress of *Bogland Studies, Irish Idylls*, etc.

Barlow, Sir Thomas (1845–), physician-extraordinary to Queen Victoria, Edward vii., and George v.; president Royal Coll. of Physicians, 1910–15; baronet, 1900.

Bar'nabas, the Apostle, a Levite of Cyprus named Joses; sold his land and gave the money to the Apostles; was the uncle of Mark; accompanied Paul on his first missionary journey; sailed with Mark to Cyprus, where he is said to have died as a martyr. (See *Acts* 15.) The apocryphal Epistle of Barnabas is found in the *Codex Sinaiticus*; Harnack gives its date as about 130.

Barnaby, Sir Nathaniel (1829–1915), Brit. naval architect; *b.* Chatham; director of naval construction, 1870–85; one of founders of Institute of Naval Architects; knighted, 1895.

Bar'nard, Lady Anne (1750–1825), Scot. poetess; daughter of 5th Earl of Balcarres; married Andrew Barnard, colonial secretary at Cape of Good Hope; chiefly remembered for her ballad, 'Auld Robin Gray,' and her *Letters* from the Cape.

Barnard, Edward Emerson (1857–1923), Amer. astronomer; discovered Jupiter's fifth satellite.

Barnar'do, Thomas John (1845–1905), Irish philanthropist; opened 'Dr. Barnardo's Home,' at Stepney, 1867, to shelter and train homeless children; and afterwards established 111 similar refuges, besides village home at Barkingside for girls.

Barnat'o, Barnett Isaacs (1852–97), S. African diamond merchant; *b.* London; built up Barnato Diamond Mining Co. at Kimberley, ultimately amalgamated with De Beers group; committed suicide at sea.

Barn'by, Sir Joseph (1838–96), Eng. composer and conductor; *b.* York; head of Guildhall School of Music, 1892; works include *Rebekah*, an oratorio, anthems, songs, and many hymn tunes.

Barnes, Ernest William (1874–), Eng. divine; had distinguished mathematical career at Cambridge. Appointed Bishop of Birmingham, 1924. An active opponent of the Anglo-Catholic party. Has written much on scientific, philosophical, and theological subjects.

Barnes, Rt. Hon George Nicoll (1859–), Brit. statesman; began life as working engineer; M.P. for division of Glasgow, 1906–22; first minister of pensions, 1916; Labour minister in war cabinet, 1917; Brit. representative of Labour at Peace Conference; C.H., 1920.

Barnes, WILLIAM (1800–86), Dorsetshire poet; successively lawyer's clerk, schoolmaster, and clergyman; pub. *Poems of Rural Life in the Dorset Dialect* (1844), *Hwomely Rhymes* (1859), etc. His poems are exquisitely finished idylls.

Barnett, JOHN FRANCIS (1837–1916), Eng. composer; *b.* London; first cantata, *The Ancient Mariner*, appeared in 1867. Other works include *Raising of Lazarus* (1876).

Barnett, SAMUEL AUGUSTUS (1844–1913), Eng. clergyman and philanthropist; canon of Bristol, 1893, and of Westminster, 1906; devoted to amelioration of conditions in Whitechapel, assisted by Toynbee; one of founders of Toynbee Hall; wrote, with his wife, *Practicable Socialism* (1893).

Barnfield, RICHARD (1574–1627), Eng. poet; *b.* Norbury, Staffs; wrote *The Affectionate Shepherd* (1594), *Cynthia* (1598), *The Passionate Pilgrim* (1599); some of his songs were long attributed to Shakespeare.

Barnum, PHINEAS TAYLOR (1810–91), Amer. showman; *b.* Bethel, Conn.; toured with 'General Tom Thumb' in U.S.A. and England, and with Jenny Lind in U.S.A.; with Bailey, launched 'The Greatest Show on Earth,' with which he toured the world.

Barocchio (*ba-rok'ē-ō*), GIACOMO (1507–73), called DA VIGNOLA, Ital. architect; *b.* Vignola, near Modena; succeeded Michelangelo as architect of St. Peter's, 1564; designed numerous other buildings in Rome.

Baro'da, MAHARAJAH GAEKWAR SIR SAYAJI RAO III. (1863–), Ind. ruler; regrettable incident at Delhi durbar caused his loyalty to be impugned; during Great War was generous supporter of Brit. Government. One of the most progressive rulers in India. The Maharanee has written *The Position of Women in Indian Life.*

Baron, BERNHARD (1850–1929), millionaire tobacco merchant and philanthropist; *b.* in Russia; taken to U.S.A. to avoid conscription; at first lived in great poverty; invented cigarette-making machine, and sold it in England for £160,000; bought and developed Carreras Tobacco Co.; gave large sums to hospitals and charities.

Barr, AMELIA EDITH (1831–1919), Eng. novelist; *b.* Ulverston; went with husband to U.S.A., where she wrote novels, including *Jan Vedder's Wife* (1885), *The Maid of Maiden Lane* (1900), and *The House on Cherry Street* (1909).

Barr, ARCHIBALD (1855–1931), Scot. engineer and inventor; prof. of civil engineering at Leeds and at Glasgow; numerous inventions include range-finders, electrical fire-control instruments for warships, and the optophone, for enabling the blind to read books by sound.

Barr, ROBERT (1850–1912), Scot. novelist; *b.* Glasgow; schoolmaster at Windsor, Canada; returned to England, 1881, and with Jerome K. Jerome founded the *Idler* (1892).

Barras', PAUL FRANÇOIS JEAN NICOLAS, VICOMTE DE (1755–1829), Fr. Jacobin statesman; brought about fall of Robespierre, and had a share in early advancement of Bonaparte. Wrote *Mémoires.*

Barrès, MAURICE (1862–1923), Fr. novelist and publicist; *b.* Charmes (Vosges); member of Fr. Academy; an individualist, his works teach the importance of patriotism; wrote an excellent diary of the war (Aug. to Oct.

1914); author of *Le Jardin de Bérénice, Colette Baudoche, Les Déracinés, L'Appel au Soldat, Un Jardin sur l'Oronte.*

Barrett, ELIZABETH. See BROWNING, E. B.

Barrett, SIR WILLIAM FLETCHER (1844–1925), Brit. scientist; prof. of physics, Royal Coll. of Science, Dublin, 1873–1910; principal founder of Soc. for Psychical Research.

Barrett, WILSON (1846–1904), Eng. actor and dramatist; *b.* in Essex; established reputation as exponent of emotional drama in *The Silver King*; one of his own plays, *The Sign of the Cross*, was very popular.

Barrie, SIR JAMES MATTHEW (1860–), Scot. novelist and dramatist; *b.* Kirriemuir; made his reputation with sketches and novels of Scot. life, *Auld Licht Idylls* (1888), *A Window in Thrums* (1889), *The Little Minister* (1891), etc., and plays of a delicate fancy and whimsical satire —*e.g. The Admirable Crichton* and *Quality Street* (1902); *Peter Pan* (1904); *What Every Woman Knows* (1908); *Dear Brutus* (1918); *Mary Rose* (1920); baronet, 1913; Lord Rector, St. Andrews Univ., 1919; O.M., 1922; chancellor of Edinburgh Univ., 1930.

Barrière (*bä-rē-er'*), THÉODORE (1823–77), Fr. dramatist; created character of *raisonneur* or moralizing chorus; produced *Manon Lescaut*, etc.

Barrington, GEORGE (1755–*c.* 1840), Irish author and pickpocket; *b.* Maynooth; after career of crime was transported to Botany Bay; on voyage discovered and disclosed conspiracy to seize ship, and obtained warrant of emancipation. Works include *A Voyage to Botany Bay* (1801), *History of New Holland* (1808); author of the oft-quoted line, 'We left our country for our country's good.'

Barrington, JOHN SHUTE, 1ST VISCOUNT (1678–1734), Eng. polemical and theological writer; helped to secure Scot. Presbyterian support for union of the two kingdoms; gained favour of George I. by his *Dissuasive from Jacobitism*; represented Berwick-on-Tweed, 1715–22, but was expelled House for connection with lottery.

Bar'ros, JOÃO DE (1496–1570), Port. historian, the 'Livy of Portugal'; famed for his *Decades*, a monumental work on history of Portuguese in India.

Barrow, ISAAC (1630–77), Eng. mathematician and divine; first Lucasian prof. of mathematics at Cambridge, 1663, but gave up chair to his pupil Isaac Newton, 1669; master of Trinity Coll., 1672; a remarkable preacher.

Barrow, SIR JOHN (1764–1848), Eng. statesman; *b.* in Lancs; secretary to the Admiralty for forty years; was in China and S. Africa as secretary to Brit. ambassador; actively promoted Arctic exploration; a founder of Royal Geographical Soc.

Barry, SIR CHARLES (1795–1860); *b.* London; architect of Houses of Parliament, King Edward VI. Grammar School, Birmingham, etc.; knighted 1852; buried in Westminster Abbey.

Barry, JAMES (1741–1806), Irish artist; *b.* Cork; decorated hall of Soc. of Arts with six pictures representing *Human Culture*; prof. of painting to Royal Academy, 1784–99.

Barry, SIR JOHN WOLFE WOLFE-(1836–1918), civil engineer; *b.* London; son of Sir Charles Barry; constructor of Kew, Blackfriars, and Tower Bridges over R. Thames; of docks at Middlesbrough, Newport, and Barry, etc.

Barry, SIR REDMOND (1813–80), Australian judge of Irish birth; first solicitor-general for Victoria, and afterwards judge;

first chancellor of Melbourne Univ., which he founded.

Barry, SPRANGER (1719–77), Irish actor; *b.* Dublin; a rival of Garrick, over whom, though inferior as an actor, he possessed the advantage of a tall and handsome person.

Barry Cornwall. See PROCTER, BRYAN WALLER.

Barrymore, ETHEL (Mrs. R. G. COLT) (1879–), Amer. actress; *b.* Philadelphia; has played leading rôles in England and U.S.A.; opened Ethel Barrymore Theatre, New York, 1928. Her brother, JOHN BARRYMORE (1882–), has achieved success as a Shakespearian actor in Britain and U.S.A., and as a film actor.

Bart, JEAN (1651–1702), Fr. naval officer; son of a fisherman of Dunkirk; first served in Dutch navy under de Ruyter, later entered Fr. service; by sheer force of character and bravery rose to highest rank; made a daring raid on Eng. coast, 1692.

Bar'tels, HANS VON (1856–1913), Ger. artist; *b.* Hamburg; prof. of painting at Munich, 1891; best work consists of stormy seascapes and scenes of work of fishing people.

Barth (*bärt*), HEINRICH (1821–65), Ger. explorer and writer; *b.* Hamburg; accompanied Richardson on Brit. Government expedition to W. Sudan; his *Travels* (new ed. 1890) still the standard work on N. and Central Africa; prof. of geography, Berlin, 1862.

Barth, KARL (1886–), Ger. theologian; prof. of theology at Bonn, 1930. Was retired, 1934, for his opposition to Nazi control of German Church. Introduced a new spirit into theology by emphasizing the sovereignty of God, and the part that God plays in revealing Himself to man.

Barthélemy (*bär-tāl-mē'*), AUGUSTE MARSEILLE (1796–1867), Fr. poet; *b.* Marseilles; along with Méry wrote satires on Bourbon monarchy, *Napoléon en Egypte*, *L'Insurrection*, etc.

Barthélemy, JEAN JACQUES (1716–95), Fr. scholar; *b.* in Provence; his great work was *Voyage du Jeune Anacharsis en Grèce.*

Barthélemy Saint-Hilaire, JULES (1805–95), Fr. philosopher and republican statesman; *b.* Paris; prof. of anc. philosophy, Coll. de France, 1838; author of a great annotated trans. of Aristotle and other works.

Barthez (*bär-tā'*), PAUL JOSEPH (1734–1806), Fr. physician; prof. of medicine and chancellor of univ. of Montpellier; chief work, *Science de l'Homme.*

Bartholdi (*bär-tol-dē'*), FRÉDÉRIC AUGUSTE (1834–1904), Fr. sculptor; *b.* Colmar, Alsace; *Statue of Liberty* (New York harbour) and *Lion of Belfort* are among his best-known works.

Bartholomé (*bär-tol-o-mā'*), PAUL ALBERT (1848–1928), Fr. painter and sculptor; chief work, *Monument aux Morts*, Père Lachaise, Paris; hon. R.A., 1921.

Barthol'omew, ST., one of the twelve Apostles, sometimes identified with Nathanael; festival, Aug. 24.

Barthol'omew, JOHN (1831–93), Scot. cartographer; *b.* Edinburgh; founded Edinburgh Geographical Institute.

Barthou (*bär-too'*), LOUIS (1862–1934), Fr. statesman and author; prime minister, May to Dec. 1913; senator, 1922; minister of foreign affairs, 1934; assassinated at Marseilles. Author of *Mirabeau* (1913); *Les Amours d'un poète* (1919), etc.

Bartók, BÉLA (1881–), Hungarian musician; *b.* in Transylvania; collected folk music and traditional melodies; works include *Bluebeard's Castle* (1918) and *The Miraculous Mandarin*; prof. of music, Budapest.

Bar'toli, Adolfo (1833–94), Ital. author; prof. of literary history, Florence; wrote *Storia della Letteratura Italiana*, the first critical history of Ital. literature.

Bartolini (*bär-tō-lē'nē*), Lorenzo (1777–1850), Ital. sculptor; *b.* near Florence. His bust of his patron Napoleon is famous.

Bartolomme'o di Paghola, Fra (1475–1517), Ital. painter; *b.* near Florence; famous for magnificent altar-pieces; introduced the jointed lay-figure; his masterpiece is figure of St. Mark, in Florence.

Bartolozzi (*bär-tō-lōt'sē*), Francesco (1727–1815), Ital. engraver; *b.* Florence; lived in London, 1764–1802; well-known works include *Clytie*, the *Virgin and Child* after Dolci, and engravings of pictures by Cipriani and Angelica Kauffmann.

Bar'ton, Andrew (*d.* 1511), Scot. naval hero, one of a famous family of seamen in reign of James iv.; instrumental in creating a Scot. navy.

Barton, Bernard (1784–1849), the 'Quaker poet'; *b.* Carlisle; friend of Southey, Hogg (the Ettrick Shepherd), and Lamb; author of *Household Verses*, etc.

Barton Clara (1830–1912), Amer. philanthropist; *b.* Oxford, Mass.; nursed the wounded in Civil War and Franco-Prussian War; first president of Amer. Red Cross, 1881; performed field duties during Span.-Amer. War and S. African War.

Barton, Rt. Hon. Sir Edmund (1849–1920), Australian statesman; *b.* Sydney; largely instrumental in securing the Federation Act of 1900; prime minister of Australia, 1901–3; senior puisne judge of High Court of Australia, 1903.

Barton, George Aaron (1859–), theologian; *b.* in Quebec; Director of Amer. School of Oriental Study and Research in Palestine, 1902–3; prof. of Semitic languages, Univ. of Pennsylvania, since 1922; publications include *Royal Inscriptions of Sumer and Akkad* (1927).

Barye (*bä-rē'*), Antoine Louis (1796–1875), great Fr. sculptor; *b.* Paris; chiefly animal studies; his *Lion Struggling with Serpent* (1832) and *Lion Resting* (1847) now in the Tuileries.

Bashkirt'seff, Marie (1860–84), Russ. painter and diarist; *b.* Poltava; her *Jean et Jacques*, *The Umbrella*, and *The Meeting* now in the Luxembourg; chiefly remembered for her *Journal*, begun at twelve, and for her *Letters*, under a feigned name, to Guy de Maupassant.

Basil the Great, St. Basil (329–79), bishop of Cæsarea in Cappadocia, one of most eminent Gr. fathers; resolute opponent of Arianism; believed that work and usefulness could be carried on in conjunction with saintliness and austerity; founded a monastic order, since known as Basilian Monks.

Baskerville, John (1706–75), Eng. printer; *b.* in Worcestershire; greatly developed art of typography; examples of his Bible, Prayer Book, and Lat. classics much valued.

Bass, George (*d.* 1812 ?), Eng. explorer; *b.* in Lincs; spent five years exploring and mapping Australian coast; circumnavigated Tasmania along with Flinders.

Bass, Michael Thomas (1799–1884), brewer, politician, philanthropist; worked actively to abolish imprisonment for debt, and took keen interest in welfare of working-classes.

Bassan'o, Jacopo da Ponte (1510–92), Ital. painter; his altar-piece, *The Nativity*, highly praised by Lanzi; National Gallery contains two of his portraits.

Bastard of Orleans. See Dunois, Jean.

Bas'tian, Adolph (1826–1905),

Ger. ethnologist; world-wide traveller; wrote *Die Völker des östlichen Asien* (1866–71), etc.

Bastien-Lepage (*bäs-tyan'-le-päzh'*), JULES (1848–84), Fr. painter; *b.* Damvillers, Meuse; painted portraits, landscapes, and historical pictures, including *The Hayfield, Sarah Bernhardt, Joan of Arc listening to the Voices, The Thames at London.*

Bataille (*bä-tī'ye*), HENRI (1872–1922), Fr. lyric poet and playwright; *b.* Nîmes; main theme is the dawn and death of the passion of love; among his works are *La Femme Nue* (1908), *La divine tragédie* (1916).

Batemans, THE, a famous Amer. theatrical family. HEZEKIAH LINTHICUM BATEMAN (1812–75); *b.* Baltimore; introduced Henry Irving to London in *The Bells.* His wife, SIDNEY FRANCES (1823–81), was the first to bring over to this country an Amer. company with an Amer. play, *The Danites.* Two daughters, KATE and ELLEN, achieved success on the stage.

Bates, HARRY (1850–99), Eng. sculptor; *b.* Stevenage, Herts; pupil of Rodin; A.R.A., 1892; some of his works, purchased by the Chantrey Trustees, are now in the Tate Gallery; most famous statue, *Love and Life.*

Bates, HENRY WALTER (1825–92), Eng. naturalist; *b.* Leicester; explored Amazon with Alfred Russel Wallace, 1848–59; author of *The Naturalist on the Amazons* (1863).

Bath, WILLIAM PULTENEY, 1ST EARL OF (1684–1764), Brit. statesman; took prominent part against Dr. Sacheverell; led opposition to Walpole; lost influence on accepting peerage, 1742.

Bathsheba, wife of Uriah the Hittite, and afterwards of David; mother of Solomon (1 Kings 1).

Batman, JOHN (1800–40), is generally regarded as founder of Victoria, Australia; *b.* Parramatta; settled in Tasmania; in 1835 acquired from natives the site of Melbourne and district.

Batten, HARRY MORTIMER (1888–), author and naturalist; among publications are *Romances of the Wild* and *Birds of our Gardens.*

Battenberg. See under CARISBROOKE and MILFORD HAVEN.

Batthyanyi (*bot'yon-yē*), anc. family of Hungarian nobles. PRINCE KARL JOSEPH (1697–1772), Austrian field-marshal, distinguished in War of Austrian Succession. COUNT CASIMIR (1807–54), follower of Kossuth, and Hungarian foreign minister. COUNT LOUIS (1809–49), premier of first constitutional ministry, 1848; condemned to death by the Austrians, but took his own life.

Batu Khan (*d.* 1255), Mongol chief, grandson of Jenghiz Khan; burnt Moscow and overran Russia, Poland, Hungary, and Silesia, 1235–41; settled in lower Volga basin.

Baudelaire (*bōd-lār'*), CHARLES PIERRE (1821–67), Fr. poet; *b.* Paris; admirer of Poe, many of whose works he translated; his poems, though morbid, had a profound influence on later Fr. poetry; pub. *Les Fleurs du Mal, Les Paradis Artificiels* (inspired by De Quincey), *L'Art Romantique,* etc.

Baudrillart (*bōd-rē-yär'*), HENRI JOSEPH LÉON (1821–92), Fr. political economist; *b.* Paris; prof. of political economy at Ecole des Ponts et Chaussées from 1881; author of *Manuel d'Economie Politique,* etc.

Bauhin (*bō-an'*), GASPARD (1560–1624), botanist; *b.* Basle, of Fr. descent; called 'the Linnæus of the 16th cent.'; his lifework was the *Pinax.*

Baumann (*bou'man*), OSKAR (1864–99), Austrian traveller; *b.* Vienna; expeditions to Congo, Fernando Po, Kilimanjaro, and L. Victoria; pub. accounts of these.

Baumgarten (*boum'gar-ten*), Alexander Gottlieb (1714–62), Ger. philosopher; first used the term 'æsthetics' for the theory of the beautiful; pub. *Ethica Philosophica* (1740), *Æsthetica* (1750), etc.

Baumgärtner (*boum'gert-ner*), Andreas, Baron von (1793–1865), Austrian scientist and statesman; prof. of physics at Vienna, 1817–33; director of imperial porcelain factories; afterwards held various state appointments; devoted later years to study of meteorology.

Baumgärtner, Karl Heinrich (1798–1886), Ger. physician; prof. of medical clinics at Freiburg, 1824–62; made important discoveries in embryology and the circulation of the blood.

Baur, Ferdinand Christian (1792–1860), Ger. theologian; *b.* Stuttgart; prof. of theology at Tübingen; wrote numerous works on Church history, Biblical criticism, and the philosophy of religion.

Bautain (*bō-tan'*), Louis Eugène Marie (1796–1867), Fr. philosopher; prof. of philosophy, Strasbourg; opposed atheistic tendency of the philosophy of his day; pub. *Psychologie Expérimentale* (1839), *Philosophie Morale* (1840), etc.

Bax, Arnold Edward Trevor (1883–), Eng. composer; *b.* London; his music is modern in outlook with mystical atmosphere; works include symphonies, choral works, chamber music, etc.

Bax, Clifford (1886–), Eng. dramatist, brother of above. Plays include *Poetasters of Ispahan* (1912), *Insect Play* (1923), and *Rose without a Thorn* (1931).

Bax, Ernest Belfort (1854–1926), Eng. Socialist and author; *b.* Leamington; assisted Morris in founding Socialist League, 1885; active member of Social Democratic Federation.

Baxter, Sir David (1793–1872), Scot. philanthropist; linen manufacturer, Dundee; presented Baxter Park to Dundee; left £600,000 for charitable purposes.

Baxter, Richard (1615–91), Eng. Puritan preacher; *b.* Rowton, Salop; during Civil War was chaplain in Parl. army; strongly opposed execution of Charles i., and favoured the Restoration; persecuted by Judge Jeffreys. He was noted for the saintliness of his life, and in spite of ill-health was the author of about 170 works, of which the best known is his *Saints' Everlasting Rest* (1650).

[*The Autobiography of Richard Baxter*, by J. M. Lloyd (1925).]

Bayard (*bä-yär'*), Pierre du Terrail, Chevalier de (1473–1524), Fr. military commander; *b.* Dauphiné; perfect example of chivalrous knight—the *Chevalier sans peur et sans reproche*; accompanied Charles viii. of France into Italy, and greatly distinguished himself in all the Fr. wars; taken prisoner at Battle of Spurs, 1513, but immediately set at liberty; conferred knighthood on Francis i. after victory of Marignano; mortally wounded in defending passage of the Sesia against the Milanese.

Bayard (*bī'ard*), Thomas Francis (1828–98), Amer. democratic statesman and diplomatist; *b.* Wilmington, Delaware; was first Amer. ambassador to Great Britain, 1893–97.

Bayliss, Sir William Maddock (1866–1924), distinguished Eng. physiologist; *b.* Wolverhampton; researches, resulting in many discoveries, carried on in London Univ., 1888–1923; pub. *Principles of General Physiology* (1914); awarded Copley Medal of Royal Soc., 1919.

Bayliss, Sir Wyke (1835–1906), Eng. painter; *b.* Madeley, Salop; president of Royal Soc. of Brit. Artists, 1888–1906; notable works,

Trèves Cathedral; St. Mark's, Venice; The Cathedral, Amiens.

Bayly, ADA ELLEN. See LYALL, EDNA.

Baynes (*bānz*), THOMAS SPENCER (1823–87), Eng. philosopher and man of letters; *b.* Wellington, Somerset; educated Edinburgh Univ.; ed. *Edinburgh Guardian* (1850–52); assistant editor of *Daily News* (1858); prof. of logic at St. Andrews, 1864; ed. *Encyclopædia Britannica* (9th ed., 1873).

Bazaine (*bä-zān'*), FRANÇOIS ACHILLE (1811–88), Fr. marshal; *b.* Versailles; rose from ranks; made general in Crimean War; chief commander in Franco-Ger. War; was sentenced to 20 years' detention for capitulating at Metz, but escaped, 1874, and died in Spain.

Bazin (*bä-zan'*), RENÉ FRANÇOIS NICOLAS MARIE (1853–1932), Fr. novelist; *b.* Angers; upholder of the old ways and stands resolutely for patriotism; among works, *L'Ame Alsacienne, Le Blé qui lève, Récits du Temps de la Guerre,* and *Le Conte du Triolet.*

Beach, SIR M. E. H. See ST. ALDWYN, VISCOUNT.

Beaconsfield, BENJAMIN DISRAELI, EARL OF (1804–81), Eng. statesman and novelist; *b.* London; son of Isaac Disraeli (author of *Curiosities of Literature,* etc.), who abandoned Judaism, and Benjamin was baptized into the Church of England, 1817; trained as a lawyer but turned attention to literature; achieved considerable success with *Vivian Grey* (1826); became society dandy; health breaking down, he travelled abroad for some years, reappearing as unsuccessful Radical candidate for High Wycombe, 1832; attacked Liberals in *Letters of Runnymede* (1836); Conservative M.P. for Maidstone, 1837; maiden speech a disastrous failure, but memorable for prediction, 'The time will come when you will hear me.' In 1839 married Mrs. Wyndham Lewis, whose fortune relieved his pecuniary embarrassments. At first a follower of Peel, but went over to the Protectionists; chancellor of the exchequer under Lord Derby, 1852, again 1858–9 and 1866; prime minister for a short time, 1868, and again took office, 1874–80; introduced Reform Bill of 1867; consolidated Brit. power in East by purchasing Suez Canal shares, 1875; added title of 'Empress of India' to Queen Victoria, and was created Earl of Beaconsfield, 1876. Disraeli was undoubtedly one of the greatest statesmen of his time; a master of epigram and a brilliant debater. His many novels remain as valuable pictures of the times in which he lived; best are *Coningsby, Sybil, Tancred,* and *Lothair.*

[*Benjamin Disraeli, Earl of Beaconsfield* (2 vols. 1929), by Buckle and Monypenny.]

Beale, DOROTHEA (1831–1906), Eng. educationist; tutor at Queen's Coll., London, 1849–54; became principal of Ladies Coll., Cheltenham, 1858, and made it the best girls' secondary school in England; founded St. Hilda's Hall, Oxford, for women students.

Beardsley, AUBREY VINCENT (1872–98), black-and-white decorative artist; *b.* Brighton; his work, superb in technique, influenced the æsthetic movement of late 19th cent.

Beaton, or BETHUNE, DAVID (*c.* 1494–1546), Scot. cardinal; *b.* in Fife; for years virtually ruled Scotland, and was a strong advocate of Franco-Scot. alliance; persecuted Protestants, and condemned George Wishart to be burned; was murdered at St. Andrews Castle.

Beattie, JAMES (1735–1803), Scot. poet; *b.* Laurencekirk; prof. of moral philosophy, Marischal College, Aberdeen; best-known poem, *The Minstrel.*

Beatty, DAVID, 1ST EARL OF THE NORTH SEA (1871–1936), Brit. admiral; *b.* in Ireland; served in Sudan, 1896–8; in China, 1900; naval secretary to first lord of Admiralty, 1912; commanded 1st Battle-cruiser Squadron, 1913–16; fought battle of Dogger Bank, 1915; sighted von Hipper's five battle cruisers, 1916, and gave chase, thus opening the battle of Jutland, in which he played a leading part; appointed to command the Grand Fleet, 1916–19; lord rector of Edinburgh Univ., 1917; admiral of the fleet, 1919–36; awarded O.M., 1919, an earldom and grant of £100,000; first sea lord, 1919–27.

Beau Brummell. See BRUMMELL.

Beaufort (*bō'fort*), HENRY, CARDINAL (1377–1447), legitimized son of John of Gaunt and Catherine Swynford; three times chancellor; cardinal, 1426; led crusade against Hussites in Bohemia; crowned Henry VI. King of France, 1431; instrumental in arranging peace between England and France, 1444.

Beauharnais (*bō-är-nā'*), Fr. noble family. ALEXANDRE (1760–94), Vicomte de Beauharnais, married Josephine Tascher de la Pagerie, afterwards first wife of Napoleon; served Revolution as general of Army of Rhine, 1792, but was executed; daughter, HORTENSE, married Louis Bonaparte, and was mother of Napoleon III.; son, EUGÈNE DE BEAUHARNAIS (1781–1824), Fr. soldier, stepson and favourite of Napoleon I.; served in Napoleon's wars, and became prince of the empire and viceroy of Italy; brave and skilful general; retired to Munich after the fall of Napoleon.

Beaumarchais (*bō-mär-shā'*), PIERRE AUGUSTIN CARON DE (1732–99), Fr. dramatist; *b.* Paris; wrote the famous comedies, *Le Barbier de Séville* (1773), and *Le Mariage de Figaro* (1778); was a witty adventurer and a great favourite in France; made a fortune by selling muskets to Amer. insurgents against Britain.

Beaumont (*bō'mont*), FRANCIS (1584–1616), and FLETCHER, JOHN (1579–1625), Eng. dramatists. Beaumont, son of Sir Francis Beaumont, *b.* Grace Dieu, Leicestershire; educated at Oxford; entered Inner Temple; made the acquaintance of Ben Jonson, and formed a friendship with Fletcher. The two poets lived together until Beaumont's marriage in 1613. Beaumont was buried in Westminster Abbey. Fletcher, son of Richard Fletcher, afterwards Bishop of London; *b.* Rye; educated Cambridge; drifted into the service of the theatre; died of the plague. Of the fifty plays attributed to the two dramatists, *The Maid's Tragedy*, *Philaster*, *The Knight of the Burning Pestle*, and *The Faithful Shepherdess* (by Fletcher alone) are considered the finest examples, and rank only below the masterpieces of Shakespeare. Probably Beaumont had the loftier genius, while Fletcher had more constructive ability and excelled in wit and fancy. They were sometimes associated with other dramatists—*e g.* Shakespeare, Massinger, and Jonson. *The Two Noble Kinsmen*, sometimes attributed to Shakespeare, was largely the work of Fletcher, who collaborated with Massinger in Shakespeare's *Henry VIII.*

Beaumont, SIR JOHN (1583–1627), Eng. poet; *b.* in Leicestershire; brother of Francis Beaumont, the dramatist; works include *Metamorphosis of Tobacco*, *Bosworth Field*, and several sacred pieces.

Beau Nash. See NASH, RICHARD.

Beauregard, PIERRE GUSTAVE TOUTANT (1818–93), Amer. Confederate general; *b.* New Orleans; received surrender of Fort Sumter, 1861.

Beaverbrook, RT. HON. SIR WILLIAM MAXWELL AITKEN, 1ST BARON (1879–), Brit. financier and politician; *b.* Newcastle, New Brunswick; controlled enterprises in Canada and W. Indies; Conservative M.P. for Aston-under-Lyne, 1910–16; private secretary to Bonar Law, 1911; Can. 'Eye Witness' during Great War; raised to peerage, 1917; chancellor of the Duchy of Lancaster and minister of information in 1918; as newspaper proprietor exerted great influence; championed cause of Empire Free Trade, 1930; author of several political books.

Beazley, SIR CHARLES RAYMOND (1868–), Eng. geographer and historian; *b.* Blackheath; prof. of history, Birmingham Univ.; wrote *Voyages of Elizabethan Seamen, Dawn of Modern Geography, Nineteenth Century Europe.*

Bebel (*bā'bel*), FERDINAND AUGUST (1840–1913), Ger. Socialist; *b.* Cologne; a most influential member of Social Democratic party; deprecated useless strikes; in 1870 urged government not to annex an acre of Fr. soil, and was imprisoned for high treason.

Beccafu'mi, DOMENICO DI PACE (1486–1551), Ital. artist; *b.* near Siena; son of a peasant; displayed talent for art from earliest years; famous for share in designing magnificent pavement in cathedral at Siena.

Beccaria (*bek-ä-rē'ä*), CESARE BONESANA (1735–94), Ital. political reformer and economist; *b.* Milan; his work had a lasting influence, through Jeremy Bentham, on the Eng. legal code.

Bechstein (*bech'stīn*), KARL (1826–1900), Ger. pianoforte-maker; *b.* Gotha; his well-known instruments are of singularly full and powerful tone.

Becke, GEORGE LOUIS (1855–1913), Australian author; *b.* Port Macquarie, New S. Wales; celebrated for graphic stories of the South Seas.

Becker, WILHELM ADOLF (1796–1846), Ger. classical scholar; prof. of archæology at Leipzig; author of studies of daily lives of anc. Romans and Greeks.

Becket, THOMAS (1118–70), Eng. churchman, son of a London merchant; accompanied Archbishop Theobald to Rome, 1143; made Chancellor of England, 1155, and became chief adviser to Henry II.; lived in great magnificence, and encouraged the king in all his warlike enterprises. In 1162 appointed Archbishop of Canterbury; from this time led ascetic life, and became the Church's enthusiastic champion; refused his assent to the Constitutions of Clarendon, and was exiled, but returned in 1170; some hasty words spoken by Henry II. led to his murder in Canterbury Cathedral. Canonized 1172. His shrine became noted place of pilgrimage.

Beckford, WILLIAM (1709–70), Eng. merchant; M.P. for City of London and twice lord mayor; a strong supporter of John Wilkes; opposed George III.'s encroachments on city's privileges.

Beckford, WILLIAM (1760–1844), Eng. author; son of above; inherited a great fortune, much of which he squandered; famous as author of *Vathek* (1782), a mysterious Oriental romance.

Becquerel (*bek-rel'*), distinguished Fr. family of scientists. (1) ANTOINE CÆSAR (1788–1878), physicist; prof. of physics in Paris; made many important discoveries in magnetism and electrochemistry. (2) ALEXANDRE EDMONDE (1820–91), his son, was also prof. of physics in Paris; made valuable researches on light. (3) ANTOINE HENRI (1852–1908), son of (2); discoverer of radioactivity; joint winner of Nobel prize, 1903.

Bed'does, THOMAS LOVELL (1803–49), Eng. dramatic poet; *b.* Clifton; nephew of Maria Edgeworth; author of *The Improvisatore*, *The Bride's Tragedy*, and *Death's Jest-Book*; plays are inspired by the Elizabethans, and some of his lyrics are of considerable beauty.

Bede, or BÆDA (*c.* 673–735), Eng. monk; usually called 'the Venerable Bede'; in early youth was placed under care of Benedict Biscop, Abbot of Wearmouth; later under that of Ceolfrith, Abbot of Jarrow, where he spent remainder of his life, and was buried; his bones were removed to Durham during the 11th cent.; author of the *Ecclesiastical History of the English Nation*, written 731; has been called 'the father of Eng. history'; was undoubtedly the most learned Englishman of his time; works are chief source of O.E. history; wrote also a *History of the Abbots*, and a scientific treatise, *De Natura Rerum*, based on Pliny and Isidore.

Bede, CUTHBERT (1827–89), pseudonym of EDWARD BRADLEY, Eng. clergyman and humorist; *b.* Kidderminster; author of *Adventures of Mr. Verdant Green, an Oxford Freshman.*

Bedford, JOHN PLANTAGENET, DUKE OF (1389–1435), third son of Henry IV.; on Henry V.'s death, 1422, became regent of England; continued Henry's work of conquest in France, forming an alliance with the Duke of Burgundy; stemming the tide of disasters which followed the siege of Orleans, he crowned Henry VI. king of Paris, 1431; died at Rouen.

Bedford, FRANCIS RUSSELL, 4TH EARL OF (1593–1641), leader of the Parliamentarians, dying in the middle of the struggle; played a great part in the drainage of the Fens, called the Bedford Level.

Bedford, FRANCIS RUSSELL, 5TH DUKE (1765–1802), a friend of George IV. Pioneer in scientific agriculture and stock-breeding.

Bédier (*bā-dyā*), CHARLES MARIE JOSEPH (1864–), Fr. writer and member of Fr. Academy, 1920; *b.* Paris; prof. of Mediæval Fr. language and literature at Coll. de France; has rendered invaluable service to Fr. literature and mediæval studies generally by researches into origin of *Chansons de Geste*; works include *Les Légendes Epiques*.

Beebe, CHARLES WILLIAM (1877–), Amer. ornithologist; *b.* Brooklyn, New York; organized collection of birds in New York Zoo; expeditions to S. America and Asia, and the Sargasso Sea, are described in *Jungle Days* (1925), *Beneath Tropic Seas* (1928), etc.

Beecham, SIR THOMAS (1879–), Eng. musical conductor and operatic impressario; *b.* Liverpool; introduced Russ. ballet into England, 1911; has devoted his life and fortune to the establishment of opera in Britain and to the spread of musical culture.

Beecher, HENRY WARD (1813–87), Amer. preacher; *b.* Connecticut; brother of Harriet Beecher Stowe; pastor of Plymouth Congregational Church, Brooklyn; advocated abolition of slavery; sermons marked by great originality and eloquence; ed. *Christian Union*; twice visited England, and attracted vast audiences; pub. *Seven Lectures to Young Men* (1844), *Life Thoughts* (1858), *Life of Christ* (1871), etc.

Beechey, FREDERICK WILLIAM (1796–1856), Eng. explorer; *b.* London; served in navy and in explorations with Franklin and Parry; pub. (1831) *Voyage to the Pacific and Bering's Strait to Co-operate with the Polar Expeditions, 1825–28*; rear-admiral, 1854.

Beechey, Sir William (1753–1839), Eng. artist; portrait-painter to Queen Charlotte; R.A. and knighthood, 1798.

Beeching, Henry Charles (1859–1919), Eng. clergyman and poet; Dean of Norwich, 1911; pub. *In a Garden and Other Poems, Provincial Letters and Other Papers*; produced editions of several standard poets.

Beerbohm, Max (1872–), Eng. essayist and caricaturist; *b.* London; half-brother of Sir Herbert Tree; literary work is marked by whimsical humour; as a caricaturist he is a master of biting portraiture; publications include *The Works of Max Beerbohm, The Happy Hypocrite, The Poets' Corner, Fifty Caricatures* (1913), and *The Dreadful Dragon of Hay Hill* (1928).

Beethoven (*bā'tō-ven*), Ludwig van (1770–1827), Ger. composer; *b.* Bonn; son of a tenor singer at the Elector of Cologne's court; suffered dire poverty in early years; began musical training at the age of five. By 1781 Beethoven had acted as deputy court organist; in 1783 he was made cymbalist (practically conductor) at the Bonn theatre, and in 1784 was given a court appointment. In 1787 he visited Vienna, where he received a few lessons from Mozart; returned to Bonn and became the chief support of his father's household. Through the friendship of Count Waldstein the elector was induced to send Beethoven again to Vienna, 1792, where he made his home for the remainder of his life. There he placed himself under the tuition of Haydn, but was dissatisfied with his progress, and took lessons from Schenk, and studied counterpoint later with Albrechtsberger, and the violin with Schuppanzigh. Though a man of generous and noble character, he frequently treated his friends with inconsiderate rudeness, probably owing to the deafness which afflicted him before he was thirty years of age, and became total by 1822. Yet some of his greatest compositions belong to this period. To Beethoven's first period belong: first two symphonies, first ten sonatas (including *Pathétique* (1799) and *Moonlight*), string trios, first six string quartets, *Mount of Olives* (oratorio), and most of the sets of variations for pianoforte. Second period includes most of his greatest works—*e.g. Kreutzer* Sonata (violin and piano) (1803); 3rd *Eroica* Symphony (1804); *Fidelio* (opera) (1805); *Appassionata* Sonata, 4th Symphony, and 32 Variations in C minor for Pianoforte (1806); C minor (5th), and *Pastoral* (6th) Symphony (1807); and G minor Pianoforte Concerto (1807); Violin Concerto and *Lebewohl* Sonata (1809); music to *Egmont* and trio in B♭ (1810); Symphonies 7 and 8 (1812). To the last period belong 9th (*Choral*) Symphony (1823 onwards); last four pianoforte sonatas, last four string quartets, *Missa Solemnis* two overtures, and other minor works. His earlier works were akin to Mozart and Haydn; his later compositions marked entirely new departures, characterized by amazing individuality and classical beauty.

[*Beethoven and his Nine Symphonies* (1896), by Sir G. Grove; *Life of Beethoven* (revised Eng. trans. 1921), by A. W. Thayer; *Beethoven* (1927), by W. J. Turner.]

Beets (*bāts*), Nicolaas (1814–1903), Dutch author; *b.* Haarlem; prof. of theology at Utrecht Univ.; famous as author of *Camera Obscura*, a collection of tales and sketches, largely of peasant life, distinguished for their humour and fidelity.

Be'gas, Karl (1794–1854), Ger. painter; *b.* near Aachen; a leader of the 'Nazarenes,' or Ger.

pre-Raphaelites; painted *The Resurrection*, etc.

Begas, Reinhold (1831–1911), Ger. sculptor, son of Karl Begas; *b.* Berlin; his *Borussia*, *Schiller*, *Neptune* fountain, and other statues adorn Berlin.

Begbie, Edward Harold (1871–1929), Eng. author and journalist; an enthusiast for social reform, the subject of *Broken Earthenware* (1910), and many other books. Under pseudonym of 'A Gentleman with a Duster' wrote *The Mirrors of Downing Street*, etc. (1920–22).

Behaim (*bā'hēm*) or Behem, Martin (?1436–1506), Ger. geographer; *b.* Nürnberg; voyaged to west coast of Africa with Port. expeditions; improved nautical instruments, drew fine maps, and constructed celebrated Nürnberg globe.

Behm (*bām*), Ernst (1830–84), Ger. geographer and statistician; *b.* Gotha; founded *Geographisches Jahrbuch*; joint compiler of *Bevölkerung der Erde* (1872–84).

Behmen, Jacob. See Boehme.

Behn (*bān*), Mrs. Aphra (1640–89), novelist and dramatist; *b.* in Kent; first Eng. professional authoress; visited S. America in childhood, and hence her best novel, *Oroonoko*; employed by Charles II. as a spy in Holland; plays include *The Rover.* Work lively, witty, and coarse.

Behring (*bē'ring*), Emil von (1854–1917), Ger. physician and bacteriologist; discovered antitoxin for diphtheria and tetanus; director of Hygienic Institute, Marburg, 1895–1917; Nobel prizeman (med.), 1901.

Beilby, Sir George Thomas (1850–1924), Scot. scientist; *b.* Edinburgh; an authority on coal economy, also on shale oil industry, and founder in this country of synthetic production of alkali cyanides; established Fuel Research station at Greenwich; knighted, 1916; appointed fuel director, 1917.

Beilstein (*bīl'stīn*), Friedrich Konrad (1838–1907), Russ. chemist; prof. of chemistry, St. Petersburg Technological Institute, 1866–96; his *Handbuch der Organischen Chemie* is famed.

Beit, Alfred (1853–1906), S. African financier and philanthropist; *b.* Hamburg; diamond merchant, Kimberley, director of De Beers, friend of Cecil Rhodes: founded chair of colonial history, Oxford; left bequests to univs. of Johannesburg, Hamburg, and London.

Beit, Sir Otto (1865–1930), brother of above; noted philanthropist; *b.* Hamburg; established Beit Memorial Fellowship for Medical Research.

Beith, John Hay, c.b.e. (1876–), pen-name Ian Hay, Scot. novelist and playwright; author of many pleasing novels, beginning with *Pip* (1907), and *The First Hundred Thousand* (1915); plays include *Tillie of Bloomsbury* (1919), and *Mr. Faint-Heart* (1931).

Bek, Antony (*d.* 1311), Eng. ecclesiastic; Bishop of Durham, 1283, and chief adviser in Scot. affairs to Edward I.; made sovereign of Isle of Man by Edward II.

Beke, Charles Tilstone (1800–74), Eng. explorer; *b.* London; travelled in Abyssinia, Syria, Palestine, and Egypt, and pub. books on his travels.

Bekh'terev, Vladimir Mikhailovich (1857–1927), Russ. physician; *b.* in Viatka province; pioneer in psycho-physiological researches; writings include *General Basis of the Reflex Action of Man.*

Bela. (1) III., King of Hungary (*d.* 1196), a great statesman, whose court was one of the most brilliant in Europe; assisted the Serbs to institute a native dynasty. (2) IV., Hungarian king

(1235–70), in whose reign occurred the Tatar invasion of Hungary.

Bela Kun. See KUN, BELA.

Belasco, DAVID (1853–1931), Amer. dramatist; *b.* San Francisco; controlled many theatres in U.S.A.; wrote and produced *Zaza* (1896), *The Girl of the Golden West* (1905), etc.

Belcher, SIR EDWARD (1799–1877), Brit. admiral, led unsuccessful expedition in 1852 in search of Franklin; wrote *Last of the Arctic Voyages* (1855), etc.

Belgiojoso (*bel-jō-yō'sō*), CRISTINA, PRINCESS OF (1808–71), Ital. patriot; *b.* Milan; ardent supporter of Cavour; founded patriotic journal *Italia*; wrote several historical works.

Belgran'o, MANUEL (1770–1821), Argentine patriot and statesman; *b.* Buenos Aires; played a leading part in Argentina's struggle for freedom from Span. rule.

Belisa'rius (*c.* 505–65), greatest general of Byzantine Empire; won famous victories against Vandals and Ostrogoths of Africa and Italy; accused of conspiring against the emperor; died in disgrace.

Bell, ACTON, CURRER, AND ELLIS. See BRONTË.

Bell, ALEXANDER GRAHAM (1847–1922), scientist; *b.* Edinburgh; went to Canada, 1870; to Boston, 1872; inventor of the telephone, 1876, photophone, 1880, and gramophone, 1887.

Bell, ANDREW (1753–1832), Scot. clergyman and educationist; *b.* St. Andrews; superintendent of school in Madras; introduced monitorial system of education; founded Madras Coll., St. Andrews, etc.; buried in Westminster Abbey.

Bell, SIR CHARLES (1774–1842), Scot. anatomist; *b.* Edinburgh; discovered the function of the nerves; prof. of anatomy, Royal Coll. of Surgeons, London.

Bell, GERTRUDE MARGARET LOWTHIAN (1868–1926), Eng. traveller; *b.* Durham; travelled in Persia, Syria, Palestine, and Arabia; services in Mesopotamia during Great War were invaluable; secretary to high commissioner, Iraq, 1920–6; did much archæological work, and founded Baghdad museum.

[*Letters of Gertrude Bell* (1927).]

Bell, HENRY (1767–1830), Scot. engineer; *b.* in W. Lothian; constructed first steamship, the *Comet*, a 30-ton vessel, to ply on the Clyde, 1812.

Bell, JOHN (1811–95), Eng. sculptor; *b.* in Suffolk; works include the *Wellingtom Monument* at Guildhall and *Guards' Memorial*, Waterloo Place, London; was a promoter of the Great Exhibition of 1851.

Bell, JOHN JOY (1871–1934), Scot. humorous writer; *b.* Glasgow; author of *Wee Macgreegor* (1902), *Oh Christina!* (1909), etc. Also *The Glory of Scotland* (1932).

Bell, JOHN KEBLE (1875–1928), Eng. novelist and dramatist; pen-name KEBLE HOWARD; *b.* Basingstoke; plays include *The Smiths of Surbiton* (1922), and *Lord Babs* (1925); autobiography, *My Motley Life* (1927).

Bell, SIR JOSEPH (1837–1911), famous Edinburgh surgeon, whose power of accurate deduction is said to have suggested Conan Doyle's 'Sherlock Holmes.'

Bell'amy, EDWARD (1850–98), Amer. author; *b.* in Massachusetts; his socialistic romance, *Looking Backward* (1888), caused the formation of many 'Nationalist' clubs in U.S.A.

Bell'armine, ROBERT (1542–1621), Ital. cardinal; *b.* in Tuscany; great Jesuit theologian; befriended Galileo in Rome.

Bellay (*be-lā*), JOACHIM DU (1524–60), Fr. poet; *b.* near Angers; one of famous group of poets, the Pléiade; wrote famous prose work *Deffense et Illustration de la Langue françoyse* (1549); poetical works include *Recueil de Poésie* and *L'Olive.*

Belle-Isle (*bel-ēl'*), CHARLES LOUIS AUGUSTE FOUQUET, DUC DE (1684–1761), Fr. soldier and statesman; distinguished in wars of Span. and Austrian successions; marshal of France, 1741, duke and peer, 1748, and minister of war, 1757; established Order of Merit, 1759.

Bell'enden, JOHN (*fl.* 1533), Scot. poet and translator in service of James v.; wrote *History and Chronicles of Scotland* (1536), a trans. from Boece's *Historia Scotorum.*

Bellenden, WILLIAM (*b.* 1555), Scot. classical scholar; prof. at Paris Univ.; authority on Cicero.

Belli, GIUSEPPE GIOACHINO (1791–1863), Ital. poet; *b.* Rome; remembered as author of numerous masterly sonnets.

Bellini (*bel-ē'nē*), a family of celebrated Venetian painters. (1) JACOPO (1400–70), father-in-law of Mantegna; one of his sketch-books is in Brit. Museum. (2) GENTILE (1426–1507), son of Jacopo; his masterpiece, *The Preaching of St. Mark,* is at Milan. (3) GIOVANNI (1428–1516), brother of Gentile, founder of Venetian school; master of Titian, Giorgione, and Tintoretto; finest works, *Christ at Emmaus* (Venice), *The Transfiguration* (Naples), and *Coronation of the Virgin* (Pesaro).

Bellini, VINCENZO (1801–35), Sicilian operatic composer, of European fame; best-known opera, *La Sonnambula* (in which both Patti and Albani made their début in England).

Bellman, KARL MIKAEL (1740–95), Swed. poet; *b.* Stockholm; received patronage of Gustavus III.; pub. *Fredmans Epistlar* (1790), and *Fredmans Sånger* (1791).

Bello (*bel'yō*), ANDRÉS (1781–1865), Venezuelan poet and scholar, founded univ. in Santiago, 1843, and was its first rector.

Belloc, HILAIRE (1870–), Eng. author, of Fr. descent; *b.* St. Cloud, France; educated Oxford; naturalized, 1902; M.P., 1906–10; author of poems, satirical novels, books of travel, history, etc.; keen student of military matters; strong supporter of Roman Catholic Church; works include *The Bad Child's Book of Beasts* (1896); *The Path to Rome* (1902); *History of England* (in 5 vols.); *Charles I.* (1933).

Belloy (*bel-wä'*), PIERRE LAURENT BUIRETTE DE (1727–75), Fr. historical dramatist; *b.* in Auvergne; chief works, *Zelmire* (1760), and *Le Siège de Calais* (1765).

Below, OTTO VON (1857–), Ger. soldier; *b.* Danzig; led troops brilliantly at battle of Tannenberg, E. Prussia, 1914; commanded army on Baltic flank; in command of Ger. troops operating with Bulgarians, 1916; sent to Italy, and broke Ital. lines at Caporetto, 1917; led the army that failed to take Arras, March 1918; retired 1919.

Belshaz'zar (6th cent. B.C.), Babylonian general, son of King Nabonidos, not of Nebuchadnezzar, as stated in Book of Daniel; made last resistance of Babylonia to Cyrus. (See Dan. 5.)

Belzoni (*bel-tsō'nē*), GIOVANNI BATTISTA (1778–1823), Ital. Egyptologist; *b.* Padua; pioneer in Egyptian archæological discovery.

Bem, JOSEF (1795–1850), Polish soldier; *b.* Tarnov; fought in Polish war of independence, 1830; served under Kossuth against Austrians; adopted Mohammedanism, and became Turk. governor of Aleppo.

Bem'bo, PIETRO, CARDINAL (1470–1547), Ital. poet; *b.* Venice; reputed as the principal man of letters of his day.

Benavente, JACINTO (1866–), Span. playwright; *b.* Madrid; left study of law for literature; has written *El Nido Ajeno* (1894), *La Gata de Angora* (1900), *La Malquerida* (1913); Nobel prize for literature, 1922.

Ben'bow, JOHN (1653–1702), Eng. admiral; *b.* Shrewsbury; sent to W. Indies to settle disputes with Spaniards over the Scot. Darien settlement; fought Fr. squadron, 1702, off St. Domingo.

Benck'endorff, COUNT ALEXANDRE (1849–1917), Russ. diplomatist; *b.* Berlin; ambassador to Great Britain, 1903–17; had a large share in forming the Triple Entente (Great Britain, France, and Russia).

Benc'zur, JULIUS (1844–1920), Hungarian painter; director of Budapest Academy; painted *The Departure of Ladislaus Hunyady, The Baptism of St. Stephen, King of Hungary*, etc.

Benda, JULIEN (1868–), distinguished Fr. essayist and novelist; *b.* Paris; opponent of Bergson; chief work, *Trahison des Clercs* (1927).

Benedek (*bā'ne-dek*), LUDWIG AUGUST VON (1804–81), Austrian general; *b.* in Hungary; distinguished in Galician, Hungarian, and Ital. campaigns. Hampered by staff intrigues, was defeated at Sadowa, 1866.

Benedet'ti, VINCENT, COUNT (1817–1900), Fr. diplomatist; *b.* in Corsica; ambassador at Berlin, 1864–70; at declaration of Franco-Prussian War defended his policy successfully in *Ma Mission en Prusse* (1871).

Benedict, name of fifteen popes and one antipope. BENEDICT XV., GIACOMO DELLA CHIESA (1854–1922); Archbishop of Bologna, 1907; cardinal, May 25, 1914; pope, Sept. 3, 1914; first years of his pontificate extraordinarily difficult owing to complications of the Great War, during which he remained neutral.

The antipope PEDRO DI LUNA was known as Benedict XIII.; elected by cardinals of Avignon, 1394; maintained a struggle against each pope in turn from Urban VI. to Martin V.

Benedict, ST. (480–543), founder of the order of Benedictines; *b.* in Umbria, Italy; author of *Regula Monachorum* (*c.* 515), which became the standard rule of the Western monastic orders.

Benedict, SIR JULIUS (1804–85), musical composer; son of Jewish banker of Stuttgart; settled in London, 1835; associated with grand opera at Drury Lane and other theatres; operas include *The Lily of Killarney*, his greatest success.

Benedict Biscop (628–690), Eng. churchman; made several visits to Rome; founded a monastery at Jarrow, 682; associated with Bede at Jarrow; remarkable for learning and influence on eccles. architecture.

Beneke (*bā'nek-e*), FRIEDRICH EDUARD (1798–1854), Ger. philosopher; *b.* Berlin; held that the best approach to philosophy is through psychology; most important work, *Lehrbuch der Psychologie als Naturwissenschaft* (1833).

Benes (*ben-esh'*), EDUARD (1884–), Czech statesman; prof. of sociology at Prague, 1921; went to Paris, 1915, and urged the formation of an independent Czecho-Slovak state; premier, 1921–2; president, 1935. Pub. *Bohemian Case for Independence* (1917), *My War Memoirs* (1928), etc.

Benfey (*ben'fī*), THEODOR (1809–81), Ger. philologist; *b.* near Göttingen; greatest work is his *Sanskrit-English Dictionary* (1866).

Benjamin ('son of the right hand'), youngest son of Jacob and Rachel. (See Genesis.)

Benjamin, JUDAH PHILIP (1811–84), Anglo-Amer. statesman and lawyer; *b.* St. Thomas, W. Indies; Confederate secretary of state, 1862–5; escaped to England and called to bar, 1866; Q.C., 1872; his work, generally known as *Benjamin on Sales* (1868), is a classic.

Bennett, Enoch Arnold (1867–1931), Eng. novelist and playwright; *b.* Hanley; abandoned law for literature, 1893; several of his novels describe life in the Potteries ('Five Towns') with consummate realism. Best known novels include *Anna of the Five Towns* (1902), *The Old Wives' Tale* (1908), *Clayhanger* (1910), *The Card* (1911), *Riceyman Steps* (1923), and *Imperial Palace* (1930). Among his plays are *Milestones* (1912, with E. Knoblock), and *The Great Adventure* (1913).

Bennett, James Gordon (1841–1918), Amer. journalist; *b.* New York; proprietor of *New York Herald*, founded by his father, 1835; fitted out, in conjunction with the *Daily Telegraph*, Stanley's expedition to find Livingstone, 1874. Donor of cup competed for annually by motorists.

Bennett, Richard Bedford (1870–). Canadian statesman; *b.* in New Brunswick. Practised as a lawyer; entered parl., 1911; director-general of National Service, 1917; leader of Conservative Party since 1927; prime minister, 1930–5.

Bennett, Sir William Sterndale (1816–75), Eng. musical composer; *b.* Sheffield; founded Bach Soc.; principal of Royal Academy of Music from 1868; composed overtures, cantatas, anthems, etc.

Ben'nigsen, Levin August Theophil, Count von (1745–1826), Russ. general; *b.* Brunswick; gov.-gen. of Lithuania, 1801; checked Napoleon at Eylau, 1807; fought at Borodino, 1812, and shared in victory over Napoleon at Leipzig, 1813; created Count the same day.

Benoît (*be-nwä'*), Peter Léonard Leopold (1834–1901), Flem. composer; *b.* Harlebeke, Belgium; director of Antwerp Conservatory.

Benson. (1) Edward White (1829–96), Archbishop of Canterbury; *b.* Birmingham; headmaster of Wellington Coll., 1859–72, and Bishop of Truro, 1877–82. (2) Arthur Christopher (1862–1925), author, son of above; Master at Eton Coll., 1885–1903; Master of Magdalene, Cambridge, 1915; best-known works, *House of Quiet*, *The Upton Letters*, and *From a College Window*; collaborated with Lord Esher in *Selections from the Correspondence of Queen Victoria* (1907); his *Hugh, Memoirs of a Brother* (1915), is an account of (4). (3) Edward Frederic (1867–), novelist, son of (1); first success was the society novel *Dodo* (1893); other works include *The Luck of the Vails* (1901), *The Osbornes* (1910), *Thorley Weir* (1913), *David Blaize* (1916), *David of Kings* (1924), *As We Were* (1930). (4) Robert Hugh (1871–1914), author and R.C. priest; son of (1); wrote *The Light Invisible*, *By What Authority?*, *The Queen's Tragedy*, *A Mirror of Shalott*, *The Necromancers*, *The Dawn of All*.

[*Memoir*, by A. C. Benson.]

Benson, Sir Frank R. (1858–), actor-manager; *b.* in Hants; with his wife, Miss Constance Featherstonhaugh, produced Shakespeare's plays; trained many leading actors and actresses; knighted 1916; directed annual festivals at Shakespeare Memorial Theatre, Stratford-on-Avon, from 1888.

Bent, James Theodore (1852–97), Eng. traveller; *b.* near Leeds; with his wife made extensive journeys in Asia Minor, S. Africa, and Arabia. Wrote *The Ruined Cities of Mashonaland* (3rd ed. 1895), etc.

Bentham, GEORGE (1800–84), Eng. botanist, nephew of Jeremy Bentham; *b.* near Portsmouth; in collaboration with Sir Joseph Hooker wrote *Genera Plantarum,* a masterpiece of systematic botany.

Bentham, JEREMY (1748–1832), Eng. writer on law and political economy; *b.* London; called to bar, but refused to plead; gave himself up to philosophical writing, publishing *Fragment on Government, or a Comment on the Commentaries* (1776), in opposition to Blackstone; enjoyed a wide European reputation; wrote *Defence of Usury* (1787), and *Principles of Morals and Legislation* (1789); established *Westminster Review* (1823). Bentham was a follower of Adam Smith; belonged to rationalist-utilitarian school of philosophy, and adopted as motto, 'the greatest happiness of the greatest number.' His *Principles of Penal Law* foreshadowed modern principles of punishment.

[*Jeremy Bentham* (1922), by Graham Wallas.]

Bentinck, WILLIAM, 1ST EARL OF PORTLAND (?1649–1709), diplomatist and friend of William III., whose marriage he arranged; *b.* in Overyssel, Holland; took part in negotiations which led to Peace of Ryswick, 1697, and the two Partition Treaties, 1698–1700.

Bentinck, LORD WILLIAM CAVENDISH (1774–1839), gov.-gen. of India, 1827–35; introduced important reforms into Ind. administration.

Bentinck, WILLIAM GEORGE FREDERIC CAVENDISH (1802–48), commonly called Lord George Bentinck; prominent sportsman and politician; promoted enfranchisement of Irish and Jews; opposed Free Trade, and was formidable opponent of Peel.

Bentinck, WILLIAM HENRY CAVENDISH, 3RD DUKE OF PORTLAND (1738–1809), Whig statesman; lord-lieutenant of Ireland, 1782; prime minister of coalition government, 1783; Fr. Revolution forced him to join Pitt; again prime minister, 1808–9.

Bentley, RICHARD (1662–1742), Eng. classical scholar and textual critic; *b.* Oulton (Yorks); educated Cambridge; accompanied a pupil to Oxford, where he became noted for his learning, and delivered the Boyle lectures on the *Evidences of Natural and Revealed Religion*; took holy orders. His famous *Dissertation on the Epistles of Phalaris* (1699) established his reputation as the greatest scholar of his age; in 1700 he was appointed master of Trinity Coll., Cambridge; in 1717 regius prof. of divinity. A man of overbearing temper, his controversies gave rise to Swift's *Battle of the Books,* and he was satirized by Pope in *The Dunciad*; pub. various annotated editions of the classics, including Terence and Horace, and of Milton's *Paradise Lost.*

[*Life* (1882), by R. C. Jebb (Eng. Men of Letters); vol. ix. of *Cambridge History of Literature.*]

Benvenu'to (1481–1559), Ital. painter, known as Tisio da Garofalo; his *Vision of St. Augustine* is in National Gallery, London.

Benvenuto Cellini. See CELLINI, BENVENUTO.

Béranger (*bā-ron-zhā'*), PIERRE JEAN DE (1780–1857), Fr. songwriter; *b.* Paris. He was made a small allowance by Lucien Bonaparte, and later procured a clerkship in the univ.; the *Petit Homme Gris* (1812) and *Roi d'Yvetot* (1813) made his name familiar throughout France; his songs were collected into a volume (1815); for a second volume (1821) he was imprisoned; wrote also *Chansons Nouvelles* (1825) and *Chansons Inédites* (1828); for publication of latter, containing his democratic and anti-papal views, he was fined and again imprisoned; *Dernières Chansons* (1857) was his last vol. His songs were witty, full of high feeling and pathos, and by them Béranger acquired a great political influence and an unrivalled hold on the hearts of the Fr. people.

Berchem (*berch'em*), or BERGHEM, NICOLAAS (1624–83), Dutch painter; *b.* Haarlem; generally painted Ital. scenery, with ruins and figure groups; pictures by him are in Wallace Collection and many continental galleries.

Berchtold (*berch'tolt*), LEOPOLD, COUNT VON (1863–), Austrian diplomatist; *b.* Vienna; ambassador to Russia, 1906; Austro-Hungarian foreign minister, 1912; after first Balkan War, 1912, prompted Bulgaria to attack Serbia; following the Serajevo incident, 1914, presented the fatal ultimatum to Belgrade; resigned office, 1915.

Berenga'ria OF NAVARRE married (1191) Richard I. of England.

Berenga'rius OF TOURS (998–1088), Fr. theologian; came into conflict with papal see by denying transubstantiation.

Beresford, LORD CHARLES WILLIAM DE LA POER, 1ST BARON (1846–1919), Brit. admiral and politician; *b.* in Ireland; famous for gallantry in *Condor* at bombardment of Alexandria, 1882, and in Nile Expedition, 1884–5; admiral, 1906; commander of Mediterranean Fleet, 1905–7; commander of Channel Fleet, 1907–9; M.P. (Unionist) on five occasions, 1874–1916; peerage, 1916; keen naval critic.

Beresford, JOHN DAVYS (1873–), Eng. novelist; *b.* near Peterborough; trained as architect; works include *The Hampdenshire Wonder* (1911), *Love's Pilgrims* (1923), *Real People* (1929).

Beresford, WILLIAM CARR BERESFORD, VISCOUNT (1768–1854), Brit. general; illegitimate son of George de la Poer Beresford, 1st Marquess of Waterford; distinguished in Peninsular War; viscount, 1823; general, 1825.

Bergerac (*berzh'räk*), SAVINIEN CYRANO DE (1620–55), Fr. soldier, novelist, and dramatist; wrote plays on classical model and scientific romantic stories; notorious for reckless bravery, duels, and free thinking; subject of a very popular play by Rostand.

Berg'haus, HEINRICH (1797–1884), Ger. geographer and cartographer; *b.* Cleve; conducted geographical school at Potsdam; chief work, *Physikalischer Atlas* (1838–48); shared in preparation of Stieler's Atlas.

Berghem. See BERCHEM.

Bergson, HENRI (1859–), Fr. philosopher; *b.* Paris; prof. at Collège de France; exponent of the philosophy of change. According to this philosophy duration, change, and movement comprise not only reality, but the whole and only reality. In particular, life is essentially identical with time and change, and it is this which constitutes the universe. This reality is apprehended by us not through the intellect, but through intuition, which gives us a direct knowledge of the reality which consists of life. The purpose of intellect is to give us views, of certain limited aspects of reality, which are of importance only in so far as they are of service to life. His philosophy is embodied in three works, *Time and Freewill* (1888), *Matter and Memory* (1896), *Creative Evolution* (1907). Elected to Fr. Academy, 1914; Nobel prize for literature, 1927.

[*Henri Bergson* (1919), by H. W. Carr.]

Bering, VITUS (1680–1741), Dan. explorer; employed by Peter the Great; discovered and explored Bering Sea and Strait; died on Bering I.

Berkeley (*bärk′li*), George (1685–1753), Irish philosopher; *b.* near Kilkenny; friend of Steele, Swift, Addison, etc. In 1709 he wrote his *Essay towards a New Theory of Vision*, showing that the immediate objects of sight are all mind-dependent appearances, which form what is practically a natural language; in *A Treatise on the Principles of Human Knowledge* (1710) he advanced the theory that the actuality of the seen world depends on its being perceived, and that this involves the assumption of creative Eternal Reason. Resolving to establish a centre of Christian civilization in Bermuda, he went to Rhode I., 1728, but, as promised grant was not paid, returned 1731; made Bishop of Cloyne, 1734; resigned bishopric, 1752, and died at Oxford. His last word in philosophy is found in *Siris* (1744), a most curious and profound book on metaphysics.

[Revised complete ed. of his works by Campbell Fraser (Oxford, 4 vols. 1901).]

Berkeley, Miles Joseph (1803–89), Eng. botanist; *b.* in Northants; founder of Brit. mycology (scientific fungus study).

Berlichingen (*ber-lich-ing′en*), Goetz (or Gottfried) von (1480–1562), Ger. robber knight; *b.* in Württemberg; lost hand in war and wore iron substitute, still preserved; his autobiography, ed. by Pistorius, 1731, inspired Goethe's drama, *Goetz von Berlichingen* (trans. by Scott, 1799).

Berlioz (*ber-lē-ō′*), Hector (1803–69), Fr. musical composer; *b.* near Grenoble; pioneer of the Romantic movement in music. His compositions include *Benvenuto Cellini, La Damnation de Faust, Roméo et Juliette, Béatrice et Bénédict*, which are the glories of Fr. music; had a supreme command of orchestration, and in many respects resembled Wagner.

Bernadotte. See Charles xiv. of Sweden.

Bernard, St., of Clairvaux (1090–1153), Fr. monastic reformer; *b.* near Dijon; entered monastery of Citeaux, *c.* 1112; helped to found monastery of Clairvaux, where life was rigidly ascetic; supported election of Innocent ii. to Papacy, 1130; rebuilt Clairvaux, 1135; preached Second Crusade, 1146. His influence in Europe was enormous, his greatness being due to personality and character; great opponent of Abélard, and strongly conservative; believed heresy should be met by argument, but advocated persecution rather than allow it to spread. Writings include many hymns still in use.

[*Life of St. Bernard* (1863), by J. C. Morison.]

Bernard, St., of Menthon (923–1008), founder of monasteries and hospices on passes of Alps (Great and Little St. Bernard); feast, June 15.

Bernard of Morlaix (or Cluny), Fr. Benedictine monk of 12th cent., author of long poem *De Contemptu Mundi*, the source of several well-known hymns, *e.g.* 'Jerusalem the Golden.'

Bernard, Claude (1813–78), Fr. physiologist; *b.* near Villefranche; noted for researches on poisons, functions of pancreas, liver, and vaso-motor system.

Bernard, John Henry (1860–1927), Brit. scholar and preacher; *b.* in India; Bishop of Ossory, 1911; Archbishop of Dublin, 1915; Provost of Trinity Coll., Dublin, 1919; his statesmanship was of value to Irish Convention, 1917–18; ed. *Kant's Critical Philosophy* (along with Sir John Mahaffy).

Berners, John Bourchier, 2nd Baron (1467–1533), Eng. author and diplomatist; lord chancellor, 1516; deputy of Calais, 1520; noted for trans. of *Froissart* (1523–

5), *The Golden Book of Marcus Aurelius*, etc.

Berners (or BARNES), DAME JULIANA (*fl.* first half of 15th cent.), author of famous *Boke of St. Albans* (1486), a treatise on hawking, hunting, and heraldry; said to have been prioress of Sopwell Nunnery.

Bernhard, DUKE OF SAXE-WEIMAR (1604–39), Ger. general; *b.* Weimar; assisted Gustavus Adolphus to win battle of Lützen; won many battles for French against the Emperor.

Bernhardi, FRIEDRICH VON (1849–1930), Ger. soldier and writer; *b.* St. Petersburg; served in Franco-Ger. War, 1870–1, and in Great War; best known by his *Germany and the Next War* (1912), in which he advocated the doctrine 'world power or downfall.'

Bern'hardt, SARAH (1845–1923), famous Fr. actress; *b.* Paris; of Jewish descent; made début at Comédie Française, 1862; her golden voice and dramatic power soon established her reputation as the greatest actress of her day; awarded Cross of Legion of Honour, 1913; acted even after amputation of a leg, 1915.

[*Ma Double Vie* (autobiography, 1907; Eng. trans., 1908).]

Ber'ni, FRANCESCO (1497–1535), Ital. poet; canon in cathedral at Florence; stands easily at head of Ital. comic poets; chiefly known for rewriting of Boiardo's *Orlando Innamorato*. His verse is known as Bernesque.

Bernini (*ber-nē'nē*), GIOVANNI LORENZO (1598–1680), Ital. artist; *b.* Naples; chiefly celebrated as architect and sculptor; designed Barberini Palace and colonnade of St. Peter's at Rome.

Bernoulli (*ber-noo-lyē'*), or BERNOUILLI, eminent family of Basle, Switzerland; refugees from Antwerp, remarkable for their scientific ability, especially in mathematics. (1) JACQUES (1654–1705) extended the use of the calculus and determined various curves; prof. and rector, Basle Univ. (2) JEAN (1667–1748), his brother, discovered exponential calculus and curve of swiftest descent; prof. in Groningen; succeeded (1) in Basle. (3) NICOLAS (1695–1726), eldest son of (2), prof. of mathematics in St. Petersburg. (4) DANIEL (1700–82), son of (2), gained international recognition, sharing prize of Académie des Sciences, Paris, with Maclaurin and Euler; prof. of mathematics, St. Petersburg; prof. of physics in Basle. (5) JEAN (1710–90), youngest son of (2), succeeded his father in Basle. (6) NICOLAS (1687–1759), son of (3); met Halley and Newton in England; prof. of mathematics in Padua; afterwards prof. of logic in Basle. (7) JEAN (1744–1807), son of (5); astronomer-royal at Berlin; afterwards mathematical director of the Akademie. (8) JACQUES (1759–89), brother of (7); succeeded (4) in chair of experimental physics in Basle; afterwards prof. of mathematics, St. Petersburg.

Bernstein, EDUARD (1850–1932), Ger. social democrat, politician; *b.* Berlin; lived in London, 1888–1901; was a leading member of Reichstag; author of many works on socialism.

Bernstein, HENRI (1876–), Fr. playwright; *b.* Paris; has attained great success, especially with *La Rafale* (1905), *Le Secret* (1913), and *Le Venin* (1927).

Bernstorff, ANDREAS PETER, COUNT VON (1735–97), Dan. statesman; *b.* Hanover; renewed friendship between England and Denmark; introduced many reforms, including abolition of serfdom.

Bernstorff, CHRISTIAN GÜNTHER, COUNT VON (1769–1835), Dan. statesman; *b.* Copenhagen; ambassador successively to Sweden,

Austria, and Germany; transferred allegiance to Prussia; made Prussian foreign minister, 1818–32.

Bernstorff, Johann Hartwig Ernst, Count von (1712–72), great Dan. statesman; called by Frederick the Great 'the Oracle of Denmark'; very successful minister for foreign affairs.

Bernstorff, Johann Heinrich, Count von (1862–), Ger. diplomatist; *b.* London; secretary to Ger. embassy, London, 1902–6; Ger. ambassador at Washington, U.S.A., 1908–17, until the entrance of the U.S.A. into the Great War; ambassador to Constantinople, 1917–18; president of Ger. League of Nations Union. Pub. *My Three Years in America* (1920).

Berruguete (*ber-oo-gā'tā*), Alonzo (*c.* 1480–1561), Span. painter and architect; *b.* near Valladolid; studied under Michelangelo; his masterpiece is archbishop's stall in Toledo Cathedral, representing *The Transfiguration*, worked in marble.

Berry, Charles Ferdinand, Duc de (1778–1820), second son of Charles x. of France; assassinated at the opera; memoirs written by Chateaubriand; his wife, Caroline Ferdinande Louise, Duchesse de Berry (1798–1870), suffered imprisonment (1832) for stirring up revolt against Louis Philippe in Vendée.

Bertha. (1) St. Bertha (*d.* early 7th cent.), wife of Ethelbert of Kent; persuaded him to accept Christianity. (2) 'Bertha au grand pied' (Bertha Greatfoot, *d.* 783), wife of Pepin the Short and mother of Charles the Great; subject of early literature. (3) Sister of Charles the Great and mother of Roland in Arthurian romances. (4) Wife of Rudolf ii. of Burgundy; subject of many anecdotes; *d. c.* 1000.

Berthelot (*bert-lō'*), Marcellin Pierre Eugène (1827–1907), distinguished Fr. chemist and statesman; prof. of organic chemistry at Paris; minister of foreign affairs, 1895; wrote *Sur la Force de la Poudre et des Matières Explosives.*

Berthier (*ber-tē-ā'*), Pierre Alexandre (1753–1815), Prince of Neuchâtel, marshal of France; *b.* Versailles; Napoleon's chief of staff, 1796–1814; went over to the Bourbons, 1814.

Berthollet (*ber-tō-lā'*), Claude Louis, Count (1748–1822), Fr. chemist; *b.* near Annecy; accompanied Napoleon to Egypt; was the first to analyse ammonia; discovered chlorate of potash.

Berthon, Edward Lyon (1813–99), Eng. clergyman; *b.* London; invented two-bladed propeller and collapsible boats; latter used in Africa by General Gordon and by Selous.

Bertie, Francis Leverton, 1st Baron Bertie of Thame (1844–1919), Brit. ambassador to Paris, 1905; rendered great service in the growth of the Entente Cordiale.

Bertillon (*ber-tē-yōn*), Alphonse (1853–1914), Fr. criminologist; *b.* Paris; invented the 'Bertillon system' of measurement for identification of criminals; also a handwriting expert.

Bertin (*ber-tan*), Louis François (1766–1841), Fr. journalist; *b.* Paris; founded the *Journal des Débats*, which was carried on by his family.

Bertrand (*ber-tron*), Henri Gratien, Comte (1773–1844), Fr. general; *b.* Châteauroux; friend of Napoleon i., whom he accompanied to Elba and St. Helena, and in 1840 brought his remains to France.

Bertrand, Jacques Louis Napoleon (1807–41), Fr. poet; *b.* in Piedmont; wrote *Gaspard de la Nuit* and *Fantaisies à la Manière de Rembrandt et de Callot.*

Bertrand, Louis (1866–), Fr. writer; prof. of rhetoric in Algiers, 1891–1900; wrote *Pépète le Bien-Aimé* (1904); his *L'Invasion* was crowned by Fr. Academy; wrote also *Saint Augustin* (1913) and *Louis XIV* (1923); member of Fr. Academy, 1925.

Bervic (*ber-vēk'*), Charles Clément Balvay (1756–1822), Fr. engraver; *b.* Paris; famous for portrait of Louis xvi., also for the *Laocoon.*

Berwick (*ber'ik*), James Fitz-James, Duke of (1670–1734), natural son of James ii., and marshal of France; *b.* in France; served at Battle of Boyne, 1690; established his fame by winning battle of Almanza, 1707.

Berze'lius, Jons Jakob (1779–1848), Swed. chemist; prof. of chemistry, Stockholm; experiments in electrolysis resulted in his theory of chemical proportions and determination of atomic weights; discovered many of the elements; pioneer of organic chemistry.

Bes'ant, Mrs. Annie, *née* Wood (1847–1933), Eng. theosophist; *b.* London; associated with Charles Bradlaugh, 1874–88, in his free-thought campaigns; early member of the Fabian Soc.; became a theosophist in 1889; spent much time in India, where she founded Central Hindu Coll., Benares, 1898, and was strong supporter of Ind. Home Rule; numerous works on theosophy, social and religious questions, include *Reincarnation, Theosophy and the New Psychology*, etc.

Besant', Sir Walter (1836–1901), Eng. writer; *b.* Portsmouth; prof. at Royal Coll., Mauritius, 1861–7; wrote many novels, at first in collaboration with James Rice, *e.g. Ready-money Mortiboy* and *The Golden Butterfly*. After Rice's death wrote *All Sorts and Conditions of Men* (which led to erection of People's Palace in east end of London), *Dorothy Forster*, etc., and works on London.

Beskow (*bes'kov*), Bernhard von, Baron (1796–1868), Swed. poet and historian; *b.* Stockholm; secretary of Swed. Academy; works include dramatic and lyrical poems, memoir of Gustavus iii., etc.

Besnard (*bes-när'*), Paul Albert (1849–1934), Fr. painter; *b.* Paris; works include frescoes at the Sorbonne and twelve 'Stations of the Cross' in the chapel of Berck Hospital.

Bes'sel, Friedrich Wilhelm (1784–1846), Ger. astronomer; *b.* Minden; introduced the heliometer and correction for personal equation, 1823; invented *Bessel's Functions*, of importance in mathematical physics.

Bes'semer, Sir Henry (1813–98), Eng. engineer and inventor; *b.* in Herts; famous for his steel-manufacturing process, which revolutionized the industry.

Bessières (*bes-yer'*), Jean Baptiste (1768–1813), Duke of Istria and marshal of France; distinguished cavalry officer in Napoleonic wars; commanded Imperial Guard in retreat from Moscow.

Best, William Thomas (1826–97), Eng. organist; *b.* Carlisle; revolutionized musical life of Liverpool by his recitals, especially of Bach's works.

Betham-Edwards, Matilda Barbara (1836–1919), Eng. novelist; *b.* in Suffolk; writer on Fr. life.

Bethlen de Bethlen, Stephen, Count (1874–), Hungarian statesman; led successful opposition to Bolshevist revolution, 1918–19, and to the attempt of King Charles to resume power; prime minister, 1921–31.

Bethmann-Hollweg (*bāt'man hol'vāg*), Theobald von (1856–1921), Ger. statesman; *b.* near Berlin; educated at Bonn Univ., where he became a friend of the

Kaiser; Prussian home secretary, 1905, vice-chancellor, 1907, and imperial chancellor, 1909–17; shortly after outbreak of the Great War defended Ger. invasion of Belgium on ground that 'necessity knows no law.' Credited with referring to the guarantee of Belgian neutrality as 'a scrap of paper.' Was suspected of showing undue deference to the U.S.A.; declined to define Germany's war aims, and in 1917 was dismissed by the Kaiser at the instigation of the military party. Pub. (1919) a volume of *Memoirs*.

Bet'terton, THOMAS (*c.* 1635–1710), Eng. actor; *b.* London; said to have introduced movable scenery into England; famed as Shakespearian actor; buried in Westminster Abbey.

Betty, WILLIAM HENRY WEST (1791-1874), well known as 'young Roscius,' or the boy actor; *b.* Shrewsbury; Pitt adjourned the House to allow members to see his Hamlet; retired with large fortune, 1812.

Beulé (*bu-lā'*), CHARLES ERNEST (1826–74), Fr. archæologist and politician; *b.* Saumur; discovered the propylæa of the Acropolis at Athens; was minister of the interior in 1873.

Beust (*boist*), FRIEDRICH FERDINAND, COUNT VON (1809–86), Austrian statesman, and chancellor of the Austrian Empire; *b.* Dresden; secured the emperor's coronation as King of Hungary; removed religious disabilities, and organized national defence; dismissed, 1871; subsequently ambassador to Britain and France.

Bewick (*bū'ik*), THOMAS (1753–1828), Eng. wood engraver; *b.* near Newcastle-on-Tyne; famous woodcuts are prized by collectors; his *British Birds* (1804) is especially esteemed.

Beyers (*bī'ers*), CHRISTIAN FREDERICK (1869–1914), S. African general; one of ablest strategists among Boer commanders during S. African War; chairman of Vereeniging Peace Conference; speaker of Transvaal Republic, 1906; was one of chief plotters of S. African rebellion, Oct. 1914; defeated by Botha near Rustenburg; was shot while crossing Vaal R.

Beyle, MARIE HENRI. See STENDHAL.

Be'za, THEODORE (1519–1605), Genevan reformer and theologian; *b.* in Burgundy; succeeded Calvin as head of Protestant Church in Geneva, 1564; wrote many religious works, including most of Huguenot Psalter, 1562; revised Huguenot Bible; presented uncial N.T. in MS. (*Codex Bezæ*) to Cambridge Univ.

Bezold (*bā'tsolt*), WILHELM VON (1837–1907), Ger. meteorologist; *b.* Munich; prof. of meteorology and director of Meteorological Institute, Berlin.

Bhandarkar, DEVADATTA RAMKRISHNA (1875–   ), Ind. archæologist; prof. of Ancient Indian History and Culture, Calcutta Univ., since 1917; author of numerous works on Ind. history and archæology.

Bhau Daji (1822–74), Hindu physician; *b.* in Goa; practised medicine in Bombay; author of many papers on Ind. antiquities; discovered preparations of great use in treatment of leprosy.

Bhownagree, SIR MANCHERJEE MERWANJEE (1851–1933), Parsee journalist and politician; *b.* Bombay; called to Eng. bar, 1885; helped to establish constitution in Bhaunagar; Conservative M.P. for Bethnal Green, 1895–1906; wrote *History of the Constitution of the East India Company* (1871), *Loyalty of India* (1916).

Bibes'co, LADY ELIZABETH ASQUITH, PRINCESS, Eng. novelist; younger daughter of Earl of Oxford and Asquith; married Antoine Bibesco, a Romanian prince, 1919. Works include *I Have Only Myself to Blame* (1921), *Portrait of Caroline* (1931).

Bichat (*bē-shä'*), MARIE FRANÇOIS XAVIER (1771–1802), Fr. anatomist and physiologist; *b.* in Jura; his *Anatomie Générale* created a revolution in methods of research.

Bickerdyke, JOHN, pseudonym of CHARLES HENRY COOK (1858–1933), Eng. writer on sport; *b.* London; author of *Angling in Salt Water, Wild Sports in Ireland,* etc.

Bickerstaffe-Drew, MONSIGNOR COUNT FRANCIS BROWNING DREW (1858–1928), Eng. R.C. prelate and writer; *b.* Leeds; senior chaplain to the forces at Malta and at Salisbury Plain; served in Great War, 1914–15, being twice mentioned in dispatches; under pseudonym 'John Ayscough' wrote several romances; in *French Windows* records personal war experiences.

Bidder, GEORGE PARKER (1806–78), Eng. engineer; *b.* in Devon; calculating prodigy; assisted George Stephenson; designed Victoria Docks (London) and the first railway swing bridge; was a founder of Electric Telegraph Co.

Biddle, JOHN (1615–62), 'father of Eng. Unitarianism'; *b.* in Gloucestershire; several times imprisoned for opinions; befriended by Cromwell; died in prison.

Bielski (*byel'ski*), MARTIN (1495–1576), Polish historian; wrote a history of Poland, the first historic work printed in Polish.

Big'elow, JOHN (1817–1911), Amer. diplomat and author; *b.* Malden, New York; proprietor and editor of New York *Evening Post*; U.S.A. minister to France, 1864–7; secretary of state of New York, 1875–7; author of *Life of Benjamin Franklin,* etc.

Bigelow, POULTNEY (1855–), Amer. journalist and author, son of above; *b.* New York; voyaged round world in a sailing ship, 1875–6; a celebrated canoe traveller; has written travel books, also *Memoirs* (1928).

Bikaner (*bē-kan-ēr'*), SIR GANGA SINGH, MAHARAJAH OF (1880–), Ind. statesman and soldier; served in Great War; member of Imperial Conferences, 1917 and 1919; first chancellor of Chamber of Princes, 1921–6; A.D.C. to King George V. since 1910.

Bilderdijk (*bil-der-dīk'*), WILLEM (1756–1831), Dutch poet; *b.* Amsterdam; pub. collections of love songs, 1781 and 1785; a didactic poem, *Maladies of the Learned* (1807), etc.

Billings, JOSH. See SHAW, HENRY W.

Billroth (*bil'rōt*), ALBERT CHRISTIAN THEODOR (1829–94), Ger. surgeon; prof. of surgery at Zürich, 1860, and Vienna, 1867; made a member of the Austrian House of Peers, 1887; one of the greatest surgeons of his time; ambulance system largely due to him.

Bilney, THOMAS (*c.* 1495–1531), Eng. martyr; opposed saint and relic worship; burned at the stake in London.

Bil'se, OSWALD FRITZ (1878–), Ger. soldier; dismissed the service for his book, *Life in a Garrison Town.*

Binet (*bē-nā'*), ALFRED (1857–1911), Fr. psychologist; *b.* Nice; director of physiological psychology at the Sorbonne; an eminent experimental psychologist; roused much keen discussion by his 'Metrical Scale of Intelligence.'

Binger (*ban-zhā'*), LOUIS GUSTAVE (1856–), Fr. explorer and author; *b.* Strasbourg; explored Fr. W. Africa; director of Fr. Colonial Department, 1898–1907.

Binnie, SIR ALEXANDER RICHARDSON (1839–1917), Eng. civil engineer; *b.* London; constructed Nagpore waterworks (India), Blackwall tunnel, etc.

Binyon, LAURENCE (1869–), Eng. poet; *b.* Lancaster; won Newdigate prize, 1890; keeper of prints and drawings, Brit. Museum; retired 1933; volumes of verse include *London Visions, The Praise of Life, Odes, Porphyrion and Other Poems, The Death of Adam,* and *Poems of Nizami*; author of excellent books on Brit. and Oriental art.

Biot (*bē-ō'*), JEAN BAPTISTE (1774–1862), Fr. scientist; *b.* Paris; prof. of physics, Coll. de France; made first balloon ascent for scientific purposes, 1804; with Arago made meridian measurements; was first to investigate phenomena of mirage; invented polarimeter.

Birch, SAMUEL (1813–85), Eng. Egyptologist and archæologist; *b.* London; keeper of Egyptian and Assyrian antiquities, Brit. Museum; founded Soc. of Biblical Archæology, 1870.

Birch-Pfeiffer (*bērch-pfī'fer*), CHARLOTTE (1800–68), Ger. actress and dramatist; *b.* Stuttgart; wife of Christian Birch, the Dan. historian; acted chiefly in Court Theatre, Berlin; plays include a version of *Jane Eyre.*

Bird, EDWARD (1772–1819), Eng. genre painter; *b.* Wolverhampton; R.A., 1815; works include *Good News, The Village Politicians, Chevy Chase.*

Bird, ISABELLA. See BISHOP, ISABELLA.

Bird, WILLIAM. See BYRD.

Birdwood, SIR GEORGE CHRISTOPHER MOLESWORTH (1832–1917), Anglo-Indian official; *b.* in India; his sympathy with the Ind. people gave him great influence over them; went to England in ill-health, 1868; served in India Office, 1871–1902; one of founders of 'Primrose Day'; author of many books on India.

Birdwood, SIR WILLIAM RIDDELL (1865–), Brit. field marshal; served in several Ind. expeditions and S. African War; military secretary to Lord Kitchener; during Great War won fame in Gallipoli Campaign, 1915, as the 'hero of Anzac'; commanded the Australian and New Zealand Army Corps, and later the 5th Army in France; received a baronetcy and grant of £10,000, 1919; Northern Command in India, 1920–4; commander-in-chief of army in India, 1925–30.

Birkbeck, GEORGE (1776–1841), Eng. physician; *b.* Settle, Yorks; prof. of natural philosophy, Anderson's Coll., Glasgow; founded the London Mechanics' Institute, now known as Birkbeck Coll.; made a constituent coll. of London Univ., 1920.

Birkenhead, FREDERICK EDWIN SMITH, LORD (1872–1930), Brit. lawyer and politician; *b.* Birkenhead; called to bar at Gray's Inn, 1899; Conservative M.P. for Walton Division, Liverpool, 1906–19; prominent in the Ulster movement against Irish Home Rule, 1914; knighted on becoming solicitor-general, 1915; attorney-general, 1915–19; baronet, 1919; during Great War saw service in France with the Ind. Corps; lord chancellor, 1919–22; responsible for Law of Property Act, 1922; secretary for India, 1924–28; left politics for commercial life, 1928; author of several books on international law; *Law, Life, and Letters* (1927), etc.

Birmingham, G. A. See under HANNAY, JAMES OWEN.

Birney, JAMES GILLESPIE (1792–1857), Amer. anti-slavery politician, son of a slave-owner of Kentucky; freed his own slaves, 1834; joined Amer. Anti-Slavery Soc., 1834.

Biron, ARMAND DE GONTAUD, BARON DE (1524–92), Fr. soldier and favourite of Henry III.; marshal of France, 1576; joined Henry of Navarre, 1589, and fell at siege of Epernay.

Birrell, AUGUSTINE (1850–1933), Eng. essayist and politician; *b.* near Liverpool; Quain prof. of law, Univ. Coll., London, 1896–9; Liberal M.P. for W. Fife, 1889–1900, and for N. Bristol, 1906–18; president of Board of Education, 1905–7; secretary for Ireland, 1907–16; under his régime Irish Univ. Act, Irish Land Act, and Home Rule Act were carried; resigned on outbreak of Dublin rebellion, 1916; witty speaker, an essayist of delightful style; writings include *Obiter Dicta*, *Life of Charlotte Brontë*, *Men, Women, and Books*, *Frederick Locker-Lampson*, and *Et Cetera.*

Bishop, SIR HENRY ROWLEY (1786–1855), Eng. composer; *b.* London; musical director at Covent Garden, Drury Lane, and Vauxhall; prof. of music at Edinburgh, 1841, and Oxford, 1848; knighted 1842, being the first musician to receive that honour; chiefly remembered by settings of Shakespeare's songs, and popular ballads such as 'My pretty Jane,' 'Home, sweet Home,' and 'Should he Upbraid.'

Bishop, ISABELLA, *née* BIRD (1832–1904), Eng. traveller and author; *b.* in Yorks; wrote books of high value to travellers; journeyed extensively in Asia; deeply interested in Christian missions, and founded numerous hospitals and orphanages in China; in 1901 rode 1000 miles in Morocco.
[*Life*, by Stoddart (1906).]

Bishop, WILLIAM AVERY (1894–), Canadian airman; Lieut.-Col., R.F.C.; officially credited with bringing down seventy-two Ger. machines, and unofficially with over a hundred. V.C., 1917.

Bismarck, OTTO EDUARD LEOPOLD, PRINCE VON (1815–98), Ger. statesman responsible for the foundation of the Ger. Empire; *b.* Schönhausen, Brandenburg; represented lower nobility in Estates-general, 1847; sat for Brandenburg, 1849; Prussian representative in Federal Diet, 1851–8; became convinced that only by 'blood and iron' could Germany be welded into a national state; ambassador at St. Petersburg, 1858, and at Paris, 1862; prime minister, Sept. 1862, and ruled for four years, depending on the king's confidence; aided Russia during Polish rebellion; opposed Augustenburg claims to Schleswig and Holstein, and went to war with Denmark, 1864.

The war of 1866 with Austria left Prussia supreme in Germany. He became sole responsible minister in confederation of N. Ger. states. After 1870 he controlled foreign policy and played foremost rôle in events leading up to Franco-Ger. War. Victory in this war enabled Bismarck to establish a new Ger. Empire with the King of Prussia as emperor. This new Empire, proclaimed at Versailles in 1871, included both North and South Ger. States, and excluded Austria.

In his domestic policy after 1871 Bismarck was strongly anti-Socialist, but passed many measures improving the lot of the workers, and introducing important commercial changes. From 1872–9 he was engaged in a struggle with the R.C. hierarchy, but in the end was forced to repeal much of his anti-Catholic legislation. In foreign policy after 1871 he aimed at a league of the three Emperors of Germany, Austria, and Russia, but conflict of interest between Russia and Austria broke the scheme. As an 'honest broker' presided at Congress of Berlin, 1878, which laid down settlement of Near East. In 1879 he forced on his sovereign Dual Alliance with Austria, and later Triple Alliance including Italy. In 1884, however (renewed in 1887), Bismarck, behind the back of Austria, concluded 'reinsurance treaty' with Russia, the existence of which was not revealed till 1896. In 1884, too, he reluctantly embarked on programme of colonial expansion. Bismarck was 'dropped' by William II., 1890. He profoundly distrusted the impulsiveness of the new sovereign. Until his death he resided mainly at his country estate of Friedrichsruh, near Hamburg.

[*Memoirs* (trans. by A. J. Butler under title *Bismarck: the Man and the Statesman*, 1898); *Bismarck and German Unity* (1923), by E. Munroe Smith; *Bismarck*, by E. Ludwig (Eng. trans. 1927).]

Bissell, GEORGE EDWIN (1839–1920), Amer. sculptor; *b.* in Connecticut; served during Civil War, 1862–3; works include monuments in U.S.A., statues of Abraham Lincoln at Edinburgh, and of Burns and Highland Mary at Ayr.

Bissolat'i, LEONIDA (1857–1920), Ital. Socialist statesman; *b.* Cremona; ed. of Socialist paper *L'Avanti*, 1892. Formed Socialist Reformist party, 1911, which advocated intervention in Great War; member of cabinet, 1916–18; opposition to annexation of Alto Adige and Dalmatia compelled his retirement, 1918.

Bizet (*bē-zā'*), GEORGES, pseudonym of ALEXANDRE CÉSAR LÉOPOLD (1838–75), Fr. composer; *b.* near Paris; gained the Grand Prix de Rome, 1857; experienced many struggles and privations during his musical career; produced several operas, which achieved little success, and the charming incidental music to Daudet's *L'Arlésienne* (1872). His masterpiece, *Carmen* (1875), has retained its popularity.

Bjerregaard (*byer'eg-ard*), HENRIK ANKER (1792–1842), Norweg. poet; author of Norweg. national anthem, *Sönner af Norge.*

Björnson (*byĕrn'son*), BJÖRNSTJERNE (1832–1910), Norweg. poet, novelist, and dramatist; *b.* in Österdal; son of a Lutheran pastor; one of the outstanding personalities of Norway; many of his novels have enjoyed a European reputation; first work was *Synnöve Solbakken* (1857), followed by *Arne* (1858), *A Happy Boy* (1860), *The Fisher Maiden* (1868), and numerous others. His plays include *Sigurd the Bastard*, *Sigurd the Crusader*, *Mary Stuart*, *The Newly Married*, *Beyond our Powers*, ranging from poetic tragedy to comedy and social drama; in 1870 issued *Poems and Songs* and *Arnljot Gelline*, including his famous ode *Bergliot*; awarded Nobel prize for literature, 1903; later work propagated his Radical, social, and religious views.

[Critical *Studies* (1899), by G. Brandes; *Works*, preface by Gosse (1895).]

Blache (*bläsh*), VIDAL DE LA (1845–1918), Fr. geographer; *b.* in Hérault; prof. of geography at Paris; founder, 1891, and ed. of *Annales de Géographie*; works include *Tableau Général de la Géographie de France* (1903), and an *Atlas Général* (1894).

Black, ADAM (1784–1874), Scot. publisher; *b.* Edinburgh; founder of firm of A. and C. Black, which acquired, 1827, the copyrights of the *Encyclopædia Britannica* and Scott's Waverley Novels; twice lord provost, and M.P. for Edinburgh, 1856–65.

Black, JOSEPH (1728–99), Scot. chemist and physician; *b.* Bordeaux; prof. of chemistry, Edinburgh, 1766; did pioneer work on carbon dioxide, and propounded theory of 'latent heat,' which gave first impulse to Watt's improvements on the steam-engine.

Black, WILLIAM (1841–98), Scot.

novelist; *b.* Glasgow; excelled in descriptions of W. Highland scenery; pub. *A Daughter of Heth, A Princess of Thule*, etc.; lighthouse to his memory, 1901, at Duart Point (Sound of Mull).

Blackburn, COLIN BLACKBURN, BARON (1813–96), Brit. judge; *b.* in Selkirkshire; lord of appeal, 1876; noted authority on common law; author of the *Law of Sales*.

Blackie, JOHN STUART (1809–95), Scot. scholar and writer; *b.* Glasgow; prof. of Greek, Edinburgh Univ., 1852–82; pub. *Homer and the Iliad* (1866), *Lay Sermons* (1881), etc.

Blackmore, RICHARD DODDRIDGE (1825–1900), Eng. novelist; *b.* in Berks; author of *Lorna Doone* (1869), a romance of Exmoor, and other novels.

Black Prince, EDWARD, PRINCE OF WALES (1330–76), eldest son of Edward III.; distinguished himself in Fr. wars, especially at Crécy, 1346, and Poitiers, 1356; expedition into Spain, 1367, on behalf of Pedro the Cruel, ruined his health, and he returned to England, 1372.

Blackstone, SIR WILLIAM (1723–80), a distinguished writer on Eng. law; *b.* London; judge of the Common Pleas, principal of New Inn Hall, Oxford; his *Commentaries* have formed the basis of nearly all modern works of the kind.

Blackwood, JOHN (1818–79), Scot. publisher, son of William Blackwood; *b.* Edinburgh; ed. *Blackwood's Magazine*, which was founded by his father; discovered George Eliot, all of whose novels but one he published.

Blackwood. WILLIAM (1776–1834), Scot. publisher; *b.* Edinburgh; started as a bookseller, later founding publishing firm of William Blackwood and Sons; pub. first number of *Blackwood's Magazine* (1817); among contributors were Scott, Lockhart, Wilson, De Quincey, Hogg, and John Galt.

Blaikie, WILLIAM GARDEN (1820–99), Scot. divine; *b.* Aberdeen; prof. of pastoral theology, New Coll., Edinburgh, 1868–97; moderator of Free Church Assembly, 1892. Books include *Heroes of Israel, Thomas Chalmers*, etc.

Blaine, JAMES GILLESPIE (1830–93), Amer. statesman; *b.* in Pennsylvania; speaker of House of Representatives, 1869–75; secretary of state, 1881, and 1889 to 1892; programme was 'national expansion' and 'participation in world-politics'; in 1884 was unsuccessful Republican candidate against Cleveland for presidency of U.S.A.

Blair, HUGH (1718–1800), Scot. divine, prof. of rhetoric and belles-lettres in Edinburgh Univ.; much admired as an elegant preacher.

Blair, ROBERT (1699–1746), Scot. poet and divine; *b.* Edinburgh; author of *The Grave*, illustrated in 1804–5 by William Blake.

Blake, ROBERT (1599–1657), Brit. admiral and founder of Britain's naval supremacy; *b.* Bridgwater; sat in Long Parliament, 1640, and fought on Parliamentary side in Civil War; defeated Royalist fleet off Malaga, 1650; commanded Brit. fleet against admirals van Tromp, de Witt, and de Ruyter, and severely defeated the Dutch off North Foreland, 1653; destroyed Span. treasure fleet at Tenerife, 1657; died at sea, and buried in Westminster Abbey.

Blake, WILLIAM (1757–1827), Eng. poet, artist, and mystic; son of a London hosier; trained as an engraver; exhibited at Royal Academy *The Death of Earl Godwin* (1780); pub. *Songs of Innocence* (1789) and *Songs of Experience* (1794), the text and designs for both being engraved by himself, and afterwards hand-coloured; later, he pub. his mystical works—part prose, part verse—which include *The Gates of Paradise*, *The Marriage of Heaven and Hell*, etc. In art his inventive genius finds its culmination in the illustrated *Book of Job*, Dante's *Poems*, and Blair's *Grave*, and in the *One Hundred and Fourteen Designs for Gray's Poems*, discovered 1919; his mysticism in art and literature, labelled madness by his age, is now better understood.

Blakiston, THOMAS WRIGHT (1832–91), Eng. soldier and explorer; *b.* Lymington; during Chin. War, 1859, charted upper waters of Yang-tse-Kiang; studied ornithology of Japan; pub. *Five Months on the Yangtze* (1862).

Blanc (*blon*), LOUIS (1811–82), Fr. publicist and historian; *b.* Madrid; founder of *Revue du Progrès* (1839), in which appeared his chief Socialistic work, *L'Organisation du Travail*; president of Government Labour Commission, 1848; member of National Assembly, 1871; pub. *Histoire de la Révolution Française* (12 vols. 1847–62), also *Histoire de la Révolution de 1848*.

Bland. (1) HUBERT (1856–1914), Eng. Socialist and journalist; dramatic and art critic to *Daily Chronicle*; wrote articles to *Sunday Chronicle* from 1889 till 1914; pub. volumes of essays; was an original member of Fabian Soc. (2) MRS. HUBERT BLAND (Edith Nesbit) (1858–1924), wife of above; poet and novelist; noted for capable novels with child characters.

Bland-Sutton, SIR JOHN (1855–), Brit. surgeon; *b.* London; authority on diseases of women; president Royal Coll. of Surgeons, 1923–6; baronet, 1925.

Blane, SIR GILBERT (1749–1834), Brit. physician; *b.* in Ayrshire; accompanied Admiral Rodney as medical attendant; discovered the efficacy of lime juice in combating scurvy.

Blanqui (*blon-kē'*), JÉRÔME ADOLPHE (1798–1854), Fr. economist; *b.* Nice; head of Ecole de Commerce, Paris; pub. numerous valuable works upon economic subjects; advocated Free Trade.

Blanqui, LOUIS AUGUSTE (1805–81), Fr. politician; *b.* near Nice; founded Société Républicaine Centrale; uncompromising advocate of Communism; spent nearly half his life in prison.

Blasco Ibañez, VICENTE. See IBAÑEZ.

Bla'sius, or BLAISE, ST., bishop of Sebaste (Sivas), Asia Minor; martyred under Diocletian, 316, and traditionally said to have been tortured with wool-combing instruments; regarded as patron saint of wool-combers.

Blass, FRIEDRICH (1843–1907), Ger. classical scholar; prof. at Kiel and later at Halle; greatest work, *Die Attische Beredsamkeit* (1868–80); numerous critical editions of Gr. authors.

Blatchford, ROBERT (1851–), Eng. Socialist and journalist (pseudonym 'Nunquam'); *b.* Maidstone; founded the *Clarion*; author of *Merrie England*, *God and my Neighbour*, *My Eighty Years* (1931), etc.

Blavat'sky, MADAME HELENA PETROVNA (1831–91), Russ. theosophist; claimed to have been initiated into esoteric Buddhism, and to have the power of communicating with the unseen world; travelled widely; founded, in America, the Theosophical Soc., 1875; wrote *Isis Unveiled* (1877), and *Key to Theosophy* (1889).

Bleek (*blāk*), WILHELM HEINRICH IMMANUEL (1827–75), Ger. philologist; *b.* Berlin; spent much time in S. Africa and pub. *Vocabulary of the Mozambique Language*, *Comparative Grammar of the S. African Languages*, and other philological works.

Bleibtreu (*blīb'troi*), GEORG (1828–92), Ger. painter of battle scenes; painting is vigorous and powerful, and colouring brilliant; paintings include *Battle of Waterloo, Capitulation of Sedan.*

Blenkinsop, JOHN (1783–1831), Eng. inventor; *b.* near Leeds; his cogwheel locomotive engine was the forerunner of Stephenson's *Rocket.*

Blériot (*blā-rē-ō'*), LOUIS (1872–), Fr. aviator and inventor; *b.* Cambrai; was the first, 1909, to fly the Eng. Channel on a monoplane (38 min.).

Blessington, MARGUERITE, COUNTESS OF (1789–1849), Irish writer and woman of fashion; *b.* in Tipperary; her second husband was Earl of Blessington; after his death, 1829, she lived under the protection of Count d'Orsay; travelled much on the Continent, and made the acquaintance of Lord Byron; her Paris and London houses attracted most of the notabilities of the period; ostracized because of d'Orsay affair, and loaded with debt, fled to Paris, 1849; ed. *The Book of Beauty* and *The Keepsake*, pub. *Conversations with Lord Byron* (1834).

Blicher (*blich'er*), STEEN STEENSEN (1782–1848), Dan. national poet and novelist; *b.* Viborg; skilfully describes rural types of Jutland.

Bligh (*blī*), WILLIAM (1754–1817), Eng. admiral; *b.* Plymouth; commanded the *Bounty*, 1787; at Tahiti his crew mutinied and cast him adrift; sailed *c.* 4,000 miles in open boat to Timor; governor of New South Wales, 1805–8, but deposed for tyrannous conduct and sent back to England.

Bliss, FREDERICK JONES (1859–), Amer. archæologist; *b.* in Syria; explorer to Palestine Exploration Fund, 1890–1900; on commission for anc. buildings in Syria and Palestine, 1919; author of *Excavations in Palestine*, etc.

Bloch, CARL HENRIK (1834–90), Dan. painter and etcher; portrayed peasant life; painted humorous side of monastic life; his *Christian II.* and *Samson and the Philistines* are in the Royal Gallery, Copenhagen.

Bloch, JEAN DE (1836–1902), Polish banker and railway constructor; best-known book is *The War of the Future* (1898), in which he predicts that modern wars must result in economic exhaustion and stalemate.

Blok, ALEXANDER (1880–1921), Russ. poet, *b.* St. Petersburg; Bolshevist revolution inspired his greatest poem, *The Twelve* (1918), trans. into English; dramas are *The Fair Booth* and *The Rose and the Cross.*

Blok, PETRUS JOHANNES (1855–1929), Dutch historian, prof. at Leyden till 1925; works include *Geschiedenis van het Nederlandsche Volk* (8 vols. Eng. trans.).

Blomefield (*bloom'fēld*), FRANCIS (1705–52), topographer, rector of Fersfield, Norfolk; wrote *History of Norfolk*; discoverer of the famous *Paston Letters.*

Blomfield (*bloom'fēld*). (1) SIR ARTHUR WILLIAM (1829–99), Eng. architect; designed many churches, Law Courts branch in Fleet Street, etc. (2) SIR REGINALD (1856–), Eng. architect, nephew of (1); *b.* in Kent; designed many country houses; R.A., 1914; prof. of architecture, Royal Academy, 1906–10; principal architect of Imperial War Graves Commission; recent works include bridge at Stratford-on-Avon and the Menin Gate; author of standard works on architecture.

Blom'maert, PHILIP (1808–71), Flem. author; *b.* Ghent; devoted himself to revival of national language and spirit; author of *History of the Belgians.*

Blom'mers, BERNARDUS JOHANNES (1845–1914), Dutch artist; works include landscapes, interiors, and scenes of peasant and fisher life; painted *Girl Knitting*, *Mother's Joy*, *Shrimpers*.

Blondin (*blōn-dan'*), CHARLES (1824–97), stage-name of JEAN FRANÇOIS GRAVELET, Fr. acrobat and tight-rope walker; crossed Niagara Falls, 1859, on a tight rope in five minutes; afterwards performed the feat blindfold in a sack, trundling a wheelbarrow; again on stilts; and yet again with a man on his back, sitting down in middle to eat his lunch.

Bloomer, AMELIA JENKS (1818–94), Amer. dress reformer; *b.* in New York state; pioneer of the women's dress-reform movement (hence ' bloomers ').

Bloomfield, ROBERT (1766–1823), Eng. poet; *b.* in Suffolk; pub. verse dealing with rural life; best-known poem, *The Farmer's Boy*, was illustrated by Bewick.

Blouet, PAUL. See MAX O'RELL.

Blount, THOMAS (1618–79), Eng. antiquary; *b.* in Worcestershire; author of the *Boscobel* tract (1651) describing the adventures of Charles II. after Worcester.

Blow, JOHN (1648–1708), Eng. composer and organist; *b.* in Notts; organist of Westminster Abbey, 1669–80; composer to the Chapel Royal, 1699; wrote many anthems, choral odes, etc.

Blowitz (*blō'vits*), HENRI GEORGES STEPHAN ADOLPHE DE (1825–1903), Anglo-Fr. journalist; *b.* in Bohemia; settled in Marseilles; chief Paris correspondent of the *Times* from 1873; was a force in journalistic and diplomatic circles, and influenced international affairs; pub. *My Memoirs* (1903).

Blücher (*blooch'er*), GEBHARD LEBERECHT VON (1742–1819), Prince of Wahlstadt, Prussian general; *b.* Rostock; one of leaders of Prussian war-party, 1805–6; commander-in-chief of Silesian army during War of Liberation; field-marshal, 1813; defeated by Napoleon at Ligny, 1815; made decisive advance at Waterloo; shrewd, vigorous, upright in character; known as ' old Marshal Vorwärts.'

Blum (*bloom*), LÉON (1872–), Fr. politician and literary critic; *b.* Paris; supported Jaurès in favour of Dreyfus; opposed Fr. occupation of Ruhr after Great War; as leader of Socialists kept Herriot ministry in power, 1924–5. An attack was made on his life by Royalists, 1936.

Blu'menbach, JOHANN FRIEDRICH (1752–1840), Ger. naturalist; prof. of natural history, anatomy, and medicine at Göttingen; founded science of anthropology; pub. *Handbuch der Naturgeschichte* (1780), etc.

Blunden, EDMUND CHARLES (1896–), Eng. writer; his service in Great War inspired his poem *Shepherd*, which gained Hawthornden prize, 1922, and his famous prose *Undertones of War* (1928); prof. of Eng. literature, Tokyo Univ., 1924–7; fellow and tutor, Oxford, since 1931; *Collected Poems* (1930).

Blunt, WILFRID SCAWEN (1840–1922), Eng. poet, traveller, and publicist; *b.* in Sussex; travelled with his wife in N. Africa, Arabia, and Mesopotamia; upheld Arabi Pasha, 1882; wrote fine sonnets as well as lyrical verse; pub. *Poetical Works*, *Secret History of British Occupation of Egypt*, *The Land War in Ireland*; and *My Diaries* in 1919–20. His wife, LADY ANNE BLUNT, a granddaughter of Lord Byron, wrote *Bedouins of the Euphrates* and a *Pilgrimage to Nejd*.

Bluntsch'li, JOHANN KASPAR (1808–81), Swiss jurist; *b.* Zürich; prof. of constitutional law at Munich, 1848, and Heidelberg, 1861; helped to organize Ger.

House of Representatives, 1862, and to found Ghent Institute of International Law, 1873; represented Germany at Brussels conference on laws of war, 1874.

Boabdil′, more correctly ABU ABDALLAH, the last of the Moorish kings of Granada (1482–92); surrendered the city to Ferdinand and Isabella, 1492; killed in Africa.

Boadice′a, or BOUDICCA (*d.* A.D. 62), Brit. queen; her husband Prasutagus ruled the Iceni, inhabiting E. Anglia, and upon his death his dominions were seized by the Romans; roused by the indignities she and her people had suffered, Boadicea raised an army and seized in turn Colchester, St. Albans, and London, slaughtering some 70,000 of the invaders; was eventually defeated; put an end to her life by poison.

Boaz, a Bethlehemite who married Ruth (see Book of Ruth), an ancestor of David.

Bocage (*bo-käzh′*), MANOEL MARIA BARBOSA DE (1765–1805), Port. poet; *b.* Setubal; second only to Camoens; excelled in the sonnet; his *Obras Poeticas* appeared in 1875.

Boccaccio (*bo-kä′chō*), GIOVANNI (1313–75), Ital. poet, novelist, and scholar; *b.* Paris; taken in infancy to Florence; was sent to Naples, 1328, where he commenced to write poetry, and fell deeply in love with Maria, the illegitimate daughter of King Robert of Naples and Sicily, whom he afterwards celebrated in his writings under the name of 'Fiammetta.' In 1342 he returned to Florence, formed a close friendship with Petrarch, and acted as Florentine ambassador at Rome, Avignon, Ravenna, and Brandenburg. In 1358 he completed his great prose masterpiece, the *Decameron.* This work sets forth how, during the plague of 1348, seven court ladies and three gentlemen seek refuge in a country villa, where, to while away the time, they relate tales. These tales number one hundred, and though many of them are very indelicate in subject, the *Decameron* has a place amongst the greatest books the world has seen. There is scarcely an Eng. poet, from Chaucer to Keats, Tennyson, and Swinburne, who has not drawn on the stores of Boccaccio.

[*Boccaccio as Man and Author* (1894), by J. A. Symonds; *Life* (1910), by E. Hutton.]

Boccherini (*bok-ā-rē′nē*), LUIGI (1743–1805), Ital. composer; *b.* Lucca; visited Paris, Madrid, and Prussia; noted as 'cellist, and his violoncello works are still standard; his works show him a master of chamber music.

Bochart (*bō-shär′*), SAMUEL (1599–1667), Fr. scholar; *b.* Rouen; a noted authority on Oriental languages, and wrote, amongst other works, *Hierozoicon,* a treatise on scriptural and fabulous animals.

Boch′mann, GREGOR VON (1850–), Russ. painter; *b.* in Estonia; works include *A Church in Esthonia, Dockyards in Holland, The Fish Market at Reval.*

Böck′lin, ARNOLD (1827–1901), Swiss artist; *b.* Basle; famous for his realistic treatment of the weird and of mythological subjects, including *Battle of the Centaurs, Prometheus, Ulysses and Calypso.*

Bocskay (*bochs′koi*), STEPHEN (1557–1606), prince of Transylvania; *b.* Cluj; led insurrection in Hungary, and was proclaimed prince; supposed to have been poisoned by his chancellor.

Bo′de, JOHANN ELERT (1747–1826), Ger. astronomer; *b.* Hamburg; pub. astronomical almanacs and maps. *Bode's Law* is an empirical formula denoting relative distances of the planets.

Bode, WILHELM VON (1845–1929), Ger. art critic; *b.* in Brunswick; director of Prussian royal museums, 1905–20; authority on Dutch and Flem. painting.

Bo′denstedt, FRIEDRICH MARTIN VON (1819–92), Ger. poet and translator; prof. of language and literature, Munich; his *Die Lieder des Mirza Schaffy* (1851), a volume of original verse with a Pers. atmosphere, met with great success; trans. Shakespeare's sonnets, and (with others) a complete edition of the plays.

Bodin (*bō-dan′*), JEAN (1530–96), Fr. author, lawyer, and political philosopher; *b.* Angers; king's attorney at Laon, 1576; secretary to Duc d'Alençon, 1581; pub. several works, of which the most important is the *Six Livres de la République* (1576), the earliest treatise on political science.

Bodley, JOHN EDWARD COURTENAY (1853–1925), Eng. student of foreign politics, especially of France. His most important work is *France* (2 vols. 1898).

Bodley, SIR THOMAS (1545–1613), Eng. diplomatist; *b.* Exeter; minister at The Hague, 1588–96; founded Bodleian library at Oxford, and left most of his fortune to it.

Boece (*bois* or *bō-ēs′*), HECTOR (*c.* 1465–1536), Scot. historian; *b.* Dundee; prof. at Montaigu Coll., Paris, and friend of Erasmus; first principal of Aberdeen Univ., 1494; wrote *History of Scotland.*

Boehm (*bĕm*), or BEHMEN, SIR JOSEPH EDGAR (1834–90), Eng. sculptor; *b.* Vienna; R.A., 1882; executed statues of Queen Victoria (Windsor), Carlyle (Chelsea), Dean Stanley (Westminster), Wellington (Hyde Park Corner), etc.; appointed sculptor-in-ordinary to Queen Victoria; designed Jubilee coinage, 1887.

Boehme (*bĕ-me*), JAKOB (1575–1624), Ger. philosopher and mystic; son of a Silesian peasant; conceived a profound mystic sense of God in nature. His first work, *Aurora* (1612), tries to explain the origin of things. His writings have exercised considerable influence on European thought.

Boerhaave (*boor′hä-ve*), HERMANN (1668–1738), Dutch physician; successively prof. of medicine and botany, prof. of chemistry, and rector of Leyden Univ., where Peter the Great was one of his pupils; leading physician of 18th cent.

Boëthius (*bō-ē′thi-us*), ANICIUS MANLIUS SEVERINUS (*c.* 480–524), Rom. statesman and philosopher; won favour of Theodoric the Ostrogoth, and became consul, 510; condemned for treason towards end of Theodoric's reign; in prison wrote his famous *De Consolatione Philosophiæ*, for centuries one of the great textbooks of moral wisdom. Put to death, 524; regarded as a martyr some centuries after his death. Wrote several commentaries, a textbook on music, and trans. into Latin some of Aristotle's chief works.

[*Boëthius, an Essay* (1891), by H. F. Stewart.]

Bogar′dus, JAMES (1800–74), Amer. mechanician; *b.* Catskill, New York; invented the dry gas meter, and instruments for deep-sea soundings, making postage stamps (Brit. Government's prize, 1839), engraving medals, pressing glass, etc.

Bögh (*bĕg*), ERIK (1822–99), Dan. dramatist and journalist; *b.* Copenhagen; besides dramatic works produced volumes of verse; ed. *Folkets Avis* (1860–77), the most popular journal in Denmark.

Bogue (*bōg*), DAVID (1750–1825), Scot. Congregational minister; *b.* in Berwickshire; one of founders of London Missionary Soc., 1795, Brit. and Foreign Bible Soc., and Religious Tract Soc.

Bo′hemond I. (1056–1111), prince of Antioch; son of Robert Guiscard of Normandy; a leader of the First Crusade, he showed great gallantry in the capture of Antioch, of which he made himself prince.

Bohn (*bōn*), Henry George (1796–1884), Eng. publisher; *b.* London; commenced, in 1846, to publish the famous 'Bohn Libraries' of standard works and translations, which extended to nearly 800 vols.

Bohr, Niels Henrik David (1885–), Dan. scientist; *b.* Copenhagen; studied in Denmark and England; prof. of physics, Univ. of Copenhagen, since 1916; authority on structure of the atom; Nobel prize, 1922.

Bohtlingk (*bet'link*), Otto (1815–1904), Sanskrit scholar; *b.* St. Petersburg; studied in Germany; greatest work is Sanskrit Dictionary, in collaboration with two friends (1853–75).

Boiardo (*bō-yär'dō*), Matteo Maria, Count of Scandiano (1434–94), Ital. poet; his epic, *Orlando Innamorato* (1495), a rehandling of the Charlemagne legend, was the model for Ariosto's *Orlando Furioso.*

Boieldieu (*bō-yel-dyū'*), François Adrien (1775–1834), Fr. composer; *b.* Rouen; produced numerous operas and musical pieces which achieved considerable popularity, including *Le Calife de Bagdad, Jean de Paris,* and *La Dame Blanche* (the White Lady of Scott's *Monastery*).

Boileau-Despréaux (*bwä-lō' dā-prā-ō'*), Nicolas (1636–1711), Fr. poet and critic; *b.* Paris; studied for the Church and for the bar, but eventually devoted himself to literature, and became arbiter of literary taste in Europe; joint historiographer-royal with Racine, 1677; poems include the mock epic *Lutrin,* and *Art Poétique* (1674), his most important work; defended the usages of the classic writers against the moderns in the famous *Querelle.* His writings exercised considerable influence on the work of Pope and other Eng. authors.

Boissy d'Anglas (*bwä-sē' dän-glas'*), François Antoine, Comte de (1756–1826), Fr. statesman; *b.* in Ardèche; helped to overthrow Robespierre, 1794; president of Convention, 1795; member of Committee of Public Safety and subsequently of Council of Five Hundred; proscribed Sept. 1797; lived in England until the Consulate; member of Tribunate, 1801; senator and a count under Napoleon; created peer by Louis XVIII.

Boito (*bō-ē'tō*), Arrigo (1842–1918), Ital. composer and poet; *b.* Padua; his opera, *Mefistofele,* was a failure at Milan in 1868, but successful at Bologna, 1875; won distinction as a writer of libretti; author of the books of Verdi's *Otello* and *Falstaff,* Ponchielli's *La Gioconda,* etc.

Bojer (*bō'yĕr*), Johan (1872–), Norweg. novelist and dramatist; *b.* near Trondhjem; works include *The Power of a Lie* (crowned by the Fr. Academy), *The Great Hunger,* and other realistic studies of Norweg. peasant life; among his plays are *The Eyes of Love* and *Brutus.*

Bok, Edward William (1863–1930), Amer. ed.; *b.* in Holland; emigrated to U.S.A., 1869; ed. *The Ladies' Home Journal* (1889–1919); founded Amer. Peace Award, 1923, of $100,000 for American who should submit the most practical plan for world peace; works include *The Americanization of Edward Bok* (1922), and *Perhaps I am* (1928).

Boldrewood, Rolf (1826–1915), pseudonym of Thomas A. Browne, Anglo-Australian novelist; *b.* London; settled in Victoria, 1844; novels deal with life in the early bush-ranging days; best known is *Robbery under Arms.*

Boleslas, Boleslaus, or Boleslav, the name of several early kings of Poland, of whom the most important were: (1) I. (*d.* 1025), called 'the Great,' who made Poland a powerful state, and established a native church. (2) II., 'the Bold' (1039–81), exiled in 1079. (3) III. (1086–1139), devoted his life mainly to subjugation of Pomerania.

Boleyn (or BULLEN) (*bool'en*), ANNE (*c.* 1507–36), second wife of Henry VIII. of England, daughter of Sir Thomas Boleyn, and niece of Duke of Norfolk. Henry married her secretly in Jan. 1533; birth of Princess (afterwards Queen) Elizabeth, Sept. 1533, instead of desired son, disappointed Henry, who soon tired of his wife; she was imprisoned in the Tower on charges of immorality, condemned, and beheaded on Tower Green.

Bolingbroke (*bol'ing-brook*), HENRY ST. JOHN, VISCOUNT (1678–1751), Eng. statesman and writer; *b.* London; entered Parliament, 1701; war secretary, 1704; and secretary of state, 1710; created Viscount Bolingbroke, 1712; proceeded to France, and had a responsible share in the Peace of Utrecht, 1713; superseded Oxford in leadership of Tories; his plans for a Jacobite restoration were upset by Queen Anne's sudden death; dismissed from office by George I., and joined the Pretender in France, but was pardoned, 1723, and returned to London; on death of George I. joined opposition round Frederick, Prince of Wales, but returned to France, 1734; came back to England, 1742, but did not support '45 rebellion. He was an eloquent and plausible debater, but a superficial and unscrupulous statesman. His writings include the *Patriot King*, which inspired the political ideas of Bute and George III.

Bolivar (or *bol-ē'var*), SIMON (1783–1830), S. American patriot, known as 'the Liberator'; *b.* Caracas, Venezuela; leader of cause of independence of Span. colonies in S. America; aided rebellion at Caracas, 1810; Venezuela declared its independence, 1811; war began, 1812; after varying success, Bolivar defeated Spaniards at Barcelona, 1817, and finally routed Spaniards at Carabobo, 1821; Venezuela and New Granada were united to form 'Republic of Colombia,' under Bolivar's presidency, 1821. He also liberated Ecuador and Peru; Upper Peru became a separate state called Bolivia, in honour of Bolivar, who became dictator; Bolivian code was adopted as constitution of Peru, and Bolivar declared president for life, 1826.

[*Simon Bolivar* (1921), by G. Sherwell.]

Bologna (*bō-lō'nya*), GIOVANNI DA (1524–1608), Fr. sculptor; *b.* Douai; lived chiefly in Italy; employed by the Medicis; most celebrated work, *The Rape of the Sabines*, in the Loggia dei Lanzi, Florence.

Bon'aparte, or BUONAPARTE (Ital. form). The Bonaparte family consisted of: (1) CHARLES BONAPARTE (1746–85), father of Napoleon I., descendant of Ital. family settled in Corsica; occupied position at court of Ajaccio. (2) NAPOLEON I. (see under Napoleon) was the second son; he had four brothers and three sisters. (3) JOSEPH (1768–1844), eldest brother; on Napoleon's rise to power was appointed commissary-general; ambassador to Pope, 1797; King of Naples, 1806–8; King of Spain, 1808–13. In Spain endeavoured to thwart Napoleon, but retired from Madrid after his defeat at Vittoria, 1813; lieut.-gen. of France, 1814; after final fall of Napoleon went to U.S.A., but returned to Florence, 1832. (4) LUCIEN (1775–1840), Prince of Canino, third son of (1): president of Council of Five

Hundred and minister of interior, 1799; ambassador to Madrid, 1800; estranged from Napoleon, 1803; lived for some years in Italy; offered Napoleon his help during the Hundred Days; died at Rome. (5) LOUIS (1778–1846), favourite brother of Napoleon; accompanied him during Ital. campaign, 1796–7; general, 1804; governor of Paris, 1805; married Hortense de Beauharnais, daughter of Josephine; King of Holland, 1806–10; abdicated in favour of his son. For his son, see NAPOLEON III. (6) JEROME (1784–1860), youngest brother of Napoleon, King of Westphalia, 1807–13; took part in Russ. campaign, 1812; commanded a division at Waterloo; subsequently a marshal of France and president of senate. (7) CAROLINE (1782–1839), youngest sister of Napoleon, married Joachim Murat, King of Naples, 1808–13.

[*Napoléon et sa Famille* (Paris, 1897–1900), by F. Masson; *Napoleon's Brothers* (1909), by Atteridge; *Marriages of the Bonapartes* (1881), by D. A. Bingham.]

Bon′ar, HORATIUS (1808–89), Scot. divine and hymn writer; *b.* Edinburgh; moderator of Free Church Assembly, 1883; best-known hymns, 'I heard the Voice of Jesus say,' 'Thy way, not mine, O Lord,' and 'A few more years shall roll.'

Bonaventu′ra, ST. (1221–74), Ital. Franciscan theologian and mystic; educated Paris; general of Franciscan Order, 1256; called 'The Seraphic Doctor'; a follower of Plato rather than of Aristotle; a profound philosopher and theologian; canonized 1482.

Bond, SIR EDWARD AUGUSTUS (1815–98), Eng. librarian; *b.* Hanwell; appointed chief librarian, Brit. Museum, 1878; ed. a series of Anglo-Saxon charters; with Maunde Thompson founded Palæographical Soc.; K.C.B., 1898.

Bond, SIR ROBERT (1857–1927), Newfoundland statesman; son of merchant from Torquay, England; *b.* St. John's; studied law at Edinburgh Univ.; entered legislature, 1882; colonial secretary, 1889–97; played important part in negotiations with France and U.S.A. over fisheries question, 1890–1914; prime minister, 1900–9.

Bond, WILLIAM CRANCH (1789–1859), Amer. astronomer; *b.* Portland, Maine; director of Harvard Univ. observatory; one of earliest to photograph celestial bodies, 1848; discovered eighth satellite of Saturn, 1848, and invented an astronomical chronograph, 1850.

Bondfield, MARGARET GRACE (1873–), Eng. politician; *b.* in Somerset; chairman, Trades Union Congress, 1923; M.P. for Northampton, 1923–4, and parliamentary secretary to Ministry of Labour; M.P. for Wallsend, 1926–31, and minister of labour, 1929–31; labour adviser to International Labour Conference, Geneva, 1921–27; first Brit. woman cabinet minister.

Bone, HENRY (1755–1834), Eng. enamel-painter; *b.* Truro; private and historical portraits and classical subjects; royal enamel-painter, 1801; R.A., 1811.

Bone, MUIRHEAD (1876–), Scot. etcher and painter; *b.* Glasgow; a leading master of dry-point; official artist on western front and with the fleet, 1916–18; famous etching, *The Great Gantry, Charing Cross*; has illustrated several books.

Boner, ULRICH (14th cent.), Swiss fabulist; *b.* Berne; compiled oldest book of fables in German, his *Edelstein*, to serve as a 'talisman' against evils and errors of the world.

Bonheur (*bo-nĕr′*), ROSA (1822–99), Fr. artist; *b.* Bordeaux; famous for masterly painting of animals; *Attelage Nivernais* (1848) now in the Luxembourg; *Horse Fair* (1853) in New York, a replica being in National Gallery.

Bo'ni, GIACOMO (1859–1925), Ital. archæologist; *b.* Venice; director of excavations in Forum and Palatine, Rome, where his work won him European renown; appointed senator by Signor Mussolini, 1923.

Bon'iface, ST. (680–754), the 'Apostle of Germany'; *b.* in Devon; began missionary labours in Frisia, 718, where tribes were still heathen; founded famous monastery of Fulda; organized eccles. system of Germany; bishop of Mainz and archbishop of all Germany, 746–54; resigned to return to evangelization of Frisians; massacred by heathen.

Boniface V., POPE (619–25), interested himself in the conversion of England; established the right of asylum in churches.

Boniface VIII., POPE (1294–1303), determined to be temporal as well as spiritual head of Christendom; intervened unsuccessfully when Edward I. was at war with Scotland.

Bon'ington, RICHARD PARKES (1801–28), Eng. artist; *b.* near Nottingham; best-known paintings, *Henry IV. and the Spanish Ambassador,* and *Francis I. and the Duchesse d'Etampes,* noted for brilliancy of colouring; over thirty works are in the Wallace Collection, and one in the National Gallery.

Bonivard (*bō-nē-vär'*), FRANÇOIS (1493–1570), prior of Geneva; imprisoned in Chillon for six years by order of Charles III. of Savoy; released when Chillon fell into hands of Bernese, 1536; took refuge at Geneva, accepted the Reformation. His career adapted by Byron in his *Prisoner of Chillon.*

Bonnat (*bo-nä'*), LÉON JOSEPH FLORENTIN (1833–1922), Fr. painter; *b.* Bayonne; studied in Spain and Paris; noted for portraits, including Victor Hugo, Thiers, Pasteur, Dumas, Renan, and Carnot.

Bonner, EDMUND (?1500–69), Bishop of London; was Wolsey's chaplain; chosen to advocate Henry VIII.'s divorce cause before the Pope; deprived of his see under Edward VI., but restored by Mary; savagely persecuted Protestants; refused to take the oath of supremacy under Elizabeth; died in prison.

Bon'ney, THOMAS GEORGE (1833–1923), Eng. geologist and clergyman; *b.* Rugeley; emeritus prof. of geology at Univ. Coll., London; best-known works include *The Story of Our Planet, Volcanoes,* and *The Present Relations of Science and Religion.*

Bonnivet (*bo-nē-vā'*), GUILLAUME GOUFFIER, SEIGNEUR DE (1488–1525), Fr. courtier and soldier; favourite of Francis I.; admiral of France, 1515; commanded the army of Navarre, 1521; served in Italy, 1523–5, and was killed at Pavia; famed for his wit, handsome person, and licentious life.

Bono'mi, GIUSEPPE (1739–1808), Eng. architect, of Ital. parentage; *b.* Rome; famous works include Rosneath Castle, Dumbartonshire; Dale Park, Sussex; and other erections in the Grecian style.

Bonstet'ten, CHARLES VICTOR DE (1745–1832), Swiss author; *b.* Berne; held advanced liberal opinions; friend of the Eng. poet Gray, and Madame de Staël; best-known work, *L'Homme du Midi et l'Homme du Nord* (1824), is a study of the influence of climate on peoples.

Boole, GEORGE (1815–64), Eng. mathematician and logician; *b.* Lincoln; prof. of mathematics, Queen's Coll., Cork, 1849; pub. treatise on *Differential Equations* (1859), and on *Calculus of Finite Differences* (1860), etc.; principal work as a logician was the *Laws of Thought* (1854).

Boone, DANIEL (1734–1820), famous Amer. pioneer; *b.* in Pennsylvania; one of the founders of Boonesboro, Kentucky; a well-known hunter, and expert in Indian matters.

Boorde (or BORDE), ANDREW (*c.* 1490–1549), Eng. physician and traveller; *b.* in Sussex; wrote *The Fyrst Boke of the Introduction of Knowledge* (1547), an account of his European travels, and *Itinerary of Europe*, the first printed handbook of Europe.

Booth, BARTON (1681–1738), Eng. actor; educated Trinity Coll., Cambridge; achieved greatest successes as Cato, Hotspur, Brutus, King Lear, Othello, 'the gay Lothario,' and ghost in *Hamlet*; buried in Westminster Abbey.

Booth, RT. HON. CHARLES (1840–1916), a pioneer in statistical sociology; *b.* Liverpool; partner of shipping firm of Booth and Co.; wrote books on old age pensions, also *Life and Labour of the People in London* (16 vols. 1891–1903).

Booth, EDWIN THOMAS (1833–93), Amer. actor; *b.* in Maryland; made his first appearance at Boston, 1849. His striking personality and the charm of his elocution made him one of greatest Shakespearian actors Amer. stage has produced.

Booth, JOHN WILKES (1839–65), Amer. actor, younger brother of above; became a Secessionist plotter, 1863; shot President Lincoln, 1865, and refusing to surrender, was himself shot.

Booth, WILLIAM, 'GENERAL' BOOTH (1829–1912), founder of Salvation Army; *b.* Nottingham; in 1865 established the Christian Mission in the East End of London, out of which developed the Salvation Army. As 'General' he became prominent in Eng. life, and his army spread almost over the whole world; organized Rescue, Maternity, Prison-gate, and Children's Homes, Slum Posts, Shelters for Homeless, Food Depots, Labour Bureaux, and Farms at home and abroad. His *In Darkest England and the Way out* (1890) proposed remedies for poverty and vice.

[*Life of General Booth* (2 vols. 1920), by Harold Begbie.]

Booth, W. BRAMWELL (1856–1929), eldest son of above; 'general' of Salvation Army, 1912. In 1929 the Salvation Army demanded democratic control, and compelled him to retire.

Boothby, GUY NEWELL (1867–1905), novelist; *b.* in S. Australia; lived in England from 1894; wrote sensational novels, including *The Beautiful White Devil* and *Dr Nikola*.

Borchgrevink (*borch'grev-ink*), CARSTEN EGEBERG (1864–1934), Antarctic explorer; *b.* Christiania (Oslo); emigrated to Australia, 1888; commanded Southern Cross expedition, 1898; returned to Norway; wrote *First on the Antarctic Continent*, etc.

Bordeaux, HENRY (1870–), Fr. novelist, critic, and dramatist; *b.* in Haute-Savoie; member of Fr. Academy; served in Great War; wrote *Les Derniers Jours du Fort de Vaux* and *Les Captifs délivrés*, etc.; author of *Vies Intimes*, *La Vie au Théâtre* (critical works); *L'Ecran brisé* and *Un Médecin de Campagne* (plays); many of his novels have been trans. into English.

Bor'den, SIR ROBERT LAIRD (1854–), Can. statesman; *b.* Grand Pré, Nova Scotia; admitted to Can. bar, 1878; M.P. for Halifax, Nova Scotia, 1896; became leader of Conservative opposition, 1901; opposed Laurier's proposal for reciprocity with U.S.A., and became premier, 1911, when Laurier government was defeated; brought forward bill, 1913 (rejected by senate), for

Can. contribution of three battleships to Brit. navy; during Great War zealously supported imperial government, and was the first overseas minister to be summoned to a meeting of the Brit. cabinet; enforced conscription law; represented Canada at the Paris Peace Conference, 1919; retired from premiership, 1920.

Bordet (*bor-dā'*), JULES (1870–), Belgian physiologist; *b.* Soignies; prof. of bacteriology, Brussels Univ.; introduced method of diagnosis of microbes by serums; discovered microbe of whooping cough; Nobel prize for medicine, 1919.

Borgia (*bor'jä*), CESARE (1476–1507), son of Rodrigo Borgia, Pope Alexander VI.; *b.* Rome; created cardinal, 1493; released from eccles. vows, 1498; went on diplomatic mission to France, and married sister of King of Navarre; returned to Italy and overran Romagna, overcoming opposition by treachery and assassination; as Duke of Romagna, proved an able administrator and patron of the arts, but was hated for his licentiousness and cruelty. The death of his father, 1503, ended his power; was arrested by Pope Julius II.; sent as a prisoner to Spain; escaped to Navarre, and was killed while besieging castle of Viana. Is the extreme example of corruption of Ital. Renaissance; on his career Machiavelli based callous precepts of *The Prince* (1535).

Borgia, LUCREZIA (1480–1519), sister of above; puppet of the schemes of her father and brother; her third husband was Alfonso d'Este, Duke of Ferrara; in high repute at death as patroness of culture, but her name afterwards became synonymous, probably unjustly, with all the crime and licentiousness of the time.

Borgognone (*bor-gō-nyō'nā*), AMBROGIO (*c.* 1445–1523), Ital. painter and architect; masterpiece is celebrated façade of the Certosa, near Pavia; in painting followed school of Mantegna; works full of devotional sentiment.

Boris III. (1894–), Tsar of Bulgaria; *b.* Sofia; succeeded to throne on abdication of his father, Ferdinand, in Oct. 1918.

Bor'is Godunov' (*c.* 1551–1605), Tsar of Russia; rose to power under Ivan the Terrible, who married his son, Theodore, to Irene, sister of Boris; became omnipotent as guardian of Theodore, and succeeded him as tsar, 1598; a pacific, prudent ruler.

Boro'din, ALEXANDER PORFYRIEVICH (1834–87), Russ. composer; *b.* St. Petersburg; trained in medicine; a brilliant executant on several instruments; compositions distinctly Russ. in character, and consist of symphonies, string quartets, songs, and an opera, *Prince Igor*.

Borough (*bŭr'o*), STEVEN (1525–84), Eng. navigator; *b.* in Devon; accompanied Sir Hugh Willoughby in his search for a northern passage to Cathay, 1553; discovered Kara Strait, 1556. His brother, WILLIAM (1536–99), commanded *Lion* in Drake's Cadiz expedition, 1587.

Bor'row, GEORGE HENRY (1803–81), Eng. author and philologist; *b.* in Norfolk; son of a soldier; apprenticed to a solicitor; in 1824 went to London and worked as a publisher's hack; entered the employment of the Bible Soc., 1833, and was sent to Russia, and afterwards to Spain; in Spain associated with the Zincali; returned to England, 1839, and in 1841 pub. *The Zincali, or The Gipsies in Spain*, an exhaustive work on the gipsy languages; this was followed by *The Bible in Spain* (1843), which made him famous, *Lavengro* (1851), *The Romany Rye* (1857), *Wild Wales* (1862), and a gipsy word-book, *Romano Lavo Lil* (1874).

[*George Borrow* (1912), by E. Thomas.]

Bosanquet (*bō'san-ket*), BERNARD (1848–1923), Eng. philosopher; *b.* in Northumberland; lecturer at Univ. Coll., Oxford, 1871–81; prof. of moral philosophy, St. Andrews, 1903–8; Gifford lecturer, 1911–12; author of *Logic, or Morphology of Knowledge*; *History of Æsthetic*; *Knowledge and Reality*, etc.

Bosboom - Toussaint (*bos'bōm too-san*), ANNA LUISE (1812–86), Dutch novelist; *b.* Alkmaar; famous as a writer of historical stories.

Bos'cawen, SIR EDWARD (1711–61), Brit. admiral; co-operated with Amherst in capture of Louisburg and Cape Breton, 1758; destroyed the Fr. Toulon squadron in Lagos Bay, 1759.

Bos'covich, ROGER JOSEPH (1711–87), Ital. mathematician; *b.* Ragusa; prof. of mathematics at Padua, 1764–70; his chief works deal with the mathematics of astronomy.

Bose, SIR JAGADIS CHANDRA (1858–), Ind. scientist, studied in Calcutta and Cambridge; pioneer and leading authority on plant life; prof. of physical science, Calcutta Univ., 1885–1915; founder and director of Bose Research Institute, Calcutta; inventor of delicate instruments, such as crescograph, for measuring and recording movements in plant growth; many works include *Growth and Tropic Movements of Plants* (1929).

Bossuet (*bos-wā'*), JACQUES BENIGNE (1627–1704), Fr. theologian and orator; *b.* Dijon; ordained 1652; came to Paris, 1659, and became famous as a preacher; tutor to the dauphin, son of Louis XIV., 1670; a firm believer in absolutism in Church and State, which he defended in his *Discours sur l'Histoire Universelle.* He applauded the Revocation of the Edict of Nantes; he defended the liberties of the Fr. Church against the Papacy in the *Defensio Cleri Gallicani*, over which subject he was involved in a bitter controversy with Fénelon and the Ultramontanes; one of the greatest figures of the monarchy of Louis XIV.

[*Bossuet: a Study* (1921), by Ella K. Sanders.]

Boston, THOMAS (1676–1732), Scot. theologian; *b.* Duns; his famous *Human Nature in its Fourfold State* (1720) exerted powerful influence on religious life in Scotland.

Bos'well, JAMES (1740–95), Scot. author; son of Alexander Boswell of Auchinleck, subsequently Lord Auchinleck; *b.* Edinburgh; educated at Edinburgh Univ.; called to the Eng. and Scot. bar, and practised with little success; travelled, 1763, across Europe to Corsica, where he met Paoli, the Corsican leader; pub. *An Account of Corsica* (1768); during visits to London had met Dr. Johnson frequently after 1763; travelled with him in Scotland, 1773, and recorded journey in *Journal of a Tour in the Hebrides* (1786); succeeded to his father's estate, 1782. Greatest work is *The Life of Samuel Johnson, LL.D.* (1791), one of the masterpieces of Eng. literature. He was vain and addicted to drunkenness, but possessed a distinct genius for hunting down celebrities, and had, as Goldsmith said, 'the faculty of sticking.'

[*Life of Boswell* (1896), by W. K. Leask.]

Botha (*bō'ta*), LOUIS (1863–1919), S. African soldier and statesman; *b.* Greytown, Natal; a member of the first Volksraad of the Transvaal; succeeded General Joubert as commander of the Transvaal Boers during S. African War, 1899–1902, in which he greatly distinguished himself;

premier of Transvaal, 1907–10; first prime minister of Union parliament, 1910; warmly espoused Brit. cause in Great War, subdued S. African rebellion, 1914, and commanded the Union forces in S.W. Africa, receiving the surrender of the Germans, July 9, 1915; represented S. Africa at the Paris Peace Conference, 1919; noted for integrity, sincerity, and chivalry.

[*General Botha* (1924), by Earl Buxton.]

Both'well, JAMES HEPBURN, 4TH EARL OF (*c.* 1536–78), lord high admiral of Scotland, 1556; one of chief advisers of Mary Queen of Scots, and, after murders of Rizzio, 1566, and Darnley, 1567, obtained complete ascendancy over her; created Duke of Orkney and Shetland, and married Mary, 1567. Nobles revolted, and after meeting at Carberry Hill Bothwell was driven into exile; became leader of band of pirates, and was imprisoned in Zealand till his death; Mary divorced him, 1570.

Bot'ta. (1) CARLO GIUSEPPE GUGLIELMO (1766–1837), Piedmontese historian; became naturalized Fr. citizen; rector of Rouen Univ., 1817–22; pub. (1824) *History of Italy from 1789–1814.* (2) PAUL EMILE (1802–70), archæologist, son of above; *b.* Turin; discovered palace of Sargon (722–705 B.C.) and other fine specimens of Assyrian architecture.

Bottesini (*bot-e-zē'nē*), GIOVANNI (1823–89), celebrated Ital. double-bass player; *b.* in Lombardy; was also composer and conductor.

Botticelli (*bot-e-chel'ē*), SANDRO (1444–1510), Ital. artist of the Florentine school; real name was Alessandro di Mariano di Vanni dei Filipepi; *b.* Florence; son of a tanner; apprenticed at fifteen to a goldsmith; developed artistic ambitions, and entered the studio of Fra Lippo Lippi, 1460, where his famous picture, *The Adoration,* now in the National Gallery, was painted; found favour in the eyes of the Medici family, and his progress was continuous for many years; his subjects are drawn almost entirely from classic and Scriptural sources; other famous pictures include *Spring, The Birth of Venus, Mars and Venus, Pallas and the Centaur, The Nativity,* and numerous Madonnas.

[*Life* (1908), by Herbert P. Horne.]

Bouchardon (*boo-shär-dōn'*), EDMÉ (1698–1762), Fr. sculptor; *b.* Chaumont; great works include the Fountain of Grenelle, in Paris, and *Cupid fashioning a Bow out of the Club of Hercules,* in the Louvre.

Boucher (*boo-shā'*), FRANÇOIS (1703–70), famous Fr. painter; *b.* Paris; court painter to Louis XV.; an artist of great facility, known for his voluptuous style as 'Anacreon of painting'; specimens of work in Louvre (Paris) and Wallace Collection (London).

Boucher de Crèvecour de Perthes (*boo-shā' de krev-koor' de pert*), JACQUES (1788–1868); Fr. archæologist; *b.* in Ardennes; discovered worked flints in valley of R. Somme; wrote on Stone Age and prehistoric man.

Boucicault (*boo'sē-kō*), DION (1822–90), Irish dramatist and actor; *b.* Dublin; acted in England and U.S.A.; popular and successful plays include *The Colleen Bawn, Arrah-na-Pogue,* and *The Shaughraun.*

Bougainville (*boo-gan-vēl'*), LOUIS ANTOINE DE (1729–1811), Fr. navigator; *b.* Paris; entered army, 1753, and served in Seven Years' War; accomplished first Fr. circumnavigation of the world, 1766–9; field-marshal in army, 1780; vice-admiral, 1791; under Napoleon a senator and count of the empire.

Bough (*bō*), SAMUEL (1822–78), Brit. landscape painter; *b.* Carlisle; self-taught, but a master of effect in light and shade; excelled chiefly in water colour; pictures include *Shipbuilding at Dumbarton* and *Borrowdale*.

Boughton (*bō'ton*), George Henry (1833–1905), Anglo-Amer. painter; *b.* near Norwich, England; illustrated *The Scarlet Letter*, *Rip Van Winkle*; collaborated with E. A. Abbey in *Sketching Rambles in Holland*; R.A., 1896.

Bouguereau (*boog-rō'*), Guillaume Adolphe (1825–1905), Fr. artist; *b.* La Rochelle; a versatile painter in many styles, but chiefly known for somewhat heavy treatment of classical subjects and the nude.

Boulanger (*boo-lon-zhā'*), George Ernest Jean Marie (1837–91), Fr. general and agitator; *b.* Rennes; director of infantry at War Office, 1882; war minister, 1886–7; created the 'Boulangist' democratic agitation which threw France into confusion; took up a command at Clermont-Ferrand, 1887; insubordination led to loss of this post, 1888; elected deputy for Paris, 1889, but, accused of monarchical intrigues and misapplying public funds, he fled; committed suicide at Brussels, 1891.

Boul'ger, Demetrius Charles (1853–1928), Eng. historian and traveller; established *Asiatic Quarterly Review* (1885); authority on Asiatic and Belgian and Congo problems; works include *Histories* of China, India, and Belgium, *Lives* of Gordon and Sir Stamford Raffles.

Boulle (*bool*), André Charles (1642–1732), Fr. cabinet-maker, whose Boulle (or Buhl) inlaid work became famous; did much decoration in marquetry, inlaid panelling, etc., for the court of Louis XIV.

Boul'ton, Matthew (1728–1809), Eng. engineer and inventor; *b.* Birmingham; was partner of James Watt; designed machinery for stamping coinage.

Bouras'sa, Henri (1868–), Fr.-Can. politician; *b.* Montreal; trained for law and became journalist; M.P., 1896–9, resigned as protest against Can. participation in Boer War; M.P. 1900–8; opposed conscription during Great War; M.P. 1925–35.

Bourbak'i, Charles Denis Sauter (1816–97), Fr. soldier; *b.* Pau; won distinction in Algeria, Crimea, and Italy; in Franco-German War, 1870, commanded Imperial Guard in Bazaine's army; escaped from Metz, and was given command of Army of East to relieve Belfort; his army was cornered against Swiss frontier; attempted suicide, was carried across border, and interned in Switzerland; held military posts till 1881.

Bourbon (*boor-bōn'*), Fr. family, figuring in history from 9th cent. In 1272, a younger son of Louis IX. of France obtained the lordship of Bourbon in Berry by marriage with the heiress. In the person of Henry IV. the Bourbons ascended the throne of France, 1589, and the War of the Span. Succession resulted in establishment of Bourbons on throne of Spain. The Bourbons fell in France, 1791, and were expelled from their various Span. and Ital. possessions by Napoleon; restored 1815; younger Orleanist branch replaced elder in France, 1830–48, when they were expelled; driven from Naples 1860, Spain 1868–74. The elder branch died out with the Comte de Chambord, 1883, and the Orleanists again became sole hope of the Fr. monarchists.

Bourchier (*bou'cher*), Arthur (1864–1927), Eng. actor-manager *b.* in Berks; a most versatile actor Lessee of Garrick Theatre, and afterwards of the Strand; his numerous successes included *Henry VIII.* and *Treasure Island*.

Bourchier, THOMAS (?1404–86), Eng. ecclesiastic; Archbishop of Canterbury, 1454; lord chancellor, 1455; cardinal, 1467; crowned Edward IV., Richard III., and Henry VII.

Bourdaloue (*boor-dä-loo'*), LOUIS (1632–1704), Fr. Jesuit; *b.* Bourges; famous preacher at court of Louis XIV.; man of fine character and great oratorical power; much revered by all classes.

Bourgelat (*boorzh-lä'*), CLAUDE (1712–79), Fr. veterinary surgeon and pioneer of veterinary science in Europe; founder of veterinary schools at Lyons, 1761, and at Alfort, near Paris, 1765.

Bourgeois (*boor-zhwä'*), LÉON VICTOR AUGUSTE (1851–1925), Fr. statesman and eminent writer; *b.* Paris; a leader of Radical party; held office in eight cabinets; prime minister, 1895–6; minister of labour and social reform, 1912–13; of labour, 1917; president of Senate, 1920–3; accomplished orator and writer; author of an epoch-making book, *La Solidarité*; appointed to represent France on Council of League of Nations, Oct. 1919; awarded the Nobel Peace Prize, 1920.

Bourget (*boor-zhā*), PAUL CHARLES JOSEPH (1852–1935), Fr. novelist, critic, and poet; *b.* Amiens; produced numerous novels in various styles; a master of psychological analysis; most justly celebrated work is *Physiologie de l'amour moderne* (1890). Works include *Un Crime d'Amour*, *Mensonges*, *Le Disciple*, *Drames de Famille*, *Le démon du midi*, *Conflicts intimes*, *Le Danseur Mondain*, *Nos Actes nous suivent*. Also occupied a high position as a critic—*e.g. Etudes et Portraits*; descriptive powers shown in *Sensations d'Italie*.

Bourmont (*boor-mōn'*), LOUIS AUGUSTE VICTOR, COMTE DE GHAISNES DE (1773–1846), marshal of France; served with army of *émigrés* (1792–3); fled to Portugal and joined Fr. army of invasion; subsequently became a general in imperial army; deserted Napoleon before the battle of Ligny; war minister, 1829; commanded Algiers expedition, 1830; refused oath of allegiance to Louis Philippe, and retired to Portugal; returned to France after general amnesty, 1840.

Bourne, FRANCIS (1861–1935), R.C. archbishop of Westminster, and head of R.C. Church in England; *b.* London; Bishop of Southwark, 1897; archbishop, 1903; cardinal, 1911.

Bourne, HUGH (1772–1852), founder of Eng. Primitive Methodists from Wesleyan Methodists, 1811; *b.* in Staffs; before his death his followers numbered some 110,000.

Bourne, VINCENT (1695–1747), Eng. Lat. poet; a master at Westminster School; famous for the exquisite grace of his Lat. poems, which have received high praise from Cowper, Lamb, and others.

Bourrienne (*boo-rē-en'*), LOUIS ANTOINE FAUVELET DE (1769–1834), Fr. diplomatist; *b.* Sens; educated at Brienne with Napoleon; private secretary to Napoleon in Ital. campaign, 1798; Fr. envoy to Hamburg, 1805–10; dismissed for bribery and corruption; joined Royalists, 1814; chiefly remembered for his *Mémoires*.

Bouts, DIERICK (also called STUERBOUDT and THIERRY DE HAARLEM), Dutch artist (*c.* 1400–75); municipal painter at Louvain; painted many Biblical and historical pictures.

Bout'well, GEORGE SEWALL (1818–1905), Amer. statesman; *b.* Brookline, Massachusetts; originally a democratic leader, became a republican, 1854; representative in Congress, 1863–9; was one of seven who conducted impeachment of President Johnson; secretary of treasury, 1869–73); senator, 1873–7; opposed acquisition of the Philippines.

Bouvet (*boo-vā'*), François Joseph (1753–1832), Fr. admiral; captain and rear-admiral, 1793; dismissed for failure to land General Hoche in Ireland, 1796; restored to service by Napoleon.

Bouvier (*boo-vēr'*), John (1787–1851), Amer. judge and legal writer; *b.* in France; emigrated to U.S.A., 1802; *Bouvier's Law Dictionary* is still a standard work.

Bov'ill, Sir William (1814–73), Eng. judge; *b.* Barking; great authority on commercial law; assisted in passing the Partnership Law Amendment Act, usually known as Bovill's Act; solicitor-general, 1866; judge at first Tichborne trial.

Bow'dich, Thomas Edward (1790–1824), Eng. author; *b.* Bristol; spent some years on the Gold Coast; arranged treaty by which Brit. company obtained control of coast natives; his criticism of administration of Gold Coast led Britain to take over control of colony.

Bowd'ler, Thomas (1754–1825), Eng. ed. and philanthropist; *b.* near Bath; an M.D. of private fortune; notorious as ed. of *The Family Shakespeare* (1818), in ten vols., in which all words and expressions were omitted which might offend the prudish sense, hence the word 'bowdlerize.'

Bowdoin (*bō'dn*), James (1726–90), Amer. separatist in War of Independence; one of founders and first president of Amer. Academy of Arts and Sciences. His son, James Bowdoin (1752–1811), was generous benefactor of Bowdoin Coll. (named in honour of father).

Bowen (*bō'en*), Charles Synge Christopher Bowen, Baron (1835–94), Eng. judge; *b.* in Gloucestershire; distinguished in Tichborne case; lord of appeal in ordinary, 1893; great lawyer, but more brilliant wit; trans. *Eclogues* and part of *Æneid* of Virgil; wrote legal studies.

Bowen, Francis (1811–90), Amer. philosophic writer; *b.* in Massachusetts; prof. of natural religion at Harvard, 1853–89; ed. *N. American Review* (1843–54); wrote *A Treatise on Logic* (1864), *American Political Economy* (1870), and numerous other works.

Bowen, Sir George Ferguson (1821–99), Brit. colonial statesman; *b.* in Ireland; governor successively of Queensland, New Zealand, Victoria, Mauritius, and Hong-Kong; did much to reconcile Maoris to Brit. rule.

Bow'er, Walter (?1385–1449), Scot. chronicler; *b.* Haddington; abbot of Inchcolm; continued the narrative of Fordun's history (*Scotichronicon*) to 1437; abridged it as *Book of Cupar*.

Bowles (*bōlz*), Thomas Gibson (1844–1922), Eng. politician and author; Conservative M.P., 1892–1906, and afterwards Liberal M.P., 1910–1916; was an authority on maritime law.

Bowles, William Lisle (1762–1850), Eng. poet and antiquary; *b.* in Northants; canon, Salisbury Cathedral; his *Fourteen Sonnets on Picturesque Spots* (1789) influenced Coleridge and Wordsworth, and prepared the way for the romantic revival.

Bowley (*bō'li*), Arthur Lyon (1869–   ), Eng. statistician; *b.* Bristol; prof. of statistics, London Univ., 1915; works include standard treatise *Elements of Statistics*, and books on economics.

Bowman (*bō'man*), Isaiah (1878–   ), Amer. geographer; *b.* in Canada; director of Amer. Geographical Soc. since 1915; leader of several expeditions to S. America; works include *The New World* (1926) and *The Pioneer Fringe* (1931).

Bow'ring, Sir John (1792–

1872), Eng. linguist (knew 100 languages); *b.* Exeter; first ed. of *Westminster Review* (1824); M.P., 1835–7 and 1841–9; strong opponent of Corn Laws; governor of Hong-Kong, 1854; ordered the much criticized bombardment of Canton, 1856.

Boyce (*bois*), WILLIAM (1710–79), Eng. composer; son of a London cabinet-maker; master of the king's band, and organist of the Chapel Royal; celebrated for his church services and anthems—*e.g.* *By the Waters of Babylon*; pub. a valuable work on *Cathedral Music* (1760–78).

Boyd, ANDREW KENNEDY HUTCHISON (1825–99), Scot. divine, commonly referred to as A.K.H.B.; *b.* in Ayrshire; author of *Recreations of a Country Parson*, etc.

Boyd. (1) ROBERT, LORD BOYD (*d. c.* 1470), Scot. statesman; regent during minority of James III., and arranged his marriage with Margaret of Norway which secured Orkney and Shetland Is. for Scotland. (2) ROBERT, 4TH LORD (*d.* 1590), joined Protestants, but later supported Queen Mary; banished for share in Raid of Ruthven, 1583.

Boyd, ZACHARY (?1585–1653), Scot. Protestant theologian; twice rector of Glasgow Univ.; preached against Cromwell during his occupation of city, 1650; author of *Zion's Flowers*, metrical versions of Scripture known as *Boyd's Bible*.

Boy'dell, JOHN (1719–1804), Eng. engraver and publisher; *b.* in Shropshire; famous for his illustrated ed. of Shakespeare's works; Lord Mayor of London, 1790.

Boyer (*bwä-yā'*), JEAN PIERRE (1776–1850), president of republic of Haiti, 1818–43; *b.* Port-au-Prince; a mulatto, educated in France; ruled with judicious firmness, but was forced to flee the country; *d.* Paris.

Boyle, ROBERT (1626–91), Eng. natural philosopher; son of Richard Boyle, Earl of Cork; *b.* in Ireland; studied natural sciences, and made important researches in pneumatics (*Boyle's law*); a founder of the Royal Soc. and an East India Co. director; instituted 'Boyle Lectures' for defence of Christian religion; works include *Seraphic Love*, *Hydrostatical Paradoxes*, *Experiments touching Colour*.

Boylesve (*bwä-lev'*), RENÉ (1867–1926), Fr. novelist; depicts the bourgeois life of Touraine with subtle instinct and delicate irony; member of Fr. Academy; among his works are *Le Médecin des Dames de Néans*, *Mlle. Cloque*, *La Becquée*, and *L'Enfant à la Balustrade*.

Boz. See DICKENS, CHARLES.

Brace, CHARLES LORING (1826–90), Amer. philanthropist and author; *b.* in Connecticut; founded New York Children's Aid Soc. and other organizations.

Brace'girdle, ANNE (?1663–1748), Eng. actress; chiefly remembered in connection with Congreve's comedies; buried in Westminster cloisters.

Brac'ton, HENRY DE (*d.* 1268), Eng. judge and priest; archdeacon of Barnstaple and chancellor of Exeter Cathedral, 1264; wrote treatise on laws and customs of England.

Bradbury, JOHN SWANWICK, 1ST BARON (1872–), Eng. civil servant; *b.* in Cheshire; joint permanent secretary to the treasury, 1913; signature appeared on first treasury notes, 1914; principal Brit. representative on Reparations Commission, 1919–25; peerage, 1925.

Brad'dock, EDWARD (1695–1755), Brit. general; *b.* in Scotland; sent to Virginia in command of forces operating against the French on R. Ohio; ambushed during attempt, with Washington, to capture Fort Duquesne, and was mortally wounded.

Brad'don, MARY ELIZABETH

(1837–1915), Eng. novelist; *b.* London; made her name with *Lady Audley's Secret* (1862); a prolific writer of popular novels; married the publisher, John Maxwell; her son is the novelist W. B. Maxwell.

Brad'ford, JOHN (1510–55), Eng. Prot. martyr; *b.* Manchester; converted to Protestanism by Latimer; chaplain to Edward VI., 1553; during Mary's reign was committed to the Tower, tried for heresy, and burnt at Smithfield.

Bradford, WILLIAM (1590–1657), a leader of the Pilgrim Fathers; *b.* in York; sailed in *Mayflower*, 1620; elected governor of Plymouth colony, 1621; wrote *History of Plimouth Plantation.*

Bradlaugh (*brad'law*), CHARLES (1833–91), Eng. freethinker and politician; *b.* London; enlisted as a soldier; later was employed in a solicitor's office; began his platform campaign as a Radical and freethinker, 1858; ed. of *National Reformer*; elected M.P. for Northampton, 1880; refused to take the oath in Parliament, was excluded twice, each time being re-elected, and in 1886 was permitted to take his seat; by his efforts the Affirmation Bill was passed.

Brad'ley, ANDREW CECIL (1851–1935), Eng. critic; prof. of Eng. literature, Glasgow Univ., 1889–1900, and prof. of poetry at Oxford, 1901–6; author of *Shakespearean Tragedy* (1904) and *Oxford Lectures on Poetry* (1909).

Bradley, EDWARD. See BEDE, CUTHBERT.

Bradley, GEORGE GRANVILLE (1821–1903), Eng. divine and schoolmaster; headmaster of Marlborough; master of Univ. Coll., Oxford, 1870; Dean of Westminster, 1881–1902; revised *Arnold's Introduction to Latin Prose Composition.*

Bradley, HENRY (1845–1923), Eng. philologist; *b.* Manchester; senior ed. of Oxford Eng. Dictionary from 1915; ed. of early texts and author of *The Making of English.*

Bradley, JAMES (1693–1762), Eng. astronomer; *b.* in Glos; discoverer of 'aberration of light'; prof. of astronomy, Oxford, 1721; lecturer on experimental philosophy, 1729; Astronomer-Royal at Greenwich Observatory, 1742–52.

Brad'shaw, GEORGE (1801–53), Eng. printer and publisher; *b.* in Lancs; originator of railway guides; began issue of *Bradshaw's Railway Time-Tables* in 1839.

Bradshaw, HENRY (1831–86), Eng. scholar, antiquary, and librarian; *b.* London; fellow of King's Coll., Cambridge; made a special study of Celtic, and discovered MS. of the famous *Book of Deer* (1857).

Bradshaw, JOHN (1602–59), Eng. judge; *b.* in Cheshire; called to bar, 1627; presided over 'High Court of Justice' which tried Charles I.; president of council of state, 1649; commissioner of great seal, 1659; a zealous republican; body disinterred at Restoration and gibbeted.

Bra'dy, NICHOLAS (1659–1726), Irish divine; chaplain to William III., Queen Mary, and Queen Anne; wrote, with Tate, metrical version of Psalms, 1696.

Braga, THEOPHILO (1843–1924), Port. statesman and author; *b.* in Azores; first provisional president of republic, 1910–11; chief work, *Historia da Literatura Portugueza* (20 vols. 1870–80).

Bragg. (1) SIR WILLIAM HENRY (1862–), Eng. scientist; *b.* in Cumberland; prof. of mathematics and physics, Adelaide Univ., S. Australia, 1886–1908; Leeds Univ., 1909–15; London Univ., 1915–23; specialist in X-rays and radio-activity; along with his son has investigated methods of sound-ranging; has written many scientific works; Nobel prize, 1915; K.B.E., 1920; President Brit. Association, 1928;

O.M., 1931. (2) WILLIAM LAWRENCE (1890–), son of above; *b.* Adelaide, S. Australia; prof. of physics, Victoria Univ. of Manchester, since 1919; Nobel prize, 1915, along with father, with whom much of his work has been done; pub. papers on crystal structure; F.R.S., 1921.

Bra'ham, JOHN (1774–1856), Eng. tenor vocalist; *b.* London; studied in Italy, and on return had no rival as a tenor for over forty years; composer of 'Death of Nelson' and 'All's Well.'

Brah'e, PER, COUNT (1602–80), Swed. chancellor; *b.* near Stockholm; served with Gustavus Adolphus in army; as gov.-gen. of Finland, 1637–40 and 1648–54, gained great honour; entirely reformed system of government; introduced postal system; founded Åbo Univ., 1640.

Brahe, TYCHO (1546–1601), Dan. astronomer; *b.* in Scania, S. Sweden, then a Dan. province; discovered new star in Cassiopeia whilst resident in Germany, 1572; director of observatory of Uraniborg, 1576–97; after death of Frederick II. and subsequent friction with Christian IV. he removed to Prague, 1597, where he worked in conjunction with Kepler; chief work, *Astronomiæ Instauratæ Progymnasmata.*

[*Life* (1890), by Dreyer.]

Brahms, JOHANNES (1833–97), Ger. composer; *b.* Hamburg; an austere classicist; only since his death has he taken a foremost place among composers; wrote symphonies, concertos, Hungarian dances, songs, and practically every musical form but the dramatic, all marked by skilful technique and greatness of rhythm; attains highest point in his *Lieder* and choral works, among which are well known *Schicksalslied*, *Rinaldo*, and *Triumphlied.*

[*Brahms* (1911), by J A. F. Maitland.]

Braid, JAMES (1870–), Scot. golfer; *b.* in Fife; five times open champion of Great Britain, 1901, 1905, 1906, 1908, 1910; winner of Fr. championship, 1910, and of many tournaments; holed out in one stroke on fourteen occasions; expert golf-course architect; professional to Walton Heath Golf Club.

Braid'wood, THOMAS (1715–1806), Scot. educationist; opened at Edinburgh, 1760, the first school in Great Britain for the education of the deaf and dumb; removed to London, 1783.

Braille (*brāl*), LOUIS (1809–52), Fr. educationist; *b.* near Paris; blind from third year; as teacher of blind adapted and improved alphabet invented by Fr. officer called Barbier, 1829–34.

Braithwaite, JOHN (1797–1870), Eng. engineer; devised the donkey engine, 1822, and first practical steam fire-engine.

Bram'ah, JOSEPH (1748–1814), Eng. mechanician; *b.* in Yorks; invented the hydraulic press, machine for printing bank-notes, etc.

Braman'te, DONATO (1444–1514), Ital. architect; *b.* in Urbino; employed by Popes Alexander VI. and Julius II.; commissioned to rebuild St. Peter's, which, begun in 1506, was completed after his death by Michelangelo and others.

Brampton, BARON. See HAWKINS, SIR HENRY.

Brand. (1) SIR JAN HENDRIK (1823–88), S. African politician; *b.* Cape Town; called to Eng. bar, 1849; president of Orange Free State from 1863; maintained policy of friendliness towards Britain. (2) SIR CHRISTOPHER JOSEPH QUINTIN (1893–), S. African airman; nephew of (1); came to England, 1915, and joined the Air Force; during air raid on England brought down a Gotha. With Pierre van Ryneveld was first to accomplish flight from England to Cape Town.

Bran'dan (or Brendan), St. (*d.* 578), Irish Benedictine abbot of Clonfert (Galway); became confused with a legendary hero who sailed to an island paradise in the neighbourhood of the Canaries or the W. Indies; 'St. Brandan's Isle' was long believed in by geographers.

Bran'des, Georg Morris Cohen (1842–1927), Dan. literary critic; *b.* Copenhagen, of Jewish parentage; established European reputation by brilliant critical writings, including studies of Shakespeare, Ibsen, Anatole France; work of high merit is *Main Streams in Nineteenth Century Literature* (1886–1906); also wrote on *The World at War, Voltaire, Cæsar, Goethe,* and *Michael Angelo.*

Bran'dis, Christian August (1790–1867), Ger. philologist; prof. of philosophy at Bonn, 1821; author of several authoritative philological and philosophical works.

Brandl, Alois Leonhard (1855–), Austrian critic of Eng. literature; *b.* Innsbruck; has written on Coleridge, Shakespeare, etc.; ed. Schlegel and Tieck's Shakespeare.

Brangwyn, Frank (1867–), Eng. artist; *b.* Bruges; of Welsh extraction; pupil of William Morris; travelled in East; noted for breadth of style and sumptuous sense of colour; R.A., 1919; works include *Modern Commerce* and *Trade on the Beach.*

Brant, Joseph, or Thayendanegea (1742–1807), famous Mohawk Amer. Ind. chief; fought with English against French; became colonel and missionary of Church of England; said to be ablest of all Ind. leaders.

Bran'ting, Karl Hjalmar (1860–1925), Swed. statesman; *b.* Stockholm; first Socialist deputy to Riksdag, 1896; during Great War stood decisively for neutrality; later formed three ministries; Nobel Peace Prize, 1921; supported League of Nations.

Brantôme (*bron-tōm'*), Pierre de Bourdeille, Seigneur and Abbé de (*c.* 1540–1614), Fr. historian, soldier, and courtier; chamberlain to Charles IX. and Henry III., enjoyed patronage of Catherine de' Medici; travelled extensively from Scotland to Morocco; his *Mémoires* appeared after his death.

Brassey. (1) Thomas (1805–70), Eng. railway contractor; *b.* near Chester; constructed numerous railways at home and abroad; said to have left £7,000,000. (2) Thomas, 1st Earl (1836–1918), son of (1); M.P. for Hastings, 1868–85; civil lord of admiralty, 1880–4, and secretary, 1884–5; peerage, 1886. Sailed round world in famous yacht *Sunbeam.* He founded and ed. *Naval Annual.*

Bratian'u. (1) Jon Constantin (1821–91), Romanian statesman; *b.* Pitesti; leader in Romanian revolt, 1848; helped to establish Romanian kingdom; minister, 1866–70 and 1876–88. (2) Jon (1864–1927), Romanian statesman, son of above; secretary for foreign affairs, 1904; prime minister, 1909–11, 1914–18, 1918–19, and from 1922; brought Romania into the Great War, 1916; delegate to Peace Conference, 1919.

Brax'field, Robert Macqueen, Lord (1722–99), famous Scot. judge; *b.* in Lanarkshire; lord justice clerk from 1788; earned epithet of 'hanging judge' by his merciless sentences. Prototype of 'Weir of Hermiston' in R. L. Stevenson's novel.

Bray, Thomas (1656–1730), Eng. divine; *b.* in Shropshire; helped to found S.P.C.K., 1698, and the S.P.G., 1701; organized a scheme for providing public libraries.

Brazza (*brät'sä*), Pierre Paul François Camille, Count Savorgnan de (1852–1905), Fr. explorer and colonial commissioner; b. on board ship in Rio de Janeiro harbour; explored Ogowe R., W. Africa, 1875–8; sent on political mission to the Congo, 1880–2; appointed commissary-general of Fr. W. Africa, 1886, and governor, 1888–98; returned to Africa, 1905, to inquire into alleged ill-treatment of natives; died in Senegal.

Breadal'bane, JOHN CAMPBELL, 1ST EARL (1635–1717); responsible with Sir John Dalrymple for Glencoe massacre, 1692.

Breakspear, NICHOLAS. See ADRIAN.

Breasted, JAMES HENRY (1865–1935), Amer. Orientalist; *b.* in Illinois; prof. of Egyptology and Oriental history, Chicago Univ., since 1905; leader of expeditions to Egypt and the Near East; works include *A History of Egypt* (1905) and *The Conquest of Civilization* (1926).

Breitmann, HANS. See LELAND, CHARLES GODFREY.

Bremer, FREDRIKA (1801–65), Swed. novelist; *b.* near Åbo; her earlier stories, of a simple, idyllic character, trans. into English by Mary Howitt; later devoted her attention to the emancipation of women, and dealt with this in her novels, *Hertha* (1856) and *Father and Daughter* (1858).

Brendan, ST. See BRANDAN.

Bren'nan, LOUIS (1852–1932), Irish engineer; *b.* Castlebar; inventor of a torpedo and of gyroscopic mono-rail; superintendent of the government Brennan torpedo factory, 1887–96; Air Ministry research work, 1919–26.

Brentan'o, CLEMENS (1778–1842), Ger. poet and novelist; *b.* Ehrenbreitstein; brother of Goethe's friend, Bettina von Arnim; author of some charming short stories which have been trans. into English.

Brentano, LUDWIG JOSEPH ('LUJO') (1844–1931), Ger. economist; *b.* Aschaffenburg; studied labour conditions in England, 1868; chief work, *Die Arbeitergilden der Gegenwart* (1871–2), is study of evolution of trade unions from mediæval gilds; prof. of political economy, Munich, 1891–1914; pacifist; Nobel prize, 1927.

Brent'ford, WILLIAM JOYNSON-HICKS, 1ST VISCOUNT (1865–1932), Eng. Conservative politician; held various offices, including Home Office, 1924; opposed revision of Eng. Prayer Book, 1928; peerage, 1929.

Breton (*bre-tōn'*), JULES ADOLPHE AIMÉ LOUIS (1827–1906), Fr. artist; *b.* in Pas-de-Calais; secured a high reputation by his landscapes and rustic scenes—*e.g. Return of the Gleaners, St. John's Feast, Potato Harvest, The Fountain.*

Bret'on, NICHOLAS (*c.* 1545–1626), Eng. poet; *b.* London; poems include *A Flourish upon Fancie* and *The Passionate Shepherd*; wrote some charming lyrics.

Breton' de los Herre'ros, MANUEL (1796–1873), Span. dramatist; *b.* in Logroño; wrote upwards of 300 plays, many of great comic power.

Bretschneider (*bret-shnī'der*), KARL GOTTLIEB (1776–1848), Ger. theologian; *b.* in Saxony; superintendent-general at Gotha from 1816; argued against Johannine authorship of the gospel and epistles.

Breughel (*bruch'el*) (or BRUEGHEL), PIETER (1525–69), noted Dutch genre painter; *b.* near Breda; chief works are *The Village Fair* and *The Shepherd,* both in Vienna. His son, PIETER THE YOUNGER (1564–1638), was less talented in same line; younger son, JAN (1568–1625), was famous landscape painter and engraver, and father of JAN THE YOUNGER (1601–78), painter of same school.

Breun, JEAN E., COMTE DE L'HÔPITAL (1862–1921), Eng. portrait painter; gold medal Paris Salon for *Cold Steel* (1892); painted Princess Victoria of Wales, Sir Redvers Buller, W. G. Grace, Madame Patti, etc.

Brew'er, EBENEZER COBHAM (1810–97), Eng. clergyman; *b.* London; author of *Dictionary of Phrase and Fable* (1870), *The Reader's Handbook*, etc.

Brew'ster, SIR DAVID (1781–1868), Scot. natural philosopher; *b.* Jedburgh; principal of united colleges of St. Salvator and St. Leonard, St. Andrews, 1838, and of Edinburgh Univ., 1859; one of the founders of the Brit. Association, 1831; invented the kaleidoscope, improved the stereoscope, and made many discoveries in science of optics; wrote *Life of Newton*, etc.

Brialmont (*brē-äl-mōn'*), HENRI ALEXIS (1821–1903), Belgian military engineer; *b.* Venlo (Holland); planned and carried out fortifications (Antwerp, Namur, Liége) for defence of Belgium; retired 1887; wrote elaborate work on fortification, *Les Régions fortifiées* (1890), in which he maintained that concrete and armoured forts were proof against high-explosive shells, a thesis proved false in the Great War.

Bri'an (926–1014), surnamed BORU, King of Ireland, 'the Alfred of Irish history'; defeated Dan. host at Clontarf, 1014, but was killed after the battle.

Briand (*brē-on'*), ARISTIDE (1862–1932), Fr. statesman; *b.* Nantes; eleven times premier; entered Chamber of Deputies, 1902; brought forward proposals for separation of Church and State (became law 1905); first Socialist prime minister of France, 1909; during Great War was premier, 1915–17; retired from public activities, 1917–20; as prime minister, 1921, engaged in application of Treaty of Versailles especially on question of repara tions; took great interest i League of Nations; signed Lo carno pact; received Nobel Peac Prize, 1926; planned Unite States of Europe, 1930. Fron 1925–32 controlled Fr. foreig policy as minister of foreig affairs, and was associated wit every peace proposal.

Bride, ST. See BRIDGET, ST.

Bridge, SIR FREDERICK (1844–1924), Eng. musician and com poser; *b.* Oldbury; King Edwar prof. of music, London Univ., fron 1902; organist at Westminste Abbey, 1875–1918; pub. accoun of career, *A Westminster Pilgrin* (1919).

Bridges, ROBERT (1844–1930) Eng. poet; *b.* Isle of Thanet poet laureate from 1913; O.M. 1929; formerly physician, an practised at various London hos pitals; retired 1882; wrote man vols. of poems in experimenta metres; pub. *Poetical Work* (1898–1905), *The Spirit of Ma* (1916), an anthology in English an French, *October and other Poem* (1920), *New Verse* (1925), an *The Testament of Beauty*, issue on his eighty-fifth birthday, prob ably his greatest work; his poetr is appreciated by a limited bu cultured class; prose works in clude essays on *Milton's Prosody*, *John Keats*, and *The Necessity o Poetry*.

Bridget, ST., or ST. BRIDE, popular Irish saint of 5th cent.

Brid'get, ST. (1302–73), founded *Bridgettines* (Augustinian Order) in Sweden; lived in Rome from 1350; order spread to other lands.

Bridgewater, FRANCIS EGERTON, 3RD DUKE OF (1736–1803); pioneer in inland navigation in England; with aid of Brindley, made canals from Worsley to Manchester and from Manchester to Liverpool.

Bridg'man, LAURA DEWEY (1829–89), Amer. deaf mute; was

also blind, and deprived of smell and almost of taste; carefully taught in blind asylum of Boston, her mind developed in spite of her affliction.

Bri′erly, Sir Oswald Walters (1817–94), Eng. artist; spent much time in sea travel, and thus gave realism to his marine pictures; most famous are *The Retreat of the Spanish Armada* (1871) and *The Loss of the 'Revenge'* (1877).

Brieux (*brē-ĕ′*), Eugene (1858–1932), Fr. dramatist; *b.* Paris; plays deal mainly with social abuses; member of Fr. Academy; plays include *Les Avariés* (1901) ('Damaged Goods'), *L'Enfant* (1923), and *La Famille Lavolette* (1926); Bernard Shaw's *Three Plays by Brieux* (1916) contain *La Femme Seule, La Robe Rouge*, and *Les Remplaçantes*.

Briggs, Henry (1561–1630), Eng. mathematician; *b.* near Halifax; prof. of geometry, Gresham Coll., 1596–1619; Savilian prof. of astronomy, Oxford; originator of 10 as best base for logarithms.

Bright, Sir Charles Tilston (1832–88), Eng. telegraph engineer; *b.* in Essex; laid first cable between Scotland and Ireland and first Atlantic cable, 1858; knighted 1858; M.P., Greenwich, 1865–8.

Bright, John (1811–89), Brit. statesman and orator; *b.* Rochdale; son of a Quaker cotton manufacturer; while in his father's cotton mill he took great interest in public questions, and after a foreign tour, 1835, became a prominent member of the Anti-Corn-Law League, and joined Cobden in Free Trade agitation; entered Parliament, 1843; a great master of oratory, he also advocated electoral reform and religious freedom; opposed the Crimean War, 1854; M.P. for Birmingham, 1857; his name is closely associated with Reform Bills of 1859–67; president of Board of Trade, 1868; supported disestablishment of Irish Church, 1869, and Irish Land Act, 1870, and became chancellor of duchy of Lancaster, 1873; unable to support government's Egyptian policy, he retired, 1882; strenuously opposed Gladstone's Home Rule Bill, 1886; lord rector of Glasgow Univ., 1880.

[*Life of John Bright* (1913), by G. M. Trevelyan.]

Bright, Richard (1789–1858), Eng. physician; *b.* Bristol; M.D. of Edinburgh Univ., 1812; researches led to discovery of connection between dropsy and kidney disease; papers on 'Bright's Disease' made him famous.

Bril (*brēl*), Paul (1554–1626), Flem. painter; *b.* Antwerp; painted frescoes at Vatican, Lateran, etc.; assisted his brother Matthew (1550–84), to whose post and pension in the Vatican he succeeded.

Brillat-Savarin (*brē-yä′ sä-vä-rän′*), Anthelme (1755–1826), Fr. gastronomist; *b.* in Ain; member of Court of Cassation, 1797; his *Physiologie du Goût* is a lively and humorous work on the art of dining.

Brin (*brēn*), Benedetto (1833–98), Ital. naval designer and organizer; *b.* Turin; minister of marine for nearly twenty years; contributed powerfully to creation of shipbuilding yards and engineering works in Italy; virtual founder of Ital. navy.

Brind′ley, James (1716–72), Eng. engineer; *b.* in Derbyshire; associated with Duke of Bridgewater in canal construction; Barton aqueduct over Mersey his greatest achievement; also constructed the Grand Trunk Canal between Trent and Mersey; in all superintended construction of over 365 miles of canal.

Brink, Bernhard ten. See Ten Brink.

Bris′bane, Sir Thomas Mak-

DOUGALL (1773–1860), Scot. colonial governor and astronomer; *b.* in Ayrshire; governor of New South Wales, 1821–5; founded observatories at Parramatta, and, on his return, at Makerstoun in Scotland; president of Brit. Association, 1834.

Brisson (*brē-sōn'*), EUGÈNE HENRI (1835–1912), Fr. Radical statesman; *b.* Bourges; prime minister, 1885 and 1898; president of the Chamber, 1894–98 and 1906; exposed Panama scandals, and insisted on revision of Dreyfus case.

Brit'ton, JOHN (1771–1857), Eng. antiquary; *b.* in Wilts; wrote numerous popular topographical works, including *The Beauties of England and Wales, The Architectural Antiquities of Great Britain.*

Broad'bent, SIR WILLIAM HENRY (1835–1907), Eng. physician; *b.* near Huddersfield; attended Queen Victoria, Edward VII., and George V. (when Prince of Wales); an authority on paralysis; wrote valuable memoir, *On the Cerebral Mechanism of Speech and Thought.*

Broad'wood, ROBERT GEORGE (1862–1917), Brit. soldier; *b.* in Sussex; served in Egypt and in S. African War; commanded in China, 1906; when Great War broke out was in command of troops in E. Anglia; died from wounds received in action.

Bro'ca, PAUL (1824–80), Fr. surgeon, pathologist, and anthropologist; *b.* in Gironde; prof. of surgical pathology, Paris, 1867; discovered seat of speech in 'convolution of Broca'; founded Paris Anthropological Soc., 1859; regarded as originator of science of craniology.

Brock, SIR ISAAC (1769–1812), Brit. soldier; *b.* Guernsey; lieut.-gov. of Upper Canada, 1803; in war with U.S.A., 1812, captured Hull's army; killed at battle of Queenstown; 'hero of Upper Canada.'

Brock, SIR THOMAS (1847–1922), Eng. sculptor; *b.* Worcester; R.A., 1891; principal works are *The Moment of Peril*, memorials to Lord Leighton and Queen Victoria, *Eve*, and *Edward, the Black Prince.*

Brock'haus, FRIEDRICH (1772–1823), Ger. publisher; *b.* Dortmund; completed the issue of the *Konversations Lexikon* (1810–11; 14th ed. 1904), besides numerous other bibliographical and historical works.

Brod, MAX (1884–), Ger.-Czechoslovak novelist, poet, and dramatist; *b.* Prague; novels include *The Redemption of Tycho Brahe, Reubini*, and *Three Lovers*; chief drama, *Lord Byron*; writes in German.

Bro'die. (1) SIR BENJAMIN COLLINS (1783–1862), Eng. surgeon; *b.* in Wilts; prof. of comparative anatomy and physiology at Royal Coll. of Surgeons, London; first president of General Medical Council. (2) SIR BENJAMIN COLLINS (1817–80), son of above, Eng. chemist; did important work on carbon, sulphur, phosphorus, and iodine; prof. of chemistry at Oxford, 1865.

Brodie, WILLIAM (*d.* 1788), known as 'Deacon Brodie'; Scot. criminal; *b.* Edinburgh; cabinetmaker in Edinburgh Lawnmarket; though posing as a man of high character, committed numerous daring burglaries, for which he was hanged.

Broglie (*brō-yē'*), Fr. noble family who emigrated from Piedmont, 1643, when they assumed title of Comtes de Broglie. Distinguished members are: (1) VICTOR MAURICE (1647–1727), marshal of France (1724). (2) FRANÇOIS MARIE (1671–1745), marshal of France (1734), Duc de Broglie (1742). (3) VICTOR FRANÇOIS (1718–1804), marshal of France (1759), became an *émigré* at the Revolution. (4) CHARLES FRANçois (1719–81), distinguished diplomatist. (5) Victor Claude (1757–94), *maréchal de camp*, Revolutionist and Jacobin, but executed in the Terror. (6) Achille Charles Léonce Victor (1785–1870), statesman, attempted to keep France both from reaction and from violent democracy; strengthened country by friendship with Britain. (7) Jacques Victor Albert (1821–1901), statesman and historian; member of Fr. Academy, 1862; held political office, 1871–7; later devoted himself to historical work. (8) Louis Victor, Prince de (1892–), scientist; *b.* Dieppe; awarded Nobel prize, 1929, for discovery of undulatory nature of electrons.

Broke (*brook*), Sir Philip Bowes Vere (1776–1841), Brit. naval commander; *b.* near Ipswich; fought single-ship duel in *Shannon* against *Chesapeake*, which he boarded and captured, 1813; rear-admiral, 1830.

Brome, Richard (*d.* 1652), Eng. dramatist; servant, and afterwards friend, of Ben Jonson; wrote about fifteen comedies, including *The Northern Lass*, *The Court Beggar*, *The City Wit*, and *A Jovial Crew*; *Collected Works* pub. in 1873.

Brongniart (*brön-yär'*), Adolphe Theodore (1801–76), Fr. botanist; *b.* Paris; director of Museum of Natural History, 1833; wrote important work on fossil plants, 1828–37; founded and was first president of Fr. Botanical Soc., 1854.

Bron'të, Charlotte (1816–55), Emily (1818–48), and Anne (1820–49), Eng. novelists; *b.* in Yorks; daughters of Rev. Patrick Brontë, incumbent of Haworth, Yorkshire; children were left motherless at an early age; their brother, Branwell (1817–48), turned out a waster. Charlotte mothered the family, and in their lonely life the three girls found solace in literary composition. Their first venture was a volume of *Poems*, under the pseudonyms Currer, Ellis, and Acton Bell, 1846, which cost them £50, and only one or two copies were sold. The sisters next applied themselves to novel-writing.

Charlotte wrote *The Professor*, which, however, proved too short for the publishers to whom it was offered, and it did not appear in print until after her death; wrote also *Jane Eyre* (1847), which at once achieved a popular success, followed by *Shirley* (1849), and by *Villette* (1852); married, 1854, her father's curate, Rev. A. Nicholls, but died in the following year. Emily was the author of *Wuthering Heights* (1848); and Anne pub. *The Tenant of Wildfell Hall* and *Agnes Grey* (1848). The novels of Charlotte and Emily Brontë and the poems of Emily hold a high place in Eng. literature.

[*Life of Charlotte Brontë* (1902 ed.), by Mrs. Gaskell; also later ones by Birrell (1887), Shorter (1906), and May Sinclair (1912).]

Brooke, Henry (1703–83), Irish author; *b.* in Co. Cavan; now chiefly remembered by his novel, *The Fool of Quality* (1765–70).

Brooke. (1) Sir James (1803–68), Brit. colonial governor; *b.* near Bath; servant of E. India Co.; aided sultan's forces to reduce revolted tribes of Sarawak, 1839–41; ruled as Rajah of Sarawak, 1841–6; island of Labuan purchased for Brit. colony, and Brooke made governor, 1847; charged with maladministration, but exonerated, 1851. (2) Charles Johnson (1829–1917), nephew of above; succeeded his uncle as rajah, 1868; his rule was successful example of peaceful and beneficent despotism; Sarawak became Brit. protectorate, 1888. (3) Sir Charles Vyner (1874–) succeeded his father as rajah in 1917.

Brooke, Rupert (1887–1915), Eng. poet; *b.* Rugby; travelled on Continent, U.S.A., Canada, and South Seas, 1911–13. Served in Great War, and died on Fr. hospital ship at Lemnos. His *Letters* and his *Poems* pub. 1918 in collected ed. with memoir; had remarkable poetic gift, but output small.

Brooke, Stopford Augustus (1832–1916), Irish clergyman and man of letters; *b.* in Donegal; seceded from Church of England and became Unitarian minister; wrote *Life and Letters of F. W. Robertson*, *Primer of Eng. Literature*, etc.

Brooks, Charles William Shirley (1816–74), Eng. novelist; *b.* London; educated for the law, but adopted journalism; on the staff of *Morning Chronicle*, *Illustrated London News*, and *Punch*; as ed. of *Punch*, 1870, started well-known series of articles 'The Essence of Parliament.'

Brooks, Phillips (1835–93), Amer. bishop and author; *b.* Boston; a dominating force among all classes in Massachusetts; best-known works are *The Influence of Jesus* and *Literature and Life*.

Brougham and Vaux (*broom and vō*), Henry Peter Brougham, 1st Baron (1778–1868), Eng. lord chancellor; *b.* Edinburgh; admitted to Scot. bar, 1800; contributed articles to *Edinburgh Review*; settled in London, 1805; called to Eng. bar, 1808; entered Parliament, 1810, and carried a bill making slave-trading felony. In 1816 became a prominent Opposition member, defeated Income Tax Bill, and zealously advocated extension of popular education. His management of Queen Caroline's case, 1820, won him fame; introduced a great scheme of law reform, 1828; returned for York, 1830, and was made lord chancellor. Brougham was excluded from reconstructed Whig government, 1835; *d.* at Cannes. Versatile, egotistical, turbulent, he is chiefly remembered as a law reformer.

[*Brougham's Life and Times* (1871), by himself; *Lord Brougham and the Whig Party* (1927), by A. Aspinall.]

Brought'on, John Cam Hobhouse, Baron (1786–1869), politician; *b.* Bristol; M.P. for Westminster, 1820; supported Reform party in Parliament; secretary for war, 1832; confined himself mainly to literary work after 1852; had two great admirations, one for Napoleon and the other for his friend Byron; arranged poet's funeral, 1824, and carried out burning of his memoirs; wrote *Recollections of a Long Life* (new ed. 1909).

Broughton, Rhoda (1840–1920), Eng. novelist; *b.* near Denbigh; wrote numerous novels, including *Cometh up as a Flower*, *Second Thoughts*, *Dear Faustina*, *Between Two Stools*, *The Devil and the Deep Sea*.

Brouwer (*brou'er*), Adrian (1606–38), Dutch artist, many of whose works are at Munich; *A Sleeping Boor* is in the Wallace Collection; *d.* Antwerp.

Brown, Sir Arthur Whitten (1886–), Brit. airman; *b.* Manchester; served in France, 1915; wounded and taken prisoner; interned Switzerland; repatriated, 1917. With Sir John Alcock made first transatlantic flight in aeroplane, June 1919; knighted 1919.

Brown. (1) Ford Madox (1821–93), Eng. artist; *b.* Calais; some of his best-known pictures are *Christ washing Peter's Feet*, *Romeo and Juliet*, and *Chaucer at the Court of Edward III*. Was pioneer of Pre-Raphaelite movement, though not a member of the brotherhood. Much of his best work is in Manchester Art Gallery and in Town Hall. (2)

Oliver Madox (1855–74), son of above, showed astonishing precocious genius, exhibited pictures, and pub. a novel, *Gabriel Denver*.

Brown, Hon. George (1818–80), Can. reforming statesman; *b.* Edinburgh; emigrated 1838; helped to bring about federation of British North America.

Brown, George Douglas (1869–1902), Scot. novelist; *b.* in Ayrshire; wrote *The House with the Green Shutters* (1901), a counterblast to the sentimental 'kailyard' school.

Brown, John (1800–59), Amer. abolitionist; *b.* in Connecticut; organized plot to free slaves of Virginia, and seized Harper's Ferry, 1859; wounded, tried by court-martial, and hanged; subject of popular song during Civil War, 'John Brown's Body.'

Brown, John (1810–82), Scot. physician and essayist; *b.* Biggar; author of *Horæ Subsecivæ* (1858–61), *Rab and His Friends* (1859), *Marjorie Fleming* (1863), etc.

Brown, Sir John (1816–96), Eng. steel manufacturer; *b.* Sheffield; invented the conical steel buffer spring, 1848; started the Atlas Works, Sheffield, where up to 1863 he had sheathed with iron armour three-fourths of the whole Brit. navy.

Brown, Lancelot (1715–83), best known as 'Capability Brown'; *b.* in Northumberland; founder of the modern Eng. style of landscape gardening; laid out the grounds at Kew and Blenheim.

Brown, Peter Hume (1850–1919), Scot. historian; *b.* in E. Lothian; prof. of anc. Scot. history in Edinburgh Univ. from 1901; historiographer-royal from 1908; an impartial historian; works include *Life of George Buchanan*, *Early Travellers in Scotland*, *Life of John Knox*, *History of Scotland*, *The Youth of Goethe*.

Brown, Robert (1773–1858), Scot. botanist; *b.* Montrose; naturalist on scientific expedition to Australia, 1801–5; president Linnean Soc., 1849–53; keeper botanical collection at Brit. Museum, 1827–58.

Brown, Thomas (1778–1820), Scot. philosopher; *b.* in Kirkcudbrightshire; succeeded Dugald Stewart as prof. of moral philosophy at Edinburgh, where he achieved great popularity as a lecturer; his *Lectures on the Philosophy of the Human Mind* had an extensive circulation.

Brown, Thomas Edward (1830–97), Manx poet and schoolmaster; *b.* Douglas, Isle of Man; master at Clifton Coll., 1863–92; author of *Fo'c'sle Yarns* (1881), *The Doctor and other Poems* (1887), *The Manx Witch* (1889), *Old John* (1893); many of his racy narrative poems are written in Manx.

Brown, Sir William (1784–1864), Liverpool linen manufacturer and banker; *b.* Ballymena; erected public library and museum at Liverpool; M.P. for S. Lancashire, 1846.

Browne, Charles Farrar (1834–67), better known as Artemus Ward, Amer. humorist; *b.* in Maine; his lectures in America and Europe were famed for their raciness and originality. Pub. *Artemus Ward, his Book* (1862), *Artemus Ward in London* (1867), etc.

Browne, Edward Granville (1862–1926), Oriental scholar; *b.* in Glos; travelled in Persia, 1887–8; prof. of Arabic, Cambridge Univ.; works include *The Literary History of Persia*, and *Materials for the Study of the Babi Religion*.

Browne, Hablôt Knight (1815–82), Eng. artist; better known as Phiz; *b.* London, of Huguenot descent; met Dickens, 1836, and became illustrator of the *Pickwick Papers* and other works of Dickens, besides novels of Ainsworth, Lever, and Smedley.

Browne, SIR JAMES CRICHTON. See CRICHTON-BROWNE.

Browne, ROBERT (1550–1633), founder of extreme Puritan sect, especially obnoxious to Queen Elizabeth; the *Brownists* formed first Dissenting body, that of the Independents.

Browne, SIR SAMUEL JAMES (1824–1901), Brit. general, served during Ind. Mutiny, and received V.C.; invented the 'Sam Browne belt.'

Browne, SIR THOMAS (1605–82), Eng. author and physician; *b.* London; practised medicine at Norwich, 1637; author of *Religio Medici* (1643), *Pseudodoxia Epidemica* (1646), *Hydriotaphia or Urn-Burial* (1658). Amid the distractions of the Civil War he preserved a singularly contemplative mind, which he exhibited in his works written in an elaborate and rich style.

[*Life*, by Gosse (1905).]

Browne, THOMAS A. See BOLDREWOOD, ROLF.

Browning, ELIZABETH BARRETT (1806–61), Eng. poetess; *b.* Durham; was an invalid from an early age; developed a remarkable aptitude for study, especially in Gr. poetry and philosophy; at the age of ten she began to write verse, and pub. two vols. of *Collected Poems* (1844). In 1846 she married secretly Robert Browning, whose poetry she had already admired; went to Pisa, and later settled at Florence. Her health greatly improved after her marriage. *Sonnets from the Portuguese*, written before her marriage, appeared in 1850, *Casa Guidi Windows* (1851), and *Aurora Leigh* (1856); she pub. her collected poems under the title, *Poems before Congress* (1860). Though her work is often slipshod, and her rhyming far from perfect, she is undoubtedly one of the greatest of Eng. women poets; *Sonnets from the Portuguese*, *Aurora Leigh*, *Lady Geraldine's Courtship*, and many of her shorter lyrical pieces have secured a lasting place in Eng. literature.

[*E. B. Browning* (Eminent Women Series, 1888), by J. H. Ingram.]

Browning, OSCAR (1837–1923), Eng. historian; *b.* London; master at Eton, 1860–75; lecturer in history, Cambridge Univ., 1891–1909; works include *History of England* (4 vols. 1890), *Dante, Life and Works* (1891), *Napoleon, the First Phase* (1905), and *Memories of Later Years* (1923).

Browning, ROBERT (1812–89), Eng. poet; *b.* London; pub. his first poem, *Pauline*, anonymously in 1833; two years later issued *Paracelsus*, a long dramatic poem, which met with little success, but found appreciative readers in Wordsworth, Carlyle, and other men of letters; pub. *Strafford* (1837) and *Sordello* (1840); these were followed by *Bells and Pomegranates* (1841), *A Blot on the 'Scutcheon* (1843), *Luria*, and *A Soul's Tragedy* (1846). In 1846 he married Elizabeth Barrett, and went to live in Italy, returning to England after his wife's death, 1861. *Men and Women* appeared (1855), *Dramatis Personæ* (1864), *The Ring and the Book* (1868–9), *Balaustion's Adventure* (1871), *Fifine at the Fair* (1872), *Red-cotton Night-cap Country* (1873), *The Inn Album* (1875), *Pacchiarotto* (1876), *La Saisiaz* (1878), *Dramatic Idylls* (1879–80), and *Asolando* (1889), pub. on his death-day.

The obscurity of his earlier poems, such as *Sordello*, and the general ruggedness of diction of the greater part of his work, undoubtedly militated against Browning's popularity, but what he lacks in poetical form he makes good in thought and vigour of expression. His profound knowledge of the mind and heart of man, his fearless optimism, his manliness, his tenderness, and his humour give him a very high place among Eng. poets.

[*Robert Browning* (1890), by E. Gosse; *Poetry of Robert Browning* (1902), by Stopford Brooke; *Browning* (English Men of Letters, 1908), by G. K. Chesterton.]

Brown-Séquard (*sā-kär'*), CHARLES EDWARD (1817–94), physiologist; *b.* Mauritius; studied medicine in Paris; prof. of physiology and neuropathology at Harvard and Paris; did valuable research on spinal cord, internal secretions, etc.

Bruce, or BRUS, Scot. dynasty; descended from Robert de Bruis, who came over with Conqueror from Normandy; branch obtained lordship of Annandale, Scotland; from latter descended ROBERT DE BRUS, claimant of Scot. crown, and his grandsons, ROBERT I. and EDWARD BRUCE (*d.* 1318), the latter of whom assisted in establishing Scot. independence; he was crowned King of Ireland, 1316, and killed at Dundalk. Robert Bruce's son reigned as DAVID II.; his grandson as ROBERT II., first of Stewart line. For ROBERT THE BRUCE, see ROBERT I.

Bruce, SIR DAVID (1855–1931), Eng. army physician; *b.* Melbourne, Australia; served with R.A.M.C. in Malta, Egypt, and S. Africa; specialist in tropical diseases; discoveries included transmission of Malta fever by goats' milk, and of sleeping sickness by tsetse fly; chairman of Trench Fever Committee during Great War; president, Brit. Association, 1924.

Bruce, JAMES (1730–94), Scot. African explorer and archæologist; *b.* in Stirlingshire; travelled in N. Africa and the Near East; explored Abyssinia; discovered source of Blue Nile, 1768–70, and, 1772, its confluence with White Nile. Wrote *Travels.*

Bruce, MICHAEL (1746–67), Scot. poet; *b.* in Kinross-shire; schoolmaster; fame rests on *Ode to the Cuckoo*; *Poems on Several Occasions,* pub. by John Logan in 1770.

Bruce, ROBERT. See ROBERT I.

Bruce, RT. HON. STANLEY MELBOURNE (1883–), Australian statesman; *b.* Melbourne; called to bar, Middle Temple, 1907; served in Great War; entered Commonwealth parliament, 1918; has held many offices; prime minister, 1923–9; represented Australia at League of Nations, 1921, and at Imperial Conferences, 1923 and 1926; high commissioner for Australia in London since 1933.

Bruce, WILLIAM SPEIRS (1867–1921), Scot. polar explorer and oceanographer; *b.* London; leader of *Scotia* expedition to Weddell Sea, 1902–4; discovered Coats Land; scientific work of great value; explored Spitsbergen between 1898 and 1919; wrote *Polar Exploration* (1911).

Bruch (*brooch*), MAX (1838–1920), Ger. musician; *b.* Cologne; conductor of the Liverpool Philharmonic, 1880–2; composed music for Schiller's *Jungfrau von Orleans,* and many other pieces, including *Odyssey.*

Brummell, GEORGE BRYAN (1778–1840), known as 'Beau Brummell,' Eng. leader of fashion; *b.* London; educated at Eton and Oxford; patronized by George IV., then Prince of Wales; in matters of dress was followed by all society till 1816. Died in an asylum at Caen.

Bruneau (*broo-nō'*), ALFRED (1857–1934), Fr. composer; *b.* Paris; operas include *Kerim* (1887), *Le Rêve* (1891), *L'Attaque du Moulin* (1893), *Le Roi Candaule* (1920), and *Le Jardin du Paradise* (1923); has also written collections of songs.

Brunel. (1) SIR MARC ISAMBARD (1769–1849), civil engineer; *b.* Normandy; on account of royalist opinions was expelled in 1793; settled in U.S.A.; established arsenal at New York; came to England, 1799, and was employed by the government in construction of his machine for making pulley blocks; built Thames tunnel (opened 1843), assisted by his son. (2) ISAMBARD KINGDOM (1806–59), Eng. civil engineer; son of above; *b.* Portsmouth; designed Clifton Suspension Bridge (completed 1864); engineer to Great Western Rly., 1833–46; introduced broad gauge; constructed *Great Western*, first steamship to cross Atlantic, 1838, and *Great Eastern* (launched 1858); also docks at Monkwearmouth, Plymouth, and Milford.

Brunelleschi (*broo-nel-les'kē*), FILIPPO (1379–1446), Ital. architect; *b.* Florence; revived the classic style in Italy; most of his great work was executed in Florence, and includes the Pitti Palace, the great cupola of cathedral of Santa Maria del Fiore, the Capella del Pazza; one of first to bring laws of perspective into practical use.

Brunetière (*broon-tyār'*), FERDINAND (1849–1906), Fr. critic and historian of literature; *b.* Toulon; ed. of *Revue des Deux Mondes*; author of *Etudes Critiques* (1880–98), *Histoire et Littérature* (1884–87), *Questions de Critique* (1889–90), *Honoré de Balzac* (1906).

Brün'now, FRANZ FRIEDRICH ERNST (1821–91), Ger. astronomer; *b.* Berlin; director, Observatory of Ann Arbor, Michigan, 1854–63; astronomer-royal for Ireland, 1865.

Bru'no, ST. (?1030–1101), founder of Carthusians; *b.* Cologne; after some years at Reims retired to mountains near Grenoble, and founded the Carthusian Order, 1084; erected other monasteries in Calabria, Italy.

Bruno THE GREAT (925–965), Archbishop of Cologne and Duke of Lorraine; chancellor to his brother, the Emperor Otto the Great, 940; reformed chancery, and purified monastic life; noted church builder; canonized 1628.

Bruno, GIORDANO (*c.* 1550–1600), Ital. philosopher; *b.* near Naples; Dominican friar in youth, but fled to Geneva, 1576, on account of religious opinions; proceeded to Toulouse and to Paris, 1580, where he lectured on philosophy and attacked Aristotelians; visited England, 1583, where he met Sir Philip Sidney; in 1586, prof. at Wittenberg; returned to Italy, 1592; imprisoned by Inquisition, and burnt as a heretic in Rome; his philosophy tends towards pantheism, and influenced the thought of Descartes, Spinoza, etc.

Bruns'wick, FRIEDRICH WILHELM, DUKE OF (1771–1815), was 'Brunswick's fated chieftain' of Byron's *Childe Harold*; deprived of his duchy by Napoleon, he organized the 'Black Brunswickers'; killed at Quatre Bras.

Brus'silov, ALEXEI ALEXIVITCH (1853–1926), Russ. general; belonged to old Russ. noble family; fought in Russo-Turk. War, 1877–78; in Great War commanded the Russ. army which invaded Galicia and crossed Carpathians; after the Russ. revolution he succeeded Alexeieff, 1917, as generalissimo, and conducted temporarily successful offensive.

Brutus. (1) LUCIUS JUNIUS, nephew of Tarquinius Superbus; helped to overthrow the Tarquin monarchy and became one of first consuls, 509 B.C. (2) MARCUS JUNIUS (85–42 B.C.), the great patriot of Shakespeare's *Julius Cæsar*; deeply loved by Cæsar, but joined in his assassination, 44; after defeat by Augustus, he slew himself at Philippi.

Bry'an, WILLIAM JENNINGS

(1860–1925), Amer. orator and politician; *b.* in Illinois; sprang into note by speeches in favour of bimetallism; thrice nominated for presidency by Democratic party, 1896, 1900, and 1908, and thrice defeated; organized volunteer regiment in Span.-Amer. War, but advocated an anti-imperial policy; supported President Wilson's successful candidature, 1912, and became secretary of state for foreign affairs; resigned, 1915, owing to difference of opinion on *Lusitania* note; ardent prohibitionist; as Fundamentalist acted for prosecution in famous Dayton trial, 1925.

Bryant, WILLIAM CULLEN (1794–1878), Amer. poet and journalist; *b.* in Massachusetts; abandoned legal profession in 1829 to become ed. of the *New York Evening Post*; may be regarded as the pioneer of Amer. poets, his first considerable poem, *Thanatopsis*, appearing in 1817; trans. Homer's *Iliad* and *Odyssey*.

Bryce, JAMES, 1ST VISCOUNT (1838–1922), statesman and man of letters; *b.* Belfast; regius prof. of civil law at Oxford, 1870–93; M.P., 1880; under-secretary for foreign affairs in Gladstone's ministry, 1886; chancellor of the duchy, 1892; president of Board of Trade, 1894; strenuous supporter of Home Rule; chief secretary for Ireland, 1905–6; Brit. ambassador to U.S.A., 1907–13; won golden opinions and promoted cordial relations between U.S.A. and Britain; one of the first fellows of the Brit. Academy, 1902; peerage, 1914; awarded O.M.; G.C.V.O., 1917. His works include *The Holy Roman Empire* (1862), *The American Commonwealth* (1888), *Impressions of S. Africa* (1897), *Studies in History and Jurisprudence* (1901), *Studies in Contemporary Biography* (1903), *The Hindrances to Good Citizenship* (1909), *S. America: Observations and Impressions* (1912), and *Modern Democracies* (1921).

[*James Bryce* (1927), by H. A. L. Fisher.]

Bu'cer, MARTIN (1491–1551), Ger. reformer; *b.* in Alsace; a Dominican who was converted to Protestantism by Luther, and afterwards made Strasbourg a centre of Prot. learning; refused to sign the Augsburg Interim, 1548, and fled to England, where he became prof. at Cambridge.

Buch (*booch*), CHRISTIAN LEOPOLD VON, BARON (1774–1853), Ger. geologist and geographer; travelled through Europe, making special study of volcanic rocks; regarded by Humboldt as 'the greatest geologist of our century.'

Buchan (*bŭch'an*), ALEXANDER (1829–1907), Scot. meteorologist; *b.* in Kinross-shire; one of the promoters of the Ben Nevis observatory, 1883; wrote the *Handy Book of Meteorology*, and some of the 'Challenger' reports.

Buchan, JOHN, BARON TWEEDSMUIR (1875–), novelist and historian; *b.* Perth; called to bar, 1901; on headquarters staff in France, 1916–17; M.P. Scot. Universities, 1927–35; gov.-gen. of Canada, 1935; author of *John Burnet of Barns*, *The Thirty-Nine Steps*, *Greenmantle*, *Witch Wood*, and other novels; of biographical studies *The Marquis of Montrose* (1928) and *Sir Walter Scott* (1932); and of *A History of the Great War* (1921–2); prose is distinguished for strength, lucidity, and unpretentious dignity.

Buchanan (*buk-an'an*), GEORGE (1506–82), Scot. humanist and reformer; *b.* in Stirlingshire; fled from Scotland, 1539, during persecution of Lutherans, and became prof. of Lat. at Bordeaux (where Montaigne was his pupil); Scaliger declared that 'in Lat. poetry Buchanan leaves all Europe behind'; imprisoned in Portugal by Inquisition, 1551; tutor to

Mary Queen of Scots, 1562; tutor to James VI., 1570; wrote democratic political treatise, which was twice condemned by Parliament and publicly burned by Univ. of Oxford, 1683; pub. *History of Scotland*, valuable as material for his own times, 1582; a scholar and writer of first rank.

[*Life* (1890), by P. Hume Brown.]

Buchanan, James (1791–1868), 15th president, U.S.A.; *b.* in Pennsylvania; barrister, 1812; member of congress, 1821–31; ambassador to St. Petersburg, 1832–3; in senate, 1833–45, as democrat; secretary of state, 1845–9; minister to Great Britain, 1853–6; president, 1856–61; favoured the maintenance of slavery.

Buchanan, Robert Williams (1841–1901), Eng. poet, novelist, and dramatist; *b.* in Staffs; first vol. of verse, *Undertones* (1863); *Complete Poetical Works* (1901); numerous novels include *The Shadow of the Sword* and *God and the Man*; also a successful playwright.

Büchner (*booch'ner*), Eduard (1860–1917), Ger. chemist; prof. of chemistry successively at Tübingen, Agricultural Coll., Berlin, Breslau Univ., and Würzburg Univ.; famous for investigations on fermentation; Nobel prizeman, 1907.

Buck, Dudley (1839–1909), Amer. composer; *b.* in Connecticut; organist at Chicago, Boston, and New York; operas include *Serapis* and *Deseret*; cantatas, *Columbus, Golden Legend,* and *Light of Asia.*

Buck, Leffert Lefferts (1837–1909), Amer. engineer; *b.* in New York state; captain in Civil War; rebuilt suspension bridge at Niagara Falls, etc.

Buck'ingham, George Villiers, 1st Duke of (1592–1628), Eng. statesman; *b.* in Leicestershire; created earl, 1617, marquess, 1618, and Duke of Buckingham, 1623; lord high admiral, 1619; supported Span. party, but after disastrous visit to Madrid, 1623, headed popular movement against Spain, and strove for a Fr. alliance. On James's death, 1625, Buckingham and Charles resolved to fight Spain, but their attempts failed disgracefully; Parliament demanded Buckingham's dismissal, but Charles stood by his minister, who was assassinated by a discontented subaltern at Portsmouth, while preparing an expedition to relieve La Rochelle.

Buckingham, George Villiers, 2nd Duke of (1628–87); son of above; fought for the king in Civil War; present at battle of Worcester, 1651; imprisoned on suspicion of organizing a Presbyterian plot against government, 1657–9; restored to favour at Restoration; succeeded Clarendon as chief minister; tenure of office chiefly marked by scandals and intrigues; separated from Whigs on Exclusion question; restored to king's favour, 1684, but took no part in public life after James II.'s accession; volatile, insincere man, the 'Zimri' of Dryden's *Absalom and Achitophel*; wrote occasional verses and satires, also witty comedies, including *The Rehearsal* (1671).

Buckingham, James Silk (1786–1855), Eng. author and journalist; *b.* near Falmouth; went to India and founded the *Calcutta Journal* (1818); returned to England and started the *Athenæum* (1828); M.P. for Sheffield, 1832–7; wrote numerous books of travel.

Buck'land, Francis Trevelyan (1826–80), Eng. naturalist; *b.* Oxford; authority on fish culture; works include *Curiosities of Natural History, Natural History of British Fishes*; founded *Land and Water* (1866).

Buckland, William (1784–1856), geologist; *b.* Tiverton; Dean of

Westminister, 1845; gave immense stimulus to the study of palæontology.

Buck'le, GEORGE EARLE (1854–1935), author; *b.* near Bath; ed. of the *Times*, 1884–1912; undertook completion of Monypenny's *Life of Disraeli*, vols. iii.–vi. (1914–20); ed. *The Letters of Queen Victoria* (1926–30).

Buckle, HENRY THOMAS (1821–62), Eng. historian and sociologist; *b.* Lee, Kent; travelled on Continent and in Egypt and Syria; famous chess-player; pub. two vols. of his great work, *History of Civilization* (1857–61); death at Damascus stopped its completion.

Buck'ley, ARABELLA BURTON (MRS. FISHER) (1840–1929), Eng. naturalist; *b.* Brighton; secretary to Sir Charles Lyell, 1864–75; lecturer on natural science, 1876–83; expounded the charms of science for the young in several works—*e.g.* *The Fairyland of Science*; *Eyes and No Eyes* (1901).

Buckley, DONAL (1877–), gov.-gen. of Irish Free State since 1932; *b.* Maynooth; educated Belvedere Coll., Dublin; took part in Easter Rebellion, 1916. Sinn Fein M.P., 1918; member of Dail, 1919–23, 1927–32.

Buck'master, STANLEY OWEN, 1ST BARON OF CHEDDINGTON (1861–1934), Liberal M.P., 1906–13; solicitor-general, 1913; director of Press Bureau, 1914–15; created peer, 1915; lord chancellor, 1915–16; member of Inter-allied Conference on Finance and Supplies; chairman of Political Honours Review Committee, 1924.

Buddha, 'the enlightened one' (*c.* 560–480 B.C.), the founder of Buddhism, a purified form of Hinduism; son of a chief of N. India; as a child received the name Gautama; is also known as Prince Siddhartha; in twenty-ninth year saw visions which led him to devote himself to religion and philosophy; after birth of son parted from sleeping wife and babe, renounced wealth and power, and became a homeless wanderer, practising rigorous asceticism for six years; underwent fierce temptation from demon of wickedness; sat for six weeks plunged in abstraction under the Bodhidruma (' tree of intelligence,' Bo Tree), and so attained perfect wisdom, and received name of 'Buddha.' He proclaimed thereafter the equality and brotherhood of man, and that the great end of existence was to attain extinction of personality (*Nirvana*) by self-sacrifice, contemplation, and suppression of all passion.

Budge, SIR ERNEST A. WALLIS (1857–1934), Eng. orientalist; *b.* in Cornwall; keeper of Egyptian and Assyrian Antiquities, Brit. Museum, 1893–1924; conducted excavations at Nineveh and at Der in Mesopotamia, 1891; numerous works include *Egyptian Sculptures*, *Tutankhamen*, and *George of Lydda, the patron saint of England* (1930).

Buffon (*boo-fōn'*), GEORGE LOUIS LECLERC, COMTE DE (1707–88), Fr. naturalist; *b.* in Burgundy; early abandoned law for natural sciences; appointed member of Academy and superintendent of Jardin du Roi (now Jardin des Plantes), 1739; enjoyed favour of Louis XV. and XVI.; produced, with assistance of Daubenton, his great work, *Histoire Naturelle* (1749 *et seq.*).

Bugeaud de la Piconnerie (*boo-zhō' de lä pē-kon-rē'*), THOMAS ROBERT, DUC D'ISLY (1784–1849), Fr. soldier; *b.* Limoges; served in Napoleonic campaigns; field-marshal, 1831; won distinction in Algeria, being gov.-gen., 1840–6; marshal of France, 1843; commanded the army of the Alps, 1848–9.

Bugge (*boog'e*), SOPHUS (1833–1907), Norweg. philologist; prof.

of philology at Christiania; ed. the *Elder Edda*, *Gamle Norska Folkeviser* (folk songs), etc.

Buisson (*bwē-sōn'*), FERDINAND EDOUARD (1841–1932), Fr. educationist; *b.* Paris; prof. of education, Sorbonne, 1896–1901; deputy, 1902 and 1906; strong supporter of League of Nations; Nobel Peace Prize, 1927.

Bull, JOHN (1563–1628), Eng. composer; *b.* in Somerset; organist of Hereford Cathedral, Queen Elizabeth's chapel, and prof. of music at Gresham Coll., London; organist of cathedral at Antwerp, 1617; has been claimed as composer of the National Anthem.

Bull, OLE BORNEMANN (1810–80), Norweg. violinist; *b.* Bergen; attained European celebrity, and had immense success in America.

Bullen (*bool'en*), FRANK THOMAS (1857–1915), Eng. writer of sea stories; *b.* London; served before the mast as a boy; junior clerk in Meteorological Office; books include *The Cruise of the Cachalot* and *With Christ at Sea.*

Buller (*bool'er*), CHARLES (1806–48), lawyer and politician; *b.* Calcutta; accompanied Lord Durham to Canada, 1838; the Durham report (recommending a system of federation of the Can. colonies) was attributed to him; became judge-advocate-general and chief poor-law commissioner.

Buller, SIR REDVERS HENRY (1839–1908), Brit. general; *b.* in Devon; distinguished himself in Kaffir and Zulu wars (gained V.C.) and in Sudan; appointed commander-in-chief of Brit. troops in S. African War, 1899; repulsed at Colenso, and superseded by Lord Roberts; as commander of Natal army finally relieved Ladysmith.

Bull'ock, SHAN F. (1865–1935), Irish novelist; *b.* in Fermanagh; author of *The Awkward Squads*, *The Ring o' Rushes*, *The Loughsiders*, *Gleanings*, etc.; novels are keenly observant studies of Irish life, full of a kindly humour.

Bülow (*bū'lō*), BERNHARD HEINRICH KARL MARTIN, PRINCE VON (1849–1929), Ger. statesman; *b.* in Holstein; served in Fr.-Ger. War, 1870; entered diplomatic service, 1873; secretary of the Berlin Congress, 1878; first secretary of the embassy at Paris, 1880, and at St. Petersburg, 1883; minister at Bucharest, 1888, and ambassador at Rome, 1894–7, when he was appointed Prussian minister of state; made count, 1899; chancellor of the Ger. Empire and prime minister of Prussia, 1900; raised to rank of prince, 1905; resigned office, 1909; after outbreak of Great War acted as Ger. ambassador at Rome, but failed to prevent Italy's intervention; retired to Switzerland. Pub. *Imperial Germany* (1912), and *Memoirs* (4 vols., 1930–1).

Bülow, FRIEDRICH WILHELM, COUNT OF DENNEWITZ (1755–1816), Prussian general; created count for great victory at Dennewitz, 1813, repelling Marshal Ney. At Waterloo he was in command of Blücher's division, which saved the day.

Bülow, HANS GUIDO VON (1830–94), Ger. pianist and conductor; *b.* Dresden; studied under Hauptmann, Liszt, and Wagner; was a pianist of the first rank, and obtained fame throughout Europe and America as a conductor; married the daughter of Liszt, but the union was afterwards dissolved, and the lady married Wagner.

Bulwer-Lytton. See LYTTON.

Bun'bury, HENRY WILLIAM (1750–1811), Eng. caricaturist; *b.* in Suffolk; celebrated comic artist, praised by Sir Joshua Reynolds.

Bunsen (*boon'sen*), CHRISTIAN CHARLES JOSIAS, BARON VON (1791–1860), Ger. diplomatist;

b. in Waldeck; Prussian envoy to papal court; rest of his official life was spent as ambassador to Britain; recalled by Bismarck, on outbreak of Crimean War, for giving impression that Germany might join Britain and France; sat in Prussian Upper House as Baron von Bunsen, 1858. Strongly evangelical, he revived the Ger. liturgy and hymn book, and wrote *The Church of the Future* (1845) and *God in History* (1857).

Bunsen, ROBERT WILHELM VON (1811–99), Ger. chemist; *b.* Göttingen; successively chemistry prof. at Marburg, Breslau, and Heidelberg; famous as the founder, with Kirchoff, of spectrum analysis; inventor of Bunsen burner; designed electric cell bearing his name.

Bunt′ing, JABEZ (1779–1858), Eng. Methodist divine; *b.* Manchester; known as 'Second founder of Methodism,' transforming it into a self-governing Church; president of Wesleyan Coll. at Hoxton, 1835.

Bun′yan, JOHN (1628–88), Eng. religious leader and writer; *b.* near Bedford, of humble parentage; served in parliamentary army during Civil War; married in 1648, gradually gave up his amusements and dancing, and preached the gospel; Nonconformist preaching was not tolerated, and in 1660 he was imprisoned in Bedford jail, where he wrote *Grace Abounding to the Chief of Sinners*, describing his own religious conflicts; released in 1672, and again imprisoned for a short time in 1675. In 1678 appeared his *Pilgrim's Progress* (the second part appearing in 1684); before his death it was read widely in England, New England, and among foreign Protestants; the allegory has appealed to successive generations of readers; though he sometimes feared persecution, he was never again imprisoned. He was pastor of the Bedford Church for sixteen years; pub. *The Life and Death of Mr. Badman* (1680), *The Holy War* (1682), and more than fifty other works.

[*John Bunyan* (1885), by Rev. J. Brown.]

Bur′bage. (1) JAMES (*d.* 1597), Eng. actor and manager; built the Shoreditch Theatre, 1576, the earliest in London, and the Blackfriars Theatre, 1596. (2) RICHARD (1567–1619), son of above; most famous actor of his day, excelling especially in Richard III. and other tragic parts; pulled down the Shoreditch Theatre and erected the Globe, in the proprietorship of which he was associated with Shakespeare and others.

Bur′bank, LUTHER (1849–1926), Amer. horticulturist; *b.* in Massachusetts; in his nursery garden in California produced many new varieties of plants—*e.g.* Burbank potatoes, Shasta daisy, stoneless plum, and pineapple quince; wrote *How Plants are trained to work for Man* (1921).

Burck′hardt, JACOB (1818–97), Swiss authority on art; *b.* Basle; wrote *Der Cicerone: eine Anleitung zum Genuss der Kunstwerke Italiens* (1855), *Die Cultur der Renaissance in Italien* (1860), etc.

Burckhardt, JOHN LEWIS (1784–1817), Swiss explorer and student of Oriental life and language; *b.* Lausanne; explored north-east interior of Africa; made pilgrimage to Mecca; bequeathed his collection of Oriental MSS. to Cambridge Univ.

Bur′der, GEORGE (1752–1832), Eng. Congregationalist minister; *b.* London; chief founder of Religious Tract Soc., 1799, and of Brit. and Foreign Bible Soc., 1804.

Bur′dett, SIR FRANCIS (1770–1844), Eng. Radical politician; advocated parl. reform, removal of R.C. disabilities, ballot, universal male suffrage, etc.; twice imprisoned for political reasons.

Burdett-Coutts, ANGELA GEORGINA, BARONESS (1814–1906), English philanthropist; *b.* London; daughter of above; on inheriting £2,000,000 from her grandfather, took additional name Coutts; married William Lehman Ashmead Bartlett, 1881; founder of many charitable institutions.

Burg'er, GOTTFRIED AUGUST (1748–95), Ger. poet; *b.* near Halberstadt; author of famous ballad *Lenore* (1773), trans. into English by Sir Walter Scott.

Burger, SCHALK WILLIAM (1852–1918), Transvaal statesman; *b.* Lydenburg; president of republic, 1900; served under Botha in war of 1899–1902; upheld loyalty to Britain during the Great War.

Bur'gess, JOHN BAGNOLD (1829–97), Eng. genre painter; *b.* London; excelled in Span. subjects; best works are *Stolen by Gypsies*; *Spanish Mendicant Students*.

Burgess, THOMAS W. (1873–1926), Brit. swimmer; first to swim Channel, 1911, since Captain Webb in 1875.

Burgh (*bŭrg*), HUBERT DE (*d.* 1243), Eng. chief justiciar, 1215–31; held important offices under John, and received custody of Arthur of Brittany, whom he is said to have preserved from being blinded, 1201; repulsed Fr. invasion, 1217; ruled kingdom in minority of Henry III., dismissing foreign mercenaries.

Burghley (or BURLEIGH) (*bŭr'lĭ*), WILLIAM CECIL, BARON (1520–98), Eng. statesman; *b.* Bourne; M.P. for Stamford, 1547; fought at Pinkie Cleugh; made chief secretary of state on accession of Elizabeth; from this time his policy was the queen's; master of court of wards, 1561; lord high treasurer, 1572; claim to fame is that of successful administrator, his spy system being the only blot on his administration. (See also CECIL.)

[*Life of Burghley* (1904), by Dr. Jessopp.]

Burgoyne (*bŭr-goin'*), JOHN (1722–92), Brit. general, politician, and playwright; caused general outcry by surrendering to Amer. forces at Saratoga, 1777; wrote several dramas, including *The Maid of the Oaks* and *The Heiress.*

Bu'rian, STEPHEN, BARON, OF RAJECZ (1851–1922), Austro-Hungarian statesman; *b.* near Bratislava; consul at Moscow; minister at Athens, and afterwards administrator of Bosnia-Herzegovina; appointed foreign minister by Count Tisza, 1915, but failed to prevent Italy joining the Allies; unsuccessfully approached other Central Powers with peace proposals, 1916; remained in retirement till 1918, only remaining in power for a short time, and being succeeded by his opponent, Count Andrassy, who accepted the terms of peace.

Burke, EDMUND (1729–97), Brit. statesman, writer, and orator; *b.* Dublin; educated Trinity Coll., Dublin, 1743–8; entered Middle Temple, London, 1750, but abandoned law for literary work; wrote *A Vindication of Natural Society*, a satire upon Bolingbroke, and a *Philosophical Inquiry into the Origin of our Ideas on the Sublime and Beautiful* (1756). Became secretary to the prime minister, Lord Rockingham, 1765; entered parliament, 1766, and drew up all the principal protests of the Whig party, 1767–82. In *Thoughts on the Cause of the Present Discontents* (1770) he defended party government; won over Charles James Fox to Whig party; M.P. for Bristol, 1774–80, for Malton, 1780–94. During struggle with Amer. colonies, showed unrivalled knowledge of Amer. questions; as paymaster of the forces under Rockingham,

1782, introduced great financial reform; on Rockingham's death, July 1782, Burke and Fox joined North in coalition against Shelbourne. On failure of coalition Pitt accepted the premiership. Burke soon engaged in his famous impeachment of Warren Hastings. His *Reflections on the French Revolution* (1790), followed by his *Appeal from the New to the Old Whigs*, greatly influenced Eng. opinion; he viewed the Revolution with misgivings from the first. This attitude finally led to his rupture with Fox, 1791. At close of 1794 Burke left Parliament. He wrote against Pitt's anxiety for peace with France in *Letters on a Regicide Peace* (1796). A self-confident statesman and political genius, champion of the old order of Europe, Burke, despite some eccentricities, was the greatest orator and political thinker of his day.

[*Select Works of Burke* (1897), Clarendon Press; *Memoir of the Life and Character of Edmund Burke* (1824), by Sir James Prior; *Edmund Burke* (1879), by John Morley; *The Political Philosophy of Edmund Burke* (1913), by John McCunn.]

Burke, Sir John Bernard (1814–92), Eng. genealogist; *b.* London; son of John Burke, whose work he continued as the compiler of *Burke's Peerage*, pub. annually since 1847; Ulster king-at-arms, 1853; knighted, 1854.

Burke, Robert O'Hara (1820–61), Australian traveller; *b.* in Ireland; educated Belgium; captain in Austrian army; member of Royal Irish Constabulary, 1848; police inspector at Melbourne, 1853; led ill-fated expedition with Wills across Australian continent, 1860–1; died of starvation on return journey.

Burke, William (1792–1829), Irish murderer; implicated, 1827–29, with William Hare in a series of murders in an Edinburgh lodging-house; the victims were suffocated ('burked'), and their bodies sold for anatomical purposes; Hare turned king's evidence, and Burke was hanged.

Burleigh. See Burghley.

Bur'naby, Frederick Gustavus (1842–85), Eng. soldier and traveller; *b.* Bedford; entered Royal Horse Guards, 1859; made an adventurous journey on horseback to Khiva, 1875–6, recorded in *A Ride to Khiva*; made several aeronautical ascents, and crossed Channel in a balloon, 1882; engaged in Suakin campaign, 1884, and wounded at El-Teb; killed at Abu Klea (Nile Expedition).

Bur'nand, Sir Francis Cowley (1836–1917), Eng. humorist; *b.* London; ed. of *Punch,* 1880–1906; knighted, 1902.

Burne-Jones, Sir Edward Burne, Bart. (1833–98), Eng. artist; *b.* Birmingham; educated Oxford, where he formed a friendship with William Morris; studied under D. G. Rossetti. He used his wide knowledge of classics in his pictures, decorative work, and stained-glass designs. His best-known paintings include *King Cophetua and The Beggar Maid* (1884). He exercised a strong influence upon the art of his time.

[*Memorials of Edward Burne-Jones* (1904), by Lady Burne-Jones; *Life* (1894), by Julia Cartwright.]

Burnes (*bŭrnz*), Sir Alexander (1805–41), Scot. traveller; *b.* Montrose; entered E. India Co., 1821; made extensive journeys through Afghanistan to Bokhara and Persia, accounts of which he pub., 1834; assassinated at Kabul.

Bur'net, Gilbert (1643–1715), Anglican bishop and historian; *b.* Edinburgh; prof. of divinity at Glasgow, 1669; received preferments from Charles ii., but later lost Court favour; settled in Holland and joined party of William of Orange, on whose accession he was made Bishop of Salisbury; mainly responsible for establishment of Queen Anne's Bounty; chiefly remembered for his *History of My Own Times.*

Burnet, JOHN (1863–1928), Scot. classicist; *b.* Edinburgh; prof. of Greek, St. Andrews Univ., 1892–1926; works include *Early Greek Philosophy* (1892), *Greek Philosophy* (1914).

Burnett, FRANCES ELIZA HODGSON (1849–1924), Eng.-American novelist; *b.* Manchester; went to U.S.A., 1865; author of many novels; her greatest success was *Little Lord Fauntleroy*, a children's romance of real life.

Bur'ney, CHARLES (1726–1814), Eng. musician; *b.* Shrewsbury; won fame as an organist; wrote operatic pieces, sonatas, concertos, etc.; chiefly remembered for his *History of Music* (1776–89). His life written by his daughter Fanny, Mme. d'Arblay.

Burney, FANNY. See under D'ARBLAY.

Burn'ham. (1) EDWARD LEVY LAWSON, 1ST BARON (1833–1916), ed. and proprietor of *Daily Telegraph*; *b.* London; organized, with Mr. Gordon Bennett, H. M. Stanley's African expedition, 1874–77; sent expeditions to Nineveh, to Kilimanjaro, and from Cape to Cairo; began many charitable schemes, such as the Prince of Wales's Hospital Fund; peerage, 1903. (2) HARRY LAWSON WEBSTER LAWSON (1862–1933), 1ST VISCOUNT (created 1919); president of Empire Press Union, 1916–28; four times M.P. between 1885 and 1916; presided over committee on teachers' salaries, 1919, and produced the 'Burnham scale'; president of Birkbeck Coll., London Univ., from 1929.

Burnham, FREDERICK RUSSELL (1861–), Amer. scout; *b.* in Minnesota; entered service of Brit. S. Africa Co. and fought against Matabele, etc.; summoned by Lord Roberts from America for special service during Boer War, when he was awarded the D.S.O.; explorations in tropical Africa and in Mexico; author of *Scouting on Two Continents* (1926).

Burns, SIR GEORGE (1795–1890), Brit. shipowner; *b.* Glasgow; one of founders of the Cunard line of steamships; created baronet, 1889.

Burns, RT. HON. JOHN (1858–), Brit. Labour politician; *b.* London; worked as an engineer; imprisoned, 1887, for asserting right to hold mass meetings in Trafalgar Square; a leader of the great dock strike, 1889; M.P. for Battersea, 1892–1918; president of Local Government Board, with seat in cabinet, 1905–14 (first Labour M.P. with cabinet rank); resigned on the war question.

Burns, ROBERT (1759–96), greatest of Scot. poets; *b.* Jan. 25 at Alloway, near Ayr; son of William Burness, a small farmer; went to school at the age of six, and was afterwards taught by a tutor named Murdoch; through his father's influence he steeped his mind in the Eng. classics. At fifteen he became his father's assistant, and led for ten years a life of hard toil. For some years after his father's death in 1784 he and his brother Gilbert stuck to farming at Lochlea and at Mossgiel, but misfortune attended their efforts. During this period were written such masterpieces as *The Jolly Beggars*, *Hallowe'en*, *Holy Willie's Prayer*, *The Cottar's Saturday Night*, *The Holy Fair*, *Scotch Drink*, *Address to the Deil*, *To a Mouse*, *To a Mountain Daisy*. Though these poems greatly increased his reputation they did little to provide a means of livelihood. To mend his fortunes he booked a passage for

Jamaica, but on the successful publication of the first Kilmarnock edition of his works, 1786, changed his mind. He visited Edinburgh, where he was lionized; in 1788 he married Jean Armour, and took Ellisland farm, near Dumfries, where he lost what little capital he had. Here he wrote *Tam o' Shanter* and *Auld Lang Syne*. Soon after he became an exciseman at Dumfries, where he died.

Burns's first vol. of poems brought him the admiration of Edinburgh society. Scott minutely describes Burns, particularly mentioning his poetic and glowing eye, his simplicity and dignity. It may be noted that though, like Shakespeare, Burns borrowed from other writers, he was no plagiarist, but used and adapted his material to express his own individuality and original point of view. To Robert Fergusson, in particular, he owed a large debt, which he acknowledged by placing a memorial stone over his grave.

[The authoritative ed. of the *Poetry of Robert Burns* is that of W. E. Henley and T. F. Henderson (with Memoir), known as the 'Centenary Burns' (4 vols., 1896–97); study by Carlyle in his *Essays*; 'Some Aspects of Robert Burns,' in R. L. Stevenson's *Familiar Studies of Men and Books*; *The Life of Robert Burns* (1930), by Catherine Carswell.]

Burr, AARON (1756–1836), Amer. statesman, vice-president, 1801–1805, and leader of famous 'Burr conspiracy'; admitted to bar, 1782; attorney-general of New York State, 1789–91; U.S.A. senator, 1791–7; identified himself with Democratic Republicans. Endowed with intellectual gifts of high order, and a politician of consummate ability, he was an intriguer and a profligate.

Bur'ritt, ELIHU (1810–79), Amer. humanitarian; *b.* in Connecticut; a blacksmith who made himself master of a great number of languages; lectured throughout America and Europe on peace and universal brotherhood.

Burroughs (*bŭr'ōz*), JOHN (1837–1921), Amer. poet and naturalist; *b.* in New York State; successively teacher, government clerk, and farmer; publications include *Whitman* (1896), *Ways of Nature* (1905), *Bird and Bough* (poems, 1906), and *The Breath of Life* (1915).

Burrows, RONALD MONTAGU (1867–1920), Eng. scholar and archæologist; *b.* Rugby; principal of King's Coll., London, from 1913; carried out excavations in Greece, 1895–6, and 1905–7; his best-known work is *The Discoveries in Crete* (1907); other works include contributions to Gr. archæology and scholarship, and political studies of modern European problems. One of founders of Anglo-Hellenic League, 1913, and was largely instrumental in retaining for Britain the friendship of Greece during the Great War.

Bur'ton, JOHN HILL (1809–81), Scot. historian and advocate; *b.* Aberdeen; wrote *Life of David Hume* (1846), *The Book Hunter* (1862), *The Scot Abroad* (1864), and *History of Scotland* (1870).

Burton, SIR RICHARD FRANCIS (1821–90), Eng. explorer and orientalist; *b.* in Herts; joined Ind. army, 1842, and applied himself to study of oriental life and languages; made pilgrimage to Mecca, 1853; explored interior of Somaliland, 1854, and lakes of Central Africa, 1857–8; Brit. consul at Fernando Po, Santos, Damascus, and Trieste; wrote many vols. on his travels; his trans. of *Arabian Nights* (pub. 1885–8) shows his intimate knowledge of Eastern life.

[*Life* (1893), by wife.]

Burton, ROBERT (1577–1640), Eng. writer; *b.* in Leicestershire; educated at Oxford and held studentship at Christ Church till death; *The Anatomy of Melancholy* (1621), his *magnum opus*, is full of erudition and quotation.

Bu′ry, JOHN BAGNAL (1861–1927), Eng. historian; prof. of modern history, 1893–1902, and of Greek, 1898–1902, Trinity Coll., Dublin; succeeded Acton as prof. of modern history at Cambridge, 1902; an authority on history of the Eastern Empire; works include *History of Later Roman Empire* (1889), *Life of St. Patrick* (1905), and *The Idea of Progress* (1920); standard ed. of Gibbon's *Decline and Fall* (6 vols., 1896–1900).

Bus′by, RICHARD (1606–95), Eng. schoolmaster and clergyman; *b.* in Lincs; successful headmaster of Westminster School; notorious for his flogging; boasted that he had birched sixteen living bishops.

Busch, JULIAN HERMANN MORITZ (1821–99), Ger. publicist—'Bismarck's Boswell'; *b.* Dresden; entered government service, and identified himself with Prince Bismarck's life and aims; his works on Bismarck excited wide interest.

Busk, GEORGE (1807–86), Eng. surgeon, zoologist, anthropologist, and palæontologist; *b.* St. Petersburg; Hunterian prof. of comparative anatomy and physiology, Royal Coll. of Surgeons, London, 1856–9; pub. *Report on Polyzoa collected by H.M.S. 'Challenger'* (1884–6).

Busk, HANS (1815–82), Eng. lawyer; organizer of army volunteer system, and author of *Navies of the World* (1859).

Bus′ken-Huet, CONRAD (1826–86), Dutch author and critic; *b.* The Hague; wrote *Lidewijde*, a novel, and several series of criticisms pub. under the title of *Literary Fantasies*.

Buso′ni, FERRUCCIO BENVENUTO (1866–1924), Ital. pianist and composer; *b.* near Florence; prof. at Moscow Imperial Conservatory, 1890, and at Boston (U.S.A.), 1891; wrote compositions for piano and an opera, *Die Brantwahl* (1913).

Butcher, SAMUEL HENRY (1850–1910), Brit. classical scholar; *b.* Dublin; prof. of Greek, Edinburgh Univ., 1882–1903; M.P. for Cambridge Univ., 1906–10; pub. (with Andrew Lang) *Prose Translation of the Odyssey*, and wrote on Gr. subjects in general.

Bute, JOHN STUART, 3RD EARL OF (1713–92), Brit. prime minister; *b.* Edinburgh; succeeded to earldom, 1723; gained the favour of Frederick, Prince of Wales, 1747, and obtained great influence over his son, on whose accession as George III., 1760, he rose to power; prime minister, 1761. His Scot. nationality, advocacy of royal supremacy, and peace policy, made him very unpopular; resigned 1763, and withdrew from court. Of dilettante temperament, and inexperienced in politics, his ministry was marked by gross corruption and intimidation.

But′ler. (1) GEORGE (1774–1853), headmaster of Harrow and dean of Peterborough; father of (2) GEORGE (1819–90), principal of Liverpool Coll. and writer on theological subjects, and of (3) HENRY MONTAGU (1833–1918), headmaster of Harrow and master of Trinity Coll., Cambridge, from 1886, and chaplain-in-ordinary to the king from 1912.

Butler, JOSEPH (1692–1752), Anglican theologian; *b.* in Berks; prebendary of Rochester, 1736; Bishop of Bristol and Dean of St. Paul's, 1740; Bishop of Durham, 1750; fame rests on his *Analogy of Religion* (1736), and his *Sermons* (in Rolls Chapel); his *Analogy* is regarded as one of the greatest intellectual achievements of Anglicanism.

Butler, MRS. JOSEPHINE ELIZABETH (1828–1906), Eng. author, wife of George Butler, canon of Winchester; *b.* in Northumberland; a leader in women's movements, such as rescue, higher education, and Married Women's Property Act.

Butler, SAMUEL (1612–80), Eng. satirical poet; *b.* in Worcestershire; became a justice's clerk, and was subsequently in the service of the Countess of Kent, John Selden, Sir Samuel Luke, the Earl of Carbery, and the Duke of Buckingham; while in their service had unique opportunities of observing men and manners, and this wide knowledge of life makes his famous doggerel satire, *Hudibras* (1663–78), lastingly attractive; it consists of some ten thousand verses, and though perhaps little read now, its witty passages have become merged in everyday language.

Butler. (1) SAMUEL (1774–1839), Eng. ecclesiastic and scholar; as headmaster raised Shrewsbury School to a high state of efficiency; Bishop of Lichfield, 1836; ed. works of Æschylus, and pub. a *Sketch of Modern and Ancient Geography* (1813). (2) SAMUEL (1835–1902), Eng. essayist, satirist, and miscellaneous writer; *b.* in Notts; grandson of the above, whose *Life* he wrote; lived in New Zealand, 1859–64, and used this experience in his Utopian romance *Erewhon* (Nowhere) (1872); his novel, *The Way of All Flesh*, was pub. in 1903.

Butler. (1) SIR WILLIAM FRANCIS (1838–1910), Brit. soldier and traveller; *b.* in Tipperary, I.F.S.; served in Red River expedition, 1870–1, Ashanti, 1873–4, Zulu War, 1879–80, and Egyptian and Sudan campaigns; commander-in-chief in S. Africa, 1898; author of *The Great Lone Land* (1872), and other works. (2) LADY BUTLER (*née* ELIZABETH THOMPSON) (1844–1933), wife of above; *b.* Lausanne; painted many famous battle-pictures; studied in Italy; most popular are *The Roll Call, The Dawn of Waterloo.*

Butt, DAME CLARA (1873–1936), Eng. contralto; *b.* in Sussex; made her début at performance of *Orfeo*, Lyceum Theatre, London, 1892; figured prominently at oratorio and ballad concerts; married Kennerley Rumford, the singer, 1900. During Great War, as result of her concerts, over £70,000 was distributed among war charities.

Butt, ISAAC (1813–79), Irish Nationalist leader; *b.* in Donegal; a prominent lawyer; engaged in all leading cases bearing upon Irish affairs; entered Parliament, and rose to front rank amongst Irish Protestants; inaugurated Home Rule movement at Dublin, 1870, and for some time was its leader.

Bux'ton. (1) SIR THOMAS FOWELL (1786–1845), Eng. brewer and philanthropist; *b.* in Essex; married to Hannah, sister of Elizabeth Fry; M.P. for Weymouth, 1818–37; devoted himself to prison reform and abolition of slavery in the Brit. colonies. (2) SYDNEY CHARLES, 1ST EARL, 1920 (1853–1934), grandson of (1); Eng. Liberal statesman; under-secretary for colonies, 1892–5; introduced penny postage to U.S.A. and Can. magazine post; postmaster-general, 1905–10; president Board of Trade, 1910–14; high commissioner and gov.-gen. of S. Africa, 1914–20.

Bux'torf, JOHANNES (1564–1629), Ger. Heb. scholar; *b.* in Westphalia; prof. in Basle Univ.; author of *Manuale Hebraicum et Chaldaicum* (1602), *Synagoga Judaica* (1603), and similar works.

Buys-Ballot (*boiz-bä-lō'*), CHRISTOPH HEINRICH DIEDRICH (1817–90), Dutch meteorologist; *b.* in Zeeland; prof. at Utrecht; enunciated, 1857, *Buys-Ballot's law* dealing with the relation of wind direction to barometric pressure.

By, JOHN (1781–1836), Eng. soldier and engineer; served in Peninsular War; constructed Rideau Canal between St. Lawrence and Great Lakes, 1827–32; his camp, Bytown, was renamed Ottawa.

Byng (*bing*), GEORGE. See TORRINGTON, VISCOUNT.

Byng, JOHN (1704–57), Brit. admiral; *b.* Wrotham; during Seven Years' War was sent to relieve Minorca, which the French had attacked; he withdrew without fighting a battle; in consequence, Fort St. Philip surrendered; he was tried and shot, as Voltaire said, 'pour encourager les autres.'

Byng, JULIAN, 1ST VISCOUNT OF VIMY (1862–1935), Brit. soldier, son of 2nd Earl of Strafford; served in Sudan expedition, 1884, and S. African War, 1899–1902. In Great War served in France and Dardanelles; in 1916 commanded Can. Corps ('Byng Boys'), which he led at capture of Vimy Ridge, 1917; succeeded Allenby in command of the 3rd Army, and played a prominent part in final Allied offensive; created a baron and voted grant of £30,000, 1919; gov.-gen. of Canada, 1921–26; commissioner of Metropolitan Police, 1928–31; field-marshal, 1932.

Byrd (*bird*), REAR-ADMIRAL RICHARD EVELYN (1888–), Amer. aviator and explorer; *b.* in Virginia; went to Greenland under auspices of National Geographical Soc., 1925; from Spitsbergen, May 9, 1926, reached and circled North Pole; flew across Atlantic, 1927; during Antarctic expedition, 1928, flew over South Pole; further Antarctic exploration, 1933–4.

Byrd, WILLIAM (1543–1623), Eng. composer; organist at Lincoln, 1563; shared with Tallis the post of organist to the Chapel Royal; composed masses, part-songs, madrigals, etc.

By'rom, JOHN (1692–1763), Eng. poet and stenographer; *b.* near Manchester; a fellow of Trinity Coll., Cambridge; F.R.S., 1724; besides writing numerous poems and hymns, including 'Christians, Awake,' was the inventor of a system of shorthand.

By'ron, GEORGE GORDON, 6TH LORD (1788–1824), Eng. poet; *b.* London. His father married Catherine Gordon of Gight, a small Scot. heiress, and squandered all her fortune. After his father's death, 1791, Byron, who was lame from his birth, lived with his mother (a violent, foolish woman) chiefly in Aberdeen; educ. at Harrow and Trinity Coll., Cambridge, where he led a very riotous life. Fell in love with Mary Chaworth, but was rejected — a disappointment that affected his life. In 1807 he pub. *Hours of Idleness*, which was 'cut up' by Brougham in the *Edinburgh Review*; Byron retaliated with *English Bards and Scotch Reviewers* (1809), and then set out on a tour through Europe; on his return he issued, 1812, the first two cantos of *Childe Harold*, describing his travels, and 'found himself famous.' For the next few years he was the darling of London society, contracting numerous liaisons with married women; pub. *The Giaour* (1813), *The Corsair* and *Lara* (1814), and *The Siege of Corinth* (1816). Married Miss Milbanke, an heiress, 1815, but a year later his wife left his house; the reasons for this separation are not known. Cast off by society, Byron settled near Geneva, where he came under the influence of Shelley, and formed an intimacy with Mrs. Shelley's step-sister, Claire Clairmont, who became the mother of

Allegra Byron; at Geneva wrote canto iii. of *Childe Harold* (*The Prisoner of Chillon*), and began *Manfred*; went to Milan, thence to Venice, where he spent two years of dissipation, and wrote *Mazeppa*, and the first two cantos of *Don Juan*, his masterpiece.

From his life in Venice he was rescued in 1819 by the Countess Guiccioli, with whom he lived for the next four years at Ravenna, Pisa, and Genoa; continued *Don Juan* and wrote several plays, and his burlesque of Southey, *The Vision of Judgment* (1821). In 1822 he entered into partnership with Leigh Hunt in editing *The Liberal*, which proved a failure. In 1823 took up the cause of Greek independence, and sailed to Missolonghi, where he died of fever. Byron's poems show not only sympathy with the stormy side of nature, but also great powers of wit and satire.

[*The Poetical Works of Lord Byron* (1905), with Memoir by E. H. Coleridge; *Letters and Journals of Lord Byron*, ed. by Thomas Moore; *Byron* (reprint 1924), by E. C. Mayne; *Byron*, by André Maurois (1930.)]

Byron, HENRY JAMES (1834–84), Eng. dramatist and actor; *b.* Manchester; first ed. of ***Fun***; achieved remarkable success with *Our Boys*, which had a run of over four years, 1875–9.

Byron, HON. JOHN (1723–86), Eng. vice-admiral; grandfather of the poet; sailed round the world with Anson; the elements were generally unfavourable to his naval engagements, and he gained the sobriquet of 'Foul-Weather Jack'; governor of Newfoundland, 1769.

C

Caballero (*cä-bäl-yār'ō*), FERNAN (1796–1877), pseudonym of CECILIA FRANCISCA JOSEFA BÖHL DE FABER, Span. novelist; *b.* in Switzerland; author of numerous historical and other stories; most famous work, *La Gaviota*—'The Seagull'—(1849).

Cabell', JAMES BRANCH (1879–), Amer. author; *b.* Richmond, Virginia; noteworthy volumes include *Jurgen* (1919), *Beyond Life* (1919), *Figures of Earth* (1921), and *The Silver Stallion* (1926).

Ca'ble, GEORGE WASHINGTON (1844–1925), Amer. novelist; *b.* New Orleans; made reputation by truthful and humorous sketches of the Latin quarter of New Orleans and of Southern plantation life; books include *Old Creole Days* (1879), *The Grandissimes* (1880), *Dr. Sevier* (1884), *Kincaid's Battery* (1908).

Cab'ot. (1) JOHN (1450–98), Ital. navigator; *b.* Genoa; naturalized at Venice, 1476; came to England, *c.* 1484; subsequently sailed from Bristol, 1497, under letters patent from Henry VII.; sighted Cape Breton Island and coasted for a considerable distance; in 1498, on second expedition, reached east coast of Greenland and Labrador. (2) SEBASTIAN (*c.* 1476–1557), son of above; probably took part in 1498 expedition; explored in E. and S. America for Spain; returned to England, 1549, and became governor of London Co. of Merchant Adventurers, 1551.

[*John and Sebastian Cabot: the Discovery of North America*, by Beazley (1898).]

Cabral′ (or CABRERA), PEDRO ALVAREZ (*c.* 1467–*c.* 1520), Port. navigator and discoverer; planted Port. flag in Brazil, which he called Santa Cruz, 1500.

Cad′bury, GEORGE (1839–1922), Eng. manufacturer and philanthropist; *b.* Edgbaston, of Quaker parents; developed large chocolate-making business; a social pioneer, founding model village at Bournville.

[*Life*, by A. G. Gardiner (1923).]

Cade, JACK (*d.* 1450), Eng. rebel; leader of the Kentish insurgents, 1450; marched on London with 20,000 men, and after defeating Henry VI.'s forces entered the city; driven out of London by the citizens within a few days, his followers dispersed, and he became a wanderer; was captured, and died of wounds received in the struggle.

Cadell′, FRANCIS (1822–79), Scot. naval officer; *b.* Cockenzie; explored Murray, Edward, and Darling rivers, Australia; murdered by crew while sailing to Spice Islands.

Cadell′, ROBERT (1788–1849), Scot. publisher; *b.* Cockenzie; partner in house of Constable, Edinburgh, which he resuscitated after its failure, 1825; publisher of Scott's later works.

Cador′na, COUNT LUIGI (1850–1928), Ital. marshal; *b.* Pallanza; commander-in-chief on Italy's entrance into Great War; showed great strategic skill, but after disaster of Caporetto, 1917, was superseded and appointed to represent Italy on Allied War Council at Versailles; the foremost Ital. military figure of Great War.

Cadoudal′, GEORGES (1771–1804), Fr. royalist leader; *b.* in Brittany; during Revolution organized Chouan rebellion in support of royalists; executed for conspiracy.

Caed′mon (*c.* 660), first Eng. poet; known to us from Bede's *Ecclesiastical History*, which tells us that he was a herdsman of the monastery at Whitby, and mentions the religious themes on which he wrote; none of his poems can be identified with certainty; of the so-called Caedmon poems only one MS. exists, dating from 10th cent., and containing poems usually entitled *Genesis*, *Exodus*, *Daniel*, *Christ and Satan*.

Cæsar, GAIUS JULIUS (102–44 B.C.), Rom. general and statesman; in early youth led a life of pleasure, but saw active service in the East. Though of patrician blood, sided with democratic party in the civil strife at Rome, held offices of curule ædile, pontifex maximus, and prætor; in 60 B.C. formed with Pompey and Crassus the First Triumvirate, a dictatorship aiming at the overthrow of the reactionary Senate; was elected consul, 59 B.C.; secured government of Gaul for five years (afterwards extended to 49 B.C.); during Gallic wars landed in Britain in 55 B.C., and again in 54 B.C.; subdued Gaul and made it a Rom. province.

The Triumvirate ended with the death of Crassus in battle, 53 B.C.; Pompey now sided with the Senate and became hostile to Cæsar, who definitely defied the Rom. authority by crossing the Rubicon with his army, 49 B.C. In the war which followed Pompey was defeated and killed, 48 B.C. Victories in Africa and Spain left Cæsar master of the Empire. As dictator he reorganized the state, extended local self-government, encouraged agriculture, and reformed provincial administration; his government gradually tended towards undisguised absolutism, and he was assassinated on the Ides of March, 44 B.C. Among his murderers was his friend Brutus. Cæsar was a skilful orator and a great writer. As a brilliant and original soldier, a forceful administrator and great statesman, he paved the way for the new monarchy at Rome.

[*Julius Cæsar* (1892), by W. Warde Fowler; *The Roman Republic and the Founder of the Empire* (1923), by T. Rice Holmes.]

Cagliari (*käl-yär'i*), PAOLO. See under VERONESE.

Cagliostro (*käl-yōs'trō*), ALESSANDRO, COUNT (1743–95), Ital. charlatan; *b.* Palermo; real name, GIUSEPPE BALSAMO; travelled widely, making money by alchemy; arrested for fraudulent practices and for heresy, he died in prison.

Cagnola (*kän-yō'la*), LUIGI (1762–1833), Ital. architect; *b.* Milan; designed the magnificent Arco della Pace, Milan, etc.

Caillaux (*kä-yō'*), JOSEPH MARIE AUGUSTE (1863–), Fr. statesman; early entered Parliament, and soon obtained high position; noteworthy for his financial and administrative ability; premier 1911, but conduct of Franco-Ger. Morocco crisis led to his fall. Again held portfolio of finance, 1913, but murder by his wife of ed. of *Figaro* drove him from office. At outbreak of Great War held office again, but subsequently was suspected of defeatism, and in 1918 was arrested and sentenced to three years' imprisonment and deprivation of civic rights for ten years; obtained benefit of amnesty in 1924; held office again in 1925, 1926, and since 1932.

Caillie (or CAILLÉ) (*kä-yā'*), RENÉ AUGUSTE (1799–1838), Fr. traveller; *b.* Poitou; penetrated to Timbuktu, 1827–8; pub. *Journal of Travels through Central Africa.*

Caine, SIR THOMAS HENRY HALL (1853–1931), Eng. novelist and dramatist; *b.* of mixed Manx and Cumberland parentage at Runcorn; works include *The Deemster* (1887), *The Bondman* (1890), *The Manxman* (1894), *The Christian* (1897), *The Eternal City* (1901), *The White Prophet* (1909), *The Woman Thou gavest me* (1913), and *The Woman of Knockaloe* (1923); several of these dramatized and filmed. Dramas include *The Iron Hand* (1916) and *The Prime Minister* (1918).

Caird, EDWARD (1835–1908), Scot. philosopher; was prof. of moral philosophy, Glasgow Univ., and afterwards master of Balliol, 1893–1907; exercised great influence on Brit. philosophy and theology through his lectures and writings on Neo-Hegelianism.

[*The Life and Philosophy of Edward Caird*, by Sir Henry Jones and J. H. Muirhead (1921).]

Cairnes, JOHN ELLIOT (1823–75), Irish political economist; *b.* in County Louth; prof. of political economy at Dublin, Queen's Coll., Galway, and Univ. Coll., London; works include, besides essays, *The Slave Power* (1862), and *Some Leading Principles of Political Economy Newly Expounded* (1874).

Cairns, HUGH M'CALMONT CAIRNS, 1ST EARL (1819–85), Brit. politician; *b.* in County Down; entered Parliament, 1852, and held various offices; lord chancellor, 1868; created earl, 1878; a fine parliamentary orator and the leading lawyer of his time.

Cairns, JOHN (1818–92), Scot. theologian; prof. of apologetics, and afterwards principal of the United Presbyterian Theological Hall at Edinburgh.

Caius (*kēz*), JOHN (1510–73), Eng. physician; *b.* Norwich; studied divinity at Cambridge; visited Italy, 1533, and studied medicine; practised in London, and became president of Coll. of Physicians; enlarged his old college, 1557, renaming it Gonville and Caius Coll.; a pioneer in the study of anatomy.

Cal'decott, RANDOLPH (1846–86), Eng. artist; *b.* Chester;

attained fame by humorous drawings in *Graphic*; noted for his illustrations to Washington Irving's books, etc.

Cal'der, SIR ROBERT (1745–1818), Brit. admiral; *b.* Elgin; encountered Villeneuve, 1805, captured two enemy ships, but did not next day resume action; court-martialled and reprimanded; nevertheless had forced Villeneuve to retreat to Cadiz, and thus had foiled Napoleon's invasion project.

Calderon (*käl-dā-ron'*), PHILIP HERMOGENES (1833–98), Anglo-Fr. painter of Span. parentage; *b.* Poitiers, but educated from his twelfth year in London; R.A., 1867; keeper of Royal Academy, 1887. Best-known works, *Broken Vows, His Most Noble, High, and Puissant Grace, Ruth and Naomi.*

Calderon de la Barca (*käl-dā-rōn' dā lä bär'ka*), PEDRO (1600–81), Span. dramatist; *b.* Madrid; was patronized by Philip IV.; a prolific writer (about 120 of his plays are still extant); his works are noteworthy for their beautiful poetry, their sense of dramatic form, and their lofty moral standard; his plays include *El Magico Prodigioso* (partly trans. by Shelley), *La Vida es sueño, El Principe Constante, La Dama Duende, El Medico de su Honra, El Mayor Monstruo los celos, El Alcalde de Zalamea,* and his sacred plays *Autos Sacramentales*; Eng. trans. include one by Denis MacCarthy (6 vols., 1853–73), *Eight Plays of Calderon,* by E. Fitzgerald (1853); *Select Plays of Calderon,* by Norman Maccoll (1888).

Caleb, one of the spies sent by Moses to spy out land of Canaan (Num. 14).

Calig'ula, GAIUS CÆSAR (A.D. 12–41), succeeded Tiberius as Rom. emperor (A.D. 37); tyrannical, cruel, profligate; insane; insisted on divine honours; was assassinated.

Calixtus, or CALLISTUS, name of three popes. I. (217–22), Bishop of Rome and martyr; originally a slave; catacombs on Appian Way, of which he had charge, still bear his name. II. (1119–24), a Burgundian, displaced the anti-pope, Gregory VIII.; concluded with emperor, Henry V., the important Concordat of Worms, 1122. III. (1455–8), a Spaniard (ALFONSO DE BORGIA), owed his elevation to Alfonso V. of Aragon; annulled sentence against Joan of Arc.

Call'aghan, SIR GEORGE (1852–1920), Brit. admiral; *b.* London; commanded naval brigade for relief of Peking, 1990; commander-in-chief of home fleet, 1911–14; commander-in-chief at Nore, 1915–18; admiral of the Fleet, 1917.

Callcott (*kol'kut*). (1) SIR AUGUSTUS WALL (1779–1844), Eng. landscape painter; R.A., 1810; knighted, 1827, for his *Raffaelle and the Fornarina,* exhibited in 1837. (2) JOHN WALL (1766–1821), Eng. composer and organist; brother of (1); composer of glees and canons.

Call'es, PLUTARCO ELIAS (1877–), Mexican statesman; *b.* Guaymas, Sonoro, Mexico; of humble birth; after varied career as schoolmaster, soldier, and social reformer, appointed governor of his native province; president of Mexico, 1924–8; term of office marked by disputes with U.S.A. and R.C. Church.

Callisthenes (*kal-is'then-ēz*) (*c.* 360–328 B.C.), Gr. historian; pupil of Aristotle; accompanied Alexander the Great into Asia, and wrote an account of the expedition, also histories of the wars of the period.

Callot (*kä-lō'*), JACQUES (1592–1635), *b.* Nancy; Fr. engraver; studied at Florence; won European fame by his series of engravings, such as *The Miseries* *of War, The Nobles, The Gipsies,* describing with fidelity the manners of his time.

Calonne (*kal-on'*), CHARLES ALEXANDRE DE (1734–1802), Fr. statesman; *b.* Douai; minister of finance under Louis XVI.; his proposal to abolish the immunity from taxation of the nobles, magistrates, and clergy was so ill received that the king dismissed and exiled him, 1787.

Calvaert (*käl-värt'*), DENIS (DIONISIO FIAMMINGO) (*c.* 1540–1619), Flem. painter; *b.* Antwerp; founder of school of Bologna, master of Guido Reni and Domenichino.

Calvé, EMMA (1866–), Fr. soprano operatic singer; *b.* Decazeville; appeared, 1882, in Gounod's *Faust* (Brussels); sang at Covent Garden in *Cavalleria Rusticana*, 1892; most brilliant success was in *Carmen.*

Cal'verley, CHARLES STUART (1831–84), Eng. poet and scholar; *b.* Martley, Worcestershire; brilliant univ. career both at Oxford and Cambridge; pub. *Verses and Translations* (1862), *Verse Translation of Theocritus* (1869), *Fly-Leaves* (1872). As a writer of light verses and parodies he is unsurpassed.

Cal'vin, JOHN (1509–64), Prot. Reformer; *b.* Noyon, Picardy; was appointed, 1521, to a chaplaincy in Noyon cathedral; later continued his education in Paris; in 1527 received the curacy of St.-Martin-de-Marteville, and later that of Pont-l'Évêque; then decided to withdraw from Church; studied law at Orléans and later at Bourges; here also began to study Greek under Melchior Wolmar, and first imbibed doctrines of Reformation; in 1531 was again in Paris. When persecution of Protestants began, he had to flee to Basle, where he wrote his *Institutes of the Christian Religion* (1540). His influence with the Reformers now became supreme; in 1536 he moved to Geneva, where he was followed by his chief supporters; here issued a Prot. Confession of Faith, which enforced a strict morality; within two years, owing to reaction against his severe rule, Calvin had to take refuge in Strasbourg, where he was appointed pastor of a church and prof. of theology; in 1540 attended Diet of Worms, and in 1541 that of Ratisbon, where he was introduced to Melanchthon; returned to Geneva, 1541, where, except for brief interval, he lived for rest of his life.

Besides his great *Institutes,* he pub. valuable commentaries on nearly all the books of the Bible. He differs from Luther in his emphatic assertion of predestination, and in maintaining the purely symbolic nature of the elements used in communion. He demanded for the Church control over the whole lives of the people. Through John Knox his influence penetrated to Scotland.

[*Life,* by Walker (1906); *Life and Times,* by Penning (Eng. trans. 1912).]

Cal'vo, CARLOS (1824–1906), Argentine historian and jurist; *b.* Buenos Aires; wrote authoritative histories of S. Amer. republics; ambassador at Berlin, 1885, and at Paris, 1899–1905; pub. *Dictionnaire du Droit International* (1885), etc.

Cam (*kän*), or CÃO, DIOGO (*fl.* 15th cent.), Port. explorer; continued work of Prince Henry the Navigator; discovered R. Congo *c.* 1482; afterwards explored W. African coast to lat. 21° 50' s.

Cambacérès (*kan-bas-a-res'*), JEAN JACQUES RÉGIS DE, DUKE OF PARMA (1753–1824), Fr. statesman; *b.* Montpellier; represented nobles in Legislative Assembly, 1792; on Committee of Public Safety, 1793; second consul,

1799; later arch-chancellor of empire and president of Senate; under his direction Fr. *Code Civile* was prepared; Duke of Parma, 1808.

Cambon (*kän-bon'*), JULES MARTIN (1845–1935), Fr. diplomat; *b.* Paris; gov.-gen. of Algeria, 1891; ambassador at Washington, 1897, Madrid, 1902, and Berlin, 1907; arranged Morocco agreement of 1909 and 1911; largely owing to him France was prepared when Great War broke out; general secretary at Fr. Foreign Office, 1915; president of Council of Ambassadors, 1920.

Cambon, PIERRE JOSEPH (1756–1820), Fr. financier and statesman; *b.* Montpellier; member of Legislative Assembly, 1791, and of Convention, 1792; in finance was supreme, but by his independence incurred hatred of Robespierre; at restoration exiled; died in Belgium.

Cambon, PIERRE PAUL (1843–1924), Fr. diplomat; *b.* Paris; brother of Jules Martin Cambon; ambassador at Madrid, 1886, Constantinople, 1890, and London, 1898–1920; did much to cement the *entente* between France and Great Britain.

Cam'bridge, GEORGE WILLIAM FREDERICK CHARLES, DUKE OF (1819–1904), Brit. soldier; *b.* Hanover; cousin of Queen Victoria; present at Alma, Balaklava, Inkerman, and Sevastopol; was field-marshal in 1862; general commanding-in-chief, 1856–87; commander-in-chief, 1887–95.

[*Memoir*, by Sheppard (1906).]

Cambyses (*kam-bī'sēz*), son of Cyrus the Great, founder of Pers. Empire; succeeded his father *c.* 529 B.C., conquered Egypt in 525, and after unsuccessful attempt against Ethiopia, died in Syria.

Cam'den, CHARLES PRATT, 1ST EARL (1714–94), lord chancellor of England; attorney-general, 1757; chief justice of the Common Pleas, 1762; president of Council, second Rockingham administration; raised to peerage, 1786; chiefly remembered for his bold championing of John Wilkes.

Camden, WILLIAM (1551–1623), Eng. antiquary and historian; *b.* London; headmaster Westminster School, 1593; Clarencieux king-at-arms, 1597; great work, the *Britannia*, a survey of Brit. Isles (in Latin, trans. into Eng. 1610); wrote also *Remaines concerning Britain* (1605), and *Annales of Queen Elizabeth's Reign* (1615).

Camerar'ius, RUDOLF JAKOB (1665–1721), Ger. physician and botanist; *b.* Tübingen; laid foundation of sexual theory of plants in *Epistola de sexu Plantarum* (1694).

Cam'eron, SIR DAVID YOUNG (1865–), Scot. painter and etcher; *b.* Glasgow; R.S.A., 1918; R.A., 1920; knighted, 1924; royal painter and limner in Scotland from 1932. His pictures and etchings are to be found in many public galleries at home and abroad; with William Strang, illustrated with etchings *The Compleat Angler* (1902).

Cameron, RICHARD (*c.* 1648–80), Scot. Covenanter; *b.* Falkland, Fife, where he became schoolmaster; preached in Clydesdale and Annandale; took refuge in Holland, 1678–80; on return, issued, with others, the Sanquhar Declaration; slain in skirmish at Aird's Moss.

[*Richard Cameron*, by Prof. Herkless (1896).]

Cameron, VERNEY LOVETT (1844–94), Brit. traveller; *b.* Dorsetshire; was first European to cross Africa from east to west, 1873–75; pub. *Across Africa* (1877), and, with Sir Frederick Burton, *To the Gold Coast for Gold* (1883).

Cammaerts, EMILE (1878–), Belgian author; *b.* Brussels;

settled in England, 1908; trans. vols. of Ruskin into French; author of *Belgian Poems* (1915), *New Belgian Poems* (1917), *Messines and other Poems* (1918), *Poèmes Intimes* (1922), *Les Bellini* (1927), etc.

Camoens (*kä'mō-ens*) (or CAMÖES), LUIS DE (1524–80), Portugal's greatest poet; *b.* Lisbon, of noble descent; graduated at Coimbra Univ.; removed to Lisbon and fell in love with Donna Caterina de Ataide, but her father forbade their union. Camoens remained true to her, and celebrated his love in his poems. Banished from Lisbon, he entered the army, and at Ceuta lost his right eye in a skirmish. He returned to Lisbon in 1550, and seems to have led a disorderly life; was imprisoned for assault upon a royal servant; was released on volunteering for service in India, 1553. In India wrote his masterpiece, *The Lusiads*, on the explorations of Vasco da Gama. Returned to Lisbon, 1570; the poem appeared, 1572, and was an immediate success. But the remainder of Camoens's life was passed in poverty, and he died of plague in a public hospital.

[Translation of *The Lusiads*, by Burton (1884); *Camoens: Life and Lusiads* (1881).]

Campanel'la, TOMMASO (1568–1639), Ital. philosopher and poet; was for some time a Dominican; opposed Scholasticism, and devoted to study of nature; imprisoned twenty-seven years as rebel against Span. tyranny in Naples; liberated in 1629; found a patron in the Pope, and later in Richelieu.

[Sonnets trans. into English by J. A. Symonds (1878); *Campanella and his Poetry*, by E. G. Gardner (1923).]

Campbell (*kam'bel*), SIR COLIN, BARON CLYDE (1792–1863), Brit. soldier; as commander-in-chief during Ind. Mutiny he relieved Lucknow, pacified N. India, and organized successful campaign in central districts.

Campbell, GORDON (1886–), Scot. sailor; served in Great War and was awarded V.C., 1917, for his exploits with 'Mystery Ships'; rear-admiral, and retired, 1928. M.P. for Burnley since 1931.

Campbell, JOHN FRANCIS (1821–85), Scot. writer, known as 'Campbell of Islay'; author of *Popular Tales of the West Highlands* (1860–2), best collection of genuine Gaelic folk-tales; inventor of sunshine recorder.

Campbell, SIR MALCOLM (1885–), Brit. motorist; *b.* Chislehurst; created world's motor speed record on land (301 m.p.h.) on Daytona Beach, Florida, 1935.

Campbell, MRS. PATRICK (BEATRICE STELLA TANNER), (1865–), Eng. actress; first success at Adelphi Theatre, 1892; created the part of *Second Mrs. Tanqueray* (1893) at St. James's. Has played with Beerbohm Tree, Forbes-Robertson, and Sarah Bernhardt. Toured U.S.A. Created Eliza Doolittle in *Pygmalion*, by Bernard Shaw (1914).

[*My Own Life* (1922).]

Campbell, REGINALD JOHN (1867–), Eng. preacher; *b.* London; succeeded Dr. Parker at City Temple, 1903; pub. *The New Theology* (1907), which aroused controversy; entered Church of England, 1915; vicar of Christ Church, London, 1917–21; canon of Chichester, 1930.

Campbell, ROY (1902–), S. African poet; *b.* Natal; educated Oxford; *The Flaming Terrapin* (1924) established his reputation; *Wayzgoose* (1928) is a satire on the minor writers of his native country.

Campbell, THOMAS (1777–1844), Scot. poet; *b.* Glasgow; settled in Edinburgh, 1797. *The Pleasures* *of Hope* appeared in 1799. Its success was immediate. His patriotic lyrics, 'Ye Mariners of England' and 'The Battle of the Baltic,' are amongst the finest in the language.

[*Thomas Campbell,* by J. C. Hadden (1899).]

Campbell, WILLIAM WILFRED (1860–1919), Can. poet; *b.* in Ontario; works, which show a strong love of Nature and a fervid patriotism, include *Collected Poems* (1905) and *Poetic Tragedies* (1908).

Campbell - Bannerman, SIR HENRY (1836–1908), Brit. statesman; *b.* Glasgow; M.P. for Stirling Burghs from 1868 to death; held various important state offices in successive Liberal governments between 1870 and 1895, including War Office, 1892–95; strongly disapproved of Boer War, which caused split in Liberal party, and won him much unpopularity, but after crushing defeat of the Unionists, 1906, he became prime minister, and held office till 1908. Chief features of his administration were granting of constitution and responsible government to Transvaal, and the Trades Dispute Act, 1906.

[*Life,* by J. A. Spender (1923).]

Campeggio (*käm-ped'jō*), LORENZO (1464–1539), Ital. cardinal; *b.* Milan; made Bishop of Salisbury by Henry VIII.; was also Archbishop of Bologna; chiefly notorious for his connection with the divorce of Catherine of Aragon.

Camphausen (*kamp'hou-zen*), WILHELM (1818–85), Ger. artist; *b.* Düsseldorf; famous for his battle pictures; also portraits of modern Ger. celebrities.

Cam'pion, EDMUND (1540–81), Eng. Jesuit; *b.* London; took orders in the Church of England, but in 1571 joined the Jesuits; was sent with Robert Parsons to conduct a mission in England, 1580, and drew crowds to his meetings; executed at Tyburn; beatified 1886.

Campion, THOMAS (1567–1620), Eng. poet and musician; *b.* London; his several *Bookes of Ayres* (words and music by himself) constitute his title to be considered in the front rank of Jacobean lyric poets; also wrote number of masques.

Campoamor y Campoosorio (*käm-pō-a-mor ē käm-po-o-sō'rē-ō*), RAMON DE (1819–1901), Span. poet; *b.* in Asturias; claimed to be the creator of two new kinds of poetry—the *dolora,* a poem illustrating some moral or philosophical idea, and the *peuqeño poema,* a kind of novel in verse; his best productions are undoubtedly his lyrical works, such as *Obras Poeticas* (1900), marked by polished diction and subtle thought.

Campomanes (*käm-pō-män'es*), PEDRO RODRIGUEZ, CONDE DE (1723–1802), Span. statesman and economist; *b.* Asturias; pub. *Discurso sobre el Fomento de la Industria Popular* (1774); was founder of Span. National Bank, and opened ports to foreign trade.

Cam'pos, ARSENIO MARTINEZ DE (1831–1900), Span. general; *b.* Segovia; restored Alfonso XII. to Span. throne; during minority of Alfonso XIII. was trusted adviser of queen-regent.

Canale (*kä-nä'le*) (or CANALETTO), ANTONIO (1697–1768), architectural painter of Venice. National Gallery, London, has ten of his Venetian pictures; other examples are in the Wallace Collection, and at Edinburgh and Dublin.

Candace (*kan'da-sē*), hereditary title of queens of Meroë in Upper Nubia; specifically applied (1) to a queen who twice invaded Egypt in 22 B.C. and was twice defeated by Rom. general Petronius, and (2) to the Queen of Ethiopia whose treasurer Philip converted to Christianity (Acts 8).

Cand'lish, Robert Smith (1806–73), Scot. theologian; *b.* Edinburgh; prof. of divinity, New Coll., Edinburgh, and some time principal. One of leaders of the Disruption party, 1843.

Can'ning, George (1770–1827), Eng. statesman; *b.* London; educated Eton and Oxford; M.P. for Newport, Isle of Wight, 1794; made reputation by speeches in support of abolition of slave trade; foreign secretary, 1807; president of Board of Control, 1816; foreign secretary and leader of House of Commons, 1822; prime minister, in succession to Lord Liverpool, 1827; one of the most brilliant and witty orators of his time; his fame as a statesman rests chiefly on his foreign policy, 1822–7, when he exerted all his influence in support of all national and liberal movements in Europe.

[*Canning and his Times*, by Marriott (1903); *George Canning*, by H. W. V. Temperley (1905).]

Cannizzaro (*kä-nēt-sä'rō*), Stanislao (1826–1910), Ital. chemist; *b.* Palermo; prof. of chemistry, Alexandria, Genoa, Palermo, and Rome; chief work lay in establishing difference between atomic and molecular weights.

Can'o, Alonzo (1601–67), Span. painter, sculptor, and architect; *b.* Granada; court painter to Philip IV.; most of his pictures are in Seville.

Cano, Juan Sebastian del (*d.* 1526), Span. circumnavigator of the globe; sailed with Magellan, after whose death he commanded expedition from Philippines home, 1521–2.

Cano'va, Antonio (1757–1822), Ital. sculptor; *b.* near Treviso; revived the art of classic sculpture. First great work was *Dædalus and Icarus*. Went to Rome, 1780, and produced *Theseus vanquishing the Minotaur*, *Psyche and the Butterfly*, *Perseus with the Head of Medusa* (Vatican). He modelled a statue of Napoleon, and in 1815 obtained the restoration of the Ital. treasures removed by the latter; created Marquess of Ischia, 1816. After 1819 he executed some of his greatest works. *Hercules and Lichas* ranks as his most sublime achievement, *Hebe* his most graceful work, and the monument to the Archduchess Maria Christina his finest. The Louvre in Paris has his celebrated *Cupid and Psyche*.

[*Canova*, by A. G. Meyer (1898).]

Canrobert (*kon-rō-bār'*), François Certain (1809–95), Fr. marshal; *b.* in Lot; commanded division at the Alma, and was afterwards commander-in-chief of Fr. army; distinguished himself at Magenta and Solferino, afterwards at Wörth and Gravelotte.

Cantemir (*kan'te-mēr*), Demetrius (1673–1723), prince of Moldavia and historian; prince of Moldavia for one year; on his defeat by the Turks, 1711, he retired to live in Russia; an expert in the chief Oriental languages; works include *History of the Growth and Decay of the Ottoman Empire* (Eng. trans. by N. Tindal, 1756) and *Descriptio Moldaviæ* (1769), the first description of Moldavia.

Can'ute the Great, or Cnut (*c.* 995–1035), King of England; son of Sweyn Forkbeard of Denmark. On the death of his father, 1014, who had compelled the English to accept him as king, the English restored Ethelred. Canute at once made war upon Ethelred, who died 1016, and continued the struggle against Edmund Ironside, his successor. Upon Edmund's death, 1017, Canute was accepted as King of all England. He became King of Denmark on his brother's death, 1019, acquired the throne of Norway by conquest, 1028, and received the homage of the

King of Scotland, 1031. He ruled England as a native ruler, conciliating the clergy by his liberality, and securing his position still further by the creation of a standing army. The four earldoms, Wessex, Mercia, East Anglia, Northumbria, were formed by him, 1017.

Capablanc'a, JOSÉ R. (1888–), chess player; *b.* Cuba; educated Cuba and Columbia Univ., New York; chess champion of the world, 1921–7; author of *My Chess Career* and *Chess Fundamentals* (1921).

Capek' (*chap'ek*), KAREL (1890–), Czech dramatist and novelist; *b.* Bohemia; plays include his 'robot' play, *R.U.R.* (Eng. trans. 1923), and *The Life of the Insects* (Eng. trans. 1923), both satirical, the one of the mechanical tendency of civilization, the other of modern society; novels include *Painful Tales* (1920), a collection of short stories, and *Krakatit* (Eng. trans. 1925); other works include *Letters from England* (1927), *The Gardener's Year* and *Letters from Spain* (1931).

Caprivi (*kä-prē'vē*), GEORG LEO VON, COUNT (1831–99), Ger. soldier and statesman; *b.* Charlottenburg; served with distinction in Dan., Austrian, and Franco-Ger. campaigns; succeeded Bismarck as chancellor and foreign minister, 1890.

Caracal'la, MARCUS AURELIUS ANTONINUS (A.D. 186–217), Rom. emperor; son of Septimius Severus; noted for his cruelties and extravagance; ravaged Mesopotamia and destroyed tombs of Parthian kings; built Arch of Septimius Severus in Forum.

Carac'tacus, or CARADOC, Brit. chieftain who held Rom. invaders at bay (*c.* A.D. 48–50), but was later taken prisoner and sent to Rome.

Caran d'Ache (*kä-rän d'ash*) (1858–1909), pseudonym of EMMANUEL POIRÉ, Fr. caricaturist; *b.* Moscow; contributed political cartoons to *Figaro*; won great fame by *L'Epopée*, a series of over 2,000 portraits of the celebrated men who helped to win Napoleon's victories; during the Panama scandal his *Carnet de chèques* made a great sensation.

[*Causeries Caran D'Ache*, by W. H. Anstie (1925).]

Car'digan, JAMES THOMAS BRUDENELL, 7TH EARL OF (1797–1868), Brit. soldier; *b.* Hambleden, Bucks; of an overbearing temper, but of undoubted courage, he led the famous charge of the 'Light Brigade' at Balaklava.

Carducci (*kar-doo'chē*), GIOSUÈ (1836–1907), one of greatest Ital. poets; *b.* Val-di-Castello, Tuscany; prof. of literature, Bologna; followed classic tradition; his *Hymn to Satan* marks his strong republican convictions; other poetic works include *Decennali* (1871), *Nuove Poesie* (1873), and *Odi barbare* (1877–89); his lyrical verse has not been surpassed since Catullus.

[*Giosuè Carducci*, by Orlo Williams (1914); *L'uomo Carducci*, by E. Papini (1918).]

Card'well, EDWARD, VISCOUNT (1813–86), Eng. statesman; *b.* Liverpool; as secretary for war, 1868, proved himself a great military reformer, instituting short-service system and army reserve.

Carew (*kā'ri* or *kar-oo'*), RICHARD (1555–1620), Eng. antiquary and translator; *b.* in Cornwall; trans. first five cantos of Tasso's *Jerusalem Delivered* (1594), and pub. *Survey of Cornwall* (1602).

Carew, THOMAS (1595–*c.* 1639), Eng. poet; *b.* in Kent; abandoned law for court employment, and was much favoured by Charles I.; one of most brilliant of Cavalier poets, he will live by virtue of a few incomparable lyrics.

Ca'rey, HENRY (*d.* 1743), Eng.

poet and musician; chiefly remembered for his songs, of which 'Sally in our Alley' is best known; authorship of 'God Save the King' claimed for him, but without good grounds.

Carey, WILLIAM (1761–1834), Eng. missionary; *b.* in Northants; one of founders of the Baptist Missionary Soc.; went as missionary to India; trans. Bible into Sanskrit, Punjabi, Bengali, and other languages and dialects, of which he compiled dictionaries.

[*Life*, by G. Smith (1884).]

Cargill (*kar-gil'*), DONALD (1610–81), Scot. Covenanter; *b.* Rattray, Perthshire; minister of Barony parish, Glasgow, 1655, but ejected 1660; became field preacher, was wounded at Bothwell Bridge, and joined Richard Cameron in issuing Sanquhar Declaration; executed in Edinburgh, 1681.

Carisbrooke, ALEXANDER ALBERT MOUNTBATTEN, 1ST MARQUESS OF (1886–), eldest son of Princess Beatrice, youngest daughter of Queen Victoria, and Prince Henry of Battenberg; entered army, 1911, and served during Great War (1914–18). Assumed surname of Mountbatten and created Marquess of Carisbrooke, 1917.

Carlén (*kar-lān'*), EMILIA (1807–92), Swed. novelist; *b.* Strömstad; works include *Gustaf Lindorm* (1853), *Professor's Favourites* (1843), *The Maiden's Tower* (1853).

[*Autobiography* (1878).]

Carleton, WILLIAM (1794–1869), Irish novelist; *b.* Clogher, Tyrone; remembered for his *Traits and Stories of the Irish Peasantry* (1830–33); one of the most realistic of Irish writers.

Carlile, WILSON (1847–), Eng. churchman and social worker; *b.* Brixton; founder of Church Army, a working man's mission for rescue of outcasts of society; appointed prebendary of St. Paul's Cathedral, 1906, Companion of Honour, 1926.

Carlos, DON (1545–68), son of Philip II. of Spain, was of vicious character and feeble intellect; imprisoned by his father, and died mysteriously. He has been made the theme of many dramas, including Schiller's famous tragedy *Don Carlos*.

Carlos I. (1863–1908), King of Portugal; succeeded, 1889; determined to assert power of crown, suspended the constitution, 1907, and appointed a dictator; was assassinated in Lisbon, together with his eldest son, Louis, 1908.

Carlyle, ALEXANDER (1722–1805), Scot. preacher; *b.* Dumfriesshire; minister of Inveresk, 1748–1805; his *Autobiography* is valuable commentary on life of his period; friend of Adam Smith, David Hume, etc.

Carlyle, THOMAS (1795–1881), Scot. historian, essayist, and philosopher; *b.* Ecclefechan, Dumfriesshire; educated at parish school, Annan Academy, and Edinburgh Univ.; intended entering the ministry, but abandoned the idea, and became mathematical master at Annan Academy, and later in Kirkcaldy, where he formed a lasting friendship with Edward Irving. In 1818 Carlyle returned to Edinburgh, where he studied law. He next embarked upon a literary career; wrote articles for *Edinburgh Encyclopædia*, trans. Legendre's *Geometry*, and also wrote his *Life of Schiller*, and trans. Goethe's *Wilhelm Meister*. He visited London and Paris, making the acquaintance of Coleridge, Hazlitt, and others. In 1826 he married Jane Baillie Welsh, 1801–66, and set up house in Edinburgh, where he became a contributor to *Edinburgh Review*. Two years later Carlyle moved to his wife's small estate at Craigenputtock, Dumfriesshire, and wrote *Sartor Re-*

sartus. In 1834 the Carlyles settled finally at Cheyne Row, Chelsea. His masterly *French Revolution* was published 1837, *Sartor Resartus* (1838), *Chartism* (1839), *Heroes and Hero-Worship* (1841), *Past and Present* (1843), *Oliver Cromwell* (1845), *Latter-Day Pamphlets* (1850), *Frederick the Great* (1858–65). In 1865 Carlyle was elected lord rector of Edinburgh Univ.; the sudden death of his wife, 1866, overshadowed the rest of his life. Carlyle exercised a most powerful influence upon the literary, ethical, and political views of his time. His work is remarkable for its qualities of humour, sarcasm, and profound insight, and its vivid and picturesque style. Carlyle was often irritable, hasty, and inconsiderate, afflicted as he was by chronic dyspepsia, yet these defects scarcely served to hide a noble and tender nature.

[*Reminiscences of Carlyle*, ed. by Norton (1887); *Life*, by Froude (1882–4), by R. Garnett (1887), and by D. A. Wilson (6 vols., 1923–); *Guide to Carlyle*, by A. Ralli (1920).]

Carman, WILLIAM BLISS (1861–1929), Can. poet; *b.* Fredericton, N. Brunswick; vols. of verse include *Low Tide on Grand Pré* (1893), *Ballads of Lost Haven* (1897), *Pipes of Pan* (1903–5), *Later Poems* (1921).

Carmen Sylva. See ELIZABETH of Romania.

Carnegie, ANDREW (1835–1919), Scot.-Amer. millionaire and philanthropist; *b.* Dunfermline; emigrated to Pennsylvania. Through his business ability in the iron and steel industries, oil, railways, etc., he rose from poverty to great wealth. He devoted a large part (estimated at £70,000,000) of his fortune to useful purposes, including gifts of public libraries throughout Britain and America; church organs to Scot. churches; swimming baths; a large grant to Scot. universities; provided pensions for professors in U.S.A., Canada, and Newfoundland; founded Carnegie Institutes, Pittsburgh and Washington; 'Hero Funds'; a palace at The Hague for the Court of Arbitration; and numerous minor benefactions in America and Dunfermline. Author of several works, including *Triumphant Democracy* (1886), *Gospel of Wealth* (1900), and *Problems of To-day* (1908).

[*Life*, by Alderson (1902).]

Carnot (*kär-nō'*), LAZARE NICOLAS MARGUERITE (1753–1823), Fr. general; *b.* in Côte-d'Or; organizer of victory for revolutionary armies in early days of Revolution; voted for death of king, and as minister of war chose Bonaparte for Ital. campaign; afterwards opposed him; minister of interior during Hundred Days; spent his later years in scientific study.

Carnot, MARIE FRANÇOIS SADI (1837–94), president of Fr. republic; *b.* Limoges; minister of public works, 1880; minister of finance, 1885; president, 1887. His term of office, which included the opening of the Paris Exhibition, 1889, proved very popular. He was assassinated by an Ital. anarchist at Lyons.

Carnot, NICHOLAS LÉONARD SADI (1796–1832), Fr. physicist; *b.* Paris; founded science of thermo-dynamics; author of *Réflexions sur la Puissance motrice du Feu* (1824).

Carol, KING OF ROMANIA. See under CHARLES.

Caroline, AMELIA ELIZABETH (1768–1821), queen of George IV., was daughter of Duke of Brunswick. She and her husband separated soon after their marriage, and on his accession George had her name omitted from the liturgy and unsuccessfully attempted to procure a divorce; she was excluded from the coronation ceremony, and died nineteen days later, the object of much popular sympathy.

Caroline Wilhelmina OF ANSPACH (1683–1737), George II.'s queen; supported Sir Robert Walpole and was a patron of literature and the Church.

Carolus-Duran (*kär'o-lus-doo-rän*), pseudonym of CHARLES AUGUSTE EMILE DURAND (1837–1917), famous Fr. portrait painter; established studio in Paris, which attracted many brilliant pupils, including J. S. Sargent; painted *St. Francis of Assisi*, *L' Assassiné*, *Lady with the Glove*, a portrait of his wife, etc.

Carpaccio (*kar-pat'cho*), VITTORE (*c.* 1450–*c.* 1522), Venetian painter, extolled by Ruskin; finest works: *The Presentation in the Temple*, the *St. Ursula* series, and that of Saints *Tryphon*, *Jerome*, and *George*.

Carpenter, EDWARD (1844–1929), democratic author and poet; *b.* Brighton; became fellow and lecturer at Trinity Hall, Cambridge, but abandoned these appointments on adopting Socialist views; eventually exercised a very wide influence; his writings include *Towards Democracy* (1883; enlarged ed. 1902), *Love's Coming of Age* (1896), and *My Days and Dreams*, an autobiography (1916).

Carpenter, MARY (1807–77), Eng. social reformer; *b.* Exeter; founder of reformatory schools in England; devoted her life to the service of destitute children, and was largely instrumental in securing the passing of the Juvenile Offenders Act, 1854.

Carpentier (*kar-pän-tyā'*), GEORGES (1894–), Fr. boxer; *b.* Lens; in 1913 fought Bombardier Wells, defeating him sensationally in 72 seconds; knocked out Joe Becket, 1910; defeated by Jack Dempsey, 1921.

Carpini (*kär-pē'nē*), JOANNES DE PIANO (13th cent.), priest and explorer; sent in 1245 by Pope Innocent IV. on mission to the Mongols; his account of his journey, partly made use of by Hakluyt, 1598, is contained in his *Liber Tartarorum*.

Carracci (*kär-ä'chē*), LUDOVICO (1555–1619), and his nephews, AGOSTINO (1557–1602) and ANNIBALE (1560–1609), Ital. artists; *b.* Bologna; founders of Eclectic school; their work is distinguished by correct technique, large design, and fine figure-drawing; nine works by Ludovico are in National Gallery.

Carranza (*kär-änt'za*), VENUSTIANO (1859–1920), President of Mexico; *b.* in Coahuila; in 1911 became governor of his native state; after murder of President Madero, 1913, and the fall of his successor Huerta, Carranza became provisional president, and established his capital at Hermosillo; moved his government to Vera Cruz, 1914, and recognized as president, 1915, though not formally elected till 1917; rebellion broke out under Obregon, 1920, and Carranza was treacherously shot.

Carrel', ALEXIS (1873–), Fr. surgeon; *b.* Lyons; went to America and carried on research at univ. of Chicago; appointed member of Rockfeller Institute for Medical Research, 1912; Nobel Prize in physiology and medicine, 1912; during Great War, with Henry D. Dakin, devised a scheme for the sterilization of extensive wounds, known as '*La Méthode d'irrigation intermittente Carrel*'; awarded the Nordhoff Jung Cancer Prize, 1931.

Carrick, THOMAS (1802–75), Eng. miniature painter; *b.* near Carlisle; was first a chemist, but gave this up for miniature painting; had many distinguished sitters, including Sir Robert Peel, Wordsworth, Longfellow, and Carlyle.

Carroll, LEWIS. See DODGSON, CHARLES.

Carson, EDWARD HENRY, BARON (1854–1935), Irish Unionist politician and leader; *b.* Duncairn, County Antrim; M.P., 1892–1918; solicitor-general, 1900–6; attorney-general, 1915; first lord of Admiralty, 1917; member of War Cabinet, 1917–18; leader and inspirer of Ulster Anti-Home Rule campaign against the Parliament Act, 1912–13; accepted reluctantly Home Rule Bill of 1920.

Carstares, WILLIAM (1649–1715), Scot. statesman and preacher; *b.* Cathcart, Glasgow; went to Utrecht and became confidant of William of Orange and court chaplain; most influential person in Scot. affairs from 1688 till 1702; later principal of Edinburgh Univ., and a strong promoter of the Union.

Carte, RICHARD D'OYLY (1844–1901), Eng. theatrical manager and producer; *b.* Soho, London; produced at Savoy Theatre Gilbert and Sullivan's comic operas, ably assisted by his wife.

Carter, HOWARD (1873–), Eng. Egyptologist; *b.* Swaffham; on staff of Egyptian Archæological Survey; subsequently carried out explorations on behalf of Earl of Carnarvon. Discovered tomb of Tut-ankh-Amen, 1923.

Car'teret, SIR GEORGE (1610–80), Eng. royalist; *b.* Jersey; as lieut.-gov. of Jersey carried on campaign against Commonwealth until compelled to surrender, 1651. After the Restoration was rewarded by grants of land in America. New Jersey was named in his honour.

Carteret, JOHN. See GRANVILLE.

Cartier (*kär-tyā'*), SIR GEORGES ETIENNE (1814–73), Can. statesman; *b.* Quebec; from 1858–62 was, with Sir John Macdonald, joint premier of Canada; secured entry of Quebec into federation, 1867; promoted Grand Trunk and Can. Pacific Rys.

Cartier, JACQUES (1491–1557), Fr. navigator; *b.* St. Malo; the 'Columbus' of Canada; made three voyages to America in 1534, 1536, and 1541, in the course of which he discovered the St. Lawrence R., and explored it as far as the site of Montreal.

Carton, RICHARD CLAUDE (formerly CRITCHETT) (1853–1928), Eng. dramatist; *b.* London; wrote chiefly comedies, best known including *The Home Secretary*, *Lord and Lady Algy*, and *Lady Huntworth's Experiment*.

Cartwright, EDMUND (1743–1823), Eng. clergyman and inventor; *b.* Marnham, Notts; invented the power-loom, for which Parliament voted him £10,000; also a wool-combing machine; pub. two vols. of poems.

Caruso (*kä-roo'sō*), ENRICO (1874–1921), Ital. operatic tenor; *b.* Naples; first great success in *La Bohème* at Monte Carlo, 1898; performed in many cities of Europe and America; possessed a voice of wonderful quality, sweetness, and power.

Carvajal, ANTONIO FERNANDEZ (*d.* 1659), Port. Jew; was the first naturalized Eng. Jew, and was often employed by Cromwell; may be called the founder of Jewish community in England.

Ca'ry, HENRY FRANCIS (1772–1844), Eng. author and translator; *b.* Gibraltar; famous for trans. of Dante's *Divina Commedia* (1805–14).

[*Memoir*, by son (1847).]

Casabian'ca. (1) RAPHAEL, COMTE DE (1738–1825), Fr. general; served under the revolutionary government in Italy, 1794–8; rejoined Napoleon during the Hundred Days. (2) LOUIS (1762–98), nephew of the above; succeeded Admiral Brueys in command of *Orient* at battle of the Nile. His son, Jacques, aged ten, was hero of Mrs. Hemans's poem.

Casals, PABLO (1876–), violoncellist and composer; *b.* near Barcelona, where he made his first public appearance in 1889; first Eng. appearance, 1898, since when he has acquired world-wide reputation; has pub. two symphonic poems and chamber music.

Casaubon (*ka-saw'bon*), ISAAC (1559–1614), Swiss classical scholar; *b.* Geneva, of Huguenot parentage; prof. of Greek at Geneva and Montpellier; librarian in Paris to Henry IV., 1598; came to London, and was made prebendary of Canterbury, 1610. His merits as a commentator are very great. He ed. Aristotle, Theophrastus, Strabo, Theocritus, Suetonius, etc.

[*Life*, by Mark Pattison (1875; 2nd ed. by H. Nettleship, 1892).]

Casement, ROGER DAVID (1864–1916), Brit. consular servant; *b.* Kingstown, Ireland; served in Port. E. and W. Africa, Fr. Congo, San Paulo, Rio de Janeiro; exposed infamous conditions of rubber industry in Congo and Peru; knighted 1911; during Great War was in Germany urging Irish prisoners to serve against Britain; captured off coast of Kerry, tried for high treason, and executed.

Casimir-Périer (*ka-si-mēr-per-yā'*), JEAN PAUL PIERRE (1847–1907), Fr. statesman; *b.* Paris; prime minister and minister for foreign affairs, 1893–4; president 1894, after assassination of President Carnot, but resigned six months later.

Cas'lon, WILLIAM (1692–1766), the first great Eng. typefounder; *b.* Cradley, Worcestershire; employed by most of the leading publishers of his time because of the clearness and legibility of his type, which he modelled after the Elzevir pattern.

Cassel, SIR ERNEST JOSEPH (1852–1921), financier; *b.* Cologne; financed the great Assuan dam in Egypt, the Swed. railways, the Central London Tube Ry.; assisted in negotiating three state loans for Mexico, and raised a loan for China after the war with Japan; contributed generously to various charities.

Cassell, JOHN (1817–65), Eng. publisher; *b.* Manchester; self-educated; went to London, 1836; set up as tea and coffee merchant, 1847, and 1850 turned publisher; founder of Cassell, Petter, and Galpin, now Cassell and Co., Ltd.

Cassius, GAIUS (*d.* 42 B.C.), Rom. prætor; member of a plebeian family which had once held patrician rank; one of the murderers of Julius Cæsar.

Cassivellaunus (*käs-i-vel-ou'nus*), Brit. chieftain, ruling country north of Thames; offered a valiant defence to Julius Cæsar during his second invasion, 54 B.C.; compelled to capitulate and promise tribute to the conqueror.

Castelar (*käs-tā-lär'*), EMILIO (1832–99), Span. statesman; *b.* Cadiz; prof. of history and philosophy, univ. of Madrid, 1856–65, being removed for his republican sympathies; defeated in rising of 1866, he escaped to France, returning 1868; assisted in downfall of King Amadeus, 1873, and appointed dictator by the Cortes; compelled to resign, 1874; publications include *La Formula del Progreso, Historia del Movimiento Republicano en Europa.*

Castell'o-Branco, CAMILLO, VISCOUNT OF CORREIA-BOTELHO (1825–90), Port. author, most national of modern Port. writers; produced over 200 vols., chiefly novels.

Castelnau (*käs-tel-nō'*), EDOUARD DE CURIÈRES DE (1851–), Fr. soldier; *b.* in Aveyron; fought in Franco-Prussian War, 1870–1; at outbreak of the Great War took command of the army of Lorraine, subsequently transferred to 7th Army, and conducted Fr. offensive in Champagne, 1915; was entrusted with defence of Verdun; towards close of the war became commander of the eastern army group, and was present at the entry of the French into Strasbourg, 1918.

Castiglione (*käs-tēl-yō'nā*), BALDASSARE (1478–1529), Ital. diplomatist and author; *b.* near Mantua; known as 'the perfect courtier'; sent by Duke of Urbino on a mission to Henry VII. of England. He wrote Latin and Ital. poems of rare quality, and *Il Cortegiano* (1528), one of the greatest prose works of the 16th cent., describing the ideal Ital. gentleman of the Renaissance (trans. 1928).

Castlereagh (*kas'el-rā*), VISCOUNT. See LONDONDERRY, 2ND MARQUESS OF.

Catena (*kä-tā'nä*), VINCENZO DI BIAGIO (*c.* 1470–1531), Ital. painter; *b.* Venice; pupil of Giovanni Bellini; painter of portraits and of religious pictures; among his works are *Virgin and Child* (Walker Gallery, Liverpool), *St. Jerome in his Study* and *Madonna and Child with kneeling Warrior* (National Gallery).

Catesby, ROBERT (1573–1605), Eng. conspirator; *b.* Lapworth, Warwickshire; of good family and abilities; organized the Gunpowder Plot, 1605; on discovery he attempted to escape, but was overtaken and shot.

Cathcart'. (1) WILLIAM SCHAW, 1ST EARL (1755–1843), Brit. general; *b.* Petersham, Surrey; served in America, Flanders, and Germany; commander-in-chief in Ireland, 1803; commanded Copenhagen expedition, 1807; ambassador to Russia, 1813–14. (2) SIR GEORGE (1794–1854), Eng. soldier; son of above; *b.* London; Wellington's aide-de-camp at Quatre Bras and Waterloo; governor and commander-in-chief of Cape Colony, 1852–3; served in Crimea, and was killed at Inkerman.

Cath'er, WILLA SIBERT (1876–), Amer. author; *b.* in Virginia; associate-editor, *McClure's Magazine* (1906–12); *O Pioneers!* (1913) established her reputation; subsequent vols. are *My Antonia* (1918), *One of Ours* (1922), *A Lost Lady* (1923), *The Professor's House* (1925), *Death comes for the Archbishop* (1927), *Shadows on the Rock* (1931), and *Obscure Destinies* (1932).

Catherine OF ALEXANDRIA, ST. (4th cent.), upbraided the Emperor Maximinus for his cruelties and worship of false gods; martyred at Alexandria, bound to a 'spiked wheel,' with which she is commonly represented; her feast day is Nov. 25.

Catherine OF ARAGON (1485–1536), first wife of Henry VIII.; daughter of Ferdinand and Isabella of Castile and Aragon; married, when sixteen, Arthur, Prince of Wales, who died 1502; subsequently married his brother, Henry VIII., 1509, to whom she bore six children, Queen Mary I. being the only one who survived. In 1529 Henry began to doubt legality of papal dispensation which had enabled him to marry Catherine. When the Pope would not grant a divorce, the king broke with Rome, and Cranmer in 1533 declared the parties no longer man and wife.

[*Divorce of Catherine of Aragon*, by Froude (1891); *Wives of Henry VIII.*, by M. Hume (1905).]

Catherine OF BRAGANZA (1638–1705), queen-consort of Charles II. of England; daughter of John IV. of Portugal, who settled Bombay upon her at her marriage; returned to Portugal, 1692. She had no children.

Catherine OF SIENA, ST. (1347–80), dedicated herself to the religious life from her seventh year; took a prominent part in the religious controversies of her day; she nursed the plague-stricken, and was venerated for her gentleness; 'one of the most wonderful women that have ever lived.'

[*Saint Catherine of Siena*, by E. G. Gardner (1907).]

Catherine OF VALOIS (1401–37), queen-consort of Henry V. of England; daughter of Charles VI. of France; in accordance with Treaty of Troyes she married Henry, 1420. After Henry's death, 1422, she married Owen Tudor, by whom she had three sons, one of whom, Edmund, was the father of Henry VII.

Catherine I. (1680–1727), Empress of Russia; daughter of a peasant; mistress, then wife, of Peter the Great. After his death, 1725, she became empress in her own right.

Catherine II. (1729–96), Empress of Russia, generally called CATHERINE THE GREAT, was a daughter of Prince of Anhalt-Zerbst; married Archduke Peter of Russia, 1745, who frequently ill-treated her. Catherine's immoralities soon became as flagrant as those of her husband. On his accession to the throne, 1761, he tried to divorce her, but failed because of her power with the clergy. Peter was murdered, 1762, and Catherine was declared empress. She governed with great ability, her greatest service to her country being the consolidation and extension of the empire. Her reign is second only to that of Peter the Great in importance.

[*Memoirs of the Empress Catherine II.* (Eng. trans. 1859); *Romance of an Empress*, by Waliszewski (1893; 14th ed. 1902).]

Catherine de' Medici (*mā'dē-chē*) (1519–89), Queen of France; daughter of Lorenzo de' Medici; wife of Henry II. and mother of Francis II., Charles IX., and Henry III. During the rule of her three sons she was all-powerful. An inveterate foe of Protestants; responsible for murder of Admiral de Coligny and massacre of St. Bartholomew; was fearless, treacherous, and relentless, but a great patron of the arts.

[*Catherine de' Medici and the French Reformation*, by E. Sichel (1905); *Catherine de' Medici*, by P. Van Dyke (1923).]

Catilina (*kä-ti-lē'nä*) (or CATILINE), LUCIUS SERGIUS (*c.* 108–62 B.C.), Rom. conspirator; member of an impoverished patrician family; organized a revolutionary plot, 63 B.C., frustrated by the vigilance of Cicero. He fell in the conflict.

Ca'to. (1) MARCUS PORCIUS (234–149 B.C.), the Censor; Rom. statesman; capable and efficient soldier; consul, 195; resisted foreign influences in Rome, and earnestly desired a return to the simplicity and severity of ancient Rom. life. Of his writings only his *De Rustica* is extant. (2) MARCUS PORCIUS (95–46 B.C.) of Utica, grandson of above; a Stoic distinguished for stern morality in a corrupt age. In the war between Cæsar and Pompey attached himself to cause of latter, and finding position hopeless at Utica, advised surrender of city, and stabbed himself; he is subject of a tragedy by Addison.

Cats, JACOB (1577–1660), Dutch poet; *b.* Zeeland; familiarly known as 'Father Cats'; ambassador to London, 1627; was knighted by Charles I. Author of several vols. of poetry, moral and didactic in tone.

Cattermole, GEORGE (1800–68), Eng. artist; *b.* near Diss, Norfolk; chiefly known as a water-colour painter and book illustrator; illustrated Britton's *English Cathedrals* (1816); Waverley Novels; *Master Humphrey's Clock* (1840–41), etc.

Catull'us, GAIUS VALERIUS (*c.* 87–54 B.C.), great Rom. lyric poet; his works consist of 116 poems, greater number being brief lyrics. Perhaps most perfect are addressed to Clodia, sister prob ably of Publius Clodius Pulcher, whom he immortalized as 'Lesbia.'

[*Poems*, trans. by Sir William Morris (1929); *Catullus and his Influence*, by K. P. Harrington (1923).]

Caulaincourt (*kō-lan-koor'*), ARMAND AUGUSTIN LOUIS, MARQUIS DE (1772–1827), Fr. general and statesman; rose to eminence under Napoleon, who made him Duke of Vicenza. Accompanied the emperor in the Russ. campaign. Foreign minister during Hundred Days. His memoirs appeared as *Souvenirs du Duc de Vicence* (1837–40).

Cavagnari (*kä-vän-yä'rē*), SIR PIERRE LOUIS NAPOLEON (1841–79), Brit. military administrator; *b.* Stenay (France), naturalized as Englishman, 1857, and entered East India Co.'s service; deputy-commissioner of Peshawar, 1877; appointed government resident at Kabul, where he was murdered by Afghans.

Cavaignac (*kä-vān-yäk'*), LOUIS EUGÈNE (1802–57), Fr. general; *b.* Paris; won distinction in Algeria, where he was appointed gov.-gen., 1848. Returning to Paris in same year, having been elected to the National Assembly, he quelled formidable insurrection (June 23–26). He was a candidate for the presidency of the republic, but was defeated by Louis Napoleon.

Cavalier (*kä-väl-yā'*), JEAN (1681–1740), Fr. Prot. leader; in 1702 headed revolt of Protestants of Cevennes against Louis XIV., and by his military genius won extraordinary success; later joined Eng. service, fought at Almanza, 1707, became general, and was appointed lieut.-gov. of Jersey.

Cav'an, FREDERICK RUDOLF LAMBART, EARL OF (1865–), Brit. soldier; served in S. African War; in Great War commanded 14th Corps, Brigade of Guards (subsequently Guards Division); was in charge of operations on the Piave front, 1918. Appointed to Aldershot command, 1920; chief of Imperial General Staff, 1922–26; field-marshal, 1932.

Cave, EDWARD (1691–1754), Eng. publisher; *b.* Newton, Warwickshire; founded, 1731, and ed. (as 'Sylvanus Urban, Gent.') the *Gentleman's Magazine*. He gave Dr. Johnson his first literary employment.

Cave, GEORGE, 1ST VISCOUNT (1856–1928), K.C., 1901; M.P., 1906–19; solicitor-general, 1915–16; home secretary, 1916–19; carried through Representation of People Act; lord of appeal, 1919; lord chancellor, 1922–24, and again from Nov. 1924.

Cavell, EDITH LOUISA (1865–1915), Eng. nurse; *b.* Swardeston, Norfolk; became head of Birkendael Medical Institute, Brussels, 1907; continued her work during Ger. occupation of Belgium; with others she formed organization for helping Allied soldiers to escape into Holland; denounced by a renegade, sentenced to death and shot; Amer. minister pleaded for her life in vain. Her body was removed to Norwich Cathedral, 1919. A statue in her memory stands in St. Martin's Lane, London.

Cavendish, LORD FREDERICK (1836–82), Brit. statesman, second son of 7th Duke of Devonshire; chief secretary for Ireland, 1882; assassinated in Phœnix Park, Dublin.

Cavendish, GEORGE (1500–62 ?), Eng. historian; in service of Cardinal Wolsey, 1526–30, and wrote his life (pub. 1641), the only authentic record of many contemporary events; MS. was probably used by Shakespeare for his part of *Henry VIII.*

Cavendish, HENRY (1731–1810), Eng. chemist and physicist; enormously wealthy, he devoted his life to scientific study and research; discovered hydrogen, 1766; demonstrated composition of water and of nitric acid; determined density of the earth.

[*The Scientific Papers of the Honourable Henry Cavendish, F.R.S.*, in 2 vols., ed. by Sir J. Larmor and Sir Edward Thorpe (1921).]

Cavendish (or CANDISH), THOMAS (1560–92), Eng. navigator; sailed with Grenville to Virginia, 1585; sailed from Plymouth, 1586, and was third circumnavigator of the globe.

Cavour (*kä-voor'*), CAMILLO BENSO, COUNT (1810–61), Ital. statesman; *b.* Turin; educated for army, but his Liberal opinions proving incompatible with a military career, he retired, 1831; took up agriculture, and did much to improve economic conditions of Piedmont; in 1847 founded a newspaper, *Risorgimento*, to advocate his ideas of constitutional and social reform; entered politics, 1848, and was successively minister of agriculture, commerce, marine, and finance; became premier, 1851. In 1858 he entered into a secret treaty with Napoleon III. with a view to driving the Austrians out of Italy; he encouraged the efforts of Garibaldi, and lived to see what had been the dream and struggle of his life—a united Italy.

[*Life and Times*, by W. R. Thayer (1911); *Cavour*, by G. M. Paléologue (1926).]

Caxton, WILLIAM (*c.* 1422–91), first Eng. printer; *b.* in the Weald of Kent; apprenticed to a London mercer; went to Bruges, and became governor of the Eng. Merchant Adventurers in the Low Countries; entered the service of Margaret, Duchess of Burgundy, sister of Edward IV.; learned the art of printing; returned to England, 1476, and set up his printing-press in the Almonry of Westminster. His first book printed in England was the *Dictes and Sayings of the Philosophers* (1477); but he had already printed in English at Bruges the *Recuyell of the Historyes of Troye* (1474), and the *Game and Playe of Chesse.* He printed the principal works of Chaucer, Gower, Lydgate, and Sir Thomas Malory's *Morte d'Arthur*, and was himself a busy translator.

[*Life and Typography of William Caxton*, by W. Blades (1861–63).]

Cay'ley, ARTHUR (1821–95), Eng. mathematician; *b.* Richmond, Surrey; senior wrangler, Cambridge, 1842; prof. of mathematics, Cambridge, 1863–95; his papers prove him to be one of the greatest of mathematicians.

Cazin (*ka-zan'*), JEAN CHARLES (1840–1901), Fr. landscape artist; *b.* in Pas-de-Calais; best-known works, *Flight into Egypt*, *Ishmael*, *Dusk*, and *A Dead City.*

Cecil, noble Eng. family. WILLIAM CECIL, Lord Burghley, Queen Elizabeth's great minister (see BURGHLEY), married (1) Mary Cheke, through whom are descended the Marquesses of Exeter; (2) Mildred Cooke, through whom are descended the Marquesses of Salisbury, 1605.

Cecil OF CHELWOOD, EDGAR ALGERNON ROBERT, 1ST VISCOUNT (1864–), third son of 3rd Marquess of Salisbury; K.C., 1900; M.P. E. Marylebone, 1906–10, Hitchin Division, 1911–23; during Great War was minister of blockade, 1916–18; has devoted himself mainly to the cause of World Peace; strong advocate of the League of Nations, on the Council of which he has frequently served; was awarded the Wilson Peace Prize of £5,000, 1924.

Cecil, Lord Hugh Richard Heathcote (1869–), fifth son of 3rd Marquess of Salisbury; fellow of Hertford Coll., Oxford; M.P. Greenwich, 1895–1906, Oxford Univ. since 1910; lieutenant, R.F.C., 1915; P.C., 1918; distinguished for high Christian idealism; one of most influential private members of House of Commons.

Cecilia, St., patron saint of the blind and of music; festival, Nov. 22; said to have suffered martyrdom in Sicily, *c.* 176.

Cellini (*chel-ē'nē*), Benvenuto (1500–71), Ital. artist, metalworker and sculptor; *b.* Florence; apprenticed to a goldsmith; showed great genius as a metalworker under patronage of Pope Clement VII., but his penchant for brawling led to his constant change of domicile, and he lived at Paris, Siena, Pisa, Rome, and Florence, changing his profession as often as his place of residence. His greatest work as sculptor is the bronze group, *Perseus holding the Head of Medusa*, in the Loggia dei Lanzi, Florence. His brilliant *Autobiography* is an admirable picture of the man and of the Renaissance times.

[*Life*, by J. A. Symonds (5th ed. 1903), including trans. of Cellini's *Autobiography*.]

Celsius (*sel'si-us*), Anders (1701–44), Swed. physicist; *b.* Uppsala, where he was prof. of astronomy, 1730–44; measured arc of the meridian in Lapland; devised centigrade thermometer; wrote works on astronomy.

Cenci (*chen'chē*), Beatrice (1577–99), Ital. girl, famous for her tragic history; *b.* Rome. Her father, Francesco Cenci, a man of great wealth and an adjudged criminal, after treating his family with great cruelty, particularly his wife and daughter, was murdered by assassins hired by his wife Lucrezia, Beatrice, and his son Giacomo, who were executed by order of Pope Clement VIII. Beatrice is immortalized in Shelley's tragedy *The Cenci.*

Centlivre (*sent-lē'ver*), Susan (*c.* 1667–1723), Eng. dramatist; some of her comedies are still played; among the best are *The Gamester* (1705), *The Busybody* (1709), and *The Wonder! A Woman keeps a Secret* (1714).

Cernuschi (*cher-noo'shē*), Henri (1821–96), Ital. economist; *b.* Milan; spent most of life in France; specialist on bimetallism (the term was coined by him).

Cervan'tes Saave'dra, Miguel de (1547–1616), Span. novelist, dramatist, and poet; *b.* Alcalá de Henares, near Madrid; entered service of Cardinal Acquaviva, and went with him to Rome. Enlisted, 1570, as a private soldier, serving under Don John of Austria; wounded at battle of Lepanto, 1571, took part in naval battle off Navarino, 1572, and was at the capture of Tunis, 1573. When returning to Spain, 1575, the fleet in which he sailed was captured by Algerine pirates, and Cervantes became the slave of a Gr. renegade. After five years his family secured his freedom by ransom. Being crippled, he was unable for military service, and turned to literature. His first publication was a pastoral romance, *Galatea* (1585). At this time he married. He now produced between twenty and thirty plays, but achieved little success. He was appointed deputy-purveyor to the fleet at Seville, 1587, and then collector of revenues in Granada, 1594. In 1597 he was imprisoned at Seville because of a monetary deficiency, but was eventually released. It is believed that during his imprisonment his world-famous romance, *Don Quixote*, was begun. The first part was pub. at Madrid, 1605. It was a satire upon the romances of the period, and met with instant success. The second part appeared in 1615, and contains the author's most mature work.

[*Complete Works*, ed. J. Fitzmaurice-Kelly (1901–6); *Lives*, by J. Fitzmaurice-Kelly (1913), A. F. Calvert (1905), and R. Schevill (1919).]

Cerve'ra, Pascual Cervera y Topete (1839–1909), Span. admiral; *b.* Medina-Sidonia; commanded a squadron in Span.-Amer. War, 1898, which was destroyed at Santiago de Cuba. He was afterwards tried, but was acquitted.

Cespedes (*thās'pe-thāz*), Pablo de (1538–1608), Span. artist and poet; *b.* Cordoba; a fine specimen of his work is a *Last Supper*. He also wrote a poem on *The Art of Painting*, considered the best didactic verse in Spanish.

Cezanne (*se-zän'*), Paul (1839–1906), Fr. painter; *b.* Aix-en-Provence; one of the leaders of the revolutionary movement in art; after passing through a phase of impressionism evolved a style of his own. His work shows strength and harmony of colour, and attempts to express the depth of modelling absent from the work of the impressionist; since his death his fame has been steadily growing.

Chabrier (*shab-rē-ā'*), Alexis Emmanuel (1841–94), Fr. composer. Of his operas *Gwendoline* was produced at Brussels, 1886, and *Le Roi malgré lui* at the Opéra-Comique, 1887.

Chadwick, Sir Edwin (1800–90), Eng. social reformer; *b.* near Manchester; assistant to Jeremy Bentham; assisted in drafting Poor Law report, 1834; issued report on 'Sanitary Condition of the Labouring Population,' 1842; was commissioner of Board of Health, 1848–54; formed Social Science Association, 1878.

Chaillé Long (*shä-yā' long*), Charles (1842–1917), Amer. soldier, explorer, and diplomat; *b.* in Maryland; joined army of Khedive of Egypt, 1869, and was chief of staff to General Gordon in Egyptian Sudan; navigated the unknown Victoria Nile, and solved the problem of the Nile sources; retired from army, 1877; U.S.A. consul-general and secretary of legation to Korea, 1887–9.

Chaliapin (*shäl-yä'pin*), Fyodor Ivanovich (1873–), Russ. singer; *b.* Kazan; made his first public appearance in opera in Tiflis, 1892; joined the Russ. Imperial Troupe, 1895, and later sang at the Imperial Opera House, St. Petersburg; appeared in London, 1913; till 1921 remained in Russia; has since appeared frequently both in London and in America; now resident in France; has superb bass voice and fine dramatic powers. Pub. memoirs *Man and Mask* (1932).

Chalmers, George Paul (1833–78), Scot. painter; *b.* Montrose; his best works are *The End of the Harvest* (1873), *Running Water* (1875), and *The Legend* (National Gallery, Edinburgh).

Chalmers, James (1841–1901), Scot. missionary; *b.* Ardrishaig, Argyll; laboured under London Missionary Soc. at Raratonga, S. Pacific, and at New Guinea, where R. L. Stevenson met him; killed by cannibals.

[*Autobiography and Letters* (1902).]

Chalmers, Thomas (1780–1847), eminent Scot. divine; *b.* Anstruther; ministered at Kilmany (Fife) and later at Glasgow, where he became a noted preacher, and was singularly successful in dealing with the problem of poverty, his experiments suggesting the methods now followed by modern social agencies; prof. of moral philosophy at St. Andrews, 1823, and of divinity at Edinburgh, 1828; chief promoter and first moderator of Free Church of Scotland, 1843.

[*Memoirs*, by W. Hanna (4 vols., 1849–52); *Life*, by Mrs. Oliphant (1893).]

Chamberlain. (1) JOSEPH (1836–1914), Brit. statesman; *b.* London; joined his cousin, Joseph Nettlefold, in a screw-making business in Birmingham; retired from business, 1874, and devoted his energies to public work; as mayor of Birmingham, 1873–6, transformed the city, municipalized gas and water supply, erected improved municipal buildings, abolished much slum property, laid out open spaces for recreation; returned unopposed as M.P. for Birmingham as John Bright's colleague, 1876. He entered Gladstone's cabinet as president of Board of Trade, 1880. Objecting to Gladstone's Home Rule policy he resigned his seat in the cabinet, 1886, and became leader of the 'Liberal Unionists.' In 1895 he became colonial secretary in Lord Salisbury's cabinet, and advocated old age pensions. As a strong believer in imperial federation he 'breathed a new spirit' into the colonial office. He conducted negotiations with the S. African republics previous to the war of 1899–1902. When Balfour became premier, 1902, Chamberlain again became colonial secretary, but withdrew, 1903, having adopted 'Tariff Reform,' which divided the Unionist party. In 1906 he ceased to take an active part in public life owing to illness. He was instrumental in founding Birmingham Univ., 1900, and became its first chancellor.

[*Life*, by Viscount Milner (1912) and by J. L. Garvin (1932).]

(2) (JOSEPH) AUSTEN (1863–), Eng. statesman, eldest son of above; M.P. for E. Worcestershire, 1892–1914, and W. Birmingham since 1914; has been civil lord of Admiralty, financial secretary to Treasury, postmaster-general, chancellor of Exchequer, 1903–6, secretary of state for India, 1915–17; member of war cabinet, 1918; again chancellor of Exchequer in 1919. He was secretary for foreign affairs, 1924–29, and was largely responsible for the Treaty of Locarno, 1925, which did much for post-war reconciliation. For his services in the cause of peace he received the Garter and was awarded the Nobel Prize, 1925.

(3) (ARTHUR) NEVILLE (1869–), Brit. statesman; second son of (1); lord mayor of Birmingham, 1915–16; M.P. since 1918; during Great War acted as director-general of National Service, 1916–17; has since held various cabinet offices in the Conservative governments of 1922–4 and 1924–9, including Ministry of Health, 1923 and 1924–9, when he was responsible for Housing and Rent Restriction Acts, Rating and Valuation, and Pensions Acts; established himself as capable administrator; chancellor of the Exchequer in National Government since 1931, and was responsible for the Tariff Act of 1932.

Chambers, SIR EDMUND KERCHEVER (1866–), Eng. scholar; *b.* Berkshire; chief works authoritative on their subject are *The Medieval Stage* (1903) and *The Elizabethan Stage* (1923); other works include *Shakespeare: A Survey* (1925) and *William Shakespeare* (2 vols., 1930).

Chambers. (1) WILLIAM (1800–83), Scot. publisher; *b.* Peebles; with his brother Robert founded firm, W. and R. Chambers; began publication of *Chambers's Journal*, 1832; famed for public munificence; twice Lord Provost of Edinburgh. (2) ROBERT (1802–71), Scot. author and publisher, brother of above; *b.* Peebles; opened a bookstall in Edinburgh, 1818; later joined (1) as partner; author of *Traditions of Edinburgh* (1824), *History of the Rebellions in Scotland* (1828), *Book of Days* (1862–4). An ardent geologist, his *Vestiges of the Natural History of Creation* (1846) anticipates many of the theories of Darwin.

[*Memoirs* (13th ed. 1884).]

Chambers, Sir William (1726–96), Brit. architect; *b.* Stockholm; educated in England; spent some years in China, acquiring a knowledge of the art and architecture of that country; later studied architecture in Paris and Italy. He designed many houses for the nobility, the buildings at Kew (of which the pagoda remains), and Somerset House, 1775.

Chambord (*shon-bor'*), Henri Charles Dieudonné, Comte de (1820–83), son of Duc de Berri; grandson of Charles x.; *b.* Paris; claimed Fr. crown and title of Henry v.; married Archduchess Maria Theresa, but had no issue.

Chamfort (*shon-for'*), Sebastien Roch Nicolas (1741–94), Fr. author; *b.* in Auvergne; took active part in the Revolution; is chiefly remembered by his *Maximes et Pensées.*

Chamisso (*shä-mē'sō*), Adalbert von (1781–1838), Ger. poet and botanist; *b.* in Champagne; his lyrical poems were set to music by Schumann. He wrote *Peter Schlemihl* (1814), a weird tale (trans. into Eng.), and numerous botanical treatises.

Champlain (*shon'plan'*), Samuel de (1567–1635), Fr. explorer and first Fr. governor of Canada; *b.* near Rochefort; explored St. Lawrence, 1603; founded Quebec, 1608; discovered Lake Champlain, 1609, and established thriving fur trade; made trading settlement, 1611, at Mount Royal (Montreal). Was carried as prisoner to England on Brit. capture of Quebec, 1629, but when Treaty of St. Germain, 1632, restored Fr. Can. possessions, resumed post as governor.

[*Life*, by Dionne (1905), and by Flenly (1924); *Champlain's Voyages*, by A. N. and E. G. Bourne (1906).]

Champollion (*shon-pol-yon'*), Jean François (1790–1832), Fr. Egyptologist; *b.* at Figeac, Lot; prof. of Egyptology, Coll. de France, 1831; a pioneer in study of Egyptian hieroglyphics; discovered the twenty-five letters mentioned by Plutarch in the Rosetta inscription; pub. *Précis du Système Hiéroglyphique*, etc.

Chancellor, Richard (*d.* 1556), Eng. navigator; commanded the *Bonaventure* in the search for a N.E. Passage to India under Sir Hugh Willoughby. He sailed to Russia, went overland to Moscow, and his friendly reception caused Queen Mary to dispatch an embassy there, and later to establish the Muscovy Trading Co.

Chan'dos, Sir John (*d.* 1369), Eng. military commander; fought at Cambrai, 1337, Crécy, 1346, Poitiers, 1356, where he saved life of the Black Prince. He was held in great estimation by Edward iii., who made him a Knight of the Garter and seneschal of Poitou. He was killed at Lussac

Chandragup'ta (*c.* 316–292 b.c.), first Emperor of India of the Maurya dynasty, whose dominions extended from the Hindu-Kush to the Bay of Bengal.

Chang Chih-tung (1837–1909), Chin. statesman and scholar; *b.* in province of Chihli; intensely patriotic, but quite unpractical; unrivalled in his knowledge of the Chin. classics; his *China's Only Hope* had great influence on the 1898 Reform movement, and produced complete revolution in Chin. education.

Chang Tso-Lin (1873–1928),

Chin. military leader; *b.* in province of Fengtien; of humble origin, became leader of Manchurian brigands and supported the Japanese during Russo-Jap. War; military governor of Fengtien, 1913; a strong supporter of the new republic in China; governor of Manchuria, 1918, and made it best-governed province of China.

Channing, WILLIAM ELLERY (1780–1842), Amer. Unitarian preacher and author; *b.* Newport, Rhode Island; noted for his denunciation of war and slavery, and his advocacy of all social reforms; visited England, 1822–23, and became friend of Wordsworth and Coleridge.

Chantrey, SIR FRANCIS LEGATT (1782–1841), Eng. sculptor; *b.* near Sheffield; as a wood-carver in his early years acquired a knowledge of painting and sculpture; exhibited a head of Satan at the Royal Academy, 1808, and quickly rose to fame; R.A., 1818; knighted, 1835. One of his finest conceptions is his well-known *Sleeping Children* in Lichfield Cathedral. Among his best-known works are his statues of George Washington, at Boston, George III., in London Guildhall, Pitt, in Hanover Square, London. Chantrey left the bulk of his fortune in trust to the Royal Academy for the 'purchase of works of fine art' by Brit. artists, or by foreign artists who have completed their work within the United Kingdom.

[*Life*, by A. J. Raymond (1904).]

Chapelain (*shäp-lan'*), JEAN (1595–1674), Fr. critic and poet; *b.* Paris; played a great part in founding the Academy, and in the establishment in Fr. drama of the rules of the 'three unities.' His best work was *Sentiments de l'Académie sur le Cid.*

Chaplin, CHARLES SPENCER (1889–), film actor and producer; *b.* London; visited U.S.A., 1910, with touring company and began his film career at Hollywood; his first film, 1913, was an immediate success, and before long his eccentric costume and mannerisms were familiar in every country in the world. Among his most successful films have been *Shoulder Arms* (1918), *The Kid* (1921), *The Gold Rush* (1925), and *City Lights* (1931).

Chapman, FRANK MICHLER (1864–), Amer. ornithologist; *b.* at Englewood, New Jersey; curator of Department of Ornithology in Amer. Museum of Natural History, New York, since 1908; has done much collecting in Canada, Mexico, W. Indies, and S. America; publications include *Bird Life, a Guide to the Study of our Common Birds* (1897), *The Economic Value of Birds to the State* (1903), *The Travels of Birds* (1916).

Chapman, GEORGE (1559–1634), Eng. dramatist and translator; plays include *Bussy d'Ambois*, *Eastward Hoe* (with Ben Jonson). His greatest work is a trans. of the *Iliad* (1611); also the *Odyssey* (1616).

Chapone, HESTER (1727–1801), Eng. letter-writer and essayist; *b.* at Twywell, Northants; admirer and correspondent of Samuel Richardson; her *Letters on the Improvement of the Mind* (1772) had great vogue in female educational circles.

Chappell, WILLIAM (1809–88), Eng. musical antiquary, partner in Messrs. Chappell and Co., music publishers; noted for collections—*Popular Music of the Olden Time* (1855–9) and *Roxburghe Ballads* (1869); pub. also *History of Music* (1874).

Chaptal (*shäp-täl'*), JEAN ANTOINE, COMTE DE CHANTELOUP (1756–1832), Fr. chemist and statesman; *b.* Nogaret, Lozère; prof. of chemistry, Montpellier,

1781; minister of interior, 1800–4, minister of commerce, 1811; founded Fr. Chamber of Commerce; began canalization of Fr. rivers; introduced the metric system of weights and measures; made valuable investigations in alum and soda.

Chapu (*shä-poo'*), HENRI (1833–91), Fr. sculptor; *b.* in Seine-et-Marne; while essentially modern in his treatment, did not discard classical traditions. The most typical examples of his work are his *Princess Hélène at the Tomb of the Duc d'Orléans*, at Dreux, and *Youth*, a memorial to Henri Regnault.

Charcot (*shär-kō'*), JEAN BAPTISTE ETIENNE AUGUSTE (1867–), Fr. explorer; *b.* Neuilly; studied medicine but turned to Antarctic exploration; leader of Fr. expeditions, 1903–5 and 1908–10; accounts of these expeditions will be found in his *La Français au Pôle Sud* (1905) and '*Le Pourquoi pas?' dans Antarctique* (1910).

Charcot, JEAN MARTIN (1825–93), Fr. physician; *b.* Paris; prof. of pathological anatomy, Univ. of Paris, 1860; made valuable investigations on neurology, hypnotism, etc.; best-known works are *Leçons sur les maladies du système nerveux* (5 vols., 1872–93) and *Leçons du mardi à la Salpêtrière* (2 vols., 1889–90); extraordinarily successful and influential as a teacher.

Chard, JOHN ROUSE MERRIOTT (1847–97), colonel and V.C.; *b.* near Plymouth; the defender of Rorke's Drift in the Zulu War, 1879. His action saved Natal from invasion.

Chardin (*shär-dan'*), JEAN BAPTISTE SIMÉON (1699–1779), Fr. painter; *b.* Paris; departed from tradition of his time by painting domestic subjects, such as *Le Bénédicité*; noted also for his still-life paintings.

Chardin, SIR JOHN (1643–1713), Fr. traveller, son of a Paris jeweller; travelled as a gem-dealer in Persia; settled in London, 1681; knighted by Charles II., and appointed court jeweller; buried in Westminster Abbey.

Charlemagne (*shärl-män'*), CHARLES THE GREAT, or CHARLES I. (742–814), King of the Franks and Emperor, and perhaps greatest figure of the Middle Ages; son of Pepin the Short; on death of his brother Carloman, 771, became sole King of the Franks. In 772 began his thirty years' warfare against the Saxons. Went to the aid of Pope Adrian I. against the Lombard king. Crossed the Alps and conquered Lombardy, 774, which he added to his possessions. He won a victory over the Saxons, who acknowledged him as their king; was called to Spain, 778, as intermediary between the Moors and Arabs, and secured considerable territory. On Christmas Day, 800, Charlemagne was crowned Emperor by Pope Leo III., thus originating the Holy Rom. Empire. Devoted rest of his life to consolidation of his empire, codification of the laws, and encouragement of education under Alcuin; buried at his capital, Aachen. As a soldier his successes were due rather to his ability as an organizer than to personal brilliance in the field. His exploits, real and imaginary, are the subject of an extensive cycle of romance.

[*Life*, by Hodgkin (1897); *Charlemagne, Charles the Great, The Hero of Two Nations*, by H. W. C. Davies (1900).]

Charles I. (1600–49), King of Great Britain and Ireland; second son of James I.; *b.* Dunfermline; succeeded 1625, and married Henrietta Maria of France in the same year. His belief in the divine right of kings involved him in a struggle with Parliament. He was forced to accept a Petition of Right, which protested against forced loans, arbitrary imprisonment, etc. Dissolving Parliament in 1629, Charles attempted absolute rule for eleven years, raising money by exactions such as ship money, and also compelling Calvinists to conform to Episcopacy. This latter policy led to rebellion in Scotland, 1639. Advised by Strafford, he summoned a Parliament (Short Parliament, 1640), which refused supplies, and was dissolved; but in the same year he again summoned Parliament (Long Parliament). Charles consented to various reforms, and was forced to sign a bill of attainder against Strafford, who was beheaded, 1641. A massacre of Protestants in Ireland evoked from the Commons the Grand Remonstrance. Following an attempt to arrest five members in the House of Commons, 1642, civil war broke out. The first two campaigns were indecisive. In 1644 the Parliamentary army, remodelled by Cromwell, and aided by a Scot. army, inflicted a severe defeat on the Royalists at Marston Moor, and in 1645 the cause of Charles received its death-blow at Naseby. In 1646 Charles sought the protection of the Scots, who surrendered him to the Eng. Parliament. After three years in prison, he was finally tried and executed, 1649, meeting his fate with dignity. Charles was a pattern of all the private virtues, but in public affairs he was weak, obstinate, and tortuous in his methods.

[*Life*, by E. B. Chancellor (1886); *The Royal Martyr*, by C. W. Coit (1925).]

Charles II. (1630–85), King of Great Britain and Ireland; son of Charles I.; *b.* London; after Civil War retired to France; landed in Scotland, 1650, and, having signed the Covenants, was crowned at Scone, 1651. Charles marched into England, but was defeated at Worcester, fled to France, and wandered over W. Europe till the Restoration, 1660. His attempt to procure religious toleration was unsuccessful. Episcopacy was re-established in Scotland and the Covenanters persecuted. He dismissed his great minister Clarendon to satisfy popular discontent at the Dutch War, 1665–7. Clarendon was succeeded by the Cabal ministry, during which was made the secret Treaty of Dover that bound Charles hand and foot to Louis XIV. An Exclusion Bill was introduced debarring Rom. Catholics from reigning, but Charles's astuteness secured its defeat. He died a Rom. Catholic. He was profligate, untrustworthy, thoroughly insincere; but he knew when to bend to public opinion, and this pliability, coupled with geniality and an air of frankness, secured his popularity, and this despite the fact that his reign was probably one of the worst in Eng. history.

[*Charles II.*, by O. Airy (1904).]

Charles I., HOLY ROM. EMPEROR. See CHARLEMAGNE.

Charles II., THE BALD (823–77), Holy Rom. Emperor and King of the West Franks; son of Louis the Pious; succeeded 843; nominal ruler of Aquitaine and Brittany.

Charles III., THE FAT (832–88), Holy Rom. Emperor and King of the West Franks, nephew of Charles the Bald; was crowned Rom. emperor by Pope John VIII. in 881, but was deposed by his nobles, 887.

Charles IV. (1316–78), Holy Rom. Emperor and King of Bohemia; fought at Crécy, 1346, where his father, King John, was killed; largely extended Bohemian territory; noted for the wisdom of his government; founded first Ger. univ. at Prague, 1348, and promoted agriculture and industry.

Charles V. (1500–58), Holy Rom. Emperor and King of Spain (Charles I.); *b.* Ghent; son of Philip of Burgundy and Joanna, daughter of Ferdinand and Isabella. From his father he inherited the Low Country dominions and Burgundy, and through his mother inherited Spain and Naples. On the death of Ferdinand, 1516, Charles was recognized as joint ruler of Spain with his mother; and on the death of his paternal grandfather, the Emperor Maximilian, in 1519, he was elected Emperor of Germany. Charles was now the most influential political figure of his time, and the rivalry between himself and Francis I. of France dominated the history of W. Europe. The French were driven out of Italy. In 1525 Francis again entered Italy, but was taken prisoner at Pavia, and was only released on resigning all his claims and pretensions. In this year, 1526, Charles married Isabella, sister of John III. of Portugal. Like his son, Philip II., Charles was a relentless opponent of Lutheranism. The Peace of Augsburg, 1555, however, compelled him to acquiesce in the establishment of Protestantism over the greater part of Germany. This blow to his hopes, and his declining health, led to his abdication in favour of his son Philip, 1556, and he retired to the monastery of San Yuste, in Estremadura.

[*History of Emperor Charles V.*, by Robertson; *Life*, by E. Armstrong (2 vols., 1902).]

Charles VI. (1685–1740), Holy Rom. Emperor; son of Emperor Leopold I.; his claim to the throne of Spain brought about the War of the Span. Succession. He was proclaimed emperor, 1711, on the death of his brother, Joseph I. A campaign against Turkey ended disastrously. He secured the succession to his daughter, Maria Theresa, by the Pragmatic Sanction.

Charles VII. (1697–1745), Holy Rom. Emperor; son of Elector Maximilian Emmanuel of Bavaria, whom he succeeded, 1726; was one of the claimants in the War of the Austrian Succession. Elected emperor, 1742, but was eventually driven even from Bavaria; restored by Frederick the Great, but died a few months later.

Charles III., THE SIMPLE (879–929), King of France; son of Louis 'the Stammerer'; chiefly notable for the treaty, 911, by which he conferred upon Rollo the hereditary dukedom of Normandy. His nobles revolted, and Charles was imprisoned till his death.

Charles IV., THE FAIR (1294–1328), King of France; youngest son of Philip IV.; succeeded his brother, Philip V., 1322; hampered by lack of revenue, he put public offices to auction. Aided his sister Isabella in the overthrow of her husband, Edward II. of England. Was the last of the direct line of Capetian kings.

Charles V., THE WISE (1337–80), King of France; son of John II., who was captured at Poitiers, 1356. Acted as regent during his father's captivity, came to the throne, 1364, and cleared the country of mercenaries by dispatching them against the English in Spain; drove the English out of the greater part of France. Charles gave France a navy, encouraged commerce, restricted the power of the nobles, built the Bastille, erected palaces, and made a valuable collection of books and articles of vertu.

Charles VI., LE BIEN-AIMÉ (1368–1422), King of France; son of Charles V.; succeeded his father when twelve; married Isabeau of Bavaria, 1385, and was crowned in 1389. Henry v. of England revived the Eng. claim to Fr. throne, won the victory of Agincourt, 1415, and compelled Charles to sign Treaty of Troyes. Charles was subject to fits of insanity, and during the latter part of his reign the country was distracted by civil war between the Burgundians and the Armagnacs.

Charles VII., THE INDOLENT, later the VICTORIOUS (1403–61), King of France; son of Charles VI.; his title to the throne of France was disputed by Henry VI. of England, until the successes of Joan of Arc eventually gave Charles rule over the entire kingdom. It is to his lasting shame that he made no effort to save Joan from her fate.

Charles VIII. (1470–98), King of France; son of Louis XI.; succeeded at age of thirteen; married Duchess Anne of Brittany, 1491, thus adding Brittany to Fr. kingdom; was vain and worthless king; invaded Italy, but was forced to retire, though he won during his retreat a brilliant victory at Fornovo, 1495.

Charles IX. (1550–74), King of France; third son of Henry II. and Catherine de' Medici; succeeded his brother, Francis II., 1560. His mother persuaded him to sanction the Massacre of St. Bartholomew. Remorse for this act probably shortened his life.

Charles X. (1757–1836), King of France; reigned 1824–30; younger brother of Louis XVI. and Louis XVIII.; before accession known as Comte d'Artois. His youth was marked by dissipation; succeeded Louis XVIII., but his short reign involved him in frequent troubles with his people; abdicated, 1830.

Charles I. OF SPAIN. See CHARLES V.

Charles II. (1661–1700), King of Spain; son of Philip IV.; was feeble-minded; the last Habsburg to occupy the Span. throne. His death without issue led to the War of the Span Succession.

Charles III. (1716–88), King of Spain; son of Philip V. and Elizabeth Farnese; succeeded his brother, Ferdinand VI., 1759; opposed England during Seven Years' War and Amer. War of Independence; showed a progressive domestic policy; introduced many reforms; expelled the Jesuits, reduced the Inquisition to inactivity; encouraged trade, and built many of the finest buildings of Spain.

Charles IV. (1748–1819), King of Spain; second son of Charles III. and Maria Amelia of Saxony; was probably the most foolish king of Spain; was practically a puppet in the hands of his wife, Maria Luisa of Parma, and her favourite, Emmanuel Godoy, who ruled the country. His fleet was destroyed at Trafalgar. He abdicated at Napoleon's suggestion, accepted a pension, and died at Rome.

Charles IX. (1550–1611), King of Sweden; son of Gustavus Vasa; was recognized as king in 1600; crowned 1607; engaged in wars with Russia and Denmark, which were continued by his son, Gustavus Adolphus. He aimed at the foundation of a great Prot. kingdom. A hard but capable ruler, he was hated by the nobility, but beloved by the common folk.

Charles X. (1622–60), King of Sweden; son of John Casimir of Zweibrücken and Catherine, daughter of Charles IX.; succeeded his cousin, Queen Christina, 1654. In 1655 overran Poland; later compelled the Elector of Brandenburg to surrender Pomerania; subsequently defeated the Poles in battle of Warsaw, July 28–30, 1656. Invaded Denmark, crossing both the Great and Little Belt over the ice with a large army, and forced the cession of great territories. Later, when attacking Copenhagen, he was beaten off; when preparing for a further war he died suddenly at Gothenburg.

Charles XI. (1655–97), King of Sweden; only son of Charles x. and Hedwig-Leonora of Holstein-Gottorp; was four years of age at his father's death. When he came of age, 1672, he threw himself diligently into the business of administration; after several reverses, won three great victories over Danes; curbed the power of the nobles; reformed finance, trade, church government, and education. At his death Sweden was stronger and richer than ever before.

Charles XII. (1682–1718), King of Sweden; son of Charles xi.; succeeded 1697. Russia, Denmark, and Poland combined in 1699 against him, but he landed near Copenhagen, and compelled the Dan. king to sue for peace. Next, with about 9,000 men, he routed 50,000 Russians at Narva, 1700. Then he proceeded against Poland, and dethroned Augustus ii. Invaded Russia, but was defeated at Poltava by Peter the Great, 1709, and took refuge in Turkey; returned to Sweden, but was killed while invading Norway. Charles had many characteristics which rendered him popular with the Swed. people. He was brave, despised rank, and shared with his soldiers all the hardships of war, but was absolutely callous, caring for nothing but military glory.

[*Lives*, by Bain (1895) and E. Godley (1928).]

Charles XIII. (1748–1818), King of Sweden and Norway; son of Adolphus Frederick, King of Sweden; acted as regent for his nephew, Gustavus iv., 1792–6, but had little real power; though elected king, 1809, all power was in the hands of Bernadotte (later Charles xiv.). In 1814 he became first king of a united Norway and Sweden.

Charles XIV. (1763–1844), King of Sweden and Norway; was a Frenchman whose name was Jean Baptiste Bernadotte; won speedy promotion during progress of Fr. Revolution; commander of army in La Vendée, 1800–1; made marshal of France under the empire; governor of Hanover, 1804–5. He was elected Crown Prince of Sweden and adopted as heir by Charles xiii., whom he succeeded, 1818; under his wise rule the financial condition of the country greatly improved.

Charles XV. (1826–72), King of Sweden and Norway; son of Oscar i.; succeeded 1859; made many reforms in administration; attempted to bring about closer union between Norway and Sweden and Denmark; attained eminence both as poet and artist.

Charles I. (1226–85), King of Naples and Sicily and Count of Anjou; son of Louis viii. of France, and brother of St. Louis; accompanied the latter on Sixth Crusade; received crown of Naples and Sicily from Pope Clement iv., 1266; made himself by conquest one of most powerful European sovereigns. But his greed, ambition, and cruelty raised up enemies everywhere. Died while preparing to crush rebellion in Sicily.

Charles, or Carol (1839–1914), King of Romania; Prince of Hohenzollern-Sigmaringen; elected Prince of Romania, 1866; proclaimed king, 1881, and by his administration greatly improved prestige of his country; married Princess Elizabeth of Wied, 1869, better known as 'Carmen Sylva'; was averse to hostile action against Germany in Great War.

Charles, Count of Valois (1270–1325), Fr. military leader;

distinguished himself in wars in Guienne and Flanders. His son became King of France as Philip VI., founding the Valois dynasty, 1328–1498.

Charles Albert (1798–1849), King of Sardinia; succeeded 1831; was liberally inclined, and hostile to Austria, though Mazzini distrusted him. He declared war on Austria, but was defeated at Novara, 1849, and abdicated in favour of his son, Victor Emmanuel, afterwards first King of Italy.

Charles Augustus (1757–1828), Grand-duke of Saxe-Weimar; patron of art, science, and letters; intimate friend of Goethe; first Ger. ruler to give subjects a constitution, 1816.

Charles Edward Stewart, PRINCE (1720–88), 'THE YOUNG PRETENDER,' son of James, 'Old Pretender'; *b.* at Rome; attempted, with Fr. help, invasion of England, but was driven back by storm, 1744; landed in Scotland, 1745, and obtained support of many Highland chiefs; defeated Cope at Prestonpans; took Carlisle; reached Derby; compelled to retreat by desertion of troops; marched north, defeating Hawley at Falkirk; was utterly defeated at Culloden by Duke of Cumberland, 1746. After five months' wandering escaped to France, whence he was expelled, 1748; wandered over Europe intriguing, but meeting with no success; married Louise of Stolberg, 1772; separated, 1784; *d.* Rome. Charles was brilliant, versatile, and courageous, but profligate; romantic interest attached to his name has formed subject of many Highland poems.

[*Lives*, by A. C. Ewald (2 vols., 1875), and C. S. Terry (1900).]

Charles Louis (1771–1847), Archduke of Austria, third son of Emperor Leopold II.; governor of Netherlands, 1790; fought at Jemappes and Neerwinden against French; appointed field-marshal to command the Austrian army of the Rhine, 1796, and had a series of remarkable victories. Appointed to command of Austrian forces; reorganized the army, and defeated Jourdan, but was beaten by Moreau near Zurich, and resigned. In 1805 again took command, and beat Masséna at Caldiero. He was now regarded by Napoleon as the greatest of his adversaries; he again commanded in 1809, and defeated Napoleon at Aspern. At Wagram he was wounded and defeated. An armistice followed, and resigning his command, he retired into private life, 1809.

Charles Martel, *i.e.* 'THE HAMMER' (*c.* 688–741), Frankish ruler; son of Pepin II.; mayor of the palace under the last Merovingian kings; was grandfather of Charlemagne; stemmed tide of Moslem conquest at Tours, 732, therefore regarded as the saviour of Christendom.

Charles the Bold (1433–77), Duke of Burgundy; son of Philip the Good; succeeded to the duchy in 1467. His ambition was to throw off allegiance to France and to restore the anc. kingdom of Burgundy, a policy which led to constant conflict with Louis XI. Successful at first, he was finally defeated and killed at Nancy.

[*Life*, by Putnam (1908).]

Charles, ELIZABETH (1828–96), Eng. novelist; *b.* Tavistock; wrote about fifty books, including *The Chronicles of the Schönberg-Cotta Family* (1864), which enjoyed an immense vogue.

Charlevoix (*shär-le-vwä'*), PIERRE FRANÇOIS XAVIER DE (1682–1761), Fr. Jesuit missionary and historian; *b.* St. Quentin; travelled in America and elsewhere. Writings include *Histoire de la Nouvelle France*, a work of great importance for Can. history.

Charpentier (*shär-pon-tyā'*), GUSTAVE (1860–), Fr. composer; *b.* in Lorraine; studied violin; best-known work, the romantic opera *Louise.*

Chartier (*shär-tyā'*), ALAIN (*c.* 1392–*c.* 1430), Fr. poet; *b.* Bayeux; was secretary to Charles VII.; famous for his poems, *Le Lay des Quatre Dames, La Belle Dame sans Merci,* etc. A prose work, *Le Curial,* was trans. by Caxton.

Chase, SALMON PORTLAND (1808–73), U.S.A. statesman; secretary of treasury under Lincoln (1861–64), and his most trusted adviser; chief justice from 1864; active supporter of anti-slavery movement; his banking law, 1863, is the basis of U.S.A. system.

Chastelard (*shät-lär'*), PIERRE DE BOSCOSEL DE (1540–63), Fr. poet; *b.* in Dauphiné; accompanied Mary Stewart to Scotland; nourished a hopeless passion for the queen, and having twice been discovered hiding in her room, was arrested and hanged.

Chateaubriand (*shä-tō-brē-on'*), FRANÇOIS RENÉ, VICOMTE DE (1768–1848), one of the greatest masters of Fr. prose; *b.* St. Malo; on outbreak of Revolution went to America to discover N.W. Passage; after arrest of Louis XVI. returned to France and joined the *émigrés*; left for dead at siege of Thionville, but revived and escaped to London, where he lived by teaching , here he wrote the romance *Atala* and his prose poem *Les Natchez,* which deal with Red Indian life; another story, *René,* appeared 1802. Though at first a sceptic, Chateaubriand's chief work, *Le Génie du Christianisme,* is a vindication of Christianity. Travelling in the Holy Land, he produced his *Itinéraire de Paris à Jérusalem,* and *Les Martyrs,* a prose epic of the days of Diocletian. He held diplomatic appointments under Napoleon, and later was ambassador at London, Berlin, and Rome.

[*Complete Works,* with introductory study by Sainte-Beuve (20 vols., 1858–61); *Mémoires* (trans. 1903).]

Chatham, WILLIAM PITT, 1ST EARL OF (1708–78), Brit. statesman; *b.* Westminster; entered army, but in 1735 became M.P. for Old Sarum, and in the Commons vigorously attacked Walpole. Later he became vice-treasurer of Ireland, and then paymaster-general. In 1756 he was appointed secretary of state and leader of the House, and though dismissed in 1757 was reinstated as practical though not nominal head of the government. The administration of 1757–61 is famous in Brit. history for the successes of Wolfe in Canada and Clive in India, and for the conduct of the Seven Years' War in which Pitt supported Frederick the Great. Went to the House of Lords as Earl of Chatham, 1766; resigned office, 1768, but appeared in House of Lords again, 1770; before his death vigorously opposed government policy towards America. A great orator and of unimpeachable integrity; in purely domestic politics he was not a success; in foreign affairs, however, he revived the glory of Britain, and may be regarded as our first real Imperialist.

[*Lives,* by B. Williams (2 vols., 1913) and A. von Ruville (Eng. trans., 3 vols., 1907); *Early Life of Chatham,* by Lord Rosebery (1910).]

Chatrian. See under ERCKMANN.

Chatterji, BANKIM CHANDRA (1838–94), Ind. novelist; his chief work is *Ananda Math,* containing a famous song, *Bande Mataram,* which has become the recognized war-song of the extremist party in Bengal.

Chatterton, THOMAS (1752–70), Eng. poet; *b.* at Bristol. When the new bridge was opened at Bristol, 1768, Chatterton wrote an alleged description of the opening of the earlier bridge by a 15th cent. monk, Thomas Rowley. Shortly afterwards he submitted to Horace Walpole specimens of poems by Rowley, which he claimed to have discovered in a muniment chest of the Church of St. Mary Redcliffe. Walpole at first wrote to him in a most courteous manner, but when some of his friends pronounced them to be forgeries, treated the boy with silent contempt and neglect. The poet quitted Bristol for London, 1770, where he slowly starved and committed suicide. Chatterton's work is very unequal, but some of his ballads and lyrics are amongst the most precious things of their kind in Eng. literature. Amongst these are *The Bristowe Tragedy*, *The Balade of Charitie*, and the Minstrel's Song in *Ælla*. His influence upon Coleridge and Keats was very considerable.

[*Poetical Works* (Aldine ed., ed. by W. W. Skeat, 1871); *Lives*, by Masson (1874), Russell (1909), Ingram (1910).]

Chaucer, GEOFFREY (*c.* 1340–1400), the first great Eng. poet; son of a London vintner. In 1357 was page to the Duchess of Clarence. During the war with France was captured, 1359, but was ransomed, 1360. Six years later he married a certain Philippa, a lady attending the Duchess of Lancaster. In 1367 he was a valet to the king, and later esquire. Subsequently was frequently employed in diplomatic missions abroad. He was appointed comptroller of the customs of wool, skins, and leather in 1374, and comptroller of petty customs of the Port of London, 1382; other offices followed. Thus he occupied a position of honour during the greater portion of his life. He was buried in Westminster Abbey. His works include *The Book of the Duchess*, *The House of Fame*, *Troilus and Criseyde*, *The Legend of Good Women*, and probably the *Romaunt of the Rose*. The work upon which his fame chiefly rests is *The Canterbury Tales*, begun probably about 1373, and left incomplete at his death. The various tales are remarkable for their lyrical and decorative qualities, the knowledge of life which they display, keen insight into character, playful satire, and joyous humour. Besides an absolute poetic position irrespective of date, Chaucer is important for his influence on language and metre. There were many dialects of English, and this first great vernacular literature helped to create a central speech. In prosody Chaucer gave an example of the first regular verse, the octosyllabic, and later the decasyllabic couplet.

[*Works*, ed. by Skeat (1894–5); *Works*, Globe ed., ed. Pollard (1899); *Lives*, by Ward (1879), and Legouis (1913).]

Chavannes (*shä-vän'*), PUVIS DE. See PUVIS DE CHAVANNES.

Chebishev, PAFNUTIY LVOVICH (1821–94), a renowned Russ. mathematician; *b.* Borovsk; pub. researches on prime numbers, rectilinear motion, theory of integrals, etc.

Cheke, SIR JOHN (1514–57), Eng. classical scholar, first regius prof. of Greek, Cambridge, 1540. Amongst his pupils were Roger Ascham, and Prince Edward from 1542 till after his accession.

Chek'hov, ANTON PAVLOVICH (1860–1904), Russ. dramatist and novelist; *b.* Taganrog; studied medicine and graduated, 1884, but took to literature; even during student days pub. many short stories; his plays include *Ivando* (1887), *Uncle Vanya*

(1899), *The Three Sisters* (1901), and his masterpiece, *The Cherry Orchard* (1904); among his best tales are *A Dreary Sky* (1889), *The Teacher of Literature* (1894), *The New Villa* (1899), and *The Bishop* (1902).

[*Tales*, trans. in 13 vols., and *Plays*, trans. in 2 vols., by C. Garnett (1916–23); *Life and Letters*, trans. by Koteliansky and Tomlinson (1925).]

Chelmsford, FREDERIC JOHN NAPIER THESIGER, 1ST VISCOUNT (1868–1933), Brit. statesman; governor of Queensland, 1905–9, and of New S. Wales, 1909–13; served with army in India on outbreak of Great War; Viceroy of India, 1916–21; his period of office was associated with the introduction of dyarchy in Ind. government, the Montagu-Chelmsford reforms; while these measures were accepted by moderate opinion, they were opposed by Gandhi and his extremist followers.

Chemnitz (*kem'nitz*), MARTIN (1522–86), Ger. Lutheran divine; lecturer at Wittenberg, then pastor at Brunswick; wrote against Calvinistic doctrine of the Eucharist, and helped to maintain dogmatic standards in Lutheranism.

Chénier (*shān-yā'*), ANDRÉ MARIE DE (1762–94), Fr. poet; *b.* Constantinople; greatest Fr. lyrical writer of 18th cent.; wrote *La Jeune Tarentine* and other poems in manner of Theocritus. In 1790 he took part in Revolution, and wrote *Ode* in praise of Charlotte Corday; arrested and guillotined by the Jacobins. In prison wrote famous *Jeune Captive*.

Cheops (*kē'ops*) (Gr. form of KHUFU), an Egyptian king; founder of the 4th dynasty; he was the builder of the first or Great Pyramid; date, according to some, 3969–3908 B.C.

Cherbuliez (*sher-bool-yā'*), CHARLES VICTOR (1829–99), Fr. novelist and essayist; *b.* Geneva; in the front rank of Fr. novelists, his best works include *Le Roman d'une honnête Femme* (1866), *Miss Rovel* (1875), *La Ferme du Choquard* (1883).

Cherubini (*kā-roo-bē'nē*), MARIA LUIGI CARLO ZENOBIA SALVATORE (1760–1842), Ital. composer; *b.* at Florence; visited London, and appointed composer to the king, 1784–5; finally settled in Paris as director of the Conservatoire; fame now rests chiefly upon his sacred compositions; *Requiem in C minor* is his masterpiece.

Chéruel (*shā-roo-el'*), PIERRE ADOLPHE (1809–91), Fr. historian; *b.* Rouen; prof. of history successively at Rouen, Strasbourg, and Poitiers; works include *Histoire de France pendant la Minorité de Louis XIV.*, *Histoire de France sous le Ministère de Mazarin.*

Ches'elden, WILLIAM (1688–1752), Eng. anatomist and surgeon; *b.* Somerby, Leicestershire; friend of Newton and of Pope; wrote *Anatomy of the Human Body* (1713).

Ches'ney. (1) FRANCIS RAWDON (1789–1872), Brit. general; *b.* County Down, Ireland; explored Suez, 1829, and proposed construction of canal; afterwards explored Western Asia and Mesopotamia, and proved practicability of overland route to India. (2) CHARLES CORNWALLIS (1826–76), Brit. colonel; *b.* County Down; nephew of (1); writer on military tactics and strategy; prof. of military history at Sandhurst, 1858; best known for his *Waterloo Lectures* (1868). (3) SIR GEORGE TOMKYNS (1830–95), Brit. general; *b.* Tiverton; brother of (2); distinguished in Ind. Mutiny; originated many reforms in military administration; wrote novels and valuable book on *Indian Polity* (1868).

Chesterfield, PHILIP DORMER STANHOPE, 4TH EARL OF (1694–

1773), Eng. statesman and author; *b.* London; became earl, 1726; ambassador to The Hague, 1728; lord-lieutenant of Ireland, 1744, where he ruled with firmness and moderation; and secretary of state, 1746–8. His *Letters to his Son* are famous. They are frank and cynical, but full of wisdom and wit. Dr. Johnson's letter declining his patronage is well known. Wrote also *Letters to his Godson* (pub. 1890).

Chesterton, GILBERT KEITH (1874–), Eng. author; *b.* London; has written critical works, novels, poems, and miscellaneous works; a journalist of distinction, art and literary critic, brilliant satirist, and paradoxical writer; his best criticism includes monographs on Browning (1903), Dickens (1906), and *The Victorian Age in Literature* (1913); novels include *The Napoleon of Notting Hill* (1904), *The Man who was Thursday* (1908), *The Innocence of Father Brown* (1911); poetical works, *New and Collected Poems* (1927).

Chetham, HUMPHREY (1580–1653), Eng. merchant; *b.* Manchester; founder of Chetham's Hospital, Manchester, for poor boys, and of the famous library connected with it.

Chetwode, SIR PHILIP WALHOUSE (1869–), Brit. general; saw service in Burma and S. Africa. In Great War rendered valuable service during retreat from Mons, and later in Egypt and Palestine; deputy-chief, Imperial General Staff, 1920–2; adjutant-general, 1922–3; commander-in-chief, Aldershot command, 1923–7; commander-in-chief of army in India since 1930; field-marshal, 1933.

Chevalier (*shev-al'yā*), ALBERT (1851–1923), comedian of great originality; *b.* London; originally appeared on legitimate stage; was then connected with the music halls; wrote his own sketches and songs, of which 'My Old Dutch' is a typical example; toured England and America with his own entertainment. Has pub. *Before I Forget* (1901) and *Uninitiated* (1906).

Chevalier, MICHEL (1806–79), Fr. economist; *b.* Limoges; prof. of political economy, Coll. de France; advocate of Free Trade; helped to arrange famous commercial treaty between England and France, 1860.

Chevreul (*she-vrool'*), MICHEL EUGÈNE (1786–1889), Fr. chemist; *b.* Angers; prof. of organic chemistry, and director of Paris Natural History Museum; celebrated for his researches on colours, fats, and saponification.

Chevrillon (*she-vrē-yon'*), ANDRÉ (1864–), Fr. man of letters and member of Fr. Academy, 1920; *b.* in Charente; works include *Romantic India* (1891), *Britain and the War* (1916), *Three Studies in English Literature* (1925).

Cheyne (*chān*), THOMAS KELLY (1841–1915), Eng. theologian, one of the pioneers of O.T. criticism in Britain; joint ed. of the *Encyclopædia Biblica* (1899–1903); prof. of interpretation of Holy Scripture, Oxford, 1885–1908; books include *The Prophecies of Isaiah* (1880–1), *The Origin and Contents of the Psalter* (1891), *Jewish Life after the Exile* (1898).

Cheyne, SIR WILLIAM WATSON (1852–1932), prof. of clinical surgery, King's Coll., London; *b.* Shetland; authority on antiseptic surgery; was consulting (civil) surgeon to the forces in S. Africa, 1900–1; president of the Royal Coll. of Surgeons, 1914–17, and temporary surgeon-general R.N. during the Great War; Lister Memorial medallist and prizeman, 1924.

Chiang Kai-Shek (1886–), Chin. general; *b.* Ningpo; became commander of Nationalist army, 1925; waged a successful war with Chên Chiung-ming which led to formation of a Nationalist administration at Wu-chang, 1926; president of Chin. National Government, 1928–31.

Chicheley (*chich'e-li*), HENRY (1364–1443), Eng. prelate and diplomatist; *b.* Northants; Archbishop of Canterbury, 1413; famed for his educational foundations, such as St. Bernard's Coll. (superseded by St. John's) and All Souls' Coll., Oxford.

Chiche'rin, GEORGIY VASILEIEVICH (1872–), Russ. statesman; *b.* province of Tambov; entered diplomatic service, but becoming involved in the revolutionary movement, resigned; during Great War was active in peace movements in Great Britain; after Bolshevik revolution, 1917, was imprisoned in Brixton, but in 1918 was exchanged for the Brit. ambassador in Russia; foreign secretary to the Soviet Republic, 1918–28.

Child, FRANCIS JAMES (1825–96), Amer. scholar; *b.* Boston; prof. of Early English at Harvard; his *English and Scottish Popular Ballads* (1882–98) are the authoritative collection.

Child, SIR JOSIAH (1630–99), Eng. merchant and economist; *b.* London; director and afterwards governor of the East India Co.; wrote *New Discourse of Trade,* in which he affirms that high wages are the surest indication of a country's prosperity.

Childers, HUGH CULLING EARDLEY (1827–96), Brit. statesman; *b.* London; spent early years in Australia and was a member of first cabinet of Victoria; on return entered Parliament; as first lord of the Admiralty, 1868–71, was the first to advocate the two-power standard.

Childers, ROBERT ERSKINE (1870–1922), Irish politician; author of a brilliant novel, *The Riddle of the Sands* (1903), dealing with Germany's preparations for war; served in Air Force during Great War; became involved in Irish politics, supported Republican party, and was executed for treason against the newly formed Free State.

Chippendale, THOMAS (*c.* 1718–79), Eng. cabinetmaker; *b.* Otley; the most famous of his period; his *Gentleman and Cabinet Maker's Director* (1754) shows examples of his work in Louis XV., Chin., and Gothic styles.

Chirol, SIR VALENTINE (1852–1929), journalist and traveller, director of the foreign department of the *Times,* 1899–1912; travelled in Asiatic Turkey, Persia, and Far East; a recognized authority on Eastern questions.

Chisholm (*chiz'um*), GEORGE GOUDIE (1850–1930), Scot. geographer; *b.* Edinburgh; lecturer and reader in geography at Edinburgh Univ., 1908–23; did much to give geography an important place both in education and commerce; his *Handbook of Commercial Geography* is the recognized authority on its subject.

Chladni (*chläd'nē*), ERNEST FLORENS FRIEDRICH (1756–1827), Ger. physicist; *b.* Wittenberg; his work, *Die Akustik* (1802), is the basis of the mathematical theory of sound.

Choate (*chōt*), JOSEPH HODGES (1832–1917), U.S.A. lawyer and diplomatist; *b.* Salem, Mass.; ambassador to Britain, 1899–1905; famous after-dinner speaker and wit; wrote *The Two Hague Conferences, Abraham Lincoln* (1910), *American Addresses* (1911).

Chodowiecki (*kō-dō-vyets'ki*), DANIEL NICOLAS (1726–1801), Ger. miniature painter and engraver of Polish descent; *b.* Danzig; director Berlin Academy, 1797; his works number more than 3,000, the chief being the picture, *Jean Calas and his Family*.

Choiseul (*shwä-zool'*), ÉTIENNE FRANÇOIS, DUC DE (1719–85), Fr. statesman; minister of foreign affairs, 1758–61, 1766–70; aimed at uniting France and Spain against England, and achieved 'Family Compact'; encouraged expulsion of Jesuits; brought about the annexation of Corsica, and the union of Lorraine with France.

Chopin (*shō-pan*), FRÉDÉRIC FRANÇOIS (1810–49), Polish composer and pianist; *b.* near Warsaw; settled in Paris, 1831, where he enjoyed friendship of George Sand, Heine, Berlioz, and Liszt; his compositions (mostly for pianoforte) have marked Polish characteristics, and are full of originality and lyric beauty; wrote sonatas, ballads, études, nocturnes, preludes, polonaises, valses, etc.

[*Life*, by Niecks (1888).]

Chosroes I. (*kos'rooz*), King of Persia (531–79); defeated the Romans under Belisarius, and afterwards the Turks; a wise ruler, tolerant of Christianity though himself a Zoroastrian.

Chosroes II., King of Persia (590–628); grandson of above; conquered Jerusalem, and took away the 'true cross'; was defeated by Heraclius, and afterwards deposed and killed by his nobles.

Chrétien de Troyes (*krā-tyän de trwä'*) (12th cent.), Fr. poet; *b.* in Champagne; left a series of romances, *Érec et Enide*, *Cligés*, *Lancelot*, *Yvain*, *Perceval*, in which the principal cycles of Arthurian legend were standardized as great dramatic stories.

Christian II. (1481–1559), King of Denmark, Norway, and Sweden; succeeded his father as King of Denmark and Norway, 1513; defeated the Swedes at Uppsala, 1520, and became king of that country; was responsible for massacre known as 'Stockholm Blood Bath.' A strong and able monarch, his autocracy and partiality for the lower classes offended his people, and he was deposed in 1531, spending his later years in prison.

Christian III. (1503–59), King of Denmark and Norway from 1533; was a strong Lutheran, and won from Charles V. the profitable Peace of Spires, 1544. He was a capable ruler.

Christian IV. (1577–1648), King of Denmark and Norway from 1588; fostered Dan. navy and promoted commerce; as champion of Protestantism against Empire was utterly defeated by Tilly, 1626, and only saved by alliance with Sweden. In later years he fought against Sweden, 1643–5, and was compelled to surrender much territory; was founder of Christiania (Oslo); one of the most popular Dan. kings.

Christian IX. (1818–1906), King of Denmark; came to throne, 1863; lost Schleswig-Holstein to Prussia by war of 1864. His second son, George, became King of Greece, 1863, and his eldest daughter, Alexandra, married Edward VII.

Christian X. (1870–   ), King of Denmark; came to throne, 1912. Iceland was acknowledged as a separate kingdom, and 'King of Iceland' incorporated in king's title, 1919.

Christina (1626–89), Queen of Sweden, daughter of Gustavus Adolphus; succeeded 1632, and took the reins of government in 1644; encouraged science and literature; able and brilliant, but self-willed; abdicated in 1654, and died forgotten at Rome, 1689.

Chris'tison, SIR ROBERT (1797–1882), Scot. physician, toxicologist, and medical jurist; *b.* Edinburgh; prof. of forensic medicine, 1822, of medicine and therapeutics, 1832, in Edinburgh Univ.; made important researches in toxicology and pathology.

Christopher, St., patron saint of ferrymen; reputed to be a native of Syria; his name is derived from the well-known legend of his carrying the Christ child across a stream. Said to have been martyred under Emperor Decius, *c.* 250 A.D.; commemorated in the Rom. Church on July 25 and in the Gr. Church on May 9.

Christop'oulos, Athanasios (1772–1847), Gr. poet; *b.* Macedonia; his poems, which earned him wide popularity, include *Erotica*, and a tragedy, *Achilles*.

Christy, Henry (1810–65), Eng. ethnologist; travelled extensively, and made splendid archæological collection (now in Brit. Museum).

Chrysostom (*kris'os-tom*), or St. John Chrysostom, 'the golden-mouthed' (*c.* 345–407), the greatest of the Gr. Fathers of the Church; *b.* Antioch; lived some time as a recluse in the desert; then deacon and priest at Antioch; Bishop of Constantinople, 398, but exiled, 404; his numerous works include *De Sacerdotio*, a treatise on the priesthood, and many *Homilies* on books of the Bible.

[*Lives*, by W. R. W. Stephens (1871) and R. W. Bush (1885).]

Chubb, Charles (*d.* 1845), Eng. locksmith, made improvements on locks patented by his brother, Jeremiah; invented burglar and fireproof safes. Further improvements were made on his locks, etc., by his son, John Chubb, 1816–72.

Chulalongkorn I. (1853–1910), King of Siam; succeeded 1868; abolished slavery; encouraged development of army and navy, roads and railways, schools and hospitals; introduced many other improvements and reforms; visited Queen Victoria, 1897.

Church, George Earl (1835–1910), Amer. geographer; *b.* New Bedford, Mass.; explored the Amazon, 1868–79; authority on geography of S. and Central America.

Church, Sir Richard (1784–1873), Brit. soldier, and liberator of Greece; *b.* Cork, the son of a Quaker; served against Napoleon; entered Neapolitan service, 1817, and suppressed brigandage; on rising of Greeks against Turks, 1827, became Gr. generalissimo; later helped to overthrow King Otho, 1843; made general of Gr. army, 1854.

Church, Richard William (1815–90), Anglican ecclesiastic; *b.* Lisbon, and spent early years in Florence; fellow of Oriel, 1838; dean of St. Paul's, 1871, where he reorganized the cathedral, and became one of the most prominent High Churchmen of his day.

[*Life and Letters*, by M. C. Church (1895).]

Churchill, Charles (1731–64), Eng. satirist and clergyman; author of *The Rosciad* (1761), brilliant but merciless satire on contemporary stage; in *The Cheat* he attacked Dr. Johnson as Don Pomposo; friend of John Wilkes.

Churchill, Lord Randolph Henry Spencer (1849–95), Brit. statesman; son of 6th Duke of Marlborough; M.P. for Woodstock, 1874, as an independent Conservative; formed 'Fourth Party,' *c.* 1880; pioneer of 'Tory Democracy'; secretary of state for India, 1885, in Salisbury administration; chancellor of the Exchequer, 1886, and leader of the House of Commons; resigned owing to differences with his colleagues; travelled in S. Africa for health reasons, 1891; re-elected to Parliament, 1893; opposed Irish Home Rule Bill, but soon afterwards died.

[*Life*, by Winston Spencer

Churchill (1906); *Monograph*, by Lord Rosebery (1906).]

Churchill, WINSTON, Amer. writer (1871–); *b.* St. Louis; his romantic tales of Amer. history are his most popular works, and include *Richard Carvel* (1899), *The Crisis* (1901), *The Crossing* (1904); later works are *A Modern Chronicle* (1910), *The Inside of the Cup* (1913), and *The Dwelling Place of Light* (1917).

Churchill, WINSTON LEONARD SPENCER (1874–), Brit. statesman; elder son of Lord Randolph Churchill; educated Harrow and Sandhurst; entered army, 1895, served with the Span. forces in Cuba, 1895, with British in Ind. frontier wars, 1897–8, in Sudan, 1899, and S. African War, 1899–1902, where he was captured by the Boers, but escaped. Conservative M.P. for Oldham, 1900; became under-secretary for colonies in Liberal administration, 1905; on appointment as president of the Board of Trade, 1908, was defeated at N.W. Manchester, but returned for Dundee; home secretary, 1910; first lord of the Admiralty, 1911–15. The readiness of the fleet at outbreak of Great War, 1914, was largely due to his exertions. Directed expedition to Antwerp, 1914, and was a keen advocate of the Dardanelles expedition, 1915. He was chancellor of the duchy of Lancaster in first Coalition government, but resigned, Nov. 1915, and for a spell saw active service in France. In July 1917 he became minister of munitions in Lloyd George Coalition government, and later secretary for war and for air, 1918–21, for the colonies, 1921–22, till fall of Coalition. Severing his connection with the Liberals, he rejoined Conservative party, 1924, and became chancellor of the Exchequer, 1924–9. A brilliant writer, he is author of *The Story of the Malakand Field Force* (1898), *The River War* (1899), *Savrola* (1900—a novel), *Life of Lord Randolph Churchill* (1906), *My African Journey* (1908), *The World Crisis* (4 vols., 1923–9), *My Early Life* (1930), *Thoughts and Adventures* (1932), etc.

Cialdini (*chäl-de'ne*), ENRICO (1811–92), Ital. soldier and diplomatist; *b.* Castelvetro; served in Crimea, 1855; defeated Garibaldi at Aspromonte, 1862; viceroy of Naples, 1862; ambassador to Paris, 1876.

Ciamician (*chäm-ēch'ē-än*), GIACOMO LUIGI (1857–1922), Ital. chemist; *b.* Trieste; prof. of chemistry, Padua, 1887–9, and at Bologna, 1889–1922; made important researches in organic chemistry and in the chemical action of light.

Cibber, COLLEY (1671–1757), Eng. actor and dramatist; *b.* London; manager of Drury Lane, 1711; poet laureate, 1730, and, as such, attacked by Pope in the *Dunciad*; Cibber's *Apology* (1740) is a most entertaining autobiography; made many adaptations from Shakespeare; own plays include *Love's Last Shift, The Careless Husband, She Would and She Would Not.*

Cicero (*sis'er-ō*), MARCUS TULLIUS (106–43 B.C.), Rom. orator, philosopher, and statesman; *b.* Arpinum. Served under Sulla in Civil War, 89 B.C. His legal work began in 81 B.C.; in 80 he defended S. Roscius, who was accused of parricide. In 70 he prosecuted Gaius Verres for his oppression of Sicily. In 66 he was prætor; in 63 he became consul, and suppressed the Catiline conspiracy. Owing to the scheming of P. Clodius was obliged to go into exile in 58. He returned to Italy next year. In 52 he defended Milo for the murder of Clodius. In 50 he became governor of Cilicia, where he suppressed a revolt. He returned to Rome in 49 at outbreak of Civil War; after some hesitation he threw in his lot with Pompeius. After battle of Pharsalia went to Rome in 47, as Cæsar was anxious to be on friendly terms with him. He was much distressed at the death of his daughter, Tullia, in 46. After Cæsar's murder he joined the Republican party, was among those proscribed, and was killed near Formiæ, Dec. 7, 43. Cicero's works are more extensive than those of any other anc. writer. His *Letters* are most valuable both for revealing his personality and for the history of his times. His speeches are numerous, many of them of great political importance. His chief oratorical works are the *Brutus* and *De Oratore*. He wrote also many philosophical and political works, *e.g.* the *De Finibus, De Natura Deorum, De Officiis, De Senectute*, and *De Amicitia*.

[*Life*, by J. L. Strachan-Davidson (1894).]

Cid (*sid*; Span. pron. *thēth*), THE, hero of Span. history and romance. The original Cid (Rodrigo Diaz de Bivar), *b. c.* 1030, was a Castilian noble, fighting now for Moslems, now for Christians, but always for his own hand; died at Valencia, 1099. In the *Poem of the Cid*, written forty years later, and in subsequent Span. literature, he appears as the glorified and ideal knight of Spain; subject of Corneille's play, 1636.

Cimabue (*chēm-a-boo'e*), GIOVANNI (1240–1302), Ital. artist; *b.* Florence; called the 'Father of Ital. Painting' and spoken of as the greatest artist of his time, but much of the work attributed to him has been proved to be by other painters; he was the master of Giotto; among works attributed to him are mosaics at Pisa and frescoes at Florence, which are world famous.

Cimon (*sī'mon*) (*c.* 507–449 B.C.), Athenian statesman and general; fought against Persians at Salamis; persuaded Athens to help Sparta in putting down Helots' revolt; the ignominious dismissal of his force by the Spartans aroused the anger of the Athenians against him, and he was ostracized, 461.

Cincinnat'us, LUCIUS QUINTIUS (*fl.* 458 B.C.), hero of early Rome; twice dictator; won signal victory over the Æquians; famed for simplicity of life.

Cin'na, LUCIUS CORNELIUS, Rom. patrician; follower of Marius; elected consul, 87 B.C.; killed by mutineers, 84 B.C., when undertaking an expedition against Sulla. His daughter, Cornelia, married Julius Cæsar.

Cipriani (*chē-pri-än'i*), GIOVANNI BATTISTA (1727–85), Ital. artist and engraver; *b.* Florence, but spent most of his life in England, where he did much decorative work; helped to institute Royal Academy.

Clairaut (*klā-rō'*), ALEXIS CLAUDE (1713–65), Fr. mathematician and astronomer; *b.* Paris; author of *Théorie de la Figure de la Terre* and *Théorie de la Lune*; accompanied Maupertius to Lapland to measure the meridian; predicted the return of Halley's comet in 1759.

Clapperton, HUGH (1788–1827), Scot. explorer; *b.* Annan, Dumfriesshire; from 1822 explored N. and Central Africa.

Clare, JOHN (1793–1864), Eng. peasant poet; *b.* near Peterborough; author of *Poems of Rural Life* (1820), *The Village Minstrel, The Rural Muse*, etc.; died insane.

[*Poems*, ed. by E. Blunden and A. Porter (1920); *Life*, by J. W. and Anne Tibble (1932).]

Clare, JOHN FITZGIBBON, 1ST EARL of (1749–1802); lord chancellor of Ireland, 1789; opposed Grattan, yet held that England had no right to make laws for Ireland; was strongly against the Catholics and concessions generally.

Clarendon, EDWARD HYDE, 1ST EARL OF (1609–74), Eng. statesman and historian; educated at Oxford; called to bar, 1633; opposed the king's absolutism, and supported Strafford's overthrow, but took the king's side during Civil War. He left England in 1648, and was one of Charles II.'s advisers in exile. He was created earl at the Restoration. His daughter Anne married the Duke of York (afterwards James II.). Always favoured moderation, and did not support such measures of religious intolerance as are contained in the Clarendon Code. He was partly responsible for the defeat of the Eng. fleet by the Dutch in the Medway, 1667; fell from power, being deprived of all his offices, and went into exile; died at Rouen, a disappointed man. His *History of the Rebellion in England* is noteworthy for its wonderful series of portraits of contemporary statesmen.

[*Lives*, by T. H. Lister (1838) and Sir Henry Craik (1911).]

Clarendon, GEORGE WILLIAM FREDERICK VILLIERS, 4TH EARL OF (1800–70), Brit. statesman and diplomatist; *b.* London; entered diplomatic service, and as minister to the Court of Spain, 1833, distinguished himself by his handling of the question of the Span. succession; as viceroy of Ireland, 847–52, he guided that country successfully through a very troubled period of her history; as foreign secretary in 1853, and again in 1865, he played a leading part in the Crimean negotiations, the Austro-Prussian War of 1866, and the Alabama dispute.

Claretie (*klär-tē'*), JULES ARSÈNE ARNAUD (1840–1913), Fr. man of letters; *b.* Limoges; member of Fr. Academy; dramatic critic; director of the Comédie-Française, 1885–1913. His novels include *Noris*, *Le Petit Jacques*, and *Les Huit Jours du Petit Marquis*; *Œuvres Complètes* (1897–1904).

Claribel, pseudonym of CHARLOTTE ALINGTON BARNARD (1830–69), Eng. poet and song-writer; *b.* London. Many of her ballads, such as 'Come back to Erin,' achieved popularity.

Clark, SIR ANDREW (1826–93), Scot. physician; *b.* Aberdeen; pathologist to Haslar Naval Hospital; practised in Aberdeen and London; president of Royal Coll. of Physicians, 1888–93.

Clark, FRANCIS EDWARD (1851–1927), Amer. clergyman; *b.* in Canada; founded, 1881, World's Christian Endeavour Union.

Clark, JOHN BATES (1847–), Amer. economist; *b.* Providence, Rhode Island; prof. of political economy, Minnesota, 1877, and at Columbia Univ., 1895–1923; author of many works on economics.

Clark, JOSIAH LATIMER (1822–98), Eng. inventor and electrician; *b.* Great Marlow, Bucks; made improvements in telegraphs, submarine cables, etc.

Clarke, CHARLES COWDEN (1787–1877), Eng. author and scholar; *b.* Enfield; author of *Shakespeare's Characters* (1863), etc. His wife, MARY COWDEN CLARKE (1809–98), compiled a *Concordance to Shakespeare* (1844–5), and wrote *Girlhood of Shakespeare's Heroines*.

Clarke, EDWARD DANIEL (1769–1822), Eng. traveller and mineralogist; *b.* Willingdon; travelled in Europe, Palestine, and Egypt, collecting statues, MSS., etc.; prof. of mineralogy at Cambridge, 1808; pub. works on travel and archæology.

Clarke, RT. HON. SIR EDWARD GEORGE (1841–1931), Eng. lawyer and politician; *b.* London; called to the bar, 1864; entered Parliament, 1880; solicitor-general, 1886; privy councillor, 1908; retired from practice, 1914. Wrote books on varied topics, including *Easy Shorthand* (1907), *The New Testament: the Authorized Version corrected* (1913), *The Story of My Life* (1918), *Benjamin Disraeli, the Romance of a Great Career* (1926).

Clarke, SAMUEL (1675–1729), Eng. divine and philosopher; *b.* Norwich; among most important works are his Boyle Lectures, *A Demonstration of the Being and Attributes of God* (1704) and *The Evidences of Natural and Revealed Religion* (1705), and his correspondence with Leibniz, 1717.

Clarke, WILLIAM BRANWHITE (1798–1878), Eng. geologist; *b.* Suffolk; studied the geology of Suffolk and Dorsetshire; emigrated to New South Wales and became the founder of Australian geology; discovered gold, 1841, tin, 1849, and diamonds, 1859, in Australia.

Clarkson, THOMAS (1760–1846), Eng. anti-slavery agitator; *b.* Wisbech; travelled to collect evidence on subject; in 1789 went to France to urge his anti-slavery propaganda; after abolition of slave trade, 1807, became vice-president of Anti-Slavery Soc., 1823; following Emancipation Bill, 1833, took part in other philanthropic schemes.

Claude Lorrain (CLAUDE GELÉE) (1600–82), Fr. landscape artist; *b.* Chamagne, Lorraine; excelled in representing the sky in all its varying shades and lights, and in the delicacy and harmony of his colouring; his engravings are also excellent. Examples of his work are to be found in all the principal galleries of Europe.

Claudel (*klō-del'*), PAUL (1868–), Fr. poet, dramatist, and diplomat; *b.* Villeneuve-sur-Fère; has filled many diplomatic posts; was ambassador to the U.S.A., 1927–33, to Belgium, 1933–35; considered one of greatest Catholic writers of France, he has found inspiration in the Bible, Æschylus, and Rimbaud; among his poetical works are *Cinq Grandes Odes* (1910), *Corona Benignitatis Dei* (1915); his dramas, probably his best work, include his great trilogy, *L'Otage* (1911), *Le Pain Dur* (1918), and *Le Père Humiliè* (1919).

Claudian'us, CLAUDIUS (*c.* 396), last Rom. poet; *b.* Alexandria; wrote the *Rape of Proserpine,* also panegyrics.

Claudius, APPIUS CLAUDIUS CÆCUS, Rom. censor, 312 B.C.; consul, 307 and 296 B.C.; prætor, 295 B.C. Constructed Appian Way. Forced senate to reject peace terms of Pyrrhus.

Claudius, MARCUS AURELIUS, Rom. emperor (A.D. 268–70); defeated Goths—hence assumed the title Gothicus.

Claudius, TIBERIUS CLAUDIUS DRUSUS NERO GERMANICUS (10 B.C.–A.D. 54), Rom. emperor; son of Drusus, and nephew of Emperor Tiberius; emperor, A.D. 41; conquered S. Britain, 43; said to have been poisoned by his wife, Agrippina, mother of Nero.

Clausel (*klō-zel'*), BERTRAND, COUNT (1772–1842), Fr. soldier; *b.* in Ariège; served in the Revolutionary and in Peninsular campaigns; after Restoration, served under the Bourbons; marshal of France, 1835.

Clausen (*klō'sen*), SIR GEORGE (1852–), Eng. landscape artist; *b.* London; devotes himself to painting impressions of rural life and study of sunlight direct from nature; R.A., 1908.

Clausewitz (*klow'ze-vēts*), KARL VON (1780–1831), Prussian general; *b.* near Magdeburg; fought in Rhine campaign, 1793–94; in campaign of Jena, 1806; a prisoner two years; helped to reorganize Prussian army, 1809–12; fought for Russia in 1812, and then served in Prussian army in Waterloo campaign; wrote important military work, *Vom Kriege*, an exposition of the philosophy of war.

Clausius (*klow'zē-oos*), RUDOLF JULIUS EMMANUEL (1822–88), Ger. physicist; *b.* Köslin; prof. of physics at military school in Berlin, 1850, univ. of Zürich, 1855, Würzburg, 1867, Bonn, 1869; founder of the science of thermodynamics; formulated many new physical theories.

Clay, FREDERIC (1838–89), Eng. composer of operas and songs; *b.* Paris. His most popular songs are, 'I'll sing thee Songs of Araby' and 'The Sands o' Dee.'

Clay, HENRY (1777–1852), U.S.A. statesman; *b.* in Virginia; entered legal profession, 1797; was elected to Senate, 1806; to House of Representatives, 1811; served as Speaker several times; helped to urge on the war with Britain in 1812. Was a pioneer of Protection. As regards slavery he took a middle ground, so that he was mistrusted by slaveholders and abolitionists alike. This position later enabled him to play the part of mediator between North and South, and he became known as 'the great pacificator.' He was a great orator and immensely popular.

Clays, PAUL JEAN (1819–1900), Belgian marine painter; *b.* Bruges; helped to establish modern Belgian school of art; among his works are *Dutch Boats in the Flushing Roads*, *The Port of Antwerp*, and *The Open North Sea*.

Cleanthes (*klē-an'thēz*) (3rd cent. B.C.), poet and philosopher; *b.* Assos; worked as drawer of water by night to earn fee as pupil of Zeno, whom he succeeded, 263 B.C.

Clearchus (*klē-ar'-chus*) (*fl.* 5th cent. B.C.), Spartan leader; governor of Byzantium when citizens opened their gates to Alcibiades, 409 B.C. Leader of the famous Ten Thousand, whose retreat is immortalized in the *Anabasis* of Xenophon.

Cleisthenes (*klīs'the-nēz*) (*fl.* 500 B.C.), Athenian statesman; began his democratic reforms, *c.* 508 B.C.; divided Attica into three regions—the city, coast, and inland; and each of these into ten groups or *trittyes*. Formed Council of Five Hundred, with definite administrative functions. He further carried out franchise reforms, and introduced 'ostracism.' He prepared the way for the glory of Athens under Pericles.

[*History of Greece*, by J. B. Bury.]

Clemenceau (*klā-mon-sō'*), GEORGES BENJAMIN EUGÈNE (1841–1929), Fr. statesman; *b.* in Vendée; went to U.S.A., 1865, to study social conditions; returned in 1870, and practised as a physician in Montmartre. Elected a member of the National Assembly, 1871; member of the Chamber of Deputies, 1876, finally leader of the Extreme Left. He was defeated at the election of 1893, but in 1900 was elected a senator. He took a prominent part in the Dreyfus case, pleading his cause ably in *L'Aurore*, which he ed., 1903–7. In May 1906 he became minister of the interior, and then prime minister until 1909. He founded *L'Homme Libre* (1913), which, owing to difficulties with the censorship during the Great War, he rechristened *L'Homme Enchaîné*. The wrecker of many ministries, 'the Tiger' again became premier in Nov. 1917, and his conduct of affairs largely contributed to the victory of France and her Allies. Ardently defended all the claims of France at the Peace Conference at Paris. He demitted office, 1920. Retiring into private life, he visited Egypt, India, and America, and spent his last years in study and writing.

His works include *La Mêlée Sociale* (1895), *Le Grand Pan* (1896), *Les Plus Forts* (1898), *Les Requins* (play), *Grandeurs et Misères d'une Victoire* (1929), *Au Soir de la Pensée* (1929).

[*Clemenceau: The Events of his Life as told by himself to his former secretary, Jean Martet*, trans. by M. Waldman (1930); *The Tiger: Georges Clemenceau, 1841–1929*, by G. Adam (1930).]

Clemens, SAMUEL LANGHORNE. See TWAIN, MARK.

Clement, name of fourteen popes. CLEMENT I., ST., said to have been a bishop in Rome (*c.* A.D. 96). His name is associated with a letter addressed by the Christian Church in Rome to the Church in Corinth in the attempt to act as peacemaker in some troubles and disputes on the subject of ejected bishops. CLEMENT IV., GUI FOULQUES (1265–8), Fr. soldier and lawyer; ordained after death of his wife; supported Charles of Anjou against Manfred; encouraged the researches of Roger Bacon. CLEMENT V., BERTRAND DE GOUTH (1305–14), Archbishop of Bordeaux; removed the papal residence to Avignon, 1309; consented to suppression of Templars, 1311. CLEMENT VII., GIULIO DE' MEDICI (1523–34), Florentine; pronounced against Henry VIII.'s divorce from Catherine of Aragon, 1534, and excommunicated Henry. In his time Rome was sacked by the Germans, 1527. CLEMENT XII., LORENZO CORSINI (1730–40), Florentine; elected at 78; issued first papal decree against Freemasons, 1738. CLEMENT XIV., GIOVANNI VINCENZO ANTONIO GANGANELLI (1769–74), Franciscan Italian; of humble birth; agreed to suppress Jesuits, 1773.

Clement OF ALEXANDRIA (*b. c.* 150), one of the most brilliant of the Gr. Fathers, was head of the Alexandrian school. Writings include *A Word of Exhortation to Greeks* (*i.e.* Gentiles), in which he dwells on the antecedents to Christianity in the better types of paganism; *The Schoolmaster*; and *Patchwork* (*Stromateis*), a guide to deeper Christian philosophy; also wrote a commentary on the Scriptures, but this survives only in fragments.

Clemen'ti, MUZIO (1752–1832), Ital. pianist and composer; *b.* Rome; settled in England, and founded pianoforte firm, afterwards Collard and Collard; his pianoforte studies, *Gradus ad Parnassum*, are still in high favour; buried in Westminster Abbey.

Cleomenes I. (*klā-om'en-ēz*), King of Sparta; reigned 520–488 B.C.; did much to strengthen power of Sparta. CLEOMENES III., King of Sparta; his reign (235–219 B.C.) was marked by the restoration of the constitution of Lycurgus and the conquest of nearly all Arcadia, 226. Defeated by Antigonus of Macedonia, he fled to Egypt and committed suicide.

Cle'on (*d.* 422 B.C.), Athenian statesman; headed opposition to Pericles in 430; after Pericles's death became democratic leader; displayed enmity against Athenian nobility and against Sparta; captured Spartans in Sphacteria, 425; killed at Amphipolis.

Cleopat'ra (69–30 B.C.), Queen of Egypt; succeeded her father, Ptolemy Auletes XIII.; fascinated Julius Cæsar and then Mark Antony, at whose death she killed herself by the bite of an asp. A woman of great ability and boundless ambition; of pure Macedonian descent, and therefore no darker than a Greek; had three children by Antony.

Clerk-Maxwell. See MAXWELL, JAMES CLERK.

Clermont - Ganneau (*kler - mon gä-nō'*), CHARLES SIMON (1846–1923), Fr. oriental scholar; *b.* Paris; in Palestine discovered the 'stele' of Mesha which bears the oldest known Semitic inscription, 1870; leader of archæological expeditions to Palestine, Red Sea, and Syria; became director of the École des Langues Orientales and prof. at the Coll. de France; appointed consul-general, 1896, and minister-plenipotentiary, 1906; works include *Palestine Inconnu* (1886) and *Receuil d'Archéologie orientale* (1885–1924).

Cleveland, John (1613–58), Eng. Cavalier poet; devoted adherent of Charles I.; his poems were more highly esteemed by his contemporaries than Milton's; best known are *The Rebel Scot, Smectymnuus*, and *Rupertismus*.

Cleveland, Stephen Grover (1837–1908), president of U.S.A.; *b.* New Jersey; called to the bar, 1859; Democratic candidate and governor of Erie county, 1882; president, 1885–9. He set himself to reform the tariff, and being again nominated for the presidency, was defeated largely on that issue; elected again, 1893–7. His second term of office was marked by a financial crisis and a dispute with Great Britain regarding Venezuela boundary.

Clifford, Sir Hugh (1866–), Brit. colonial governor; *b.* London; Brit. resident in Pahang, Malay States, 1896–9; governor of Gold Coast, 1912–19, of Nigeria, 1919–25, of Ceylon, 1925–7, and of Straits Settlements till 1929. A voluminous and interesting writer, his works include *Studies in Brown Humanity* (1898), *Malayan Monochromes* (1913), *The Further Side of Silence* (1916), *In Days that are Dead* (1926), *Bush-Whacking and other Asiatic Tales and Memories* (1929).

Clifford, John (1836–1923), Eng. Baptist minister and Nonconformist leader; *b.* Sawley; prominent in the movement known as 'passive resistance,' 1902, and in the disestablishment campaign.

Clifford, Thomas (1630–73), Eng. politician; *b.* in Devon; strong supporter of royal prerogative; member of Cabal ministry, and instrumental with Arlington in arranging Secret Treaty of Dover.

Clinton, Sir Henry (*c.* 1738–95), Brit. soldier; fought in Seven Years' War and in Amer. War of Independence; commander-in-chief of forces in N. America, 1778; governor of Gibraltar, 1794.

Clive, Catherine (1711–85), best known as Kitty Clive, Eng. comedy actress; acted under Cibber and Garrick at Drury Lane; friend of Horace Walpole; praised by Dr. Johnson.

Clive, Robert, Baron Clive of Plassey (1725–74), Brit. soldier and administrator; *b.* near Market Drayton. At school he was unruly, and at eighteen was sent to India as a writer in the E. India Co., 1744. He joined the Company's army in 1747, and won great distinction at the siege of Arcot, 1751. After a three years' visit to England returned as governor of Fort St. David, 1756. Following on the 'Black Hole of Calcutta,' Clive defeated Suraj-ud-Dowlah's troops in the great victory of Plassey, 1757, and ultimately established Brit. supremacy in Bengal. Returned to England, 1760; he was created baron, 1762. He sailed again for India, 1765, to effect reforms in the administration of Bengal. His health obliged him to return to England, and there violent attacks were made on him, occasioned by his reforms and cutting down of illicit gains. He defended himself vigorously, and the House of Commons unanimously exonerated him, but morbid depression overcame him and he committed suicide. Clive ranks high as a Brit. empire-builder, basing the Brit. Empire in India on a territorial rather than a commercial system.

Clodd, EDWARD (1840–1930), Eng. rationalist and writer on folk-lore; works include *Childhood of the World* (1873), *Myths and Dreams* (1885), *Story of Primitive Man* (1895), *Memoirs* (1916), and *Occultism* (1922).

Cloots (*klōts*), JEAN BAPTISTE DU VAL DE GRÂCE, BARON DE (1755–94), Fr. Revolutionist, known as 'Anacharsis Cloots'; *b.* near Cleves; violent anti-Christian; member of Convention, 1792; was guillotined through Robespierre's influence.

Close, MAXWELL HENRY (1822–1903), Irish clergyman and geologist; *b.* Dublin; leading authority on glacial geology of Ireland; also interested in archæology and the Irish language.

Clotilde, ST. (475–544), daughter of Chilperic, King of Burgundy; married Clovis, King of Franks, whom she helped to convert to Christianity; she was canonized a few years after death.

Clouet (*kloo-ā'*), FRANÇOIS (*d.* 1572), Fr. miniature artist; court painter to Francis I., Henry II., and Charles IX.; executed portraits of Henry II. and Mary Queen of Scots.

Clough (*kluf*). (1) ARTHUR HUGH (1819–61), Eng. poet; *b.* Liverpool; spent childhood in S. Carolina; educated at Rugby and Oxford, where he met Matthew and Thomas Arnold; head of Univ. Hall, London, 1849–51, and later an examiner in the Education Office; chief poem, *The Bothie of Tober-na-Vuolich*, an account of a student's reading party; wrote also *Amours de Voyage*, *Dipsychus*, and many exquisite lyrics. Arnold's *Thyrsis* was written in his memory.

[*Monographs*, by S. Waddington (1883) and J. L. Osborne (1920).]

(2) ANNE JEMIMA (1820–92), Eng. educationist, sister of (1); *b.* Liverpool; principal, first hostel for women students, Cambridge, which developed into Newnham Coll.

Clo'vis I. (*c.* 465–511), King of the Franks; conquered Seine country, 486; married Clotilde, 493; was baptized, 496; defeated Visigoths; became champion of orthodox faith against the Arians.

Clowes (*klouz*), SIR WILLIAM LAIRD (1856–1905), Eng. naval historian; *b.* London; naval correspondent to the *Times*, 1890–95, also to the *Standard* and *Daily News*; sometimes wrote under the pen-name of 'Nauticus.' His chief historical work, written in collaboration with others, was *The Royal Navy* (7 vols.).

Cluseret (*kloo-se-rā'*), GUSTAVE PAUL (1823–1900), Fr. officer and revolutionary; *b.* Paris; left the Fr. army, joined Garibaldi in Italy, 1860, and entered the service of the North in the Amer. War, 1861; later joined the Fenians, and returned to Paris as revolutionary journalist, 1868. Expelled from France, he fought with the Turks against Russia, 1878, and on his return to France was elected a deputy.

Clyde, BARON. See CAMPBELL, COLIN.

Clyde, RT. HON. JAMES AVON, LORD (1863–), Scot. advocate; *b.* Dollar; called to the Scot. bar, 1887; K.C., 1901; solicitor-general for Scotland, 1905–6; dean of the Faculty of Advocates, 1915–18; lord advocate, 1916–20; lord president of the Court of Session, 1920.

Clynes, RT. HON. JOHN ROBERT (1869–), Brit. statesman; *b.* Oldham; for many years an artisan, and secretary of the Oldham Trades and Labour Council for twenty-one years; M.P. for N.E. Manchester (Platting division), 1906–31, and since 1935. President of the National Union of General and Municipal Workers; was parl. secretary to Ministry of Food, 1917–18; food controller,

1918–19; lord privy seal and deputy leader of Commons, 1924, and home secretary, 1929–31.

Cnut. See CANUTE.

Coates, ALBERT (1882–), Eng. conductor and composer; *b.* Leningrad, of Eng. parents; educated in England; studied music in Germany; became conductor of the Imperial Orchestra in Russia; returned to England, 1919, as conductor for Sir Thomas Beecham.

Coats, JAMES (1774–1857), founder of famous thread works, Paisley, now J. and P. Coats, Ltd. The family have been distinguished for their philanthropy.

Cobbe, FRANCES POWER (1822–1904), Eng. author; *b.* Dublin; interested herself in social questions; advocated women's suffrage; wrote *The Duties of Women* (1881; new ed., 1905), and a fascinating *Autobiography* (1894).

Cobbett, WILLIAM (1763–1835), Eng. radical reformer; *b.* Farnham; served in army, 1784–91; went to Philadelphia, 1792, where he attacked Amer. institutions and was fined; returned to England, 1800; developed Radical views, which he expounded in his weekly *Political Register* from 1802; imprisoned, 1809–11, for protesting against flogging of militia; M.P. for Oldham, 1830 and 1834; pub. *The Poor Man's Friend, Rural Rides, The Curse of Paper Money,* etc.; and originated Hansard's *Debates* and Howell's *State Trials*; a good stylist and vigorous and original controversialist.

[*Lives,* by L. Melville (1913) and G. D. H. Cole (1924).]

Cobden, RICHARD (1804–65), Brit. statesman and apostle of free trade; *b.* near Midhurst; started business as a cotton printer in Manchester, 1830; pub. *England, Ireland, and America, by a Manchester Manufacturer* (1835); travelled in U.S.A. and the East; M.P. for Stockport, 1841; engaged in Anti-Corn Law agitation; recognized by Peel as the man to whom repeal of Corn Laws was due; next gave himself to cause of international peace; opposed Crimean War; attacked Brit. action in China and lost seat; arranged famous commercial treaty between England and France, 1860.

[*Speeches,* ed. J. Bright and J. E. Thorold Rogers (1870); *Life,* by J. Morley (1882).]

Cobham, SIR ALAN JOHN (1894–), Brit. aviator; served in Great War in Air Force; a pioneer in civil and commercial aviation; winner of King's cup for air racing, 1924. Most notable flights, London–Cape Town and back, 1926; England–Australia and back, 1926; commander-pilot of flying boat expedition that flew round the entire African continent. Has written *My Flight to the Cape and Back, Australia and Back,* and *Twenty Thousand Miles in a Flying Boat.*

Cochrane, ROBERT, EARL OF MAR (*d.* 1482), Scot. architect and courtier; favourite of James III.; probably builder of Parliament House and Chapel Royal at Stirling; his elevation to the earldom of Mar, 1479, aroused the jealousy of the nobles, who later seized and hanged him.

Cochrane, THOMAS. See DUNDONALD, EARL OF.

Cockburn (*kō'burn*), SIR ALEXANDER JAMES EDMUND (1802–80), lord chief-justice of England; nephew of Sir George Cockburn; educated Cambridge; called to bar, 1829; Q.C., 1841; M.P. for Southampton, 1847; solicitor-general, 1850; attorney-general, 1851; chief-justice of Common Pleas, 1856; was a brilliant orator, and earned a high reputation as a judge.

Cockburn, ALISON (1713–94),

Scot. poetess; *b.* in Selkirkshire; wrote version of 'Flowers of the Forest,' beginning 'I've seen the smiling of Fortune beguiling.'

Cockburn, Sir George (1772–1853), Brit. admiral; *b.* London; was in command at capture of Martinique, 1809; in his ship *Northumberland* conveyed Napoleon to St. Helena, 1815; admiral of the fleet, 1851.

Cockburn, Henry Thomas, Lord (1779–1854), Scot. judge; *b.* Edinburgh; shared with Jeffrey the leadership of the Scot. bar; solicitor-general for Scotland, 1830; author of *Life of Lord Jeffrey* (1852), and *Memorials of My Time* (1856), a fine picture of Edinburgh society.

Cockburn, Hon. Sir John Alexander (1850–1929), statesman; *b.* near Duns; went to S. Australia and entered on political career; prime minister and chief secretary, 1889–90; minister of education and agriculture, 1893–98; Australian representative in various federal and international conferences; pub. *Australian Federation* (1901).

Cocker, Edward (1631–75), an Eng. teacher who compiled the famous Cocker's *Arithmetick* (1678); hence the phrase 'according to Cocker.'

Cock'erell, Charles Robert (1788–1863), Eng. architect; *b.* London; travelled in Greece and assisted in excavations at Ægina; R.A., 1829, and architect to Bank of England, 1836; president Royal Institute of Architects; built a wing of Univ. Library and the Fitz-William Library, Cambridge; completed St. George's Hall, Liverpool.

Cod'rington, Sir Edward (1770–1851), Brit. admiral; *b.* Doddington; entered navy, 1783; served in war with France, at Trafalgar, off Spain, in America, and in Greek War of Independence fought the battle of Navarino, 1827; admiral, 1837.

Cody, Samuel Franklin (1861–1913), Anglo-Amer. aviator; *b.* Texas; settled in London; invented a man-lifting kite; built a successful biplane, 1909; became adviser to the War Office in aeronautical matters; was killed in a flying accident at Farnborough.

Cody, William Frederick (1846–1917), Amer. scout and showman; *b.* in Iowa; known as 'Buffalo Bill,' from supplying over 4,000 buffaloes for food for the labourers on the Kansas Pacific Ry.; served as scout in Ind. troubles, 1874–6; rose to be a magistrate, senator, and brigadier-general; in 1883 organized his famous 'Wild West Show,' and travelled with it throughout America and Europe.

Coehoorn (*koo'hōrn*), Menno, Baron van (1641–1704), Dutch soldier and military engineer; *b.* Leeuwarden; distinguished himself under Marlborough, especially at Namur, 1692, and at capture of Bonn and siege of Huy, 1703; wrote works on fortification.

Cohn, Ferdinand Julius (1828–98), Ger. botanist; *b.* Breslau; improved the miscroscope and made outstanding discoveries in plant and animal cell theory; practically the founder of the science of bacteriology.

Coke, Sir Edward (1552–1634), Eng. lawyer and politician; *b.* Mileham, Norfolk; called to bar, 1578; elected M.P. and speaker, 1593; attorney-general, 1594; chief-justice of Common Pleas, 1606; vigorously defended the common law against royal prerogative; offended king, and was imprisoned, 1621; re-entered Parliament, 1625, and retired in 1629; famous as a legal writer.

Coke, Thomas William, Earl of Leicester (1752–1842), pioneer of Eng. agriculture; educ. at Eton. On his estate in Norfolk introduced methods of arable farming and stock-breeding.

Colbert (*kol-bār'*), JEAN BAPTISTE (1619–83), Fr. statesman; *b.* Reims. In 1651 he was employed by Cardinal Mazarin. After Mazarin's death, 1661, entered employment of Louis XIV. He reformed the burdensome taxation, making it juster and more economical. He did much to raise the prosperity of France, strengthened the navy, and was interested in literature and art. His condemnation of men to be galley slaves is a serious blot on his character.

Colchester, CHARLES ABBOT, 1ST BARON (1757–1829), Eng. politician; *b.* Abingdon; M.P., 1795; carried Act for taking first census of population, 1801; speaker of House of Commons, 1802–17.

Cole, VICAT (1833–93), Eng. artist; *b.* Portsmouth; R.A., 1880; painted Thames and Surrey scenes; one of his largest pictures, *The Pool of London,* is in Tate Gallery.

Colenso, JOHN WILLIAM (1814–83), Anglican ecclesiastic and mathematician; *b.* St. Austell; pub. well-known textbooks on arithmetic and algebra; first Bishop of Natal, 1853; trans. N.T. into Zulu; a pioneer in the 'Higher Criticism'; pub. works on Pentateuch which aroused a storm of protest.

Colepeper (or CULPEPPER), JOHN, 1ST BARON (*d.* 1660), Eng. politician; first opposed Charles I., but changed from fear of revolution; chancellor of Exchequer, 1642; fought at Edgehill in Civil War; accompanied Charles II. into exile.

Coleridge (*kōl'rij*), HARTLEY (1796–1849), Eng. poet; eldest son of S. T. Coleridge; *b.* Clevedon; educated at Oxford; became writer for magazines and a schoolmaster at Ambleside; lacking stability, he failed in all his occupations. In his poetry he showed kinship to Wordsworth, and left several sonnets of high quality; one of the most brilliant conversationalists of his day.

[*Memoir,* by Derwent Coleridge (1851).]

Coleridge, HERBERT (1830–61), Eng. philologist; first general ed. of *Oxford English Dictionary.*

Coleridge, JOHN DUKE, 1ST BARON (1820–94), lord chief-justice of England; grand-nephew of S. T. Coleridge; *b.* Ottery St. Mary; educated at Eton and Oxford; called to the bar, 1846; Liberal M.P. for Exeter, 1865; greatly distinguished himself in Tichborne trial; chief-justice of Common Pleas and baron, 1873; lord chief-justice, 1880; a great orator and scholar.

[*Life and Correspondence,* by E. H. Coleridge (1904).]

Coleridge, SAMUEL TAYLOR (1772–1834), Eng. poet, philosopher, and critic; *b.* Ottery St. Mary, where his father was vicar; educated at Cambridge; got into debt and enlisted, but was bought off. Coleridge and Southey married two sisters (Sara and Edith Fricker), and proposed to found a 'pantisocratic' settlement in America, but the scheme was abandoned. At Nether Stowey, Somerset, Coleridge and Wordsworth planned their joint work, the *Lyrical Ballads* (1798), to which Coleridge contributed *The Ancient Mariner* and other poems; here also he wrote the first part of *Christabel,* and *Kubla Khan* (pub. 1816). An earlier vol., *Poems on Various Subjects,* had appeared in 1796. Coleridge acted for some time as Unitarian preacher. He spent a year in Germany, where he studied metaphysics. In 1799 he was in London, writing for the *Morning Post*; made his home at Keswick, 1800; went to Malta in search of health, 1804; afterwards travelled in Italy. In 1808 he lectured on Shakespeare in

London. His later publications include *Biographia Literaria, Sibylline Leaves, Aids to Reflection, The Constitution of Church and State.* In 1796 he had become a victim to opium, and was long dependent for money upon the generosity of friends. Coleridge has left us poetry, small in quantity, but of the noblest quality. No finer ballad poetry was ever written than *The Ancient Mariner; Christabel* and *Kubla Khan* are works of the highest metrical and imaginative beauty. His exposition of poetic theory in *Biographia Literaria* is the clearest statement of the principles followed by all great poets.

[*Life*, by J. Dykes Campbell (1894); *Letters*, ed. by E. H. Coleridge (1895); *Monograph*, by Traill.]

Coleridge, SARA (1802–52), Eng. poetess and miscellaneous writer; daughter of S. T. Coleridge; *b.* Keswick; trans. several foreign authors; wrote *Pretty Lessons in Verse for Good Children*, and a fairy tale, *Phantasmion.*

Coleridge-Taylor, SAMUEL (1875–1912), Brit. musical composer; *b.* London; son of Eng. mother and W. African father; his works include chamber music, songs, and cantatas; his *Hiawatha* trilogy is universally regarded as a work of genius; early death cut short promising career.

Col'et, JOHN (1467–1519), Eng. Renaissance scholar; lectured on theology at Oxford; refounded St. Paul's School, 1512; an earnest reformer and a zealous exponent of the new learning.

Coligny (*kō-lēn'yē*), GASPARD DE (1519–72), Fr. Huguenot leader; *b.* Châtillon-sur-Loing, Loiret; of noble Burgundian family; famous as military reformer; admiral of France, 1552. On capture of St. Quentin, 1557, by the Spaniards was imprisoned, but later ransomed; he had now become a Huguenot. On death of Louis, Prince of Condé, he became leader of Protestant armies; after Peace of St. Germain, 1570, he became favourite of Charles IX. Through the machinations of the queen-mother, Catherine de' Medici, the Massacre of St. Bartholomew took place, in which Coligny was slain.

[*Gaspard de Coligny, Admiral of France*, by A. W. Whitehead (1904); *L'Amiral de Coligny*, by C. Merki (1909).]

Colleoni (*kol-ā-ō'nē*), BARTOLOMEO (1400–75), Ital. mercenary, generalissimo of the Venetian land forces, 1455; his equestrian statue in Venice, by Verrocchio, is said to be the finest in the world.

Collet'ta, PIETRO (1775–1831), Ital. soldier and historian; *b.* Naples; served under Ferdinand of Naples, 1798, and under Joseph Bonaparte, 1806; wrote standard history of the Kingdom of Naples.

Colley, SIR GEORGE POMEROY (1835–81), Brit. soldier; *b.* Ireland; commanded in Natal, 1881, and was killed at Majuba Hill.

[*Life*, by Sir W. Butler (1899).]

Collier, JEREMY (1650–1726), Anglican ecclesiastic; *b.* Cambridgeshire; staunch Tory and supporter of Stewart cause, for which he suffered imprisonment; wrote numerous works; in his famous *Short View of the Immorality and Profaneness of the English Stage* (1698) he attacked the contemporary stage, in particular censuring Dryden, Wycherley, and Congreve.

Collier, HON. JOHN (1850–1934), Brit. painter, second son of Lord Monkswell; *b.* London; highly popular for his problem pictures or such as represent some dramatic incident; his portraits are, however, his best work; his paintings include *The Last Voyage of Henry Hudson* (1881), *Sentence of Death* (1908); among his portraits are those of Prof. Ray Lankester (1904) and Lord Alverstone (1912).

Collier, John Payne (1789–1883), Eng. man of letters; *b.* London; Elizabethan student; notorious as forger of 17th cent. annotations to Shakespeare folio.

Colling, Charles (1751–1836), and Robert (1749–1820), Eng. cattle-breeders; *b.* near Darlington; improved shorthorn breed by scientific breeding.

Collings, Rt. Hon. Jesse (1831–1920), Eng. politician; *b.* Exmouth; M.P., 1880–1918; a strong advocate of land reform as a means of checking rural depopulation, he was the mover of the 'three acres and a cow' amendment which turned Lord Salisbury out of office, 1886, and was responsible for the Allotments Act, 1887, and the Small Holdings Act, 1892.

Collingwood, Cuthbert Collingwood, Baron (1750–1810), Brit. naval commander; *b.* Newcastle-on-Tyne; served in Amer. War, 1774; was at the battle of Cape St. Vincent, 1797; vice-admiral, 1799; celebrated for his part in the victory of Trafalgar, where he led one line of ships in *Royal Sovereign.*

Collins, Anthony (1676–1729), Eng. deist; *b.* Hounslow; educated at Cambridge; intimate friend of Locke; advocated free-thinking as a cure for atheism.

Collins, Michael (1890–1922), Irish politician; *b.* near Clonakilty; fought in rebellion during Easter week, 1916; arrested, but liberated, 1917; Sinn Fein member for Cork, 1918; declared for Irish Republic, and became virtual dictator; £10,000 offered for his arrest, 1920; took a prominent part in negotiations leading to a truce with Britain, 1921, and the establishment of the Irish Free State; on the death of Griffith, first president, he became head of state. While fighting irreconcilables in Munster he was ambushed and shot, 1922.

Collins, William (1721–59), Eng. poet; *b.* Chichester; best remembered for his *Odes* (1746), which, though they met with no acceptance in his own day, show him to have been one of the greatest lyric writers of the 18th cent.

Collins, William Wilkie (1824–89), Eng. novelist; *b.* London; achieved popular success with *The Woman in White, The Moonstone,* etc.; a first-class story-teller to whom subsequent writers of mystery tales owe much.

Collot d'Herbois (*kol-ō'der-bwä'*), Jean Marie (1750–96), Fr. revolutionist; *b.* Paris; a prominent Jacobin; president of Convention, 1793; the most sanguinary of the characters in power during the Terror.

Colman, St. (*d.* 676), Bishop of Lindisfarne, 661; then in Iona and Ireland; argued in favour of Celtic Church at Synod of Whitby when the Rom. Church triumphed.

Colman. (1) George (1732–94), Eng. dramatist and scholar; *b.* Florence; wrote *The Clandestine Marriage, The Jealous Wife,* etc.; also trans. from Terence and Horace. (2) George, the Younger (1762–1836), Eng. dramatist; son of above; author of *The Heir at Law* and other popular and amusing dramas; examiner of plays, 1824–36.

Colman, Samuel (1832–1920), Amer. landscape painter; *b.* Portland, Maine; one of the founders and first president of Amer. Water-colour Soc., 1866. His works include *The Ships of the Western Plains* and *The Spanish Peaks, Colorado.*

Colomb, Philip Howard (1831–99), Brit. vice-admiral and inventor; *b.* in Scotland; served in Burmese and Crimean Wars; recognizing the difference steam power made to naval warfare, he invented system known as Colomb's flashing signals, devised new tactics, and expounded his theories in *Naval Warfare* (1891).

Colon'na, VITTORIA (1490–1547), Ital. poetess; *b.* Marino; her poems were inspired partly by devotion to her husband's memory and partly by her powerful religious convictions; held in great estimation by Michelangelo.

Colston, EDWARD (1636–1721), Eng. philanthropist; *b.* Bristol; made enormous sums of money in trade; endowed Queen Elizabeth's hospital; spent over £70,000 on philanthropy.

Colt, SAMUEL (1814–62), Amer. inventor of the revolver; *b.* Hartford, Connecticut; made the first model as a boy; patented, 1835. In 1847 the Amer. government ordered a supply for the Mexican wars; subsequently millions were manufactured in Colt's factories.

Columba, ST., also known as ST. COLM and ST. COLUMCILLE (521–97), Celtic missionary to Scotland; of royal birth; *b.* in Donegal; spent early life in Ireland; in 563 came to evangelize Scotland, founding monastery at Iona, where he died; worked among the Picts, and made Iona the religious centre of Scotland. The Church which he founded in Scotland differed from the Church of Rome in various points of doctrine and ceremonial.

[*Life*, by Adamnan, ed. by J. T. Fowler (1894); *Makers of the Scottish Church*, by Beveridge (1908).]

Colum'ban (or COLUMBA'NUS), ST. (543–615), *b.* in Leinster; preached in Switzerland and Italy; founded monastery of Bobbio in Apennines.

Columbus, CHRISTOPHER, CRISTOFERO COLOMBO, or CRISTOBAL COLON (*c.* 1446 or 1451–1506), discoverer of America; *b.* Genoa; son of a wool-weaver. Made many voyages, and gradually formed the idea of discovering a western passage to Asia; like others of his time, he believed Asia stretched farther eastwards than it does. After many disappointments, gained the support of Queen Isabella of Castile, and set sail on his first voyage on Aug. 3, 1492, with three ships. On Oct. 12 they first came to land at the Bahama Islands (Watling I.), and spent three months in the W. Indies. He then returned, and was welcomed by Ferdinand and Isabella. On a second voyage in 1493 he discovered more islands, and founded the city of Isabella in Hispaniola (Haiti). Returning to Cadiz in 1496, he again set sail, 1498, discovering Trinidad and the estuary of the Orinoco. Failed in governing his new Span. colonies, and fell from court favour; on his return in 1500 was welcomed again. He set out on his fourth and last voyage in 1502, sailing, among other places, to Cuba and Jamaica. He returned in 1504, and died two years later at Valladolid. His remains, transferred from one place to another, are now in Seville Cathedral.

[*Lives*, by Fernando Columbus (Eng. ed. 1867), by C. R. Markham (1892); *History of the New World called America*, vol. i., by E. J. Payne (1892).]

Colvin, SIR SIDNEY (1845–1927), Eng. literary and art critic; *b.* London; Slade prof. of fine art at Cambridge, 1873–85; keeper of prints and drawings at the Brit. Museum, 1884–1912; had wide knowledge of art and letters; among his numerous works are *Walter Savage Landor* (1881), *Keats* (1887), *John Keats, his Life and Poetry*, etc. (1917), *Letters of Keats* (1887); ed. R. L.

Stevenson's *Works* (Edinburgh ed., 1894–7), and the *Vailima Letters* (1898) of Stevenson, addressed to him.

Come'nius (or KOMENSKI), JOHN AMOS (1592–1670), Czech scholar and educational reformer; *b.* in Moravia; 'elder' of Moravian Brethren, 1632; remembered for his *Didactica Magna*, elaborating his theory of education.

Comines, or COMMINES (*ko-mēn'*), PHILIPPE DE (*c.* 1445–1509), Fr. historical writer; adherent of the court of Charles the Bold of Burgundy and later of Louis XI. and Charles VIII. of France; 'father of modern history'; author of *Mémoires* (1464–83 and 1494–5).

Comparet'ti, DOMENICO (1835–1927), Ital. scholar and senator; his masterpiece is *Virgil in the Middle Ages*, one of the most fascinating of erudite works (1872); also wrote *The Traditional Poetry of the Finns* (Eng. trans. 1898).

Compayré, JULES GABRIEL (1843–1913), Fr. educationist; *b.* Albi; inspector-general of public education, 1905; his *L'Evolution morale et intellectuelle de l'Enfant* and *Cours de pédagogie théorique et pratique* are classics of education.

Compton, ARTHUR HOLLY (1892–), Amer. physicist; *b.* in Ohio; prof. of physics, Chicago Univ., since 1923; made noteworthy investigations on X-rays; Nobel Prize in Physics, 1927; publications include *Secondary Radiations produced by X-rays* (1922), and *X-rays and Electrons* (1926).

Compton, HENRY (1805–77), Eng. comedian; celebrated as a Shakespearian clown. His son EDWARD (1854–1918) formed the Compton Comedy Company, 1881.

Comte (*kont*), AUGUSTE (ISIDORE MARIE AUGUSTE FRANÇOIS XAVIER) (1798–1857), Fr. philosopher; *b.* Montpellier; educated at Ecole Polytechnique, but quarrelled with the authorities; went to Paris, 1816, where he lived by teaching mathematics; was friendly with Saint-Simon, who influenced his speculations; in 1826 had attack of insanity, but recovered; pub. first vol. of *Positive Philosophy* in 1830, the sixth and last coming out in 1842; pub. his *Positivist Calendar* (1849), an imitation of the Catholic Calendar of Saints, and *Positive Polity* (1851–54). In his lectures Comte promulgated his new 'Religion of Humanity.' The *Catechism of Positivism* was pub. in 1852. Comte aimed at adapting the methods and principles of the mediæval Church to new social conditions for a Religion of Humanity. In his later works he raises humanity to the place held by God in monotheism. Amongst other ideas, he believed in the enormous importance of women in the social state. His system of positivism influenced J. S. Mill and other Eng. philosophers, but despite its brilliance and suggestiveness on many points, has not as a whole won very wide acceptance.

[*Comte's Theory of Man's Future* (1877), *Comte, the Man and the Founder* (1891), *Comte's Life and Work* (1892), by H. D. Hutton; *Comte, Mill, and Spencer*, by J. Watson (1895 and 1899); *Auguste Comte*, by A. A. L. Seillière (1924).]

Comyn, JOHN (*d.* 1306), Scot. baron, known as 'Red Comyn'; after battle of Falkirk was made 'Guardian' of Scotland; surrendered to Edward I., 1304; murdered by Robert Bruce in the Minorite Friary, Dumfries.

Condé (*kon-dā*), LOUIS I. DE BOURBON, 1ST PRINCE OF (1530–69), Fr. military leader; younger brother of King of Navarre; head of the Huguenot party; opposed Catherine de' Medici; took part in Prot. rising, and was killed at battle of Jarnac.

Condé, LOUIS II. DE BOURBON,

PRINCE OF (1621–86), Fr. general; *b.* Paris; great-grandson of above; known as 'the Great Condé.' As Duc d'Enghien won decisive battle of Rocroi against Spain, 1643, and great victories against Empire, 1644–6; succeeded as prince in 1646, and his great territories and abilities made him a dangerous noble; supported regency against the Fronde, 1649, but was arrested, 1650; new Fronde obtained his release, and he led armies against government, 1651–58; was pardoned by Louis XIV., and distinguished himself in his wars; his fame chiefly rests on spirited conduct in battle and his absolute control of men.

[*The Great Condé and the Period of the Fronde*, by Fitzpatrick (1874); *Life*, by Lord Mahon (1845).]

Condillac (*kon-dē-yäk'*), ETIENNE BONNOT DE (1715–80), Fr. philosopher; *b.* Grenoble; follower of Locke and friend of Rousseau; wrote *Essai sur l'Origine des Connaissances Humaines*; *Traité des Sensations* is his greatest work. He contends that everything is due to sensation, and nothing to heredity. His work influenced subsequent Eng. philosophers, though it was severely criticized in the 19th cent. Time has shown, however, that his ideas agree with the psycho-physiological discoveries of modern times.

Condorcet (*kon-dor-sā'*), MARIE JEAN ANTOINE NICOLAS CARITAT, MARQUIS DE (1743–94), famous Fr. mathematician, philosopher, and revolutionary publicist; *b.* Ribemont, Picardy; assisted with Fr. *Encyclopédie*; became member of Fr. Academy, 1782; wrote, 1785, an essay on the laws of probability, *Vie de Turgot* (1786), *Vie de Voltaire* (whose disciple he in many ways was), 1787; and while concealed in Paris during Terror wrote his *Progrès de l'Esprit Humain*, which traces the development of the human race towards ultimate perfection; member of Legislative Assembly, 1790; drew up memorandum for calling of National Convention, of which he was member; opposed execution of king and many other acts of Convention, and was proscribed.

[*Critical Miscellanies*, by Lord Morley (1871–7); *Life*, by J. F. E. Robinet (1895); *Condorcet et la Révolution française*, by Cahen (1904).]

Confucius (*con-fū'shi-us*), Romanized form of Kung fu-tsze (*c.* 551–478 B.C.), Chin. philosopher and reformer; *b.* in Shantung. In 531 he began to teach; visited the imperial court, where he continued his own 'school of thought'—'how to get through life like a courteous gentleman.' He was made chief magistrate of city of Chung-tu *c.* 504, and exercised universal influence, but the hostility of external foes forced him to withdraw from Chung-tu. His attempts to persuade princes to become model rulers failed, and, although he wandered throughout China and won great fame, he remained in private life. No philosophical writings by Confucius are known, but his disciples collected his sayings. These form three of the four classics of China. He taught veneration of past and imitation of antique virtues, superiority to ambition, charity, forgiveness, repentance. He was founder of Chin. philosophy, although his disciples complained that he left them no word on the nature or end of man. His *Spring and Autumn*, a brief abridgment of Chin. history, is regarded as a Chin. classic. He was buried in Kung cemetery, adjoining Kiuh-fow, where his descendants (said to number 50,000) still dwell.

[*The Ethics of Confucius*, by M. M. Dawson (1915).]

Congreve, WILLIAM (1670–1729), Eng. dramatist; *b.* Bardsey, Yorkshire; defended morality of stage against Jeremy Collier; plays include *Old Bachelor* (1693), *The Double Dealer* (1694), *Love for Love* (1695), *The Mourning Bride* (1697), *The Way of the World* (1700); wrote some masques and artificial lyrics. He was the greatest of Restoration dramatists, a master of dialogue and intrigue.

[*Life*, by E. Gosse (1881; new ed 1924); *Complete Works*, ed. by M. Summers (4 vols., 1923).]

Conington, JOHN (1825–69), Eng. classical scholar; *b.* Boston, Lincs; prof. of Latin, Oxford, 1854. The labour of his life was his verse translation of Virgil (1868); trans. *Odes and Satires* of Horace, etc., into Eng. verse.

Connaught (*kon'ot*). (1) ARTHUR WILLIAM PATRICK ALBERT, DUKE OF (1850–), third son of Queen Victoria; entered the army, 1868; commanded 1st Brigade in Egypt, 1882, and was present at Tel-el-Kebir; represented Edward VII. at Delhi Durbar, 1903; in 1910 opened first Union Parliament, S. Africa. As gov.-gen. of Canada, 1911–16, was very popular. Represented King George in India at inauguration of Provincial Legislative Councils, 1920. (2) PRINCE ARTHUR OF (1883–), son of above; entered Hussars, 1901, and served during Great War; frequently represented the king on ceremonial occasions. Gov.-gen. of the Union of S. Africa, 1920–3. He married the Duchess of Fife, 1913.

Con'nolly, JAMES (1870–1916), Irish revolutionary leader; *b.* near Clones; founded Irish Socialist Republican Party; organized strike of transport workers in Dublin, 1913; during Great War joined with Sinn Fein and acted as commander-in-chief in rebellion of 1916; captured, and shot for treason.

Con'nor, RALPH (1860–), pseudonym of CHARLES W. GORDON, Can. clergyman and novelist; *b.* Glengarry, Ontario; author of tales mostly dealing with the miners and lumbermen of the Far West, to whom for some years he acted as missionary; served as chaplain to the Can. forces during the Great War; works include *The Sky Pilot*, *Black Rock*, *The Man from Glengarry*, *Treading the Winepress*, and *The Runner*.

Con'olly, JOHN (1794–1866), Eng. physician; *b.* in Lincolnshire; founded Brit. Medical Association; while resident physician at Hanwell, 1839, introduced modern treatment of insane.

Conrad II. (*c.* 990–1039), Holy Rom. Emperor, 1027; extended boundaries of Germany by conquering Burgundy, 1032; reunited Italy and Germany.

Conrad III. (1093–1152), first Ger. monarch of the house of Hohenstaufen, elected by the anti-papal Ger. princes. In his reign the war-cries of 'Guelph' and 'Ghibelline' were first heard at the siege of Weinsberg, 1140, the former being papalist, the latter imperialist. He headed the unsuccessful crusade of 1147.

Conrad, JOSEPH (1857–1924), Eng. novelist; *b.* in the Ukraine, of a Polish family; full name, JOSEPH THEODORE CONRAD KORZENIOWSKI. He went to sea at an early age, became a master in the Eng. merchant service, and after retiring pub. *Almayer's Folly* (1895). This was followed by *An Outcast of the Islands* (1896), *The Nigger of the Narcissus* (1897), *Lord Jim* (1900), *Youth* (1902), *Typhoon* (1903), *Nostromo* (1904), *Chance* (1914), *The Arrow of Gold* (1919), *Rescue* (1920), and *The Rover* (1923). Though he did not learn English till he was twenty, he was a master of style; he is unsurpassed as a novelist of the sea, but it is due to his power of interpreting the inmost life that he stands in the front rank of modern European novelists.

[*Joseph Conrad*, by Ford Madox Ford (1924); *Joseph Conrad, Life and Letters*, by G. Jean-Aubry (1927).]

Con'radin OF SWABIA (1252–68), King of Jerusalem and Sicily; last Hohenstaufen emperor; excommunicated, 1267; beheaded by Charles of Anjou.

Consal'vi, ERCOLE, CARDINAL (1757–1824), Ital. statesman and ecclesiastic; *b.* Rome; chamberlain of Pope, 1783; organized papal army to meet armies of Fr. Revolution; imprisoned in castle of St. Angelo, 1798; deported to Naples, and escaped; plenipotentiary at Congress of Vienna; recovered Papal States for the Vatican.

Conscience (*kon'syans*), HENDRIK (1812–83), probably the greatest of Flem. novelists; *b.* Antwerp; works include *The Lion of Flanders* (1838), *Blind Rosa* (1850), *Rikketikketak* (1851), and *The Miser* (1853).

Considérant (*kon-sē-dā-rän'*), VICTOR PROSPER (1808–93), Fr. Socialist; *b.* in Jura; founded a Socialist colony at La Réunion, Texas, but the Amer. Civil War ruined the project; wrote Socialistic works.

Constable, ARCHIBALD (1774–1827), Scot. publisher; *b.* Carnbee, Fife; publisher of *Edinburgh Review* from 1802, and a number of Sir Walter Scott's poems and most of his prose works; his failure, with that of Ballantyne and Co., involved Scott in heavy financial loss.

[*Archibald Constable and his Literary Correspondents*, by T. Constable (1873).]

Constable, JOHN (1776–1837), Eng. artist; *b.* East Bergholt, Suffolk; in early years worked with his father as a miller; first exhibited at the Royal Academy, 1802; R.A., 1829. Became one of England's greatest landscape artists. Amongst most famous works are *Flatford Mill, The Leaping Horse, The Cornfield,* and *The Hay Wain.*

[*Memoirs of the Life of John Constable*, by C. R. Leslie (1843); *Constable and his Influence on Landscape Painting*, by C. J. Holmes (1902).]

Constant (*kon-stän'*), JEAN JOSEPH BENJAMIN (1845–1902), Fr. painter and writer on art; *b.* Paris; distinguished painter of Oriental subjects and portrait painter. Portraits include *Queen Victoria, Queen Alexandra, Pope Leo XIII.*

Constant de Rebecque (*kon-stän' de re-bek'*), HENRI BENJAMIN (1767–1830), Fr. writer on politics and religion; *b.* Lausanne; member of coterie of Madame de Staël; opposed to Napoleon, but later drew up *L'Acte additionnel aux Constitutions*, 1814, in his favour; won fame as orator in Chamber of Deputies, 1819. His chief work is *De la Religion* (1825–31); he also wrote a celebrated novel, *Adolphe* (1816).

Constantine, name of many Rom. emperors. CONSTANTINE I., THE GREAT (*c.* 280–337), son of Emperor Constantius I.; *b.* Nish; was proclaimed *Augustus* by army at York on his father's death, 306, but waited six years before seizing supreme power. Christianity was made the state religion after traditional vision of Constantine of a flaming cross before the battle of Milvian Bridge, 312. He removed the capital, 330, from Rome to Byzantium (Constantinople). In his reign Rom. republic became absolute despotism, Constantine settling the succession on his family, creating new nobility, and leaving the mere shadow of power to senate. His son, CONSTANTINE II. (312–40), acquired name *Alemannicus* from victories over Alemanni. CONSTANTINE V. (emperor, 740–75); held synod, 754, forbidding image-worship, and exiled monks as upholders of same, with result that Rom. Church permanently severed connection with Constantinople. CONSTANTINE VII. (905–59), *Porphyrogenitus* (born in the purple), Byzantine emperor and writer of important books of history, war, law, agriculture, etc. CONSTANTINE X. (1059–67) finally lost Ital. possessions; inroads of Turks and Magyars took place during his reign. CONSTANTINE XIII. (1394–1453), *Palæologus*, the last emperor of the East; reigned from 1448–53; he made a heroic but unsuccessful defence of Constantinople against the Turks.

Constantine I. (1868–1923), King of Greece; *b.* Athens; succeeded to the throne, 1913, on the assassination of his father, King George; was successful commander during second Balkan War; proved an autocratic king. As brother-in-law of the Kaiser, his sympathies were with the Central Powers during Great War. This resulted in the blockade of Greece by the Allies, and the expulsion of the king through the action of Venizelos, 1917. He was succeeded by his second son, Alexander, who died 1920. Constantine returned, but was forced to abdicate, 1922, and died in exile.

Constantine Pavlovich (1779–1831), Russ. grand-duke; *b.* Tsarskoye Selo; second son of Tsar Paul I. of Russia; commander-in-chief in Poland; he aimed at founding a Polish dynasty; renounced claim to the throne of Russia; forced to fly during insurrection at Warsaw, 1830.

Constan'tius, name of three Rom. Emperors. (1) FLAVIUS VALERIUS (*c.* A.D. 250–306), father of Constantine the Great; re-established order in Britain; routed the Alemanni; succeeded to the empire, 305; died at York. (2) FLAVIUS JULIUS (317–61), third son of Constantine the Great, ruled jointly with Constantine II. and Constans; waged unsuccessful war with Persia. (3) CONSTANTIUS III., Emperor of West for seven months in A.D. 421; was preparing to make war on Theodosius II., Emperor of the East, when he died.

Conti, NICCOLO DE' (early 15th cent.), Venetian trader and traveller; explored India and Malay Archipelago; his account of Ind. life, manners, and customs is remarkable for his time.

Conway of Allington, WILLIAM MARTIN, LORD (1856–   ), Eng. mountaineer and historian of art; *b.* Rochester; prof. of art at Univ. Coll., Liverpool, 1885–8, and Slade prof. of fine art at Cambridge, 1901–4; has written many books on art. Made a number of first ascents of the Himalayas, explored Spitsbergen, traversed the whole of the Alps, and surveyed the Bolivian Andes and Tierra del Fuego. His travels are described in his various books, including *The Alps from End to End, The First Crossing of Spitsbergen, The Bolivian Andes.* M.P. for Eng. Univs., 1918–31.

Conybeare (*kun'i-bār*), WILLIAM DANIEL (1787–1857), Eng. geologist; *b.* London; first to describe *Plesiosaurus*; pub. numerous research memoirs and *Outlines of the Geology of England and Wales*; Wollaston medallist, Geological Soc., 1844.

Cook, ARTHUR JAMES (1884–1931), Eng. Socialist and Labour leader; *b.* Wookey, Somerset; worked as miner in Wales; became general secretary of Miners' Federation of Great Britain, 1924; took prominent part in coal strike of 1926, and general strike which followed.

Cook, CHARLES HENRY. See BICKERDYKE, JOHN.

Cook, SIR EDWARD TYAS (1857–1919), Eng. journalist; *b.* Brighton; succeeded W. T. Stead as ed. of *Pall Mall Gazette*, 1890; ed. *Westminster Gazette*, 1893–6, and the *Daily News*, 1896–1901; wrote *Life of Ruskin* (1911). Chief of Press Bureau during Great War.

Cook, ELIZA (1818–89), Eng. verse writer; *b.* Southwark; her lyrics include the well-known poem, 'The Old Arm-Chair.'

Cook, JAMES (1728–79), Eng. navigator and explorer; *b.* in Cleveland, Yorks; apprenticed to shipowners of Whitby; entered navy, 1755; charted St. Lawrence R. and coasts of Newfoundland, 1759–67; in command of *Endeavour*, which sailed for S. Pacific to observe transit of Venus, 1768; explored coasts of New Zealand and E. Australia, of which he took possession in name of Britain; as commander of *Resolution*, 1772, made a marvellous voyage of discovery in the S. Pacific; commanded an expedition to find N.W. Passage from the Pacific end, discovering Sandwich Is., surveying west coast of N. America, and sailing through Bering Strait; his precautions prevented usual heavy death-roll from scurvy; on his return journey was killed at Hawaii; was the greatest of Brit. maritime discoverers, alike for his qualities as observer, as organizer, and as commander.

[*Captain James Cook, the Circumnavigator*, by A. Kitson (1907); *Captain Cook, Explorer and Navigator*, by Y. G. Rowe (1928).]

Cook, SIR JOSEPH (1860–), Australian statesman; *b.* Silverdale, Staffs; emigrated to Australia, 1885; entered New South Wales Legislature, and held various government posts; elected to the Commonwealth Parliament in 1901; prime minister, 1913–14; represented Australia at Peace Conference, 1919; high commissioner of Australia in London, 1924–7.

Cook, THOMAS (1808–92), Eng. excursion agent; *b.* Melbourne, Derbyshire; founder of famous tourist agency; ran first excursion train in England, 1841, between Leicester and Loughborough.

Coolidge, CALVIN (1872–1933), Amer. statesman; *b.* Plymouth, Vermont; practised as lawyer; was mayor of Northampton and governor of Massachusetts (two terms), 1919–20; vice-president U.S.A., 1921, and president, 1923, on the death of Harding; re-elected, 1925–9; during his tenure of office America enjoyed unexampled prosperity, and he was pressed to stand for a third term of office, but declined.

Cooper, ASHLEY. See under SHAFTESBURY.

Cooper, SIR ASTLEY PASTON (1768–1841), Eng. surgeon; *b.* Brooke, Norfolk; prof. of comparative anatomy to Royal Coll. of Surgeons, 1813; president Royal Coll. of Surgeons, 1827 and 1836; performed famous operation of tying the abdominal aorta for aneurism, 1817; author of several surgical and anatomical works.

Cooper, JAMES FENIMORE (1789–1851), Amer. novelist; *b.* Burlington, New Jersey; famous for his 'Leather-Stocking' series of tales. *The Deerslayer*, *Last of the Mohicans*, *The Pathfinder*, *The Pioneers*, and *The Prairie*, which have been trans. into many languages, reveal great inventive faculty, and picturesque and descriptive gifts.

Cooper, PETER (1791–1883), Amer. inventor and philanthropist; *b.* New York; introduced new processes for obtaining iron; constructed first locomotive in America, 1830; established, 1850,

Cooper Union in New York for advancement of art and science.

Cooper, SAMUEL (1609–72), Eng. miniature painter; *b.* London; painted portraits of most of the celebrated people of his time, including Cromwell, Milton, and Charles II., which show him to be the greatest of all miniature painters.

Cooper, THOMAS (1805–92), Chartist poet and lecturer; *b.* Leicester; arrested for sedition; wrote his *Purgatory of Suicides* in jail, in which he discussed social and religious problems; was the original of Kingsley's *Alton Locke.*

Cooper, THOMAS SIDNEY (1803–1902), Eng. artist; *b.* Canterbury; R.A., 1867; famous for cattle studies; work was done in fine Flem. style.

Coornhert (*kōrn'hert*), DIRCK VOLKERTSEN (1522–90), Dutch poet and writer; *b.* Amsterdam· his prose helped to lay foundations of Dutch literary language. Wrote poems, plays, and theological and controversial treatises. His masterpiece was *Zedekunst,* an ethical treatise.

Coote, SIR EYRE (1726–83), Brit. general; *b.* Limerick; distinguished himself in India, in Seven Years' War, and, 1781, defeated Hyder Ali at Porto Novo.

Cope, SIR ARTHUR STOCKDALE (1857–), Eng. artist; R.A., 1910; chiefly a portrait painter, his best work includes portraits of King George, Kitchener, the ex-Kaiser Wilhelm, Sir W. Harcourt, Edward VII.

Cope, SIR JOHN (*d.* 1760), Eng. general; remembered for his ignominious defeat by Prince Charles Edward at Prestonpans, 1745, celebrated in the well-known song, 'Hey, Johnnie Cope, are ye waukin' yet?'

Coper'nicus (or KOPPERNIGK), NICOLAUS (1473–1543), Polish astronomer; *b.* Thorn; studied at Cracow, Bologna, Padua, and Ferrara; undertook the duties of physician administrator of a diocese and other public work. At the same time he created a new conception of the universe by his theory, enunciated in his treatise *De Revolutionibus Orbium Cœlestium* (pub. 1543), that the earth and other planets revolve round the sun.

[*Life,* by Leopold Prowe.]

Cop'ley, JOHN SINGLETON (1737–1815), Anglo-Amer. artist; *b.* Boston, Mass.; settled in England, 1775; painted portraits and historical subjects; R.A., 1783. His *Death of Chatham* is his most famous picture.

Coppée (*ko-pā'*), FRANÇOIS EDOUARD JOACHIM (1842–1908), Fr. poet; *b.* Paris; member of Fr. Academy; was a prolific writer of poetry, plays, and novels, some of his work being marred by excessive sentimentality.

Coquelin (*kōk-län'*). (1) BENOÎT CONSTANT (1841–1909), greatest Fr. actor of modern times; *b.* Boulogne; called 'Coquelin *aîné*'; shone in comedy and farce. (2) ALEXANDRE (1848–1909), brother of (1); called 'Coquelin *cadet*'; also won fame as an actor and writer of monologues. (3) JEAN (1865–), Fr. actor, son of (1); created rôle of Ragueneau in Rostand's *Cyrano de Bergerac* and of Talleyrand in *Plus que reine.*

Coram, THOMAS (1668–1751), Eng. philanthropist; *b.* Lyme Regis; became sea captain; settled in New England; returning to England, established the Foundling Hospital, 1740.

Corday d'Armont (*kor-dā' där-mon'*), MARIE ANNE CHARLOTTE (1768–93), heroine of Fr. revolution, better known as Charlotte Corday. Of noble family of Normandy; absorbed Rom. republican ideas and, to save her country from the Terrorists, assassinated Marat; was guillotined.

Corelli, Arcangelo (1653–1713), Ital. violinist and composer; travelled widely and established great reputation both for his playing and his compositions, the chief of which was his *Concerti Grossi*, or Twelve Concertos.

Corelli, Marie (1864–1924), Eng. novelist; *b.* in Italy; her first story, *A Romance of Two Worlds*, 1886, brought her immediate fame, while her later stories achieved wide popularity. Among these may be mentioned *The Sorrows of Satan* (1895), *The Master Christian* (1900), and *Temporal Power* (1902).

Coriola'nus, Gaius (Gnæus) Marcius, general in mythical period of Rom. history. The legend that he received his surname owing to his capture of Corioli from the Volscians is recounted in Plutarch's *Lives* and Shakespeare's *Coriolanus*.

Cork, Richard Boyle, 1st Earl of (1566–1643), Eng. statesman; *b.* Canterbury; bought in 1602 Sir Walter Raleigh's Irish lands (12,000 acres) in Cork, Waterford, and Tipperary, and developed their resources, building roads and fortresses, and encouraging industry and agriculture; created Earl of Cork, 1620, and lord high treasurer, 1631; his predominance in Ireland ended with Strafford's appointment as lord deputy; father of Robert Boyle, 1627–91.

Cornar'o, Caterina (1454–1510), Queen of Cyprus by bequest of husband, James III., who died 1473; Venetian republic compelled her to abdicate, and annexed Cyprus, 1489.

Corneille (*kor-nā'*), Pierre (1606–84), Fr. dramatist and poet; *b.* Rouen; educated for the bar, but eventually devoted his attention to play-writing; entered service of Cardinal Richelieu to aid him in writing plays. Corneille could not rest satisfied with such employment, and he left the cardinal's service. His *Médée* appeared in 1635, and met with some acceptance; but *Le Cid* (his masterpiece), produced in the following year, achieved immediate success, notwithstanding the jealous efforts of Richelieu to damn the play. It was followed by *Horace* and *Cinna* in the same year, 1640, *Polyeucte* and *La Mort de Pompée* (1643). In 1643, also, appeared *Le Menteur*, a comedy which is the equal of many of Molière's. He was associated with Molière in the writing of *Psyché* (1671), which contains some of his finest lyrical work. Corneille was the father of Fr. drama—one of the greatest of Fr. tragic writers, and a pioneer of Fr. comedy. His genius was essentially romantic. His great work brought him little monetary return, and in his later years he was superseded in public favour by Racine.

[*Life*, by Lanson (1898).]

Corneille, Thomas (1625–1709), Fr. dramatist; brother of Pierre Corneille; wrote about forty plays, the best of which are probably *Ariane* and *Le Comte d'Essex*.

Corne'lia (2nd cent. B.C.), daughter of Scipio Africanus; famous as the mother of the Gracchi, the famous reformers. Exemplified the virtues of the best type of Rom. matron.

Corne'lius, Peter von (1783–1867), Ger. artist; *b.* Düsseldorf, founder of the Munich school, which was enormously influential in Ger. art.

Cornelius Nepos. See Nepos, Cornelius.

Cornwall, Barry. See under Procter, Bryan Waller.

Cornwallis. (1) Charles, 1st Marquess (1738–1805), British general; *b.* London; with his surrender of Yorktown in 1781, Amer. War of Independence ended. Did good work as gov.-gen. of India, 1786–93, and as Viceroy of Ireland, 1798–1801. (2) SIR WILLIAM (1744–1819), Brit. admiral, brother of (1); served under Hood and Rodney, and distinguished himself in the wars against the French; vice-admiral, 1794; admiral, 1799.

Corot (*ko-rō'*), JEAN-BAPTISTE CAMILLE (1796–1875), Fr. artist; *b.* Paris; one of the most individual and poetical of landscape painters; examples of his work are in the Louvre, the Wallace Collection, and the Glasgow Gallery, his best pictures including *Une Matinée* (1850), *Macbeth* (1859), *Le Lac* (1861), *L'Arbre brisé* (1865), *Pastorale - Souvenir d'Italie* (1873), and *Biblis* (1875).

Correggio (*kor-ed'jō*), ANTONIO ALLEGRI (1494–1534), Ital. artist; *b.* Correggio, Modena; unequalled in flesh painting, and, apart from the Venetians, the greatest colourist of the Ital. schools; works mostly executed at Padua, Parma, and at Correggio. Padua and Parma have still some of his magnificent frescoes. The National Gallery, London, contains his *Ecce Homo, Cupid, Mercury and Venus,* and other pictures.

[*Lives,* by C. Ricci (1896), H Thode (1898), and T. Sturge Moore (1906).]

Cort, CORNELIS (1536–78), Dutch engraver; *b.* Hoorn; head of a famous school of engraving at Rome; engraved Titian's and Raphael's pictures.

Cort, HENRY (1740–1800), Eng. inventor of a purifying process for iron called 'puddling,' 1784; also contrived a method by which puddled balls of ore were rolled into bars.

Cor'tes, HERNANDO (1485–1547), Span. soldier; *b.* Medellin, Estremadura; assisted in conquest of Cuba, 1511; took charge of colonists sent to Mexico, 1519; founded Vera Cruz; was worshipped as god by subjects of Montezuma, Emperor of Mexico; seized Montezuma, and finally subdued Mexico in 1521; developed mining and agricultural interests of the country; discovered Lower California, 1536. Grasping and cruel, but with military genius and initiative, Cortes was an important builder of Span. colonial empire.

[*Lives,* by Sir A. Helps (1871), and H. D. Sedgwick (1927).]

Cortot (*kor-tō'*), ALFRED (1877–), famous pianist; *b.* Nyon, Geneva; studied music at Paris Conservatoire; became choral director at Bayreuth; produced Wagner's 'Ring' at Paris, 1902; first appearance in England, 1914; one of greatest of living pianists.

Co'ry, WILLIAM JOHNSON (1823–92), Eng. poet; *b.* in Devon; author of *Ionica,* a volume of exquisite verse.

Cor'yate, THOMAS (? 1577–1617), Eng. traveller; *b.* Somersetshire; noted pedestrian, who travelled widely both in Europe and the East; pub. *Coryate's Crudities* (1611), an account of a walking tour undertaken in 1608.

Cosgrave, WILLIAM THOMAS (1880–). Irish politician; *b.* Dublin; became Sinn Fein member of Dublin Corporation, 1913, acting as chairman of the finance committee, 1916–22; took part in Easter rising, 1916; Sinn Fein M.P., 1918–22; took a large share in the negotiations leading to formation of Irish Free State, 1922, and on the death of Michael Collins in the same year became president, and held office till 1932; his government was marked by moderation, good sense, and courage.

Costa, LORENZO (1460–1535), Ital. painter; *b.* Ferrara, but lived chiefly in Bologna and Mantua; excelled in landscape backgrounds and architectural details; London National Gallery has his *Enthroned Madonna and Child.*

Costa, Sir Michael Andrew Agnus (1808–84), composer and conductor; *b.* Naples; settled in England, 1830; composed opera *Don Carlos* (1844), oratorios *Eli* (1855) and *Naaman* (1864).

Costan'zo, Angelo di (*c.* 1507–91), Ital. historian and poet; wrote valuable history of Naples, his native town, 1581–2.

Costello, Louisa Stuart (1799–1870), Brit. miniature painter and author; protégée of Thomas Moore and Sir W. Scott; pub. *Songs of a Stranger, A Pilgrimage to Auvergne,* etc.

Coster, Laurenz Janszoon (*c.* 1370–1440), native of Haarlem; claimed by Dutch, in opposition to Gutenberg, as the inventor of printing by movable types.

Cotes, Roger (1682–1716), Eng. mathematician; *b.* Burbage, Leicestershire; friend of Newton; first Plumian prof. of astronomy and natural philosophy at Cambridge, 1706.

Cotman, John Sell (1782–1842), Eng. landscape painter; *b.* Norwich; also famed for his architectural etchings; illustrated Dawson Turner's *Architectural Antiquities of Normandy* (1822).

Cotta, Johann Friedrich, Baron Cotta von Cottendorf (1764–1832), noted Ger. publisher; *b.* Stuttgart; great-grandson of founder of the publishing firm; friend and publisher of Goethe and Schiller; founder of *Allgemeine Zeitung* and other noted periodicals.

Cottet (*ko-tā'*), Charles (1863–1925), Fr. artist; *b.* Le Puy; painted portraits, landscapes, and Breton fisher scenes; his masterpiece is the triptych in the Luxembourg, 1898.

Cotton, Charles (1630–87), poet and translator; *b.* Beresford, Staffs; friend of Izaak Walton; contributed treatise on fly-fishing to fifth ed. of *Compleat Angler*; made standard trans. of Montaigne's *Essays.*

Coué (*koo-ā'*), Emile (1857–1926), Fr. psychotherapeutist; *b.* Troyes; engaged in business as a chemist for many years; studied hypnotism and autosuggestion, and came to believe in their value in the cure of disease; established a free clinic at Nancy, 1910, and after the War lectured widely, both in Europe and America, on his favourite theme, 'Every day and in every way I am getting better and better.'

Coulomb (*koo-lon'*), Charles Augustin de (1736–1806), Fr. physicist; *b.* Angoulême; served in corps of engineers, Martinique; invented torsion balance for measuring electrical attraction; gave his name to the *Coulomb*, the quantity of electricity conveyed by a current of one ampère in a second.

Couper'us, Louis (1863–1923), Dutch novelist; *b.* at The Hague; his first novel, *Eline Vere* (1889), established his fame; later became known as one of the greatest of European novelists; works, most of which have been trans. into English by A. Teixeira de Mattos, include *Small Souls* (1914), *The Later Life* (1915), *The Twilight of the Souls* (1917), *Dr. Adriaan* (1918), *Old People and the Things that Pass* (1919), and *The Law Inevitable* (1921).

Courier (*koo-re-ā'*), Paul Louis (1772–1825), Fr. Hellenist and pamphleteer; *b.* Paris; imbibed ideals of Gr. republics, and laid aside his noble title 'de Méré'; works valuable for style and record of manners.

Cousin (*koo-zän'*), Jean (1500–90), Fr. artist; *b.* Soucy; famed for subject pictures, including the *Last Judgment* (Louvre); painted glass in chapel at Vincennes; also sculptor and wood-engraver.

Cousin, Victor (1792–1867), Fr. philosopher; *b.* Paris; founder of modern Eclectic School; identified with struggles for civil and intellectual liberty. Suspended from his professorship at the Sorbonne, 1821, for liberal opinions; replaced 1828, and lectured on Hegel to crowded assemblies; became minister of public instruction, and between 1831 and 1848 laid foundations of modern elementary education in France; gave great impetus to the study of philosophy in France. Chief works, *Translations of Plato*, in 13 vols.; essays on Abélard, Pascal, Locke; *Hist. of Philosophy.*

[*Lives*, by J. Simon (1887), and J. Barthélemy St. Hilaire (1895).]

Cousins, SAMUEL (1801–87), Eng. mezzotint engraver; *b.* Exeter; executed engravings of *Lady Acland and Children* and *Master Lambton* (Lawrence); first R.A. engraver, 1855; left £15,000 to Academy for poor artists.

Coutts, THOMAS (1735–1822), Brit. banker; *b.* Edinburgh; carried on a banking business in London; amassed a large fortune; a keen business man, noted for his generosity; his second wife was the well-known actress, Harriet Mellon, who bequeathed her wealth to his grandchild, afterwards the Baroness Burdett Coutts.

[*Coutts and Co.*, by R. Richardson (1900); *Life of Thomas Coutts*, by E. H. Coleridge.]

Coverdale, MILES (1488–1568), Eng. reformer and translator of Bible; *b.* Yorkshire; his trans. of Bible was pub. in 1535; parts subsequently incorporated in A.V.; famous preacher under Edward VI.; made Bishop of Exeter in 1551; deposed under Mary.

[*History of English Bible Translation*, by Conant (1910); *The Bible by Coverdale*, by F. Fry (1867).]

Coward, NOEL (1899–), Eng. dramatist and actor; *b.* London; acted in *The Goldfish*, 1910, and in his own plays, which include *The Vortex*, *Fallen Angels*, *The Queen was in the Parlour*, *Bitter Sweet* (an operetta), and *Cavalcade*, mainly dealing with modern society life and manners.

Cow'en, SIR FREDERIC HYMEN (1852–1935), Brit. composer and conductor; *b.* Kingston, Jamaica; conductor of Covent Garden Promenade Concerts, 1880, London Philharmonic Concerts, 1888–92, Manchester and Liverpool Philharmonic Concerts, 1896, and Scot. Orchestra, 1900–10. Works include *Rose Maiden* (1870), *Ruth* (1887), *Coronation Ode* (1902), *John Gilpin* (1904), *Suite of English Dances* (1905), *The Veil* (1910), and many songs. Pub. reminiscences, *My Art and My Friends* (1913).

Cow'ley, ABRAHAM (1618–67), Eng. poet and essayist; *b.* London; he is chiefly remembered by his *Pindaric Odes* and some fine elegies; and his prose essays, distinguished by directness and simplicity, continue to hold a high place in Eng. literature.

Cowper (*koop'er*), WILLIAM (1731–1800), Eng. poet; *b.* Great Berkhamsted; educated for the bar; early developed symptoms of insanity, which rendered a settled occupation impossible. He subsequently retired to the village of Olney (Bucks), where the good genius of his life was Mary Unwin, widow of a friend. He collaborated with the Rev. John Newton in writing the *Olney Hymns* (1779). In this environment he amused himself with his tame hares and other pets. In 1780, at the suggestion of Mrs. Unwin, he turned to secular poetry, and in 1782 pub. a vol. containing *Table Talk*, which was received with little enthusiasm. A new friendship with Lady Austen resulted in his next vol., 1785, which contained *The Task*, the ballad of *John Gilpin*, and other poems, and was an instantaneous success. His verse fills the transition period between the classicism of Pope and the nature poetry of Wordsworth, and therefore Cowper stands as a landmark in Eng. literature. In addition, he was a great letter-writer.

[*Life and Letters*, by R. Southey (1834–7); *Life*, by Goldwin Smith (Eng. Men of Letters, 1880); *The Stricken Deer*, by David Cecil (1929).]

Cowper-Temple, WILLIAM FRANCIS, LORD MOUNT TEMPLE (1811–88), Eng. politician; *b.* in Herts; nephew of Lord Melbourne and stepson of Lord Palmerston; M.P., 1835–80; Baron, 1880; as commissioner of works, 1860–6, prevented enclosure of common lands; in Education Act of 1870 inserted clause giving parents right to withdraw children in elementary schools from religious instruction, and prohibiting the teaching of denominational religion in a school provided by a public authority (Cowper-Temple clause).

Cox, DAVID (1783–1859), Eng. landscape artist; *b.* near Birmingham; son of a blacksmith; found most of his subjects at Bettws-y-Coed in N. Wales; his best works are in water colours. His *Hayfield* sold for £2,950 in 1875.

Cox, SIR GEORGE WILLIAM (1827–1902), Eng. mythologist; *b.* Benares; voluminous author, his works including *Mythology of the Aryan Nations* (1870), *Introduction to the Science of Comparative Mythology and Folk-lore* (1881). He was strongly influenced by the ideas of Max Müller, but was the ablest of the older school of comparative mythologists.

Cox, HAROLD (1859–), Eng. politician and journalist; educated Cambridge; worked as an agricultural labourer for a time to gain insight into the conditions of labouring life; Liberal M.P. for Preston, 1906–10; ed. *Edinburgh Review*, 1912–29; member of the Bryce Commission on Ger. Outrages, 1915, of the Committee on Public Retrenchment, 1916, and the Royal Commission on Decimal Currency, 1919.

Cox, SAMUEL (1826–93), Eng. Baptist preacher; *b.* London; founded *The Expositor* (1875), the first 20 vols. of which were almost entirely his own work.

Coxe, WILLIAM (1747–1828), Eng. traveller and historian; wrote *Memoirs of Sir Robert Walpole* (1798), and a *History of the House of Austria* (1807).

Cox'well, HENRY TRACEY (1819–1900), Eng. aeronaut; *b.* in Kent; his balloon ascent with Glaisher, 1862, to a height of 7 miles created a record.

Crabbe, GEORGE (1754–1832), Eng. poet; *b.* Aldeburgh, Suffolk; befriended by Burke, Fox, and others; took orders, and devoted his leisure to production of poetry. His *Parish Register*, *The Borough*, *The Village*, *The Library*, and other works, are marked by homely realism, of which he was a master.

[*Lives*, by his son, George Crabbe (1834), and Canon Ainger (Eng. Men of Letters, 1902).]

Cradock, SIR CHRISTOPHER (1862–1914), Brit. admiral; *b.* Hartforth, Yorks; took part in the Sudan campaign of 1891, and was present with the Brit. naval brigade at the relief of Peking, 1900, being promoted captain for his great daring; later, led the allied forces for the relief of Tientsin; rear-admiral, 1910. In August 1914 he set sail to protect the southern trade routes menaced by the Ger. admiral von Spee. Though the enemy fleet was more powerful than his own, Cradock gave battle off Coronel, Nov. 1, 1914, was defeated, and went down in his flagship, the *Monmouth*.

Craig, EDWARD GORDON (1872–), Eng. stage designer; son

of Ellen Terry; formed a school for the Art of the Theatre in Florence, 1913; produced numerous plays both on the Continent and in England; wrote *The Art of the Theatre* (1911), *Towards a New Theatre* (1913), etc., and has exercised a strong influence on modern stage craft.

Craig, JOHN (*c.* 1512–1600), Scot. Calvinist; became Knox's colleague, 1563, and took important part in the abolition of Episcopacy and drawing up of National Covenant, 1580–1.

Craigavon, JAMES CRAIG, 1ST VISCOUNT (1871–), Irish politician; served in S. African War; entered Parliament, 1906; strongly opposed Home Rule for Ulster; treasurer of household under Coalition Government, 1916; financial secretary to Admiralty, 1920. Became first prime minister of Northern Ireland, 1921.

Craig'ie, PEARL MARY TERESA (1867–1906), Anglo-Amer. novelist and dramatist; *b.* Boston, U.S.A.; wrote under name of JOHN OLIVER HOBBES; works include *Some Emotions and a Moral* (1891), *The Herb Moon* (1896), *The School for Saints* (1897), *The Dream and the Business* (1906).

Craigie, SIR WILLIAM A. (1867–), Scot. philologist; *b.* Dundee; prof. of Anglo-Saxon, Oxford, 1916–25; prof. of English, Chicago, since 1925; joint ed. of *Oxford English Dictionary*; compiled *Dictionary of the Older Scottish Tongue* (1931), etc.

Craigmyle OF CRAIGMYLE, THOMAS SHAW, BARON (1850–), Scot. lawyer; *b.* Dunfermline; called to Scot. bar, 1875; solicitor-general for Scotland, 1894–5; lord advocate, 1905–9; lord of appeal, 1909–29; author of *Letters to Isabel* (1921), *The Other Bundle* (1927), *The Trial of Jesus Christ* (1928), and *Leicester, a Historie* (1931).

Craik, DINAH MARIA MULOCK, MRS. (1826–87), Eng. novelist; *b.* Stoke-on-Trent; wrote *John Halifax, Gentleman* (1857), and numerous other stories, as well as serious studies and some verse.

Craik, RT. HON. SIR HENRY (1846–1927), Scot. writer and publicist; secretary of the Scotch Education Department, 1885–1904; M.P. for Glasgow and Aberdeen Universities, 1906–18, and for the Scot. universities, 1918–27; author of *Life of Swift* (1882), *English Prose Selections* (1893–6), *A Century of Scottish History* (1901), and *Life of Edward, First Earl of Clarendon* (1911).

Cranach (*kran'a*ch), LUCAS (1472–1553), Ger. artist; court painter at Wittenberg, of which town he became burgomaster; formed a friendship with Luther, of whom he painted several portraits. His subjects are chiefly scriptural, marked by force and originality; he excelled in portraiture. Examples of his work are to be seen at Berlin, Munich, and the London National Gallery.

[*Lukas Cranach*, by Muther (1902).]

Crane, STEPHEN (1870–1900), Amer. novelist; *b.* Newark, New Jersey; *The Red Badge of Courage* (1895) is a series of war sketches which won him immediate fame; war correspondent in the Greco-Turk., 1897–8, and Span.-Amer., 1898, wars; other works include *The Open Boat and Other Tales of Adventure* (1898), and *The Monster* (1899).

Crane, WALTER (1845–1915), Eng. artist; *b.* Liverpool; chiefly famous for decorative work and book illustrations; successful writer and lecturer upon art; notable pictures include *The Bridge of Life* (a fine allegorical canvas).

[*The Art of Walter Crane*, by P. G. Konody (1902).]

Cranmer, THOMAS (1489–1556), Eng. ecclesiastic; *b.* in Notts; reader in divinity in Jesus Coll., Cambridge, and univ. examiner in theology; expressed opinion that Henry VIII. should take advice of universities as to validity of his marriage with Catherine of Aragon. Summoned by the king, Cranmer was employed in obtaining opinions in favour of divorce; made Archdeacon of Taunton; married, 1532; Archbishop of Canterbury, 1533; pronounced king's marriage invalid, May 23, 1533; helped to enforce king's supremacy over Church; declared king's marriage with Anne Boleyn invalid, 1536; carried out his Prot. views under Edward VI.; after signing recantations under Mary, was martyred, thrusting offending hand first into flames. He is famous as compiler of the first Book of Common Prayer.

[*Lives*, by Canon Mason (1897), A. D. Innes (1900), and A. F. Pollard (1904).]

Crashaw, RICHARD (*c.* 1613–49), Eng. poet; *b.* London; son of a Puritan preacher; joined R.C. Church; his *Steps to the Temple* (1646) and other religious poems show much genuine poetry.

Crassus, MARCUS LICINIUS (*c.* 115–53 B.C.), Rom. general and statesman; became richest man in Rome; as prætor crushed the revolt of Spartacus, 71; elected consul, 70; with Cæsar and Pompey formed first triumvirate; he obtained command of Syria for five years, 55; invaded Parthia, but was defeated and slain at Carrhae.

Crawford, FRANCIS MARION (1854–1909), Amer. novelist; *b.* in Italy, and thoroughly Italian in literary spirit; was a journalist in India for a time, and in early novels paints Oriental life. Among his many novels are *Saracinesca*, *Sant' Ilario*, and *A Cigarette-maker's Romance.*

Creasy, SIR EDWARD (1812–78), Eng. historian; *b.* Bexley; prof. of history, London Univ.; author of *Fifteen Decisive Battles of the World*, and other historical works.

Crébillon (*krā-bē-yon'*), PROSPER JOLYOT DE (1674–1762), Fr. tragic dramatist; *b.* Dijon; wrote *Atrée et Thyeste*, *Rhadamiste et Zénobie*, *Pyrrhus*, *Catilina*, *Le Triumvirat*, etc. His son, CLAUDE (1707–77), was a novelist and playwright.

Creech, THOMAS (1659–1700), Eng. scholar; *b.* Blandford, Dorset; noted for classical translation, especially verse translation of Lucretius.

Creech, WILLIAM (1745–1815), Edinburgh publisher and lord provost; made his shop and breakfast room the resort of celebrities. Pub. the second ed. of poems of Robert Burns.

Creevey, THOMAS (1768–1838), Eng. Whig politician; *b.* Liverpool; *Creevey Papers* (ed. by Sir Herbert Maxwell, 1903) give an excellent picture of life of late Georgian period.

Creighton (*krī'ton*), MANDELL (1843–1901), Eng. historian; *b.* Carlisle; joint founder of *English Historical Review*, 1886; prof. of eccles. history, Cambridge, 1884; Bishop of Peterborough, 1891; Bishop of London, 1897; author of *Tudors and the Reformation*, *Age of Elizabeth*, *Wolsey*, and a monumental *History of the Papacy.*

[*Life and Letters of Mandell Creighton*, by his wife (2 vols., 1903).]

Crémieux (*krā-mū'*), ISAAC MOÏSE, commonly called ADOLPHE (1796–1880), Fr. lawyer and statesman; *b.* Nîmes; when minister of justice, 1848, abolished death penalty for political offences; in 1870 conferred Fr. citizenship on Jews of Algeria.

Cres'pi, DANIELE (1590–1630), Ital. painter of Milan; his colouring in oil and fresco occasionally recalls Titian; his best works are *Pictures of the Life of St. Bruno*, *The Descent from the Cross* (both in Milan).

Creswick, THOMAS (1811–69), Eng. landscape painter; *b.* Sheffield; illustrated Gray's *Elegy*, Milton's *L'Allegro*, and Goldsmith's *Deserted Village*.

Crewe, ROBERT OFFLEY ASHBURTON CREWE-MILNES, MARQUESS OF (1858–), Brit. statesman; *b.* London; son of Lord Houghton, and son-in-law of Lord Rosebery; has held many important offices in the Liberal and Coalition governments, including lord-lieutenant of Ireland, 1892–5; lord president of the Council, 1905–8, 1915–16; secretary of state for colonies, 1908–10; secretary of state for India, 1910–15; ambassador to France, 1922–8; has written *Stray Verses* (1889–90) and *Life of Lord Rosebery* (1931).

Cribb, TOM (1781–1848), Eng. pugilist; defeated great boxers of his day, including Molineux, an Amer. negro; was one of pugilists (dressed as pages) at George IV.'s coronation; in 1821 was given title 'Champion of England' for life; noted for his fair play and integrity.

Crichton (*krī'ton*), JAMES, 'THE ADMIRABLE CRICHTON' (*c.* 1560–1582), Scot. scholar, whose versatility has become proverbial; *b.* in Dumfriesshire; son of Robert Crichton, lord advocate of Scotland; tradition states that he successfully carried on a debate in twelve languages in Paris, and next day won a match in a tournament; outstanding philosopher, mathematician, theologian; composer of Lat. verses; a fine swordsman; a man of great beauty; killed in a street brawl.

[*James Crichton of Eliock*, by D. Crichton (1911).]

Crichton-Browne, SIR JAMES (1840–), Brit. physician; authority on mental and nervous disorders and public health; has written many medical works and also various volumes of reminiscences.

Cris'pi, FRANCESCO (1819–1901), Ital. statesman; *b.* Sicily; took side of popular party in Sicilian revolution, 1848, in Mazzini plot at Milan, 1853, and in Garibaldi movement, which he organized, 1860, as minister of interior, 1877, secured the accession of Humbert I. as king of a united Italy, and worked to make Rome the capital; prime minister, 1887, when Italy entered Triple Alliance, and again, 1893–5, but resigned after Ital. defeat at Aduwa in Abyssinia.

Crispin, ST., the patron saint of shoemakers. According to legend, two Rom. brothers, Crispin and Crispinian, settled at Soissons, in Gaul, and were beheaded, 287, for preaching the gospel. During their mission they supported themselves as shoemakers. The battle of Agincourt was fought on St. Crispin's Day, Oct. 25, 1415.

Croce (*krō'chā*), BENEDETTO (1866–), Ital. philosopher; *b.* in Aquila; declared inseparable alliance of history and philosophy. Of his numerous publications the following have been trans. into English: *Æsthetic* (1902), *Logic* (1905), *Theory of History* (1916), *Problems of Æsthetic* (1910), *Goethe* (1919), *Ariosto, Shakespeare, and Corneille* (1920), *Autobiography* (1927).

Crockett, SAMUEL RUTHERFORD (1860–1914), Scot. novelist; *b.* in Galloway; became minister of the Free Church, but eventually abandoned the ministry for a literary career; a prolific writer, his works include *The Stickit Minister* (1893), *The Raiders* (1894), *Men of the Moss Hags* (1895).

Crœsus (*krē'sus*), King of Lydia (reigned 560–546 B.C.), proverbially wealthy. He subdued the whole of Ionia, but was finally overcome by Cyrus, King of Persia.

Croft, or CROFTS, WILLIAM (1678–1727), Eng. organist and composer; *b.* in Warwickshire; wrote anthems, sonatas for the flute, and theatrical music; organist of Westminster Abbey, from 1708.

Crofts, ERNEST (1847–1911), Eng. painter of historical subjects; *b.* Leeds; R.A., 1896; largest work a panel, *Queen Elizabeth opening the First Royal Exchange*; other works include *On the Morning of the Battle of Waterloo, Cromwell at Marston Moor, Charles I. on his way to the Scaffold, Napoleon and the Old Guard at Waterloo*; some of his frescoes are in the palace of Westminster.

Croker, JOHN WILSON (1780–1857), Brit. Conservative statesman and writer; *b.* Galway; said to have introduced word 'Conservatives'; wrote condemnation of Keats's *Endymion* for *Quarterly Review*; ed. Boswell's *Life of Johnson*; also *Stories for Children from the History of England*, which suggested Scott's *Tales of a Grandfather.*

Croker, THOMAS CROFTON (1798–1854), Irish antiquary and humorous writer; *b.* Cork; pub. *Fairy Legends, Popular Songs of Ireland*, etc.

Croll, JAMES (1821–90), Scot. scientist; *b.* in Perthshire; keeper of Andersonian Museum, Glasgow; appointed to Scot. Geological Survey; his most noted book is *Climate and Time* (1875).

Crome, JOHN (1768–1821), Eng. landscape artist; *b.* Norwich; known as 'Old Crome'; founder of Norwich School of Artists, 1805. His pictures include *Mousehold Heath* and *Bruges.* His son, JOHN BERNAY CROME (1794–1842), was a landscape painter of similar style.

Cromer, EVELYN BARING, 1ST EARL (1841–1917), Brit. statesman and ambassador; *b.* Norfolk; famous for his work in Egypt when he held the offices of commissioner of Egyptian public debt, 1877–9, controller-general, 1879–80, Brit. minister plenipotentiary, 1883–1907. Upon his advice Egypt surrendered the Sudan, but recovered it through Kitchener's campaign, 1896–8. He reorganized Egyptian education, finance, irrigation, and general administration, and on resigning received the thanks of Parliament and a grant of £50,000, besides the O.M. Was appointed chairman of the Dardanelles Inquiry Commission, 1916. Works include *Modern Egypt* (2 vols., 1908), *Ancient and Modern Imperialism* (1910), and *Political and Literary Essays* (1908–13).

Crompton, SAMUEL (1753–1827), Eng. cotton spinner; *b.* in Lancs; invented spinning-mule for muslin yarns, and thus practically created the Brit. muslin trade, 1779.

Cromwell, OLIVER (1599–1658), Lord Protector of the Commonwealth of England; *b.* Huntingdon. Early showed popular sympathies in public life at Huntingdon and Ely; was member for Cambridge in Short and Long Parliaments, 1640. He was foremost in securing military forces of country for Parliament. Cromwell commanded under Essex at Edgehill, 1642; organized 'the Ironsides' from men 'who made some conscience of what they did'; distinguished himself at Winceby, 1643; commanded left wing at Marston Moor. A dispute now arose as to ultimate aim of the war. The army, composed of Puritans of various new sects, sided with Cromwell, who persuaded Parliament to pass 'Self-denying Ordinance,' 1645, for remodelling army. Sir Thomas Fairfax was appointed general, and Cromwell (exempted from new law) lieut.-general, and the king was utterly defeated at Naseby, 1645. A quarrel ensued between army and Parliament, and the army seized the king, 1647. On flight of Charles to Carisbrooke, Cromwell forced Parliament to abandon attempt at compromise; and, exasperated by second Civil War which followed, he denounced the king, and secured his execution, 1649. Pride's 'Purge' made Independents supreme, and Parliament became Cromwell's instrument. Appointed lord-lieutenant and commander-in-chief for Ireland, Cromwell ruthlessly subdued Drogheda and Wexford, 1649, and made himself master of Ireland. Cromwell was then made commander-in-chief against party of Charles II. in Scotland, 1650; great victories of Dunbar, Sept. 3, 1650, and Worcester, Sept. 3, 1651, ended Civil War. Long Parliament was dismissed by Cromwell, 1653, and he as commander-in-chief became dictator and protector, 1653. Peace was made with Holland; England acquired a great name in Europe, and a large party besought Cromwell to become king; Cromwell refused the title owing to army's objection. He was buried in Westminster Abbey, but his body was exhumed and hanged after the Restoration.

[*Cromwell's Letters and Speeches*, by Carlyle; *Lives*, by Lord Morley, C. H. Firth, F. Harrison, and John Buchan.]

Cromwell, Richard (1626–1712), son and successor of Oliver Cromwell; Lord Protector of England, 1658–9, he lacked capacity for ruling, and, being violently opposed by army, was forced to resign.

Cromwell, Thomas, Earl of Essex (*c.* 1485–1540), Eng. statesman; *b.* London; son of a blacksmith and fuller; after a varied career entered Wolsey's service; remained faithful to Wolsey after his fall. He guided Henry VIII. in his divorce proceedings against Catherine of Aragon, getting Parliament to pass the Act of Supremacy, 1534. Thereafter he was Henry VIII.'s chief minister, his policy being to secure absolute power for the king; secured revenue by suppression of monasteries; created Earl of Essex, 1540. He was executed on the failure of Henry's marriage with Anne of Cleves, which he had brought about.

[*Life and Letters of Thomas Cromwell*, by R. B. Merriman (1902).]

Cro'nin, Archibald Joseph (1897–   ), Scot. author; *b.* in Dumbartonshire; practised medicine; his novels, *Hatter's Castle* (1931), *Three Loves* (1932), and *The Stars look Down* (1934), are realistic studies of Scot. life.

Cronje (*krōn'ye*), Piet Arnoldus (1840–1911), Boer general; *b.* Transvaal; commanded Boer force which compelled the surrender of the Jameson raiders at Krugersdorp, 1896; in S. African War defeated British at Magersfontein, 1899; captured at Paardeberg, 1900.

Crookes, Sir William (1832–1919), Eng. chemist and physicist; discovered the element thallium, invented the radiometer, and investigated electric discharges in exhausted tubes; conducted researches on the composition of rare earths, artificial production of diamonds, and the fixation of atmospheric nitrogen, etc. Was a keen student of spiritualism. Received numerous honours, scientific and public; O.M., 1910.

Crooks, Will (1852–1921), Labour leader and politician; elected to the London County Council, 1892; mayor of Poplar, 1901; M.P. for Woolwich from 1901 (except from Jan.–Dec. 1910); advocated the establishment of industrial arbitration courts. During the Great War he did useful service to the cause of recruiting; P.C., 1916.

Crowe. (1) SIR JOSEPH ARCHER (1825–96), Eng. art critic; *b.* London; studied painting; war correspondent during Crimean War; consul-general in Leipzig, 1860–72, and in Düsseldorf, 1872–80; best known for his histories of art, written in collaboration with Giovanni Battista Cavalcaselle, which have become classics. (2) SIR EYRE (1864–1925), Brit. diplomat, son of (1); *b.* Leipzig; entered the Foreign Office, 1885; assistant under-secretary of state for foreign affairs, 1912; permanent under-secretary of state for foreign affairs, 1920; his Memorandum on Ger. foreign policy did much to influence the Brit. Cabinet when the Great War broke out; took part in the Paris Peace Conference as minister-plenipotentiary.

Crowther, SAMUEL ADJAI (1810–91), African native bishop, 1864, of Niger territories; *b.* near Dahomey; eloquent preacher; trans. Bible and Prayer Book into Yoruba dialect.

Cruden, ALEXANDER (1701–70), Scot. scholar; *b.* Aberdeen; author of *Concordance* to the Bible, 1737.

Cruikshank, GEORGE (1792–1878), Eng. artist, caricaturist, and book illustrator; *b.* London; renowned for his illustrations to Dickens, Ainsworth, Lever, etc.; later works definitely moral in purpose, such as the temperance series, *The Bottle, The Drunkard's Children*, and *The Worship of Bacchus*.

Cudworth, RALPH (1617–88), Eng. divine and philosopher; *b.* in Somersetshire; the greatest of the Cambridge Platonists. His chief works were *The True Intellectual System of the Universe* (1678) and *Treatise concerning Eternal and Immutable Morality.* He sought to confute the philosophy of Atheism.

Cullen, PAUL (1803–78), Irish ecclesiastic; *b.* Prospect, County Kildare; Archbishop of Armagh, 1849, of Dublin, 1852; cardinal, 1866; he opposed extreme Nationalists and sided with Brit. Government against Fenians.

Cumberland, RICHARD (1631–1718), Eng. divine and philosopher; *b.* London; became Bishop of Peterborough. His *De Legibus Naturæ Disquisitio Philosophica* (1672) anticipated utilitarian school in its enunciation of the public good as the end of morality, and opposed the doctrines of Hobbes.

Cumberland, RICHARD (1732–1811), Eng. dramatist; *b.* Cambridge; filled numerous government appointments; plays, which number fifty-four, and are chiefly sentimental comedies, include *The West Indian* (his best), *The Wheel of Fortune*, etc.; wrote also novels, poems, and essays; his *Memoirs* (1806) are of value.

Cumberland, WILLIAM AUGUSTUS, DUKE OF (1721–65), Brit. general, son of George II.; distinguished himself at Dettingen, 1743, and Fontenoy, 1745; put down the 'Forty-five' rebellion, winning the battle of Culloden, 1746, and so sternly stamped out revolt that he earned the nickname 'Butcher'; fell into disgrace through misfortunes in Seven Years' War, but ultimately regained popularity.

Cummings, BRUCE (1889–1917), known by his pseudonym of 'W. N. P. BARBELLION,' Eng. zoologist and man of letters; *b.* Barnstaple; won fame with his *Journal of a Disappointed Man* (1917), written in a clear, vigorous style. Pub. posthumously were his *Enjoying Life, and Other Literary Remains* (1919) and *A Last Diary* (1920).

Cunard', SIR SAMUEL (1787–1865), Anglo-Can. engineer and shipowner; *b.* Halifax, Nova Scotia; one of the founders of the Brit. and N. Amer. Steam Packet Co. (afterwards the Cunard Co.); first established steam postal communication between England and America.

Cunningham, ALLAN (1784–1842), Scot. lyric poet and man of letters; *b.* Keir, Dumfriesshire; pub. *Songs, chiefly in the Rural Dialect of Scotland, Songs of Scotland, Ancient and Modern*, etc., among the best known of which are his version of 'My Ain Countree' and 'A Wet Sheet and a Flowing Sea.'

Cunningham, WILLIAM (1805–61), Scot. divine; *b.* Hamilton; took a leading part in pre-Disruption controversy and in formation of the Free Church; first prof. of Church History and Divinity, New Coll., Edinburgh, 1843; principal, 1847.

Cunningham, WILLIAM (1849–1919), Brit. political economist; *b.* Edinburgh; prof. of economics at King's Coll., London, 1891–7; pub. authoritative works on the growth of Eng. industry and commerce, also wrote on social and political subjects.

Cunninghame Graham, ROBERT BONTINE (1852–1936), Scot. author and Socialist; *b.* London; critic of modern civilization; spent early life in Argentine; travelled, particularly in Spanish-speaking countries; M.P. for N. Lanarkshire, 1886–92; writer of essays, biographies, and travel-sketches noted for their style and originality; his works include *Mogreb el Acksa* (1898), *A Vanished Arcadia* (1901), *Hernando de Soto* (1902), *His People* (1906), *The Conquest of the River Plate* (1924), *The Horses of the Conquest* (1930), and *Writ in Sand* (1932).

[*Cunninghame Graham: His Life and Works*, by H. F. West (1932).]

Curel, FRANÇOIS DE (1854–1928), Fr. dramatist; *b.* Metz; member of Fr. Academy; his plays deal with social problems and difficult situations of ordinary life; among his successes were *Le Repas du Lion* (1898), *Terre Inhumaine* (1923), and *La Vi-veuse et le Moribond* (1926).

Curie (*koo-rē'*), PIERRE (1859–1906), and his wife, MARIE SKLODOWSKA (1867–1934), Fr. physicists; Pierre Curie was born at Paris; became prof. of physics at Sorbonne, 1900; his wife, born at Warsaw, had been his pupil. While investigating Becquerel radiations from uranium they jointly discovered polonium and radium, 1898; in 1903 they shared the Nobel Prize for physics with Henri Becquerel; Madame Curie succeeded her husband as director of physics at Faculty of Sciences, Paris, and in 1911 received the Nobel Prize for chemistry; on behalf of women of U.S.A. President Harding presented her with a gramme of radium in recognition of her services to science, 1921.

Currie, SIR ARTHUR WILLIAM (1875–1933), Can. soldier; *b.* in Ontario; commanded 1st Can. Division, 1914–17, in Great War, and a Can. Corps in France, 1917–19; principal of M'Gill Univ. from 1920.

Currie, SIR DONALD (1825–1909), Scot. shipowner; *b.* Greenock; established Castle Line to India and S. Africa, afterwards amalgamated with Union Line as Union Castle.

Currie, JAMES (1756–1805), Scot. physician; *b.* in Dumfriesshire; promoted hydrotherapy and was first to make systematic record of clinical observations with thermometer; also remembered as first editor of Burns, 1800.

Curtis, GEORGE WILLIAM (1824–92), Amer. author; *b.* Providence, Rhode Island; ed. *Harper's Monthly* and *Harper's Weekly*;

wrote several books of travel and some verse.

Curt'ius, Ernst (1814–96), Ger. historian; *b.* Lübeck; prof. at Berlin Univ.; made excavations in Greece for Ger. Government; wrote numerous archæological works and a *History of Greece.*

Curtius, Marcus, Rom. legendary hero. A chasm having opened in the Forum, the soothsayers declared that it could only be filled by throwing into it Rome's best treasure; Curtius, crying that the greatest treasure of Rome was a brave citizen, leaped on horseback into the chasm, which immediately closed.

Curwen, John (1816–80), Eng. Nonconformist preacher; *b.* Heckmondwike; promulgator of Tonic Sol-Fa musical system, and founder of Tonic Sol-Fa Coll.; author of *People's Service of Song,* etc.

Curzon of Kedleston, George Nathaniel, 1st Earl (1859–1925), Brit. statesman; *b.* Kedleston, Derbyshire; Conservative M.P. for Southport, 1886–98; under-secretary for India, 1891–2; under-secretary for foreign affairs, 1895–8; viceroy of India, 1899–1905, during which time occurred the Tibet expedition, 1904, and partition of Bengal; opposition of Kitchener in 1905 on question of dual control of Ind. army led to his resignation; chancellor of Oxford Univ., 1907; created earl, 1911; leader of House of Lords, 1916; president of Air Board and member of Imperial War Cabinet, 1916; foreign secretary, 1919–24; in 1923 he succeeded in modifying Fr. action in Germany regarding reparations; might have become prime minister in that year had he not been in Upper House; travelled extensively in Central Asia, Persia, etc.; author of *Problems of the Far East* (1894), *Principles and Methods of University Reform* (1909), *Modern Parliamentary Eloquence* (1913), *War Poems* (1915), *British Government in India* (1925), etc.

[*Life,* by Lord Ronaldshay (3 vols., 1928).]

Cuthbert, St. (*d.* 687), Scot. saint; *b.* probably in Northumbria; joined Melrose Abbey, becoming prior; later prior of Lindisfarne, Bishop of Hexham, and Bishop of Lindisfarne; lived as a hermit on Farne Is.; converted Scotland, from Forth to Tweed, to Christianity. His remains are in Durham Cathedral.

[*Life,* by Bede; also modern *Lives,* by A. C. Fryer (1880) and C. Eyre (1887).]

Cuvier (*koo-vyā'*), Georges Leopold Chrétien Frédéric Dagobert (1769–1832), Fr. anatomist; *b.* Montbéliard; assistant, later prof., in the Jardin des Plantes, Paris; made painstaking researches in comparative anatomy and palæontology, especially of molluscs and vertebrates and fossil reptiles and mammals. His *Le Règne Animal* was long the standard work on zoology.

Cuyp (*koip*), Albert (1620–91), Dutch artist; *b.* Dordrecht; famous for pastoral scenes, executed with striking simplicity. Among his best works are *Banks of a Lake* and *The Meuse near Dort.*

Cynewulf (*kin'e-woolf*) (*fl.* 750), O.E. vernacular poet; author of four poems, *Christ, Juliana, Elene,* and *The Fates of the Apostles*; poetry shows feeling for nature, especially in its stormy moods.

Cyprian (*sip'ri-an*), St. (*c.* 200–258), Bishop of Carthage; converted from paganism to Christianity; made bishop *c.* 248–9; after various conflicts between Christians and the state, he was beheaded by order of the Emperor Valerian. Cyprian was more of a Church leader than a theologian, his interest being mainly in discipline and organization.

Cyrano de Bergerac. See BERGERAC, SAVINIEN CYRANO DE.

Cyril, ST. (1) Bishop of Jerusalem (*c.* 315–86); famed for his writings, which are of the greatest value for students of creeds and liturgies. (2) Bishop of Alexandria (*c.* 376–444). As patriarch of Alexandria expelled Jews, and in zeal against heretics is said to have instigated murder of Hypatia; defeated Nestorius at Council of Ephesus, 431; wrote commentaries, etc.

Cyrus, name of two great Pers. rulers. (1) THE GREAT, founder of Pers. empire; overthrew King of the Medes, 549 B.C., and became sole ruler of Medes and Persians; defeated Crœsus of Lydia, and annexed Lydia, 546; overran Asia Minor; captured Babylon, 539, when Belshazzar was put to death. His domain extended from the Ægean to Afghanistan; was killed in battle with Scythians, 528. (2) THE YOUNGER, younger son of Darius II. of Persia; in Peloponnesian War gave important help to Spartans, who assisted him in attempt to overturn government of brother, Artaxerxes, in which his army, the famous Ten Thousand of Xenophon, won the battle of Cunaxa, at which Cyrus was slain.

Czartoryski (*chăr-tō-ris'kē*), ADAM GEORG, PRINCE (1770–1861), Polish statesman; *b.* Warsaw; supported rising of Kosciuszko; family estates were confiscated; afterwards gained favour of Tsar, was present at Austerlitz, 1805, and held various government appointments. In revolution of 1830 was appointed president of provisional government, but resigned and served as a private soldier; exempted from amnesty, he emigrated to France.

Czernin (*cher'nēn*), OTTOKAR, COUNT (1872–), Austro-Hungarian statesman; *b.* Vienna; minister at Bucharest, 1913–16, where he laboured unsuccessfully to prevent Romania's entry into the Great War; foreign minister, 1916–18; resigned owing to differences with the Emperor. His *Memoirs* (1919), in which he lays chief blame for the war on the Prussian militarists, shed the first authentic light on Austro-Ger. relations during the Great War.

Czerny, GEORGE. See KARAGEORGE.

Czerny (*cher'nē*), KARL (1791–1857), Austrian composer and pianist; *b.* Vienna; pupil of Beethoven; teacher of Liszt; still well known by his manuals for learning music.

D

D'Ab'ernon, EDGAR VINCENT, 1ST VISCOUNT (1857–), Brit. diplomatist; *b.* Slinfold, Sussex; financial adviser to Egyptian Government, 1883–9; governor of the Imperial Ottoman Bank, Constantinople, 1889–97; M.P., 1899–1906; created peer, 1914; chairman of Central Control Board (Liquor Traffic) during Great War; ambassador to Germany, 1920–6. Author of *A Grammar of Modern Greek* (1881), *An Ambassador of Peace* (1929–31), *The Eighteen Decisive Battles of the World* (1931).

D'Ache, CARAN. See CARAN D'ACHE.

Dacier (*dă-syā'*), ANDRÉ (1651–1722), Fr. classical scholar; *b.* Castres, Languedoc; librarian at the Louvre, 1694; ed. *Festus* and *Verius Flaccus*, and made numerous translations. His wife, ANNE LEFEVRE (1654–1720), trans. the *Iliad* and the *Odyssey* into prose.

Da Cos'ta, ISAAK (1798–1860), Dutch poet; *b.* Amsterdam; among works are *Poëzy* (1821), *God met ons* (1826), *Festliedern* (1828), *Hagar* (1852).

Da Gama. See GAMA.

Dag'obert I. (*d.* 639), Merovingian king; succeeded as king of the Franks, 628; curbed disorder of nobles and Church, encouraged art, sent out Christian missionaries, made alliance with Byzantine empire.

Daguerre (*dä-gär'*), LOUIS JACQUES MANDÉ (1789–1851), Fr. painter of panoramic views; *b.* Cormeilles, Seine-et-Oise; invented the diorama, and later the *daguerreotype*, the forerunner of modern photography

Dahl (*däl*), VLADIMIR IVANOVICH (1801–72), Russ. author and philologist (pen-name, KAZAK LUGANSKY); wrote novels of high value for study of Russ. songs and folklore.

Dahl'gren, KARL FREDRIK (1791-1844), Swed. poet of a humorous, realistic, and idyllic character; best-known piece, *The Zephyr and the Girl.*

Dahl'mann, FRIEDRICH CHRISTOPH (1785–1860), Ger. historian and politician; *b.* Wismar; held various professorships; stirred up feeling in Schleswig-Holstein hostile to Denmark; banished, 1837, for supporting constitutional reform in Hanover; attempted to bring about union of Germany, 1849; wrote valuable historical works.

Daim'ler, GOTTLIEB (1834–1900), inventor; *b.* near Württemberg; made the first motor-bicycle, 1885; produced first petrol-driven car, 1887, the forerunner of the modern Daimler car.

Dal'berg, name of Ger. noble family. Prominent members were JOHANN (1445–1503), founded first Gr. chair at Heidelberg. KARL THEODOR ANTON MARIA (1744–1817), last prince-archbishop of Mainz and important statesman of Empire. WOLFGANG HERIBERT VON (1750–1806), patron of Schiller.

Dalcroze. See JAQUES-DALCROZE.

Dale, DAVID (1739–1806), Scot. manufacturer and philanthropist; *b.* Stewarton, Ayrshire; established mills at New Lanark, and first turkey-red dyeworks in Scotland; founder and chief pastor of old Independents. Father-in-law of Robert Owen.

Dalen (*dä'len*), NILS GUSTAF (1869–   ), Swed. scientist; *b.* Stenstorp; has invented numerous improvements in hot-air turbines, air compressors, and milking machines; devised automatic lighting of unmanned lighthouses; Nobel Prize in Physics, 1912.

Dalhousie (*dal-hou'zi*), 10TH EARL AND 1ST MARQUESS OF, JAMES ANDREW BROUN-RAMSAY (1812–60), Brit. administrator; *b.* Dalhousie Castle, near Edinburgh; president of Board of Trade, 1845–6. As gov.-gen. of India, 1847–56, annexed Punjab, Kingdom of Pegu, Nagpur, and Oudh; introduced numerous reforms, including system of post offices and telegraphs, railways, canals, bridges, and metalled roads. Created marquess, 1849.

[*Life*, by Lee-Warner (1904).]

Dal'in, OLOF VON (1708–63), Swed. man of letters; *b.* Vinberg, Holland; ed. *Den Svenska Argus* on the model of Addison's *Spectator*, and wrote a history of Sweden.

Dal'linger, WILLIAM HENRY (1842–1909), Eng. Wesleyan minister and scientist; *b.* Devonport; made microscopic researches on little-known 'monads' or 'flagellates'; four times president of Royal Microscopical Soc.

Dallmeyer (*däl′mī-er*), JOHN HENRY (1830–83), Anglo-Ger. optician; *b.* in Westphalia; settled in London, 1851; manufactured telescopes; was authority on photographic lenses.

Dal′ton, JOHN (1766–1844), Eng. chemist and physicist; *b.* near Cockermouth; became a teacher in Manchester in 1793; from 1787 kept meteorological observations until the day before his death. In 1794 wrote a paper on colour-blindness, with which he was afflicted, and pub. numerous papers on the properties of gases. His most important work, however, is his enunciation of the atomic theory; F.R.S., 1822.

[*John Dalton and the Rise of Modern Chemistry,* by Roscoe (1895).]

Dalyell, or DALZELL (*dē-el′*), THOMAS (*c.* 1599–1685), Scot. soldier; *b.* near Linlithgow; served with Tsar of Russia against Turks and Tatars; commander-in-chief in Scotland, 1666; defeated Covenanters at Rullion Green; raised the Scots Greys, 1681.

Damien (*dä-myan′*), 'FATHER' JOSEPH (1840–89), Belgian missionary; *b.* near Louvain; went to minister to the lepers of Molokai, Hawaii, 1873; died of leprosy; eulogized by R. L. Stevenson.

[*Father Damien,* by Clifford (1889).]

Damocles (*dam′ō-klēz*) (4th cent. B.C.), flatterer at court of Dionysius of Syracuse, who at a banquet suspended a sword above Damocles' head by a single hair, to show how close death is to earthly felicity.

Da′mon (*c.* 400 B.C.), Pythagorean philosopher; famed for devotion to his friend Phintias (or Pythias), in whose place he became hostage to Dionysius of Syracuse.

Dampier (*dam′pēr*), WILLIAM (1652–1715), Eng. navigator and author; *b.* East Coker, Somerset; buccaneer on Span. Main; commander of Eng. voyage of discovery to Australia, 1699; surveyed east coast of New Guinea; master of expedition, 1708–11, which rescued Alexander Selkirk.

Dan, elder of two sons of Jacob and Bilhah (Gen. 30); ancestor of the tribe of Dan.

Dana (*dā′nä*), CHARLES ANDERSON (1819–97), Amer. journalist; *b.* in New Hampshire; ed. *Tribune*; assistant secretary for war, 1864–5; proprietor of the New York *Sun,* 1868; ed. *New American Cyclopædia,* 1857–63, and *American Cyclopædia,* 1873–6.

Dana, JAMES DWIGHT (1813–95), Amer. geologist; *b.* Utica, New York; mathematical teacher, U.S.A. navy; geologist to U.S.A. exploring expedition to southern seas under Wilkes, 1838; prof. of natural history and geology at Yale Coll., 1850; wrote numerous works, including *Manual of Geology.*

Dana, RICHARD HENRY (1815–82), Amer. author; *b.* Cambridge, Mass.; wrote *Two Years before the Mast*; was an authority on maritime law.

Dancourt (*dän-koor′*), FLORENT CARTON (1661–1725), Fr. actor and dramatist; *b.* Fontainebleau; wrote some sixty plays illustrating contemporary social history; best play *Le Chevalier à la Mode* (1687).

Dan′dolo, name of noble Venetian family. ENRICO (*c.* 1120–1205), elected doge 1193, turned aside Fourth Crusade to capture Constantinople; rewarded with Crete and other possessions of Gr. Empire. ANDREA (1307–54), doge 1343–54, a famous administrator, was eulogized by Petrarch.

Dandolo, VINCENZO, COUNT (1758–1819), Ital. scientist; *b.* Venice; governor of Dalmatia, 1805–9; improved the sanitary, agricultural, and educational condition of the people.

Daniel, chief character of biblical Book of Daniel; Jewish captive who rose to importance in Babylonian court. See Dan. 1–6.

Daniel, SAMUEL (1562–1619), Eng. poet; *b.* near Taunton; author of the *Complaynt of Rosamund, Delia* (sonnets), a verse history of the Wars of the Roses and court masques; championed poetry in *The Defence of Ryme.*

Daniell, JOHN FREDERIC (1790–1845), Eng. physicist; *b.* London; invented *Daniell cell*, a pyrometer, a hygrometer, etc.; first prof. of chemistry, King's Coll., London, 1831.

Dan'necker, JOHANN HEINRICH VON (1758–1841), Ger. sculptor; *b.* Stuttgart; *Ariadne on the Panther* (at Frankfurt) is his best-known work.

D'Annunzio (*dä-noon'tsē-ō*), GABRIELE, PRINCE MONTE NEVOSO (1864–), Ital. poet, novelist, dramatist, and soldier; *b.* Pescara, Abruzzi; son of Duchessa Maria Gallese of Rome; his novels were placed on the *Index Expurgatorius* by the Vatican in 1911; most of his novels and plays have been trans. into English. During War advocated Italy's intervention, and became national idol; served in army and navy, and proved himself a daring airman. After armistice carried out a dramatic coup by seizing Fiume for Italy. Created prince, 1924.

Dante Alighieri (*dän'tā al-ē-gyā'-rē*) (1265–1321), greatest Ital. poet; *b.* Florence; Dante is an abbreviation of Durante. Little is known of his early life. At the age of nine he first met Beatrice, who is believed to have been the daughter of Folco Portinari; she married Simone de' Bardi, and died, 1290, aged 25. In 1283 the poet began to write the noble lyrics inspired by his love for Beatrice, which he included in *Vita Nuova* (*New Life*). The death of Beatrice was followed by a period of bitter depression, and Dante appears to have plunged into dissipation. A period of military service ensued. About 1298 he married Gemma, daughter of Manetto Donati. Dante took an active part in the government of Florence, but his party was overthrown by the nobles in 1301, and in 1302 he was banished. From 1302–10 Dante wandered over Italy, spending much time at Verona, and commenced to write his *Convivio* (*Banquet*) and *De Vulgari Eloquentia.* A fresh sentence of banishment, 1311, prevented his return to Florence. His closing years were happily spent under the patronage of Can Grande della Scala at Verona, and of Guido da Polenta at Ravenna. During this period his *Divina Commedia* was written, and other works continued. He died and was buried at Ravenna. The greatest poet Italy has produced, he was supreme as an epic poet, but also distinguished as a lyric writer, as is shown in his *Canzoniere* and the lyrical portions of the *Vita Nuova.* In his epic masterpiece, the *Divina Commedia*, man's life after death is portrayed, the poet describing his visions of hell, purgatory, and the heavens, under the guidance first of Virgil and then of Beatrice.

[Complete Eng. trans. of Dante's works in 'Temple Classics'; also trans. of the *Divine Comedy* by Cary, Longfellow, and Plumptre.]

Danton (*dän-ton'*), GEORGES JACQUES (1759–94), Fr. revolutionist; *b.* Arcis-sur-Aube; became president of Cordeliers' Club, an extreme antimonarchical and anti-aristocratic body; appointed minister of justice, and afterwards member of the Convention; voted for execution of king; fanned rage of populace against Girondists; made Committee of Public Safety supreme and army efficient. 'Reign of Terror' now passed out of Danton's control. At first protected by Robespierre, he was subsequently abandoned, and guillotined.

[*Life*, by Belloc.]

D'Arblay (*där'blā*), MADAME (FANNY BURNEY) (1752–1840), Eng. novelist and diarist; *b.* King's Lynn; self-educated; helped to develop Eng. novel as form of literature by *Evelina* (1778), *Cecilia* (1782); in service of Queen Charlotte, 1785–91; began her *Diary*, 1768.

Dari'us, name of several anc. Pers. rulers. (1) DARIUS I., THE GREAT (*d.* 485 B.C.), seized throne, 521 B.C.; extended territories to Caucasus; great lawgiver and organizer; led expedition to Europe; great defeat of his general at Marathon, 490 B.C. (2) DARIUS OCHUS (*r.* 424–405 B.C.); made alliance with Sparta against Athens. (3) DARIUS CODOMANNUS, beaten at Issus and Arbela, 331, by Alexander the Great.

Darling, CHARLES JOHN, 1ST BARON (1849–), judge of King's Bench Division, 1897–1923, distinguished for his wit; author of *A Prisoner's Garden and other Verses* (1926), etc.

Darling, GRACE HORSLEY (1815–42), Eng. heroine; *b.* Bamborough; daughter of keeper of Longstone lighthouse (Farne Is.); shared in rescue of shipwrecked crew of *Forfarshire*, 1838; died of consumption.

Darn'ley, HENRY STEWART, LORD (1545–67), Scot. noble; *b.* Temple Newsam, Yorks; great-grandson of Henry VII.; son of Earl of Lennox; married Mary Queen of Scots, 1565; father of James VI.; assisted in murder of Riccio; murdered at Kirk o' Field, Edinburgh.

Dar'win, CHARLES ROBERT (1809–82), Eng. naturalist; *b.* Shrewsbury; grandson of Dr. Erasmus Darwin, and of Josiah Wedgwood. Studied medicine in Edinburgh Univ., 1825–7; entered Christ's Coll., Cambridge, 1828, with the intention of becoming a clergyman. Became naturalist for the survey expedition of H.M.S. *Beagle*, 1831–6. On this celebrated voyage, Darwin made observations which laid the foundations for his subsequent work. On his return to England pub. the scientic results of the voyage: *Journal of a Naturalist* (1839), *Structure and Distribution of Coral Reefs* (1842), *Geological Observations* (1844 and 1846). In 1839 he married his cousin, Emma Wedgwood, and settled at Down, in Kent, where, in spite of persistent ill-health, he pursued the researches which led to the enunciation of his famous theories regarding natural selection and the origin of man. His essay, *On the Tendency of Species to form Varieties, etc.*, together with an essay by Alfred Russel Wallace, who had arrived at the same conclusions, was read at a memorable meeting of the Linnean Soc., 1858. This communication, followed by the publication of *On the Origin of Species by Means of Natural Selection*, aroused wild enthusiasm, and at the same time bitter opposition. *The Variation of Animals and Plants under Domestication* (1868) and *The Descent of Man* (1871) were other proofs of the vast amount of material Darwin had collected. He pub. various works on the fertilization of plants and their movement. Always a reverent searcher after truth, he gave a new impetus and direction to scientific investigation.

[*The Life and Letters of Charles Darwin, including an Autobiographical Chapter*, by Francis Darwin (1887).]

Darwin, ERASMUS (1731–1802), Eng. physician and poet; *b.*

Elton, Notts; practised at Lichfield and Derby. By his first marriage he was grandfather of Charles Darwin; by his second, of Francis Galton. He anticipated in part the theory of evolution propounded by Lamarck, and by his grandson.

Darwin, Sir Francis (1848–1925), Eng. botanist and biographer; *b.* Down, Kent; son of Charles Darwin; F.R.S.; president of Brit. Association, 1908; knighted, 1913. Wrote *Life and Letters of Charles Darwin* (1887).

Darwin, Sir George Howard (1845–1912), Eng. astronomer; *b.* Down, Kent; second son of Charles Darwin; Plumian prof. of astronomy at Cambridge, 1883; president Brit. Association, 1905; wrote on the tides, 1898, and on periodic orbits, etc.

Dasent (*dā'sent*), Sir George Webbe (1817–96), Eng. Scandinavian scholar; *b.* St. Vincent, W. Indies; did much to familiarize Brit. readers with Scandinavian and Icelandic sagas; pub. *Story of Burnt Njal, Popular Tales from the Norse*, etc.

Dass, Petter (1647–1708), Norweg. poet; *b.* Isl. of Nord Herö; son of Peter Dundas, a Scot. merchant in Bergen; chief work *The Trumpet of Nordland* (pub. 1739); 'father' of modern Norweg. poetry.

Daubeny (*dōb'nē*), Charles Giles Bridle (1795–1867), Eng. scientist; *b.* Stratton, Glos; prof. of chemistry, 1822, and of botany, 1834, at Oxford; pub. *Active and Extinct Volcanoes* (1826); president Brit. Association, 1856.

Daudet (*dō-dā'*), Alphonse (1840–97), Fr. novelist; *b.* Nîmes; served as usher in a school, as described in *Le Petit Chose*; became journalist, and after hard struggle achieved fame with *Fromont Jeune et Risler Aîné, Jack, Numa Roumestan, Sapho*, the brilliant, humorous *Tartarin* stories, *Lettres de mon Moulin*, and *Contes du Lundi*; noted as a stylist; his play, *L'Arlésienne*, with Bizet's music, is still a favourite. One of the greatest Fr. novelists of the later 19th cent.

[*Life*, by L. A. Daudet (1898).]

Daudet, Léon (1867–), Fr. man of letters and Royalist agitator; *b.* Paris; son of Alphonse Daudet; ed. of *L'Action Française*; his most popular work is *Les Morticoles*, 1894, a satire on physicians.

Daumier (*dō-myā'*), Honoré (1808–79), Fr. caricaturist; *b.* Marseilles; contributor to *Charivari*, and also a serious artist.

Daun (*doun*), Leopold Josef, Count von (1705–66), Austrian general; inflicted first defeat suffered by Frederick the Great, at Kolin, 1757, and was principal opponent to Prussia during Seven Years' War.

Dav'enant, Sir William (1606–68), Eng. poet and dramatist; *b.* Oxford; poet laureate, 1638; fought on Royalist side in Civil War; suffered imprisonment; wrote *Gondibert*, an epic poem, and plays.

David (Heb. 'beloved') (*fl. c.* 1000 B.C.), most famous King of Israel; son of Jesse of Bethlehem in Judah; kept his father's sheep; his slaying of Goliath is described in 1 Samuel 17 and 18; he relieved the madness of King Saul by means of his harp; became royal favourite and formed classic friendship with king's son Jonathan. His popularity roused the jealousy of Saul, and resulted in his exile; found refuge in cave of Adullam. On Saul's death David became King of Judah; captured Jerusalem from Jebusites. Was the author of several of the psalms.

[See Books of Samuel, Kings, and Chronicles.]

David (or DEWI), ST. (*c.* 6th cent.), Welsh patron saint; Bishop of St. Davids; canonized in 12th cent.; festival, March 1.

David I. (1084–1153), King of Scots; son of Malcolm Canmore and Margaret; introduced feudalism into Scotland; encouraged the development of the burghs; his endowments of bishoprics and abbeys earned for him the title, 'Ane sair sanct for the crown.' Invaded England in support of Matilda, and was defeated in Battle of the Standard, 1138.

David II. (1324–71), King of Scotland, 1329; *b.* Dunfermline; son of Robert the Bruce; taken prisoner by English at Neville's Cross, 1346; released, 1357, on promise of ransom of 100,000 merks; unable to raise this sum, could only reign as vassal of Edward III.

David I. OF WALES (*d.* 1203), lord of dist. round Snowdon; called by one chronicler 'king.' DAVID II. (*c.* 1208–46), Prince of N. Wales, half-brother of above; forced to do homage to Henry III. DAVID III. (*d.* 1283), last native prince of Wales; nephew of David II., revolted against Edward I. and fell into his hands; was tried and executed.

David (*dä-vēd'*), FÉLICIEN CÉSAR (1810–76), Fr. composer; achieved fame with *Le Désert*, a symphonic ode, 1844, and later composed comic operas and oratorios.

David, JACQUES LOUIS (1748–1825), Fr. painter; *b.* Paris; one of the outstanding figures in the history of modern painting; helped in revolt against light and frivolous style of Louis XV.; took prominent part in Fr. Revolution; was court painter to Napoleon; exiled after Waterloo. Among most famous pictures are *The Grief of Andromache, The Coronation of the Empress Josephine, Madame Récamier.*

David, PIERRE JEAN, or DAVID D'ANGERS (1789–1856), Fr. sculptor; *b.* Angers; famed for his busts and medallions; executed pediment of Panthéon, Paris.

Davids, THOMAS WILLIAM RHYS (1843–1922), Eng. Orientalist; *b.* Colchester; prof. of comparative religion in Manchester Univ., 1904–15; wrote several works on Buddhism. Married Caroline Foley, who was also an authority on Buddhism.

Davidson, ANDREW BRUCE (1831–1902), Scot. pioneer of Bible criticism; *b.* Kirkhill, Aberdeenshire; prof. of Oriental languages, New Coll., Edinburgh; member of O.T. Revision Committee; author of commentary on Job (unfinished), *Outlines of Hebrew Accentuation* (1861), etc.

Davidson, JOHN (1857–1909), Scot. poet, dramatist, and novelist; *b.* Barrhead; won distinction with *Fleet Street Eclogues, Ballads and Songs*, etc.

Davidson, RANDALL THOMAS, 1ST BARON (1848–1930), Brit. divine; *b.* Edinburgh; Bishop of Rochester, 1891–5, of Winchester, 1895–1903; Archbishop of Canterbury, 1903–28; was leading protagonist of Church reform, and a trusted leader in all questions of social reform. Closely associated with proposal to revise Prayer Book. Works include *The Testing of a Nation* (1919), *Occasions* (1925).

Davies (*dā'vis*), SIR HENRY WALFORD (1869–), Eng. musician; *b.* Oswestry; prof. of music, Wales Univ. Coll., Aberystwith, 1919–26; director of music, National Council of Music, since 1919; organist of St. George's Chapel, Windsor, 1927–32; master of music to the King, 1934; a noted composer. Pub. *The Pursuit of Music* (1935).

Davies, SIR JOHN (1569–1626), Eng. poet; *b.* Tisbury, Wilts; author of *Orchestra*, poem in praise of dancing; *Nosce Teipsum,* philosophical poem; *Hymns to Astræa*; held several political posts in Ireland, and was a founder of the Soc. of Antiquaries.

Davies, SARAH EMILY (1830–1921), Eng. educationist; *b.* Southampton; assisted to found Girton Coll., Cambridge, 1867; Mistress of Girton, 1873–5; secretary of Girton, 1882–1904; wrote *The Higher Education of Women.*

Davies, WILLIAM HENRY (1871–), Brit. poet; *b.* Newport, Mon.; lived as tramp in U.S.A., and later as pedlar in England. His poems show delight in Nature and the simple things of life; his first vol. of poems was *The Soul's Destroyer* (1907); other works include *New Poems, Collected Poems, Nature Poems, Songs of Joy, The Hour of Magic*, also in prose, *The Autobiography of a Super-Tramp* (1908), and some essays.

Davis, HENRY WILLIAM CARLESS (1874–1928), Brit. historian; *b.* Stroud, Glos; prof. of modern history, Manchester, 1921–5; at Oxford from 1925; director of *Dictionary of National Biography*, 1902–28; authority on mediæval history. Works, *England under the Normans and Angevins* (1905), *Mediæval Europe* (1911), *Mediæval England* (1924.)

Davis, JEFFERSON (1808–89), Amer. statesman; *b.* Fairview, Kentucky; became a cotton planter and a model slave-owner. Member of U.S.A. senate, 1847; secretary for war, 1853–7; resigned from Senate in support of the claims of the Southern States, and was elected president of Southern Confederacy, 1861; on outbreak of Civil War organized efficient army under every disadvantage. His military tactics were not always wise, however, and he laid himself open to charge of autocracy; it was proposed to supersede him shortly before the end of the war, but General Lee refused to become dictator; was taken prisoner, 1865, but released two years later.

[*A Memoir*, by Mrs. Davis (1890).]

Davis, JOHN (*c.* 1550–1605), Eng. navigator and explorer; *b.* near Dartmouth; sought unsuccessfully N.W. Passage to East, passing through the strait now called Davis Strait, 1587; invented quadrant.

Davis, RICHARD HARDING (1864–1916), Amer. novelist; *b.* Philadelphia; ed. *Harper's Weekly*, 1892–4; was correspondent for various papers; most of his novels are on martial themes.

Davis, THOMAS OSBORNE (1814–45), Irish poet and journalist; *b.* Mallow, County Cork; a founder of Young Ireland party; author of *Poems, Literary and Historical Essays.*

Davis, WILLIAM MORRIS (1850–1934), Amer. geologist and geographer; *b.* Philadelphia; prof. of physical geography, Harvard, 1890; travelled extensively on scientific expeditions; author of numerous works on geology, meteorology, and physical geography.

Davitt (*dä'vit*), MICHAEL (1846–1906), Irish agitator and journalist; *b.* Straide, County Mayo; became Fenian, 1865; associated with Parnell, 1879–90; thrice imprisoned for sedition; M.P., 1892–3, 1895–9; author of *Fall of Feudalism in Ireland* (1904), etc.

Da'vy, SIR HUMPHRY (1778–1829), Eng. chem.; *b.* Penzance; apprenticed to a surgeon; educated himself in natural philosophy and chemistry; became superintendent of Dr. Beddoes' medical 'Pneumatic Institution' at Bristol, where he investigated the physiological properties of nitrous oxide (laughing gas); prof. of chemistry, Royal Institution, London; took up agricultural chemistry; main researches were in electro-chemistry; isolated potassium and sodium, and other elements; proved that diamond is pure carbon. In 1816 invented miner's safety-lamp. President of Royal Soc., 1820–7.

[*Humphry Davy, Poet and Philosopher*, by Thorpe.]

Dawes (*dauz*), CHARLES GATES (1865–), Amer. lawyer, financier, and statesman; *b.* Marietta, Ohio; served in Great War, 1917–19; chairman, Allied Reparations Commission, Paris, 1924 (report known as 'Dawes Plan'); Nobel Peace Prize, 1925; vice-President, U.S.A., 1925–9; ambassador to Great Britain, 1929–32; author of works on money and banking, and *A Journal of the Great War* (1921).

Dawes, WILLIAM RUTTER (1799–1868), Eng. astronomer; *b.* London; observations of Mars, Jupiter, and Saturn were epoch-making; discovered dusky ring of Saturn, 1850; made micrometrical measurements of double stars.

Dawkins, SIR WILLIAM BOYD (1837–1929), Eng. scientist; *b.* near Welshpool; prof. of geology and palæontology at Owen's Coll., Manchester, 1872; did research work on cave-dwellers; discovered prehistoric remains at Mendip.

Dawson of Penn, BERTRAND EDWARD DAWSON, 1ST BARON (1865–), British physician; physician, London Hospital, 1906; served in Great War, 1914–18; physician in ordinary to King George V. from 1907–36, and to Prince of Wales from 1923; authority on diabetes and gastric troubles; pub. *The Diagnosis and Operative Treatment of Diseases of the Stomach* (1908), etc.

Dawson. (1) SIR JOHN WILLIAM (1820–99), Canadian geologist; *b.* Pictou, Nova Scotia; made geological researches with Sir Charles Lyell in Nova Scotia; prof. of geology and principal of M'Gill Univ., Montreal, 1855–93; first president of Royal Soc. of Canada; F.R.S., 1891; an opponent of Darwinism. (2) GEORGE MERCER (1849–1901), son of above; geologist and naturalist to N. Amer. Boundary Commission; director, Geological Survey of Canada, 1895; in charge of Yukon expedition, 1887; Dawson City owes its name to him; on Bering Sea Arbitration Board, 1891; president of Royal Soc. of Canada, 1893.

Day, JOHN (1574–1640?), Eng. dramatist; *b.* Cawston, Norfolk; collaborated with Dekker and other writers of his time; best known by his *Parliament of Bees*, an allegorical masque.

Deák, FERENCZ (1803–76), Hungarian statesman, became representative to Diet, 1832; brought about reconciliation with Austria; minister of justice, 1848, but resigned when Kossuth succeeded Batthyanyi. During war of independence Deák lived in retirement. He was returned to power in 1861, and opposed extremists; drew up address to Emperor demanding constitution of 1848, return of exiles, etc.; repeated demand, 1866, when Austria was forced to concede it.

Deakin (*dē'kin*), ALFRED (1856–1919), Australian statesman; *b.* Melbourne; elected to Victorian Legislative Assembly, 1878; a promoter of federation; elected to Federal Parliament, 1901; prime minister of Commonwealth, 1903–4, 1905–8, and 1909–10, and afterwards leader of Federal opposition, ill-health compelling him to retire, 1912; attended Colonial Conference, 1887. Wrote works on irrigation.

Dear'mer, PERCY (1867–), Eng. clergyman and author; *b.* London; prof. of eccles. art, King's Coll., London, 1919; canon of Westminster, 1931; a voluminous writer on Church matters, including liturgy, carols, hymns, etc.

De Bary, HEINRICH ANTON (1831–88), Ger. botanist; *b.* Frankfurt; prof. of botany, Freiburg, 1855; Halle, 1867; Strasbourg, 1872; founder of modern mycology; wrote standard work on potato disease, 1861, *Comparative Anatomy of Ferns and Phanerogams* (1877), *Lectures on Bacteria* (1885), etc.

Deb'orah, Israelite heroine of period of Judges; joined Barak to deliver Israel from yoke of Canaanites (Judges 4 and 5).

Debrett', JOHN (*d.* 1822), Eng. compiler and publisher of the *Peerage* known by his name.

Debussy (*de-boo-sē'*), CLAUDE ACHILLE (1862–1918), Fr. composer; *b.* St. Germain-en-Laye; pioneer of musical modernism; exercised powerful influence on art of his time; setting of Maeterlinck's *Pelléas et Mélisande* established his fame; notable also for orchestral and piano music.

De Candolle (*cän-dol'*), AUGUSTIN PYRAME (1778–1841), Swiss pioneer of systematic botany; *b.* Geneva; prof. of botany at Montpellier, 1808–16, at Geneva, 1816–41; inspired the finest work of descriptive botany yet produced—*Prodromus Systematis Naturalis.*

Decius (*dē'shi-us*), CAIUS MESSIUS QUINTUS TRAJANUS (201–51), Rom. emperor of Illyrian extraction; did much to retard advance of Goths; died in battle against them; was great persecutor of Christians.

Deep'ing, GEORGE WARWICK (1877–), Eng. novelist; *b.* Southend; gave up medical practice for literature; served in Great War; best-known novels include *Sorrel and Son, Old Pybus, Exiles, The Road.*

Defoe (*de-fō'*), DANIEL (1661–1731), Eng. author and pamphleteer; *b.* London; son of butcher; educated at a Dissenting academy; Jacobite plots against William III. gave occasion to his pamphlet, *A New Discovery of an Old Intrigue* (1691). A born pamphleteer, he wrote naturally and forcibly; pub. *The Shortest Way with the Dissenters* (1702), and was convicted of seditious libel, fined, pilloried, and imprisoned. Harley sent him to Scotland, 1706, to promote Union of the Parliaments. Between 1704 and 1713 Defoe carried on his famous *Review*, written entirely by himself; later wrote for the *Mercator.* In 1719 he achieved success with *Robinson Crosoe*, one of the masterpieces of Eng. prose. Other works of high literary quality are *Captain Singleton, Moll Flanders, Colonel Jack, Roxana, Journal of the Plague Year*, and *Memoirs of a Cavalier.*

[*Life*, by Wilson, Hazlitt, Masefield, Minto.]

Degas (*de-gä'*), HILAIRE-GERMAINE EDGARD (1834–1917), Fr. painter; *b.* Paris; delineator of night and sporting life; among pictures are *Steeplechase, Portraits of Criminals, Races, The Rehearsal*, etc.

Dehan, RICHARD. See GRAVES, C. I. M.

Dek'ker, THOMAS (*c.* 1570–1641), Eng. dramatist and pamphleteer; *b.* London; pamphlets include *The Wonderful Year, The Gull's Hornbook*, etc.; chief plays, *The Shoemaker's Holiday, Old Fortunatus, The Honest Whore, The Witch of Edmonton*, and others in collaboration with Webster, Massinger, Chettle, Ford, and Middleton; writing prolific and unequal, but of high emotional quality.

De la Beche (*bāsh'*), SIR HENRY THOMAS (1796–1855), Eng. geologist; *b.* Jamaica; F.R.S., 1819; induced government to establish Geological Survey of Great Britain (director, 1835), Museum of Practical Geology and Royal School of Mines; president of Geological Soc., 1847; author of *The*

Geological Observer, and numerous research memoirs.

Delacroix (*de-lä-krwä'*), FERDINAND VICTOR EUGÈNE (1798–1863), Fr. historical painter; *b.* near Paris; leader of Fr. romantic school; painted *Barque of Dante*, *Massacre of Chios*, *Cromwell at Windsor Castle*, etc.

De la Mare, WALTER (1873–), Eng. poet and novelist; *b.* Charlton, Kent; known by his *Collected Poems 1901–18* and *Poems for Children* (1930). His prose works include *Henry Brocken* (1904), *The Return* (1910), and *Memoirs of a Midget* (1921). His poetry has the high seriousness of great verse.

Delambre (*de-län'br*), JEAN BAPTISTE JOSEPH (1749–1822), Fr. astronomer; *b.* Amiens; assisted in measurement of meridional arc between Dunkirk and Barcelona; prof. of astronomy, Coll. de France.

Delane (*de-lān'*), JOHN THADDEUS (1817–79), ed. of the *Times*, 1841–77; *b.* London; raised paper to level of an international institution.

De la Rive (*rēv'*), AUGUSTE ARTHUR (1801–73), Swiss physicist; *b.* Geneva; prof. of physics at Geneva, 1823; investigated various electrical phenomena; invented electroplating.

Delaroche (*de-lä-rosh'*), HIPPOLYTE, known as PAUL (1797–1856), Fr. historical painter of romantic school; *b.* Paris; among his historical subjects are *The Princes in the Tower*, *Execution of Lady Jane Grey*, *Murder of Duke of Guise*, *Death of Queen Elizabeth.*

De la Rue (*roo'*), WARREN (1815–89), Brit. chemist and astronomer; *b.* Guernsey; made researches on solar physics and astronomical photography; invented photoheliograph; founder of well-known firm of stationers.

Delavigne (*de-la-vēny'*), JEAN FRANÇOIS CASIMIR (1793–1843), Fr. dramatist and poet; *b.* Havre; finest lyric *La Toilette de Constance*; song *La Parisienne* (1830) rivalled in popularity *La Marseillaise*; chief plays *Les Vêpres Siciliennes*, *L'Ecole des Vieillards*, *Louis XI.*

Del'brück, HANS (1848–1929), Ger. historian; *b.* on isl. of Rügen; prof. of modern history, univ. of Berlin, 1855; his most notable work is a glorification of war; has written extensively on military tactics and responsibility for Great War.

Delcassé (*del-kas-ā'*), THÉOPHILE (1852–1923), Fr. statesman; *b.* in Ariège; colonial minister, 1894–5; minister for foreign affairs, 1898–1905; arranged the differences with Great Britain over the Fashoda Affair, 1898; placed Franco-Russ. alliance on a secure basis; established the *Entente Cordiale* with Great Britain, 1904; difficulties between France and Germany over Morocco led to his retirement; minister of marine, 1911–13; ambassador at Petrograd, 1913–14; minister for foreign affairs, Aug 1914–15.

Delibes (*de-lēb'*), CLÉMENT PHILIBERT LEO (1836–91), Fr. composer; *b.* St. Germain du Val; best opera, *Lakmé*; ballets include *Sylvia* and *Coppélia.*

Delille (*de-lēl'*), JACQUES (1738–1813), Fr. poet; *b.* in Auvergne; won fame by trans. of *Georgics* (1769); acclaimed as greatest living poet; *Les Jardins* (1782) confirmed his reputation; trans. Milton's *Paradise Lost* (1805) and the *Æneid.*

Delisle (*de-lēl'*), JOSEPH NICOLAS (1688–1768), Fr. astronomer; *b.* Paris; founded observatory in St. Petersburg (Leningrad); naval astronomer in Paris; discovered method for calculating transit of Mercury and Venus.

Delitzsch (*dā'lich*), FRANZ (1813–90), Ger. theologian; *b.* Leipzig;

one of the greatest Hebraists of 19th cent.; author of many theological works; one of founders of higher criticism. His son, FRIEDRICH (1850–1922), was well-known Oriental scholar.

De'lius, FREDERICK (1862–1934), Brit. composer; *b.* Bradford; an outstanding personality of modern musical world; C.H., 1929; wrote *In a Summer Garden, Over the Hills and Far Away* (overture), *Life's Dance* (symphonic poem), *Appalachia* (opera), *Village Romeo and Juliet*, etc.

Della Gherardesca Ugolino. See UGOLINO, DELLA GHERARDESCA.

Della Rob'bia. (1) LUCA (1399–1482), Ital. sculptor; *b.* Florence; trained as goldsmith; turned to sculpture; executed much fine work in marble, bronze, and terra-cotta reliefs; much of it done for cathedral at Florence; held very high position in Florentine art; his relief work gave name to style known as 'Della Robbia ware.' (2) ANDREA DELLA ROBBIA (1435–1525), nephew of (1), continued his work, and, with several other members of same family, achieved distinction.

De Long, GEORGE WASHINGTON (1844–81), Amer. explorer; *b.* New York; in *Jeannette* sailed through Bering Strait and to north of Siberia; caught in ice pack and vessel was crushed; perished on return journey by sledge and boat up the Lena.

Deluc', JEAN ANDRÉ (1727–1817), Swiss meteorologist and geologist; *b.* Geneva; settled in England, 1773; invented a hygrometer, and devised first correct rules for measuring heights by barometer; discovered dry pile or electric column.

Deme'trius, name of two Macedonian kings. (1) DEMETRIUS I. (337–283 B.C.), the 'besieger,' established supremacy over Greece and Macedonia, seizing throne, 294; attempted conquest of Asia; died a prisoner. (2) DEMETRIUS II. (*r.* 239–229 B.C.), son of Antigonus Gonatas; reign marked by first Rom. interference.

Demetrius, name of two kings of Syria. (1) DEMETRIUS SOTER (*r.* 162–150 B.C.), grandson of Antiochus the Great; sovereignty recognized by Rome; defeated by the Jews under Judas Maccabæus; killed in battle against Alexander Balas, who usurped the throne. (2) DEMETRIUS NICATOR (?164–125 B.C.), son of above; recovered kingdom from Balas with assistance of Philometor, King of Egypt; captured by Mithridates, 140, and held captive for ten years; restored, but during civil war was killed.

Democ'ritus (460–370 B.C.), one of greatest Gr. philosophers; anticipated atomic theory of matter, holding that matter is composed of atoms always in motion; attempted to explain colour. In ethics he anticipated Epicurus.

De Moivre (*mwävr*), ABRAHAM (1667–1754), Fr. mathematician; *b.* Vitry, Champagne; fled to England after revocation of Edict of Nantes, 1685; intimate friend of Newton; famed for theorem known by his name; pub. *The Doctrine of Chances* (1716), and other papers.

De Morgan. (1) AUGUSTUS (1806–71), Eng. mathematician; *b.* Madura, India; prof. of mathematics at London Univ., 1828–31 and 1836–66; did much for the development of formal logic and for introduction of metric system; chief works, *Formal Logic*; *Elements of Arithmetic, Alegbra, Trigonometry*; treatises on *Differential and Integral Calculus*. (2) WILLIAM FREND (1839–1917), Eng. novelist and potter; son of above; *b.* London; invented new processes in lustre ware; pub. his first novel, *Joseph Vance* (1906), when sixty-six—a long, leisurely, humorous book reminiscent of Dickens. Other novels include *Alice-for-Short* (1907), *It Never can Happen Again* (1909), and *A Likely Story* (1911).

Demosthenes (*dē-mos'the-nēz*) (*c.* 384–322 B.C.), Gr. statesman and orator; studied law, and devoted energies to oratory, at first being very bad and meeting with derision; entered political life, 354; set himself to revive best spirit and traditions of Gr. life; believed Athens was rightful leader of Greece. Demosthenes tried to stir up his fellow-citizens against Philip of Macedon; delivered his *First Philippic* while Philip was still a foreign foe outside Greece; his *Second* and *Third Philippics* when Philip was a power in Greece itself. From 338 to 322 he worked loyally for Athens in her internal affairs; his speech *On the Crown* is the greatest of this period. After the death of Alexander the Great Demosthenes was condemned to death; fled to Ægina, then to Calauria, and committed suicide. His fame as an orator and a stylist has been almost unquestioned, and he is reckoned supreme among Gr. orators.

[*Demosthenes*, by S. H. Butcher (1881).]

Demp'sey, WILLIAM HARRISON (JACK) (1895–), Amer. boxer; *b.* in Colorado; world's heavyweight champion, 1919–27; among others, defeated Carpentier, 1922; defeated by Gene Tunney.

Denham (*den'am*), SIR JOHN (1615–69), Eng. poet; *b.* Dublin; author of *Cooper's Hill* (1642), the earliest purely descriptive poem in English, and a fine elegy on Cowley.

Denikin (*den-ē'kin*), ANTON (1872–), Russ. soldier; son of a serf; chief of general staff with Alexeieff and Brussilov; in Great War was commander-in-chief on western front, 1917; after Revolution commander-in-chief on south-west front when Kornilov advanced against Kerensky, 1917. On death of Kornilov took over command of White army which fought the Bolsheviks; defeated, 1920; fled to Constantinople.

Den'is (Fr. *de-nē'*), ST. (3rd cent.), short for Dionysius, patron saint of France; first bishop of Paris; evangelized Gauls; on arrival in Paris was tortured and put to death, 272 or 290; feast day, 9th Oct.

Dennery (*de-ner-ē'*), ADOLPHE PHILIPPE (1811–99), Fr. playwright and novelist; *b.* Paris; wrote libretto of Gounod's *Faust*, 1856; most of work done in collaboration with others.

Denning, WILLIAM FREDERICK (1848–1931), Eng. astronomer; *b.* near Radstock, Somerset; made important discoveries of comets and meteoric showers; discoverer of the new star in Cygnus, 1920.

Depretis (*dā-prā'tēs*), AGOSTINO (1813–77), Ital. statesman; *b.* Mezzana Corte, Stradella; member of Young Italy party opposed to Austrian control; sent on mission by Cavour, 1860, to proclaim the Ital. constitution in Sicily; three times premier of united Italy; though extravagant in administration introduced many reforms.

De Quincey (*dē kwin'si*), THOMAS (1785–1859), Eng. essayist: *b.* Manchester; educated at grammar school there and at Oxford. At Oxford he became a victim to the opium habit, with disastrous effects upon his future career. About 1807 he made the acquaintance of Wordsworth, Coleridge, Lamb, and others, settled at Grasmere, ed. a local paper, and contributed to *Blackwood's Magazine.* In 1828 he removed to Edinburgh, where, and at Lasswade, he spent the greater part of his life. His *Confessions of an English Opium-Eater* appeared in the *London Magazine*, 1821, and was followed by critical writings and biographical studies in various journals. His reading was very extensive, and he had great intellectual endowments. He was one of the greatest English stylists, and excelled in impassioned ornate prose; but his work is marred by digression.

[*Life* (English Men of Letters), by Masson (1881).]

Derby, EARL OF, title of Stanley family since 1485. EDWARD GEOFFREY SMITH STANLEY, 14TH EARL (1799–1869); *b.* Knowsley; strong supporter of Reform Bill; secretary for Ireland, 1830; colonial secretary, 1841; became earl, 1851; thrice prime minister, 1852, 1858, 1866. EDWARD HENRY STANLEY, 15TH EARL (1826–93); first secretary of state for India, 1858; foreign secretary, 1866 and 1874; colonial secretary, 1882–5. FREDERICK ARTHUR STANLEY (1841–1908), 16TH EARL; gov.-gen. of Canada, 1888–93. EDWARD GEORGE VILLIERS STANLEY, 17TH EARL (1865–); postmaster-general, 1903–5; director-general of recruiting, 1915, and responsible for 'Derby Scheme' of voluntary enlistment; secretary for war, 1916–18 and 1922–4; ambassador to France, 1928. Noted patron of the turf.

Déroulède (*dā-roo-lād'*), PAUL (1846–1914), Fr. poet, dramatist, and politician; *b.* Paris; served in Franco-Ger. war; wrote patriotic poems, *Chants du Soldat*, *Vive la France*; also dramas, *L'Hetman*, *La Moabite*.

De Ruyter (*roi'ter*) (more correctly RUIJTER), MICHAEL ADRIANZOON (1607–76), Dutch admiral; *b.* Flushing; served with Tromp in first Dutch war with England, 1653; assisted Danes against Swedes, 1659; in second Dutch war defeated Eng. fleet at N. Foreland, 1665; sailed up the Thames and burned shipping, 1667; in third Dutch war he fought combined Fr. and Eng. fleets at Sole Bay, 1672.

[*Life*, by Milne (1896).]

Descartes (*dā-cärt'*), RENÉ (Latinized as CARTESIUS) (1596–1650), Fr. philosopher; *b.* La Haye, Touraine; settled in Paris, 1625, but from 1629 to 1649 resided principally in Holland. In 1636 his first published work appeared, *Discours de la Méthode*, accompanied by three scientific treatises as illustrations of the method expounded; *Meditationes de Prima Philosophia*, in 1641; *Principia Philosophiæ*, in 1644; the last of his chief works, *Traité des Passions de l'Ame*, in 1649. In the same year he went to Sweden on the invitation of Queen Christina, but after some four months at Stockholm he died. Descartes was the first influential thinker of modern times who sought to work out a philosophical system (Cartesianism) in independence of scholastic tradition and theological dogma. Seeking some indubitable and fundamental certainty, he found it in his famous 'Cogito, ergo sum,' a proposition which it is impossible to doubt. In mathematics Descartes was the founder of analytical geometry—*i.e.* the application of algebra to geometry.

[*The Philosophical Works of Descartes*, by Haldane and Ross (1911, 1912).]

Deschamps (*dā-shän'*), EMILE (1791–1871), Fr. poet; *b.* Bourges; wrote with La Touche verse comedies, and with his brother ANTONY (1800–69) established the critical journal *La Muse Française*; trans. Shakespeare's *Romeo and Juliet* and *Macbeth*; wrote operatic libretti.

Deschamps, EUSTACHE, known also as MOREL (*c.* 1346–*c.* 1410), Fr. poet; *b.* in Champagne; his poems give pictures of the lawlessness, ruin, vices, and miseries of the Hundred Years' War.

Deschanel (*dā-shä-nel'*), PAUL EUGÈNE LOUIS (1856–1922), Fr. statesman; *b.* Brussels; entered the Chamber of Deputies in 1885 as republican; soon known as brilliant speaker; vice-president, 1896; president, 1898–1902 and 1912–20; member of Academy, 1899; president of the Fr. republic, Jan.–Sept. 1920. Died as result of a fall from a train. Wrote on colonial questions, orators, and statesmen.

Deshoulières (*dā-zoo-lyār'*), ANTOINETTE DU LIGIER DE LA GARDE (1638–94), Fr. poetess; *b.* Paris; renowned for wit, poetic talents, and beauty; figured among the *précieuses*; wrote songs, ballads, madrigals, etc., her idylls being of lasting merit.

Deside'rius (*fl.* 756–774), last King of Lombardy; conquered, 774, by Charlemagne, who annexed his kingdom.

Desmond, GERALD FITZGERALD, 15TH EARL OF (*d.* 1583); Irish leader; imprisoned in London, 1562; returned to Ireland, 1564; spent most of his life plotting and in rebellion; murdered at Glanaginty, and estates forfeited.

Desmoulins (*dā-moo-lan'*), LUCIE SIMPLICE CAMILLE BENOÎT (1760–94), Fr. revolutionary journalist; *b.* Guise, Picardy; wrote articles urging abolition of monarchy; pub. weekly *Les Révolutions de France et de Brabant* (1789–91); became member of Cordeliers Club and a follower of Danton; elected to National Convention, 1793; first a friend of Robespierre, but later incurred his enmity; guillotined same day as Danton, 1794. His wife shared his fate.

[*Desmoulins and his Wife*, by Claretie (Eng. trans. 1876).]

De Soto (*dā sō'tō*), FERNANDO (1496–1542), Span. explorer; *b.* Badajoz; took part in Pizarro's conquest of Peru; discovered the Mississippi.

Des Periers (*dā per-yā'*), BONAVENTURE (*c.* 1500–1544), Fr. author; secretary to Marguerite, Queen of Navarre, 1536; possibly wrote *The Heptameron*; his *Nouvelles Récreations et Joyeux Devis* show humour and narrative ability.

Despréaux. See BOILEAU-DESPRÉAUX.

De Tabley, JOHN BRYNE LEICESTER WARREN, 3RD BARON (1835–95), Eng. poet; pub. his first collections, 1859–68, under pseudonyms of 'G. F. Preston' and 'William Lancaster'; *Philoctetes* (1866); *Poems Dramatic and Lyrical* (1893), with a second series, 1895, comprise the best of his work.

Detaille (*de-tä'ē*), JEAN BAPTISTE (1848–1912), Fr. artist; *b.* Paris; excelled in military and historical pictures—*e.g.* *The Dream* (Luxembourg), *The Passing Regiment*, *The Conquerors*, *Salute to the Wounded*, etc.; equestrian portrait of King Edward VII.

Deus Nogueira Ramos (*dā'oosh nō-gā'ra rä'mosh*), JOÃO DE (1830–96), greatest Port. lyric poet of his century; *b.* Messines, Algarve; early won renown for verses circulated in MS.; greatest work, *Flores do Campo* (1869).

De Vale'ra, EAMON (1882–), Irish politician; *b.* New York (father Spanish, mother Irish); educated in Dublin; became a teacher of mathematics, French, and Latin; commandant in Irish National Rebellion, 1916; captured and sentenced to death; death sentence commuted; raised funds in America, 1919–20, for Irish Republican Government; chancellor of National Univ. of Ireland since 1921; president of Sinn Fein party, 1917–26; leader of Fianna Fail party since 1926; president of Irish Free State, 1932.

De Vere, AUBREY THOMAS (1814–1902), Irish poet; *b.* Curragh Chase, County Limerick; author of *Legends of St. Patrick* (1872),

Foray of Queen Mœve (1882), *Legends of the Saxon Saints* (1879), and fine blank verse poems. His *Recollections* appeared in 1897.

Devonshire. (1) SPENCER COMPTON CAVENDISH, 8TH DUKE OF (1833–1908), Brit. statesman; *b.* Holker Hall, N. Lancs; long known as the Marquis of Hartington, one of the most prominent statesmen of the Victorian era; successively lord of the Admiralty, under-secretary for war, war secretary, and postmaster-general, 1863–74; chief secretary for Ireland, 1871; on Gladstone's retirement became leader of Liberal party; on fall of Beaconsfield government, 1880, invited to form a ministry; stood aside in favour of Gladstone, but split with him over Home Rule, 1886; strongly opposed Chamberlain's Tariff Reform proposals; won great respect for his sterling personal integrity. (2) VICTOR CHRISTIAN WILLIAM CAVENDISH, 9TH DUKE OF (1868–), nephew of (1); represented W. Derbyshire, 1891–1908; financial secretary to Treasury, 1903–5; gov.-gen. of Canada, 1916–21; colonial secretary, 1922–4.

De Vries (*de vrēz'*), HUGO (1848–1935), Dutch botanist; *b.* Haarlem; prof. of botany, Amsterdam, 1881–1918; from researches in plant evolution, formulated theory of mutation; works, *Intercellular Pangensis* (1889), *The Mutation Theory* (1901), *Plant Breeding* (1907).

Dew'ar, SIR JAMES (1842–1923), Brit. chemist and physicist; *b.* Kincardine-on-Forth; prof. of natural philosophy, Cambridge, 1875; of chemistry, Royal Institution, London, 1877; F.R.S., 1877; with Abel invented cordite; name chiefly associated with liquefaction of gases and researches on electrical and other properties of matter at lowest temperatures; in 1898 liquefied hydrogen; invented Dewar flask, precursor of Thermos flask; president Brit. Association, 1902; knighted, 1914.

De Wet, CHRISTIAN (1854–1922), Orange Free State general and politician; *b.* Leeuwkop, Orange Free State; famed for guerrilla tactics during S. African War, 1899–1902; when responsible government was granted he became minister of agriculture, but supported General Hertzog in his policy of separation, 1912–13; early in Great War, Oct. 1914, led a revolt, but was met and routed by Botha; captured and condemned to six years' imprisonment and fine of £2,000; released after six months.

Dewey, GEORGE (1837–1917), Amer. naval officer; *b.* Montpelier, Vermont; fought in Civil War, 1861–5, and Span.-Amer. War, 1898; on May 1, 1898, defeated enemy in Manila Bay; admiral of the navy, 1899; from 1900 was president of general board of navy.

Dewey, JOHN (1859–), Amer. philosopher, psychologist, and educationist; *b.* Burlington, Vermont; teacher of philosophy at Univ. of Minnesota, 1888–89, Michigan, 1889–94, Chicago, 1894–1904, and director, School of Education, Chicago; prof. of philosophy, Columbia Univ., New York, 1904–1932; has carried out important researches in education, and has written much on philosophy.

Dewey, MELVIL (1851–1931), Amer. librarian; *b.* Adams Center, New York; state director of libraries, 1904–6; devised *Decimal Classification* for libraries and perfected a cataloguing system known by his name.

De Windt (*de vint*), HARRY (1856–1933), explorer and journalist; *b.* Paris; made overland journey from Paris to New York, 1901–2; wrote numerous books on his travels, including *My Restless Life* (1909).

De Witt (*de vit*), JAN (1625–72),

Dutch statesman; *b.* Dort; grand pensionary of Holland, 1653–72. Resolutely opposed house of Orange; did much for Holland in commercial struggle with England; secured Triple Alliance with England and Sweden against France, 1668. When Louis XIV. declared war on Holland, 1672, the people unanimously placed William III. at head of affairs, and De Witt and his brother CORNELIUS (1623–72) were cast into prison, from which they were taken by the infuriated mob and literally torn to pieces.

[*Administration of De Witt*, by Geddes (1879).]

D'Eyncourt (*dān'kurt*), SIR EUSTACE HENRY WILLIAM TENNYSON (1868–), director of Brit. naval construction, 1912–23; responsible for changes of design leading to increased speed and additional protection of battleships; did valuable work in connection with introduction of tanks; knighted, 1917; F.R.S., 1921; baronet, 1930.

Dhuleep (or DHULIP) **Singh** (*doo-lēp' sing*) (1837–93), Maharajah of the Sikhs; succeeded to throne, 1843, with mother as regent; rose against British, and was defeated; concluded Treaty of Lahore, 1846. Punjab was ruled by British in his name until second Sikh War, 1848–9; after victory of Gujarat, Dhuleep was deposed and pensioned; afterwards spent most of his life in England; attempted to return to India; visited Russia, where he denounced British Government; settled in Paris.

Diaz (*dē'ats*), ARMANDO (1861–1928), Ital. soldier; *b.* Naples; in Great War replaced Cadorna as commander-in-chief, 1917; cleared N. Italy of the Austrians and forced their surrender, 1918; Fascist minister of war till 1924; marshal, 1924.

Diaz (*dē'as*) (DE NOVAES), BARTHOLOMEU (*c.* 1455–1501), Port. navigator; sailed to Gold Coast, 1481; first to round Cape of Good Hope, 1488, reaching as far east as Great Fish R.; sailed to Brazil, 1500; lost in a storm near Cape of Good Hope.

Diaz (*dē'as* or *dē'ath*) (JOSÉ DE LA CRUZ), PORFIRIO (1830–1915), Mexican soldier and statesman; *b.* Oaxaca; studied for priesthood, then took up law; distinguished himself against Fr. troops sent to Mexico to uphold the claim of Maximilian. After prolonged struggle became president of Mexico, 1877–80 and 1884–1911; greatly increased prosperity of Mexico, but was overthrown in a revolution, 1911; retired to Paris.

[*Life*, by Mrs. Alec Tweedie (1906).]

Diaz de la Peña (*dē-äz' de la pen'yä*), NARCISSE VIRGILE (1807–76), Fr. painter; *b.* Bordeaux; noted for his Fontainebleau landscapes, *Sunset in the Forest, The Storm, The Forest of Fontainebleau*, etc.

Dib'din. (1) CHARLES (1745–1814), Eng. musician, dramatist, and song writer; *b.* Southampton; wrote thirty plays and 1,400 songs, among the latter 'Poor Jack' and 'Tom Bowling.' (2) THOMAS FROGNALL (1776–1846), Eng. bibliographer, nephew of above; *b.* Calcutta; established fame with *Bibliomania* (1809); founder and vice-president of Roxburghe Club, 1812; rector of St. Mary's, Bryanston Square, London.

Dicey (*dī'se*), EDWARD JAMES STEPHEN (1832–1911), Eng. author and journalist; *b.* in Leicestershire; wrote especially on foreign politics; ed. of *The Observer*, 1870–89.

Dickens, CHARLES (1812–70), Eng. novelist; *b.* Portsea; son of an improvident father, the original of Mr. Micawber. Family removed to Chatham, 1816, then settled in Camden Town, 1823.

His childhood may be studied in *David Copperfield*, in *Great Expectations*, and in *Dombey and Son*. Dickens was practically self-educated. As a youth he became a lawyer's clerk, but turned to journalism. He soon made a position for himself, first as parliamentary reporter, later as a writer of sketches, collected and pub. under the title of *Sketches by Boz* (1836). He began the production of *The Pickwick Papers* in periodical numbers in 1836, and practically the whole of the reading public of England fell under the sway of *Pickwick*. In that year he married Catherine Hogarth, from whom he separated in 1858. Pickwick was followed by *Oliver Twist* (1837), *Nicholas Nickleby* (1838), *Old Curiosity Shop* and *Barnaby Rudge* (1840), *Martin Chuzzlewit* and *A Christmas Carol* (1843), *Dombey and Son* (1846), *David Copperfield* (1849), *Bleak House* (1852), *Tale of Two Cities* (1859), *Great Expectations* (1860), *Our Mutual Friend* (1864), *Edwin Drood* (1870; unfinished), etc. Besides novel-writing, Dickens ed. the magazines *Household Words* and *All the Year Round*, and gave readings from his works, which realized large sums. In 1842 he visited the U.S.A. His *American Notes* (1842) gave much offence to Americans. Though Dickens was one of the greatest realists in picturing the conditions of life in his time, his genius was essentially humorous and fantastic. His imagination found free scope not only in fantasies like *The Chimes* and *A Christmas Carol*, but still more in wonderful beings such as Quilp, Mrs. Gamp, the Wellers, and Mrs. Micawber.

[*Life*, by Forster (new ed., 2 vols., 1927), and by Chesterton (1906).]

Dick'inson, EMILY (1830–86), Amer. poet; *b*. Amherst, Massachusetts; after an unhappy love affair lived as a recluse; her poems, not pub. till after her death, reveal her as one of the great Amer. poets.

Dick'see, SIR FRANCIS BERNARD (FRANK) (1853–1928), Brit. artist; *b*. London; gold medal of Royal Academy for *Elijah confronting Ahab and Jezebel in Naboth's Vineyard* (1876); R.A., 1891; one of best of 'symbolic' school. President of Royal Academy, 1924–8; among works are *La Belle Dame sans Merci*, *Passing of Arthur*, *Harmony*, *The Two Crowns*.

Diderot (*dē-drō'*), DENIS (1713–84), Fr. author and encyclopædist; *b*. Langres; wrote several philosophic essays directed against the Church, and was imprisoned for his *Lettre sur les Aveugles* (1746); on his release became ed. of a projected Encyclopædia; first vol. pub. 1751. He was assisted by D'Alembert and a host of other writers, but a great part of it was written by himself. Its speculative spirit was feared by the eccles. party, and by their means it was suppressed in 1759, but it was afterwards continued. Diderot also wrote plays, novels, philosophical works, and art criticisms, and shone as a letter-writer; one of the greatest thinkers, writers, and conversationalists of 18th cent.

[*Life*, by Morley (1878).]

Didon (*dē-don'*), HENRI (1840–1900), 'Le Père Didon,' Fr. preacher and author; *b*. Trouvet, Isère; joined Dominicans, 1862; became one of the leading preachers of his day; his discourse on the 'Indissolubility of Marriage' brought upon him the censure of Rome and his withdrawal to a Corsican monastery for eighteen months; subsequently visited Palestine for material for his *La Vie de Jésus* (1890).

Diemen (*dē'men*), ANTHONY VAN (1593–1645), Dutch admiral and administrator; *b.* near Utrecht; gov.-gen. of Dutch E. Indies, 1636; Tasmania was originally named Van Diemen's Land, after him, by Tasman, 1642.

Diesel (*de'zel*), RUDOLF (1858–1913), Ger. engineer; *b.* Paris; educated Augsburg and Munich; inventor of Diesel oil engine, 1893–8.

Diez (*dēts*), FRIEDRICH CHRISTIAN (1794–1876), Ger. philologist; *b.* Giessen, Hesse-Darmstadt; prof. of modern literature, Bonn, 1830; specialist in Provençal language. Chief works, *Poesie der Troubadours* (1826), *Leben und Werke der Troubadours* (1829), and *Grammatik der romanischen Sprachen* (1836–44).

Dig'by, SIR KENELM (1603–65), Eng. philosopher and poet; imprisoned for Royalist intrigues, 1642; helped to found Royal Soc.; his *Private Memoirs* (1629) are half biographical, half romantic.

Dilke, SIR CHARLES WENTWORTH (1843–1911), Eng. politician; *b.* London; M.P. for Chelsea, 1868–86; under-secretary for foreign affairs, 1880–2; president, Local Government Board, 1882–5; appeared as co-respondent in a divorce case, 1885, and though he maintained his innocence, he withdrew into private life; M.P. for Forest of Dean, 1892. Dilke was proprietor of the *Athenæum* and *Notes and Queries*, and author of *Greater Britain* (1868), *Problems of Greater Britain* (1890), and, with Mr. Spenser Wilkinson, *Imperial Defence* (1897) and *The British Empire* (1899).

[*Life*, by Gwynn and Tuckwell (1917).]

Dill'mann, CHRISTIAN FRIEDRICH AUGUST (1823–94), Ger. theologian and Orientalist; *b.* in Württemberg; prof. of philosophy, Kiel, 1852; of theology at Giessen, 1864, and at Berlin, 1869; regarded as first Ethiopian scholar of his time; compiled catalogues of Ethiopic MSS. in Brit. Museum and Bodleian, 1848, also of those at Copenhagen, 1857, and Berlin, 1878

Dill'on, EMILE JOSEPH (1854–1933), Brit. author and journalist; *b.* in Ireland; studied at various foreign univs.; special correspondent of *Daily Telegraph* for thirty-three years. An authority on foreign affairs; played an influential part in Russ. politics.

Dillon, JOHN (1851–1927), Irish Nationalist statesman; *b.* New York; M.P. for Tipperary, 1880–3, and E. Mayo, 1885–1918; active promoter of Land League, National League, 'Plan of Campaign,' and United Irish League; suspended from the House on three occasions and four times imprisoned. He visited Australia, New Zealand, and U.S.A., collecting funds for the Irish Nationalist cause. Opposed Parnell after the O'Shea divorce case. Throughout Great War supported Brit. Government; succeeded John Redmond as leader of Irish Nationalist party, 1918; lost his seat the same year, and took no further part in politics.

Din'dorf, KARL WILHELM (1802–83), Ger. Hellenist; *b.* Leipzig; produced many accurate texts and elucidated the dramatic poetry of Greece. Edited Aristophanes, Sophocles, Euripides, Æschylus, Homer, and Demosthenes.

D'Indy. See INDY.

Ding'aan (*d.* 1840), King of the Zulus; murdered the Boer leader Retief and sixty companions, and made havoc of the Boer settlers; beaten by Boers at Blood R., Dec. 16, 1838, on *Dingaan's Day*; ultimately driven out by Pretorius and Panda; captured and put to death.

Diocle'tian, or GAIUS AURELIUS VALERIUS DIOCLETIANUS (A.D. 245–313), Rom. emperor, 284–305; reorganized government of empire; built the great baths in Rome;

conducted last great persecution of Christians; abdicated owing to illness.

Diogenes (*dī-oj′en-ēz*) (*c.* 412–323 B.C.), Gr. 'cynic' philosopher; *b.* Sinope; he practised most rigid asceticism; took up abode in a tub or rather huge bowl; captured by pirates and became a slave in Corinth, where he spent rest of life; impressed Alexander the Great by his personality.

Di′on (*c.* 408–353 B.C.), Tyrant of Syracuse, follower of Plato; banished from Syracuse by Dionysius the younger, he returned and captured the city; was assassinated.

Dion Cass′ius (*c.* A.D. 155–235), Rom. historian; *b.* Nicæa, Bithynia; wrote *History of Rome* to period of Agrippa's death, A.D. 10.

Dion Chrysostomus (*kris-os′to-mus*) (A.D. 50–117), most eminent of Gr. rhetoricians; called the 'Golden-mouthed'; *b.* Prusa; his orations, written in Attic Greek, were distinguished by a clear and graceful style.

Dionysius (*dī-ō-nish′i-us*). (1) THE ELDER (430–367 B.C.), Tyrant of Syracuse; fought four wars with Carthaginians, and conquered much of S. Italy. (2) THE YOUNGER (*c.* 396–330 B.C.), son of above; succeeded his father, 367; supplanted by Dion, A.D. 356.

Dionysius Areopagit′icus (Acts 17:34), an Athenian converted by St. Paul; supposed author of several theological works which exercised considerable influence on the thought of the West.

Dionysius of Halicarnass′us, Gr. rhetorician and historian of age of Augustus; one of the greatest of Gr. literary critics.

Disraeli, BENJAMIN. See BEACONSFIELD.

Disraeli (*diz-rā′li*), ISAAC (1766–1848), Eng. author; *b.* Enfield; belonged to a family of Span. Jews; father of Earl of Beaconsfield; author of *Curiosities of Literature, Calamities of Authors,* etc.

Dit′tersdorf, KARL DITTERS VON (1739–99), Austrian musician; *b.* Vienna; brilliant violinist; composed oratorios and operas, including *Doktor und Apotheke.*

Di′ver, MRS. (KATHERINE HELEN) MAUD (1867–), Brit. novelist; *b.* in India, and spent most of her early life there; embodied much of her experience in her novels, which include *Captain Desmond, V.C.* (1907), *The Great Amulet* (1908), *Desmond's Daughter* (1916), *Siege Perilous* (1924).

Dixon, WILLIAM MACNEILE (1866–), prof. of English at Glasgow Univ., 1904–1935; *b.* in India; prof. of English, Birmingham, 1894–1904; has written *English Poetry from Blake to Browning, A Tennyson Primer, In the Republic of Letters, Hellas revisited,* etc.

Dobbie, SIR JAMES JOHNSTON (1852–1924), Scot. chemist; *b.* Glasgow; director, Royal Scot. Museum, 1903–9; F.R.S., 1904; principal of the Government laboratories, London, 1909–20; wrote largely on alkaloids and absorption spectra of organic compounds.

Dobell′, SYDNEY THOMPSON (1824–74), Eng. poet and critic; *b.* Cranbrook, Kent; belonged to 'Spasmodic school'; works include *The Roman* (1850), and *Balder* (1853).

Dob′son, HENRY AUSTIN (1840–1921), Eng. poet and essayist; *b.* Plymouth; principal clerk, marine department, Board of Trade, 1884–1901; won reputation by poems contributed to Anthony Trollope's magazine, *St. Paul's,* and with verse in old Fr. forms—*e.g.* villanelle, rondeau, ballade, and triolet; poetry marked by daintiness of form and expression; pub. *Collected Poems, Fielding, Horace Walpole, Steele, Goldsmith, Richardson, Fanny Burney,*

Eighteenth Century Vignettes, At Prior Park and Other Papers, etc.

Dodd, WILLIAM (1729–77), Eng. clergyman; *b.* Bourne, Lincs; wrote two comedies and compiled *Beauties of Shakespeare.* Executed for forgery.

Doddridge, PHILIP (1702–51), Eng. Nonconformist minister; *b.* London; pastor at Northampton, 1729; wrote *The Rise and Progress of Religion in the Soul*, and hymns, including 'O God of Bethel.'

Dodgson (*doj'son*), CHARLES LUTWIDGE, pseudonym LEWIS CARROLL (1832–98), Eng. humorist and mathematician; *b.* Daresbury, Cheshire; mathematical lecturer, Christ Church, Oxford, 1855–81; author of the great classics for children, *Alice's Adventures in Wonderland* and *Through the Looking-Glass*; also the humorous poem, *The Hunting of the Snark*, as well as mathematical works, including *Euclid and his Modern Rivals.*

[*Life and Letters of Lewis Carroll*, by Collingwood (1898).]

Dod'sley, ROBERT (1703–64), Eng. author, bookseller, and publisher; *b.* Mansfield, Notts; author of *Cleone* and other successful plays; founded the *Annual Register* (1759) leading publisher of his day.

Doggett, THOMAS (*d.* 1721), Irish actor; founded, 1715, sculling match for 'Doggett's Coat and Badge,' open to all Thames watermen.

Dohrn (*dōrn*), ANTON (1840–1908), Ger. zoologist; *b.* Stettin; founded famous Zoological Station, Naples, 1870; wrote books on origin of vertebrates, etc.

Dolabel'la, PUBLIUS CORNELIUS (*d.* 43 B.C.), Rom. general; married Tullia, Cicero's daughter; seized consulship, 44 B.C.; notorious for profligacy and perfidy; killed by one of his own soldiers.

Dollfuss, ENGELBERT (1892–1934); Austrian statesman, of peasant origin; educ. at Vienna and Berlin univs.; rose to be chancellor, 1932; forcibly crushed socialist rebellion, 1933; opposed Nazi movement for union with Germany; assassinated by Austrian Nazis.

Döllinger (*del'ing-er*), JOHANN JOSEPH IGNAZ VON (1799–1890), Ger. theologian; *b.* Bamberg, Bavaria; prof. of theology at Munich, 1826; one of most learned and able of those who opposed papal declaration of infallibility at Vatican Council of 1870; refused to submit, and was excommunicated; wrote many works on Church history and doctrine.

[*Life*, by Friedrich (1899–1901).]

Dolomieu (*dō-lō-mye'*), DÉODAT GUY SILVAIN TANCRÈDE GRATET DE (1750–1801), Fr. geologist; *b.* Dolomieu, Isère; travelled widely on geological expeditions; wrote several scientific works, and was first to describe rocks of Tyrol as magnesian limestone—now called *dolomite* after him

Domenichino (*dō-men-ē-kē'nō*), ZAMPIERI (1581–1641), Ital. artist; *b.* Bologna; famed for landscapes and frescoes; works include *Communion of St. Jerome, Adam and Eve, Martyrdom of St. Agnes, Death of Adonis.*

Dom'ett, ALFRED (1811–87), Brit. poet and statesman; *b.* Camberwell Grove, Surrey; premier of New Zealand, 1862; friend of Browning, and subject of his poem *Waring*; wrote *Ranolf and Amohia* (1872) and *Flotsam and Jetsam* (1877).

Dom'inic, ST. (1170–1221), founder of Dominican Order; *b.* Calaroga, Old Castile. From 1204–15 he devoted himself to the Albigensian heretics of Languedoc, preaching and teaching, and not resorting to the violence of later Inquisition; closing years occupied in establishing his order; canonized by Gregory IX., 1234.

[*Life*, by Jarrett (1924).]

Domitian (*dō-mish'i-an*), or TITUS FLAVIUS DOMITIANUS AUGUSTUS, Rom. emperor (*r.* A.D. 81–96); *b.* Rome; son of Vespasian; succeeded his brother Titus; attempted some reforms, but personally vicious; killed by his officers.

Donaldson, SIR JAMES (1831–1915), Scot. educationist; *b.* Aberdeen; rector, Royal High School, Edinburgh, 1866; prof. of Latin, Aberdeen, 1881–6; principal of St. Salvator and St. Leonard's, St. Andrews, 1886–90; principal and vice-chancellor of St. Andrews Univ., 1890; author of many notable works on theology and Church history.

Donatell'o (DONATO DI BETTO BARDI) (1386–1466), Ital. sculptor; *b.* Florence; perhaps the greatest master of the Early Tuscan school. His fame rests mainly upon his statues in Florence —*e.g. St. George* and *David.*

[*Life*, by Maud Cruttwell (1911).]

Donat'i, GIOVANNI BATTISTA (1826–73), Ital. astronomer; *b.* Pisa; discovered six comets, 1854–64, and the gaseous composition of comets by spectroscopy, 1864.

Donizet'ti, GAETANO (1797–1848), Ital. composer; *b.* Bergamo; prof. of counterpoint, Naples; very rapid and prolific opera writer; over sixty operas, some of which rank among best of Ital. style; most successful, *Lucia di Lammermoor*, *The Daughter of the Regiment*, and *La Favorita.*

Donnay', MAURICE CHARLES (1859–), Fr. dramatist; *b.* Paris; *La Bascule*, *L'Autre Danger*, *Amants*, *La Chasse à l'Homme*, and *L'Assemblée des Femmes*, are among his plays, which deal mostly with questions of the time.

Donne (*don*), JOHN (1573–1631), Eng. poet and clergyman; *b.* London; brought up as R.C.; studied law; accompanied Essex to Cadiz and Azores, 1596–7; changed his faith, pub. his anti-Catholic *Pseudo-Martyr*, was ordained, and became chaplain to James I., and afterwards Dean of St. Paul's, 1621; powerful and popular preacher; pub. several vols. of sermons; deservedly famed for religious poems, elegies, satires, epigrams, etc.; style frequently crabbed, laboured, and artificial, but verse shows passion and imagination; accounted greatest of the 'Metaphysical Poets.'

[*Life and Letters of Donne*, by Gosse (1899); ed. of *Poems*, by Grierson (1912).]

Doré (*dō-rā'*), LOUIS CHRISTOPHE GUSTAVE PAUL, usually GUSTAVE DORÉ (1833–83), Fr. artist; *b.* Strasbourg; successful landscape painter and sculptor, but reputation rests on his illustrations of the Bible, Dante, Rabelais, Balzac, Cervantes, Milton, etc.

[*Life*, by Jerrold (1891).]

Doria (*dō'rē-ä*), ANDREA (1466–1560), Genoese admiral and general; served both Charles V. and Francis I.; drove French from Genoa, 1528; famous for naval exploits against Turk. corsairs; maintained Genoese republic until his death.

D'Orsay, ALFRED GUILLAUME GABRIEL, COUNT (1801–52), Fr. man of fashion and London dandy; *b.* Paris; close friend of Countess of Blessington; author, painter, and sculptor; Director of Fine Arts in Paris, but died a few days after appointment.

[*D'Orsay, or The Complete Dandy*, by Shore (1911).]

Dor'set, THOMAS SACKVILLE, EARL OF (1530–1608), Eng. poet and statesman; *b.* in Sussex; wrote *A Mirror for Magistrates*, and, with Norton, *Gorboduc, or Ferrex and Porrex* (the first Eng. tragedy); created earl, 1604.

Dos'so Dos'si, name adopted by GIOVANNI DE LUTERO (1479–1542), Ital. painter; *b.* near

Mantua; works, noted for their fine colour, include *Circe, Adoration of the Magi, Madonna and Saints.* His masterpiece is great altarpiece at Ferrara.

Dost Mohammed Khan (1793–1863), Afghan ruler from 1809; surrendered to Brit. forces, 1840; hostile again, 1846; made alliance with Britain, 1855.

Dostoievski (*dō-stō-yev'ski*), FEODOR MIKHAILOVITCH (1818–81), famous Russ. novelist; *b.* Moscow; prisoner in Siberia, 1849–53; wrote very powerful stories dealing with peasant life and social problems, including *Letters from the Underworld* (1864), *Crime and Punishment*, his masterpiece (1866), *The Gambler* (1867), *The Idiot* (1868–9), *The Demons* (1871), *The Brothers Karamazov* (1880).

[*Life*, by Gide (Eng. trans. 1925).]

Doughty (*dow'ty*), CHARLES MONTAGU (1843–1926), Eng. traveller and author; *b.* Theberton Hall, Suffolk; travelled in N. Africa, Syria, Palestine, Arabia; chief work is *Travels in Arabia Deserta* (1888); his poetry includes *The Dawn in Britain* (1906), *The Titans* (1916), and *Man-Soul* (1920).

Douglas (*dug'las*), FAMILY OF, famous in Scot. history, dates from 12th cent. (1) SIR JAMES, 'the Good' (1286–1330), commanded part of Bruce's army at Bannockburn, 1314; killed in Spain while carrying Bruce's heart to Palestine. (2) WILLIAM, 6TH EARL (*c.* 1423–1440), was murdered along with his brother in Edinburgh Castle, 1440. This incident, known as the 'Black Dinner of the Douglases,' broke the family's power, and its lands were forfeited. (3) WILLIAM, 8TH EARL (*c.* 1425–1452), restored the power of the 'Black Douglases,' and James II., alarmed at the strength of the family, treacherously murdered him at Stirling, 1452. The 'Red Douglases'—the Angus branch of the family—were granted the Douglas lands. (4) ARCHIBALD, 5TH EARL OF ANGUS (1449–1514). When the nobles met to plot against James III.'s favourite, Cochrane, and, like mice in fable, hesitated to 'bell the cat,' Douglas volunteered, thus earning nickname 'Bell the Cat.' (5) GAVIN, or GAWAIN (*c.* 1474–1522), poet and bishop; third son of (4); provost of St. Giles, Edinburgh, 1501; Bishop of Dunkeld, 1515–20; pub. first Eng. trans. of Virgil's *Æneid* (with prologues of his own); allegorical poems, *King Hart* and *The Palice of Honour*; one of leading poets in Middle Scots; best work in prologues to *Æneid.*

Douglas, GEORGE. See BROWN, GEORGE DOUGLAS.

Douglas, SIR GEORGE BRISBANE SCOTT (1856–1935), Scot. author; *b.* Gibraltar; lecturer in Scot. literature at Glasgow Univ., 1911; author of *New Border Tales, Poems of a Country Gentleman, Life of James Hogg, History of the Border Counties*, etc.; also ed. *The Scottish Minor Poets.*

Douglas, STEPHEN ARNOLD (1813–61), Amer. statesman; *b.* in Vermont; judge of supreme court of Illinois, 1841–3; leader of Democratic party, an opponent of Lincoln. He secured the passing of a bill which permitted each state to settle the question of slavery for itself. Strongly opposed secession of southern states during Civil War.

Doulton, SIR HENRY (1820–97), Eng. potter; head of the famous Lambeth firm of drainpipe and Doulton ware manufacturers.

Doumer (*doo-mer'*), PAUL (1857–1932), Fr. politician and author; *b.* Aurillac; son of a navvy; minister of finance, 1895–6; gov.-gen. of Indo-China, 1897–1902; held many important offices, and became president of the Senate, 1927–31, and of the Fr. Republic, 1931; assassinated, May 1932; author of *L'Indo-Chine Française*, *Livre de mes Fils*, etc.

Doumergue (*doo-merg'*), GASTON (1863–), Fr. politician and lawyer; *b.* Aigues-Vives, Gard; minister for colonies, 1902–5; attracted notice by his Military Service Bill, 1910; premier, 1913–14, and 1934; president of senate, 1923; president of Republic, 1924–31 (first Protestant president).

Dow, GERARD (1613–75), Dutch painter; *b.* Leyden; pupil of Rembrandt; devoted himself at first to portraits, later to Scriptural events; greatest work, *The Woman Sick of the Dropsy*.

Dow'den, EDWARD (1843–1913), Irish scholar and man of letters; *b.* Cork; prof. of Eng. literature at Trinity Coll., Dublin, from 1867; wrote *Shakespeare, his Mind and Art* (1875), and numerous other works of high literary quality and criticism. His ed. of *Shelley* (1890) is specially noteworthy.

Dowie, JOHN ALEXANDER (1848–1907), Scot.-Amer. religious leader; *b.* Edinburgh; preached 'Divine healing'; founded Zion City on Lake Michigan, 1901, and there organized the Christian Catholic Church; deposed from authority by Zionites, 1906.

Doyle (*doil*), SIR ARTHUR CONAN (1859–1930), English novelist; *b.* Edinburgh; nephew of Richard Doyle; studied medicine at Edinburgh under Dr. Joseph Bell, from whom he drew character of Sherlock Holmes. Produced *A Study in Scarlet*, *Micah Clarke*, *The Sign of Four*, and *The White Company* while in medical practice; leaped into fame with *The Adventures of Sherlock Holmes* (1891), followed by *The Memoirs of Sherlock Holmes* and *The Return of Sherlock Holmes*. Other novels include *Rodney Stone* and *Adventures of Brigadier Gerard*. His *Great Boer War* (1900) became a standard work. Was an active propagandist of spiritualism; knighted 1902.

Doyle, SIR FRANCIS HASTINGS CHARLES (1810–88), Eng. poet; *b.* Nunappleton, Yorks; won much popularity with his military and heroic ballads, such as 'A Private of the Buffs' and 'The Loss of the Birkenhead.'

Doyle, RICHARD (1824–83), Eng. black-and-white artist; *b.* London; on staff of *Punch*, 1843–50, and designed its cover; illustrated Dickens and Thackeray.

Drachmann (*drach'män*), HOLGER HENRIK (1846–1908), Dan. poet and dramatist; *b.* Copenhagen; wrote poems of fisher life, love lyrics, and several plays.

Drake, ADMIRAL SIR FRANCIS (*c.* 1545–95), famous Eng. seaman; *b.* in Devon; took part in expeditions to Spanish Main under Hawkins; did great damage to Span. trade and shipping in S. America, 1572–3; first Englishman to sail round world, 1577–80; 'singed the King of Spain's beard' by burning shipping in Cadiz harbour, 1587; helped to defeat Armada, 1588; died at sea off Nombre de Dios.

[*Life*, by Benson (1927).]

Draper. (1) JOHN WILLIAM (1811–82), Anglo-Amer. scientist; *b.* St. Helens; emigrated to U.S.A.; prof. of chemistry, and later president of medical school, New York Univ. Improved Daguerre's process of photography, and took the first human likeness. (2) HENRY (1837–82), son of above; *b.* New York; prof. of physiology at univ. of New York, 1860–6; constructed telescope, with which he photographed lunar, stellar, and solar spectra.

Dray'ton, MICHAEL (1563–1631), Eng. poet; *b.* Hartshill, Warwickshire; wrote *Polyolbion* (1613), a gazetteer of England in verse,

The Barons' Wars, England's Heroical Epistles, Nymphidia; ballad of 'Agincourt,' and the great sonnet, 'Since there's no help, come let us kiss and part.'

[*Life*, by Elton (1905).]

Dreiser (*drī'ser*), THEODORE (1871–), Amer. author; *b.* Terre Haute, Indiana, of poor parents; ed.-in-chief of Butterick publications, 1907–10; a realistic but clumsy novelist; works include *Sister Carrie* (1900), *Jennie Gerhardt* (1911), *The Financier* (1912), *The Genius* (1915), *The Hand of the Potter*, a tragedy (1918), *An American Tragedy* (1925), *Dawn* (1931).

Dreyfus (*drī'fus*), ALFRED (1859–1935), officer of Fr. army; *b.* Mulhouse, of Jewish parentage; was arrested, 1894, on charge of betraying military secrets to Germany; found guilty and sent to Ile du Diable, his condemnation being due to his unpopularity and to antisemitic feeling. After long agitation, which even endangered the republic, his innocence was completely established, 1906. Served in Great War; afterwards lived in retirement.

Drinkwater, JOHN (1882–), Eng. poet, critic, and playwright; *b.* Leytonstone; manager of Birmingham Repertory Theatre; works include *Poems* (1908–14), containing all he wishes to preserve from his earlier volumes; *Collected Poems* (1923); among his plays are *Cophetua* (1911), *Rebellion* (1914), *Abraham Lincoln* (1918), *Oliver Cromwell* (1921), *Mary Stuart* (1922), and *Bird in Hand* (1928); critical studies of William Morris and Swinburne, and *The Pilgrim of Eternity* (1925), *Mr. Charles, King of England* (1926), *All About Me* (1928), *Pepys* (1930).

Driver, SAMUEL ROLLES (1846–1914), Eng. Hebraist and O.T. scholar; *b.* Southampton; prof. of Hebrew in univ. of Oxford, and canon of Christ Church; member of O.T. Revision Co.; wrote commentaries on nearly half O.T.; works include *Introduction to the Literature of the Old Testament*; ed. the Variorum Bible; joint ed. of *A Hebrew and English Lexicon of the Old Testament, Modern Research as Illustrating the Bible.*

Droeshout (*droos'hout*), MARTIN (1601–51), Eng. engraver; *b.* London; remembered chiefly for his engraved portrait of Shakespeare prefixed to the first folio edition; almost certainly a copy of only portrait of Shakespeare made during poet's lifetime.

Drouais (*droo-ā'*), FRANÇOIS HENRI (1727–75), Fr. portrait painter; *b.* Paris; study of Marie Antoinette is at S. Kensington; other portraits, *Madame de Pompadour* (Orleans), *Comte d' Artois et Madame Clothilde* (Louvre).

Droysen (*droi'sen*), JOHANN GUSTAV (1808–84), Ger. historian; *b.* Treptow, Pomerania; prof. of history, Kiel, Jena, and Berlin; wrote *Geschichte Alexanders des Grossen, Geschichte des Hellenismus,* and *Geschichte der preussischen Politik*

Droz (*drō*), ANTOINE GUSTAVE (1832–95), Fr. author; *b.* Paris; wrote series of articles for *La Vie Parisienne*, portraying manners, follies, and vices of Parisian society; these were collected and pub. as *Monsieur, Madame et Bébé* (1866).

Drummond, HENRY (1851–97), Scot. theologian, evangelist, and scientist; *b.* Stirling; prof. of natural science, Free Church Coll., Glasgow; first attracted attention by his *Natural Law in the Spiritual World* (1883); explored Lake Nyasa district, and wrote *Tropical Africa* (1888); his Lowell lectures at Boston, 1893, were pub. as *The Ascent of Man.*

[*Life*, by G. A. Smith (1898).]

Drummond, HON. SIR JAMES

ERIC (1876–), half-brother and heir-presumptive to the 15th Earl of Perth; held various posts in Brit. Foreign Office; first secretary-general of League of Nations, 1919–33; ambassador to Italy since 1933.

Drummond, WILLIAM, 'of Hawthornden' (1585–1649), Scot. poet; *b.* Hawthornden, near Edinburgh; devoted life to literature; chief poems, *Tears on the Death of Meliades* (Prince Henry of Wales), *Forth Feasting, Flowers of Sion*; prose works, *A Cypresse Grove* (1623), *History of Scotland* (1655); corresponded with Michael Drayton and Ben Jonson, and entertained the latter at Hawthornden, 1619; their *Conversations*, discovered in Advocates' Library, Edinburgh, were pub 1842.

Drury, ALFRED, Eng. sculptor; *b.* London; R.A., 1913; executed colossal statues of Queen Victoria for Bradford and Portsmouth, 1903; decoration for front of Victoria and Albert Museum, 1909; numerous statues, busts, and war memorials.

Dru'sus, MARCUS LIVIUS, Rom. statesman; tribune with Gaius Gracchus, 122 B.C.; consul, 112; fought in Macedonia. His son, of same name, was tribune, 91 B.C.; reformed senate; murdered, 91 B.C.

Drusus, NERO CLAUDIUS (38–9 B.C), son of Livia, and younger brother of Emperor Tiberius; Rom. general; fought in Ger. campaign, 12–9 B.C., and pushed forward frontier as far as the Elbe; married Antonia, daughter of Mark Antony; his sons were Emperor Claudius and Germanicus.

Drusus Cæsar (*d.* A.D. 23), son of Emperor Tiberius; consul, A.D. 14 and 21; married his cousin Livia, sister of Germanicus; poisoned by Tiberius's favourite minister, Sejanus.

Dry'den, JOHN (1631–1700), Eng. poet and dramatist; *b.* Aldwinkle; son of Northamptonshire rector; educated Westminster, and Trinity Coll., Cambridge; poet laureate and historiographer royal, 1670. Dryden began his career as poet with *Heroic Stanzas on the Death of Oliver Cromwell* (1658), followed by *Astræa Redux* (1660), in celebration of the Restoration; *Annus Mirabilis*, commemorating the events of 1666; *Absalom and Achitophel*, political satire (1681); *The Medal*, and *MacFlecknoe*, a satire on Shadwell (1682); *Religio Laici* (1683); and *The Hind and the Panther*, a defence of Church of Rome (1687). The strong, vigorous English of these poems, and their satirical quality, give Dryden very high rank amongst Eng. poets. He was a voluminous dramatist, and his dramatic work is characterized by the immorality of the age. His best-known play is *All for Love*. The lyrical poems, *Ode for St. Cecilia's Day*, and *Alexander's Feast*, written in his later years, increased his fame. His *Essay on Dramatic Poesy* (1668) is valuable for its critical qualities. In poetry Dryden marks the establishment of the classical school, and in prose the transition from elaborate construction to the more supple and practical modern style.

[*Life*, by Saintsbury (1881).]

Du Barry (*bä-rē*), MARIE JEANNE VAUBERNIER, COMTESSE (1746–93), mistress of Louis XV. of France; *b.* Vaucouleurs; after death of Louis, 1774, lived for fifteen years at his Château de Luciennes; at Revolution fled to England, 1792, but returning, was guillotined.

Du Bellay, JOACHIM. See BELLAY, JOACHIM DU.

Dubois (*doo-bwa'*), FRANÇOIS CLÉMENT THÉODORE (1837–1924), Fr. composer; *b.* Rosney, Marne; honorary director of the National Conservatoire of Music; wrote operas, ballets, *suites d'orchestre*, etc.

Dubois, Paul (1829–1905), Fr. sculptor and painter; *b.* Nogent-sur-Seine; among his statues are *Chanteur Florentin* (1865), *Jeanne d'Arc* (1895), at Reims, and *Le Connétable de Montmorency* at Chantilly, and *Tombeau du Général Lamoricière. Mes Enfants* (1876) is the best example of his portraiture.

Du Camp (*kän'*), Maxime (1822–94), Fr. author and traveller; *b.* Paris; travelled through Asia Minor, Greece, and other countries; pub. works on his travels.

Du Chaillu (*shä-yoo'*), Paul Belloni (1835–1903), Fr. traveller and author; *b.* New Orleans; educated, Paris; made numerous discoveries in zoology, anthropology, and geography in his extensive African travels.

Duchenne (*doo-shen'*), Guillaume Benjamin (1806–75), Fr. physician; *b.* Boulogne; first to apply electricity in muscular and nervous diseases; founder of electro-therapeutics.

Duclaux (*doo-klō*), Agnes Mary Frances, *née* Robinson (1857–), Anglo-French poetess and biographer; *b.* Leamington; her second husband was Emile Duclaux (1901), director of Pasteur Institute, Paris; pub. *Collected Poems* (1902); chief prose works, *Life of Renan* (1897), *Life of Racine* (1925).

Dud'dell, William du Bois (1872–1917), Brit. electrical engineer; *b.* London; constructed an oscillograph and discovered the "singing arc."

Dudevant, Mme. See under Sand, George.

Dudley, Robert. See Leicester, Earl of.

Duff, Alexander (1806–78), first Church of Scotland missionary to India, 1829; *b.* near Pitlochry; established missionary schools and colleges; later was appointed prof. of evangelistic theology in Free Church of Scotland, 1867.

Duff'erin and Av'a, Frederick Temple Hamilton Temple Blackwood, Marquess of (1826–1902), Brit. diplomatist; *b.* Florence; created Earl of Dufferin, 1871; gov.-gen. of Canada, 1872; ambassador to Russia, 1879, Turkey, 1881; commissioner in Egypt, 1882–3; viceroy of India, 1884–8; created Marquess of Dufferin and Ava, 1888; ambassador to Rome, 1888, Paris, 1892–6; a gifted diplomat.

Duffy, Sir Charles Gavan (1816–1903), Irish politician and colonial statesman; *b.* in Co. Monaghan; founded the *Nation* (1842), in which appeared his *Ballad Poetry of Ireland*; five times tried for treason between 1848 and 1849, but each time discharged. M.P. for New Ross, 1852; a promoter of Tenant League and Independent Irish party; on disruption of latter, 1855, emigrated to Australia; prime minister of Victoria, 1871–72, and speaker of Legislative Assembly, 1877.

Dug'dale, Sir William (1605–86), Eng. antiquary; *b.* near Coleshill; pub. *Monasticon Anglicanum, Antiquities of Warwickshire, History of St. Paul's Cathedral,* etc. Was made Norroy and Garter Principal King of Arms, 1677.

Du Guesclin (*doogā-klan'*), Bertrand (*c.* 1320–80), famous Fr. soldier; *b.* Dinan; fought at first for Charles of Blois, then for Fr. king; fought against English in France from 1356; twice captured and ransomed; Constable of France, 1370; recovered Poitou, Auvergne, and Guyenne from the English.

Duhamel (*doo-ă-mel'*), Georges (1884–), pseudonym of Denis Thévenin, Fr. author; *b.* Paris; practised as doctor; has written poems, plays, war books, *Vie des Martyrs* (1916), *Civilisation* (1917), and novels.

Dujardin (*doo-zhär-dan'*), FELIX (1801–60), Fr. biologist; *b.* Tours; prof. at Rennes, 1842; first to identify protoplasm; discovered rhizopods; wrote *Natural History of Infusoria* (1841).

Dulac', EDMUND (1882–), Brit. artist; *b.* Toulouse; naturalized, 1912; paints portraits and has illustrated numerous books, including *The Arabian Nights*, *Omar Khayyam*, Andersen's *Fairy Tales*, *Tanglewood Tales*, etc.

Dumas (*doo-ma'*). (1) ALEXANDRE (*Père*) (1802–70), Fr. novelist and dramatist; *b.* Villers-Cotterets (Aisne); son of a general; grandson of a marquess and Haitian negress; came to Paris, 1823; became clerk in bureau of Duke of Orleans; took to play-writing, his first play being *Henri III. et sa Cour* (1829). It is, however, as the author of romances that Dumas attained world-wide fame. The three books of the D'Artagnan cycle, *The Three Musketeers*, *Twenty Years After*, and *The Vicomte de Bragelonne*, with the three of the Valois cycle and *Monte Cristo*, have given him a lasting reputation. The wit, the glorious spirits, the brilliance, the movement are all Dumas's own.

[*Life*, by Davidson (1902).]

(2) ALEXANDRE (*Fils*) (1824–95), Fr. novelist and dramatist; *b.* Paris; natural son of (1); achieved success with *La Dame aux Camélias* (1848), which he afterwards dramatized. Produced among other dramas the famous plays, *Diane de Lys*, *Le Demi-Monde*, and *L'Affaire Clémenceau*. The ready wit and repartee keep many of his plays still popular.

Dumas, JEAN BAPTISTE ANDRÉ (1800–84), Fr. chemist; *b.* Alais; acquired wide reputation by researches on isomerism, the law of substitutions, the atomic weights of elements; as minister of agriculture, 1850–1, organized excellent system of agricultural instruction. Author of *Leçons sur la Philosophie Chimique* (1837), etc.

Du Maurier (*doo-mō-ryā*), GEORGE LOUIS PALMELLA BUSSON (1834–96), Eng. black-and-white artist and novelist; *b.* Paris; analytical chemist in early life; later adopted profession of art, achieving fame as *Punch* artist and book illustrator; wrote three novels: *Peter Ibbetson*, *Trilby*, and *The Martian*; *Trilby* was successfully dramatized. His son, SIR GERALD (1873–1934), was a well-known actor-manager.

Dumont D'Urville (*doo-mon' door-vēl'*), JULES SÉBASTIEN CÉSAR (1790–1842), Fr. navigator; *b.* in Normandy; was in charge of expedition to Polynesia to discover traces of La Pérouse, 1826–9; explored Antarctic regions, discovering various islands, 1837–40.

Dunbar, PAUL LAURENCE (1872–1906), Amer. Negro poet and novelist; *b.* Dayton, Ohio; his *Lyrics of Lowly Life* were well received; also wrote novels and volumes of verse, *Poems of Cabin and Field*, etc.

Dunbar, WILLIAM (*c.* 1465–1530), chief of the old Scot. poets or 'makaris'; probably *b.* in East Lothian; was for a time a begging friar; *The Thistle and the Rose* is an allegory in honour of the marriage of James IV. and Margaret Tudor; in *The Dance of the Seven Deadly Sins* he is far ahead of the Chaucerians in imagination and realism; his *Lament for the Makaris* manifests his lyrical power. These qualities, along with his whimsical humour and biting satire, make him the greatest Brit. poet between Chaucer and Spenser.

Dun'can I. (*d.* 1040), King of Scotland; succeeded Malcolm II., 1034; defeated by Danes, and was slain by Macbeth, who usurped the throne.

Duncan, ADAM, 1ST VISCOUNT (1731–1804), Brit. admiral; *b.* Lundie, Angus; as commander-in-chief of North Sea fleet quelled mutiny of the Nore, and won battle of Camperdown, 1797, for which he was created viscount.

Duncan, THOMAS (1807–45), Scot. artist; *b.* Kinclaven, Perthshire; skilled portrait painter; R.S.A., 1830; A.R.A., 1843; best-known pictures are *Prince Charlie entering Edinburgh*, and *Charles Edward asleep after Culloden.*

Duncker (*doong'ker*), MAXIMILIAN WOLFGANG (1811–86), Ger. historian; *b.* Berlin; prof. of history successively at Halle and Tübingen; director of State archives, 1867–74; chief work, *Geschichte des Alterthums* (1852–57).

Dundas', HENRY, 1ST VISCOUNT MELVILLE (1742–1811), Brit. politician; practised at Scot. bar; M.P. for Midlothian, 1774–90, for Edinburgh, 1790–1802; created viscount, 1802; as solicitor-general, lord advocate, and dispenser of patronage, 1784–93, was virtually king of Scotland; secretary for war, 1794–1801; treasurer of navy, 1782, 1783–1800; first lord of Admiralty, 1804–5; impeached for malversation, but technically acquitted.

Dundee, JOHN GRAHAM OF CLAVERHOUSE, VISCOUNT (*c.* 1649–89), Scot. soldier; entered Dutch service, and saved William of Orange's life at Seneff, 1674; returning to Scotland, 1677, was charged with suppression of Covenanters, by whom he was defeated at Drumclog, 1679; after Bothwell Brig, 1679, harried the Covenanters in s.w. counties; at revolution of 1688 Claverhouse supported James II., and was created Viscount Dundee; he was killed in the moment of victory at the battle of Killiecrankie.

[*Life*, by Terry (1905).]

Dundon'ald, THOMAS COCHRANE, 10TH EARL OF (1775–1860), Brit. admiral; *b.* Annsfield, Lanarkshire; one of the most daring of Brit. naval officers, 1800–1; M.P. for Honiton, 1806; attacked naval abuses; was condemned and cashiered for alleged fraud on Stock Exchange, 1814; was in naval service of Chile, 1817–22, Brazil, 1823–5, Greece, 1825–8, and reinstated in Brit. navy, 1832; admiral, 1851.

Dunedin, ANDREW GRAHAM MURRAY, 1ST VISCOUNT (1849–), Scot. lawyer and statesman; *b.* Edinburgh; called to bar, 1874; M.P. for Bute, 1891–1905; solicitor-general for Scotland, 1891–2, and 1895–6; lord advocate, 1896–1903; secretary for Scotland, 1903–5; lord president of Court of Session, 1905–13; lord of appeal in ordinary, 1913–32; a most learned and brilliant lawyer.

Dunfermline, SIR ALEXANDER SETON, 1ST EARL OF (?1555–1622), Scot. statesman; intended for Church, but turned to law; lord president of Court of Session, 1593; guardian to second son (afterwards Charles I.) of James VI.; commissioner for union with England; chancellor, 1604–8; created earl, 1606.

Dunlop', JOHN BOYD (1840–1921), Scot. inventor; *b.* Dreghorn, Ayrshire; veterinary surgeon, Belfast, 1867; invented pneumatic tyre for tricycle, 1887, pioneer of Dunlop pneumatic rubber tyre.

Dunne, FINLEY PETER (1867–), Amer. journalist; associate ed. *The American Magazine* (1906); author of the 'Mr. Dooley' series of humorous Irish-Amer. sketches.

Dunois (*doo-nwa'*), JEAN, COMTE DE (1403–68), Fr. general; commonly known as 'Bastard of Orleans'; defended that city till arrival of Joan of Arc, 1429; accompanied her to Reims; thereafter swept English from N. France, and from Bordeaux and Bayonne.

Dunra'ven and Mount-Earl,

WINDHAM THOMAS WYNDHAM-QUIN, EARL OF (1841–1926), Eng. politician and sportsman; *b.* Adare Abbey, Limerick; war correspondent in Abyssinian and Franco-Prussian wars; under-secretary for colonies, 1885 and 1886–7; propounded devolution scheme for Ireland; senator of Irish Free State; was an enthusiastic yachtsman; twice tried to win the America Cup.

Dunsa'ny, EDWARD JOHN MORETON DRAX PLUNKETT, 18TH BARON (1878–), Irish dramatist and soldier; served in Boer War and Great War; plays include *The Glittering Gate* (1909), *The Gods of the Mountain* (1911), *A Night at an Inn* (1916), *If* (1921), *Mr. Faithful* (1927); has also written numerous tales.

Duns Scotus, JOHN (1265 or 1275–1308), mediæval Scot. schoolman and critical theologian; *b.* Duns; studied at Oxford and Paris; engaged at Paris in famous controversy with St. Thomas Aquinas over Immaculate Conception, reason, and revelation.

Dun'stan, ST. (924–988), Eng. churchman; *b.* near Glastonbury; as abbot of Glastonbury, from 945, made the monastery a famous centre of learning. Had great influence in the reigns of Edred and Edgar; became Archbishop of Canterbury, 961; greatly extended the power of the Church and purified its administration.

Dun'sterville, LIONEL CHARLES (1865–), Brit. general, served in N.W. Frontier (India) and China; during Great War commanded brilliant expedition to Baku, Jan. to Sept. 1918. Is the original of Kipling's 'Stalky'; pub. *The Adventures of Dunsterforce* (1920), *Stalky's Reminiscences* (1928), and *More Yarns* (1931).

Dupleix (*doo-plā'*), JOSEPH FRANÇOIS (1697–1763), Fr. administrator; *b.* Landrecies; gov.-gen. of all Fr. establishments in India, 1742; tried to establish Fr. supremacy in India, but was frustrated by Clive; recalled, 1754.

[*Life*, by Martineau (3 vols. 1920–7).]

Dupont (*doo-pon'*), PIERRE (1821–70), Fr. song-writer; *b.* Lyons; son of blacksmith; popular songs include 'Le Chant des Ouvriers,' 'Le Pain,' etc.

Dupré (*doo-prā'*), JULES (1811–89), Fr. landscape painter of romantic school; *b.* Nantes. Examples of work are *Morning, Evening*, and *River Scene*.

Dupuy de Lôme (*doo-pwē' de lōm'*), STANISLAS CHARLES HENRI LAURENT (1816–85), Fr. naval constructor; *b.* near Lorient; invented method of converting sailing battleships into steamships; introduced building of 'ironclads' into France.

Durán (*doo-ran'*), AGUSTIN (1789-1862), Span. critic and man of letters; *b.* Madrid; chief librarian, Madrid, 1854; remembered for his collection of anc. Span. ballads and plays.

Durand, CHARLES AUGUSTE EMILE. See CAROLUS-DURAN.

Durand (*dū-rand'*), RT. HON. SIR HENRY MORTIMER (1850–1924), Brit. diplomat; political secretary to Roberts during Kabul campaign, 1879; foreign secretary in India, 1884–94; envoy to Afghanistan, 1893; minister at Tehran, 1894–1900; and ambassador at Washington, 1903–6; author of lives of his father, Sir George White, etc.

D'Urban, SIR BENJAMIN (1777–1849), Brit. soldier-administrator; fought in Peninsular War; while governor of Cape Colony, 1834–8, abolished slavery, leading to Great Trek of Dutch farmers. Durban, Natal, is named after him.

Dü'rer, ALBRECHT (1471–1528), Ger. artist and engraver; *b.* Nuremberg; apprenticed to the painter Wolgemut, then travelled for several years, finally settling in his native town. Among his most famous paintings are the *Feast of the Rosary, The Crucifixion, Madonna and Child, SS. John and Peter, SS. Paul and Mark,* and many portraits; his copperplates, for which he is still more famous, include *St. Jerome in his Study*; *Knight, Death, and the Devil*; *Adam and Eve*; *Death's Coat-of-Arms*; he also produced numerous sets of woodcuts. His writings include *The Art of Mensuration,* and other scientific works. Dürer's work is the culminating point of mediæval Ger. art; his painting is distinguished by mastery of composition, grasp of character, and forcible colouring.

[*Dürer*, by Furst; *Life,* by L. Cust (1897).]

D'Ur'fey, TOM (1653–1723), Eng. song-writer and dramatist; many songs set to music by Purcell, Blow, and Farmer; pub. *Wit and Mirth, or Pills to Purge Melancholy* (1684–1720); plays, *Love for Money, The Fond Husband,* etc.

Dur'ham, JOHN GEORGE LAMBTON, 1ST EARL OF (1792–1840), Brit. statesman; *b.* London; helped to frame great Reform Bill; ambassador to Russia, 1832 and 1835–7; created earl, 1837; gov.-gen. of Canada, 1838; wrote valuable *Report on the Affairs of British North America,* which opened the modern era of colonial government by establishing local autonomy.

[*Life and Letters of the First Earl of Durham,* by S. J. Reid (1906).]

Duse (*doo'zā*), ELEANORA (1859–1924), famous Ital. actress; *b.* in Lombardy; appeared in all the capitals of Europe; scored her first success as Juliet; famed for her realistic impersonations.

Dutt (*doot*), MICHAEL MADHU SUDAN (1824–73), Ind. poet; *b.* in Bengal; greatest poet of his age and country; wrote several plays; fame rests on beautiful blank-verse epic, *Meghanad-Badha.*

Dutt, ROMESH CHUNDER (1848–1909), Ind. publicist; *b.* Calcutta; entered Ind. Civil Service by competition; acting commissioner, Bardwan, 1894; revenue minister of Baroda, 1909. Author of many works on India.

Dvorák (*dvor'zhăk*), ANTONÍN (1841–1904), Bohemian composer; *b.* Mülhausen, Bohemia; choral works include *Stabat Mater* and *The Spectre's Bride.* Director of the Conservatoire of Music, New York, 1892–5; director of Prague Conservatory, 1901.

Dyce (*dīs*), ALEXANDER (1798–1869), Eng. dramatic ed., critic, and clergyman; *b.* Edinburgh; curate at Nayland, Suffolk; ed. Shakespeare and other Elizabethan dramatists, also Kemp's *Nine Daies' Wonder.*

Dyce, WILLIAM (1806–64), Scot. artist and lecturer; *b.* Aberdeen; prof. of art, King's Coll., London, 1844; R.A., 1848; *Descent of Venus, Bacchus, Madonna and Child,* etc.; his Arthurian frescoes are in House of Lords, King's Robing-Room.

Dyck, VAN. See VAN DYCK.

Dyer, JOHN (*c.* 1700–58), Brit. poet; *b.* Aberglasney, Caermarthen; wrote *Grongar Hill* (1726), *Ruins of Rome* (1740), *The Fleece* (1757).

Dyer, REGINALD EDWARD HENRY (1864–1927), Brit. general; *b.* Simla; served in many campaigns in India from 1886; during Great War was in command of Infantry Brigade on Persian frontier. In 1919 quelled rebellion at Amritsar by firing on the crowd; commission of inquiry condemned his action, and he was asked to resign; an Eng. judge subsequently upheld his conduct as necessary for security in India.

Dyke, SIR WILLIAM HART (1837–

1931), Eng. politician; *b.* in Kent; chief secretary for Ireland, 1885–6; vice-president of Committee of Council on Education, 1887–92; responsible for Act which gave free education to England, Wales, and Ireland.

Dykes, JOHN BACCHUS (1823–76), Eng. church-music composer; a founder of Cambridge Univ. Musical Soc.; has written popular church music; joint compiler of *Hymns Ancient and Modern.*

Dy'moke, name of Eng. family who, by ownership of manor of Scrivelsby, Lincolnshire, have held hereditary right of champion at coronation of King of England since reign of Richard II.

Dy'son, SIR FRANK WATSON (1868–), Brit. astronomer; *b.* Ashby-de-la-Zouch; chief assistant at Greenwich Observatory, 1894–1905; astronomer-royal for Scotland, 1905–10; astronomer-royal, Greenwich, 1910–33; has pub. many mathematical and astronomical papers.

E

Ealdhelm (*ald'helm*), or ALDHELM (*c.* 640–709), Saxon churchman and scholar; one of most learned men in England; Abbot of Malmesbury, 676; Bishop of Sherborne, 705; his Lat. works have been preserved, but his Old Eng. poetry has perished.

[*Life of St. Ealdhelm*, by Wildman (1905).]

Ear'hart, AMELIA (1899–), Amer. airwoman; *b.* in Kansas; served with Can. V.A.D. during Great War; was the first woman to fly Atlantic (from Newfoundland to Wales), 1928, and was the first woman to make a solo crossing of the Atlantic, 1932. Married George Palmer Putnam, 1931.

Earl, MAUD, Eng. animal painter; *b.* London; among chief works exhibited at Royal Academy are *In the Drifts, Old Benchers, A Cry for Help, The Dog of War, The End of the Expedition, The Dogs of Death* (1900), etc.

Earle, JOHN (*c.* 1601–65), Eng. churchman; *b.* York; dean of Westminster, 1660; Bishop of Worcester and Salisbury, 1662; wrote *Microcosmographie* (1628), and the Lat. trans. of *Eikon Basilike* (1649).

Earle, JOHN (1824–1903), Eng. philologist; *b.* Elston, Devon; rural dean of Bath, 1873–7; prof. of Anglo-Saxon, Oxford, 1849–54 and 1876–1903; did much to encourage study of that language in England, and pub. texts.

Earlom (*er'lom*), RICHARD (1743–1822), Eng. mezzotint engraver; *b.* London; engraved *Liber Veritatis* (from drawings of Claude Lorraine); also Hogarth's *Marriage à la Mode.*

East, SIR ALFRED (1849–1913), Eng. landscape painter and etcher; *b.* Kettering; R.A., 1913; knighted, 1910. Among his best pictures are *Passing Storm, The Nene Valley, The Silent Somme,* and *Autumn*; wrote *The Art of Landscape Painting in Oil Colour.*

East'lake, SIR CHARLES LOCK (1793–1865), Eng. artist; *b.* Plymouth; R.A., 1850; Director of National Gallery, 1855; painted *Christ lamenting over Jerusalem, Byron's Dream,* etc.; pub. *Materials for a History of Oil Painting,* and trans. Goethe's *Theory of Colours.*

East'man, GEORGE (1854–1932), Amer. inventor; *b.* Waterville, New York; invented first roll photographic film and the Kodak camera. During his lifetime gave large sums for the advancement of education.

Eberhard (*ā'ber-hart*), CHRISTIAN AUGUST GOTTLOB (1769–1845), Ger. poet and philosopher; *b.* near Wittenberg; principal works are poem *Hannchen und die Küchlein* (1822), and an epic on the creation, *Der erste Mensch und die Erde* (1828).

Ebers (*ā'berz*), GEORG MORITZ (1837–98), Ger. Egyptologist and historical novelist; *b.* Berlin; prof. of Egyptology at Leipzig, 1870–89; wrote *Ägypten und die Bücher Moses* (1867–8), and several novels dealing with Egypt.

Ebert (*ā'bert*), FREDRICH (1870–1925), first president of Ger. republic, 1919–25; son of a Heidelberg tailor; ed. Socialist newspaper *Bürgerzeitung* (1897); throughout Great War was a leading member of Majority Socialist party; took firm stand against military rising of 1920; later accused of treason, but emerged with honour.

Eck, JOHANN MAIER VON (1486–1543), Ger. theologian; *b.* Eck, Swabia; leading upholder of Catholic doctrine against Luther; pub. *Opera contra Lutherum* (1530–35).

Eck'ermann, JOHANN PETER (1792–1854), Ger. author; *b.* Winsen, Hanover; friend and secretary of Goethe; his *Gespräche mit Goethe* (1836–48) has been widely translated.

Eck'ersberg, CHRISTOFFER VILHELM (1783–1853), Dan. realistic painter; *b.* Warnitz; painted sea-pieces, battle-pieces, and portraits; created 'Danish colour'; prof. and subsequently director of Copenhagen Academy.

Eck'hart, JOHANNES (*c.* 1260–*c.* 1327), Ger. Dominican theologian ('Meister Eckhart'); *b.* near Gotha; follower of Aristotle and the Neoplatonists; suspected of unorthodoxy, and summoned before Inquisition at Cologne; collected writings pub. in *Deutsche Mystiker* (1857).

Eddington, SIR ARTHUR STANLEY (1882–), prof. of astronomy, Cambridge Univ., since 1913, and director of the observatory since 1914; *b.* Kendal; F.R.S., 1914; knighted, 1930. Wrote *Report on the relativity theory of gravitation* (1918), *The Internal Constitution of the Stars* (1926), *Stars and Atoms* (1927), *The Nature of the Physical World* (1928), etc.

Eddy, MRS. MARY BAKER G. (1821–1910), founder of the Christian Science movement, which she declared to be divinely revealed to her; became pastor of first 'Church of Christ Scientist' (1879); built up one of the largest and most powerful organizations in America. Principal work, *Science and Health* (1875).

Eden, ROBERT ANTHONY (1897–), British statesman; educ. Eton and Oxford; served in Great War; M.P. since 1923. Achieved an international reputation by his work at Geneva; Lord Privy Seal, 1934–5; Minister for League of Nations Affairs, 1935; Foreign Secretary since 1935.

Edgar THE PEACEFUL (944–975), Eng. king, son of Edmund I.; succeeded his brother Edwy, 959; at Chester received homage of eight sub-kings, including those of Scotland and Strathclyde; outstanding figure in his reign was Dunstan, Archbishop of Canterbury.

Edgar Atheling (*c.* 1058–1125), Eng. prince, grand-nephew of Edward the Confessor, and heir to the Eng. throne; after defeat of Harold at Senlac, took refuge in Scotland, and finally submitted to the Conqueror.

Edgeworth, MARIA (1767–1849), Irish novelist; *b.* Black Bourton, Oxfordshire; daughter of Richard Lovell Edgeworth of Edgeworthstown, Co. Longford, Ireland, who exercised great influence on her writing. Novels, including *Castle Rackrent* (1800), *The Absentee*, *Ormond*, and *Garry Owen*, are full of vivacity and realistic Irish characterization, and their success inspired Scott's Waverley Novels. Wrote also *The Parent's Assistant*, *Moral Tales for Young People*, *Early Lessons*, etc.

[*Life*, by Lawless; *Maria Edgeworth: Chosen Letters*, by F. V. Barry (1931).]

Edison, THOMAS ALVA (1847–1931), Amer. inventor; *b.* Milan, Ohio, of Dutch and Scottish descent; began life as a railway newsboy, then became telegraph operator. Among his many inventions were the phonograph, cinematograph, incandescent electric lamp, carbon telephone transmitter, multiplex telegraphic system, electric pen, improved electric traction. During his lifetime patented over a thousand inventions.

[*Life*, by Dyer and Martin (2 vols. 1910).]

Edmund, ST. (EDMUND RICH) (*d.* 1240); distinguished ascetic, scholar, and preacher; *b.* near Oxford; Archbishop of Canterbury, 1233; opposed foreign favourites of Henry III.; returned to monastic life, 1240; canonized, 1247.

Edmund (*fl.* 855–70), King of East Anglia; said to have been martyred by Danes; canonized; interred at 'Bury St. Edmunds.'

Edmund I. (*d.* 946), King of the English; succeeded his half-brother Athelstan, 941; a successful warrior and energetic ruler.

Edmund Ironside (*c.* 981–1016), King of the English, son of Ethelred the Unready, whom he succeeded, 1016; was defeated by Canute at Assandun (Ashington in Essex) and was forced to divide the country.

Edward THE CONFESSOR (*d.* 1066), King of England, son of Ethelred II.; succeeded Hardicanute, 1042; married Edith, daughter of Earl Godwin; his reign was peaceful, and he himself a religious man; brought Norman influences into England.

Edward THE ELDER (*d.* 924), King of the Angles and Saxons; son of Alfred the Great, whom he succeeded in 901; warred successfully against Danes, and was recognized as overlord of Britain.

Edward THE MARTYR (963–78), King of England, 975–8; succeeded his father, Edgar the Peaceful; control of country was in hands of Dunstan; murdered at instigation of his stepmother.

Edward I. (1239–1307), King of England; *b.* Westminster; succeeded his father, Henry III., 1272, while on crusade; fought in civil war against Simon de Montfort, 1264–5. In his reign, one of the most important in Eng. history, many enactments regulating the tenure of land were passed; power of Pope checked; Jews expelled; Wales conquered, and an unsuccessful attempt made to subdue Scotland. Was creator of Eng. parliament.

[*Edward I.*, by Tout (1888).]

Edward II. (1284–1327), King of England; succeeded his father, Edward I., 1307; fell under power of his favourite, Piers Gaveston; was defeated at Bannockburn, 1314. Alienated every one by his misgovernment. The queen, Isabella of France, plotted against him; he was deposed and murdered in Berkeley Castle.

Edward III. (1312–77), King of England; succeeded his father, Edward II., 1327. In 1337 declared war against France ('the Hundred Years' War') and won the battles of Crécy, 1346, and Poitiers, 1356. Scots were defeated at Neville's Cross, 1346, and their king, David II., taken prisoner. England was ravaged by the Black Death in 1349. The reign was marked by an extension of popular liberties wrung from the king in return for money for carrying on Fr. wars. Noteworthy also were Wyclif's attempt to reform the Church, and the establishment of the House of Commons as a separate body.

[*History of Edward III.*, by Mackinnon (1900).]

Edward IV. (1442–83), King of England; *b.* Rouen; son of Richard, Duke of York, whose claim to throne caused Wars of Roses; succeeded on deposition of Henry VI., 1461, and reigned till his death, except during Henry's short restoration, 1470–1; he was a firm ruler and good soldier, but not of noble character.

Edward V. (1470–83), King of England; son of Edward IV.; along with his brother was murdered in Tower of London by order of his uncle, Richard III.

Edward VI. (1537–53), King of England and Ireland; *b.* Greenwich; son of Henry VIII. and Jane Seymour; succeeded his father, 1547. His reign was marked by religious strife.

Edward VII. (1841-1910), ALBERT EDWARD, eldest son of Queen Victoria and Prince Albert; King of Great Britain and Ireland; Emperor of India; *b.* Buckingham Palace. As Prince of Wales travelled extensively, visiting Canada and U.S.A., 1860, India, 1875. In 1863 he married Alexandra, the King of Denmark's eldest daughter; became king, Jan. 22, 1901. Notable events of his reign were end of S. African War, 1902, and formation of Union of S. Africa, 1909–10; House of Lords crisis, 1909–10; Anglo-Japanese Alliance, 1902; cementing of *Triple Entente* with France and Russia, 1904–10. During his reign earned the title of 'Edward the Peacemaker' by his tact and diplomacy; he was a good sportsman, a man highly endowed with common sense and *savoir-faire*, and a conscientious and successful ruler.

[*Life*, by Sir Sidney Lee (2 vols. 1928).]

Edward VIII. (1894–), King of Great Britain, Ireland, and the Brit. Dominions beyond the Seas, Emperor of India; eldest son of George V.; *b.* White Lodge, Richmond Park; educ. at Osborne Coll. and Dartmouth; joined cruiser *Hindustan* as midshipman, 1911; lieutenant, 1913; captain, 1919. On accession of George V. was created Prince of Wales and Earl of Chester. Studied at Magdalen Coll., Oxford, as an ordinary undergraduate.

On outbreak of Great War, 1914, he received a commission in the Grenadier Guards. Was on the staff of Sir John French, was in Egypt with the Mediterranean Expeditionary Force, paid three visits to Italy, and was with Brit. army at the entry into Valenciennes, Nov. 7, 1918.

In 1919 he sailed for Canada, visited important cities, and also toured the more outlying parts. From Canada he proceeded to U.S.A., visiting Washington and New York. In both countries he was welcomed with enthusiasm.

In 1920 he sailed for Australasia, calling at Barbados, Panama, San Diego, Hawaii, and Fiji on his way to New Zealand. He next toured Australia for three months. On his return journey he visited Samoa, Mexico, and the Brit. W. Indies, being received everywhere with enthusiasm and goodwill. In 1921 he paid a state visit to India and then proceeded to Japan; in 1925 he visited West and South Africa, and East Africa in 1928. His tours of the Dominions Overseas and of the home industrial regions have been of imperial and world-wide significance, and he has been well called 'the greatest ambassador of the Brit. Empire.' In 1928 he received the new title of Master of the Merchant Navy and Fishing Fleets. He became king, Jan. 1936.

Edward, PRINCE OF WALES. See BLACK PRINCE.

Edwards, ALFRED GEORGE (1848–), Welsh churchman; *b.* Llanymawddwy; headmaster, Llandovery Coll., 1875–85; Bishop of St. Asaph, 1889; first Archbishop of Wales, 1920–34; works, *The Church in Wales* (1888), *Commonsense Patriotism* (1894), *Landmarks in Welsh Church History* (1912), *Memories* (1927).

Edwards, AMELIA ANN BLANDFORD (1831–92), Eng. novelist and Egyptologist; *b.* London; founder of Egyptian Exploration Fund; pub. *A Thousand Miles up the Nile* (1877), *Pharaohs, Fellahs, and Explorers* (1891), and novels, *Debenham's Vow*, etc.

Edwards, JOHN PASSMORE (1823–1911), Eng. philanthropist; *b.* near Truro; proprietor and ed. of the *Echo*, the first halfpenny newspaper; M.P., 1880–5; endowed libraries, hospitals, and Passmore Edwards Settlement and other homes.

Edwards, JONATHAN (1703–58), Amer. theologian; *b.* East Windsor, Conn.; pastor of Congregational Church at Northampton, Mass., 1727; missionary to Indians, 1750; president of Princeton Coll., 1757; author of many books; a man of great learning and deep piety; a vigorous defender of Calvinistic theology.

Edwin, or EDWINE (585–633), King of Northumbria; extended kingdom to the Forth; reputed founder of Edinburgh; defeated and slain by Penda, King of Mercia.

Eeckhout (*ek'hout*), GERBRAND VAN DEN (1621–74), Dutch artist; *b.* Amsterdam; pupil of Rembrandt; chief subjects are biblical, including *Christ in the Temple*, *Haman and Mordecai*, etc.

E'gan, PIERCE (1772–1849), Eng. sporting writer; *b.* London; his *Days and Nights of Jerry Hawthorne and Corinthian Tom*, illustrated by Cruikshank, probably inspired Dickens's *Pickwick Papers*.

Egbert (reigned 802–839), King of Wessex; chosen king while a refugee at court of Charlemagne; subdued Britons of Cornwall, overthrew supremacy of Mercia, made Northumbria submit, and assumed title of Bretwalda, or overlord of the whole of England; finally overthrew the Danes at Hengestdune in Cornwall, 837.

Eg'mont, LAMORAL, COUNT OF (1522–68), Flem. soldier; *b.* in Hainault; helped to arrange marriage between Philip II. of Spain and Mary of England; opposed autocratic rule of Philip in the Netherlands, and became a popular hero; was treacherously seized and beheaded along with Count Horn by the Duke of Alva.

Ehrlich (*ār'lich*), PAUL (1854–1915), Ger. scientist; *b.* in Silesia; director of Royal Institute for Experimental Therapeutics at Frankfurt-on-Main; Nobel Prize for medicine (with Metchnikoff), 1908; his greatest triumph, discovery of salvarsan and neosalvarsan.

Eichendorff (*ī'chen-dorf*), JOSEPH VON (1788–1857), Ger. poet; *b.* near Ratibor; served in Prussian army, 1813–15; his lyrics have secured him his chief fame; he also wrote romances, plays, trans. Calderon's religious plays, and produced critical works on Ger. literature.

Eiffel (*ī'fel*), ALEXANDRE GUSTAVE (1832–1923), Fr. engineer; *b.* Dijon; made bridges over Garonne and Douro; designed locks for Panama Canal; best-known work, Eiffel Tower, Paris, 1889.

Einhard (*īn'hart*), HEINHARDUS, or EGINHARDUS (*c.* 770–840), biographer and friend of Charle-

'magne; one of the most brilliant disciples of Alcuin; abbot of Mühlheim; his great work is *Vita et gesta Caroli Magni* (*c.* 821; Eng. trans., 1877).

Einstein (*īn'stīn*), ALBERT (1879–), Ger.-Swiss physicist; *b.* Ulm; studied at Zürich; became nationalized as Swiss, 1900; prof. at Zürich, 1910; prof. at Prague, 1911; returned again to Zürich; prof. of physics, Berlin, 1914. He enunciated his epoch-making theory of Relativity in a paper read to Berlin Academy, 1915; pub. his work on the subject, 1920; Nobel Prize, 1921. An ardent Zionist, he was exiled from Germany, 1933, and finally settled in U.S.A. as prof. of mathematics, Princeton, N.J.

Eisner (*īz'ner*), KURT (1867–1919), Bavarian socialist leader; *b.* Berlin; of Jewish descent; wrote for many papers, including *Frankfurter Zeitung*; joint ed. of *Vorwärts*; opposed to Great War. Organized bloodless revolution which led to abdication of King of Bavaria, Nov. 1918, and was the signal for general revolution throughout Germany; was the first Premier of the Bavarian Republic, but was assassinated by reactionaries.

Eldon, JOHN SCOTT, 1ST EARL OF (1751–1838), Eng. lawyer; Lord Chancellor, 1799, and 1801–21; violently conservative, he conducted high treason prosecutions against Horne Tooke, etc.; opposed emancipation of Catholics, and abolition of capital punishment for minor offences.

El'gar, SIR EDWARD (1857–1934), Brit. musician; *b.* near Worcester; prof. of music, Birmingham Univ., 1905–8; O.M., 1911; Master of the King's Musick, 1924; numerous and varied compositions include his great choral work, *The Dream of Gerontius*; also *The Apostles, In the South,* and *Pomp and Circumstance* marches. Best-known melody, *Land of Hope and Glory.* Elgar stands first among Brit. composers of modern times.

Elg'in and Kincar'dine, THOMAS, EARL OF (1766–1841), Brit. diplomatist; while envoy-extraordinary at Constantinople he brought the famous Elgin Marbles from Greece (now in Brit. Museum).

Eli (*ē'lī*), high priest and judge of Israel, judged Israel forty years. (See 1 Sam. 1–4).

Elias (*ē-lī'as*), LEVITA (1469–1549), Jewish grammarian; *b.* Neustadt, Bavaria; compiled first dictionary of Hebrew language, and trans. the psalms into German.

Elijah (*ē-lī'jä*), O.T. prophet; the most impressive figure among the Hebrew seers; appears suddenly in 1 Kings 17. His life's work was a contest with the cult of Baal, favoured by Ahab and Jezebel, during which he overcame the prophets of Baal on Mount Carmel. (See 1 Kings 17–19 and 21; 2 Kings 1–2.)

El'iot, GEORGE (1819–80), Eng. novelist, pen name of MARY ANN EVANS; *b.* on a Warwickshire farm. In 1849 produced a trans. of Strauss's *Life of Jesus,* and in 1851 became assistant ed. of *Westminster Review.* Amongst her friends were Herbert Spencer, Carlyle, and George Henry Lewes; with the last-named she formed an irregular connection which lasted until his death in 1878. Lewes undoubtedly inspired much of her work. She married J. W. Cross in 1880. Her first effort in fiction was *Amos Barton,* which appeared in *Blackwood's* in 1857, and was followed by *Scenes of Clerical Life* (1858). *Adam Bede* (1859) met with instant success. Then came *The Mill on the Floss* (1860), *Silas Marner* (1861), *Romola* (1863), *Middlemarch* (1872), and other novels. Her place is amongst the greatest writers of Eng. fiction. She excelled as a painter of middle-class life and character, and her work is marked by much pathos and humour.

[*Lives*, by J. W. Cross, Sir Leslie Stephen, Mathilde Blind, Oscar Browning.]

Eliot, SIR JOHN (1592–1632), Eng. statesman; *b.* Port Eliot, Cornwall; leader of House of Commons, 1626, and was foremost in impeachment of Buckingham; vigorous upholder of Petition of Right; strongly opposed to tonnage and poundage; imprisoned, and died, in Tower.

Elisha (*e-lī'shä*), O.T. prophet, successor of Elijah, with whom he is closely associated. (See 2 Kings 2–9.)

Elizabeth (1533–1603), Queen of England and Ireland; daughter of Henry VIII. and Anne Boleyn; *b.* London; imprisoned in the Tower for suspected complicity in Wyat's rebellion, 1554; succeeded Mary, 1558. She supported the Reformation mainly from policy; aided the reformers in Scotland and on the Continent. By her diplomacy she kept England at peace for twenty-five years. R.C. plots against her led her in 1587 to consent to the execution of Mary, Queen of Scots. The Elizabethan age is one of the most glorious in Eng. history; the exploits of her great captains, such as Drake, Frobisher, Hawkins, and Raleigh, prepared the way for the defeat of the Spanish Armada, 1588, and made England mistress of the seas. The names of Spenser, Marlowe, Shakespeare, and Bacon exemplify the extraordinary outburst of literary activity to which she gave her patronage. She was amenable to flattery, but the execution of Essex showed that courtiers dared not presume on her favour. Though autocratic she showed wisdom in her choice of counsellors, such as Cecil, and knew when to yield to Parliament. Her rule was based not on arbitrary powers but on the trust reposed in her by her subjects.

[*Queen Elizabeth*, by Creighton (1896), by Neale (1934).]

Elizabeth (1596–1662), eldest daughter of James I. of England; married, 1613, Frederick V., Elector Palatine and King of Bohemia; was mother of Sophia, wife of Ernest, Elector of Hanover, mother of George I.

Elizabeth, AMÉLIE EUGÉNIE (1837–98), Empress of Austria and Queen of Hungary; daughter of Duke Maximilian of Bavaria; married Emperor Francis Joseph II. of Austria; murdered at Geneva.

Elizabeth, PAULINE ELIZABETH OTTILIE LOUISE (1843–1916), Queen of Romania, known in literary world as 'Carmen Sylva'; did much for higher education of women and philanthropic objects; wrote plays, poems, novels, essays, etc.; works include the poems *Sappho* and *Hammerstein*; *Les Pensées d'une Reine*, *A Romanian Vendetta*, etc.

Elizabeth Petrovna (1709–62), Empress of Russia; daughter of Peter the Great; *b.* near Moscow; succeeded 1741; obtained from Sweden part of Finland; during Seven Years' War successfully opposed Frederick the Great. Had serious faults, but was a capable ruler.

Ella. See ÆLLA.

Ell'iot, JANE (1727–1805), Scot. poetess; *b.* in Teviotdale; daughter of Sir Gilbert Elliot; remembered for her ballad 'The Flowers of the Forest.'

Elliott, EBENEZER (1781–1849), Eng. poet; *b.* Masborough, Yorks; 'Corn-law Rhymer'; ardent chartist; pub. *Corn-law Rhymes* (1831), and other volumes dealing with working-class life.

Ell'is, HENRY HAVELOCK (1859–), Eng. psychologist; *b.* Croydon; spent much of boyhood at sea; qualified as a doctor, but turned to literary and scientific work. His greatest work is *Studies in the Psychology of Sex* (in 6 vols.); also noted for the literary charm of his occasional writings.

Elman, MISCHA (1892–), Russ. violinist; *b.* Stalnoje, Kiev, of Jewish parents; won extraordinary success as a boy; was pupil of Auer and Fidelmann; appeared in London, 1905; naturalized as U.S.A. citizen, 1920; regarded as one of the greatest violinists.

Elphinstone (*el'fin-stōn*), WILLIAM (1431–1514), Scot. statesman and prelate; rector of Glasgow Univ., 1474; Bishop of Ross, 1481; ambassador to England, 1484; Bishop of Aberdeen and lord high chancellor, 1488; founded King's Coll., Aberdeen, and built bridge over Dee; helped to introduce printing into Scotland.

Em'erson, RALPH WALDO (1803–82), Amer. essayist, poet, and philosopher; *b.* Boston, Mass.; educated Harvard; a teacher for three years, then entered Unitarian ministry; gave up the ministry, 1832, and devoted himself to writing and lecturing. He twice visited England, and formed friendships with Carlyle, Coleridge, Wordsworth, and other authors. His philosophic creed was broad and sincere, but was suggestive rather than systematic. In his essays his style is brilliant and epigrammatic. His verse never appealed to a wide public, for though it is full of the essence of poetry, the form is rugged and unmusical.

[*Life*, by Van Wyck Brooks (1927).]

Emine'scu, MICHAIL (1849–89), Romanian poet; *b.* in Moldavia; greatest of 19th cent.; librarian of Jassy Univ., 1874; chief poems, *Venera si Madona* and *Epigonii.*

Emin Pasha (EDUARD SCHNITZER) (1840–92), Ger. traveller and administrator; *b.* Oppeln; entered Egyptian medical service, 1876; was an invaluable ally of Gordon, who appointed him governor of the Equatorial Province of the Sudan, 1878; isolated for years after Gordon's death; Stanley relieved him, 1888; he entered Ger. service and returned to Equatoria, where he was killed; did valuable work in African flora and fauna, in road surveys, and by abolishing slavery.

Em'met, ROBERT (1778–1803), Irish rebel patriot; *b.* Dublin; joined the exiled leaders of United Irishmen on the Continent, and, returning, planned Irish rebellion, which, however, ended in futile riot in Dublin, 1803; Emmet escaped, but later was arrested, tried, and hanged.

Empedocles (*em-ped'ō-klēz*) OF AGRIGENTUM (probably *c.* 490–430 B.C.), democrat, philosopher, and physician; wandered through Gr. cities, preaching the ascetic life. He regarded all things as composed of earth, air, fire, and water, mingled by Love or separated by Strife. According to tradition threw himself into Etna.

Encke (*eng'ke*), JOHANN FRANZ (1791–1865), Ger. astronomer; *b.* Hamburg; investigated several comets, and his name was given to one.

En'nius, QUINTUS (239–170 B.C.), Lat. poet; *b.* Rudiae, Calabria; regarded as inventor of the 'satire'; greatest work is *Annales.*

Entrecasteaux (*ontr-käs-tō'*), JOSEPH ANTOINE BRUNI D' (1739–93), Fr. navigator; famed for his surveys of New Caledonia, Tasmania, etc.; D'Entrecasteaux Archipelago, east of New Guinea, commemorates him.

En'ver Pasha' (1881–1922), Turk. statesman; prominent among the Young Turks who brought about the deposition of

Abdul Hamid, 1909. In 1912 he headed the movement against the cession of Adrianople to the Bulgarians, and occupied Adrianople, 1913. Became minister of war, 1913, and brought Turkey into the Great War on side of Central Powers. After Turkey's surrender he fled to Germany, and later Russia, where he was killed in rebellion against the Soviets.

Epaminon'das (*c.* 418–362 B.C.), Theban general and statesman; expelled Spartan garrison, 379 B.C.; defeated Spartans at Leuctra, 371, and Mantinea, 362; did much for Thebes politically, and developed military strategy.

Epicte'tus, Stoic philosopher of 1st cent. A.D.; a freed slave; expelled from Rome, along with other philosophers, by Domitian; settled and taught at Epirus. His stoicism approaches the spirit of Christianity. His *Discourses* were written down by a pupil.

Epicu'rus (341–270 B.C.), Gr. philosopher; *b.* Samos; settled in Athens, and formed a society of friends. His distinctive doctrine was that welfare consists in pleasure; pleasures of the mind and of friendship rank above those of the body. Far from being 'epicures,' members of the society, in its earlier days, led frugal and abstemious lives.

Epstein (*ep'stīn*), JACOB (1880–), sculptor; *b.* New York of Russ.-Polish parents; settled in London, 1905; executed figures to decorate the building of the Brit. Medical Association, Strand, London. Among other works are tomb of Oscar Wilde, Paris, *Rima*, *Christ*, *Night* and *Day*, *Genesis*, bust of Einstein. Most of his work excited much controversy.

Eras'mus, DESIDERIUS (1466–1536), Dutch scholar and theologian; *b.* Rotterdam; educated in monastic schools. In 1498 he paid a visit to England, studied Greek at Oxford, and formed a close friendship with Sir Thomas More; spent several years in France, the Netherlands, and in Italy, where he made the acquaintance of the Venetian printer Aldus Manutius; became tutor to the Archbishop of St. Andrews, son of James IV. of Scotland. He spent the years 1509–14 in England; latter part of his life was spent at Basle. Of his many publications the best known is his famous satire, the *Praise of Folly*. Erasmus remained faithful to the Church of Rome, but criticized the vice and ignorance of the Romish clergy, while at the same time he directed satire against Luther. His writings were marked by perfect sanity and broadness of view, and his influence was very widespread both as critic and theologian. During his lifetime he was unquestionably the intellectual dictator of his age.

[*Life*, by P. Smith (1923).]

Eras'tus, THOMAS (1524–83), Ger.-Swiss theologian of Heidelberg and Basle; *b.* Baden, Switzerland; supporter of Zwingli; maintained that Christians should be punished by civil law and not by excommunication. Hence the term 'Erastianism'—the subordination of Church to State.

Eratosthenes (*e-ra-tos'the-nēz*) OF ALEXANDRIA (*c.* 276–*c.* 194 B.C.), Gr. mathematician and scientist; *b.* Cyrene; superintendent of Alexandrian library; computed earth's circumference, and was the founder of scientific chronology and geography.

Erck'mann, ÉMILE (1822–99), and **Chatrian** (*sha-trē-on'*), LOUIS GRATIEN (1826–90), Fr. novelists, both born in Alsace, who collaborated in writing popular military stories and plays, including *Le Juif polonais* (1869) (adapted as *The Bells* on Eng. stage).

Er'icsson, JOHN (1803–89), Swed.-Amer. naval inventor; *b.*

in Wermland, Sweden; lived in England, 1826–39, and competed with Stephenson in locomotive competition; settled in America, 1839; applied screw to steam navigation; built turreted battleship *Monitor*, 1861, and invented steam fire-engine.

Erigena (*e-rij'e-nä*), JOHANNES SCOTUS (*c.* 815–877), mediæval theologian, forerunner (or one of founders) of scholasticism; controlled Palatine Academy at Paris. He developed in his *De Divisione Naturæ* a philosophical system closely akin to neo-Platonism.

[*John the Scot*, by Gardiner (1900).]

Ern'le, ROWLAND EDMUND PROTHERO, BARON (1851–), Eng. politician and author; *b.* Clifton-on-Teme; ed. *Quarterly Review* (1894–9); M.P. for Oxford Univ., 1914–19; president of board of agriculture, 1916–19. An authority on agricultural questions. Pub. *Life of Dean Stanley*, *Psalms in Human Life*, *English Farming*, *Pleasant Land of France*, etc. Created baron, 1919.

Er'skine, EBENEZER (1680–1756), Scot. churchman; *b.* Chirnside; minister of Portmoak, 1703, of Stirling, 1731; suspended for upholding that people should choose their pastors; originator of the Secession Church, 1733.

Erskine, HENRY (1746–1817), Scot. lawyer; *b.* Edinburgh; lord advocate, 1783 and 1806; famed for oratory and wit; pub. *The Emigrant, an Eclogue* (1773), and other poems.

Erskine, JOHN (1695–1768), Scot. jurist; prof. of Scots law, Edinburgh, 1737; his *Principles of the Law of Scotland* and his *Institutes of the Law of Scotland* are still the standard works.

Erskine, THOMAS, 1ST BARON (1750–1823), Brit. lawyer; *b.* Edinburgh; son of 10th Earl of Buchan; noted for several famous defences, including Captain Baillie, Admiral Keppel, Lord George Gordon, and Tom Paine; M.P. for Portsmouth, 1785; chancellor to Prince of Wales; lord chancellor, 1806–7.

Er'vine, ST. JOHN GREER (1883–), Brit. dramatist and author; *b.* Belfast; forsook business for literature; manager of Abbey Theatre, Dublin, 1915; wounded in Great War; dramatic critic; author of plays, biographies, and novels.

Erzberger (*erts'berg-er*), MATTHIAS (1875–1921), Ger. politician; *b.* in Württemberg; became leader of Centre or R.C. party in Reichstag; during Great War was author of famous Reichstag resolution in favour of peace without annexations, 1917; member of inner cabinet, 1918; chief Ger. representative on Armistice commission; minister of finance, 1919. Was cordially hated by the capitalists, militarists, and Protestants, and was assassinated.

E'sau, son of Isaac and twin brother of Jacob, who robbed him of his birthright. (Gen. 25–27.)

Esher, REGINALD BALIOL BRETT, 2ND VISCOUNT (1852–1930), Eng. politician and author; *b.* London; M.P. for Penryn and Falmouth, 1880–5; held many important offices; chairman of War Office Reconstitution Committee, 1904. Among publications are *To-day and To-morrow*, *The Influence of King Edward*, *The Tragedy of Kitchener*, *Ionicus*, etc.

Es'march, JOHANNES FRIEDRICH AUGUST VON (1823–1908), Ger. army surgeon; *b.* in Schleswig-Holstein; surgeon-general, Franco-Prussian War, 1870–1; authority on hospital management and first-aid appliances.

Es'sex. (1) ROBERT DEVEREUX, 2ND EARL OF (1567–1601), favourite of Queen Elizabeth; *b.* in Herefordshire; earl marshal,

1597; lord deputy of Ireland, 1599; failed to quell Tyrone's rebellion, condemned for treason, and executed. (2) ROBERT DEVEREUX, 3rd earl (1591–1646), son of (1); lieutenant-general of the army sent against Scot. Covenanters, 1639; commanded Parliamentary army in Civil War until passing of Self-Denying Ordinance, 1645.

Estella, MARQUÉS DE. See PRIMO DE RIVERA.

Eth'elbald, King of Wessex; son of Ethelwulf; fought against Danes at Aclea, 851; reigned 856–860.

Ethelbert, or ÆTHELBERT (552–616), King of Kent; married Bertha, daughter of Charibert, King of Soissons; converted to Christianity by St. Augustine; first to write Saxon laws—*dooms*.

Etheldreda, ST., or ÆTHELDREDA (630–79), abbess of Ely, which she founded, 673; name corrupted into St. Audrey, and further into 'tawdry'; Ely Cathedral is built over her tomb.

Eth'elfrith, King of Northumbria; succeeded 593; repelled the Scots at Daegsastan, 603; defeated Welsh at Chester, 614.

Eth'elred I., King of Wessex and Kent (reigned 866–871); son of Ethelwulf; harassed by Danes during all his reign.

Eth'elred II. (THE UNREADY), King of the English (reigned 979–1016); continually troubled by Dan. invasions, led chiefly by Sweyn and Canute; policy of buying off Danes only procured short periods of peace.

Eth'elstan. See ATHELSTAN.

Eth'elwulf (reigned 839–858), King of West Saxons; father of Alfred the Great; reign taken up with contests with Danes.

Eth'erege, SIR GEORGE (1635–91), Eng. dramatist; a courtier and man of fashion. In his plays, *Love in a Tub*, *She Would if She Could*, and *The Man of Mode*, he inaugurated the comedy of intrigue.

Et'ty, WILLIAM (1787–1849), Eng. historical painter; *b.* York; great colourist; untiring student of anatomy; A.R.A., 1824; R.A., 1828; his *Youth on the Prow and Pleasure at the Helm* (Tate Gallery, London), and the *Judiths* in the National Gallery, Edinburgh, are fine examples of his work.

Eucken (*oi'ken*), RUDOLF CHRISTOPH (1846–1926), Ger. philosopher; *b.* in E. Friesland; prof. of philosophy, Jena, 1874–1920; Nobel Prize for literature, 1908. His philosophy is an interpretation of life as a whole, in which religion plays a predominant part; action, not contemplation, is the essential feature of spiritual life.

[*Eucken: a Philosophy of Life*, by A. J. Jones (1912).]

Euclid (*ū'klid*), Gr. mathematician of 3rd cent. B.C.; nothing known of his life except that he taught mathematics at Alexandria; immortalized by *Elements of Geometry* (13 books). It is not possible to say how far Euclid's works were original, but some of his propositions were certainly discovered by his Gr. predecessors. Also the author of *Data*, *Divisions of Superficies*, *Porisms*, etc.

[*Euclid: his Life and System*, by T. Smith (1902).]

Eugene, PRINCE (FRANÇOIS EUGÈNE, PRINCE DE SAVOIE) (1663–1736), Austria's most famous general; *b.* Paris; entered service of Emperor Leopold I.; defeated Turks at Zenta, 1697; fought in War of Span. Succession, 1699; co-operated with Marlborough at Blenheim, 1704; fought against French at Cassano, 1705; governor of Milan, 1707; fought at Oudenarde, 1708, and Malplaquet, 1709; continued war against France when Britain had withdrawn from alliance; returned to Vienna, 1714; defeated Turks with great slaughter in battle of Belgrade, 1717; vicar-general of Italy, 1724. He was a daring commander, reckless of his soldiers' lives, but equally so of his own.

[*Prince Eugene*, by Malleson.]

Eugénie (*ū-zhā-nē'*), MARIE EUGÉNIE IGNACE AUGUSTINE DE MONTIJO (1826–1920), empress of the French, *b.* Granada; of Span., Ital., and Scot. descent; married Napoleon III., 1853; after revolution following Franco-Prussian War retired to Chislehurst, Kent, with deposed emperor and son, 1871; afterwards lived at Farnborough and Cap Martin; her son, the Prince Imperial, was killed while serving as volunteer in the Brit. force in Zululand, 1879.

[*Recollections o, the Empress Eugénie*, by A. Filon (1920).]

Euler (*oi'ler*), LEONHARD (1707–83), Swiss mathematician; *b.* Basle; prof. at St. Petersburg, 1730; at Berlin, 1741–66. His name is perpetuated in various mathematical formulæ. Euler chiefly worked at problems left by Newton.

[*Life*, by Rudio (1884).]

Euripides (*ū-rip'i-dēz*) (480–406 B.C.), Gr. tragic dramatist; *b.* Phlya, Attica; was an athlete and a painter; subsequently turned to dramatic work; said to have written about ninety plays; gained first prize at age of thirty-nine, and four times subsequently. Unlike his great contemporaries Æschylus and Sophocles, he appears to have taken no part in public affairs. In later life he made his home at the court of Archelaus, King of Macedon, and tradition attributes his death to jealous enemies. His extant works include: *Alcestis, Medea, Hippolytus, Hecuba, Andromache, Supplices, Ion, Heraclidæ, Troades, Helena, Phœnissæ, Orestes, Bacchæ, Iphigenia in Aulis, Hercules Furens, Iphigenia in Tauris, Electra,* and *The Cyclops.* Euripides ranks below Æschylus and Sophocles, but his plays served as the model for later writers.

[*Euripides and His Age*, by Gilbert Murray (1914).]

Euse'bius OF CÆSAREA (264–340), Bishop of Cæsarea; *b.* in Palestine; great Christian scholar and prolific writer; his *Ecclesiastical History*, tracing history of Christian Church from beginning to triumph of Constantine, was written *c.* 326; his *Life of Constantine* carries on the story.

Eutro'pius (*fl. c.* 350–78), Rom. historian; his *Breviarium Historicæ Romanæ* covers history of city from its foundation to his own day, and was for long a favourite school textbook.

Evans, SIR ARTHUR JOHN (1851–), Eng. archæologist; *b.* Nash Mills, Herts; son of Sir John Evans; made important archæological discoveries in Balkans; excavated anc. sites in Crete, and in excavating palace of Knossos discovered the pre-Phœnician script; honorary keeper of Ashmolean Museum, Oxford, since 1908; extraordinary prof. of prehistoric archæology; author of *Antiquarian Researches in Illyricum, Cretan Pictographs and Præ-Phœnician Script, The Palace of Minos*, etc.

Evans, EDWARD RATCLIFFE GARTH RUSSELL (1881–), Brit. sailor and explorer; entered navy, 1897; served in relief ship to *Discovery* Expedition, 1902–4; second in command to Captain Scott in Antarctic Expedition, 1909–13; in command on Captain Scott's death. During Great War, in 1917, when H.M. destroyers *Swift* and *Broke* engaged six Ger. destroyers, he commanded the latter ship, which sank two and torpedoed a third. Commanded Royal Australian Navy, 1929–31; commander-in-chief, The Nore, since 1935. Author of *Keeping the Seas* (1920),

South with Scott (1921), *To Sweep the Spanish Main* (1930).

Evans, Sir John (1823–1908), Eng. archæologist and geologist; was the president of Geological Soc., the Soc. of Antiquaries, the Numismatic Soc., and the Brit. Association; author of standard works of antiquarian interest.

Evelyn (*ev'e-lin*), John (1620–1706), Eng. diarist and author; *b.* near Dorking; his famous *Diary*, covering period 1640–1706, remained in MS. until 1818, and is a grave and dignified autobiography and commentary on current affairs. He was one of the founders, and for some time secretary, of the Royal Soc.

Ev'erest, Sir George (1790–1866), Brit. geographer and surveyor; *b.* Gwerndale, Breconshire; on Ind. Survey, 1816–43; measured meridional arc of India; Mount Everest named after him.

Ewald (*ā'vält*), Georg Heinrich August von (1803–75), Ger. theologian and Oriental scholar; *b.* Göttingen; prof. of philology, Göttingen, 1827–37; Tübingen, 1838; of theology, 1841; recalled to Göttingen, 1848. His *History of People of Israel*, finished 1859, shows great learning.

Ewald (*ā'väld*), Johannes (1743–81), Dan. poet; *b.* Copenhagen; his masterpieces of lyrical and dramatic poetry made him the first poet of his age and country; among his notable works are the lyrical drama *The Fishers*, containing the Dan. national song, his dramatic poem *Adam and Eve*, and a tragedy, *Rolf Krage*. He performed for Dan. literature what Goethe, Wordsworth, etc., did later for other literatures of Europe.

Ewart (*ū'art*), James Cossar (1851–1933), Scot. zoologist; *b.* Penicuik, Midlothian; regius prof. of natural history, Edinburgh, 1882–1927; authority on zebras; author of *Locomotor System of the Echinoderms* (1881), *On the Preservation of Fish* (1887), *Penicuik Experiments* (1899), *On a Prejvalsky Hybrid* (1907), etc.

Ewing (*ū'ing*), Sir James Alfred (1855–1935), Scot. physicist and civil engineer; *b.* Dundee; prof. of applied mechanics, Cambridge, 1890–1903; director of naval education, 1903–16; principal of Edinburgh Univ., 1916–29; president of Brit. Association, 1932. In Great War did brilliant work in intercepting and deciphering enemy code messages. Published *The Steam Engine and other Heat Engines* (1894), *The Strength of Materials* (1899), *Thermodynamics for Engineers* (1920), *The Physicist in Engineering Practice* (1923), etc.

Ewing, Juliana Horatia Orr (1841–85), Eng. writer for children; *b.* in Yorks; daughter of Mrs. Gatty. Her works include *Jan of the Windmill* (1876), *Jackanapes* (1884), etc.

Eyck (*īk*), Hubert van (*c.* 1370–1426) and Jan van (*c.* 1389–1440), Flem. artists; founders of early Flem. school; court painters of Philip, Duke of Burgundy; subjects are chiefly Scriptural, and, apart from the general excellence of their work, the brothers are credited with the invention of oil-painting, colours having been previously mixed with gums. Examples of their works are in the London National Gallery, and at Bruges, Ghent, Antwerp, Paris, and other continental cities. Their sister, Margaret van Eyck, was also a painter of eminence.

[*The Van Eycks and their Followers*, by Conway (1921).]

Eyre (*ār*), Edward John (1815–1901), Brit. administrator and explorer; *b.* Hornsea; proved the practicability of an overland route between S. and W. Australia; author of *Expeditions into Central Australia* (1845); governor of Jamaica, 1862–5; superseded for stern measures taken to suppress a rebellion; tried and acquitted.

Eze'kiel, Heb. prophet; of priestly descent; carried off to captivity in Babylonia, 597 B.C.; prophesied for about twenty-two years. See book of Ezekiel.

Ez'ra, 'the Scribe,' one of the Jewish captives in Babylon under Artaxerxes I.; obtained, 458 B.C., edict empowering him to repatriate a band of fellow-exiles in Jerusalem. See books of Ezra and Nehemiah.

F

Fa'ber, FREDERICK WILLIAM (1814–63), Eng. theologian and hymn-writer; *b.* Calverley, Yorks; follower of Newman, went over to R.C. Church, 1845; founded, 1844, religious community at Birmingham, branch established in London, 1849, removed to Brompton, 1854; author of hymns, 'O Paradise, O Paradise,' 'O Saviour, bless us ere we go,' 'Pilgrims of the Night,' etc.

Fab'er. (1) JOHN (?1660–1721), Dutch artist; *b.* The Hague; settled in London; famed for pen portraits on vellum, and engravings. (2) JOHN, 'The Younger' (?1695–1756), son of (1), a still more famous engraver; produced over 400 engravings of portraits.

Fa'bius, QUINTUS FABIUS MAXIMUS, Rom. dictator, 221 B.C.; wore out Hannibal and saved the state by masterly tactics, drawing on the Carthaginians and refusing to fight; hence called *Cunctator* ('delayer').

Fabre (*fäbr*), JEAN HENRI (1823–1915), Fr. entomologist; *b.* in Aveyron; was teacher for some time, and then devoted himself to study of the life and habits of insects; wrote *Annales des Sciences naturelles* (1855–8), and in 10 vols. *Souvenirs entomologiques* (1879–1907).

Faed (*fād*), THOMAS (1826–1900), genre painter; *b.* Burley Mill, Kirkcudbrightshire; excelled in domestic scenes; R.A., 1864; among his celebrated pictures are *Scott and his Friends at Abbotsford* and *The Mitherless Bairn.*

Faguet (*fä-gā'*), EMILE (1847–1916), Fr. critic and literary historian; *b.* La Roche-sur-Yon; prof. at Sorbonne, 1897; member of Academy, 1900; pub. studies of great Fr. writers 16th to 19th cent., also history of Fr. literature.

Fahrenheit (*fä'ren-hīt*), GABRIEL DANIEL (1686–1736), Ger. scientist; *b.* Danzig; introduced use of mercury and new scale for thermometers; improved the hygrometer; F.R.S., 1724.

Fairbairn, ANDREW MARTIN (1838–1912), Scot. Congregationalist theologian; *b.* Inverkeithing; principal of Mansfield Coll., Oxford, 1886–1909; wrote *Studies in Religion,* etc.

Fairbairn, SIR WILLIAM (1789–1874), Scot. civil engineer; *b.* Kelso; improved mill works and water wheels; established shipbuilding yard at Millwall, London; built one of first iron ships; erected Conway and Menai Straits tubular bridges, 1845 (with Robert Stephenson); made steam boiler improvements.

Fairfax, EDWARD (*c.* 1580–1635), Eng. poet; *b.* Leeds; remembered for translation of Tasso's *Gerusalemme Liberata.*

Fairfax, THOMAS, 3RD BARON FAIRFAX OF CAMERON (1612–71), Eng. soldier; *b.* near Otley,

Yorks; commander-in-chief of Parliamentary army in Civil War; defeated Charles I. at Naseby, 1645; opposed king's execution.

Falconer, HUGH (1808–65), Scot. botanist; *b.* Forres; advised tea planting and growing cinchona bark in Ind. Empire; saved teak forests from reckless felling; F.R.S., 1845; superintendent of Calcutta botanic garden and prof. of botany, 1847; interested in palæontology.

Falconer, WILLIAM (1732–69), Brit. poet and sailor; *b.* Edinburgh; author of *The Shipwreck* (1763) and the *Universal Marine Dictionary* (1769), in which *retreat* is defined as 'a French manœuvre, not properly a term of the British marine.'

Falguière (*făl-gyār'*), JEAN ALEXANDRE JOSEPH (1831–1900), Fr. sculptor; *b.* Toulouse; famed for his *Vainqueur au Combat de Coqs* (Luxembourg).

Falkenhayn (*fal-ken-hīn'*), ERICH VON (1861–1922), Ger. general; *b.* Thorn; Prussian minister of war, 1913; after battle of the Marne (Sept. 1914) succeeded von Moltke as chief of general staff; responsible for first battle of Ypres (Nov.–Dec. 1914); prepared great onslaught on Verdun, which destroyed his reputation; in 1916 commanded offensive against Romania. Wrote *General Headquarters 1914–16 and its Critical Decisions* (Eng. trans. 1919)

Fallières (*fal-yer'*), CLÉMENT ARMAND (1841–1931), Fr. politician; *b.* Mézin, Lot-et-Garonne; son of blacksmith; under-secretary to the interior, 1880–2; prime minister for twenty-two days, Jan. 1883; twice minister of public instruction and twice minister of justice; senator, 1890; president of senate, 1899; re-elected eight times; president of republic, 1906–13.

Fallopius (*făl-ō'pē-us*), or FALLOPIO, GABRIELLO (1523–62), Ital. anatomist; prof. of anatomy in Pisa, and afterwards in Padua; made several anatomical discoveries relating to the inner ear, the ethmoid bone, and the abdomen; *Fallopian Tubes* perpetuate his name.

Fantin-Latour (*făn-tan'-lă-toor'*), IGNACE HENRI JEAN THÉODORE (1836–1904), Fr. painter; *b.* Grenoble; best works comprise portrait groups, such as *Autour du Piano*, and delicate flower studies.

Far'aday, MICHAEL (1791–1867), Eng. physicist; *b.* Newington, Surrey; originally a bookbinder's apprentice; appointed assistant in the Royal Institution laboratory on recommendation of Sir Humphry Davy, 1813; Fullerian prof. of chemistry, 1833; experimented on the diffusion and liquefaction of gases and on the alloys of steel. His great discovery was the induction of electric currents; was first to recognize the chemical decomposition set up by an electric current, and to detect the rotation of the plane of polarized light in a magnetic field.

[*Michael Faraday,* by S. P. Thompson (1898).]

Farina (*fă-rē'nă*), SALVATORE (1846–1918), Ital. novelist; *b.* in Sardinia; author of *Il Signor Io, Amore Bendato, Il Numero 13,* etc. His books, full of clever characterization and humour, have earned him the title of 'Italian Dickens.'

Farjeon (*făr'jun*), BENJAMIN LEOPOLD (1838–1903), Brit. novelist; *b.* London; settled in Dunedin, New Zealand; ed. and joint-proprietor of *Otago Daily Times*; returned to England and produced mystery tales, such as *Great Porter Square, The House of White Shadows*, etc.

Far'man, HENRY (1874–), Fr. aviator; *b.* Paris; son of Eng. journalist; designed and flew first biplane; made first cross-country flight from Châlons to Reims, 1908; first aviator to fly 100 miles; established factory at Buc.

Farnborough, SIR THOMAS ERSKINE MAY, 1ST BARON (1815–86), Brit. historian; *b.* London; authority on constitutional law; wrote *A Treatise on the Law Privileges, Proceedings, and Usage of Parliament* (1844), and *Constitutional History of England.*

Farnese (*fär-nā'se*), Ital. family which governed Parma 200 years. Alexander Farnese became Pope Paul III., 1534; formed Parma and Piacenza into duchy; gave large properties to his natural children, of whom best known is Pierluigi, afterwards Duke of Parma, whose son, Ottavio, was father of famous general Alexander Farnese. Line became extinct in 1731.

Far'nol, JOHN JEFFERY (1878–), Brit. novelist; scene painter in New York for two years; author of numerous romantic novels, including *The Broad Highway, The Money Moon, The Amateur Gentleman,* etc.

Farquhar (*fär'kär*), GEORGE (1678–1707), Eng. dramatist; *b.* Londonderry; last of the Restoration tradition; plays include *Love and a Bottle, The Constant Couple, The Twin Rivals, The Beaux' Stratagem,* etc.

Farquharson (*fär'kar-son*), JOSEPH (1846–1935), Scot. artist; *b.* Edinburgh; R.A., 1915; famed for winter scenes with sheep; his *Joyless Winter Day* was purchased for Chantrey Collection.

Far'rar, FREDERIC WILLIAM (1831–1903), Eng. divine and author; *b.* Bombay; headmaster of Marlborough Coll., 1871; rector of St. Margaret's and canon of Westminster, 1876; Dean of Canterbury, 1895. His school tales *Eric* (1858) and *St. Winifred's* (1859) were immensely popular; fame rests chiefly on his *Life of Christ* (1874) and *Life of St. Paul* (1877); ardent temperance and social reformer.

[*Life,* by R. Farrar (1904).]

Faucit (*fau'sit*), HELENA SAVILLE (1820–98), Eng. actress and author; *b.* London; famous for Shakespearian impersonations; married Sir Theodore Martin, 1851; wrote *On Some of Shakespeare's Female Characters,* etc.

Faure (*fōr*), FRANÇOIS FÉLIX (1841–99), Fr. statesman; *b.* Paris; minister of marine, 1894; president of republic, 1895–99; cemented Franco-Russian alliance, 1897.

Fauré (*fō-rā*), GABRIEL URBAIN (1845–1924), Fr. composer; *b.* in Ariège; pupil of Saint-Saëns, he was successively organist at St. Sulpice, St. Honoré, and the Madeleine in Paris; prof. of harmony at the Conservatoire, 1896; director, 1905–20; noted for his songs; also wrote some orchestral works, music to a number of plays, the cantata *The Birth of Venus,* etc.

Faust, JOHANN. See FUST.

Faustina (*fos-tī'na*) (A.D. 104–141), wife of Emperor Antoninus Pius. Her daughter, Faustina (*d.* 175), was wife of Emperor Marcus Aurelius.

Favart (*fä-vär'*), CHARLES SIMON (1710–92), Fr. dramatist; *b.* Paris; son of a pastry-cook; director of the Opéra Comique; most successful works are *Annette et Lubin, Le Coq du Village, Ninette à la Cour, Les Trois Sultanes,* etc.

Fawcett (*fau'set*). (1) HENRY (1833–84), Eng. political economist; *b.* Salisbury; educated King's Coll. School, London, and Cambridge; lost eyesight, 1858; prof. of political economy, Cambridge, 1863; M.P. for Brighton, 1865; took leading part in movements for abolition of religious tests at universities, compulsory education, preservation of commons and open spaces; his enthusiasm for India gained for him title of 'member for Hindustan'; worked for representation of women in political affairs; postmaster-general, 1880; initiated parcel post, sixpenny telegrams, savings bank, and postal orders.

[*Life*, by Leslie Stephen (1885).]

(2) MILLICENT GARRETT (1847–1929), G.B.E., 1925, wife of above; *b.* Aldeburgh; did much work in connection with education of women and the women's suffrage movement; pub. *Political Economy for Beginners*, *Janet Doncaster* (a novel), *Life of Queen Victoria*, etc. Her daughter, Philippa Garrett Fawcett, was senior wrangler.

Fawkes (*fauks*), GUY (1570–1606), Eng. conspirator; *b.* York; became zealous Catholic, acting as agent of Span. party in England; fought for Spain in Netherlands; at Catesby's invitation assisted in Gunpowder Plot; arrested in cellar beneath Parliament House, 1605; was hanged. Guy Fawkes Day (Nov. 5) is still observed.

Fayrer (*fā'rer*), SIR JOSEPH (1824–1907), Eng. physician; *b.* Plymouth; surgeon in Lucknow Residency during the Mutiny, 1857; prof. of surgery in Calcutta Medical Coll., 1859; president India Office Medical Board, 1874; authority on poisonous snakes of India; wrote *Thanatophidia of India* (1872), *Epidemiology of Cholera* (1888), etc.

Fechner (*fech'ner*), GUSTAV THEODOR (1801–87), Ger. psychologist; *b.* Gross-Särchen; founder of psycho-physics; enunciated psycho-physical ('Fechner's') law of relation between stimulus and sensation; pioneer in experimental psychology.

Fehrenbach (*fā-ren-bäch*), KONSTANTIN (1852–1926), Ger. statesman; *b.* in Bavaria; lawyer in Freiburg; president of Bavarian Second Chamber, 1907–9; member of Reichstag, 1903; president, 1918; chancellor, 1920; conducted negotiations with Allies, 1920–1.

Feisal (*fī-zal'*), or FAISAL (1885–1933), King of Iraq; *b.* Taïf; third son of Hussein, King of Hejaz; direct descendant of Mohammed; educated at Constantinople. During Great War, with T. E. Lawrence, led Arab revolt, and carried Arab arms to Damascus, 1917. Commanded Arab forces with Allenby's army till 1918. Visited Paris and London as his father's representative to the Peace Conference; crowned King of Syria, March 1920, but left Damascus in July; elected, by plebiscite, King of Iraq, 1921.

Fell, JOHN (1625–86), Eng. ecclesiastic; *b.* Longworth, Berks; dean of Christ Church, Oxford, and Bishop of Oxford, 1676; royalist in Civil War; restored many of the coll. buildings; founder of the Oxford Press; name associated with rhyme beginning, 'I do not love thee, Dr. Fell.'

Fénelon (*fān-lon'*), FRANÇOIS DE SALIGNAC DE LA MOTHE (1651–1715), Fr. ecclesiastic and author; *b.* in Périgord; tutor to Duke of Burgundy, 1689; Archbishop of Cambrai, 1703; was involved in prolonged theological controversy with Bossuet; wrote didactic novel *Télémaque*; other works include a treatise on *Education of Girls*, *Dialogues of the Dead*, and *Maxims of the Saints.* He was notable for the dignified austerity of his life and his benevolence.

[*Life*, by Lord St. Cyres (1906).]

Fenwick (*fen'ik*), ETHEL GORDON (1857–), Brit. nurse and journalist; *b.* Spynie House, Morayshire; matron, St. Bartholomew's Hospital, London, 1881–87; ed. of *British Journal of Nursing* (1893); founded the British Nurses' Association and the International Council of Nurses.

Ferdinand I. (1865–1927), King of Romania; *b.* Sigmaringen, Prussia; succeeded his uncle, King Carol, in Oct. 1914; married Princess Marie, daughter of the Duke of Edinburgh. He was unswerving in his loyalty to the Allied cause during Great War. He initiated a system of peasant proprietorship, as well as universal suffrage. The provinces of Bukovina, Bessarabia, Banat, and Transylvania were added in 1918, and in 1922 Ferdinand was crowned King of Greater Romania.

Ferdinand I. (1861–), formerly Tsar of the Bulgarians; elected Prince of Bulgaria, 1887, but in 1908 he was proclaimed tsar, his sovereignty being recognized by the powers, 1909. In 1912 attacked Turkey, and in 1913 was fighting his former allies over the division of the spoil. In the early stages of the Great War he intrigued with both sides; in Sept. 1915 mobilized his army, took sides with Germany, and attacked the hard-pressed Serbians; in Sept. 1918 the Bulgarian army was defeated, and Ferdinand abdicated in favour of the Crown Prince Boris.

Ferdinand I., THE GREAT (*c.* 1000–65), first King of Castile; became also King of Leon, 1038; extended his possessions by victories over the Moors.

Ferdinand II. (1136–88), King of Castile and Leon; waged constant wars with the Moors; founded the order of St. James of Compostella.

Ferdinand III., THE SAINT (1199–1252), King of Castile and Leon; secured the throne of Castile in opposition to his father, Alfonso IX. of Leon, 1217, after whose death he became King of Leon, 1230, the two kingdoms never being thereafter separated; won many successes against the Moors.

Ferdinand V. OF CASTILE AND LEON and II. OF ARAGON, 'THE CATHOLIC' (1452–1516), married Isabella of Castile, succeeding to the throne of Castile with her, 1474, and on the death of his father, John I., to the throne of Aragon, thus becoming the first king of united Spain, 1479. He defeated the Moors, annexing Granada, their last stronghold, 1492, conquered Naples, 1502, and seized Navarre, 1512. He united the whole of Spain under his sway, and, influenced by his wife, forwarded the voyages of Columbus.

[*History of Reign of Ferdinand and Isabella*, by Prescott.]

Ferdinand VI. (1713–59), King of Spain, 1746; effected a revival in Span. art, literature, and science, and attempted to develop the resources of the country.

Ferdinand VII. (1784–1833), King of Spain; proclaimed king, 1808, but was dethroned by Napoleon; restored to throne, 1814, ruled despotically, re-established the Inquisition, and by his misgovernment lost all the Span.-Amer. colonies. His setting aside of the Salic law in favour of his daughter, Isabella II., led to the Carlist War.

Ferdinand I. (1503–64), Holy Rom. Emperor; brother of Charles V.; claimed the crowns of Bohemia and Hungary in his wife's right. Bohemia he secured, 1526, but was unsuccessful in Hungary against John Zapolya. He pursued a conciliatory policy towards the Protestants, and, after succeeding Charles V. as emperor, 1558, vainly pressed a policy of reforms in the Church.

Ferdinand II. (1578–1637), Holy Rom. Emperor, grandson of Ferdinand I.; became King of Bohemia, 1617, of Hungary, 1618, and emperor, 1619. His deposition in Bohemia, 1618, in favour of the elector-palatine led to the Thirty Years' War. His religious fanaticism, as instanced by the Edict of Restitution, 1629, reclaiming for the Church all secularized lands, and his lack of statesmanship, involved his dominions in disaster and misery.

Ferdinand III. (1608–57), Holy Rom. Emperor, son of Ferdinand II.; defeated Swedes at Nördlingen, 1634; succeeded his father, Ferdinand II., 1637; continued Thirty Years' War till 1648, when a series of disasters forced him to make peace; arranged Polish Alliance to combat Sweden.

Ferdinand I. (1751–1825), King of the Two Sicilies; third son of Charles III. of Spain; became King of Sicily and Naples, 1759. Influenced by his wife, Maria Carolina, a sister of Marie Antoinette, he waged war against France, but was driven from his throne, 1798. After Austerlitz, Napoleon conquered Naples and gave it to Joseph Bonaparte. Ferdinand again fled, but was restored in 1815, and with the help of Austria set up a despotic monarchy.

Ferdinand II. (1810–59), King of the Two Sicilies; grandson of preceding; began his reign, 1830, by granting Neapolitans a constitution, but, influenced by his wife, Theresa of Austria, he revoked his promises. Revolts broke out, and were suppressed with ruthless cruelty. His merciless bombardment of Palermo and Messina, 1849, earned him the name of 'King Bomba.'

Fer'guson, ADAM (1723–1816), Scot. philosopher and historian; *b.* Logierait, Perthshire; prof. of natural philosophy, Edinburgh, 1759; of moral philosophy, 1764; wrote *History of the Roman Republic*, and several philosophical works.

Ferguson, PATRICK (1744–80), Scot. inventor and soldier; *b.* Pitfour, Aberdeenshire; invented breech-loading rifle, 1776, which could be fired seven times a minute.

Ferguson, SIR SAMUEL (1810–86), Irish poet and antiquary; *b.* Belfast; deputy-keeper of the Irish Records, 1867; wrote famous ballad *The Forging of the Anchor*, and *Lays of the Western Gael* (1865), etc.

Fergusson, ROBERT (1750–74), Scot. poet; *b.* Edinburgh; his poems exercised a marked influence on Burns, who borrowed from him the measure since known as the 'Burns stanza.'

Fergusson, SIR WILLIAM (1808–77), Scot. surgeon; *b.* Prestonpans; prof. of surgery in King's Coll., London, 1840–70; renowned for his conservative surgery, such as excision of joint instead of amputation of limb; invented many surgical instruments; wrote *Progress of Anatomy and Surgery in the Nineteenth Century* (1867), etc.

Ferish'ta, MOHAMMED KASIM HINDU SHAH (*c.* 1550–1612), Pers. historian, author of the *Rise of the Mohammedan Power in India* (Eng. ed. 1829).

Fermat (*fer-mä'*), PIERRE (1601–65), Fr. mathematician; *b.* near Montauban; with Pascal discovered certain properties of numbers; regarded as having initiated the differential calculus; name perpetuated in *Fermat's Last Theorem*; wrote *De Maximis et Minimis.*

Fernan'dez (or *fer-nän'deth*), JUAN (1536–76), Span. navigator; discovered, 1572, off Chilean coast the two islands which bear his name; discovered St. Felix and St. Ambrose Islands, 1574.

Fer'rar, NICHOLAS (1592–1637), Eng. theologian; *b.* London; after busy commercial life, formed religious community, 1625, at Little Gidding, Huntingdonshire, which taught, doctored, and nursed the villagers.

[*Life*, by Skipton (1907).]

Ferrar'a, ANDREA (*fl.* 16th cent.),

Italian whose name is found on many claymores and broadswords, but whose history is obscure. His swords were common in Scotland and in S. and W. Europe.

Ferreira (*fer-rā'rä*), ANTONIO (1528–69), Port. poet; *b.* Lisbon; prof. at Coimbra; called the 'Portuguese Horace'; besides sonnets and other poems, wrote *Castro*, the first Port. tragedy.

Ferrier, SIR DAVID (1843–1928), Scot. physician; *b.* Aberdeen; prof. of forensic medicine, King's Coll., London, 1872–89; prof. of neuropathology, 1889–1928; F.R.S., 1876; studied physiology of the brain and founded science of neurology; chief works, *Functions of the Brain* (1876), and *Regional Diagnosis of Cerebral Disease* (1910).

Ferrier, SUSAN EDMONSTONE (1782–1854), Scot. novelist; *b.* Edinburgh; pub. anonymously *Marriage* (1818), *The Inheritance* (1824), and *Destiny* (1831). Her books are full of humour and lively descriptions of Scot. life and character. Her *Recollections of Visits to Ashiestiel and Abbotsford* describes her friendship with Scott from 1811–31.

Ferry (*fā-rē'*), JULES FRANÇOIS CAMILLE (1832–93), Fr. statesman; *b.* Saint Dié, Vosges; member of National Defence Government, 1870, and mayor of Paris; elected to Chamber of Deputies, 1873; introduced bill, 1879, against Jesuit instruction, which eventually led to expulsion of that order from France; premier, 1880, and again, 1883; responsible for present form of primary education in France, and for the foundations of Fr. colonial empire.

Festus, PORCIUS, Rom. procurator of Judæa, before whom St. Paul was tried in A.D. 62 (Acts 25).

Fétis (*fā-tēs'*), FRANÇOIS JOSEPH (1784–1871), Belgian composer and musical historian; *b.* Mons; prof. Paris Conservatoire; founder of *Revue Musicale* (1827); pub. *Histoire Universelle de la Musique*, etc.

Fet'tes, SIR WILLIAM (1750–1836), Scot. merchant and contractor; *b.* Edinburgh; amassed great wealth and bequeathed bulk of fortune to build Fettes Coll., Edinburgh, a school of Eng. public-school type.

Feuchtwanger (*foicht'vang-er*), LION (1884–), Ger. author; *b.* Munich; of Jewish origin; famous, especially, for his historical novels, *Jew Süss*, *The Ugly Duchess*, *Josephus*, *The Oppermanns*, etc.; has also written poems and dramatic pieces. Exiled from Germany, 1933.

Feuerbach (*foi'er-băch*), ANSELM (1829–80), Ger. painter; *b.* Speyer; leader of the Ger. classic school; among works are *Iphigenia in Tauris*, *Orpheus and Eurydice*, *Hafiz at the Well*, *Medea*, *The Judgment of Paris*, etc.

Feuillet (*fĕ-yā'*), OCTAVE (1821–90), Fr. novelist and dramatist; *b.* Saint-Lô; member of Fr. Academy; noted for purity of style and able delineation of society life during Second Empire; chief novels, *Histoire de Sibylle*, *Monsieur de Camors*, *Julia de Trécœur*, and *Le Roman d'un Jeune Homme Pauvre* (dramatized 1858), etc.

Fib'iger, JOHANNES (1868–1928), Dan. pathologist; prof. at Copenhagen Univ; noted for work in connection with cancer in rats and cockroaches; Nobel Prize, 1927.

Fichte (*fich'te*), JOHANN GOTTLIEB (1762–1814), Ger. philosopher; *b.* Rammenau, Saxony; son of a ribbon-weaver; studied theology at Jena and Leipzig; prof. at Jena, 1794–99; dismissed on charge of atheism. He delivered his famous addresses to the Ger. people in Berlin after the battle of Jena; rector of new Berlin Univ., 1810–12. In philosophy he was influenced by Kant. Taking self-consciousness as the basis of certitude, Fichte's aim is to show how all phenomena have their circle within the ego. He distinguishes between two egos, so to speak, the absolute ego and the individual ego, and the attempt to distinguish the two leads to mystification. Fichte opened an epoch in Ger. thought which found its culmination in Hegel. Chief works, *Critique of Revelation*, *Theory of Knowledge*, *Foundation of the Laws of Nature*, *System of Moral Philosophy*, etc.

[*Fichte* (Philosophical Classics, 1881), by Adamson.]

Field, CYRUS WEST (1819–92), Amer. capitalist; *b.* Stockbridge, Mass.; planned first Atlantic cable, whch was laid, 1866, after several failures.

Field, EUGENE (1850–95), an Amer. writer and bibliophile; *b.* St. Louis; on staff of *Chicago Daily News*, where he made a reputation by his charming poems of childhood; wrote *Love Songs of Childhood* (1894), etc.

Fielding, HENRY (1707–54), Eng. novelist and miscellaneous writer; *b.* near Glastonbury; educated at Eton and Leyden. Between 1730 and 1736 he produced a number of plays long since forgotten; subsequently studied law, and became a magistrate. His first novel, *Joseph Andrews* (1742), was originally intended as a parody of Richardson's *Pamela*. It was followed by other notable productions, including his powerful satire, *Jonathan Wild the Great* (1743), *Tom Jones* (1749), *Amelia* (1751), and numerous other works. Fielding ranks amongst the greatest of Eng. novelists. He was well acquainted with worldly society, and had himself acquired that experience, particularly of the seamy side of life, which he exhibited in his novels with so sure a touch. His characters are always drawn with a masterly hand, and his style is bracing and vigorous.

[*Life*, by Austin Dobson (English Men of Letters).]

Fildes (*fīldz*), SIR LUKE (1844–1927), Eng. artist and book illustrator; *b.* Liverpool; A.R.A., 1879; R.A., 1887; illustrated magazines and books, including *Edwin Drood*. Among his pictures are *A Casual Ward*, *The Widower*, *The Doctor* (his best-known picture), etc. He also painted portraits of King Edward VII. and Queen Alexandra.

Fill'an (or FAELAN), ST., name of two saints whose lives are legendary, supposed to have come to Scotland from Ireland; commemorated on Jan. 9 and June 20.

Fil'mer, SIR ROBERT (*d.* 1653), Eng. political writer; *b.* East Sutton, Kent; royalist in civil war; wrote the *Patriarcha*, defending divine right of kings.

Findlay, JOHN RITCHIE (1824–98), Scot. newspaper proprietor and philanthropist; *b.* Arbroath; became proprietor of the *Scotsman*; was generous patron of Scot. National Gallery, and presented Scot. National Portrait Gallery to the public.

Fin'sen, NIELS RYBERG (1860–1904), Icelandic anatomist; *b.* Thorshavn, Faroe Islands; demonstrated at Copenhagen Univ. that biological processes are affected by violet and ultra-violet rays of spectrum; applied light rays to such diseases as lupus, favus, ringworm, smallpox, etc.; instrumental in founding Light Institute at Copenhagen, 1896; invented Finsen lamp; Nobel Prize, 1903.

Fiorenzo (*fē-ō-ren'zo*) **di Lorenzo** (*c.* 1440–1522), Ital. painter; *b.* Perugia; one of most distinguished painters of Umbrian school. Little is known of his life; authentic works include a beautiful *Nativity*, *Adoration of the Shepherds*, and *Adoration of the Magi*.

Firdausi (*fēr-dou'sē*), or FIRDOUSI (ABÚ-'L KÁSIM MAUSÚR) (*c.* A.D. 940–1020), Pers. poet; sometimes called 'the Homer of Persia,' and the greatest poet of his country. Spent thirty years writing his great epic, *Shah Náma*, founded on the history of the Pers. kings; disappointed by the reward given by the Sultan, spent many years in exile at Baghdad, where he composed another famous poem, *Yusuf and Zuleika*, dealing with the loves of Joseph and Potiphar's wife.

Firth, SIR CHARLES HARDING (1857–), Eng. historian; *b.* Sheffield; Regius prof. of modern history in Oxford Univ., 1904–25; F.B.A., 1903; has written largely on the period of the Civil War and the Commonwealth.

Fischer (*fish'er*), EMIL (1852–1919), Ger. chemist; *b.* Euskirchen; prof. of chemistry in Berlin; Nobel Prize, 1902; prepared dyestuffs, etc., but his greatest work was the synthesis of the simplest proteins from amido-acids.

Fisher, RT. HON. ANDREW (1862–1928), Australian statesman; *b.* Kilmarnock, Scotland; emigrated 1885; Labour member of Queensland Parliament, 1893; minister of railways; elected to Commonwealth Parliament, 1900; minister of trade and customs, 1904; leader of his party, 1907; premier three times, 1908–9, 1910, 1914–15; P.C., 1911; High Commissioner for Australia, 1916–21.

Fisher, HERBERT ALBERT LAURENS (1865–), Eng. statesman and historian; *b.* London; vice-chancellor of Sheffield Univ.; president of Board of Education, 1916–22, and carried the Education Act of 1918; warden, New Coll., Oxford, 1925; author of *A Political History of England* (1906), *The Republican Tradition in Europe* (1911), *The Common Weal* (1924), *Life of Lord Bryce* (1926), *History of Europe* (1935).

Fisher, JOHN (*c.* 1469–1535), Eng. churchman; *b.* Beverley; chancellor of Cambridge Univ., and Bishop of Rochester, 1504; supported new learning; held Church to be supreme; opposed Henry VIII.'s divorce from Catherine of Aragon; cardinal, 1535; beheaded; canonized, 1935.

Fisher OF KILVERSTONE, JOHN ARBUTHNOT, 1ST BARON (1841–1920), admiral of the fleet; commanded *Inflexible* at Alexandria, 1882; lord of the Admiralty, 1892–7, and after holding various commands became first sea lord, 1904–10 and 1914–15, resigning in 1915 on the question of the Dardanelles expedition; initiated the Dreadnought policy, and thereby created a revolution in naval shipbuilding; O.M., 1905; peerage, 1909; pub. the highly fulminatory works *Memories* (1919) and *Records* (1919).

Fitzgerald (*fits-jer'ald*), EDWARD (1809–83), Eng. man of letters; *b.* Bredfield, Suffolk; trans. some dramas of Calderon; wrote several miscellaneous works; was a delightful letter-writer, and secured world-wide fame by his paraphrase of *Omar Khayyám* (1859).

[*Life*, by A. C. Benson (1905).]

Fitzherbert, MARIA ANNE, *née* SMYTHE (1756–1837), secretly married after death of second husband to George IV., when Prince of Wales, in 1785; a Roman Catholic; marriage invalidated by Royal Marriages Act. In Parliament Fox denied the marriage, which, on the break with Princess Caroline, was resumed by papal permission, but finally ended in 1803.

Fitzroy, ROBERT (1805–65), Brit. admiral, hydrographer, and meteorologist; *b.* Ampton Hall, Suffolk; surveyed coasts of Patagonia and Tierra del Fuego; commanded surveying expeditions of *Adventure* and *Beagle*, being accompanied by Darwin on latter;

governor of New Zealand, 1843–5; meteorologist to Board of Trade, 1854; pub. *Weather Book* (1863); weather forecasts are based on his system of storm warnings.

Flaccus, QUINTUS HORATIUS. See HORACE.

Flammarion (*flä-mä-rē-ōn'*), CAMILLE (1842–1925), Fr. astronomer; *b.* Montigny-le-Roi, Haute-Marne; famous for observations on double stars, star-drift, and common proper motion; great reputation as lecturer; chief work, *Popular Astronomy.*

Flamsteed, JOHN (1646–1719), first astronomer-royal of England; *b.* near Derby; appointed by Charles II. 'astronomical observator' to the king, 1675; formed first trustworthy catalogue of fixed stars, and supplied lunar observations by means of which Newton verified his lunar theory.

Flaubert (*flō-bār'*), GUSTAVE (1821–80), Fr. novelist; *b.* Rouen. His works, most of which have been trans. into English, are either realistic novels or historical romances, and include *Madame Bovary, Bouvard et Pécuchet, Salammbô, L'Education sentimentale, Trois Contes,* etc.; a slow, careful writer; one of the greatest Fr. stylists.

Flax'man, JOHN (1755–1826), Eng. sculptor; *b.* York; employed as a designer by Wedgwood, 1775–87. In 1782 he began to devote himself to statuary and monumental sculpture, and established his fame as the greatest of Eng. classical sculptors; his designs in illustration of Homer, Æschylus, and Dante are also famous; R.A., 1800.

Fleck'er, JAMES ELROY (1884–1915), Brit. poet; *b.* London; entered consular service, 1910; pub. book of verse same year, and *The Golden Journey to Samarkand* (1913). Died of consumption at Davos. After his death appeared *The Old Ships*; his *Hassan*, a spectacular, Oriental play, pub. 1922, was produced 1923.

Fleck'noe, RICHARD (*c.* 1600–*c.* 1678), Eng. poet and dramatist; satirized by Dryden in *Mac-Flecknoe.*

Flem'ing, DAVID HAY (1849–1931), Scot. historian; *b.* St. Andrews; an authority on Reformation and Covenanting period; chief works, *Mary Queen of Scots* (1897), *The Reformation in Scotland* (1910), *Critical Reviews relating chiefly to Scotland* (1912); founder of Knox Club.

Fleming, SIR JOHN AMBROSE (1849–), Eng. electrical engineer; *b.* Lancaster; prof., Univ. Coll., London, 1885–1926; has done important research work in electricity, especially in connection with wireless telegraphy and telephony; invented thermionic valve, 1904, and oscillating valve detector.

Fleming, MARGARET (1803–11), known as 'Pet Marjorie,' the youngest poetess of fame; friend of Sir Walter Scott; wrote verses before the age of eight. See Dr. John Brown's *Pet Marjorie.*

Flers (*flār*), MARQUIS ROBERT DE (1872–1927), Fr. man of letters; *b.* Pont l'Évêque; member of Fr. Academy, 1920; wrote *Entre Cœur et Chair,* a book of travel, *Vers l'Orient,* crowned by the Academy, etc., and, in collaboration, plays such as *L'Amour veille, Le Retour, Les Nouveaux Messieurs,* etc.

Fletcher, ANDREW (1655–1716), OF SALTOUN, Scot. politician; *b.* Saltoun, E. Lothian; he took part in Monmouth's rising, 1685; afterwards travelled; returned to Scotland, 1689; prominent in politics from 1703 to 1707, opposing the union of Scotland and England; closing years devoted to improvement of Scot. agriculture.

Flet'cher. (1) GILES (*c.* 1584–1623), Eng. poet; rector of Alderton, Suffolk; notable preacher; chief poem, *Christ's Victory* (1610). (2) PHINEAS (1582–1650), Eng. poet; *b.* Cranbrook; brother of (1); rector of Hilgay, Norfolk; best-known poem, *The Purple Island.*

Fletcher, JOHN (1579–1625). See BEAUMONT.

Fleury (*fler-ē'*), ANDRÉ HERCULE DE (1653–1743), Fr. cardinal and statesman; *b.* Lodève, Hérault; bishop of Fréjus, 1698; cardinal, and first minister to Louis XV., 1726; put France on sound financial basis, gave her good roads, and increased her prosperity.

Flin'ders, MATTHEW (1774–1814), Eng. hydrographer and discoverer; *b.* Donnington, Lincs; entered navy, 1789; surveyed great part of Australian coast, 1795–9, discovering Bass Strait, and circumnavigating Tasmania; led expedition to explore Australian coast, 1801; on return was wrecked, and imprisoned at Mauritius six years; returned to England, 1810; pub. *Voyage to Terra Australis* (1814).

Flood, HENRY (1732–91), Irish politician; *b.* near Dublin; elected to Irish Parliament, 1759; became leader of national party; looked on as a renegade on accepting office of vice-treasurer of Ireland, 1775, and superseded by Grattan as party leader; helped to organize Irish Volunteers, 1778; entered Brit. Parliament, 1783, but made no particular mark there.

Florian (*flō-ryän'*), JEAN PIERRE CLARIS DE (1755–94), Fr. pastoral poet, fabulist, and romancer; *b.* near Sauve, Gard; member of Fr. Academy, 1788; chiefly remembered for his *Fables* (1792).

Flor'io, GIOVANNI (*c.* 1553–1625), Eng. writer; *b.* London; of Waldensian parentage; famous for his translation of Montaigne's *Essays.*

Foch (*fosh*), FERDINAND (1851–1929), famous Fr. soldier; *b.* Tarbes; educated at Metz; joined army during Franco-Prussian War; entered artillery school and passed out with distinction; Staff College lecturer on military history, strategy, and applied tactics, 1885; wrote standard books on tactics; colonel, 1903; general commanding 13th Infantry Division, 1907. In Great War he commanded 9th Army at first battle of Marne (Sept. 1914), and stopped Ger. advance on Paris. Again distinguished himself during first battle of Ypres. In great Somme offensive of 1916 the Fr. armies co-operated with the Brit. under his direction. Finally, in March 1918, he was appointed generalissimo of the Allied armies in France. The turning-point came in July at the second battle of the Marne, and thereafter he struck blows which demoralized the Ger. armies and forced them to sue for an armistice. Marshal of France, 1918; Brit. field-marshal, 1919; O.M., 1918. His marvellous success was due to his mastery of technique, quick perception, genius for co-ordination, capacity for envisaging the situation in a comprehensive fashion, allied with the virtue of 'calculated tenacity.'

Fogazzaro (*fog-at-sär'ō*), ANTONIO (1842–1911), Ital. novelist; *b.* Vicenza; in addition to poems wrote *Malombra* (1882), *Daniele Cortis* (1887), *Piccolo Mondo antico* (1896), and *Il Santo* (1906).

Fok'ker, ANTHONY HERMAN GERARD (1890–), Dutch inventor; *b.* in Java; built the famous Fokker aeroplanes for Germans during the Great War; retired to Holland after war, and established factories; announced invention of a wireless-directed bomber, 1919; director of Dutch and American aircraft corporations.

Fo'ley, JOHN HENRY (1818–74), Irish sculptor; *b.* Dublin; his

Youth at the Stream, 1844, led to commissions for the statues of *Hampden* and *Selden* for Houses of Parliament; R.A., 1858. Amongst his statues are those of *Goldsmith* and *Burke* (in front of Trinity Coll., Dublin), *Prince Consort* (Hyde Park), and *Sir James Outram*, in Calcutta.

Fontaine, J. DE LA. See under LA FONTAINE.

Fontane, THEODOR (1819–98), Ger. novelist and poet; *b.* Neu-Ruppin, Brandenburg; wrote numerous ballads on England, Scotland, and Prussia; his historical novel *Vor dem Sturm* (1878) was followed by *Stine*, *Effi Briest*, etc., novels of contemporary manners and life.

Foote, SAMUEL (1720–77), Eng. actor and dramatist; *b.* Truro; achieved success by marvellous powers of mimicry of well-known characters of the day. Wrote many plays popular in their day. Friend of Dr. Johnson and Garrick.

Forbes, DUNCAN, of Culloden (1685–1747), Scot. judge and statesman; *b.* near Inverness; prominent anti-Jacobite; supported government in 1715 and 1745; lord advocate, 1725; president Court of Session, 1737. It was at his suggestion that Highland regiments were formed in the Brit. army.

Forbes, JAMES DAVID (1809–1868), Scot. physicist; *b.* Edinburgh; F.R.S., 1832; prof. at Edinburgh, 1833–59; principal of United Coll., St. Andrews, 1859–68; made important contributions to knowledge of heat and glaciers.

Forbes, STANHOPE ALEXANDER (1857–), Brit. painter; *b.* Dublin; studied at Royal Academy, London, also in Paris; settled in Newlyn, Cornwall; R.A., 1910. Some of his best pictures are *The Fish Sale*, *Forging the Anchor*, and *The Smithy*.

Forbes-Robertson, SIR JOHNSTON (1853–), Brit. actor; *b.* Aberdeen; intended for artistic career, turned to acting in 1874; played with the Bancrofts, Hare, Modjeska, Irving, and Mary Anderson. Began management on his own account, 1895, playing Romeo to the Juliet of Mrs. Patrick Campbell; produced *Hamlet* with great effect, 1897. In Jerome's *Passing of the Third Floor Back* he had extraordinary success both in Britain and America.

Ford, EDWARD ONSLOW (1852–1901), Eng. sculptor; *b.* Islington; R.A., 1895; first important statue was that of *Sir Rowland Hill* (Royal Exchange); executed long series of busts of men of the time—*Millais*, *Huxley*, *Herbert Spencer*, *Orchardson*, etc.—and produced small replicas. His *Gladstone* and *Gordon* are well known.

Ford (formerly HUEFFER), FORD MADOX (1873–), Eng. author; has written numerous novels and books of verse, biographies, etc.; collaborated with Conrad in *The Inheritors* and *Romance*.

Ford, HENRY (1863–), Amer. engineer and inventor; *b.* near Dearborn, Michigan; organizer of Ford Motor Co. at Detroit, Michigan, U.S.A.; deeply interested in welfare of his workers; in 1915 carried party of peace advocates to Europe, but plan met with no success. On entrance of America into the war (March 1917) he placed his works at disposal of government; manufactured motor engines, aeroplanes, etc., forgoing all profits; in various other ways assisted vigorously in prosecution of the war. Has established large motor works at Dagenham since the war.

[*My Life and Work* (1922), *To-day and To-morrow* (1926), both by Ford and Crowther.]

Ford, JOHN (1586–*c.* 1640), Eng. dramatist; *b.* Ilsington, N. Devon; studied law, but eventually devoted himself to drama.

There is much that is repulsive in his plays, but they are distinguished by great intensity of passion and literary quality. His plays include *'Tis Pity She's a Whore*, *The Lover's Melancholy*, and *Perkin Warbeck*; author, with Dekker and Rowley, of *The Witch of Edmonton*.

Forrest OF BUNBURY, BARON (RT. HON. SIR JOHN FORREST) (1847–1918), Australian statesman and explorer; commanded expedition in search of Dr. Leichhardt, 1869; first premier of W. Australia, 1890–1901; minister of defence under the Commonwealth, 1901–3; minister of home affairs, 1903–4. In 1917 he became treasurer of Commonwealth War Government; created baron, 1918. Wrote *Explorations in Australia* (1876) and *Notes on Western Australia* (1884–7).

Forster, JOHN (1812–76), Eng. biographer and ed.; *b.* Newcastle-on-Tyne; son of cattle-dealer; wrote biographies of Goldsmith and Landor, and standard *Life of Charles Dickens* (1872–4).

Forster, WILLIAM EDWARD (1818–86), Eng. statesman; *b.* in Dorsetshire of Quaker parents; member of Gladstone's cabinet from 1870; carried Education Bill of 1870, by which School Boards were established. Chief Secretary for Ireland, 1880; took strong line against Land League, and proclaimed it illegal.

Fortuny (*fŏr-too'nē*) **y Carbo,** MARIANO JOSÉ MARIA (1838–74), Span. painter; *b.* Reus, Catalonia; one of most remarkable artists of modern times; famous for canvases in which gorgeous blaze of colour is subtly interblended with sunlight; among works are *The Serpent Charmer*, *The Arabian Fantasia*, *The Spanish Marriage*, and *The Garden of a Poet*; also distinguished etcher.

Fos'colo, UGO (1778–1827), Ital. author and patriot; *b.* Zante, Ionian Islands; prof. of eloquence, Pavia, 1809; opposed to Austrian rule in Italy; took refuge in England, 1816, and *d.* there; among works are *Letters of Jacopo Ortis* (1798), *Carme sui sepolcri* (1807), *Ricciarda*, and translations of *Callimachus* and Sterne's *Sentimental Journey*.

Fos'dick, HARRY EMERSON (1878–), noted Amer. preacher; *b.* Buffalo; Baptist minister, 1904–15; prof. of theology, Union Theological Seminary, New York, since 1915; pastor, Park Avenue Baptist Church, since 1925. Pub. many works on religious subjects.

Foster, SIR MICHAEL (1836–1907), Eng. physiologist; *b.* Huntingdon; prof. of physiology, Univ. Coll., London, 1869, and at Cambridge, 1883–1903; president Brit. Association, 1899; secretary of Royal Soc., 1881–1903; author of standard *Text-book of Physiology*.

Foster, MYLES BIRKET (1825–99), Eng. artist; *b.* North Shields; began as wood-engraver, and made first success by illustrating *Evangeline* (1850) and *Hyperion* (1852); produced *The Rhine and its Scenery* (2 vols.); chiefly celebrated for his water-colour drawings of Eng. country life.

Foster, STEPHEN COLLINS (1826–64), Amer. song-writer; *b.* Pittsburgh; remembered for his Negro songs, *e.g.* *Old Folks at Home*; *Massa's in the Cold, Cold Ground*; *My Old Kentucky Home*, etc.

Foster, VERE (1819–1900), Eng. philanthropist; *b.* Copenhagen; visited Ireland during potato famine, 1847, and thereafter devoted himself to amelioration of Irish people; encouraged emigration; pub. copy-books inaugurating Civil Service style of handwriting.

Foucault (*foo-kō'*), JEAN BERNARD LÉON (1819–68), Fr. physicist; *b.* Paris; investigated intensity of sun's light; invented the gyroscope and the Foucault polarizer; set up monster pendulum in Pantheon, Paris, 1851, to demonstrate diurnal motion of the earth.

Fouché (*foo-shā'*), JOSEPH, DUKE OF OTRANTO (1763–1820), Fr. politician; *b.* near Nantes; prominent in Jacobin movement; quarrelled with Robespierre; chief of police, 1799, continuing in office under Napoleon; deprived of office, 1810, and sent to Rome as titular governor. After Napoleon's fall, Fouché became minister of police; retired, 1816, and died in exile.

Fourier (*foo-ryā'*), FRANÇOIS MARIE CHARLES (1772–1837), Fr. social philosopher; *b.* Besançon; developed theory of social reorganization. His scheme (a failure when tried in 1827 at Condé-sur-Vesgre) was to divide society into autonomous sections of about 1,700 persons living in common building, with fixed amount of arable land attached; members to choose their own employment and receive minimum wage.

Fourier, JEAN BAPTISTE JOSEPH (1768–1830), Fr. mathematician; *b.* Auxerre; served in Egypt under Bonaparte; chief works, *Analyse des Equations déterminées* and *Théorie Analytique de la Chaleur*, in the latter of which he suggested what are now known as *Fourier's Series.* His discoveries had far-reaching effects on mathematical physics.

Fowler, ELLEN THORNEYCROFT (HON. MRS. FELKIN) (*d.* 1929), Eng. novelist; elder daughter of first Viscount Wolverhampton; began with verses; novels include *Concerning Isabel Carnaby, A Double Thread, The Farringdons, Ten Degrees Backward,* etc., all characterized by smart dialogue and epigram.

Fowler, SIR JOHN (1817–98), Eng. civil engineer; *b.* near Sheffield; built Manchester, Sheffield, Lincolnshire Rly., and London Metropolitan Rly.; co-operated with Sir Benjamin Baker in designing Forth Bridge, 1883–90.

Fowler, JOHN (1826–64), Eng. inventor; *b.* Melksham, Wilts; invented steam plough and a steam cultivator.

Fox, CHARLES JAMES (1749–1806), Whig statesman, son of Lord Holland; *b.* Westminster; educated Eton and Oxford; great gambler in early days; M.P., 1768; junior lord of Admiralty, 1770–2; opposed Royal Marriage Act, thus incurring dislike of George III.; junior lord of Treasury, 1773; quarrelled with Lord North and joined Opposition, 1774; became Whig leader, and opposed Lord North's policy towards the American colonists; foreign secretary under Rockingham, 1782; formed unpopular coalition with Lord North. Whigs were defeated, 1784; for twenty-two years Fox remained out of office, and was rival of Pitt, the prime minister; opposed free trade with Ireland, 1785, and commercial treaty with France, 1787; prominent in impeachment of Warren Hastings; advocated removal of religious disabilities and abolition of slave trade; opposed Pitt's policy during Fr. Revolution, which he upheld. After Pitt's death, 1806, Fox became foreign secretary, but died a few months afterwards, and was buried in Westminster Abbey. A brilliant orator with charming personality, his powerlessness as a statesman was due partly to the reputation gained by his early excesses, partly to long-continued disfavour of George III.

Fox, GEORGE (1624–91), founder of Soc. of Friends; *b.* Drayton, Leicestershire; son of weaver; began to preach in 1647, advocating doctrine of 'the Light within'; frequently imprisoned for his opinions. Made missionary travels in Scotland, Ireland, W. Indies, America, and Holland; founded schools; wrote famous *Journal*.

[*Life*, by Hodgkin (1896).]

Fox, HENRY. See HOLLAND, BARON.

Fox, RICHARD (*c.* 1448–1528), Eng. churchman and statesman; *b.* near Grantham; lord privy seal and principal secretary to Henry VII.; Bishop of Exeter, Bath and Wells, Durham, and Winchester in succession; arranged marriage of James IV. of Scotland and Henry's daughter Margaret; chancellor of Cambridge Univ., 1500; founded Corpus Christi Coll., Cambridge, 1515–16; built and endowed schools.

Foxe, JOHN (1516–87), Eng. ecclesiastic; *b.* Boston; chiefly remembered by his *Acts and Monuments* (1563), better known as *Foxe's Book of Martyrs*.

Fragonard (*frä-gō-när'*), JEAN HONORÉ (1732–1806), Fr. painter; *b.* Grasse; son of a glover; chiefly known for love scenes and beauty of colour; among works are *Serment d'Amour*, *Le Verrou*, *La Culbute*, and *The Swing*.

Frampton, SIR GEORGE JAMES (1860–1928), Eng. sculptor; R.A., 1902; knighted, 1908; president Royal Soc. of Brit. Sculptors, 1911–12; introduced polychromatic effects into Brit. sculpture; designed many medals; several statues of Queen Victoria, also one of Queen Mary; Peter Pan (Kensington Gardens); Edith Cavell Memorial, London, etc.

France (*fräns*), ANATOLE (1844–1924), JACQUES ANATOLE THIBAULT, the greatest figure in modern Fr. literature; *b.* Paris; son of a bookseller; used his knowledge of Gr. and Rom. antiquities in many of his stories; turned in 1876 from poetry to prose, the pure mirror of Fr. intellect, wit, and urbanity. Amongst his most famous works are *Le Crime de Sylvestre Bonnard* (1881); *Le Livre de mon Ami* (1885); *Thaïs* (1890); *Les Opinions de M. Jérôme Coignard* (1893); *Le Lys Rouge* (1894); *Pierre Nozière* (1899); *Sur la Pierre blanche* (1905); *Vie de Jeanne d'Arc* (1908); *Les Sept Femmes de la Barbe Bleue* (1909); *La Revolte des Anges* (1914); *Le Petit Pierre* (1918); *La Vie en Fleur* (1922). He made the largest contribution to humanist criticism since Voltaire.

[*Life*, by J. L. May (1924); *Conversations avec Anatole France*, by N. Ségur (1925).]

Franchet d'Esperey, LOUIS FÉLIX MARIE FRANÇOIS (1856–), Fr. general; *b.* in Algeria; became prominent as leader of Fr. troops in Algeria; in Great War commanded 1st Fr. Army Corps at Charleroi, and 5th Fr. Army at the battles of the Marne and Aisne; commanded the Allied armies in the Balkans, 1918, and forced Bulgaria to sue for peace. He was one of the signatories of the Armistice, Sept. 29, 1918. Marshal of France, 1921.

Francis OF ASSISI, ST. (FRANCIS BERNARDONE) (*c.* 1181–1226), founder of Franciscan Order; *b.* Assisi; in youth prominent among young men of fashion; taken captive and imprisoned in war with Perugia, 1201; spiritual experiences during illness resulted in complete change of life; devoted himself to religion, and became beggar, taking 'Lady Poverty' as his spouse, and formed new order, 1210; went as pilgrim to Holy Land, 1219–20. His mysticism, poetry, simplicity, gaiety, and love of nature have won him permanent and universal sympathy. Canonized 1228.

Francis OF SALES, ST. (1567–1622), son of Savoyard noble; studied law at Padua, 1588; ordained, 1592, as provost of chapter of Geneva; conducted mission in Chablais with great success, 1593; bishop of Geneva,

1602; founded the Order of the Visitation, 1610; died much revered, and was canonized, 1665; chief work, *Introduction à la Vie dévote* (1608).

Francis I. (1494–1547), King of France, succeeded Louis XII., 1515; conquered Milan in battle of Marignano, 1515; bitter rival of Emperor Charles V.; failed to gain England's support at Field of Cloth of Gold, 1520; defeated and taken prisoner at Pavia, 1525; resigned Ital. possessions by Treaty of Madrid, 1526; persecuted the Reformers (massacre of Waldenses, 1545), but promoted the Renaissance, and founded the Collège de France.

Francis II. (1544–60), King of France; *b.* Fontainebleau; married Mary Stewart, Queen of Scots, 1558; died after reigning about one year.

Francis II. (1768–1835), last Emperor of Holy Rom. Empire; *b.* Florence; in wars against Napoleon lost Netherlands, Lombardy, Venetia, and other provinces; became Francis I. of Austria, 1804; renounced Holy Rom. Empire, 1806; his daughter, Marie Louise, married Napoleon, 1810; after battle of Leipzig regained Lombardy, Galicia, and Venetia, by Treaty of Vienna, 1815.

Francis II. (1836–94), last Bourbon King of Naples and Sicily; defeated by Garibaldi, 1860–1, after which Naples was united to Italy.

Francis, SIR PHILIP (1740–1818), Brit. politician and writer; *b.* Dublin; first clerk in War Office, 1762; member of Council of Bengal, 1773; bitter opponent of Warren Hastings; M.P. with short intervals from 1784 to 1807; reputed author of *Letters of Junius*.

Francis Ferdinand, ARCHDUKE OF AUSTRIA (1863–1914), nephew of Emperor Francis Joseph; *b.* Graz; became heir to Dual Monarchy, 1889; regarded as strong man of Austria; credited with desire to extend Austrian territory to Salonica; his murder at Serajevo, June 28, 1914, precipitated the Great War.

Francis Joseph (1830–1916), Emperor of Austria and King of Hungary; succeeded uncle, Ferdinand, 1848. His reign of sixty-eight years witnessed enormous changes in his empire. In 1848 Austria was at the head of the Ger. Confederation, its influence was predominant in Italy, and Hungary was compelled to unite with Austria. Both Italy and Hungary rebelled, but the insurgents were crushed, and reactionary principles triumphed, with the entire approval of the emperor. In 1859 a successful Ital. revolt forced Austria to surrender Lombardy. In 1866 Austria was routed by Prussia and excluded from the Ger. Confederation; in the same year Austria lost her Ital. possessions, and in 1867 Hungary was recognized as a separate entity, and the Emperor of Austria was crowned King of Hungary. In 1882 Germany, Austria, and Italy formed the Triple Alliance.

During Francis Joseph's reign numerous tragedies afflicted his house: his brother Maximilian was shot in Mexico, 1867; the Crown Prince Rudolph committed suicide, 1889; and the Empress Elizabeth was fatally stabbed at Geneva, 1898. The annexation of Bosnia and Hercegovina in 1908 created distrust of Austria in the Balkans, and led to the assassination of Archduke Francis Ferdinand, heir to the throne, the outbreak of the Great War, and the downfall of the Austrian Empire.

[*The Habsburg Monarchy*, by Wickham Steed (1913).]

Franck (*fränk*), CÉSAR (1822–

90), Fr. musician; *b.* Liége; prof. of organ at Paris Conservatoire, 1872; famous teacher; was one of the great influences in modern music; compositions include *Les Béatitudes* (an oratorio), *Hulda* and *Ghiselle* (operas), symphonies, cantatas, sonata for violin and piano, and songs.

Frankland, Sir Edward (1825–99), Eng. chemist; *b.* near Lancaster; first prof. of chemistry, Owens Coll., Manchester, 1851; prof. at Royal Institution, 1863, and Royal School of Mines, 1865–85; investigated organic metallic bodies, and introduced idea of valency of atoms from observation of saturation capacity of metallic bodies; investigated the contamination of water supplies; associated with Sir Norman Lockyer in spectroscopic researches which proved gaseous character of sun's photosphere, and identified helium in the sun.

Franklin, Benjamin (1706–90), Amer. statesman, diplomatist, and author; one of the heroes of Amer. War of Independence; *b.* Boston, Massachusetts; began life as a working printer; established in Philadelphia one of earliest circulating libraries in America, 1731; postmaster at Philadelphia, 1737, and about same time organized first police force and fire company in the colonies. In conjunction with others he established an academy, opened 1751, which became univ. of Pennsylvania. Served as member of General Assembly of Pennsylvania for thirteen years. His famous experiment proving identity of lightning and electricity was made in 1752, and gave him a great reputation as a man of science. He resided in England as agent for four of the colonies, 1757–62, and protested against claim of Britain to tax her colonies; returned to Philadelphia, 1775, and became prominent member of insurrectionary government in America; in 1776 was sent on mission to France, and in 1778 managed to induce Fr. Government to form alliance against Britain. Returning to America, he was elected president of Supreme Executive Council of Pennsylvania; re-elected, 1786–7. His last public act was to address a petition to Congress for abolition of slavery, 1790. His many-sided genius was eminently practical, and in science and politics he worked for the good of the many.

[*Life*, by himself (ed. 1888), Parton (1864), Morse (1889).]

Franklin, Sir John (1786–1847), Eng. Arctic explorer; *b.* Spilsby, Lincolnshire; early resolved to be a sailor; commanded overland expedition from Hudson Bay to Arctic Sea, 1819; commander, 1821; post rank of captain, 1822; headed another overland expedition, 1826, and traced N. Amer. coast as far as 149° 37′ W. long.; knighted, 1829; lieutenant-governor of Van Diemen's Land (Tasmania), 1836–43, fostering social and political advancement of colony; died during ill-fated expedition for discovery of N.W. Passage to Pacific. The ships were last seen on July 26, 1845, by a whaler in Baffin Bay. Within the next twelve years thirty-nine expeditions were sent out in search of Franklin's party, but without success till 1857, when M'Clintock discovered traces and records of the expedition.

[*Life*, by Traill (1896).]

Franz Josef. See Francis Joseph.

Fraser, Sir John Foster (1868–), Brit. traveller and author; *b.* Edinburgh; in 1896 made bicycle tour round world; in 1901 crossed Siberia and Manchuria; toured Canada and U.S.A., 1902–4; visited Balkan states, 1905, Russia, 1906, Sahara, 1910, and subsequently Australasia, Panama, and Argentina. On all these countries he has written graphic books.

Fraser, SIMON, LORD LOVAT. See LOVAT.

Fraunhofer (*froun'hō-fer*), JOSEPH VON (1787–1826), Ger. optician; *b.* Straubing, Bavaria; invented many optical instruments, especially in regard to telescopic prisms; discovered 'Fraunhofer's lines' in solar spectrum.

Frazer, SIR JAMES GEORGE, O.M. (1854–), Brit. writer on mythology and comparative religion; *b.* Glasgow; chiefly known by his epoch-making work, *The Golden Bough* (1890), which revolutionized popular ideas on mythology and the religions of savages. Pub. *Folklore in the Old Testament* (1918), *Sir Roger de Coverley and Other Literary Pieces* (1920), etc.; F.R.S., 1920; O.M., 1925.

Frederick I. (OF HOHENSTAUFEN), BARBAROSSA (*c.* 1123–90), Emperor of Holy Rom. Empire; endeavoured to appease territorial feuds in Germany; undertook first Ital. expedition, 1154; received Lombard crown at Pavia; crowned emperor, 1155, by Adrian IV.; married Beatrice of Burgundy, 1156. Diet at Besançon, 1157, saw rupture of alliance between Pope and Emperor. During second Ital. expedition, 1158–62, Milan was destroyed. After Adrian's death, 1159, Frederick set up anti-pope, captured Rome, but was defeated at Legnano, 1176; submitted to Pope, 1177; secured union of empire and Sicily by Treaty of Augsburg, 1184; drowned in Cilicia, 1190, while on crusade. A brilliant statesman and brave general.

Frederick II. (1194–1250), Emperor of Holy Rom. Empire; *b.* near Ancona; grandson of Frederick I.; crowned King of Sicily, 1198; King of Germany, 1212; elected emperor, in opposition to Otto IV.; strove to make himself despotic in Sicily; founded Naples Univ., 1224; quarrelled with Pope about separation of Sicily from empire, and excommunicated, 1227; on crusade, 1228–9, and secured Jerusalem; made peace with Pope at San Germano, 1230; renewed breach with Pope, 1239; Council of Lyons, 1245, deposed him, and hence war broke out; till his death was engaged in struggle with the Pope. Though not a great soldier, he was brilliant, versatile, and a shrewd, crafty statesman.

Frederick III. (1415–93), Duke of Styria and Carinthia; son of Ernest of Habsburg; *b.* Innsbrück; elected Emperor of Holy Rom. Empire, 1440; acquired Austria, 1463; driven from Vienna, 1485, by Hungarians; an inefficient ruler, and a cautious, timid diplomatist. The marriage of his son Maximilian to Mary of Burgundy made the Habsburgs one of the great dynasties of Europe.

Frederick I. (1657–1713), first King of Prussia; son of Frederick William, the Great Elector; *b.* Königsberg; became Elector Frederick III. of Brandenburg, 1688; aided William III. in carrying out revolution of 1688; founded Halle Univ., 1694; received title of king, 1700, from emperor in order to secure his services in War of Span. Succession.

Frederick II., THE GREAT (1712–86), King of Prussia; son of Frederick William I., who conceived intense dislike for him and treated him harshly; served in Polish Succession War; devoted himself largely to literature, 1735–40; succeeded to the throne, 1740, and inherited a well-administered, skilfully organized despotism. Prussians invaded Silesia, 1740, an aggression which was unjustifiable but successful; by Treaty of Breslau Austria yielded to Prussia Upper and Lower Silesia; in second Silesian war Frederick confirmed his hold on Silesia by Treaty of Dresden, 1745; at outbreak of Seven Years' War, 1756, became Britain's ally; overran Saxony, 1756, thus anticipating attack of his enemies, Austria and Russia. Frederick fought tenaciously, but only the death of Elizabeth of Russia and the exhaustion of France enabled him to retain the dominions he had won. In 1772 he obtained Polish Prussia and part of Great Poland; in Bavarian Succession War, 1777–9, he successfully contested Habsburg claims; formed League of Princes, 1785. An opportunist, a philosopher despot, a great administrator, cynical, selfish, industrious, tolerant, Frederick made his country the first of Ger. states. [*History of Frederick the Great*, by Carlyle (1872); *Frederick the Great and Rise of Prussia*, by Reddaway (1904).]

Frederick III. (1831–88), King of Prussia and Ger. Emperor; *b.* Potsdam; married Princess Victoria of Great Britain, 1858; a strong Liberal; distinguished himself in war with Denmark and in Austrian war of 1866 and Franco-Prussian War, 1870–71; acted as regent, 1878; succeeded, March 1888, but, already smitten with mortal disease, reigned only three months.

Frederick I. (*c.* 1372–1440), Elector of Brandenburg; founder of the greatness of House of Hohenzollern; noted military leader and administrator.

Frederick I. (1370–1428), Elector and Duke of Saxony; received his electorate in return for services against Hussites, who, however, finally defeated him at Aussig, 1426; founded Leipzig Univ., 1409; secured duchy of Saxe-Wittenberg, 1423.

Frederick III., THE WISE (1463–1525), Elector of Saxony; succeeded, 1486; was offered the imperial crown, but refused, and supported election of Charles V.; founded univ. of Wittenberg, 1502; patron and protector of Luther and Melanchthon.

Frederick V. (1596–1632), Elector Palatine of Rhine; married Elizabeth, daughter of James I. of England; elected King of Bohemia, 1619; driven from Bohemia and Palatinate, 1620; father of Sophia, who married Elector of Hanover and became mother of George I. of Britain.

Frederick VIII. (1843–1912), King of Denmark, eldest son of Christian IX.; *b.* Copenhagen; succeeded, 1906; married Princess Louise, daughter of Charles XV. of Sweden, 1869; in 1905 his second son, Charles (married to Princess Maud, daughter of Edward VII.), was chosen King of Norway under title Hakon VII.

Frederick William, THE GREAT ELECTOR (1620–88); *b.* Berlin; succeeded as Elector of Brandenburg, 1640; reorganized army and finances; created a navy, and established a colony in Africa; definitely annexed E. Pomerania, 1653, and was acknowledged sovereign over Prussia; won battle of Fehrbellin, 1675, over Swedes. He added greatly to the wealth of his country by encouraging settlement of Flemings and Huguenots, and was the real founder of Prussian state.

Frederick William I. (1688–1740), King of Prussia, father of Frederick the Great; succeeded his father Frederick I., 1713; gave Prussia a compact political organization, efficient civil service, well-filled treasury, and well-drilled army; fought at Malplaquet under Marlborough, 1709; obtained greater part of Gelderland, 1713, and part of Pomerania, 1720; assisted Russia in Polish Succession War, 1734–5; encouraged agriculture and colonization. A conscientious, thrifty administrator, strong-willed and passionate, he made Prussia a military bureaucracy.

Frederick William II. (1744–97), King of Prussia; *b.* Berlin; succeeded his uncle Frederick the Great, 1786, whose policy he reversed; left his country bankrupt, his army weakened, and the monarchy dishonoured; patronized Beethoven and Mozart.

Frederick William III. (1770–1840), King of Prussia; *b.* Potsdam; succeeded, 1797; defeated by Napoleon at Jena, 1806; had to surrender great part of his dominions by Treaty of Tilsit, 1807; compelled to join Napoleon in war against Russia; subsequently ally of Emperor Alexander of Russia.

Frederick William IV. (1795–1861), King of Prussia; succeeded, 1840; centralized government and pursued policy of religious toleration; behaved irresolutely in Berlin Revolution, 1848; refusal of imperial crown, April 1849, postponed union of Germany; attacked by paralysis, 1857, and his brother became regent.

Freeman, EDWARD AUGUSTUS (1823–92), Eng. historian; *b.* Harborne, Staffordshire; devoted his life to literary work; regius prof. of modern history, Oxford, 1884; spent much time abroad after 1886, owing to ill-health; died of smallpox at Alicante. An indefatigable writer and great investigator; wrote *History of the Norman Conquest, Historical Essays, William Rufus, History of Sicily* (unfinished), etc.

Frémiet (*frā-myā'*), EMMANUEL (1824–1910), Fr. sculptor; *b.* Paris; first attained distinction by studies of animals; his statues include *Joan of Arc* (1874 and 1889), *Condé, Velasquez,* etc.; colossal figure of *Fredinand de Lesseps* (1900), at entrance to Suez Canal.

Fré'mont, JOHN CHARLES (1813–90), Amer. explorer; *b.* Savannah, Georgia; made five important journeys to the western seaboard; in 1842, with Kit Carson as guide, explored country between the Missouri and Rocky Mountains; in 1843 reached the tide water of Columbia R., and finally the Sacramento valley; in 1845 surveyed California; served in U.S.A. Senate, 1849, and was governor of Arizona, 1878–81.

French, JOHN DENTON PINKSTONE, 1ST EARL OF YPRES (1852–1925), Brit. field-marshal; *b.* Ripple, Kent; served in navy, 1866–70; joined army, 1874; with Nile expedition, 1884–5; commanded cavalry with Sir George White's force in Natal, 1899; won battle of Elandslaagte; appointed to command of cavalry division, 1900; relieved Kimberley; forced Cronje into trap at Paardeberg; appointed to command in S. Transvaal. On return from S. Africa commanded 1st Army Corps at Aldershot, 1901–7; chief of imperial general staff, 1911–14; field-marshal, 1913; commander of the Expeditionary forces in France, 1914–15. After disastrous battle of Loos, 1915, was retired in favour of Sir Douglas Haig; commander-in-chief of troops stationed in U.K., 1915–18; lord-lieutenant of Ireland, 1918–21; O.M., 1917; earldom, 1921. Pub. *1914* (in 1919), a justification of his war record, which was severely criticized.

Frere (*frēr*), SIR HENRY BARTLE EDWARD (1815–84), Brit. administrator; *b.* Clydach, Breconshire; governor of Bombay, 1862. After work in Zanzibar connected with slave trade, became High Commissioner of S. Africa, 1877; made premature attempt to unite S. Africa; failure culminated in Zulu War; recalled, 1881.

Freshfield, DOUGLAS WILLIAM (1845–1934), Eng. explorer and mountaineer; first to climb Kazbek in the Caucasus; pub. map of region; explored Kanchenjunga at high level (*c.* 1899), and subsequently Armenia, Corsica, Apennines, and most parts of the Alps. President of Royal Geographical Soc., 1914–17; ed. of *Alpine Journal* (1872–80).

Fresnel (*frā-nel'*), AUGUSTIN JEAN (1788–1827), Fr. scientist; *b.* Broglie, Normandy; introduced compound lenses as substitutes for mirrors in lighthouse work; studied aberration of light and polarized rays.

Freud (*froid*), SIGMUND (1856–), Austrian psychologist; *b.* Freiberg, Moravia; of Jewish parents; qualified as doctor, and specialized in study of nervous and mental diseases; prof. of neurology, Vienna Univ., since 1902; founded psycho-analysis, the science which investigates the subconscious mind, stressing the importance of dreams and of sex as a clue to this; his numerous books expounding his theories have been widely translated.

Freycinet (*frā-sē-nā'*), CHARLES LOUIS DE SAULCES DE (1828–1923), Fr. statesman; *b.* in Ariège; in Franco-Ger. War, 1870–1, was head of military department under Gambetta; entered Senate, 1876; held various offices, including premiership four times; as minister of war, 1888–93, reorganized Fr. army administration. Member of Fr. Academy from 1890.

Freytag (*frī'täg*), GUSTAV (1816–95), Ger. novelist and dramatist; *b.* Kreuzburg, Silesia. His play *Die Journalisten* (1854) was one of the best comedies of the century; won wider fame as novelist with *Soll und Haben* (1855), *Die Verlorene Handschrift* (1864), etc. See his autobiography, *Reminiscences of my Life.*

Friedel (*frē-del'*), CHARLES (1832–99), Fr. chemist; *b.* Strasbourg; prof. at Sorbonne of mineralogy, 1876–84; of organic chemistry, 1884–99; synthesized benzene homologues, ketones, and aldehydes; formed minerals artificially; wrote on crystallography and organic chemistry.

Frith, WILLIAM POWELL (1819–1909), Eng. painter; *b.* Aldfield, Yorks; R.A., 1852; noted for historical and genre subjects and portraits; painter of *Derby Day*; wrote *Autobiography* (1887).

Fro'bisher, SIR MARTIN (?1535–94), Eng. navigator; *b.* in Yorkshire; first Englishman to attempt N.W. Passage to Cathay. Sailed in command of small expedition in 1576; reached Labrador; following year set out with larger expedition, but returned on account of discovery of supposed gold ore in Frobisher Strait; made another attempt in 1578; with Drake made expedition to W. Indies, 1585; distinguished himself against Span. Armada, 1588; knighted for services; mortally wounded during assault on fort near Brest.

[*Life*, by Jones (1878); and Hakluyt Soc., *Three Voyages of Frobisher* (1867).]

Fröding (*fre'ding*), GUSTAV (1860–1911), Swed. poet; his lyrics are fresh and musical. His collections include *Guitarr och Dragharmonika* (1891), *Räggler å Paschaser* (1895), and *Nytt och Gammalt* (1897).

Froe'bel, FRIEDRICH WILHELM AUGUST (1782–1852), Ger. educationist; *b.* in Thuringia; father of the 'kindergarten'; worked with Pestalozzi; devoted himself to the training of children before they attained the age of seven; opened first kindergarten at Blankenburg, Thuringia, 1837; trained women teachers; labours interrupted by edict, 1852, forbidding establishment in Prussia of schools on his principles; basis of Froebel system is development through voluntary activity; object of all training, to assist mind and body to develop along the lines of natural growth.

Froissart (*frwä-sär'*), JEAN (1338–1410?), chronicler; *b.* Valenciennes; travelled in England and Scotland, 1361; afterwards in W. Europe. In 1372 he began the writing of his famous *Chroniques*, which describe events in Western Europe from 1326 to 1400. Though historically unreliable, it presents a picture of the time unrivalled in its vivid colour and its charm.

[*Froissart*, by de Lettenhove (1858).]

Fromentin (*frō-mon-tan'*), EUGÈNE (1820–76), Fr. artist and writer; excelled in Algerian subjects; he wrote well-known autobiographical novel *Dominique*, and *Les Maîtres d' Autrefois*, a subtle and critical study of the Dutch and Flem. painters.

Frontenac (*frōnt-nak'*), LOUIS DE BUADE, COMTE DE (1620–98), Fr. colonial administrator; governor of Canada, 1672; recalled, 1682, owing to quarrels with Church; sent back to Canada, 1689, and warmly welcomed by colonists; repulsed attack on Quebec by the English, 1690; conducted campaign against Iroquois.

Froude (*frood*), JAMES ANTHONY (1818–94), Eng. historian; *b.* Dartington, Devon; educated at Westminster and Oxford; fellow of Exeter Coll., 1842; came under influence of Tractarian movement; became a sceptic, and after publication of *Nemesis of Faith* (1848) was forced to resign fellowship; contributed largely to *Westminster Review* and *Fraser's Magazine*; ed. Mrs. Carlyle's *Letters*, and wrote *Life of Carlyle*, which gave rise to much controversy. His most important work, *History of England*, deals with the Reformation period. Prof. of modern history, Oxford, 1892; historical work characterized by brilliant style, attractive narrative, but by partiality and inaccuracy.

[*Life*, by Herbert Paul (1906).]

Fry, ELIZABETH (1780–1845), Eng. social reformer; *b.* Norwich; a Quaker; promoted prison reform; secured great improvements in hospital system and in treatment of the insane.

Fry, ROGER ELLIOT (1866–1934), Eng. post-impressionist artist and author; *b.* London; professor of fine art at Cambridge from 1933. Most notable achievements are *Early Morning near Cagnes*; *Convent, Venice*; *The Reader*; *La Diligente*. Author of *Giovanni Bellini* (1899), *Cézanne* (1927), etc.

Fryatt, CHARLES (1872–1916), master of Great Eastern packet *Brussels*; captured and court-martialled by Germans for trying to ram U-boats, and shot (July 27, 1916) at Bruges. His body was re-interred, 1919, at Dovercourt.

Fryxell (*frooks'el*), ANDERS (1795–1881), Swed. historian; pastor of Sunna; pub. valuable *Swedish Grammar* (1824), and exhaustive history of Sweden (46 vols., 1823–79).

Fu'ad I. (1868–1936), King of Egypt; *b.* Gizeh; succeeded his brother as Sultan of Egypt, 1917; proclaimed king after expiration of Brit. protectorate, Feb. 1922.

Fugger (*fook'er*), famous Ger. family of merchants and bankers founded by Johann Fugger (1348–1409), a weaver of Graben, near Augsburg. They rendered great services to Habsburgs; made large loans to Maximilian I. and Charles V., under whom family reached zenith of its power and wealth.

Full'er, THOMAS (1608–61), Eng. divine, biographer, and historian; during Civil War supported king; royal chaplain at Restoration; wrote *Worthies of England, Church History of Britain*, etc. His style, usually called 'quaint,' is full of wit and humour.

Fulton (*fool'ton*), ROBERT (1765–1815), Amer. engineer; *b.* in Pennsylvania; began life as a miniature portrait and landscape painter; came to England, 1787; invented and launched the steamship *Clermont* at New York, 1807—an epoch-marking event in steam navigation; built first steam warship, 1814; invented submarine, 1801, in France.

Fur'ley, SIR JOHN (1836–1919), Eng. philanthropist; *b.* Ashford, Kent; one of original founders of Red Cross organization, 1870; director of ambulances in France during Franco-Prussian War; during Great War designed huts, hospital trains, etc. Knighted, 1899.

Fur'niss, HARRY (1854–1925), Brit. caricaturist; *b.* Wexford; illustrated *Punch's* 'Essence of Parliament' and numerous books, including whole of Dickens and Thackeray.

Fur'nivall, FREDERICK JAMES (1825–1910), Eng. scholar and philologist; *b.* Egham; founded the Early Eng. Text, Chaucer, Browning, and other societies; one of originators of Oxford *New English Dictionary.*

Furse, CHARLES WELLINGTON (1868–1904), Eng. painter of many-sided talent; *b.* London; painted excellent portraits and sporting pictures. Well-known works include *Return from the Ride*, in the Chantrey collection, and *Diana of the Uplands.*

Fuseli (*foo'ze-li*), HENRY (1741–1825), Swiss artist and art critic; *b.* Zurich; studied in Italy; settled in England; R.A., 1790; prof. of painting at Academy, 1799; illustrated Shakespeare and Milton; his *Lectures on Painters* are of great critical value.

Fust (*foost*), or FAUST, JOHANN (*c.* 1400–66), Ger. printer; for some time associated with Gutenberg; there has been controversy as to which of them invented printing; Fust seems to have advanced capital to Gutenberg, and, litigation ensuing, Fust commenced with his son-in-law Schöffer a separate printing house.

Fyt (*fit*), JOHANNES (1609–61), Belgian painter; *b.* Antwerp; noted for animal scenes—*e.g. Dead Game and Fruit, Dead Snipe with Ducks, Hunted Roedeer with Dogs*, etc.

G

Gaboriau (*gä-bō-rē-ō'*), ÉMILE (1835–73), French novelist; *b.* in Charente-Inférieure; noted for his sensational detective and criminal stories.

Gad'e, NIELS WILHELM (1817–90), Dan. composer; *b.* Copenhagen; gained prize for *Echoes of Ossian* (1841); wrote symphonies, overtures, orchestral pieces, and songs; originator of modern Scandinavian school of music.

Gage, LYMAN JUDSON (1836–1927), Amer. financier; *b.* De Ruyter, New York State; president of first National Bank, 1891 secretary of U.S.A. Treasury, 1897–1902.

Gainsborough, THOMAS (1727–88), Eng. artist; *b.* Sudbury; son of a small tradesman; studied engraving, and set up as a portrait and landscape painter, 1743, at Ipswich, and later at Bath and London. He was one of original members of Royal Academy, 1768, but, offended by bad position given to his *Three Princesses* (1784), withdrew, and never exhibited again. He may be called the father of modern Eng. painting. The greatest colourist of the early Eng. school, he was absolutely true to life and nature, and essentially English in sentiment. He painted over 300 canvases, 220 of which were portraits. The National Gallery contains his portrait of Mrs. Siddons, and some of his finest landscapes.

[*Lives*, by Sir W. Armstrong (1898 and 1904), by Mrs. A. Bell (1902), and R. Gower (1903).]

Gaird'ner, JAMES (1826–1912), historian; *b.* Edinburgh; deputy keeper of public records, 1859–93; pub. *Letters and Papers of the Reign of Henry VIII.* (25 vols., completed 1910; first four with Dr. Brewer), also similar collections of reigns of Richard III. and Henry VII., and *Lollardy and the Reformation in England* (1908–11).

Gais'ford, THOMAS (1779–1855), Eng. classical scholar; *b.* Ilford, Wilts; regius prof. of Greek and curator of the Bodleian Library, Oxford; Gaisford prize for Gr. verse and prose was founded in his memory, 1856.

Gaius (*gī'us*), Roman jurist; author of the *Institute*, an exposition of Rom. law, a treatise on the Edicts of the Magistrates, and Commentaries on the Twelve Tables; written between A.D. 130 and 180.

Gaius Cæsar. See CALIGULA.

Galba, SERVIUS SULPICIUS (B.C. 3–69 A.D.), emperor of Rome, 68–9; had distinguished career as prætor, consul, and governor of Gaul, Africa, and Spain; was proclaimed emperor on death of Nero, and his short reign ended in disaster.

Ga'len (or GALENUS), CLAUDIUS (*c.* A.D. 130–*c.* 200), celebrated ancient medical writer; *b.* Pergamum, Asia Minor; his writings were the guide for physicians for several centuries; one of the founders of science of anatomy.

Galile'o Galile'i (1564–1642), Ital. astronomer and physicist; *b.* Pisa. While a student he enunciated the law of swings of a pendulum. In 1588 he became lecturer at Pisa Univ. At this period he invented the hydrostatic balance. Owing to the hostility of the ecclesiastics and the loss of court favour, he quitted Pisa, and obtained the professorship of mathematics in Padua Univ., 1592–1610. In 1609 he constructed a telescope, on the model of that of Hans Lippershey of Middelburg in Holland, and with it discovered four satellites of Jupiter. The uneven configuration of the surface of the moon was demonstrated; and he detected sun-spots. The astronomer was invited to Florence, 1610, by his patron, Cosimo, Grand-duke of Tuscany. Continued advocacy of Copernican principles, and disquisitions on their Scriptural significance, brought him under the ban of the Church, and he was cited to appear before the Inquisition, 1616, and was ordered to discontinue his teaching. In 1632 appeared his *Dialogues on the Systems of the World*; summoned to Rome by Pope Urban VIII., and dreading imprisonment, Galileo publicly abjured his own philosophy, and, among other penalties, suffered detention, and his book was prohibited. At the close of 1633 he was allowed to return to Florence, where he lived in seclusion until his death.

[*Complete Works*, ed. by A. Favaro (20 vols.); *Lives*, by Viviani (1654), T. H. Martin (1868), Favaro (1882), and J. J. Fahie (1903).]

Gall, ST. (554–*c.* 645), saint; *b.* in Ireland; settled near Lake Constance and evangelized neighbouring country; founded monastery of St. Gall.

Galland (*gä-lon'*), ANTOINE (1646–1715), Fr. Orientalist and numismatist; *b.* in Picardy; travelled through Asia Minor, copying inscriptions and collecting coins, etc.; prof. of Arabic at Collège de France, 1709; pub. first European trans. of the *Arabian Nights*.

Gallatin (*gäl'a-tin*), ALBERT (1761–1849), notable Amer. statesman; *b.* Geneva; was one of founders of Anti-Federalist party (afterwards the Republican); secretary of Treasury, 1801; minister to France, 1816; retired from public life, 1827.

Galli-Curci (*gal-ē-koor'chē*), AMELITA (Mme. HOMER SAMUELS), (1889–), Italian coloratura soprano; *b.* Milan; made her début at Rome, 1909; toured in S. America and visited U.S.A. in 1918, where she won immediate success, and where she settled.

Gallieni (*gal-ē-ān'ē*), JOSEPH SIMON (1849–1916), Fr. general; *b.* in Haute-Garonne; fought in Franco-German War, 1870–1; reorganized administration of Madagascar, 1896–1905; governor of Paris, Sept. 1914; played important part in first battle of the Marne by rushing reserves from Paris in every available taxi and motor-bus; minister of war, 1915; resigned, 1916; marshal (posthumously), 1921.

Gallienus (*gal-ē-ā'nus*), PUBLIUS LICINIUS EGNATIUS, Roman emperor from A.D. 253; notorious for his debauchery; killed by his soldiers, 268.

Gall'io, JUNIUS ANNÆUS, proconsul of Achaia (A.D. 53–4); mentioned in Acts 18 : 12–17. His name has become a synonym for easy-going indifference.

Gals'worthy, JOHN (1867–1933), Eng. novelist and playwright; *b.* Coombe, Surrey; called to the bar, 1890; spent much of his early manhood in travel; first attracted attention with *The Island Pharisees* (1904), a criticism of Eng. character, society, and institutions; in succeeding novels he showed himself skilled in the analysis of character and social relationships; plays display the same qualities. Awarded the Nobel Prize for literature, 1932. His best known work, *The Forsyte Saga* (1922), includes *The Man of Property* (1906), *In Chancery* (1920), and *To Let* (1921), and was followed by the trilogy *A Modern Comedy* (1929), including *The White Monkey* (1924), *The Silver Spoon* (1926), and *Swan Song* (1928); other novels are *The Country House* (1907), *Fraternity* (1909), *The Patrician* (1911). His plays include *The Silver Box* (1906), *Strife* (1909), *Justice* (1910), *The Skin Game* (1920), *Loyalties* (1922), *The Forest* (1924), and *The Roof* (1929).

[*John Galsworthy*, by S. Kaye-Smith (1916); *Trois Études Anglaises*, by A. Chevrillon (1924).]

Galt, JOHN (1779–1839), Scot. novelist; *b.* Irvine; writer of stories dealing with Scottish life and character; his masterpiece is *Annals of the Parish.*

Galt'on, SIR FRANCIS (1822–1911), Eng. anthropologist; *b.* Birmingham; cousin of Charles Darwin; made explorations in S.W. Africa and other countries; investigated meteorological conditions, being the first to establish the theory of anticyclones; made important researches in anthropology and heredity; founded the science of eugenics, and endowed a chair in London Univ.

[*Memories of my Life* (1908).]

Galvan'i, LUIGI (1737–98), Ital. physiologist; *b.* Bologna; lecturer on anatomy at Bologna, 1762; investigated action of electricity on muscles of animals, hence the term galvanic.

Gama, VASCO DA (1469–1524), Port. navigator; *b.* Sines; discovered the Cape route to India, 1498; founded Port. colonies on E. African coast; made a second voyage to Calicut, 1502; appointed

Viceroy of Portuguese India, 1524, but died soon after.

Gamaliel, a Pharisee mentioned in Acts 5 : 34; taught St. Paul (Acts 22 : 3). His grandson GAMALIEL II. helped to revive Judaism after fall of temple.

Gambetta, LÉON (1838–82), Fr. statesman; *b.* Cahors; sat in Assembly, 1869, as a republican; supported Franco-Prussian War, and after Sedan continued a wonderfully inspiring resistance; chiefly responsible for securing constitution of Feb. 1875; invented Fr. policy of opportunism; was opponent of clericalism, and became head of 'Le Grand Ministère,' Nov. 1881; advocated co-operation with Britain in Egypt, but was prevented from developing policy by his death.

Gandhi (*gän'dē*), MOHANDAS KARAMCHAND (1869–), Hindu nationalist leader, commonly known as MAHATMA GANDHI; *b.* Porbandar, Kathiawar; studied in London and called to the bar; while in S. Africa, 1893–1914, championed the cause of the Asiatics there; served with the Red Cross during the S. African War; returned to India and advocated a policy of non-co-operation and passive resistance, which in 1920 led to serious disorders; was arrested, 1922, and sentenced to six years' imprisonment, but was released in less than two years. After a period of eclipse he regained his power, and in pursuance of his policy infringed the Salt Law, 1930, and was again imprisoned, but released in 1931; attended Round Table Conference in London; returned to India, and resumed opposition to government; was arrested, 1932, and while in prison began 'fast unto death' to secure more favourable social and political conditions for the 'Untouchables'; his fast ended when agreement was reached between caste Hindus and the Untouchables. A man of high ideals, he has often set in motion forces beyond his power to control.

Garay (*gor'oi*), JÁNOS (1812–53), Hungarian poet, dramatist, and author; his most widely known works are a romance in verse, *Frangepán Kristófné* (1846), and historical poem, *Szent László* (1852).

Garcia (*gär-thē'-a*). (1) MANOEL DEL POPOLO VICENTE (1775–1832), Span. tenor singer and musical composer; *b.* Seville; great successes in opera in Paris and Italy. (2) MANOEL (1805–1906), son of above; won a brilliant reputation as teacher of singing in Paris and London; was author of *Mémoire sur la Voix Humaine* (1840), etc.; inventor, 1854, of laryngoscope.

Garcilaso de la Vega. See under VEGA.

Garden, MARY (1877–), Amer. singer; *b.* Aberdeen, Scotland; received her musical training in Chicago, and later in Paris; had great success in England, the Continent, and New York; was general manager of the Chicago Opera Co., 1921–3.

Gardiner, ALFRED G. (1865–), Eng. journalist; *b.* Chelmsford; ed. of *Daily News*, 1902–19; author of biographies of Sir William Harcourt and George Cadbury, 1923; his *Prophets, Priests, and Kings*, *Pillars of Society*, and *War Lords* give pen-portraits of contemporary celebrities; under name of 'Alpha of the Plough' has written a series of interesting and entertaining essays.

Gardiner, SAMUEL RAWSON (1829–1902), Eng. historian; *b.* Alresford, Hampshire; fellow of All Souls, 1884, and Merton, 1892; subsequently prof. of modern history, King's Coll., London. A careful and impartial writer, his great work is *History of England from the Accession of James I. to the Outbreak of the Civil War* (10 vols., new ed., 1883–4).

[*Life*, by H. B. Learned (1902).]

Gardiner, STEPHEN (?1483–1555), Eng. bishop; *b.* Bury St. Edmunds; became secretary to Cardinal Wolsey; won Henry VIII.'s favour for his services in connection with the king's divorce; bishop of Winchester, 1531, but deprived of his see and imprisoned in Edward VI.'s reign for his adherence to Romish doctrines; liberated under Mary, and made lord chancellor; he opposed the persecutions of the reign.

Gardner, ERNEST ARTHUR (1862–), English archæologist; *b.* London; director of Brit. School of Archæology at Athens, 1887–95; prof. of archæology, London Univ., 1896–1929; author of *Ancient Athens* (1902), *Catalogue of Ancient Sculpture*, collected by him (1921), *The Art of Greece* (1925).

Gardner, PERCY (1846–), Eng. numismatist, archæologist, and theological writer; *b.* London; works include *New Chapters in Greek History* (1892), *Evolution of Christian Ethics* (1918), *Modernism in the English Church* (1926), and *The Interpretation of Religious Experience* (1931).

Garfield, JAMES ABRAM (1831–81), president, U.S.A.; *b.* in log-cabin in Ohio; after early struggle became prof. of ancient languages at Hiram Coll., Ohio; in Civil War was promoted major-general for bravery at Chickamauga, 1863; entered Congress, 1864, and in 1880 was elected president; shot by madman in 1881.

[*Life and Letters*, by T. C. Smith (1925).]

Garibal'di, GIUSEPPE (1807–82), Ital. patriot and revolutionary; *b.* Nice. Came under influence of Mazzini, and was involved in futile revolt at Genoa, 1834; escaped to S. America; assisted Rio Grande in revolt against Brazil, and was the moving spirit in securing independence of Uruguay. Returning to Italy, 1848, he heroically defended Roman republic against French and Austrian forces, and after fall of Rome conducted wonderful retreat through Central Italy; escaped to America, but returned to island of Caprera in 1854. Though indignant at cession of Savoy and Nice to France he supported King of Sardinia in his revolt against Austria, 1859, and cleared Austria out of a large part of Alpine Italy. In May 1860 sailed with his famous 'Thousand' to aid the Sicilian revolt against Francis of Naples, and by end of July had completed conquest of Sicily; crossed to mainland, occupied Naples, and accompanied Victor Emmanuel in his state entry into that city, returning to Caprera next day. He made three unsuccessful attempts to capture Rome, in 1862 and 1867 (twice), and took part in war of 1866, defeating Austrians on three occasions; in 1874 he was elected to Italian Parliament as deputy for Rome; after hesitation, accepted a well-merited pension.

[*Autobiography* (trans. 1889); *Garibaldi's Defence of the Roman Republic* (1907), *Garibaldi and the Thousand* (1909), and *Garibaldi and the Making of Italy* (1911), by G. M. Trevelyan.]

Garland, HAMLIN (1860–), Amer. author; *b.* W. Salem, Wis.; devoted himself principally to fiction, presenting forceful pictures of development of Middle West; among his later books are *Son of the Middle Border* (1914), *A Daughter of the Middle Border* (1922), *The Book of the American Indian* (1923), and *Trail Makers of the Middle Border* (1927).

Gar'nett, RICHARD (1835–1906), Eng. librarian and miscellaneous writer; *b.* Lichfield; keeper of printed books, Brit. Museum, 1890–9; pub. poems, biographical works, and volumes of literary criticism.

Garnier (*gärn-yā'*), CLÉMENT

Joseph (1813–81), Fr. economist; *b.* Beuil, Alpes-Maritimes; established association for advocacy of free trade; senator, 1876; pub. *Richard Cobden, les Ligueurs et la Ligue* (1846), etc.

Garrick, David (1717–79), Eng. actor and dramatist; *b.* Hereford; was a pupil of Samuel Johnson, with whom, in 1737, he went to London; appeared at Goodman's Fields as Richard III., 1741, achieving immediate success; became joint proprietor of Drury Lane Theatre, 1747, where during thirty years he commanded unvarying popularity and unrivalled success; retired, 1776; was buried in Westminster Abbey. Garrick elevated the whole tone of the stage, substituted for the old stilted and declamatory style one more vivacious and natural, and greatly increased the popularity of Shakespearian performances. He was author of plays, prologues, epilogues, and miscellaneous pieces.

[*Lives*, by Percy Fitzgerald (1868; later ed. 1899), and by J. Knight (1894); *Garrick and his Circle*, by Mrs. Parsons (1906).]

Garrison, William Lloyd (1805–79), Amer. reformer, and leader of Abolitionists in anti-slavery struggle; *b.* Newburyport, Mass.; imprisoned and pursued with incessant threats by slave-owners; founded and ed. the *Liberator* (1831); president of Amer. Anti-Slavery Soc. During his last years he supported various reforms, especially prohibition.

[*Life*, by sons, W. P. and F. J. Garrison.]

Garstang, John (1876–), Brit. archæologist; *b.* Blackburn; conducted valuable researches into Rom. remains in Britain; also leader of archæological expeditions in Egypt, Nubia, Palestine, and other parts of Near East; prof. of archæology, Liverpool Univ., since 1907; works include *Roman Ribchester* (1911), *The Land of the Hittites* (1911), *The Hittite Empire* (1929), *The Foundations of Bible History* (1931), and *Reports on the Excavation of Jericho* (1932–4).

Garvin, James Louis (1868–), Brit. journalist and publicist; *b.* Birkenhead; was leader writer on *Newcastle Chronicle* (1891–9), ed. of *Outlook* (1905) and of *Pall Mall Gazette* (1912–15), also of *Observer* since 1908; author of *Economic Foundations of Peace* (1919), and *Life of Joseph Chamberlain* (1932); ed.-in-chief of 14th ed. of *Encyclopædia Britannica.*

Gascoigne (*gas-koin'*), George (*c.* 1525–77), Eng. poet; served as soldier of fortune in Low Countries, and was taken prisoner; associated with Leicester in entertainment of Elizabeth at Kenilworth; original works include *A Hundred Sundry Flowers* and *The Steele Glas*—one of the earliest Eng. satires. His poetry is marked by considerable originality.

[*Works*, ed. by J. W. Cunliffe (1907); *Life*, by F. E. Schelling (1894).]

Gas'kell, Elizabeth Cleghorn Stevenson, Mrs. (1810–65), Eng. novelist; *b.* London; spent early life at Knutsford, Cheshire (the original of 'Cranford'), and her married life at Manchester; *Mary Barton*, her first novel, pub. anonymously, 1848, met with instant success; *Cranford* (1853) is a series of exquisite studies of village life; also wrote *Life of Charlotte Brontë* (1857).

[*Mrs. Gaskell and Knutsford*, by J. A. Payne (1905), and *Mrs. Gaskell*, by E. K. Chadwick (1913).]

Gasquet, Francis Aidan (1846–1929), R.C. historian; *b.* London; superior of Downside Benedictine Monastery, Somerset, 1878–84; cardinal, 1914; prefect of the Vatican archives; president International Commission for the Revision of the Vulgate; author of *Henry VIII. and the English Monasteries*

(1888–89), *Pope Gregory the Great* (1904), *Monastic Life in the Middle Ages* (1922), *His Holiness Pope Pius XI.* (1922).

Gaster, Moses (1856–), Romanian philologist and Heb. scholar; *b.* Bucharest; lecturer, univ. of Bucharest, 1881–5, but expelled for agitating on behalf of Jews; proceeding to England, was appointed Ilchester lecturer at Oxford, 1886, and since 1887 has been chief rabbi of the Sephardi communities in England; vice-president Anglo-Jewish Society; author of numerous publications.

Gat'acre, Sir William Forbes (1842–1906), Brit. general; *b.* near Stirling; served in Ind. and Burmese wars, 1888–95; commanded Brit. brigade at Omdurman, 1898. In S. African War commanded 3rd Infantry Division, which suffered reverse at Stormberg, 1899; failed to relieve Reddersburg, and was recalled, 1900.

Gatling, Richard Jordan (1818–1903), Amer. inventor; *b.* in N. Carolina; invented various kinds of agricultural machinery, and later his well-known machine-gun, now superseded by more recent makes.

Gatty, Margaret Scott, Mrs. (1809–73), Eng. writer for children; *b.* in Essex; best-known work, *Parables from Nature.*

Gauguin (*go-gän'*), Paul (1848–1903), French post-impressionist painter; *b.* Paris; educated at Lima and Orleans; abandoned banking to take up art; settled in Tahiti, 1891, living with the natives and making studies of native life; influenced work of subsequent Fr. painters.

Gaunt, John of. See under Lancaster.

Gauss (*gows*), Karl Friedrich (1777–1855), Ger. mathematician; *b.* Brunswick; won early reputation by his *Disquisitiones Arithmeticæ* (1801), a standard work on the theory of numbers; director of the observatory, Göttingen, 1807; in conjunction with Weber erected a magnetic observatory, 1833.

Gautama. See Buddha.

Gautier (*gō-tyā'*), Théophile (1811–72), Fr. author and poet; disciple of Victor Hugo and the Romantic School; prolific writer of travel books, criticism, and feuilletons; chief poetical work, *Emaux et Camées* (1856 and 1872); best novels, *Mademoiselle de Maupin* (1835) and *Le Capitaine Fracasse* (1863).

Gay, John (1685–1732), English poet; *b.* Barnstaple; his most successful works were his *Fables* (1727) and *The Beggar's Opera* (1728)—a Newgate pastoral. Other writings include *Rural Sports, Trivia, The Shepherd's Week,* also some plays and miscellaneous poems.

Gay-Lussac (*gā loo-säk'*), Joseph Louis (1778–1850), Fr. physicist; *b.* St. Léonard, Haute-Vienne; prof. of physics at the Sorbonne, and of chemistry at the Jardin des Plantes; investigated properties of gases, hygrometry, capillarity, and stated the law of volumes of combination of gases, and improved the processes for the manufacture of sulphuric and oxalic acids.

Ged, William (1690–1749), inventor of stereotyping; *b.* Edinburgh; in 1725 patented his invention for printing from casts taken from set type; two prayer-books and an ed. of Sallust were the only fruits of his method during his lifetime; from patriotic motives he refused repeatedly to sell his invention to the Dutch.

Geddes, Andrew (1783–1844), Scot. artist; *b.* Edinburgh; gained great success as a portrait painter; A.R.A., 1832; works include *Discovery of the Regalia of Scotland in 1818* and *Christ and the Woman of Samaria* (1841).

Geddes, JENNY (*fl.* 1637), according to tradition, a 'kail-wife' or vegetable seller in the High Street of Edinburgh, who, when Archbishop Laud's service-book was being used for the first time in St. Giles' Cathedral, July 23, 1637, flung a stool at the head of the Bishop of Edinburgh and caused a riot.

Geddes, SIR PATRICK (1854–1932), Brit. biologist and sociologist; *b.* Perth; prof. of botany at Univ. Coll., Dundee, and of sociology and civics, Bombay Univ.; organized univ. halls at Edinburgh and Chelsea; pioneer in town-planning, city improvement, and educational work; wrote on botany, evolution of cities, and, with J. Arthur Thomson, on the evolution of sex; knighted, 1932.

Geijer (*yī'er*), ERIK GUSTAF (1783–1847), Swed. historian and poet; *b.* Ransäter, Värmland; graduated at univ. of Uppsala, and was prof. of history there, 1817–46; pub. *History of the Swedes* (1832–6), a masterpiece of modern history.

Geikie (*gē'kā*). (1) SIR ARCHIBALD (1835–1924), Scot. geologist; *b.* Edinburgh; joined Geological Survey, 1855; director, Geological Survey for Scotland, 1867–81; prof. of geology, Edinburgh University, 1871–81; director-general of Geological Survey of U.K., 1881–1901; president of Royal Soc., 1908–13; made special study of microscopic petrography; publications include *The Ancient Volcanoes of Great Britain*, *The Founders of Geology*, *The Scenery of Scotland*, and *Scottish Reminiscences*. (2) JAMES (1839–1915), Scot. geologist, brother of (1); *b.* Edinburgh; succeeded his brother as prof. of geology at Edinburgh Univ., 1882. A specialist in influence of glacial action, he published *The Great Ice Age*, *Prehistoric Europe*, and *Outlines of Geology*, etc.

Gel'lius, AULUS (*fl.* A.D. 130–180), Lat. grammarian; *b.* Rome; wrote *Noctes Atticæ*, chiefly valuable as containing extracts from Gr. and Rom. writers no longer extant.

Genée-Isitt, MADAME ADELINE (1878–), Dan. operatic dancer; *b.* Aarhus; appeared successively in Berlin, Copenhagen, Paris, and London; married F. S. N. Isitt, 1910; retired from the stage, 1914; president of the Association of Operatic Dancing of Great Britain, 1928.

Geneviève (*zhen'e-vēv*), SAINTE (*c.* 422–512), patron saint of Paris, which she protected against Attila and the Huns; what is now the Panthéon was erected as a church in her honour.

Genghiz Khan. See under JENGHIZ KHAN.

Genlis (*zhän-lēs'*), STÉPHANIE FÉLICITÉ DUCREST DE SAINT-AUBIN, COMTESSE DE (1746–1830), Fr. writer; *b.* Autun; lady-in-waiting to Duchess of Chartres, and tutor to her sons, one of whom, Louis Philippe, became King of France; after Revolution, passed through many vicissitudes; best-known works are *Mademoiselle de Clermont* (1802) and *Mémoires* (1825).

Genseric (*jen'ser-ik*), more correctly GAISERIC, greatest king of Vandals (428–77); invaded Africa, 429, and gained possession of Rom. provinces, also of Carthage, 439; seized Rome, 455; carried off empress and her two daughters; Western emperor Majorian fitted out fleet, but it was destroyed by Genseric, as was also expedition of Leo, Eastern emperor, 477. Genseric died in possession of all his conquests.

Gentile (*jen-tē'lā*), GIOVANNI (1875–), Ital. philosopher; *b.* Castelvetrano, Sicily; prof. of philosophy, Rome, 1918; founded *Giornale critico della filosofia italiana*, 1920; has written many books on religion, education, and philosophy; minister of education, 1922–4.

Geoffrey (*jef'rĭ*) OF MONMOUTH (*c.* 1100–54), Welsh chronicler, and Bishop of St. Asaph, 1152; his *Historia Britonum*, a romance tracing descent of Britons from Brut, son of Æneas, is a source of Arthurian legends and stories of Cymbeline and King Lear.

Geoffroy Saint-Hilaire (*zhō-frwaw' san-tē-lār'*). (1) ÉTIENNE (1772–1844), celebrated Fr. zoologist; famous for his theories of anatomical relationships between different types of animals. (2) ISIDORE (1805–61), Fr. zoologist, son of above; assisted and finally succeeded his father; writings include *Histoire générale et particulière des Anomalies de l'Organisation chez l'Homme et les Animaux* (1832–7).

George, ST., patron saint of England, Aragon, and Portugal; feast day, April 23; probably came from Asia Minor; lived in Nicomedia; arrested as a Christian under anti-Christian laws of Diocletian, and was tortured, A.D. 303; dragon usually associated with him is later legendary embellishment; canonized, 1222, and finally recognized as patron of England by Edward III., 1349.

George I. (1660–1727), Elector of Hanover and King of Britain; succeeded to Brit. throne, 1714, as grandson of Elizabeth, daughter of James I. This new dynasty successfully withstood Jacobite rebellion of 1715; intensely German in sentiment, he regarded England as means for the aggrandizement of Hanover; he left the government in the hands of the Whig statesmen, especially Walpole; owing to his frequent absences on the Continent and to his inability to speak English, the power of the cabinet was enormously strengthened.

George II. (1683–1760), King of Britain; succeeded, 1727; married Caroline of Brandenburg-Anspach, who kept Walpole in power, despite the king's aversion to him. War of Austrian Succession, 1740–8, and Jacobite rebellion, 1745–6, occurred in this reign, which also saw beginnings of Seven Years' War; George was thoroughly German in habits, self-centred and avaricious, but prudent and business-like; he showed bravery at battle of Dettingen, 1743.

George III. (1738–1820), King of Britain, grandson of George II.; succeeded to throne, 1760; married Charlotte Sophia of Mecklenburg-Strelitz; was determined to destroy Whig oligarchy, and by aid of a party formed by him, known as 'King's Friends,' he brought about resignation of Pitt. After a succession of short-lived ministries, he formed a ministry under Lord North, and from 1770 till 1782 the government was in accordance with his own wishes. For the policy which led to Declaration of Independence of U.S.A., 1776, he was largely responsible. After his unconstitutional rejection of Fox's India Bill, 1783, he entrusted the government to William Pitt the younger, who remained in power during the struggle against French Republic. In 1801 parliaments of England and Ireland were united. During struggle with Napoleon, 1803–15, George had the support of the country, but while issue was still in doubt he became permanently insane, 1811. George was not eminently wise as a king, but he was hard-working and disinterested; he prided himself on being English, and this, coupled with his exemplary domestic life, helped him to retain the esteem of his subjects. His reign was marked by great imperial and industrial development.

George IV. (1762–1830), King of Great Britain and Ireland; son of George III.; acted as prince regent from 1811, and succeeded, 1820. In 1795, after previous secret marriage with Mrs. Fitzherbert, he married Caroline of Brunswick, whom he endeavoured to divorce, 1820, but failed largely owing to public hostility. During his reign the progress which had set in on conclusion of Fr. war was continued. Largely through Canning's foreign policy, Great Britain assumed commanding position on Continent. In home affairs reforms were effected, and the Catholic Emancipation Bill was passed, 1829. George's levity and profligacy, and his treatment of Queen Caroline, made him most unpopular.

George V. (1865–1936), King of Great Britain; second son of Edward VII.; *b.* at Marlborough House, June 3; entered navy, 1877; served on the *Britannia* training-ship; midshipman, 1883; lieutenant, 1885; commander of gunboat *Thrush*, 1890. Left service, 1892, when he became heir-apparent on the death of his elder brother, Duke of Clarence. As Duke of York entered House of Lords, 1893; married Princess Victoria Mary of Teck, 1893; their children were: (1) Edward (now Edward VIII.); (2) Albert, Duke of York; (3) Mary, Princess Royal; (4) Henry, Duke of Gloucester; (5) George, Duke of Kent; (6) John (*d.* 1919). In 1901, on his father's accession, he was created Prince of Wales. During tour of the colonies in the *Ophir*, opened first Commonwealth Parliament, 1901. On May 6, 1910, King George ascended the throne. On Dec. 12, 1911, His Majesty was proclaimed Emperor of India in person at Delhi Durbar. During Great War he laboured incessantly for his country, making frequent visits to Fr. front and great munition and industrial centres. In 1917 the family name of the King was changed to Windsor by Royal proclamation. A grave illness in 1928 evoked spontaneous demonstration of sympathy and concern from all his subjects. In 1935 the silver jubilee of his reign was celebrated enthusiastically throughout the Empire.

George I. (1845–1913), King of Greece; son of Christian IX. (Denmark); elected after expulsion of Otto I., 1863; co-operated in policy of a league of Balkan states; assassinated at Salonica.

George, DAVID LLOYD. See LLOYD GEORGE.

George, HENRY (1839–97), American economist; *b.* Philadelphia; founder of 'single tax' movement in America, and 'Taxation of Land Values' movement in Great Britain; supporter of Irish Land League; pub. *Progress and Poverty* (1879), *Irish Land Question* (1881), *A Perplexed Philosopher* (1893).

Gérard (*zhā-rär'*), FRANÇOIS PASCAL, BARON (1770–1837), Fr. artist; *b.* Rome; studied at Paris under David; his portraits of Madame Bonaparte, 1799, and others placed him in forefront of contemporary painters; his historical paintings include *La Bataille D'Austerlitz* (1810), and *Entrée de Henri IV. à Paris* (1814).

Gerard', JAMES WATSON (1867–), Amer. lawyer; *b.* in New York state; ambassador to Germany, 1913–17; recalled when U.S.A. entered Great War. Published *My Four Years in Germany* (1917), etc.

Gerhardt (*gār'härt*), ELENA (1885–), German singer; *b.* Leipzig; studied at Leipzig Conservatorium and under Nikisch, the famous conductor; one of the greatest *lieder* singers in the world.

Gerhardt, PAUL (1607–76), German Lutheran hymn-writer; *b.* in Saxony; author of 123 hymns, among which is 'Befiehl du deine Wege,' translated by Wesley in 'Commit thou all thy griefs.'

German, Sir Edward (1862–), Eng. musical composer; *b.* Whitchurch, Shropshire; director of music at Globe Theatre, 1889; soon devoted himself entirely to musical composition; works include the operas *Nell Gwynn* (1900), *Merrie England* (1902), *A Princess of Kensington* (1903), and *Tom Jones* (1907); his coronation march and hymn were performed at coronation of George v., 1911.

German'icus Cæsar (15 B.C.–A.D. 19), Rom. general; son of Nero Claudius Drusus; adopted by Emperor Tiberius; consul A.D. 12; subsequently commanded eight legions on Rhine, distinguishing himself against Germans; rousing Tiberius's jealousy, was sent to East; death probably due to poisoning.

Gérôme (*zhā-rōm'*), Jean Léon (1824–1904), French painter and sculptor; *b.* in Haute-Saône; painter of historical, classical, and Eastern subjects; his *Ave, Cæsar! morituri te salutamus* is well known.

Geron'tius (360–413), Byzantine general; dethroned Constantine iii., 408, and besieged Byzantium; his troops mutinied and he committed suicide; subject of poem by Cardinal Newman, set to music by Sir Edward Elgar.

Gerry, Elbridge (1744–1814), American politician; *b.* Marblehead, Mass.; vice-president U.S.A., 1812; term 'gerrymander' coined when he rearranged political districts in favour of his party.

Gerstenberg, Heinrich Wilhelm von (1737–1823), Ger. poet; *b.* Tondern, Schleswig; wrote the dramatic work *Ugolino*, and was a pioneer of the *Sturm-und-Drang* school.

Gervex (*zher-vā'*), Henri (1852–1929), Fr. artist; *b.* Paris; his earlier works were classic studies, of which *Bacchantes and Satyr* (Luxembourg Gallery) is a notable example; his later pictures include *The Coronation of Nicholas II.*, *Dr. Péan at the Salpêtrière*, *Return from the Ball.*

Gervinus (*ger-fē'noos*), Georg Gottfried (1805–71), Ger. literary historian; *b.* Darmstadt; prof. at Göttingen, 1835; wrote *Händel und Shakespeare* (1849–52, Eng. trans. by F. E. Bunnet, 1863, later ed. 1877), once a classic amongst Shakespearian commentaries.

Gesenius (*ge-sēn'i-oos*), Heinrich Friedrich Wilhelm (1786–1842), Ger. Oriental scholar; *b.* Nordhausen, Hanover; inaugurated the scientific method of Semitic philology.

Ghazal'i (or Ghazzali), Abu Hamid Mohammed ibn-Ahmed, Al (1058–1111), Oriental philosopher, commonly known as Algazel; represents critical side of Arab. philosophy; chief work, *Overthrow of the Philosophers.*

[Autobiography, *Confessions of Al-Ghazzali*, trans. by C. Field (1909).]

Ghiberti (*gē-ber'tē*), Lorenzo (1378–1455), most notable Ital. sculptor and metal worker of 15th cent.; *b.* Florence; renowned for his bronze doors of the Baptistery, Florence, said by Michelangelo to be worthy the gates of Paradise; he wrote autobiographical *Commentaries.*

Ghirlandajo (*gēr-län-dä'yō*), a family of Florentine artists. The most accomplished were (1) Domenico (1449–94), surnamed *Il Ghirlandajo* from early employment in making jewelled garlands; famed for his frescoes and portraits; had as pupil Michelangelo. (2) Ridolfo (1483–1561), son of (1); oil painter; executed large scenic canvases for public occasions; was patronized by Medici family.

Ghose (*gōz*), Lalmohun (1849–

1909), Ind. lawyer and politician; *b.* Krishnagar, Bengal; called to Eng. bar, 1873; practised as lawyer in India; member of Bengal Legislative Council, 1892–95; president of Ind. National Congress, 1903; did much for the advance of Ind. interests along constitutional lines.

Gibb, ROBERT (1845–1932), Scot. painter and Royal limner for Scotland; *b.* Laurieston; keeper of National Gallery of Scotland, 1895–1907; well known for military pictures, among which are *The Retreat from Moscow*, *The Thin Red Line*, *Hougomont* (1815).

Gibbon, EDWARD (1737–94), English historian; *b.* Putney; went to Oxford Univ., 1752. Temporarily converted to the Church of Rome, he was placed by his father under the tutelage of a Calvinist minister of Lausanne, and in 1754 returned to Protestantism; fell in love with Mlle. Suzanne Curchod, the future Madame Necker, but on command of his father broke off the engagement; returned to England, 1758. During Seven Years' War became captain in Hampshire Militia, 1759; during 1763–5 toured the Continent; at Rome first conceived his immortal work, the *Decline and Fall of the Roman Empire* (1764), first vol. of which appeared in 1776. The famous chapters 15 and 16, with their cynical account of the growth of Christianity, produced a great clamour. Meanwhile he had been elected M.P. for Liskeard, and afterwards for Lymington, his parliamentary career lasting from 1774–83. From 1779–80 was at the Board of Trade and Plantations, with a sinecure salary of £800 a year. The second and third vols. of his history were issued in 1781; retired to Lausanne, 1783, where last three vols. of his history were written and pub. in 1788. His *Memoirs* came out in 1789. He returned to England, 1793, and died at London.

His style is stately, and though occasionally monotonous, is in keeping with the subject. The vast range, learning, and insight of Gibbon's work place it among the great works of history.

[*The Decline and Fall of the Roman Empire*, ed. by J. B. Bury, 7 vols. (1909–13); *Memoirs*, ed. by Lord Sheffield; *Gibbon*, by Morison (English Men of Letters Series, 1887).]

Gibbons, GRINLING (1648–1721), Anglo-Dutch wood-carver and sculptor; *b.* Rotterdam; executed Whitehall statue of James II., and monument to Newton in Westminster Abbey; chiefly celebrated for beauty and delicacy of his wood-carving, of which the choir stalls at St. Paul's Cathedral and the archiepiscopal throne at Canterbury are examples.

Gibbons, JAMES (1834–1921), Amer. Rom. Catholic prelate; *b.* Baltimore; became Bishop of Richmond, Virginia, 1872, and Archbishop of Baltimore and Primate of U.S.A., 1877; cardinal, 1886; was keenly interested in labour problems; publications include *The Faith of our Fathers*, *Our Christian Heritage*, and *The Ambassador of Christ*.

Gibbs, SIR PHILIP (1877–), war correspondent and novelist; entered journalism, 1902; war correspondent with Bulgarian army, 1912, and on Western Front in Great War; author of several books about the Great War, and novels, including *The Street of Adventure* (a sketch of life in Fleet Street), *The Middle of the Road*, *The Anxious Days*, and *Blood Relations*. Knighted, 1920.

Gibson, CHARLES DANA (1867–), Amer. black-and-white artist and book illustrator; *b.* Roxbury, Mass.; the creator of the 'Gibson girl'; also famed for series of drawings, such as *The Education of Mr. Pipp.*

Gibson, JOHN (1790–1866), British sculptor; *b.* Conway; studied under Canova at Rome; famed for beauty of his classical subjects, such as *The Tinted Venus, Pandora, Mars and Cupid.*

Gibson, WILFRID (1878–), Eng. poet; engaged in social work and served in the ranks during Great War; poems chiefly deal with humble folks and their lives in the great industrial centres; works include *Daily Bread* (1910), *Thoroughfares* (1914), *Friends* (1916), *Neighbours* (1920), *Collected Poems, 1905–25* (1926).

Gide (*zhēd*), ANDRÉ PAUL GUILLAUME (1869–), Fr. man of letters; *b.* Paris; works, which display exquisite talent, include *Les Cahiers d'André Walter* (1891), *Paludes* (1895), *Le Roi Candaule* (1901), *L'Immoraliste* (1902), *La Porte Etroite* (1909), *Isabelle* (1911), *La Symphonie pastorale* (1919), *Caractères* (1925), and *La Retour du Tchad* (1928).

Gideon, the warrior-judge who delivered Israel from the Midianites (Judges 5–8).

Gifford, ADAM (1820–87), Scot. judge; *b.* Edinburgh; called to the bar, 1849; judge of Court of Session, 1870. Bequeathed £80,000 to the four Scot. universities for the foundation of lectureships in natural theology (*Gifford Lectures*).

Gilbert, SIR ALFRED (1854–1934), Eng. sculptor; *b.* London; studied under Boehm and later at Paris, his style exhibiting the influence of Fr. 'modernity' and a profound study of Florentine art of the 15th and 16th centuries; R.A., 1892; prof. of sculpture at the Royal Academy, 1900–9; among his chief works are the *Clarence Memorial* (Windsor), the *Fawcett Memorial* (Westminster Abbey), *Queen Victoria Monument* (Winchester), the *Shaftesbury Fountain* (*Eros*, London).

Gilbert, SIR HUMPHREY (*c.* 1539–83), Eng. navigator; *b.* near Dartmouth; half-brother of Sir Walter Raleigh, with whom he set sail on a fruitless voyage of discovery, 1578; took possession of Newfoundland, 1583, but was drowned on his way home.

Gilbert, SIR JOHN (1817–97), Eng. historical painter and illustrator; *b.* London; president Water-colour Soc., 1871; R.A., 1876; amongst his pictures are *Richard II. resigning the Crown, Agincourt, Naseby*; illustrated many Brit. classics.

Gilbert, SIR JOSEPH HENRY (1817–1901), Brit. chemist; *b.* Hull; along with Sir J. B. Lawes of Rothamsted he did valuable research work in agricultural chemistry; instituted nitrogen treatment of soil; experiments described in *Agricultural Investigations at Rothamsted* (1895).

Gilbert, WILLIAM (1540–1603), physician to Queen Elizabeth; *b.* Colchester; a careful and accurate chemist; studied terrestial magnetism and wrote earliest treatise on magnetism; invented the terms 'electric force' and 'electricity.'

Gilbert, SIR WILLIAM SCHWENCK (1836–1911), Eng. playwright and humorist; *b.* London; won distinction with his *Bab Ballads*; became world-famous as librettist in conjunction with Sir Arthur Sullivan; their comic operas include *H.M.S. Pinafore, The Pirates of Penzance, Patience,* and the immortal 'Savoy' series—*Iolanthe, The Mikado, The Yeomen of the Guard, The Gondoliers,* etc. His ability as a versifier was almost unsurpassed.

[*W. S. Gilbert*, by E. A. Browne (1907); *Gilbert and Sullivan and their Operas*, by Cellier and Bridgeman (1914).]

Gildas (516?–70), earliest Eng. historian; wrote *De Excidio et Conquestu Britanniæ*; the sole authority for Brit. history during the 5th cent.

Giles (GIL, or GILLES), ST. (*fl.* 6th or 7th cent.), abbot who founded hermitage of St. Giles, France, and patron of lepers, cripples, and beggars; festival, Sept. 1.

Giles, ERNEST (1839–97), Australian explorer; *b.* Bristol, but went early to Melbourne; crossed from Adelaide to Perth, 1874–6, and led other expeditions which discovered L. Amadeus, etc., and confirmed belief of arid nature of interior; author of *Australia Twice Traversed* (1889), etc.

Giles, HERBERT ALLEN (1845–1935), Brit. Oriental scholar; was in consular service in China; prof. of Chinese at Cambridge Univ.; did much to arouse interest in China; awarded Triennial Gold Medal of Royal Asiatic Soc., 1922; member of Fr. Academy, 1924; among his numerous works are *Chinese Sketches, A Chinese-English Dictionary, A Chinese Biographical Dictionary, A History of Chinese Literature.*

Gill, SIR DAVID (1843–1914), Scot. astronomer; worked in private observatory of Lord Lindsay at Dunecht, Aberdeenshire; Royal astronomer at Cape of Good Hope, 1879–1907; made important investigations in stellar parallax; international chart of heavens largely due to him.

Gill, ERIC (1882–), Eng. sculptor; *b.* Brighton; apprenticed as an architect but ultimately turned to sculpture; one of finest of living sculptors; pub. his views on his art in *Id quod visum placet, A Practical Test of the Beautiful* (1926), and *Christianity and Art* (1927); sculptures include *A Crucifix* (1910), *Torso* (1912), *The Stations of the Cross* (1913), *Deposition* (1924), *Christ driving the Moneylenders out of the Temple* (1922–3), and *Prospero and Ariel,* Broadcasting House (1933).

Gillray, JAMES (1757–1815), Eng. caricaturist; *b.* Chelsea; began life as engraver, and after hard struggles became one of England's greatest comic artists; works are remarkable for exquisite finish; the chief butts of his satire, apart from social follies, were George III. and Napoleon.

Gilman, DANIEL COIT (1831–1908), Amer. educationist; first president Johns Hopkins Univ., Baltimore, U.S.A., 1875–1902; exercised a marked influence on education in America.

Ginkel (*ging'kel*), GODART VAN (1630–1703), 1st Earl of Athlone; Dutch soldier; came to England with William of Orange; reduced Ireland to submission, 1691.

Ginsburg, CHRISTIAN DAVID (1831–1914), rabbinical scholar; *b.* Warsaw; one of the original members of committee for revision of Eng. version of O.T.; works include *The Kabbalah* (1865), *The Massorah, The Moabite Stone* (1871), and *Critical Text of the Hebrew Bible* (new ed. 1911).

Giolitti (*jol-ē'tē*), GIOVANNI (1842–1928), Ital. statesman; *b.* Mondovi, Piedmont; head of the Ital. Treasury, 1889; four times premier between 1892 and 1914, when he was practically ruler of Italy; broke power of Socialism; became Conservative, and later Radical-Socialist; strove to keep Italy out of the Great War, 1915; again premier, 1920; re-elected, 1921, but resigned shortly after.

Giordano (*jor-dän'ō*), LUCA (1632–1705), Italian painter; *b.* Naples; nicknamed *Fapresto* ('Look Alive') from his speed with his brush; spent years at Span. court. His best work is the *Nativity* (Madrid).

Giorgione (*jor-jō'ne*) (*c.* 1477–1511), Venetian painter; one of the supreme colourists of the

Renaissance; works flooded with sunshine, and noted for splendour of their backgrounds; chief are *Madonna* (Castelfranco), *The Sleeping Venus* (Dresden), *Fête Champêtre* (Louvre), *Family of Giorgione* (Venice).

Giotto (*jot'ō*), AMBROGIO DI BONDONE (1267?–1337), Italian artist and architect; *b.* near Florence; pupil of Cimabue; called the 'father of modern painting'; first to break away from eccles. convention; executed famous mosaic, the *Navicella*, in vestibule of St. Peter's, Rome, but worked chiefly in fresco—greatest series found in Arena Chapel, Padua, and on ceiling of lower church of St. Francis, Assisi, where he depicted Franciscan allegories, *Poverty*, *Chastity*, and *Obedience*; equally renowned as an architect; designed exquisite campanile and façade of Santa Maria del Fiore at Florence.

Giral'dus Cambren'sis (*c.* 1146–1220), Welsh historian; *b.* in Pembrokeshire; entered the priesthood; wrote *Topographia Hibernica*, *Itinerarium Cambriæ*—works of considerable value. *Works* pub. in 8 vols. (1861–91).

Girardon (*zhē-rär-don'*), FRANÇOIS (1628–1715), Fr. sculptor; *b.* Troyes; worked at decoration of palace at Versailles and the Trianon palace under Le Bonn; his masterpiece is the *Tomb of Richelieu* in the Sorbonne (Paris).

Gissing, GEORGE ROBERT (1857–1903), Eng. novelist of realistic school; *b.* Wakefield; typical works are *Demos*, *The Nether World*, *New Grub Street*, *Born in Exile*, *The Odd Women*, all depicting sordid monotony of lower middle-class and working-class life. *The Private Papers of Henry Ryecroft* is to some extent autobiographical; wrote also an appreciation of *Charles Dickens* and collection of charming travel-sketches, *By the Ionian Sea*; his own story is told by Morley Roberts in *The Private Life of Henry Maitland*.

Giulio Romano (*joo'lē-ō rō-män'ō*) (GIULIO DI PIETRO FILIPPO DE' GIANNUZZI) (*c.* 1492–1546), Ital. artist and architect; *b.* Rome; pupil and assistant of Raphael; along with his fellow-pupil, Penni, completed Raphael's unfinished frescoes in the Vatican, the *Battle of Constantine* and the *Apparition of the Cross* being entirely his; afterwards entered service of Duke of Mantua, and rebuilt cathedral of Mantua.

Gladstone, HERBERT JOHN, VISCOUNT (1854–1930), Eng. statesman, youngest son of W. E. Gladstone; *b.* London; history lecturer at Keble Coll., Oxford, 1877–1880; financial secretary to War Office, 1886; under-secretary to Home Office, 1892–4; first commissioner of works, 1894–5; chief Liberal whip, 1899–1905, and home secretary, 1905–10; was appointed first gov.-gen of Commonwealth of S. Africa, being raised to the peerage on appointment; author of *W. E. Gladstone* (1918) and *After Thirty Years* (1928).

Gladstone, JOHN HALL (1827–1902), Eng. chemist and physicist; *b.* London; studied under Liebig at Giessen; Fullerian professor of chemistry, Royal Institution, 1874–7; first president of Physical Soc., 1874; president of the Chemical Soc., 1877–9; author of *Life of Faraday*, *The Chemistry of Secondary Batteries*, etc.

Gladstone, WILLIAM EWART (1809–98), Brit. statesman; *b.* Liverpool of Scot. parents; educated at Eton and Oxford; entered Parliament, 1832, as Tory member for Newark, and soon made his mark in the House; held various offices in Sir Robert Peel's government from 1834; his criticism of Disraeli's budget, 1852, caused the downfall of Lord Derby's Tory administration; was chancellor of the Exchequer in 1852, resigned 1855, and for some years remained out of office.

In 1859 he joined the Liberal ministry of Lord Palmerston as chancellor of the Exchequer, and devoted himself to remission of taxation and sweeping tariff clear of duties; in 1865 became leader of House of Commons under Earl Russell; in 1866 he introduced a Reform Bill which was defeated; but the succeeding Tory government, led by Disraeli, brought in household suffrage. Gladstone brought forward a series of resolutions in favour of disestablishing the Irish Church, and defeated the government; the Liberals returned to power, 1868, Gladstone becoming prime minister; after disestablishing the Church of Ireland and passing Land Bill he brought in a bill dealing with Irish univ. education, but was defeated, and retired into private life.

Emerging from retirement he denounced Disraeli's foreign and colonial policy, particularly with regard to the Bulgarian atrocities, and in 1880 returned to power, having been elected for Midlothian, and immediately set himself to deal with Ireland; the Land League was suppressed and its leaders imprisoned, and a coercion bill was carried through. In foreign policy his government was severely criticized in consequence of the murder of General Gordon, and was defeated, 1885. After a short Conservative administration Gladstone came into power again in 1886, and his Home Rule Bill resulted in a split in Liberal party and in defeat of government. Aided by Liberal Unionists, Conservatives came back into office. Prime minister for the fourth time, 1892, Gladstone again introduced a Home Rule Bill which was passed by Commons but rejected by Lords, and his speech against the upper chamber was his last in the House, as shortly thereafter he resigned. He died at Hawarden, and was buried in Westminster Abbey. Gladstone was a brilliant departmental head, a magnificent party leader and orator, and probably the greatest parliamentarian since Pitt.

[*Lives*, by J. Morley (1903), Barnett Smith (1879), G. W. E. Russell (1891), and H. Paul (1901).]

Glas, John (1695–1773), Scot. cleric; *b.* Auchtermuchty, Fife; ordained in 1719; founded Prot. sect known as Glassites or Sandemanians, aiming at independence of Church government and simplicity of doctrine, expounding his ideas in *Testimony of the King of Martyrs* (1729).

Glazounow (*gla-zoo'nov*), Alexander Constantinovich (1865–1936), Russ. composer; *b.* Leningrad; studied under Rimsky-Korsakov; first symphony played at Weimar, 1884; conducted in London, 1897; director of St. Petersburg Conservatoire, 1906; works include *Stenka Razin*, *The Kremlin*, a symphonic poem, *The Sea*, an orchestral fantasia, and *Chant du Menestrel.*

Gleig (*gleg*), George Robert (1796–1888), Brit. author and soldier; *b.* Stirling; served in Peninsular War, 1813–14, and in America, 1814; later took holy orders, and became chaplain-general of forces, 1844, and inspector-general of military schools, 1846; pub. *History of India* (1830–5); *Lives of Military Commanders* (1831); and biographies of Warren Hastings, Clive, and Wellington.

Glendower (*glen'door*), Owen (*c.* 1359–1415), Welsh hero; claimed descent from Llewellyn and from ruling princes of Wales; opposed Henry iv., assumed title of Prince of Wales, and gave his rebellion character of national movement for Welsh independence; defeated in 1405 by Prince Henry, whose capture of Harlech in 1409 ended the war.

Gloucester (*glos'ter*), HUMPHREY, DUKE OF (1391–1447), Eng. soldier; son of Henry IV. and Mary de Bohun; present at Agincourt, 1415; regent during Henry V.'s absence in France, 1421, 1422; protector during Henry VI.'s minority; patron of learning.

Gloucester, THOMAS OF WOODSTOCK, 1ST DUKE OF (1355–97), Eng. statesman; youngest son of Edward III.; practically ruled England from 1386–9; arrested on charge of plotting against his nephew, Richard II., in 1397, and put to death.

Gluck (*glook*), CHRISTOPH WILLIBALD (1714–87), Ger. composer; *b.* in Upper Palatinate; studied at Vienna and Milan; first great operas of new type, *Orfeo* (1762) and *Alceste* (1769), in which he adapted music to the dramatic situations expressed in the libretto. Under patronage of Marie Antoinette attained remarkable success with *Iphigénie en Aulide* (1774), and *Armide* (1777). His greatest and last work, *Iphigénie en Tauride* (1779), secured him complete victory over his Ital. rival Piccini.

Gmelin (*gmā'len*), name of distinguished family of Ger. scientists, the most prominent of whom was LEOPOLD (1788–1853), chemist; *b.* Göttingen; prof. of medicine and chemistry at Heidelberg, 1817–51; author of classic *Handbuch der Chemie* (1817–19, Eng. trans. 1848), and discoverer of potassium ferricyanide.

Gneisenau (*gnī'ze-now*), AUGUST WILHELM ANTON, COUNT NEITHARDT VON (1760–1831), Prussian field-marshal; *b.* in Prussian Saxony; fought on Brit. side in Amer. War of Independence; took part in occupation of Poland, 1793–4; fought at Jena, 1806; was Blücher's chief of staff in Waterloo campaign.

Gneist (*gnīst*), HEINRICH RUDOLF HERMANN FRIEDRICH VON (1816–95), Ger. jurist; *b.* Berlin; prof. of jurisprudence, Berlin, 1844; senior judge of supreme court, 1875. A great admirer of England and her institutions; among his most important works are *History of English Constitution* and *History of the English Parliament*.

Gobineau (*gōb-ē-nō'*), JOSEPH ARTHUR, COMTE DE (1816–82), Fr. diplomat and author; *b.* Paris; diplomatic service, 1849–76; voluminous author; fame rests chiefly on *L'Inégalité des Races Humaines*, *Nouvelles Asiatiques*, *Souvenirs de Voyage*, and *La Renaissance*, all of which have been trans. into English.

Godard (*gō-där'*), BENJAMIN LOUIS PAU (1849–95), Fr. composer; *b.* Paris; wrote operas *Dante*, *La Vivandière*, and *Jocelyn*, the dramatic symphony *Le Tasse*, and many charming songs.

Godfrey OF BOUILLON (*c.* 1060–1100), Fr. knight, a leader of First Crusade, 1096; captured Jerusalem, 1099; became virtual ruler of Jerusalem; died after defeating invasion from Egypt; hero of Fr. mediæval romance poems, such as *Chanson de Jérusalem*.

Godi'va (1040–80), Saxon lady; wife of Leofric, Earl of Mercia and overlord of Coventry; at her husband's challenge, she rode naked through the town to secure for inhabitants relief from taxation he had imposed; a procession commemorating the event, and instituted 1678, forms part of annual fair of Coventry.

Godol'phin, SIDNEY, EARL OF (*c.* 1645–1712), Eng. politician; *b.* in Cornwall; page to Charles II., 1662; P.C. and lord of Treasury,

1679–1710; promoted Anglo-Scot. Union; dismissed from office, 1710.

[*Life*, by Hugh Elliot (1888).]

Godunov, BORIS. See BORIS GODUNOV.

God'win, or GODWINE (*c.* 990–1053), Earl of Wessex; justiciar under Canute; assisted in restoration of Edward the Confessor, 1042, who married Godwin's daughter; exiled, 1051, owing to his opposition to Edward's policy; returned and forced the king to reinstate him with full honours; father of Harold.

Godwin. (1) WILLIAM (1756–1836), Eng. revolutionary writer; intellectual leader of philosophic Radicals, whose principles he enunciated in *Inquiry concerning Political Justice* (1793); failed as a book publisher, but held sinecure government post till his death; pub. *History of the Commonwealth*; *Caleb Williams*, a novel; and various other works. (2) MARY WOLLSTONECRAFT (1759–97), Eng. writer, wife of (1); pioneer of woman's movement; pub. *Vindication of the Rights of Women* (1792) and *Original Stories for Children*, illustrated by Blake; her daughter Mary became Shelley's wife.

Godwin-Austen, HENRY HAVERSHAM (1834–1923), Eng. soldier and military surveyor; *b.* Teignmouth; rendered great service by his surveys in Kashmir, 1857, Ladakh, 1862, and Bhutan, 1863–65; had charge of survey operations in the Garo, Khasi, N. Cachar, and Naga Hills, and Manipur, 1866–76; made many remarkable ascents in the Himalayas; Mt. Godwin-Austen (K^2) was named in his honour.

Goebbels, PAUL JOSEPH (1897–), German politician; minister for propaganda since 1933; was a leader in anti-semitic movement.

Goes (*goos*), HUGO VAN DER (*c.* 1420–82), Flem. artist; *b.* Ghent; painter of famous triptych now in the Uffizi Gallery, Florence, and of side panels of an altar-piece, introducing portraits of James III. and his queen, Margaret of Denmark, now in Holyrood Palace.

Goethals (*gō'thälz*), GEORGE WASHINGTON (1858–1928), U.S.A. army engineer; *b.* Brooklyn; chief engineer of Panama Canal, 1907, which he completed, 1914, and subsequently, 1914–17, was first civil governor of Canal zone, being promoted major-general, 1915; received many academic honours and medals.

Goethe (*gĕ'tĕ*), JOHANN WOLFGANG VON (1749–1832), Ger. poet, dramatist, philosopher, and scientist; *b.* Frankfurt-on-Main; at Leipzig studied law, 1765–8, and wrote vol. of lyrics, *Annette*, and two plays. Returned to Frankfurt an invalid; graduated as doctor of law at Strasbourg, 1771. At Strasbourg became a leader in the 'Sturm und Drang' movement. At Wetzlar, 1772, he became friends with Kestner, whose fiancée, Charlotte Buff, is immortalized in *Die Leiden des jungen Werthers* (1774), which made him world-famous. In 1773 the historical drama *Götz von Berlichingen* (first really great work) appeared. In 1775 Goethe wrote the *Faust* of the 'Sturm und Drang' period. From 1775 he lived in Weimar, first as the guest of Duke Karl August, holding several responsible government posts; formed intimate friendship with Frau von Stein; ennobled, 1782. To the Weimar period belong dramas, *Egmont*, *Die Geschwister*, *Iphigenie* (prose version), *Harzreise im Winter*, *Briefe aus der Schweiz*, etc. The spell of an Ital. visit, 1786–8, and the Greek ideals of harmony and restraint, are seen in *Die Italienische Reise* (pub. 1816–17); *Iphigenie* (poetical version, 1787) and *Torquato Tasso* (1790), by many reckoned as his masterpieces. In 1794 Goethe formed deep and lasting friendship with Schiller, contributing to his journal, 1795–6, *Wilhelm Meisters Lehrjahre*, one of the most influential of his works. He was director of Weimar Court Theatre, 1791–1817. His *Hermann und Dorothea* (narrative poem) and some of his finest ballads appeared in 1798. In 1806 Goethe married his mistress, Christiane Vulpius. To his later years belong first part of *Faust* (1808), which established his reputation as the greatest poet of his time; *Die Wahlverwandtschaften* (novel, 1809); autobiographical *Dichtung und Wahrheit* (1811); *Wilhelm Meisters Wanderjahre* (romance, 1821); and *Faust* (second part, 1833).

Of handsome presence and amazing versatility, Goethe ranks as one of the most universally gifted of writers, distinguished in letters, philosophy, science, and politics, a profound thinker and a great lyric poet.

[*Lives*, by G. H. Lewes (1873), H. Düntzer (Eng. trans. 1908), A. Bielschowsky (Eng. trans. 1905–8), P. Hume Brown (1920), and J. G. Robertson (1927).]

Gogh (chōch), VINCENT WILLEM VAN (1853–90), Dutch artist; *b.* Brabant; one of the leaders of the Post-Impressionist school; painted figures, still-life, and landscapes; works include *The Potato Eaters*, *The Restaurant on Montmartre*, and *Mairie au 14 juillet*.

Go'gol, NIKOLAI VASILIEVICH (1809–52), Russ. novelist; *b.* in Poltava; well known for his Cossack tales and novels exposing the abuses of officialdom; achieved fame with his *Evenings in a Farm* (1831–4), and *Mirgarod*, the latter including *Taras Bulba*; other works are, *The Government Inspector*, a satirical comedy, and his novel, *Dead Souls*.

Goldie, SIR GEORGE DASHWOOD TAUBMAN (1846–1925), Eng. administrator; *b.* Isle of Man; entered the Royal Engineers; travelled widely in Africa, and visiting the Niger region in 1877, conceived the idea of adding it to the Brit. Empire; charter granted to Royal Niger Co., 1886; territory finally transferred to Britain, 1900.

Goldo'ni, CARLO (1707–93), Ital. dramatist; *b.* Venice; took his degree in law, but had a passion for playwriting; founded the modern school of Ital. comedy; went to Paris, 1761, and met with success there; in great favour with the king, who granted him a pension.

[*Memoirs* (Eng. trans. 1877).]

Goldschmidt. See LIND, JENNY.

Goldsmith, OLIVER (1728–74), Brit. poet, dramatist, and man of letters; son of an Irish clergyman; *b.* Pallas, Longford; educated Trinity College, Dublin; studied medicine at Edinburgh and Leyden. Wandered on foot over Europe, and in 1756 turned bookseller's hack in London; after severe struggles began to be known in literary society, and made the acquaintance of Johnson, Burke, Reynolds, Garrick, and others. Plain in appearance and marked with smallpox, generous to a fault, extremely foolish in most of his actions, lacking in the ability to take care of money, nevertheless beloved by everybody. His *Vicar of Wakefield* (1766) is one of the masterpieces of Eng. fiction; equally noteworthy are his plays, *She Stoops to Conquer* (1773) and *The Good-natured Man*; his poems, *The Deserted Village* and *The Traveller*; wrote many other works — histories, biographies, essays, and poems. Johnson said of him that he 'left scarcely any style of writing untouched, and nothing that he did not adorn.'

[*Lives*, by J. Foster (1848), A. Dobson (1888), and R. A. King (1910).]

Goldstücker (*gōlt'stook-er*), THEODOR (1821–72), Ger. Sanskrit scholar; *b.* Königsberg; of Jewish extraction; prof. of Sanskrit at Univ. Coll., London, 1852–72; founder of the Sanskrit Text Soc., 1866.

Goliath, Philistine giant who challenged army of Israel; slain with a sling and a stone by David. See 1 Sam. 17.

Gollancz (*gol'ans*), SIR ISRAEL (1863–1930), Eng. man of letters; *b.* London; lecturer in English, Cambridge, 1896–1906; prof. of English, King's Coll., London, 1906–30; first secretary of the Brit. Academy, 1902; an authority on Shakespeare and Old Eng. literature.

Golovnin (*gō-lōv-nēn'*), VASILY MICHAILOVICH (1776–1831), Russ. naval commander and navigator; *b.* in Ryazan province; surveyed coast of Kamchatka and N.W. America, 1807; taken prisoner by the Japanese, 1810; returned to Russia, 1814; circumnavigated the globe, 1817–8; wrote *Narrative of my Captivity in Japan*, also *Journey Round the World.*

Goltz, BARON KOLMAR VON DER (1843–1916), Ger. soldier, commonly known as GOLTZ PASHA; *b.* Bielkenfeld, E. Prussia; was wounded in Austrian War, 1866; staff officer in Franco-Ger. War, 1870–71; lecturer on military history at Berlin, and wrote his classic works, *Rossbach and Jena* and *A Nation in Arms* (1883); reorganized the Turk. army, 1883–95; retired from Prussian army with rank of field-marshal, 1913. In the Great War was governor of Brussels, Sept.–Oct. 1914, and supervised the defences of the Dardanelles and the Turk. campaign. He died the day after the fall of Trebizond.

Gomme (*gom*), SIR GEORGE LAURENCE (1853–1916); Eng. folklorist; *b.* London; founder and subsequently president of Folklore Soc.; numerous publications on folklore.

Gompers, SAMUEL (1850–1924), Amer. labour leader; *b.* London; son of a Dutch Jew; emigrated to America, 1863; president of Amer. Federation of Labour from 1882 till his death, except in 1894; champion of labour legislation; president of International Commission on Labour Legislation of Paris Peace Conference, 1919; president International Labour Conference, Washington, 1919.

Goncharov (*gon-chä-rof'*), IVAN ALEXANDROVICH (1812–91), Russ. novelist; *b.* Simbirsk; held posts in finance and postal departments; went as secretary to Admiral Putiatin, 1856, to open commercial relations with Japan; works include *A Common Story*, *Oblomov*, his masterpiece, and *The Precipice.*

Goncourt (*gon-koor'*), EDMOND DE (1822–96), and JULES DE (1830–70), brothers; Fr. authors; the first-named *b.* Nancy, the second at Paris; collaborated as historians of the 18th cent., and as critics of Japanese art. As the originators of naturalism they shared with Gustave Flaubert the earliest place in the Fr. realistic school. Among their histories are *Portraits intimes du XVIIIe siècle*, *L'Art du XVIIIe siècle*, and *Journal des Goncourt*; their novels include *Sœur Philomène*, *Renée Mauperin*, and *Manette Salomon.* Edmond was founder of the Goncourt prize awarded annually to an author of talent not yet publicly recognized.

[*Lives*, by Delzant (French; 1889), Belloc-Lowndes and Shedlock (English; 1895).]

Gonzag'a, Ital. family, rulers of Mantua from 1328 to 1708. GIOVANNI FRANCESCO II. obtained marquisate for military services to Emperor Sigismund, 1433; and LUIGI, 1568–91, surrendered his marquisate to his brother and entered the Soc. of Jesus, being eventually canonized as St. Aloysius.

Goodall, FREDERICK (1822–1904), Eng. artist; *b.* London; R.A., 1863. A visit to Egypt, 1857–9, strongly influenced his work, and his Eastern and Scriptural pictures proved very popular.

Goodsir, JOHN (1814–67), Scottish anatomist; *b.* Anstruther; studied dentistry; curator of museum of Royal Coll. of Surgeons, Edinburgh, and, 1846, prof. of anatomy at Edinburgh Univ.; carried out researches on structure of the tissues, being one of the first to recognize importance of cell life.

Goossens (*goos'ens*), EUGENE (1893–), Eng. composer and conductor; *b.* London, of Belgian parentage; educated at Bruges Conservatoire and Royal Coll. of Music, London; has conducted many of the leading orchestras in this country and in America; his compositions include *Five Impressions of a Holiday* (1915), *Rhapsody* (1916), and *The Eternal Rhythm* (1920).

Gorchakov, or GORTSCHAKOV, ALEXANDER MICHAELOVITCH (1798–1883), the most distinguished member of Russ. princely family; ambassador to Württemberg and Austria; foreign minister, 1856; chancellor, 1863; for some time most powerful minister in Europe. To same family belong ANDREAS IVANOVITCH (1768–1855), who fought against Napoleon; MIKHAIL (1795–1861), Russ. commander-in-chief who conducted defence of Sevastopol; and PETER DMITRIEVITCH (1790–1868), who was in command of a division at Alma and Inkerman.

Gordian'us, name of two Rom. emperors. (1) MARCUS ANTONIUS GORDIANUS AFRICANUS (A.D. 159–238), emperor only for a month. (2) MARCUS ANTONIUS GORDIANUS, grandson of above; emperor, 238; inflicted defeat on Persians; assassinated, 244.

Gordon, ADAM LINDSAY (1833–70), national poet of Australia; *b.* Fayal (Azores); educated at Cheltenham, Woolwich, and Oxford. Went to S. Australia, 1853; coming into a legacy, entered Parliament, but gave up his seat to plunge heavily into steeplechasing; becoming involved in monetary difficulties he shot himself. His last and best volume is *Bush Ballads and Galloping Rhymes* (1870). Other successful publications include *Sea Spray and Smoke Drift* and *Ashtaroth.*

[*Poems*, ed. by F. M. Robb (1912); *Adam Lindsay Gordon*, by E. Humphries and D. Sladen (1912).]

Gordon, CHARLES GEORGE (1833–85), Brit. soldier and administrator; *b.* Woolwich; served in Crimea, 1854–5; joined military expedition to China, 1860; during Taiping rebellion took command of some Chin. troops, trained by European and Amer. officers; relieved Chansu, 1863; reorganized his troops, named 'ever victorious'; final suppression of rebellion largely due to his leadership; refused all pecuniary rewards from Chin. emperor. On returning home Gordon became commanding royal engineer at Gravesend, and supervised construction of forts to defend Thames; devoted means and spare time to philanthropy. Entering service of Khedive of Egypt in 1873, for nearly seven years (the last three as governor of the Sudan) he laboured to establish law and order in Upper Nile district; resigned, 1880, but returned to Sudan at request of Brit. Government, 1884, to arrange withdrawal of Egyptian garrisons in danger owing to the Mahdi's rebellion; was shut up in Khartoum by rebels; bravely defended city for a year, but was treacherously killed two days before the arrival of relief force under Wolseley. 'Chinese Gordon' lives as a national hero, thanks to his gallantry, his integrity as administrator, his piety, and his tragic fate.

[*Modern Egypt*, by Lord Cromer (1908); *Lives*, by Sir W. F. Butler (1889) and Bernard M. Allen (1931); *The Journals of Major-General Gordon at Khartoum* (1885).]

Gordon, CHARLES W. See CONNER, RALPH.

Gordon, LORD GEORGE (1751–93), son of Duke of Gordon; *b.* London; fanatical leader of Gordon Riots, 1780—a violent protest against the removal of R.C. disabilities; arrested, tried for treason, but acquitted; afterwards joined the Jewish faith; died in Newgate.

Gordon, SIR JOHN WATSON. See WATSON-GORDON, SIR JOHN.

Gordon, PATRICK (1635–99), Russian general, of Scot. birth; rose to high military rank under Peter the Great.

Gordon-Cumming, ROUALEYN GEORGE (1820–66), Scot. traveller and hunter; detailed his experiences in *Five Years of a Hunter's Life in South Africa* (1850).

Gore, CHARLES (1853–1932), Eng. theologian; canon of Westminster, 1894–1902; held successively bishoprics of Worcester, 1902–4, Birmingham, 1905–11, and Oxford, 1911–19; leader of High Church party in Church of England; numerous publications include *The Incarnation* (1891), *The Body of Christ* (1901), *The New Theology and the Old Religion* (1908), *Belief in God* (1921), *Christ and Society* (1928), and *The Philosophy of the Good Life* (1930).

Gor'gas, WILLIAM CRAWFORD (1854–1920), Amer. surgeon; *b.* Mobile; as chief sanitary officer in Havana, 1898–1902, cleared the city of yellow fever. In Panama Canal zone exterminated yellow fever and bubonic plague, and reduced malaria, typhoid, and dysentery by 50 per cent.

Görgei (*ger'gī*), ARTHUR (1818–1916), Hungarian patriot; fought for Hungarian revolution, 1848–9, winning numerous successes, 1848–49; became dictator on Kossuth's resignation, 1849; surrendered before combined Austrian and Russ. force at Vilagos, 1849, and was confined at Klagenfurt for twenty years.

Göring, HERMANN (1893–), German general and politician. Was noted flying officer during Great War; minister for air since 1933. Intimately associated with Hitler and Nazi movement.

Gor'ky, MAXIM (1868–), pseudonym of ALEXEY MAXIMOVICH PESHKOV, Russ. writer; *b.* Nijni-Novgorod (now Gorky); in early life an ikon painter, pedlar, scullery boy, baker's apprentice, etc.; travelled widely in E. and S. Russia; became journalist, and by his tale *Chelkash* (1895) established himself as a writer of intense realism. Always a revolutionist, repeatedly imprisoned, he supported the Soviet government; works include *My Fellow Traveller* and *Twenty-six Men and a Girl* (1902), *Childhood* (1915), *In the World* (1917), *Reminiscences of my Youth* (1924), *Fragments from my Diary* (1924), and *The Magnet* (1931).

Gorst, SIR JOHN ELDON (1835–1916), Eng. statesman; *b.* Preston; called to the bar, 1865, and entered Parliament; became a member of the Fourth Party; was solicitor-general, 1885–6, under-secretary for India, 1886–91, and financial secretary to the Treasury, 1891–2; represented Britain at the Berlin Labour Congress, 1890, and the Labour Commission, 1891–3, was largely due to his initiative. Author of *The Children of the Nation* (1907) and *New Zealand Revisited* (1908).

Goschen (*gō'shen*), GEORGE JOACHIM, VISCOUNT (1831–1907), Brit. statesman; *b.* London; grandson of Leipzig bookseller (1752–1828) of same name; first lord of Admiralty, 1871; opposed Home Rule and joined Unionists; chancellor of Exchequer, 1887–92; carried out conversion of National Debt, 1888; again first lord of Admiralty, 1895–1900; resolute supporter of Free Trade.

Gosling, HARRY (1861–1930), Eng. Labour leader; *b.* London; for many years a Thames waterman and lighterman; became president of Transport and General Workers Union; entered Parliament, 1923; minister of Transport and Paymaster-General, 1924–9; made Companion of Honour, 1917; wrote *Up and Down Stream* (1927), a volume of reminiscences.

Goss, SIR JOHN (1800–80), Eng. composer; *b.* Fareham; chorister of the Chapel Royal, 1811–16; organist of St. Luke's, Chelsea, 1824, and of St. Paul's Cathedral, 1838; his works include anthems, hymns, and glees.

Gosse (*gos*), SIR EDMUND (1849–1928), Eng. critic and miscellaneous writer; assistant librarian in the Brit. Museum, 1867–75; translator to the Board of Trade, 1875–1904; librarian at the House of Lords, 1904–14; he gained many foreign distinctions and pub. numerous works on Eng. and foreign literature, notably Ibsen's works; works include *Collected Poems* (1896), *History of Eighteenth Century Literature* (1889), *History of Modern English Literature* (1897), *Lives* of John Donne, Sir Thomas Browne, Swinburne, Ibsen, etc.; *Leaves and Fruit* (1927); *Father and Son* (1907), his most noted book, was crowned by French Academy.

Gottschall (*got'shäl*), RUDOLF VON (1823–1909), Ger. author; *b.* Breslau; wrote epics, dramas, novels, etc.; plays include *Pitt and Fox, Amy Robsart*, and *Mazeppa*; novels include *Welke Blätter, Das Goldene Kalb*, and *Die Tochter Rübezahls.*

[Autobiography, *Aus meiner Jugend* (1898).]

Gottsched (*got'shed*), JOHANN CHRISTOPHE (1700–66), Ger. literary critic; *b.* near Königsberg; sought to reform the drama along the lines of pseudo-classicism. His literary influence was destroyed by criticism of Lessing. His wife, LUISE ADELGUNDE VICTORIA, *née* KULMUS (1713–62), wrote original comedies of merit.

Gough (*goff*), SIR HUBERT DE LA POER (1870–), Brit. general; educated at Eton and Sandhurst; joined 16th Lancers, 1889, served in Tirah expedition, 1897–8, S. African War, 1899–1902; during the Great War commanded 5th Army, 1916–18; he was recalled after the Germans had broken through his sector of the front.

Gough, HUGH, VISCOUNT (1779–1869), Brit. general; *b.* Limerick; served in Peninsular War; commanded in China, 1842, and successfully conducted Mahratta war, 1843, and Sikh war, 1845–9; field-marshal, 1862.

[*Life*, by R. S. Rait (1903).]

Goujon (*goo-zhon'*), JEAN (*c.* 1510–*c.*1566), French sculptor; *b.* Paris; employed on decoration of Rouen Cathedral and on restorations of Saint-Germain-l'Auxerrois; he designed the façade at the Louvre, the Henri II. staircase, etc.; finest sculptures include the *Fontaine des Innocents* and *Dianne Chasseresse.*

Gould (*goold*), SIR FRANCIS CARRUTHERS (1844–1925), Eng. caricaturist; *b.* Barnstaple; joined Stock Exchange; caricatured for *Truth, Pall Mall Gazette*, and *Westminster Gazette*, of which last he became assistant ed.; author and illustrator of *Picture Politics, The Modern Froissart, Who killed Cock Robin?*, etc.

Gould, JAY (1836–92), Amer. financier and railway proprietor; *b.* Roxbury, New York; after various employments turned his attention to railway speculation and eventually controlled 10,000 miles; by 1908 the 'Gould group' included over 19,000 miles; was instrumental in combining the telegraph companies into the Western Union, 1881, and securing control of elevated railway of New York.

Gounod (*goo-nō'*), CHARLES FRANÇOIS (1818–93), Fr. composer; *b.* Paris; won Grand Prix de Rome, 1839; studied sacred music in Rome, especially Palestrina and Bach; first opera, *Sappho* (1851); *Faust* (1859), most popular work and long the standard type of Fr. opera; *Philémon et Baucis* (1860); *La Reine de Saba* (1862); *Mireille* (1864); *Romeo and Juliet* (1867). Gounod wrote during the later part of his life two oratorios, *The Redemption* and *Mors et Vita*; a master of orchestration; romantic in style, with great dramatic passion.

Gouraud (*goo-rō'*), HENRI JOSEPH EUGÈNE (1867–), Fr. soldier; *b.* Paris; had brilliant career in Morocco; was youngest commander of high rank in Fr. army at outbreak of Great War; commander of Fr. Expeditionary Force at Dardanelles, 1915, where he lost an arm; drove Germans out of Champagne, 1918; high commissioner of Syria and Cilicia, and commander of army of Levant, 1919; military gov. of Paris since 1923.

Gourgaud (*goor-gō'*), GASPAR, BARON (1783–1852), Fr. soldier; *b.* Versailles; distinguished for personal devotion to Napoleon, and shared exile at St. Helena till the jealousy of fellow-attendants caused his departure; wrote *Campagne de 1815*, *Journal inédit de Sainte-Hélène*, etc.

Gow, ANDREW CARRICK (1848–1920), Eng. artist; *b.* London; R.A., 1891; painter of costume subjects; among his principal pictures are *Relief of Leyden* (1876), *After Waterloo* (1890), *Queen Victoria's Diamond Jubilee* (for the City Corporation), etc.

Gow, NEIL (1727–1807), Scot. violinist and composer of dance music; *b.* near Dunkeld; did valuable work in preserving old Scot. melodies.

Gower, JOHN (*d.* 1408), Eng. poet; b. (probably) in Kent; of good family; called by his friend Chaucer 'the moral Gower.' His Eng. poem, *Confessio Amantis*, consists of love stories and meditations. He also wrote in Lat. *Vox Clamantis*, dealing with the Peasants' Revolt; and in Fr. *Speculum Meditantis*, a poem on the nature of man.

Gowrie, JOHN RUTHVEN, 3RD EARL OF (1577–1600), Scot. noble; central figure of so-called Gowrie Conspiracy, a plot to dethrone or assassinate James VI., who was lured to Gowrie's house in Perth, 1600. Gowrie and his brother Alexander were seized by the king's followers and slain on the spot. Existence of plot has never been authoritatively established.

[*James VI. and the Gowrie Mystery*, by A. Lang (1902).]

Goya y Lucientes (*gō'yä ē loo-thē-en'tes*), FRANCISCO JOSÉ DE (1746–1828), Span. painter; *b.* near Saragossa; on his return from Rome, 1774, he was appointed painter-in-ordinary to Charles IV., of whom he painted one of his best portraits; most of his paintings are in Spain, but the National Gallery, London, has a fine collection of his etchings and aquatints.

Goyen (*goi'en*), JAN JOSEPHSZOON VAN (1596–1656), Dutch artist; *b.* Leyden; a famous master of landscape, his favourite subjects being Dutch scenes and views of the Rhine.

Gracchus (*grak'oos*), plebeian Rom. family of *gens* Sempronia, of which most noted members were TIBERIUS SEMPRONIUS and GAIUS SEMPRONIUS, generally known as the *Gracchi*. Tiberius Sempronius (*c.* 167–133 B.C.) fought under Scipio against Carthaginians; became tribune, 133, when he passed agrarian law, allotting public lands to the poor; killed by patricians headed by Scipio Nasica. Gaius (158–121 B.C.) became tribune, 123; introduced many reforms, passed corn law, and re-established agrarian law; rejected for tribunate, 121; escaped from ensuing riots, but was found dead next day; like his brother, of lofty character, an ardent reformer, and a fine orator.

Grace, WILLIAM GILBERT (1848–1915), Eng. cricketer; *b.* Downend, Gloucestershire; was for some forty years engaged in first-class cricket, and was known as England's 'champion'; an excellent all-round cricketer; highest score in first-class cricket was 344; scored over 100 runs on 126 occasions; in eight seasons scored over 1,000 runs and took over 100 wickets, in two of these seasons scoring over 2,000 runs; a doctor by profession; recipient of a national testimonial, 1896, of £10,000.

Graham, SIR GERALD (1831–99), Brit. general; *b.* Acton, Middlesex; distinguished himself in Crimean War and China War of 1860; commanded in Egyptian War at Tell-el-Kebir; wrote *Last Words with Gordon* (1887).

Graham, JOHN. See DUNDEE, VISCOUNT.

Graham, STEPHEN (1884–), Eng. author; has travelled widely in different parts of the world, but chiefly in Russia; works include *A Vagabond in the Caucasus, Undiscovered Russia, With Poor Emigrants to America* (1914), *Private in the Guards* (1919), *Children of the Slaves* (1920), *The Lay Confessor* (1928), and *Stalin* (1931).

Graham, THOMAS (1805–69), Brit. physicist and chemist; *b.* Glasgow; master of the mint, 1855–69; investigated molecular physics and the diffusion of gases; he divided substances into crystalloids and colloids, and investigated their behaviour towards membranes; he also discovered polybasic acids, and obtained three acids from phosphoric anhydride; to him we owe the introduction of bronze coinage.

Grahame, KENNETH (1859–1932), Eng. author; *b.* Edinburgh; secretary to the Bank of England; retired, 1908. Wrote three classics for children, *The Golden Age, Dream Days,* and *The Wind in the Willows.*

Grahame-White, CLAUDE (1879–), Brit. aviator and aeronautical engineer; a pioneer of petrol-driven car; was first Englishman to obtain aviator's certificate; afterwards established a flying school at Pau, 1909, and won many prizes, including the Gordon-Bennett international trophy. He has written many books on aviation.

Grainger, PERCY ALDRIDGE (1883–), Australian pianist and composer; *b.* Melbourne; received musical education mainly in Germany; noted for his collection of folk-songs; compositions include *Molly on the Shore, Shepherd's Hey, Hill Songs,* and *Marching Song of Democracy.*

Gramont (*grä-mon'*), ANTOINE ALFRED AGÉNOR, DUC DE (1819–80), Fr. statesman and diplomat; *b.* Paris; ambassador to Italy, 1857, and Austria, 1861; foreign minister, 1870; did much to precipitate Franco-German War.

Gramont, PHILIBERT, COMTE DE (1621–1707), Fr. courtier; a favourite of Louis XIV.; was exiled, and appeared at the court of Charles II. of England; famous *Mémoires de la Vie du Comte de Gramont* were compiled by his brother-in-law, A. Hamilton.

Granby, JOHN MANNERS, MARQUIS OF (1721–70), Eng. soldier; served at Culloden, 1746; his exploits at Minden, 1759, and afterwards as commander-in-chief of the Brit. forces in Germany during Seven Years' War, made him the popular hero of England.

Grant, SIR ALEXANDER (1826–84), Brit. educationist; *b.* New York; held various educational appointments in India, and was principal of Edinburgh Univ., 1868–84. It was mainly through his energies that the New Edinburgh Medical School was built.

Grant, SIR FRANCIS (1803–78), Brit. artist; *b.* Edinburgh; his *Equestrian Group of Queen Victoria and Others* brought him fame, and he became the fashionable portrait painter of Britain; president of Royal Academy, 1866.

Grant, JAMES (1822–87), Scot. novelist; *b.* Edinburgh; author of *The Romance of War, The Yellow Frigate*, and other lively historical and military novels; also *Old and New Edinburgh* (1884–7).

Grant, JAMES AUGUSTUS (1827–92), Scot. soldier and explorer; *b.* Nairn; served during Indian Mutiny and Abyssinian Expedition, 1868; was associated with Speke in exploration of sources of the R. Nile, 1860–3.

Grant, SIR JAMES HOPE (1808–75), Brit. general; *b.* Perthshire; brother of Sir Francis Grant; served with distinction against Chinese, 1839–42, and Sikhs, 1845–6 and 1848–9; took a leading part in suppressing Mutiny, and commanded expedition against China, 1860–1; commander-in-chief of army of Madras, 1861; was one of most notable strategists of his time.

Grant, ULYSSES SIMPSON (1822–85), Amer. soldier and statesman; president of U.S.A.; *b.* at Point Pleasant, Ohio; served in Mexican War, 1846–8. Soon after outbreak of Civil War, 1861, Grant became brigadier-general; took Paducah, 1861; captured Fort Donelson, 1862, in which year he was defeated at Shiloh; successfully besieged Vicksburg, and defeated Confederates at Chattanooga, 1863; appointed commander-in-chief, 1864, and fought great number of severe actions, his method being to wear down his opponents by sheer weight of numbers. Finally defeated Confederates at Five Forts, 1865, after which their surrender at Appomattox ended the war. After Lincoln's assassination he became war minister during Johnson's presidency; elected president in 1868, and re-elected in 1872. During his administration the *Alabama* dispute with Britain was settled. He was overtaken by financial misfortune in 1884, to remedy which he wrote his *Personal Memoirs*, which proved an enormous success.

Granville, JOHN CARTERET, EARL (1690–1763), English politician; supported George I. against Jacobites; ambassador to Sweden, 1719; lord-lieutenant of Ireland, 1724–30; secured recall of patent for 'Wood's halfpence'; opposed Walpole's peace policy; president of council, 1751–63.

Granville-Barker, HARLEY GRANVILLE (1877–), actor, playwright and theatrical manager; *b.* London; introduced plays of Ibsen and Shaw to British public; as a dramatist remarkable for combination of literary idealism and realism; works include *The Voysey Inheritance* (1905), *Waste* (1917), etc.

Gratianus (*grä-shi-än'oos*) (359–83), Rom. emperor, whose weakness led to revolts; rebellion of Maximus in Britain and Gaul ended in his assassination.

Grattan, HENRY (1746–1820), Irish orator and statesman; *b.* Dublin; called to Irish bar, 1772; entered Irish Parliament, 1775; as leader of national party, advocated removal of Brit. authority, his attitude leading to enrolment of 80,000 Irish volunteers; Britain was compelled to yield to Irish demands, 1779, and Ireland obtained legislative independence; for this service Grattan received grant of £50,000; in 1800 he opposed bill for Union of Great Britain and Ireland; afterwards sat in the United Parliament, 1808, and worked unceasingly for Catholic emancipation; as a statesman he was broad-minded, disinterested, and patriotic; as an orator, brilliant, witty, and remarkably eloquent.

Grätz (*grets*), HEINRICH (1817–91), Jewish historian; *b.* Posen; prof. in Jewish Theological Seminary, Breslau, 1854, and in Breslau Univ., 1869; his *Geschichte der Juden* (11 vols., 1853–75), a standard work on its subject, has been trans. into English.

Graves. (1) ALFRED PERCEVAL (1846–1931), Irish writer; *b.* Dublin; inspector of schools, 1875–1910; author of 'Father O'Flynn'; contributed largely in prose and verse to *Punch* and other periodicals; collected folk-songs, and took a prominent part in Irish renaissance; pub. *To Return to all that* (1930), an autobiography. (2) ROBERT RANKE (1895–), Brit. writer; *b.* London; son of (1); served in Great War; pub. *Collected Poems* (1927); his autobiography, *Good-bye to all that* (1929), deals largely with his war experiences; also pub. vols. of critical essays, *The Real David Copperfield* (1932), *I, Claudius* (1933), and *Claudius the God* (1934).

Graves, CLOTILDE INEZ MARY, pseudonym RICHARD DEHAN (1863–1932), Brit. novelist and dramatist; *b.* co. Cork; plays include *Puss in Boots* (1888) and *A Maker of Comedies* (1903); her novels include *The Dop Doctor* (1910), *The Sower of the Wind* (1927), and *The Man in the Mask* (1931).

Gray, THOMAS (1716–71), Eng. poet; *b.* London; educated Eton and Cambridge; spent two years abroad with Horace Walpole, and afterwards returned to Cambridge. He declined the laureateship; prof. of modern history at Cambridge from 1768. His poems include 'Ode on a Distant Prospect of Eton College' (1747) and 'Pindaric Odes'; in 1750 he completed the famous 'Elegy written in a Country Churchyard.' He was a noted letter-writer and a sound scholar. No one who published so little holds so high a place in literature.

[*Lives*, by E. Gosse, 'Eng. Men of Letters,' 1889), and D. C. Tovey (1890).]

Greeley, HORACE (1811–72), Amer. journalist and politician; *b.* Amherst; editor of the *New Yorker*, the *Jeffersonian*, and the *Log Cabin;* founded the *New York Tribune*, 1841, which soon acquired great influence; was one of first advocates of emancipation of slaves.

[*Lives*, by Jas. Parton, L. U. Reaves, L. D. Ingersoll, and F. N. Zabriskie.]

Green, JOHN RICHARD (1837–83), Eng. historian; *b.* Oxford; vicar of Stepney, 1865; librarian at Lambeth, 1869; historical works: *A Short History of the English People* (1874), on which his fame chiefly rests, *The Making of England* (1882), and *The Conquest of England* (1883), completed by his wife. He conceived history as the story of a people's political and social development.

Green, THOMAS HILL (1836–82), Eng. philosopher; *b.* Birkin, Yorks; educated at Rugby and Oxford; prof. of moral philosophy,

1878–82; his *Prolegomena to Ethics* and lectures on the *Principles of Political Obligation* were pub. after his death. Green was perhaps the most important Eng. philosopher of his day, and led the reaction against Hume and Herbert Spencer.

[*Works*, ed. by R. L. Nettleship (3 vols., 1888).]

Greenaway, KATE (1846–1901), Eng. artist; *b.* London; noted for her delightful drawings of children. Wrote much of the verse and prose in some of the books which she illustrated.

Greene, ROBERT (*c.* 1560–92), Eng. dramatist and pamphleteer; *b.* Norwich; educated Oxford and Cambridge; travelled on the Continent; subsequently settled in London. His plays, including *Friar Bacon*, are distinguished by their humour, and are invaluable as pictures of Elizabethan life. His prose writings are innumerable, and upon one of these, *Pandosto, the Triumph of Time*, Shakespeare founded *The Winter's Tale*. He also wrote some delightful lyrics, and *A Groat's-worth of Wit*, partly autobiographical, the epilogue a violent attack on Shakespeare.

[*Plays and Poems*, ed. by Churton Collins (1905).]

Greenwood, FREDERICK (1830–1909), Eng. journalist; *b.* London; ed. of *Cornhill*, 1864–8, later of *Pall Mall Gazette* and *St. James's Gazette;* one of greatest and most influential journalists of 19th cent.; learning that a Fr. syndicate meant to purchase Suez Canal shares held by Khedive, he conveyed the information direct to Lord Derby, which resulted in Britain's purchase.

Greet, SIR PHILIP BEN (1856–), Eng. actor-manager; organized 'Woodland players' for performance of Shakespearian plays out of doors; joint producer of the morality play *Everyman*; has made a feature of Shakespearian plays for young people at the 'Old Vic,' London.

Grégoire (*grā-gwär'*), HENRI (1750–1831), Fr. statesman and ecclesiastic; *b.* near Lunéville; Bishop of Blois, 1791–1801; took important part in abolishing royal power, 1792, but opposed execution of the king; did much for education in France; largely through his influence the works of art in Paris were saved during the reign of terror.

[*Mémoires* (1837); *Lives*, by A. Debidour (1881) and L. Maggiolo (1884).]

Gregory, name borne by sixteen popes. Most important were: GREGORY I., ST., surnamed THE GREAT (*c.* 540–604); *b.* Rome; elected Pope, 590; with him begins the temporal sovereignty of the papacy; distinguished by his missionary zeal, he sent Augustine to England; his struggle with John of Constantinople widened breach between Eastern and Western Churches; writings include *Liber Pastoralis*, trans. into Anglo-Saxon by order of Alfred the Great; in music his name is associated with *Gregorian chants.* GREGORY VII., HILDEBRAND (*c.* 1020–85), *b.* Tuscany; he did most to establish eccles. supremacy of the Papacy, and increased the importance of its temporal power; before his election as Pope in 1073 he had directed the policy of the four preceding popes. On being deposed by the Emperor Henry IV. because of his prohibition of imperial investitures, Gregory retaliated by excommunicating the emperor, and compelled him to do penance at Canossa, 1077. The dispute was subsequently renewed, and Henry besieged and captured Rome. Liberated by Robert Guiscard, Gregory retired to Salerno. Canonized in 1729. GREGORY IX. (*d.* 1241) was elected Pope, 1227. He excommunicated Emperor Frederick II.,

1227, for refusing to join crusade; but peace was restored by submission of emperor. The dispute was renewed, and emperor again excommunicated, 1239. Frederick was marching towards Rome when Gregory died. GREGORY XI. (1330–78), *b.* Limousin; elected Pope, 1370; retransferred the papal see from Avignon to Rome, 1377; tried to suppress heresy and to reform religious orders. GREGORY XIII. (1592–85), *b.* Bologna; elected Pope, 1572; founded Jesuit Coll. at Rome; reformed Calendar, 1582; approved massacre of St. Bartholomew. GREGORY XVI. (1765–1846), *b.* Belluno; elected Pope, 1831; an autocrat, he discouraged democracy on principle, although he encouraged learning and fine arts; favoured Jesuits.

Gregory OF NAZIANZUS, ST. (*c.* 329–*c.* 389), one of the four fathers of the Eastern Church; archbishop of Constantinople, 378; resigned appointment and returned to Asia, 381; his famous five discourses on the Trinity gained for him the title of 'Theologus.'

Gregory OF NYSSA, ST. (*c.* 331–*c.* 396), a copious writer, strictly orthodox, on the subjects of Trinity and Incarnation; described as 'a father of fathers'; a constructive and speculative theologian; chief work, *Twelve Books against Eunomius.*

Gregory OF TOURS, ST. (538–94), 'father of French history'; Bishop of Tours, 573; took part in various political quarrels of Merovingian kings; wrote several theological works, but greatest work is *History of the Franks*, chief authority for history of Gaul in 6th cent.

Gregory, Scot. family famous in medicine and science. (1) JAMES (1638–75), *b.* Aberdeen; invented Gregorian telescope, 1661; was first prof. of mathematics, Edinburgh, 1674. (2) DAVID (1661–1708), *b.* Aberdeen; nephew of (1), whom he succeeded in chair of mathematics, Edinburgh; later was prof. of astronomy, Oxford. (3) JOHN (1724–73), grandson of (1); *b.* Aberdeen; was prof. of medicine at Aberdeen, 1755, and Edinburgh, 1766. (4) JAMES (1753–1821), eldest son of (3); *b.* Aberdeen; succeeded father in chair at Edinburgh; compounded 'Gregory's powder'; wrote on philosophical and medical subjects. (5) WILLIAM (1803–58), son of (4); prof. of chemistry, Glasgow, 1837, Aberdeen, 1839, and Edinburgh, 1844; was pupil of Liebig; wrote *Outlines of Chemistry* (1845).

[*The Academic Gregories*, by A. G. Stewart (Famous Scots Series, 1896).]

Gregory, ISABELLA AUGUSTA PERSSE, LADY (1852–1932), Irish playwright and authoress; *b.* co. Galway; married Sir W. H. Gregory, 1880; stimulated national drama in Ireland and fostered interest in its folklore; works include *Cuchulain of Muirthemne* (1902), *Gods and Fighting Men* (1904), *Seven Short Plays* (1909), *Irish Folk History Plays* (1912), and *The Dragon* (1920).

Greiffenhagen (*grī′fen-häg-en*), MAURICE (1862–1931), Brit. artist; R.A., 1922; head of life department, Glasgow School of Art, 1906; many of his works are in leading collections, and include *The Idyll*, *The Judgment of Paris*, *Women by a Lake*, *Dawn.*

Grenfell, BERNARD PYNE (1869–1926), Eng. Egyptologist; *b.* Birmingham; made several important discoveries with A. S. Hunt of anc. papyri, including that of the *Logia*, or *Sayings of our Lord.*

Grenfell, GEORGE (1849–1906), Eng. explorer; *b.* near Penzance; sent by the Baptist Missionary Soc. to the Cameroons, 1874; surveyed about 2,000 miles of Upper

Congo; served on royal commission for delimitation of frontier between Congo state and Port. territory (1891–3).

[*Life*, by G. Hawker (1909).]

Grenfell of Kilvey, Francis Wallace, 1st Baron (1841–1925), Brit. field-marshal; *b.* London; served in wars in S. Africa and Egypt from 1878; was sirdar and commander-in-chief of the Egyptian army, 1885–92; commanded forces in Egypt, 1897–8; governor of Malta, 1899–1903; commander of forces in Ireland, 1904–8; created peer, 1902; field-marshal, 1908.

Grenfell, Sir Wilfred Thomason (1865–), Brit. medical missionary; *b.* Parkgate, Cheshire; fitted out first hospital ship for the North Sea Fisheries; went to Labrador, 1892, where he has built hospitals, established orphanages and schools, and organized industrial schemes; has received numerous honours both from America and Britain; works include *Labrador Days* (1921) and *Labrador Looks at the Orient* (1928); knighted, 1927; lord rector of St. Andrews Univ., 1929–31.

Grenville, George (1712–70), Brit. prime minister, 1763; attacked liberty of press in Wilkes's case, 1764; passed the Stamp Act, 1765, the immediate cause of America's secession.

Grenville, Sir Richard (*c.* 1541–91), Eng. mariner; as commander of *Revenge* had celebrated fight against fifteen Span. ships; died shortly after action.

Grenville, William Wyndham, Baron (1759–1834), Brit. politician; son of George Grenville; formed 'All the Talents' ministry, 1806, which abolished slave trade; was strong advocate of R.C. emancipation.

Gresham, Sir Thomas (1519–79), Eng. merchant; helped to consolidate and improve Eng. trade by building the Royal Exchange, 1566–71; devoted much of his wealth to educational and charitable purposes; founder of Gresham College.

Gresset (*grā-sā'*), Jean Baptiste Louis (1709–77), Fr. poet; *b.* Amiens; whilst teaching in Jesuit college at Rouen pub. his poem *Vert Vert* (1734), which brought him immediate fame; also wrote *La Chartreuse* (1734), the satire *L'Abbaye* (1741), and plays, the most successful of which was *Le Méchant* (1747).

Grétry (*grā-trē'*), André Ernest Modeste (1741–1813), Belgian musical composer; *b.* Liége; studied in Rome and Paris; gained fame for his comic operas, of which he wrote over fifty.

Greuze (*grooz*), Jean Baptiste (1725–1805), Fr. artist; *b.* near Mâcon; established his claims as painter with his first picture, *The Bible Reading*. His reputation rests largely on his portraits and single heads, especially those of young women and girls.

[*J. B. Greuze*, by Normand (1892).]

Grev'ille, Charles Cavendish Fulke (1794–1865), Eng. author; clerk of the Council in Ordinary for nearly forty years. His *Memoirs* (1875–87) are valuable for the contribution which they make to the social and official life of 19th cent.

Grévy (*grā-vē'*), François Paul Jules (1807–91), Fr. statesman; *b.* Mont-sous-Vaudrey, Jura; president of National Assembly, 1873; president of republic, 1879, and 1885–7; he was noted for his sagacity and patriotism.

[*Lives*, by Barbou (1879) and Bertrand (1892).]

Grey, Albert Henry George, 4th Earl (1851–1917); Brit. administrator; sat in Parliament, 1880–6; friend of Cecil Rhodes; administrator of Rhodesia, quelling Matabele rising, 1896–7; gov.-gen. of Canada, 1904–11.

Grey, CHARLES, 2nd EARL GREY (1764–1845), Brit. statesman; *b.* Falloden, Northumberland; first lord of Admiralty, 1806; after Fox's death became foreign secretary in 'All the Talents' ministry; succeeded to earldom, 1807; prime minister, 1830; his ministry produced the Reform Bill, which was carried, 1832, by Grey's obtaining royal permission to create sufficient peers to ensure its passing.

[*Life of Grey*, by Hon. C. Grey (1861).]

Grey OF FALLODON, EDWARD, 1ST VISCOUNT (1862–1933), Brit. statesman, grandson of Sir George Grey; educ. Winchester and Oxford; Liberal member for Berwick-on-Tweed, 1885–1916; under-secretary for foreign affairs, 1892–5, with Rosebery as his chief; secretary of state for foreign affairs, 1905–16, receiving in 1912 the honour of K.G. During his tenure of office the Triple Entente was developed; in 1907 he concluded Anglo-Russian agreement, which settled outstanding Asiatic rivalries, and added to his reputation during Morocco crisis, 1909, and by inducing the belligerents in the Balkan War to sign the Peace of London, May 30, 1913. He made earnest but unsuccessful efforts to preserve peace after the Austrian ultimatum to Serbia, 1914; later he paved the way for Italy's entry into Great War. Owing to failing eyesight entered House of Lords as viscount, 1916. On Asquith's resignation, Dec. 1916, he retired from Foreign Office and became ardent advocate of the League of Nations; went to U.S.A. on a special mission, 1919; lord rector of Edinburgh Univ., 1920, and chancellor of Oxford Univ., 1928. Was a noted tennis player, angler, and student of bird life. His publications include *Twenty-five Years, 1892–1916* (1925), *Fallodon Papers* (1926), and *Charm of Birds* (1927).

Grey, SIR GEORGE (1812–98), Brit. colonial administrator; *b.* Lisbon; led exploring expeditions in N.W. and W. Australia, 1837–38; governor of S. Australia, 1841, of New Zealand, 1846, conciliating the Maoris; governor of Cape Colony, 1854–61, when he tried to federate S. African states; again governor of New Zealand, 1861, speedily terminating second Maori War; premier of New Zealand, 1877–9.

[*Lives*, by G. C. Henderson (1907) and J. Collier (1909).]

Grey, LADY JANE (1537–54), the 'nine days' queen' of England; granddaughter of Henry VIII.'s sister, Mary; married Lord Guildford Dudley, whose father, the Duke of Northumberland, influenced Edward VI. to nominate Lady Jane as his successor; on his death, 1553, she was proclaimed queen. Meanwhile Mary, daughter of Henry VIII., rallied her supporters and caused Lady Jane and her husband to be thrown into the Tower, where they were beheaded.

Grey, ZANE (1875–   ), Amer. novelist; *b.* Zanesville, Ohio; practised as dentist in New York, 1898–1904; devoted himself to Wild West fiction; works include: *The Lone Star Ranger, The Rainbow Trail, Wildfire, The Vanishing American.*

Griboyedov (*grē-bō-yă'dof*), ALEXANDER SERGIEVICH (1795–1829), Russian dramatist; *b.* Moscow; secretary to the Russ. embassy in Persia and in Georgia; famed for satirical drama, *Goré et Uma* ('The Mischief of Being Clever'), dealing with Moscow official life.

Grieg (*grēg*), EDVARD HAGERUP (1843–1907), Norweg. composer and pianist; *b.* Bergen; studied at Leipzig and Copenhagen; his numerous compositions include many *Lieder, Melodien,* and *Volks-Lieder,* with sonatas and other pianoforte pieces; his best-known work is the *Peer Gynt* suite.

[*Lives*, by H. T. Finck (1906) and R. H. Stein (1921).]

Griffith, ARTHUR (1872–1922), Irish politician; *b.* Dublin; a compositor by trade; became leading member of various nationalist organizations; founded Sinn Fein movement; in 1899 began publication of a newspaper to propagate his views; imprisoned several times as a rebel between 1916 and 1920; acted as leader in negotiations with Brit. government, 1921, which resulted in treaty establishing I.F.S., of which he was first president.

Griffith, SIR RICHARD JOHN (1784–1878), Irish geologist; *b.* Dublin; carried out boundary survey of Ireland; pub. geological map of Ireland. Originator of method of land valuation in Ireland known as 'Griffith's Valuation.'

Grillparzer (*gril'pärt-ser*), FRANZ (1791–1872), Austria's greatest dramatist and poet; *b.* Vienna; his plays include *Sappho* (1818), *Das Goldene Vliess* (1821), *König Ottokars Gluck und Ende* (1825), *Des Meeres und der Liebe Wellen* (1831). His lyric poetry is of high literary quality. He wrote also a prose romance, *Der Arme Spielmann* (1848), and some literary criticisms. Eng. trans. of several of his plays have appeared.

Grimaldi (*grē-mäl'dē*), JOSEPH (1779–1837), Eng. clown; one of the greatest drolls known to the Eng. stage; wrote *Memoirs*, ed. by Charles Dickens (1838).

Grimm, JAKOB LUDWIG KARL (1785–1863) and WILHELM KARL (1786–1859), Ger. philologists and folklorists; brothers, *b.* Hanau; after holding various library appointments, were called to Berlin by Frederick William IV., and both made professors at the univ. and members of the Academy of Sciences, 1841; here spent the remainder of their lives; collaborated in the world-renowned collection of fairy tales *Kinder- und Hausmärchen* (1812–15), and many learned volumes on the German languages such as *Geschichte der Deutschen Sprache* (1848), and mythological works such as *Deutsche Mythologie* (1835), etc. Jakob propounded the theory of 'consonant shift,' known as Grimm's Law, in his *Deutsche Grammatik* (1819), a pioneer work on philology.

[*Die Brüder Grimm*, by C. Francke (1899).]

Grimthorpe, EDMUND BECKETT, 1ST BARON (1816–1905), *b.* near Newark; authority on clocks and bells; designed, with Airy, the astronomer-royal, 'Big Ben' on the Houses of Parliament; restored at his own expense St. Albans Cathedral, from 1877.

Gringore (*gran-gōr'*), or GRINGOIRE, PIERRE (*c.* 1480–1539), Fr. satiric poet and dramatist; *b.* Caen; able political and social critic; author of satirical comedies directed against Pope Julius II., the enemies of Louis XII., and the vices of society.

Grolier (*grō'lyā*), JEAN DE SERVIER, VICOMTE D'AGNISY (1479–1565), Fr. book collector; *b.* Lyons; owned sumptuous library, rich in the finest examples of binding; many fine examples now in Brit. Museum and the Bibliothèque Nationale, Paris.

[*Recherches sur Jean Grolier*, by Leroux de Lincy (1866).]

Groome, FRANCIS HINDES (1851–1902), Eng. man of letters; *b.* Monk Soham, Suffolk; made a special study of gipsies, and was one of the founders of the Gipsy Lore Society; author of *Two Suffolk Friends* (1895), *Gipsy Folk Tales* (1898), etc.; ed. *Ordnance Gazetteer of Scotland*, etc.

Groot (*grōt*), GERHARD (1340–84), Dutch mystic; was distinguished scholar of Paris; canon at Utrecht, and afterwards Carthusian missionary preacher; founded at Deventer the 'Brethren of the Common Life,' a community without vows, of which Thomas à Kempis was a member, and wrote a life of the founder.

Gros (*grō*), ANTOINE JEAN, BARON (1771–1835), Fr. painter; *b.* Paris; attached to Napoleon's headquarters as military painter, 1796, gaining fame by his portrayal of outstanding incidents in Napoleon's career.

Grose (*grōs*), FRANCIS (*c.* 1730–1791), Eng. antiquary; *b.* Greenford, Middlesex; pub. *Antiquities of England and Wales* (1776–87), *of Scotland* (1789–91), *of Ireland* (1791).

Grosseteste (*grōs'test*), ROBERT (*c.* 1175–1253), philosopher and writer; *b.* Suffolk; educated a Oxford, and became one of the outstanding teachers there; Bishop of Lincoln, 1135; frequently embroiled in disputes with the Pope and the king about his eccles. rights; wrote commentaries on Aristotle, poems in Fr., and works on husbandry.

Grossmith. (1) GEORGE (1847–1912), Eng. actor; *b.* London; leading actor in Gilbert and Sullivan operas, 1877–89; composed numerous songs and nautical sketch; author (with his brother, Weedon Grossmith) of *The Diary of a Nobody* (1894). (2) GEORGE (1874–1935), son of above; musical comedy actor; author of many revues; advisory director to B.B.C.

Grote, GEORGE (1794–1871), Eng. historian; *b.* near Beckenham; became banker, but studied history and philosophy; pub. his famous *History of Greece* (1846–56); also wrote *Plato and other Companions of Socrates* (1865) and *Aristotle* (1872).

Grotius (*grō'shi-us*), HUGO, or HUIG VAN GROOT (1583–1645), Dutch jurist; *b.* Delft; sent to England to make arrangements concerning Greenland whale fisheries, 1613. In the religious disputes in Holland composed edict counselling toleration, which aroused such resentment that he was sentenced to lifelong confinement; but his wife, who shared his imprisonment, contrived his escape. Going to Paris, he later held the post of Swed. ambassador to France. His most celebrated works are *De Jure Belli et Pacis* (1625; Eng. trans. 1853), a great treatise on jurisprudence, and *Annales et Historiæ de Rebus Belgicis*, an historical work. He was one of the greatest men of his age, and a scholar of the first rank.

[*Life*, by C. Butler (1826).]

Grouchy (*groo-shē'*), EMMANUEL, MARQUIS DE (1766–1847), Fr. officer in republican army; *b.* Paris; distinguished at Hohenlinden, Wagram, and in Russia in 1812; marshal, 1814, defeated Blücher at Ligny, but failed to come to Napoleon's relief at Waterloo; retired to U.S.A. in 1815, but returned to France in 1819.

Grove, SIR GEORGE (1820–1900), Eng. civil engineer and ed; *b.* Clapham; secretary Crystal Palace, 1852–73, where he organized famous concerts; established the Palestine Exploration Fund, 1865; ed. *Macmillan's Magazine*, 1868–83; first director Royal Coll. of Music, 1882; ed. famous *Dictionary of Music and Musicians.*

Grove, SIR WILLIAM ROBERT (1811–96), Eng. judge and scientist; *b.* Swansea; constructed platinum-zinc voltaic cell and first employed incandescent electric lamps.

Grundtvig (*groont'vig*), NIKOLAI FREDERIK SEVERIN (1783–1872), Dan. theologian, historian, and author; *b.* in Zealand; a staunch upholder of freedom in religion and politics, he helped to bring about many reforms both in church and state; made bishop, 1861; an authority on Northern mythology and Anglo-Saxon; works include *Northern Mythology* (1808), *Songs for the Danish Church* (1837–41).

Guérin (*gā-răn'*), PIERRE NARCISSE, BARON (1774–1833), Fr. classical and historical painter, influenced by David; *b.* Paris; director Fr. school, Rome, 1822; first success *Marcus Sextus*; other works, *Andromache*, *Clytemnestra*, *Æneas and Dido* (all in the Louvre), etc.

Guesclin, BERTRAND DU. See DU GUESCLIN.

Guest, LADY CHARLOTTE (1812–95), collector of fans and china; *b.* in Lincolnshire; trans. various old Welsh MSS., and named them *The Mabinogion* (1838–49).

Guest, EDWIN (1800–80), Eng. antiquary; *b.* King's Norton; friend of Goethe; helped to found Philological Soc., 1842; works include *A History of English Rhythms* (1838), *Julius Cæsar's Invasion of Britain.*

Guicciardini (*gwē-chär-dē'nē*), FRANCESCO (1483–1540), Italian statesman and historian; *b.* Florence; held various offices in papal service and under Medici; retired 1537, and spent his remaining years in writing *Istoria d'Italia* (1561–4), dealing with the years 1492–1530, a masterly work for its spirit of detachment and the importance of the period.

Guido d'Arezzo (*gwē'dō dä-ret'sō*), or GUIDO ARETINUS (*c.* 990–1050), Fr. Benedictine monk and musician; birthplace uncertain; sometimes called the father of modern music; invented *Harmonic* or *Guidonian Hand*; was first to use stave with lines and spaces, and invented the names ut, re, mi, fa, sol, la, for the first six notes of the scale.

Guido Reni (1575–1642), Ital. painter, of Bologna; pupil of the Carracci; lived twenty years in Rome, and enjoyed patronage of Pope Paul V.; earlier works include *Crucifixion of St. Peter* (in the Vatican) and *Massacre of the Innocents* (Bologna); later, adopted soft and graceful style—to this period belong the *Nativity* in choir of S. Martino, Naples, and the large fresco, *Aurora and the Hours*, on ceiling of Rospigliosi Palace, Rome (considered his masterpiece).

Guinness. (1) SIR BENJAMIN LEE (1798–1868), Dublin brewer; lord mayor of Dublin, 1851; M.P. for Dublin from 1865; restored St. Patrick's Cathedral at a cost of £150,000. (2) EDWARD CECIL, son of above. See IVEAGH.

Guiscard (*gēs-kär'*), ROBERT (1015–85), Norman conqueror of Sicily; *b.* Coutances; Count of Apulia, 1057; reduced cities of Sicily, 1061–72; drove Henry IV. from Rome and restored Pope, 1083–4; died at Cephalonia while preparing to march on Constantinople.

Guise (*gēz* or *givēz*), DUKEDOM OF, Fr. noble family founded by CLAUDE OF LORRAINE, 1ST DUKE (1496–1550), who served with distinction in Italy under Francis I., and later in Luxembourg, 1542; his daughter Mary married James V. of Scotland. FRANCIS, 'LE BALAFRÉ,' 2ND DUKE (1519–63), son of Claude, defended Metz against Charles V., 1552, and took Calais, 1558; was leader of Catholics against Huguenots, whom he defeated at Dreux, 1562; was assassinated. CHARLES (1524–74), brother of Francis, entered the Church, and became cardinal of Lorraine. HENRY, 3RD DUKE (1550–88), son of Francis, also surnamed 'Le Balafré,' defeated Huguenots at Jarnac and Moncontour, 1568, and formed Catholic League, 1576; shared in instigating Massacre of St. Bartholomew, 1572, and opposed Henry of Navarre; was assassinated.

Title became extinct at death of Mary, Duchess of Guise, 1688.

Guitry (*gwē-trē'*). (1) LUCIEN GERMAIN (1860–1925), Fr. actor; *b.* Paris; made début in *La Dame aux Camélias*, 1878, and appeared in many rôles, including *Chantecler* in Rostand's play, 1910; one of the most noted players of his day. (2) SACHA (1885–), Fr. dramatist and actor, son of (1); *b.* St. Petersburg; a dramatist of great versatility, displaying genius for light comedy and for serious and moving scenes; plays include *Jean de la Fontaine*, *L'Illusioniste*, *Mon Père avait Raison*, *Les Nuées d'Aristophane*, and *Petite Hollande*.

Guizot (*gē-zō'*), FRANÇOIS PIERRE GUILLAUME (1787–1874), Fr. statesman and historian; *b.* Nîmes, of Huguenot stock; educated at Geneva and Paris; prof. of modern history at Sorbonne, 1812. Secretary-general of interior under Louis XVIII., 1814, but retired after Napoleon's escape from Elba, 1815. After final defeat of Napoleon, he obtained office under Ministry of Justice; as minister of education, 1832–6, he had principal share in development of education in France. Ambassador to Britain, 1840, but recalled to France to form cabinet; became foreign minister, and in 1847 premier; remained in office till the revolution of 1848, when he escaped to England. He wrote *Histoire de la Révolution d'Angleterre*, *Histoire de la Civilisation en France*, *Histoire de la Civilisation en Europe*, etc.

Gunter, EDMUND (1581–1626), Eng. mathematician; *b.* Hertfordshire; became prof. of astronomy, Gresham Coll., London, 1619; invented Gunter's chain for land measurement, Gunter's line, a quadrant, and Gunter's scale for working navigation problems.

Gurney, EDMUND (1847–88), Eng. philosopher and scientist; *b.* Hersham; educated Cambridge; one of founders of Soc. for Psychical Research; with Myers and Podmore ed. *Phantasms of the Living*.

Gurney, SIR GOLDSWORTHY (1793–1875), Eng. inventor; *b.* near Padstow; produced oxy-hydrogen blowpipe, and the 'Drummond' light (lime-magnesia); applied steam-blast to steamboats; ran steam carriage to Bath and back; superintended lighting and ventilation of Houses of Parliament, 1854–63.

Gustavus I., VASA (1496–1560), King of Sweden; fought against Danes, and after various battles expelled them from Sweden; crowned King of Sweden, 1523. Established Lutheran religion, freed country from restrictions of Hanseatic League, laid foundations of navy, crushed peasant revolts and established law and order. Diet declared crown hereditary in his house, 1560.

Gustavus II., ADOLPHUS (1594–1632), King of Sweden; grandson of Gustavus I.; the champion of Protestantism in the Thirty Years' War. He succeeded his father, Charles IX., in 1611, reorganized the government, and waged successful wars against Denmark, Russia, and Poland, 1611–29. In 1630 he crossed to Germany, on invitation of Prot. princes; captured Stettin, but failed to prevent sack of Magdeburg, 1631; defeated Tilly at Breitenfeld, 1631, and again in 1632. Wallenstein now replaced Tilly, but after checking Gustavus at Nuremberg, was decisively beaten at Lützen, Nov. 1632, where Gustavus fell. Gustavus won his victories by recognizing value of musketry, and by employing smaller and more mobile formations than those hitherto used.

Gustavus III. (1746–92), King of Sweden; succeeded, 1771; overthrew the tyranny of the nobles by a *coup d'état*, 1772. He carried out various reforms, encouraged literature and art, and developed trade; increased naval strength, and established religious toleration. Gustavus warred against Catherine II. of Russia, 1788–90, and at the naval battle of Svensksund decisively defeated the Russians; tried to form league against Jacobins; assassinated, 1792.

Gustavus IV. (1778–1837), King of Sweden; son of Gustavus III.; succeeded, 1792; joined European coalition against Napoleon; deposed as insane, 1809.

Gustavus V. (1858–), King of Sweden; succeeded father, Oscar II., 1907; married Princess Victoria of Baden, 1881.

Gutenberg (*goo'ten-berg*), JOHANNES (*c.* 1398–1468), Ger. printer; *b.* Mainz; entered into partnership with Johann Fust, who furnished the capital to start a printing business. Gutenberg is credited with the invention of printing by movable types, *c.* 1454. The principal works attributed to him are: *The Bible of 36 Lines, The Bible of 42 Lines* (known as Mazarin Bible), and *Catholicon* (a Latin dictionary).

Guthrie, SIR JAMES (1859–1930), Scot. artist, of Glasgow school; *b.* Greenock; painted open-air subject-pictures, such as *Sheep-shearing, Schoolmates. The Highland Funeral, To Pastures New,* and portraits of outstanding merit; R.S.A., 1892; president R.S.A., 1902–19; R.A., 1911.

Guthrie, THOMAS (1803–73), Scot. preacher and philanthropist; *b.* Brechin; seceded at Disruption, 1843, becoming minister of St. John's Free Church, Edinburgh; promoted establishment of industrial schools for destitute children. See *Autobiography*, with a *Memoir* by his sons (1874–5).

Guthrie, THOMAS ANSTEY. See under ANSTEY, F.

Gutzkow (*goots'kō*), KARL FERDINAND (1811–78), Ger. novelist and dramatist; *b.* Berlin; his successful plays include *Uriel Acosta, Richard Savage,* and *Zopf und Schwert*; his novels, *Die Ritter vom Geiste, Der Zauberer von Rom*; a prominent figure in the 'Young Germany' movement.

Guy, THOMAS (1644–1724), Eng. philanthropist and bookseller; *b.* Southwark; obtained from Oxford Univ. the privilege of printing Bibles; amassed fortune; founded Guy's Hospital, 1721, which he endowed.

Guyot (*gē-ō'*), YVES (1843–1928), Fr. journalist and publicist; *b.* Dinan; first to cast suspicion upon verdict in notorious Dreyfus trial; pub. several works on Socialism; member of Chamber of Deputies, 1885–92; minister of public works, 1889–92.

Guzman-Blanco, ANTONIO (1829–99), Venezuelan statesman; *b.* Carácas; was elected president of assembly which transformed Venezuela into a confederation on a democratic basis, 1870–89.

Gwyn, NELL or ELEANOR (1650–87), Eng. actress; originally an orange-seller; famed for her performances in comedy; mistress of Charles II.; had two sons, one of whom became Duke of St. Albans.

H

Haakon (*haw'kon*), or HACO, name of several kings of Norway. HAAKON I., *the Good* (915–61), passed his youth in England, and on return to Norway dethroned his brother Eric; defeated Danes, and was converted to Christianity; killed in battle. HAAKON IV.

(1204–63) won over-lordship of Iceland and Greenland; was defeated by Alexander III. at Largs, Scotland, 1263, and died in Orkneys on way home. HAAKON VII. (1872–), son of King Frederick VIII. of Denmark, became King of Norway on its separation from Sweden, 1905; married Princess Maud, daughter of Edward VII.

Haase (*hä'ze*), HUGO (1863–1919), Ger. Socialist; *b.* Allenstein, E. Prussia; of Jewish extraction; studied law; entered Reichstag, 1897; became president of Social Democratic party; during Great War as pacifist seceded from main body of Socialist party, 1915; one of authors of revolution which brought about abdication of the Kaiser; co-operated with Majority Socialists in formation of a People's Government; shot on steps of Reichstag by a Viennese.

Habak'kuk, one of the twelve 'minor prophets' of O.T.; personal life practically unknown; supposed to have been a member of temple choir; best authorities give date of book which bears his name as 600 B.C.

Habibullah Khan (1872–1919), Amir of Afghanistan; succeeded to throne, 1901; became friendly with Ind. Government as result of visit to India, 1907; during Great War kept country neutral; assassinated.

Habs'burg, or HAPSBURG, Ger. noble family, deriving name from castle of Habsburg on R. Aar, built *c.* 1020. Rudolph of Habsburg, who became Holy Roman emperor in 1273, acquired Austria; from 1438 the imperial title remained practically hereditary in house of Habsburg. Family was remarkable for its acquisition of territories in the east; Maximilian, by marriage with Mary of Burgundy, 1477, established his family as great European power. In reign of Charles V. Spain was united to empire; when he abdicated, 1556, it was transferred to his son Philip, while the empire passed to his brother Ferdinand. Family thus divided into Spanish (elder) and Austrian (younger) branches. Span. line became extinct with the death of Charles II. of Spain, 1700. Male line of Austrian Habsburgs became extinct with death of Charles VI., 1740; he had previously, by the Pragmatic Sanction, secured succession to his daughter, Maria Theresa. She married Francis of Lorraine, who became emperor in 1745. Henceforth Habsburg-Lorraine family were Holy Roman emperors till 1806, and from 1804 till conclusion of Great War, 1918, emperors of Austria.

Hack'er, ARTHUR (1858–1919), Brit. artist; *b.* London; a celebrated figure painter; R.A., 1910; R.I., 1918; among his pictures are *Her Daughter's Legacy, Pelagia and Philammon, Christ and the Magdalen.*

Hac'o. See HAAKON.

Hading (*ä-dän'*), JANE (1864–), stage name of JEANNE ALFRÉDINE TRÉFOURET, famous Fr. comedienne; *b.* Marseilles; achieved great success in *Le Maître de Forges, La Châtelaine, Le Demi-monde,* etc.; toured with Coquelin in U.S.A.

Had'ley, ARTHUR TWINING (1856–1930), Amer. educationist; *b.* New Haven; prof. of political economy, Yale Univ., 1886–99; president of Yale Univ., 1899–1921; chairman of the Railroad Securities Commission of the U.S.A., 1910–11; numerous publications on educational and civic subjects.

Had'ow, SIR WILLIAM HENRY (1859–), Eng. musician and educationist; *b.* in Gloucestershire; principal of Armstrong Coll., Newcastle, 1909–19; vice-chancellor of Sheffield Univ., 1919–30; during Great War directed army education schemes; served on numerous education committees; has written chamber music and songs, but best known for works on musical history; ed. *Oxford History of Music.*

Ha'drian, or PUBLIUS ÆLIUS HADRIANUS (A.D. 76–138), Rom. emperor; distinguished himself in Dacian war; succeeded Trajan as emperor, 117; restored Assyria and Mesopotamia to Parthians; travelled extensively throughout empire; visited Britain and constructed famous wall from the Solway to the Tyne, 122. From 123 to 126 lived at Athens; founded Ælia Capitolina on site of Jerusalem; remaining years of life spent partly at Rome, partly at his villa at Tibur; built castle of St. Angelo, Rome, as imperial mausoleum, 135; founded Athenæum; a patron of arts; a great emperor who spent his life in service of state.

Haeckel (*hek'el*), ERNST HEINRICH (1834–1919), Ger. biologist; *b.* Potsdam; prof. of zoology at Jena from 1865. Pub. masterly monographs on several divisions of lower forms of life; propounded his 'fundamental biogenetic law'—that the development of the individual is a recapitulation of the development of the race; this theory won wide acceptance among naturalists, and with modifications still lies at the base of all zoological classifications; more popular works include *Natural History of Creation, The Last Link,* and *The Riddle of the Universe.*

Hafiz' (*d. c.* 1389), greatest Pers. lyric poet; real name was MOHAMMED SHAMS UD-DIN; *b.* and *d.* at Shiraz; little known of his life; his book, or *Diwan,* consists of *ghazals* (short odes), impregnated with Sufi philosophy; they are known by heart in Persia. Eng. trans. by McCarthy, G. L. Bell, and others.

Ha'gar, an Egyptian woman, Sarah's handmaiden, and mother of Abraham's eldest son Ishmael. See Gen., ch. 16 and 21.

Haggai (*hag'ī*), first Hebrew prophet after return from the exile, and writer of O.T. book of Haggai; purpose of book to inspire returned exiles to rebuild temple.

Hag'gard, SIR HENRY RIDER (1856–1925), Eng. novelist; *b.* in Norfolk; secretary to governor of Natal, 1875; member of special commission to the Transvaal, 1877; returned to England and became barrister, 1884; investigated agricultural conditions in England, 1901–2; travelled round world as member of Dominions Royal Commission, 1912–17; most famous novels include *King Solomon's Mines* (1886), *She* (1887), *Allan Quatermain* (1887). He has also written on land questions.

Hahnemann (*hä'ne-män*), SAMUEL CHRISTIAN FRIEDRICH (1755–1843), Ger. physician; *b.* in Saxony; made researches on drugs and their effects, and introduced the homœopathic method of treatment; driven from Leipzig by jealous colleagues; settled in Paris.

Haidar Ali (*hī'der*), or HYDER ALI (*c.* 1720–82), Mohammedan Indian; *b.* in Mysore; the most formidable enemy of the British in India; won command of army of Mysore; dethroned the rajah and proclaimed himself sultan; allying himself with French, 1780, overwhelmed two Brit. detachments near Madras, and threatened extinction of E. India Co.; Sir Eyre Coote, with the aid of the fleet, overcame his force in a series of battles, 1780–1.

Haig OF BEMERSYDE, DOUGLAS HAIG, 1ST EARL (1861–1928), Scot. soldier; *b.* Edinburgh; served in Sudan and S. African War; inspector-general of cavalry, India, 1903–6; chief of staff, India, 1909–12; general officer commanding, Aldershot, 1912–14.

At outbreak of Great War was placed in command of the 1st Army; during first battle of Ypres rendered distinguished services, and on Dec. 15, 1915, succeeded Viscount French as commander-in-chief of the Brit. forces in France. Much of the success of the Allies was due to his co-operation with the French, and to his acceptance of Foch as generalissimo. Field-marshal, 1917. His brilliant advance of Aug. 1918 was followed by victory. In 1919 received O.M., an earldom, £100,000, and the thanks of Parliament. After the war zealously championed the ex-soldier, for whom he founded Brit. Legion. Buried in Dryburgh Abbey.

Hakluyt (*häk'loot*), RICHARD (*c.* 1553–1616), Eng. geographer and ecclesiastic; *b.* London; held several livings and became archdeacon of Westminster, 1603; early devoted to study of navigation; intimate friend of Drake, Raleigh, Gilbert, and others; one of the first promoters of colonization of Virginia; buried in Westminster Abbey. His monumental work, *The Principall Navigations, Voiages, Traffiques, and Discoveries of the English Nation*, was pub. 1589–1600; unpublished MSS. afterwards used by Samuel Purchas in his *Pilgrims*.

Haldane. (1) JOHN SCOTT (1860–1936), Brit. physiologist; *b.* Edinburgh; brother of 1st Viscount; conducted public health investigations for government departments; C.H., 1928; publications include *Organism and Environment* (1917), *The New Physiology* (1919), and *The Philosophical Basis of Biology* (1931). (2) JOHN BURDON SANDERSON (1892–   ), Brit. scientist; son of (1); served in Great War; reader in biochemistry, Cambridge Univ., 1922–33; prof. of genetics, Univ. Coll., London, since 1933. Works include *Dædalus* (1924), *Possible Worlds* (1927), *Animal Biology* (with J. S. Huxley, 1927), *The Causes of Evolution* (1932).

Haldane OF CLOAN, RICHARD BURDON, 1ST VISCOUNT (1856–1928), Brit. statesman and philosopher; *b.* Edinburgh; educated Edinburgh and Göttingen; called to Eng. bar, 1879; Gifford lecturer in St. Andrews Univ., 1902–4; M.P. for Haddingtonshire, 1885–1911; counsel for United Free Church before House of Lords, 1904; secretary of state for war, 1905–12, and established the Territorial System, and practically created Brit. Expeditionary Force, 1914; lord chancellor, 1912–15 and 1924; an admirer of philosophic Germany; resigned in cabinet crisis of May 1916, but continued to act as a member of judicial committee of the Privy Council, and in a variety of ways assisted in the prosecution of the war; was an enthusiast for education; wrote *Essays on Philosophical Criticism* (with Prof. Seth), *Education and Empire* (1902), *The Pathway to Reality* (1905), *The Reign of Relativity* (1921), and *The Philosophy of Humanism* (1922).

[*R. B. Haldane: An Autobiography* (1929).]

Hale, EDWARD EVERETT (1822–1909), Amer. author and clergyman; *b.* Boston; devoted himself to the anti-slavery interest; wrote short tales, including *The Man Without a Country* and *Ten Times One is Ten* (1870), etc.

Hale, SIR MATTHEW (1609–76), famous Eng. judge and chief justice; *b.* in Gloucestershire; counsel for Archbishop Laud; judge in Court of Common Pleas, 1653; chief baron of Exchequer, 1660; chief justice of England, 1671; wrote numerous works on law and history.

Hales, STEPHEN (1677–1761), curate of Teddington, Middlesex, and natural philosopher; F.R.S.,

1717; made investigations in plant and animal physiology, etc.

Halévy (*ă-lā-vē'*) (1) or LEVI, JACQUES FRANÇOIS FROMENTAL ÉLIE (1799–1862), Fr. composer; prof. at Paris Conservatoire; chief operas, *La Juive, l'Eclair*, and *Valentine d'Aubigny*. (2) LUDOVIC (1834–1908), Fr. dramatist and novelist, nephew of (1); *b.* Paris; chiefly associated with Henri Meilhac; they wrote the libretti for operas by Offenbach and Bizet, *Froufrou*, and other plays; Halévy's successful novels include *L'Abbé Constantin, La Famille Cardinal*, and *Criquette*.

Halibur'ton, THOMAS CHANDLER (1796–1865), Canadian judge; *b.* in Nova Scotia; wrote droll sketches celebrated for knowledge of human nature—*e.g. The Clockmaker, or Sayings and Doings of Sam Slick of Slickville; The Attaché, or Sam Slick in England;* settled in England, 1856; M.P. for Launceston, 1859–63.

Hal'ifax, CHARLES MONTAGU, EARL OF (1661–1715), Eng. politician and poet; *b.* in Northants; a lord of Treasury, 1692; raised loan of £1,000,000, creating the National Debt; carried through Paterson's scheme for founding Bank of England, 1694; chancellor of Exchequer, 1694; reformed coinage, 1695; first lord of Treasury, 1697 and 1714; collaborated with Prior in poem, *Country Mouse and City Mouse*.

Halifax, EDWARD FREDERICK LINDLEY WOOD, VISCOUNT (1881–), Brit. statesman; *b.* in Yorks; educated at Eton and Oxford; Unionist M.P. for Ripon, 1910–25; president of Board of Education, 1922–4; minister of agriculture, 1924–5; created Lord Irwin, 1935. As viceroy of India, 1926–31, favoured further progress of India towards dominion government. President of Board of Education, 1932–5; succeeded his father as Viscount, 1934; secretary of state for war, 1935; Lord Privy Seal since 1935.

Halifax, GEORGE MONTAGUE DUNK, 2ND EARL OF (1716–71), Brit. administrator; president, Board of Trade, 1748; lord-lieutenant of Ireland, 1761; secretary of state, 1762–5; Halifax, Nova Scotia, named after him.

Halifax, GEORGE SAVILE, 1ST MARQUESS OF (1633–95), Eng. politician and author; opposed Exclusion Bill, 1679; lord privy seal, 1682; under James II. became president of Council, 1685, but shortly afterwards was dismissed from office; one of commissioners sent by James II. to arrange terms with William of Orange; held office as lord privy seal in early part of William's reign; retired, 1690.

Hall, BASIL (1788–1844), Brit. naval officer and explorer; *b.* Edinburgh; wrote *Voyages and Travels* (1831–40) and other books of travel, also numerous scientific and miscellaneous works.

Hall, CHARLES FRANCIS (1821–71), Amer. explorer; *b.* in New Hampshire; his expedition of 1864 spent five years among Eskimos and obtained information of fate of Franklin's party; commanded U.S.A. Polar Expedition, 1871, and reached 82° 11′ N.; pub. *Arctic Researches and Life among the Esquimaux* (1864).

Hal'lam, HENRY (1777–1859), Eng. historian; *b.* Windsor; careful investigator; produced work incisive, judicious, and accurate; chief works include *View of the State of Europe during the Middle Ages, Constitutional History of England, Introduction to the Literature of Europe*. The death of his son Arthur Henry Hallam (1811–33) inspired Tennyson's *In Memoriam*.

Hallé (*hăl'ā*), SIR CHARLES (1819–95), pianist and conductor; *b.* in Westphalia; settled in England, 1848; knighted, 1888; married Madame Norman-Neruda, famous violinist; developed chamber music in London from 1852; established Hallé concerts, Manchester, 1857.

Hal'ler, ALBRECHT VON (1708–77), Swiss poet, physiologist, and botanist of extraordinarily varied gifts; *b.* Berne; prof. of medicine, anatomy, botany, and surgery at univ. of Göttingen, 1736–53; returned to Berne, and served as magistrate there; works fill over 200 vols., and include *Die Alpen*, a poem pub. in his *Gedichte* (1732), *Bibliotheca Medica*, and three philosophical romances.

Halley (*hal'i*), EDMUND (1656–1742), Eng. astronomer; *b.* London; made stellar observations at St. Helena, 1676–8; promoted publication of Newton's *Principia*; investigated variation of compass in the Atlantic; discovered comet which bears his name, 1682, and correctly predicted its return in 1759; prof. of geometry, Oxford, 1703; astronomer-royal, 1720.

Hal'liwell-Phil'lipps, JAMES ORCHARD (1820–89), Eng. Shakespearian scholar; *b.* London; pub. 16 vols., with critical notes of the folio ed. of Shakespeare, 1853–65; wrote *Life of Shakespeare* (1848), *History of New Place* (1864).

Hals, FRANZ (*c.* 1580–1666), Dutch painter; *b.* Antwerp; settled in Haarlem, 1616; famed for portrait groups, such as the *Arquebusiers of St. George*, and other guild companies—archers, civic guards, etc.; Wallace Collection, London, has his *Laughing Cavalier*, and National Gallery, Edinburgh, *The Burgomaster and his Wife*.

Hals'bury, HARDINGE STANLEY GIFFARD, 1ST EARL OF (1823–1921), Brit. Conservative statesman; *b.* London; solicitor-general, 1875–80; M.P. for Launceston, 1877–85; lord chancellor, 1895–1905; baron, 1885; earl, 1898. Was engaged in Tichborne trial; gave judgment in House of Lords, 1904, in favour of Free Church of Scotland against the United Free Church; led extreme 'Die-Hard' party in Lords against Parliament Bill.

Hamil'car Barc'a (*d.* 228 B.C.), Carthaginian general; father of Hannibal; maintained Carthaginian rule against Romans in Sicily during first Punic War, 247–241 B.C.; successfully opposed Romans in Spain, *c.* 237–228; fell in battle; great military genius.

Ham'ilton, Scot. family, descended from Walter Fitz-Gilbert, a supporter of Bruce. SIR JAMES HAMILTON, founder of fortunes of house, became Lord Hamilton in 1445; married secondly Mary, daughter of James II., and thus made Hamiltons important in Scot. history. JAMES, 1ST DUKE (1606–49), served under Gustavus Adolphus, 1631; took part in disputes between Charles I. and Covenanters; deserted royalist cause and threw in his lot with Argyll, but was subsequently restored to royal favour; commanded Scots army in England in support of king, 1648, but was defeated and captured by Cromwell at Preston, and executed in the following year.

Hamilton, ALEXANDER (1757–1804), American statesman and author; *b.* Nevis, Brit. W. Indies; Washington's aide-de-camp, 1777–81; secretary of Treasury under Washington, 1789–95, and displayed great financial talent; after Washington's death became commander-in-chief, and one of leaders of Federalist party; he was mortally wounded in a duel with Aaron Burr. Author of *The Federalist*, a series of brilliant essays on Amer. constitutional law; his *Report on Manufactures* is still quoted by advocates of protective tariff.

Hamilton, EMMA, LADY (*c.*

1765–1815), Englishwoman of humble birth but extraordinary beauty; wife of Sir William Hamilton, Brit. ambassador at Naples, and mistress of Lord Nelson; subject of nearly fifty portraits by Romney.

Hamilton, Sir Ian Standish Monteith (1853–), Brit. general; *b.* in Corfu; fought under Roberts in Afghanistan, 1878–80; wounded at Majuba, 1881; with Wolseley's expedition for relief of Gordon, 1884–5; took part in Burmese expedition, 1886–7, etc. In S. African War was chief of staff of Natal relief force under Sir G. White; was through siege of Ladysmith; chief of staff to Kitchener, 1901; inspector-general of overseas forces, 1910–15. In Great War commanded land forces of Gallipoli Campaign, 1915; relieved of his command in Oct. 1915; G.C.M.G., 1919. Lord rector of Edinburgh Univ., 1932–5. A man of wide culture and literary gifts. Pub. *A Ballad of Hadji* (1887), *A Staff Officer's Scrap-Book* (1906), and *Gallipoli Diary* (1920).

Hamilton, Patrick (? 1504–28), Scot. martyr; studied at univs. of Paris and Louvain; avowed follower of Luther, 1526, and fled from Scotland to Germany to escape inquisition of Beaton; met Luther; returned to St. Andrews, condemned for heresy, and burned at the stake.

Hamilton, Sir William (1788–1856), Scot. philosopher; *b.* Glasgow; prof. of civil history, Edinburgh Univ., 1821, and of logic and metaphysics, 1836; contributed famous article on the 'Philosophy of the Unconditioned' to the *Edinburgh Review* (1829); pub. *Discussions on Philosophy, Literature, and Education* (1852–53); ed. Reid's *Works* (1846); *Lectures on Logic and Metaphysics* appeared posthumously; his theory of the relativity of knowledge influenced Herbert Spencer and Huxley.

Hamilton, Sir William Rowan (1805–65), Irish mathematician; *b.* Dublin; brilliant scholar; prof. of astronomy, Dublin, 1827, and afterwards astronomer-royal for Ireland; knighted, 1835; president Royal Irish Academy, 1837; helped to prove 'undulatory theory of light'; invented the calculus of quaternions.

Ham'ley, Sir Edward Bruce (1824–93), Brit. soldier and author; *b.* in Cornwall; served in Crimean War; appointed a prof. at Sandhurst, 1859, and afterwards acted on frontier commissions in Bulgaria, Armenia, and Greece; commanded a division in Egyptian War, 1882, the non-recognition of his services in which led to a somewhat painful controversy with Lord Wolseley; M.P. for Birkenhead, 1885–92; pub. *The Operations of War* and *The War in the Crimea.*

Ham'mond, John Lawrence le Breton (1872–), Eng. journalist and historian; ed. *The Speaker,* 1899–1906; secretary Civil Service Commission, 1907–13; served in Great War; joint-author with his wife of *The Village Labourer, The Town Labourer,* etc., a series of authoritative vols. on the Industrial Revolution.

Hamp'den, John (1594–1643), Eng. statesman; *b.* London; entered Parliament, 1621; refused to pay ship-money, 1637; was a determined opponent of Charles I., and a member of Short and Long Parliaments; shared in prosecution of Strafford; one of five members impeached by Charles in 1642. On outbreak of Civil War raised troops for Parliament; mortally wounded at Chalgrove Field; universally esteemed for his modesty, charity, and bravery.

Ham'sun, Knut (1859–),

Norweg. author; till 1889 served successively as clerk, farm-worker, schoolmaster, and tram-conductor in U.S.A.; his novel *Sult*, trans. *Hunger* (1899), is a grimly powerful description of slow starvation; Nobel Prize for literature, 1920. Other works include *Siesta* (1897), *Kratskow* (1904), *Growth of the Soil* (1920), and *Vagabonds* (1931).

Handel, GEORGE FREDERICK (1685-1759), Anglo-Ger. composer; *b.* Halle; showed musical precocity; appointed organist at cathedral, Halle, and studied law at univ., 1702; joined opera orchestra, Hamburg, 1703; visited Italy, 1706, where he became friend of Scarlatti and Corelli; appointed *capellmeister*, Hanover, 1710; offended Elector of Hanover, but on latter's accession as George I. was reconciled; director of music to Duke of Chandos, 1718; directed Ital. Opera for Royal Academy of Music, London, 1720; settled in England, becoming naturalized, 1726; lost eyesight towards end of life.

Handel was a man of independent and upright character and artistic temperament; was one of the finest organ and harpsichord players of his time, and worked with remarkable rapidity; his great oratorio *The Messiah* was written in three weeks. To his Eng. period belong over forty operas and his greatest oratorios, including *Saul*, *Israel in Egypt* (1738); *Samson*, *Messiah* (1741); *Joseph* (1743); *Judas Maccabæus* (1746); *Joshua* (1747); *Jephthah* (1751).

[*Life*, by R. A. Streatfeild (1909).]

Hank'ey, SIR MAURICE PASCAL ALERS (1877–), Brit. soldier; joined Royal Marine Artillery, 1895; appointed to Naval Intelligence Dep., 1902–6; secretary to Committee of Imperial Defence, 1912; during Great War was appointed secretary to War Cabinet, 1916; Brit. secretary at Peace Conference, 1919; received a grant of £25,000 and the G.C.B.; clerk of Privy Council since 1923; G.C.M.G., 1929.

Han'nay, CANON JAMES OWEN, pen-name GEORGE A. BIRMINGHAM (1865–), Irish ecclesiastic and humorist; rector of Westport, co. Mayo, 1892–1913, and of Mells since 1924; best-known books: *Spanish Gold, The Simpkins Plot, The Lost Tribes, Bindon Parva, A Wayfarer in Hungary, Fed Up*, etc.; plays include *General John Regan.*

Han'nen, JAMES, BARON (1821–94), Eng. judge; *b.* London; presided over Parnell Commission, 1888; lord of appeal, 1891; acted as arbitrator in the Bering Sea seal fisheries question, 1892.

Han'nibal (*c.* 247–183 B.C.), Carthaginian general; son of Hamilcar; one of the greatest military geniuses of antiquity; carried on second Punic War against Rome; took Saguntum, 218, marched from Spain into Gaul, and led his troops over Alps into Italy in space of five months; maintained war for fifteen years; won great victories at Trasimene Lake, 217, and Cannæ, 216; took Tarentum, 212; failed to capture Rome, 211; compelled to withdraw to Carthage, and finally defeated by Scipio at Zama, 202 B.C.; fled to Syria and Asia Minor; poisoned himself to prevent his being surrendered to Romans.

Han'nington, JAMES (1847–85), Eng. missionary; *b.* in Sussex; first bishop of Equatorial E. Africa; murdered by Mwanga, King of Uganda; distinguished for his individuality and strength of character.

Han'no 'the Great' (3rd cent. B.C.), Carthaginian general, known to history as antagonist of Hannibal; leader of aristocratic party in Carthage.

Hanotaux (*a-nō-tō'*), GABRIEL

(1853–), Fr. statesman and author; *b.* in Aisne; minister for foreign affairs, 1894–8; elected to Academy, 1897; author of important works on Fr. history.

Han'sard, LUKE (1752–1828), Eng. printer; *b.* Norwich; printed the *Journals of the House of Commons* (1774–1828); Official Reports of parliamentary debates, etc., are still known as 'Hansard.'

Han'som, JOSEPH ALOYSIUS (1803–82), Eng. inventor and architect; *b.* York; invented, 1834, the cab which bore his name; founded, 1842, *The Builder* journal; architect of Birmingham Town Hall, Plymouth Cathedral, etc.

Harcourt, SIR WILLIAM GEORGE GRANVILLE VENABLES VERNON (1827–1904), Brit. statesman; *b.* York; solicitor-general, 1873; secretary of state under Liberal government, 1880; chancellor of Exchequer, 1886 and 1892–5; his chief claim to fame rests on his Death Duties budget, 1894, a great financial achievement. Leader of Opposition, 1895–8, and continued to be prominent parl. figure. His political letters to the *Times* signed 'Historicus' were pub. in book form, 1863.

Har'den, MAXIMILIAN (1862–1927), Ger. journalist and publicist; *b.* Berlin; founded famous weekly review *Die Zukunft*; caused great sensation by exposure of court scandals, 1907; stood trial, and drove his accusers from public life; his paper was suppressed on several occasions during Great War because of its criticisms of Ger. administration.

Har'denberg, KARL AUGUST VON, PRINCE (1750–1822), Prussian statesman; *b.* in Hanover; made minister of state and member of Prussian cabinet by Frederick William III., 1791; concluded treaty of Basel, 1795; first minister, 1803; dismissed through Napoleon's influence, 1806, but succeeded Stein as chancellor of state, 1810; largely helped to negotiate treaty of Paris, 1814; sat at Congress of Vienna; carried out many social and educational reforms and reorganized army.

Har'dicanute, or HARTHACNUT (*c.* 1019–42), son of Canute; on father's death became King of Wessex, 1035, and King of England on death of his half-brother Harold, 1040. A cruel and oppressive king.

Har'die, JAMES KEIR (1856–1915), Brit. Labour leader; *b.* in Lanarkshire; worked in coal mines between ages of 7 and 24; one of first Labour M.P.'s, 1892–5, and from 1900; one of founders of Independent Labour Party, 1893; proprietor and ed. of *Labour Leader*; visited India and Australia, 1907; leader of Labour party in House of Commons, 1906–15.

Har'ding, WARREN GAMALIEL (1865–1923), Amer. Republican statesman; *b.* in Ohio; president, Harding Publishing Co., Ohio, publishers of *Star* newspaper; lieutenant-governor of Ohio, 1904–6; member of U.S.A. senate, 1915–21; President of U.S.A. from 1920; convened Washington Conference on limitation of armaments, 1921; died in office.

Hardinge (*här'ding*) OF LAHORE, HENRY, 1ST VISCOUNT (1785–1856), Brit. field-marshal; *b.* Wrotham; distinguished in Napoleonic wars; M.P. for Durham, 1820; secretary for war, 1828; chief secretary for Ireland, 1830; gov.-gen. of India, 1844–7; fought in second Sikh War, 1845–6; viscount, 1846; commander-in-chief of British army, 1852–6; field-marshal, 1856.

Hardinge OF PENSHURST, CHARLES, 1ST BARON (1858–), Brit. diplomat; grandson of above; *b.* London; entered diplomatic service, 1880; secretary of legation to Tehran, 1896; ambassador to Russia, 1904–6; permanent under-secretary for foreign affairs, 1906–10 and 1916–18; viceroy of India, 1910–16; ambassador in Paris, 1920–22; created baron, 1910; K.G., 1916.

Har'dy, THOMAS (1840–1928), Eng. novelist and poet; *b.* near Dorchester; trained as an architect; first achieved fame with his 'Wessex' novels, including *Under the Greenwood Tree* (1872), *Far from the Madding Crowd* (1874), *The Return of the Native* (1878), *The Mayor of Casterbridge* (1886), *Tess of the d'Urbervilles* (1891), and *Jude the Obscure* (1895); thereafter he devoted himself entirely to poetry, and pub. *Wessex Poems* (1898), *The Dynasts* (1903–8), a Napoleonic drama and his most outstanding work in poetry, and several vols. of lyrical poems; later vols. include *Selected Poems* (1916), *Moments of Vision* (1917), *Winter Words* (posthumously pub., 1928); definitive Wessex ed. of his works pub. 1912; O.M., 1910; interred in Westminster Abbey.

[*Life of Thomas Hardy*, by his wife, Florence Emily Hardy (2 vols., 1928, 1930).]

Hardy, SIR THOMAS MASTERMAN (1769–1839), Brit. vice-admiral and friend of Nelson; *b.* in Dorset; captain of *Victory* at Trafalgar, where Nelson died in his arms; governor of Greenwich Hospital from 1834.

Hardyng, JOHN (1378–?1465), Eng. chronicler; served in family of Hotspur, earl of Northumberland, whose death he witnessed at battle of Shrewsbury, 1403; constable of Warkworth Castle, 1405; present at Agincourt, 1415; prepared documents relating to feudal status of Scotland; his *Chronicle* of Eng. history, without literary merit, deals with affairs up to 1461.

Hare, AUGUSTUS JOHN CUTHBERT (1834–1903), Eng. biographer and miscellaneous writer; *b.* Rome; educated Harrow and Oxford; author of *Memorials of a Quiet Life*, *Walks in Rome*, *Story of My Life* (6 vols.), and many other descriptive works.

Hare, SIR JOHN (1844–1921), Eng. actor; *b.* in Yorks; first appearance on stage, Liverpool, 1864; distinguished for highly finished representations of old men; a theatrical manager from 1875; knighted, 1907.

Hare, WILLIAM. See under BURKE, WILLIAM.

Har'graves, EDMUND HAMMOND (1816–91), discoverer of Australian goldfields; *b.* in Hants; joined merchant service; landed in Australia, 1832; became pastoral farmer; went gold-digging in California, 1849; returned to Australia and found gold in Macquarie valley, 1851; granted £10,000 as commissioner of crown lands, 1853, and an annuity, 1877, by New S. Wales.

Har'greaves, JAMES (*d.* 1778), handloom weaver; *b.* in Lancs; invented the spinning-jenny, *c.* 1764; was persecuted by fellow-workmen, who thought his invention would upset labour conditions; partner in a small cotton mill near Nottingham after 1770.

Harīrī (*hä-rē'rē*), ABU MOHAMMED ALQASIM-IBN-ALI, AL- (1054–1122), Arabic author; *b.* Basra; wrote in verse valuable works on grammar and literature; greatest work: *Mákámat*, a collection of tales in rhyme, regarded in East as second only to Koran.

Hark'ness, EDWARD S. (1874–), Amer. financier; *b.* Cleveland, Ohio; made fortune in Amer. railways; his numerous philanthropic gifts include founding of Pilgrim Trust of £2,000,000 to mark Britain's acceptance of financial burdens in Great War.

Har'land, HENRY (1861–1905), Amer. author; *b.* St. Petersburg; best-known novels, *The Cardinal's*

Snuffbox (1900) and *My Friend Prospero* (1904).

Harley, ROBERT. See OXFORD, EARL OF.

Harmsworth, ALFRED CHARLES. See NORTHCLIFFE, LORD.

Harmsworth, HAROLD SIDNEY. See ROTHERMERE, LORD.

Har'nack, ADOLPH VON (1851–1930), Ger. Church historian; *b.* in Estonia; prof. at Leipzig, Giessen, Marburg, and Berlin; general director of Royal Library, Berlin, 1905–21; his historical insight gained him world-wide reputation; publications include *History of Christian Dogma*, *What is Christianity?* and *The Sayings and Discourses of Jesus.*

Har'old I., HAREFOOT (*d.* 1040), King of England; succeeded Canute, 1035; opposed by his half-brother Hardicanute; chosen to rule north of Thames, and became king of all England, 1037.

Harold II. (*c.* 1022–66), King of England; son of Earl Godwin; Earl of Wessex, 1053; elected king, 1066; routed and killed his brother Tostig and Harold Hardrada of Norway at Stamford Bridge, 1066; defeated and slain at Hastings by William the Conqueror; last of the Saxon kings.

Harold III., HARDRADA (1015–66), King of Norway, brother of St. Olaf; fled to Constantinople, where as captain of Byzantine Varangian guards won many victories over Saracens; succeeded to throne of Norway, 1047; failed to subdue Denmark; killed at Stamford Bridge fighting against Harold of England.

Haroun-al-Raschid (*hä-roon'-äl-ra-shēd'*) (763–809), caliph of Baghdad; famed for greatness of his empire, the splendour of his court, and his patronage of learning and letters; one of the greatest princes of his day; best known from his association with the *Arabian Nights.*

Harpignies (*är-pēn-yē'*). HENRI JOSEPH (1819–1916), Fr. landscape painter; *b.* Valenciennes; gave up business career and studied art in Paris and Italy, 1846–52; visited Italy with Corot, 1860; best-known pictures, *Evening* (1866), *Le Saut du Loup* (1873), *The Rising of the Moon* (1884).

Har'raden, BEATRICE (1864–), Eng. novelist; *b.* London; best-known books: *Ships that Pass in the Night* (1893), *The Fowler* (1899), *Interplay* (1908), *Where your Treasure is* (1918).

Har'riman, EDWARD HENRY (1848–1909), Amer. railway magnate and capitalist; with his associates bought Union Pacific Railway, 1893; obtained control of Southern Pacific Railway, 1900; in six years spent £40,000,000 improving these lines; finally controlled some 70,000 miles of railway.

Har'rington, JAMES (1611–77), Eng. political philosopher; *b.* in Northants; chief work *Oceana*, in which he propounded a scheme for an oligarchical republic on the Venetian model, 1656.

Har'ris, SIR AUGUSTUS HENRY GLOSSOP (1852–96), Eng. actor and dramatist; part author of *The World* (1880) and *Cheer, Boys, Cheer* (1895); was manager of Her Majesty's, Covent Garden, Drury Lane, and the Olympic theatres.

Harris, GEORGE ROBERT CANNING, 4TH BARON (1851–1932), politician and famous cricketer; *b.* in Trinidad; captained Kent cricket eleven for 13 years; played for England *v.* Australia, 1879, 1880, and 1884; under-secretary for India, 1885–6; for war, 1886–89; governor of Bombay, 1890–5; lord-in-waiting to Queen Victoria, 1895–1900.

Harris, JAMES RENDEL (1852–), Eng. Biblical scholar; *b.* Plymouth; made researches in the East, and discovered, 1889, an important Syriac MS. of 7th cent.

in a convent on Mt. Sinai; lecturer in Palæography, Cambridge Univ., 1893–1903; curator of MSS., John Rylands Library, Manchester, 1918–25; works include *Teaching of the Apostles* (1887), *Origin of the Doctrine of the Trinity* (1919), *Tenedos* (1930).

Harris, JOEL CHANDLER (1848–1908), Amer. novelist and folklorist; *b.* in Georgia; his reputation was established by *Uncle Remus* (1880), which appealed not only to children but to students of folklore.

Har'rison, BENJAMIN (1833–1901), president of U.S.A.; settled as lawyer in Indianapolis; distinguished himself in Union army in Civil War; president, 1889–93, when the Bering Sea question was settled; chief council for Venezuela in arbitration of boundary dispute with Britain, 1899.

Harrison, FREDERIC (1831–1923), Eng. jurist, critic, and philosopher; *b.* London; called to bar, 1858; prof. of jurisprudence, Inns of Court, 1877–89; helped to codify Eng. law; leader of Eng. Positivism; studied Labour problems; distinguished literary critic and historian. Works include *Oliver Cromwell* (1888), *The Creed of a Layman* (1907), *Autobiographic Memoirs* (1911), *Among My Books* (1912), *The Positive Evolution of Religion* (1912), *Obiter Scripta* (1919).

Harrison, WILLIAM HENRY (1773–1841), president U.S.A.; *b.* in Virginia; served in army, 1791–8; governor N.W. Territory, 1798, Indiana, 1801; fought against Britain in war of 1812; president, 1841, for one month.

Harry, BLIND (HENRY THE MINSTREL), minstrel of Scot. court in latter part of 15th cent.; name occurs in Dunbar's famous *Lament for the Makaris* (1508); wrote long epic poem called *William Wallace*, of importance in history of verse.

Harte, FRANCIS BRET (1839–1902), Amer. novelist, poet, and humorist; *b.* Albany, New York; ed. *The Overland Monthly*; prof. of literature, univ. of California, 1870–1; U.S.A. consul in Glasgow, 1880–5; lived in London from 1885. Prolific writer; among best-known works are *The Luck of Roaring Camp, Truthful James* ('Heathen Chinee').

Harty, SIR HERBERT HAMILTON (1880–), Brit. composer and conductor; *b.* in co. Down; one of most brilliant conductors in England; permanent conductor of Hallé Orchestra, Manchester, 1920–33; conductor of London Symphony Orchestra, 1933. Has written songs and orchestral works.

Harvey, SIR GEORGE (1806–76), Scot. painter; *b.* near Stirling; one of founders of Royal Scot. Academy, and became its president, 1864; noted for figure pictures illustrative of Scot. life.

Harvey, SIR JOHN MARTIN (1863–), Eng. actor-manager; *b.* in Essex; managed Lyceum, Prince of Wales's and other theatres, and Covent Garden Opera House; toured America with Sir Henry Irving; best-known part is that of Sydney Carton in *The Only Way*.

Harvey, WILLIAM (1578–1657), Eng. physician; *b.* Folkestone; discoverer of circulation of blood; appointed to St. Bartholomew's Hospital, 1609; Lumleian lecturer at College of Physicians, 1615; lectured on theory of movements of the heart and circulation of the blood; essay on subject pub. 1628.

Ha'stings, FRANCIS RAWDON, 1st MARQUESS (1754–1826), Brit. soldier and administrator; *b.* in Ireland; fought in Amer. war, 1775–82; gov.-gen. of Bengal, and commander-in-chief of India, 1813; established Brit. supremacy and extended her territory in India; annexed Singapore by purchase, 1819.

Hastings, JAMES (1852–1922), Scot. Biblical scholar; *b.* Huntly; founder, 1889, and ed. *Expository Times*; ed. *Dictionary of the Bible*, etc.; was ed. of *Encyclopædia of Religion and Ethics.*

Hastings, WARREN (1732–1818), Brit. administrator; *b.* in Oxfordshire; entered East India Co.'s service, 1750; held various important posts, finally becoming gov.-gen. of India, 1773; members of council were inimical to him, and condemned all his measures. Between 1777 and 1785 he conducted war against Mahrattas and against Haidar Ali; suppressed insurrection of Rajah of Benares; caused begums of Oudh to give up land and treasure, 1780, some of which he afterwards restored; returned to England, 1785, and was impeached by Burke in a famous speech, 1786, for oppression, maladministration, and corruption; the trial lasted seven years, after which he was acquitted, 1795. Costs of trial swallowed up his entire fortune, but he subsequently received a pension from East India Co. The consolidation of the Ind. Empire was largely due to his administrative genius.

Hathaway, ANNE (1556–1623). See SHAKESPEARE.

Hat'ton, SIR CHRISTOPHER (1540–91), lord chancellor of England; *b.* in Northants; favourite of Queen Elizabeth; member of Fotheringay commission which tried Mary Queen of Scots; a friend and patron of letters.

Hatton, JOHN LIPTROT (1809–86), Eng. composer; *b.* Liverpool; practically self-taught; musical director of Princess Theatre, London; wrote operetta *Queen of the Thames* (1843), and about three hundred popular songs, including 'To Anthea,' 'Simon the Cellarer.'

Hauch (*hou*ch), JOHANNES CARSTEN (1790–1872), Dan. poet; prof. of Scandinavian literature, Kiel, 1846, and prof. of æsthetics, Copenhagen, 1851; most successful work consists of nine historical tragedies, 1849–52.

Hauptmann (*houpt'män*), GERHART (1862–), Ger. poet and dramatist; *b.* in Silesia; works include historical and realistic dramas and comedies; among works are *Einsame Menschen* (1891), *Die Weber* (1892), a study of conditions of life among hand-weavers of Silesian mountains, *Und Pippa Tanzt* (1906), a masterly fairy tale, and *The Island of the Great Mother* (1926); Nobel Prize for literature, 1912.

Haussmann (*ōs-män*), GEORGES EUGÈNE, BARON (1809–91), Fr. magistrate; *b.* Paris; prefect of the Seine; devoted his attention to improvement of Paris by widening streets, constructing boulevards, etc. The tremendous cost (£35,000,000) led to much adverse criticism; forced to resign, 1870.

Hav'elock, SIR HENRY (1795–1857), Brit. soldier; *b.* Sunderland; distinguished himself in Afghan and Sikh wars; during Indian Mutiny relieved Cawnpore, 1857; advanced to relieve Lucknow, entered that city, but was himself besieged; co-operated successfully with Sir Colin Campbell, who commanded relieving army, but died as withdrawal from Lucknow commenced.

Hawke, EDWARD, LORD (1705–81), Brit. admiral; *b.* London; entered navy, 1720; commander, 1733; in action off Toulon, 1744, gained reputation as fearless officer; defeated squadron of Fr. ships off Cape Finisterre, 1747; admiral, 1757; greatest achievement was victory at Quiberon Bay, 1759.

Haw'ker, ROBERT STEPHEN (1803–75), Eng. poet; *b.* in Devon; vicar of Morwenstow, Cornwall; became a R.C. twelve hours before he died; wrote Cornish poems and ballads. His best-known poem is 'And shall Trelawney die?'

Hawkins, Sir Anthony Hope. See Hope, Anthony.

Hawkins, Sir Henry, Baron Brampton (1817–1907), Eng. judge; *b.* in Herts; called to the bar, 1843; Q.C., 1858; prosecuting counsel in Tichborne trial, 1874; peerage, 1899; author of *Reminiscences* (1904).

Hawkins, or Hawkyns, Sir John (1532–95), Eng. seaman; *b.* Plymouth; first Englishman to visit Guinea coast on slaving expeditions, 1562; M.P. for Plymouth, 1572; fought against Armada, 1588, rendering valuable service, for which he was knighted; *d.* off Porto Rico while in command of expedition to W. Indies.

Hawk'shaw, Sir John (1811–91), Eng. engineer; *b.* in Yorks; constructed many railways at home and abroad; made Severn Tunnel, 1887; reported favourably on Suez Canal scheme, 1863, and unfavourably on Panama scheme, 1879; completed Amsterdam ship-canal, 1876.

Haw'thorne, Nathaniel (1804–64), Amer. author; *b.* Salem, Mass.; a great imaginative writer, and one of the greatest Amer. novelists; associated with Emerson and Thoreau; held positions in Customs service; Amer. consul at Liverpool, 1853–7. His outstanding work, *The Scarlet Letter* (1850), achieved world-wide popularity; other works are *Twice-told Tales* (1837), *The House of the Seven Gables* (1851), *The Wonder Book* and *Tanglewood Tales* (1851–3), which retell the old classical legends for children, *The Blithedale Romance* (1852).

[*Nathaniel Hawthorne* ('English Men of Letters,' 1879), by Henry James.]

Haw'trey, Sir Charles Henry (1858–1923), Eng. actor-manager and playwright; *b.* Eton, his production of *The Private Secretary* (1884) and *A Message from Mars* (1899) achieved remarkable success; knighted, 1922.

Hay, Ian. See Beith, J. H.

Hay, John (1838–1905), Amer. politician and author; *b.* in Indiana; secretary and friend of Abraham Lincoln; held diplomatic posts, 1865–70, at Paris, Vienna, and Madrid; assistant secretary of state for U.S.A., 1879–81; ambassador to Great Britain, 1897–8; secretary of state at Washington, 1898–1905; wrote *Pike County Ballads* (1871), *Castilian Days* (1891), and collaborated in *Life of Lincoln* (1890).

Hayash'i, Tadasu, Count (1850–1913), Jap. statesman and diplomatist; *b.* Tokyo, leading figure in movement which gave rise to modern Japan; envoy extraordinary to China, 1895–6; envoy to Russia, 1897–9; minister to Britain, 1900–6; recalled after Russo-Jap. war to become minister of foreign affairs; created viscount, 1902, for services in connection with Anglo-Jap. treaty; count, 1907.

Haydn (*hī'dn*), Franz Joseph (1732–1809), Austrian composer; *b.* near Vienna; joined St. Stephen's cathedral choir, Vienna, 1740; conductor of Count Morzin's band, 1759; among his pupils was Beethoven; greatly influenced his friend Mozart; a master of melody and generally regarded as the creator of the symphony; compositions include symphonies, quartets, and numerous trios, operas, and oratorios, best-known oratorio being *The Creation.*

Hay'don, Benjamin Robert (1786–1846), Eng. painter; *b.* Plymouth; first exhibited at Royal Academy, 1807; excessively vain; spent his life struggling against debt; committed suicide; best-known pictures, *The Judgment of Solomon* (1814),

Christ's Entry into Jerusalem (1820).

Haynau (*hī'nou*), JULIUS JAKOB, FREIHERR VON (1786–1853), Austrian soldier; *b.* Cassel; natural son of William I., Elector of Hesse; entered Austrian service, 1801, and became field-marshal, 1844; crushed revolution in Italy, 1848, and Hungary, 1849; incurred public dislike by his cruelty.

Hay'ter, SIR GEORGE (1792–1871), Eng. historical painter; *b.* London; miniature painter to Princess Charlotte, 1816; studied in Italy, 1816–31; court painter to Queen Victoria, 1841; knight, 1842; principal pictures, *The Trial of Queen Caroline* and *Queen Victoria taking the Coronation Oath.*

Haz'litt, WILLIAM (1778–1830), Eng. critic and essayist; *b.* Maidstone; friend of Charles Lamb; first became known by his *Characters of Shakespeare's Plays,* 1817; other publications include *Table Talk* (1822), *The Spirit of the Age* (1825), and *Life of Napoleon* (1828–30); in some respects the greatest of English critics (' the critics' critic ').

[*William Hazlitt* (' English Men of Letters,' 1902), by Augustine Birrell.]

Hazlitt, WILLIAM CAREW (1834–1913), Eng. bibliographer; grandson of above; *b.* London; barrister, Inner Temple, 1861; principal works include *Bibliographical Collections and Notes* (8 vols., 1876–1904), *Memoirs of William Hazlitt* (1867), *Faiths and Folklore* (1905).

Head'lam, ARTHUR CAYLEY (1862–), Eng. divine; *b.* in Durham; rector of Welwyn, Herts, 1896–1903; ed. of *Church Quarterly Review,* 1901–21; principal of King's Coll., London, 1903–12, and prof. of dogmatic theology, 1903–16; regius prof. of divinity, Oxford, and canon of Christ Church, 1918–23; Bishop of Gloucester since 1923; writings include *History, Authority, and Theology* (1909), *The Study of Theology* (1918), *The New Prayer Book* (1927).

Healy, TIMOTHY MICHAEL (1855–1931), Irish politician and lawyer; *b.* Bantry; called to Irish bar, 1884; Q.C., 1899; bencher, Gray's Inn, 1910; M.P., 1880–1918; with William O'Brien founded Independent Nationalist party; resourceful, eloquent, and ironically witty debater; became one of bitterest opponents of Parnell; secured insertion of ' Healy clause ' (that in future no rent should be chargeable on tenants' improvements) in Land Bill of 1881; first gov.-gen. of Irish Free State, 1922; resigned, 1927; pub. *Letters and Leaders of My Day* (1928).

Hearn, LAFCADIO (1850–1904), a writer on Japan; *b.* Ionian Islands, of Irish and Ger. parentage; some years a journalist in America; subsequently naturalized in Japan, where he married Jap. wife and turned Buddhist; works, which vividly portray Jap. character and social conditions, include *Glimpses of Unfamiliar Japan* (1894), and *Japan: an attempt at Interpretation* (1904).

Hearn'shaw, FOSSEY JOHN COBB (1869–), Eng. historian; *b.* Birmingham; prof. of history, Hartley Univ. Coll., Southampton, 1900–10, Armstrong Coll., Univ. of Durham, 1910–12, and Univ. of London, 1913–34; works include *England in the Making* (1913), *Democracy and British Empire* (1921), *The ' Ifs ' of History* (1929).

Hearst, WILLIAM RANDOLPH (1863–), Amer. journalist and newspaper proprietor; *b.* San Francisco; owns and edits a number of New York, Chicago, Boston, and Western papers of what is known as the ' Yellow Press.'

Heath'field, George Augustus Eliott, Lord (1717–90), Brit. general; *b.* in Roxburghshire; fought at Dettingen and Fontenoy, and through Ger. campaign of 1759–61; governor of Gibraltar, 1775, and defended it against the French and Spaniards during the famous siege, 1779–83; Baron of Gibraltar, 1787.

Heat'on, Sir John Henniker (1848–1914), Eng. politician; *b.* in Kent; landowner and part proprietor of newspapers in Australia; M.P. for Canterbury, 1885–1910; carried imperial penny postage scheme, 1898; introduced telegraphic money orders in England.

He'ber, Reginald (1783–1826), Eng. hymnologist; *b.* in Cheshire; second bishop of Calcutta, 1823; pub. first volume of hymns, 1812, which included 'From Greenland's icy mountains' and other well-known favourites.

Hedin (*he-dēn'*), Sir Sven Anders (1865–), Swed. Asiatic explorer; *b.* Stockholm; travelled extensively in the East; first gained reputation by crossing the Pamirs in the depth of winter, 1893; crossed the Takla-Makan desert, nearly losing his life, 1895; floated down the Tarim, 1899; found evidences of Chin. civilization of 3rd cent. on shores of Lobnor; subsequently explored in Persia and Tibet; discovered a great range in north of Himalayas, 1907–8; works include *Trans-Himalaya* (1909–13), *My Life as an Explorer* (1925), and *Lop-nov* (1931).

Heem (*hām*), Jan Davidsz van (*c.* 1603–83), Dutch painter; *b.* Utrecht; greatest master of flower and fruit painting of his school.

Heemskerk (*hāmz'kerk*), Maerten Jacobsz or Maerten van Veen (1498–1574), Dutch religious painter of Ital. school; *b.* Heemskirk, near Alkmaar; principal works were burnt at Haarlem, 1572, when city was sacked by the Spaniards; many specimens of his work in continental galleries.

Hegel (*hā'gel*), Georg Wilhelm Friedrich (1770–1831), Ger. philosopher; *b.* Stuttgart; lecturer at Jena, Heidelberg, and Berlin; intimate friend of Schelling's, and collaborated with him; founder of absolute idealism, a development of the idealistic element of Kant's philosophy; it denies the materialistic interpretation of nature, lays stress on the evolutionary character of the universe, and maintains that this evolution is by conflict, so that ideas which seem contradictory are in fact complementary. His chief work, in which his theory is most fully developed, is his *Logic.* One of the greatest of Ger. philosophers, he has had an enormous influence on later philosophy, not only in Germany but also in France and Britain.

Heidenstam (*hī'den-stam*), Carl Gustaf Werner von (1859–), Swed. man of letters; *b.* in Orebro; one of most brilliant figures in modern Swed. literature; works are ideal, romantic, and full of imagination; Nobel Prize for literature, 1916; publications include *Endymion, Hans Alienus, Karolinerna*, famous romance of Charles XII.; also poems and historical tales.

Heifetz (*hī'fets*), Jascha (1901–), Russ. violinist; *b.* Vilna; had great success during world tours; settled in New York.

Heine (*hī'ne*), Heinrich (1797–1856), Ger. poet; *b.* Düsseldorf of Jewish parents; studied law at Bonn, Göttingen, Berlin; adopted Christianity, 1825; pub. *Reisebilder* (1826), *Buch der Lieder* (1827), which made him the most popular poet of Germany; visited England, 1827; settled in Paris, 1831; to this period belong *Französische Zustände* (1831–2), *Der Salon* (1834), *Ludwig Börne* (1840), *Die Romantische Schule*

(1836) (prose works); *Atta Troll* (1847), *Romanzero* (1851), and *Letzte Gedichte und Gedanken* (1853, 1855), rank among his finest poetical works; bedridden from 1848 to 1856; belongs partly to Romantic movement, partly to 'Young Germany' revolt; great lyric writer, marred at times, however, by cynicism and sentimentality.

Hel'ena, St. (*c.* 247–328), wife of Roman emperor Constantius I., and mother of Constantine the Great; accepted Christianity and made pilgrimage to Jerusalem, where she is said to have discovered the Cross and built the churches of the Holy Sepulchre and Nativity.

Heliogab'alus, or Elagabalus (*c.* 205–222), Roman emperor, 218–222; original name was Varius Avitus Bassianus, which was changed when he became priest to sun-god Elagabal; notorious for debauchery; assassinated during mutiny.

Hel'ler, Stephen (1815–88), Hungarian pianist and composer; *b.* Budapest; distinguished himself at an early age; works are marked by charm and delicacy; *Nuits Blanches*, *Dans les Bois*, etc., are well known.

Helm'holtz, Hermann von (1821–94), Ger. scientist; *b.* Potsdam; prof. of physiology in Heidelberg, and later of physics in Berlin; gave a new direction to physiological research in seeing and hearing, his *Sensations of Tone* and his *Physiological Optics* being epoch-making works; created a new field in hydrodynamics by investigations on vortex motion, and contributed to theory of electrodynamics; by his inspiration Hertz discovered the Hertzian waves of wireless telegraphy.

Héloïse. See under Abélard.

Helps, Sir Arthur (1813–75), Eng. essayist and historian; *b.* Streatham; clerk to Privy Council, 1860–75; author of *Friends in Council*, *Companions of my Solitude*, *Conquerors of the New World*, etc.

Helvétius (*el-vā-sē-oos'*), Claude Adrien (1715–71), Fr. philosopher; *b.* Paris; wrote *De l'Esprit* (1758), in which he reduces intellectual activity to physical sensation, and finds prime motive of conduct in self-gratification; also teaches that all men are born equal in faculty; book evoked storm of abuse; was censured by Diderot and refuted by Rousseau in his *Emile*.

He'mans, Felicia Dorothea Browne, Mrs. (1793–1835), Eng. poetess; *b.* Liverpool; pub. many books of verse popular at the time; much of her work appeals to the heart rather than the intellect, but such lyrics as 'The Better Land,' 'The Graves of a Household,' 'Casabianca,' and 'The Homes of England,' are still well known.

Hen'derson, Alexander (1583–1646), Scot. divine; *b.* in Fife; held living of Leuchars, Fife, 1614–39; rector of Edinburgh Univ. from 1640; chaplain to Charles I., 1641; helped to draft National Covenant and Solemn League and Covenant; real successor of John Knox in organizing Presbyterianism.

Henderson, Rt. Hon. Arthur (1863–1935), Brit. Labour leader; *b.* Glasgow; served apprenticeship as moulder in Newcastle; held various positions in Trade Union movement; mayor of Darlington, 1903; M.P. for Barnard Castle, 1903–18; chairman of parliamentary Labour party, 1908–10 and 1914–17; P.C., 1915; joined first Coalition government as president of Board of Education, 1915–16; paymaster-general and Labour adviser to government, 1916; member of war cabinet, 1916–17; went on government mission to Russia, 1917; defeated at general election, 1918; elected for Widnes, 1919; home secretary first Labour government, 1924; secretary of state for foreign affairs, 1929–31; president of League of Nations Disarmament Conference, 1932–3.

Henderson, SIR DAVID (1862–1921), Brit. soldier; *b.* Glasgow; served with distinction in Sudan, 1898, and in S. African War, 1899–1900; director-general of military aeronautics, 1913–18; his administration much criticized, but a commission of inquiry rebutted charges made against him; during Great War promoted lieut.-general; K.C.V.O., 1919.

Hen'ley, WILLIAM ERNEST (1849–1903), Eng. critic and poet; *b.* Gloucester; a lifelong invalid; his long friendship with R. L. Stevenson began in Edinburgh Infirmary; went to London, 1877; ed., in turn, of *London* (1877–8), *Magazine of Art* (1882–6), *Scots* (afterwards *National*) *Observer* (1888–93), and *New Review* (1893–8); works include *Book of Verses* (1888), *English Lyrics* (1897), *Views and Reviews—Literature* (1890), *Views and Reviews—Art* (1902), *Centenary Burns* (with T. F. Henderson, 1896–7), and plays *Admiral Guinea* (1892) and *Macaire* (1895), in collaboration with R. L. Stevenson.

Henner (*en-ār'*), JEAN JACQUES (1829–1905), Fr. painter; *b.* in Alsace; noted for his figure drawing; Grand Prix de Rome, 1858; works include *Biblis changée en Source* (1867) and *Chaste Suzanne* (1865).

Henriett'a Mari'a (1609–1666), daughter of Henry IV. of France; married Charles I. of Britain, 1625, on his promise to relieve R.C.'s; supported him in quarrels with Scots and Eng. parliament; raised funds on continent for prosecution of Eng. Civil War; retired to France, 1644, and continued to support her husband till his execution, 1649; returned to England after Restoration, 1660; *d.* in France.

Henry I., BEAUCLERC (1068–1135), King of England; youngest son of William the Conqueror; succeeded in 1100; defeated elder brother Robert at Tenchebrai, 1106, and took possession of the duchy of Normandy; defeated conspiracies by Fr. king in favour of Robert's son, 1119. Henry's son William was drowned in *White Ship*, 1120. Instituted exchequer; championed interests of nation against dominance of Norman barons.

Henry II. (1133–89), King of England; son of Matilda and Geoffrey Plantagenet; grandson of Henry I.; held large Fr. possessions; succeeded Stephen, 1154; at first supported by his minister, Becket, whom he created archbishop; quarrelled with Church, issued Constitutions of Clarendon, 1164, which Becket opposed; after latter's murder, 1170, Henry had to make various concessions to Church; conquered Ireland, 1172; crushed barons' rebellion, 1173, and reduced their power; obtained overlordship of Scotland by Treaty of Falaise, 1174; sons intrigued against him towards end of reign.

Henry III. (1207–72), King of England; succeeded his father, King John, 1216; attempted unsuccessfully to regain Fr. possessions; favouritism towards foreign adventurers and misrule generally aroused hostility of barons, who compelled him to assent to Provisions of Oxford, 1258, subsequent annulment of which resulted in outbreak of Barons' War under Simon de Montfort; Henry was defeated at Lewes, 1264, but Prince Edward defeated barons at Evesham, 1265; thenceforth Henry was a cipher.

Henry IV. (1367–1413), BOLINGBROKE, King of England; son of

John of Gaunt; helped Richard II. to suppress Gloucester's rebellion, 1397, but was banished, 1398; on Richard II.'s seizing his estates, Henry invaded England, overcame Richard, and became first Lancastrian king, 1399; routed the Percies, who had joined Glendower's revolt, at Shrewsbury, 1403; crushed Scrope's rebellion, 1405; captured Prince James of Scotland, 1406; subdued the Percies, 1408, and ended Welsh rebellion; persecuted Lollards.

Henry V. (1387–1422), King of England; son of Henry IV.; succeeded, 1413; repressed the Lollards; claimed Fr. throne, invaded France, and won battle of Agincourt, 1415; married Princess Catherine of France; attained regency of France and succession to Fr. crown by Treaty of Troyes, 1420; spent remaining years in suppressing Fr. risings against Eng. rule. An able general, his internal administration was marked by a love of justice and order.

Henry VI. (1421–71), King of England; son of Henry V.; succeeded, 1422; crowned King of France, 1431, but gradually lost Fr. possessions following Joan of Arc's campaign; suppressed Cade's rebellion, 1450; Henry became insane, 1453, but recovered; Wars of Roses began, 1455; resulted, 1461, in Henry's defeat, when Edward IV. became king; Henry was murdered in Tower, 1471; founded Eton School, and King's Coll., Cambridge.

Henry VII. (1457–1509), King of England; founder of Tudor line; son of a half-brother of Henry VI.; married Edward IV.'s daughter Elizabeth; defeated Richard III. at Bosworth Field, 1485, and became king; instituted Court of Star Chamber, 1487; suppressed Lambert Simnel's rebellion, 1487; supported Brittany against France; formed alliance with Span. and Ger. kings, and invaded France, 1492; concluded commercial treaty with Flanders, 1496; overthrew Perkin Warbeck's insurrection, 1497; amassed large fortune; strengthened crown at expense of nobles.

Henry VIII. (1491–1547), King of England; second son of Henry VII.; succeeded in 1509, and married Catherine of Aragon, his brother's widow; invaded France, winning Battle of Spurs, 1514; held conclave with Francis I. at Field of Cloth of Gold, 1520, but sided with Francis' rival, Charles V.; made peace with France in 1527. Wolsey's failure to obtain the papal decree for Henry's divorce led to his downfall; Henry disavowed the papal supremacy in England, and, with Cromwell's aid, broke with Rome and established himself as head of Eng. Church; divorced Catherine, 1533, and married Anne Boleyn, who was beheaded, 1536; dissolved monasteries, and put down Pilgrimage of Grace, 1537; married Jane Seymour, their son afterwards becoming Edward VI.; subsequent wives were Anne of Cleves, Catherine Howard, and Catherine Parr; incorporated Wales, 1536; later years marked by wars with France and Scotland; led expedition to France; took Boulogne, 1544.

Henry I., THE FOWLER (*c.* 876–936), King of Germany; was Duke of Saxony and succeeded Conrad I., 919; acquired Lorraine, 923; defeated Slavs, Danes, Hungarians.

Henry II., THE SAINT (973–1024), Holy Roman emperor; succeeded Otto III., 1002; King of Italy, 1004; crowned emperor at Rome, 1014; waged intermittent war with Poland, 1002–18; liberated Bohemia from Polish yoke, 1004; concluded peace at Bautzen, 1018; supported Benedict VIII. against Greeks, 1021.

Henry III., THE BLACK (1017–56), Holy Roman emperor; son of Conrad II.; Ger. king, 1028; forced Bretislaus of Bohemia to acknowledge his suzerainty, 1041; defeated Hungarians, 1045, and reinstated Peter of Hungary; crowned emperor, 1039, by Pope Clement II., whose election he had obtained; alienated nobility by support of clergy; built Worms, Mainz, and Spires cathedrals.

Henry IV. (1050–1106), Holy Roman emperor; succeeded his father, Henry III., as king and emperor, 1056; deposed and defeated Otto of Bavaria, 1071; waged war against Saxony and Thuringia, 1073–88; came into conflict with Pope Gregory VII., who forced him to do penance at Canossa, 1077; Henry subsequently repudiated his vow of obedience, deposed Pope, and elected antipope, Clement III.; invaded Italy, 1081; took Rome, 1082; was crowned emperor, 1084; later years marked by further disputes with popes and Ger. princes; abdicated, 1105.

Henry V. (1081–1125), Holy Roman emperor and Ger. king; son of Henry IV.; subdued Robert of Flanders, 1106; reign marked by dispute with Pope; took him prisoner, 1111; was excommunicated, 1112; ban removed and dispute settled by Concordat of Worms, 1122.

Henry VI. (1165–97), Holy Roman emperor; son of Frederick I.; elected Ger. king, 1169; married Constance, heiress to throne of Sicily, 1186; emperor, 1191; succession to Sicily opposed by Tancred, after whose death Henry became king; coalition formed against him in Germany, 1191, but he put down all opponents both there and in Italy; held Richard Coeur de Lion captive, 1193–4.

Henry VII. (*c.* 1269–1313), Holy Roman emperor; son of Henry III., Count of Luxembourg; elected Ger. king, 1308; emperor, 1309; tried to unite Germany and Italy, and was crowned at Milan, 1311; died in Italy while attempting to establish imperial authority.

Henry I. (*c.* 1005–60), King of France, 1031; waged war unsuccessfully with Odo, Count of Blois, and William, Duke of Normandy.

Henry II. (1519–59), King of France, 1547; married Catherine de' Medici; persecuted Protestants; took Metz, Toul, Verdun, from Emperor Charles V.; recovered Boulogne, 1550, and Calais, 1558; accidentally killed in tournament at Paris.

Henry III. (1551–89), King of France; reign marked by war between Catholics and Huguenots (massacre of St. Bartholomew, 1572); also by struggle between king and Duke of Guise, ending in murder of latter, 1588; very dissolute; was assassinated; ended Valois line.

Henry IV., HENRY OF NAVARRE (1553–1610), King of Navarre, 1572, and of France from 1589; leader of Huguenots; married Margaret of Valois, sister of Charles IX., 1572; had to fight Spain and the Catholic League, winning battles of Arques, 1589, and Ivry, 1599; turned R.C., 1593; passed Edict of Nantes in favour of Huguenots, 1598; developed agriculture and commerce; introduced silk industry; carried out financial reforms; assassinated by Ravaillac.

Henry THE LION (1129–95), Duke of Saxony and Bavaria; married Matilda of England, 1168; greatly extended his domains in Germany; refused to aid Emperor Frederick I. in Ital. campaign, 1176; banned by emperor, 1180; submitted, 1181; obtained Brunswick and Lüneberg; rebelled against Henry VI.; founded Munich; encouraged development of Hamburg and Lübeck.

Henry THE MINSTREL. See HARRY, BLIND.

Henry THE NAVIGATOR (1394–1460), Port. prince; *b.* Oporto; son of John I. of Portugal and Philippa, John of Gaunt's daughter; served with great distinction at siege of Ceuta, 1415; took keen interest in navigation and discovery; sent expeditions along the west coast of Africa at his own expense; colonized Madeira Islands and Azores; constructed an observatory at Sagres, near Cape St. Vincent; in later years again distinguished himself in the field in Morocco, and took Alcazar the Little, 1458.

Henry, JOSEPH (1799–1878), Amer. scientist; *b.* Albany, New York; developed electro-magnet; prof. of physics, Princetown univ., 1832, where he worked out principle of telegraph relay instrument; first secretary of Smithsonian Institution, 1846; as chairman of Lighthouse Board improved lighting and signalling of lighthouses; made researches in meteorology, and was a founder of U.S.A. Weather Service.

Henry, O. See under PORTER, WILLIAM SYDNEY.

Henry, PATRICK (1736–99), Amer. orator and statesman; *b.* in Virginia; became a lawyer, 1760, and in 1763 acquired sudden fame as orator against unjust taxation; carried the Virginian vote for independence, 1776; governor of Virginia, 1776–9 and 1784–6, and sat in its Legislature, 1780–4 and 1786–90.

Henryson, ROBERT (*c.* 1430–1500), Scot. poet; probably schoolmaster in Dunfermline; wrote *The Moral Fables of Æsop, Orpheus and Eurydice, The Want of Wise Men,* and *The Testament of Cresseid.*

Henschel, SIR GEORGE (1850–1934), baritone singer, composer, and conductor; *b.* Breslau; naturalized Englishman, 1890; first appearance as pianist, 1862, as vocalist, 1866; settled in London, 1878, and succeeded Jenny Lind at the Royal Coll. of Music, 1886–88; founder and first conductor of London Symphony Concerts; retired from singing, 1914; his compositions include songs, vocal studies, an opera, a comic opera, a *Requiem Mass, Stabat Mater,* and *Te Deum.*

Henson, HERBERT HENSLEY (1863–), Eng. churchman; *b.* London; vicar of Barking, 1888–95; dean of Durham, 1912–18; Bishop of Hereford, 1918–20; Bishop of Durham, 1920; noted for his liberal theological views; works include *Puritanism in England* (1912) and *Disestablishment* (1929).

Henty, GEORGE ALFRED (1832–1902), Eng. war correspondent and author; *b.* near Cambridge; went to Crimea, 1854; witnessed Italo-Austrian War, 1859; was with Garibaldi in the Tirol, 1860; accompanied Prince of Wales to India, 1876; newspaper correspondent during Franco-German War, 1870–1, and Turco-Serbian War, 1876; wrote about 80 books for boys.

Hep'plewhite, GEORGE (*d.* 1786), Eng. furniture maker; contemporary with Chippendale, but his work was of a lighter and more elegant character; painted designs upon satinwood were a feature of many of his productions; probably opened his business in Cripplegate, London, 1760–70.

Heracli'tus (*c.* 540–475 B.C.), Gr. philosopher; *b.* Ephesus; of aristocratic birth; called 'the weeping philosopher'; did much for study of metaphysics; thought 'everything is and is not,' and that in diversity true unity was to be found; fire is the original principle, and out of it the soul was created.

Heracli'us (*c.* 575–641), Byzantine emperor; beset by Avars from Danube, and by Persians in East; made treaty with Avars,

620; defeated Persians, 627–8; lost Syria and Egypt to Arabs.

Her′bart, JOHANN FRIEDRICH (1776–1841), Ger. philosopher; *b.* Oldenburg; prof. at Göttingen, 1805–9, and Königsberg, 1809–33, then again at Göttingen; importance of his work lies in his employment of mathematical symbols to express processes of psychology; his doctrine of apperception has exercised a powerful influence on education.

[*The Meaning of Education as interpreted by Herbart* (1907), by F. H. Hayward.]

Her′bert, ALAN PATRICK (1890–), Eng. author; called to the Bar, 1918; member of *Punch* staff; works include *Trials of Topsy, Water Gipsies,* a novel, and the musical comedy *Tantivy Towers*; M.P. for Oxford Univ., 1935.

Herbert, GEORGE (1593–1633), Eng. ecclesiastic and poet; *b.* in Wales; younger brother of Lord Herbert of Cherbury; public orator at Cambridge, 1619; ordained priest, 1630, with a living in Wilts; his works include *The Temple* (1633) and his deeply spiritual *Sacred Poems and Private Ejaculations* (1634).

Herbert OF CHERBURY, EDWARD, LORD (1583–1648), Eng. philosopher, historian, and diplomatist; *b.* in Salop; fought in Netherlands, 1610–14; ambassador to France, 1617–24; being imprisoned by Parliament, 1642, took no part in Civil War; author of *De Veritate,* an important metaphysical work, *De Religione Gentilium,* a comparative history of religion, and other philosophical treatises.

Herbert OF LEA, SIDNEY, 1ST LORD (1810–61), Eng. statesman; *b.* Richmond, Surrey; M.P. for S. Wilts, 1832–60; secretary to Board of Control, 1834–5; secretary to the Admiralty, 1841–5; secretary for war, 1852–5; during Crimean War sent Florence Nightingale to Crimea; colonial secretary, 1855; again secretary for war, 1859–60; responsible for transfer of Ind. army to crown control; peerage, 1860.

Her′der, JOHANN GOTTFRIED VON (1744–1803), Ger. poet, critic, and philosopher; studied medicine and theology at Königsberg, 1762–64; teacher at Riga, 1764–9; after travelling in Germany, France, England, and Holland, became an intimate friend of and greatly influenced Goethe; court preacher at Weimar from 1776; works include *Volkslieder* (1778–9; songs and ballads), *Vom Geist der Hebräischen Poesie* (1782), and *Ideen zur Philosophie der Geschichte der Menschheit* (1785–94), prose works; trans. the Span. romances of the *Cid.*

Herd′man, ROBERT (1829–88), Scot. artist; *b.* in Perthshire; studied in Scotland and Italy; leading portrait painter; principal pictures include *After the Battle, Landless and Homeless,* and a portrait of Lady Shand.

Herdman, SIR WILLIAM ABBOTT (1858–1924), naturalist; *b.* Edinburgh; son of above; prof. of natural history, Liverpool, 1881–1919, and of oceanography, 1919–21; assisted in establishing marine biological station at Port Erin, Isle of Man, and sea-fish hatchery near Barrow.

Her′eward the Wake (*fl. c.* 1070), Saxon patriot who defied authority of William I., and was in possession of the Isle of Ely in 1070; when finally overcome by William he succeeded in escaping; legend asserts that he was subsequently reconciled with William.

[*Hereward the Wake* (1866), by Charles Kingsley.]

Her′iot, GEORGE (1563–1624), Scot. goldsmith; popularly known as 'Jingling Geordie'; accompanied court of James VI. to London, 1603; acquired considerable wealth, and bequeathed residue of his fortune to endow Heriot's Hospital, now George Heriot's School, Edinburgh.

Herk'omer, Sir Hubert von (1849–1914), portrait and subject painter; *b.* in Bavaria; became naturalized Englishman; exhibited *After the Toil of the Day* at Royal Academy, 1873; R.A., 1890; founded school of art at Bushey, 1883; best pictures include *The Last Muster*, *On Strike*, and portraits of Ruskin, Wagner, and Tennyson.

He'ro of Alexandria (1st or 2nd cent. B.C.), mathematician; probably Egyptian, but wrote in Greek; invented a water-clock, a hydraulic organ, and a compressed-air catapult, and studied the determination of areas, volumes, and heights.

Her'od. (1) The Great (*d.* 4 B.C.), King of Judæa (40 B.C.); after severe struggle, made himself master of Jerusalem; rebuilt Cæsarea, the temple at Jerusalem, and restored Samaria; ordered massacre of innocents (see Matt. 2). (2) Antipas, son of Herod the Great, tetrarch of Galilee and Peræa, 4 B.C–39 A.D.; beheaded John the Baptist; to him Pilate sent Jesus. (3) Agrippa I., son of Aristobulus, a favourite of Emperor Caligula; one of most powerful kings of East; executed Apostle James, imprisoned Peter; eaten of worms (Acts 12 : 23). (4) Agrippa II., son of (3); took side of Rome when Jews began war with Rome, 67; after capture of Jerusalem, 70, retired to Rome; before him and Festus St. Paul made his defence at Cæsarea (Acts 25 and 26).

Herod'otus (*c.* 484–*c.* 425 B.C.), Gr. historian; *b.* in Asia Minor; known as the 'father of history'; travelled for many years in Egypt, Babylon, Greece, and Italy, and his descriptions of the events of the period are invaluable; main subject of his work was the uprising of the Greeks against the Persians.

Herrera (*ār-rā'rā*), Francisco (1576–1656), Span. painter; *b.* Seville; pupil of Luis Fernandez; chiefly noted for his *St. Basil* in the Louvre, Paris, and *Apotheosis of San Hermangildo* and *Vision of San Basilio* in the museum at Seville; a skilled worker in bronze and sculptor. His son Francisco (1622–85) became an accomplished painter of still-life, and later of portraits.

Her'rick, Robert (1591–1674), Eng. poet; *b.* London; son of a goldsmith; apprenticed to his father's trade, but subsequently took orders at Cambridge and became rector of Dean Prior, Devon; prolific writer of exquisite lyrics dealing with love and country life; best works are *Noble Numbers* (1647) and *Hesperides* (1648).

Herriot (*er-ē-ō'*), Edouard (1872–), Fr. statesman; *b.* Troyes; was in turn university prof., lecturer, and journalist; mayor of Lyons, 1905; senator, 1912; minister of public works, 1916–17; deputy of Rhone department, 1919; leader of Radical party; premier and minister of foreign affairs, 1924, when he strongly supported peace policy; resigned over financial policy, 1925; minister of public instruction, 1926–8; prime minister and minister of foreign affairs, 1932.

Herschel (*her'shel*). (1) Friedrich Wilhelm (1738–1822), better known as Sir William Herschel, astronomer; *b.* Hanover; trained as a musician; to escape military service came to England, 1757; organist at Bath; studied the stars with a 7-foot telescope of his own construction; later constructed a 20-foot and a 40-foot instrument; discovered the planet Uranus, 1781, and also two of the satellites of Saturn; astronomer to George III.; presented to Royal Soc. a catalogue of 5,000 nebulæ and star clusters which he had discovered, 1802; knighted, 1816. (2) CAROLINE LUCRETIA (1750–1848), most famous woman astronomer; *b.* Hanover; sister of (1); came to England, 1772, and was appointed his assistant when he became astronomer-royal; discovered eight comets and many nebulæ and star clusters. (3) SIR JOHN FREDERICK WILLIAM (1792–1871), Eng. astronomer; son of (1); read for the bar, but never practised; resided, 1834–8, at Cape Town; set up an observatory, and enormously extended knowledge of the southern skies; returned to England, 1838, publishing the result of his survey of the skies; pub. *Outlines of Astronomy* (1849).

Hert'ling, GEORG, COUNT VON (1843–1919), Ger. writer and politician; *b.* Darmstadt; prof. of philosophy, univ. of Munich; wrote historical and philosophical works; entered Reichstag, 1875; employed by Bismarck during the Kulturkampf to secure concessions from Rome; leader of the Catholic centre; president of the council and minister of foreign affairs in Bavaria, 1911; later laboured for supremacy of Prussia; Ger. chancellor, 1917, and made treaties of Brest-Litovsk and Bukharest; retired, 1918.

Hertz, HEINRICH RUDOLPH (1857–94), Ger. physicist; *b.* Hamburg; prof. of physics, Bonn, 1889; demonstrated the similarity between electro-magnetic, light, and heat waves, and worked at electric discharges in gases; wireless telegraphy is a practical application of his investigations; important writings include *Electric Waves* (1893), *Miscellaneous Papers* (1896), and *Principles of Mechanics* (1899).

Hert'zog, JAMES BARRY MUNNIK (1866–), S. African politician and soldier; *b.* in Cape Province; a Free State general in S. African War; as minister of education, 1907, urged rights of Dutch language in Orange Free State; minister of justice in first Union Cabinet, 1910–12; anti-imperial views caused his omission from cabinet of 1912; leader of Nationalist party; opposed S. African intervention in European war; minister of native affairs, 1924–9; prime minister since 1924; minister of external affairs, 1929; formed Coalition government with Smuts, 1933.

Hervieu (*ăr-vyĕ'*), PAUL ERNEST (1857–1915), Fr. psychological novelist and dramatist; *b.* Paris; called to the bar, 1877; great originality and charm of style; novels include *Diogène-le-Chien* (1882), *Flirt* (1890), *L'Armature* (1895); plays include *Les Paroles restent* (1892), *La Course du Flambeau* (1901), *Le Dédale* (1903), *Le Réveil* (1905), and *Connais-toi* (1909); works deal chiefly with sex problems.

Herzen (*hert'sen*), ALEXANDER (1812–70), Russian critic and publicist; *b.* Moscow; exiled to Siberia, 1834; returned to Moscow, 1840, but left Russia, 1847; in London pub. two Russian periodicals, the *Polar Star* and the *Bell* (*Kolokol*); espoused Polish cause, 1863, losing all influence in Russia; *Memoirs* (Eng. trans., 1924–7).

Herzl, THEODOR (1860–1904), Jewish politician; *b.* Budapest; founder of Zionist movement; long on staff of Viennese *Neue Freie Presse*; in 1896 produced *Der Judenstaat,* advocating founding of autonomous Jewish state.

He'siod (*c.* 8th cent. B.C.), one of earliest Gr. poets; *b.* Ascra, in Bœotia; poems are *Works and Days,* a didactic work on peasant life, and *Theogony,* an account of the origin of the gods and heroes.

[Eng. trans. of poems, by A. W. Mair, 1908.]

Hew'art, GORDON, 1ST BARON (1870–), Brit. politician and lawyer; *b.* Bury; for some years a journalist; called to bar, 1902; Liberal M.P. for Leicester, 1913–22; solicitor-general, 1916–19; attorney-general, 1919–22; privy councillor, 1918; lord chief-justice since 1922.

Hew'ins, WILLIAM ALBERT SAMUEL (1865–1931), Brit. politician and economist; *b.* near Wolverhampton; prof. of economic science, King's Coll., London, 1897–1903; Unionist M.P. for Hereford, 1912–18; strong advocate of Tariff Reform.

Hew'lett, MAURICE HENRY (1861–1923), Eng. novelist and poet; *b.* Addington, Kent; keeper of Land Revenue Records and Enrolments, 1896–1900; pub. essays, *Earthwork out of Tuscany* (1894); then *Songs and Meditations* (1897); first novel, *The Forest Lovers* (1898), followed by *Richard Yea-and-Nay*, *The Queen's Quair*, *Halfway House*, and many others; poems include *Song of the Plow.*

Heyden (*hī'den*), JAN VAN DER (1637–1712), Dutch painter, chiefly of architecture; *b.* Gorinchem; sometimes collaborated with Adrian van der Velde, who supplied figures for his pictures; *View of the Town Hall, Amsterdam*, and *A Street in Cologne* are among his masterpieces.

Heyse (*hī'ze*), PAUL JOHANN LUDWIG (1830–1914), Ger. poet, dramatist, and novelist; *b.* Berlin; renowned for his *Novellen* (short stories); has also written fine lyrics, narrative poems, and plays; Nobel Prize, 1910.

Hey'wood, JOHN (*c.* 1497–*c.* 1580), Eng. dramatist and epigrammatist; famed for his *Interludes*, which link the morality plays to modern drama; chief of these are *The Play of Love* and *The Play of the Wether*; author also of many noted epigrams.

Heywood, THOMAS (*c.* 1570–*c.* 1650), Eng. dramatist, of voluminous output; *b.* in Lincs; excelled in domestic plays, which were praised by Lamb; chief of these are *A Woman Killed with Kindness*, *Fair Maid of the Exchange*, and *Love's Mistress*; also wrote an *Apology for Actors.*

Hezeki'ah (*fl. c.* 700 B.C.), King of Judah, son and successor of Ahaz; influenced by the prophet Isaiah, was active in carrying out reforms; improved position of Jerusalem as a stronghold, and delivered his country from the Assyrians.

Hib'bert, ROBERT (1770–1849), Eng. merchant; *b.* in Jamaica; founder of Hibbert Trust for the 'spread of Christianity in its most simple and intelligible form.' The Hibbert Lectures and *Hibbert Journal* have been maintained since 1878 by this Trust.

Hich'ens, ROBERT SMYTHE (1864–), Eng. novelist and journalist; *b.* in Kent; gave up music for literature; won recognition with *The Green Carnation* (1894); other novels include *An Imaginative Man*, *Flames*, *The Woman with the Fan*, *The Garden of Allah* (1905; dramatized 1920), *Bella Donna* (1909), and *The God within Him* (1926).

Hicks, SIR EDWARD SEYMOUR (1871–), English actor and author; *b.* in Jersey; joined Gaiety company, 1893; chiefly associated with his wife, Ellaline Terriss; has made successful tours in U.S.A. and S. Africa; author of over 60 plays; kt., 1935.

Hicks, WILLIAM (1830–83), an Anglo-Egyptian general, known as HICKS PASHA; served through Ind. Mutiny and in Abyssinian War, 1867–8; entered Egyptian army, 1882, and was made pasha by Khedive; commander-in-chief against Mahdi, 1883; his force was ambushed and massacred at Kashgil.

Hicks-Beach, SIR MICHAEL. See ST. ALDWYN, VISCOUNT.

Hil'ary, ST. (*d.* 367), Bishop of

Poitiers, known as the 'Hammer of the Arians'; wrote famous treatise on the Trinity; his day is Jan. 13.

Hil'da, St. (614–680), founder, 658, and first abbess of Whitby; patroness of Cædmon; baptized by Paulinus; took the veil, *c.* 647; abbess of Hartlepool, 649; her effigy appears on anc. seal of Hartlepool.

Hildebrand, Pope. See under Gregory.

Hill, George Birkbeck Norman (1835–1903), Eng. author; *b.* in Middlesex; made special study of 18th cent. literature, and is recognized as a leading authority on life and works of Dr. Johnson.

Hill, Octavia (1838–1912), Eng. social reformer; *b.* London; laboured with Ruskin to improve working-class dwellings; helped to institute Charity Organization Soc., etc.

Hill, Sir Rowland (1795–1879), Brit. statesman; *b.* Kidderminster; in early life a successful schoolmaster; invented rotary press for printing newspapers; originator of penny postage (adopted 1839), and inventor of adhesive stamp; secretary to postmaster-general, 1846.

Hill'el (*c.* 70 B.C.–*c.* A.D. 10), famous Jewish rabbi; *b.* in Babylonia; his gentler view of the law was opposed to that of Shammai; author of some sayings proclaiming the duty of love to one's neighbour, and of others emphasizing the value of learning; collected the *Mishnah*, or oral traditions of the law.

Hil'ler, Ferdinand (1811–85), musical conductor, pianist, and composer; *b.* Frankfurt-on-Main; founder and director of Conservatorium, Cologne; wrote chamber music, two oratorios, six operas, etc.; greatest work is oratorio *Die Zerstörung Jerusalems.*

Hin'denburg, Paul von (1847–1934), German soldier; *b.* Posen; served in Austrian campaign, 1866, and in Franco-Ger. War, 1870–1; specialized on topography of E. Prussia; retired, 1911. On outbreak of Great War, 1914, re-commissioned as commander-in-chief, with Ludendorff, against Russians in E. Prussia; won decisive victory over Russians at Tannenberg, Aug. 1914; made field-marshal, and placed in chief command of the Austro-Ger. forces on Eastern front; occupied Warsaw, May 1915, and Russians were driven back to the Pripet marshes; his spectacular advances gave frenzied delight to the Ger. people; was appointed, 1916, chief of the general staff, and brought with him his faithful lieutenant, Ludendorff, who was the brains of the combination; was forced by Somme battles to retreat to the 'Hindenburg Line,' which was broken Sept. 1918; retained his chief command until June 1919; after period of retirement accepted office as president of Ger. Republic, 1925; re-elected, 1932; wrote *Out of My Life* (1920).

Hipparchus (*hi-pär'kus*), greatest astronomer of anc. times, sometimes called 'the father of astronomy'; lived and worked in Rhodes during 2nd cent. B.C.; constructed first star catalogue (1,080 stars), and discovered precession of equinoxes; founder of trigonometry, and employed theory of eccentrics and epicycles to explain planetary motion.

Hip'per, Franz, Rear-admiral von (?1866–1932), Ger. sailor; *b.* in Upper Bavaria; entered navy, 1881; during Great War bombarded Scarborough and Hartlepool, 1914; commanded Ger. fleet at battle of Dogger Bank, 1915, and played important part at Jutland battle, 1916; commander-in-chief of High Seas fleet, 1918, and arranged surrender of Ger. navy, 1918.

Hippocrates (*hi-pok'ra-tēz*) (*b.* 460 B.C.), Gr. philosopher and physician; a descendant of Æsculapius; *b.* Cos; called 'father of medicine,' and first to treat it scientifically; a firm believer in recuperative force of nature; wrote *Prognostics*, *Epidemics*, *Aphorisms*.

Hippolytus (*hi-pol'i-tus*) (*d.* 235), writer of early church; quarrelled with Calixtus I.; chief work, *A Refutation of all the Heresies*, known as the *Philosophumena*; wrote also *Christ and Antichrist*.

Hirsch, MAURICE, BARON DE (1831–96), Jewish capitalist and philanthropist; *b.* Munich; endowed the *Alliance Israélite Universelle*, 1889; gave £500,000 for establishment of schools in Galicia and Bukovina; founded Jewish Colonization Association, to benefit persecuted Jews.

Hit'ler, ADOLF (1889–), Ger. politician; *b.* in Upper Austria; served in architect's office; founded 'Hitler's Volunteers' to oppose Social Democrats; started a revolt in Bavaria, 1923, but failed and was imprisoned; National Socialists, or 'Nazis,' rose to power under his leadership, 1930–2; was elected chancellor of the Reichstag, 1933, and established virtual dictatorship, adopting a strong anti-semitic policy. Succeeded Hindenburg as president with title of *Führer*. His book *Mein Kampf* (1925) is autobiographical.

Hoadly (*hōd'li*), BENJAMIN (1676–1761), Eng. prelate; bishop successively of Bangor, Hereford, Salisbury, and Winchester; engaged, 1717, in famous Bangorian controversy with the High Churchmen as to extent of eccles. authority.

Hoare, SIR SAMUEL (1880–), Eng. politician; educ. Harrow and Oxford; M.P. for Chelsea, 1910; sec. of state for air, 1922–24 and 1924–29; sec. of state for India, 1931–5; foreign secretary, 1935.

Ho'bart Pasha, AUGUSTUS CHARLES HOBART-HAMPDEN (1822–86), Brit. sailor; *b.* in Leicestershire; served with distinction in Crimean War, retiring with captain's rank; during Amer. Civil War commanded a blockade runner for Confederate states, describing his adventures in *Never Caught* (1867); joined Turk. navy and became admiral of Sultan's fleet, commanding Black Sea Fleet in Russian war of 1878.

Hob'bema, MEYNDERT (*c.* 1638–1709), Dutch landscape painter; *b.* Amsterdam; ranks with Cuyp and Ruysdael; his painting of peaceful landscapes unsurpassed; *The Avenue of Middelharnis*, *Showery Weather*, and others, are in National Gallery, London.

Hobbes (*hobz*), JOHN OLIVER. See CRAIGIE, P. M. T.

Hobbes, THOMAS (1588–1679), Eng. philosopher; *b.* Malmesbury; educated at Oxford; tutor in Cavendish family and remained in their service practically all his life. His fame is highest as a political philosopher; lived abroad, 1640–51, and devoted his attention to his great book *Leviathan*, in which he anticipated later thinkers in believing that government was for the benefit of the people as a whole; he believed that the civil power residing in the people was absolute. He laid foundation on which political philosophers of the 19th cent. were to build.

[*Hobbes* (1904; 'English Men of Letters'), by Sir Leslie Stephen.]

Hobbs, JOHN BERRY (1883–), Eng. cricketer; *b.* Cambridge; played for Surrey, 1905–32; played in Test Matches against Australia since 1907; established many batting records, including record aggregate of runs and record number of centuries.

Hobhouse, LEONARD TRELAW-

NEY (1864–1929), Eng. sociologist; on editorial staff of *Manchester Guardian*, 1897–1902, and *Tribune*, 1906–7; prof. of sociology, London Univ., from 1907; works include *The Labour Movement* (1893), *Democracy and Reaction* (1904), and *Principles of Sociology* (1924).

Hock'ing, JOSEPH (1855–), Eng. novelist; *b.* in Cornwall; land surveyor, 1878; entered Nonconformist ministry, 1884; travelled in Near East, 1887; retired, 1910; books include *Zillah* (1892), *All Men are Liars* (1895), *And shall Trelawney Die?* (1897), *The Path of Glory* (1917), *The Man who was Sure* (1931).

Hocking, SILAS KITTO (1850–1935), Eng. novelist; brother of above; *b.* in Cornwall; Nonconformist minister, 1870–96; devoted himself to literature; among novels are *God's Outcast* (1898), *The Beautiful Alien* (1916), *Watchers in the Dawn* (1920), *The Mystery Man* (1930).

Hod'son, WILLIAM STEPHEN RAIKES (1821–58), Brit. soldier; *b.* near Gloucester; served in first Sikh War, 1845; commanded Native Guides in the Punjab, 1852; dismissed on charges of fraud, 1855, but exonerated; on outbreak of Mutiny raised body of cavalry, known as Hodson's Horse; at fall of Delhi slew Mogul princes, which again subjected him to criticism; killed during attack on Lucknow.

Ho'fer, ANDREAS (1767–1810), Tirolese patriot; when Napoleon transferred Tirol from Austria to Bavaria headed Tirolese revolt, and thrice drove out French and Bavarians; ruled three months, then was forced to flee; was betrayed and shot.

Hoff'mann, AUGUST HEINRICH, commonly called HOFFMANN VON FALLERSLEBEN (1798–1874), Ger. poet and philologist; *b.* in Hanover; his revolutionary *Unpolitische Lieder* (1840–1) cost him his post as prof. of German at Breslau; noted for his collections of Ger. children's songs, folk-songs, etc.; verse collections include *Rheinleben* and a selection of *Gedichte*; philological works include *Deutsche Philologie* (1836) and *Horæ Belgicæ* (1830–62).

Hoffmann, ERNST THEODOR WILHELM (1776–1822), Ger. writer and musical composer; *b.* Königsberg; studied law, but led precarious career as musician, caricaturist, scene painter, story writer, etc.; finally resumed legal profession in Berlin; one of the master novelists of Ger. romantic school; chief novels trans. into Eng., such as *The Serapion Brethren*, *Weird Tales*, etc.; chief opera, *Undine*.

Hofmann, AUGUST WILHELM VON (1818–92), Ger. chemist; *b.* in Hesse; pupil of Liebig; prof. Royal Coll. of Chemistry, London, 1845, and at Berlin, 1865, where his researches and those of Perkins brought the coal-tar products under notice, and practically revolutionized the art of dyeing.

Hofmeyr (*hof'mīr*), JAN HENDRIK (1845–1909), S. African politician and journalist; *b.* Cape Town; leader for many years of the Cape Dutch party or Afrikander Bond; supported Cecil Rhodes till Jameson Raid, 1895; tried to influence Kruger and prevent outbreak of war; supported federation of S. African colonies.

Ho'garth, WILLIAM (1697–1764), Eng. painter and engraver; *b.* London; set up in business as an engraver; achieved first success with a series of six paintings representing *The Harlot's Progress* (1731), shortly afterwards engraved by himself; this series was followed by eight scenes depicting *The Rake's Progress* (1735), *Marriage à la Mode*, *Industry and Idleness*, *The Stage Coach*, *The March to Finchley*, portraits of

Garrick, Lavinia Fenton, scriptural pieces, etc. He achieved immediate success with his engravings, but his original paintings, apart from portraiture, found little appreciation, many remaining unsold at the time of his death; they are now recognized as masterpieces. His closing years were embittered by a quarrel with Wilkes and the poet Churchill

Hogg, JAMES (1770–1835), a Scot. poet and prose writer, known as 'the Ettrick Shepherd'; *b.* in Selkirkshire. His education was very meagre; from age of six was employed as a shepherd. He made the acquaintance of Sir Walter Scott; pub. *The Queen's Wake* (1813), which showed that he possessed genius of a high order; *The Brownie of Bodsbeck* (1818), a Covenanting story, is his best prose work; 'Bonnie Kilmeny' assures him a place among the poets; collected works pub. in 2 vols. (1865).

Hogg, QUINTIN (1845–1903), Eng. philanthropist; *b.* London; founder and president of the London Polytechnic, which provided educational facilities and rational amusements for young men and women; an extensive travelling agency was also established in connection with the institute.

Hohenlohe-Schillingsfürst (*hō-en-lō'e shil'ings-foorst*), CHLODWIG KARL VIKTOR, PRINCE VON (1819–1901), Ger. statesman; *b.* in Bavaria; after Sadowa appointed chief minister of Bavaria, 1866–70; advocated alliance of Bavaria with Prussia in Franco-German War; ambassador to Paris, 1874–85; governor of Alsace-Lorraine, 1885–94; imperial chancellor, 1894–1900; *Memoirs* (1906) incurred severe condemnation of Kaiser on account of their frank and damaging revelations.

Hohenzollern (*hō'en-tsol-ern*), name of Ger. imperial family; derived from castle in Swabia; first came into prominence, 1415, when one of its members became Elector of Brandenburg; in 1701 Frederick III., Elector of Brandenburg, became first King of Prussia, and in 1871 William I., seventh King of Prussia, became first Ger. emperor; his grandson, ex-Kaiser William II., abdicated at end of the Great War, 1918.

Holbein (*hol'bīn*). (1) HANS, THE ELDER (*c.* 1460–1524), Ger. painter; *b.* Augsburg; painted chiefly religious subjects; examples at Basle, Munich, and Augsburg, also at Hampton Court; the St. Sebastian altar-piece at Munich is his masterpiece. (2) HANS, THE YOUNGER (1497–1543), Ger. painter, son of (1); *b.* Augsburg; after assisting his father, joined painters' guild of Basel, 1519; engaged in portraiture, mural decoration, and the production of wood-cuts, including celebrated *Dance of Death*; visited London, 1526, with introduction from Erasmus to Sir Thomas More, and finally settled there; court painter to Henry VIII., 1532; died of plague; ranks among greatest of Ger. mediæval painters; works include *The Ambassadors* (National Gallery, London), *Anne of Cleves* (Louvre, Paris), and numerous private portraits.

Hol'den, SIR ISAAC (1807–97), Brit. inventor; *b.* near Paisley; after a life of struggle, invented a wool-comber, 1847, and established near Paris a wool-combing industry; eventually concentrated his business at Bradford, where it became the largest wool-combing establishment in the world; M.P. for Knaresborough, 1865–8, and for other constituencies, 1882–95; baronet, 1893.

Hole, WILLIAM (1846–1917), Scot. painter, etcher, and mural decorator; *b.* Salisbury; settled in Edinburgh; R.S.A., 1889; chief works: *Prince Charlie's Parliament*, *The Night's Catch*, etc.; also *The Life of Jesus of Nazareth*, a series of eight water-colour paintings; series of historical paintings in Scot. National Portrait Gallery, 1900, and municipal buildings, Edinburgh, 1903.

Hol'inshed (or HOLLINGSHEAD), RAPHAEL (*d. c.* 1580), Eng. chronicler; wrote *Chronicles of England, Scotland, and Ireland* (pub. 1578), from which Shakespeare's Eng. historical plays were largely drawn.

Holl, FRANK (1845–88), Eng. artist; *b.* London; R.A., 1883; achieved distinction as painter of genre subjects; among his notable portraits are Gladstone, Chamberlain, Bright, Wolseley, and Roberts.

Hol'land, HENRY FOX, 1ST BARON (1705–74), Brit. Whig politician; *b.* Chiswick; father of Charles James Fox; held various offices of state; leader of Lower House and secretary of state, 1755, 1762; paymaster-general, 1757.

Holland, HENRY SCOTT (1848–1918), Eng. clergyman; canon of Truro, 1882–4; canon and precentor of St. Paul's Cathedral from 1884 to 1910, then prof. of divinity and canon of Christ Church, Oxford; a leading preacher and theologian of Church of England; works include *Logic and Life, On Behalf of Belief, Vital Values, Fibres of Faith,* and *A Bundle of Memories.*

Holland, SIR THOMAS ERSKINE (1835–1926), Eng. jurist; Vinerian reader of Eng. law, and prof. of international law and diplomacy, Oxford, 1874–1910; protested strongly against the ratification of the Declaration of London, 1911; ed. the *Institutes of Justinian* (1873), and wrote *Elements of Jurisprudence, The Laws and Customs of War on Land, War and Neutrality,* etc.

Hol'loway, THOMAS (1800–83), Eng. patent medicine manufacturer; *b.* Devonport; made large fortune from pills and ointment, and built Holloway Coll. for Women, at Egham, Surrey, 1887.

Holmes (*hōmz*), OLIVER WENDELL (1809–94), Amer. author and physician; *b.* Cambridge, Mass.; educated at Harvard; practised medicine at Boston; prof. of anatomy at Harvard, 1847–82; pub. *The Autocrat of the Breakfast Table* (1858), followed by the *Professor* (1860) and *Poet* (1871) of the same series; other important works include two novels, *Elsie Venner* (1861) and *The Guardian Angel* (1868), *Our Hundred Days in Europe* (1887), and several collections of poems. His poetry is graceful and ingenious; as a prose essayist he ranks high.

Holst, GUSTAV (1874–1934), Eng. composer; *b.* Cheltenham; has written works for orchestras, part songs, operas, etc.; best-known works: *The Planets*, an orchestral suite; *Hymn of Jesus*, choral and orchestral work; *The Perfect Fool*, an opera.

Holstein (*hōl'stīn*), FRIEDRICH VON (1837–1909), Ger. politician; counsellor to Ger. foreign office, 1878–1906; power behind the throne in foreign affairs; largely responsible for Germany obtaining Kiaochou and Samoa; opposed increase of Ger. fleet.

Holyoake (*hōl'i-ōk*), GEORGE JACOB (1817–1906), Eng. journalist and pioneer of co-operative movement in England; *b.* Birmingham; an advocate of secularism—a system of moral culture without regard to religious beliefs; works include autobiography (1892) and *History of the Rochdale Pioneers* (1857–92).

Home, JOHN (1722–1808), a Scot. dramatist and clergyman; *b.* Leith; his play, *Douglas*, was produced in Edinburgh, 1756, with great success, and at Covent Garden, 1757; resigned his charge and became secretary to Lord Bute; tutor to Prince of Wales (George III.).

Ho'mer, according to tradition, was the author of the two greatest epic poems of Greece, the *Iliad* and the *Odyssey*, the former describing the siege of Troy and the latter the wanderings of Odysseus for ten years after Troy had fallen. Varying accounts are given of Homer's birthplace and the time when he lived. The strongest tradition says that he was born at Chios, that he was blind, and that he wandered from city to city reciting his poems, none of which he committed to writing. His period seems to be somewhere between 1100 B.C. and 900 B.C. How much of the *Iliad* and *Odyssey* can be ascribed to this traditional figure is a problem which is entirely unsolved. The poems as they now stand are undoubtedly the product of various ages, ranging from prehistoric times up to about 600 B.C. They were recited at many Gr. festivals, and Virgil modelled on them his own epic poem the *Æneid*. Other poems, the Homeric *Hymns* and the *Thebaid*, have been ascribed to Homer, but are certainly of different authorship from that of the two great epics.

Hono'rius, name of several popes. (1) HONORIUS I. (625–638), tried unsuccessfully to persuade Brit. Church to observe Easter according to Roman custom; was excommunicated after death for his support of Monothelite heresy. (2) HONORIUS II. (1124–30), sanctioned order of Knights Templars; contended unsuccessfully with Roger of Sicily. (3) HONORIUS III. (1216–27), authorized orders of St. Dominic and St. Francis; supported Henry III. of England against France; opposed the Albigenses. (4) HONORIUS IV. (1285–7), supported Charles of Anjou against Peter of Aragon, who had taken Sicily and imprisoned the king.

Honorius, FLAVIUS (384–423), W. Roman emperor from 395; reign marked by Gothic invasions and sack of Rome, 410; persecuted pagans and abolished the gladiatorial combats; his reign saw the practical loss to the empire of Spain, Gaul, and Britain.

Hooch (*hōch*), PIETER DE (1629–*c.* 85), Dutch painter of interiors; *b.* Rotterdam; obtains wonderful effects of material, reflections of light in pots and pans, and subtle expression in countenances.

Hood, HON. HORACE LAMBERT ALEXANDER (1870–1916), Brit. admiral; *b.* London; entered navy, 1883; served on Nile during Sudan operations, 1898, and in Somaliland, 1904; naval attaché at Washington, 1907–8; in command of Royal Naval Coll., Osborne, 1910–14. On outbreak of Great War commanded Dover patrol; perished in battle of Jutland, 1916, when his flagship *Invincible* was sunk.

Hood, SAMUEL, 1ST VISCOUNT HOOD (1724–1816), Brit. admiral; *b.* in Somerset; after service in N. America, and in the W. Indies, distinguished himself against the French at Martinique, 1781, St. Kitts and Dominica, 1782; in command of Mediterranean fleet, 1793; captured Toulon, 1793, and took Corsica, 1794.

Hood, SIR SAMUEL (1762–1814), Brit. naval commander; cousin of above; served in W. Indies and in Mediterranean, 1793; present at Santa Cruz, 1797, and battle of the Nile, 1798; commanded *Venerable* at Algeciras and Gibraltar, 1801; defeated French in W. Indies, 1802, at Rochefort, 1805; took Madeira, 1807; aided Sweden against Russia, 1808.

Hood, THOMAS (1799–1845), Eng. humorist and poet; *b.* London; educated as engraver; life was a long struggle with ill-health and debt; sub-ed. of *London Magazine*, 1821; pub. *Odes* *and Addresses to Great People* (1825), *Whims and Oddities* (1826); launched *Hood's Comic Annual*, 1830; pub. 'The Song of the Shirt' in *Punch*, 1843; at heart a serious writer, noted for his kindly nature.

[*Life and Times of Thomas Hood* (1907), by Walter Jerrold.]

Hook, THEODORE EDWARD (1788–1841), Eng. novelist, dramatist, and wit; son of a London composer; accountant-general of Mauritius, 1813–17, but owing to the defalcations of an assistant was imprisoned; ed. of *John Bull*, a Tory organ, 1820; his *Sayings and Doings* (1824–8) were highly popular; novels include *Jack Brag* and *Gilbert Gurney*; famed for improvisations and practical jokes.

Hook′er, SIR JOSEPH DALTON (1817–1911), Eng. botanist and traveller; *b.* in Suffolk; accompanied Ross on his Antarctic expedition as surgeon and botanist; travelled in India, Syria, and Morocco; succeeded his father as director of Kew Gardens, 1865; pub. *Genera Plantarum* and a *Flora of the British Isles*, still a standard work; O.M., 1907; a friend of Darwin and Huxley.

Hooker, RICHARD (1553–1600), Eng. theologian; *b.* near Exeter; educated at Oxford; received the living of Drayton-Beauchamps (Bucks); master of the Temple, 1585; subsequently held livings at Boscombe (Wilts) and Bishopsbourne (Kent); remarkable for his sweetness and dignity of character. His *Laws of Ecclesiastical Polity* is a masterpiece of theological reasoning and eloquence.

[*Life* (1907), by Vernon Staley.]

Hoop′er, JOHN (*c.* 1495–1555), Prot. martyr; *b.* in Somerset; went to Switzerland during the last years of Henry VIII.; returned, 1549; reforming preacher under Edward VI.; Bishop of Gloucester, 1550; imprisoned on Mary's accession, 1553; burned at the stake in Gloucester, 1555; called 'the father of Nonconformity.'

Hoov′er, HERBERT CLARK (1874–), Amer. statesman; *b.* in Iowa; educated at Stanford Univ., California; in charge of U.S.A. Geological Survey of Sierra Nevada Mts., 1895; took up mining engineering in California, Australia, and China; in the Great War was organizer and chairman of Amer. Commission for Relief in Belgium, superintending provision of food for more than 10,000,000 people in Belgium and N. France; in April 1917 went to America to become food administrator; secretary of trade and commerce, 1920–8; though for a time a Democrat, eventually became a Republican; president of U.S.A., 1929–33.

Hope, ANTHONY (1863–1933), pseudonym of SIR A. H. HAWKINS, Eng. novelist; barrister, Middle Temple, 1887; achieved distinction in romantic style with *The Prisoner of Zenda* and *Rupert of Hentzau*, and in light modern comedy with *The Dolly Dialogues* and similar works; later books include *The God in the Car*, *Quisanté*, *Tristram of Blent*, *Intrusions of Peggy*, *Second String*, etc.; author of several plays; pub. autobiography, 1927.

Hop′kins, SIR FREDERICK GOWLAND (1861–), Eng. biochemist; *b.* Eastbourne; educated London Univ.; prof. of biochemistry, Cambridge Univ., since 1914; Royal Medal, 1918; Copley medal, 1926; Nobel Prize for medicine, 1929; has done valuable research work in proteins.

Hop′kinson, JOHN (1849–98), Eng. electrical engineer; *b.* Manchester; senior wrangler, Trinity Coll., Cambridge, 1871; practised as consulting engineer in London from 1878; head of Siemens Laboratory at King's Coll., London, 1890; author of many scientific papers dealing with electricity and magnetism, dynamos, etc.; accidentally killed in Alps.

Hor'ace, QUINTUS HORATIUS FLACCUS (65–8 B.C.), Roman poet; *b.* Venusia, in Apulia; educated at Rome and Athens; at Athens joined Brutus, and fought at Philippi as tribune. His homestead appears to have been twice confiscated, but his patron Mæcenas bestowed on him the beloved Sabine farm; at Virgil's death, 19 B.C., Horace became chief court poet and voiced the ideals of Augustus. His *Satires* employ ridicule and not invective; the *Epistles* are similar to the *Satires*, but wider in their choice of subjects, and even more good-humoured in tone; *Epodes* are less delicate in sentiment, less restrained in passion; *Ars Poetica* and 2nd book of the *Epistles* are poetic treatises on literary art and criticism; the *Odes*, his lyrical poems, are his greatest work, and are polished, chaste, and perfect in expression.

[*Horace and the Elegiac Poets* (1899), by Sellar.]

Horne, SIR HENRY SINCLAIR, 1ST BARON (1861–1929), Brit. general; *b.* in Caithness; served in S. African War; in Great War was promoted major-general, 1914; made general for services at Vimy and Arras, 1917; invented the 'creeping barrage'; did brilliant work in closing part of war; baron, 1919; granted £30,000, and received thanks of Parliament; held East command, 1919–23; retired, 1926.

Horne, RT. HON. SIR ROBERT STEVENSON (1871–), British statesman; *b.* in Stirlingshire; educated at Glasgow Univ.; called to bar, 1896; during Great War was assistant inspector-general of transportation, 1917; director of Admiralty Labour Department, 1918; Coalition Unionist M.P. for Hillhead div. of Glasgow, 1918; minister of labour, 1919–20; president of Board of Trade, 1920; chancellor of Exchequer, 1921–2.

Hor'nel, EDWARD ATKINSON (1864–1933), Scot. artist; *b.* in Australia; studied at Edinburgh and Antwerp; influential member of the Kirkcudbright school of painters; visited Japan and the East; his work is decorative in design and distinctive in its colour; many of his works purchased for public collections.

Hor'ner, FRANCIS (1778–1817), Brit. politician and economist; Whig M.P., 1806; chairman of Bullion Committee, 1810; one of founders of and contributors to *Edinburgh Review*.

Hor'niman, ANNIE ELIZABETH FREDERICKA (1860–), pioneer in modern drama production; *b.* London; managed Avenue Theatre, London, and Abbey Theatre, Dublin; in 1908 bought Gaiety Theatre, Manchester, and started first Eng. repertory theatre.

Hor'nung, ERNEST WILLIAM (1866–1921), Eng. novelist and journalist; *b.* Middlesbrough; years spent in Australia, 1884–6, coloured much of his work, as in *A Bride from the Bush* (1890), *The Boss of Taroomba* (1894); best known as creator of *Raffles*, gentleman burglar, and tales of a similar type.

Hor'rocks, JEREMIAH (1617–41), Eng. astronomer; *b.* near Liverpool; first to show how moon follows Kepler's laws; revised Kepler's tables; predicted and first observed transit of Venus; first to make tidal observations.

Horsley, JOHN CALLCOTT (1817–1903), Eng. painter; *b.* London; painted frescoes for the Houses of Parliament, 1845–8; R.A., 1856; principal pictures include *Rent Day at Haddon Hall, The Chess Players, The Healing Mercies of Christ.*

Hors'ley, SIR VICTOR ALEXAN-

DER HADEN (1857–1916), Eng. surgeon and neurologist; *b.* London; prof. of pathology at Univ. Coll., London, 1893–6; emeritus prof. of clinical surgery and consulting surgeon at Univ. Coll. Hospital, 1906–16; famous for valuable researches in cerebral localization; leader of a medical movement against the use of alcohol; during Great War served in Mesopotamia, 1915–16, and died there of heat stroke.

Hortense (*or-täns'*), EUGÉNIE BEAUHARNAIS (1783–1837), daughter of Empress Josephine by her first marriage; *b.* Paris; married Louis Bonaparte, who became King of Holland in 1806; mother of Napoleon III.

Horthy de Nagybanya (*hor'tē de nozh'bän-yo*), NICHOLAS VITÉZ, ADMIRAL (1868–), Hungarian statesman; joined navy, 1886; during Great War took part in naval raids and was wounded; after mutiny at Cattaro, 1918, commanded Austro-Hungarian sea forces; created Hungarian national army after revolution, Oct. 1918, and entered Budapest, whereupon Romanians withdrew; regent of Hungary since 1920.

Hor'ton, ROBERT FORMAN (1855–1934), Eng. Congregational minister; lecturer in history, New Coll., Oxford; minister, Lyndhurst Road Church, Hampstead, 1880–1930; chairman of Congregational Union of England and Wales, 1903; author of many theological and devotional works; *Autobiography* (1917).

Hosea (*hō-zē'a*) (*fl.* 8th cent. B.C.), first in order among the twelve 'minor' prophets of the Bible; prophesied from end of reign of Jeroboam II. till extinction of northern kingdom; used his own experience to illustrate the tragedy which was being enacted in the nation.

Hotspur. See under PERCY, SIR HENRY.

Houdon (*oo-dōn'*), JEAN ANTOINE (1740–1828), Fr. sculptor; *b.* Versailles; gained Prix de Rome, 1761; remained in Rome ten years; there executed statue of St. Bruno; visited U.S.A., 1785, to make statue of Washington; among his works are busts of Turgot, Rousseau, Lafayette, Mirabeau, and Napoleon.

Houghton (*hou'ton*), RICHARD MONCKTON MILNES, 1ST BARON (1809–85), Eng. poet and critic; *b.* London; M.P., 1837–63; peerage, 1863; pub. poetical works under various titles, 1834–44; *Collected Poems* (1876), *Life and Letters of Keats* (1848). A generous patron of poets and authors.

House, EDWARD MANDELL (1858–), Amer. statesman; *b.* Houston, Texas; educated at Cornell Univ.; actively interested in Democratic politics; nominated, 1912, Woodrow Wilson for presidency; subsequently Wilson's intimate adviser, and special representative to European governments, 1915–17; appointed to represent U.S.A. at Versailles Peace Conference; helped to draft League of Nations covenant and mandates system; a 'power behind the scenes' in both U.S.A. and pan-American politics.

[*The Intimate Papers of Colonel House* (1926–8), by C. Seymour.]

Hous'man. (1) ALFRED EDWARD (1859–1936), Eng. poet and classical scholar; prof. of Latin at Univ. Coll., London, 1892–1911, and at Cambridge from 1911; ed. many Latin texts; best-known poems, *A Shropshire Lad* (1896) and *Last Poems* (1892). (2) LAURENCE (1865–), Eng. writer and artist of extraordinary versatility and charm; brother of (1); book illustrator; author of *An Englishwoman's Love Letters*, *A Modern Antæus*, *Sabrina Warham*, and *Thimblerigg*; poems include *Spikenard* and *The Love Concealed*; plays include *Prunella*, *Angels* *and Ministers*, and *Little Plays of St. Francis*.

Houssaye (*oo-sā'*) Arsène (1815–96), Fr. novelist and poet; *b.* in Aisne; novels include *Les Filles d'Eve*, *La Couronne de Bluets*; poetry, *Cent et un Sonnets*; dramas, critical and historical works. His son Henry (1848–1911) wrote valuable works on Napoleon's campaigns.

How'ard, old English family, said to have been settled in Norfolk in 10th cent. In 1483 Sir John Howard was created Duke of Norfolk and Earl Marshal of England, an office hereditary in the family ever since. The first duke was killed at Bosworth and attainted; but his son Thomas won battle of Flodden, and regained the dukedom in 1514; third duke was uncle of Anne Boleyn and Catherine Howard; his grandson and successor was beheaded for plotting in favour of Mary Queen of Scots, 1572. The family regained dukedom from Charles II. Bernard Marmaduke Fitzalan-Howard, 16th Duke of Norfolk (1908–), is premier duke of England and head of English R.C.'s. The Earls of Effingham, Suffolk, and Carlisle are of same stock.

Howard, Catherine (1521–42), fifth queen of Henry VIII.; daughter of Lord Edmund Howard; married Henry in 1540; charged with unfaithfulness, and beheaded in Tower.

Howard, John (1726–90), Eng. philanthropist; *b.* London; as high sheriff of Bedford, 1773, inspected the prison, and, finding many abuses both there and in other Eng. jails, devoted his life to securing reforms in prison management. He visited prisons of many European countries, which he described, with those of England, in his *State of Prisons* (1777). He also carried out researches on the plague.

Howard of Effingham, Charles, 2nd Baron (1536–1624), Eng. admiral; ambassador to France, 1559; one of commissioners for trial of Mary Queen of Scots, 1586; as Lord High Admiral commanded fleet against Span. Armada; with Essex, 1596, joined expedition against Cadiz; created Earl of Nottingham, 1597; held many offices under James I.

Howe, Elias (1819–67), Amer. inventor; *b.* in Massachusetts; granted patent, 1846, for sewing-machine.

Howe, Joseph (1804–73), Canadian politician; *b.* near Halifax, Nova Scotia; shared in obtaining responsible administration for Nova Scotia, and did much to establish and improve its government; provincial secretary of state for Nova Scotia in Dominion government, 1869–72; governor, 1873.

Howe, Julia Ward (1819–1910), Amer. author and philanthropist; *b.* New York; associated with her husband, Dr. S. G. Howe, in editing *Boston Commonwealth*, and in numerous philanthropic movements; wrote 'The Battle-hymn of the Republic,' besides several vols. of verse.

Howe, Richard, 1st Earl (1726–99), Brit. admiral; *b.* London; treasurer of navy, 1765–70; served in war of Amer. Independence; relieved Gibraltar, 1782; first lord of Admiralty, 1783–8; defeated French off Cape Ushant —'the glorious first of June,' 1794; helped to end mutiny at Spithead, 1797.

Howe, William Howe, 5th Viscount (1729–1814), Brit. soldier; brother of above; distinguished himself at capture of Quebec, 1759; fought in Amer. War of Independence till 1778, when he was relieved at his own request, his military conduct having been severely criticized in England; conduct approved after parliamentary inquiry; general, 1793.

How'ells, William Dean (1837–1920), Amer. novelist and author; *b.* in Ohio; worked as compositor, reporter, editor in various newspaper offices; U.S.A. consul at Venice, 1861–5; ed. of *Atlantic Monthly*, 1866–81; prolific and versatile author; produced some seventy books; his novels, which portray a faithful picture of Amer. life and character, include *Their Wedding Journey* (1871), *The Lady of the Aroostook* (1878), *The Leatherwood God* (1916).

Howitt, William (1792–1879), Eng. author; *b.* in Derbyshire; wrote *History of Priestcraft, Rural and Domestic Life in Germany, Visits to Remarkable Places*, etc.; lived in Australia, 1852–4. His wife, Mary (1799–1888), wrote novels and children's poems, trans. Hans Andersen; joint-author with her husband of numerous works.

Hrdlicka (*hurd-lits'ka*), Ales (1869–), Amer. anthropologist; *b.* in Bohemia; emigrated to New York, 1882; graduated in medicine; did research work in insanity, 1894–6; anthropologist in many expeditions, 1898–1913; founder and ed. of *American Journal of Physical Anthropology* since 1918; an authority on ancient man; curator, Smithsonian Institute, since 1910.

Huc (*ook*), Evariste Régis (1813–60), Fr. R.C. missionary and traveller; *b.* Toulouse; went to China as missionary; journeyed from Peking to Lhasa, 1844–6; wrote *Souvenirs d'un Voyage dans la Tartarie, le Thibet, et la Chine* (1851–2) and *L'Empire Chinois* (1855).

Hud'son, George (1800–71), Eng. financier; *b.* near York; called 'railway king'; promoted railway extensions in England; acquired large fortune, subsequently lost.

Hudson, Henry (*d.* 1611), Brit. explorer; attempted to discover north-east passage to Pacific, 1607; in 1609 explored Hudson R.; sailed, 1610, to Hudson Strait and Bay in search of north-west passage; crew mutinied, and Hudson and others were cast adrift and never heard of again.

Hudson, William Henry (1841–1922), Brit. naturalist; *b.* near Buenos Aires; lived in England after 1870; civil pension in 1901 helped to relieve his poverty; wrote *The Purple Land* (1885), *Green Mansions* (1904), *Afoot in England* (1909), *British Birds* (1895), *Birds of La Plata* (1920), and *A Hind in Richmond Park* (1922). Bird sanctuary in Hyde Park established in his memory.

Hueffer, F. M. See Ford, F. M.

Huerta, Victoriano (1854–1916), Mexican president and generalissimo; of Indian parentage; became general, 1901; after resignation of Diaz, 1911, entered service of President Madero; combined with General Felix Diaz to make Madero a prisoner, upon which he became interim president. He incurred odium in U.S.A. for his share in murder of Madero, and this led to protracted conflict with America. After his confirmation in the office of president, Carranza and Villa headed rebellion against him. Repudiated the National Debt, thereby precipitating anarchy only remedied by Amer. intervention. Resigned, 1914, and took up residence in U.S.A.; arrested for violating Amer. neutrality, but died before being brought to trial.

Hug'gins, Sir William (1824–1910), Eng. astronomer; *b.* London; pioneer in stellar spectroscopy and photography; made many striking discoveries relative to origin, constitution, and condition of the heavenly bodies; produced *Atlas of Representative Stellar Spectra*; O.M., 1902.

Hughes (*hūz*), CHARLES EVANS (1862–), Amer. lawyer and public official; *b.* in New York state; practised law in New York; governor of New York state, 1907–8 and 1909–10; defeated by Wilson for presidency of U.S.A., 1916; secretary of state, 1921–5; chairman of international conference on limitation of armaments, 1921; chief justice of supreme court, 1930; wrote *The Pathway of Peace* (1925).

Hughes, HUGH PRICE (1847–1902), Brit. Wesleyan minister; *b.* Carmarthen; founded *Methodist Times,* 1885; started West London Mission, 1887; president of Wesleyan Conference, 1898; first president, 1896, of the National Free Church Council.

Hughes, SIR SAM (1853–1921), Can. soldier and public official; *b.* in Ontario; educated at Toronto Univ. and Royal Military School; lecturer in English in Toronto Collegiate Institute, 1875–85; served during Fenian raid, 1870; lieutenant-colonel, 1897; served in South African War; member of Dominion Parliament, 1892–1921; minister of militia and defence, 1911–16. On outbreak of Great War organized Canadian troops, whom he accompanied to France; major-general, 1914; knighted, 1915.

Hughes, THOMAS (1822–96), Eng. author; *b.* Uffington, Berks; joined Christian Socialist movement, 1848, and was one of founders and principals of Working Men's Coll., London. Pub. anonymously *Tom Brown's School Days* (1857), which was an instant success, and *Tom Brown at Oxford* (1861); M.P., 1865–74; presided at first Co-operative Congress, 1869.

Hughes, RT. HON. WILLIAM MORRIS (1864–), Australian statesman; *b.* in Wales; went to Australia, 1884, and entered politics as member of the Legislative Assembly of New South Wales, 1894, a position he resigned on becoming member of the Federal Parliament; devoted himself to the interest of Labour; attorney-general in various Labour administrations; minister for external affairs, 1921–23; prime minister, 1915–23; defeated twice on subject of conscription; represented Commonwealth at Imperial War Cabinet, 1918; Australian delegate to Peace Conference.

Hu'go, VICTOR MARIE (1802–85), Fr. author; *b.* Besançon; travelled with his father, General Count Hugo (1774–1828), through Spain and Italy during Napoleonic campaigns; intermittently educated in Paris; private and public life were troubled from outset; nearly all his children died in his lifetime. Entered Parliament after revolution of 1848; became ardent Republican, and after *coup d'état* of 1851 retired to Channel Islands until 1870; returned to Paris, and took deep interest in politics, working for abolition of capital punishment, etc. He was buried in the Panthéon as perhaps the greatest figure in Fr. literature.

Hugo was the great leader of Romantic school of Fr. literature; his poems, dramas, and romances, on every subject, aroused unbounded enthusiasm; his dramas —*Hernani* (1830), *Le Roi s'amuse* (1832), *Lucrèce Borgia* (1833), etc., and novels, *Le Dernier Jour d'un Condamné* (1829), *Notre-Dame de Paris* (1831), *Les Misérables* (1862), *Les Travailleurs de la Mer* (1866), *L'Homme qui Rit* (1869), were epoch-making, and were only surpassed in greatness by his lyrics. One of the main features of his writing was frequent use of *motif* of oppressed virtue and evil fate; this 'eternal note of sadness' is one of the charms of Hugo.

[*A Study of Victor Hugo* (1886), by Swinburne; *Victor Hugo* (1921), by Mme. Dudaux. An ed.

of the *Œuvres Complètes* of Victor Hugo is pub. by Nelson in 51 vols.]

Hulse, JOHN (1708–90), Eng. divine; *b.* Middlewich; bequeathed funds to univ. of Cambridge to provide the Hulsean Prize for a dissertation, and for four annual Hulsean Lectures on the evidences of the Christian religion.

Hum'bert I. (1844–1900), King of Italy, son of Victor Emmanuel II.; succeeded, 1878; supported Triple Alliance and also maintained friendly relations with Britain; assassinated by anarchist Bresci.

Hum'boldt, FRIEDRICH HEINRICH ALEXANDER, BARON VON (1769–1859), Ger. naturalist and explorer; *b.* Berlin; explored R. Orinoco, the Andes, R. Amazon, and Mexico; introduced guano into Europe. In 1817 delineated isothermal lines; wrote accounts of the natural history of the regions he explored, and many works on natural history; made a journey to Siberia in 1829, during which he determined the height of the plateau, and discovered diamonds in the gold washings of the Ural. In 1845 began his classic work *Kosmos*, in which are embodied the results of his observations.

[*F. H. Alexander von Humboldt, Naturalist* (2 vols., 1873), ed. by C. C. Bruhns, trans. by J. and C. Lassell; *A. von Humboldt* (1900), by S. Günther.]

Humboldt, KARL WILHELM, BARON VON (1767–1835), Ger. statesman and philologist; brother of above; as Prussian minister of public instruction established univ. of Berlin, 1809; retired from politics, 1819; works lay down certain basic principles of modern comparative philology.

Hume, DAVID (1711–76), Scot. historian and philosopher; *b.* Edinburgh; educated at Edinburgh Univ.; in 1739 pub. first two vols. of *Treatise of Human Nature*, which was a failure; tried, unsuccessfully, to secure chair of moral philosophy at Edinburgh, 1744; librarian at Advocates' Library, Edinburgh, 1751; his *Philosophical Essays* (later called *Inquiry Concerning Human Understanding*) were pub. in 1748, and *Political Discourses* in 1751; then he pub. a *History of England* (1754–56); *Natural History of Religion* appeared in 1757; under-secretary of state to the Home Department, 1766.

Hume's philosophy carried Locke's account of the origin of knowledge to its logical conclusion. He set up as a general test for all ideas that they must originate in impressions, otherwise they have no real meaning, but are merely illusions. Thus the theory of casual connection is resolved into a mere blind belief engendered by custom. The outcome of such criticism applied to the fundamental concepts on which knowledge rests was total scepticism.

[*Life and Correspondence of David Hume* (1846), by J. H. Burton; *Hume* ('English Men of Letters,' 1878), by T. Huxley.]

Humperdinck (*hoom'per-dink*), ENGELBERT (1854–1921), German composer; *b.* near Bonn; prof. at Berlin; wrote *Hänsel und Gretel*, a fairy opera which brought him world-wide fame.

Hunt, JAMES HENRY LEIGH (1784–1859), Eng. poet and essayist; *b.* Southgate; educated Christ's Hospital; ed. the *Examiner*, 1808, a Radical newspaper, founded by his brother; fined and imprisoned, 1813, for two years for pub. uncomplimentary article on Prince Regent; pub. best-known poem, *The Story of Rimini* (1816); other journalistic ventures were *The Indicator* (1818), *The Companion* (1828), *The Tatler* (1830), and *Leigh Hunt's London Journal* (1834); original works include *Lord Byron* *and his Contemporaries* (1828), *Imagination and Fancy*, *Wit and Humour*, *The Town*, *Men, Women, and Books*; *Autobiography*, pub. 1850; intimately associated with Keats, Byron, and other poets of the day; fame rests chiefly upon his genial essays.

Hunt, WILLIAM HOLMAN (1827–1910), Eng. artist; *b.* London; formed friendship with Millais, and became one of founders of Pre-Raphaelite Brotherhood; earlier pictures dealt chiefly with historical subjects, but later he became recognized as greatest of modern religious artists; works include *The Light of the World*, *The Scapegoat*, *The Hireling Shepherd*, *The Shadow of Death*, and *The Triumph of the Innocents*; brought into modern art a new note of spiritual emotion.

Hunter, JOHN (1728–93), Scot. anatomist and surgeon; *b.* in Lanarkshire; discovered the circulation in the human placenta, 1754, the method of tying the artery above the disease in aneurism, 1785, etc. His museum in Leicester Square, London, was bought by the nation and opened in 1813, when the Hunterian orations began.

Hunter, WILLIAM (1718–83), Scot. anatomist and obstetrician, elder brother of John Hunter; first prof. of anatomy to Royal Academy, 1768; his collection of specimens forms Hunterian Museum at Glasgow Univ.; great work, *The Human Gravid Uterus* (1774).

Hunyadi (*hoon'yod-i*), JANOS (*c.* 1387–1456), Hungarian soldier and politician; *b.* in Transylvania; instrumental in obtaining Ladislaus of Poland's election as King of Hungary; defeated Turks at Hermannstadt and near Iron Gates of Danube, 1442; he was defeated at Varna, 1444, when the king was slain; during heir's minority Hunyadi acted as regent; he was defeated by Turks at Kossovo, 1448; accomplished relief of Belgrade from the Turks, 1456; died three weeks later of plague.

Hurd, SIR ARCHIBALD (1869–), Eng. journalist and writer on naval matters; on editorial staff of the *Daily Telegraph*, 1899–1928; joint-ed. of *Brassey's Naval Annual*, 1920–8; author of official *History of the Merchant Navy in the War*.

Hus'kisson, WILLIAM (1770–1830), Brit. financier and politician; *b.* in Worcestershire; secretary of Treasury, 1804; president Board of Trade, 1823; colonial secretary, 1827; advocated free trade, and secured reduction of import duties; killed at opening of Liverpool and Manchester Railway.

Huss, JOHN (*c.* 1369–1415), Bohemian reformer; at Prague Univ. came under influence of Wyclif's writings; came into conflict with R.C. Church; forbidden to preach, and finally excommunicated; went to Council of Constance to defend his views, 1414, having been granted a safe conduct, but was tried and condemned, and refusing to recant was burned at the stake; prepared the way for the Reformation.

Hussein (*hoo-sīn'*) **ibn Ali** (1856–1931), first King of the Hejaz, 1916–24; *b.* Constantinople; lived, 1890–1908, as an honoured prisoner at Constantinople; after Turk. revolution, 1908, appointed Grand Sherif and Emir of Mecca, and gained great influence over surrounding Arab tribes; led Arab revolt against Turkey; was proclaimed King of Hejaz, 1916, and set himself vigorously to organize new kingdom; represented at Peace Conference by Feisal, 1919; abdicated, 1924, in favour of his son Ali, and retired to Cyprus, 1925.

Hut'ton, JAMES (1726–97), Scot. geologist; *b.* Edinburgh; successively a doctor and a farmer; pub., 1795, *The Theory of the Earth*, first attempt to explain geological history of earth scientifically; substituted, for cataclysmal changes, the processes of aerial denudation, oceanic deposition, and gradual upheaval.

[*The Founders of Geology* (1897), by Sir A. Geikie.]

Huxley. (1) THOMAS HENRY (1825–95), great Eng. zoologist and biologist; *b.* Ealing; assistant-surgeon on H.M.S. *Rattlesnake*; during four years' cruise in Australian seas studied the surface fauna of the ocean; gave up medical for biological science; palæontologist and lecturer on natural history at the Royal School of Mines, 1854–85; laboured strenuously, in popular lectures and 'Lay Sermons,' to make abstruse science—the evolution theory of Darwin in particular—clear to the people; member of Fisheries Commission and of London School Board; a constant critic of political and social progress, and a bitter opponent of all narrowness of thought; made zoology a practical training instead of a book study; in addition to printed lectures and essays wrote many masterly general works—*e.g. Man's Place in Nature*, *Lessons in Elementary Physiology*, *Physiography*, *Anatomy of the Invertebrates*, and *Scientific Memoirs* (ed. Ray Lankester). (2) LEONARD (1860–1933), journalist and author; son of (1); ed. of *Cornhill Magazine*, 1901–33; chief work *The Life and Letters* of his father. (3) JULIAN SORELL (1887–), biologist and writer; son of (2); demonstrator in zoology, Oxford Univ., 1919–25; took part in univ. expedition to Spitsbergen, 1921; prof. of zoology, King's Coll., London, 1925–7; Fullerian prof. of physiology, Royal Institution, 1926–9; visited E. Africa to advise on native education, 1929; pub. *Essays of a Biologist* (1923), *The Stream of Life* (1926), *Animal Biology* (1927, with J. B. S. Haldane), *Africa View* (1931), *What Dare I Think?* (1931), etc. (4) ALDOUS (1894–), novelist; son of (2); first attracted attention with *Antic Hay* (1923); other novels include *Point Counterpoint* (1928), *Brief Candles* (1930), and *Brave New World* (1932); also pub. poems, including *Leda* (1920), and essays.

Huygens (*hī'gens* or *hoi'gens*), CHRISTIAN (1629–95), Dutch mathematician; *b.* The Hague; improved telescope lenses; was first to show that Saturn's rings surround planet; made first pendulum clock, 1657; founder of undulatory theory of light; explained reflection and refraction, and double refraction in uniaxial crystals; discovered polarization of light.

Hyde, DOUGLAS (1860–), Irish literary historian, poet, and folklorist; *b.* in co. Roscommon; known as 'An Craoibhin Aoibhinn' (Delightful Little Branch); has played large part in the Celtic revival; founder of Gaelic League, and president up to the rise of Sinn Fein, 1915; senator, Irish Free State, 1925; works include *Literary History of Ireland* (1899), *Love Songs of Connacht* (1906), and short plays for Irish-speaking actors.

Hyde, EDWARD. See CLARENDON, EARL OF.

Hyder Ali. See HAIDAR ALI.

Hynd'man, HENRY MAYERS (1842–1921), Eng. author and Socialist leader; *b.* London; correspondent of *Pall Mall Gazette* in Austro-Ital. War, 1866; friend of Cavour and Garibaldi; founded Social Democratic Federation, 1881; tried for sedition along with John Burns and others, 1885, but acquitted; bitterly opposed S. African War, but took popular side in Great War; pub.

many Socialistic works, also *The Record of an Adventurous Life* (1911).

Hyne, CHARLES JOHN CUTCLIFFE WRIGHT (1866–), Eng. novelist; *b.* in Glos; has travelled over the world; creator of 'Captain Kettle,' a character second only in popularity to Sherlock Holmes.

I

Ibáñez (*i-ban'yeth*), VICENTE BLASCO (1867–1928), Span. novelist; *b.* Valencia; political agitator; exiled; imprisoned frequently; best-known books, *The Shadow of the Cathedral*, *Blood and Sand*, and *The Four Horsemen of the Apocalypse*.

Ibn Batuta (ABU ABDULLAH MOHAMMED) (1304–1378), Moslem traveller; *b.* Tangier; made pilgrimage to Mecca four times; between 1325 and 1355 visited, among other places, Near East, India, China, Sumatra, Spain, travelling more than 75,000 miles.

Ibn Sa'ud (ABDUL AZIZ IBN ABDULRAHMAN IBN FAISAL IBN SA'UD) (*c.* 1889–), King of Hejaz and Nejd; *b.* Riyadh; recovered Nejd for family and became ruler, 1901; extended his conquest till in 1926 was proclaimed King of Hejaz, in 1927 King of Nejd, and in 1932 of these united kingdoms known as Saudi Arabia. Friendly to Britain during Great War; has done much to improve his territory.

Ib'sen, HENRIK (1828–1906), Norweg. dramatist and poet; *b.* Skien, s. Norway; apprentice to a chemist at Grimstad; wrote blank-verse plays and took part in stage-management (1850 onwards) at Bergen. *The Vikings of Helgeland*, a romantic dramatic poem, 1858, was refused by managers. His first great protest against social conventions was *Love's Comedy*; *Brand*, a beautiful lyric against moral deadness, appeared in 1866; its theme was repeated in the greater *Peer Gynt*, with its marvellous songs. From this time Ibsen's position in literature was assured. He now substituted analysis and irony for lyrical attacks on middle-class vices. *The Pillars of Society* (1877) was an exposure of the *bourgeoisie*; *A Doll's House* (1879), *Ghosts* (1881), *Hedda Gabler* (1890), and other plays, discuss the position of women in social life; in *An Enemy of the People* (1882) he shows up the cowardice of public opinion; in *The Wild Duck* (1884) the attempts of reformers are ironically ridiculed. *The Master Builder* (1892) is perhaps his chief work. Ibsen's plays revolutionized dramatic art by their realism and their consummate mastery of stage technique.

[*The Quintessence of Ibsenism*, by Bernard Shaw (1892); *Life*, by Edmund Gosse (1908).]

Ida (*d.* 559), first King of Bernicia; ascended throne, 547, on foundation of kingdom; built fortress at Bamborough.

Ignatius (*ig-nā'-shi-us*) (*d. c.* A.D. 117), one of apostolic fathers; very little known of him; epistles preserved in three recensions; Ignatius defends Episcopacy and protests against Docetism and Judaizing tendencies in Church.

[*Apostolic Fathers*, by Lightfoot (1889).]

Ignatius de Loyola. See LOYOLA, IGNATIUS OF.

im Thurn, SIR EVERARD (1852–

1932), Brit. colonial administrator; curator Brit. Guiana Museum, 1877–82; lieut.-governor and colonial secretary, Ceylon, 1901–4; governor of Fiji and high commissioner of the W. Pacific, 1904–10; president Royal Anthropological Institute; did much exploring in Brit. Guiana; first to ascend Roraima.

Indy (*an-dē'*), PAUL MARIÉ THÉODORE VINCENT D' (1851–1931), Fr. musical composer; *b.* Paris; his music did not suit popular taste of his day; chief works: *Le Chant de la Cloche*, *Le Forêt Enchantée* (symphonic poem), *Fervaal*, and *L'Etranger*, operas, much chamber music, and biographies of Beethoven and Franck.

Inge (*ing*), WILLIAM RALPH (1860–), Eng. churchman; *b.* Crayke, Yorks; educated Eton and Cambridge; master at Eton, 1884–8; Lady Margaret prof. of divinity, Cambridge, 1907–11; Dean of St. Paul's, 1911–33; Gifford lecturer at St. Andrews, 1917–18. Numerous works include *The Philosophy of Plotinus* (1918), *Outspoken Essays* (1919 and 1922), *Lay Thoughts of a Dean* (1926), *The Church in the World* (1927), *Christian Ethics and Modern Problems* (1930). He has been dubbed by newspaper writers 'the Gloomy Dean' because he faces problems of the age without undue optimism.

Ingelow (*in'je-lō*), JEAN (1820–97), Eng. poetess and novelist; *b.* Boston, Lincs; her *Poems* (1863) contain 'The High Tide on the Coast of Lincolnshire, 1571,' her best-known poem. Her novels include *Off the Skelligs* (1872), *Fated to be Free* (1875), and *Sarah de Berenger* (1880).

Ing'emann, BERNHARD SEVERIN (1789–1862), Dan. novelist and poet; *b.* in Falster; numerous poems, including historical epics 'Valdemar the Great,' and 'Queen Margaret'; chief historical novels, *Valdemar Seier* (1826), *Erik Menved's Childhood* (1828), *King Erik* (1833), and *Prince Otto of Denmark* (1835).

Ingoldsby, THOMAS. See BARHAM, RICHARD HARRIS.

Ingres (*ang'r*), JEAN AUGUSTE DOMINIQUE (1780–1867), Fr. historical painter; *b.* Montauban; director of Fr. school at Rome, 1834–41; settled in Paris, and became leader of the classical school as opposed to the romanticists under Delacroix. His works include *Virgil reading the Æneid*, the *Odalisque*, *La Source*, and numerous portraits of celebrities.

Innocent, the name of thirteen Popes. INNOCENT I., native of Albano; became Pope, 402; vigorously enforced celibacy of clergy and supremacy of Roman see; *d.* 417; was canonized. INNOCENT III. (Lotario de' Conti di Segni, 1160–1216); *b.* Anagni; succeeded Celestine III., 1198. Under his rule papal power reached its highest point. He excommunicated the kings of England, France, and Spain, and laid these countries under interdict; he was equally zealous for reform within the Church. INNOCENT XI. (Benedetto Odescalchi, 1611–89); *b.* Como; Pope, 1676; quarrelled with Louis XIV., and elicited the famous 'declarations of the Gallic clergy.' INNOCENT XII. (Antonio Pignatelli, 1615–1700); *b.* Naples; Pope, 1691; reversed policy of Innocent XI. to some extent; reconciled to Louis XIV.

Inouyé (*ēn-ō-oo'yā*), MARQUESS KAORU (1835–1915), Jap. statesman; foreign minister, 1885; home affairs, 1892; minister plenipotentiary, Korea, 1894; introduced European innovations with some success.

Irenæ'us, ST. (*c.* 120–202), a Father of the Early Church; *b.* Smyrna; disciple of Polycarp; bishop of Lyons, *c.* 179; helped to evangelize Gaul, and mediated in dispute between Churches of East and West regarding correct date of Easter; wrote *Against the Heresies*, in which he defended Catholic doctrine and tradition; an authority on history of Christian Church in 2nd cent.

Ironside. See EDMUND IRONSIDE.

Ir'ving, EDWARD (1792–1834), Scot. preacher; *b.* Annan; educated Edinburgh Univ.; teacher at Haddington, and at Kirkcaldy, where he became a friend of Carlyle. Assisted Dr. Chalmers at St. John's Church, Glasgow; minister of Cross Street Chapel, London, 1822; attracted extraordinary crowds by his eloquence; gave way to mysticism and was deposed from the ministry, 1832; he originated community of Christians who became the Catholic Apostolic Church.

[*Reminiscences*, by Carlyle (1881); *Life*, by Oliphant (1862).]

Irving, SIR HENRY (1838–1905), (original name, JOHN HENRY BRODRIBB), Eng. actor; *b.* in Somerset; first public appearance in Sunderland, 1856. His real fame dates from his appearance, in 1871, as Mathias in *The Bells* at the Lyceum; his Hamlet stamped him as an actor of rare distinction. In 1878 he became lessee of the Lyceum, and his association with Miss Ellen Terry did much to ensure his success. Possessed of singular magnetic qualities and a wonderful poetic imagination, he stood at the head of contemporary Eng. actors; knighted, 1895.

Irving, HENRY BRODRIBB (1870–1919), Eng. actor-manager, elder son of Sir Henry Irving; *b.* London; went on stage, 1891; called to the bar, 1894; returned to stage, 1894; later formed company of his own with Miss Dorothea Baird, his wife, 1908; appeared in several of his father's most famous parts. A keen criminologist, he pub. several books on criminals and crime.

Irving, WASHINGTON (1783–1859), Amer. author; *b.* New York; first literary success, amusing sketches entitled *Salmagundi*. In 1809 appeared satirical *History of New York*, by 'Diedrich Knickerbocker,' which brought him European fame; lived mainly in England, 1815–32, and produced his famous *Sketch Book*, which contained 'Rip Van Winkle'; visited Spain, 1826–9, and wrote biography of Columbus; other works, *Astoria* (1836), *Adventures of Captain Bonneville* (1837), *Life of Oliver Goldsmith* (1849), etc. A writer of distinction and charm, he was the first Amer. man of letters to gain an international reputation.

Irwin, LORD. See HALIFAX, VISCOUNT.

I'saac ('laughter'), Heb. patriarch; son of Abraham and Sarah; married Rebekah; father of Esau and Jacob. (See Book of Genesis.)

Isaacs, JORGE (1837–95), Colombian novelist and poet; *b.* Cali; among poems are *River Moro, The Silent Night,* and *The Soldier's Tomb*; chief novel, *Maria*, the most famous S. Amer. novel.

Isaacs, SIR RUFUS. See READING, LORD.

Isabella (1451–1504), Queen of Castile and wife of Ferdinand of Aragon; *b.* Madrigal; raised tone of Castilian court, patronized literature, and financed Columbus.

Isabey (*ē-zä-bā'*), JEAN BAPTISTE (1767–1855), French painter; *b.* Nancy; portraits of Josephine, Napoleon, Louis XVIII., etc.

Isai'ah, greatest of Heb. prophets; called to prophetic office, 740 B.C.; also appears as statesman and adviser of kings; seeks to shape destinies of the nation on true religious lines; uttered some remarkable prophecies with regard to the Assyrians which received immediate fulfilment.

The Book of Isaiah, formerly considered to have been written wholly by Isaiah, is now divided by O.T. scholars into three sections, of which Section I. (Chaps. 1–35) is held to have been written mainly by Isaiah; Sections II. and III. are by other hands.

Ish′mael ('May God hear'), son of Abraham and Hagar (see Gen. 16 and 21); became founder of the Ishmaelites; through him Mohammedans trace their descent from Abraham.

Ismail (*is-mä-ēl′*) **Pasha** (1830–95), Khedive of Egypt, 1873–79, grandson of Mehemet Ali; *b.* Cairo; made Egypt virtually independent of Turkey; initiated internal reforms—roads, railways, etc.; greatest enterprise, the Suez Canal; being in financial difficulties sold shares in canal to Brit. government, 1875. His reckless expenditure led to Anglo-Fr. control; forced to abdicate in favour of Tewfik, his son, 1879.

Isocrates (*ī-sok′rä-tēz*) (436–338 B.C.), one of the ten Attic orators; teacher of rhetoric at Athens; owing to weakness of voice, composed speeches on topics of the day and pub. them in pamphlet form. Twenty-one speeches and nine letters extant; style lucid and graceful, but lacks force of Demosthenes.

Israel. See JACOB.

Israëls (*ēz-rä-āls′*), JOSEF (1824–1911), Dutch painter, of Jewish parentage; *b.* Groningen; modern painter-interpreter of Dutch fisher and peasant life; noted for human emotion and mastery of technique and colour; works include *Interior of the Orphan Asylum at Katwijk*, *The Village Poor*, *The Little Sick Nurse*, *The Cradle*, *A Frugal Meal*, etc.

Itagak′i, COUNT TAISÜKE (1837–1919), Jap. statesman; *b.* in Shikoku; ardent advocate of representative government; held several state appointments; in 1898, with Count Okuma, formed first cabinet of constitutional party; retired into private life, 1900.

Ito (*ē′to*), PRINCE HIROBUMI (1841–1909), Jap. statesman; visited Europe to study Western educational and military systems, and constitutional forms of government; became prime minister, 1886, an office which he held four times, resigning 1901; devoted his life to reorganization and reconstruction of Japan; responsible for constitution of new Japan; created prince, 1907; assassinated at Harbin.

Ivan (*ē-vän′*), or JOHN, name of several Russian rulers: IVAN I. ('Money-Bag'), Grand-duke of Vladimir (succeeded 1328); acquired Tver and other dominions; took title Grand-duke of Moscow. IVAN III., THE GREAT (1440–1505), Grand-duke of Muscovy, began to reign in 1462; abolished Tatar rule and brought provinces and principalities of Muscovy under central government; patron of art and learning. IVAN IV., 'The Terrible' (1530–84); first to assume title of Tsar; succeeded, 1533; developed art and commerce; extended his dominions; introduced many reforms; made commercial treaty with Queen Elizabeth of England; annexed Kazan, Astrakhan, and later Siberia. In his later years cruelty of his rule made his name a byword. In 1580 killed his son Ivan in a fit of rage, and passed rest of his life in sorrow for the deed.

Ivanov (*ē′van-ov*), NICHOLAS (1851–1918), Russ. general; educated under royal patronage; fought in Russo-Turk. War, 1877; distinguished himself in Russo-Jap. War, 1904. In Great War commanded Russ. armies operating in Galicia, which captured Lemberg and Przemysl (Sept. 1914); after Russ. retiral, 1915, resigned command. Took part in anti-Bolshevist movement in Ukraine; was wounded, and died at Rostov-on-Don.

Iveagh (*i'vah*) (Edward Cecil Guinness), Earl (1847–1927), for some time chief of brewing concern of Guinness Brothers, Dublin; devoted himself to public beneficence; gave £250,000 for the Jenner Institute of Preventive Medicine. Bought Ken Wood for the nation, and endowed its mansion-house as art gallery, bequeathing pictures valued at £300,000 to form nucleus for the collection.

Ives (*ivz*), Frederic Eugene (1856–), Amer. inventor; *b.* Litchfield, Conn.; paid much attention to colour photography; invented process of half-tone photo-engraving, 1886, and the photochromoscope, 1888, which reproduces natural colours. Many publications on photography.

J

Jacks, Lawrence Pearsall (1860–), British Unitarian churchman; *b.* Nottingham; first editor of *The Hibbert Journal*; prof. of philosophy, 1903–31, and principal, Manchester Coll., Oxford, 1915–31; author of *Life and Letters of Stopford Brooke* (1917), *From Authority to Freedom* (1920), *The Challenge of Life* (1924), *Heroes of Smokeover* (1926), *The Education of the Whole Man* (1931), etc.

Jack'son, Andrew (1767–1845), president of the United States; *b.* on south border of N. Carolina; as a boy fought in Amer. War of Independence; studied law, and was admitted to the bar, 1787; helped to frame constitution of Tennessee, 1796; distinguished himself in war with Britain, 1812; occupied Pensacola, and defeated British at New Orleans, 1815; first governor of Florida, 1821; president of U.S.A., 1828; reelected, 1832; founder of Democratic party and a highly popular and influential president.

Jackson, Frederick George (1860–), Eng. Arctic explorer; *b.* Alcester; travelled in Australia; crossed Siberian tundras in midwinter, 1893; led Jackson-Harmsworth Polar expedition to Franz Josef Land, 1894–7, which discovered Nansen after his expedition to the Pole in the *Fram*; served with distinction in S. African War and in early part of Great War; author of *The Great Frozen Land* (1895) and *A Thousand Days in the Arctic* (1899), etc.

Jackson, Thomas Jonathan ('Stonewall Jackson') (1824–63), Amer. soldier; *b.* Clarksburg, Virginia; served in Mexican War; taught military subjects at Lexington, 1852–61; commanded Virginian army in Civil War; defeated Federals at Cedar Mountain, Bull Run (where he obtained his nickname 'Stonewall'), and Harper's Ferry, 1862; commanded right wing at Fredericksburg, 1862; accidentally shot dead by his own men at Chancellorsville. Jackson resembled Cromwell in religious fervour and military genius.

[*Life*, by Henderson (1902).]

Ja'cob, Jewish patriarch, son of Isaac. His life is a strange blend of selfishness, duplicity, heroism, and spiritual aspiration, as indicated by his names, Jacob ('supplanter') and Israel ('prince with God'). (See Gen. 25–50.)

Jacobs, Joseph (1854–1916), folklorist and Jewish historian, *b.* Sydney, Australia; director of Bureau of Jewish Statistics; ed. of *Folklore,* the *Literary Year-book,* the *Jewish Encyclopædia,* and the *American Year-book*; works include *Celtic Fairy Tales, Indian Fairy Tales, The Jews of Angevin England,* etc.

Jacobs, William Wymark (1863–), Eng. humorous writer; *b.* London; his *Many Cargoes* (1896) brought him immediate fame; other works, *The Skipper's Wooing, Sea-Urchins, The Lady of the Barge, Odd Craft,* etc.

Jacotot (*zhä-kō-tō'*), Jean Joseph (1770–1840), Fr. educationist; *b.* Dijon; prof. of French at Louvain, where he elaborated and applied his system of *Universal Instruction* (1824).

Jacquard (*zhä-kär'*), Joseph Marie (1752–1834), Fr. mechanician and inventor; *b.* Lyons; invented Jacquard loom, which revolutionized art of weaving; pensioned by Napoleon I.

Jagellones (*yä-gel'onz*), a royal dynasty of Poland, descended from Gedimin, grand-duke of Lithuania in early 14th cent.; grand-duke Jagello obtained Polish throne by marriage, 1386; male line became extinct, 1572; supplied rulers to Lithuania, Hungary, and Bohemia.

James I. (1394–1437), King of Scotland; *b.* Dunfermline; son of Robert III.; captured by English when on his way to France, 1406; succeeded to throne, while captive in England, 1406; released, and crowned, 1424; made Parliament an efficient representative body; curbed power of nobles, and established law and order; murdered at Perth, 1437; reputed author of *King's Quair.*

James II. (1430–60), King of Scotland; son of James I.; succeeded, 1437; killed Douglas, 1452, and curbed power of that house; was killed at siege of Roxburgh Castle, 1460; strong and capable ruler, continuing his father's policy.

James III. (1451–88), King of Scotland; son of James II.; succeeded, 1460; married Princess Margaret of Denmark, 1468, and received Orkney and Shetland Is. in lieu of dowry; defeated by rebels at Sauchieburn; treacherously murdered during flight; a weak king, greatly influenced by unworthy favourites.

James IV. (1473–1513), King of Scotland; son of James III.; succeeded, 1488; married Margaret, daughter of Henry VII. of England; founded Scot. navy; subdued Lord of the Isles; as ally of France, led army against England, and was defeated and slain at Flodden. During reign literature flourished, education and general welfare of country improved.

James V. (1512–42), King of Scotland; *b.* Linlithgow; son of James IV.; succeeded, 1513; reduced the Borders to order; married Mary of Guise; his army was defeated by English at Solway Moss, 1542; died at Falkland, leaving a daughter (afterwards Mary Queen of Scots) only seven weeks old.

James I. (1566–1625), King of Great Britain and Ireland; son of Mary Queen of Scots and Darnley; *b.* Edinburgh; proclaimed James VI. of Scotland, 1567; under regents till 1581; married Anne of Denmark; curbed power of nobles in Scotland. James succeeded Elizabeth on Eng. throne, 1603. He had an obstinate belief in divine right of kings, and in duty of passive obedience on part of subjects; his reign was marked by constant struggle with Parliament, which in the following reign led to the Great Rebellion. 'The wisest fool in Christendom'; was the author of several books; much influenced by favourites.

James II. (1633–1701), King of Great Britain and Ireland; second son of Charles I.; distinguished himself in Fr. and Span. service, and in Dutch Wars; professed Roman Catholicism, 1672; succeeded brother, Charles II., 1685; put down insurrections of Monmouth and Argyll, 1685; persecuted Covenanters in Scotland; opposition to his Declarations of Indulgence, 1687 and 1688, led to William of Orange being invited to assume the crown; on his landing James escaped to France; was defeated at the Boyne, 1690; afterwards lived in France.

James, THE OLD PRETENDER (1688–1766), son of James II.; *b.* London; in rising of 1715 he landed at Peterhead; after battle of Sheriffmuir and surrender of his supporters at Preston, returned to France; married Clementina Sobieski; lived at Rome.

James. (1) HENRY (1843–1916) Amer. novelist; *b.* New York; lived in England for greater part of his life; naturalized Brit. subject, 1915; O.M., 1916; wrote many novels, short stories, and some critical works which became exceedingly popular; was a consummate artist, portraying characters which were leisured, complex, and modern. His earlier stories are American, but his later work is predominantly cosmopolitan. Works include *Roderick Hudson, Daisy Miller* (his first success), *Life of Hawthorne, The Wings of a Dove, Partial Portraits, Notes on Novelists,* and *A Small Boy.* (2) WILLIAM (1842–1910), Amer. philosopher; brother of (1); *b.* New York; prof. of philosophy at Harvard, 1881; did valuable work in analytic psychology; in philosophy rather made detached inquiries than built up any system, though he developed system of pragmatism; all his writing marked by freshness and charm; works include *Principles of Psychology* (1890), *The Will to Believe* (1897), *Varieties of Religious Experience* (Gifford Lectures, 1902), *Pragmatism* (1907), *A Pluralistic Universe* (1909).

Jameson (*jā'me-son*), SIR LEANDER STARR (1853–1917), S. African politician; *b.* Edinburgh; took medical degrees in London; went to S. Africa, where he became associated with Cecil Rhodes, and was appointed administrator of Rhodesia, 1891; after hard fighting secured submission of Matabele tribe, 1894. His famous raid into Transvaal territory, Dec. 1895, resulted in his defeat and capture at Krugersdorp; was tried in London and imprisoned; returned to S. Africa; served in S. African War; member for Kimberley in Cape Legislative Assembly, and in 1901 succeeded Rhodes as leader of Progressive party; prime minister, 1904–8, and leader of Unionist party till 1912, when he resigned, thereafter residing in England; P.C., 1907; baronet, 1911. Buried beside Rhodes on Matoppo Hills.

Jamieson (*jā'mi-son*), JOHN (1759–1838), Scot. lexicographer; *b.* Glasgow; minister in Forfar and Edinburgh, 1789–1830; author of famous *Etymological Dictionary of the Scottish Language* (1808).

Jansen (*yan'sen*), CORNELIUS (1585–1638), Dutch Catholic theologian; *b.* in Utrecht province; prof. of Scriptural interpretation, Louvain, 1630; Bishop of Ypres, 1636; pub. *Mars Gallicus*, attacking policy of Richelieu, but his great work was *Augustinus* (1640); founder of Jansenism.

Jaques-Dalcroze' (*zhäk*), EMILE (1865–), Swiss composer; *b.* Vienna; taught harmony, Geneva Conservatoire, 1891; director of Institut Jaques-Dalcroze, Geneva, since 1915; founder of musical eurhythmics, especially in connection with children; has written numerous songs, concertos, orchestral suites, symphonies, and choral works.

Jasmin (*zhäs-man'*), JACQUES (1798–1864), Provençal poet; *b.* Agen; wrote in popular speech of lower classes; last of troubadours; precursor of Mistral; best known by *Papillotos*.

Jaurès (*zhō-rāz'*), JEAN (1859–1914), Fr. Socialist writer, orator, and leader; prof. of philosophy, Toulouse Univ., 1883; elected to Chamber of Deputies, 1885; activity as historian, organizer, and orator of Socialists unceasing; did more than any other to unify Socialist groups; led Socialists in Chamber; fought hard for Dreyfus, 1902. Assassinated. Among works, *Action Socialiste*, *Histoire Socialiste*, and *Études Socialistes*.

Jay, JOHN (1745–1829), Amer. statesman; drew up constitution of New York state, 1777; chief justice of New York, 1777; entered Congress, 1778, and elected its president; diplomatic minister to Spain, 1780; helped to arrange peace with Great Britain, 1781–3; foreign secretary, 1784–9; negotiated 'Jay Treaty' with Great Britain, 1794; governor of New York, 1795–1801.

Jeans, SIR JAMES HOPWOOD (1877–), Eng. mathematician and scientist; *b.* London; second wrangler, 1898, and Smith's prizeman, Cambridge, 1900; prof. of applied mathematics, Princeton Univ., 1905–9; secretary of Royal Society, 1912–29; research associate, Mt. Wilson Observatory, since 1923; has made numerous discoveries by applying mathematics to astronomy and physics; author of *Dynamical Theory of Gases* (1904), *Problems of Cosmogony and Stellar Dynamics* (1919), *The Universe Around Us* (1929), *The Mysterious Universe* (1930), and numerous other works; knighted, 1928.

Jebavy, VACLAV (1868–1929), Czech poet; *b.* Pocatky, Bohemia; greatest modern Czech poet; author of *Secret Distances* (1895), *Dawn in the West* (1896), *Polar Winds* (1897), *Temple Builders* (1899), *The Hands* (1901).

Jebb, SIR RICHARD CLAVERHOUSE (1841–1905), Brit. classical scholar; *b.* Dundee; prof. of Greek, Glasgow, 1875–89, Cambridge, 1889–1905; knighted, 1900; M.P. for Cambridge Univ., 1891; famous for translations of Sophocles, Theophrastus, and other Gr. writers; *Essays and Addresses* (1907).

Jefferies (*jef'riz*), RICHARD (1848–87), Brit. naturalist and author; *b.* near Swindon; his *Gamekeeper at Home* (1878) showed rare powers of observation and description; pub. also *The Amateur Poacher*, *Wild Life in a Southern County*, *Hodge and his Masters*, etc.; *Field and Hedgerow* and *Toilers of the Field* were issued posthumously.

[*Life*, by E. Thomas.]

Jeff'erson, THOMAS (1743–1826), third president of U.S.A.; *b.* Shadwell, Virginia; member of continental congresses of 1775 and 1776; drew up Declaration of Independence; governor of Virginia, 1779, and conducted affairs during British invasion. Entered Congress, 1783; minister to France, 1784–9; secretary of state, 1789–94; vice-president under Adams, 1796; elected president, 1801; arranged purchase of Louisiana, 1803; carried out various reforms, and insisted on retrenchment in public expenses; waged war against Tripoli pirates; admitted Ohio to the Union; second term of office, 1805, marked by trial of Aaron Burr and abolition of slave trade. During his last years he founded the univ. of Virginia at Charlottesville.

[*Thomas Jefferson*, by D. S. Muzzey (1918).]

Jeffrey, FRANCIS, LORD (1773–1850), Scot. judge and literary critic; *b.* Edinburgh; advocate, 1794; Dean of the Faculty of Advocates, 1829; M.P. for Edinburgh, 1832; supported Reform Bill; lord advocate, 1830–4; judge of Court of Session, 1834. Chiefly remembered for his connection with *Edinburgh Review*, which he edited, 1803–29; the conduct of this magazine, and its incisive criticisms, drew out Byron's satire, *English Bards and Scotch Reviewers*; involved Jeffrey in challenge from Moore; estranged the 'Lake Poets' by repeated and bitter attacks.

[*Life*, by Cockburn.]

Jeffreys, GEORGE, 1ST BARON (1648–89), Eng. lawyer; *b.* near Wrexham; called to bar, 1668; showed great skill in cross-examination. After Monmouth's rebellion was sent, as lord chief justice, to try rebels, and at 'Bloody Assize' opened at Winchester, 1685, he condemned 320 persons to death; lord chancellor of England, 1685; secured committal of the seven bishops to Tower, 1688; after flight of James II., was arrested and sent to the Tower, where he died.

[*Life*, by H. B. Irving (1898).]

Jehosh'aphat, King of Judah (*c.* 876–851 B.C.); succeeded his father Asa; made alliance with house of Omri; conducted successful expeditions against Moab, Edom, and Ammon. (See 1 Kings 15; 2 Kings 3; 2 Chron. 17–20.)

Je'hu, King of Israel (842–815 B.C.), son of Jehoshaphat; used his power in merciless and unscrupulous manner; responsible for death of Jehoram, Ahaziah, Jezebel, and seventy descendants of royal house of Israel. (See 2 Kings 9 and 10.)

Jell'icoe OF SCAPA (JOHN RUSHWORTH JELLICOE), 1ST EARL (1859–1935), Brit. sailor; entered navy, 1872; became expert in gunnery; commander on *Victoria* when she was sunk by *Camperdown* off Tripoli, 1893; commanded Naval Brigade during relief expedition to Peking, 1900; director of Naval Ordnance, 1905–7; commanded Atlantic Fleet, 1910–11, second squadron Home Fleet, 1911–12; second Sea Lord, 1912–14. On outbreak of Great War was placed in command of the Grand Fleet; in supreme command of Brit. fleet at battle of Jutland, 1916. First Sea Lord, 1916; introduced 'protected sailings' against submarine attack; O.M., 1916; chief of Naval Staff, 1917; raised to peerage, 1918, and awarded grant of £50,000. In 1919 visited the Dominions to advise colonial authorities on naval matters; created admiral of the fleet; pub. *The Grand Fleet, 1914–16*, followed by *The Crisis of the Naval War* (1920). Gov.-gen. of New Zealand, 1920–4; president of British Legion, 1928–32.

Jenghiz (*jen'gis*) **Khan** ('perfect warrior') (1162–1227), Mongol emperor; one of world's greatest conquerors; *b.* in Mongolia; originally named Temuchin; succeeded to Mongol throne, 1175; twice overran China; his envoys to Transoxiana having been killed, he started in 1219 on his great career of conquest; looted Bukhara and Merv; conquered Herat and other towns; drove Turks into S.E. Europe, while his armies successfully ravaged S. Russia and N. India; died while overrunning China for the third time.

Jen'ner, EDWARD (1749–1823), Eng. physician; discoverer of vaccination; *b.* Berkeley, Glos; studied under John Hunter. After prolonged research, satisfied himself that cow-pox was antagonistic to smallpox; pub. result of his investigations, 1798, but met with much opposition from the public and from many members of the medical faculty; received support from many eminent physicians and surgeons. The

Royal Jennerian Soc., the national vaccine establishment, and other means, propagated the benefits of his discovery.

Jenner, Sir William (1815–98), Eng. physician; *b.* Chatham; prof. of pathology, 1849, and afterwards of clinical medicine at University Coll., London; president of Coll. of Physicians, 1881–8; physician-in-ordinary to Queen Victoria; first to distinguish typhoid from typhus fever.

Jennings, Sarah. See under Marlborough.

Jephthah (*jef'tha*), a judge of Israel; son of Gilead; sacrificed his daughter in fulfilment of a rash vow. (See Judges 11.)

Jeremi'ah, a great Heb. prophet; *b.* Anathoth; while young, called to prophetic office, 626 B.C.; prophesied under five kings. In reign of Zedekiah, the last of those kings, Jewish monarchy was overthrown; prophet permitted to remain in Judæa, but later compelled to go to Egypt, and according to tradition was stoned to death. As a religious teacher he was the first to emphasize the importance of the individual and the spiritual bond between God and man.

Jerobo'am, King of Israel in 10th cent. B.C.; led the tribes of N. Israel against Rehoboam, who was defeated. (See 2 Chron. 13.)

Jerome (*jer-ōm'*), St. (340–420), one of the greatest of Lat. fathers; distinguished scholar; founded monastery at Bethlehem, where he lived for thirty-four years. His great work was his trans. of the Bible into Latin, the Vulgate, prepared partly by trans. from the original, and partly by revision of Lat. versions already in existence.

Jer'ome, Jerome Klapka (1859–1927), Eng. humorous writer; *b.* Walsall; was successively clerk, schoolmaster, actor, and journalist; won notice with *On the Stage and Off* (1885), followed by *Idle Thoughts of an Idle Fellow* (1886), and *Three Men in a Boat* (1889), his best-known work; with Robert Barr ed. *The Idler*, 1892–7; also ed. *To-day*, 1893–97; plays include *New Lamps for Old* and *The Passing of the Third Floor Back*.

Jerome Bonaparte. See Bonapartes.

Jer'rold, Douglas William (1803–57), Brit. dramatist, wit, and man of letters; *b.* London: his melodrama, *Black-eyed Susan* (1829), was a huge success; contributed to *Punch* the *Q. Papers*, *Punch's Letters to his Son*, *Mrs. Caudle's Curtain Lectures*, etc.; ed. several papers; novels include *The Story of a Feather* and *A Man Made of Money*.

Jervis, Sir John. See St. Vincent (John Jervis), Earl of.

Jes'sel, Sir George (1824–83), Brit. judge, son of a Jewish merchant of London; called to bar, 1847; solicitor-general, 1871; master of rolls, 1873; Judicature Acts passed during his term of office. First Jew to be a Brit. judge.

Jesus Christ. Jesus is a personal name; Christ is added to identify Him with the promised Messiah. The authorities for His life are contained in the N.T. writings. Jesus was born in Bethlehem, four years before the date reckoned as the beginning of the Christian era. The national conditions were unsound, both in politics and religion, but a few men and women kept their hearts pure, and relying on the prophecies of old, waited the advent of the Messiah who should deliver their nation from the tyranny of Rome. Jesus spent His early life with His parents at Nazareth, where He learned the trade of a carpenter. At the age of twelve He went with His parents to the Passover at Jerusalem, where there seems to have dawned upon Him the consciousness of His divinity. Returning to Nazareth, He remained with His parents until, at the age of thirty, He came suddenly before the public eye. Presenting Himself to John the Baptist, He requested baptism, and received from God a direct gift of His Spirit and confirmation of His mission as the Messiah. Soon after there came the temptation to yield to the expectations of the Jewish people and establish an earthly kingdom. With His rejection of this temptation the central and distinctive idea of Christianity came into being, that victory came through service and not through assertion of self.

From this point Jesus' life was spent in public service, and falls into three divisions: (1) The year in which He was comparatively unknown, in which, however, four incidents stand out clearly—the adherence to Him of some of John's disciples; the first miracle at Cana of Galilee; the cleansing of the temple; and His interview with Nicodemus. (2) The year in which He came into prominence and was favourably received by the people, in which the chief incidents were these: Jesus returned into Galilee; visited Nazareth, and declared Himself the Messiah; made Capernaum His centre; preached with power and authority; wrought miracles and taught by parables; and ordained the twelve disciples. (3) The year in which His influence seemed to weaken, in which the outstanding events were: the breach between Him and the Pharisees; the animosity of the Herodians, the scribes, and Sadducees; the adherence of the common people until their overtures to have Him crowned king were rejected; the confession of His disciples that He was the Christ, the Son of the living God; His declaration that the cross was an essential part of His ministry; the raising of Lazarus; the triumphal entry into Jerusalem; the institution of the Lord's Supper; the agony in Gethsemane; His betrayal, His trial; and then the crucifixion, the resurrection, and ascension (A.D. 29).

The burden of Jesus' message was, 'The kingdom of God is the will of the heavenly Father enthroned in the hearts of men,' in which there always lay the thought of Himself as the power which was to endow men with the spiritual gifts necessary to their admission to the kingdom. Men were to know God as the God and Father of the Lord Jesus Christ, and would find Him to be a God whose love was over all His works, and whose fatherhood was apparent. By prayer from hearts which have been purified through repentance and sincere desire of a better life, His kingdom will come, and the reward of men will be fellowship with God.

[*Lives*, by Farrar, Edersheim, Cunningham Geikie; *Jesus of Nazareth*, by Gore (1929); *Everyman's Life of Jesus*, by Moffatt (1930).]

Jevons, William Stanley (1835–82), Eng. political economist and logician; *b.* Liverpool; assayer to Mint, Sydney, 1854–9; prof. of political economy, Owens Coll., Manchester, 1866, and Univ. Coll., London, 1876; drowned while bathing; emphasized doctrine of utility and mathematical aspects of economics; pub. *Pure Logic* (1864), *Theory of Political Economy* (1870); in philosophy, *The Substitution of Similars* (1869), etc.

Jiménez. See Ximenez.

Jo'ab, son of Zeruiah, David's sister; commander-in-chief of army during most of David's reign. (See 2 Sam. and 1 Kings.)

Joachim (*yō'ă-chĕm*), Joseph (1831–1907), Hungarian violinist and composer; *b.* near Bratislava; of Jewish parentage; director of concerts at court of Hanover, 1853–66; married famous contralto, Amalia Weiss; director of Berlin High School of Music, 1868; appeared annually in London from 1844 with his famous 'Berlin Quartet'; foremost violinist of his day; works include overtures, piano and violin pieces, etc.; greatest work, *Hungarian Concerto* for violin and orchestra.

[*Life of Joachim*, by Moser (1899).]

Joan of Arc, St. (Fr. *Jeanne d'Arc*), 'The Maid of Orleans' (1412–31), Fr. patriot; *b.* Domrémy; urged by heavenly 'voices' to deliver France from the English, she sought out Charles, the dauphin, and convinced him of her mission; entrusted with leadership of the army, she relieved Orleans (then besieged by English), 1429, and the dauphin was crowned at Reims. Joan's task being in her own view accomplished, she wished to return home, but was dissuaded by the dauphin. Disaster now overtook her; an attack on Paris failed, and she was wounded; in 1430 she was captured by the Burgundians, handed over to the English, and, after a mockery of trial before the Bishop of Beauvais, was burned as a heretic at Rouen; beatified in 1909; canonized at Rome, May 1919.

[*Vie de Jeanne d'Arc*, by Anatole France; *The Maid of France*, by Andrew Lang; *St. Joan*, by Bernard Shaw.]

Jo'ash. (1) King of Judah (*c.* 836–796 B.C.), crowned at age of seven; restored temple, but relapsed into idolatry. (See 2 Chron. 22 and 24.) (2) King of Israel (*c.* 798–782 B.C.); daring and able ruler. (See 2 Kings 13 : 14.)

Jo'el, one of the 'minor' prophets; wrote book which bears his name about 500 B.C.

Joffre (*zhofr*), Joseph Jacques Césaire (1852–1931), Fr. soldier; Marshal of France (title in abeyance since 1871 revived for him in 1916); *b.* in Pyrénées-Orientales; son of a cooper; was lieutenant of engineers in war of 1870–1; served in Indo-Chinese campaign, 1885. In 1892 began construction of Fr. military road from the Senegal to the Niger; name became known to public when he occupied Timbuktu, 1894; received Legion of Honour; brigadier-general in command of artillery, 1901; governor of Lille and general of division, 1905; commander of Second Army at Amiens, 1909. In 1911 he was appointed chief of General Staff, an appointment implying supreme command in time of war. Commander-in-chief of Fr. armies on outbreak of Great War; through the black period of the long retreat of the Allies (Aug.–Sept. 1914) he remained cool and unflurried, and organized 'miracle of the Marne,' which checked the Ger. advance. Retired, Dec. 1916; became chief technical adviser to Allied forces; went to America with Viviani and others on special mission, 1917; O.M., 1919. Distinguished for simplicity of character and life, alertness and clearness of mind, organizing power, and sound common sense.

John, the Apostle, son of Zebedee, a Galilean fisherman; came under influence of John the Baptist; attached himself to Jesus as permanent disciple; became one of twelve apostles; associated after Ascension with Peter; banished to Patmos by Roman emperor; released and probably lived at Ephesus; traditional author of St. John's Gospel, the three epistles of John, and Book of Revelation.

John the Baptist, in N.T., son of Zacharias and Elisabeth; 'forerunner' of Jesus; preached repentance and baptized in the wilderness; baptized Jesus; imprisoned and slain by order of Herod.

John (1167–1216), King of England; *b.* Oxford; youngest son of Henry II.; succeeded his brother, Richard I., 1199; murdered nephew Arthur, 1203; lost Anjou, Normandy, Maine, Touraine; quarrelled with Pope over Langton's election as Archbishop of Canterbury and was excommunicated; signed Magna Carta, 1215; 'the worst king England ever had.'

John III., SOBIESKI (1624–96), King of Poland; had share in driving Charles XII. from Poland; saved Poland from Cossacks and Tatars, and afterwards from Turks; elected king, 1674; gained brilliant victory over Turks, who were besieging Vienna, 1683; freed Hungary from Turk. domination; efforts to reform his own country were frustrated by the nobles.

John, the name of twenty-two popes and one anti-pope.

John, AUGUSTUS EDWIN (1878–), Brit. artist; *b.* Tenby, Wales; R.A., 1928; renowned as portrait painter; has painted many celebrities, including Lord Fisher, Mr. Lloyd George, Lord Robert Cecil, Sir Robert Borden, Emir Feisal, etc.

John, SIR WILLIAM GOSCOMBE (1860–), Brit. sculptor; *b.* Cardiff; R.A., 1909; statues of King Edward VII., W. E. H. Lecky, Mr. Lloyd George, Viscount Wolseley, etc.

John of Gaunt. See under LANCASTER.

John of Salisbury (*c.* 1115–80), Eng. author and churchman; *b.* Salisbury; secretary to Theobald, Archbishop of Canterbury, and to Thomas Becket; bishop of Chartres, 1176; wrote *Policraticus*, *Metalogicus*, *Historia Pontificalis*, and lives of St. Anselm and St. Thomas of Canterbury.

John'son, ANDREW (1808–75), president of U.S.A.; *b.* Raleigh, N. Carolina; entered Congress, 1843; governor of Tennessee, 1853; senator, 1857; prominent anti-secessionist; remained loyal to Federal government during Civil War; military governor of Tennessee, 1862. On Lincoln's assassination, 1865, became president; opposed enfranchisement of Negroes; impeached by Congress, 1868, for violating Tenure of Office Act, which had been passed despite his veto in 1867, but acquitted; retired, 1869.

Johnson, SAMUEL (1709–84), Eng. man of letters; *b.* Lichfield; son of a bookseller; educated Lichfield, Stourbridge, and Oxford; left Oxford, 1731, without a degree. In 1735 he married a Birmingham widow, Mrs. Porter, who died in 1752. Till 1762 he had a severe struggle with destitution; after failing as a schoolmaster, started journalism in London in connection with Cave's *Gentleman's Magazine*, on which he was parliamentary reporter. Pub. poem *London* (1738); started, 1747, work on his famous *Dictionary of the English Language*; then followed *Vanity of Human Wishes* (1749), his tragedy of *Irene*, staged by Garrick (1749), *The Rambler* (1750–2), the novel *Rasselas* (1759), and the periodical essay paper *The Idler* (1758). In 1762 he was given a royal pension of £300 a year. In 1763 began his friendship with Boswell; founded Literary Club, 1763, with Burke, Boswell, Reynolds, Garrick, Gibbon, and Goldsmith among its members, and Johnson's famous literary dictatorship began. He now began to travel with newly-made friends—Mr. and Mrs. Thrale. In 1773 he visited Scotland with Boswell. The rest of his life was embittered by ill-health and the death or defection of many of his friends. The chief fruits of this later period were the *Journey to the Western Islands*, and the *Lives of the Poets* (1781), his greatest work; buried in Westminster Abbey.

[*Life* by Boswell; *Six Essays on Johnson* by Raleigh (1910).]

Johnston, SIR HARRY HAMILTON (1858–1927), Eng. traveller, administrator, and writer; *b.* Kennington; explored the R. Congo, 1883; led Kilimanjaro scientific expedition, 1884; vice-consul in Cameroon, 1887; explored lakes Nyasa and Tanganyika, 1889; helped to establish Brit. Central African Protectorate, of which he became consul-general, 1891; commissioner in Uganda, 1899–1901; K.C.B., 1896; author of many books on Africa. Remarkable for versatility, he exhibited at Royal Academy, and also wrote *The Gay Dombeys* (1919), and *Mrs. Warren's Daughter* (1920).

Johnston, MARY (1870–), Amer. novelist; *b.* Buchanan, Virginia; novels are chiefly on historical subjects, and include *The Old Dominion*, *By Order of the Company* (1908), *The Slave Ship* (1925), *The Great Valley* (1926), *The Exile* (1927).

Jokai (*yō'kī*), MAURUS (1825–1904), Hungarian writer of prolific output; *b.* Komarom; took active part in Hungarian revolution, 1848–9; wrote sixty romances in Magyar; entered Parliament and supported Tisza, 1875–90.

Jo'nah ('dove'), Heb. prophet (2 Kings 14 : 25), native of Gath-hepher in Galilee, foretold victories of Jeroboam II. The Book of Jonah is an O.T. parable of which Jonah is made the hero.

Jon'athan, eldest son of Saul, remembered mostly for warmth and disinterestedness of his friendship with David; perished in battle with Philistines at Gilboa (1 Sam. 14; 2 Sam. 1).

Jones, SIR EDWARD BURNE. See BURNE-JONES, SIR EDWARD.

Jones, SIR HENRY (1852–1922), Brit. philosopher; *b.* in N. Wales; son of shoemaker; educated Glasgow Univ.; prof. of philosophy and political economy at Bangor, and of logic and metaphysics at St. Andrews Univ; prof. of moral philosophy, Glasgow Univ., 1894–1922; deeply interested in social reforms. Among his works are *Browning as a Religious and Philosophical Teacher*, and *Idealism as a Practical Creed.*

Jones, HENRY ARTHUR (1851–1929), Eng. dramatic author; *b.* Grandborough, Bucks; made first definite success with *The Silver King* (1882), followed by *Saints and Sinners* (1884), *Judah* (1890), *The Crusaders* (1891), *The Lie* (1914), etc.; also produced long series of comedies, and pub. *Renascence of the English Drama* (1895), etc.

Jones, INIGO (1573–1652), famous Eng. architect; *b.* London; son of cloth-worker; studied in Italy; arranged scenery for Jonson's court masques, and, quarrelling with Jonson, was satirized by him in *Bartholomew Fair*; surveyor-general of royal buildings, 1619–22; designed banqueting hall at Whitehall, 1619–22.

Jones, ROBERT TYRE (1902–), Amer. golfer; *b.* Atlanta, Georgia; won National Amateur Championship five times, National Open Championship four times, Brit. Open Championship three times, Brit. Amateur Championship once, and numerous other tournaments.

Jones, SIR WILLIAM (1746–1794), Brit. scholar; *b.* London; judge at Calcutta, 1783; founded Bengal Asiatic Society, 1784; pioneer in study of Sanskrit language and literature; author of *Digest of Hindu Laws*, *Persian Grammar*, and trans. *Institutes of Manu*.

Jonson, BEN (1573–1637), Eng. dramatist and poet; *b.* London·

educated at Westminster School; for short time followed his step-father's trade of bricklaying, but abandoned it for the army; served in campaigns in Netherlands; returned to London; became actor-playwright, sometimes working with Dekker, Porter, and others; was tried for killing fellow-actor in duel; pleaded benefit of clergy, escaped death, but was branded and property confiscated, 1598.

His first play, *Every Man in his Humour*, was staged about 1596, taken over by Shakespeare in 1598, and produced at Globe Theatre—a bright play, abounding in variety of interest; its sequel is *Every Man out of his Humour*. Then followed several comedies, including *Cynthia's Revels* (1600), *The Poetaster* (1601, in which his dramatic rivals were satirized), *Volpone* (1605), *Epicene* (1609), *The Alchemist* (1610). *Sejanus* (1603) and *Catilina* (1611) are two rather dull tragedies. *The Alchemist* is his masterpiece. Jonson wrote about forty charming masques, mostly in collaboration with Inigo Jones. His poems range from graceful lyrics to scurrilous epigrams. Of his songs, 'Drink to me only with thine eyes' is still popular. His last years were spent in poverty and disease; his tomb in Westminster Abbey bears inscription, 'O Rare Ben Jonson.'

[*Ben Jonson*, by Gregory Smith (1919).]

Jordan, David Starr (1851–1931), Amer. naturalist; *b.* Gainesville, New York; prof. of zoology, Indiana Univ., 1879–85, and president, 1885–91; first president of Leland Stanford Jr. Univ., 1891–1913; chancellor, 1913–16. Author of numerous books on natural history, especially fishes, and on world problems.

Jo'seph. (1) Son of Jacob and Rachel; sold into Egypt; rose to position of eminence; saved Egypt during famine, and brought his father and brethren to Egypt (see Genesis 37–50). (2) Joseph, husband of Mary, the mother of Jesus; descendant of King David.

Joseph II. (1741–90), Holy Rom. emperor; *b.* Vienna; emperor, 1765; shared authority in Austria with his mother, Maria Theresa, who retained supreme power; signed treaty for partition of Poland, 1772; opposed Frederick the Great; succeeded to Austrian throne, 1780; established religious toleration; abolished serfdom; subordinated Church to State.

Josephine (1763–1814), Empress of the French; *b.* Martinique; married Vicomte Beauharnais, 1779, who died, 1794; became first wife of Napoleon Bonaparte, 1796; crowned empress, 1804; divorced, 1809, to enable Napoleon to marry Marie Louise of Austria.

Jose'phus, Flavius (*c.* A.D. 37–*c.* 100), Jewish soldier and historian; a Pharisee; leader in Galilean revolt, A.D. 66; captured and spared by Vespasian; marched, as interpreter to Titus, against Jerusalem, A.D. 70; subsequently resided at Rome; wrote *Jewish Antiquities* and *The Jewish War*, both valuable historical documents.

Josh'ua, son of Nun; succeeded Moses as leader of Israelites; completed invasion of Canaan; a bold and intrepid leader. (See Book of Joshua.)

Josi'ah, King of Judah (*c.* 639–608 B.C.), son of Amon; reign marked by suppression of idolatry; during renovation of temple rediscovered Book of the Law; killed at Megiddo fighting against King of Egypt. (See II Kings 22, 23.)

Jó'sika (*yō-shē'kō*), Miklos, Baron (1794–1865), Hungarian novelist; *b.* Torda, Transylvania; historical romances include *The Last of the Batoris* (1837), *Abafi* (1843), *Esther* (1853), etc.

Joule (*jowl*), James Prescott

(1818–89), Eng. physicist; *b.* Salford; pupil of Dalton; did important work on magnetism in its relation to current electricity; most important discovery was the mechanical equivalent of heat in 1843; later, improved on his original calculation; practical unit of energy named after him.

Jovia'nus, FLAVIUS (*c.* 331–64), Rom. emperor; succeeded Julian the Apostate, 363, whose pagan policy he reversed, making the Christian religion the state religion.

Jow'ett, BENJAMIN (1817–93), Anglican scholar and divine; *b.* Camberwell; educated Oxford; prof. of Greek, 1855; Master of Balliol, 1870; suspect on account of his liberal views in theology; had enormous influence in Oxford; vice-chancellor of univ., 1882; best known for translations of Plato, Aristotle, and Thucydides.

[*Life and Letters*, by Abbott and Campbell (2 vols. 1897).]

Joyce, JAMES (1882–), Irish writer; *b.* Dublin; has pub. poems, essays, and novels; his best-known work, *Ulysses* (1922), marked a definite break from the traditional form of the novel.

Joynson-Hicks. See BRENTFORD.

Juarez (*hu-ä'reth*) BENITO PABLO (1806–72), Mexican president; *b.* in Oaxaca; of Ind. parentage; after holding various offices, elected president, 1858; declared war on France, 1862; in 1864 Maximilian was crowned emperor, and Juarez driven northwards; emperor captured and executed, 1867, and Juarez remained constitutional president till his death.

Ju'das Iscar'iot, the disciple of Jesus Christ who betrayed Him; overcome with remorse, committed suicide (Matt. 27 : 3; Acts 1 : 18).

Judas Maccabæ'us (*d.* 161 B.C.), Jewish revolutionary and patriot; delivered Jews from Syrian yoke in reign of Antiochus Epiphanes; afterwards purified temple and attacked neighbouring tribes, obtaining full religious liberty for Jews; was finally defeated and slain at Elasa by Bacchides. A great general, he is one of the most heroic figures in history of Israel. (See *Book of Maccabees.*)

Judd, JOHN WESLEY (1840–1916), Eng. geologist; *b.* Portsmouth; prof. of geology, 1876–1905, and dean of Royal Coll. of Science, London, 1895–1905; pub. *Geology of Rutland* (1875), *Volcanoes* (1878), *The Student's Lyell* (1896), *The Coming of Evolution.*

Jugur'tha (2nd cent. B.C.), King of Numidia; aided Scipio in conquest of Numantia, 134 B.C.; waged war with success against Romans, 110; subsequently defeated by Quintus Metellus; finally captured by Marius and put to death at Rome, *c.* 104.

Ju'lian the Apostate (331–63), Rom. emperor; *b.* Constantinople; nephew of Constantine the Great; gained great victory over Alemanni, 357; reduced Frankish tribes to submission; emperor, 361; tolerated all religions, but preferred paganism; killed, 363, during invasion of Persia. Remarkable as last champion of paganism, he was a ruler of ability.

Julius, name of three popes. JULIUS I., elected 337; supported Athanasius in Arian dispute. JULIUS II. (1443–1513), pope 1503; banished Cæsar Borgia from Italy; arranged League of Cambrai against Venice, 1508; concluded Holy League against France, 1511; initiated Vatican museum, and laid foundation stone of St. Peter's; encouraged fine arts and literature. JULIUS III. (1487–1555), pope 1550; favoured Jesuits.

Jung (*yoong*), CARL GUSTAV (1875–), Swiss psychologist; *b.* Basle; specialist in nervous and mental diseases; originally a disciple of Freud, now rejects much of the sex element in Freud's theories. Writings include *Psychology of the Unconscious*, *Papers on Analytical Psychology*.

Ju'nius, pseudonym of contributor of *Letters of Junius* to *Public Advertiser*, London, 1769–72; attacked George III. and his ministers; identified with several politicians, especially Sir Philip Francis, enemy of Warren Hastings, but indisputable proof is lacking.

Jusserand (*zhoo-ser-an'*), JEAN ADRIEN ANTOINE JULES (1855–1932), Fr. author and diplomatist; *b.* Lyons; consul in London, 1878; minister at Copenhagen, 1890; ambassador to U.S.A., 1902–25; brilliant critic of Eng. literature; pub. *A Literary History of the English People* (1895–1904), *With Americans of Past and Present Days* (1916), *The School of Ambassadors and Other Essays* (1924), *American Sentiment during the War* (1931), etc.

Justin'ian I., FLAVIUS ANICIUS JUSTINIANUS (483–565), BYZANTINE emperor; *b.* in Illyria; of barbarian extraction; adopted by his uncle, Justin I., whom he succeeded, 527; aided by his two great generals, Belisarius and Narses, who subdued the Vandals and Ostrogoths in Africa and Italy, he restored these countries to Byzantine empire; war against Chosroes of Persia was unsuccessful; strengthened frontiers of empire; built Church of St. Sophia. An orthodox Christian, he showed severity to Christian sectaries, Jews, and pagans.

Justinian is best known for thorough revision of whole system of law which he caused to be made; *Corpus Juris Civilis*, or Justinian Code, constituted Rom. law in Europe for next four centuries.

[*Age of Justinian and Theodora*, by Holmes (1905).]

Justin Martyr (*fl.* 2nd cent.), one of 'apostolic fathers'; *b.* Nablus, Samaria; lived at Ephesus; after being Stoic and Pythagorean, was converted to Christianity; went to Rome, where he was martyred *c.* A.D. 148; his *Apology* meets pagan attacks on Christianity; *Dialogue with Trypho the Jew* maintains claims of Christianity as against Judaism.

Ju'venal, full name DECIMUS JUNIUS JUVENALIS (*c.* A.D. 60–140), Rom. satirical poet; *b.* Aquinum; successful as amateur declamator; banished, possibly to Egypt, at advanced age. His *Satires*, sixteen in number (collected into five books), were probably composed between 100 and 130, and deal mainly with abuses prevalent in Domitian's reign.

K

Kane, ELISHA KENT (1820–57), Amer. explorer; *b.* Philadelphia; surgeon to first, commander of second, expedition in search of Franklin; wrote accounts of both enterprises.

Kant, IMMANUEL (1724–1804), Ger. philosopher; founder of transcendental or critical philosophy; *b.* Königsberg; prof. of philosophy, Königsberg, 1770–97; of frail constitution, prolonged life by adherence to strict routine. Chief works, *Kritik of Pure Reason* (1781), *Theory of Ethics*, *Prolegomena*, *Kritik of Judgment*.

His philosophy investigates the limits of reason. A distinction must be made between phenomena and noumena (things-in-themselves). Of the latter we can know nothing. Knowledge, however, is possible so long as the reason confines itself to phenomena, which must therefore conform to the laws of the constitution of the mind. Kant shows the necessity of the truths of spatial and temporal relations upon which the mathematical sciences depend, and the laws, such as that of causality, upon which the physical sciences depend.

In his ethics, all that is good is the good will. His Categorical Imperative is never to act otherwise than so that I could will that my maxim should become a universal law. This law is not an object of the senses, so that the moral law thus affirms a double system of nature—sensible, and super-sensible, *i.e.* according to laws belonging to the autonomy of pure reason. Kant postulates immortality to secure perfect accordance with the moral law, and the existence of God to secure happiness proportionate to virtue.

[*The Philosophy of Kant*, by Adamson (1879); *Life of Kant*, by Stuckenberg (1882).]

Karageorge, name given to GEORGE CZERNY (1766–1817), founder of Serbian independence; leader of revolutionary party, 1804; expelled Turks and captured Belgrade in 1806; struck such terror into his foes that they called him *Karageorge* (' Black George '), a term since adopted as designation of Serbian dynasty; made peace with Turkey, 1812, and Turks reoccupied Serbia, 1813; assassinated; a fierce, barbarous leader, but a genius.

Karl I. (1887–1922), last Emperor of Austria-Hungary; reigned from death of Francis Joseph (his grand-uncle) in 1916 until 1918; reign opened during Great War. Continued disasters in Italy and disaffection in his army compelled him to ask for an armistice (Oct. 30, 1918); abdicated Nov. 12, 1918.

Kar′olyi, MICHAEL, COUNT (1875–), Hungarian democratic statesman, of pacifist principles. During Great War was entrusted with abortive Austro-Hungarian peace overtures to Allies through Switzerland, 1917. When Dual Monarchy realized its defeat he was called upon to form a ministry, Nov. 1918; later in same month he became provisional president of Hungarian republic. His endeavours to restore order being frustrated by Bolshevist propaganda, he resigned, 1919. Now one of editors of Paris *Monde.*

Kauffmann (*kouf′män*), ANGELICA (1741–1807), Swiss painter; *b.* Coire; worked first in Italy, afterwards in London, where she attained fame for her classic and mythological pictures and her portraits; was friend of Reynolds and Goldsmith; one of the earliest of the Royal Academicians.

Kaulbach (*koul′bach*), WILHELM VON (1805–74), Ger. painter; *b.* Arolsen; director of Munich Academy, 1849–74; among his numerous works are *Narrenhaus, Destruction of Jerusalem, Battle of the Huns*, etc.

Kay, JOHN (*d.* 1764), Eng. inventor; *b.* near Bury; chief of his inventions was his fly-shuttle, which greatly improved the weaving of cloth.

Kaye-Smith, SHEILA (MRS. PENROSE FRY), Eng. novelist; *b.* St. Leonards-on-Sea; her works, mainly dealing with Sussex, include *Sussex Gorse* (1916), *Joanna Godden* (1921), *The George and the Crown* (1925), *The Village Doctor* (1929), *Susan Spray* (1931), *The Children's Summer* (partly autobiographical, 1932), etc.

Kean, EDMUND (1787–1833), Eng. actor; *b.* London; son of a strolling actress; after playing in various touring companies, appeared at Drury Lane as Shylock,

1814, and had instant success; equally popular in America; broke down while acting Othello, and died shortly afterwards; the greatest tragedian of his time.

Kear′ton, CHERRY (1871–), naturalist, photographer, author; *b.* Thwaite, Yorks; first to illustrate natural history books wholly by photographs, and to make cinematograph records of big game in natural surroundings; author of *Wild Life across the World, My Animal Friendships, The Island of Penguins*, etc.

Kearton, RICHARD (1862–1928), Brit. field naturalist and author; brother of above; *b.* Thwaite, Yorks; originally a farmer; among works are: *Birds' Nests; Eggs and Egg Collecting; Wild Life at Home: how to Study and Photograph it; Our Rarer British Breeding Birds; Wonders of Wild Nature*, etc.

Keats, JOHN (1795–1821), Eng. poet; *b.* London; son of livery-stable keeper; apprenticed to surgeon, 1810; became dresser at Guy's Hospital, 1816; abandoned medicine for literature and became one of the foremost Eng. poets. His first poems were pub., 1817, with the encouragement of Shelley; *Endymion* appeared, 1818; *Lamia, Hyperion*, and other poems, 1820; was attacked by various journals, notably *Quarterly Review*; driven from England by consumption, he died in Rome. Much of Keats's poetry is immature both in thought and style, but such poems as *La Belle Dame sans Merci, The Ode on a Grecian Urn, To a Nightingale*, and his sonnets, are unsurpassable. His influence on later Eng. poetry has been almost incalculable.

[*Life*, by Sir Sidney Colvin (1887).]

Ke′ble, JOHN (1792–1866), Eng. priest and poet; *b.* Fairford, Glos; took double first at Oxford; was ordained, 1816; tutor of Corpus Christi, 1818; retired, 1823; pub. *Christian Year*, a book of meditations in verse for holy days, 1827; prof. of poetry at Oxford, 1831–41. His univ. sermon on 'National Apostasy,' 1833, started Tractarian movement; closely associated with Newman and Pusey, with whom he issued *Tracts for the Times*; vicar of Hursley, Hants, from 1835; Keble Coll., Oxford, was founded in his memory, 1869.

Keene, CHARLES SAMUEL (1823–91), Eng. black-and-white artist; contributed to *Punch* from 1851; also illustrated Douglas Jerrold's *Curtain Lectures*, Charles Reade's *Cloister and the Hearth*, etc.; ranks among best 19th cent. etchers.

Keith (*kēth*), SIR ARTHUR (1866–), Scot. anthropologist; *b.* Aberdeen; prof. of comparative anatomy, Royal Institution, 1917–23; president, British Association, 1927; F.R.S., 1913; rector, Aberdeen Univ., 1930–3; expert on prehistoric man as reconstructed from fossil remains; author of *Introduction to Study of Anthropoid Apes* (1896), *Human Embryology and Morphology* (1901), *Ancient Types of Man* (1911), *Concerning Man's Origin* (1927), etc.

Kekulé (*kā′koo-lā*), FRIEDRICH AUGUST (1829–96), eminent Ger. chemist; *b.* Darmstadt; prof. of chemistry, Ghent, 1858, and at Bonn, 1865–96; famous for his 'ring' structure theory of benzene and his views on the linking of atoms; wrote *Lehrbuch der organischen Chemie.*

Keller, HELEN ADAMS (1880–), Amer. blind deaf-mute; *b.* in Alabama; attack of scarlet fever, when she was two years old, left her without sight, smell, or hearing; educated at home by Miss Anne M. Sullivan, and at various schools; learned to read, write, and talk; graduated from Radcliffe Coll., 1904; knows several languages; LL.D., Glasgow, 1932; author of *The Story of my Life* (1902), *The World I Live in* (1910), and *My Religion* (1927).

Kell'ogg, FRANK BILLINGS (1856–), Amer. statesman and lawyer; *b.* Potsdam, New York; ambassador to Britain, 1923–5; secretary of state, U.S.A., 1925–29. Took the initiative in securing signature of Powers to Peace Pact, 1928.

Keltie, SIR JOHN SCOTT (1840–1927), Brit. geographer; *b.* Dundee; librarian, 1885–92, and secretary, 1892–5, of Royal Geographical Soc.; ed. (jointly) *Geographical Journal*, 1915–17; kt., 1918. From 1880 ed. *The Statesman's Year Book;* author of *The Partition of Africa*, etc.

Kel'vin, WILLIAM THOMSON, BARON (1824–1907), most eminent physicist of his time; *b.* Belfast; educated Glasgow and Cambridge; studied at Paris under Regnault; prof. of natural philosophy, Glasgow, 1846–99. His work covered every branch of physics; did valuable work in thermo-dynamics; made submarine telegraphy a possibility; invented sounding apparatus, pressure gauge, tide gauge, and made great improvements in mariner's compass; knighted, 1866; president Royal Soc., 1890; peer, 1892; O.M., 1902; chancellor of Glasgow Univ., 1904.

[*Life*, by Gray (1908); Thompson (1910); Russell (1912).]

Kemble, Eng. theatrical family. JOHN PHILIP (1757–1823); *b.* Prescot; first London appearance was as Hamlet in Drury Lane, 1783; leading tragedian of his day. His brother CHARLES (1775–1854), *b.* Brecon; succeeded best in second parts when John played first—*e.g.* Laertes, Cassio, Macduff. FRANCES ANNE, 'Fanny' (1809–93), daughter of Charles; *b.* London; noted for her rendering of tragic parts and her Shakespearian readings. Her sister ADELAIDE (1814–79) was a distinguished operatic performer and author of some tales.

Kemp, GEORGE MEIKLE (1795–1844), Scot. architect; *b.* in Midlothian; son of a shepherd; worked as carpenter, millwright, and draughtsman; designed famous Scott monument, Edinburgh.

Kempis, THOMAS À (THOMAS HAMMERKEN) (1379–1471), religious writer; *b.* Kempen, near Cologne; received orders at Augustinian convent of Mount St. Agnes, Zwolk; became priest, 1413, and lived in a convent till death. Most famous work is his *Imitation of Christ*, which has been trans. into nearly every language.

Kemp-Welch, LUCY ELIZABETH (1869–), Eng. artist; *b.* Bournemouth; especially famous as painter of animals, more particularly horses; exhibited in Royal Academy from 1894; president of Soc. of Animal Painters (formed 1914). Among her paintings are: *Horses bathing in the Sea, The Riders, Colt-hunting in the New Forest*, and *Forward the Guns.*

Ken, THOMAS (1637–1711), Eng. prelate and hymn-writer; *b.* Little Berkhampstead, Herts; Bishop of Bath and Wells, 1684; one of the seven bishops who resisted Declaration of Indulgence, 1688; refused, nevertheless, to take oath to William III.; deposed, 1691.

Kendal. (1) WILLIAM HUNTER (1843–1917), stage name of WILLIAM HUNTER GRIMSTON, well-known actor and actor-manager. (2) DAME MARGARET BRUNTON ROBERTSON ("Madge") (1849–1935), famous actress; wife of (1), with whom she toured America, 1889–95.

Kennedy, BENJAMIN HALL (1804–89), Eng. schoolmaster; *b.* near Birmingham; headmaster at Shrewsbury, 1836–66; prof. of Greek, Cambridge, and Canon of Ely, 1867; best-known work, *Public School Latin Grammar.*

Kennedy-Fraser, MRS. MARJORY (1857–1930), collector of Celtic music; *b.* Perth; devoted her life to collecting Hebridean folksongs; pub. *Songs of the Hebrides,* and *A Life of Song,* an autobiography.

Kenneth I., MAC ALPIN (*d. c.* 860), Scot. king; defeated Picts, and united Picts and Scots; frequently invaded Northumbria. KENNETH II. (*d.* 995), son of Malcolm I.; overran Northumbria to the Tees; Central Scotland was consolidated under his rule; killed by his own followers.

Ken'tigern, or MUNGO, ST., Scot. saint; *fl.* 6th cent.; founded monastery in Glasgow; Bishop of Cumbria, 543; said to have done missionary work in Galloway, and north of Firth of Forth; *c.* 584 was visited by St. Columba.

Kep'ler, JOHANN (1571–1630), Ger. astronomer; *b.* near Weil, Württemberg; prof. of astronomy at Graz, 1593; owing to religious persecutions accepted Tycho Brahe's invitation to Prague, to assist in preparation of Rudolphine tables; succeeded Tycho as imperial astronomer; his great work, *The New Astronomy: Commentaries on the Motions of Mars* (1609), forms the basis of physical astronomy. In it he enunciated his first two laws relating to the motion of the planets. The third law was contained in *The Harmonies of the World* (1619), dedicated to James I.

[*Life*, by Müller (1903).]

Ker, WILLIAM PATON (1855–1923), Brit. man of letters; *b.* Glasgow; educ. there and at Oxford; prof. of Eng. literature and history in Univ. Coll. of S. Wales, Cardiff, 1883–9, at Univ. Coll., London, 1889–1922; from 1920 prof. of poetry at Oxford. Author of *Epic and Romance, The Dark Ages, Sturla the Historian,* etc.

Kerensky (*kā'ren-ski*), ALEXANDER FEODOROVICH (1881–), Russ. revolutionary leader; *b.* in Tashkent; practised law; elected to Duma as Socialist-Labour deputy, 1913. After Russ. Revolution, 1917, became minister of justice under Prince Lvov, and then as minister of war strove to stop disaffection in the army; became premier two months later, but was unable to stop the tide of Bolshevik revolution, and fled the country; settled in Paris.

Ker'nahan, COULSON (1858–), Brit. novelist and critic; *b.* Ilfracombe. Among his works are *A Dead Man's Diary; A Book of Strange Sins; Scoundrels and Co.; A World without a Child; The Child, the Wise Man, and the Devil;* and *Begging the Moon's Pardon.*

Keyes (*kēz*), SIR ROGER (1872–), Brit. admiral; entered navy, 1885; in charge of submarine service, 1910–14; chief of staff E. Mediterranean squadron at Dardanelles and Gallipoli, 1915; rear-admiral, 1917; commanded Dover Patrol and operations for blocking Zeebrugge and Ostend; admiral of the fleet, 1930. M.P. for N. Portsmouth, 1934.

Khufu. See CHEOPS.

Kil'ligrew, THOMAS (1612–83), Eng. dramatist; *b.* London; built first Theatre Royal, Drury Lane, 1663; famous as a wit.

King, WILLIAM LYON MACKENZIE (1874–), Canadian statesman; *b.* Berlin (now Kitchener), Ontario; entered Canadian parliament as Liberal, 1908; leader of Liberal party from 1919; prime minister, 1921–June 1926, September 1926–30, and since 1935. Represented Canada at Imperial Conferences, 1923 and 1926.

King'lake, ALEXANDER WILLIAM (1809–91), Eng. historian; *b.* Taunton; made extended tour in East, 1835–6, which he described in *Eothen*; from Lord Raglan's papers compiled *The Invasion of the Crimea* (8 vols., 1863–87).

Kings'burgh, John Hay Athole Macdonald, Lord (1836–1919), Scot. judge; *b.* Edinburgh; solicitor-general for Scotland, 1876–80; dean of faculty of advocates, 1882–85; lord advocate, 1885–8; lord justice-clerk of Scotland, 1888–1915. Through his influence post cards came into use in Great Britain; pioneer of volunteering and motoring.

King'sley. (1) Charles (1819–75), Eng. clergyman and novelist; *b.* Holne, Dartmoor: educated at Cambridge; rector of Eversley, Hampshire, 1844; prof. of modern history, Cambridge, 1860–69; Canon of Westminster from 1873. Pub. *Andromeda and Other Poems* (1858), which included some excellent songs and ballads. His first novels, *Alton Locke* and *Yeast*, show Kingsley's 'Christian Socialism.' His romances and novels, *Hypatia*, *Westward Ho! Two Years Ago*, and the inimitable *Water Babies*, are famous.

[*Kingsley's Letters and Memoirs*, ed. by his wife (1877).]

(2) Henry (1830–76), Eng. author, younger brother of (1); *b.* Barnack, Northants; spent five years in Australia, and depicted life in the goldfields in *Geoffrey Hamlyn*; wrote novels, *Ravenshoe*, *The Hillyars*, *The Burtons*. (3) Mary Henrietta (1862–1900), Eng. author; niece of Charles and Henry; *b.* London; travelled in Africa and wrote *Travels in West Africa*, *West African Studies*, and *The Story of West Africa*, valuable studies of folklore, anthropology, and primitive religions; died while acting as nurse in S. African War.

King'ston, William Henry Giles (1814–80); *b.* London; Eng. writer boys' stories—*e.g. Peter the Whaler*, *The Three Midshipmen*; wrote over 120 books of healthy tone and vigorous action.

Ki'pling, Rudyard (1865–1936), Eng. poet and novelist; *b.* Bombay; educated at the United Service Coll., Westward Ho, England; made use of his experiences there in his *Stalky and Co.* (1899), a tale of schoolboy life; went to Lahore as sub-ed. of the *Civil and Military Gazette*, 1882, and remained in India till 1889; subsequently travelled extensively before settling down in England; a voluminous writer. *Plain Tales from the Hills*, *Soldiers Three*, *Under the Deodars*, *Wee Willie Winkie*, and *The Phantom 'Rickshaw*, pub. 1887–9, gave Kipling his place among the world's great short-story writers. He gained an equal reputation from his poems which appeared in *Barrack-room Ballads* (1892), *The Seven Seas* (1896), and *The Five Nations* (1903). Wrote a number of charming books, ostensibly for children, including *The Jungle Books* (1894–5), *Captains Courageous* (1897), *Kim* (1901), *Puck of Pook's Hill* (1906), *Rewards and Fairies* (1910). Other volumes include *The Light that Failed* (1891), *Many Inventions* (1893), *Actions and Reactions* (1909), *A Diversity of Creatures* (1917), *Letters of Travel* (1920), and *Thy Servant a Dog* (1930). Kipling has greatly extended literary art by new types of character and novel forms of presentation; he shows an absolute command of style and all its resources. Awarded Nobel prize for literature, 1907; rector, St. Andrews Univ., 1922–5.

Kisfaludy (*kish'fo-looj*), Karoly (1788–1830), Hungarian author; *b.* near Raab; put new life and power into Magyar literature by his war songs, folk-tales, and dramas.

Kitchener of Khartoum, Horatio Herbert, Earl (1850–1916), Brit. soldier and administrator; *b.* Ballylongford, Ireland; educated in France; entered Woolwich, 1868; during Franco-

Prussian War served with Chanzy's army for short time; joined Palestine Survey, 1874–8. After survey work in Cyprus, 1878–82, received cavalry command in Egyptian army; took part in Nile Expedition, 1884–5, for relief of Gordon; commandant of Suakin, 1886–8. Appointed sirdar (commander-in-chief) of Egyptian army, 1890; reconquered the Sudan; at Omdurman, 1898, completely destroyed the power of Mahdism. For his services he was created a peer, and awarded the sum of £30,000. In the Fashoda Affair, 1898, he showed himself a diplomat of real ability. During visit to England on conclusion of Sudan campaign, he raised £100,000 to found a coll. at Khartoum in memory of Gordon.

During the South African War, 1900, he was chief of staff to Lord Roberts, becoming commander-in-chief, 1900–2. At end of this war was made a viscount and received grant of £50,000. From 1902–9 he was commander-in-chief in India, and reorganized the army; his conflict with Lord Curzon, the viceroy, led to the latter's resignation; field-marshal, 1909; consul-general of Egypt, 1911–14; O.M., P.C., and lord rector of Edinburgh Univ., 1914.

On outbreak of Great War he was appointed secretary for war, and raised and equipped large voluntary forces. On June 5, 1916, he embarked on the *Hampshire* for Russia; the vessel struck a mine off the Orkney Is. and Kitchener lost his life. A chapel was erected in St. Paul's to his memory, 1925.

[*Life of Lord Kitchener*, by Sir George Arthur (3 vols., 1920).]

Klaproth (*kläp'rōt*), MARTIN HEINRICH (1743–1817), Ger. chemist; *b.* Wernigerode; professor of chemistry, Berlin, 1810; discovered uranium, zirconium, cerium, and titanium.

Kling'er, FRIEDRICH MAXIMILIAN VON (1752–1831), Ger. dramatist and novelist; *b.* Frankfurt-on-Main; of humble parents; curator of Dorpat Univ., 1803–17; dramas include *Sturm und Drang* (1776), which gave its name to the movement, *Medea in Korinth* and *Medea auf dem Kaukasos* (1791), etc.; romances include *Der Weltmann und der Dichter* (1798), etc.

Klop'stock, FRIEDRICH GOTTLIEB (1724–1803), Ger. poet; *b.* Quedlinburg; studied theology at Jena and Leipzig; lived in Copenhagen, 1751–70; was the first genuine Ger. poet of 18th cent.; aimed at giving the Ger. nation a Christian epic, viz. *Der Messias* (in 4 vols.); wrote numerous odes, lyric poetry, and several dramas.

Kluck (*klook*), ALEXANDER VON (1846–1934), German soldier; *b.* Münster, Westphalia; fought as lieutenant in Franco-Prussian War; during Great War commanded 1st Army which formed the right of the German front advancing upon Paris and the Marne valley, and caused the Brit. retreat from Mons, but was defeated at battle of Marne; wounded, 1915; retired, 1916. Pub. *March to Paris*, 1920.

Kneller (*nel'er*), SIR GODFREY (1646–1723), portrait painter; *b.* Lübeck; studied under Rembrandt; court painter to Charles II. of England, retaining this position into reign of George I. Among his most famous works are *Celebrities of the Kit-Cat Club*, *Beauties of the Court of William III.*, and a series of admirals.

Knight, DAME LAURA, British artist; first woman R.A., 1936; famous for her circus subjects; D.B.E., 1929.

[*Autobiography* (1936).]

Knox, EDMUND GEORGE VALPY (1881–), pen-name EVOE, Eng. humorist and author; educated Rugby and Oxford; editor of *Punch* since 1932; has written much in humorous vein, and ed. *Anthology of Humorous Verse.*

Knox, John (1513–72), Scot. reformer; probably *b.* Haddington; took orders as secular priest; came under influence of George Wishart. When St. Andrews was taken by the French, 1547, he was taken prisoner and sentenced to labour in the Fr. galleys; released two years later, became minister at Berwick, and afterwards at Newcastle. On accession of Mary I. of England took refuge on the Continent; came much in contact with Calvin at Geneva; returned, 1556, and took up permanent abode in Scotland, 1559; strengthened Protestant enthusiasm, and inaugurated a more thoroughgoing reform, securing the help of England against Fr. influence. Knox became minister at Edinburgh, 1560; the death of the queen regent gave another blow to Rom. Catholicism; Protestantism was formally installed as the established religion of the country, 1561; the *First Book of Discipline* drawn up. The revival of old dissensions took place on return of Mary, but the victory was to remain with Knox, largely through the queen's ill-fortune. After the murder of Rizzio, Knox withdrew for safety to Ayrshire; wrote *History of Reformation*; retired to St. Andrews, 1569, but returned to Edinburgh in 1572, the year of his death. Knox was unequalled as a social reformer; his theological position was that of Calvin.

[*Works*, ed. by David Laing (1846–8); *Life of Knox*, by McCrie; *John Knox and the Reformation*, by Andrew Lang.]

Koch (*ko*ch), Robert (1843–1910), German bacteriologist; *b.* Klausthal, Hanover; prof., Berlin Univ., and director of Institute of Hygiene, 1885; famous for his discoveries and isolation of the bacilli of anthrax, Asiatic cholera, and tuberculosis, and for his modes of preventive inoculation; Nobel prize for medicine, 1905.

Kock, Charles Paul de (1794–1871), Fr. novelist; *b.* Paris; pub. about one hundred novels, in which, in witty, vulgar, and realistic fashion, he described low and middle-class life in Paris. His works include *Georgette, Gustave,* and *André le Savoyard.*

Koltchak (or Kolchak), Alexander Vasilievich (1875–1920), Russ. admiral and soldier; in 1903 crossed the Arctic from the Lena to Bennet I. for the relief of Baron Tol, who had wintered there, but found no trace of explorer. During Russo-Jap. War he distinguished himself in the defence of Port Arthur. During Great War was given independent command in the Baltic, and later promoted vice-admiral and commander of the Black Sea fleet. After revolution, 1917, was leader of the Whites, or Anti-Bolshevists; virtual leader of Russia. In Jan. 1920 an anti-Koltchak revolution broke out at Vladivostok, and on Jan. 24 Koltchak surrendered to the revolutionaries at Irkutsk, and was shot.

Kosciuszko (*kos-i-us'ko*), Tadeusz (1746–1817), Polish patriot and general; *b.* in Lithuania; served in U.S.A. army under Washington; in 1794 led rising for Polish independence, but was finally defeated and captured; released by Paul I., 1796; spent twenty-one years in America, France, and Switzerland.

[*Life*, by Michelet (1863).]

Kossuth (*kosh'oot*), Lajos (1802–94), noted Hungarian patriot; *b.* Monok, Hungary; imprisoned in 1838 for circulating reports of debates in National Diet; after release ed. the *Pesti Hirlap*, a party periodical, for several years, and, 1847, entered Diet and became leader of the National League which aimed at Hungarian independence of Austria. In 1848 the Diet declared independence of Hungary, and appointed Kossuth governor. After suppression of the revolt by Emperor of Austria, he had to take refuge in Turkey, and subsequently lived in England and Italy, his hostility to Austria preventing him from taking advantage of general amnesty. Author of *Memories of My Exile.*

Kotzebue (*kot'se-boo*), AUGUST FRIEDRICH FERDINAND VON (1761–1819), Ger. dramatist; *b.* Weimar; held high official post in Russ. service; director of Viennese Burgtheater, 1798; assassinated. Wrote over 200 plays; *Menschenhass und Reue* was for long the most popular play in Germany and England.

Kras'sin, LEONID BORISOVICH (1870–1927), Russ. Soviet minister; *b.* Siberia, of bourgeois family; studied engineering; accompanied Lenin and Trotsky to Brest-Litovsk to negotiate treaty with Germany, 1918; commissary of food in Red Army, and later minister of commerce and industry; came to London, 1920, as president of Soviet commercial mission; represented Soviet interests in Paris and in London, 1925–26.

Kreisler (*krīz'ler*), FRITZ (1875–), world-famous violinist and composer; *b.* Vienna; received musical education at Vienna and Paris; has appeared in all the great cities of the world; during Great War served in Austrian army and was wounded.

Krogh, SCHACK AUGUST STEENBERG (1874–), Dan. physiologist; *b.* Grenaa; prof. at Copenhagen Univ., 1916; Nobel prize for medicine, 1920; author of *The Respiratory Exchange in Animals and Man* (1916) and *The Anatomy and Physiology of Capillaries* (1922).

Kropot'kin, PETER ALEXEIEVICH, PRINCE (1842–1921), Russ. author and revolutionary; *b.* Moscow; made geographical survey of Manchuria, 1864; visited Switzerland, 1872, and joined the International Working Men's Association; subsequently became an anarchist and was frequently arrested. Made his home in England from 1886, but returned to Russia after the revolution, 1917. Among numerous publications are *Fields, Factories, and Workshops* (1899), *Memoirs of a Revolutionist* (1900), *The Desiccation of Asia* (1904), *Russian Literature* (1905), *Modern Science and Anarchism* (1912), etc.

Kruger (*kroo'ger*), STEPHANUS JOHANNES PAULUS (1825–1904), president of Transvaal; *b.* Colesberg, Cape Colony; took part in Great Trek, 1836; rapidly rose to power in Transvaal; led Boers in 1881, when they asserted their independence, and became president, 1883; re-elected, 1888, 1893, 1898. His rooted hostility to the British and Uitlanders generally precipitated S. African War, 1899–1902. He fled to Europe, 1900, first settling in Holland, and lastly at Mentone. Imbued with strong puritanical spirit, he was an ardent Dutch-Afrikander patriot, and a 'slim' diplomatist; pub. *Memories* (1902).

Krylov (*krē'lof*), IVAN ANDREEVICH (1768–1844), famous Russ. fabulist; *b.* Moscow; in addition to writing dramas, he translated some of La Fontaine's fables and pub. (1809) his own *Fables.*

Kubelik (*koo'be-lik*), JAN (1880–), Bohemian violinist; *b.* near Prague; gave first recital in 1898; has since given recitals throughout the world; violinist, royal court of Romania; works include three violin concertos.

Kublai Khan (*koob'lī*) (1216–94), grandson of Jenghiz Khan; emperor of the Mongols; succeeded as khan, 1259; invaded China, 1267; established Mongol dynasty; extended conquests over Cochin China, Tibet, and beyond the Ural Mts. westward, thus creating one of largest empires ever known.

Kun (*koon*), BELA (1886–), Hungarian communist leader; a Russ. Jew; *b.* near Györ; organized a revolutionary rising in Budapest, Feb. 1919, and established a Soviet government; concluded military alliance with Russ. Soviets; government overthrown in Aug.; fled to Vienna; ultimately settled in Moscow, 1928.

Kuroki, TAMESADA, COUNT (1844–1923), Jap. general; *b.* Satsuma; won distinction in Chino-Jap. War, 1894; commanded 1st Army in Russo-Jap. War, 1904–5; created count for his services.

Kuropat'kin, ALEXEI NICOLAEVICH (1848–1921), Russ. general; *b.* Pskov; chief of staff in Russo-Turk. War, 1877–8; commander-in-chief during first part of Russo-Jap. War, but relieved at his own request, 1905; at outbreak of the Great War was commander-in-chief of Manchurian army, and, in 1916, was appointed commander-in-chief on northern front; gov.-gen. of Turkistan, 1916; after Russ. revolution became a teacher in a village school.

Kyd, THOMAS (1558–94), Eng. dramatist; *b.* London; most important works are *The Spanish Tragedy* and *Cornelia.*

Kyrle (*kerl*), JOHN (1637–1724), 'the Man of Ross'; *b.* in Gloucestershire; spent greater part of his life at Ross, Herefordshire; devoted his money to building churches and hospitals; the Kyrle Soc. was founded, 1877, to ameliorate the lives of the poor.

L

Labori (*lä-bor-ē'*), FERNAND GUSTAVE GASTON (1860–1917), Fr. advocate; *b.* Reims; won fame by his brilliant defence of Zola, and by his conduct of the Dreyfus appeal; counsel for the defence in the trial of Mme. Caillaux, etc.

Labouchere (*lä-boo-shār'*), HENRY DUPRÉ (1831–1912), Eng. journalist; *b.* London; after a career in the diplomatic service, entered parliament, and in 1876 founded and became editor of *Truth,* a society journal which exposed many social and other scandals.

La Bruyère (*lä broo-yār'*), JEAN DE (1645–96), Fr. essayist and novelist; *b.* Paris; treasurer of finances at Caen, 1675–87; tutor to Duke of Bourbon, 1684–6; his *Caractères* (1688) contained 420 separate *caractères* or portraits; the eighth ed., pub. before the author's death, contained 1,120 *caractères*; admitted to Fr. Academy, 1693; depicted his acquaintances with such skill as to win immediate renown; some of his wit still keeps its savour.

Lafayette (*lä-fā-yet'*), MARIE JOSEPH PAUL ROCH YVES GILBERT MOTIER, MARQUIS DE (1757–1834), Fr. soldier and statesman; *b.* in Auvergne; assisted Amer. colonists in their war with England, 1777–81; imbibed republican views, and in Fr. Revolution led minority of nobility in States-General to join the Tiers-Etat, June 25, 1789; after fall of Bastille became commander-in-chief of National Guard; commanded an army during war with Austria, 1792; was captured by Austria and imprisoned for five years. At restoration, 1815, he became a prominent supporter of liberal ideas; was commander of National Guard in revolution of 1830.

[*Mémoires* (1837–8); *Lives*, by B. Tuckerman (1889) and E. Charavaray (1895).]

La Fontaine (*läfon-tān'*), JEAN DE (1621–95), Fr. poet and fabulist; *b.* Château-Thierry, Champagne; educated for church but turned to law; first book of his *Contes* (1664) won him popularity, increased by the second book, and above all by his *Fables* (12 vols.), which began to appear in 1866 and which have been widely translated. He contrived to make the fable a vehicle for poetry, satire, and comedy, selecting his subjects from Æsop or the old Fr. *fabliaux*; wrote in lively, concise, and beautiful language.

Lagerlöf (*lä-ger-loov'*), SELMA (1858–), Swed. novelist; *b.* in Vermland; won immediate fame with *Gösta Berlings Saga* (1891), a modern treatment of old legends; in *Antikrist's Mirakler* (1897) pleaded for Christian socialism; other works include *Nils Holgerssons underbara resa* (2 vols., 1906–7), *Kejseren af Portugalien* (1914), and *Charlotte Löfvensksöld* (1925); awarded Nobel prize for literature, 1909; first woman member of Swed. Academy, 1914.

Lagrange (*lä-gronzh*), JOSEPH LOUIS, COMTE (1736–1813), Fr. mathematician; *b.* Turin; prof. of geometry at Turin Royal Artillery School at age of eighteen; appointed by Frederick the Great to succeed Euler as director of Berlin Academy, 1766; went to Paris, 1787, becoming prof. of geometry at the Polytechnic School, 1797; his chief works are *Calcul des Variations* (1762), *Mécanique Analytique* (1788), and *Théorie des Fonctions Analytiques* (1797), all marked by originality and power.

La Halle. See ADAM DE LA HALLE.

Lally-Tollendal (*lä-lē' tol-on-däl'*), THOMAS ARTHUR, COMTE DE (1702–66), Fr. general; served in the Jacobite expedition to Scotland, 1745; commander-in-chief in the E. Indies, 1756; forced to surrender Pondicherry, 1761; on return to France tried and beheaded, supposedly for treachery.

Lalo', EDOUARD (1823–92), Fr. composer; *b.* Lille; wrote two operas, *Fiesque* (1867) and *Le Roi d'Ys* (1888), besides chamber music, concertos, and symphonies, which exercised a strong influence on the work of subsequent Fr. composers.

Lamarck (*lä-märk'*), JEAN BAPTISTE PIERRE ANTOINE DE MONNET, CHEVALIER DE (1744–1829), eminent Fr. zoologist; *b.* in Picardy; educated Amiens; occupied important scientific posts in Paris, where he died; chief works are *Philosophie Zoologique* (1809) and *Historie des Animaux sans Vertèbres* (7 vols. 1815–22); a precursor of Darwin, he is best known for the doctrine called *Lamarckism*, which attempts to explain evolution by assuming that acquired characteristics are hereditary.

[*Lamarck*, by E. Perrier (1925).]

Lamartine (*lä-mär-tēn'*), ALPHONSE MARIE LOUIS DE PRAT DE (1790–1869), Fr. poet; *b.* Mâcon; a pioneer of Romantic school; most of his poetry was pub. in the early years of his life, including *Premières Méditations Poétiques* (1820), *Nouvelles Méditations Poétiques* (1823), *Harmonies Poétiques et Religieuses* (1830), *Jocelyn* (1836), *La Chute d'an Ange* (1838), and *Recueillements Poétiques* (1839); played a notable part in politics, especially in revolution of 1848, when he showed great gifts of eloquence and was member of Executive Committee; under empire sank into comparative poverty; wrote many prose works during these years, including *Trois mois au Pouvoir* (1848), *Raphael* (1849), *Confidences* (1849), *Geneviève* (1850), and *Nouvelles Confidences* (1851).

[*Lives*, by C. de Pomairoles (1890), E. Deschanel (1893), and H. R. Whitehouse (1918).]

Lamb, CHARLES (1775–1834), Eng. essayist; *b.* London; educated Christ's Hospital, where he formed friendship with Coleridge; held clerkship in South Sea House and India House; never married, but devoted his life to his sister Mary, who was subject to fits of insanity; dabbled in verse and journalism; with Mary wrote *Tales from Shakespeare* (1807); pub. *Specimens of English Dramatic Poets* (1808); contributed essays on wide variety of subjects, under name *Elia*, to *London Magazine* (1820–2). Lamb is one of the most lovable characters and writers in Eng. literature. He counted among his friends all the great writers of his day. His essays are written in a style mingling quaintness and delicacy, humour and pathos. He ranks high as a literary critic and letter-writer.

[*Life and Works*, by A. Ainger (1899–1900); *Life*, by E. V. Lucas (1921).]

Lambert, JOHN (1619–83), Eng. soldier; *b.* Yorkshire; during Civil War fought on Parliamentary side at Marston Moor, Preston, Dunbar, and Worcester; during Commonwealth period rose to high importance in Parliamentary councils; after Restoration was banished to Guernsey.

Lancaster, JOHN OF GAUNT, DUKE OF (1340–99), a son of Edward III.; *b.* Ghent; served in Spain, 1367, France, 1369; after second marriage, with Constance of Castile, assumed title King of Castile; towards close of Edward III.'s reign he attained great power in England; supported Wyclif; after Richard's accession, supported king; unsuccessfully invaded Castile, 1387; Duke of Aquitaine, 1390; governed Aquitaine, 1395.

Lancaster, JOSEPH (1778–1838), Brit. educationist; *b.* London; opened free school for poor children in London; his "system" (consisting mainly in teaching by monitors, mechanical drills, no corporal punishments, but a graded system of ranks, badges, etc., as rewards) had great success; later went to America, where his system was also adopted.

Land′er, RICHARD LEMON (1804–34), Eng. explorer; *b.* Truro; accompanied Clapperton's Niger expedition, 1825; along with his brother JOHN (1807–39) he explored lower reaches of Niger, and proved that it flows into Bight of Benin; killed by natives. Pub. *Journal* (1832).

Land′or, WALTER SAVAGE (1775–1864), Eng. prose-writer and poet; *b.* Warwick; educated at Rugby and Cambridge; headed volunteer force, raised at his expense, in Peninsula, 1808; travelled in Europe for several years; finally settled at Florence; friend of Southey and Browning. His works are distinguished by purity of style and delicacy of diction. Best-known works are his *Poems*, *Imaginary Conversations* (1824–9), and *Pericles and Aspasia* (1836).

[*Lives*, by J. Forster (1869) and S. Colvin (English Men of Letters) (1881).]

Landseer, SIR EDWIN HENRY (1802–73), Eng. animal painter; son of an engraver; *b.* London; exhibited at Royal Academy when thirteen; patronized by Queen Victoria; R.A., 1831; knighted, 1850; dogs and deer his favourite subjects, and Scot. highlands the scene of some of his best pictures; bronze lions of Nelson Memorial, Trafalgar Square, 1867, were his work.

Lane, Edward William (1801–76), Brit. Arabic scholar; went to Egypt for health reasons; pub. *Manners and Customs of the Modern Egyptians* (1836), trans. *The Thousand and One Nights* (recognized as finest version of *Arabian Nights*), and compiled famous *Arabic Lexicon*.

Lane, Ralph Norman Angell. See Angell, Norman.

Lane-Poole, Stanley (1854–1931), Eng. historian and Orientalist; *b.* London; early turned his attention to Arabic; prof. of Arabic, Trinity Coll., Dublin, 1898–1904; pub. *Catalogue of Oriental and Indian Coins* for Brit. Museum (14 vols. 1875–92), also *Art of the Saracens* (1886); travelled much and wrote many books, including *Egypt in the Middle Ages* (1901), *Story of Cairo* (1902), *The Thousand and One Nights* (3 vols. 1906), *Mediæval India from Contemporary Sources* (1916), *Watson Pasha* (1919).

Lan′franc (1005–89), Archbishop of Canterbury; *b.* Pavia; began life as jurist, teaching at Paris, Bologna, and Avranches; entered church, 1042, and became successively abbot of Bec, 1045, and of Caen, 1066; Archbishop of Canterbury, 1070–89; reorganized Eng. church and improved its discipline and education.

Lang, Alexander Matheson, Brit. actor; *b.* Montreal; has acted with Sir F. Benson, Mrs. Langtry, and Ellen Terry, etc.; appeared in *Mr. Wu*; produced *The Wandering Jew* (1920), *Christopher Sly* (1922), *Such Men are Dangerous* (1928), etc.

Lang, Andrew (1844–1912), Scot. scholar; *b.* Selkirk; was a graceful poet, admiring and practising Old Fr. forms; wrote a *History of Scotland* (4 vols., 1900–7), and many other historical works; trans. (with Butcher) the *Odyssey*. with Leaf and Myers the *Iliad*; authority on folklore.

Lang, Cosmo Gordon (1864–), Anglican divine; *b.* Aberdeen; educated at Glasgow and Oxford; after holding various appointments became canon of St. Paul's, 1901–8; hon. chaplain to Queen Victoria; Archbishop of York, 1908–28; Archbishop of Canterbury, 1928; chairman of committee of Lambeth Conference, 1920; protagonist among supporters of Prayer Book measure. Has pub. several devotional and ecclesiastical books.

Langland (or Langley), William (*c.* 1332–*c.* 1400), reputed author of *The Vision of Piers Plowman*; *b.* in Shropshire; received monastic education; destined for priesthood, but married; lived precariously by chanting psalms for souls of departed. The poem attributed to him is allegorical, the Plowman a personification of Christ; writer is in deadly earnest, and attacks contemporary abuses in Church and State. The poem shows transition from O.E. to modern prosody.

Langley, Samuel Pierpoint (1834–1906), Amer. astronomer; *b.* Roxbury, Mass.; prof. of astronomy, Pennsylvania, 1867; secretary of Smithsonian Institute, 1887; invented the bolometer with which he explored the infrared solar spectrum, 1881; his aeronautical experiments showed the practicability of aviation, 1896.

Langton, Stephen (*d.* 1228), Eng. prelate; educated in France, where he became chancellor of Paris univ.; appointed Cardinal and Archbishop of Canterbury by Innocent III. against the wishes of King John; a strong supporter of the barons against the king.

Langtry, Lillie (Emily Charlotte Le Breton), Lady de Bathe (1852–1929), Eng. actress; *b.* Jersey, hence known as the 'Jersey Lily'; married Edward Langtry, 1874; society beauty; was for long one of leading Eng.

actresses. Married Gerald de Bathe, 1899.

Lankester, SIR EDWIN RAY (1847–1929), Brit. zoologist; *b.* London; prof. at London, 1874–90, and Oxford, 1891–8; director of natural history section of Brit. Museum, 1898–1907; president Brit. Association, 1906; works include *Extinct Animals* (1905), *Kingdom of Man* (1907), *Science from an Easy Chair* (1910, 1912), etc.

Lansbury, RT. HON. GEORGE (1859–), English Socialist; formerly ed. of the *Daily Herald*; member of Church Socialist League; M.P. Bow and Bromley, 1910–12, and since 1922; member of Royal Commission on Poor Law, L.C.C., etc.; mayor of Poplar, 1919–20; visited Russia to inspect Bolshevism at work, 1920; First Commissioner of Works in Labour Ministry, 1929–31; leader of the Opposition, 1931–1935; author of *What I saw in Russia* (1920), *My Life* (1928), etc.

Lansdowne, HENRY CHARLES KEITH PETTY-FITZMAURICE, 5TH MARQUESS OF (1845–1927); Eng. statesman; lord of Treasury, 1869–72; under-secretary for war, 1872–4; under-secretary for India, 1880; gov.-gen. of Canada, 1883–88; gov.-gen. of India, 1888–93; secretary for war, 1895–1900; foreign secretary, 1900–5; minister without portfolio, 1915–16; resigned office with end of Asquith régime; his letter to *Daily Telegraph* advocating a negotiated peace, 1917, caused strong protest.

Lansing, ROBERT (1864–1928), Amer. lawyer and public official; *b.* Watertown, N.Y.; after 1892 served U.S.A. government as counsel and technical expert in such cases as Bering Sea Claims Commission, 1896–7, Alaskan Boundary Tribunal, etc.; in July 1915 succeeded W. J. Bryan as secretary of state; one of the five delegates appointed by America to negotiate peace at Paris, 1918–19; resigned, 1920.

Lâo-tse (*lä-ō-tsā'*) (*b.* 604 B.C.), Chin. philosopher, founder of Taoism; *b.* in dist. of Ch'û; keeper of archives at imperial court; reputed author of *Tao-teh-king*, which teaches that the right course of conduct consists in the abnegation of self, simplicity, humility, and compassion.

Laplace (*lä-pläs'*), PIERRE SIMON, MARQUIS DE (1749–1827), Fr. mathematician and astronomer; *b.* in Normandy; prof. of mathematics at Ecole Militaire de Paris, 1767; pub. *Exposition du Système du Monde* (1796), in which his famous 'Nebular Hypothesis' appeared; this work, along with his *Traité de Mécanique Céleste* (5 vols. 1799–1825), gives him a foremost place among astronomers.

La Rochefoucauld (*lä rōsh-foo-kō'*), FRANÇOIS, DUC DE (1613–80), Fr. author; *b.* Paris; descendant of one of greatest Fr. families. As Prince de Marsillac spent first part of his life in plots against Richelieu and Mazarin; retired to his castle, where he wrote his *Memoirs*; at fifty returned to society at Madame de Sablé's *salon*. For ten years composed his famous *Maximes* (1665), which still retain charms of wit, paradox, and sense of spacious intellect.

Larsen, KARL HALFDAN EDWARD (1860–1931), Dan. novelist and humorist, one of the finest of Dan. stylists; *b.* Rendsborg; wrote *Modet og den blank Klinge*, account of a Span. tour, and *Poetisk Tyskland*. His *Dr. Ix* (1898) attacks the hyperæstheticism of the time.

La Salle, RENÉ ROBERT CAVELIER, SIEUR DE (*c.* 1643–87), Fr. traveller; *b.* Rouen; went to Canada, 1666, and from 1679 explored Great Lakes, the Ohio, and Mississippi, descending the last to Gulf of Mexico, 1682, naming province through which it flowed

Louisiana; returned, 1684, to found port at mouth of stream; small colony failed, and La Salle was murdered by a follower.

[*Journeys of La Salle*, by I. J. Cox (1922), *The Discovery of the Great West*, by F. Parkman (1869).]

Las Cas'as, BARTOLOMÉ DE (1474–1566), Span. prelate; *b.* Seville; joined an expedition of Columbus to the W. Indies, 1498–1500; called 'Apostle of the Indians'; endeavoured to secure better treatment of Indians by Spain; Bishop of Chiapa (Mexico), 1544–7; wrote *General History of the Indians*, etc.

Lasker, EMANUEL (1868–), Ger. chess player; *b.* Berlinchen; defeated Blackburne, 1892, and Steinitz, 1894; first prizes in tournaments in several cities, 1892–1900. Renounced title of Champion of the World to Capablanca, 1920.

Lassalle (*lä-säl'*), FERDINAND (1825–64), Ger. Socialist; *b.* Breslau; one of the founders of the Social Democratic party in Germany; a follower of Marx, but an ardent Nationalist; founded *Allgemeiner Deutscher Arbeiterverein*; pub. *A System of Acquired Rights* (1861), and many political pamphlets; died as result of duel; life story forms basis of Meredith's novel, *The Tragic Comedians.*

[*Lives*, by H. Oncken (1904) and G. Brandes (1900).]

László de Lombos, PHILIP ALEXIUS (1869–), Hungarian portrait painter; *b.* Budapest; naturalized Brit. subject; studied at Budapest, Munich, and Paris; has painted Pope Leo XIII., King Edward VII., Queen Alexandra, King of Portugal, ex-Kaiser Wilhelm II., ex-President Roosevelt, etc., and has received numerous honours and distinctions from various courts; president of the Royal Society of British Artists, 1930.

Lat'imer, HUGH (*c.* 1485–1555), Eng. reformer; *b.* in Leicestershire; educated at Cambridge; took holy orders and preached against eccles. abuses; Bishop of Worcester, 1535–9; in 1546–7 he was imprisoned in the Tower; again imprisoned after Mary's accession in 1553; burned at stake with Ridley. Stands high among the world's reformers.

Laud, WILLIAM (1573–1645), Archbishop of Canterbury; *b.* Reading; one of the advisers of Charles I. from 1625 to 1629; uniformity in the Church was the object of his heart; he compelled the bishops to retire to their sees, and improved the fabrics of the churches. His attempt to introduce a service book and canons into Scot. Church drove the Presbyterians into opposition to the crown. He was impeached for treason on opening of Long Parliament, and beheaded.

Lauder, SIR HARRY MACLENNAN (1870–), Scot. vocalist and comedian; *b.* Portobello; was a mill boy, then miner; became vocalist and made hit at London Pavilion; has attained unprecedented success on music-hall stage by dint of healthy sentiment and clean humour; writes and composes his own songs; knighted, 1919; autobiography, *Roamin' in the Gloamin'* (1928).

Lauderdale, JOHN MAITLAND, 1ST DUKE OF (1616–82); *b.* Lethington, E. Lothian; a zealous Covenanter, but after surrender of Charles I., 1547, a loyal supporter of the king; taken prisoner at Worcester, 1651; after Restoration made Secretary of State for Scotland; notorious for the severity of his administration of the laws against the Covenanters; member of Cabal ministry.

Laurier (*lō-rē-ā'*), SIR WILFRID (1841–1919), Can. statesman of Fr. extraction; *b.* St. Lin, Quebec; called to bar, 1864; entered

Dominion House of Commons, 1874; minister of inland revenue, 1877; leader of Liberal party, 1891; prime minister (first Fr.-Can. to hold the office), 1896; inaugurated Brit. preferential tariff, 1897; devoted himself to development of Canada; returned to power in 1900, 1904, and 1908; leader of Opposition from 1911; though out of office throughout the Great War, supported the Allied cause in every way possible; a courteous opponent, fine scholar, rare orator, and upright statesman.

Lavater (*lä-fä'tär*), JOHANN KASPAR (1741–1801), Ger. poet, physiognomist, and mystic; *b.* Zürich; author of *Swiss Lays*, *Christliche Lieder*, and *Jesus Messias*; great work *Physiognomische Fragmente* (1775–8), trans. into most European languages.

La'very, SIR JOHN (1856–), Brit. painter; *b.* Belfast; studied at Glasgow, London, and Paris; R.A., 1921; early pictures include *Two Fishers* (1883), *Tennis Party* (1887), and *Visit of Queen Victoria to the Glasgow Exhibition* (1888). Other notable pictures are *Mother and Son*, *White Feathers*, *A Lady in Black*, and many portraits, including those of the king and the queen.

Lavisse (*lä-vēs'*), ERNEST (1842–1922), Fr. historian; *b.* in Aisne; prof. of modern history, Sorbonne, 1888; member of Fr. Academy; works include *Trois empereurs d'Allemagne* (1888), *La Jeunesse du grand Frédéric* (1891, Eng. trans. 1891); ed. and part author of *Histoire générale* (12 vols., 1893–1901), and a monumental *Histoire de France*.

Lavoisier (*lä-vwäz-yā'*), ANTOINE LAURENT (1743–94), Fr. chemist; *b.* Paris; laid the foundations of quantitative chemistry by use of balance; proved indestructibility of matter; he employed Priestley's discovery of oxygen, and Cavendish's of the compound nature of water, to overthrow phlogiston theory, and establish true theory of combustion; showed nature of diamond, introduced system of chemical classification and nomenclature; executed by Revolutionists.

Law, ANDREW BONAR (1858–1923), Brit. statesman; *b.* in New Brunswick; educ. in Glasgow, where he became an iron merchant; Conservative M.P. for Glasgow, 1900; a protagonist of tariff reform; parl. secretary to the Board of Trade, 1902–6; leader of the Opposition, 1911–15. On formation of first Coalition became secretary of state for the colonies, 1915–16. In the first Lloyd George ministry he was chancellor of the Exchequer and leader of the House, 1916–18; also a member of the War Cabinet. Plenipotentiary to the Peace Conference, 1919. After the general election of Dec. 1918, became lord privy seal and leader of the House. Played conspicuous part in Home Rule Act, 1920. On resignation of Lloyd George, 1922, he formed entirely Conservative government. In Nov. was returned with strong majority. Resigned for health reasons, 1923, and died same year.

Law, JOHN, 'of Lauriston' (1671–1729), Scot. economist; *b.* Edinburgh; in 1694 he slew his antagonist in a duel and fled to Holland, and became interested in finance; served in France under the regent, 1715, and propounded a scheme to get the country out of financial difficulties. A bank was started, of which Law became director, and a company was formed to develop the Mississippi Valley, 1717. A tremendous boom resulted, but this 'Mississippi Scheme' collapsed, 1720, when Law, who had been popular, became detested. He left France, and died in poverty.

[*Life*, by Winston-Glynn (1908).]

Law, WILLIAM (1686–1761), Eng.

divine; *b.* Kings Cliffe, Northants; acted as private tutor; his writings, now religious classics, include *A Serious Call to a Devout and Holy Life* (1729).

Lawes (*lawz*), HENRY (1596–1662), Eng. musician; *b.* Dinton, Wilts; became a gentleman of the chapel royal, 1626; composed music for many songs and for several masques, including Milton's *Comus* (1634).

Lawes, SIR JOHN BENNET (1814–1900), Eng. agriculturist; *b.* near St. Albans; studied chemistry; experimented for more than fifty years on his estate at Rothamsted on the effect of various manures; began the manufacture of superphosphate as manure, 1843; left the bulk of his fortune for the maintenance of Rothamsted as an experimental farm.

Lawrence, DAVID HERBERT (1885–1930), Brit. novelist; *b.* Eastwood, Notts; after short period as clerk and schoolmaster turned to writing; his first books, *The White Peacock* (1911), *The Trespasser* (1912), and *Sons and Lovers* (1913), established him as one of the most original of 20th century writers; many of his books are overweighted with a study of sex problems; works include the following vols. of poetry: *Amores* (1916), *Look! We have come Through* (1917), *Birds, Beasts, and Flowers* (1925); and the following novels: *Kangaroo* (1923), *St. Mawr* (1925), *The Plumed Serpent* (1926), *Lady Chatterley's Lover* (1928), and *The Escaped Cock* (1930).

Lawrence. (1) SIR HENRY MONTGOMERY (1806–57), Brit. soldier and politician; *b.* in Ceylon; served in first Burmese War, 1824–6, first Afghan War, 1838, and in Sikh War, 1845–8; first administrator in Punjab after annexation, 1849; fortified Lucknow in Mutiny, enabling Residency to withstand a four months' siege; fell on second day of defence. (2) JOHN LAIRD MAIR, 1ST BARON LAWRENCE (1811–79), Brit. soldier-administrator; *b.* Richmond, Yorks; brother of (1); aided in annexation of Punjab, 1849, of which he was lieut.-gov. when Mutiny broke out; having won devotion of Sikhs, raised 59,000 men to replace the mutinied regiments; called the 'saviour of India'; pensioned by government and E. India Co.; baronet, 1858; viceroy, 1863; baron, 1869.

Lawrence, SIR THOMAS (1769–1830), Eng. portrait painter; *b.* Bristol; succeeded Reynolds as limner to the king, and had a greater vogue than any portrait painter of his time; R.A., 1794; knighted, 1815; president, Royal Academy, 1820–30; among his famous portraits are *Countess of Derby* and *Master Lambton.*

Lawrence, THOMAS EDWARD (1888–1935), Eng. archæologist, linguist, and soldier; *b.* Tremadoc; studied at Oxford; spent much time in the Near East in archæological excavation. In Great War was the moving spirit in organizing Arab campaigns against the Turks, and placing Feisal on the throne of Iraq; during the campaigns won an almost legendary reputation as a skilful and daring leader; accompanied Brit. delegation to Peace Conference, 1919, and was adviser on Arabian affairs, 1921–22; disgusted at what he considered the unfair treatment of the Arab claims he gave up all official rank and decorations, and served in the Royal Air Force and in the Tank Corps as a mechanic under the name of Thomas Edward Shaw, 1922–33; wrote *The Seven Pillars of Wisdom* (1926) and *Revolt in the Desert* (1927); died after motoring accident.

Lawson, SIR WILFRID (1829–1906), Brit. politician and temperance advocate; introduced Permissive Bill, 1864; carried Local

Option resolutions, 1880; opposed Boer War; president of United Kingdom Alliance; had reputation as a wit, and pub., with Sir F. C. Gould, *Cartoons in Rhyme and Line* (1904).

[*Memoir*, by G. W. E. Russell (1909).]

Lay'amon, Eng. poet-chronicler and priest of 12th cent., lived at Ernley on the Severn. His *Brut* is a poetical paraphrase of Wace's chronicle, *Brut d'Angleterre*, with additions of his own; of great linguistic value.

Lay'ard, SIR AUSTIN HENRY (1817–94), Brit. archæologist and diplomatist; *b.* Paris; conducted important excavations near Nineveh, 1845–7, discovering palaces of Esarhaddon and Sennacherib, etc.; afterwards entered Parliament; ambassador at Madrid, 1869–77, Constantinople, 1877–80; pub. *Nineveh and its Remains* (1848–49), and *Discoveries in the Ruins of Nineveh and Babylon* (1855).

Leacock, STEPHEN BUTLER (1869–), humorist and economist; *b.* in Hants; head of department of Political Economy, McGill Univ., Montreal, till 1935; best known for his humorous writings, such as *Literary Lapses* (1910), *Nonsense Novels* (1911), *Sunshine Sketches of a Little Town* (1912), *Arcadian Adventures with the Idle Rich* (1914), *Frenzied Fiction* (1917), etc. Has also written serious works, including *The Unsolved Riddle of Social Justice* (1920).

Leader, BENJAMIN WILLIAMS (1831–1923), Eng. landscape painter; *b.* Worcester; first picture, *Cottage Children blowing Bubbles* (1854); R.A., 1898; specialized in mountain and river scenery of N. Wales and Scotland.

Lear, EDWARD (1812–88), Eng. artist, writer, and traveller; *b.* London; wrote *The Book of Nonsense* (his still famous work) for Lord Derby's grandchildren; pub. also *Journal of a Landscape Painter in Corsica* (1870), etc.

Le Brun (*le brun'*), MADAME, MARIE LOUISE ELISABETH VIGÉE (1755–1842), Fr. portrait painter; received into the Academy at twenty-eight; escaped to Italy during Revolution, 1789; returned the year after Napoleon became first consul; painted many of the great personages of the time, including Marie Antoinette, the Prince of Wales, Byron, etc.

Lecky, WILLIAM EDWARD HARTPOLE (1838–1903), Irish historian and man of letters; *b.* near Dublin; chief work, *History of England in the Eighteenth Century* (1878–90); wrote also *History of European Morals*, *Democracy and Liberty*, *The Map of Life*.

Lecocq (*le-kok'*), ALEXANDRE CHARLES (1832–1918), Fr. composer; *b.* Paris; wrote comic operas, including *La Fille de Madame Angot* (1873), *Girofle-Girofla* (1874), *La Marjolaine* (1877), *Le Cygne* (1899).

Lee, ARTHUR HAMILTON, 1ST VISCOUNT LEE OF FAREHAM (1868–), Eng. politician; *b.* Bridport; president of Board of Agriculture and Fisheries, 1919–21; first lord of Admiralty, 1921–22; gave Chequers estate to the nation, 1921, as country residence for Brit. prime ministers.

Lee, ROBERT EDWARD (1807–70), Amer. Confederate general in civil war; *b.* Stratford, Virginia; in campaign of 1862 proved himself to be a great leader and a consummate soldier; invaded Maryland and won battles of Fredericksburg and Chancellorsville; his defeat at Gettysburg proved to be a turning point in the war; opposed to Grant, 1864, he was invested at Richmond and eventually forced to surrender; one of the greatest soldiers of the 19th cent.

[*Lives*, by F. Lee and by Sir F. Maurice.]

Lee, Sir Sidney (1859–1926), Eng. man of letters; *b.* London; ed. of *Dictionary of National Biography*, 1891; prof. of Eng. language and literature, Univ. of London, 1913–24; works include *Life of Shakespeare* (1898), *Life of Queen Victoria* (1902), *Great Englishmen of the Sixteenth Century* (1904), *Shakespeare and the Italian Renaissance* (1915), *Life of King Edward VII*. (2 vols. 1927).

Leech, John (1817–64), Eng. caricaturist; *b.* London; fellow-pupil with Thackeray at Charterhouse; pub. at eighteen *Etchings and Sketchings*, by A. Pen, Esq.; joined staff of *Punch*, 1841, with which his name is inseparably connected; illustrated A'Beckett's *Comic History of England* and Hood's *Comic Annual*, etc.

Le Gallienne (*le gal-ē-en'*), Richard (1866–), Eng. author and poet; *b.* Liverpool; his works include *The Quest of the Golden Girl* (1896); *The Life Romantic* (1901), *Vanishing Roads* (1915), *Pieces of Eight* (1918), *The Romantic '90's* (1926), and *The Magic Seas* (1930).

Legendre (*le-zhond'r*), Adrien Marie (1752–1833), Fr. mathematician; *b.* Toulouse; prof. of mathematics at École Militaire and École Normale, Paris; greatest work is *Traité des Fonctions Elliptiques* (1825–32); others include *Nouvelles Methodes pour la Determination des Orbites des Comètes* (1806), in which he invented the rule of the 'least square of errors.'

Legros (*le-grō'*), Alphonse (1837–1911), Fr. painter, etcher, and sculptor; *b.* Dijon; Slade prof. of fine arts, Univ. Coll., London, 1876–93; naturalized Englishman, 1881; his *Amende Honorable* and *Le Christ Mort* are in the Luxembourg; sculptures include fountains in bronze and granite at Welbeck Abbey, 1902.

Leibniz, or Leibnitz (*līb'nits*), Gottfried Wilhelm (1646–1716), Ger. scholar; *b.* Leipzig; entered univ. there, 1661, early showing his genius. He invented a calculating machine, and discovered the differential and integral calculus, and then studied economics, politics, and history. Most of his philosophical work was done after 1690. In 1710 he pub. his *Essai de Théodicée sur la Bonté de Dieu, la Liberté de l' Homme, et l' Origine du Mal*, the greatest of his philosophical works, and in 1714 *La Monadologie* and *Principes de la Nature et de la Grâce.*

The central point of his philosophy is his doctrine of substance. Leibniz believed the universe to be composed of centres of force (monads), without extension but with some of the attributes of spiritual being, such as feeling; space, matter, and motion have accordingly no ultimate existence. His theology is theistic, and he believes in the goodness of God, who is the 'harmony' of all things; the problem of evil he strives in vain to solve.

[*Critical Exposition of the Philosophy of Leibniz*, by Bertrand Russell (1900).]

Leicester (*les'ter*), Robert Dudley, Earl of (*c.* 1531–88), Eng. statesman and courtier; favourite of Queen Elizabeth; suspected of compassing death of his wife, Amy Robsart, in order to marry the queen; entertained Elizabeth at Kenilworth for seventeen days at a cost of £60,000; created earl, 1564; commanded unsuccessful expedition to Low Countries, 1585, when his nephew, Sir Philip Sidney, fell at Zutphen; central figure in Sir Walter Scott's *Kenilworth.*

Leicester, T. W. Coke, Earl of. See Coke, T. W.

Leighton (*lā'ton*), Frederick Leighton, Baron (1830–96), Eng. painter and sculptor; *b.* Scarborough; his first Royal Academy picture, *Cimabue's Madonna carried in Procession through Florence*, was purchased by Queen Victoria; career thereafter one of unbroken success; president of Royal Academy and knighted, 1878; baronet, 1886; peerage, 1896; among classical works are *Clytemnestra*, *The Last Watch of Hero*, *The Garden of the Hesperides*, etc.; other works: *Wedded*, *Dante in Exile*, *Paolo e Francesca*, etc.

[*Lives*, by E. Rhys (1900) and Mrs. R. Barrington (1906).]

Leland (*lē'land*), CHARLES GODFREY (1824–1903), Amer. author; *b.* Philadelphia; after 1869 lived mostly in England; pub. two important books on the Eng. gipsies, 1873, 1882; best known as author of highly amusing *Hans Breitmann's Ballads*, dialect poems in Pennsylvanian Dutch-English.

Leland (*lel'and*), JOHN (*c.* 1506–52), Eng. antiquary; *b.* London; appointed by Henry VIII. 'King's Antiquary,' and made six years' tour of Eng. cathedrals, priories, and abbeys; MSS. of this journey in Bodleian Library were ed. by Thomas Hearne, 1710–12, as *Itinerary of John Leland*.

Lely (*lē'li*), SIR PETER (1617–80), Dutch-Eng. portrait painter; *b.* in Westphalia; came to England, 1641; painted portrait of Oliver Cromwell; court painter to Charles II.; the beauties of the court of Charles II. at Hampton Court are typical works.

Leman, COUNT MATHIEU (1852–1920), Belgian general; military gov. of Liége at outbreak of Great War; noted for defence of Liége from Aug. 4–15, 1914; captured and imprisoned in Germany; created count, 1919.

Lenglen, SUZANNE (1899–), Fr. lawn-tennis player; *b.* Compiègne; gained Fr. championship at St. Cloud, 1914. At Wimbledon won Ladies Singles Championship, 1919–23 and 1925; won for France ladies singles and (with Max Decougis) mixed doubles at Olympic Games, 1920; gave up amateur status, 1926.

Lenin, name adopted by VLADIMIR ILITCH ULIANOV (1870–1924), Russ. Soviet leader; *b.* Simbirsk; entered Kazan Univ., but was expelled for participating in an anti-government students' riot. In 1887 his brother Alexander was executed for complicity in plot against life of Alexander III. In 1891 Lenin attended law and economic classes in St. Petersburg Univ.; four years later he went to Germany; on his return in the same year he was arrested on account of his Socialistic activities, and exiled for three years to E. Siberia; released in 1900, again went abroad, and for next seventeen years was a revolutionary leader. Appeared in Petrograd in Oct. 1917, and with Trotsky brought about fall of Kerensky, and set up a Soviet Republic. His immense labours in this connection wore him out and brought about his early death. His creed is set forth in his book, *The State and Revolution* (Eng. trans. 1919), in which he regards the state as a *bourgeois* conception, an instrument for exploiting the oppressed classes. He was opposed to violence, but admitted that violence was necessary to achieve Communism. The transition stage he described as 'the Dictatorship of the Proletariat.' He showed himself ruthless in attempting to force his Marxian dogma upon Russia and the whole world.

[*Lives*, by L. Trotsky (Eng. trans. 1925) and N. Bucharin (1924); *Leninism*, by J. Stalin (Eng. trans. 1928).]

Leonardo da Vinci (*lā-ō-när'dō dä vin'chē*) (1452–1519), Ital. painter, sculptor, architect, engineer, poet, and mathematician; one of the 'supermen' of history; *b.* near Florence; studied art under Verrocchio and was patronized by Lorenzo de' Medici; his *Adoration of the Kings* and *Medusa's Head* belong to this period; settled in Milan, 1482, where he painted *Our Lady of the Rocks* and his world-famous *Last Supper*, besides devising an irrigation scheme for the plains of Lombardy; returned to Florence, 1499, and was commissioned, along with Michelangelo, to decorate the council hall of the Signoria; architect and engineer to Duke of Romagno (Cæsar Borgia), 1502; completed *Mona Lisa* (1504), one of the most famous pictures in the Louvre; finally entered service of Francis I. of France, 1516, for whom he designed a palace at Amboise and projected a great canal between the Loire and the Saône. Leonardo wrote a *Trattato della Pittura* (pub. 1561), and left numberless MSS. dealing with anatomy, astronomy, physics, geology, etc., while throughout his life he made eager experiments in the art of flying. A portrait of Leonardo from his own hand is in the Royal Library at Turin.

[*Lives*, by E. Müntz (Eng. trans. 1898), E. McCurdy (1904 and 1907).]

Leoncavallo (*lā'on-ka-vä'lō*), RUGGIERO (1858–1919), Ital. operatic composer; *b.* Naples; his operas, *I Pagliacci* and *La Bohème*, were great successes.

Leonidas (*le-on'id-as*) (*fl.* 491–480 B.C.), King of Sparta; during great Persian invasion under Xerxes held Thermopylæ against Persians till taken by treachery; pattern of bravery.

Leopardi (*lā-ō-pär'dē*), COUNT GIACOMO (1798–1837), Ital. writer; *b.* in Ancona province; studied the classics and became one of most brilliant scholars of the day; a martyr to ill-health, he led an unhappy life in various Ital. towns till he found refuge in the home of a friend at Naples where he spent his last years; all his work, whether prose or verse, is tinged with pessimism, but in style and form it is practically flawless, and has had great influence on subsequent writers.

[*Poems*, ed. by G. Mestica (1886); *Prose Works*, ed. by G. Carducci (1898–1900); *Lives*, by Annovi (1898) and Casario (1902).]

Le'opold I., GEORGE CHRISTIAN FREDERIC (1790–1865), King of the Belgians, son of Francis, Duke of Saxe-Coburg; *b.* Coburg; fought for Russia against Napoleon, 1813, and entered Paris with allied sovereigns; married Princess Charlotte, daughter of George IV. In 1830 declined crown of Greece; next year was elected first king of the Belgians; married (2nd wife) Louise, daughter of Louis Philippe; bore title 'Juge de Paix de l'Europe' for his good offices as umpire in international disputes; was warm friend and adviser of Queen Victoria.

Leopold II., LOUIS PHILIPPE MARIE VICTOR (1835–1909), King of the Belgians; *b.* Brussels; succeeded his father, Leopold I., 1865; in 1884 was recognized as King of the Congo Free State; the treatment of the natives there roused world-wide indignation, and the state was annexed to Belgium, 1908; gave royal assent to Army Bill of 1909, under which first step was taken in building up a national army. Strong ruler, but lived a loose life; was succeeded by his nephew, King Albert.

Lep'idus, MARCUS ÆMILIUS (*d.* 13 B.C.), one of triumvirs with Augustus and Antony; after battle of Philippi 'this slight unmeritable man' received government of Africa; tried to secure Sicily for himself; overcome by Octavian; retired into private life.

Le Queux (*le kū'*), WILLIAM

TUFNELL (1864–1927), Eng. novelist and traveller; *b.* London; author of mystery and spy stories such as *Secrets of Monte Carlo* (1899), *German Spies in England* (1915), *Blackmailed* (1927).

Lermontov, MIKHAIL YUREVICH (1814–41), Russ. poet; *b.* Moscow; wrote great lyrics, *Ismail-Bey*, *Valerik*, and *A Hero of our Time* (novel); killed in duel.

Le Sage (*le säzh*), ALAIN RÉNÉ (1668–1747), Fr. author; *b.* in Brittany, was in youth employed on farm; for forty years fought against poverty, translating and doing other work; pub. *Crispin Rival de son Maître*, a little play in prose (1707); *Le Diable boîteux*, which won him fame (1707); *Turcaret* (1709), a severe satire on financiers. His novel, *Gil Blas* (1715–35), a great comic masterpiece, setting of which is in Spain, belongs to all times and all countries.

Leslie, ALEXANDER. See LEVEN, EARL OF.

Leslie, DAVID, LORD NEWARK (*d.* 1682), Scot general; *b.* in Fife; served under Gustavus Adolphus; returned to Scotland to aid Covenanters against Charles I., serving under Alexander Leslie, Earl of Leven, at Marston Moor, 1644; defeated Montrose at Philiphaugh, 1645; commanded Scot. army against Commonwealth, being defeated by Cromwell at Dunbar and Worcester; created Lord Newark, 1661.

Les'seps, FERDINAND, VICOMTE DE (1805–94), Fr. diplomat; *b.* Versailles; employed in consular service, 1825–48; retired from diplomatic service, 1849; conceived project of making Suez Canal; introduced scheme, 1854, obtaining concession from Said Pasha; company organized, 1858; work begun, 1859; canal opened, 1869; received Grand Cross of Legion of Honour. Undertook Panama Canal, 1881, on insufficient money; was charged with fraud and condemned, but sentence of imprisonment not carried out.

[*Life and Enterprises of F. de Lesseps*, by G. B. Smith (1895).]

Les'sing, GOTTHOLD EPHRAIM (1729–81), Ger. critic and dramatist; *b.* Kamenz; studied theology and philology at Leipzig; journalist and critic in Berlin, 1748–55; to this period belong his critical writings and *Miss Sara Sampson* (tragedy); lived in Leipzig, 1755–8; returned to Berlin and wrote *Fabeln* and *Philotas* (tragedy) (1759), and his share of the *Briefe, die neueste Litteratur betreffend* (1759–65). In Breslau, 1760–5, wrote parts of his great critical work, *Laokoon* (1766), and fine comedy, *Minna von Barnhelm* (1767); court librarian at Wolfenbüttel, 1770–81. Three of his best works belong to these years—viz. *Wie die Alten den Tod gebildet* (1769), *Emilia Galotti* (tragedy) (1772), and the great drama, *Nathan der Weise* (1779). His views on the progressive nature of religion were summed up in *Die Erziehung des Menschengeschlechts* (1780). A man of grand sincerity and fearlessness, with unique critical and creative powers, Lessing is the greatest Ger. writer between Luther and Goethe.

[*Lives*, by J. Sime (1877), T. W. Rolleston (1889), and R. M. Werner (1917).]

Lettow-Vorbeck, PAUL VON (1870–), Ger. soldier; fought in China, 1900–1, and in Ger. S.-W. Africa, 1904–6; appointed to command of forces in Ger. E. Africa, 1914; resisted all efforts to 'round up' his forces during four years of tropical fighting; surrendered at Armistice, 1918; pub. *My Reminiscences of East Africa* (1920).

Leven, ALEXANDER LESLIE, 1ST EARL OF (*c.* 1580–1661), Scot. soldier; *b.* Coupar-Angus; distinguished himself in service of Charles IX. and Gustavus Adolphus of Sweden; commanded Scots army against Charles I., 1640; took Edinburgh Castle; in Civil War commanded Scots army at Marston Moor, 1644; took Newcastle; played merely nominal part in campaign of Dunbar, 1650.

Lever, CHARLES JAMES (1806–72), Irish novelist; *b.* Dublin; physician; entered consular service; died while consul at Trieste; had a European reputation for generosity, extravagance, and eccentricity; novels include *Charles O'Malley* and *Harry Lorrequer*, which are full of excellent fun; later he essayed continental scenes and topics, but not with the same success.

Leverhulme (*lē'ver-hūm*), WILLIAM HESKETH LEVER, LORD (1851–1925), Brit. captain of industry; *b.* Bolton; entered his father's grocery business, in 1877 purchased a soapworks at Warrington, and gradually extended it into a world-wide business centred in the model village of Port Sunlight, Cheshire; a strong advocate of co-partnership in industry; purchased isl. of Lewis, 1918, and attempted unsuccessfully to develop industry there; baron, 1917; viscount, 1922.

Leverrier (*le-vār-yā'*), URBAIN JEAN JOSEPH (1811–77), Fr. astronomer; *b.* St. Lô; known chiefly for brilliant investigation of perturbations of orbit of Uranus, 1846. Adams treated same problem independently, 1845, which led to discovery of planet Neptune by Galle of Berlin.

Lewes (*loo'es*), GEORGE HENRY (1817–78), Eng. journalist and philosopher; *b.* London; abandoned medicine and the stage for literature; pub. *Biographical History of Philosophy* (1845–6), *Life of Goethe* (1855); his best philosophical work was *Problems of Life and Mind.* His connection with George Eliot lasted from 1854 till his death; founded and ed. *Fortnightly Review* (1865–6).

Lewis, SIR GEORGE CORNEWALL (1806–63), Eng. politician and writer; *b.* London; chancellor of Exchequer, 1855; home secretary, 1859; war secretary, 1861. Ed. of *Edinburgh Review*, 1852–5; author of *Essays on the Administrations of Great Britain from 1783–1830, The Government of Dependencies*, etc.

Lewis, MATTHEW GREGORY (1775–1818), Eng. author; *b.* London; wrote famous romance, *Ambrosio, or The Monk* (1795), which led to his being known as 'Monk' Lewis; other works include *The Castle Spectre* (1798) and *The Bravo of Venice* (1804); two voyages to the W. Indies led to publication of *The Journal of a West Indian Proprietor* (1833).

Lewis, SINCLAIR (1885–), noted Amer. author; *b.* in Minnesota; educated at Yale; became reporter; the publication of his novel *Main Street* (1920) at once established his reputation; his subsequent novels, *Babbitt* (1922), *Arrowsmith* (1924), *Elmer Gantry* (1927), *The Man who knew Coolidge* (1928), and *Dodsworth* (1929), have substantiated the impression made by *Main Street*; awarded Nobel prize for literature, 1930.

Leyden (*lā'den*), JOHN (1775–1811), Scot. poet and Orientalist; *b.* Denholm, Roxburghshire; friend of Sir Walter Scott, whom he helped with his *Minstrelsy*; held governmental positions in India.

Lichnowsky (*lēch-nov'ski*), KARL MAX (1860–1928), Ger. diplomatist; *b.* in Upper Silesia; ambassador to London, 1912–14; disapproved of Ger. war policy; wrote account of his mission to London, which compelled him to leave Germany; returned after revolution; opposed terms of Peace Treaty, 1919.

Liddell, HENRY GEORGE (1811–98), Eng. classical scholar; *b.* near Bishop Auckland; headmaster of Westminster School, 1846–55; was Dean of Christ Church, Oxford, 1855–91; famous, with Dean Scott, for the standard *Greek Lexicon*.

Liddon, HENRY PARRY (1829–90), Eng. theologian; *b.* N. Stoneham, Hampshire; prof. of exegesis at Oxford, 1870–82, and from 1870 canon of St. Paul's; in close sympathy with Oxford movement, but considered that the action of the extreme ritualists imperilled its progress.

Liebermann (*lē'ber-man*), MAX (1847–1935), Ger. painter; *b.* Berlin of Jewish parents; studied art at Weimar, and in 1875 visited Barbizon, where he came under the influence of Millet, Corot, and Daubigny; most famous as a portrait painter; works include *An Asylum for Old Men*, *The Cobbler's Shop*, *The Flax Spinners*, *The Netmenders*, *The Seamstress*, and *Dutch Orphan Girls*.

[*Life*, by H. Rosenhagen (1900).]

Liebig (*lē'big*), JUSTUS VON, BARON (1803–73), Ger. chemist; *b.* Darmstadt; prof. of chemistry at Giessen, 1824–52, at Munich, 1852–73; laid the foundations of organic analysis; discovered chloroform, 1832; made valuable contributions to the chemistry of agriculture and physiology, and established by analysis the nutritive values of foods; a well-known extract of beef is prepared from his prescription.

[*Life*, by W. A. Shenstone (1895); *Famous Chemists*, by Tilden (1921).]

Liebknecht (*lēp'knecht*), KARL (1871–1919), Ger. Socialist; *b.* Leipzig; son of WILHELM LIEBKNECHT (1826–1900), one of the founders of the Ger. Socialist party; barrister in Berlin; after imprisonment for 'seditious propaganda' entered lower house of Prussian Diet, 1908; violently opposed to Ger. war party; during Great War served in labour battalion on Western front; expelled from Socialist party and from Reichstag, 1916; arrested for organizing May Day celebrations in Berlin, convicted of attempted high treason, and sentenced to four years' penal servitude; released, 1918; became leader with Rosa Luxemburg of Spartacus party and was prominent in Ger. revolution; killed under obscure circumstances.

Lightfoot, JOSEPH BARBER (1828–89), Eng. theologian; *b.* Liverpool; after brilliant scholastic career at Cambridge, took orders, and finally became Bishop of Durham, 1879; his best-known works were his commentaries on the Epistles of St. Paul and his editions of the Apostolic Fathers.

[*Life*, by B. F. Westcott (1894).]

Li Hung Chang (*lē hoong chäng*) (1823–1901), Chinese statesman; *b.* Hofei; associated with Gordon in suppressing Taiping rebellion, 1863; later, governor of Kiang-su; viceroy of Hu-kwang, 1867, Chihli, 1870; conducted Chin. foreign affairs for many years.

Lilly. See LYLY.

Lilye, or LILY, WILLIAM (*c.* 1468–1522), Eng. grammarian; *b.* Odiham, Hants; first headmaster of St. Paul's School, 1510; part author, with Erasmus, of the Eton Latin Grammar.

Liman von Sanders (*lē'man fōn sänd'ers*), OTTO (1855–1929), Ger. soldier; *b.* in Prussia; sent to Constantinople at head of 'military commission,' 1913; organized Turk. forces on Ger. model; at outbreak of Great War supervised defences of Dardanelles, and directed operations against Allies in Gallipoli, and subsequently in Syria.

Linacre (*lin'ā-ker*), or LYNAKER,

THOMAS (*c.* 1460–1524), Eng. humanist and physician; *b.* Canterbury; studied at Oxford, Bologna, and Padua; court physician to Henry VIII.; took orders and became prebend of York, 1518; first teacher of Greek at Oxford, having Erasmus and Sir Thomas More among his pupils; founder of Royal Coll. of Physicians.

[*Life*, by N. Johnson (1835).]

Lincoln, ABRAHAM (1809–65), president of U.S.A.; *b.* near Hodgenville, Kentucky; had little schooling; brought up on father's farm; journeyed to New Orleans as employee on flatboat, 1828; clerk of store at New Salem, 1831; turned attention to law and politics; served in Black Hawk Ind. War, 1832; postmaster of New Salem, 1833; member of the Illinois legislature, 1834–40; admitted to bar, 1836; member of Congress, 1846; opposed to slavery; retired from political affairs, 1852. When slavery question was reopened, Lincoln again entered public life, 1854; became leader of opposition in Illinois; met Douglas in public discussions; nominated for senate by Republicans, 1858; made a great speech against slavery in New York, 1860; elected president, 1860.

On outbreak of Civil War, 1861, Lincoln proclaimed blockade of southern ports, and arranged for raising of large army and navy; saving of the Union, even more than destruction of slavery, was his aim; proclaimed freedom of slaves in rebel states, 1863; measure abolishing slavery in U.S.A. ultimately passed, 1865. During the Civil War he preserved friendly relations with foreign states, thus preventing outside complications; made famous speech dedicating battlefield of Gettysburg as soldiers' cemetery, 1863; announced willingness to stop war on submission of rebels to national authority of Union constitution. Re-elected president in 1864, he held conference with Confederate Commissioners, 1865, but his terms were rejected; war ended two months later, 1865. Assassinated at Washington, April 14. He was one of the greatest of Americans, simple and unaffected in manner; tolerant and honourable in character. His public life was devoted to the good of his fellow-men.

[*Lives*, by J. G. Nicolay and J. Hay (1890), W. H. Herndon and J. W. Weik (1890), I. M. Tarbell (1917), Lord Charnwood (1917), and N. W. Stephenson (1922).]

Lind, JENNY (1820–87), Swed. soprano singer; 'the Swedish nightingale'; *b.* Stockholm; studied at Stockholm and Paris; after great success on Continent, visited London, 1847, and America, 1850, and was received with extraordinary enthusiasm; retired from operatic stage, and became concert singer, 1849; married Otto Goldschmidt, and became naturalized Brit. subject, 1859; teacher of singing, Royal Coll. of Music, London, 1883–6. Noted also for her fine character and generosity.

Lindau (*lin'dou*), PAUL (1839–1919), Ger. dramatist and novelist; *b.* Magdeburg; among his plays are *Maria und Magdalena* (1872), *Gräfin Lea* (1879), *Der Abend* (1896), *Der Herr im Hause* (1899), and *So ich dir* (1903); one of the wittiest and most polished Ger. writers of his time.

Lindbergh (*lind'berg*), CHARLES AUGUSTUS (1902–), Amer. aviator; *b.* Little Falls, Minnesota; joined the Air Service of U.S.A. army, then was employed as pilot on the St. Louis–Chicago route. He made first solo flight across Atlantic, 1927, flying from New York to Paris in 33½ hours. Infant son kidnapped and killed, 1932; left U.S.A., 1935.

Lindsay, SIR D. See LYNDSAY.

Lingard (*ling'gärd*), JOHN (1771–1851), Eng. historian; *b.* Winchester; author of *History of England to 1688*, an able history from R.C. standpoint.

Linlithgow, JOHN ADRIAN LOUIS HOPE, EARL OF HOPETOUN and 1ST MARQUESS OF (1860–1908), Scot. statesman; governor of Victoria, 1889; first gov.-gen. of Australia, 1901; secretary of state for Scotland, 1905; created marquess, 1902.

Linnæus (*lin-ē'us*) (VON LINNÉ), CARL (1707–78), great Swedish botanist; *b.* Råshult; studied medicine and acted as assistant in botany; travelled in Lapland, Holland, France, and England; after his return to Sweden practised as physician; became prof. of medicine and of botany at Uppsala, where he died; made remarkable classification of plants, founded on the characters of the stamens, and was the author of numerous works on botany.

Lippi (*lēp'ē*), the name of two Florentine painters, father and son. (1) FRA FILIPPO, known as 'Fra Lippo Lippi' (*c.* 1406–69), prior of Santa Margherita at Prato; often censured for his irregularities, yet one of the greatest painters of his age; frescoes dealing with lives of St. Stephen and St. John in Prato Cathedral are considered his best. (2) FRA FILIPPINO (1460–1504), painted chiefly easel pictures, but executed also celebrated frescoes in Brancacci Chapel, Florence, and at Bologna and Rome.

Lippmann (*lip'man*), GABRIEL (1845–1921), Fr. physicist; *b.* in Luxembourg; prof. of mathematical physics, 1883–6, and of experimental physics at the Sorbonne, Paris, 1886–1921; invented the capillary electrometer, a method of colour photography, and, during Great War, apparatus to enable navigators to detect the presence of submarines; awarded Nobel Prize for physics, 1912.

Lipton, SIR THOMAS JOHNSTONE (1850–1931), Brit. merchant; *b.* Glasgow; began business with a small provision shop, and soon had shops all over the British Isles. Devoted to yacht-racing, he made five attempts to capture the America Cup.

Lis'ter, JOSEPH, 1ST BARON (1827–1912), Eng. surgeon; *b.* Upton, Essex; prof. of surgery, Glasgow Univ., 1860, Edinburgh Univ., 1869, and King's Coll., London, 1877–93. Influenced by Pasteur's discoveries Lister began his important work on the cause and prevention of septic infection of wounds. This speedily led to his employing antiseptics in all surgical operations, soon adopted by surgeons everywhere. He was president of Brit. Association, 1896, and of Royal Soc., 1895–1900; bart., 1893; baron, 1897.

[*Collected Papers* (2 vols. 1909); *Lives*, by R. J. Godlee (1924), W. Cheyne (1925), and A. Turner (1927).]

Liszt, FRANZ (1811–86), Hungarian composer and pianist, greatest virtuoso of his time; *b.* Raiding, Hungary; studied in Vienna, and was strongly influenced by Paganini, Chopin, and Berlioz; held concerts all over Europe, 1839–48; became conductor of Court Theatre at Weimar, where he befriended Wagner and gave performances of his works; his daughter, Cosima, became Wagner's wife; resigned, 1861; took minor orders in Church of Rome, 1865, and was known as Abbé Liszt; creator of the symphonic poem; his *Hungarian Rhapsodies* are still unrivalled.

Littleton, SIR THOMAS (*c.* 1407–81), Eng. jurist; remembered chiefly for his work on *Tenures* (first ed., 1481).

Littré (*lē-trā'*), MAXIMILIEN PAUL EMILE (1801–81), Fr. philosopher and philologist; *b.* Paris; became partial follower of Comte; his elaborate Fr. dictionary appeared, 1863–72; supplement in 1878; pub. *Auguste Comte et la Philosophie Positive* (1863).

Litvinov, MAXIM (*lit-vē'nof*) (former name FINKELSTEIN) (1876–), Russ. politician; *b.* Bielostok; joined Communist party, 1898; arrested, 1901, and escaped, 1903. After Russ. revolution was appointed Soviet agent to Great Britain, but was expelled, 1918. Soviet delegate to various congresses; since 1929 commissar for foreign affairs.

Livingstone, DAVID (1813–73), Scot. missionary and African explorer; *b.* Blantyre, Scotland, of humble parents; worked in cotton factory at age of ten; qualified as doctor; appointed missionary by London Missionary Soc. to Bechuanaland, 1840; began explorations, 1849; discovered Lake Ngami; traversed Africa from the Zambezi to the Congo, 1853–4, and gained much valuable information about the country; visited England, 1856, and received many honours; wrote his book, *Missionary Travels and Researches in South Africa* (1857); resigned from London Missionary Soc., and was appointed chief of expedition to explore the Zambezi; discovered Lake Nyasa, 1859. In 1864 he again visited England to expose atrocities of Port. slave-traders, and to arouse interest in the establishment of a mission. Pub. *The Zambezi and its Tributaries* (1865); returned to Africa, 1866, and began search for the sources of the Nile; and after being lost sight of for five years, was discovered in great straits at Ujiji by Stanley, 1871. Livingstone determined to complete his explorations, and proceeded along east side of L. Tanganyika; reached Chitambo's village, south of L. Bangweulu, where he died; his body was taken to England, and buried in Westminster Abbey. During his three long journeys Livingstone opened up vast tracts to missionary enterprise and colonization, made many discoveries, and was the first European to traverse the whole length of L. Tanganyika. His *Last Journals* were ed. by Horace Waller, 1874.

[*How I found Livingstone,* by H. M. Stanley (1872); *Lives,* by W. G. Blaikie (1880) and C. J. Finger (1928).]

Liv'y, TITUS LIVIUS (59 B.C.–A.D. 17), Rom. historian; *b.* Padua; lived chiefly in Rome; sympathized with Pompey in civil war; befriended by Augustus, although republican in politics; his great work, *History of Rome,* deals with history of Rome from landing of Æneas to 9 B.C.; written in 142 parts or *libri,* of which 35 are still extant, while epitomes of most of others are also in existence.

Llewelyn (*loo-el'in*), name of several Welsh princes. (1) LLEWELYN THE GREAT (*d.* 1240), Prince of N. Wales; annexed S. Wales, and maintained independence of united territories; eventually submitted to Henry III. (2) LLEWELYN AP GRUFFYDD (*d.* 1282), grandson of above; succeeded his uncle, David II., 1246; revolted from his allegiance, but made peace with Henry III.; twice refused homage to Edward I., and went to war, 1276, but was defeated, and signed Treaty of Conway, 1277; again revolting, fell in battle.

Lloyd, EDWARD (1845–1927), Eng. tenor; *b.* London; had first great success at Gloucester Musical Festival, 1871; from 1888 till 1900 was principal tenor at Handel festivals.

Lloyd, GEORGE AMBROSE LLOYD, 1ST BARON (1879–), Brit. colonial governor; travelled extensively in the East; served in

Gallipoli and Mesopotamia during Great War; governor of Bombay, 1918–23; high commissioner for Egypt, 1925–9; baron, 1925.

Lloyd, MARIE (1870–1922), Eng. music-hall artiste; appeared in Drury Lane pantomimes, 1891–3, and thenceforward occupied a place in the forefront of her profession, specializing in songs of Cockney humour.

Lloyd George, RT. HON. DAVID (1863–), Brit. statesman; *b.* Manchester, of Welsh parentage; educated at Llanystymdwy School; qualified as solicitor, 1884; Liberal M.P. for Carnarvon boroughs since 1890; speedily acquired reputation as fearless debater and impassioned orator; pronounced opponent of S. African War; president of Board of Trade, 1905–8; chancellor of Exchequer, 1908–15; his Budget of 1909 with its proposals for land taxation was thrown out by House of Lords, and led to general election, 1910; introduced the National Insurance scheme, 1911. During Great War, as minister of munitions, 1915–16, he displayed remarkable organizing ability and ceaseless energy; dissatisfied with the conduct of the war, he proposed a small war cabinet; this led to the resignation of Asquith, and Lloyd George took his place, holding office, 1916–22.

The first years of his premiership were devoted entirely to war; he believed in unified command for the allied armies, and achieved this in 1918 when Foch became generalissimo. At the general election, Dec. 1918, was returned to power with a huge majority; acted as principal Brit. representative at Peace Conference, 1919–20; introduced negotiations leading to formation of the Irish Free State, 1921; this settlement alienated much Conservative support and brought about his resignation, 1922. He then became a leader of the Liberal opposition in Parliament though never entirely in sympathy with the views of the whole party at any time; in the general election of 1931 stood practically alone, and returned to Parliament, after long illness, as the leader of no party. Published his *War Memoirs* (1933 and 1934).

Locke (*lok*), JOHN (1632–1704), Eng. philosopher; *b.* in Somerset; son of a Puritan who fought in Civil War; educated at Westminster School, and Christ Church, Oxford. Was influenced by the philosophy of Descartes. Secretary to Lord Ashley (later Earl of Shaftesbury), 1668–81. He was in France from 1675–9. Suspected by the government, he fled to Holland, and returned to England, 1689. In his later years he mostly studied theology. His chief works are *Letters on Toleration* (1685, etc.), *Two Treatises on Government* (1689), *Essay Concerning Human Understanding* (1690), and *Thoughts on Education* (1693). His *Essay on Human Understanding* became famous during his lifetime, and by it he is mostly remembered.

He argues against the doctrine of innateness of our ideas, for we must go back to experience for everything. Despite this he does not entirely deny the existence of intuitive knowledge, which, unless we give way to utter scepticism, is inevitable in pure mathematics and religion.

[*Lives*, by H. R. Fox Bourne (2 vols. 1876), T. Fowler (Eng. Men of Letters, 1880), and A. C. Fraser (1890).]

Locke, WILLIAM JOHN (1863–1930), Eng. novelist; *b.* in Barbados; secretary, Royal Institute of Brit. Architects, 1897–1907; author of *The Beloved Vagabond* (1906; dramatized 1908), *Simon the Jester* (1910), *The Fortunate Youth* (1914), *The Wonderful Year* (1916), *The Rough Road* (1919), etc.

Lockhart (*lok'art*), John Gibson (1794–1854), Scot. writer, son-in-law and biographer of Sir Walter Scott; *b.* Cambusnethan; ed. *Quarterly Review* (1825–53); besides the *Life of Scott* (his masterpiece), wrote *Peter's Letters to his Kinsfolk* (1819), lives of Burns and Napoleon, and novels, *Adam Blair*, etc.

[*Life*, by A. Lang (2 vols. 1897).]

Lockhart, William Ewart (1846–1900), Scot. painter, chiefly of Span. subjects; *b.* Annan; settled in London, 1887; by royal command painted Jubilee celebration, Westminster Abbey, 1887; other works include *The Cid and the Five Moorish Kings*, *The Orange Harvest*, and *Majorca*.

Lock'yer, Sir Joseph Norman (1836–1920), Eng. astronomer; *b.* Rugby; director of Solar Physics Observatory, London, 1885–1913; president of Brit. Association, 1903–4; chief of Eng. Government Eclipse expeditions, 1870–1905; initiated spectroscopic observation of sun-spots; founded *Nature* (1869), and wrote many astronomical works.

[*Life*, by T. M. and W. L. Lockyer (1928).]

Lodge, Henry Cabot (1850–1924), Amer. political leader and historian; *b.* Boston; prof. of Amer. history, Harvard, 1876–9; republican member of Congress, 1887–93; senator from 1893; joint-editor *North American Review* (1874–6) and *International Review* (1879–82); works include *Life and Letters of George Cabot* (1877), *Short History of the English Colonies in America* (1881), *Story of the American Revolution* (1898), *War Addresses* (1917), etc.

Lodge, Sir Oliver Joseph (1851–), Brit. physicist; *b.* Penkhull, Staffs; prof. of physics, Liverpool Univ., 1881–1900, and principal of Birmingham Univ., 1900–19; president of the Brit. Association, 1913–14. Was a pioneer in many departments of physics, including wireless telegraphy, and for his work received Albert Medal of Royal Soc. of Arts, 1919. A student of psychical phenomena, he was president of Society for Psychical Research, 1901–4. His works—scientific, psychical, sociological—include *Pioneers of Science*, *Signalling across Space without Wires*, *Raymond, or Life and Death*, *Modern Scientific Ideas*, *Evolution and Creation* (1927), *The Reality of a Spiritual World* (1930), *Beyond Physics* (1930), and an autobiography, *Past Years* (1931).

Lodge, Thomas (*c.* 1558–1625), Eng. dramatist, poet, and pamphleteer; *b.* West Ham; author of *A Defence of Plays*; wrote satires and exquisite lyrical verse; his romance, *Rosalynde*, is source of Shakespeare's *As You Like It*.

Loisy (*lwä-sē'*), Alfred Firmin, Abbé (1857–), Fr. R.C. theologian; *b.* in Lorraine; prof. of history of religions, Collège de France, since 1909–32; wrote *L'Evangile et l'Eglise* (1902) in answer to Harnack's *What is Christianity?*; pub. *Autour d'un petit livre*, *Le Quatrième Evangile* (1903); *Les Evangiles synoptiques* (1908); *Les Actes des Apôtres* (1920), *L'Apocalypse de Jean* (1923), etc.; several of his works condemned by papal see, 1903–4; excommunicated, 1908.

Lombro'so, Cesare (1836–1909), Ital. criminologist; *b.* Verona; prof. of psychiatry at Pavia, 1862; prof. of forensic medicine and psychiatry, and afterwards of criminal anthropology, at Turin; propounded the theories that the criminal was a special type, and that genius is generally accompanied by signs of physical degeneration, theories not altogether accepted.

London, Jack (1876–1916), Amer. novelist; *b.* San Francisco; after an adventurous youth, went as war correspondent to Japan, Korea, and Manchuria, 1904, and to Mexico, 1914. Among his numerous works are *The Call of the Wild, White Fang, Adventure, The Valley of the Moon*, and *Island Tales.*

Londonderry, ROBERT STEWART, 2ND MARQUESS OF (1769–1822), better known as Viscount Castlereagh, Brit. statesman; *b.* in Ulster; suppressed Irish rebellion of 1798; after Irish Union with Britain, 1800, held many high offices and took prominent part in defeating the schemes of Napoleon; secured appointment of Wellesley as commander-in-chief in Portugal, 1809; planned the ill-fated Walcheren expedition, 1809; represented U.K. at Congress of Vienna, 1814, and on Napoleon's final defeat arranged terms of peace; broke down under strain of office and committed suicide.

[*Lives*, by Sir A. Alison (1861), Lady Londonderry (1904), and A. Hassall (1909).]

Long, WALTER HUME, 1ST VISCOUNT (1854–1924), Brit. politician; *b.* Bath; Conservative M.P. for N. Wilts, 1880; held many important offices, including that of chief secretary for Ireland, 1905–6; secretary of state for the colonies, 1916–18; first lord of the Admiralty, 1919–21.

Longfellow, HENRY WADSWORTH (1807–82), Amer. poet; *b.* Portland, Maine; educated at Bowdoin Coll., Brunswick; friend of Hawthorne and Emerson; prof. of modern languages at Bowdoin, 1829, at Harvard, 1836–54; travelled to Europe several times, and was popular in England. His earlier poems are natural and fresh. All through his works the religious element bulks large. His greatest poems are *Evangeline,* written in Eng. hexameters (1847), and *Hiawatha* (1855), an Indian legend; other poems are *Voices of the Night,* including 'The Psalm of Life' (1839); *Ballads and Other Poems,* including 'The Wreck of the Hesperus,' 'Excelsior,' and 'The Village Blacksmith' (1841); *The Spanish Student,* a drama (1843); *The Golden Legend* (1851); *Miles Standish* (1858); *Tales of a Wayside Inn* (1863–74); trans. of Dante's *Divina Commedia* (1871).

Longinus (*lon-jī′nus*), CASSIUS (*c.* A.D. 213–73), Gr. rhetorician and philosopher of Athens, put to death for inciting Zenobia, Queen of Palmyra, to throw off her allegiance to Rome. The treatise, *On the Sublime,* formerly ascribed to him, is probably earlier.

Loraine, ROBERT (1876–1935), Brit. actor; achieved success as D'Artagnan in *The Three Musketeers,* John Tanner in *Man and Superman,* etc.; served in S. African War; took to aviation, 1910; during Great War served in Royal Flying Corps, 1914–18, and received the M.C., 1916; afterwards promoted lieut.-col.; D.S.O., 1917.

Loreburn, ROBERT THRESHIE REID, EARL (1846–1923), Brit. jurist and politician; *b.* Corfu; called to the bar, 1871; Q.C., 1882; Liberal M.P. for Hereford, 1880, and Dumfries, 1885–1905; solicitor-general, 1894, and later in the year attorney-general; lord chancellor, 1905–12; baron, 1906; earl, 1911; author of *Capture at Sea* (1913) and *How the War Came* (1919).

Lor′imer. (1) JOHN HENRY (1856–), Scot. painter; *b.* Edinburgh; R.S.A., 1900; among his pictures are *The Ordination of Elders, Portrait of Colonel Anstruther-Thomson, Benedicite* (all in the Luxembourg, Paris), and *The Eleventh Hour* (Philadelphia Art Gallery). (2) SIR ROBERT STODART (1864–1929), Scot. architect; *b.* Edinburgh; brother of (1); was architect of the Chapel of the Knights of the Thistle, St. Giles' Cathedral, and of the world-famous

Scottish National War Memorial, Edinburgh. R.S.A., 1921.

Loti (*lō-tē'*), PIERRE, pseudonym of LOUIS MARIE JULIEN VIAUD (1850–1923), Fr. novelist and member of Academy; *b.* Rochefort; one of the finest of modern Fr. prose writers; excels in impressionistic description; works include *Mon Frère Yves* (1883), *Pêcheur d'Islande* (1886), his most popular work, describing life among the Breton fishermen, *Madame Chrysanthème* (1887), *Fantôme d'orient* (1892), *Ramuntcho* (1897), *L'Inde (sans les Anglais)* (1903), *Pèlerin d'Angkor* (1912), *Le Château de la Belle au Bois Dormant* (1916).

Lotze (*lōt'se*), RUDOLPH HERMANN (1817–81), Ger. philosopher; *b.* Bautzen; studied medicine and philosophy at Leipzig Univ.; prof. of philosophy at Göttingen, 1844–81; philosophical works include *Mikrokosmos* (1856–64), *Logik* (1874), and *Metaphysik* (1879); his philosophy represents a reaction against the unduly abstract and logical character of Hegelian idealism.

[*Lotzes Philosophie*, by E. von Hartmann (1888); *The Philosophy of Lotze*, by H. Jones (1895), and *Lotze's Theory of Reality*, by E. E. Thomas (1921).]

Loubet (*loo-bā'*), EMILE FRANÇOIS (1838–1929), Fr. statesman; *b.* in Drôme; became deputy, 1876; minister of public works, 1887, prime minister, 1892, and president of the senate, 1895; president of republic, 1899–1906; his administration was marked by the settlement of the Dreyfus affair, the disestablishment of the Church, and the *Entente Cordiale* with Great Britain.

Louis IX. (ST. LOUIS) (1215–70), King of France; succeeded, 1226; put down rising of nobles, 1242; vowed to undertake crusade, 1244; sailed for Egypt, 1248; defeated and taken prisoner at Mansura, 1250; after his release, spent four years in the Holy Land; on return made treaties with England and Aragon; set out on a second crusade, but died from plague in Tunis; canonized, 1297; a wise and just ruler; founded Sorbonne Univ.

[*Memoirs of the Sire Jean de Joinville* (Eng. trans. by J. Hutton, 1868); *Life*, by F. Perry (1901).]

Louis XI. (1423–83), King of France; twice rebelled against his father, Charles VII.; married Margaret, daughter of James I. of Scotland; succeeded, 1461; tried to curb power of barons, who formed league with Charles the Bold, Duke of Burgundy, and rose in revolt, 1465; yielded to nobles' demands; subdued Normandy, 1467; taken prisoner by Charles of Burgundy at Péronne, 1468; Charles the Bold defeated and killed at Nancy, 1477; by Treaty of Arras, 1482, Louis obtained Burgundy, Picardy, and other provinces; increased power of crown by masterly but unscrupulous diplomacy.

Louis XII. (1462–1515), King of France; called *Le Père du Peuple*; succeeded, 1499; conducted wars in Italy; married, 1499, Anne of Brittany, and added Brittany to Fr. crown; married, 1514, Henry VIII.'s sister Mary.

Louis XIII. (1601–43), King of France; son of Henry IV.; succeeded, 1610. Queen-mother, Marie de' Medici, governed during minority, but was superseded by Richelieu, who became minister, 1624, henceforth ruling France. Reign marked by civil war, plots, and struggle with Protestants.

Louis XIV. (1638–1715), King of France, the 'Grand Monarch'; succeeded, 1643; after Mazarin's death, 1661, Louis assumed government, and the Fr. monarchy reached its zenith. He encouraged Colbert's financial schemes; gained prestige in Dutch wars, 1667–78. His later years were marked by influence of Mme. de Maintenon, whom he secretly married, 1684, and under whose influence he revoked Edict of Nantes, 1685. The wars of Grand Alliance, 1688–97, and Span. Succession, 1700–13, put an end to the prosperity of his reign. A profound believer in divine right of kings, he declared *L'Etat, c'est moi*; his ostentatious despotism finally led to universal opprobrium. His reign was the Augustan age of Fr. literature and fine arts.

Louis XV. (1710–74), King of France; succeeded great-grandfather, Louis XIV.; reign was marked by War of Austrian Succession, 1741–8, and Seven Years' War, 1756–63; in the latter the French lost India and Canada. His reign weakened France at home and abroad, and, helped by the *philosophes* and *encyclopédistes*, prepared way for Fr. Revolution.

Louis XVI. (1754–93), King of France; grandson of Louis XV.; succeeded, 1774; encouraged Turgot's reforms; was later influenced by his wife, Marie Antoinette. His reign was marked by the outbreak of the Fr. Revolution, 1789, precipitated by the extravagance of court and ministry. Louis was deposed and executed, 1793. Well-intentioned though weak, he reaped what others had sown.

Louis XVII. (1785–?95), titular King of France; son of Louis XVI.; never reigned; imprisoned in Temple, 1792; whether he died or escaped is still uncertain.

Louis XVIII. (1755–1824), King of France; younger brother of Louis XVI.; fled from France during Revolution, 1791; established headquarters at Coblenz; declared himself regent, 1793, king, 1795; life marked by travels and plots; served with Condé, 1796; refused to abdicate in Napoleon's favour. After latter's defeat, 1814, Louis returned to Paris as king; promised to grant constitution; fled on Napoleon's return; again restored, 1815.

Louise, CAROLINE ALBERTA, PRINCESS (1848–), Duchess of Argyll, fourth daughter of Queen Victoria, married, 1871, the Marquess of Lorne, afterwards 9th Duke of Argyll, who died in 1914.

Louis Philippe I. (1773–1850), King of France; cousin of Louis XVI.; fought in revolutionary army; left France, 1793; returned, 1814; became associated with Liberal party; lieut.-general of France, 1830. On deposition of Charles X., Louis Philippe was proclaimed 'King of the French,' 1830; put down Louis Napoleon's rising at Boulogne, 1840. Extension of franchise was demanded by people, 1847; followed by revolution, 1848, when he had to abdicate and flee to England.

Lovat (*luv'at*), SIMON FRASER, 12TH BARON (*c.* 1667–1747), Scot. Jacobite; for compelling dowager Lady Lovat to marry him was outlawed, 1701; went to France, and later to England, taking part in various Jacobite intrigues, and more than once playing traitor; supported the rising of 1745; taken prisoner after Culloden and executed.

Lovelace, RICHARD (1618–58), Eng. Cavalier poet; *b.* Woolwich; his 'To Althea from Prison' and 'To Lucasta on going to the Wars' are reckoned among the finest lyrics in the language.

Lover, SAMUEL (1797–1868), Irish novelist, song-writer, and painter; *b.* Dublin; became popular first as a miniature painter in London; his best-known novel is the amusing *Handy Andy*. Among his songs may be mentioned 'Rory O'More,' 'Molly Bawn,' and 'The Four-leaved Shamrock.'

Low, SIR SIDNEY (1857–1932),

Brit. historian and journalist; *b.* Blackheath; lecturer on imperial and colonial history, King's Coll., London; ed. *St. James's Gazette* (1888–97). Works include *The Governance of England* (1904), *Political History of the Reign of Queen Victoria* (1907), *De Quincey* (1911), *The British Constitution* (1928), *Indian States and Princes* (1929).

Lowe, ROBERT. See under SHERBROOKE.

Lowell (*lō'el*), JAMES RUSSELL (1819–91), Amer. poet, essayist, and diplomatist; *b.* Cambridge, Mass.; admitted to the bar, but followed literature; pub. vol. of verse, 1841; married Maria White, 1844, and adopted her abolitionist views; pub. satirical *Biglow Papers* and *A Fable for Critics*, also second series of poems, and *Vision of Sir Launfal* (1848); travelled in Europe, and afterwards succeeded Longfellow as prof. of modern languages at Harvard, 1856–76; first ed. of the *Atlantic Monthly* (1857–61); U.S.A. minister to Spain, 1877–80, and to Britain, 1880–5, where he was singularly popular. Among his literary essays are *My Study Windows*, *Fireside Travels*, *The Cathedral*, *Heartsease and Rue*.

Lowther, J. W. See ULLSWATER, VISCOUNT.

Loyo'la, IGNATIUS DE (INIGO LOPEZ DE RECALDE) (1491–1556), Span. nobleman; founder of the Jesuits; *b.* in Guipuzcoa; followed career of soldier; came under influence of Christianity; spent ten months in a cave, practising austerities, and composed book of *Spiritual Exercises*; studied at Alcala, Salamanca, and Paris; gathered a small band of companions, later forming the Society of Jesus. At Montmartre they took vows which bound them to place themselves at the disposal of the reigning pontiff; welcomed at Rome by Paul III., who approved the new order, 1540; the following year he was elected first general of the order, which office he retained till his death; canonized in 1628.

Lubbock, JOHN. See AVEBURY.

Lucan (*loo'kan*), MARCUS ANNÆUS LUCANUS (A.D. 39–65), Rom. poet of Silver Age; *b.* Cordoba, Spain; his literary success arousing Nero's jealousy, he conspired against the emperor; when the plot was detected, he was put to death; only surviving work is the *Pharsalia*, which tells the story of the civil war between Cæsar and Pompey, but is unfinished.

Lucas (*look'as*), EDWARD VERRALL (1865–), Eng. man of letters; *b.* Brighton; has ed. works of Charles and Mary Lamb; pub. many vols. of charming essays, including books on travel such as *A Wanderer in Holland*, and on art criticism as in *A Wanderer among Pictures*; also many humorous writings, including his contributions to *Punch*.

Lucas, JOHN SEYMOUR (1849–1923), Eng. historical and portrait painter; *b.* London; R.A., 1898. Among his pictures are *William the Conqueror granting the First Charter to the City of London*, *Reception of the Moorish Embassy*, and *Flight of the Five Members*.

Lucian (*loosh'yan*) (*c.* A.D. 125–*c.* 190), Gr. writer of the Silver Age; *b.* Samosata, Syria; wrote numerous treatises and dialogues, mostly satires. Best-known work is his *True History*, which inspired Rabelais, Swift, and Voltaire. In *De Morte Peregrini* Lucian shows knowledge of Christianity, which he treats with scant respect. Other well-known dialogues include the *Piscator* and *Hermotimus*.

Lucil'ius, GAIUS (*c.* 180–103 B.C.), Rom. satirist; *b.* Suessa; served under Scipio, and, despite his humble origin, lived on friendly terms with Scipio and Lælius;

regarded as the first great Rom. satirist.

Lucre'tius, TITUS CARUS (*c.* 98–55 B.C.), Rom. poet; his poem, *De Rerum Natura,* one of the greatest philosophical poems in the world, treats of Epicurean philosophy. According to tradition, he was poisoned by love-potion.

Lucull'us, LUCIUS LICINIUS (*c.* 110–56 B.C.), one of the greatest orators, governors, and generals of Rome; subject of one of Plutarch's *Lives*; consul, 74; leader of forces against Mithridates; rescued Rom. governor of Bithynia and conquered Pontus, 74–72; recalled by enemies at home; retired to a life of luxury.

Lucy, SIR HENRY (1845–1924), Brit. journalist and author; *b.* Crosby; the 'Toby, M.P.,' of *Punch,* 1881–1916; author of *Memories of Eight Parliaments, Sixty Years in the Wilderness, Nearing Jordan,* and *The Diary of a Journalist.*

Ludendorff (*loo'den-dorf*), ERICH (1865–), Ger. soldier; *b.* in Posen; joined the Prussian infantry. At outbreak of Great War he was commander at Strasbourg; appointed deputy chief of staff of the 2nd Army, showed much initiative in the siege of Liége. Next he was appointed chief of staff of the 8th Army in E. Prussia, under Hindenburg. Together they won the battle of Tannenberg. When Hindenburg was appointed chief of the general staff, 1916, Ludendorff accompanied him as first quartermaster-general. With the tremendous effort made in 1918 to achieve a final decision in the West, the name of Ludendorff will ever be connected. After the Allied successful counter-attack, Aug. 1918, he tendered his resignation, and on Oct. 25 was relieved of his office. After the armistice fled to Sweden, but returned to Germany, 1919; in 1920 he played an inglorious part in 'putsch' designed to overthrow the republic, and since then has lived in retirement. His experiences are recounted in *My War Memories.*

Ludwig (or LOUIS) **I.** (1786–1868), King of Bavaria; *b.* Strasbourg; succeeded, 1825; improved financial affairs; encouraged learning and art; aided Greece in struggle for independence, his son becoming King of Greece, 1832; gave largely to charitable objects; influenced in political matters by dancer, Lola Montez; at revolution of 1848 had to abdicate.

Ludwig (or LOUIS) **II.** (1845–86), King of Bavaria, grandson of above; succeeded, 1864; opposed Prussia in war of 1866, but aided Prussia against France, 1870–1; offered imperial crown to William of Prussia, 1871. Friend of Wagner; interested in art, literature, and philosophy; built many magnificent castles and Bayreuth theatre; ultimately became insane; was deposed, 1886; drowned himself a week later.

Lugard (*loo-gärd'*), FREDERICK DEALTRY, 1ST BARON (1858–), Eng. colonial governor; served in Afghan War, 1879–80, and in Sudan and Burma; administrator of Uganda, 1889–92; high commissioner of N. Nigeria, 1900–6; governor of Hong-Kong, 1907–12; governor of both N. and S. Nigeria, 1912, with a view to federating the Protectorates; gov.-gen. of Nigeria, 1914–18; G.C.M.G., 1911; author of *Our East African Empire* (1893).

Luke, ST., a Gentile connected with Antioch, where he was a physician; accompanied St. Paul on some of his missionary journeys, and was associated with him till St. Paul's death. He was the author of the gospel which bears his name and the Acts of the Apostles.

Luther (*loo'ther*), MARTIN (1483–

1546), leader of the Prot. Reformation in Germany; *b.* Eisleben; educated at Franciscan seminary, Magdeburg, at Eisenach, and at univ. of Erfurt; entered convent of Augustinian monks at Erfurt, 1505, where he fell into state of profound melancholy; eventually found sense of pardon and forgiveness; ordained priest, 1507; appointed prof. at univ. of Wittenberg, 1508; visited Rome, and on his return attracted much attention by preaching and teaching against the sale of pardons authorized by Pope Leo x. and conducted by his emissary Tetzel; publicly protested against the practice by nailing to the church door at Wittenberg his ninety-five theses, 1517, which may be reckoned as the beginning of the Reformation. The Pope sent legate to meet him at Augsburg, but he refused to recant; engaged in disputes with Eck, a Catholic controversialist, the result of which was a stronger opposition to Rome; pub. his famous treatises *An Address to the Nobility of the German Nation*, *On the Liberty of the Christian Man*, and *The Babylonian Captivity of the Church.* A papal bull against Luther was published in Germany, but he burned it along with the decretals which declared the Pope's supremacy. He was summoned to Diet of Worms, 1521; refused to retract anything, and was condemned; was taken for safety by the Elector of Saxony to the castle of Wartburg, where wrote pamphlets and completed translation of N.T. The reforming movement spread peacefully, but disorders sprang up among both nobles and peasants. Luther condemned all excesses, sometimes in violent language, and sought to vindicate the law on the one hand and condemn tyranny on the other. A period of controversy followed. He broke with Erasmus and quarrelled with Zwingli on the sacramental question. His *Table Talk*, *Letters*, *Sermons* are well known.

[*Lives*, by Melanchthon (1545), Michelet (Eng. trans. 1846), and J. Mackinnon (4 vols. 1925–30); *History of the Reformation*, by T. M. Lindsay (1909).]

Lut′yens, Sir Edwin Landseer (1869–), Eng. architect; *b.* London; R.A., 1920; designed Hampstead Garden Suburb; planned the new city of Delhi, 1912; architect of the London cenotaph, 1919, and for Imperial War Graves Commission.

Luxemburg, Rosa (1870–1919), Ger. Socialist; *b.* in Russ. Poland; settled in Germany about 1895; with Karl Liebknecht founded Spartacus League; she was frequently imprisoned. After Revolution she was killed in obscure circumstances for her supposed share in inciting rioting.

Lvoff (or Lvov), Prince George (1861–1925), Russian statesman; served for several years on various peasant committees at Moscow, Tula, and elsewhere; took active part in first Duma, 1905, in which he became a leader of Constitutional Democratic party; appointed prime minister in first revolutionary government, March 1917, and resigned in July because of differences with the Socialists. Imprisoned by Bolshevists, but escaped. Died in Paris.

Ly′all, Edna (1857–1903), pseudonym of Ada Ellen Bayly, Eng. novelist; *b.* Brighton; came into prominence with publication of *Donovan* (1882) and *We Two* (1884); other works include *In the Golden Days*, *Derrick Vaughan*, and *Doreen.*

Lyautey (*lē-ō-tē′*), Louis Hubert Gonzague (1854–1934), Fr. soldier and administrator; *b.* Nancy; entered cavalry and had brilliant career in Indo-China, Madagascar, and Africa; in 1912 was appointed resident-general in Morocco; a gifted administrator, he succeeded in pacifying that country; during Great War was for short time war minister, but was reappointed to Morocco, 1917, and made himself master of the Atlas, 1920–4; marshal of France, 1921; a member of the Fr. Academy, his writings include *Lettres de Tonkin et de Madagascar, 1894–9* (1920), and *Paroles d'action, 1900–26* (1927).

[*Marshal Lyautey*, by André Maurois (1931).]

Lycur'gus. (1) Spartan lawgiver; according to tradition, probably lived *c.* 9th cent. B.C.; was son of royal house; sometime regent for nephew; said to have travelled, and, on returning, introduced reforms in constitution which made Sparta a strong united state. (2) Athenian orator and statesman (*c.* 396–325 B.C.); one of the ten Attic orators.

Lydgate (*lid'gāt*), JOHN (*c.* 1373–*c.* 1450), Eng. poet; *b.* Lydgate, near Newmarket; probably educated at Benedictine monastery, Bury St. Edmunds, and at univs. of Oxford and Cambridge, as well as abroad; a voluminous writer, who took Chaucer as his model, his works include *The Falls of Princes*, *The Complaint of the Black Knight*, *The Temple of Glass*, and a trans. of the *Troy Book*, written at the command of the Prince of Wales, afterwards Henry V.

Lyell (*lī'el*), SIR CHARLES (1797–1875), Brit. geologist; *b.* Forfar; son of Charles Lyell, a noted botanist; educ. Oxford; called to bar, 1825; commenced to study geology as hobby; specialized in marine remains of Tertiary period; greatest work, *Principles of Geology*; also wrote *The Antiquity of Man* (1863), etc.; strong upholder of Darwin's theories; sometimes called 'father of modern geology.'

[*Charles Lyell and Modern Geology*, by T. G. Bonney (1895).]

Lyly (*lĭl'i*), LILLY, or LYLIE, JOHN (*c.* 1553–1606), Eng. dramatist; *b.* Kent; educated Oxford; famous as inventor of Euphuism, a brilliant experiment in a new variety of prose, receiving its name from his novels *Euphues, the Anatomy of Wit* (1579), and *Euphues and his England* (1580); the style is marked by artificial cadence, peculiar similes drawn from the natural history of the day, and excessive alliteration. His plays are important for their fine lyrics and brilliant wit; best known are *Endymion*, *Midas*, and *Love's Metamorphosis*.

Lynd, ROBERT (1879–), Brit. essayist and critic; *b.* Belfast; has pub. many vols., principally essays, including *Home Life in Ireland*, *The Art of Letters*, *Dr. Johnson and Company*, *The Green Man*, and *It's a Fine World*. Literary editor of *News Chronicle*; one of the most delightful essayists of to-day.

Lyndhurst (*lind'hurst*), JOHN SINGLETON COPLEY, BARON (1772–1863), Brit. statesman; *b.* Boston, Mass.; solicitor-general, 1819–24; one of the counsel at trial of Queen Caroline; attorney-general, 1824–6; master of rolls, 1826–7; lord chancellor, 1827, 1834, 1841–6; noted for probity, ability, and polish.

Lyndsay (or LINDSAY), SIR DAVID, OF THE MOUNT (*c.* 1490–*c.* 1555), Scot. poet; *b.* Cupar, Fife; Lyon King-of-arms; famous for *Ane Pleasant Satyre of the Thrie Estatis*, a 'morality' play satirizing Church and State; other works: *The Testament of Squyer Meldrum*, a biography in verse, and *Ane Dialog betwix Experience and ane Courtier*, a history of the world; works are characterized by great command of versification, keen satire, and a decided genius for low humour and delineation of character.

Lysan'der (*d.* 395 B.C.), Spartan

general; ended Peloponnesian War, after defeating Athenian fleet at Ægospotami, by capture of Athens, 405; slain in attack on Thebes; despotic and unscrupulous.

Lys'ias (*c.* 459–*c.* 380 B.C.), Attic orator; son of wealthy Syracusan, friend of Socrates; settled in Athens, 413, as shield manufacturer; narrowly escaped death at the hands of the Thirty, 404; fled from Athens, but returned, 403; lived by writing speeches for litigants. Greatest exponent of 'plain' type of rhetoric as opposed to 'grand'; most celebrated of his thirty-four extant speeches is *Against Eratosthenes.*

Lytton, EDWARD GEORGE EARLE LYTTON BULWER, 1ST BARON (1803–73), Eng. writer; *b.* London; played prominent part in society; early writings in verse; *Pelham* (1828) established his popularity as novelist; series of brilliant novels followed, including *Eugene Aram, Paul Clifford,* and *Godolphin*; in *The Last Days of Pompeii* and *Rienzi* he showed power of sustaining interest in historical fiction; his three chief plays, *Lady of Lyons, Richelieu, Money,* had great success. Prominent Liberal politician; secretary of state for colonies, 1858–9; baron, 1866.

Lytton, EDWARD ROBERT BULWER, 1ST EARL (1831–91), Eng. poet and statesman; son of above; *b.* London; literary pseudonym 'Owen Meredith'; minor poet of considerable merit; held various posts as ambassador; viceroy and gov.-gen. of India, 1878–80; started system of 'famine insurance'; satisfactorily conducted Afghan War, 1878–9; introduced reforms in taxation and administration, severely criticized at time; created earl, 1880.

M

Mabuse (*mä-booz'*), JAN, properly YENNI GOSSAERT (*c.* 1470–1532), Flem. painter; *b.* Maubeuge (Mabuse); studied at Antwerp; among best-known works are *St. Luke painting the Virgin, Adam and Eve,* and several *Madonnas.*

Macad'am, JOHN LOUDON (1756–1836), Scot. inventor of 'macadamized' roads; *b.* Ayr; put his theory into practice at Bristol, 1815; made general surveyor of roads, and given grant of £10,000, 1827.

MacAlister, SIR DONALD (1854–1934), Brit. physician; *b.* Perth; educated at Aberdeen and Cambridge; senior wrangler and first Smith's prizeman, 1877; held many important medical appointments; principal of Glasgow Univ., 1907–29; gold medallist of Royal Geographical Soc.; author of several medical treatises; knighted, 1908; baronet, 1924.

Macaulay, THOMAS BABINGTON, 1ST BARON (1800–59), Eng. historian and Whig statesman; *b.* in Leicestershire; son of Zachary Macaulay, leader of slavery abolitionists; a precocious child; twice won chancellor's medal for poems at Cambridge; called to bar, 1826; became connected with *Edinburgh Review,* 1825; secretary to Board of Control, 1832; legal adviser to Supreme Council in India, 1834–8; secretary for war, 1839–41. His *Lays of Ancient Rome* appeared in 1842, and his *Essays* in 1843. He was paymaster-general of forces,

1846–7, but retired from political life and devoted himself to his famous *History of England from the Accession of James II*. He had great power of felicitous epigram and of giving personality to historical characters, but weakness for sweeping statements, and wrote as an avowed partisan. Peer, 1857.

[*The Life and Letters of Lord Macaulay* (1876), by Sir G. O. Trevelyan.]

Macbeth′, King of Scotland (*c.* 1040–58); ruler of Moray, succeeded to throne by slaying King Duncan; a sagacious and popular monarch; picture of his character given by Shakespeare—based upon Holinshed's *Chronicles*—is quite misleading; defeated and slain by Malcolm, son of Duncan.

Maccabæus, JUDAS. See JUDAS MACCABÆUS.

M'Cabe (*mä-kāb′*), JOSEPH (1867–), author and lecturer; ordained R.C. priest, 1890; left Church in 1896, and became private secretary, lecturer, journalist, and author; pub. *Twelve Years in a Monastery* (1897), *St. Augustine and his Age* (1902), *The Soul of Europe* (1915), *A Century of Stupendous Progress* (1925), etc.; trans. Haeckel's *Riddle of the Universe*.

M'Car′thy, JUSTIN (1830–1912), Irish novelist and politician; *b.* Cork; parl. reporter for *Morning Star*, 1860; ed., 1864; toured U.S.A. for three years; M.P. for Longford and chairman of the Home Rule party, 1890–6; novels include *Dear Lady Disdain* (1875) and *The Dictator* (1893); also wrote *A History of Our Own Times* (new ed. 1882–1905). His son, JUSTIN HUNTLY MCCARTHY (1860–1936), was a dramatist, novelist, and historian.

Macchiavelli. See under MACHIAVELLI.

M'Clellan, GEORGE BRINTON (1826–85), Amer. general; *b.* Philadelphia; commanded Union army early in Civil War; formed Army of the Potomac; driven back by Confederates at Fair Oaks; won battle of Antietam, 1862; delayed to pursue Confederates; relieved of chief command; resigned, 1864.

M'Clin′tock, SIR FRANCIS LEOPOLD (1819–1907), naval officer and arctic explorer; *b* Dundalk; entered navy, 1831; served in four arctic expeditions, 1848–59; in the last discovered fate of Franklin's expedition; K.C.B., 1891.

M'Cor′mack, JOHN (1884–), Irish tenor; *b.* Athlone; studied in Milan; first Eng. appearance was at Covent Garden, 1907, in *Cavalleria Rusticana*; toured U.S.A. and Australia; became naturalized American, 1919.

M'Crie (*mak-ree′*), THOMAS (1772–1835), Scot. historian and divine; *b.* Duns; wrote accounts of Reformation in Scotland, Italy, and Spain; also wrote standard *Life of John Knox* and *Life of Andrew Melville*.

MacCunn′, HAMISH (1868–1916), Scot. composer; *b.* Greenock; chiefly remembered for his overture *Land of the Mountain and the Flood*, and the cantatas *Lord Ullin's Daughter*, *Bonny Kilmeny*, and *The Cameronian's Dream*. Was a successful conductor of opera.

Macdon′ald, FLORA (1722–90), Scot. heroine; *b.* in S. Uist; aided Prince Charles Edward to escape from Benbecula to Skye, 1746, taking him with her in guise of an Irish spinning maid (Betty Burke). Married Macdonald of Kingsburgh; emigrated to America, 1774, but returned, 1779.

[*Life* (1901), by A. Macgregor.]

Macdonald, GEORGE (1824–1905), Scot. novelist and poet; *b.* Huntly; novels, *David Elginbrod*, *Alec Forbes of Howglen*, *Robert Falconer*, *Malcolm*, display great knowledge of north-east

Scotland; also author of *Poems*, and the striking *Phantastes, a Faerie Romance*.

Macdonald, Sir Hector Archibald (1852–1903), Brit. soldier; *b.* in Ross-shire; served in Afghan War, 1879–80, being raised from the ranks for brilliant service; in Boer War, 1881, and in Sudan campaigns, 1885–98, distinguishing himself at Omdurman; commanded Highland Brigade in S. Africa from 1899; afterwards held commands in India; committed suicide in Paris.

Macdonald, James Ramsay (1866–), Brit. statesman; *b.* Lossiemouth, of humble parents; worked as pupil-teacher, clerk, then secretary; joined Independent Labour Party, 1894; secretary of Labour party, 1900–12; M.P. for Leicester, 1906–18, for Aberavon, 1922–9, for Seaham, 1929–35, for Scottish Univs. since 1936; chairman of I.L.P., 1906–9; leader of Labour party, 1911–14; first Socialist prime minister, Jan.–Nov. 1924; prime minister, 1929, and again in national government, 1931–5; strong supporter of League of Nations; has travelled widely. Pub. *Socialism and Society, Labour and the Empire, The Social Unrest, National Defence*, etc.

Macdonald, Sir John Alexander (1815–91), Can. statesman; *b.* Glasgow, Scotland; went to Canada, 1820; called to bar, 1836; member of Can. Assembly, 1844; subsequently commissioner of crown lands; leader of Liberal-Conservative party; prime minister, 1857; took chief part in carrying out scheme resulting in creation of Dominion of Canada, of which he became first premier, 1867; again premier, 1878; established system of protection; carried out construction of Can.-Pacific Rly.

[*Life* (1894), by Joseph Pope.]

Macdonald, Sir J. H. A. See Kingsburgh, Lord.

Macdonnell, Alastair Ruadh. See Pickle the Spy.

MacDowell (*mak-dou'ell*), Edward Alexander (1861–1908), Amer. composer and pianist; *b.* New York; studied in Paris and Frankfurt; prof. of music, Columbia Univ., 1896–1904; mind gave way, 1905. Compositions include sonatas, orchestral suites, including the *Indian Suite*, songs, and pianoforte pieces. Ranks at the head of Amer. composers.

Macfar'ren, Sir George Alexander (1813–87), Eng. musical composer; *b.* London; prof. of Royal Academy of Music, 1837, and principal, 1876; works include *Chevy Chase*, produced at Leipzig by Mendelssohn; *May Day*, a cantata; and *Robin Hood*, his best opera.

MacGill, Patrick (1890–), Irish author; *b.* Donegal; worked as navvy, etc.; wounded at Loos, 1915; afterwards in Intelligence Department at War Office; author of *Songs of the Dead End, The Red Horizon, Soldier Songs*, etc.

MacGillivray (*mä-gil'vrā*), James Pittendreigh (1856–), Scot. sculptor and artist; *b.* in Aberdeenshire; R.S.A., 1901; King's Sculptor in Ordinary for Scotland since 1921; principal works are Burns statue, Irvine; Knox Memorial, St. Giles' Cathedral, Edinburgh; National Memorial to W. E. Gladstone, Edinburgh; portrait busts of Thomas Carlyle and David Masson; pub. poems, *Pro Patria* (1915), *Bog Myrtle and Peat Reek* (1922).

MacGregor, John (1825–92), Scot. traveller, known as Rob Roy MacGregor; *b.* Gravesend; navigated, 1865, in his *Rob Roy* canoe many of the rivers of Europe, the Red Sea, and part of Palestine; devoted proceeds of his books and lectures (more than £100,000) to philanthropy; author of *A Thousand Miles in the Rob Roy Canoe*.

M'Gregor, Robert. See under Rob Roy.

Machiavelli (*mak-i-a-vel'i*), Niccolo (1469–1527), Florentine statesman and author; second chancellor and secretary at Florence, 1498–1512; for a time in exile, then racked and imprisoned on suspicion of conspiracy, 1513; on release, retired to his country villa, and wrote his famous books. His experience among subtle, worldly people accounts for the urbanity, cynicism, and wide knowledge of his books; he practically abandoned the Christian standard, and thus, throughout 16th cent., 'Machiavellianism' was synonymous with everything evil. The *Prince* (*Il Principe*, 1532) deals with the founding of a new state, and suggests as model the duchy of Romagna, as founded and governed by Cesare Borgia; the *Arte della Guerra* (1521) upholds the idea of an armed people; other works include *Mandragola* (1524) and *Istorie Fiorentine* (1531).

[*Machiavelli* (1897), by John Morley; *Niccolo Machiavelli e i suoi Tempi* (Eng. trans. 1878), by P. Villari.]

Mac'intosh, Charles (1766–1843), Scot. chemist; *b.* Glasgow; invented waterproof materials and patented 'mackintosh' cloth, 1823; F.R.S., 1823.

M'Ken'na, Rt. Hon. Reginald (1863–), Eng. barrister and politician; *b.* London; Liberal M.P. for N. Monmouthshire, 1895–1918; financial secretary of the Treasury, 1905; president of Board of Education, 1907–8; first lord of the Admiralty, 1908–11; home secretary, 1911–15; chancellor of the Exchequer, 1915–16, and won fame for budget of Sept. 1915; retired from politics to take up chairmanship of Midland Bank, 1919.

M'Kenna, Stephen (1888–), Eng. novelist; attached to Intelligence Section, War Trade Intelligence Department, 1915–19; member of government mission to U.S.A., 1917; novels include *Sonia* (1917), *Ninety-six Hours' Leave* (1917), *Midas and Son* (1919), and *Dermotts Rampant* (1931).

Mack'ensen, August von (1849–), Ger. soldier; *b.* near Wittenberg; served during Franco-Prussian war; elevated to peerage, 1899; in Great War he achieved a reputation almost rivalling that of Hindenburg, who selected him to carry out great drive against Russians, 1915; completed the conquest of Serbia, 1915–16, and had charge of offensive against Romania, 1916–17; after Armistice was interned till 1919.

Macken'zie, Sir Alexander (?1755–1820), Scottish explorer; *b.* Stornoway; entered service of fur-trading North-West Co., Toronto, 1779; discovered, named, and followed to its mouth the Mackenzie River, 1789; first European to cross the Rockies, 1792–3; knighted, 1802.

Mackenzie, Sir Alexander Campbell (1847–1935), Scot. composer; *b.* Edinburgh; principal of Royal Academy of Music, 1888–1924, and conductor, Philharmonic Soc., 1892–9; works include *Jason*, a dramatic cantata (1882); *Colomba*, a lyrical drama (1883); *The Rose of Sharon*, an oratorio (1884); *Veni, Creator* (1891); *His Majesty*, comic opera (1897); *Scottish Rhapsodies*.

Mackenzie, Compton (1883–), Eng. novelist; *b.* West Hartlepool; son of Edward Compton the actor; war correspondent, 1915; director, Ægean Intelligence Service, 1917; Lord Rector of Glasgow Univ., 1931–4. Works include *Carnival* (1912), *Sinister Street* (1913–14), *Guy and Pauline* (1915), *Sylvia Scarlett* (1918), *Poor Relations* (1919), *Fairy Gold* (1926), and *Our Street* (1931).

Mackenzie, HENRY (1745–1831), Scot. novelist; a leading figure in old Edinburgh literary life; one of the first to appreciate Burns in print; his *Man of Feeling* (1771) was popular in its day.

Mackenzie, SIR MORELL (1837–92), English physician; *b.* Leytonstone; distinguished throat specialist; attended crown prince (afterwards Frederick III.) of Germany, 1887, differing from Ger. doctors in diagnosis; censured by Coll. of Surgeons for publishing his reply to Ger. physicians.

Mackenzie, WILLIAM LYON (1795–1861), Can. politician and journalist; *b.* near Dundee; emigrated to Canada, 1820; ed. of *Colonial Advocate*, 1824–33, opposing the government; M.P. for York, Canada, 1828; several times expelled, but re-elected until writ was suspended; organized rebellion of Upper Canada, 1837–8; lived in U.S.A. till 1849.

M'Kin'ley, WILLIAM (1843–1901), president of U.S.A.; *b.* in Ohio; served in Civil War as volunteer; called to bar, 1867; member of Congress, 1876; leader of Republican party in house of representatives, 1889; introduced M'Kinley Bill, 1890, providing for higher duties on various imports, and treaties of reciprocity; governor of Ohio, 1891, 1893–5; president, 1896; declared war against Spain, 1898; annexed Hawaii, 1898, and some of the Samoan isles, 1899; re-elected republican president, 1900; shot at Buffalo by anarchist.

Mack'lin, CHARLES (*c.* 1699–1797), Irish actor and playwright; first appeared on stage in Bristol; was at Drury Lane, 1733–48; last appearance at Covent Garden, 1789; reckoned one of best actors of his day.

Maclar'en, CHARLES (1782–1866), Scot. ed.; *b.* in East Lothian; mainly self-educated; one of joint-founders and editor of *Scotsman*, 1817; editor of 6th ed. of *Encyclopædia Britannica* (1823).

Maclaren, IAN. See WATSON, JOHN.

Maclay, JOSEPH PATON, 1ST BARON, 1922 (1857–   ), Scot. shipowner; shipping controller, 1916–21; member of war cabinet, 1918; keenly interested in philanthropic institutions.

Macleod, FIONA. See SHARP, WILLIAM.

Macleod (*mak-loud'*), JOHN JAMES RICKARD (1876–1935), Scottish physiologist; *b.* near Dunkeld; prof. of physiology, Cleveland, Ohio, 1903–18, and Toronto Univ., Canada, 1918–28; with Dr. Banting discovered insulin and shared Nobel Prize, 1923; F.R.S., 1923; regius prof. of physiology, Aberdeen, from 1928.

Macleod, NORMAN (1812–72), Scot. preacher and author; *b.* Campbeltown; minister of Barony Church, Glasgow, from 1851; ed. of *Good Words* from 1860; author of *Reminiscences of a Highland Parish*, etc.

Maclise (*mak-lēz'*), DANIEL (1806–70), Irish historical and genre painter; *b.* Cork; won fame with *All-Hallow Eve*, 1833; painted frescoes—*Death of Nelson*, etc.—for House of Lords; works are familiar through engravings.

MacMahon (*mäk-mä'on*), MARIE EDMÉ PATRICE MAURICE DE, DUKE OF MAGENTA (1808–93), Fr. soldier of Irish descent; *b.* near Autun; served in Algeria, 1825–55; captured Malakoff works, Crimean War, 1855; won battle of Magenta, 1859, and was made duke and marshal on the field; gov.-gen. of Algeria, 1864–70; commander in Alsace, but was forced to capitulate at Sedan; president of Fr. republic, 1873–9.

Macneill (*mak-nēl'*), JOHN GORDON SWIFT (1849–1926), Irish politician; *b.* Dublin; prof. of constitutional and criminal law at

King's Inn, Dublin, 1882–8; prof. of constitutional law in National Univ. of Ireland, 1909; nationalist M.P. for S. Donegal, 1887–1918; author of *The Irish Parliament* (1885), *The Constitutional and Parliamentary History of Ireland* (1917), *What I have Seen and Heard* (1925).

Macpher'son, JAMES (1736–96), Scot. poet; *b.* in Inverness-shire; pub. *Fingal* and *Temora*, purporting to be translations from original Gaelic of Ossian, but believed to be largely his own poems, interwoven with fragments of Gaelic legend.

Macready (*mak-rē'di*), WILLIAM CHARLES (1793–1873), Eng. actor and manager; *b.* London; favourite parts were Macbeth and Werner. See his *Diary and Reminiscences* (1875).

MacTag'gart, WILLIAM (1835–1910), Scot. painter; *b.* Campbeltown; one of leaders of Scot. impressionist school; noted as a brilliant colourist and as a painter of fisher-folk and children; R.S.A., 1870; best works include *Harbour Bar, Through Wind and Rain, Summer Breezes,* and *Dora.*

MacWhir'ter, JOHN (1839–1911), Scot. painter; *b.* near Edinburgh; R.A., 1893; excelled as a landscape painter, especially of the rugged beauty of the Highlands; his *June in the Austrian Tyrol* is in the Tate Gallery; other works are *The Lord of the Glen, The Silver Strand, The Three Graces*; wrote *Landscape Painting in Water Colour* (1901).

Mad'ison, JAMES (1751–1836), fourth president, U.S.A.; *b.* in Virginia; entered Congress, 1779; tried to establish right of Congress to tax imports; member of house of delegates, Virginia, 1784; shared in drafting Virginian constitution; again member of Congress, 1789; advocated Amer. intervention in aid of France against Britain, 1793; retired from Congress, 1797; secretary of state, 1801; president, 1808; tried to coerce Britain and France by commercial restrictions; subsequently declared war, 1812; retired, 1817.

[*Life* (1902), by Gaillard Hunt.]

Mæcenas (*mē-sē'nas*), GAIUS CILNIUS (*c.* 73 B.C.–8 B.C.), Rom. patron of letters; chief administrator at Rome during conflict between Octavian and Antony; *c.* 16 B.C. fell into disfavour with Augustus and retired from public life; to him both Horace and Virgil largely owed their fame and the privilege of imperial favour.

Maeterlinck (*mä-ter-link*), COUNT MAURICE (1862–), Belgian author; *b.* Ghent; writings deeply imbued with mysticism; *Pelléas et Mélisande* (1892) was his first great drama; other notable works are *Le Trésor des Humbles* (1896), setting forth his conception of the dim, mysterious life of the soul; *Douze Chansons* (1897), a book of verse; *La Vie des Abeilles* (1901), his best prose work, a delightful mixture of philosophy and natural history; *L'Oiseau bleu* (*The Blue Bird*) (1909), a symbolical play for children; *The Unknown Guest* (1916); *The Burgomaster of Stilemonde* (1918); *Les Sentiers dans la Montagne* (1919); and *The Magic of the Stars* (1930); Nobel Prize, 1911; count, 1932.

Magellan (*ma-jel'an*) (*Port.* MAGALHAES), FERDINAND (*c.* 1470–1521), Port. navigator; did good service to Portugal, but was ill rewarded, and entered service of Charles V.; sailed down east coast of America, 1519; turned into strait now called after him, 1520; crossed and named Pacific Ocean, 1521, undergoing terrible sufferings; treacherously slain in Philippines. One of his vessels reached Spain, 1522, being the first to circumnavigate the globe.

Mahaf'fy, SIR JOHN PENTLAND (1839–1919), Irish scholar of remarkable versatility; *b.* in Switzerland; studied at Dublin; took orders, and devoted himself to tutorial work; prof. of ancient history at Dublin, 1871–99; president of Royal Irish Academy, 1911–16; provost of Trinity Coll., Dublin, from 1914; works include *History of Classical Greek Literature* (1880), *The Silver Age of the Greek World* (1906), and *Empire of the Ptolemies* (1896); a famous conversationalist, he wrote *The Art of Conversation* (1889).

Mahan', ALFRED THAYER (1840–1914), Amer. naval officer and historian; *b.* in New York; president of Naval War Coll.; member of Naval War Board during war with Spain, 1898; rear-admiral (retired), 1906; author of important books on naval history; obtained immediate renown with *Influence of Sea Power upon History* (1890); other notable works are *Influence of Sea Power on French Revolution and Empire* (1892), and *Life of Nelson* (1897).

[*Life* (1920), by Charles Carlisle Taylor.]

Mahomet. See MOHAMMED.

Mahomet Ahmed. See MOHAMMED AHMED.

Maine (*mān*), SIR HENRY JAMES SUMNER (1822–88), Scot. jurist; *b.* Kelso; regius prof. of civil law, Cambridge, 1847–54; called to bar, 1850; great work on *Ancient Law* appeared, 1861; legal member of council in India, 1862–9; corpus prof. of jurisprudence, Oxford, 1869–78; Whewell prof. of international law, Cambridge, 1887; other works include *Early Law and Custom* (1883) and *International Law* (1888).

Maintenon (*mant-nōn'*), FRANÇOISE D'AUBIGNÉ, MADAME DE (1635–1719), second wife of Louis XIV. of France; married the poet Scarron, 1651, and was head of literary *salon* till his death, 1660; governess to children of king by Madame de Montespan; bough estate of Maintenon; marquise 1678; married king, *c.* 1685; founded school of St. Cyr; devout, she tried to restrain licence of court; had great political influence; author of often-published letters.

Mait'land, FREDERIC WILLIAM (1850–1906), Eng. historian; *b.* London; prof. of Laws of England, Cambridge, from 1888; wrote *Justice and Police* (1885), *Domesday Book and Beyond* (1897), *English Law and the Renaissance* (1901), *Life of Leslie Stephen* (1906).

Maitland, SIR RICHARD, LORD LETHINGTON (1496–1586), Scot. lawyer, poet, antiquary, and historian; lord of session, 1561–84; keeper of the Great Seal, 1562–7; made famous collection of Scot. poetry; his poems and *History of the House of Seaton* pub. by Maitland Club (1829 and 1830).

Maitland OF LETHINGTON, WILLIAM (*c.* 1528–73), Scot. statesman; son of above; secretary to Mary Queen of Scots; supported Lords of the Congregation; involved in murder of Rizzio and of Darnley; finally joined Kirkaldy of Grange in defence of Edinburgh Castle for the queen.

Malcolm III. (*mal'kŭm*) (*d.* 1093), Scot. king; known as CANMORE (' big head '); succeeded Macbeth, 1054; second wife was Margaret, sister of Edgar Atheling, in whose support he invaded England, 1070; did homage to William the Conqueror at Abernethy, 1072; killed near Alnwick during raid into England.

Malesherbes (*mäl-zerb'*), CHRÉTIEN GUILLAUME DE LAMOIGNON DE (1721–94), Fr. statesman; *b.* Paris; minister of state to Louis XVI., 1775; introduced reforms, and helped to establish the *Encyclopédie*; pleaded for king before Convention of 1793; guillotined.

Mal'et, LUCAS (1852–1931), pen-name of MRS. MARY ST. LEGER HARRISON, Eng. novelist, daughter of Charles Kingsley; *b.* in Hants; novels include *The Wages of Sin* (1891), *The Gateless Barrier* (1900), and *The History of Sir Richard Calmady* (1901).

Malherbe (*mäl-erb'*), FRANÇOIS DE (1555–1628), Fr. poet and critic; *b.* Caen; regarded as founder of classical school, and called by Romantics 'The tyrant of words and syllables'; *Œuvres Complètes*, ed. by Lalanne.

Mal'lock, WILLIAM HURRELL (1849–1923), Eng. author; *b.* in Devon; wrote on religious, philosophical, and social questions; works include *The New Republic* (1877), *Social Reform* (1914), *Memoirs of Life and Literature* (1920).

Malone (*ma-lōn'*), EDMOND (1741–1812), Irish author and critic; *b.* Dublin; well known in literary circles of London from 1777; noted Shakespearian student; his ed. of *Shakespeare* (1790) was result of long research; pub. works of Dryden, 1800.

Mal'ory, SIR THOMAS (*fl.* 1470), Eng. translator and compiler of *Morte d'Arthur*; M.P. for Warwickshire; the *Morte d'Arthur* is a magnificent prose epic of Fr. Arthurian romance.

Malpighi (*mäl-pē'gē*), MARCELLO (1628–94), Ital. anatomist and physiologist; *b.* near Bologna; founder of the science of histology; first to observe circulation of blood in capillaries; demonstrated structure of the lung, structure of secreting glands, and anatomy of brain and spinal cord.

Mal'thus, THOMAS ROBERT (1766–1834), Eng. economist; *b.* in Surrey; educated at Cambridge; ordained, 1797; famous for his *Essay on the Principle of Population* (1798), a work which caused great controversy; economists regard Malthus's chief proposition, that population tends to increase faster than the means of subsistence, as really original.

Man'deville, SIR JOHN (*d.* 1371), Eng. traveller, author or supposed author of a famous book of travels pub. in Fr. during latter half of 14th cent.; real author probably Jean de Burgoyne (*d.* 1373), a physician of Liége; writer may have travelled in Near East, but for account of Farther East is undoubtedly indebted to other earlier works.

Manet (*mä-nā'*), EDOUARD (1832–83), Fr. realistic painter; *b.* Paris; his novel treatment of his *Olympia,* which reveals endeavour to give purity of outline, awoke bitter hostility; deeply influenced the development of Fr. art.

Man'gan, JAMES CLARENCE (1803–49), Irish poet; *b.* Dublin; *Poems* ed. by D. J. O'Donoghue in 1903; wrote also *The Poets and Poetry of Munster* (1849).

Mangin (*mon-jan'*), CHARLES MARIE EMMANUEL (1866–1925), Fr. soldier; *b.* in Moselle; on staff of Marchand's Fashoda mission, 1897; took prominent part in conquest of Morocco, 1911–13; brigadier-general, 1913; during Great War commanded a division at battle of the Marne; at Verdun, 1916, recaptured Douaumont and Vaux; defeated the enemy north of Château-Thierry, July 1918; after the Armistice commanded Allied armies of occupation.

Mann, HORACE (1796–1859), Amer. educationist; *b.* in Mass.; secretary of Massachusetts Board of Education, 1837–48; his school system became model for other states; president of Antioch Coll., Ohio, from 1853; wrote *Lectures on Education* (1840), etc.

Mann, THOMAS (1875–), Ger. novelist; *b.* Lübeck; first great success *Buddenbrooks* (1903). Other works, *Death in Venice* (1912), *The Magic Mountain* (1925), etc.; ranks high among Ger. novelists.

Mann, Tom (1856–), Eng. Labour leader; *b.* in Warwickshire; took leading part in organization of dock labourers after strike of 1889; member of Royal Commission on Labour, 1892; active in labour agitation in Australia, 1906, and in Brit. transport and railway strikes, 1911.

Man'ning, Henry Edward (1808–92), Eng. cardinal; *b.* in Herts; educated Harrow and Oxford; ordained, 1832; parish clergyman from 1833; supported Tractarian movement and won name for eloquence; received into R.C. Church, 1851, ordained, and spent some time in Rome; founded Congregation of Oblates of St. Charles at Bayswater, 1857; Archbishop of Westminster, 1865; cardinal, 1875. Keenly interested in social questions; wrote several devotional works.

[*Henry Edward Manning, his Life and Labours* (1921), by Shane Leslie.]

Manoel' II. (1889–1932), ex-King of Portugal, son of King Carlos I.; succeeded to throne on assassination of his father and elder brother, 1908; after revolution, 1910, republic was proclaimed; with the queen-mother took refuge in England; married Princess Augusta Victoria of Hohenzollern, 1913.

Mans'field, Katherine (1890–1923), pseudonym of Kathleen Beauchamp; Eng. short-story writer; *b.* Wellington, New Zealand; settled in London, 1903; married J. Middleton Murry, 1913; lived in various parts of Europe from 1917 in search of health; works include *Bliss* (1920) and *The Garden Party* (1922); her *Journal* (1927), *Letters* (1928).

Mantegna (*man-tān'ya*), Andrea (1431–1506), Ital. painter and engraver; *b.* near Vicenza; before leaving Padua *c.* 1459 executed the *Eremitani* frescoes in chapel of S. Cristoforo, and the *Agony in the Garden*; afterwards lived chiefly at Mantua, where the *Madonna della Vittoria*, the *Triumph of Cæsar*, and other great works, were produced.

[*Mantegna* (Masterpieces in Colour), by Mrs. Bell.]

Manu'tius, Aldus, or Manuzio, Aldo (1450–1515), Ital. printer and distinguished Gr. scholar; tutor of Alberto Pio, a prince of Carpi, who supplied him with funds for establishing the *Aldine Press* at Venice, 1480; pub. *Aldine editions* of the Gr. classics, renowned for beautiful type and accuracy.

Manzo'ni, Alessandro Francesco Tommaso Antonio (1785–1873), Ital. poet and novelist; *b.* Milan; pub. tragedy, *Il Conte di Carmagnola* (1819); popular lyric, *Il Cinque Maggio*, on death of Napoleon, 1821; and great novel *I Promessi Sposi* (1827). Verdi's *Requiem* was written in his honour.

Mar, John Erskine, Earl of (1675–1732), Scottish Jacobite; favoured Union of 1707, and made a privy councillor; lost post under George I., and went to Scotland; raised standard of old Pretender at Braemar, 1715, and fought battle of Sheriffmuir; fled to France; accepted pension from George I.

Marat (*mä-rä'*), Jean Paul (1743–93), Fr. revolutionist; *b.* in Switzerland; became a distinguished physician; wrote *Philosophical Essay on Man*, and various scientific works; during Revolution ed. *L'Ami du Peuple*, which attacked many powerful public bodies; twice fled to London, 1790–2; sat in Commune, Aug. 1792; deputy for Paris in Convention; engaged in successful struggle with Girondins, 1793; assassinated by Charlotte Corday.

Marchand (*mar-shän'*), Jean

BAPTISTE (1863–1934), Fr. soldier; commanded Fr. troops at Fashoda, 1898; general in Great War; retired, 1919; Grand Cross Legion of Honour, 1920.

Marco'ni, GUGLIELMO (1874–), Ital. scientist; *b.* Bologna; inventor of a system of wireless telegraphy; established wireless communication between England and France, 1899, and between Canada and England, 1902; made agreement, 1904, with Brit. Post Office for transmission of wireless messages, and invented persistent-wave system, 1906; established public wireless service between Britain and America, 1907; developed wireless telephony; a member of Ital. Senate; Nobel Physics Prize, 1909; hon. G.C.V.O., 1914; plenipotentiary delegate to Peace Conference, 1919; marchese, 1929.

Marcus Aurelius. See AURELIUS.

Margaret, ST. (*c.* 1045–93), Queen of Scotland; *b.* in Hungary; wife of Scot. king, Malcolm Canmore; did much for Scotland by introducing various religious customs, the observance of Sunday, and stricter marriage laws; her charity was unbounded; canonized, 1250.

Maria Theresa (*mä-rē'ä tä-rā'zä*), (1717–80), Archduchess of Austria, Queen of Hungary and Bohemia, Empress of Holy Rom. Empire; daughter of Emperor Charles VI.; married, 1736, Francis of Lorraine (emperor, 1745); mother of Marie-Antoinette; succeeded her father, 1740, by virtue of Pragmatic Sanction; attacked by Prussia, Spain, and Bavaria, but won recognition in War of Austrian Succession; sought in vain to recover Silesia from Prussia in Seven Years' War; restored unity to Austrian dominions.

[*Life* (1897), by J. F. Bright.]

Marie-Antoinette (*mä-rē' än-twä-net'*), JOSÈPHE JEANNE (1755–93), Queen of France; youngest daughter of Emperor Francis I. and Maria Theresa; *b.* Vienna; married Louis, afterwards Louis XVI., 1770; her extravagance and unconventionality alienated people; nicknamed 'the Austrian'; led opposition to Revolution; sought to win Mirabeau, and after his death determined to escape; fled with king to Varennes, 1791; brought back, and tried to bring about foreign invasion; after popular attack on Tuileries was imprisoned, 1792; tried and guillotined.

[*Marie Antoinette* (1910), by H. Belloc.]

Ma'rius, GAIUS (155–86 B.C.), Rom. general; served under Scipio Africanus; tribune of the commons, 119; prætor, 115; served in Spain and Africa, and ended war by capture of Jugurtha; consul from 104 to 100; crushed Teutones and Cimbri, 102–101; led an attempt at a democratic reform, but failed at last moment; outlawed when Sulla seized Rome, 88; returned to Rome during revolution of Cinna; organized wholesale massacre of his opponents; died after being consul for seventeen days.

Mark, ST., originally named John, author of St. Mark's Gospel; most likely a convert of St. Peter, and witness of some events of the Passion Week; chosen by Barnabas and Paul to act as their assistant, but returned to Jerusalem; accompanied Barnabas to Cyprus; later became reconciled with Paul. His Gospel gives Peter's reminiscences of Jesus. According to tradition, founded the church at Alexandria.

Mark'ham, SIR CLEMENTS ROBERT (1830–1916), Eng. traveller and geographer; *b.* near York; served in navy, 1844–52; took part in Franklin search expedition, 1850–1; visited Peru, 1852, and introduced cinchona plant into India, 1859–62; president of

Royal Geographical Soc., 1893–1905; instrumental in fitting out Arctic expedition under Sir George Nares, 1874, and National Antarctic expedition under Captain R. F. Scott, 1900–4; a voluminous writer.

Mark Twain. See under TWAIN, MARK.

Marl'borough, JOHN CHURCHILL, 1ST DUKE OF (1650–1722), Eng. general; *b.* in Devon; served with distinction under Turenne, 1672; married Sarah Jennings, confidante of Princess Anne, 1678; gained victory for King James at Sedgemoor, 1685; subsequently attached himself to William of Orange, who made him Earl of Marlborough; distinguished in wars in Ireland and the Low Countries, 1689–92; imprisoned for treason, 1692; communicated with banished king concerning Brest affair, 1694; on Anne's accession became captain-general of army; commanded Brit. and Dutch armies in War of Span. Succession; duke, 1702; won brilliant victories at Blenheim, 1704, Ramillies, 1706, Oudenarde, 1708; captured Lille, 1708; battle of Malplaquet less decisive, 1709; deprived of his commands by Tory ministry, 1712. The chief motive of his career was self-interest, but as a general he ranks without a peer in Eng. history.

[*Duke and Duchess of Marlborough* (1914), by S. J. Reid; *A Short Life of Marlborough* (1926), by H. G. Edwards.]

Mar'lowe, CHRISTOPHER (1564–93), Eng. dramatist; *b.* at Canterbury in humble circumstances; graduated at Cambridge; possibly an actor, perhaps a soldier; led a life of great irregularity, and was killed in a brawl. He is the first great Eng. dramatist; his best-known plays were *Tamburlaine the Great* (1590), which showed the magnificent capacities of blank verse for tragedy; *Dr. Faustus* (*c.* 1588), greatly admired by Goethe; *The Jew of Malta* (1588), and *Edward II.* (1590); these plays are very unequal, passages of real strength being followed by bombastic declamations, but they show great vigour, freshness, and dramatic sense.

[*Works* (1910), ed. by C. F. T. Brooke; *Marlowe and his Associates* (1904), by J. H. Ingram.]

Marmont (*mär-mōn'*), AUGUSTE FRÉDÉRIC LOUIS VIESSE DE (1774–1852), Fr. soldier; served under Napoleon in Peninsular War and later campaigns; betrayed Napoleon at Paris, 1814; created peer of France at Restoration; went into exile with Charles x.; an able general, but self-centred; wrote valuable *Mémoires* (1856–7).

Marot (*mä-rō'*), CLÉMENT (1496–1544), Fr. poet; *b.* Cahors; attached to court of Francis I.; wounded and taken prisoner at battle of Pavia, 1525; later imprisoned in Paris for heresy, and described his imprisonment in his *L'Enfer*; distinctive style influenced Fr. literary language; *Œuvres Complètes* (1538).

[*Clément Marot* (1870), by H. Morley.]

Mar'ryat, FREDERICK (1792–1848), Eng. novelist; *b.* Westminster; spent several adventurous years in navy, 1806–30, author of well-known books of adventure for the young—*e.g. Midshipman Easy, The Phantom Ship, Masterman Ready*, and *Children of the New Forest.*

Mar'shall, ALFRED (1842–1924), Eng. economist; *b.* London; prof. of political economy at Cambridge, 1885–1908; member of Royal Commission on Labour, 1891–4; publications include *Principles of Economics* (1890), *Elements of Economics* (1891), *Industry and Trade* (1919), *Money, Credit, and Commerce* (1923).

Marshall, JOHN (1755–1835), Amer. jurist and statesman; *b.*

in Virginia; commanded in War of Independence; one of commissioners to France, 1797–8, to settle questions in dispute; was returned to House of Representatives, 1799; secretary of state, 1800–1; chief justice, 1801–35; occupied important place in history of U.S.A. law and constitution; led Supreme Court, and by many of his decisions strengthened Federalist cause; of great eloquence; author of *George Washington.*

Mar′ston, JOHN (*c.* 1575–1634), Eng. dramatist and satirist; *b.* Coventry; gave up play-writing and entered the Church; works include *The Scourge of Villainy*, *Antonio and Mellida*, *Antonio's Revenge*, *What You Will*, *The Malcontent*, and *The Dutch Courtezan*, usually considered his masterpiece; plays have much passion, but are full of horrors, blood, and bombast.

Martel. See CHARLES MARTEL.

Mar′tial, MARCUS VALERIUS MARTIALIS (A.D. 43–*c.* 104), Lat. epigrammatist; *b.* in Spain; came to Rome *c.* 63; as panegyrist of the emperors was rewarded lavishly; Trajan, however, was proof against his flattery, and the last few years of his life were passed in comparative poverty; returned to his birthplace *c.* 100. His collected epigrams consist of 14 books; his flattery is despicable and his coarseness deplorable, but his work shows polish, fancy, and keen observation.

Martin, SIR THEODORE (1816–1909), Scot. translator and man of letters; *b.* Edinburgh; married, 1851, the famous actress, Helen Faucit, of whom he wrote a memoir, 1900; with Aytoun produced the clever parodies and travesties *Bon Gaultier Ballads* (1854); trans. Goethe, Dan. plays, Dante, Schiller, and Leopardi; trans. *Odes of Horace* (1860) and *Æneid* i.–vi. (1896); wrote monumental *Life of Prince Consort* (1874–80), and *Queen Victoria as I knew her* (1908).

Martineau (*mär′ti-nō*), HARRIET (1802–76), Eng. writer; *b.* Norwich; made name by *Illustrations of Political Economy* (1831); visited America and pub. *Society in America* and *Retrospect of Western Travel*; removed to Ambleside and became friend of Wordsworth; attracted by Comte's philosophy; other works include *Feats on the Fiord*, *Eastern Life*, *Letters on the Laws of Man's Social Nature and Development*, and *Autobiography* (1877).

Martineau, JAMES (1805–1900), Eng. theologian and philosopher; brother of above; entered Unitarian ministry, 1828; pastor in Liverpool, 1832; prof. at Manchester Coll., 1840–85; pastor in London, 1859–72; wrote large number of theological and philosophical works, including *Types of Ethical Theory*, *Study of Religion*, *Seat of Authority in Religion*; several vols. of essays; ed., with Dr. Sadler, *Common Prayer*; ed. two vols. of hymns.

[*Life and Letters* (1901), by Drummond and Upton; *James Martineau* (1905), by J. E. Carpenter.]

Mar′vell, ANDREW (1621–78), Eng. poet; *b.* in Yorks; tutor to daughter of Lord Fairfax, 1650; assistant to Milton, 1657; M.P. for Hull, 1659; secretary to Lord Carlisle during his diplomatic mission, 1663–5; a zealous patriot, and although a keen Royalist in his youth, admired Cromwell; wrote *Poems* (1680–1), *Poems on Affairs of State* (1689), *The Rehearsal Transposed* (1672–3); a clever satirist and a writer of exquisite lyrics.

[*Andrew Marvell* ('English Men of Letters,' 1905), by Augustine Birrell.]

Marx, HEINRICH KARL (1818–83), Ger. Socialist; son of Jewish lawyer, convert to Protestantism; *b.* Trèves; doctor of philosophy, Berlin, 1841; met Friedrich Engels in Paris, 1844, with whom he was associated till his death; pub. Communist Manifesto (*Manifest der Kommunisten*) in 1847, and became chief ed. of the *Neue Rheinische Zeitung* at Cologne in 1848; acquitted on charge of high treason, but expelled from Prussia, 1849; shortly afterwards settled in London, where he remained for the rest of his life. He was the moving spirit in the International Working Men's Association from 1864 to 1870. His most important book, *Das Kapital* (1867), has been called the Bible of Ger. Socialists; it is a scientific study of industrial conditions, and deduces the theory of surplus value—*i.e.* that the workman's wages tend to fall to the minimum of subsistence, and that all profits, rent, and interest are part of the value which the labour of the workman has produced, and are, in fact, surplus value. This theory led to creation of a working-class Socialist party; on the Continent generally there are Marxian Socialists in every country.

[*Life* (1910), by J. Spargo.]

Mary, The Virgin, the mother of Jesus; betrothed to Joseph; told by the archangel Gabriel that she was to become the mother of the Saviour; on a visit to Bethlehem Jesus was born; after the Child's circumcision the family sojourned for a time in Egypt, and afterwards settled in Nazareth. She appears again in connection with the finding of Jesus in the temple, at the marriage at Cana, at Capernaum, at the Crucifixion, and a last glimpse is given of her in Acts 1: 14.

Mary, Queen (1867–), consort of George v.; only daughter of Duke and Duchess of Teck; married George, Duke of York, 1893; made tour with the duke through the Brit. dominions; on their return were created Prince and Princess of Wales; during autumn and winter of 1905–6 the prince and princess toured in India; crowned queen, June 22, 1911. Deeply interested in the social and moral welfare of the community, she has won the warm esteem and affection of her subjects throughout the empire.

Mary, Princess Royal and Countess of Harewood (1897–), only daughter of King George v.; served as a nurse during Great War; president of Girl Guides; married to Viscount Lascelles, 1922; created Princess Royal, 1931.

Mary I. (1516–58), Queen of England and Ireland; daughter of Henry viii. and Catherine of Aragon; *b.* Greenwich; succeeded her half-brother, Edward vi., 1553; crushed Wyatt's rebellion with great severity; had Lady Jane Grey executed, 1554; married Philip ii. of Spain, 1554; in war with France, lost Calais. During her reign England was reconciled to the Pope; heresy laws were revived, and Protestants persecuted, nearly 300 being burnt at the stake; hence epithet 'Bloody Mary.'

Mary II. (1662–94), Queen of England; daughter of James ii. by first wife; married William of Orange, 1677, with whom she became joint sovereign of U.K. in 1689.

Mary Queen of Scots (1542–87), daughter of James v. and Mary of Guise; *b.* in Linlithgow Palace; became queen when only a week old; early life was spent in France; married, 1558, to Dauphin, afterwards Francis ii. The death of her husband, 1560, led to her return to Scotland; at first she left administration of affairs in hands of Lord James Stewart, her half-brother, and of Maitland of Lethington. She married, 1565, Darnley, eldest son of the Earl of Lennox, a man of little character and ability. His share in the assassination of Rizzio, 1566, alienated his wife, but the birth of her son, afterwards James VI., brought about a temporary reconciliation; the increasing influence of Bothwell introduced a new occasion of discord. Bothwell undertook the main arrangements for Darnley's assassination, 1567; Mary's subsequent conduct seemed to prove her complicity in the murder, and after her marriage to Bothwell the chief Prot. leaders took up arms, avowedly to deliver her from him; she surrendered to them at Carberry Hill, and was escorted as a prisoner to Edinburgh; sent to Lochleven Castle, and forced to demit her crown. She escaped from Lochleven, 1568, raised an army which was defeated at Langside, and fled to England. Her remaining years were spent as a prisoner—at Sheffield, until 1583; at Wingfield, until 1585; at Tutbury, until 1586; and at Fotheringay, until her execution. That she gave her full assent to the Babington conspiracy, in the spring of 1586, is almost certain; but the Eng. Government were glad of the opportunity for obtaining a pretext for her execution. But for several months Elizabeth delayed the enforcement of the death penalty. Mary met her fate with unshaken fortitude (Feb. 8, 1587). The *Casket Letters*, which played such an important part in Mary's trial, were eight letters and some verses alleged to have been written by Mary to Bothwell. The authenticity of the letters has been a subject of great controversy.

[*Mary Stuart* (1898), by D. Hay Fleming; *The Mystery of Mary Stuart* (1901), by A. Lang; *Mary Queen of Scots* (1924), by R. H. Mahon.]

Mas'aryk, THOMAS GARRIGUE (1850–), Czechoslovak statesman: *b.* in Moravia; was a blacksmith; studied at Vienna and Leipzig; prof. of philosophy in Czech Univ., Prague, 1882; head of the Czechoslovak realistic movement in philosophy, literature, and politics; member of Parliament of Vienna, 1891–3; re-elected, 1907; resisted alike encroachments of Germany on Austria and aggressive policy of Austria in Balkans; at outbreak of Great War fled to Italy and Switzerland; lecturer in King's Coll., London. Organized the Czechoslovak movement for independence; was appointed first president of Czechoslovakia, 1918; re-elected, 1920, 1927, and 1934; resigned, 1935. Publications include *The Czech Question* (1894–6), *The Problems of Small Nations in the European Crisis* (1915), *The Making of a State* (1927), and works on philosophy.

Mascagni (*mäs-kän'yē*), PIETRO (1863–), Ital. operatic composer; *b.* Leghorn; director of Rossini conservatory at Pesaro, 1895–1903; best-known work, *Cavalleria Rusticana* (1890); others are *L'Amico Fritz* (1891), *Ratcliff* (1895), *Iris* (1898), *Isabeau* (1911), *Parisina* (1913).

Ma'sefield, JOHN (1876–), Eng. dramatist, poet, and novelist; *b.* Liverpool. Early experiences at sea and abroad are reflected in his writings, *Salt Water Ballads* (1902), *Ballads* (1903), and in novels *Captain Margaret* (1908), *Multitude and Solitude* (1909), *Sard Harker* (1924), *Odtaa* (1926), *The Bird of Dawning* (1933). Narrative poems include *The Everlasting Mercy* (1911), *The Widow in the Bye Street* (1912), *Dauber* (1913), *Reynard the Fox* (1919). *Gallipoli* (1916) and *The Old Front Line* (1917) are masterpieces of unadorned prose. Among plays are

The Tragedy of Nan (1909), *The Trial of Jesus* (1925), and *The Coming of Christ* (1928). Poet laureate since 1930.

Maskelyne (*mas'ke-lin*), NEVIL (1732–1811), Eng. astronomer-royal, 1765; *b.* London; founded *Nautical Almanac* (1767); determined the earth's density at Schiehallion, Scotland, 1774; pub. catalogue of 36 fundamental stars, 1790.

Ma'son, ALFRED EDWARD WOODLEY (1865–), Eng. novelist; *b.* Dulwich; Liberal M.P. for Coventry, 1906–10; numerous novels include *The Courtship of Morrice Buckler* (1896; dramatized 1897), *Clementina* (1901; dramatized 1910), *The Four Feathers* (1902), *The Broken Road* (1907), *At the Villa Rose* (1910; dramatized 1920), *The House of the Arrow* (1924), *No Other Tiger* (1927), *The Sapphire* (1933).

Maspero', SIR GASTON CAMILLE CHARLES (1846–1916), Fr. Egyptologist; *b.* Paris; prof. of Egyptology at Collège de France, 1874–81; director of explorations in Egypt, 1881–1914; works include *Manual of Egyptian Archæology* (1889), *Dawn of Civilization* (1891), and *Art in Egypt* (1912).

Masséna, ANDRÉ, DUKE OF RIVOLI (1756–1817), marshal of France; *b.* Nice; one of Napoleon's most skilful generals; won battle of Saorgio, 1795; commanded army in Switzerland, 1799; victorious at Zurich; defended Genoa, 1800; marshal, 1804; defeated Archduke Charles at Caldiero, 1805; served against Austria, 1809; showed brilliant leadership at Aspern-Essling; commanded in Spain, 1809–12, where he was defeated by British; subsequently commanded at Marseilles.

Massenet (*mäs-nā'*), JULES EMILE FRÉDÉRIC (1842–1912), Fr. composer; prof. of composition, Paris Conservatoire, 1878–96; took first rank with comic opera, *Le Roi de Lahore* (1877); other operas: *Manon* (1884), *Cid* (1885), *Sapho* (1897), *Le Jongleur de Notre-Dame* (1902), *Chérubin* (1905), *Don Quichotte* (1910); also oratorios, orchestral works, and pianoforte suites.

Mas'sey, RT. HON. WILLIAM FERGUSON (1856–1925), colonial statesman; *b.* in Ireland; emigrated to New Zealand, 1870; entered New Zealand Parliament, 1894; held office as minister of lands, labour, agriculture, industries, and commerce; prime minister, 1912–25; P.C., 1914; representative of New Zealand at Imperial War Cabinet and Conference, 1917–18; plenipotentiary to Paris, 1919, and Imperial Conferences, 1921 and 1923.

Massinger (*mas'in-jer*), PHILIP (1583–1640), Eng. dramatist; collaborated with Fletcher, Dekker, and Tourneur; chief plays: *The Virgin Martyr* (with Dekker), *The Duke of Milan*, *A New Way to Pay Old Debts*, *The Bashful Lover*.

Mas'son, DAVID (1822–1907), Scot. man of letters; *b.* Aberdeen; prof. of Eng. literature, Edinburgh Univ., 1865–95; ed. *Macmillan's Magazine*, 1858–65; chief work, *Life of Milton* (1859–80); wrote also *De Quincey* (1885), *Edinburgh Sketches* (1892).

Matil'da, or MAUD (1102–67), daughter of Henry I. of England; married first, 1114, Emperor Henry V., and second, 1128, Geoffrey Plantagenet; on death of Henry I. contested throne with her cousin Stephen, who had become king; civil war, 1139–47, ended in agreement that Matilda's son should succeed Stephen as Henry II.

Matsukat'a, MASAYOSKI, PRINCE (1835–1924), Jap. statesman; minister of finance, 1881; reformed currency, established Bank of Japan; regulated taxation, introducing European methods;

prime minister, 1891–2, 1896–8; minister of finance, 1898–1900; keeper of privy seal, 1917–22; on demitting office created a prince.

Matsys (*mät-sīs'*), or MASSYS, QUENTIN (1466–1530), Flem. artist; studied at Antwerp; best known for religious pictures, but also ranks high for his genre pieces and portraits; greatest works are *Pieta, The Burial of Christ, The Martyrdom of the Two Johns, The Enthroned Virgin*, and *Virgin in Glory*.

Matthew, ST., one of the disciples of Jesus; a tax-gatherer at Capernaum; abandoned his profession and accepted the call of Jesus; preached the gospel in Judæa; wrote a collection of the sayings of the Lord, which forms a source of the first Gospel.

Matthi'as Corvi'nus (1443–90), King of Hungary; son of John Hunyadi; *b.* in Transylvania; forced Emperor Frederick III. to resign Hungarian crown, 1463; attacked Turks, invading Bosnia, till truce of 1468; defeated Poles and Bohemians, crushed rebellion in Hungary, and again checked Turks; captured Vienna from Emperor, 1485, and made it his capital; invaded Lower Austria, 1487; a great leader, ruler, and scholar; founded univ. of Budapest.

Maude, CYRIL (1862–), Eng. actor and manager; *b.* London; played in America and England; built and was sole manager of the Playhouse, 1907–15; pub. *Reminiscences* (1927).

Maude, SIR FREDERICK STANLEY (1864–1917), Brit. soldier, son of General Sir Frederick Maude, V.C.; *b.* Gibraltar; entered army, 1884; fought in Sudan, 1885, in S. Africa, 1899–1900; military secretary to gov.-gen. of Canada, 1901–4; at War Office at various periods till 1912; in Great War served in France (severely wounded) and in Gallipoli, where he was largely responsible for its successful evacuation; transferred to Mesopotamia, where he executed brilliant campaign leading up to capture of Baghdad; died suddenly at Baghdad from cholera.

[*Life* (1920), by Major-General Callwell.]

Maugham (*mawm*), WILLIAM SOMERSET (1874–), English novelist and dramatist; *b.* Paris; gave up medicine for literature; first novel *Liza of Lambeth* (1897); his next success was a play, *The Man of Honour* (1903); other novels include *Of Human Bondage* (1916), *The Moon and Sixpence* (1919), *On a Chinese Screen* (1922), and *Ashenden* (1928); plays, *Cæsar's Wife, The Circle, Our Betters, The Letter, The Constant Wife*, etc.

Maunoury (*mō-noo-rē'*), MICHEL JOSEPH (1847–1923), Fr. general; *b.* in Eure-et-Loir; served in Franco-Prussian War and was severely wounded at Champigny, 1870; Officer of Legion of Honour, 1895; military governor of Paris, 1910; member of Conseil Supérieur de la Guerre; achieved fame in Great War as commander of the secretly assembled 6th Fr. Army, which attacked the Ger. flank in the first battle of the Marne, Sept. 1914. Posthumously marshal of France.

Maupassant (*mō-pä-son'*), HENRI RENÉ ALBERT GUY DE (1850–93), Fr. author; *b.* in Seine-Inférieure; disciple of Flaubert and of Zola; contributed to the *Soirées de Médan* the bold and original story *Boule de Suif*, an episode of the Prussian occupation of Normandy; continued to be a member of the Naturalistic school, but stood alone in grace, wit, and epigram; so Rabelaisian in matter and frankness that sale of *Une Vie* (1883) forbidden on railway bookstalls; was a master of the short story;

his cynicism, habit of jesting at all things, art, and imagination, find typical expression in the most malicious of tales, *L'Héritage.* Died insane.

[*Guy de Maupassant* (1926), by E. Boyd.]

Maurice (*maw'ris*), SIR FREDERICK BARTON (1871–), Brit. soldier; entered army, 1892; served in Tirah expedition, 1897–98, and S. African War, 1899–1900; went to France with Expeditionary Force, Aug. 1914; director of military operations, imperial general staff, 1915–18; charged the government with making misleading statements about the disposition of troops, March 1918, and was retired; principal, Working Men's College, 1922; prof. of Military Studies, London Univ., 1927; principal, East London Coll., since 1933; author of *Forty Days in 1914* (1919); *Governments and War* (1926), etc.

Maurice (*mō-rēs'*), JOHN FREDERICK DENISON (1805–72), Eng. divine; *b.* in Suffolk; ed. of the *Athenæum*; ordained in 1834; appointed prof. of moral philosophy, Cambridge, 1866; leader of Christian Socialists and joint-ed. of *Politics for the People*; founder of Working Men's Coll. and Queen's Coll. for Women, London; friend of Charles Kingsley, Thomas Hughes, etc.; wrote *The Kingdom of Christ, Religions of the World*, etc.

Maurier. See DU MAURIER.

Maurois (*mōr-wä'*), ANDRÉ, pseudonym of ANDRÉ HERZOG (1885–), Fr. author; *b.* Elbeuf; during Great War was interpreter to a Scot. division, and used his experiences in *Les Silences de Colonel Bramble* (1918) and its sequels; has written many charming essays and biographies of Shelley, Disraeli, Byron, etc.

Maury (*maw'ri*), MATTHEW FONTAINE (1806–73), Amer. hydrographer; *b.* in Virginia; served in navy, 1825–39; keeper of naval charts and instruments at Washington, 1842–61; initiated taking of systematic observations at sea, and pub. *Physical Geography of the Sea* (1856); prof. of meteorology, Lexington, 1868.

Maw'son, SIR DOUGLAS (1882–), Australian scientist and explorer; *b.* Bradford, England; went to Sydney while a child; made geological exploration of New Hebrides, 1903; scientist in Shackleton's antarctic expedition and discovered south magnetic pole, 1908; led Australasian antarctic expeditions, 1911–14 and 1929; wrote *The Home of the Blizzard* (1915); prof. of geology and mineralogy, Adelaide Univ., since 1920; knighted, 1914.

Maxen'tius, MARCUS AURELIUS VALERIUS, Rom. emperor, A.D. 306–312; defeated by Constantine at Saxa Rubra, near Rome, and drowned in the Tiber when trying to escape.

Max'im. (1) SIR HIRAM STEVENS (1840–1916), Anglo-American inventor; *b.* in Maine; prominently identified with development of electricity in U.S.A.; settled in London, 1883, became naturalized, and invented the Maxim gun, the 'pom-pom,' a smokeless powder, and new methods in manufacture of artillery; interested in improvement of flying machines; knighted, 1901; pub. *My Life* (1915). (2) HUDSON (1853–1927), Amer. inventor, brother of above; predared smokeless powder for U.S.A. government; invented 'Maximite,' a high explosive, a delay-action fuse for torpedoes, and 'motorite,' a fuel for propelling torpedoes.

Maximil'ian I. (1459–1519), Ger. emperor; *b.* Vienna; succeeded his father, Frederick III., 1493; during his reign the Swiss established their independence, 1499; joined League of Cambrai against Venice, 1508, and later

Holy League to drive French from Italy, but gained nothing; noted for attempts to reform imperial and Austrian administrations.

Maximilian I. (1756–1825), King of Bavaria; as Elector of Bavaria, 1799, encouraged trade and education, and reformed administration; helped Napoleon, who made him king, 1806; opposed Ger. federation.

Maximilian II. (1811–64), King of Bavaria; succeeded in 1848; opposed new Ger. constitution excluding Austria; supported Austria in restoring old diet.

Maximi'nus, GAIUS JULIUS VERUS, Rom. emperor (A.D. 235–238); a Goth of humble birth, his enormous stature (over 8 ft.) attracted attention of Septimius Severus, who made him one of his guards; secured election to imperial throne, and defeated Germans; a rapacious ruler; killed by his own troops.

Max-Mül'ler, FRIEDRICH (1823–1900), Anglo-Ger. Orientalist and philologist; *b.* Dessau; made special study of Sanskrit, and, coming to England, was invited by East Ind. Co. to edit the *Rig-Veda*, 1849–74; first prof. of modern languages, 1854, and of comparative philology, 1868–75, Oxford; Gifford lecturer, Glasgow Univ., 1889–93; ed. *The Sacred Books of the East*; author of *Comparative Mythology*, *History of Ancient Sanskrit Literature*, *My Autobiography*, etc.

Max O'Rell, pseudonym of PAUL BLOUET (1848–1903), Fr. author and lecturer; *b.* in Brittany; fought in Franco-Prussian war; teacher of French in St. Paul's School, London, 1876–84; pub. a witty and caustic book, *John Bull and his Island* (1883), and others in the same vein.

Max'well, SIR HERBERT EUSTACE (1845–   ), Brit. author and politician; *b.* Edinburgh; Conservative M.P. for Wigtownshire, 1880–1906; chairman of Royal Commission on Scot. Historical Monuments; works include novels, essays, biography, and history.

Maxwell, JAMES CLERK (1831–79), Scot. physicist; *b.* Edinburgh; prof. of natural philosophy, Marischal Coll., Aberdeen, 1856–60, and at King's Coll., London, 1860–5; prof. of physics, Cambridge, 1871; a great research worker; investigated composition of colour and colour vision, the kinetic theory of gases, and showed light to be an electro-magnetic phenomenon; wrote *Matter and Motion*, *Heat*, *Electricity and Magnetism*, *Scientific Papers* (8 vols.).

Maxwell, MRS. JOHN. See BRADDON.

May, PHIL (1864–1903), Eng. caricaturist, *b.* Leeds; worked three years in Australia on *Sydney Bulletin*; returning, 1888, contributed to *St. Stephen's Review*, *The Graphic*, etc.; joined staff of *Punch*; a master of line drawing; excelled in depicting London types.

Mazarin (*mä-zä-ran'*), JULES (1602–61), Fr. statesman; *b.* in Italy; won favour of Richelieu; naturalized Fr. subject, 1639; cardinal, 1641; on death of Louis XIII., 1643, became chief adviser to queen-regent, Anne of Austria; concluded Thirty Years' War by Treaty of Westphalia, 1648; prejudices against his Ital. birth and his oppressive taxation and avarice resulted in civil war known as first and second 'Frondes,' the latter headed by Condé, and Mazarin had to flee; on triumph of royalists continued foreign policy of allying Protestant Europe against Austria and Spain; in conjunction with Cromwell defeated Spaniards; greatest diplomatic triumph, the League of the Rhine, placing Rhine states under patronage of France; marriage of Louis XIV. to a Span. princess closed his career.

Mazzini (*mät-sē'nē*), GIUSEPPE (1805–72), Ital. patriot of Genoese family; founded *Indicatore Genovese*, 1828; imprisoned, 1830; exiled and, settling in Marseilles, formed secret soc. of Young Italy with organ *La Giovine Italia*; motto, *Dio e Popolo*; Mazzini was a dreamer, not an organizer; he settled in Switzerland, 1832; after various failures to provoke a rising in Italy, he fled to London, 1836; returned to Italy, 1848, and became dictator at Rome as one of triumvirs, 1849; vainly opposed the surrender of Rome to French; returned to England, 1850, and became the heart of conspiracies against Austria; responsible for outburst at Milan, 1853, and attack on Genoa, 1857; opposed action of Garibaldi and Cavour, 1859–60; refused to acknowledge monarchy; remained conspirator till death. Mazzini was the idealist and spiritual founder of United Italy.

[*Mazzini* (1903), by Bolton King.]

Medici (*mā'dē-chē*), a famous Florentine family. (1) GIOVANNI (*c.* 1360–1429), founded the family wealth by establishing banks in numerous cities; won popularity as defender of poor. (2) COSIMO (1389–1464), his son, started the literary tradition of his house and heaped up wealth, but Albizzi secured his banishment, 1433; was recalled and became supreme in Florence. Was the friend and helper of the Ital. humanists. (3) LORENZO (1449–92), grandson of (2), most famous member of family, known as 'the Magnificent'; one of most brilliant and mild despots of history; universally gifted (except as to looks) and of lordly generosity; won enthusiastic affection of Florence; assassins slew his brother, 1478, but failed to kill Lorenzo; made magnificent collection of MSS., books, and pictures. (4) GIOVANNI (1475–1521), second son of (3); became Pope, 1513, as Leo X.; patron of letters and art, employing Raphael to decorate Vatican; assisted Emperor Charles V. against France. (5) LORENZO (1492–1519), nephew of (4), re-established Medici rule in Florence, but was not absolute like his grandfather. (For his daughter, CATHERINE, see CATHERINE DE' MEDICI.) (6) GIULIO, cardinal, an illegitimate son of the house, assumed government of Florence on death of (5); became Pope as Clement VII. (See CLEMENT VII.) The Medici were expelled from Florence, 1527, but were restored by papal and imperial forces, 1530, in the person of an illegitimate descendant of (5), and the Medici ruled in Florence till 1737, when Austria annexed Tuscany, which had come to the family, 1567, and expelled the seventh and last grand-duke, Giovanni Gastone.

[*Lorenzo de' Medici* (new ed. 1890), by W. Roscoe; *Lorenzo the Magnificent* (1908), by E. L. S. Horsburgh; *Golden Age of the Medici* (1925), by S. Brinton.]

Meighen, RT. HON. ARTHUR (1874–), Can. statesman; *b.* in Ontario; called to bar, 1903; elected to House of Commons, 1908; solicitor-general, 1913; secretary of state and minister of mines, 1917; member of Imperial War Cabinet, 1918; prime minister, 1920–1; member of Imperial Privy Council, 1920; again prime minister, 1926.

Meissonier (*mā-so-nyā'*), JEAN LOUIS ERNEST (1815–91), celebrated Fr. painter; *b.* Lyons; produced dramatic and costume genre pictures, military pieces, and portraits such as that of *Dumas fils*; among sixteeen examples in Wallace Collection, London, are *The Guard Room* and *Napoleon and his Staff*.

Melanchthon (*mel-ank'thon*), PHILIP (originally PHILIP SCHWARTZERD) (1497–1560), Ger. reformer;

b. in Baden; prof. of Greek at Wittenberg, fellow-worker with Luther; drew up Augsburg Confession; contributed largely to save the Reformation from excesses; on Luther's death became leader of the Lutherans; most popular publication was *Loci Communes Rerum Theologicarum,* the first great Prot. work on dogmatic theology.

[*Life* (1902), by Georg Ellinger.]

Melba, DAME NELLIE (HELEN PORTER ARMSTRONG, *née* MITCHELL), (1861–1931) Australian singer and prima donna; *b.* near Melbourne (hence her professional name); one of the great soprano singers of the world; first great success at Covent Garden, 1888, in *Lucia di Lammermoor*; also scored great triumphs in *Romeo and Juliet* and *La Bohème*; for patriotic work during Great War created D.B.E., 1918; pub. *Melodies and Memories* (1925).

Melbourne, WILLIAM LAMB, 2ND VISCOUNT (1779–1848), British statesman; *b.* London; Irish secretary, 1827; home secretary, 1830; prime minister, 1834 and 1835–41; a polished dilettante; performed with great tact the duty of instructing and guiding Queen Victoria; tenure of office marked by moderation.

Melchett, ALFRED MORITZ MOND, 1ST BARON (1868–1930), Brit. politician; *b.* near Widnes; a Jew, son of Dr. Ludwig Mond; called to bar, 1894; Liberal M.P. for Chester, 1906–10, Swansea, 1910–23; joined Lloyd George's ministry, 1916; first commissioner of works, 1916–21; minister of health, 1921–2; M.P. for Carmarthen from 1924 till raised to peerage, 1928; managing director of Brunner, Mond, and Co.; chairman, Imperial Chemical Industries Ltd.; joined Unionist party, 1926; author of political and economic essays, *Questions of To-day and To-morrow* (1912), etc.

Mel'lon, ANDREW WILLIAM (1855–), Amer. public official; *b.* Pittsburgh; interested in many financial and industrial undertakings; secretary of the Treasury, 1921–32; achieved reduction of U.S.A. national debt, arranged war debt settlements with majority of European debtors, and advocated tax reductions to promote business.

Mel'ville, ANDREW (1545–1622), Scot. educationist and reforming ecclesiastic; *b.* in Angus; prof. of humanity, Geneva, 1568–74; principal, Glasgow Univ., 1574–80, and St. Mary's Coll., St. Andrews, 1580–4; rector, St. Andrews Univ., 1590–1; opposed Erastian policy of James I., and upheld spiritual independence of Scottish Church; summoned to London, 1607, and for his bold vehemence was imprisoned in the Tower, 1607–11; prof. of divinity, Sedan, from 1611.

Melville, HERMAN (1819–91), Amer. author; *b.* New York; sailed as cabin boy to Liverpool, 1837; schoolmaster, New York, and in Mass., 1841; went on whaler to Pacific but deserted owing to ill-treatment; ultimately joined an Amer. man-of-war. His books embody his experiences; best known are *Typee, Omoo, White Jacket,* and *Moby Dick.*

Melville, VISCOUNT. See DUNDAS, HENRY.

Mem'linc, or MEMLING, HANS (*c.* 1430–94), Flem. painter; ranks among purists of Flanders, and used oil methods of the Van Eycks; lived at Bruges from *c.* 1465; his best work, including the lovely *Shrine of St. Ursula,* is in St. John's Hospital, Bruges.

Menan'der (2nd cent. B.C.), Gr. King of Bactria; said to have been greater conqueror than Alexander the Great; Strabo states that he conquered India as far as mouth of Indus.

Menander (342–291 B.C.), Gr.

dramatist; only fragments of his work remain, but scenes from his play *Giorgos* were discovered on a papyrus; excelled in delineation of intrigue and in subtle character-drawing; closely imitated by Terence.

Men'del, Gregor Johann (1822–84), Austrian botanist; *b.* near Opava; studied at Vienna; became monk and later abbot of Augustinian monastery at Brünn; his experiments in plant hybridization, pub. 1865, were epoch-making in the science of heredity, but their value was not realized till 1901.

Mendeléeff (*myen'de-le-yef*), Dmitri Ivanovich (1834–1907), Russ. chemist; *b.* Tobolsk; prof. of chemistry, Technological Institute, St. Petersburg, 1863–6, and at St. Petersburg Univ., 1866–90; studied petroleum industry in Pennsylvania and in Caucasus, 1876; his greatest work was the enunciation of the periodic law of the atomic weights; did much valuable work also in every branch of physico-chemical science.

Men'delssohn-Barthol'dy, Felix (1809–47), Ger. composer; *b.* Hamburg; came of wealthy Jewish family, which finally adopted Christianity, his grandfather being Moses Mendelssohn (1720–86), the famous philosopher and historian; at seventeen composed the *Midsummer Night's Dream* overture; professional training at Berlin and Paris was rounded off by tours on Continent and in England, a visit to Scotland resulting in the *Hebrides* (or *Fingal's Cave*) *Overture,* while Italy produced the *Italian Symphony.* He directed the famous Gewandhaus concerts at Leipzig, and founded its Conservatoire. His incessant activity directly led to his early death. His works range over almost the entire field, from song to symphony and oratorio; a skilled pianist and organist, he wrote some splendid works for both instruments, including *Songs without Words*; his genius is best exhibited in his symphonies and two oratorios, *St. Paul* and *Elijah.* Mendelssohn falls short of the greatest composers, but atones by fine blending of the classic with the romantic.

Men'elik II. (1842–1913), Emperor of Abyssinia; succeeded, 1889; defeated Ital. army at Aduwa, 1896; owing to illness, his duties were entrusted to regent, 1909; gave Fr. and Brit. trading facilities, and aided British in Sudan War.

Men'shikov, Alexander Danilovich, Prince (*c.* 1663–1729), Russ. soldier and statesman; favourite of Peter the Great; won fame as commander-in-chief of army in war with Sweden; marshal after victory of Poltava, 1709; helped to place Catherine on throne, 1725, and Peter II., 1727; overthrown, 1727, and banished to Siberia; was extravagantly corrupt.

Merca'tor, Gerardus (1512–94), Flem. mathematician; original name was Kremer; studied at Louvain; lecturer on geography and astronomy; entered service of Charles V. of France; cosmographer to Duke of Cleves, 1552; author of method of projection known by his name, in which meridians and lines of latitude are straight and cut at right angles.

Mercier (*mer-syā'*), Désiré (1851–1926), Belgian ecclesiastic; Archbishop of Malines and cardinal from 1907; founder of *Revue Neo-scholastique.* During the Great War was uncompromising in his opposition to the Ger. invaders, and was arrested, Jan. 1915. After the war engaged in friendly discussions between leaders of Anglican and Rom. churches.

Mer′edith, GEORGE (1828–1909), Eng. novelist and poet; *b.* Portsmouth; pub. *Poems* (1851), and *The Shaving of Shagpat* (1855). The first of his great novels, *The Ordeal of Richard Feverel*, appeared in 1859; then followed *Evan Harrington* (1861), *Adventures of Harry Richmond* (1871), *Beauchamp's Career* (1875), *The Egoist* (1879), *Diana of the Crossways* (1885), *The Amazing Marriage* (1895). The poetry of his later period includes *Poems and Lyrics of the Joy of Earth* (1883), *Ballads and Poems of Tragic Life* (1887), etc. Meredith is an acknowledged master of the art of fiction, especially great as a psychologist; his poetry has also won a place not less assured, and the great sequence of sixteen-line poems, *Modern Love*, stands alone of its kind.

[*George Meredith* (1926, 'English Men of Letters'), by J. B. Priestley.]

Meredith, OWEN. See LYTTON, EDWARD ROBERT BULWER.

Mérimée (*mā-rē-mā′*), PROSPER (1803–70), Fr. novelist; *b.* Paris; a leader of Romantic movement; chief productions short stories, full of imagination, wit, and art, which place his works among masterpieces of his cent. Among his novels are *Colomba* (1830), *Carmen* (1847), *Chronique du Règne de Charles IX.* (1829), *Matteo Falcone* (1829), characterized by simplicity, frankness, and cynicism; as inspector of historical monuments of France pub. *Voyages Archéologiques*; his posthumous *Lettres à une Inconnue* produced a great sensation.

Mer′ivale, CHARLES (1808–93), Eng. historian; *b.* London; Dean of Ely from 1869; chief work, *History of the Romans under the Empire* (1850–62); pub. also *General History of Rome* (1875).

Mer′rick, LEONARD (1864–), Brit. author; *b.* London; has written numerous short stories and novels, many dealing with journalistic and theatrical life, and all distinguished by literary craftsmanship; collected ed. of his works, with introductions by some of most famous writers of the day, was issued in 1918; publications include *Conrad in Quest of his Youth*, *The Position of Peggy Harper*, *The House of Lynch*, *While Paris Laughed*, and several plays.

Mer′riman, HENRY SETON (1862–1903), pseudonym of HUGH STOWELL SCOTT, Brit. novelist; *b.* Newcastle-on-Tyne; his novels, most of which are historical romances, include *The Sowers*, *The Velvet Glove*, *Barlasch of the Guard*, and *The Vultures*.

Merriman, JOHN XAVIER (1841–1926), S. African statesman; *b.* Somerset, England; settled in S. Africa, 1861; entered politics, 1869; treasurer-general, 1890–3 and 1898–1900; drew up report on Jameson raid, 1895; became head of S. African party; prime minister and treasurer, 1908–10.

Mes′mer, FRIEDRICH ANTON (1733–1815), Austrian physician; *b.* near L. Constance; interested first in astrology and magnetism; promulgated his theory of animal magnetism or 'mesmerism' as a means of healing; had great success in Paris, but his theories were discredited by a government committee.

Metel′lus, distinguished Rom. family. (1) LUCIUS CÆCILIUS, distinguished himself in first Punic War, 251 B.C., and rescued Palladium from the flames in temple of Vesta. (2) QUINTUS CÆCILIUS, MACEDONICUS (*d.* 115 B.C.), made Macedonia a Rom. province; one of first two plebeian censors, 131. (3) QUINTUS CÆCILIUS, NUMIDICUS, consul, 109, defeated Jugurtha in Numidia. (4) QUINTUS CÆCILIUS, PIUS, fought against Marius; consul, 80.

Meth'uen, Paul Sanford Methuen, 3rd Baron (1845–1932), Brit. soldier; joined army, 1864; served in Ashanti, 1874, and Egyptian War, 1882; commanded Methuen's Horse in Bechuanaland expedition, 1884–5; commanded 1st Infantry Div. in S. African War, 1899–1902; was defeated at Magersfontein, 1899; wounded and taken prisoner, 1902. Held Eastern command, 1903–8; commander-in-chief of S. African forces, 1907–9, and governor of Natal, 1909; field-marshal, 1911; governor of Malta, 1915–19; governor and constable of the Tower from 1920.

Methu'selah, character in O.T.; lived, according to Heb. tradition, 969 years (Gen. 5 : 21–27).

Metternich (*met'er-nich*), Clemens Wenzel Lothar, Prince (1773–1859), Austrian statesman; *b.* Coblenz; ambassador to Berlin, 1803–5, to France, 1806; Austrian minister of foreign affairs, 1809; concluded a marriage alliance between Napoleon and Maria Louise of Austria, 1810; advocated playing off France and Russia against each other; induced Emperor to offer support to Napoleon, but to assure Russia of non-intervention. After retreat from Moscow, 1812, became European mediator; organized great coalition which won victory of Leipzig; presided over Congress of Vienna; secured domination of Austria in Ger. Confederation and at Congress of Aix-la-Chapelle, 1818; obtained consent of international congresses to suppress new movements in Italy. An excellent administrator, he was blind to need for reform, and opposed to changes; in revolution of 1848 he fell from power before clamour of Viennese populace; fled to England but returned, 1851.

[*Metternich* (1888), by G. B. Malleson.]

Meunier (*moo-nē-ā'*), Constantin (1831–1905), Belgian realistic sculptor and painter; *b.* Brussels; in sculpture produced a marvellous series of statuettes, illustrative of life of the mining poor in Belgium; among best of these are *Ecce Homo*, *An Old Colliery Horse*, *The Shingler*, and *Fire Damp*.

Meyerbeer (*mī'er-bār*), Giacomo, or Jakob Liebmann Beer (1791–1864), Ger. composer and pianist; *b.* Berlin; studied under Vogler; visited Italy, 1815, London, 1826; a transition composer, regarded by some as Wagner's forerunner; among operas are *Robert le Diable*, *Les Huguenots*, and *Le Prophète*.

Meynell (*men'el*), Alice (*née* Thompson) (1849–1922), Eng. poet and essayist; *b.* London; younger sister of Lady Butler; spent much of her youth in Italy; her work both in prose and verse has been acclaimed by the literary world; works include *Preludes*, *Poems*, and *Later Poems*, and her essays, *The Rhythm of Life*, *The Children*, and *London Impressions*; also pub. a *Life of Ruskin*.

[*Life* (1929), by Viola Meynell.]

Mi'cah (8th cent.), one of the twelve 'minor' prophets and author of O.T. Book of Micah; a younger contemporary of Isaiah, whose work embraced the period covered by the reigns of Jotham, Hezekiah, and Manasseh.

Michelangelo (*mī-kel-an'je-lō*), or Michael Angelo (1475–1564), Ital. sculptor, painter, architect, military engineer, and poet, the culminating genius of the Renaissance; *b.* near Arezzo; secured the patronage of Lorenzo de' Medici; after Lorenzo's death went to Bologna; returned to Florence, then went to Rome, 1496, where he executed his *Bacchus* and *Pietà*; and returned to Florence, 1501. Three years later he finished his colossal statue of *David*, painted *The Holy Family*, and at the request of Julius II. returned to Rome, 1505, and commenced a magnificent monument; the Pope grew tired of the idea, and Michelangelo fled to Florence; reconciliation between the artist and Julius took place after the latter's capture of Bologna, 1506, and he was commissioned to cast a colossal bronze statue of the Pope; after great difficulty, as he had no knowledge of metal-casting, finished the work in 1508; next painted the frescoes in the Sistine Chapel at Rome; this magnificent work took four and a half years to complete. After the death of Julius, 1513, Michelangelo continued his work on the sepulchral monument, which was again interrupted. Michelangelo continued in Florence, and in 1529 was appointed chief military engineer to defend the city from the expelled Medici; after the fall of the city he resumed work on the Laurentian Library and the Medici Chapel; went to Rome, 1534, in order to complete the Julian monument, but was ordered by the Pope to add to his Sistine frescoes another picture; this fresco, known as *The Last Judgment*, is one of the most magnificent pictures that the world has ever seen. During the later years of his life Michelangelo wrote many sonnets, principally to his friend Vittoria Colonna. In old age he became chief architect of St. Peter's, Rome, and to him is due the present design of the great dome. Michelangelo was scornful and intolerant, impetuous and violent, but mellowed in old age.

[*Michelangelo* (1911), by C. Holroyd; *Sonnets of Michelangelo and Campanella* (trans. 1878), by J. A. Symonds.]

Michelet (*mēsh-lā'*), JULES (1798–1874), Fr. historian; *b.* Paris; prof. of history at Coll. Rollin, 1821–6, and at Coll. de France, 1838–51; for a time head of historical section of archives, and lecturer under Guizot at Sorbonne; wrote *Le Prêtre, la Femme, et la Famille* (1845), *Le Peuple* (1846), *Histoire de la Révolution* (1847–53); monumental work, *Histoire de France* (pub. 1833–67); classic prose, picturesque and eloquent, but strongly partisan.

Michelson (*mī'kel-son*), ALBERT ABRAHAM (1852–1931), American physicist; *b.* in Poland; graduated from U.S.A. Naval Academy, 1873; studied at Berlin, Heidelberg, and Paris, 1880–1; after other univ. appointments became head of physics department, Chicago Univ., 1892. Awarded Nobel Prize and Copley Medal, 1907. Made important experiments in light; the negative result of his experiment, with Morley, 1887, to determine the velocity of the earth through the ether, revolutionized the theory of physics.

Mid'dleton, THOMAS (*c.* 1570–1627), Eng. dramatist; collaborated with Massinger, Rowley, Dekker, etc.; appointed city chronologist, 1620; devised many pageants and masques; best-known plays are *A Trick to Catch the Old One* (1608), *The Spanish Gipsie* (1623), *A Chaste Maid in Cheapside* (1630), *Women beware Women* (1657), and *The Witch* (1778).

Mignet (*mēn-yā'*), FRANÇOIS AUGUSTE MARIE (1796–1884), Fr. political writer, archivist, and historian; *b.* Aix; associated as journalist with Adolphe Thiers; historical works and editions of MSS. are valuable; *Histoire de la Révolution Française* (1824) is a standard work.

Mil'an I. (1854–1901), King of Serbia; succeeded, 1868; obtained Turk. recognition of Serbian independence, and assumed title of king, 1882; abdicated, 1889.

Milford Haven, LOUIS ALEXANDER MOUNTBATTEN, 1ST MARQUESS OF, formerly Prince Louis

Alexander of Battenberg (1854–1921); *b.* Graz; became a naturalized Brit. subject and joined navy, 1868; served in Egyptian War, 1882; married granddaughter of Queen Victoria, 1884; vice-admiral, 1908; commander-in-chief of Atlantic Fleet, 1908–10, and commander of 3rd and 4th Divisions of Home Fleet, 1911; first sea lord, 1912–14. At outbreak of Great War dispatched Grand Fleet to its war stations; resigned post as first sea lord in autumn of 1914 owing to Press agitation against him as of Ger. birth. At king's request, 1917, relinquished his Ger. titles, assumed name of Mountbatten, and was created marquis.

Mill, HUGH ROBERT (1861–), Scot. chemist, meteorologist, and geographer; *b.* Thurso; director of Brit. Rainfall Organization, and ed. of *British Rainfall* and *Symons's Meteorological Magazine* (1901–19); president of Royal Meteorological Soc., 1907–8, and member of Board of Trade Committee on Water Power of Brit. Isles, 1918–21; works include *The Realm of Nature* and *Life of Sir Ernest Shackleton* (1923).

Mill, JOHN STUART (1806–73), Eng. philosopher and economist; *b.* London; educated by his father, James Mill (1773–1836); historian and philosopher; served East India Co., 1823–58; contributed numerous articles to *Westminster Review*; M.P., 1865–68; author of *Logic* (1843), *Principles of Political Economy* (1848), *Liberty* (1859), *Representative Government* (1860), *Utilitarianism* (1863), *Examination of Hamilton's Philosophy* (1865). His *Principles of Political Economy*, professedly resting on Ricardo's views, depart from them at crucial points, notably in the direction of Socialism. As a philosopher his theories have not altogether stood the test of criticism, but his attitude towards philosophical problems greatly influenced his contemporaries. In his *Utilitarianism* he laid special emphasis on human reason. His *Essays on Religion* (pub. 1874) revealed a mind groping for light.

[*Life* (1882), by A. Bain.]

Millais (*mil-ā'*), SIR JOHN EVERETT (1829–96), Eng. painter; *b.* Southampton; studied at the Academy schools, and at seventeen exhibited his first picture. Joining Pre-Raphaelites, he was influenced towards imagination and symbolism, but with *The Gambler's Wife* (1869) he broke into a more original style, and his later pictures are remarkable for their technical qualities. Well-known pictures include *Christ in the House of His Parents*, *Ophelia*, *Vale of Rest*, *Rosalind and Celia*, *Boyhood of Raleigh*, *Chill October*, *Bubbles*, and portraits of many eminent men.

[*Life and Letters*, by his son, J. G. Millais.]

Miller, HUGH (1802–56), Scot. geologist; *b.* Cromarty; apprenticed to a stonemason, 1820–2; wrote verses in spare time; accountant in bank at Cromarty, 1834; ed. of *Witness*, 1839, in which paper appeared his famous articles on *The Old Red Sandstone*; wrote *My Schools and Schoolmasters* (1852); in his last days his reason failed, and he committed suicide.

Millerand (*mēl-rän'*), ALEXANDRE (1859–), Fr. statesman and lawyer; *b.* Paris; advocate at Paris Court of Appeal from 1881; for some years ed. Radical Socialist organ, *La Petite République*, and later *La Lanterne*; entered the Chamber, 1885, as a deputy for Paris, and was for some years leader of Socialist Left; eventually became an independent Socialist; a recognized authority on social reform; his appointment to Ministry of Commerce, 1899, gave him a wide field for dealing with women's work, old age pensions, etc.; minister of public works, 1909, and minister of war, 1912–13 and 1914–15; commissioner-general of Alsace-Lorraine, 1919–20; prime minister, 1920; president of Fr. republic, 1920–4; member of Senate from 1925.

Millet (*mē-yā'*), JEAN FRANÇOIS (1814–75), Fr. painter, of peasant birth; *b.* in La Manche; pupil of Delaroche in Paris; suffered privation, but steadily rejected rôle of fashionable portrait painter; retired to Barbizon, and won immortality as an interpreter of the pathos and dignity of labour; chief works, *The Angelus*, *The Sower*, *The Gleaners*, *Potato Gatherers*.

Mill'ikan, ROBERT ANDREWS (1868–), Amer. physicist; *b.* in Illinois; assistant to Michelson, and later prof. of physics, Chicago Univ.; from 1921 director of physics laboratory, Pasadena; has done pioneer work in the electron and in radiation; Nobel Prize for physics, 1923.

Mil'man, HENRY HART (1791–1868), Eng. churchman and historian; *b.* London; prof. of poetry, Oxford, 1821; Dean of St. Paul's, 1849; author of dramatic poems and hymns such as 'When our heads are bowed with woe,' etc.; chief works, *History of the Jews*, *History of Latin Christianity* (1855), and *Life of Gibbon*.

Milne, ALAN ALEXANDER (1882–), Eng. author; educated Westminster School and Cambridge; assistant ed. of *Punch*, 1906–14; in addition to his essays has written well-known books of verse for children, beginning with *When we were Very Young*; plays include *Mr. Pim passes by*, *The Dover Road*, and *The Ivory Door*; wrote *Peace with Honour* (1934).

Milne, GEORGE FRANCIS, LORD (1866–), Brit. field-marshal; entered army, 1885; served in Sudan and in S. Africa; during Great War served in France, and from 1915 in Salonika; commanded Allied forces of occupation in Constantinople; commander-in-chief Eastern Command, 1923–6; chief of Imperial General Staff since 1926; field marshal, 1928; baron, 1933.

Milne, JOHN (1850–1913), Eng. mining engineer and seismologist; *b.* Liverpool; for twenty years geologist and mining engineer to Jap. Government, establishing a seismic survey for Japan, and for the Brit. Association a seismic survey of the world; author of *Earthquakes*, *Seismology*, and *The Miner's Handbook*.

Milne-Edwards, HENRI (1800–85), Fr. naturalist; *b.* Bruges; father an Englishman; prof. of zoology, Paris; author of *Leçons sur la Physiologie et l'Anatomie Comparée de l'Homme et des Animaux* (14 vols. 1857–81); upheld doctrine of special creations as against that of evolution.

Mil'ner, ALFRED, 1ST VISCOUNT (1854–1925), Eng. statesman and administrator; *b.* Bonn; under-secretary of finance in Egypt, 1889–92; wrote *England in Egypt* (1892); chairman of Board of Inland Revenue, 1892–7; governor of Cape Colony, 1897–1901; high commissioner for S. Africa, 1897–1905; at the conference with Kruger at Bloemfontein, 1899, insisted on enfranchisement of British; governor of the Transvaal and Orange River Colony, 1901–5; created baron, 1901; viscount, 1902; showed good qualities as administrator, but roused storm at home by consenting to importation of Chin. coolies for work in mines, 1904; retired, 1905; re-entered politics as member of the War Cabinet without portfolio, 1916; conducted mission to Russia, 1917; secretary for war, 1918; secretary for colonies, 1919; head of mission to Egypt, 1920, which recommended recognition of independence of Egypt; resigned, 1921, and awarded Order of the Garter; chairman of committee to advise cabinet on tariffs, 1923; pub. *Questions of the Hour* (1923); *Credo*, pub. after his death.

Milnes, RICHARD MONCKTON. See HOUGHTON, LORD.

Milti'ades (*d.* *c.* 488 B.C.), Athenian general; ruler of Chersonese; fled to Athens on the approach of Persians, but later advised marching to Marathon, where he defeated Persians, 490.

Mil'ton, JOHN (1608–74), England's greatest epic poet; *b.* Cheapside, London; son of a scrivener; educated at St. Paul's School and Cambridge; lived at Horton, Bucks, 1632–8; travelled in Italy, 1638–9, and visited Galileo; returned to London and acted as tutor to his nephews, Edward and John Phillips; married Mary Powell, of Royalist family, 1643; she was only seventeen, and after a few weeks returned to her parents till 1645. From 1649 to 1660 he was 'secretary of foreign tongues' to the Commonwealth. In 1652 he became totally blind. In 1656 married Catherine Woodcock, daughter of a Puritan officer. At the Restoration he was arrested, but released, possibly through Marvell's influence. He married Elizabeth Minshull, 1663. During Great Plague, 1665, sought refuge at Chalfont St. Giles, Bucks; died in London, and was buried at St. Giles's, Cripplegate. His writings fall into three periods:

(1) His early poems—*e.g.* *Ode on the Nativity* (1629)—show Spenserian influence; *L' Allegro* and *Il Penseroso* show his thorough command of measure; *Comus* (1634), a masque, is full of beautiful poetry; *Lycidas*, an elegy on his friend Edward King, is one of the greatest elegies ever written.

(2) From 1640–60 Milton wrote no verse except his famous sonnets. Milton's prose was mainly controversial; wrote against Episcopacy, in 1641 and 1642; in 1643, incensed at his first wife's leaving him, wrote the *Doctrine and Discipline of Divorce*, and, while teaching his nephews, the *Tractate of Education* (1644); in same year wrote *Areopagitica*, a plea for the freedom of the Press; his *Tenure of Kings and Magistrates* (1649) defended the right to kill a 'wicked king'; *Eikonoklastes* (1649) and *Defensio Populi Anglicani* (1651) were bitter replies to Royalist pamphlets. On the approach of the Restoration Milton wrote *The Ready and Easy Way to Establish a Free Commonwealth.*

(3) His greatest poem is the epic *Paradise Lost* (1667), which deals with the Fall of Man, while *Paradise Regained* (1671) treats of Man's Redemption. These show all that is best in his poetry—the beautiful word music, the gorgeous imagery, the magnificent pageantry. The vehicle of both poems is the greatest non-dramatic blank verse ever written. His last great work is *Samson Agonistes* (1671), written on the model of Gr. tragedy.

[*Lives*, by Masson, Johnson, Mark Pattison (Eng. 'Men of Letters'), Sir Walter Raleigh; *Milton's Prosody* (1901), by R. Bridges.]

Min'to, SIR GILBERT ELLIOT, 1ST EARL (1751–1814), British statesman; *b.* Edinburgh; viceroy of Corsica, 1794–6; as gov.-gen. of India, 1807–13, made notable frontier treaties, and added Mauritius, Bourbon, Java, and Spice Islands to Brit. possessions; created earl, 1813.

Minto, GILBERT JOHN MURRAY KYNYNMOND ELLIOT, 4TH EARL (1847–1914), Brit. administrator;

b. London; served in Turk. army, 1877; in Afghan War, 1879; military secretary to gov.-gen. of Canada, 1883–5; gov.-gen. of Canada, 1898–1904; viceroy of India, 1905–10, and with Lord Morley introduced reforms in Ind. government.

Mirabeau (*mē-rä-bō'*), GABRIEL HONORÉ RIQUETI, COMTE DE (1749–91), Fr. statesman; *b.* in dep. Seine-et-Marne; his debts and disreputable behaviour repeatedly forced his father to have him imprisoned; pub. *Lettres de Cachet* (1782), protesting against this treatment, and other political pamphlets; visited England and imbibed ideas on constitutional government; employed by government on mission to Prussia, 1786–87, but failed. On outbreak of Fr. Revolution, 1789, took foremost place in States-General, and sought to establish constitutional monarchy; prevented the Assembly breaking with foreign powers, but met with growing opposition of *doctrinaire* and fanatical politicians; died prematurely worn out; was uncommonly well fitted to guide others; of uncompromising honesty and striking eloquence, he inspired tremendous loyalty.

Mistral (*mēs-träl'*), FRÉDÉRIC (1830–1914), Provençal poet, of peasant origin; started with six other Provençal poets the *Félibrige* movement, a Provençal literary revival, 1854; pub. *Mirèio* (1859), which won him fame; wrote many other poems, a Provençal dictionary (1886), *Mémoires et Récits* (1906); Nobel Prize for literature, 1904.

Mit'ford, MARY RUSSELL (1787–1855), Eng. novelist and dramatist; *b.* in Hants; wrote four tragedies, produced at Drury Lane and Covent Garden; chiefly renowned for delightful sketches, *Our Village* (1824–32); wrote also *Recollections of a Literary Life*; a brilliant conversationist and letter-writer.

Mithrada'tes, or MITHRIDATES, name of several Oriental kings; Pers. appellation signifying 'given by Mithras'—*i.e.* the sun god; the most famous being MITHRADATES VI., EUPATOR, King of Pontus, 111–64 B.C.; dangerous enemy of Rome, with whom he waged two wars, but was finally defeated by Pompey, and committed suicide; hero of eastern romance.

Miv'art, ST. GEORGE (1827–1900), Eng. biologist; *b.* London; prof. of biology in R.C. Univ. Coll., Kensington, and later, 1890–93, prof. of the philosophy of natural history, Louvain; contributed largely to controversies on Darwinism and natural selection, and was excommunicated by R.C. Church; author of *The Cat* (a monograph of great charm), *Genesis of Species*, *Nature and Thought*, *The Origin of Human Reason*, etc.

Moffat, ROBERT (1795–1883), Brit. missionary; *b.* in E. Lothian; missionary under London Missionary Soc., 1816, to S. Africa, where he laboured till 1870; trans. Bible into native tongue; missionary life spent mainly in Bechuanaland, where for a time he was assisted by his son-in-law, Dr. Livingstone.

Mohamm'ed, or MAHOM'ET (*c.* 571–632), prophet and founder of Mohammedan religion; *b.* Mecca. His marriage to the widow Khadija, whose servant he had been, gave him wealth and position. His custom was to retire to a cave on Mount Hira for meditation and prayer, and he professed to have received from the angel Gabriel a command to preach the revelation of the one true God. The Koran was delivered to him by God, and written down by his followers. He gathered round him a band of followers, including his wife, his cousin, and Abu-Bekr, afterwards his successor. He seems to have had to face opposition in Mecca, and receiving an invitation from the inhabitants of Yathrib (afterwards called Medina), he determined to flee from Mecca. The safe execution of his Flight (Hegira) taxed all his ability, but he finally arrived at Yathrib, Sept. 20, 622. From this time onwards he wielded greater and greater power; failing to bring about any understanding with the Jews in Yathrib, he crushed them by force of arms.

The new faith spread beyond Medina; converts had to declare belief in God and in Mohammed as His prophet, and to pay tribute; Mohammed started making attacks on Meccan caravans, and his victory at Badr greatly increased his reputation throughout Arabia. In the year 5 A.H. (of the new era, reckoning from the Flight) Mecca was invaded, and in 6 A.H. it was captured; little change was made in its internal government. The next step was the subjugation of Arabia; none but converts were allowed in his army. By 9 A.H. the encroachment of Islam on the Byzantine Empire had begun. His career was certainly one of the most remarkable of history; his ability was enormous; his sincerity is questioned by some.

[*Mohammed and the Rise of Islam* (1905), by D. S. Margolionth; *Life of Mahomet* (1858–61), by Sir W. Muir.]

Mohammed Ahmed Ibn Seyyid Abdullah (1848–85), Egyptian pretender; *b.* Dongola; claimed to be the Mahdi ('expected guide') who was to free Egypt from foreign rule; organized revolt of Sudan against British and Turks; Mahdists besieged and captured Khartum, 1885, and Gordon was killed.

Molière (*mōl-yer'*), pseudonym of JEAN-BAPTISTE POQUELIN (1622–73), Fr. dramatist; *b.* Paris; son of upholsterer to Louis XIII.; studied law; joined troupe of actors, 1643, and acted for twelve years in Paris, and, more successfully, in southern provinces, changing his name from Poquelin to Molière; began to write plays, and initiated modern comedy with *L'Etourdi*, acted in Lyons, and his epoch-making *Le Dépit Amoureux* at Béziers; returned to Paris, 1658, and enjoyed the patronage of Louis XIV. Molière found in the market-place and the court the types described in his plays, such as his *Bourgeois Gentilhomme* (1670). The *Précieuses Ridicules* (1659) took Paris by storm. *L'Ecole des Maris* (1661), *L'Ecole des Femmes* (1662), *Le Mariage forcé* (1664), *Don Juan* (1665), were comedies of his first manner. He borrowed some subjects from classical writers, as in the *Fourberies de Scapin* (1671). The *Femmes Savantes* (1672) continued the attack commenced in *Les Précieuses; Le Misanthrope* (1666) is perhaps the best picture of Molière's philosophy of life; *Tartuffe* (1667) is satire against hypocrisy; *L'Avare* (1668) was taken from Plautus's *Aulularia.* Whilst acting the 'Malade' in the *Malade Imaginaire*, a piece of pure and broad humour, in 1673, Molière was taken ill and carried away from the stage dying.

His contemporaries did not place Molière as high as do later critics; his excellence consists in detached observation of manners and passions, a terrible power of mockery beneath an assumed air of moral tolerance. His numerous works were produced in fifteen years, during which he had to be at once author, actor, and stage manager. He ranks among the world's greatest writers.

Mol'lison, JAMES ALLAN (1905–), Scot. airman; *b.* Glasgow; joined air force; made record solo flights from Australia to England, Aug. 1931 (8 days 14 hrs. 25 mins.), and from Ireland to New Brunswick, Canada, Aug. 1932 (30 hrs. 15 mins.); married Amy Johnson, the first woman to accomplish solo flight from England to Australia, May 1930.

Molt'ke, Helmuth Karl Bernhard, Count von (1800–91), Ger. field-marshal; *b.* in Mecklenburg; first lieutenant on general staff at Berlin, 1833; served Turkey against Mehemet Ali, 1838–9, exploring Near East and writing acute and graphic account of Turkey; pub. maps and surveys of Asia Minor, etc., and account of Russo-Turk. campaign, 1845; chief of general staff, 1857; commenced publication of military books which revolutionized art of war; wrote history of Ital. campaign, 1862; furnished plan for Dan. campaign, 1864, and rescued it from failure by personal intervention; sole controller of war against Austria, 1866, and so brought about great Prussian victory of Königgrätz; success largely helped by great railway system he organized. He was chief of general staff in Franco-Ger. War, 1870–1; won battle of Sedan, 1870, and entered Paris, 1871; field-marshal, 1871; ed. history of Franco-Ger. War; member of Reichstag, 1871.

[*Moltke* (1921), by F. E. Whitton.]

Mommsen, Theodor (1817–1903), Ger. historian; *b.* in Schleswig-Holstein; leader of modern school of research; spent early years in study of Ital. antiquities, and acquired enormous scholarship; pub. *Roman History* (1854–6); graphic in style, but disfigured by special pleading of a kind opposed to modern historical spirit; author of many works; ed. of great *Corpus Inscriptionum Latinarum.*

[*Life* (1903), by C. Bardt.]

Monbod'do, James Burnett, Lord (1714–99), Scot. judge and metaphysician; *b.* in Kincardineshire; raised to bench, 1767; first work, *Of the Origin and Progress of Language*; anticipated Darwin in regard to descent of man; Dr. Johnson visited him, 1773, and Burns saw much of him, 1787; wrote also *Ancient Metaphysics.*

Monck (or Monk), George, 1st Duke of Albemarle (1608–70), Eng. soldier and sailor; *b.* in Devon; was for some years in Dutch army; a royalist in early stages of Civil War, but after capture by Fairfax and imprisonment, 1644–46, accepted Parliamentary command in Ireland; distinguished himself under Cromwell at Dunbar, 1650, and as admiral against Dutch, 1653; instrumental in bringing about restoration of Charles II., 1660, who created him Duke of Albemarle; defeated Dutch, 1666.

Mond, Alfred. See Melchett,

Mond, Ludwig (1839–1909). Brit. chemist of Ger. birth; *b.* Cassel, of Jewish parents; did much to develop chemical industry in Britain, particularly by introduction of ammonia-soda process of manufacturing sodium carbonate, and later by production of 'producer gas' from useless slag; founder with Sir J. T. Brunner of Brunner, Mond, and Co.; founded Davy-Faraday research laboratory of the Royal Institution; bequeathed to nation some fine Ital. pictures.

Monet (*mō-nā'*), Claude (1840–1926), Fr. impressionist and open-air landscape painter; *b.* Paris; mainly influenced by Corot, Millet, Manet, Degas, and Turner; works include views of Argenteuil, of Vétheuil, of Pourville, cliffs of Etretat, cathedrals, and *Le Bassin des Nymphéas.*

Monk, General. See Monck.

Mon'mouth, James Scott, Duke of (1649–85), natural son of Charles II.; *b.* Rotterdam; married heiress of Buccleuchs, and became Duke of Buccleuch, 1663; claimed succession as Prot. heir in opposition to James, Duke of York, but king always denied his legitimacy, and York secured his exile; returned, 1679, and was openly supported by exclusionists headed by Shaftesbury; imprisoned, 1682; released, took part in Rye House Plot, and escaped to Holland, 1683; invaded England, 1685, conjointly with Argyll's invasion of Scotland; defeated at Sedgemoor, and executed.

Monro', SIR CHARLES CARMICHAEL (1860–1929), Brit. soldier; entered army, 1879; served on N.W. Frontier, India, 1879–80, and in S. African War; during Great War commanded 2nd Division in France, 1914, and in command of 3rd Army, 1915; in command of Mediterranean Expeditionary Force, 1915, carrying out, in conjunction with Admiral Wemyss, memorable evacuation from Suvla Bay; commander-in-chief of forces in India, 1916–20; governor of Gibraltar, 1923–8.

Monroe, JAMES (1758–1831), fifth president of U.S.A.; *b.* in Virginia; served in War of Independence; member of U.S.A. Congress, 1783–6, and influenced foreign policy; U.S.A. senator, 1790; minister to France, 1794–6; wrote pamphlet criticizing Washington, 1797; governor of Virginia, 1799–1802, 1810–11; carried out purchase of Louisiana from France, 1803, and of Florida from Spain, 1821; president, 1816 and 1820; promulgated Monroe Doctrine, 1823, that Amer. continents 'are henceforth not to be considered as subjects for future colonization by any European powers.'

Montagu, CHARLES. See HALIFAX, EARL OF.

Mon'tagu, RT. HON. EDWIN SAMUEL (1879–1924), Brit. politician; *b.* of Jewish parents; Liberal M.P., 1906–22; under-secretary of state for India, 1910–14; financial secretary to Treasury, 1914–16; minister of munitions and member of War Committee, 1916; secretary of state for India, 1917–22; visited India, 1917–18, and carried bill, 1919, introducing Montagu-Chelmsford reforms of Indian government.

Montagu, LADY MARY WORTLEY (1689–1762), Eng. authoress, daughter of the Earl of Kingston; *b.* in Notts; married Edward Wortley Montague, afterwards ambassador to Constantinople, whence her famous descriptive *Letters* were sent; a pioneer advocate of inoculation for smallpox; wrote occasional verse, pub. as *Court Poems* (1716).

[*Lady Mary Wortley Montagu and her Times* (1907), by G. Paston.]

Montaigne (*mon-tān'*), MICHEL DE (1533–92), Fr. essayist; *b.* in castle of Montaigne, near Bordeaux; had eccentric education; studied law, and was councillor in Parliament of Bordeaux, 1554–72; retired to Montaigne, and began to write his *Essais*; travelled through Switzerland, Germany, Italy, whence he was recalled to be mayor of Bordeaux, 1582–6. His famous *Essais* are a fine piece of moral philosophy, which showed new spaciousness of mental outlook; style characterized by freedom and ease of the Renaissance.

[*Montaigne* (1905), by Prof. Dowden; *Montaigne* (1911), by E. Sichel.]

Montcalm (*mont-kăm'*), LOUIS JOSEPH, MARQUIS DE (1712–59), Fr. soldier; *b.* near Nîmes; commander in Canada, 1756; captured Fort William Henry; held Ticonderoga against General Abercrombie's siege; fell fighting against Wolfe on Plains of Abraham, Quebec.

Montefiore (*mon-te-fē-ō're*), SIR MOSES HAIM (1784–1885), Jewish philanthropist; *b.* Leghorn; made fortune on London Stock Exchange; sheriff of London, 1837; baronet, 1846; secured better treatment for Jews in Turkey, Russia, Moldavia, and Morocco, and raised various funds for Jewish refugees.

Montespan (*mon-te-spän'*), FRANÇOISE-ATHÉNAÏS DE PARDAILLAN, MARQUISE DE (1641–1707), mistress of Louis XIV.; daughter of Duc de Mortemart; married Marquis de Montespan, 1663; had seven children by king, legitimized in 1673; superseded by Madame de Maintenon; entered convent, 1691; beautiful, witty, patron of letters.

Montesquieu (*mōn-tes-kū'*), CHARLES LOUIS DE SECONDAT, BARON DE LA BRÈDE ET DE (1689–1755), Fr. historian and philosopher; *b.* near Bordeaux; succeeded uncle as judge of supreme law court, Bordeaux, 1716; of retiring character, led uneventful life. His *Lettres Persanes* (1721), audacious, shocking, and amusing, went like wildfire; after publishing expurgated ed., was admitted to Academy, 1728; his *Grandeur et Décadence des Romains* (1734) contained brilliant generalizations on Rom. character, and his famous *Esprit des Lois* (1748) was marked by deep studies and wide travelling; was fiercely attacked by Church, hence his *Défense* (1750).

[*Montesquieu*, by Sir C. P. Ilbert.]

Montesso'ri, MARIA (1869–), Ital. educationist; *b.* Rome; first woman to graduate doctor of medicine at univ. of Rome, 1894; assistant in psychiatric clinic of her univ., and took great interest in mentally deficient children; lectures led to founding of Scuola Ortofrenica (' mind-strengthening school '), of which she was director, 1898–1900; lectured on pedagogical anthropology at univ. of Rome, 1900–7; first ' House of Childhood ' opened under her guidance, 1907; visited U.S.A., 1913, and England, 1919; government inspector of schools in Italy, 1922. Works include *Pedagogic Anthropology, Montessori Method, Advanced Montessori Method.* The Montessori System is a kindergarten system, adopted in the ' Houses of Childhood,' based on self-activity and the development of the senses; lays more emphasis on the practical than on the imaginative, and formal discipline is dispensed with.

Montezu'ma (1466–1520), last Aztec emperor of Mexico; by heavy taxation alienated his subjects; tried to buy off Cortes, and became a Span. prisoner; when capital rebelled, was brought to pacify the citizens; wounded by a stone, and soon afterwards died.

Mont'fort, SIMON DE, EARL OF LEICESTER (*d.* 1265), statesman and soldier, an important figure in the development of the Eng. constitution; a Fr. noble; came to England, 1230, becoming Earl of Leicester; married Eleanor, sister of Henry III., 1238; had several quarrels with king; opposed demand for subsidy, 1254; joined baronial opposition at Parliament of Oxford, 1258; went to war with Henry, 1263; won battle of Lewes, 1264, and established baronial control. The Parliament he summoned to assist king's council is prototype of modern Eng. Parliament; slain at Evesham.

[*Life* (1877), by Prothero.]

Montgolfier (*mōn-gol-fyā'*), JOSEPH MICHAEL (1740–1810) and JACQUES ETIENNE (1745–99), two brothers, paper manufacturers of Annonay, near Lyons; famous as inventors of first balloon.

Montrose, JAMES GRAHAM, MARQUESS OF (1612–50), Scot. Jacobite leader; signed National Covenant, but believed in subordination of Church to State; joined Royalists, 1641; created marquess, 1644;

won many brilliant victories as commander against Covenanters, 1644–5; defeated at Philiphaugh, 1645, and retired abroad; invaded Scotland, 1650; defeated at Invercarron, betrayed, and hanged.

[*Montrose* (1928), by John Buchan.]

Moody, Dwight Lyman (1837–99), Amer. evangelist; *b.* Northfield, Mass.; associated with Ira D. Sankey in revival campaigns, and in compilation of *Moody and Sankey Hymn Book*; founded Northfield Institution, 1880, for evangelical and educational work.

Moore, Albert Joseph (1841–93), Eng. decorative artist; *b.* York; exhibited in Royal Academy, 1857; specially excelled in pose and in the tones of drapery, and has been called the poet of drapery.

Moore, George (1852–1933), Irish novelist and dramatist; *b.* in co. Mayo; influenced in early life by works of Zola, Flaubert, and Maupassant; his novels, noted for their realism and admirable style, include *The Mummer's Wife* (1885), *Esther Waters* (1894), *Evelyn Innes* (1898), *Sister Teresa* (1901); *The Brook Kerith* (1916), and *The Passing of the Essenes*, a drama, are based on the Bible story; he rewrote story of *Héloïse and Abélard* (1921); *Hail and Farewell: Ave, Salve, Vale*, are autobiographical; *The Making of an Immortal* (1927) was his first successful play.

Moore, Henry (1831–96), Eng. marine painter, brother of Albert Joseph Moore; first important seascape exhibited in 1858; R.A., 1893; among his works are *Catspaw off Land* (Tate Gallery, London), *Clearness after Rain* (Grand Prix in Paris, 1889), *A Breezy Day in the Channel*, and *Shine and Shower*.

Moore, Sir John (1761–1809), Brit. general; *b.* Glasgow; officer in Amer. War, 1778–83; M.P., 1784; wounded in Corsican campaign, 1792; served in W. Indies, Ireland, Holland, and Egypt; commander-in-chief in Peninsula, 1808; conducted brilliant retreat from the French to Corunna, 1809, where he was killed in the moment of victory.

Moore, Thomas (1779–1852), Irish poet; *b.* Dublin; educated Dublin Univ., and went to London to study law; Admiralty registrar at Bermuda, but tired of the work, left a substitute, and came home; his substitute embezzled £6,000, Moore was held responsible, and to avoid arrest lived abroad; cleared off debt in time; was pensioned, and died insane. Chief poetical works: *Irish Melodies* (1807), *Lalla Rookh* (1817); prose works, *The Epicurean* (1827), a romance, *History of Ireland* (1834–46), *Life of Sheridan* (1825), and his great *Life of Byron* (1830); one of the greatest song-writers.

[*Life of Moore* (1905), by S. Gwynn.]

Moray, Earl of. See Murray.

More, Hannah (1745–1833), Eng. ethical writer; *b.* near Bristol; author of *Moral Sketches*, etc.; most popular work, *Cœlebs in Search of a Wife*; in *Village Politics* and in her *Cheap Repository Tracts* she inculcated obedience to tradition, law, and order; founded charity schools on Church lines.

More, Sir Thomas (1478–1535), Eng. writer and statesman; *b.* London; son of Justice of King's Bench, who placed him as page in household of Archbishop Morton; educated at Oxford; became M.P.; speaker of Commons, 1523; a friend of Erasmus, from whose letters we glean many details concerning his life; much against his will was made lord chancellor of England, 1529, and filled this office admirably; resigned, 1532, because of Henry VIII.'s breach with Rome; refused to acknowledge Henry's claim to title of head of Church; was imprisoned and tried for high treason, and executed. More's *Utopia* (1516) is a 16th-cent. picture of an ideal country governed by perfect laws; written in Latin, it met with instant success; his *History of King Richard III.* is an excellent example of 'classical' prose; beatified by R.C. Church, 1886; canonized, 1935.

[*Life*, by Roper, his son-in-law (1626), by Bridgett (1891), by Hutton (1895).]

Moreau (*mō-rō'*), GUSTAVE (1826–98), Fr. painter; *b.* Paris; prof. at Ecole des Beaux-Arts, Paris, 1892–8; his *Œdipe et le Sphinx* and his *Jeune Fille avec la Tête d'Orphée* provoked a great deal of criticism; best works include *Jason, Le Jeune Homme et la Mort, Moïse exposé sur le Nil.* Painted 8,000 pictures, etc., now in Moreau Gallery, Paris.

Moreau, JEAN VICTOR MARIE (1761–1813), Fr. general; *b.* Morlaix; won distinction at Tourcoing, 1795; led invasion of Germany, 1796, and made skilful retreat; implicated in Pichegru's plot against Republic; though innocent, was displaced; reinstated, 1799, and commanded in Italy; assisted Napoleon in revolution of 1799; commander of Army of the Rhine, and won battle of Hohenlinden, 1800; intrigued against Napoleon; banished; settled in U.S.A.; returned, 1813, to help allies against Napoleon; mortally wounded before Dresden.

Mor'gan, SIR HENRY (*c.* 1635–88), Welsh buccaneer; sacked Porto Bello, and put inhabitants to atrocious torture, 1668; subsequently sent to England in chains, but pardoned by Charles II.; knighted, and made governor of Jamaica, 1674.

Morgan. (1) JOHN PIERPONT (1837–1913), Amer. banker; *b.* in Connecticut; inherited great fortune from father, 1891; associated with U.S.A. Steel Trust and the Atlantic Shipping Combine; took an important part in railway construction, industrial and financial consolidation, and national and international finance; a great collector of paintings, porcelains, coins, and rare books and MSS. (2) JOHN PIERPONT (1867–), son of above; *b.* New York; succeeded his father as head of firm in New York; arranged payment of forty million dollars by U.S.A. for Fr. rights in Panama; Amer. agent for British Government during the Great War, and arranged loans to European countries; consulted on post-war questions of debt settlements; chairman of U.S.A. Steel Corporation since 1927.

Morgan, LADY, *née* SYDNEY OWENSON (*c.* 1780–1859), Irish authoress; *b.* Dublin; novels include *The Wild Irish Girl, O'Donnell,* and *Florence Macarthy*; also wrote travel books, verse, and two vols. of *Memoirs.*

Mo'rier, JAMES JUSTINIAN (1780?–1849), Brit. novelist; *b.* Smyrna; secretary of legation in Persia, 1808–15; author of *Travels in Asia Minor and Persia,* and *Hajji Baba of Ispahan* (1824), a novel of Pers. life.

Mor'land, GEORGE (1763–1804), Eng. painter; *b.* London; produced upwards of 4,000 works; lived reckless and dissolute life; celebrated for animal paintings and scenes of country life: *Inside of a Stable* (National Gallery, London), *Blind Man's Buff, The Gypsies,* etc.

Mor'ley, HENRY (1822–94), Brit. author; *b.* London; prof. of English, Univ. Coll., London, 1857–90; author of well-known *First Sketch of English Literature, Palissy the Potter, Jerome Cardan,* etc.; ed. Morley's Universal Library, Cassell's National Library, and Carisbrooke Library.

Morley OF BLACKBURN, JOHN MORLEY, 1ST VISCOUNT (1838–1923), Eng. statesman and author; *b.* Blackburn; educated Cheltenham and Oxford; called to the bar, 1873; ed. *Fortnightly Review*, 1867–83, *Pall Mall Gazette*, 1880–83, and *Macmillan's Magazine*, 1883–5; ed. 'English Men of Letters' series from 1878; M.P., 1883; secretary for Ireland, 1886 and 1892; secretary for India, 1905–10; viscount, 1908; was an honest and fearless politician, a consistent upholder of Home Rule. His *Life of Gladstone* (1903) was a masterpiece of biography; other works include studies of Burke, Voltaire, Rousseau, Cobden, Walpole, Cromwell, and a brilliant essay, *On Compromise*; O.M., 1902; pub. *Recollections* (1917).

Morley, THOMAS (1557–1604), Eng. composer, chiefly of canzonets and madrigals; organist, St. Paul's Cathedral, 1591–2, and Chapel Royal, 1592–1602; pub. *A Plaine and Easie Introduction to Practicall Musicke* (1597).

Mor'ris, EDWARD PATRICK, 1ST BARON (1859–1935), Newfoundland statesman; *b.* St. John's; called to bar; M.P. for St. John's, 1885; member of cabinet, 1889; leader of independent Liberal party, 1898–1900; leader of people's party, 1908; prime minister, 1909–18; represented colony at imperial war conference, 1917; baron, 1918.

Morris, GOUVERNEUR (1752–1816), Amer. statesman; member of New York Provincial Congress, 1776–7; helped to draft constitution of U.S.A.; chairman of committee which refused negotiations till recognition of independence, 1778; wrote pamphlets on currency and taxation, advocating decimal system and 'dollar' and 'cent' as names for units; ambassador to France, 1792–4; advised separation of northern and southern states.

Morris, SIR LEWIS (1833–1907), Eng. poet; *b.* Carmarthen; gained great popularity with *Songs of Two Worlds* (1872–5), *A Vision of Saints* (1890), *Idylls and Lyrics* (1896), *Harvest Tide* (1901), etc.; wrote lyrics on national themes.

Morris, THOMAS, 'OLD TOM' (1821–1908), Scot. golfer and club-maker; green-keeper at St. Andrews, 1863–1903; four times open champion. His son, 'Young Tom' (1851–75), was champion thrice in succession, 1868–70.

Morris, WILLIAM (1834–96), English poet, artist, and Socialist; *b.* Walthamstow; educated Oxford; architect, painter, then partner in house-decoration firm, 1861; associated in art with Burne-Jones, Ford Madox Brown, Rossetti. His first book, *The Defence of Guenevere* (1858), showed imagination and romance, and *The Life and Death of Jason* (1867) and *The Earthly Paradise* (1868–70) confirmed his greatness as poet; pub. *The Æneid of Virgil* (1876), *Sigurd the Volsung* (1877), and, with E. Magnusson, many translations of Icelandic sagas; excels as a writer of narrative poetry. Founded the Kelmscott Press, and pub. beautifully decorated trans. of sagas, Fr. romances, editions of Chaucer, Shakespeare, Shelley, etc. His Socialism was æsthetic; poverty to him meant lack of artistic joys, hence his anger against a system that entailed poverty.

[*Life* (1899), by Mackail; *The Kelmscott Press and William Morris* (1924), by Sparling.]

Morris, WILLIAM RICHARD, 1ST BARON NUFFIELD (1877–), Eng. motor manufacturer; *b.* Oxford; introduced mass production of motor cars at Cowley, near Oxford; baronet, 1929; baron, 1934.

Mor'rison, ARTHUR (1863–),

Eng. novelist, dramatist, and writer on Oriental art; *b.* in Kent; works include *Tales of Mean Streets* (1894), *A Child of the Jago* (1896), *The Green Eye of Goona* (1904), *The Painters of Japan* (1911).

Morrison, GEORGE ERNEST (1862–1920), Brit. traveller and journalist; *b.* Geelong, Australia; M.D., Edinburgh, 1887; crossed Australia on foot, from Gulf of Carpentaria to Melbourne, 1882–3; subsequent travels ranged from U.S.A. to Morocco and Far East; as special correspondent of the *Times*, 1895–1912, he made numerous journeys through China and neighbouring countries; political adviser to the president of China, 1912–20.

Morrison, ROBERT (1782–1834), Eng. missionary in China; *b.* Morpeth; went to China, 1807; translator to E. Ind. Co., 1809; great work, *Dictionary of the Chinese Language* (1815–23); wrote Chin. grammar and Chin. trans. of Bible.

Morse, SAMUEL FINLEY BREESE (1791–1872), Amer. artist and inventor; *b.* in Mass.; studied art in London; prof. of design, univ. of New York, 1835; conceived idea of a recording magnetic telegraph, and worked out a system of dots and dashes to represent numerals and letters of the alphabet (*Morse Code*).

Mo'ses, leader and legislator of Israelites; *b.* in Egypt; in Midian received divine call to deliver his people from Egypt; during forty years in the desert organized religious and social life of the nation, dying before the promised land was reached. See Book of Exodus.

Mot'ley, JOHN LOTHROP (1814–77), Amer. historian; *b.* in Mass.; U.S.A. minister, Austria, 1861–7, Great Britain, 1869–70; famous for his *Rise of the Dutch Republic* (1856); wrote also *History of the United Netherlands* (1860–8).

Mottistone, LORD. See SEELY.

Moulton (*mōl'ton*), JOHN FLETCHER, BARON (1844–1921), Eng. judge; *b.* in Salop; called to the bar, 1874; rapidly acquired a large practice, especially in patent law; judge of the Court of Appeal, 1906–12, and in 1912 a lord of appeal in ordinary, and received a life peerage; acted as chairman on many important commissions; director-general of explosives in Ministry of Munitions from 1914.

Mountbatten. See under CARISBROOKE and MILFORD HAVEN.

Mount Stephen, GEORGE STEPHEN, 1ST BARON (1829–1921), Can. banker and railway magnate; *b.* Dufftown, Scotland; emigrated to Canada, 1850; director and president of Bank of Montreal; associated with Lord Strathcona, his cousin, in railway enterprises; head of Can. Pacific Railway till 1888; one of greatest philanthropists of modern times; baronet, 1886; raised to peerage, 1891.

Mozart (*mōt'sart*), WOLFGANG AMADEUS (1756–91), Austrian composer; *b.* Salzburg; at age of six started on a three years' tour with his sister, and excited astonishment everywhere; during this tour, his first compositions were published; wrote, when only ten, an oratorio, and an opera soon after, performed in 1769; toured in Italy, 1769–71; settled in Vienna, where he wrote his three great operas, *The Marriage of Figaro* (1786), *Don Giovanni* (1787), and *The Magic Flute* (1791). At his death, leaving unfinished his famous *Requiem*, he was carried to a pauper's grave. Wrote more than 600 compositions. His genius might be described as universal, for he shone alike in opera, in orchestral and chamber music, and in sacred composition. His style is a happy mixture of Ital. joyfulness of melody with Ger. thoroughness and depth.

[*Mozart* (Masterpieces of Music Series, 1912), by Cowen.]

Muir, SIR WILLIAM (1819–1905), Scot. Arabic scholar and Ind. civil servant; *b.* Glasgow; entered Bengal civil service, 1837; lieut.-gov., N.W. Provinces, 1868; financial minister for India, 1874; on retiral, 1876, member of council for India, London; principal and vice-chancellor, Univ. of Edinburgh, 1885–1902; works include *Life of Mahomet*, *The Caliphate*, and *The Coran*.

Müller, FRIEDRICH MAX. See MAX-MÜLLER.

Mul'ready, WILLIAM (1786–1863), Irish genre painter; *b.* in co. Clare; R.A., 1816; typical works are *Idle Boys* and *Choosing the Wedding-gown*; designed 'Mulready envelope' for Sir Rowland Hill.

Mundel'la, ANTHONY JOHN (1825–97), Eng. social and political reformer; *b.* Leicester; introduced bill to make school attendance compulsory in England and Wales, 1881; president of Board of Trade, 1886 and 1892–5; reformed conditions of labour.

Mungo, ST. See KENTIGERN.

Munkacsy (*moon'kä-chē*), MICHAEL VON (1844–1900), Hungarian painter, with great power of dramatic composition; settled in Paris, 1872; works include *Christ before Pilate* (1881) and *Ecce Homo!*

Munro', NEIL (1864–1931), Scot. novelist and journalist; *b.* Inveraray; made his mark with *The Lost Pibroch* (1896), which finely interpreted the poetry of Highland character, and with a brilliant novel, *John Splendid* (1898); other works, mostly historical romances dealing with the Highlands, include *Gilian the Dreamer*, *Doom Castle*, *Children of the Tempest*, *Daft Days*, *The New Road*, and *Jaunty Jock*

Munro, ROBERT. See ALNESS, LORD.

Munthe (*moon'tē*), AXEL (1857–), author; *b.* in Sweden; naturalized Brit. subject; studied medicine in Paris, and practised there and in Rome; fought cholera epidemic at Naples, 1892, and gave his services after earthquake at Messina, 1908; served during Great War; retired to San Michele, Capri, where he established a bird sanctuary. His autobiography as told in *The Story of San Michele* (1929) had immediate success; also pub. *Memories and Vagaries* and *Red Cross and Iron Cross*.

Murat (*mū-rä'*), JOACHIM (1767–1815), King of Naples; *b.* in dep. Lot; son of innkeeper; one of constitutional guard of Louis XVI., 1791; Napoleon's first aide-de-camp; won fame as commander in Italy and Egypt; commander of consular guard, 1799; married Caroline, Napoleon's sister, 1800; governor of Paris, marshal of empire, prince, and grand admiral, 1805; commanded cavalry at Marengo, Austerlitz, Jena, etc.; became King of Naples by Napoleon's grant, 1808; led cavalry in invasion of Russia, 1812; after battle of Leipzig made treaty with Austria; on Napoleon's return from Elba, declared war on Austria, but was defeated; after Waterloo, escaped to Corsica, invaded Italy, and was captured and shot.

Mur'chison, SIR RODERICK IMPEY (1792–1871), Brit. geologist; *b.* in Ross-shire; studied rocks underlying Old Red Sandstone in Wales, 1831, and established Silurian system; later carried on researches in Scot. Highlands; one of the first to recognize importance of Devonian system; director, geological survey, 1855.

Murger (*mūr-zhā'*), HENRI (1822–61), Fr. author; *b.* Paris; after failing with a poem *Via Dolorosa*, wrote famous novel *Scènes de la Vie de Bohème* (1848), descriptive of vicissitudes of his own student life in Paris; other works include *Claude et Marianne*, *Le Bonhomme Jadis*, and *Les Nuits d'Hiver* (verse).

Murill'o, BARTHOLOMÉ ESTEBAN (1617–82), famous Span. painter; *b.* Seville; went to Madrid, 1641, and won friendship and help of Velazquez; founded Academy of Seville, 1660; painted street scenes—*Beggar Boys* and *Flower Girls*—and religious pictures; great works include *Immaculate Conception* (in Louvre) and *Pedroso* and *Holy Family* (National Gallery, London).

[*Murillo* (Masterpieces in Colour), by Bensusan.]

Murray, SIR DAVID (1849–1933), Brit. artist; *b.* Glasgow; well-known landscape painter; R.A., 1905; knighted, 1918; president of Royal Institute of Painters in Water Colours since 1917; pictures include *River Road*, *Gorse*, *Long After*, and series of pictures from Picardy, Ital. lakes, Venice, the Trossachs, Lewis, etc.

Murray, GEORGE GILBERT AIMÉ (1866–), Brit. classical scholar and author; *b.* Sydney, Australia; regius prof. of Greek at Oxford, 1908–36; author of *History of Ancient Greek Literature*, of plays *Carlyon Sahib* and *Andromache*, and of famous translations of Euripides, etc.; chairman, League of Nations Union, from 1923; pub. *The Foreign Policy of Sir Edward Grey; Faith, War, and Policy.*

Murray, SIR JAMES AUGUSTUS HENRY (1837–1915), Eng. lexicographer; *b.* near Hawick; schoolmaster, 1855–85; ed. from 1879 of the *Oxford English Dictionary*, one of the greatest philological works in any language. Other works are *The Complaynt of Scotland* (1874) and *The Romance and Prophecies of Thomas of Ercildoune* (1875).

Murray (or MORAY), JAMES STEWART, EARL OF (*c.* 1531–70), Regent of Scotland; illegitimate son of James V.; joined Lords of Congregation, 1559; created earl, 1562; opposed Mary's marriage with Darnley; regent after Mary's abdication, 1567; defeated her army at Langside, 1568; murdered at Linlithgow.

Murray, JOHN, the name of four generations of London publishers who, from 1745 onwards, have been associated with some of the greatest names in contemporaneous Eng. literature, including Byron, Jane Austen, Crabbe, Moore, and Darwin.

Murray, SIR JOHN (1841–1914), Brit. oceanographer; *b.* in Canada; one of naturalists on *Challenger* expedition, 1872–6; assisted to compile, and from 1882 edited, *Scientific Results* of expedition in 50 vols.; shared in explorations of the Faeroe Channel, 1880 and 1882; carried out a bathymetrical survey of freshwater lakes of Scotland; in 1910 investigated large part of N. Atlantic, North Sea, and Norwegian Sea, results being pub. in *The Depths of the Ocean* (1912); killed in a motor accident.

Murry, JOHN MIDDLETON (1889–), Eng. writer; *b.* London; educated Christ's Hospital and Oxford; critic on staff of various journals; married Katherine Mansfield, 1913; in Intelligence Department of War Office, 1916–19; author of *Fyodor Dostoevsky*, *Life of Jesus*, *The Son of Woman* (D. H. Lawrence), and *The Necessity of Communism*, and many critical studies.

Musset (*moo-sā'*), ALFRED DE (1810–57), Fr. poet; *b.* Paris; youngest and most poetical personality of first Romantic movement; a writer of melodious poems, small, exquisite dramatic pieces, some of them amusing comedies, and polished, harmonious prose; perfected the *Proverbe*, a short play with few characters illustrating some maxim, light, witty, graceful, piquant, both in verse and prose; works include *La Confession d'un Enfant du Siècle, Espoir en Dieu, Stances à la Malibran, Le Treize Juillet, Lettre à Lamartine,* and four poems called *La Nuit.*

Mussoli′ni, BENITO (1883–), Ital. prime minister and 'dictator'; *b.* near Forli; as a youth, and later as a schoolmaster, developed a deep interest in Socialism, becoming a trade union organizer, and being involved in Romagna agrarian conflicts, 1908; served a term of imprisonment; joined the staff of the *Popolo,* 1909, and his Marxian Socialism began to veer towards Syndicalism; after imprisonment for inciting revolt against the Tripoli campaigns of 1912, became the ed. of *Avanti!* —the official Socialist journal. At outbreak of Great War faced Socialist opposition by favouring Ital. participation; served in trenches; wounded, 1917. To combat post-war Bolshevism founded the Fascist movement at Milan, which rapidly spread, after many combats with the Communists. His reconstructive but undemocratic régime began after the march on Rome, 1922; his reforms included reorganization of Italy's economic life and the inculcation of an imperial outlook; was instrumental in founding City of the Vatican under rule of Pope, 1929.

Mus′tapha Kemal′ (1880–), president of Turk. Republic; *b.* Salonika; defended Dardanelles during Great War, and thereafter directed Turk. Nationalist movement; established himself at Ismid, Oct. 1919; Gr. and Allied troops took the field against him, 1920, but he formed new National Assembly at Angora, and for next three years was genius behind active Nationalist movement; assumed leadership in 1921 campaign against Greece; accomplished defeat of Gr. army, Treaty of Lausanne, and abolition of the Sultanate and Caliphate; appointed president of Turk. republic since 1923.

Mutsuhito (*moot-soo-hē′tō*) (1852–1912), Emperor of Japan; succeeded in 1867, and proceeded to abolish feudalism and establish strong central government; transferred capital from Kyoto to Yedo, henceforth called Tokyo ('the eastern capital'); introduced modern civilization.

Muzaff′ar-ed-Din (1853–1907), Shah of Persia; succeeded 1896; established great friendship with Russia and raised large loans; after revolution, 1906, on account of misgovernment, monarchy was made constitutional.

Myd′dleton (or MIDDLETON), SIR HUGH (*c.* 1560–1631), Eng. contractor; executed the scheme for supplying London with water from Ware, Herts, by a canal opening into New River Head, Islington.

My′ers, FREDERICK WILLIAM HENRY (1843–1901), Eng. scholar; *b.* Keswick; a founder of Soc. for Psychical Research, and ed. of its *Proceedings*; chief work, *Human Personality and its Survival of Bodily Death* (posthumous); other works, *St. Paul* (poem) and *Essays, Classical and Modern.*

Myl′lar, ANDROW (*fl.* 1503–8), first Scot. printer; printed his first book at Rouen, France, 1505; with Chepman introduced printing press to Edinburgh, where *The Maying or Disport of Chaucer* was issued, 1508 (only copy is in National Library).

N

Nachtigal (*näch'tē-gäl*), Gustav (1834–85), Ger. explorer; *b.* in Brandenburg; sent on mission, 1869, by Prussian king to Sultan of Bornu; extended his journey to central Sahara, hitherto unvisited by Europeans, finally reaching Khartum, 1874; was instrumental in adding Togoland and Cameroon to Ger. Empire, 1884.

Na'hum ('consoler') (7th cent. B.C.), O.T. minor prophet; described as belonging to Elkosh, not yet identified. The book which bears his name, most likely written immediately before the destruction of Nineveh, 607 B.C., is the call of humanity for justice in the face of oppression and tyranny.

Nairne, Carolina, Baroness (1766–1845), Scot. poetess; *b.* Gask, Perthshire; wrote many songs, including 'The Land o' the Leal,' 'The Auld Hoose,' 'The Laird o' Cockpen,' etc.

Nan'a Sah'ib (*c.* 1820–59), Ind. rebel; stirred up feeling in India against Brit. *raj*; perpetrated Cawnpore massacre during Mutiny; took refuge in Nepal, 1859, where he was probably killed.

Nan'sen, Fridtjof (1861–1930), Norweg. arctic explorer and statesman; *b.* near Oslo; led first expedition across Greenland, 1888; engaged in Polar exploration, 1893–6, in the *Fram*, and reached lat. 86° 14' N.; took part in movement for separation of Norway and Sweden, 1905; Norweg. minister to England, 1906–8; prof. of oceanography, Oslo, 1908; chairman of Norweg. association for League of Nations, 1918; successfully undertook repatriation of prisoners of war; in 1921, supported by Mr. Hoover, undertook feeding of millions of famine-stricken Russians; for this relief work received Nobel Prize, 1922, which he devoted to assisting Russia; negotiated for admission of Germany into the League of Nations, 1924; lord rector of St. Andrews Univ., 1926. Writings include *Farthest North* (1897), *Norway and the Union with Sweden* (1905), and *Through Siberia* (1914).

Na'pier. (1) Sir Charles James (1782–1853), Brit. soldier and administrator; *b.* London; present at retreat to Corunna, 1809; captured but released; defeated Amirs of Sind at Meeanee and in decisive battle of Hyderabad, 1843; remarkable personality; dashing, inspiring general. (2) Sir William Francis Patrick (1785–1860), Brit. soldier and historian; brother of (1); *b.* near Dublin; distinguished himself throughout Peninsular War, and wrote its history, pub. 1828–40; greatest military historian of England; wrote *History of the Conquest of Scinde* (1845), and *Life* (1857) of his brother.

Napier, John (1550–1617), inventor of logarithms; *b.* Merchiston Castle, Edinburgh; travelled on the Continent, probably studying at Paris; in *Mirifici Logarithmorum Canonis Descriptio* (1614), which made him famous all over Europe, he gave, among other things, a table of the logarithms of the sines of angles for every minute to 7 figures. The method of calculation was described in *Mirifici Logarithmorum Canonis Constructio* (1619) by his son Robert. In 1617 Napier pub. a method of performing multiplication and division by means of small rods, known as '*Napier's Bones*'; was probably the first to use decimal point in calculations; also known for his work on spherical trigonometry.

Napier of Mag'dala, ROBERT CORNELIS NAPIER, 1ST BARON (1810–90), Brit. soldier; *b.* in Ceylon; served in Sikh campaigns and in Ind. Mutiny; directed siege of Peking, 1860; commanded Abyssinian expedition and stormed Magdala, 1868; commander-in-chief of Ind. forces, 1870–6; field-marshal, 1883.

[*Life* (1927), by H. D. Napier.]

Napo'leon I., NAPOLÉON BONAPARTE (1769–1821), Emperor of the French; *b.* Ajaccio, Corsica; of Ital. extraction; studied at military schools of Brienne and Paris, 1779–84, and received a commission in an artillery regiment, 1785; lived chiefly in Corsica, 1789–92; went to France, 1793, joined Montagnards, and became a Jacobin. He first won military distinction at siege of Toulon, 1793; proceeded to the army of Italy, where he displayed 'transcendent merit'; was entrusted with task of suppressing the rising in Paris, 1795. As commander of the army of Italy, 1796, won a series of brilliant victories over the Austrians, and forced them to sign Treaty of Campo Formio, 1797. He returned to Paris in Nov. 1797; landed in Egypt, 1789, as a preliminary to a blow at India; took Alexandria and won the battle of the Pyramids; destruction of Fr. fleet by Nelson in Aboukir Bay completely ruined his plans; he invaded Syria, 1799, but was repulsed at Acre by Sir Sidney Smith; returned to Egypt, but hearing of the political crisis in France, returned home, Oct. 1799, and was placed at the head of the government as 'First Consul,' Nov. 1799. He now led an army over the Alps, won victory of Marengo, 1800, and signed peace of Lunéville, 1801. Bonaparte hoped to form a great coalition (Russia, Prussia, Sweden, and Denmark) against England, but at the battle of Copenhagen Nelson forced the Danes to make an armistice; and in 1802 the Peace of Amiens was signed with Britain.

Bonaparte now turned to civil affairs, and undertook the task of reconstructing Fr. institutions; founded the univ., revised judicial system, codified Fr. laws, established a complete system of local government, and created the Bank of France and the Legion of Honour; the bulk of this work done during period of peace, 1801–3. In 1803 royalist plots aroused public feeling; the plotters were arrested, and the Duc d'Enghien was executed, 1804. On May 18, 1804, Bonaparte assumed the title of Napoleon I., Emperor of the French. He now assembled a great army and flotilla at Boulogne to invade England; the Fr. and Span. fleets, however, were destroyed at battle of Trafalgar, 1805. Meanwhile Napoleon was crowned King of Italy, 1805. He swept down upon Austria, surrounded her main army at Ulm, and inflicted a terrible defeat on Russians and Austrians at Austerlitz, the first of his 'grand' battles. Austria was obliged to sign Peace of Pressburg. By it the Confederation of the Rhine was formed under his protection.

Napoleon next completely annihilated Prussia in the battle of Jena, 1806; he issued the Berlin Decree, which established a commercial blockade of Eng. goods. He now pressed on against the Russians, fought the indecisive battle of Eylau, and won decisive victory of Friedland, 1807. He then signed with Tsar Alexander I. the Treaty of Tilsit, 1807; Prussia was partitioned, and the kingdom of Westphalia was constituted for his brother Jerome.

Napoleon now compelled the

Span. king to abdicate, and made his brother Joseph king of Spain. Span. people rose in fury, and England landed troops in the Peninsula, and this Peninsular War was primary cause of Napoleon's downfall. Austria declared war; Napoleon drove Austrians from Ratisbon and occupied Vienna, 1809, lost the terrible battle of Aspern, but defeated the Archduke Charles at Wagram; in 1809 Austria signed Treaty of Schönbrunn. Napoleon now divorced Josephine de Beauharnais (whom he had married in March 1796), and espoused the Archduchess Marie Louise of Austria. In 1811 the alliance of Tilsit broke up, Tsar Alexander having gained Sweden over to his side. In 1812 Napoleon invaded Russia. There was a frightful battle at Borodino, 1812; Moscow was occupied, but set on fire by the Russians. After this Napoleon was obliged to retreat, and in the retreat practically the entire army perished.

Encouraged by this disaster, the Prussians re-entered the war, and after some reverses were joined by Austria. The French were decisively defeated at Leipzig, 1813, and in 1814 Napoleon was compelled to abdicate. He was banished to Elba, but escaped and landed in France, March 1815; France rallied to him, but his 'Hundred Days' were ended by his defeat at Waterloo, June 18, 1815. Napoleon surrendered to the English, and was banished to St. Helena, where he died, 1821. His body was conveyed to France, 1840, and laid in the Invalides in Paris.

His military genius has never been surpassed; while the Code Napoléon witnesses to the boldness and clearness of his statesmanship.

[*Life of Napoleon I.* (1902), by J. H. Rose; *Napoleon: the Last Phase* (1900), by Lord Rosebery; *Napoléon Intime* (1893), by A. Lévy; *Napoléon chez lui* (Eng. trans. 1894) and *Napoléon et sa Famille* (1897–1900), by F. Masson; *Napoleon* (1927), by E. Ludwig.]

Napoleon II., NAPOLÉON FRANÇOIS CHARLES JOSEPH (1811–32), titular emperor of French; son of Napoleon I. and Marie Louise; created 'King of Rome' at birth; on his father's downfall he withdrew to Austrian court and lived as Duke of Reichstadt.

Napoleon III., CHARLES LOUIS NAPOLÉON BONAPARTE (1808–73), last emperor of the French; son of Louis Bonaparte (brother of Napoleon I.) and of Hortense Beauharnais, daughter of Josephine. As head of the Bonaparte family made an unsuccessful attempt at Strasbourg against the government, 1836, and was deported to America; was captured in attempted invasion of France, 1840, and condemned to perpetual captivity; escaped, 1846, and lived a gay society life in London. The revolution of 1848 brought about his return; he was elected president, and, 1851, carried out a *coup d'état* overthrowing the constitution. Declared emperor, 1852. He married, 1853, Eugénie de Montijo (1826–1920). His career was crowned by Franco-British victories in the Crimea. He supported Italy in its War of Liberation, but secured the cession of Nice and Savoy to France. His later policy was not so successful; Russia was offended by his Polish policy, 1863; Mexican expeditions failed, 1863–7; republican party at home extorted concessions; and his attitude to Prussia helped to precipitate disastrous Franco-Ger. War, 1870. Napoleon surrendered at Sedan, and was deposed, 1870. He lived in England till his death.

[*Napoleon III.* (1898), by A. Forbes; *Le Second Empire* (1907), by A. Thomas.]

Nares (*nārz*), SIR GEORGE STRONG

(1831–1915), Scot. sailor; *b.* Aberdeen; took part in Franklin Search Expedition, 1852–4; commanded *Challenger* expedition, 1873–4, till he was recalled to command Arctic Expedition, 1875–76; professional officer of Board of Trade, 1879–96; vice-admiral, 1892.

Nar'ses (*c.* 472–568), statesman and general of Byzantine Empire; an Armenian; a eunuch; rose to be important official; in 'Nika' revolt, 532, saved Justinian by bribing rebel leaders; defeated Goths of Italy, 552, and Alemanni and Franks at great battle of Capua, 554.

Nash, RICHARD (BEAU NASH) (1674–1762), Eng. man of fashion; *b.* Swansea; famous for excellence of his dress, manners, and taste, as well as for his gambling and extravagance; lived chiefly at Bath, where he held sway as master of the ceremonies, 1704–20; died in poverty.

Nash, or NASHE, THOMAS (1567–1601), Eng. poet; *b.* Lowestoft; shared in Martin Marprelate controversy; wrote *Anatomie of Absurditie* (1589), *The Unfortunate Traveller* (1594), and *Isle of Dogs* (a play, now lost).

Na'smyth, JAMES (1808–90), Scot. engineer, son of Alexander Nasmyth the painter (1758–1840); *b.* Edinburgh; inventor of steam hammer, 1839; patented, 1842, his design having already been appropriated in France by the Creusot ironworks.

[*Autobiography*, ed. by Dr. Samuel Smiles.]

Nebuchadrez'zar, or NEBUCHADNEZ'ZAR, King of Babylonia, 604–561 B.C.; defeated Egyptians at Carchemish, 605; made Babylon one of the wonders of world; reduced Tyre after siege of thirteen years; captured and destroyed Jerusalem, 586 (2 Kings 21).

Neck'er, JACQUES (1732–1804), Fr. statesman; *b.* Geneva; established banking firm in Paris; director-general of finances, 1777; introduced reforms of details; dismissed, 1781; recalled owing to desperate condition of exchequer, 1788; advised summoning of states-general; failed to provide funds and resigned, 1790; his daughter was Madame de Staël.

Nehemi'ah, Jewish patriot; cupbearer to Artaxerxes during exile; gained his master's favour and was allowed to go to Jerusalem as governor, 445 B.C.; restored the walls of the city; with Ezra as colleague, began a process of drastic reforms in the life of the nation. See O.T. Books of Nehemiah and Ezra.

Nehru, PANDIT MOTILAL (1861–1931), Ind. nationalist leader; advocate in High Court, Allahabad, 1895; president, Ind. National Congress, Amritsar, 1919; supported Gandhi's non-co-operation movement, 1920, and civil disobedience policy, 1930; founded Swaraj (Home Rule) party, 1922; recommended Dominion status for India, 1925; imprisoned, 1921 and 1930.

Nelson, HORATIO, VISCOUNT (1758–1805), Brit. admiral; *b.* Burnham Thorpe, Norfolk; entered navy, 1770. After surrender of Toulon, 1793, was dispatched to Naples, and made the acquaintance of Emma, wife of Sir William Hamilton, for whom he conceived a romantic attachment which lasted all his life. Was largely instrumental in the capture of Bastia and of Calvi, where he lost his right eye, 1794. In 1796 joined Sir John Jervis, and took part in the battle of St. Vincent, 1797; in the same year failed in an attack on Santa Cruz de Tenerife, and lost his right arm; in 1798 swept the Mediterranean in search of the Fr. fleet, found it in Aboukir Bay, and completely destroyed it, for which he was created Baron Nelson of the Nile. In 1799 the French took Naples, and Nelson conveyed the king and court to Palermo, went back to punish the rebels, and returned to England in company of the Hamiltons.

In 1801 dealt heavy blow to Napoleon by victory of Copenhagen, and was made a viscount. Then he entered on the blockade of Toulon, but in 1805 Villeneuve, the Fr. commander, broke out of Toulon, and, having put Nelson on a false scent, crowded all sail for Martinique. Nelson followed to the West Indies and back to Europe, actually reaching Span. waters before his enemy. Villeneuve again put to sea, and on Oct. 21 engaged the Brit. fleet off Cape Trafalgar. As the fleets closed, Nelson hoisted on his flagship the *Victory* his famous signal, 'England expects that every man will do his duty.' Nelson was shot through the lungs and spine; his last words were: 'Thank God, I have done my duty.' He remains the greatest Brit. naval hero; displayed boldness of conception, impregnable determination, and the intuition of genius. Public career was adversely criticized only for intrigues in Naples, and for association with Lady Hamilton.

[*Life*, by Southey (1813; ed., 1922, by G. A. R. Callender), Mahan (1897), C. Wilkinson (1931).]

Nelson, Thomas (1780–1861), founder of publishing firm of Thomas Nelson and Sons. The business was established at West Bow, Edinburgh, 1798, and was greatly extended by his two sons, William (1816–87) and Thomas (1822–92); in 1850 the latter invented the first rotary printing-press.

Ne'pos, Cornelius (*c.* 99–24 B.C.), Rom. historian; works include *Chronica* (compressed history of world), *De Viris Illustribus* (lives of famous men).

Ne'ro (A.D. 37–68), Rom. emperor; *b.* Antium; adopted by Emperor Claudius, 50, who had married his mother, Agrippina; married Octavia, daughter of Claudius, 53; became emperor on murder of Claudius, 54; imprisoned Agrippina, and caused her to be murdered; secured murder of Octavia, and married Poppæa, 62; great fire nearly destroyed Rome, 64; said to have been planned by Nero, but supposition rests on no evidence; Rome splendidly rebuilt, but the cost raised revolts; conspiracy, 65, in which prætorians were implicated, led to reign of terror; Vindex revolted in Gaul and Galba in Spain, 68; Galba was declared emperor, and Nero committed suicide. He was the last of the first imperial line; noted for persecution of Christians; ranks in history as supreme type of vice and frivolity.

[*Nero* (1903), by B. W. Henderson.]

Neruda, Madame. See Hallé.

Nesbit, Edith. See Bland.

Nettle'ship, Henry (1839–93), Eng. Lat. scholar; *b.* Kettering; prof. of Latin, Oxford, 1878; authority on Virgil; pub. *Lectures and Essays* (1885).

New'bolt, Sir Henry John (1862–), Eng. author; *b.* Bilston; educ. Clifton and Oxford; barrister, 1887–99; ed. *Monthly Review*, 1900–4; knighted, 1915; chairman, committee on Teaching of English in National Education, 1919–21; C.H., 1922; official naval historian, 1923; pub. poetical collections, *Admirals All* (1897), *The Island Race* (1898), *Songs of the Sea* (1904), *Songs of the Fleet* (1910); tragedy, *Mordred*; novels, *The Old Country* (1906), *The New June* (1909); also *Book of the Long Trail* (1919), *Studies Green and Gray* (1926).

New'castle, Dukes of. (1) William Cavendish, Duke of Newcastle (1592–1676); governor of the Prince of Wales, afterwards Charles II., 1638–41; supported king in Civil War, and was general of the forces of the northern counties; created duke after the Restoration; author of poems and dramas, some in collaboration with his wife, MARGARET CAVENDISH (1624–74), famous for her *Life of William Cavendish, Duke of Newcastle* (1667), and her *Autobiography*, both excellent pictures of contemporary life. (2) THOMAS PELHAM HOLLES, Duke of Newcastle (1693–1768), Brit. statesman; used his influence on behalf of Hanoverians at death of Queen Anne, and created Duke of Newcastle, 1715; secretary of state, 1724–54; premier, 1754. (3) HENRY PELHAM FRANCIS PELHAM-CLINTON, 5th Duke of Newcastle (1811–64), Eng. statesman; M.P., 1832; succeeded to dukedom, 1857; secretary of state for the colonies, 1852, for war, 1854. Resigned owing to storm of discontent raised by privations of Brit. troops before Sevastopol; again secretary of state for colonies, 1859.

New'comb, SIMON (1835–1909), U.S.A. astronomer; *b.* in Nova Scotia; prof. of mathematics for U.S.A. navy, 1861; superintended installation of a 26-in. equatorial telescope at Washington, took part in several eclipse expeditions, and observed transit of Venus at the Cape, 1882; director of Amer. *Nautical Almanac*, 1877; prof. of astronomy in Johns Hopkins Univ., 1894–1901; wrote scientific and popular books on astronomy.

Newcom'en, THOMAS (1663–1729), Eng. engineer; *b.* Dartmouth; one of inventors of steam pumping-engine.

New'digate, SIR ROGER (1719–1806), Eng. antiquary; M.P. for Middlesex, 1741–7, and for Oxford Univ., 1750–80; interested in extension of canals and roads; studied anc. architecture; chiefly remembered as donor of Newdigate prize at Oxford Univ., 1805, for best Eng. poem on given subject.

New'man, JOHN HENRY (1801–90), Eng. cardinal; *b.* London; educated Oxford; vicar of St. Mary's, Oxford, 1828; travelled in S. Europe, and returned with the conviction that he had a mission to revive the Catholic spirit in Anglican Church; started *Tracts for the Times*; developed doubts as to midway course between Protestantism and Roman Catholicism; resigned vicarage of St. Mary's, 1843, and two years later was received into R.C. Church; established oratory at Edgbaston, 1847, and at London, 1850; rector of Catholic Univ., Dublin, 1854–8; cardinal, 1879. Newman excelled as a preacher; both as poet and as prose writer he ranks high; his contributions to *Lyra Apostolica* and his *Dream of Gerontius* are perfect in expression; wrote the well-known hymn, 'Lead, Kindly Light'; works include *The Idea of a University*, his great autobiography, *Apologia pro Vita Sua*, and *Grammar of Assent*.

[*Life* (3rd ed. 1927), by W. P. Ward.]

New'ton, SIR ISAAC (1642–1727), one of the greatest of natural philosophers; *b.* Woolsthorpe, Lincs; educated Grantham Grammar School and Cambridge; fellow of Trinity Coll., 1667; prof. of mathematics, Cambridge, 1669–71; F.R.S., 1671; M.P. for Cambridge Univ., 1689 and 1701. In 1696 he was made Warden of the Mint, and Master in 1699, and revolutionized its administration. He was elected president of the Royal Soc. annually from 1703; knighted, 1705. He was the inventor of the binomial theorem, of the method of tangents, and of the calculus (or 'fluctions,' as he called it). He enunciated the famous laws of motion now known by his name. As early as 1665 he began the investigation which led to the greatest of his discoveries, the law of gravitation and its universal application. The lack of exact measurement of the degree of latitude prevented his verification of the hypothesis till 1685. In 1666 he turned to optical research, resolved white light into its primary colours, and invented the reflecting telescope, 1668. In his researches on light he maintained that light was due to corpuscular emission and not to transmission by waves. From 1705 to 1724 he was engaged in a controversy with Leibnitz, who claimed priority in the discovery of the calculus. Newton's priority has been established, though Leibnitz's method has proved more valuable to later workers. The most famous of his writings are the three vols. of his *Principia* (*Philosophiæ Naturalis Principia Mathematica*), written between 1685 and 1687. He wrote also on historical and theological subjects, determining the date of anc. events from astronomical considerations, correcting the accepted text of the Scriptures, and giving an interpretation of the prophecies of Daniel and of the Apocalypse.

Newton, JOHN (1725–1807), Eng. divine; *b.* London; served at sea, partly in slave trade, 1736–54; friend of Wesley and Whitefield; curate of Olney, Bucks, 1764, where he formed a close friendship with Cowper, the poet, and had great influence on him; jointly pub. *Olney Hymns* (1779), including Newton's 'How sweet the name of Jesus sounds' and 'Glorious things of Thee are spoken'; lived in London from 1780; became blind.

Ney (*nā*), MICHEL (1769–1815), Fr. marshal; *b.* Saarlouis; rose from the ranks to eminence under Napoleon, and was made marshal, 1804; was largely responsible for victories of Ulm, 1805, Eylau and Friedland, 1807; took prominent part in Peninsular War and Russ. campaign. On Napoleon's abdication he submitted to Louis XVIII., but went over to Napoleon on his escape from Elba; served at Quatre Bras and Waterloo. Was arrested, tried as traitor, and shot; known as 'bravest of the brave.'

Nich'olas, ST. (*d.* 326), patron saint of Russia; Bishop of Myra in Lycia; patron saint of merchants, travellers by sea and land, children, and scholars; name survives in Santa Claus.

Nicholas, the name of five popes and one antipope, of whom following are chief: NICHOLAS I. (858–67), supported Ignatius, struggled with Lothair II. of Lorraine, and maintained right of bishops to appeal to Rome against their metropolitans. NICHOLAS III. (1277–80), settled dispute in Franciscan Order and repaired at great cost the Lateran and Vatican. NICHOLAS V. (1447–55), humanist and statesman, pope at time of Turk. capture of Constantinople.

Nicholas I. (1796–1855), Emperor of Russia; *b.* Tsarskoye Selo; succeeded his father, Alexander I., 1825; established iron despotism and elaborate spy system; dealt forcibly with question of Gr. independence in 1827; triumphed in war with Persia, 1826, and in 1828 began hostilities with Turkey, which resulted in Moldavia and Wallachia being placed under Russ. protection; crushed the Poles, 1830. Entered upon war with the Porte, 1853, and a rupture with British and French caused the Crimean War.

Nicholas II. (1868–1918), Emperor of Russia; *b.* St. Petersburg; succeeded his father, Alexander III., 1894; announced intention of following out absolutist policy of his father; made alliance with France, and originated Hague Conference for promotion of universal peace, 1899; roused Japan by his Eastern policy and sustained humiliating defeat; under pressure of popular agitation granted a constitution, 1905. On outbreak of Great War placed himself at head of enthusiastic movement of resistance to Central Powers; assumed command of armies, 1915, but distrust of the Tsarina, mismanagement of military operations, and maladministration of supplies added to general discontent. He abdicated, 1917, and retired to the Crimea; was arrested and taken to Tsarskoye Selo, removed to Ekaterinburg, and murdered, with Tsarina and his family, by Bolsheviks.

Nicholas, GRAND-DUKE (1856–1929), Russ. soldier, uncle of Tsar Nicholas II.; took part in Russo-Turk. War, 1877; president of council during revolutionary disturbances, 1905, and commander-in-chief of the Imperial Guards; at outbreak of Great War took command on Austro-Ger. front; brilliant initial success, 1914, ended in retreat and defeat, 1915; was removed from command; appointed governor of the Caucasus, 1916, and achieved military success; after Revolution, 1917, retired to Crimea; emigrated to France, 1919.

Nich'olson, JOHN (1821–57), Brit. general and administrator; *b.* Dublin; served in Sikh Wars; deputy-commissioner on the frontier after annexation of Punjab, 1849; crushed attempted mutiny of Punjab; during Ind. Mutiny led attack on Delhi; killed after entry; brilliant ruler, despotic but just; called by Lord Roberts the '*beau ideal* of a soldier and a gentleman.'

Nic'oll, SIR WILLIAM ROBERTSON (1851–1923), Scot. journalist; *b.* in Aberdeenshire; Free Church minister, Dufftown, 1874–7, Kelso, 1877–85; settled in London, and ed. *Expositor*; started *British Weekly*, 1886, and *Bookman*, 1918, ed. both till his death; knighted, 1909; works include ed. the *Expositor's Greek Testament.*

Niebuhr (*nē'boor*), BARTHOLD GEORG (1776–1831), Ger. historian; *b.* Copenhagen; held several public posts; important as author of *Roman History* (*Römische Geschichte*); originated new theory of early Rom. history, emphasized laws which control development of civilization, and founded new historical school.

Nietzsche (*nēt'shĕ*), FRIEDRICH WILHELM (1844–1900), Ger. philosopher; *b.* near Lützen; son of a clergyman; became prof. of Greek at Basle, 1869–79. His philosophical writings distinguish two essential ethical types—the weak or slaves among mankind, who elevate the virtues that suit their weakness; and the masters, or the strong, who stand above the others and have no need of their base utilitarian virtues; Christianity, as favouring the former type, should be superseded; only by the morality of the strong can men rise to the higher stage of being supermen. Became insane, 1889. Chief work, *Thus Spake Zarathustra.*

[*Life* (1895–1904; Eng. trans. 1912), by E. Förster-Nietzsche.]

Night'ingale, FLORENCE (1820–1910), Eng. pioneer of trained army nursing; *b.* Florence; studied hospital methods in Germany and Paris. When the reports of the sufferings of the troops in the Crimea reached England, she volunteered for service and sailed for Scutari; in face of military inertia completely transformed the appalling hospital conditions by her own heroic efforts; known to the soldiers as the 'Lady with the Lamp'; revolutionized hospital nursing at home; with national gift of £50,000 founded Nightingale Training Home for Nurses; pub. *Notes on Nursing* (1858); O.M., 1907.

[*Life* (1913), by Sir E. Cook.]

Nilsson, CHRISTINE, COMTESSE DE MIRANDA (1843–1921), Swed. soprano vocalist and prima donna; made début at Théâtre Lyrique, Paris, 1864; came to England, 1867; toured in America; creator of important rôles in *The Magic Flute*, *Faust*, *Lohengrin*, etc.

Nin′ian, ST. (*d.* ?432), earliest apostle of Scotland; probably *b.* in Strathclyde; established his diocese at Whithorn, Wigtownshire; built 'Candida Casa,' perhaps first stone church in Britain, 397; endeavoured to convert southern Picts.

Nivelle (*nē-vel′*), ROBERT GEORGES (1856–1924), Fr. soldier; *b.* in dep. Corrèze; during Great War distinguished himself in retreat from Charleroi, in battle of the Marne, Sept. 1914, and in defence of Verdun, 1916; succeeded Joffre as commander-in-chief of Fr. armies of North and East, 1916; undertook unsuccessful offensive on the Aisne front, 1917, and was relieved of position as generalissimo; commanded Fr. forces in N. Africa till 1919; member of Supreme War Council, 1920.

No′ah, the chief figure of the Deluge; father of Shem, Ham, and Japheth. See Gen. 5 to 9.

Nobel′, ALFRED BERNHARD (1833–96), Swed. chemist; *b.* Stockholm; invented dynamite, blasting gelatine, and smokeless powders; established international prizes (value, *c.* £8,000 each), awarded annually since 1901, for most important discoveries in (1) physics, (2) chemistry, (3) physiology or medicine; (4) literature; (5) greatest service to cause of peace during the year.

Nor′dau, MAX SIMON (1849–1923), Hungarian author; *b.* Budapest; of Jewish parentage; practised medicine in Paris from 1880; wrote series of works keenly critical of modern society, including *The Conventional Lies of Civilization* and *Degeneration*; also novels and plays. Took an active interest in the Zionist movement.

Nordenskiöld (*nor′den-shĕld*), NILS ADOLF ERIK, BARON (1832–1901), Swed. geographer and Arctic explorer; *b.* Helsingfors; member of Torell's expedition to Spitsbergen, 1858; led expeditions to same place, 1868 and 1872; navigated N.E. Passage, 1878–80; distinguished geologist and mineralogist; wrote *Voyage of the Vega* (Eng. trans. 1881).

Nordenskiöld, NILS OTTO GUSTAF (1869–1928), Swed. explorer; nephew of above; prof. of geography, Göteborg Univ., 1905; explored Tierra del Fuego, Alaska and Yukon, coast of Greenland, and the Andes; led expedition to Louis Philippe Land in Antarctic, 1901–4; author of *Antarctica*, *Die Polarwelt*, *La Terre de Feu*.

Norfolk, DUKE OF. See under HOWARD.

Nor′man, MONTAGU COLLET (1871–), Brit. banker; educ. Eton and Cambridge; entered grandfather's bank, 1890; served in S. African war and won D.S.O.; director of Bank of England, 1907; governor since 1920. Was of great assistance to the government during financial crisis, 1931.

Nor′ris, FRANK (1870–1902), U.S.A. novelist; *b.* Chicago; studied art in Paris; returned to U.S.A. and took up journalism; war correspondent in S. Africa and Cuba; novels include *The Octopus* (1901) and *The Pit* (1903), dealing with conditions of the wheat market, and *Shanghaied* (1904), pub. after his death.

North, CHRISTOPHER. See WILSON, JOHN.

North, FREDERICK, 2ND EARL OF GUILFORD (1732–92), Brit. statesman, generally known as Lord North; chancellor of Exchequer, 1767; premier, 1770; probably hastened War of Amer. Independence through his continuance of obnoxious tea duty and by other measures; was secretary of state in the Fox and North coalition ministry, 1783.

North'cliffe, ALFRED CHARLES WILLIAM HARMSWORTH, 1ST VISCOUNT (1865–1922), newspaper proprietor; *b.* Dublin; founded *Answers*, 1888, *Daily Mail*, 1896; proprietor of the *Times* from 1908, and of numerous newspapers and magazines; did much for aviation by offer of valuable prizes; chairman of Brit. War Mission to U.S.A., 1917; director of propaganda in enemy countries, 1918; viscount, 1917.

Novel'lo, VINCENT (1781–1861), Eng. musician; *b.* London; ed. sacred works of Haydn, Mozart, and other composers previously unknown in England; founded firm of Novello, Ewer, and Co., 1811.

Noyes (*noiz*), ALFRED (1880–), Eng. poet and critic; *b.* in Staffs; educated Oxford; Lowell lecturer in America on *The Sea in English Poetry* (1913); prof. of Eng. literature in Princeton Univ., U.S.A., 1914–23; began publication with *The Loom of Youth* (verse; 1902); other works include *The Flower of Old Japan* (1903), *Poems* (1904), *Drake* (epic; 1908), *A Salute from the Fleet* (1915), *Mystery Ships* (1916), *The Torch-bearers* (1922–30), *The Book of Earth* (1925), and *William Morris* (Eng. Men of Letters, 1908).

Nubar Pasha (1825–99), Egyptian statesman; *b.* Smyrna; successively secretary to Boghos, Mehemet Ali, Ibrahim Pasha, Abbas Pasha, and Said; organized railway communication between Cairo and Suez; obtained permission from sultan for completion of Suez Canal, 1863; minister of foreign affairs, 1866.

Nuffield, LORD. See MORRIS, W. R.

Nye (*nī*), EDGAR WILSON (1850–96), U.S.A. humorist; *b.* in Maine; under pseudonym 'Bill Nye,' adopted from Bret Harte's poem 'The Heathen Chinee,' he wrote *Bill Nye and the Boomerang* (1881), *The Forty Liars* (1883), *Bill Nye's Thinks* (1888), *Comic History of the United States* (1894), and *Comic History of England* (1896).

O

Oates, LAWRENCE EDWARD GRACE (1880–1912), Brit. soldier and explorer; *b.* London; educated Eton; served in S. African War, 1901; captain, 1906. Joined Captain Scott's Antarctic Expedition, 1910; was one of the party of five to reach the S. Pole, Jan. 18, 1912; on return journey 'walked willingly to his death in a blizzard to try and save his comrades.'

Oates, TITUS (1649–1705), professed discoverer of a Popish plot; *b.* Oakham; laid before Charles II. details of fictitious plot to murder him and to set Duke of York on throne, 1678. Through his accusations some thirty-five men were done to death; imprisoned for perjury, 1685, but pardoned, 1688, and pensioned.

Obadi'ah (' servant of the Lord '), O.T. prophet and author of book which bears his name; nothing known of him except from the book itself; first part of the prophecy pre-exilic, second part written during the Exile.

O'Bri'en, WILLIAM (1852–1928), Irish journalist and politician; *b.* in co. Cork; founded, 1880,

United Ireland, as organ of Land League; formed United Irish League, 1898, and promulgated its views in the *Irish People*; prosecuted many times for political offences, and spent more than two years in prison; M.P., 1883–1918, except between 1895 and 1900; latterly differed from Nationalist party, especially on its land policy; after 1910 became leader of Independent Nationalists. Writings include *Recollections* (1906) and *The Parnell of Real Life* (1926).

Oc′cleve (or HOCCLEVE), THOMAS (*c.* 1370–*c.* 1450), Eng. poet; chief work, *The Regement of Princes*, a metrical homily on conduct, dedicated to Henry V.; other works include *Moder of God*, long attributed to Chaucer.

O'Con′nell, DANIEL (1775–1847), Irish statesman, known as the 'Liberator'; *b.* in co. Kerry; famous barrister; head of anti-Union party; formed Catholic Association, 1823, which was dissolved, 1825; established society, 'Friends of Ireland,' 1829; M.P. for Dublin, 1832, and opposed Coercion Act of 1833; introduced subject of Repeal of Union, 1834, founded Repeal Association, 1840; imprisoned for conspiracy to raise sedition, 1844; opposed to militancy, and broke with Young Irish party.

[*Life*, by Dunlop (1900) and MacDonagh (1903).]

O'Con′nor, THOMAS POWER (1848–1929), Irish journalist and politician; *b.* Athlone; Nationalist M.P. from 1880; prominent member of Parnellite party; from 1885 one of M.P.'s for Liverpool; president, Irish Nationalist League, 1883; visited America, 1909, and raised £20,000 to further cause of Home Rule; founded and ed. *Star, Sun, Weekly Sun, M.A.P., T.P.'s Weekly,* and *P.T.O.*, all brilliant successes; censor of films, 1917. Works include *Lord Beaconsfield: a Biography* (1879), *The Parnell Movement* (1886), *Some Old Love Stories* (1895), and *In the Days of My Youth* (1900).

Octavianus. See AUGUSTUS CÆSAR.

Odoacer (*ō-dō-ā′ser*), FLAVIUS (*c.* 434–93), Ger. king; overthrew Romulus, last Rom. emperor of West, 476, and became practically sovereign of Italy; defeated by Theodoric, King of Ostrogoths.

Oersted (*oor′sted*), HANS CHRISTIAN (1777–1851), Dan. physicist; practical discoverer of electromagnetism; studied medicine at Copenhagen and became prof. of physics, 1806; the work of Ampère led to a full appreciation of the discoveries of Oersted.

Off′a (*d.* 796), King of Mercia from 757; waged war against Wessex, 779; constructed Offa's Dyke between mouth of R. Dee and Chepstow to confine Welsh within their own country.

Offenbach′, JACQUES (1819–80), Fr. operatic composer; *b.* Cologne; lived in Paris; best works include *Orphée aux Enfers, La Belle Hélène, Madame Favart,* and *Les Contes d'Hoffmann* (1881).

O′glethorpe, JAMES EDWARD (1696–1785), Eng. philanthropist and soldier; *b.* London; M.P., 1722; exposed infamous conditions of debtors' prisons; sailed, 1732, with 120 debtors to found colony of Georgia; general, 1745; served against Jacobites, 1745; accused of failing to pursue defeated Jacobites, but acquitted.

O'Henry. See PORTER, WILLIAM SYDNEY.

Ohm (*ōm*), GEORG SIMON (1787–1854), Ger. physicist; *b.* Erlangen; prof. of mathematics, Cologne; director of polytechnic school at Nuremberg, 1833; prof. at Munich, 1841; discovered law of electricity known as *Ohm's Law*, which shows the connection between the current, resistance, and electro-motive force.

Ohnet (*ō-nā'*), GEORGES (1848–1918), Fr. novelist; *b.* Paris; wrote popular romances of social life under title of *Les Batailles de la Vie*; these include *Serge Panine* (1881), *Le Maître de Forges* (1882), and *Volonte* (1889).

O'kuma, SHIGENOBU, MARQUESS (1838–1922), Jap. statesman; in struggle against anc. régime, 1868, advocated abolition of prevailing feudal system, and establishment of constitutional government; minister of finance, 1869–81; foreign minister, 1888–9; opened Japan to world trade; minister of agriculture and commerce, 1896–97; premier, 1898 and 1914; founded Waseta Univ. at Tokio and Jap. Women's Univ.; pub. *Fifty Years of New Japan* (1910).

Oliphant (*ol'i-fant*), LAURENCE (1829–88), Brit. author; *b.* Cape Town; wrote books of travel, including *A Journey to Khatmandu*, *The Russian Shores of the Black Sea*, and *Minnesota and the Far West*; later years devoted to occultism, dealt with in *Sympneumata*, *Scientific Religion*, and *Masollam.*

Oliphant, MRS. MARGARET OLIPHANT (1828–97), Brit. novelist and biographer; *b.* in Midlothian; daughter of Francis Wilson; a prolific writer of novels and critical sketches; most successful in depicting scenes from simple Scot. life; established reputation by *The Chronicles of Carlingford* (1862–6), and *Francis of Assisi* (1871).

Olivares (*ō-lē-vä'reth*), GASPERO DE GUZMAN, COUNT OF (1587–1645), Span. statesman; *b.* Rome; ruled Spain as chief favourite of Philip IV., 1621–43, and was made scapegoat of disasters abroad; heavy cost of wars into which he plunged Spain caused his downfall; driven from office, 1643.

Ollivier (*ō-lē-vyā'*), OLIVIER EMILE (1825–1915), Fr. statesman; *b.* Marseilles; opposed Napoleon III.'s despotism; chief instrument in obtaining constitution of 1869; held responsible for Franco-Prussian War, which overthrew his ministry.

O'man, SIR CHARLES WILLIAM CHADWICK (1860–), Eng. historian; *b.* in India; Chichele prof. of modern history, Oxford, 1905; fellow of Brit. Academy, 1905; president, Royal Historical Soc., 1917–21; M.P. Oxford Univ., 1919–35; numerous historical publications include *History of the Art of War in the Middle Ages* (1898), *History of the Peninsular War* (1902–22), *A History of England before the Norman Conquest* (1910), and *Napoleonic Studies* (1929).

Omar Khayyám (*ō'mär kī-yäm'*) (*c.* 1050–*c.* 1123), astronomer-poet of Persia; *b.* Nishapur; co-operated in reconstruction of the Pers. calendar; best known by collection of quatrains or *Rubáiyát*, comprising reflections on life and death, wine and love, and earthly delights, all coloured by a certain fatalistic pessimism (trans. by Edward Fitzgerald, 1859).

O'Neill, EUGENE GLADSTONE (1888–), Amer. dramatist; *b.* New York; educated Princeton and Harvard Univs.; tried various occupations; was a sailor for two years; started writing plays, 1919, and soon became the foremost Amer. dramatist. Plays include *Beyond the Horizon* (1919), *Emperor Jones* (1921), *The Hairy Ape* (1922), *All God's Chillun's Got Wings* (1924), *Desire under the Elm* (1924), *Lazarus Laughed* (1927), and *Mourning becomes Electra* (1931).

Opie (*ō'pi*), JOHN (1761–1807), Eng. painter; *b.* in Cornwall; went to London, 1780, where his talent was immediately recognized; his *Assassination of Rizzio*, *Mary Wollstonecraft Godwin*, *William Godwin*, and *William Siddons* are well-known examples of his work.

Orcagna (*or-kän'yä*), or ARCANUOLO ('archangel'), designations of ANDREA DI CIONE (*c.* 1316–*c.* 68), Italian painter, sculptor, and architect, of Florence; painted frescoes of Santa Maria Novella; architect of exquisite marble tabernacle of Or San Michele, Florence.

Or'chardson, SIR WILLIAM QUILLER (1835–1910), Brit. genre and portrait painter; *b.* Edinburgh; settled in London, 1863; R.A., 1877; pictures include *Napoleon on the Bellerophon, Her First Dance, Her Mother's Voice*; among portraits are *Master Baby* and *Mrs. Orchardson.*

Orczy, THE BARONESS (MRS. MONTAGU BARSTOW), Eng. novelist; *b.* in Hungary; studied painting and exhibited at the Royal Academy; won recognition with a series of detective stories known as *The Old Man in the Corner* (1905); *The Scarlet Pimpernel* (1905) had a great success. Other novels include *I Will Repay, Beau Brocade,* and *The Elusive Pimpernel.*

O'Rell, MAX. See under MAX O'RELL.

Orford, EARL OF. See WALPOLE.

Origen (*or'i-jen*) (185–254), Christian theologian, and most voluminous writer of early Christian Church; *b.* Alexandria; head of catechetical school at Alexandria, 203; diligent student of philosophy and Scripture; lived mostly in Alexandria till 231, though he journeyed in Syria and elsewhere; was ordained priest, 230, but deprived of his order; remainder of his life was spent mostly in Palestine. Of his very numerous writings, few have survived; *Hexapla,* or editions of Gr. versions of O.T., is preserved in part, and much of his commentaries on the Scriptures and some apologetic and dogmatic writings.

Orlan'do, VITTORIO EMANUELE (1860–), Ital. statesman and jurist; *b.* in Sicily; prof. of constitutional law at Palermo; minister of the interior, 1916, prime minister, 1917, and stiffened national resistance at time of disastrous defeat at Caporetto. At Peace Conference in Paris, 1919, was one of the 'Big Four'; his inability to settle Fiume question brought about fall of his ministry; ambassador to Brazil, 1920; re-elected deputy, 1924; on success of Fascists retired, 1925.

Or'pen, SIR WILLIAM (1878–1931), Brit. painter; *b.* in co. Dublin; one of artists selected by government to paint pictures of Great War; exhibition of these, 1918; among them are *Changing Billets* and *Bombing at Night*; *Signing of Peace* exhibited in Academy of 1920; other pictures include *The Fracture, A Bloomsbury Family, The Dead Ptarmigan,* and *Young Ireland.* R.A., 1919.

Orsay, COUNT D'. See D'ORSAY.

Orsini (*or-sē'nē*), FELICE, COUNT DI (1819–58), Ital. patriot; fought in war of independence, 1848; laboured with Mazzini till 1854; pub. *Austrian Dungeons in Italy* (1857); executed in Paris for attempted assassination of Napoleon III.; left *Memoirs.*

Osbourne (*oz'bŭrn*), LLOYD (1868–), U.S.A. novelist; *b.* San Francisco; stepson of Robert Louis Stevenson; resided at Samoa with Stevenson, 1887–96, collaborating with him in *The Wrong Box* (1889), *The Wrecker* (1892), *The Ebb Tide* (1894); his own works include *Love, the Fiddler* (1903), *The Kingdoms of the World* (1911), and *Peril* (1929).

Os'car II. (1829–1907), King of Sweden and Norway, 1872–1905, of Sweden, 1905–7; *b.* Stockholm; arbitrator in international affairs; gifted writer; the separation of Norway and Sweden took place in his reign.

O'Shaughnessy (*ō-shaw'nĕ-sĭ*), ARTHUR WILLIAM EDGAR (1844–

81), Eng. poet; *b.* London; sonneteer and lyrist; wrote *Epic of Women* (1870), *Music and Moonlight* (1874), *Songs of a Worker* (posthumous, 1881).

Osler, SIR WILLIAM (1849–1919), Brit. physician; *b.* in Canada; prof. of medicine in U.S.A., 1884–1904, and at Oxford from 1905; baronetcy, 1911. His publications include *Principles and Practice of Medicine*, *System of Medicine*; wrote also *Æquanimitas and Other Addresses* (1904), and *A Way of Life* (1914).

Osman' Dig'na (1836–1900), leader of Sudan tribesmen; slave-dealer at Suakin; appointed governor of E. Sudan by the Mahdi, and defeated troops sent against him, 1883–4; was defeated at El Teb by Anglo-Egyptian troops, 1884, and at Amideb by Abyssinians, 1887; carried on guerrilla war; took part in battle of Omdurman, 1898; killed at Tokar.

Ostade (*os'tä-dĕ*), name of two Dutch painters, brothers, *b.* Haarlem. (1) ADRIAN (1610–85), pupil of Franz Hals, and later influenced by Rembrandt; excelled in depicting rural life: *Rustics in a Tavern*, *The Village School*, etc. (2) ISAAC (1621–49), painted somewhat similar subjects, but chiefly out-of-door scenes—frozen canals, roadside inns, etc.

Ostwald (*ost'valt*), WILHELM (1853–1932), Ger. chemist; *b.* Riga; prof. of chemistry, Riga, 1881–7, and in Leipzig, 1887–96; pioneer in physical chemistry; discovered method of obtaining nitrogen from the air, 1900. Nobel Prize, 1909.

Os'wald, SAINT (*c.* 605–42), King of Northumbria after victory over Cædwalla, 635; embraced Christianity at Iona; settled St. Aidan at Holy I.; slain in battle against Penda, King of Mercia.

Ot'to I., or OTTO THE GREAT (912–73), Holy Rom. Emperor, son of Henry the Fowler; elected King of Germany, 936; checked Magyar invasion at battle of Lechfeld, 955; led two expeditions into Italy against Berengar, 951 and 961; crowned Emperor, 962, by Pope John XII.; succeeded in reviving empire of Charlemagne on a more stable basis.

Otto II. (955–83), Holy Rom. Emperor; succeeded his father, Otto I., 973; warred successfully against Bavaria, Denmark, and Bohemia, and checked Fr. attempts on Lorraine; made himself master of Apulia and Calabria, but was defeated by Saracens, 982.

Otto III. (980–1002), Holy Rom. Emperor, 983; son of Otto II.; crowned, 996; sought to revive Rom. greatness, but was frustrated by general revolt in Italy, 1001; a visionary, largely influenced by churchmen; Germany deteriorated during his reign.

Otto IV. (*c.* 1175–1218), Holy Rom. Emperor, son of Henry the Lion, Duke of Bavaria, and Matilda of England; elected Ger. king in opposition to Philip of Swabia, but was unable to make good his claim till Philip was murdered, 1208; crowned Emperor, 1209; excommunicated for annexation of Apulia, 1210; defeated by French at Bouvines, 1214.

Ot'way, THOMAS (1652–85), Eng. dramatist; *b.* in Sussex. His life was embittered by an unrequited passion for Mrs. Barry, the actress; wrote *The Poet's Complaint of his Muse*, the fine tragedy called *The Orphan*, and *Caius Marius*; greatest drama, *Venice Preserved* (1682).

Oudinot (*oo-dē-nō'*), CHARLES NICHOLAS (1767–1847), Duke of Reggio, 1810; Marshal of France, 1809; distinguished in revolutionary wars; led 'grenadiers of Oudinot' in chief campaigns till capitulation of Paris, 1814; submitted to Bourbons, and continued to hold high commands.

Ouida (*wē'da*), pseudonym of LOUISE DE LA RAMÉE (1839–1908), Eng. novelist; *b.* Bury St. Edmunds; lived chiefly in Florence; her novels, *Strathmore, Under Two Flags, Puck, Moths,* etc., had great popularity.

Ouless (*oo'les*), WALTER WILLIAM (1848–1934), Eng. portrait painter; *b.* St. Helier, Jersey; R.A., 1881; exhibited at Royal Academy from 1869; carried on the best traditions of Eng. portrait painting; among his works are portraits of Cardinal Newman and Darwin.

Outram (*oo'tram*), SIR JAMES (1803–63), Brit. soldier; *b.* in Derbyshire; served in first Afghan War, 1838; performed famous ride in disguise through Afghanistan, 1839; won title of 'Bayard of India' by defence of Hyderabad, 1843; distinguished in Indian Mutiny, 1857–8, being specially prominent at siege of Lucknow.

Ov'id (PUBLIUS OVIDIUS NASO) (43 B.C.–A.D. 17), Rom. poet; *b.* near Aquila; son of Rom. knight; abandoned law for poetry; for some obscure reason banished, A.D. 9, to Tomi, near mouth of Danube; spent remaining years of life there; wrote continually but vainly to friends and patrons to procure his return. In character Ovid was a genial pleasure-seeker; probably greatest master of the elegy; style smooth and pleasing. Works include the *Amores*, dealing with his relations with Corinna, who occupied his affections between his first and second marriage; *Ars Amatoria, Remedia Amoris, Medicamina formæ,* on the use of cosmetics, *Metamorphoses* (in hexameters), recounting mythical tales of transformations, *Fasti,* unfinished antiquarian calendar, *Tristia,* poems of exile, and *Epistulæ ex Ponto.*

Owen (*ō'en*), SIR RICHARD (1804–92), Eng. zoologist; *b.* Lancaster; conservator of Royal Coll. of Surgeons, and, till 1884, superintendent of the Natural History Department of Brit. Museum; a comparative anatomist of great skill; his papers, dealing with the description and classification of animals, cover a wide field; also pub. general memoirs on comparative anatomy of vertebrates.

Owen, ROBERT (1771–1858), Eng. Socialist reformer; *b.* Newtown, Montgomeryshire; served as draper's apprentice; at age of nineteen became manager, and at twenty-three partner, of cotton mill in Manchester, which he conducted with great success. His firm took over cotton mills in New Lanark, and Owen married daughter of David Dale, the former owner, 1799, and started to reform conditions of work of the hands; established schools, founded co-operative societies, and provided models for future factory management; roused strong feeling against existing conditions of labour; pub. *A New View of Society* (1813), in which he preached Socialism.

[*Life* (1925), by G. D. H. Cole.]

Oxenstjerna (*oks'en-shăr-nä*), AXEL, COUNT (1583–1654), Swed. statesman; imperial chancellor under Gustavus Adolphus, 1612; made peace with Poland, 1623; during Thirty Years' War joined Gustavus in Germany; after king's death at Lützen, 1632, was real head of Prot. cause; leader of Evangelical Union, 1633; gave Sweden new constitution, 1634; crippled Denmark in war of 1643–45; policy of later years thwarted by young Queen Christina, and Peace of Westphalia not as favourable to Sweden as he desired.

Oxford, ROBERT HARLEY, EARL OF (1661–1724), Brit. statesman; Speaker of House of Commons, 1701–5; chancellor and under-treasurer of Exchequer, 1710–11; created Baron Harley of Wigmore, Earl of Oxford, and Earl Mortimer,

1711 ; first lord of Treasury, 1711, and made Treaty of Utrecht ; impeached and imprisoned, 1715 ; acquitted, 1717, but never regained power ; highly praised by literary men, who had reason to be grateful for his liberal patronage. His character, though blackened by rivals, was without serious faults.

[*Life*, by Roscoe.]

Ox'ford and As'quith, HERBERT HENRY ASQUITH, 1ST EARL OF (1852–1928), Brit. statesman ; *b.* Morley, Yorks ; educated City of London School and Balliol, Oxford, where he became a fellow ; called to bar, 1876 ; entered House of Commons as Liberal member for E. Fife, 1886 ; home secretary in Gladstone government, 1892 ; returned to bar, 1895 ; during S. African War was vice-president of Liberal League which supported government policy ; strongest opponent of Chamberlain's tariff reform ; chancellor of Exchequer under Campbell-Bannerman, 1905–8 ; carried Old Age Pension Act, 1908 ; prime minister, 1908–16, during which he passed the Parliament Act, 1911. While attempting to give Home Rule to Ireland, the Great War broke out, 1914, and he was successful in uniting the whole nation in support of the war ; formed coalition ministry, 1915 ; alliance of Lloyd George and his followers with Unionist members of cabinet led to Asquith's resignation, 1916. In *débâcle* of Liberal party, Dec. 1918, lost seat for E. Fife. ; in 1920 returned for Paisley. Raised to peerage, 1925 ; will live in history as one of the great prime ministers. Author of several works. *Reflections* was pub. posthumously, 1928.

[*Life* (1932), by Spender and Asquith.]

Oyam'a, PRINCE IWAO (1842–1916), Jap. soldier-statesman, a Samurai of Satsuma ; attaché with Ger. army, Franco-Ger. War, 1870 ; helped to reorganize Jap. army, 1873 ; a commander during Satsuma rebellion, 1877 ; minister of war, 1880–95 ; led 2nd Army in Chino-Jap. War, 1894–5 ; field-marshal, 1898 ; chief of general staff, 1899 ; commander-in-chief in Manchuria, Russo-Jap. War, 1904–5 ; Brit. O.M., 1906 ; keeper of Privy Seal, 1914.

P

Pachmann (*pach'man*), VLADIMIR DE (1848–1933), Russ. pianist ; *b.* Odessa ; studied music at Vienna ; as an interpreter of Chopin earned a unique reputation.

Paderewski (*pad-er-ef'ske*), IGNACE JAN (1860–), Polish pianist and statesman ; *b.* in Podolia ; studied at Warsaw Conservatoire and Berlin ; first concert tour, 1878 ; taught music in Warsaw and in Strasbourg, 1878–84 ; in 1884 returned to concert platform, and made many tours in Germany, England, France, and U.S.A. ; became recognized as one of the greatest of pianists. During Great War was sent to America as plenipotentiary by the National Polish Committee ; gave numberless concerts, delivered many addresses, in effort to rouse sympathy for Polish cause. In Jan. 1919 he was made prime minister of the reconstituted Polish state ; one of Polish delegates to Peace Conference ; resigned premiership, Nov. 1919. Works include an opera, symphony, concerto, sonatas, and songs. G.B.E., 1925.

Paganini (*pä-gä-nē'nē*), NICOLO (1784–1840), Ital. violinist and composer; founder of modern school of violin-playing.

Page, THOMAS NELSON (1853–1922), U.S.A. author and diplomatist; *b.* Oakland, Virginia; excelled in depicting life in southern states; ambassador to Italy, 1913–18. Works include *In Old Virginia* (1887), *The Old South* (1892), *The Old Gentleman of the Black Stock* (1897), *The Old Dominion: her Making and her Manners* (1908), *Italy and the World War* (1920).

Page, WALTER HINES (1855–1918), U.S.A. diplomat and journalist; *b.* Cary, N. Carolina; became partner in publishing firm of Doubleday, Page, and Co.; ed. *The Forum*, New York, 1890–5; *Atlantic Monthly*, Boston, 1896–9; *World's Work*, New York, 1900–13; ambassador in London, 1913–18; endeavoured to promote Anglo-American unity. Author of *The Rebuilding of Old Commonwealths* and *The Southerner* (a novel).

[*Life and Letters of W. H. Page* (1922–5), by Hendrick.]

Paget (*päj'et*), SIR JAMES (1814–99), Brit. surgeon; *b.* Yarmouth; lecturer, St. Bartholomew's Hospital, and warden of its coll., 1843–51; prof., Coll. of Surgeons, 1847; F.R.S., 1851; baronet, 1871; pres., Royal Coll. of Surgeons, 1873; great surgeon, pathologist, and physiologist; discovered parasite *Trichina spiralis*. Author of *Lectures on Surgical Pathology*.

Pain, BARRY (1865–1928), Eng. journalist and humorous author; ed. of *To-day*, 1897; served in R.N.V.R., 1915–16; pub. *Playthings and Parodies* (1892), *The Gifted Family* (1909), *One Kind and Another* (1914), *The Problem Club* (1919), *This Charming Green Hat Fair* (1925), *Essays of To-day and Yesterday* (1926), etc.

Paine, THOMAS (1737–1809), Eng. author and agitator; *b.* Thetford, Norfolk; went to Philadelphia, 1774, where he pub. *Common Sense* (1776), advocating Amer. independence; returned to England, 1787, and pub. *The Rights of Man*, a reply to Burke's *Reflections on the French Revolution*; prosecuted for sedition and fled to France; secretary to Convention, 1793; on fall of Girondists was imprisoned for ten months, during which he completed *The Age of Reason*; died in America.

Painlevé (*pän-le-vā'*), PAUL (1863–1933), Fr. statesman and mathematician; *b.* Paris; prof. at Sorbonne; minister of instruction and inventions, 1915; prime minister and minister of war, Sept.–Dec. 1917; advisory director-general to Chin. Government railways, 1920; premier, minister of war, and minister of finance, 1925; air minister, 1930–1 and from 1932. Author of numerous mathematical works and *Life* of Nurse Cavell.

Palestrina (*pä-les-trē'nä*), GIOVANNI PIERLUIGI DA (1526–94), Ital. composer; *b.* Palestrina; director of sacred music at the Vatican, 1551, when he wrote an epoch-making set of Masses; music director at the Lateran, 1555, at S. Maria Maggiore, 1561. The prevalent Church music being condemned by Council of Trent, 1562, Palestrina was commissioned to reform it, and wrote his classic *Marcellus Mass*.

Pa'ley, WILLIAM (1743–1805), Eng. theologian; *b.* Peterborough; archdeacon of Carlisle, 1782; rector of Bishop Wearmouth, 1795; famed for his *Evidences of Christianity* (1794); wrote also *Horæ Paulinæ* (1790), *Natural Theology* (1802), etc.

[*Life*, by G. W. Meadley (1809).]

Palgrave, FRANCIS TURNER (1824–97), Eng. critic and poet;

b. Great Yarmouth; served in Education Office, Whitehall, till 1884; prof. of poetry at Oxford, 1885–95; a great friend of Tennyson; compiled his well-known anthology, *Golden Treasury of English Lyrics* (1861 and 1897). Author of many vols. of verse.

Palissy (*pä-lē-sē′*), BERNARD (1510–89), Fr. potter; settled at Saintes, near Rochefort, 1538; laboured sixteen years to discover secret of enamel manufacture; appointed 'inventor of rustic pottery' to the king; established workshop in Paris, 1564. He was an advanced thinker and lecturer on natural philosophy. Imprisoned in the Bastille as a Huguenot, and died there.

Palmer, EDWARD HENRY (1840–82), Brit. Orientalist; *b.* Cambridge; son of schoolmaster; engaged in survey of Sinai, 1869; prof. of Arabic at Cambridge, 1871–81; perished in expedition sent to win over tribes from Arabi Pasha; wrote *Oriental Mysticism* (1867), *Desert of the Exodus* (1871), *Dictionary of the Persian Language* (1876), *Arabic Grammar* (1874), etc.

Palm′erston, HENRY JOHN TEMPLE, VISCOUNT (1784–1865), Brit. statesman; *b.* Broadlands, Hants; succeeded father in peerage, 1802; secretary of war, 1809–28; adhered to Canning, and warmly supported policy of aiding revolution abroad; deserted Tory party. Minister of foreign affairs under Whig government of Earl Grey, 1830–41; made alliance with Louis Philippe, thus ending long enmity of England and France; actively assisted in establishing Belgian kingdom. Under Lord John Russell he again became foreign minister, 1846–51; dismissed by Queen Victoria, 1851, for unauthorized action with regard to France; home secretary in Aberdeen administration, 1852. When the Aberdeen government came to grief over the Crimean War, Palmerston formed an administration, 1855, which carried the country through the war, and remained premier till 1858, and again 1859–65. He was not an impressive personality, but was skilful and very popular.

[*Life,* by Dalling and Ashley (1870–76); *Life,* by Guedalla (1926).]

Pal′udan-Mül′ler, FREDERIK (1809–76), Dan. poet; *b.* in Fünen; greatest work, *Adam Homo,* an epic; also wrote idylls, prose romances, etc.

Panizzi (*pä-nēt′se*), SIR ANTHONY (1797–1879), Eng. librarian; *b.* Brescello, Modena; settled in England, 1823; prof. of Italian, Univ. Coll., London, 1828; keeper of printed books, Brit. Museum, 1837; principal librarian, 1856–66; responsible for principles of cataloguing, and designed the new library and reading-room.

Pank′hurst, MRS. EMMELINE (1858–1928), Brit. militant suffragist; *b.* Manchester; one of founders of Women's Social and Political Union, 1903; strong advocate of votes for women; several times imprisoned; able speaker and lecturer.

Paolo Veronese. See VERONESE, PAOLO.

Papin (*pä-pan′*), DENIS (1647–*c.* 1712), Fr. physicist; *b.* Blois; settled in London, 1707; invented safety valve and the Papin digester; discovered principle of siphon.

Papini (*pä-pē′nē*), GIOVANNI (1881–   ), Ital. essayist and critic; *b.* Florence. At first a sceptical and cynical essayist, his *Life of Christ* (1921) was an entirely sympathetic study, and aroused wide interest. Wrote *St. Augustine* (1929), etc.

Paracel′sus, or PHILIPPUS AUREOLUS THEOPHRASTUS BOMBASTUS VON HOHENHEIM (1493–1541),

Swiss physician and naturalist; *b.* Einsiedeln. After a period of wandering became town physician at Basle, 1526; lectured also in the univ., but was compelled to leave the city; again led wandering life until 1541, when he settled at Salzburg. He emphasized importance of direct observation of nature, discovered hydrogen, and introduced many chemical remedies.

Park, MUNGO (1771–1806), Scot. African explorer; *b.* Foulshiels, Selkirkshire; became a surgeon; sent by African Association to explore valley of Niger, 1795; returning, settled as doctor at Peebles, 1801; undertook second W. African expedition, 1805; drowned at Boussa; author of famous *Travels* (1799); *Journal of a Mission to the Interior* (pub. 1815).

[*Mungo Park and the Niger*, by J. Thomson (1890).]

Parker, SIR GILBERT (1862–1932), Eng. author and politician; *b.* Camden East, Ontario; travelled widely in South Sea Islands and Near and Far East; joint ed., *The Sydney Morning Herald*, 1886; M.P., Gravesend, 1900–18; knighted, 1902; baronet, 1915; P.C., 1916; distinguished for tales of Can. life; novels include *Pierre and his People* (1892), *When Valmond came to Pontiac* (1895), *The Seats of the Mighty* (1896), *The Battle of the Strong* (1898), etc.

Parker, SIR HYDE (1739–1807), Eng. admiral; served during Amer. and Fr. wars; commanded Baltic fleet, 1801, and vainly gave Nelson signal to withdraw at Copenhagen.

Parker, JOSEPH (1830–1902), Eng. Congregational minister and author; *b.* Hexham; son of stonemason; best known as pastor of the City Temple, London, which was built through his efforts, 1874; great preacher and philanthropist. Pub. *The People's Bible* (1885), etc.

Park'man, FRANCIS (1823–93), foremost Amer. historian; *b.* Boston; a standard authority on Ind. tribe life and on the struggle between Britain and France in N. America; trained as a lawyer, but devoted himself to exploration and historical research. His great work is *France and England in the New World* (pub. in 7 vols., 1865–92); also pub. *The Book of Roses*, still valuable.

Par'nell, CHARLES STEWART (1846–91), Irish politician; *b.* Avondale, co. Wicklow; educated Cambridge; M.P. for co. Meath, 1875–80; at once commenced policy of opposition to England; advocated Home Rule for Ireland; in 1877 developed Irish plan of parliamentary obstruction; president of National Land League, founded in 1879; M.P. for Cork, 1880–91; chairman of Nationalists in House of Commons, 1880; founded *The Irish National Newspaper and Publishing Company*, and reissued *The Flag of Ireland as United Ireland* (1881); imprisoned, 1881–82, at Kilmainham for speeches at League Convention in Dublin; acclaimed by his party as 'the uncrowned king of Ireland.' Chairman of Irish Parliamentary party, 1886, when Gladstone declared for Home Rule. In 1887 Parnell had to face charge of having been implicated in Phœnix Park murders; the evidence depended on a letter pub. in the *Times*, which was proved to be a forgery by Richard Pigott. In 1890 he was co-respondent in divorce suit by Captain O'Shea, and Gladstone insisted on his resignation from chairmanship of Irish Parliamentary party.

[*Lives*, by T. P. O'Connor (1891) and St. John Ervine (1925).]

Par'ry, SIR CHARLES HUBERT

HASTINGS (1848–1918), Eng. composer; *b.* Bournemouth; principal, Royal Coll. of Music, 1894; prof. of music, Oxford, 1899–1908; wrote *Prometheus Unbound, Lotos Eaters*, and numerous symphonies, suites, overtures, chamber music, oratorios, anthems, and songs; also *Style in Musical Art.*

Par'ry, SIR EDWARD ABBOTT (1863–), Eng. judge and author; called to the bar, 1885; judge in the county court at Manchester, 1894–1911, and at Lambeth, 1911–27; knighted, 1927; famous as author and dramatist; contributed to *Punch*; plays include *Katawampus* (1901), and *What the Butler Saw* (1905); ed. *Letters from Dorothy Osborne to Sir William Temple* (1887); wrote numerous children's books; other works include *What the Judge Saw* (1912), *The Law and the Poor* (1914), and *My Own Way* (1932).

Parry, SIR WILLIAM EDWARD (1790–1855), Eng. Arctic explorer; *b.* Bath; accompanied Ross's first expedition for discovery of N.W. Passage, 1818; commanded second expedition, 1819, and received government award of £5,000 for its scientific results; made three other Arctic expeditions; controller, steam department of navy, 1837–46; wrote *Narrative of an Attempt to reach the North Pole* (1828), etc.

Par'sons, ALFRED WILLIAM (1847–1920), Eng. painter, chiefly in water-colour; *b.* Beckington, Somerset; R.A., 1911; chief picture, *When Nature painted all Things Gay* (1887).

Parsons, HON. SIR CHARLES ALGERNON (1854–1931), Eng. engineer and inventor; *b.* London; son of third Earl of Rosse; educated at Cambridge; famous as inventor of compound steam turbine bearing his name, 1884; K.C.B., 1911; O.M., 1927; president of Brit. Association, 1919, 1920.

Part'ridge, SIR BERNARD (1861–), Eng. black-and-white artist; *b.* London; stained-glass designer and decorative painter, 1880–4; joined staff of *Punch*, 1891, and became its chief cartoonist; successful book illustrator.

Pas'cal, BLAISE (1623–62), Fr. mathematician and author; *b.* Clermont-Ferrand; at sixteen wrote treatise on conic sections; did noteworthy work in mathematics and physics. A delicate man, he retired to Port-Royal, 1655, and embraced doctrines of Jansenists; wrote in their defence against the Jesuits the famous *Lettres Provinciales* (1656–7), showing novelty and literary merit; fragments, collected as *Pensées*, another Fr. classic, give his views on Christian religion.

[*Life*, by R. H. Soltau (1927).]

Passfield, LORD. See WEBB, SIR SIDNEY.

Pasteur (*päs-ter'*), LOUIS (1822–95), Fr. chemist; *b.* Dôle, Jura; son of a tanner; prof. of physics at Dijon, 1848; prof. of physical chemistry at Strasbourg, 1852; dean of faculty of science at Lille, 1854; held various appointments in Paris from 1857 till 1888, when he became director of the Pasteur Institute; studied crystallography and laid foundations of stereochemistry; best known for his work on micro-organisms; showed that alcoholic and acetic fermentation and putrefaction are caused by living organisms, and that when these are killed or excluded decay is prevented; introduced sterilization. Made studies on wine and beer, and his researches into silkworm disease saved the Fr. silk industry. This led to investigation of the cause and means of prevention and cure of virulent diseases (*e.g.* hydrophobia), to the germ theory of disease, and the principles of preventive medicine.

[*Life*, by René Vallery-Radot (1900).]

Pa'ter, WALTER HORATIO (1839–1894), Eng. critic; *b.* London; educated at Oxford. A visit to Italy, 1865, led him to make a prolonged study of Ital. art and humanism, resulting in *Studies in the History of the Renaissance* (1873), which revealed him as a penetrating critic, with a beautiful though highly elaborated style. Other books of criticism and critical romance include *Marius the Epicurean* (1885), *Imaginary Portraits* (1887), *Appreciations* (1889), *Plato and Platonism* (1893), *The Child in the House* (1894), *Greek Studies* (1895).

[*Life*, by A. C. Benson (1906).]

Pat'erson, WILLIAM (1658–1719), Scot. financier; *b.* in Dumfriesshire; founded the Bank of England, 1694; promoter of Darien colonization scheme, 1698; supported parl. union of England and Scotland, 1707.

Pat'more, COVENTRY KERSEY DIGHTON (1823–96), Eng. poet and critic; *b.* Woodford, Essex; a librarian at Brit. Museum, 1847. His poetry shows great depth and tenderness of thought, idealizing love, and giving fine pictures of Eng. scenery and of domestic life. The best of his poems is *The Angel in the House*. His chief prose works are a *Memoir of Bryan Waller Procter* (1877), *Principle in Art* (1889), and *Religio Poetæ* (1893).

[*Life*, by Gosse (1905).]

Pa'ton, SIR JOSEPH NOEL (1821–1902), Scot. painter of historical and Shakespearian and, later, allegorical and religious subjects; *b.* Dunfermline; R.S.A., 1850; Queen's limner for Scotland, 1866; knighted, 1867. Paintings include *Quarrel and Reconciliation of Oberon and Titania*, *The Pursuit of Pleasure*, *Lux in Tenebris*.

Pat'rick, ST. (*c.* A.D. 389–461), patron saint of Ireland; subject of many legends; birthplace unknown; carried to Ireland by pirates about 405; escaped after six years, and fled to Gaul. He formed the idea of evangelizing Ireland. In 432 he was consecrated and went to Ireland; preached vigorously. To him the real conversion of Ireland is due.

[*Life*, by Bury.]

Patti, ADELINA (BARONESS CEDERSTRÖM) (1843–1919), famous soprano singer; *b.* Madrid, of Italian parents; appeared in New York, 1859, and London, 1861; equally successful in concert and opera; last public appearance, 1914.

Pat'tison, MARK (1813–84), Eng. scholar and author; *b.* Hornby; at Oxford came for a time under influence of Newman, and pub. trans. of Aquinas on *St. Matthew* (1842), and two lives of Eng. saints—*Stephen Langton* and *St. Edmund*—in the series ed. by Newman; college tutor, 1843; rector of Lincoln Coll., 1861. His writings include *The Present State of Theology in Germany* (1857), *Learning in the Church of England* (1863), *Isaac Casaubon* (1875), *Milton* (1879), etc.

Paul, THE APOSTLE, greatest figure in history of Christianity after Christ Himself; *b.* Tarsus, date unknown; a Jew and a free-born Rom. citizen; he received name of Saul and also Rom. name Paul; learned trade of tentmaker; studied under Gamaliel at Jerusalem; was the agent of Sanhedrin to exterminate Christian Church at Damascus, but on way thither had vision of Jesus which changed his career, and he became Christianity's strongest supporter. The next three years were spent in Arabia; returned to Damascus, from which he had to flee owing to opposition of Jews; went to Jerusalem and preached the gospel, supported by Barnabas. The next seven years were apparently spent in Syria and Cilicia. He was invited by Barnabas to help the Christian revival which had taken place at Antioch; was sent to Jerusalem with help to the Church there, which was suffering from famine of A.D. 44; was commissioned by the Church as apostle to Gentiles, along with Barnabas, and as a consequence made his three great missionary journeys described in Acts.

Returning to Jersalem, Paul was attacked as an opponent of tradition; obtained protection of Rom. guards; transferred for safety to Cæsarea; left in prison for two years; brought before Festus, he appealed to Rome; reached that city a prisoner, after adventurous journey by sea and land; remained at Rome, a prisoner in his own hired house, for two years. The narrative given in Acts ends here, but from other sources it is probable that he was tried and acquitted, travelled to Colossæ, Crete, Nicopolis, etc.; a second imprisonment took place, followed by trial, condemnation, and death, A.D. 64.

Paul was author of thirteen epistles contained in the N.T.; these letters or epistles emphasize the glory of God and the exaltation of Jesus Christ, His Son, the Saviour.

[*Life and Epistles of St. Paul*, by Conybeare and Howson; *St. Paul the Traveller and the Roman Citizen*, by W. M. Ramsay.]

Paul III., POPE. See FARNESE.

Pausa'nias (*d. c.* 470 B.C.), Spartan regent, 479; joint commander of Greeks with Aristides at battle of Platæa, 479; admiral, 478, against Persia; relieved Cyprus and recovered Byzantium.

Pausanias (*fl.* 2nd cent. A.D.), Gr. writer and geographer; probably a native of Lydia; visited Syria, Palestine, Egypt, Byzantium, Epirus, Italy, and greater part of Greece. Wrote *Description of Greece*.

Pav'lova, ANNA (1885–1931), Russ. dancer; *b.* St. Petersburg; first appeared on stage at Imperial Opera House, St. Petersburg; came to London, 1909, appeared at Palace Theatre, and made an instantaneous success; remained in London for some years, and subsequently toured U.S.A., etc.; recognized as finest and most original dancer of the day.

Pax'ton, SIR JOSEPH (1801–65), Eng. architect and gardener; *b.* in Bedfordshire, of poor parents; manager of Duke of Devonshire's estates in Derbyshire, 1836; designed building for Great Exhibition, 1851; knighted, 1851; also designed and had charge of erection of the Crystal Palace, 1853–4; wrote on horticulture.

Payn (*pān*), JAMES (1830–98), Eng. novelist; *b.* Cheltenham; ed. of *Chambers's Journal*, 1858–73; of the *Cornhill Magazine*, 1883–96; wrote more than a hundred novels, of which the best is *Lost Sir Massingberd* (1864).

Pea'body, GEORGE (1795–1869), Amer. philanthropist; *b.* South Danvers (now Peabody), Mass.; amassed a fortune in dry goods store; settled in London, 1837, as banker and merchant. In his lifetime gave £500,000 to London for better housing of working men, and about £2,000,000 for educational purposes in U.S.A.

Pea'cock, THOMAS LOVE (1785–1866), Eng. writer; *b.* Weymouth; friend of Shelley; abandoned business for letters; eventually obtained government post. Poems include *Palmyra*, *Philosophy of Melancholy*, and *Rhododaphne*; best novels are *Melincourt*, *Nightmare Abbey*, *Maid Marian*. His novels contain much amiable and diverting satire.

Peake, ARTHUR SAMUEL (1865–1929), Eng. theologian; *b.* Leek; prof. of Biblical exegesis, Victoria Univ., Manchester, 1904; among numerous works most notable is his *Commentary on the Bible* (1919).

Pears (*pērz*), CHARLES (1873–), Eng. artist; specialist in painting sea scenes; illustrated many books—*e.g.* Dana's *Two Years before the Mast*, Masefield's *Salt-water Ballads*, and Dickens's works; official naval artist for the Great War.

Pearse, MARK GUY (1842–1930), Eng. Wesleyan minister; *b.* Camborne; held numerous pastorates, including West London Mission, 1914; best known books are *Daniel Quorm and his Religious Notions* (1st and 2nd series; 1875–9), *Cornish Stories* (1883), and *West Country Songs* (1902).

Pearse, PATRICK H. (1879–1916), Irish rebel and author; *b.* Dublin; founded St. Enda's Coll., a secondary school for boys, where Irish nationalism was fostered; founded the New Ireland Soc., 1897; commandant-general of army of Irish Republic during rebellion, 1916; tried by court-martial, and executed. *Collected Works*, pub. in two vols. (1917 and 1918), are chiefly plays and poems.

Pear'son, SIR ARTHUR (1866–1921), Eng. publisher and philanthropist; founder and chairman of C. Arthur Pearson, Ltd.; proprietor of various newspapers until he became blind; president National Institute for the Blind; baronet, 1916; founded St. Dunstan's, for blinded soldiers.

Pearson, KARL (1857–), Eng. scientist; *b.* London; educated Cambridge; Galton prof. of eugenics and director of the Laboratory for National Eugenics, London Univ., 1911; publications include *The Ethic of Free Thought* (1887 and 1901), *National Life from the Standpoint of Science* (1901), *The Life and Letters of Francis Galton* (1915).

Peary (*pē'ri*), ROBERT EDWIN (1856–1920), U.S.A. Arctic explorer; *b.* Cresson, Pennsylvania; entered U.S.A. navy, 1881; spent some years as assistant engineer on Nicaragua Ship Canal; led several Arctic expeditions; in the last of these he reached the N. Pole, 1909, the first man to do so. By some writers doubt has been thrown on the accuracy of his observations. Wrote narratives of his travels.

Peel, ARTHUR WELLESLEY, VISCOUNT (1829–1912), Brit. Liberal statesman; youngest son of Sir Robert Peel; one of the most noted Speakers of House of Commons, 1884–95; viscount, 1895; chairman of Commission on Licensing Laws, 1896–9.

Peel, SIR ROBERT (1788–1850), Brit. statesman; *b.* near Bury; son of wealthy Lancs. cotton manufacturer; educated Harrow and Oxford. Tory member for Cashel, 1809; under-secretary for colonies, 1811; secretary for Ireland, 1812–18; home secretary, 1822; again home secretary in Wellington's Tory ministry, 1827; passed Catholic Emancipation Bill, 1829, owing to agitation in country, but steadily resisted outcry for parl. reform; Tories were forced to resign, 1830. Peel had reorganized the London police (hence slang terms, *peeler*, *bobby*); led opposition in ministries of Grey, 1832–4, and Melbourne, 1834. He became prime minister, 1834; forced to resign, 1835. The restored Whigs continued sweeping reforms, but lost favour through distress of country, misfortunes abroad, and fear of Irish secession. Conservatives returned, 1841, with Peel as prime minister. He restored order in finances, imposing income tax. Departing from Tory tradition, he was responsible for the repeal of the Corn Laws, 1846, the year he resigned; killed by fall from horse.

[*Peel, from his Private Papers*, ed. by Parker (1899).]

Peele, GEORGE (*c.* 1558–*c.* 97), Eng. dramatist; *b.* London; composer of masques and pageants;

wrote *Arraignment of Paris*, *Old Wives' Tale*, etc.

Peisistratus, or PISISTRATUS (*pi-sis'trat-us*) (*c.* 600–527 B.C.), Tyrant of Athens; cousin of Solon; of great wealth and influence. Seized the Acropolis, 560, but was expelled by Lycurgus and Megacles, but later restored, 555 or 554; again expelled, 552; returned, 541, with an army and ruled till 527; ruled as a benevolent despot, building public works and protecting democrats against aristocrats.

Pemberton, SIR MAX (1863–), Eng. author; *b.* Birmingham; educated, Cambridge; ed. *Chums*, 1892–3, and *Cassell's Magazine*, 1896–1906; has written many historical adventure novels, including *The Iron Pirate* (1893), *Kronstadt* (1898), *The Hundred Days* (1905), *War and the Woman* (1912); has also written plays.

Penn, WILLIAM (1644–1718), English colonizer; *b.* London; founder of Pennsylvania; became a Quaker, 1667; imprisoned, 1668–9, for publishing *Sandy Foundations Shaken*, and again in 1670–1; obtained grant of land in America, 1681, and sailed in 1682; became governor as well as proprietor of this new province, called Pennsylvania, after his father; made it a haven for persecuted Quakers; he proclaimed religious toleration, founded Philadelphia, and promulgated 'Great Law,' 1682, making drunkenness, swearing, etc., punishable offences; remarkable for his equitable treatment of neighbouring Ind. tribes; deprived of governorship for suspected Jacobitism, 1692, but restored 1694; imprisoned for debt, 1707, and mortgaged the colony; he was an incalculable moral force; wrote numerous pamphlets—*e.g.* *The Great Cause of Liberty of Conscience*; *No Cross, No Crown*, etc.

Pen'nell, JOSEPH (1860–1926), Amer. etcher, illustrator, and author; *b.* Philadelphia; produced a series of etchings of old Philadelphia, etc.; author—sometimes jointly with his wife (Elizabeth Robins)—and illustrator of *A Canterbury Pilgrimage*, *Life of Whistler* (1907), *Pictures of the Panama Canal* (1912), *The Wonder of Work* (1916), etc.

Pep'in (Fr. *pā-pan'*), or PIPPIN, name of several Carolingian rulers, the most prominent being PEPIN II. (*d.* 714), mayor of the palace; defeated Neustrians at Testri, and became virtual ruler of the Franks; encouraged Christianity. Was the father of Charles Martel. PEPIN III., THE SHORT (714–68), King of the Franks, younger son of Charles Martel; deposed Childeric; was crowned, 751; crossed Alps and forced Lombards to give up Ravenna and other cities to the Church, known as 'donation of Pepin,' the foundation of temporal power of the Papacy; was the father of Charlemagne.

Pepys (*pēps*), SAMUEL (1633–1703), Eng. diarist; *b.* London; educated at Huntingdon and Cambridge; clerk of the Acts of the Navy, 1660; F.R.S., 1665; secretary to the Admiralty, 1673; imprisoned in Tower, 1679, on charge of selling information to French; acquitted, but lost his post; reappointed, 1684, and held office till 1689. His *Diary*, begun in 1659, was in cipher. He wrote freely of his thoughts, his vices, his domestic affairs; he noted down all the scandal he heard. It is invaluable as a source of information concerning 17th cent. manners. It ends in 1669. It was deciphered by John Smith, rector of Baldock, Herts, and pub. 1825.

[*Memoirs of Pepys*, by Lord Braybrooke (1825); *Life, Journals, and Correspondence of Pepys*, by J. Smith (1840); *Samuel Pepys*, by Ponsonby (1928).]

Per′cy, name of famous Eng. family; most notable member was Sir Henry Percy (1364–1403), called Hotspur, eldest son of 1st Earl of Northumberland; famous in border warfare, particularly at battle of Otterburn, 1388; killed at battle of Shrewsbury.

Percy, Thomas (1729–1811), Eng. divine and collector; *b.* Bridgnorth; son of grocer; dean of Carlisle, 1778; Bishop of Dromore, Ireland, 1782; his invaluable *Reliques of Ancient English Poetry* (1765) had great influence on Sir Walter Scott.

Pereda (*pā-rā′thä*), José Maria de (1833–1906), Span. novelist, of realistic school; *b.* near Santander; excelled in descriptions of fisher life—*e.g.* *Sotileza* and *La Puchera.*

Pérez Galdos (*pā′rāth*), Benito (1845–1920), Span. novelist; in addition to stories of contemporary life, specialized in realistic historical fiction; monumental work is *Episiodios nacionales* in 46 vols.

Pergolesi (*per-gō-lā′sē*), or Pergolese, Giovanni Battista (1710–36), Ital. composer; *b.* near Ancona; of striking originality and charm; wrote operetta *La Serva Padrona*, cantata *Orfeo e Euridice*, and celebrated *Stabat Mater.*

Pericles (*per′i-klēz*) (*c.* 500–429 B.C.), Athenian statesman of 'Golden Age'; attended lectures of Anaxagoras, Damon, and Zeno, and acquired powers of oratory and cultivated well-balanced mind. On death of Aristides, *c.* 468, Pericles assumed leadership of democrats against oligarchic party under Cimon; supreme after banishment of Cimon, 461. He and Ephialtes took judicial power from Areopagus and council of 500 and gave it to *dicastai*, chosen from citizens, who received small payment. The 'age of Pericles' was the time of the supremacy of Athens in religion, art, and literature. He encouraged the work of Thucydides the historian, Phidias the sculptor, and the dramatists Sophocles and Euripedes. By 445, however, Athens was forced to abandon to Sparta the hegemony over Greece. One of the world's greatest and noblest statesmen.

[*Pericles*, by E. Abbot (1891).]

Per′kin, Sir William Henry (1838–1907), Eng. chemist; *b.* London; pupil of Hofmann; when eighteen prepared aniline black and mauve, 1856, by oxidizing aniline, laying foundation of coal-tar colour industry; also discovered a process of manufacturing alizarin, and coumarin, the first artificial perfume from coal-tar, and artificial indigo.

Pero′si, Lorenzo (1872–), Ital. priest and musical composer; became director of Sistine chapel choir, the Vatican, Rome, 1898; most famous works, *Resurrection of Lazarus* and *Passion of Christ*; also numerous masses, psalms, and motets.

Perowne (*pe-roun′*), John James Stewart (1823–1904), Eng. theologian and Heb. scholar; *b.* Burdwan, Bengal; Bishop of Worcester, 1890–1901; member of O.T. Revision Committee; ed. *Cambridge Bible for Schools.*

Perrault (*pā-rō′*), Charles (1628–1703), Fr. author; *b.* Paris; secretary and protégé of Colbert; his poem *Siècle de Louis le Grand* gave rise to famous dispute of the Ancients and the Moderns; best known for his fairy tales, *Contes des Fées*, including *Tom Thumb, Puss in Boots, Blue Beard, Little Red Riding Hood, Cinderella, The Sleeping Beauty.* A writer of exquisite prose—simple, sententious, witty.

Pershing, John Joseph (1860–), Amer. soldier; *b.* in Missouri; educated at U.S.A. Military Academy; served in campaigns against the Indians, and Span.-Amer. War, 1898; military attaché at Tokyo, 1905–6; military governor of Moro province, Philippines, 1909–13; commanded American troops in Mexico, 1916–17; in command of U.S.A. expeditionary force in France, 1917, and carried out offensive, 1918; chief of staff, 1921–4. Author of *My Experiences in the World War* (1931).

Perugino (*pā-ru-jē'nō*), properly PIETRO VANNUCCI (1446–1524), Ital. painter; *b.* in Umbria; head of Umbrian school, master of Raphael; lived in Florence, Rome, Venice, Cremona, and Perugia (his adopted city); great work, the beautiful frescoes adorning the Hall of Cambio, Perugia; assisted in decoration of Vatican, and painted *Christ giving the Keys to Peter*, Sistine Chapel, Rome; died of plague; National Gallery, London, has his *Virgin and Child, Michael*, and *Raphael*.

Pestalozzi (*pes-tä-lot'sē*), JOHANN HEINRICH (1746–1827), Swiss educational reformer; *b.* Zurich; dwelt with waifs at his farm, Neuhof, but failed owing to lack of business ability; opened school at Yverdon, 1805–25; wrote novels on educational themes: *Leonard and Gertrude* (1781), *How Gertrude teaches her Children* (1801); had great influence on educational methods. He applied psychology to teaching, and added manual to mental training.

Pétain (*pā-tän'*), HENRI PHILIPPE (1856–), Fr. soldier; *b.* Cauchy-la-Tour, Pas-de-Calais. Command 4th Brigade in the Charleroi retreat, Aug. 1914, and in Artois with great success; commanded 2nd Army, distinguished himself in Champagne offensive, 1915, and became commander of the centre group of armies. In 1916 he was given command at Verdun, and his defence of that place is one of the epics of the war. In 1917 he became commander-in-chief of the Fr. armies of the North and North-East. He was made a Marshal of France in Nov. 1918, on the day he led Fr. troops into Metz.

Peter, one of disciples of Jesus; original name Simon; name Peter, 'a rock,' given to him by Jesus; a fisherman on Lake of Galilee; called by Jesus, along with his brother Andrew, to be His disciple, and later took up work of an apostle; with John and James had intimate relation with Jesus; full of loyalty, devotion, and impetuosity of heart; affirmed his adherence to Jesus, yet at critical moment denied Him, but afterwards bitterly repented; took a leading place in Christian community after Pentecost; worked with Paul, with whom he differed regarding circumcision. According to tradition, spent his last years in Rome, and was martyred there about A.D. 64; author of first epistle of Peter.

Peter I., THE GREAT (1672–1725), Emperor of Russia; *b.* Moscow; succeeded, 1682; sole ruler on death of brother Ivan, 1696; attacked Turkey, captured Azov, 1696, and obtained port on Black Sea; travelled in Europe for two years, learning shipbuilding in Holland and England in order to found a Russ. navy; recalled by revolt of Streltzi or 'soldiery,' which he ruthlessly suppressed, 1698; defeated by Charles XII. of Sweden at Narva, 1700; founded new capital, Petersburg (Leningrad), 1703; defeated Swedes at Poltava, and seized Baltic provinces and part of Finland, 1709, thus acquiring wide seaboard; married his mistress, afterwards Catherine I.; wrested Caspian provinces from Persia, 1722. His reign was marred by acts of great cruelty, as exemplified by his execution of his son, but Russia made enormous advances.

[*Life*, by Schuyler.]

Peter I., KARAGEORGEVITCH (1844–1921), first King of the Serbs, Croats, and Slovenes; succeeded to throne of Serbia after assassination of Alexander I., 1903; fought for French in Franco-Prussian War, 1870; compelled to retreat from Serbia with his troops, Nov. 1915, and established government at Corfu. Restored to Serbia in Oct. 1918, he was in same year proclaimed king of newly formed state of Serbs, Croats, and Slovenes (Jugoslavia).

Peters (*pā'terz*), KARL (1856–1918), Ger. explorer; *b.* Neuhaus, on R. Elbe; founded the Ger. Colonization Soc., 1884; director, Ger. E. Africa Co., 1885, but dismissed on charges of cruelty to natives, 1896; led expedition for relief of Emin Pasha, 1888–90; commissioner for settling Anglo-Ger. frontier in E. Africa, 1892; explored country of the Zambezi, 1899 and 1905; pub. *The El Dorado of the Ancients* (1902), etc.

Peter the Hermit (*c.* 1050–1115), priest; *b.* Amiens; preacher of First Crusade, which he helped to lead in 1096; his army was destroyed by Turks; founded Augustinian monastery at Huy.

Petrarch (*pē'trark*), or PETRARCA, FRANCESCO (1304–74), Ital. poet and scholar; *b.* Arezzo; one of the greatest lyric poets of all time. His life was somewhat stormy, due to varied vicissitudes of Ital. political life. Destined for the law, he studied at Montpellier and Bologna, but devoted himself to classical and especially Rom. letters; in 1326 entered priesthood; travelled extensively and made valuable discoveries of manuscripts; crowned poet laureate at Rome, 1341. From 1343 he lived in Avignon and various cities of Upper Italy, searching for manuscripts.

Petrarch initiated the revival of learning in Italy. His chief works are the epic poem *Africa*, the prose historical biographies known as *De Viris Illustribus*, the prose dialogues *De Contemptu Mundi* or *Secretum*, and his famous collection of letters. His fame as a lyric poet rests on the *Canzoniere*, sonnets to the mysterious Laura (whom he met at Avignon, and whose death he laments in his *In Morte di Madonna Laura*), the lyrical story of one of the great loves of the world's literature.

[*Francesco Petrarca, Poet and Humanist* (1909), by Jerrold; *Renaissance in Italy* (vols. ii. and iv.), by Symonds.]

Petrie (*pē'trē*), SIR WILLIAM MATTHEW FLINDERS (1853–), Eng. Egyptologist; *b.* Charlton, Kent; during excavations in Egypt, 1880–1924, discovered Gr. settlements at Naukratis and Daphnæ, inscription of Israelite war at Thebes, treasure of Lahun, etc.; founded Brit. school of archæology in Egypt, 1905; prof. of Egyptology, Univ. Coll., London, 1892–1933; pub. *History of Egypt* (1894–1905), *Egypt and Israel* (1910), *Amulets* (1914), *Scarabs* (1917), *Religious Life in Ancient Egypt* (1924), etc.

Pet'tie, JOHN (1839–93), Scot. painter; *b.* Edinburgh; fine colourist; R.A., 1874; works include *The Drumhead Court-martial*, *Two Strings to her Bow*, *The Chieftain's Candlesticks*, etc.

Phædrus (*fē'drus*) (*fl.* 1st cent. A.D.), Rom. fabulist; *b.* Macedonia; came early to Italy; a slave, freed by Augustus; turned fables of his day into verse; nothing original in his work, but has often been translated.

Pheidias, or PHIDIAS (*fid'i-as*) (*c.* 490–432 B.C.), greatest sculptor of anc. Greece; *b.* Athens; executed number of splendid statues for Athens, including an ivory and gold figure of the goddess Athena. A colossal figure of Zeus at Olympia was considered his masterpiece. Superintended building of the Parthenon; fragments of his work are among Elgin Marbles in Brit. Museum.

Philip II. (382–336 B.C.), King of Macedon; father of Alexander the Great; seized throne, 359; conquered several Gr. cities on Macedonian border, and founded Philippi, 358; conquered Phocis, 346, and Thrace, 342–1; routed Athens and Thebes at Chæronea, 338, thus becoming supreme in Greece. Built up a magnificent army.

Philip I. (1052–1108), King of France; succeeded, 1060; his vassal, William, Duke of Normandy, made himself more powerful than his overlord by conquering England. Philip was excommunicated for evil living, 1094.

Philip II., or PHILIPPE AUGUSTE (1165–1223), King of France; succeeded, 1180; married Isabella of Hainaut, descendant of Carolingians; subdued Duke of Burgundy, 1186, and established strong rule; ambitious of conquering Normandy; went on Third Crusade, 1189; returned prematurely to prosecute designs against Richard of England's Fr. possessions, planning to divide them with John; united Normandy, Anjou, Touraine, and Poitou to France, 1204; defeated Emperor Otho at Bouvines, 1214, thus consolidating his power. Philip was the greatest of the Capetians; gave France unity.

[*Life*, by Hutton.]

Philip IV., LE BEL (1268–1314), King of France; succeeded, 1285; was defeated by Flemings at Courtrai, 1302, the 'Day of Spurs'; reign is chiefly remarkable for struggle with Papacy arising from Philip's taxation of clergy. Ultimately Philip seized Boniface VIII., and after his death secured election of Fr. pope, Clement V., the papacy migrating to Avignon four years later, 1309. His reign is of the greatest constitutional importance. He strengthened the royal authority, checked feudalism, supported the middle classes, and first summoned the States-General.

Philip VI. (1293–1350), King of France, nephew of Philip IV.; succeeded his cousin, Philip V., 1328; defeated Flemings at Cassel, 1328; unsuccessful against English during early stages of Hundred Years' War.

Philip II. (1527–98), King of Spain; *b.* Valladolid; married Mary of Portugal, 1543, Mary I. of England, 1554; his father, Charles V., abdicated, 1556, and Philip became chief monarch of Christendom; defeated French at St. Quentin and Gravelines; devoted himself to counter-Reformation movement; lost northern Netherlands through persecution of Protestants. The failure of his Span. Armada, 1588, marked beginning of decline of Spain; his narrow-minded bigotry proved disastrous to his country.

Philip III. (1578–1621), King of Spain, son of Philip II.; succeeded, 1598. Decline of Spain continued in his reign; Moors were expelled, 1609; alliance was made with Austrian Habsburgs, which later involved Spain in Thirty Years' War. Government was left to favourites.

Philip IV. (1605–65), King of Spain; succeeded his father, Philip III.; much under influence of Olivarez, and later of less worthy favourites; intervened in Thirty Years' War with disastrous effect; lost Portugal, 1641; was defeated by French at Rocroi, 1643, and had to cede much territory to France; largely responsible for fall of Spain.

Philip V. (1683–1746), King of Spain; grandson of Louis XIV.; founded Span. Bourbon dynasty; became king, 1700, and thus brought about Span. Succession War.

Philip the Bold (1342–1404), Duke of Burgundy, 1363; younger son of John of France; won title *le hardi* by gallantry at Poitiers, 1356; crushed large Flem. army at Rosbeck, 1382; inherited Artois, Burgundy, Flanders, etc., 1384, and developed their resources.

Philip the Good (1396–1467), Duke of Burgundy; drove bargain with France, 1435, and aided in expulsion of English; crushed Ghent rising with terrible slaughter, 1454; most powerful ruler of his time in Europe.

Philip, Sir Robert William (1857–), Scot. physician; prof. of tuberculosis, Edinburgh Univ., since 1917; founded first tuberculosis dispensary, 1887; his coordinated schemes against tuberculosis now adopted nationally.

Phillips, Stephen (1868–1915), Eng. poet and dramatist; *b.* near Oxford; his *Poems* (1897) won *Academy* first prize; other poetical works include *Marpessa* (1890), *Christ in Hades* (1896); and plays, *Paolo and Francesca, Herod, Ulysses*, etc.

Phillpotts (*fil'potz*), Eden (1862–), Eng. novelist; *b.* India; after ten years as clerk in an insurance office took to literature. Most of his novels deal with Devon, typical examples being *Children of the Mist, The American Prisoner, The Portreeve, Widecombe Fair, Old Delabole, The Spinners, Up Hill Down Dale;* his plays *The Farmer's Wife* and *Yellow Sands* scored big successes.

Philo (*fī'lō*) (*b. c.* 20 B.C.), Jewish philosopher; lived at Alexandria, forerunner of Alexandrian school. His philosophy blends Platonism and Judaism.

Philostratus (*fi-los'tra-tus*), Flavius (*c.* A.D. 170–245), Gr. rhetorician; taught at Athens and Rome; author of *Life of Apollonius of Tyana, Lives of the Sophists*, etc.

Phiz. See Browne, H. K.

Picard (*pē-kar'*), Jean (1620–82), Fr. astronomer; *b.* La Flèche, Anjou; first to measure a degree of a meridian accurately. Founded and ed. *La Connaissance des Temps*, 1679.

Picas'so, Pablo (1881–), pseudonym of Pablo Ruiz, Span. painter; *b.* Malaga; settled in Paris, 1903. Along with Georges Braque he invented Cubism, 1906–10; in 1918 reverted to painting natural forms; also a book illustrator.

Piccard (*pē-kar*), Auguste (1884–), Belgian meteorologist; *b.* Basle; prof. of meteorology, Brussels; was the first to ascend into the stratosphere by means of specially constructed balloons; made two ascents, 1931 and 1932, reaching a height of 10.07 miles; purpose of ascent was to study cosmic rays.

Piccinni (*pēt-chē'nē*), Niccola (1728–1800), Ital. opera composer; *b.* Bari; protégé of Marie Antoinette; prof. Royal School of Music, Paris, 1784; lost ground in famous contest with Gluck for the composition of an opera on *Iphigénie en Tauride*; wrote also *La Cecchina, Roland*, etc.

Pick'ford, Mary (1893–), U.S.A. film actress; *b.* Toronto, Canada; till 1913 was on legitimate stage, but then turned to film acting, in which she scored great success; became film producer, 1918.

Pickle the Spy, pseudonym of Alastair Ruadh MacDonnell or MacDonald (? 1725–61), chief of Glengarry; joined Royal Scots Guards in France, 1743; captured in Scotland while on Jacobite business; imprisoned in the Tower, 1745–7; appropriated Jacobite treasure hidden at Loch Arkaig, 1749; identified by Andrew Lang as revealer of Jacobite secrets, 1749–60.

[*Pickle the Spy* (1897) and *Companions of Pickle* (1898), by A. Lang.]

Pic′ton, Sir Thomas (1758–1815), Brit. general; *b.* in Pembrokeshire; served in W. Indies, 1794–7; governor of Trinidad; accused by enemies of cruelty to Negroes, and resigned, 1803; found guilty, 1806, but later was acquitted; served in Walcheren expedition, and was governor of Flushing, 1810; commanded under Wellington in Peninsular War; wounded at Quatre Bras, and fell at Waterloo.

Pierce (*pērs*), Franklin (1804–69), president of U.S.A.; *b.* in New Hampshire; practised as lawyer; distinguished in Mexican War, 1846–7; president, 1853–7; supported slavery; settled Mexican boundary dispute; arranged ten years' reciprocity with Canada; completed surveys for Pacific Railway. Sided with the Union, 1861.

Pi′late, Pontius, Rom. governor who authorized crucifixion of Jesus Christ; procurator of Judæa, probably from A.D. 26 to 36; deposed because of his severity, and returned to Rome; said to have committed suicide.

Pilsud′ski, Joseph Clemens (1867–1935), Polish soldier and statesman; *b.* near Vilna; for Nationalist views imprisoned in Russia and in Germany; at outbreak of Great War, invaded Russia at head of Polish Legion, 1914; head of provisional government formed when state of Poland was restored by Treaty of Versailles, 1919; president, Dec. 1919; led Poles in invasion of the Ukraine, July 1920, which resulted in Bolshevist attack on Poland; took supreme authority over Poland, 1926; prime minister, 1927–8 and 1930. Wrote considerably on military and historical subjects.

Pin′dar (*c.* 522–443 B.C.), Gr. lyric poet; *b.* at Cynoscephalæ, Bœotia; studied music and poetry at Athens; after long study wrote choral odes, and attained great fame; died, probably at Argos, at age of eighty. His poems consisted of songs in praise of gods and men, processional songs, festal songs, dirges, and pæans of victory, besides poems on other themes. A great part of his work has been lost, but the discoveries at Oxyrhynchus, 1905–7, provided several of his hitherto unknown poems.

Pinero (*pin-ăr′ō*), Sir Arthur Wing (1855–1934), Eng. dramatist; *b.* London; on stage, 1874–81; author of numerous plays and comedies, including *The Magistrate*, *The Cabinet Minister*, *Trelawney of the Wells*, *Sweet Lavender*, *The Second Mrs. Tanqueray*, *The Gay Lord Quex*, *His House in Order*, etc.; knighted, 1909.

Pinsuti (*pin-soo′te*), Ciro (1829–88), Ital. composer; *b.* near Siena; came to England, 1848, as teacher of singing; was at Royal Academy of Music, 1858–85; wrote two successful operas, a *Te Deum*, nearly 300 songs, and numerous pianoforte pieces.

Pinto, Serpa. See Serpa Pinto.

Pir′rie, William James, 1st Viscount (1847–1924), Brit. shipowner; *b.* Quebec; joined Harland and Wolff's shipbuilding establishment, Belfast, 1862; partner, 1874, and then chairman; lord mayor of Belfast, 1896–7; controller-general of merchant shipbuilding, 1918–19; created viscount, 1921.

Pisan′o, Andrea (*c.* 1270–1348), Ital. sculptor; *b.* Pontedera, Tuscany; pupil of Giovanni Pisano; goldsmith at first; did famous south bronze door of baptistery of Florence, and panel reliefs for the campanile; architect in Orvieto cathedral, 1347.

Pisano. (1) Niccola (*c.* 1227–*c.* 78), Ital. sculptor and architect; settled in Pisa, and executed marble pulpit of baptistery there; numerous religious panels; finest work is pulpit in Siena cathedral. (2) GIOVANNI (*c.* 1249–*c.* 1314), Ital. architect and sculptor; son of (1); *b.* in Pisa; began façade of Siena cathedral; worked on pulpit of Pisa cathedral, and helped his father with great fountain at Perugia.

Pit′man, SIR ISAAC (1813–97), inventor of well-known system of shorthand; *b.* Trowbridge; schoolmaster for eleven years; pub. *Stenographic Sound Hand* (1837); the *Phonetic Journal* was begun in 1842; knighted, 1894.

[*Life,* by T. A. Reed (1890) and A. Baker (1908).]

Pitt, the Elder. See CHATHAM, 1ST EARL OF.

Pitt, PERCY (1870–1932), Eng. composer and conductor; *b.* London; musical director at Covent Garden, London; conductor of Brit. National Opera Co.; helped to develop musical policy of B.B.C.; works include symphonic poems, serenades, incidental music to plays, and choral works.

Pitt, WILLIAM (1759–1806), Brit. statesman; *b.* Hayes, near Bromley; second son of 1st Earl of Chatham; called to bar, 1780; M.P., 1781; took important part in Opposition side, especially denouncing the war with the Amer. colonies; chancellor of the Exchequer, 1782–3. On fall of coalition ministry (including Fox), Pitt became prime minister; his cabinet was without ability and was opposed by House of Commons, led by Fox, but the general election, 1784, was a triumph for the government. He restored national credit by his genius for finance, lowered the tea duties, and suppressed smuggling, etc. He had already brought in bills for parliamentary reform; carried a commercial treaty with France, 1786; attempted partial abolition of slave trade, 1799; passed India Bill re-forming the E. India Co. on a new basis, 1788. War with France was declared, 1793. Pitt's war policy was designed to break the power of France on land and to maintain England's supremacy at sea. He succeeded in the latter, but failed in the former. During this period he had to pass drastic coercion laws. Induced by the Irish rebellion of 1798, Pitt passed the Act of Union, 1800, but quarrelled with the king on Catholic Emancipation, and resigned, 1801. Again called to office, 1804, he formed a new coalition, 1805, against Napoleon. Petty parliamentary attacks completed the ruin of his health, and he never recovered his spirits after news of Austerlitz. Self-contained and apparently cold of nature, Pitt was passionately patriotic and a great orator. Great as a peace minister, he abandoned all attempts at reform on the outbreak of war.

[*Life,* by Gifford (1809), Rosebery (1891), Whibley (1905), Holland Rose (1911).]

Pi′us, the name of several popes. PIUS II., pope 1458–64; author (known as Æneas Silvius) of poems, a novel, a play and a history of his own times. PIUS IV., pope 1559–65; pontificate marked by the Council of Trent. PIUS V., pope 1566–72, excommunicated Queen Elizabeth and drove the Jews from Rome. PIUS IX., pope 1846–78; during his reign Rome became the capital of Italy, and the temporal power of the papacy was lost; he re-established R.C. hierarchy in England, 1850; the infallibility of the pope was proclaimed, 1870. PIUS X., pope 1903–14; rose from the ranks of the people; opposed modernism. PIUS XI., pope 1922–   ; during his reign temporal power of popes was restored, 1929, by the establishment of the City of the Vatican.

Pizarro (*pi-zä′rō* or *pē-thär′rō*),

FRANCISCO (1475–1541), Span. conqueror of Peru; *b.* Trujillo; was with Balboa when he discovered the Pacific; landing with Almagro in Peru, he marched inland, captured the Inca Atahualpa by treachery, and strangled him, 1533. Founded Lima as new capital, 1535; the two adventurers quarrelling about their shares of land, civil war ensued, and Almagro was slain, 1538. Three years later Pizarro was assassinated by Almagrists.

[*History of the Conquest of Peru*, by Prescott.]

Planck, MAX (1858–), Ger. physicist; *b.* Kiel; prof., Kiel, 1885, Berlin, 1889; specially studied thermodynamics and enunciated 'Quantum Theory' of Radiation, 1901; Nobel Prize for physics, 1918; author of numerous scientific works.

Plantin (*plon-tan'*), CHRISTOPHE (1514–89), Fr. printer; settled in Antwerp, 1549; chief publication the *Polyglot Bible* (8 vols. 1569–73).

Pla'to (*c.* 427–347 B.C.), greatest Gr. philosopher; at age of twenty made the acquaintance of Socrates; after death of Socrates he travelled widely. About 387 B.C. he established the Academy in Athens. All Plato's philosophical writings have been preserved. They are cast in the form of dialogues, in most of which Socrates is represented as chief speaker. The slighter, so-called *Socratic*, dialogues undoubtedly come first; the first set of great constructive dialogues, viz. *Symposium*, *Phædo*, *Republic*, and *Phædrus*, come next; then come *Theætetus*, *Parmenides*, *Sophist*, *Politicus*, *Timæus* and *Philebus*, and, last of all, the *Laws*.

Plato, like Socrates, accepts the possibility of a common good. Human welfare consists in the harmonious activity of all functions of the soul under the guidance of the highest. Man, a social being, can make the best of himself only in a well-ordered state. The mass of men should be the productive workers and traders in the state. A smaller number should be the state's warriors; a very few, carefully trained, are to be the rulers of the state. They must devote themselves wholly to the public good, and therefore Plato denies them any private property and private family life.

The goal of the 'philosopher-king's' knowledge Plato calls the *Idea* (or Form) of the good. What in common parlance we call 'actual' things—the particular objects of sense-perception—are not for Plato real objects. They 'partake in' or 'copy' real Ideas or Forms more or less fully, but they always include an incalculable, material, evil element, whereas real being is free from imperfection or any unintelligibility. The Ideas constitute a rational organic system, and every member of the system derives its being and intelligibility from an ultimate principle which Plato calls 'the Good' or 'the idea of the Good.' Plato's meaning is doubtless most easily grasped if we personify the Idea of the Good as God.

Plau'tus, TITUS MACCIUS (*c.* 254–184 B.C.), comic poet and dramatist of anc. Rome; *b.* Sarsina, Umbria; pioneer of Rom. literature; twenty plays extant; imitated Gr. form, but characterization is distinctly Rom.; Latin pure and vigorous. Plays include *Miles Gloriosus*, *Captivi*, etc. Shakespeare's *Comedy of Errors* is based on his *Menæchmi*.

Playfair, LYON, 1ST BARON PLAYFAIR OF ST. ANDREWS (1818–98), Brit. chemist and politician; *b.* Meerut; prof. of chemistry, Edinburgh, 1858–68; M.P. Univs. of Edinburgh and St. Andrews, 1868–85; postmaster-general, 1873–4; chairman, Ways and Means, and deputy-speaker of

House of Commons, 1880–3; peerage, 1892; took part in royal commissions on health of towns, etc.; discovered nitroprussides; investigated blast-furnace gases, and specific gravity and atomic volume of hydrated salts.

Plim'soll, SAMUEL (1824–98), British politician—the 'sailors' friend'; *b.* Bristol; M.P., 1868; publication of *Our Seamen* (1872) led to passing of Merchant Shipping Act, 1876, which empowers Board of Trade to detain unseaworthy vessels; 'Plimsoll mark,' painted on every ship, indicates maximum load-line.

Plin'y. (1) CAIUS PLINIUS SECUNDUS, called 'the Elder' (*c.* A.D. 23–79), Rom. writer; *b.* Como; served in various campaigns; became an advocate, but retired to estate at Novum Comum (Como) and devoted himself to literature; prolific writer. His one surviving work, *Historia Naturalis*, shows encyclopædic knowledge, and is of great use regarding popular contemporary ideas; killed by eruption of Vesuvius. (2) CAIUS PLINIUS CÆCILIUS SECUNDUS (A.D. 61–*c.* 115), called 'the Younger,' Latin prose writer; nephew of above; *b.* Como; practised as pleader; military tribune in Syria, 83; consul, 100; friend of Trajan and Tacitus. His *Letters* are written in best Ciceronian style; chiefly valuable for glimpses of life of upper classes in Rome. Also wrote panegyric on Trajan.

Ploti'nus (*c.* A.D. 204–270), anc. philosopher; *b.* Lycopolis, Egypt; studied at Alexandria; travelled in East; settled in Rome, 244; founder of Neoplatonism, which combines mysticism with Plato's idealism; works and philosophy preserved by his pupil Porphyry in the *Enneads*. One of the greatest mystics and idealists.

Plumer (*ploom'er*), HERBERT CHARLES ONSLOW, 1ST BARON (1857–1932), Brit. soldier; *b.* Torquay; served in Sudan, 1884; commanded Rhodesian column in S. African War, 1899–1902; lieutenant-general, 1908. During Great War commanded 5th Army Corps in France, 1915; 2nd Army, 1915–17; general, 1916. From Nov. 1917 to March 1918 he commanded Ital. Expeditionary Force; returned to France to command 2nd Army; field-marshal, 1919. Governor of Malta, 1919–24; high commissioner for Palestine, 1925–8. Awarded G.C.M.G., G.C.B., and raised to peerage.

Plunkett, SIR HORACE CURZON (1854–1932), Irish politician; son of Lord Dunsany; *b.* in Glos; made his fortune as cattle-rancher in U.S.A.; M.P., 1892–1900; founded Irish Agricultural Organization Soc., 1894; vice-president, Department of Agriculture and Technical Instruction for Ireland, 1899–1907; commissioner, Congested Districts Board; chairman, Irish Convention, 1917–18; Senator of I.F.S., 1922–3.

Plutarch (*ploo'tark*) (*c.* A.D. 46–120), Gr. biographer; *b.* Chæronea, Bœotia; visited Italy and lectured on philosophy at Rome; renowned for his *Parallel Lives* of forty-six famous Greeks and Romans, arranged in pairs for comparison.

Pocahon'tas (1595–1617), daughter of Powhatan, an Ind. chief in Virginia; according to tradition saved life of Captain John Smith, who had been captured by Indians. Pocahontas was captured by English; married Captain Rolfe, 1614, and went with him to England, 1616; *d.* Gravesend; tomb in St. George's Church.

Po'cock, ROGER (1865–), Eng. traveller and author; raised Legion of Frontiersmen in Greenland, 1904; served in Great War; research with deep sea fisheries, 1919–21; Oxford expedition to Spitsbergen, 1923; writings include *A Frontiersman* (1903),

Jesse of Cariboo (1912), *Horses* (1917), *Chorus to Adventurers* (1931).

Poe, EDGAR ALLAN (1809–49), U.S.A. poet and prose writer; *b.* Boston; adopted by John Allan of Richmond, Virginia; educated in England and in Richmond, Virginia; entered guardian's office, then enlisted in U.S.A. army; bought out by John Allan, sent to Military Academy, but dismissed; left to his own resources and started journalism. His nature was morbid and unbalanced, partly due to inheritance and partly to poverty and lack of recognition. His best-known poems are 'The Raven,' 'The Bells,' 'Annabel Lee.' His short stories, mainly tales of horror and mystery, include *The Black Cat, The Gold Bug, The Murders in the Rue Morgue* (the pioneer of the detective story), *The Masque of the Red Death, William Wilson.*

Poincaré (*pwan-kä-rā'*), JULES HENRI (1854–1912), Fr. mathematician and physicist; cousin of Raymond Poincaré; *b.* Nancy; prof. at Paris Univ. from 1886; made original contributions to pure mathematics, astronomical mechanics, and the mathematics of physics.

Poincaré, RAYMOND (1860–1934), Fr. statesman; *b.* Bar-le-Duc; educated at Bar-le-Duc and Paris Univ.; called to bar, 1880; practised as lawyer in Paris; in 1887 entered Chamber of Deputies; held various offices, and became premier of France, 1912; president of republic, 1913–20; did much to inspire confidence in the Fr. nation during the Great War. Again premier and foreign minister, 1922–4; disagreed with Bonar Law regarding Ger. reparations, and decided to occupy the Ruhr. Premier and minister of finance, 1926–9; member of Fr. Academy, 1909. Published his *Memoirs* (in several vols. from 1926).

Poiré, EMMANUEL. See CARAN D'ACHE.

Polk (*pōk*), JAMES KNOX (1795–1849), president of U.S.A.; *b.* N. Carolina; practised as lawyer; speaker of House of Representatives, 1835; governor of Tennessee, 1839; president, 1845–9. Chief events of his presidency: settlement of Oregon boundary dispute with Great Britain; war with Mexico, 1846–7, resulting in annexation of New Mexico and California.

Poll'ard, ALBERT FREDERICK (1869–), Eng. historian; *b.* Ryde; educated Oxford; assistant editor of *Dictionary of National Biography*, 1893–1901; prof. of Eng. History, London Univ., 1903–27; director of Institute of Historical Research, 1927. His numerous historical works include *Henry VIII.* (1902), *Factors in Modern History* (1907), *The Reign of Henry VII. from Contemporary Sources* (3 vols. 1913–14), and *Wolsey* (1929).

Pollard, ALFRED WILLIAM (1859–), Eng. critic and bibliographer; *b.* London; keeper of printed books in Brit. Museum, 1919–24; prof. of Eng. Bibliography, King's Coll., London, since 1919; an authority on the bibliography of Shakespeare. Works include *Old Picture Books* (1902), *Shakespeare's Folios and Quartos* (1909), *Fine Books* (1912), etc.

Poll'ock, SIR FREDERICK (1845–), Eng. lawyer; *b.* London; prof. of jurisprudence, Univ. Coll., London, 1882; Corpus prof. of jurisprudence, Oxford, 1883–1903; fellow of Brit. Academy, 1902; judge of the Admiralty Court of Cinque Ports since 1914; ed. of *Law Reports*, and author of numerous works on law.

Po'lo, MARCO (*c.* 1254–1324), Venetian traveller; when seventeen years old accompanied his father, Nicolo, and uncle, Maffeo, on journey to the court of Kubla

Khan of Cathay (China); won favour of the Khan; remained with him till 1292; returned to Europe, reaching Venice, 1295; captured in sea-fight between Venice and Genoa, 1298, and dictated account of his travels, in French, to a fellow-prisoner; keen and truthful observer; first man to reach China by overland route.

Polybius (*po-lib'i-us*) (*c.* 204–122 B.C.), Gr. historian; *b.* Megalopolis, Arcadia; statesman of the Achæan League; one of the 1,000 Achæan hostages taken to Rome; won friendship of younger Scipio, through whom he gained access to Rom. archives; later, joined Scipio's African expedition, and saw fall of Carthage; wrote *Universal History*, of which only five books out of forty remain.

Pol'ycarp (*c.* A.D. 70–155), one of the apostolic fathers; Bishop of Smyrna for about fifty years; said to have known, and spoken with, John and other disciples; had position of great authority among the Asiatic Churches; burned to death as a martyr.

[*Apostolic Fathers*, ii., by Lightfoot.]

Pom'padour, JEANNE ANTOINETTE POISSON, MARQUISE DE (1721–64), mistress of Louis XV. of France; *b.* in Paris; became centre of brilliant intellectual and artistic circle, including Voltaire and Greuze; had great political influence.

Pompeius (*pom-pē'yus*), or POMPEY, distinguished Rom. family; noted members were: (1) GNÆUS, consul, 89 B.C.; conferred Lat. rights on all communities from the Alps to the Po. (2) GNÆUS, POMPEY THE GREAT (106–48 B.C.), aided Sulla against Marius; defeated Marians in Spain, 76–71; suppressed Mediterranean piracy; consul, 70; conquered Mithridates; annexed Syria and Palestine, 66–63; formed 'first triumvirate' with Cæsar and Crassus; defeated by Cæsar at Pharsalus, 48; murdered in Egypt.

Ponce de León (*pōn'tha dā lā-ōn'*), JUAN (*c.* 1460–1521), Span. explorer; *b.* in Leon; sailed with Columbus on second voyage to America, 1493; conquered Porto Rico, 1509; discovered Florida, 1513; *d.* in Cuba.

Pond, JOHN (1767–1836), Eng. astronomer; *b.* London; head of Greenwich observatory, 1806; F.R.S., 1807; astronomer-royal, 1811; reorganized equipment of observatory, and pub. *Greenwich Observations* (8 vols.).

Poniatowski (*pon-yä-tov'skē*), JOZEF ANTON (1763–1813), Polish prince and patriot; *b.* Warsaw; commander-in-chief against Russia, 1792; took part in Kosciuszko's rising; assisted in Napoleonic campaigns; commander-in-chief of new duchy of Warsaw; distinguished in last Napoleonic invasion of Russia; marshal after battle of Leipzig.

Poole, REGINALD LANE (1857–), Eng. historian; *b.* London; keeper of archives of Oxford Univ., 1909–27, and lecturer in Diplomatic, Oxford Univ., 1896–1927; fellow of Brit. Academy, 1904; ed. of *English Historical Review*, 1901–20. His numerous publications include *A History of the Huguenots of the Dispersion* (1880), *Wycliffe and Movements for Reform* (1889), *The Exchequer in the 12th Century* (1912), *Historical Atlas of Modern Europe* (1897–1902), etc.

Pope, ALEXANDER (1688–1744), Eng. poet; *b.* London; educated privately; showed poetic bent from an early age, and his hard study resulted in bodily deformity and bitterness of mind. *Pastorals* appeared in 1709; his *Essay on Criticism* (1711), in spite of a want of clearness, is a marvel of epigrammatic brilliance; the *Rape of the Lock* (1712), a mock-heroic poem, won him instant fame. He was occupied in translating Homer, and his *Iliad* (1715–20) and *Odyssey* (1725–6). The latter justified Bentley's remark: 'A pretty poem, but you must not call it Homer,' but the *Iliad* was far superior, and had great influence on 18th cent. poetry. Critics had been severe on him, and he retaliated with the *Dunciad* (1728). His great didactic poem, the *Essay on Man* (1732–4), and the *Moral Essays* (1731–5), are only fragments of a scheme of philosophic poems. His later works comprise *Imitations of Horace* (1733–7), *Epistle to Dr. Arbuthnot* (1735), and *Epilogue to the Satires* (1738). He also pub. his *Correspondence* (1737). He represents the culmination of the artificial school of poetry, and is unexcelled for precision, terseness, and perfection of form.

[*Life* (1880), by Leslie Stephen.]

Por'son, RICHARD (1759–1808), Eng. classical scholar; *b.* in Norfolk; of humble parentage; educated Eton and Cambridge; prof. of Greek, Cambridge, 1792; principal librarian, London Institution, 1806; did much to advance Gr. scholarship; ed. *Æschylus*, *Euripides*, etc.

Por'ter, JANE (1776–1850), Brit. novelist; *b.* Durham; friend of Sir Walter Scott; wrote historical fiction; best-known work, *The Scottish Chiefs* (1810).

Porter, WILLIAM SYDNEY (1862–1910), pseudonym O. HENRY; U.S.A. author; *b.* Greensboro, N. Carolina; during imprisonment for alleged embezzlement began writing brilliant short stories, including *The Gentle Grafter*, *Cabbages and Kings*, *Four Million*, *Roads of Destiny*, etc. His stories show acquaintance with the life of the poor in New York and of the southern and western states. They are remarkable for their humour, both of phrase and idea, and the unexpectedness of their ending.

Post'gate, JOHN PERCIVAL (1853–1926), Eng. classical scholar; prof. of comparative philology, London, 1880–1910; prof. of Latin, Liverpool Univ., 1909–20; ed. of *Classical Review*, 1899–1907; ed. many classical writers, but best known for reforming the pronunciation and teaching of Latin.

Potem'kin, GREGORY ALEXANDROVICH, PRINCE (1736–91), Russ. statesman and general; favourite of Catherine II.; retained power throughout life, skilfully guiding foreign policy of Russia; kept Prussia in check and won ports on Black Sea from Turkey; died shortly before Peace of Jassy.

Pot'ter, PAUL (1625–54), Dutch animal painter; his life-size *Young Bull* is most celebrated of all his pictures; renowned also for smaller paintings, *e.g.* *The Dairy Farm*.

Poussin (*poo-san'*), NICOLAS (1594–1665), Fr. classical, landscape, and figure painter; *b.* in Normandy; court painter to Louis XIII.; examples of work in Louvre, Paris, and National Gallery and Wallace Collection, London.

Poyn'ter, SIR EDWARD JOHN (1836–1919), Eng. historical and classical painter; *b.* Paris; R.A., 1876; director, National Gallery, London, 1894; president, Royal Academy, 1896; works include *Atalanta's Race*, *Visit to Æsculapius* (Tate Gallery), etc.; pub. *Lectures on Art* (1879, 1897).

Praed (*prād*), WINTHROP MACKWORTH (1802–39), Eng. poet and politician; *b.* London; secretary, Board of Control, 1834–5; best poems vivid, rhythmic, and imaginative; such are 'The Red Fisherman,' 'The Vicar,' 'A Letter of Advice,' etc.

Praxiteles (*praks-it'e-lēz*), greatest of Gr. sculptors of 4th cent. B.C.; most of his work lost, but marble statue of Hermes and Dionysus shows his power.

Preece, SIR WILLIAM HENRY (1834–1913), Brit. electrician; engineer-in-chief and electrician to Brit. Post Office, 1892–9; wrote (with others) *Text-book on Telegraphy* (18th ed. 1905), *The Telephone* (1889), and *Manual of Telephony* (1893).

Pres'cott, WILLIAM HICKLING (1796–1859), Amer. historian; *b.* Salem; specialized in Span. history; his *Ferdinand and Isabella* (1838) had immense success, as also *Conquest of Mexico* (1843) and *Conquest of Peru* (1847); wrote also *Charles V. after his Abdication*, and an unfinished *History of Philip II.*

[*Life* (1905), by H. T. Peck.]

Prester John, semi-mythical potentate of Middle Ages; believed to reign over a Christian kingdom in the Far East; also variously identified with a certain Mongol chief, and with the founder of the empire of the Khara-Khitai; legend of his existence proved a stimulus to mediæval exploration.

Pretender, THE. See CHARLES EDWARD STEWART, PRINCE; and JAMES, THE OLD PRETENDER.

Preto'rius, ANDRIES WILLIAM JACOBUS (1799–1853), Boer farmer and general; a leader of the Boers in Great Trek; settled in Natal, 1838; founded republic of Natal, which became Brit. colony, 1843. Headed revolts, 1848, 1851, and secured establishment of Orange Free State. His son, MARTHINIUS (*d.* 1901), became first president of Transvaal Republic, 1857–60; president of Free State, 1859–63, and of S. African Republic, 1864.

Prévost (*prā-vō'*), MARCEL (1862–), Fr. author and dramatist; *b.* Paris; member of Fr. Academy, 1909. His works include *Lettres de Femmes* (1892), *Les Demi-Vierges* (1894), *Le Jardin Secret* (1897), *Lettres à Françoise Mariée* (1908), *L'homme Vierge* (1929), etc.

Prévost d'Exiles, ANTOINE FRANÇOIS, ABBÉ (1697–1763), Fr. author; *b.* in Artois; produced 200 novels, of which *Manon Lescaut* (1733) is his masterpiece.

Prich'ard, JAMES COWLES (1786–1848), Eng. physician; *b.* Ross, Herefordshire; pioneer in anthropology and ethnology; investigated phases of insanity; author of *Physical History of Man* (1813), *Natural History of Man* (1843), *Diseases of the Nervous System*, etc.

Priest'ley, JOHN BOYNTON (1894–), Eng. author; *b.* Bradford; educated Bradford and Cambridge; novelist, essayist, and dramatist; made remarkable success with his novel, *The Good Companions* (1929); other works, *Angel Pavement* (1930), *Faraway* (1932), and *English Journey* (1934). His plays include *Dangerous Corner* (1932).

Priestley, JOSEPH (1733–1804), Eng. scientist; *b.* near Leeds; Unitarian minister in Birmingham, 1780–91, when, on account of his advanced political views, his chapel and house, books and apparatus, were burnt by the mob; later, migrated to America; renowned for his discovery of oxygen; invented the pneumatic trough; first to apply carbon dioxide in 'aerating' waters; pub. *History of Electricity* (1767), *Experiments on the Generation of Air and Water* (1793), etc.

Primo de Rivera (*prē-mo de rē-vā'ra*), MIGUEL, MARQUÉS DE ESTELLA (1870–1930), Span. soldier and political leader; *b.* Jerez; served in Philippines, 1897–1900; governor of Cadiz, 1915–16; senator for Cadiz, 1921; captain-general of Catalonia, 1922. Established a military dictatorship, 1923; reintroduced civil government, 1925, and became premier; resigned, 1930, and died two months later.

Princess Royal. See MARY, PRINCESS ROYAL.

Pringle-Pattison, ANDREW SETH (1856–1931), Scot. philosopher; *b.* Edinburgh; educated Edinburgh Univ. and in Germany. Assumed name Pringle-Pattison on succeeding to an estate in 1898. Held professorships in Cardiff, 1883–7, and in St. Andrews, 1887–91; prof. of logic and metaphysics, Edinburgh Univ., 1891–1919. Twice Gifford Lecturer, 1911–13 and 1921–3; pub. these lectures, *The Idea of God* and *The Idea of Immortality*. Other publications include *Hegelianism and Personality* and *Man's Place in the Cosmos*.

Prin'sep, VALENTINE CAMERON (1838–1904), Eng. artist and author; R.A., 1894; prof. of painting to Royal Academy; painted *Declaration of Queen Victoria as Empress of India* (1880); wrote novels and plays.

Pri'or, MATTHEW (1664–1721), Eng. poet and diplomatist; *b.* in Dorsetshire; son of joiner; helped to negotiate treaties of Ryswick, 1697, and Utrecht, 1713; commissioner of trade, 1700–7, of customs, 1711–14; impeached and imprisoned, 1715; wrote long poem, *Solomon on the Vanity of the World*, but is greatest in his 'amorous odes' and in his verses to children.

Proc'ter, BRYAN WALLER (1787–1874), Eng. poet and biographer; *b.* Leeds; metropolitan commissioner of lunacy, 1832–61; pseudonym 'Barry Cornwall'; wrote *Dramatic Scenes*, *Mirandola: a Play*, etc., memoirs of Edward Kean and of Charles Lamb, also *English Songs*; best known as song-writer.

Proc'tor, RICHARD ANTHONY (1837–88), Brit. astronomer; *b.* Chelsea; founder of *Knowledge* (1881); author of *Saturn and his System*, *Old and New Astronomy*, and popular treatises, *Half-hours with a Telescope*, *Other Worlds than Ours*, etc.

Propertius (*prō-pĕr'shius*), SEXTUS (*fl.* 28–15 B.C.), Rom. elegiac poet; *b.* near Assisi; belonged to the literary circle of Mæcenas, friend of Virgil and Ovid; four books of his verse extant, mainly to one 'Cynthia.'

Proth'ero, SIR GEORGE WALTER (1848–1922), Brit. historian; *b.* in Wiltshire; educated Eton and Cambridge; prof. of history, Edinburgh Univ., 1894–9; Rede lecturer at Cambridge, 1903, and Chichele lecturer at Oxford, 1915; director of Historical Section, Foreign Office, 1918–19. Works include *Life and Times of Simon de Montfort* (1877), *Memoir of Henry Bradshaw* (1889), *German Policy before the War* (1916); ed. of *Quarterly Review*, 1898–1922.

Proudhon (*proo-don'*), PIERRE JOSEPH (1809–65), Fr. Socialistic writer and politician; *b.* Besançon, of poor parents. Propounded his theory that society ought to rest on a basis of equality and reciprocity; his socialism was economic rather than political. Became famous with his tract, *Qu'est-ce que la Propriété?* (1840); founded paper, *Représentant du Peuple* (1847).

Proust (*proost*), MARCEL (1871–1922), Fr. novelist; *b.* Paris; attained great reputation as writer of stories of salon life. His great, leisurely series, *À la Recherche du Temps perdu*, began (1913) with *Du Côté de chez Swann*. *Du Côté de Guermantes* and *Sodome et Gomorrhe* appeared 1921; and *La Prisonnière* (1924), *Albertine Disparue* (1926), and *Le Temps retrouvé* (1926) posthumously.

Ptolemy (*tol'em-i*), name of Macedonian rulers of Egypt (323–30 B.C.). PTOLEMY I., *Soter*, became satrap of Egypt on division of kingdoms of Alexander the

Great, 323; abdicated, 285; founded museum and library at Alexandria. His son, PTOLEMY II., *Philadelphus*, developed resources of Egypt; made museum of Alexandria centre of literature and science. Rome claimed Egypt by bequest of PTOLEMY X., or Alexander II., but agreed, 51, to joint rule of PTOLEMY XII. and his sister Cleopatra. In Alexandrian War of 48–47 Ptolemy XII. died, and a younger brother, PTOLEMY XIII., was associated with Cleopatra till his death in 44. Cleopatra, and her son Cæsarion, known as PTOLEMY XIV., then ruled till both perished during Rom. attack, 30.

Ptolemy, CLAUDIUS PTOLEMÆUS, famous astronomer, geographer, and mathematician; *b.* Egypt; worked at Alexandria from A.D. 127 to 151; celebrated as author of the *Almagest*, a summary of his own and his predecessors' work in astronomy. The Ptolemaic system, which assumed that the earth was the centre of the universe, was accepted until the time of Copernicus. His *Geographike* is mainly mathematical, little attention being paid to descriptive work.

Puccini (*pōō-chē'ne*), GIACOMO (1858–1924), Ital. operatic composer; *b.* Lucca; educated under Ponchielli at Milan; prof. of composition, Milan Conservatorio, 1893. Chief works: *La Bohême* (1896), *La Tosca* (1900), *Madame Butterfly* (1904), *Gianni Schicchi* (1918), and *Turandot* (his last work, unfinished).

Pugh (*pew*), EDWIN WILLIAM (1874–1930), Brit. novelist; *b.* London; employed in a city office for eight years. Works include *The City of the World* (1912), *The Dickens Originals* (1912), *The Proof of the Pudding* (1913), *A Book of Laughter* (1916), *The World is my Oyster* (1924), *Empty Vessels* (1926).

Pugin (*pū'jin*), AUGUSTUS WELBY (1812–52), Eng. architect; *b.* London; helped to design Houses of Parliament, 1836; became R.C., and designed many R.C. churches, including cathedrals of Southwark and Killarney; pub. *True Principles of Christian Architecture* (1841).

Pu'litzer, JOSEPH (1847–1911), Amer. journalist; *b.* in Hungary; emigrated to U.S.A.; after severe struggle with poverty became newspaper proprietor; began the characteristic 'sensationalism' of the Amer. newspaper when the *New York World* passed into his hands, 1883; supported many worthy causes.

Pur'cell, HENRY (1659–95), famous Eng. musician; *b.* Westminster; organist, Westminster Abbey, 1680, Chapel Royal, 1682. *Te Deum* and *Jubilate* and *King Arthur* are among his best works; wrote also *Dido and Æneas* (opera), twelve sonatas for two violins and bass, besides anthems, songs, cantatas, etc. He has never been excelled in the simplicity, purity, and vigour of his musical works. Buried beneath the organ in Westminster Abbey.

Pusey (*pū'zi*), EDWARD BOUVERIE (1800–82), Eng. theologian; *b.* Pusey, near Oxford; prof. of Hebrew, Oxford, 1829; a leader of the Oxford Movement; author of tracts on Fasting and Baptism in celebrated *Tracts for the Times*; sought to bring Anglican Church more into harmony with Catholic traditions, but remained within the Anglican communion; wrote *Doctrine of the Real Presence*, etc.

Push'kin, ALEXANDER SERGEIEVICH (1799–1837), famous Russ. poet and author; *b.* Moscow; received post in ministry of foreign affairs, 1817; killed in duel. Pushkin wrote excellent lyrics; best works are *Eugene Onegin* and *Poltava* (narrative poems); *The Captain's Daughter*, *History of the Revolt of Pugachev* (prose works); *Boris Godunov* (tragedy); *The Prisoner of the Caucasus* (epic).

Putnam, George Haven (1844–1930), Amer. publisher; *b.* London; head of publishing house of G. P. Putnam's Sons from 1872; served in Civil War; played an important part in securing international copyright; a worker for municipal reform, free trade, civil service reform, etc. His many books include *Memories of a Publisher, 1865–1915.*

Puvis de Chavannes (*pu-vēz' de shä-vän'*), Pierre (1824–98), Fr. painter; *b.* Lyons; famous for mural decorations—*e.g.* those at Amiens Museum, *Labour* and *Repose*, *Ave Picardia Nutrix* (1865), *Ludus pro Patria* (1881); decorated Panthéon, Hôtel de Ville, and Sorbonne, Paris, staircase of fine art gallery at Lyons, Rouen Museum, the Boston (U.S.A.) library, etc.

Pym (*pim*), John (1584–1643), Eng. statesman; entered parliament, 1614; leader of Short Parliament; prominent in impeachment of Laud and Strafford; chief promoter of Grand Remonstrance; controlled parliament during Civil War.

Pyrrhus (*pir'us*) (*c.* 318–272 B.C.), King of Epirus; one of the greatest generals of the anc. world; helped Tarentum against Rome; won battle of Heraclea, 280, the first encounter of Greeks with Romans; success dearly bought—hence phrase 'a Pyrrhic victory'; decisively beaten at Beneventum, 275.

Pythagoras (*pī-thag'ō-ras*) (6th cent. B.C.), Gr. philosopher; *b.* Samos; little is known of his life; settled at Croton in S. Italy, and there founded a society, mainly of aristocrats, which came into conflict with established political custom; in 5th cent. ejected from Croton. Pythagoras believed in transmigration of souls and advocated abstinence from flesh; interested in harmonics, arithmetic, and astronomy. The proof of 47th proposition in Euclid, Book I., is attributed to him. Pythagoras left no writings.

Pytheas (*pith'e-as*) of Massilia (Marseilles) (*fl.* early 3rd cent. B.C.), Gr. navigator and astronomer; visited Britain and Thule (?Orkney or Shetland Isles); coasted N. Europe from Cadiz to mouth of Elbe; noted connection of tides with moon; among first to fix latitudes.

Q

Quain, Sir Richard (1816–98), Irish physician; *b.* in co. Cork; practised in London; physician to Brompton Hospital for Diseases of the Chest from 1855; an authority on heart disease, and author of *Dictionary of Medicine* (1875–82). His cousin, Jones Quain (1796–1865), was author of the well-known *Elements of Anatomy*, and Richard Quain (1800–87), brother of Jones, was president of Royal Coll. of Surgeons, 1868, and endowed the Quain professorships of botany, Eng. language and literature, law, and physics in Univ. Coll., London.

Quarles (*kwärlz*), Francis (1592–1644), Eng. poet; *b.* in Essex; cupbearer to Elizabeth of Bohemia, 1613; chronologer to city of London, 1639; wrote religious verse, *e.g.* *Emblems* (1635), and royalist pamphlets during Civil War.

Queens'berry, John Sholto

DOUGLAS, 8TH MARQUESS OF (1844–1900), Brit. authority on prize fighting · drew up new rules, known as 'Queensberry Rules,' to regulate fighting in prize ring.

Quesnay (*kā-nā'*), FRANÇOIS (1694–1774), Fr. physician and economist; *b.* in Seine-et-Oise; physician to Louis xv. and prof. of surgery, Paris Univ.; founded economic school of physiocrats, and wrote *Tableau Economique* (1758); referred to in Adam Smith's *Wealth of Nations.*

Quiller-Couch (*kwil'er-kooch*), SIR ARTHUR THOMAS (pseudonym 'Q') (1863–), Eng. novelist and critic; *b.* in Cornwall; prof. of Eng. literature, Cambridge, since 1912; novels include *Dead Man's Rock* (1887), *Troy Town* (1888), *The Splendid Spur* (1889), *The Ship of Stars* (1899), *Hetty Wesley* (1903), *Lady Good-for-Nothing* (1910), *Hocken and Hunken* (1912), *Nicky-Nan, Reservist* (1915), and *Foe-Farrell* (1918); ed. *Oxford Book of English Verse* and *The Oxford Book of Prose*; critical works include *On the Art of Writing* (1917), *Shakespeare's Workmanship* (1918), *The Art of Reading* (1920), *Charles Dickens and Other Victorians* (1925), and *Studies in Literature* (1918, 1922, and 1929); completed, 1897, Stevenson's romance of *St. Ives.*

Quintil'ian (MARCUS FABIUS QUINTILIANUS) (*c.* A.D. 35–96), Rom. rhetorician; *b.* in Spain; instructed the younger Pliny; favoured by Vespasian; chief work, *Institutiones Oratoriæ* (commonly called *The Institutes*), a complete system of rhetoric.

R

Rabelais (*räb-e-lā'*), FRANÇOIS (*c.* 1483–1553), Fr. writer; *b.* Chinon; studied Gr. and Lat. authors, natural history, law, mathematics; was a Franciscan monk from 1519–24, a Benedictine till 1530, then studied medicine at Montpellier, 1530, Lyons, 1532; went to Rome as medical adviser of Jean du Bellay, 1533. Rabelais pub. *Pantagruel* (1533), *Gargantua* (*c.* 1535, *et seq.*); characteristics of Rabelais' style are frankness, wonderful power of expression, pervading spirit of mockery, a simple broad humour, and coarseness. He satirizes the social life of the time, and strongly attacks the monastic system and education of his day. His influence was strong on Fielding, Smollett, and Swift. Sir Thomas Urquhart made a remarkable translation of Rabelais, 1653.

[*Lives*, by Sir W. Besant (1879), A. Tilley (Fr. Men of Letters).]

Rachmaninoff (*räch-män'ē-nov*), SERGEI VASSILIEVITCH (1873–), Russ. composer and pianist; *b.* in Novgorod; studied at St. Petersburg Conservatoire, and in 1892 won gold medal for opera *Aleko*; famous as composer and conductor; works include operas, symphonies, and pianoforte concertos, the best known of which is his *Prelude in C Sharp Minor.* Pub. *Recollections* (1934).

Racine (*rä-sēn'*), JEAN (1639–99), Fr. dramatist; *b.* La Ferté-Milon, Aisne; educated at coll. of Beauvais, and at Port-Royal. Verses on king's marriage, 1660, won for him a pension and began his fame. *La Thébaïde* (1664), his first tragedy, and *Alexandre le Grand* (1665), recalled style of Corneille. His masterpieces are

Andromaque (1667), *Britannicus* (1669), *Bérénice* (1670), *Bajazet* (1672), *Mithridate* (1673), *Iphigénie* (1675), *Phèdre* (1677). *Les Plaideurs* (1668), imitated from Aristophanes' *Wasps*, is an amusing satire on the legal profession, written in exquisite verse. At the request of Madame de Maintenon he wrote the play *Esther* (1689), and *Athalie* (1691). Racine is the greatest tragic writer of the Fr. classical school after Corneille (whom he sometimes equals).

[*Lives and Critical Studies*, by G. Larroumet (1898), J. Lemaître (1908), and M. Duclaup (1925).]

Rackham (*rak'am*), ARTHUR (1867–), Brit. artist and illustrator; drawings purchased for many national and municipal collections; excels in illustrations of books such as *Peter Pan*, *Mother Goose*, *The Tempest*, *The Compleat Angler*, etc.

Radcliffe, MRS. ANN (1764–1823), Eng. novelist; *b.* London; her command of thrilling narrative and fine descriptive power are seen to advantage in her four best novels: *The Sicilian Romance* (1790), *The Romance of the Forest* (1791), *The Mysteries of Udolpho* (1794), and *The Italian* (1797).

Radetzky (*rä-det'skē*), JOHANN JOSEF, COUNT (1766–1858), Austrian soldier; *b.* in Bohemia; distinguished in Napoleonic invasions; helped to reorganize army; commander-in-chief of army of Italy, 1831; field-marshal, 1836; crushed the Sardinian forces at Custozza, 1848, and Novara, 1849.

Rae, JOHN (1813–93), Scot. Arctic traveller; *b.* in Orkney; joined Hudson's Bay Co. as doctor, 1833; engaged in five Arctic expeditions, 1846–54, in one of which he discovered the relics of the Franklin Expedition; wrote *Narrative of the Expedition to the Shores of the Arctic Sea in 1846–7.*

Rae'burn, SIR HENRY (1756–1823), Scot. portrait painter—the Scottish Velazquez; *b.* Edinburgh; began career as a miniaturist; spent two years in Italy, then settled in Edinburgh; portraits include Lord President Dundas, Sir W. Scott, Christopher North, Mrs. R. Scott Moncrieff; R.A., 1815, knighted and made H.M. Limner for Scotland, 1822; good collections in Scot. National Gallery, Edinburgh, and in Glasgow and Tate (London) galleries.

Raemaekers (*rä'mak-ers*), LOUIS (1869–), Dutch cartoonist; *b.* Roermond; his war cartoons achieved celebrity, exhibitions of them being held in London, 1915, and elsewhere; has published *The Great War in 1916*, *The Great War in 1917*, *Devant l'Histoire* (1918), and *Cartoon History of the War* (1919).

Raffles, SIR THOMAS STAMFORD (1781–1826), Brit. administrator; *b.* at sea, off Port Morant, Jamaica; lieut.-governor of Java, 1811, after its capture from the French; ruled with conspicuous success, doing much to reform the administration and civilize the natives; governor of Sumatra, 1818–23; on his advice Singapore was purchased and occupied, 1819.

[*Memoir*, by his widow (1830); *Lives*, by D. C. Boulger (1897) and H. Egerton (1899).]

Raglan', FITZROY JAMES HENRY SOMERSET, 1ST BARON (1788–1855), Brit. soldier and diplomatist; *b.* Badminton; distinguished in wars against Napoleon, losing arm at Waterloo; commander-in-chief of Crimean army, 1854; field-marshal, 1854; died before Sevastopol, heartbroken by censures at home.

[*Invasion of the Crimea*, by A. W. Kinglake (1863–7).]

Raiffeisen (*rī-fī'zen*), FRIEDRICH WILHELM (1818–88), Ger. economist; *b.* Hamm; founder of the agricultural mutual loan societies called 'Raiffeisen Banks.' The principle has been adopted in many European countries.

Raikes (*rāks*), ROBERT (1735–1811) founder of Sunday schools; *b.* Gloucester; proprietor of the *Gloucester Journal.* His attention having been called to neglected children, he started, with the Rev. Thomas Stock, a Sunday school about 1780, which proved so successful that the idea was taken up all over the country.

Rainy, ROBERT (1826–1906), Scot. ecclesiastic; *b.* Glasgow; minister of Free Church, 1851–62; prof. of church history, 1862, and principal in New College, Edinburgh, 1874; took prominent part in the formation of the United Free Church, 1900; was thrice moderator—of the Free Church, 1887, and of the United Free Church, 1900 and 1905.

[*Lives,* by R. Mackintosh (1907) and P. Carnegie Simpson (1909).]

Rait (*rāt*), SIR ROBERT SANGSTER (1874–), Scot. historian; *b.* Aberdeen; educated Aberdeen and Oxford; tutor of New Coll., Oxford, 1903–13; prof. of Scot. history and literature, Glasgow Univ., 1913–29; Historiographer-Royal for Scotland, 1919–29; principal and vice-chancellor of Glasgow Univ. since 1929; knighted, 1933; his publications include *Scotland* in 'The Making of the Nations' series (1911), *Life in the Mediæval University* (1912), *History of Scotland* (1914), *The Parliaments of Scotland* (1924).

Rákóczy (*rä'kōt-sē*), princely Hungarian family; principal members were: (1) GEORGE I. (1591–1648), took part in rising of Gabriel Bethlen; Prince of Transylvania, 1630; went to war with Austria and won religious liberty for Hungary. (2) FRANCIS II. (1676–1735); great-grandson of (1); led Hungarian revolt, 1703, until defeated at Trencsen, 1708; retired to Poland, 1711.

Raleigh, or RALEGH (*raw'li*), SIR WALTER (1552–1618), Eng. courtier, traveller, and author; *b.* in Devon; left Oxford to aid Huguenots, 1569; took part in rising of Netherlands against Spain; sailed with his half-brother, Sir Humphrey Gilbert, 1579; served in Ireland, 1580; became personal favourite of Elizabeth; sent out several expeditions to colonize America, which failed; gave name to Virginia; is said to have introduced potato and tobacco plants into this country; in 1588 fought against the Armada; fell from favour by his marriage, 1593, but was ultimately restored; made expedition to Guiana, 1595; commanded Cadiz expedition, 1596, and attack on Azores, 1597. Imprisoned by James I., 1603, on charge of treason, Raleigh wrote in captivity his unfinished *History of the World,* in lofty prose; persuaded James I. to allow him to lead an expedition to find gold mine on Orinoco; failed to find it, burned Span. town against king's orders, and, returning, was executed.

Raleigh, SIR WALTER ALEXANDER (1861–1922), Eng. man of letters; prof. of English, 1914–22, at Oxford; works include *Style* (1897), *Shakespeare* (1907), *Romance* (1917).

Ramée, LOUISE DE LA. See OUIDA.

Ram'eses, name of several Egyptian Pharaohs. RAMESES II. (reigned 1300–1230 B.C.) is one of the greatest of Egyptian kings. He defeated a powerful coalition in Syria, and completed the conquest of Ethiopia. He is famous as the builder of the temple at Thebes, a canal between the Nile and the Red Sea, and two obelisks at Luxor. His mummy was discovered near Thebes, 1881. RAMESES III. (reigned 1180–1150 B.C.) waged successful war against the Nubians, and cleared Egypt of the sea-pirates. He built the beautiful temple of Medinet-Abu and other monumental works. Was famed for great wealth.

Ramsay. (1) ALLAN (1686–1758), Scot. poet; *b.* Leadhills; about 1718 set up as bookseller in Edinburgh; pub. *The Tea-Table Miscellany* and *The Evergreen*, collections of poems; chiefly remembered as author of *The Gentle Shepherd*, a dramatic pastoral of the realistic type. He revived vernacular poetry, and prepared the way for Fergusson and Burns.

[*Life*, by Smeaton (1896).]

(2) ALLAN (1713–84), Scot. portrait-painter; son of (1); settled in London, 1756; portrait-painter to George III., 1767.

Ramsay, SIR WILLIAM (1852–1916), Scot. chemist; *b.* Glasgow; prof. of chemistry, Univ. Coll., Bristol, 1880; prof. of chemistry, Univ. Coll., London, 1887–1913; made investigations on molecular structure of liquids; discovered, jointly with Lord Rayleigh, the element argon; also discovered helium; subsequently isolated three other gaseous elements, xenon, krypton, and neon; discovered that radium gives off helium; Nobel prize in chemistry, 1904. He pub. text-books of marked originality.

[*Life*, by Sir W. Tilden (1918).]

Ramsay, SIR WILLIAM MITCHELL (1851–), Scot. archæologist; *b.* Glasgow; prof. of humanity, Aberdeen Univ., 1886–1911); works include *The Historical Geography of Asia Minor* (1890), *The Cities of St. Paul* (1907), *Chapters from the History of Asia Minor* (1924), *Asianic Elements in Greek Civilization* (1927).

Ran'dolph, THOMAS, 1ST EARL OF MORAY (*d.* 1332), Scot. patriot; nephew and follower of Robert Bruce; captured Edinburgh Castle from English, 1314; second in command at Bannockburn, 1314; regent of Scotland, 1329–32.

Ranjit Singh (*ran'jit sing*), (1780–1839), Sikh prince who became monarch of the Punjab, and maintained its independence against Afghanistan; faithful ally of Britain; seized Lahore, 1799, Amritsar, 1802; by treaty, 1809, surrendered dist. south of Sutlej to Britain.

Ranjitsinhji (*ran-jit-sin'ji*), KUMAR SHRI, MAHARAJAH JAM SAHIB OF NAWANAGAR (1872–1933), Ind. prince; educated Rajkot, India, and Trinity Coll., Cambridge; a great cricketer, he headed batting averages for All England, 1896 and 1900, and distinguished himself in Australia, 1897–8; as Maharajah of Nawanagar, from 1906, introduced important reforms; revisited England, and played for Sussex in 1908, 1912, and 1920; during the Great War supplied troops to the government and served with them at the front, 1914–15; author of *The Jubilee Book of Cricket* (1897), etc.

Ran'ke, LEOPOLD VON (1795–1886), noted Ger. historian; *b.* in Thuringia; became schoolmaster; appointed prof. extraordinary of history at Berlin Univ., 1825. Exhibited deep insight into eccles. history, width of view, and excellent literary style; among his best-known books are *History of England, principally in the 17th century*, *History of the Reformation in Germany*, *History of the Popes in the 16th and 17th Centuries*. Ennobled in 1866.

Raphael Santi (*rä'fā-el sän'tē*) or RAFFAELLO SANZIO (1483–1520), Ital. painter, greatest of Rom. school; *b.* Urbino; studied first under Timoteo Viti; his *Vision of a Knight* (National Gallery, London) and *St. Michael and St. George* (Louvre) belong to this period; later, under Perugino, produced famous *Marriage of the Virgin*; next went to Florence and came under the influence of Leonardo da Vinci and Michelangelo ; here he began long series of Madonnas, and painted the splendid *Entombment* ; summoned to Rome by Pope Julius II., 1508 ; with the aid of his pupils he decorated the ceiling and walls of four apartments of the Vatican, the subjects depicting evolution from paganism to Christianity ; he also designed long-lost tapestry cartoons, now in S. Kensington Museum ; other works of this period were the *Sibyls* in the Chigi Chapel, portrait of Pope Julius II., and the Del Sedia and Sistine Madonnas ; died whilst painting *The Transfiguration* ; mourned by all Rome. He was distinguished for mastery of workmanship, perfection of design, harmonious beauty of expression, refinement of taste, and purity of colour.

[*Lives*, by A. Rosenberg (1906), and Venturi (1920).]

Rasmussen, KNUD JOHAN VICTOR (1879–1933), Dan. explorer ; *b.* Jakobshavn, Greenland ; of Eskimo descent on mother's side ; made many expeditions throughout Arctic regions and studied the Eskimo tribes ; author of *Greenland by the Polar Sea* (1921), and *Across Arctic America* (1927).

Rasputin, GREGORY (1871–1916), Russ. monk of semi-secret sect, who until his 34th year was a peasant. He then visited Mt. Athos, Jerusalem, and Leningrad, where he became known as a 'healer.' Obtained influence over the Tsarina, through healing Tsarevitch, and played a sinister political rôle. Lured to a supper party by a nephew of the Tsar by marriage, he was shot, and his body was disposed of beneath the ice of the Neva.

[*Life*, by L. Fülöp - Miller (1928).]

Ravel′, MAURICE (1875–), Fr. composer ; *b* in Basses-Pyrénées ; educated Paris Conservatoire ; works include opera, oratorio, chamber music, and songs. His style shows marked individuality with daring harmony, but typically French in its polish and neatness.

Raven-Hill, LEONARD (1867–), Eng. artist and cartoonist ; studied at Lambeth and at Paris ; well known for his drawings and cartoons in *Punch*, 1896–1935.

Raw′linson, HENRY SEYMOUR, 1ST BARON (1864–1925), Brit. general ; educated at Eton and Sandhurst ; served in India, Sudan, and S. African Wars ; was in high command during the whole of the Great War, his crowning exploit being the great Brit. offensive of 1918, when, with the 4th Army, he broke through the Hindenburg Line. Received a peerage and a grant of £30,000, 1919. He directed the withdrawal of Brit. forces from N. Russia, 1919 ; commander - in - chief in India, 1920.

Ray (or WRAY), JOHN (1628–1705), Eng. naturalist ; *b.* Black Notley, Essex ; 'father' of Eng. natural history ; famous for his contributions to science of botany ; his scientific work was chiefly systematic.

Rayleigh (*ray′li*), JOHN WILLIAM STRUTT, 3RD BARON (1842–1919), Eng. physicist ; *b.* Essex ; prof. of physics, Cambridge, 1879–84, and of natural philosophy at the Royal Institution, 1887–1905 ; president of the Royal Soc., 1905 ; did important work on the fundamental electrical units, in optics and capillarity, on Boyle's Law at low pressures ; discovered with Ramsay the element argon ; Nobel Prize for physics, 1904 ; wrote *Theory of Sound* (1877–8), and numerous monographs.

Reade, CHARLES (1814–84), Eng. novelist ; *b.* in Oxfordshire ; first works were dramatic, and include *Masks and Faces* (or *Peg Woffington*), *Christie Johnstone*, *Peregrine Pickle*, *The Lyons Mail* ; novels include *It is Never too Late to*

Mend, The Cloister and the Hearth (his masterpiece, dealing with the life of the father of Erasmus), *Hard Cash*, etc.; nearly all treat of social problems.

Reading, RUFUS DANIEL ISAACS, 1ST MARQUESS OF (1860–1935), Brit. statesman; *b.* London, of Jewish parents; was at sea and a stockbroker before being called to the bar; Q.C. in 1898; Liberal M.P. for Reading, 1904–13; solicitor-general, 1910, and attorney-general, 1910–13; lord chief justice, 1913–21; high commissioner and special ambassador to U.S.A., 1918; viceroy of India, 1921–6; foreign secretary, Aug.–Nov. 1931.

Réaumur (*rā-ō-mür'*), RENÉ ANTOINE FERCHAULT DE (1683–1757), Fr. scientist; *b.* La Rochelle; investigated properties of steel and iron, production of opaque glass, etc.; constructed thermometer bearing his name, in which he divided the interval between the freezing and boiling points of water into eighty degrees.

Redmond. (1) JOHN EDWARD (1851–1918), Irish politician; *b.* Ballytrent; called to Eng. bar, 1886; Nationalist M.P. from 1881; on death of Parnell, 1891, was chosen as leader of his followers, and in 1900 became leader of the reunited Irish Nationalist party; mainly owing to his efforts the Home Rule Bill of 1914 was carried; during Great War stimulated recruiting in Ireland; refused office in Asquith's Coalition Government, 1915; with the Sinn Fein movement he was out of sympathy, and condemned Irish rebellion of 1916; supported Convention of July 1917, which endeavoured to formulate a scheme of self-government for Ireland. (2) WILLIAM HOEY KEARNEY (1861–1917), Irish politician; brother of (1); Nationalist M.P. from 1883; was twice imprisoned under the Crimes Act, 1888 and 1902; served in Great War, in Royal Irish Regiment, being promoted major and mentioned in dispatches; died of wounds.

Reeves (*rēvs*), JOHN SIMS (1818–1900), Eng. tenor vocalist; *b.* Woolwich; famous in opera, as a ballad-singer, and in oratorio; last appearance, 1891.

Regnault (*ren'yō*), HENRI VICTOR (1810–78), Fr. chemist and physicist; *b.* Aix-la-Chapelle; an authority on organic chemistry, thermometry, expansion of gases, specific heats, hygrometry, steam engines, etc.

Rehan (*rē'an*), ADA (1860–1916), U.S.A. actress; *b.* Limerick, Ireland; was one of the foremost actresses in America; among the rôles by which she won fame were Katharina in *The Taming of the Shrew*, Rosalind in *As You Like It*, and Lady Teazle in *The School for Scandal*; visited England on several occasions.

Reid, SIR GEORGE (1841–1913), Scot. portrait painter; *b.* Aberdeen; R.S.A., 1878; P.R.S.A., 1891–1902; knighted, 1891; his portrait of George Macdonald (Aberdeen Univ.) is notable.

Reid, THOMAS (1710–96), Scot. philosopher; *b.* in Kincardineshire; prof. of moral philosophy, Glasgow, 1764–80; founder of Scottish 'common-sense' school. Against Berkeley and Hume, Reid affirmed doctrine of sense perception and denied that objects are perceived through ideas. Pub. *Essays on the Intellectual and Active Powers of Man* (1785 and 1788).

Reid, WHITELAW (1837–1912), U.S.A. diplomatist; *b.* Ohio; ed. *New York Tribune*, 1872; was U.S.A. minister to France, 1889–92, to Britain, 1905–13; works include *After the War* (1867), *Problems of Expansion* (1900), *The Greatest Fact in Modern History* (1906), and *American and English Studies* (1913).

Reinach (*ri'nach*), JOSEPH (1856–1921), Fr. publicist and politician; *b.* Paris; chief ed. of *République Française* from 1886; elected deputy in 1889 and in 1893; was an energetic defender of Dreyfus.

Reinhardt (*rīn-hart*), MAX (1873–), Ger. theatrical manager, a Jew; *b.* near Vienna; famous for realistic and beautiful stage productions; manager of Deutsches Theater, Berlin; went to London in 1911 and produced many plays, both there and in other foreign cities; became citizen of Czechoslovakia, 1933, owing to Nazi anti-Jewish campaign.

Réjane (*rā-zhän'*), 'GABRIELLE RÉJU,' MADAME (1857–1920), Fr. actress; *b.* Paris; made her début, 1875; among her productions have been *Ma Camarade*, *Germinie Lacerteux*, and her best, *Madame Sans-Gêne*; appeared in London, at the Gaiety, 1894, in *Madame Sans-Gêne*; made many notable tours; founded the Théâtre Réjane, 1906.

Rem'brandt (REMBRANDT HARMENS VAN RIJN) (1606–69), Dutch painter and etcher; *b.* Leyden; greatest of the Dutch school; settled in Amsterdam; *St. Paul in Prison* and *The Money Changer* are among his early works. Married, 1634, Saskia van Uylenborch, who appears in many of his pictures; after her death, 1642, his life was sombre and distressed; he became bankrupt, 1656. Rembrandt excelled in realistic portraiture and portrait groups, in depicting old age, and in effects of concentrated light; works suggest the mystery that underlies things seen. His masterpieces include *The Night Watch* (Amsterdam), *The Anatomy Lesson* (The Hague), portrait of Rembrandt's daughter-in-law, *Magdalen van Loo* (sold in 1920 for £60,000); and in landscape *The Mill* (sold in 1911 for £100,000); religious works: *Christ healing the Sick*, *Good Samaritan* (Louvre), etc.; fine collection of his etchings in Brit. Museum.

[*Lives*, by E. Mitchell (1903), G. Baldwin Brown (1907), and J. Lavan (1928).]

Renan (*rā-non'*), ERNEST (1823–92), Fr. philosopher; *b.* Tréguier, Côtes-du-Nord. He was trained for the priesthood at Saint Sulpice Seminary, left the Church because of religious doubts, and began to seek truth in science. His first work, *L'Avenir de la Science*, written at this time, was not published till 1890. He studied philosophy, theology, history of religions, and ancient languages, and did much service to Biblical criticism; his style is his great merit. His *Vie de Jésus* (1863) and *Origines du Christianisme* caused great sensation by rejection of divine elements from Christianity; his best work, partly autobiographical, is *Souvenirs d'Enfance et de Jeunesse* (1883), written in exquisitely simple style; last work, *Histoire du Peuple d'Israel* (1887–91).

[*Lives*, by W. Barry (1905) and J. M. Robertson (1924).]

Reni, GUIDO. See GUIDO RENI.

Rennie, JOHN (1761–1821), Scot. civil engineer; *b.* in E. Lothian; designed special machinery for flour mills; settled in London, 1791; constructed canals in various parts of England, built bridges, including Waterloo Bridge; London Bridge, finished after his death, was designed by him; also constructed or improved docks and harbours.

Renwick, JAMES (1662–88), Scot. Covenanter; *b.* Moniaive, Dumfriesshire; gained great reputation as field-preacher; declared a rebel by the Privy Council. Pub. the *Apologetical Declaration* (1684); captured in Edinburgh, and hanged in the Grassmarket.

Reszke (*rāsh'ke*), JEAN DE (1850–1925), Polish operatic singer; *b.* Warsaw; made his début as a baritone at Venice, 1874; appeared first as a tenor in 1879, and speedily won recognition as one of the greatest dramatic tenors.

Reuchlin (*roich'lin*), JOHANN (1455–1522), Ger. scholar; *b.* Pforzheim; revived study of Hebrew; engaged in dispute with Johann Pfefferkorn, a converted Jew, who urged destruction of all Jewish books except the Bible. Reuchlin, defending the Jewish books, came into conflict with the Inquisition, the treatment he received calling forth the indignant *Epistolæ Obscurorum Virorum*, by Ulrich von Hutten and others; greatest work, *De Rudimentis Hebraicis*; though not a Reformer, life and work influenced the Reform movement.

Reuter (*roi'ter*), PAUL JULIUS, BARON DE (1818–99), originator of Reuter's News Agency; *b.* Cassel, Germany; became naturalized Brit. subject, 1851, and established offices in London, with correspondents in all parts of the world.

Revere (*re-vēr'*), PAUL (1735–1818), Amer. patriot; *b.* Boston; became gold and silver smith, and later an engraver; was one of the leaders in the Boston Tea Party, 1773; his midnight ride to Lexington and Concord, 1775, to give warning of the British advance, is told in Longfellow's poem.

Reynolds (*ren'oldz*), SIR JOSHUA (1723–92), Eng. portrait painter; *b.* Plympton Earl, Devon; first president Royal Academy, 1768; knighted, 1769; painter to King George III., 1784; brilliant career both artistically and socially; founded Literary Club, 1764; figures much in Boswell's *Johnson*; excelled in painting children; chief works: *Mrs. Siddons as the Tragic Muse*, *Duchess of Devonshire and her Baby*, *The Age of Innocence*, and portraits of Johnson, Sterne, Burke, Goldsmith, Fox, Garrick, etc.; renowned also for literary quality of his *Discourses* (Presidential Addresses); buried in St. Paul's.

Rhodes (*rōds*), CECIL JOHN (1853–1902), Brit. colonial statesman; *b.* Bishop's Stortford; son of clergyman; sent to Natal for health, 1871; made fortune in Kimberley diamond fields; founded De Beers Mining Co., 1880; formed plan of making S. Africa British and linking it with Egypt; entered Cape politics, 1881: secured establishment of Brit. protectorate of Bechuanaland, and considerable increase of territory across Zulu border, 1884; established Brit. S. Africa Co., obtained charter for it, and built up what is now known as Rhodesia. Rhodes became prime minister at Cape, 1890; advocated policy of 'Equal rights for all civilized men south of the Zambezi,' regardless of colour; strove to conciliate the Dutch; Jameson Raid, 1895, forced him to resign, 1896; by his own personality quelled Matabele revolt, 1896; chief promoter of Cape to Cairo Railway and trans-African telegraph line; present in siege of Kimberley, 1899–1900, when his health broke down. He was buried in the Matopo Hills, Rhodesia. Public-spirited, energetic, autocratic, Rhodes was a great 'empire-maker.' By his will he left practically his whole fortune (*c.* £6,000,000) to the public service, including 175 Rhodes Scholarships (for Brit. Colonial and Amer. students) at Oxford.

[*Lives*, by Sir L. Mitchell (2 vols. 1910), A. F. B. Williams (1921), and T. G. McDonald (1927).]

Rhys (*rēs*), SIR JOHN (1840–1915), Welsh philologist; *b.* in Cardigan. Wrote standard books on Celtic literature and the Arthurian legend.

Ribot (*rē-bō'*), ALEXANDRE FÉLIX JOSEPH (1842–1923), Fr. statesman; *b.* St. Omer; as foreign minister, 1890, concluded alliance between France and Russia; premier, 1892, 1895, 1898, 1917; minister of finance, 1914–17; strongly opposed policy of retaliation against religious orders.

Ricar'do, DAVID (1772–1823), Eng. political economist, of Jewish origin; *b.* London; began life as stockbroker; pub. *High Price of Bullion a Proof of the Depreciation of Banknotes,* the first scientific treatise on currency (1809); also pub. *Principles of Political Economy and Taxation* (1817), its most important feature being doctrine of nature of rent; M.P., 1818–23.

Rice, ALICE HEGAN (1870–), U.S.A. author; *b.* in Kentucky; best known for *Mrs. Wiggs of the Cabbage Patch.*

Richard I., CŒUR-DE-LION (1157–99), King of England; third son of Henry II.; succeeded 1189; joined Third Crusade; prominent in capture of Acre, 1191; defeated Saladin at Arsuf, 1191; on way home was captured and imprisoned by Leopold of Austria; handed over to Emperor Henry VI., who released him for ransom; on return to England, 1194, crushed his brother John's intrigues; subsequently returned to Fr. dominions; killed during siege of castle of Châlus.

Richard II. (1367–1400), King of England; son of Black Prince; succeeded 1377; met rebels under Wat Tyler at Mile End and Smithfield, 1381, and ended their insurrection; deprived of absolute power by Lords Appellant, 1388; concluded peace with France, 1396; revenged himself on Lords Appellant, 1397–98, sentencing them to death or exile; captured and deposed by cousin, Henry of Bolingbroke (afterwards Henry IV.), 1399; subsequently imprisoned in Pontefract Castle, where he is supposed to have been murdered.

Richard III. (1452–85), King of England; son of Richard, Duke of York; distinguished himself at battles of Barnet and Tewkesbury; crowned 1483; shortly afterwards his nephews, Edward V. and his brother, were murdered in Tower by his orders; suppressed Buckingham's insurrection which ensued; was defeated and killed at battle of Bosworth.

Richardson, SAMUEL (1689–1761), Eng. novelist; *b.* Derbyshire; son of joiner; became printer of House of Commons Journals, and King's Printer; was made master of the Stationers' Co. Was asked to publish a 'model' letter-writer; this suggestion was the origin of his first novel, *Pamela* (1740). It was intended as a 'moral' novel, and therefore met with much ridicule, but was original and full of life. Wrote also *Clarissa Harlowe,* a somewhat tedious seven-vol. novel (1747–8), and *Sir Charles Grandison* (1753). Is called the 'father of the modern novel'; was the inspirer of Diderot and Rousseau among others; Fielding's novels were written as a counterblast to Richardson's sentimentality.

[*Life,* by A. Dobson (English Men of Letters, 1902).]

Richelieu (*rēsh-lū'*), ARMAND JEAN DU PLESSIS DE (1585–1642), Fr. statesman; *b.* Paris; Bishop of Luçon, 1607; secretary of war and foreign affairs, 1616; assisted Marie de' Medici in recovery of power, 1620; cardinal, 1622; minister of state, 1624–42. Richelieu laid foundations of France's pre-eminence; won permanent power over King Louis XIII.; secured supersession and exile of Marie de' Medici; made monarchy strong by suppression of feudal nobility; captured Rochelle, 1628, and destroyed power of Huguenots; initiated policy of opposition to Austria in Thirty Years' War, and so destroyed power of France's great rival; opposed Habsburgs in Netherlands and Piedmont, and aided revolt of Catalonia against Spain; his foreign policy was successful but immensely expensive. Founded Fr. Academy.

[*Lives*, by E. C. Price (1912), P. Denis (1913).]

Richepin (*rēsh-pan'*), JEAN (1849–1926), Fr. poet, novelist, dramatist; *b.* Algeria; member of Fr. Academy; brilliant and unconventional writer. His *La Chanson des Gueux* (1876) led to his imprisonment for 'outrage aux mœurs.' Some of his novels, including *Césarine* (1888), *Les Grandes Amoureuses* (1896), are distinguished for psychological analysis. *Miarka* (1883), *Truandailles* (1890), and *Flamboche* (1895) are realistic transcripts from life. His best work is contained in his plays: *La Glu* (1883), *Nana Sahib* (1883), *Le Chien de Garde* (1898), etc.

Richter (*rich'ter*), HANS (1843–1916), Hungarian musical conductor; *b.* Raab; conducted at Munich, Budapest, and Vienna; from 1879 up to the Great War held annual orchestral concerts in London; from 1900 conducted Hallé concerts in Manchester; noteworthy for his interpretations of Wagner, Beethoven, and Brahms.

Richter, JOHANN PAUL FRIEDRICH (1763–1825), generally known as JEAN PAUL, Ger. author; *b.* near Bayreuth; devoted himself entirely to literature; first works were satirical and unsuccessful, but with *The Invisible Lodge* (1793) he turned to purely humorous writing, and quickly attained fame; works include fine studies of humble life, such as *Dominie Wuz* (1793), probably his masterpiece, and *Quintus Fixlein* (1796); studies of the ideal as in *Hesperus* (1795), *Titan* (1803), and philosophical works. Though sometimes careless in style and form, he is noteworthy for his simplicity, kindly humour, and passionate love of nature. His popularity in Great Britain is due to Carlyle's appreciation.

Ridley, NICHOLAS (1500–55), Eng. divine and martyr; *b.* Northumberland; was chaplain to Henry VIII., 1541; Bishop of Rochester, 1547; supported Lady Jane Grey; tried as heretic under Mary, and burned at Oxford.

Riel (*rē-el'*), LOUIS (1844–85), Can. agitator; *b.* St. Boniface, Manitoba; leader of rebellion of the half-breeds, 1869–70; after its suppression fled to U.S.A.; headed a second insurrection, 1885, was captured, and executed.

Rienzi (or RIENZO) (*rē-en'zē*), COLA DI (*c.* 1313–54), Roman patriot, friend of Petrarch; *b.* Rome; was roused against nobles through the assassination of his brother; incited citizens' rising, 1347, and was made tribune; fell from power and imprisoned; released, and again in power, 1354, but murdered; is hero of poem by Byron, opera by Wagner, and of a novel by Bulwer Lytton.

Rim'sky-Korsak'ov, NICOLAS ANDREIEVICH (1844–1908), Russ. composer; *b.* in Novgorod; his first symphony (in E minor) had such success that he abandoned his career in the navy, and thereafter produced a succession of operas, symphonies, songs, pianoforte pieces, etc., which had great influence on the subsequent development of Russ. music; works include *Sadko* (1895), *The Tsar's Bride* (1899), *Le Coq d'Or* (1910), and a treatise on *The Foundations of Instrumentation.*

Ripon, GEORGE FREDERICK SAMUEL ROBINSON, 1ST MARQUESS OF (1827–1909), Brit. Liberal statesman; *b.* London; secretary for war, 1863–6; secretary of state for India, 1866; lord president of Council, 1868–

73; commissioner in *Alabama* dispute, 1871; viceroy of India, 1880–4; incurred disapproval for too liberal measures; colonial secretary, 1892–5; lord privy seal, 1905–8.

Ritschl (*rich'l*), ALBRECHT (1822–89), Ger. theologian and philosopher; *b.* Berlin. His attitude towards Christianity is to divorce it from metaphysics; thus all controversies as to the nature of the Father and Son are fruitless; spiritual experience is everything. His theology has had considerable influence.

Rivière (*riv-ē-ār'*), BRITON (1840–1920), Brit. animal painter; *b.* London; R.A., 1881; among chief works are *The Poacher's Nurse*, *The Last of the Garrison*, *Charity*, *Circe*, *Daniel*.

Rivoli, DUKE OF. See under MASSÉNA.

Rizzio, or RICCIO (*rēt'shō*), DAVID (*c.* 1532–66), Ital. musician; *b.* Turin; secretary to Mary Queen of Scots; his influence with the queen incensed the nobles, who, with Darnley, dragged him from her presence in Holyrood and murdered him.

Robbia. See DELLA ROBBIA.

Robert I., ROBERT BRUCE, or BRUS (1274–1329), Scot. king and national hero; of Norman descent. His grandfather was one of three claimants to Scot. throne on death of 'Maid of Norway.' Bruce swore fealty to Edward I., 1296, but during the next ten years he changed sides more than once. His murder of Comyn, 1306, made breach with Edward complete, and he was crowned king at Scone; was defeated at Methven, 1306. The Eng. army under Pembroke scoured Scotland for Bruce, who led wild life in hiding. The tide turned in 1307; Bruce won battle of Louden Hill; Edward I. died on his way to Scotland, and by 1313 Stirling alone held out for England; a large Eng. army under Edward II. was decisively defeated at Bannockburn, June 24, 1314, by the superior skill of Bruce. Invasions of England extorted recognition of independence of Scotland by Treaty of Northampton, 1328. Bruce died of leprosy; a wise king, a brave soldier, and a true patriot.

Robert II. (1316–90), King of Scotland; son of Walter the Steward and Robert Bruce's daughter Marjory; succeeded uncle, David II., 1371; founded Stewart dynasty; his peaceable nature was unfitted to troublous times; during his reign, 1388, English were defeated at Otterburn (Chevy Chase).

Robert I., THE DEVIL (*d.* 1035), Duke of Normandy; father of William the Conqueror; aided Edward the Confessor, and helped Henry I. of France against his rebellious subjects; died at Nicæa while returning from pilgrimage to Holy Land.

Robert Guiscard. See under GUISCARD.

Roberts OF KANDAHAR, FREDERICK SLEIGH, 1ST EARL (1832–1914), Brit. soldier; *b.* Cawnpore, India; served through the Ind. Mutiny; won V.C., 1858; served in Abyssinian expedition, 1868, and in Lushai expedition, 1871–2; led one of three columns against Amir of Afghanistan, and turned position of enemy in Peiwar Kotal Pass; promoted major-general and made K.C.B., 1878; after murder of Cavagnari, advanced on Kabul, which he occupied; heavily attacked, but made effective resistance; accomplished famous march to relief of Kandahar, 1880; received baronetcy and G.C.B., and appointed to command of Madras army. Created a peer, 1892. Finally left India, 1893. During two years of leisure wrote *Forty-one Years in India.* Field-marshal, 1895, and commander-in-chief in Ireland. Succeeded Buller, 1899, as commander-in-chief in S. African War; captured General Cronje, secured relief of Kimberley, Ladysmith, and Mafeking; occupied Pretoria, and annexed Transvaal and Orange Free State. On his return, 1901, received an earldom and the Garter. Retired, 1903, and devoted his latter years to advocacy of national service. Died during Great War when visiting Ind. troops in France.

[*Life*, by Sir S. W. Forrest (1914).]

Roberts, Sir Charles George Douglas (1860–), Canadian author; *b.* in New Brunswick; prof. of Eng. and Fr. literature and political economy in King's Coll., Nova Scotia; his works in verse include *Orion* (1880), *In Divers Tones* (1887), *The Book of the Rose* (1903), *New Poems* (1919); and in prose, *The Watchers of the Trails* (1904), *Red Fox* (1905), *The House in the Water* (1908), *Kings in Exile* (1909), *Hoof and Claw* (1913), *Wisdom in the Wilderness* (1923), *The Vagrant of Time* (1927).

Roberts, John (1847–1919), great Eng. billiards player; *b.* near Manchester; first won the championship, 1875; wrote *Billiards for Beginners* (1901), *Modern Billiards* (1902), and *The Game of Billiards* (1905).

Roberts, Morley (1857–), English novelist; *b.* London; worked in Australian bush, 1876–79; returning to England, was employed in Civil Service; travelled widely; author of *Lady Penelope* (1905), *Sea Dogs* (1910), *Hearts of Women* (1919), *Warfare in the Human Body* (1920), *Malignancy and Evolution* (1926), *The Scent of Death* (1931).

Robertson, Frederick William (1816–53), Anglican divine; *b.* London; incumbent of Trinity Chapel, Brighton; a powerful preacher and spiritual leader. His five series of sermons attracted enormous attention.

[*Life and Letters*, by S. Brooke (1865).]

Robertson, John Mackinnon (1856–1933), Scottish author and politician; *b.* Brodick, Isle of Arran; removed to London, and became editor of the *National Reformer* (1891–3), and of the *Free Review* (1893–5); Liberal M.P. for Tyneside, 1906–18; parl. secretary to the Board of Trade, 1911–15; works include *Modern Humanists* (1891), *Problem of Hamlet* (1919), *A Short History of Morals* (1920), *The Problems of the Shakespeare Sonnets* (1926), *History of Free Thought in the Nineteenth Century* (1929).

Robertson, William (1721–93), Scot. clergyman and historian; *b.* Borthwick, Midlothian; principal of Edinburgh Univ., 1762; moderator of the General Assembly, and historiographer-royal for Scotland, 1763. His writings include *History of Scotland* (1759), *History of the Reign of the Emperor Charles V.* (1769), and *History of America* (1777).

[*Life*, by Dugald Stewart.]

Robertson, Sir William Robert (1860–1933), Brit. soldier; *b.* Welbourn, Lincs; entered army as private; lieutenant in 3rd Dragoon Guards, 1888; served in Ind. frontier expeditions and in S. Africa; was assistant-director of military operations for six years; commandant of the Staff Coll., 1910–13. Quartermaster-general when the Great War began; chief of Imperial General Staff, 1915–18; general officer commanding in chief, Great Britain, 1918–19; subsequently commanded Rhine Army in Germany, 1919–20; field-marshal, 1920. Wrote *From Private to Field-marshal* (1921), *Soldiers and Statesmen, 1914–18* (1926).

Robeson (*rōb'son*), PAUL BUSTILL (1898–), Amer. Negro actor and singer; *b.* Princetown, N.J.; graduated at Rutgers Coll. with high honours; qualified for the law, but embarked on stage career, 1922; has played in London; also a successful concert-singer of Negro spirituals and songs.

Robespierre (*rōbs-pyār'*), MAXIMILIEN MARIE ISIDORE (1758–94), Fr. revolutionist; *b.* Arras; a lawyer who early imbibed the views of Rousseau; elected to states-general, 1789. In the Convention he was elected first deputy for Paris, and with Danton and Marat withstood the charge brought by the Girondists against the Jacobins of aiming at a dictatorship; urged the execution of Louis XVI.; in 1793 was elected a member of the Committee of Public Safety, and was one of the chief authors of Reign of Terror. With Danton's execution, 1794, begins the last phase of the career of Robespierre; openly declared that his aim was to extirpate the vicious and to establish a reign of virtue; carried a resolution recognizing a Supreme Being, and set up a new cult, with himself as high priest; with these views the leading men of the day had no sympathy, and they organized the revolution of 9th Thermidor (July 27, 1794) in which Robespierre fell. His speeches show him to have been a fanatic, cold-blooded but sincere; not a great administrator, nor a statesman at all. He owed his position in the main to his transparent sincerity and honesty.

[*Histoire de Robespierre*, by E. Hamel (1865–7 and 1878); *Robespierre*, by Hilaire Belloc (1901), and *Robespierre and the French Revolution*, by C. F. Warwick (1909).]

Robey (*rō'bā*), GEORGE (1869–), stage name of GEORGE WADE, Eng. comedian; one of greatest comedians on variety stage; began life as engineer; pub. various vols. of reminiscences.

Robin Hood, Eng. mediæval hero, frequently mentioned in literature from 14th cent.; probably historical character who had his headquarters in Sherwood Forest; set forth by Sir Walter Scott in *Ivanhoe.*

Robins, ELIZABETH (MRS. GEORGE RICHMOND PARKS), (1862–), author and actress; *b.* Louisville, Kentucky; an interpreter of Ibsen's plays; novels: *Below the Salt* (1896), *The Magnetic North* (1904), *The Florentine Frame* (1909), *Way Stations* (1913), *Camilla* (1918), *The Messenger* (1920), *Ancilla's Share* (1924), and *The Secret that was Kept* (1926).

Robinson, AGNES MARY F. See DUCLAUX.

Rob Roy (ROBERT M'GREGOR) (1671–1734), the Scot. Robin Hood; outlawed, 1691; organized notorious band of cattle-raiders; submitted and imprisoned, 1722; pardoned, 1727; settled at Balquhidder, Perthshire; hero of Sir Walter Scott's novel, *Rob Roy.*

Rochefoucauld. See under LA ROCHEFOUCAULD.

Rock'efeller. (1) JOHN DAVISON (1839–), U.S.A. millionaire; *b.* Richford, New York; formed first great trust, 'Standard Oil Co.,' 1870; showed much interest in educational, medical, and charitable affairs; founded and endowed the univ. of Chicago, 1890; founded the Rockefeller Institute for Medical Research, 1901. Made many gifts to educational institutions through his General Education Board and the Rockefeller Foundation for 'promoting the well-being of mankind throughout the world'; had given for philanthropic purposes up to 1927 over £100,000,000. (2) JOHN DAVISON (1874–), U.S.A. capitalist, son of above; associated with his father in various business enterprises; also connected with religious and philanthropic movements, advancing and developing his father's schemes.

Rockingham, CHARLES WATSON WENTWORTH, 2ND MARQUESS OF (1730–82), Brit. Whig statesman; premier and first lord of Treasury, 1765–6, with Burke as secretary; fell through passing repeal of Stamp Act; opposed Lord North's disastrous colonial policy, and, on his overthrow, formed second ministry, 1782; honest and high-minded, but not a great statesman.

Rodin (*rō-dan'*), AUGUSTE (1840–1917), Fr. impressionist sculptor; *b.* Paris; distinguished for busts and statues of overwhelming power, realism, and psychic perception; has also executed Biblical and symbolic groups. His works include *The Burghers of Calais* (replica in London), *The Gate of Hell, War, The Man who Awakes,* bronze *St. John the Baptist, The Thinker, Victor Hugo.*

[*Auguste Rodin,* by J. Cladel (1908; Eng. trans. 1917), and L. Benedite (1926).]

Rodney, GEORGE BRYDGES, 1ST BARON (1719–92), Brit. admiral; *b.* Walton-on-Thames; vice-admiral of Great Britain, 1781; destroyed Havre harbour, 1759; took Martinique, 1761; created baronet, 1764; won victories of Cape Finisterre and Cape St. Vincent, and relieved Gibraltar, 1780; captured St. Eustatia, 1781; defeated Fr. fleet off Leeward Islands, 1782, his crowning victory; created baron in 1782.

[*Life,* by Hannay.]

Roe, SIR THOMAS (*c.* 1581–1644), Eng. diplomatist; *b.* Low Leyton, Essex; ambassador to West Indies and Brazil, to the Great Mogul Jahangir of Agra, and to Constantinople.

Rogers, SAMUEL (1763–1855), Eng. poet; *b.* Stoke Newington; entered his father's bank, 1784; became head of the firm, 1793; famous as poet in his own day, being offered the laureateship on Wordsworth's death in 1850, and ranked by Byron above Wordsworth and Coleridge; his works are unread to-day, and even *The Pleasures of Memory,* on which his fame chiefly rests, is but a name.

Rolland (*rō-lon'*), ROMAIN (1866–), Fr. writer; *b.* Clamecy, Nièvre; prof. of art history, 1895–1910; wrote critical and historical works, but achieved reputation with his famous romance, *Jean-Christophe* (10 vols. 1904–12), the biography of a musician; has also written *Au-dessus de la Mêlée* (1915), *Les précurseurs* (1919), *Annette et Sylvie* (1922), *L'Été* (1924), *Mère et Fils* (1927), and *Goethe et Beethoven* (1931); Nobel Prize, 1915.

Rom'illy, SIR SAMUEL (1757–1818), Eng. legal reformer; *b.* London; advocated reform of the criminal law by restriction of capital punishment, and reduction of penalties for lesser crimes; wrote *Observations on the Criminal Law of England* (1810).

Rom'ney, GEORGE (1734–1802), Eng. portrait painter; *b.* Dalton-in-Furness, Lancs; rival of Reynolds; never admitted to the Academy; favourite sitter Lady Hamilton, whom he painted in more than thirty different characters; best work gives an impression of movement and elusive grace, and includes such paintings as *The Parson's Daughter, Duchess of Gordon and her Son, The Misses Beckford when Children,* and *Mrs. Yates as the Tragic Muse.*

[*Lives,* by Lord Ronald Sutherland Gower (1904), and H. Ward and W. Roberts (1904).]

Ronald, SIR LANDON (1873–), Brit. musician; *b.* London; has a wide reputation as orchestral conductor; principal, Guildhall School of Music, since 1910. Composer of numerous songs, etc.

Ronsard (*ron-sär'*), PIERRE DE (1524–85), Fr. poet; *b.* near Vendôme; chief of the *Pléiade*, which aimed at introducing the Renaissance into France. Works include *Odes* (1550), *Les Amours de Cassandre* (1552), *Le Bocage Royal* (1554), *Hymnes* (1555), *Les Discours des Misères de ce Temps* (1560), and an unsuccessful and unfinished epic, *La Franciade* (1572). Some of his sonnets are exquisite. His poetry shows rich fancy, a charming blend of mediæval and classical spirit, and beauty and variety of rhythm.

Rönt'gen, WILHELM KONRAD VON (1845–1923), Ger. physicist; *b.* Lennep; prof. of physics and mathematics, Hohenheim, 1875, and at Strasbourg, 1876, and prof. of physics at Giessen, 1879, at Würzburg, 1885, and at Munich, 1899–1920. He did valuable work in physics; best known for his discovery of the 'X' or Röntgen rays, 1895; awarded the Rumford medal of the Royal Soc., 1896; awarded Nobel Prize for physics, 1901.

Rooke, SIR GEORGE (1650–1709), Brit. admiral; *b.* near Canterbury; commanded squadron which relieved Londonderry, 1689; took part in battle of La Hogue, 1692; commanded expedition against Cadiz and destroyed Span. Plate Fleet in Vigo; captured Gibraltar, 1704.

Roon, ALBRECHT THEODOR EMIL, COUNT VON (1803–79), Prussian soldier and military author; *b.* near Kolberg, Pomerania; as minister of war, 1859–73, and of navy, 1861–71, he carried out a reorganization of the army, the value of which was shown both in the Austrian War of 1866 and in the Franco-Ger. War of 1870–1.

Roosevelt (*rō'zĕ-vell*), FRANKLIN DELANO (1882–), president of U.S.A.; *b.* New York; admitted to bar, 1907; assistant secretary of navy, 1913–20; inspector of U.S.A. naval forces in European waters, 1918; crippled by attack of infantile paralysis, 1921; democratic governor of New York State, 1928; president, 1932. Secured the repeal of Prohibition, 1933, and introduced schemes of National Recovery during financial collapse. Author of *Whither Bound?* (1926), and *The Happy Warrior* (1928).

Roosevelt, THEODORE (1858–1919), U.S.A. statesman, writer, soldier, and sportsman; president of U.S.A.; *b.* New York; educated at Harvard; member of New York State Legislature, 1882–4; civil service commissioner, 1889–95; head of police department, New York, 1895–7; assistant secretary of navy, 1897; organized and led 'Rough Riders' in Cuba during Span.-Amer. War; governor of New York State, 1898; vice-president of U.S.A. (Republican), 1901; on M'Kinley's assassination succeeded as president, 1901; president for second term, 1904–9; on retirement secured election of Taft. Came forward as independent candidate for presidentship, 1912, but without success. In 1913 headed a scientific expedition into the heart of Brazil, which explored the head-waters of a hitherto unknown tributary of the Madeira R. During Great War Roosevelt was untiring in his advocacy of Allied cause.

Roosevelt was the most prominent American of his day. America owes to him Pure Food and Drugs Act, Meat Inspection Act, Employers' Liability Act, Act to regulate railway rates, etc., and adoption of Panama Canal project. He acted as peacemaker in Russo-Jap. War, 1905. In his books he appears as a keen sportsman, rancher, student of men and of natural history. His voluminous writings include *Naval War of 1812* (1882), *Hunting Trips of a Ranchman* (1886), *Winning of the West* (4 vols. 1889–96), *American Ideals* (1897), *Autobiography* (1913), *Letters to his Children* (1919).

Root, Elihu (1845–), U.S.A. statesman ; *b.* Clinton, New York ; secretary for war, 1899–1904, and responsible for many reforms in the administration of the army ; secretary of state, 1905–9, when he did much towards the reorganization of the consular service ; awarded the Nobel peace prize, 1912, for his services in the pacification of Cuba and the Philippines, and his handling of various matters in dispute between Japan and the U.S.A. ; is a member of the permanent court of arbitration at The Hague.

Rosa, Carl August Nicholas (1843–89), operatic impresario ; *b.* Hamburg ; founded Carl Rosa Opera Co. in London, 1875, with the object of encouraging Eng. composers.

Rosa, Salvator (1615–73), Ital. painter, etcher, and poet ; *b.* near Naples ; worked in Florence and Rome ; excelled in wild and gloomy landscapes, but painted also historical subjects—*e.g. Saul and the Witch of Endor* (Louvre), *Belisarius* (Grosvenor Gallery, London), etc. ; his *Satires* appeared in 1719.

Ros'coe, Sir Henry Enfield (1833–1915), Eng. chemist ; *b.* London ; chief researches were on vanadium and the chemical action of light, but he was also notable for the stimulus he gave to the study of technical chemistry in Britain ; his *Treatise on Chemistry*, written with Schorlemmer, is a most exhaustive work ; other works include *Lessons in Elementary Chemistry*, *Primer of Chemistry*, *John Dalton.*

Rose, John Holland (1855–), Eng. historian ; *b.* Bedford ; reader in modern history, Cambridge, 1911–19 ; Vere-Harmsworth prof. of naval history, 1919–33 ; author of *The Rise of Democracy* (1897), *Life of Napoleon I.* (1902), *The Development of the European Nations, 1870–1921* (1923), etc.

Rosebery, Archibald Philip Primrose, 5th Earl of, and 1st Earl of Midlothian (1847–1929), Brit. Liberal statesman ; *b.* London ; under-secretary, Home Office, 1881–3 ; first commissioner of works, 1885 ; foreign secretary, 1886, 1892–4 ; prime minister, 1894–5, succeeding Gladstone ; resigned owing to party dissensions ; also resigned leadership of Liberal party, 1896 ; president of Liberal League, 1902, an organization of moderate members of the party ; made occasional returns thereafter to political arena as independent critic. He early advocated reform of House of Lords ; preached imperialistic ideals ; attacked both Tariff Reform and Socialistic legislation.

A devotee of local government, Lord Rosebery was first chairman of London County Council, 1889 ; he was Lord Rector of Aberdeen Univ., 1878, Edinburgh Univ., 1880, Glasgow Univ., 1899, St. Andrews Univ., 1911 ; chancellor of London Univ. An ardent sportsman, he won the Derby, 1894, 1895, 1905. A brilliant speaker, he was often called 'Orator of the Empire.' Among other literary works he wrote *Napoleon, the Last Phase* (1900), *Miscellanies Literary and Historical* (1921), and monographs on Pitt, Peel, Cromwell, Randolph Churchill, Chatham.

[*Life*, by Earl of Crewe (1931).]

Ross, Sir John (1777–1856), Brit. admiral ; *b.* in Wigtownshire ; began career of Arctic exploration, 1818, when he accompanied Parry to Baffin Bay; made a second expedition to Polar regions, 1829–33, and again in 1850 in search of Franklin; his second expedition had important scientific results recorded in his *Narrative of a Second Voyage in search of a North-West Passage* (1835).

Ross, SIR RONALD (1857–1932), Brit. physician; *b.* Almora, India; entered Ind. Medical Service, 1881, and after 1892 devoted himself to research into the causes of malaria; in 1897–8 he verified the theory that the microbes of the disease are spread by mosquitoes, and thus indicated a method of prevention which has done much to modify its ravages; received Nobel Prize for medicine, 1902; writings include *Poems*, *The Prevention of Malaria* (1910), *Memoirs* (1923), and *Studies in Malaria* (1928).

Rosse, WILLIAM PARSONS, 3RD EARL OF (1800–67), Irish astronomer; *b.* York; improved construction of reflecting telescopes; erected great telescope at his seat, Birr Castle, Parsonstown, and made many observations of nebulæ.

Rosset'ti. (1) DANTE GABRIEL (1828–82), Eng. painter and poet; *b.* London; son of Gabriele Rossetti, Ital. patriot, who had become prof. of Italian at King's Coll., London; studied art under Ford Madox Brown; first picture *The Girlhood of Mary; Virgin* (1849); followed by *The Laboratory*, a visualization of Browning's poem, and the beautiful *Ecce Ancilla Domini*; married, 1860, Elizabeth Eleanor Siddal, represented in his *Beata Beatrix* (painted in 1863, a year after her death), etc.; founded with Holman Hunt and Millais the Pre-Raphaelite Brotherhood. A series of Arthurian scenes was pub. in 1857. *Rosa Triplex*, *Dante's Dream*, *Veronica Veronese* are other well-known pictures, while his designs for stained-glass windows did much to revive interest in that art. As a writer, Rossetti was essentially mediæval and mystic. His earliest pub. poems appeared in the *Germ* (1850); his *Poems* were printed in 1870, *Ballads and Sonnets* in 1881. His scope ranges from the ethereal dreaminess of 'The Blessed Damozel' to the despairing cry of 'The Woodspurge.' A new ed. of his trans. of the early Ital. poets was pub. as *Dante and his Circle* (1874).

[*Memoir*, by W. M. Rossetti (1886; revised ed. 1911); *Lives*, by A. C. Benson ('English Men of Letters,' 1904), and E. Waugh (1928).]

(2) WILLIAM MICHAEL (1829–1919), Eng. author, brother of (1); ed. Pre-Raphaelite *Germ* (1856); assistant-secretary, Board of Inland Revenue, 1869–94; wrote *Life of Keats* (1887), *Memoir of Dante Gabriel Rossetti* (prefaced to *Collected Works*, 1886), *Some Reminiscences* (1906), *Democratic Sonnets* (1907), etc.

(3) CHRISTINA GEORGINA (1830–94), Eng. poetess; *b.* London; sister of (1); poems distinguished by metrical felicity, quiet mastery, and deep spiritual emotion; most unique is *Goblin Market* (1862); wrote also *Sing-song*, *The Prince's Progress*, *Called to be Saints*, *The Face of the Deep* (1892), *Verses* (1893), and *New Poems* (1896).

Rossini (*ros-ē'nē*), GIOACCHINO ANTONIO (1792–1868), Ital. operatic composer; *b.* Pesaro; at twenty-one *Tancredi* brought him success at Venice; in 1816 he had his crowning triumph with *The Barber of Seville*; *William Tell* was produced in 1829. Though he wrote a vast number of operas, few survive.

Rostand (*ros-ton'*), EDMOND (1868–1918), Fr. poet and dramatist; *b.* Marseilles; achieved success with verse comedy *Les Romanesques* (1894), followed by

La Princesse Lointaine, La Samaritaine, Cyrano de Bergerac (his masterpiece), *L'Aiglon, Chantecler,* and *Le Bois Sacré* (1910); member of Fr. Academy, 1902.

Rothenstein (*roth'en-stīn*), Sir William (1872–), Eng. artist; *b.* Bradford; studied at Slade School, London; was one of official painters to Brit. and Can. armies in the Great War; principal of Royal Coll. of Art, S. Kensington, since 1920; notable for his portraits, including Pater, Swinburne, Hardy, and Tagore; paintings include *The Dolls' House, Jews Mourning, Morning at Benares.* Has also written *Oxford Characters* (1896), *English Portraits* (1898), *Life of Goya* (1900), *Ancient India* (1925), and *Men and Memories* (1931–2).

Rothermere, Harold Sidney Harmsworth, 1st Viscount (1868–), younger brother of Lord Northcliffe; *b.* London; chief proprietor of *Daily Mail, Daily Mirror, Weekly Dispatch,* etc. Air minister, 1917–18; founded King Edward chair of Eng. literature, Cambridge, 1910.

Roths'child, Jewish family of bankers; founded by Mayer Amschel Rothschild (1743–1812), son of Anselm Moses Bauer; took surname from red shield, sign of his bank at Frankfurt-on-Main; the eldest of his five sons succeeded to Frankfurt bank, the others founded houses at Vienna, Paris, London, Naples. Nathan (1777–1836), founder of London house, financed England in crisis, 1813. Lionel Nathan (1808–79), his son, was largely instrumental in obtaining Jewish emancipation in Great Britain. His eldest son, Nathan (1840–1915), was created 1st Baron Rothschild, 1885.

Rouget de Lisle (*roo-zhā' de lēl*), Claude Joseph (1760–1836), Fr. poet; while captain of engineers at Strasbourg composed in a single night words and music of *La Marseillaise,* French national anthem.

Rousseau (*roo-sō'*), Jean Jacques (1712–78), Fr. philosopher and writer; *b.* Geneva; son of a watchmaker; was in turn engraver's apprentice, vagabond, candidate for holy orders, lackey, copyist of music, etc. In Madame de Warens he found a patroness and lover for some years at 'Les Charmettes.' Making his way to Paris, 1741, he associated with the *Encyclopédistes*; won Academy of Dijon's prize for *Discours sur les Arts et les Sciences,* 1749; awakened interest of Louis xv. with his opera *Le Devin du Village,* 1752; pub. *Discours sur l'Inégalité* (1754); settled in The Hermitage near Paris, a home provided by Madame d'Epinay; wrote *La Nouvelle Héloïse* (a novel) (1760), *Emile, ou de l'Education,* and *Le Contrat Social* (political) (1762). Forced on account of his deism to leave France, he wrote in Switzerland *Lettres de la Montagne*; visited England under Hume's patronage; returned to France and spent miserable years obsessed with idea of persecution; buried in Panthéon. His autobiographical *Confessions* shed much light on his irregular life and morbid character. Rousseau proclaimed the rights of individuality, denounced the evils of artificial civilization, and sought to reinstate Nature in life generally. His style was easy, simple, and clear, and effected a revolution in Fr. prose.

[*Lives,* by Saint Marc Girardin (1874) and Viscount Morley (1873; new ed. 1915).]

Rousseau, Pierre Etienne Théodore (1812–67), Fr. landscape painter; *b.* Paris; settled at Barbizon, where he produced pictures which are now considered masterpieces of Fr. landscape art: *Le Soir, L'Allée de Châtaigniers, Le Coucher du Soleil,* etc.

Roux (*roo*), PIERRE PAUL EMILE (1853–1933), Fr. bacteriologist; *b.* in Charente; assistant at Pasteur Institute on its foundation, 1888, and director, 1904–18. His discovery (in conjunction with Yersin) of diphtheric antitoxin serum made him world-famous; also investigated inoculation against tetanus and other maladies.

Rowe (*rō*), NICHOLAS (1674–1718), Eng. dramatist; *b.* Little Barford, Beds; poet-laureate, 1715; best-known plays are *Tamerlane, The Fair Penitent,* and *The Tragedy of Jane Shore*; first modern editor of Shakespeare.

Rowlandson (*rō'land-son*), THOMAS (1756–1827), Eng. caricaturist; *b.* London; pictures are of broadly humorous character, usually depicting lower orders—*e.g.* the famous Vauxhall drawing.

Rowton (*rō'ton*), MONTAGUE WILLIAM LOWRY-CORRY, BARON (1838–1903), Eng. philanthropist; *b.* London; founder, in 1892, of *Rowton Houses* in London, sometimes called 'Poor Men's Hotels,' and which proved so successful that Rowton Houses Co., Ltd., was formed, 1894.

Royden, AGNES MAUDE (1876–), Eng. Nonconformist minister; worked at the Victoria Women's Settlement, Liverpool; assistant preacher, City Temple, London, 1917–20; Companion of Honour, 1930; author of *The Church and Woman, I believe in God,* etc.; D.D., 1931.

Rubens (*roo'benz*), PETER PAUL (1577–1640), Flem. painter and diplomatist; *b.* Siegen, Westphalia; court painter to Duke of Mantua, and much influenced by Venetian masters; settled in Antwerp, 1608, and became court painter to Duke of Netherlands. In 1611 began his greatest work, *The Descent from the Cross* (Antwerp Cathedral); called in the aid of contemporary painters, such as Van Dyck, Brueghel, Teniers, Snyders, who were able to carry out his designs; the twenty-one pictures commissioned by Marie de' Medici (now in the Louvre) were completed by his 'school' at Antwerp; this method accounts, in part, for the several thousands of pictures which bear his signature. After death of his first wife, Isabella Brant, gave himself largely to diplomacy; during mission to Spain, 1628, met Velazquez, and travelled and painted with him; was sent by Philip IV. to Charles I. of England, 1629, by whom he was knighted and commissioned to decorate Whitehall banqueting hall; married, 1630, Helena Fourment, the beautiful model of so many of his later works; died at Antwerp. Rubens was great as subject painter, animal painter, portrait painter, and landscape artist; he delighted to paint the exuberance of life, and his pictures are notable for marvellous spontaneity, creative vigour, superb animation, and magnificent colouring.

[*Lives,* by R. A. M. Stevenson (1898), E. Michel (1899), H. Knackfuss (Eng. trans. 1894), and E. Dillon (1909).]

Rubinstein (*roo'bin-stīn*), ANTON (1829–94), Russ. pianist and composer; *b.* Podolia; of Jewish extraction; toured much, giving recitals; style influenced by Schubert and Mendelssohn; played with extraordinary technique and emotion; best known for his *Ocean* and *Dramatic* symphonies; songs also highly esteemed.

Runciman (*run'si-man*), WALTER (1870–), Eng. politician; *b.* S. Shields; Liberal M.P. for Oldham, 1899, Dewsbury, 1902–18, Swansea, 1924–9, St. Ives since 1929; parl. sec. Local Government Board, 1905–7, financial sec. Treasury, 1907–8, president Board of Education, 1908–11, president Board of Agriculture, 1911–14, commissioner of Woods, Forests, and Land Revenues, 1912–14, president Board of Trade, 1914–16, and in National Government, 1931.

Runeberg (*roo'ni-berg*), JOHAN LUDWIG (1804–77), Swed. poet; *b.* Jakobstadt, Finland; prof. of Latin at Borga, 1837–59; poems idyllic, patriotic, and serenely humorous; among best are *The Elk Hunters, Hanna, The Kings at Salamis, The Grave in Perrho*; his 'Vårt Land' is national hymn of Finland.

Rupert, PRINCE (1619–82), Count Palatine of the Rhine and Duke of Bavaria; *b.* Prague; nephew of Charles I.; Royalist cavalry leader in the Civil War; dismissed by the king for his surrender of Bristol; obtained command of a Royalist fleet in 1648, but had little success and retired to Germany; after Restoration returned to England and played a brilliant part as naval commander in the Dutch wars.

Ruskin, JOHN (1819–1900), Brit. art critic, writer, and social reformer; *b.* London; son of prosperous wine merchant from Scotland; educated privately, then at Oxford; from childhood was devoted to art, poetry, and science, and early became champion of J. M. W. Turner. Continental tours matured his creed as art exponent. Slade prof. of fine art, Oxford, 1869; removed from Denmark Hill, London, to Coniston, 1872, where he spent his closing years, latterly with clouded mind. His views on art, education, social, and moral questions are embodied in many books and lectures, among others *Modern Painters* (1843–60), *Seven Lamps of Architecture* (1849), *Stones of Venice* (1851–3), *Munera Pulveris* (1862–3), *Unto this Last* (1862), *Sesame and Lilies* (his most popular work, 1865), *Crown of Wild Olive* (1866), *Fors Clavigera* (1871–84). *Præterita,* his autobiography, occupied him at intervals till 1888. Ruskin's style is remarkable for its long, rhythmical sentences; he paints pictures with words, and ranks among the greatest modern prose writers. As art appreciator he was far ahead of his times, although now his message often seems obsolete; he gave art its due place in Eng. literature for the first time.

[*Lives,* by W. G. Collingwood (2 vols. 1900), Mrs. Meynell (1900), E. T. Cook (1911); *John Ruskin, Social Reformer,* by J. A. Hobson (1899).]

Russell, BERTRAND ARTHUR WILLIAM, EARL (1872–), Eng. mathematician and philosopher; grandson of Lord John Russell; lecturer, Cambridge, 1910–16; a pacifist during Great War; student of social reform; author of *Principles of Social Reconstruction* (1917), *Mysticism and Logic* (1918), *Introduction to Mathematical Philosophy* (1919), *On Education* (1926), *The Analysis of Matter* (1927), *The Conquest of Happiness* (1930), etc.

Russell OF KILLOWEN, CHARLES RUSSELL, LORD (1832–1900), lord chief-justice of England; *b.* Newry; called to the bar, 1859; entered Parliament, 1880; attorney-general in Gladstone governments of 1886 and 1892; his reputation as a pleader reached its height with his speech in defence of Parnell, 1889; appointed lord chief-justice, 1894, being first R.C. to hold that office.

[*Life,* by R. B. O'Brien (1909).]

Russell, ELIZABETH MARY ANNETTE, COUNTESS (*née* BEAUCHAMP), Eng. writer; married first Count Arnim (*d.* 1916), secondly Earl Russell (*d.* 1931). Best known for her charming *Elizabeth and her German Garden* (1898); other works include *The Caravaners* and *Father.*

Russell, George William (1867–1935), pseudonym 'A. E.,' Irish poet; *b.* Lurgan; his many works include *Homeward: Songs by the Way* (1894), *The Earth-Breath* (1897), *The Nuts of Knowledge* (1903), *New Poems* (1904), *The Candle of Vision* (1919), *The Interpreters* (1922), *Vale and other Poems* (1931), all works of remarkable beauty.

Russell, Lord John Russell, 1st Earl (1792–1878), Brit. statesman; *b.* London; started agitation for electoral reform, 1819; supported Catholic emancipation; chief promoter of Reform Bill, 1832; from 1835–66 held a succession of high offices in the state and was twice prime minister, 1846–52 and 1865–6. Wrote memoirs and historical works of some importance; solid and able, but lacked brilliance.

[*Lives*, by Sir S. Walpole (2 vols. 1891) and S. J. Reid (1895).]

Russell, Lord William (1639–83), Eng. politician; attacked policy of Cabal as member of Country party; backed Shaftesbury's opposition to Duke of York; accused of complicity in Rye-house Plot; tried for high treason, and beheaded; pious, patriotic character; revered as Prot. martyr. His devoted wife, Lady Rachel Wriothesley (1636–1723), wrote admirable *Letters*.

[*Life*, by Lord John Russell (1820).]

Russell, William Clark (1844–1911), Eng. novelist; *b.* New York; at sea eight years, wrote popular sea stories, including *Wreck of the Grosvenor* (1875), *Overdue* (1903), *The Yarn of Old Harbour Town* (1905).

Russell, Sir William Howard (1820–1907), noted Eng. war correspondent; *b.* Lilyvale, County Dublin; his letters from the Crimea to *Times* exposed bad commissariat and general mismanagement; wrote accounts of the Mutiny, Amer. Civil War, Franco-German War, Zulu campaign, etc.

Ruth'erford, Ernest, 1st Baron (1871–), Eng. physicist; *b.* Nelson, New Zealand; prof. of experimental physics and director of Cavendish laboratory, Cambridge, since 1919; a pioneer in the study of radio-activity and the structure of the atom; Nobel Prize for chemistry, 1908; o.m., 1925; his publications include *Radio-activity* (1904), *Radio-active Transformations* (1906), *Radio-active Substances and their Radiations* (1912).

Rutherford, Mark. See White, William Hale.

Rutherford, Samuel (1600–61), Scot. theologian; *b.* Roxburghshire; prof. of humanity, Edinburgh Univ., 1623–5; minister of Anwoth, 1627–36; sent to Aberdeen and forbidden to preach; prof. of divinity, St. Andrews, from 1638. An extreme Covenanter, was ultimately charged with high treason, but died before the trial. Now best known by his letters.

Ruysdael (*rois'däl*), Jakob (*c.* 1628–82), Dutch landscape painter; *b.* Haarlem; excelled in the delineation of trees and water; Hobbema was one of his pupils.

Ruyter. See De Ruyter.

S

Sabatier (*sä-bät-yā*), Paul (1858–1928), Fr. Prot. theologian; *b.* in Cévennes; vicar of Church of St. Nicholas, Strasbourg, 1885, but was expelled on political grounds by Ger. Government, 1889; then pastor at St. Cierge, but retired owing to ill-health; prof. of church history at Strasbourg Univ., 1919; author of many important theological and historical works, including *Vie de St. François* (1893), *France To-day: its Religious Orientation* (1913).

Sabatini, RAFAEL (1875–), novelist and dramatist; *b.* in Italy; naturalized Briton; his novels include *Bardelys the Magnificent* (1906), *The Shame of Motley* (1908), *The Justice of the Duke* (1912), *The Sea Hawk* (1915), *The Snare* (1917); plays include *Fugitives* and *Scaramouche.*

Sackville, THOMAS. See DORSET.

Sa'di (*sä-dē'*), or MUSHARIFF-UD-DIN-IBN-MUSLIH-UD-DIN (*c.* 1184–1292), most famous of Pers. poets; *b.* Shiraz. Greatest work is *Gulistán*, or 'Rose Garden,' a medley in prose and verse; his *Búslán*, or 'Fruit Garden,' ranks next—a poem religious in sentiment; *Diwan*, a collection of lyrical poetry, contains some of his most exquisitely impassioned and deeply pathetic pieces.

Sadler, SIR MICHAEL ERNEST (1861–), Eng. educationist; *b.* Barnsley; educated Rugby and Oxford; prof. of education, Victoria Univ., Manchester, 1903–11; vice-chancellor of Leeds Univ., 1911–23; president of the Calcutta Univ. Commission, 1917–19; master of University Coll., Oxford, 1923–34; author of *Continuation Schools in England and Elsewhere, Moral Instruction and Training, Reports on Secondary and Higher Education*, etc.

St. Aldwyn, MICHAEL EDWARD HICKS-BEACH, EARL (1837–1916), Brit. Conservative statesman; *b.* London; chief secretary for Ireland, 1874–8; secretary for the colonies, 1878–80; chancellor of the Exchequer, 1885–6 and 1895–1902; raised to the peerage, 1906, and received an earldom, 1915.

Sainte-Beuve (*sänt-boov'*), CHARLES AUGUSTIN (1804–69), French critic and guide to the Romantic movement; *b.* Boulogne-sur-Mer; started new school of criticism based on study of history and of all sources of information bearing on his subject; produced some 300 *Portraits* of literary people under various titles; chief works are *Tableau de la Poésie française au XVI. Siècle* (1828), *Histoire de Port-Royal* (1840–8), *Portraits Littéraires* (1844), *Causeries du Lundi* and *Nouveaux Lundis* (1849–69), *Chateaubriand et Son Groupe* (1860). Sainte-Beuve has a high place in the literary history of the 19th cent.

Sainte-Claire Deville (*sänt klār' de-vēl'*), HENRI ETIENNE (1818–81), Fr. chemist; *b.* St. Thomas, West Indies; devised sodium method of preparing aluminium; made researches on platinum; did pioneer work on the artificial preparation of minerals, the determination of gas densities at high temperatures, and the phenomenon of 'thermal dissociation.'

Saint-Gaudens (*sānt gaw'denz*), AUGUSTUS (1848–1907), U.S.A. sculptor; *b.* Dublin, Ireland; sprang into fame with statue of Abraham Lincoln for Lincoln Park, Chicago, a replica of which is in Canning Square, Westminster; other works include *The Puritan* (Springfield, Massachusetts), *Diana* (New York), *R. L. Stevenson Memorial* (St. Giles's Cathedral, Edinburgh), and the *Adams Memorial* (Washington), perhaps his greatest work.

Saint-Pierre (*san-pyār'*), BERNARDIN DE (1737–1814), Fr. critic and novelist; *b.* Havre; after making the acquaintance of Rousseau and d'Alembert in 1771, took up the career of letters in earnest; most famous work is *Paul et Virginie* (1787).

Saint-Saëns (*san-sa-ons'*), CHARLES CAMILLE (1835–1921), Fr. composer; *b.* Paris; organist of church of St. Méry, 1853, and of the Madeleine, Paris, 186.–77;

possessed an extraordinary musical memory and unrivalled powers of improvisation ; one of the greatest of modern organists and pianists. His operas, with the exception of *Samson et Dalila* (1877), have never become popular ; his symphonies, symphonic poems, and suites display remarkable skill in the treatment of orchestration. His works include *Harmonie et Mélodie*, *Portraits et Souvenirs*, *Problèmes et Mystères*, and *Les Idées de M. Vincent d'Indy*.

Saintsbury, GEORGE EDWARD BATEMAN (1845–1933), Eng. man of letters and critic ; *b.* Southampton ; prof. of rhetoric and Eng. literature in Edinburgh Univ., 1895–1915 ; his works consist mainly of critical essays, literary histories, and a few biographies ; the more important are *Dryden* (1881), *A Short History of French Literature* (1882), *Elizabethan Literature* (1887), *Essays in English Literature* (1890–5), *A Short History of English Literature* (1898), *A History of Criticism* (3 vols. 1900–4), *A History of English Prosody* (3 vols. 1906–10), *Prose Rhythms* (1912), *The English Novel* (1913), *The Peace of the Augustans* (1916), *A History of the French Novel* (2 vols. 1917–19), *Notes on a Cellar-Book* (1920), *Collected Essays and Papers* (4 vols. 1924), *A Last Scrap Book* (1924).

Saint-Simon (*san-se-mon'*), CLAUDE HENRI DE ROUVROY, COMTE DE (1760–1825), Fr. philosopher ; *b.* Paris ; served in America against England ; greeted outbreak of Fr. Revolution with enthusiasm ; spent his fortune on socialistic schemes ; his last work, *Nouveau Christianisme* (1825), was foundation of 19th-cent. Socialism.

St. Vincent, JOHN JERVIS, EARL (1735–1823), Brit. sailor ; *b.* in Staffs ; took part in siege of Quebec ; shared in the three reliefs of Gibraltar, 1780–2 ; commander-in-chief of the W. Indies fleet, 1793–5 ; admiral, 1795 ; won great victory off Cape St. Vincent, 1797, for which he was created earl ; served as first lord of the Admiralty, 1801–4 ; was a great naval administrator and reformer.

Sal'adin, or SALAH-ED-DIN YUSSUF-IBN-AYUB (1137–93), Sultan of Egypt and Syria ; *b.* Tekrit ; aided Noureddin in attacks on Fatimites of Egypt ; as grand-vizier defeated crusaders of Syria and Palestine ; after Noureddin's death, 1174, became Sultan of Egypt and Syria ; won great victory over Christians at Tiberias, captured Jerusalem, 1187 ; defeated by Richard I. of England, 1191–2 ; praised by Western invaders as possessor of every quality of mediæval knight-errant.

[*Life*, by S. Lane-Poole (1903) ; see also Sir Walter Scott's *Talisman*.]

Saland'ra, ANTONIO (1853–1931), Ital. statesman ; *b.* Troia, Puglia ; was premier during first eighteen months of Great War ; was responsible for Italy's declaration of neutrality, Aug. 1914, and for her declaration of war, May 1915 ; was one of Ital. delegates at Inter-Allied Peace Conference in Paris, 1919.

Salisbury (*sawlz'ber-i*), FRANK O. (1874–), Brit. portrait and figure painter ; among chief works are *Katherine of Aragon*, decorative panels for Houses of Parliament, *The Burial of the Unknown Warrior* ; portraits of the King, the Queen, the Archbishop of Canterbury, and ex-President Coolidge.

Salisbury, ROBERT ARTHUR TALBOT GASCOYNE CECIL, 3RD MARQUESS OF (1830–1903), Brit. Conservative statesman ; travelled in Australia and New Zealand, 1850–52 ; entered House of Commons, 1853, and quickly made reputation by independence of character, terse and logical speech, caustic wit, and bitter sarcasm; opposed extension of franchise and attacks on Established Church. When Gladstone roused Europe against Bulgarian 'atrocities,' 1876, Salisbury was sent as Brit. representative to a conference of the powers at Constantinople; in 1877 became foreign secretary; represented Britain with Beaconsfield at Congress of Berlin; on Beaconsfield's death became prime minister and foreign secretary, 1885–6; returned to power, 1886–92; last ministry, 1895–1902, chief event of which was S. African War.

[*Lives*, by S. H. Jeyes (4 vols. 1895–6) and G. G. Cecil (1921).)]

Sal'lust (GAIUS SALLUSTIUS CRISPUS) (86–34 B.C.), Rom. historian; tribune, 52; expelled from senate, 50; accompanied Cæsar to Africa and became governor of Numidia, 46; authentic works, *Bellum Catilinarium* and *Bellum Jugurthinum.*

Samson, the last of the tribal judges (Judges 13–16). He maintained the national feeling of the southern and eastern tribes at a period when they were almost submerged by the Philistines.

Samuel, the last judge and first prophet of Israel; born at Ramah, dedicated by his mother to priesthood; became temple attendant under Eli; received prophetic gift. He acquiesced in the people's desire for a king, when Saul was chosen; the remainder of his life was spent in retirement at Ramah, from which place he was summoned to Bethlehem to anoint David as king instead of Saul. (See 1 and 2 Samuel.)

Samuel, SIR HERBERT LOUIS (1870–), Eng. politician; *b.* Liverpool; Liberal M.P. for Cleveland, 1902–18, and for Darwen, 1929–35; quickly established a reputation in the House as a lucid debater; was chancellor of the duchy of Lancaster, 1909–10 and 1915–16, postmaster-general, 1910–14 and 1915–16, president of the Local Government Board, 1914–15, and secretary of state for home affairs, 1916; high commissioner of Palestine, 1920–5; chairman of Royal Commission on Coal Question, 1925; home secretary, National Government, 1931–2.

Sand, GEORGE (1804–76), pseudonym of ARMANDINE LUCILE AURORE DUDEVANT, Fr. novelist; *b.* Paris; brought up near La Châtre, Indre; separated from her husband, 1831, proceeded to Paris, and adopted career of letters; produced, in collaboration with Jules Sandeau, novel *Rose et Blanche*; second novel, *Indiana* (1832), written alone, under pen name 'George Sand,' aroused enormous interest and ensured the success of her literary career; was closely associated at various times with Alfred de Musset, Chopin, Balzac, and Liszt; produced a vast number of novels, psychological, socialistic, and idyllic, including *La Mare au Diable* (1846), *La Petite Fadette* (1848).

[See *The Intimate Journal of George Sand*, Eng. trans. by M. J. Howe (1929).]

Sanday, WILLIAM (1843–1920), Eng. theologian; *b.* Notts; Lady Margaret prof. of divinity and canon of Christ Church, Oxford, 1895–1919; his works include *The Gospels in the Second Century* (1876), *The Oracles of God* (1891), *The Life of Christ in Recent Research* (1907), *The Primitive Church and Reunion* (1913).

Sankey (*san'ki*), IRA DAVID (1840–1908), Amer. evangelist and hymn writer; *b.* in Pennsylvania; associated with Moody as a singer in evangelistic campaigns, and in compilation of *Sacred Songs and Solos* (1873).

Sankey, JOHN, 1ST VISCOUNT (1866–), Eng. lawyer; *b.*

Moreton, Glos; called to bar, 1892; took silk, 1909; judge of the King's Bench Division, 1914–28; chairman of Royal Commission on Coal Industry, 1919; lord-justice of appeal, 1928–9; lord chancellor since 1929.

Santayan'a, George (1863–), Amer. philosopher and poet; *b.* Madrid, of Span. parentage; graduated at Harvard Univ., 1886; was prof. of philosophy there till 1912. His works include *Sonnets and other Verses* (1894), *The Hermit of Carmel and other Poems* (1901), *The Life of Reason* (his greatest philosophical work, 1905–6), *Three Philosophical Poets—Lucretius, Dante, and Goethe* (1910), *Platonism and the Spiritual Life* (1927), *The Realm of Essence* (1928), and *The Realm of Matter* (1930).

Santos - Dumont (*-doo-mon'*), Alberto (1873–1932), Brazilian aeronaut; *b.* São Paulo; turned from coffee planting to the invention and construction of dirigible airships; in 1901 he won the Deutsch Prize at Paris, and in 1906 made a flight of some hundred feet with a flying machine not buoyed up by balloons; returned from France to Brazil, 1928; author of *My Airships* (1904).

Sappho (*saf'ō*) (*fl. c.* 600 B.C.), Gr. poetess; *b.* in Lesbos; life-story practically unknown; perhaps banished and visited Sicily; describes passion of love with unsurpassed directness of thought, force of imagery, vividness of language, and power of metre; mutilated texts of her works discovered in Egypt.

[*Sappho* (1926), by C. R. Haines.]

Sarasate (*sä-rä-sä'tā*), Pablo Martin Meliton de (1844–1908), Span. violinist; *b.* Pampeluna; studied at Paris Conservatoire; first appeared in London, 1861, and later toured throughout Europe and America.

Sardanapalus. See Assur-bani-pal.

Sardou (*sär-doo'*), Victorien (1831–1908), Fr. dramatist; *b.* Paris; succeeded best in comedies of manners; wrote *Fédora* (1882) and other plays for Sarah Bernhardt; others are *Nos Intimes* (1861), *Rabagas* (1872), *Divorçons* (1880), *Madame Sans Gêne* (1893), *Robespierre* (1902), written for Sir Henry Irving; *La Piste* (1905), and *Le Drame des poisons* (1907).

Sargent, John Singer (1856–1925), famous Anglo-Amer. portrait painter; *b.* Florence, Italy, of Amer. parents; R.A., 1897; one of the leaders in England (where he settled in 1883) of revolution in technical methods; his work shows extraordinary dexterity of execution, large disposition and balance of design; his chief works include *Carnation, Lily, Lily, Rose* (Tate Gallery), *Carmencita* (Luxembourg). From 1884 to 1910 was the most famous portrait painter of his time.

[*Lives*, by W. H. Downes (1926) and E. Charteris (1927).]

Sarto, Andrea del, or Andrea d'Agnolo (1486–1531), Ital. artist, known as 'the faultless painter'; *b.* Florence; pupil for many years of Piero di Cosimo, though more influenced by Leonardo da Vinci and Michelangelo. His *Portrait of a Sculptor*, now in the National Gallery, is one of the supreme portraits of the Ital. Renaissance. Another famous work is the *Portrait of a Lady*, supposed to have been his wife; while the known portraits of himself, no less than his *Last Supper*, are recognized masterpieces. His relations with his wife form the subject of one of Browning's best-known poems.

[*Lives*, by H. Guinness (1899) and F. Knapp (1907).]

Sassoon', Siegfried (1886–), Eng. poet and man of

letters; poems include *War Poems* (1919), *Satirical Poems* (1926), and *The Heart's Journey* (1928); prose works, *Memoirs of a Fox-hunting Man* (1928, awarded Hawthornden Prize), and *Memoirs of an Infantry Officer* (1930).

Saul, first King of Israel, son of Kish, a Benjamite. His career was spent in warfare, ending in a defeat by Philistines on Mount Gilboa. The task set before him demanded powers of organization and statesmanship which he did not possess. (See 1 Sam.)

Saussure (*sō-soor'*), HORACE BÉNÉDICT DE (1740–99), Swiss physicist and geologist; *b.* near Geneva; prof. of physics and philosophy, Geneva, 1762–88; made brilliant physical, botanical, geological, and meteorological observations in the Alps; invented the hygrometer for testing the temperature of lakes at great depths.

Savigny (*sa-vēn'yē*), FRIEDRICH KARL VON (1779–1861), Ger. jurist; *b.* Frankfurt-on-Main; prof. of law at Berlin, 1810–42; minister of justice for the revision of the law, 1842; was first to detach scientifically Roman contribution to science of jurisprudence.

Savonaro'la, GIROLAMO (1452–98), Ital. religious and political reformer; *b.* Ferrara; joined the Dominican order at Bologna, 1474; entered convent of San Marco, 1482; came into prominence at Brescia; recalled to Florence, he denounced not only sin and worldliness of the time, but government which permitted such wickedness; later he became leading spirit in new republic; strict laws were passed for repression of evil, but a reaction set in, the Medici party gained ground, and Savonarola was forbidden to preach; he refused to obey, and was excommunicated, 1497; subsequently brought to trial; imprisoned, tortured, condemned, and hanged along with two others, 1498. Though orthodox, his opposition to the corruption of the papacy links him with the precursors of the Reformation.

[*Lives*, by H. Lucas (1899), and P. Villari and E. Casanova (Eng. trans. 1899). See also *Makers of Florence*, by Mrs. Oliphant, and *Romola*, by George Eliot.]

Saxe (*saks*), MAURICE, COMTE DE (1696–1750), marshal of France; *b.* Goslar; fought in Netherlands and Russia; ruler of Courland, 1726–7; entered service of France and won fame in war of Austrian Succession; created marshal of France, 1744, for his brilliant conduct of the operations in Flanders and Holland.

Sayce (*sās*), ARCHIBALD HENRY (1845–1933), Eng. Assyriologist and philologist; *b.* near Bristol; prof. of Assyriology, Oxford Univ., 1891–1919. Works include *The Principles of Comparative Philology* (1874), *The Monuments of the Hittites* (1881), the Hibbert lectures on *Babylonian Religion* (1887), *The Higher Criticism and the Verdict of the Monuments* (1894), *Babylonians and Assyrians* (1900), *Reminiscences* (1923).

Scaligir (*skal'i-jer*), name of two great European classical scholars. (1) JULIUS CÆSAR (1484–1558), practised medicine at Agen in Guienne; first important classical works were two orations in reply to the *Ciceronianus* of Erasmus; later works include *De Causis Linguæ Latinæ, Commentarii de Causis Plantarum Theophrasti, Aristotelis Historia de Animalibus.* (2) JOSEPH JUSTUS (1540–1609), son of the above; placed himself in the front rank of European scholars with his *De Emendatione Temporum,* wherein he fixed the dates of many of the leading events of ancient history; succeeded Lipsius at univ. of Leyden, 1593–

1609; made many editions of classical authors.

Scarlatti (*skär-lä'tē*), ALESSANDRO (1659–1725), Ital. musical composer; *b.* in Sicily; lived at Naples, 1684–1702; founder of modern school of Ital. opera; examples: *Mitridate Eupatore*, *Tigrane*, *Griselda*, etc.; wrote also chamber cantatas and masses. His son DOMENICO (1683–1757) was likewise a composer of note.

Scarron (*skä-ron'*), PAUL (1610–60), Fr. comic writer; partly paralysed from age of twenty-eight; married, 1652, Françoise d'Aubigné, the future Mme. de Maintenon; created a burlesque style partly imitated from Spanish; wrote *Typhon* (1644), *Virgile travesti* (1648–53), in verse, and the *Roman Comique* (1651–7), in prose.

Schäfer. See SHARPEY-SCHÄFER.

Scharnhorst (*sharn'horst*), GERHARD JOHANN DAVID VON (1755–1813), Prussian soldier and military writer; *b.* Bordenau, near Hanover; Scharnhorst and Stein, though thwarted by Napoleon, were chief authors of reforms to which rise of Prussia was due; wrote much on war; founded Berlin Military Association.

Scheele (*shā'le*), CARL WILHELM (1742–86), Swed. chemist and pharmacist; *b.* Stralsund; member of the Swed. Academy of Sciences, 1775; working independently of Priestley, discovered oxygen; discovered chlorine, hydrochloric acid gas, oxalic, tartaric, and other organic acids; isolated glycerine and showed graphite to be carbon; great work, *Air and Fire* (1777), trans. into almost all European languages.

[*Life*, by W. A. Tilden (*Famous Chemists*, 1921).]

Scheer (*shār*), REINHARD (1863–1928), Ger. admiral; *b.* Oberkirchen; commanded battle squadron in the High Sea Fleet from beginning of Great War; commander-in-chief of Ger. navy (May 1916), and was in command at battle of Jutland; pub. *Germany's High Sea Fleet in the World War* (Eng. ed. 1920).

Scheidemann (*shīd'i-man*), PHILIPP (1865–), Ger. politician; *b.* Kassel; in 1911 became leader of Majority Socialists; subsequently vice-president of the Reichstag; secretary of state, 1918; proclaimed the Ger republic; in Feb. 1919 he became prime minister, and refusing to sign peace treaty, resigned; pub. a valuable volume of reminiscences, *Der Zusammenbruch* (1921). In exile since rise of Hitler.

Schelling (*shel'ing*), FRIEDRICH WILHELM JOSEPH VON (1775–1854), Ger. philosopher; *b.* in Württemberg; univ. teacher at Jena, 1798, and subsequently occupied chairs at different Ger. universities, notably at Munich, 1808–20 and 1827–40; a brilliant and versatile thinker; earlier philosophy is a development of that of Fichte; his later speculations chiefly concerned the philosophy of religion; chief works include *Ideas for a Philosophy of Nature* (1797), *System of Transcendental Idealism* (1800), *Lectures on the Method of Academic Study* (1803).

Schiaparelli (*skē-ä-pä-rel'ē*), GIOVANNI VIRGINIO (1835–1910), Ital. astronomer; *b.* Savigliano; was director of Brera Observatory, Milan, 1862–1900; discovered asteroid Hesperia, and made important observations on relationship between comets and meteorites; discovered 'canals' on Mars.

Schiller (*shil'er*), JOHANN CHRISTOPH FRIEDRICH VON (1759–1805), Ger. poet and dramatist; *b.* Marbach on the Neckar; first drama, *Die Räuber*, appeared in 1781, followed by the tragedies *Die Verschwörung des Fiesco zu Genua* (1784) and *Kabale und Liebe* (1784). *Don Carlos* was completed in 1787, and in the same year Schiller visited Weimar, where he began his two historical works on Thirty Years' War, and Netherlands War of Independence, which gained for him a professorship of history at Jena Univ., 1789; formed intimate and lasting friendship with Goethe, 1794. To his last period belong fine ballads (*Der Ring des Polykrates*, *Der Taucher*, *Das Lied von der Glocke*, etc.), lyrics, the great classical drama *Wallenstein* (1798–99), and dramas *Marie Stuart* (1800), *Die Jungfrau von Orleans* (1801), *Die Braut von Messina* (1803), *Wilhelm Tell* (1804). A man of fine character and a great dramatist, he ranks next to Goethe in his own period of Ger. literature.

[*Lives*, by T. Carlyle (1824), C. Thomas (1901), and J. G. Robertson (1905).]

Schlegel (*shlāg'el*), AUGUST WILHELM VON (1767–1845), Ger. critic, translator, and author; wrote an appreciation of Dante's *Divina Commedia* (1795); became acquainted with Schiller at Jena, 1796, and under his influence wrote his best ballads; trans. seventeen of Shakespeare's plays, 1797–1810; pub. a series of lectures on literature, 1809–11, under the title *Uber dramatische Kunst und Literatur*, since trans. into most European languages.

Schleiermacher (*shlī'er-mach-er*), FRIEDRICH ERNST DANIEL (1768–1834), Ger. theologian; *b.* Breslau; prof. of theology, Halle, 1804–7, and at Berlin Univ. (which he helped to found), 1810; formed independent and original conclusions in which he sought to reconcile Christianity and the philosophies then popular; his chief theological work is his *Der Christliche Glaube nach den Grundstäzen der evangelischen Kirche* (1821–2 and, with many alterations, 1830–1); in *Ueber die Religion* (1799) he attacked the rationalism of the day.

[*Life*, by W. Dilthey (1858–63, Eng. trans. by Rowan.)]

Schliemann (*shlē'män*), HEINRICH (1822–90), Ger. archæologist; *b.* Neu-Buckow, Mecklenburg-Schwerin; distinguished as the excavator of the sites of Troy and Mycenæ. The results of his work are described in Schuchhardt's *Schliemann's Excavations* (1891).

Schnitzer, EDUARD. See under EMIN PASHA.

Schomberg (*shom'berg*), FRIEDRICH HERMANN, DUKE OF (1615–90), soldier of fortune; *b.* Heidelberg; distinguished under Turenne and in Portugal, 1660–5; marshal of France, 1675, but fled at revocation of Edict of Nantes, 1685; was in service of Prince of Orange, whom he accompanied to England; captain-general of Eng. forces, 1689; slain at the battle of the Boyne.

Schopenhauer (*shō'pen-hou-er*), ARTHUR (1788–1860), Ger. philosopher; *b.* Danzig; his chief works are *The World as Will and Idea* (1819) and *The Will in Nature* (1836), but not till late in his life did these meet with much acceptance. According to him all willing comes from want and suffering, satisfaction is illusory; human life is endless pain and struggle, the human virtues are but refined egoism, and only in sympathy does the individual transcend his selfish isolation; thus sympathy is the basis of all morality.

[*Life*, by W. Wallace (1890); *Schopenhauer and his Philosophy*, by H. Zimmern (1877); *Schopenhauer's System*, by W. Caldwell (1896).]

Schreiner (*shrī'ner*). (1) OLIVE (MRS. S. C. CRONWRIGHT SCHREINER) (1859–1920), S. African novelist; *b.* in Basutoland; excels in depicting veld scenery and Dutch character; best known as author of *Story of an African Farm.* (2) WILLIAM PHILIP (1857–1919), brother of (1); S. African statesman; entered politics, 1893, and became attorney-general under Cecil Rhodes, 1887; prime minister of Cape Colony, 1898–1900. After S. African War came forward as a strong advocate of federation.

Schubert (*shoo'bert*), FRANZ PETER (1797–1828), Austrian composer; *b.* and *d.* at Vienna; began to compose at an early age, but for many years seldom managed to procure more than the bare necessaries of life; was almost entirely self-taught. Gradually his songs made an impression, and he extended his range, producing operas, cantatas, masses, symphonies, quartets, and chamber music of all kinds. His *forte,* however, was the *lied.* No fewer than 605 songs are credited to him, and he was unquestionably the most fertile and original melodist who ever lived.

[*Lives,* by E. Duncan (1905) and N. Flower (1928).]

Schulze-Delitzsch (*shoolt'se-dā-lich*), FRANZ HERMANN (1808–83), Ger. economist, a pioneer of co-operation; *b.* Delitzsch, in Prussia; founded first People's Bank, 1850; at his death there were 3,481 credit and other co-operative associations in Germany.

Schumann (*shoo'män*), ROBERT ALEXANDER (1810–56), Ger. composer; *b.* Zwickau; devoted himself almost entirely to composition and literary musical work. Beginning with songs, he gradually attempted larger forms, and his symphonies, chamber music, and numerous pianoforte works rank with the greatest productions in these forms of composition. Among his vocal works should be mentioned the cantata *Paradise and the Peri* and the opera *Genoveva.*

[*Lives,* by Wasielewski (Eng. trans. 1878), J. A. Fuller Maitland (1884); *Letters of R. Schumann,* ed. by K. Storck (Eng. trans. 1907).]

Schuster (*shoo'ster*), SIR ARTHUR (1851–1934), Eng. physicist; *b.* Frankfurt-on-Main; educated at Manchester and Heidelberg; headed the 'Eclipse' expedition to Siam, 1875; prof. of physics, Manchester Univ., 1888–1907; was president of the Brit. Association, 1915; author of *The Theory of Optics* (1909) and *The Progress of Physics* (1911).

Schweinfurth (*shvīn'foort*), GEORG AUGUST (1836–1925), Ger. traveller; *b.* Riga; between 1863 and 1888 made many journeys in Egypt and adjacent countries, the most important being that of 1868–71, in the Nile-Congo region; settled in Berlin, 1889; author of *The Heart of Africa* and *Artes Africanæ.*

Schweitzer (*shvīt'zer*), ALBERT (1875–), German theologian, musician, and medical missionary; *b.* in Alsace. Educated at universities of Strasbourg, Paris, and Berlin. As a theologian *The Quest of the Historical Jesus* was among his most notable works. Was organist of the Bach Soc., Paris, 1903–11; Gifford lecturer, 1934. Founded the medical mission of Lambaréné, Fr. Equatorial Africa. Wrote *On the Edge of the Primeval Forest,* etc.

[See *My Life and Thought: An Autobiography* (1933).]

Scipio (*sip'i-ō*), PUBLIUS CORNELIUS, AFRICANUS MAJOR (237–183 B.C.), great Rom. general; he restored Rom. courage after defeat by Hannibal, and finally defeated the Carthaginians at Zama, 202. His daughter was Cornelia, mother of the Gracchi.

Scott, CHARLES PRESTWICH (1846–1931), Eng. journalist; *b.* Bath; trained under Alexander Russell of *The Scotsman,* he joined the staff of the *Manchester Guardian*, 1871; in the following year he became its editor; under him the paper became one of the leading journals of the country.

Scott. (1) SIR GEORGE GILBERT (1811–78), Eng. architect; *b.* near Buckingham; a leading spirit in the Gothic revival; built the Albert Memorial, 1864; built or restored a vast number of cathedrals, abbeys, and churches; buried in Westminster Abbey. (2) SIR GILES GILBERT (1880–), Eng. architect; grandson of (1); noteworthy as designer of Liverpool Cathedral; R.A., 1922, he has also been responsible for many other ecclesiastical buildings. Knighted, 1924.

Scott, or SCOT, MICHAEL (*c.*1175–1234), Scot. mathematician and scholar; studied at Oxford and Paris; became astrologer to the Emperor Frederick II.; great learning gained him the reputation of being a magician, hence the many Border legends which have gathered round his name.

Scott, SIR PERCY (1853–1924), Brit. admiral; served in Ashanti War, 1873–4, Congo expedition, 1875, S. Africa, 1899–1900, and China War, 1900; gunnery expert; invented gun carriage which enabled 6-in. and 4.7-in. guns to be used in S. Africa, also night-signalling apparatus used in navy, and various appliances for improving heavy-gun shooting.

Scott, ROBERT FALCON (1868–1912), Eng. explorer; *b.* Devonport; entered the Brit. navy, 1882; became commander, 1900, and captain, 1904; was commander of two Antarctic expeditions; the first took place in 1900–4, as told in his *Voyage of the 'Discovery'* (1905). In 1910 he set out for the South Pole again, aboard *Terra Nova*; on Jan. 18, 1912, he reached the Pole, only to find that Amundsen had forestalled him by about a month. On the return journey, owing to exceptionally severe weather, to casualities to two members of the party which delayed progress, and finally to the shortage of oil left in the depôts, the whole party perished. See *Scott's Last Expedition* (2 vols. 1913).

Scott, SIR WALTER (1771–1832), Scot. novelist, poet, and man of letters; *b.* Edinburgh; sickly as child, but later an active man, though lame; educated at Edinburgh High School and Univ., studying for the bar. His first literary work consisted in translating Goethe and other Ger. poets and collecting Scot. ballads (*Minstrelsy of the Scottish Border*, 1802). In 1797 he married Charlotte Charpentier (*d.* 1826), a Fr. refugee's daughter; appointed sheriff-depute of Selkirkshire, 1799; lived at Ashiestiel, 1804–12; removed to Abbotsford, 1812. *The Lay of the Last Minstrel* (1805), *Marmion* (1808), *Lady of the Lake* (1810), *Rokeby* (1813), *Lord of the Isles* (1815), etc., placed Scott in front rank of narrative poets.

Finding his place in popular favour threatened by Byron, Scott turned to prose romance and pub. *Waverley* anonymously (1814). Other 'Waverley Novels' appeared with phenomenal success in quick succession. *Guy Mannering* (1815), *Antiquary*, *Old Mortality*, *Black Dwarf* (1816), *Rob Roy* (1817), *Heart of Midlothian* (1818), *Bride of Lammermoor*, *Legend of Montrose*, *Ivanhoe* (1819), *Monastery*, *Abbot* (1820), *Kenilworth* (1821), *Pirate*, *Fortunes of Nigel*, *Peveril of the Peak* (1822), *Quentin Durward* (1823), *St. Ronan's Well*, *Redgauntlet* (1824), *Talisman*, *The Betrothed* (1825), *Woodstock* (1826), *Fair Maid of Perth* (1828), *Anne of Geierstein* (1829), *Count Robert of Paris*, *Castle Dangerous* (1831). Other works include *Life of Napoleon* (1827), *History of Scotland* (1830), *Tales of a Grandfather* (1828–31), editions of Dryden, Swift, etc., a *Journal* (1825–32; pub. 1890), and *Familiar Letters* (pub. 1894). In 1825 the failure of his printers and publishers, Ballantyne and Constable, involved Scott as partner in debt amounting to *c.* £120,000, most of which he cleared before his death (through overwork), Sept. 21, 1832. He was buried at Dryburgh Abbey.

Scott's courageous, generous, genial character endeared him to friends and fellow-countrymen; he was an extraordinarily rapid writer, with an inexhaustible gift for character-drawing and wonderful narrative powers; his style is easy and careless, his plots diffuse. He exalted and purified the novel, and made Scotland known throughout the world.

[Standard *Life*, by Scott's son-in-law, Lockhart. Recent works are *Sir Walter Scott*, by J. Buchan (1932), and *The Letters of Sir Walter Scott, 1787–1807* (ed. by H. J. C. Grierson).]

Scribe (*skrēb*), AUGUSTIN EUGÈNE (1791–1861), Fr. playwright; *b.* Paris; wrote (with collaborators) about four hundred plays of all kinds; versatile, brilliant, but superficial. Best-known works, *Bertrand et Raton*, *Adrienne Lecouvreur*, and *Bataille de Dames*.

Scudéry (*skoo-dā-rē'*), MADELEINE DE (1607–1701), Fr. novelist; works include *Artamène ou le Grand Cyrus* (1648–53), and *Clélie* (1654–61); depicted contemporary Fr. society; wrote under the name of her brother, GEORGES DE SCUDÉRY (1601–67), dramatist of some distinction.

Seaman, SIR OWEN (1861–1936), Eng. author and humorist; joined staff of *Punch*, 1897; was ed., 1906–32; had a remarkable gift for humorous verse and parody; works include *Horace at Cambridge* (1894), *In Cap and Bells* (1899), *A Harvest of Chaff* (1904), *War Time* (1915), and *From the Home Front* (1918). Bart. 1933.

Sebastian'o del Piom'bo (1485–1547), Ital. painter; *b.* Venice; pupil of Giovanni Bellini and Giorgione; skill as a colourist won for him the friendship of Michelangelo, with whom he collaborated in three famous pictures, including *The Raising of Lazarus*, now in the National Gallery, London. He invented a method of painting on stone.

Sedgwick, ADAM (1785–1873), Eng. geologist; *b.* Dent, Yorks; Woodwardian prof. of geology, Cambridge, 1818; mapped rocks of Lake District, 1822; a pioneer in the study of rocks in Wales.

Sed'ley, SIR CHARLES (1639–1701), Eng. poet and dramatist; tragedies and comedies slight, but lyrics excellent—*e.g.* 'Phillis is my only joy'; he figures in Dryden's *Essay on Dramatic Poesy* as 'Lisideius.'

Seel'ey, SIR JOHN ROBERT (1834–95), Eng. historian; *b.* London; prof. of Latin in Univ. Coll., London, 1863, and prof. of modern history at Cambridge, 1869; his works include *Ecce Homo* (1866), an unconventional and non-theological treatment of Christianity and its founder, and *Expansion of England* (1883).

Seely, JOHN EDWARD BERNARD, 1ST BARON MOTTISTONE (1868–), Eng. politician and soldier; educated Harrow and Cambridge; entered Parliament as Conservative, 1900; changed sides during the fiscal controversy, and became Liberal under-secretary for the colonies, 1908, under-secretary for war, 1911, and secretary of state for war, 1912–14; parl. under-secretary, ministry of munitions, and deputy minister of munitions, 1918, and in 1919 under-secretary of state for Air and president of Air Council; served in S. African War and in the Great War; major-general, 1918. Wrote *Adventure* (1930), *Fear and Be Slain* (1931), both autobiographical.

Se'grave, SIR HENRY O'NEAL DEHANE (1896–1930), motor sportsman; *b.* Baltimore, U.S.A.; served in Royal Flying Corps during Great War; made numerous records in racing motor cars, culminating in speed of 231.362 miles per hour at Daytona Beach, Florida, 1929; knighted, 1929; broke world's record for motor boat on Lake Windermere, where he was accidentally killed.

Selborne, WILLIAM WALDEGRAVE PALMER, 2ND EARL OF (1859–), Eng. statesman; sat in House of Commons as Viscount Wolmer, 1885–95; seceded from Gladstone on the question of Home Rule, 1886; under-secretary for the colonies, 1895–1900; first lord of the Admiralty, 1900–5; succeeded Lord Milner as high commissioner in S. Africa, 1905–10; president of the Board of Agriculture, 1915–16.

Selden, JOHN (1584–1654), Eng. lawyer and man of letters; *b.* Salvington, Sussex; from 1623 sat in Parliament, where his opposition to the court party led to his imprisonment on several occasions; best known for his *Table Talk* (1689).

Selkirk, or SELCRAIG, ALEXANDER (1676–1721), prototype of Robinson Crusoe; *b.* Largo, Fife, where there is a statue of him as Crusoe; lived alone on Juan Fernandez, 1704–9. See his *Life and Adventures*, by Howell (1829).

Selous (*sel oo'*), FREDERICK COURTENEY (1851–1917), English traveller and big-game hunter; *b.* London; entered service of Brit. S. Africa Co., 1890, and acted as guide to pioneer expedition to Mashonaland; afterwards engaged in Matabele War; saw service in the E. African campaign, 1915–17, being killed in action; was prototype of Rider Haggard's *Allan Quatermain.*

[*Life*, by J. G. Millais (1918).]

Selwyn (*sel'win*), GEORGE AUGUSTUS (1809–78), Eng. ecclesiastic; *b.* London; Bishop of New Zealand, 1841, of Lichfield, 1868; Selwyn Coll., Cambridge, erected and endowed to his memory.

Sen'eca. (1) ANNÆUS (*c.* 54 B.C.–*c.* A.D. 39), Rom. rhetorician; *b.* Corduba; educated in rhetoric, Rome; chief works are *Suasoriæ* and *Controversiæ*, rhetorical exercises. (2) LUCIUS ANNÆUS (*c.* 5 B.C.–A.D. 65), statesman and writer; son of above; educated Rome; banished, 41; recalled, 49; became Nero's tutor; suspected of treason and ordered to commit suicide. Best-known works are the *Tragedies*, affected and pompous in style; *On Clemency*, *On Benefits*, and *Letters to Lucilius.*

Serao (*sā-rä'ō*), MATILDE (1856–1927), Ital. novelist; *b.* Patras, Greece; her novels have achieved a wide popularity for their truth to life; Eng. trans. have appeared of *Fantasy* (1891), *The Ballet Cancer* (1901), *The Land of Dockayne* (1901), *In the Country of Jesus* (1905), etc.

Ser'pa Pin'to, ALEXANDRE ALBERTO DE LA ROCHA (1846–1900), Port. explorer; crossed Africa from west to east, 1877–9, and wrote an account of his travels in *How I crossed Africa* (1881); governor of Mozambique, 1889.

Service, ROBERT WILLIAM (1874–), Can. poet; *b.* Preston, England; emigrated to Canada, and joined staff of Can. Bank of Commerce, 1905; travelled on Pacific coast and Yukon. Author of several vols. of verse, including *Songs of a Sourdough* (1907), *Ballads of a Cheechako* (1909), and *Rhymes of a Red Cross Man* (1916); also novels, including *The Pretender* (1914),

The Roughneck (1923), and *The House of Fear* (1927).

Seton-Watson, ROBERT WILLIAM (1879–), Brit. historian; specialist in European history and politics; was founder and ed. of *New Europe*; appointed Masaryk prof. of Central European History in Univ. of London, 1922; works include *Maximilian I.* (1902), *Racial Problems in Hungary* (1908), *The War and Democracy* (1914), *Rise of Nationality in the Balkans* (1917), *Europe in the Melting Pot* (1919), *The New Slovakia* (1924), *Serajevo* (1926), *A Plea for the Study of Contemporary History* (1929).

Settle, ELKANAH (1648–1724), Eng. poet and dramatist; *b.* Dunstable; his plays, *Cambyses* and *The Empress of Morocco*, enjoyed considerable popularity in his time; he is the 'Doeg' of Dryden's *Absalom and Achitophel.*

Seve'rus, LUCIUS SEPTIMIUS (A.D. 146–211), Rom. emperor; *b.* in Africa; was proclaimed emperor by his troops after death of Pertinax; defeated and killed Pescennius Niger, who had been proclaimed emperor by the Eastern legions; put down revolt of Clodius Albinus, 197; warred against Parthians and captured Babylon, Seleucia, and Ctesiphon; came to Britain and quelled revolt, and died at York.

Sévigné (*sā-vē-nyā'*), MARIE DE RABUTIN-CHANTAL, MARQUISE DE (1626–96), Fr. author, of Burgundian family; *b.* Paris; left a widow at age of twenty-five; favourite at court; devoted to her son and daughter, especially the latter, to whom she wrote her famous letters, dealing with court and society life.

Shack'leton, SIR ERNEST HENRY (1874–1922), Brit. explorer; *b.* in County Kildare; went to sea in merchant service; third lieutenant in Scott's Antarctic Expedition, 1901; commanded Antarctic Expeditions, 1907–9, 1914–16, and 1921–2; died off S. Georgia during last expedition; author of *The Heart of the Antarctic* (1909) and *South* (1919).

[*Life*, by H. R. Mill (1924).]

Shad'well, THOMAS (*c.* 1642–92), Eng. playwright; *b.* Norfolk; his plays, though successful, lack literary distinction. Satirized in *MacFlecknoe* by Dryden, whom he succeeded as poet laureate.

Shaftesbury, ANTHONY ASHLEY COOPER, 1ST EARL OF (1621–83), Brit. statesman; *b.* Wimborne, St. Giles, Dorsetshire; though on parliamentary side in Civil War supported the return of Charles II., 1660; thereafter held high office in the state, and was a member of the Cabal ministry; supported Protestant faith and opposed penal laws against the Nonconformists; created earl, 1672; passed the Habeas Corpus Act, 1679; his support of Monmouth led to his dismissal; he retired to Holland, where he died.

Shaftesbury, ANTHONY ASHLEY COOPER, 7TH EARL OF (1801–85), Eng. philanthropist; *b.* London; M.P., 1831–51; as a commissioner in lunacy, 1831–85, he effected a complete reform of the Lunacy Acts; also secured amendment of Factory Acts; obtained the passing of an Act, 1842, abolishing apprenticeship in collieries and mines, and excluding women, and boys under thirteen, from employment underground.

[*Lives*, by J. L. and B. Hammond (1923) and J. W. Bready (1926).]

Shakespeare, WILLIAM (1564–1616), Eng. dramatist and poet; *b.* Stratford-on-Avon, Warwickshire. At Stratford Grammar School he acquired 'small Latin and less Greek'; moved to London *c.* 1586, leaving behind him his wife, Anne Hathaway (*b.* 1556), whom he had married in 1582. In London, Shakespeare found employment about the theatres, and had risen by 1592 to be actor, play-adapter, and dramatist. He belonged to the company called Earl of Leicester's Men, afterwards Lord Chamberlain's Co. and King's Players.

Early Plays.—*Love's Labour's Lost* (1591) is probably the earliest of Shakespeare's plays. *Two Gentlemen of Verona* (1591) shows Shakespeare's remarkable powers of giving fresh treatment to a borrowed plot. The *Comedy of Errors* (1591) abounds in boisterous farce. In *Richard III.* (1593) he achieved a great tragedy; an even greater tragedy, *Richard II.*, followed (1593). Turning to non-dramatic poetry, he wrote *Venus and Adonis* (pub. 1593), followed, with equal success, by the *Rape of Lucrece* (1594).

Second Period.—What is generally called Shakespeare's second period lasted from *c.* 1594 to 1601. In 1597 he was sufficiently well off to buy New Place in Stratford, among his sources of income being a share in the profits of the Globe Theatre. The plays of his second period are full of exuberance; they include the beautiful *Romeo and Juliet* (in its maturer form *c.* 1594), three of his greatest romantic comedies—*The Merchant of Venice* (1594), *A Midsummer Night's Dream* (1595), and *As You Like It* (1599); the glorious dramatic histories, *Henry IV.* (two parts; 1596–8) and *Henry V.* (1599). Falstaff reappeared (tradition says at Elizabeth's command) in the *Merry Wives of Windsor* (1597). Other comedies—*All's Well that Ends Well* (1595), *Taming of the Shrew* (*c.* 1596), *Much Ado about Nothing* (1599), and *Twelfth Night* (1600)—also belong to this period.

Third Period.—*Julius Cæsar* (1600) fittingly ushers in the period of gloom and tragedy, to which belong such masterpieces as *Hamlet* (1602), *Othello* (1604), *Macbeth* (1606), *King Lear* (1606). The blow of Southampton's imprisonment, 1601, with changing political conditions, the passing of the glowing Elizabethan age, and other causes hinted at in the *Sonnets*, combined to produce a mental struggle and crisis clearly revealed in the plays mentioned and in others of sublime and almost unrelieved tragedy—*Troilus and Cressida* (1603), a cynical comedy; *Measure for Measure*, another sombre comedy; *Timon of Athens* (1608), a bitter tragedy; *Pericles* (1608); *Antony and Cleopatra* (1608) and *Coriolanus* (1609), great tragedies both.

Sonnets and Last Period.—In 1609 appeared Shakespeare's *Sonnets*—poetical gems round which much controversy has raged. Critics have disagreed as to the identity of the poet's friend 'Mr. W. H.' (who is described as the 'onlie begetter' of the Sonnets) and of the 'dark lady.' This period is marked by a calmer, happier atmosphere; the crisis is past. Prosperous days favoured the poet's closing years. His last plays, *Cymbeline* (1610), *A Winter's Tale* (1610), *The Tempest* (1611), are rich and mellow, beautiful and romantic. About 1611 Shakespeare retired to his native Stratford, where at New Place he resided till his death. He lies buried in Stratford Church. In addition to the plays mentioned, Shakespeare is believed to have collaborated with other dramatists in such plays as *Henry VIII.* (*c.* 1613) and *The Two Noble Kinsmen* (*c.* 1613).

The magnitude of Shakespeare's genius and the meagreness of the known details of his life have given rise to an enormous body of literature dealing with the man and his work. Since the *First Folio* of Shakespeare's plays (now exceedingly rare and valuable) was issued by his old colleagues, Heminge and Condell, in 1623, down to the sumptuous and scholarly editions of the 20th cent., scores of editions of Shakespeare's works have been published, and the critics, not of Britain alone, but of the whole world, have united in paying tribute to the universality and splendour of his genius. His boundless imagination rose triumphant over the limitations of the Elizabethan theatre, and refused to be restricted by classical unities and traditions. Shakespeare used blank verse with a sublimity, a harmony, a dramatic fitness which others may at times have equalled but have never excelled.

[*Life*, by Sir Sidney Lee (1925); *Shakespeare*, by W. Raleigh ('Eng. Men of Letters,' 1907); *Shakespeare's Mind and Art*, by E. Dowden (1865); *Shakespearean Tragedy*, by A. G. Bradley (1904); *William Shakespeare*, by J. Masefield (1911); *Shakespeare's Workmanship*, by Sir A. T. Quiller-Couch (1917); *Shakespeare's England* (2 vols. 1916 and 1926).]

Shannon, CHARLES HAZLEWOOD (1863–), Eng. artist; *b.* Sleaford, Lincs; R.A., 1921; studied art at Lambeth School of Art; works include *The Lady with the Green Fan, Study in Grey, Souvenir of Van Dyck, Hermes and the Infant Bacchus*, and many fine etchings.

Sharp, JAMES (1613–79), Scot. ecclesiastic; *b.* Banffshire; prof. of philosophy, St. Andrews, 1643; minister of Crail, 1648; at Restoration appointed Archbishop of St. Andrews that he might further Episcopacy in Scotland. Thenceforward took leading part in persecution of Covenanters till his assassination on Magus Muir.

Sharp, WILLIAM, pseudonym FIONA MACLEOD (1855–1905), Scot. poet, novelist, and critic; *b.* Paisley; from 1881 devoted himself entirely to literature; pub. novels, biographies, and critical works, and several volumes of poetry; pub. *Pharais* (1894), *The Sin-Eater* (1895), *The Laughter of Peterkin* (1897), *Deirdre* (1903), etc.

[*Memoir*, by his wife (2 vols. 1912).]

Sharpey-Schäfer, SIR EDWARD ALBERT (1850–1935), Brit. physiologist; *b.* London; professor of physiology, Edinburgh Univ., 1899–1932; secretary, Brit. Association, 1895–1900; as president, 1912, delivered at Dundee famous address on Origin of Life; works include an ed. of Quain's *Anatomy, Textbook of Physiology* (1898–1900), and *Essentials of Histology* (1902).

Shaw, GEORGE BERNARD (1856–), Brit. dramatist and socialist; *b.* Dublin; went to London, 1876, where he became a socialist leader and a dramatic and fine art critic. Started by writing novels which were not a success. Later began his career as a playwright which has made him world-famous. His plays, which abound in wit and irony, include *Plays, Pleasant and Unpleasant* (7 plays, 1898), *Man and Superman* (1903), *John Bull's Other Island* (1904), *Fanny's First Play* (1911), *Pygmalion* (1912), *Back to Methuselah* (1921), *Saint Joan* (1923), *The Apple Cart* (1929), *Too True to be Good* (1931), and *The Village Wooing* (1933); wrote also *Fabian Essays* (1889), *The Quintessence of Ibsenism* (1891 and 1913), *Socialism and Superior Brains* (1910), *The Intelligent Woman's Guide to Socialism and Capitalism* (1928), *Adventures of a Black Girl in search of God* (1932), etc. Nobel Prize, 1926.

Shaw, HENRY WHEELER (1818–85), Amer. humorist, known as 'Josh Billings'; author of *Essa on the Muel, bi Josh Billings* (1860), *Josh Billings, his Sayings*

(1866), *Josh Billings's Complete Works* (1876), etc.

Shaw, THOMAS. See CRAIGMYLE, BARON.

Shaw, THOMAS EDWARD. See LAWRENCE, THOMAS EDWARD.

Shelley, MARY WOLLSTONECRAFT (1797–1851), Eng. writer; *b.* London; daughter of William Godwin; second wife of the poet Shelley. She is remembered chiefly for her novel *Frankenstein* (1818). Ed. Shelley's *Poems* (1839).

Shelley, PERCY BYSSHE (1792–1822), Eng. poet; *b.* Field Place, Sussex; educated Eton and Oxford; was expelled from Oxford for a pamphlet on atheism. Soon afterwards he eloped with Harriet Westbrook, a school-friend of his sister's, and was disowned by his family; with her led a wandering life, visiting Southey at Keswick, and taking part in various political and philanthropical undertakings in Ireland and Wales. In 1813 he pub. his first poem of promise, *Queen Mab.* In 1814 he fell in love with Mary Godwin, and eloped with her to the Continent, and married her after his wife committed suicide, 1816.

On his return he pub. his first great poem, *Alastor* (1816), followed by *Revolt of Islam* (1817) in Spenserian stanza. Various circumstances drove him abroad to Italy in 1818. Here he wandered about for four years, visiting Venice, Rome, Naples, and Pisa, and here also his greatest poems were composed: *Prometheus Unbound* (1819), the finest lyrical drama in European literature, the magnificent but gloomy tragedy of the *Cenci* (1819), *Ode to the West Wind* (1819), *Witch of Atlas* (1820), *Epipsychidion* (1820), and *Adonais* (1821), an elegy on the death of Keats.

In the summer of 1822 he was drowned in the Gulf of Spezia; his body was afterwards burned in the presence of Byron, with whom he had been living, and the ashes were deposited in the Prot. cemetery at Rome. His work is inspired by an ardent love of humanity, and contains the most purely and intensely lyrical poetry of all Eng. literature.

[*Lives*, by J. A. Symonds ('Eng. Men of Letters,' 1878), E. Dowden (2 vols. 1886); *Ariel ou la vie de Shelley*, by A. Maurois (1923). *Works* (Julian ed.), ed. by R. Ingpen and W. E. Peck (1927–9).]

Shep'stone, SIR THEOPHILUS (1817–93), Eng. S. African statesman; *b.* near Bristol; Brit. resident in Kaffraria, 1839; agent in Natal, 1845; secretary for native affairs in Natal, 1856–77; proclaimed annexation of Transvaal at Pretoria, 1877; administrator of Transvaal, 1877–9; retired in 1880.

Sheraton, THOMAS (*c.* 1751–1806), Eng. furniture designer; *b.* Stockton-on-Tees; settled in London, 1790, and pub. several manuals of design. See Heaton's *Furniture of the 18th Century* (1892).

Sherbrooke, ROBERT LOWE, VISCOUNT (1811–92), Eng. statesman and orator; *b.* Bingham, Notts; chancellor of Exchequer and lord of Treasury, 1868–73; home secretary, 1873–4; little political ability; an opponent of the Reform Bill; his proposed tax on lucifer matches gave rise to riots of matchmakers, 1871; famed for wit and irony.

Sher'idan, RICHARD BRINSLEY (1751–1816), Anglo-Irish dramatist, politician, and orator; *b.* Dublin; educated Harrow; made romantic marriage with beautiful singer, Elizabeth Linley of Bath; removed to London, and with his father-in-law took Drury Lane Theatre, where *The School for Scandal* was produced, 1777, and *The Critic* (1779). Sheridan had already achieved fame with *The Rivals* (1775), and *The Duenna*

(1775), a musical comedy. Sheridan entered Parliament as a Whig; became under-secretary for foreign affairs, 1782, secretary to Treasury, 1783. Of his eloquent speeches those impeaching Warren Hastings, 1787, and vindicating the Fr. Revolution, 1794, are specially memorable. But he attained highest distinction as a playwright; in his comedies wit, humour, and sparkle have preserved their charm and freshness.

[*Lives*, by Mrs. Oliphant ('Eng. Men of Letters,' 1883) and W. Sichel (1909).]

Sher'man, William Tecumseh (1820–91), U.S.A. soldier; *b.* Lancaster, Ohio; fought in Florida and Mexico; left army to take up banking; on outbreak of Civil War, joined the North, and distinguished himself at the battle of Bull Run, 1861, and Shiloh, 1862; with Grant he did brilliant work at Vicksburg and Chattanooga; later, as general in command of Mississippi, carried out a remarkably successful campaign against Hood and Johnston, and was able also to assist Grant against Lee; became commander-in-chief of U.S.A. army, which he practically reorganized, 1869.

Shirley, James (1596–1666), Eng. poet and dramatist; *b.* London; a prolific playwright; the suppression of the theatre in 1642 broke his fortunes. Among his plays are *The Brothers*, *The Wedding*, *The Traitor*, *The Gamester*, *The Lady of Pleasure*, and *The Cardinal*.

Shorter, Clement King (1857–1926), Eng. journalist and author; *b.* London; ed. of *Illustrated London News*, 1893–1900, when he founded the *Sphere*; works include *Charlotte Brontë and her Circle* (1896), *Life of George Borrow* (1913), and *Autobiography* (1926); ed. Boswell's *Johnson* (1922) and *Complete Works of George Borrow* (1923).

Shorthouse, Joseph Henry (1834–1903), Eng. novelist; *b.* Birmingham, where he became a manufacturer of chemicals. Author of *John Inglesant* (1881), and other novels of less distinction.

Shov'ell, Sir Cloudesley (*c.* 1650–1707), Eng. admiral; *b.* Norfolk; served under Rooke at Vigo, 1702, and at Gibraltar and Malaga, 1704; as commander-in-chief of Mediterranean fleet, 1705, he co-operated with Peterborough in the taking of Barcelona; on voyage home his ship was lost with all hands.

Shrapnel, Henry (1761–1842), Eng. inventor; 'shrapnel' shell, which he invented and which was named after him, was recommended for adoption in 1803.

Shrewsbury, John Talbot, Earl of (*c.* 1390–1453), Eng. soldier; put down Irish revolt, 1414–19; famous in Fr. wars of Henry v. and Henry vi.

Sibe'lius, Jean Julius (1865–), Finnish composer; received musical education at Helsingfors, Berlin, and Vienna; compositions include symphonic poems, symphonies, chamber music, etc., among the best-known of which are *Finlandia*, *Valse Triste*, *Oceanides*, and the first Finnish opera, *The Maid in the Tower*.

Sick'ert, Walter Richard (1860–), Brit. painter and etcher; *b.* Munich; studied under Whistler; A.R.A., 1924; president of Royal Soc. of Brit. Artists since 1928; works include *The Camden Town Murder* (1906), *Ennui* (1914), *Sinn Fein* (1915), *Supper at the Casino* (1920).

Sid'dons, Sarah (1755–1831), Eng. tragic actress; *b.* Brecon; daughter of Roger Kemble. Played with Garrick's company at Drury Lane, and achieved triumph as Isabella in *The Fatal Marriage* (1782). Her most famous rôle was that of Lady Macbeth.

[*Lives*, by T. Campbell (1834),

P. H. Fitzgerald (1871), and A. Maurois (1927).]

Sidg'wick, HENRY (1838–1900), Eng. philosopher; *b.* Skipton; appointed prof. of moral philosophy, Cambridge, 1883. First president of Society for Psychical Research. Was instrumental in founding Newnham Coll., Oxford. Chief works are *Methods of Ethics, History of Ethics, Principles of Political Economy.*

[*Life*, by A. S. and E. M. S. (1906).]

Sid'ney, ALGERNON (1622–83), Eng. politician; *b.* Penshurst; younger son of Earl of Leicester and nephew of Sir Philip Sidney; during Civil War strongly supported Parliamentary party; accused of taking part in Ryehouse Plot and executed; author of *Discourses concerning Government* (printed 1698).

[See *Sidney Papers*, and *Life*, by Ewald (1873).]

Sidney, SIR PHILIP (1554–86), Eng. soldier, poet, and courtier; *b.* Penshurst; engaged in numerous diplomatic missions; enjoyed high favour at court; married Frances, the daughter of Walsingham; engaged in literary and political pursuits; appointed governor of Flushing, 1585; mortally wounded at Zutphen, where he behaved with a chivalry which has impressed itself on history. His writings include *Apologie for Poetrie* (*c.* 1581), *Arcadia* (1590), and *Astrophel and Stella* (1591), a series of sonnets to Penelope, daughter of Earl of Essex.

[*Lives*, by H. R. Fox-Bourne and J. A. Symonds ('Eng. Men of Letters,' 1886).]

Siemens (*sē'menz*), SIR WILLIAM (KARL WILHELM) (1823–83), scientist, inventor, and engineer; *b.* Lenthe, Hanover; naturalized Brit. subject, 1859; knighted, 1883; practised as engineer; made important improvements in steam engine, furnaces, telegraph, dynamo, electric lighting, locomotion, etc.

[*Life*, by Pole (1888).]

Sienkiewicz (*syen-kye'vich*), HENRYK (1846–1916), Polish novelist, of Lithuanian stock; educated at Warsaw; made reputation with short stories and studies of peasant life; awarded Nobel Prize for literature, 1905. Best-known novel, *Quo Vadis?*

Sieyès (*sē-ā-yās'*), EMMANUEL JOSEPH (1748–1836), Fr. cleric and statesman; *b.* Fréjus; deputy to States-General from Paris, 1789; urged constitution of Estates in one chamber as National Assembly; president, 1790; member of Five Hundred, and of Directory, 1799. Consul with Napoleon and Ducos, 1799; elected member of the Academy, 1830.

Si'las, or SILVANUS, a leading member of the primitive Church at Jerusalem; in the Acts of the Apostles he is known as Silas, in the epistles as Silvanus; companion of St. Paul in some of his missionary journeys.

Sim'nel, LAMBERT (*c.* 1477–1534), pretender to Eng. throne; *b.* Oxford, son of a baker; on account of his resemblance to the imprisoned Earl of Warwick, he was put forward by the Yorkist party as the real earl. Henry VII. caused the real earl to be paraded through the streets of London, but in 1487 Simnel was crowned at Dublin as Edward VI. He was taken prisoner at Stoke-on-Trent; he was appointed a scullion in the royal kitchen, and later became king's falconer.

Si'mon, SIR JOHN ALLSEBROOK (1873–), Eng. statesman and lawyer; *b.* Bath; called to the bar, 1899, and took 'silk,' 1908; Liberal M.P., 1906–18 and from 1922; solicitor-general, 1910, and attorney-general, 1913; home secretary in Coalition ministry, 1915; resigned owing to his disapproval of the Military Service Act; served as major in the Royal Air Force in France, 1917–18; spoke with remarkable effect in Parliament on illegality of General Strike, 1926; chairman Indian Statutory Commission, 1927–30; foreign secretary, 1931–5; home secretary, 1935.

Simonides of Ceos (*sim-on'id-ēz*) (*c.* 556–469 B.C.), Gr. lyric poet; *b.* in Ceos; in metre, language, and thought his poems exhibit highest Gr. genius; master of epigram; spent latter part of life in Sicily.

Simpson (*sim'son*), SIR JAMES YOUNG (1811–70), Scot. physician; *b.* Bathgate; prof. of midwifery, 1840; introduced many improvements in obstetrical methods; greatest achievement was his discovery of the anæsthetic power of chloroform; baronet, 1866.

Sims, WILLIAM SOWDEN (1858–), Amer. sailor; *b.* in Ontario; graduated at U.S.A. Naval Academy, 1880; became commander, 1907, captain, 1911, rear-admiral and vice-admiral, 1917. Shortly before U.S.A. entered the Great War, 1917, he was placed in charge of the Amer. fleet in European waters. On conclusion of the war he resumed presidency of Naval War Coll.

Sinclair, UPTON (1878–), U.S.A. author; *b.* Baltimore. His book *The Jungle* (1906) exposed practices then existing in meat-packing industry, and led to government inspection of Chicago stockyards. Other works include *King Coal* (1916), *Oil* (1927), *The Wet Parade* (1931), and *Candid Reminiscences*. Candidate for governorship of California, 1934, but not returned.

Sinha of Raipur, SATYENDRA PRASSANO, 1ST BARON (1864–1928), Ind. statesman; *b.* Raipur, Bengal; called to Eng. bar, 1886; standing counsel to government of Bengal, 1903; was the first Ind. advocate-general, 1908; president of the National Congress, 1915. attended meetings of Imperial War Cabinet, 1917, and was appointed under-secretary for India and created baron, 1918; was the first Ind. governor-general of Bihar and Orissa, 1920–21; in 1926 he was appointed to the judicial committee of the Privy Council.

Sitwell, a well-known family of English writers. (1) EDITH (1887–), *b.* Scarborough; her poems include *The Mother and Other Poems* (1915), *Clown's Houses* (1918), *The Wooden Pegasus* (1920), *Façade* (1923); prose works on *Pope* (1930) and *Victoria of England* (1936). (2) OSBERT (1892–), brother of (1); *b.* London; educated Eton; writings, mainly satirical, include *Argonaut and Juggernaut* (1919), *England Reclaimed* (1927), *Before the Bombardment* (1926), *The Man who Lost Himself* (1929), *Collected Poems* (1931). (3) SACHEVERELL (1897–), poet and prose writer; brother of (1); *b.* Scarborough; educated Eton; his poems include *The People's Palace* (1918), *The Hundred and One Harlequins* (1922), *The Thirteenth Cæsar* (1924), *The Cyder Feast* (1927), *Dr. Donne and Gargantua* (1930); prose writings include essays on art.

Skeat, WALTER WILLIAM (1835–1912), Eng. philologist; *b.* London; prof. of Anglo-Saxon, Cambridge, 1878–1912; voluminous writer and editor; issued his renowned *Etymological Dictionary* (1882).

Skel'ton, JOHN (*c.* 1460–1529), Eng. poet and satirist; probably native of Diss, Norfolk; poet laureate of Oxford Univ.; took orders, 1498, and became tutor to Henry VIII.; satirized Wolsey in *Why come ye not to Court?* and *Book of Colin Clout*; other poems are *Speak Parrot*, *Book of Philip Sparrow*; famous for his

'Skeltonic Metres.' Wrote three plays, one of which, *Magnificence*, is one of the best examples of the morality play.

Slade, Felix (1790–1868), Eng. art collector; *b.* London; devoted his wealth to acquisition of books, engravings, glass, and pottery; endowed professorships of fine art in Oxford, Cambridge, and in Univ. Coll., London.

Slatin (*slă-tēn'*), Sir Rudolf Karl von (Slatin Pasha) (1857–1932), Anglo-Austrian administrator; *b.* Austria; served in Sudan under Gordon; imprisoned for eleven years in Omdurman; inspector-general of Sudan, 1900–14; author of *Fire and Sword in the Sudan* (1896).

Sloane, Sir Hans (1660–1753), Irish physician and naturalist; *b.* Killyleagh, County Down; F.R.S., 1685; physician to governor of Jamaica, 1687, where he made collection of plants; president Royal Soc., 1727; court physician from 1716. With his and the Cottonian collection the Brit. Museum was founded, 1754.

Smart, Henry (1813–79), Eng. organist and composer; *b.* London; works include *Bertha*, an opera (1855), vocal music, part songs, and many compositions for organ.

[*Life*, by Spark (1881).]

Smeaton (*smē'ton*), John (1724–92), Eng. civil engineer; *b.* near Leeds; designed third Eddystone lighthouse; built several bridges in Scotland, and was surveyor and engineer of the Forth and Clyde Canal, 1768–90.

Smet'ana, Friedrich (1824–84), Czech pianist and composer; *b.* in Bohemia; studied at Prague and Leipzig; conductor of Philharmonic Soc., Gothenburg, 1856–61, and of National Theatre, Prague, 1866–74; wrote several operas, of which his *Bartered Bride* (1866) is the best known.

Smiles, Samuel (1812–1904), Scot. author and biographer; *b.* Haddington; first practised medicine; later took to journalism, and became known for a series of books, of which *Self-Help* (1859) had the most notable success.

Smith, Adam (1723–90), Scot. political economist; *b.* Kirkcaldy. In 1751 was appointed prof. of logic in Glasgow Univ., and in 1752 prof. of moral philosophy. In 1759 he pub. his *Theory of the Moral Sentiments*, in which he takes sympathy as the root idea in morals. In 1763 he became tutor to the young Duke of Buccleuch. In 1766 he returned to Kirkcaldy, and pub. his *Wealth of Nations* (1776). The book sprang into instant popularity. Pitt declared himself a disciple of Smith, and endeavoured, in his early career as a peace minister, to apply the principles laid down in the book, the fourth part of which deals with Free Trade principles. The influence of Adam Smith's ideas manifested themselves in the reform of the Brit. commercial system, and the repeal of the Corn Laws and the Navigation Laws.

[*Lives*, by J. A. Farrer (1881), R. B. Haldane (1887), and J. Rae (1895).]

Smith, Alexander (1830–67), Scot. poet; *b.* Kilmarnock; appointed secretary to Edinburgh Univ., 1854; with Dobell, produced *Sonnets of the Crimean War* (1855); his other works include *Edwin of Deira* (1861), *A Summer in Skye* (1865).

Smith, Mrs. Burnett. See Swan, Annie S.

Smith, Frederick E. See Birkenhead, Lord.

Smith, Sir George Adam (1856–), Scot. theologian; *b.* Calcutta; principal and vice-chancellor of Aberdeen Univ., 1909–35; moderator of the General Assembly, United Free Church of

Scotland, 1916. Ranks as one of the foremost Biblical scholars; deeply interested in social and evangelistic work. His literary works include *Book of Isaiah* (1888–90), *Historical Geography of the Holy Land* (1894), *Life of Henry Drummond* (1898), *Early Poetry of Israel* (1912), *Jeremiah* (1923), *The Kirk in Scotland* (1930).

Smith, HORACE (1779–1849), English novelist and parodist; *b.* London; collaborated with brother JAMES (1775–1839) in *Rejected Addresses* (1812), a series of parodies of contemporary poets.

Smith, JOHN (1580–1631), Eng. soldier, adventurer, and colonial administrator; *b.* Willoughby, Lincs; led life of adventure all over Europe, then went out to Virginia, 1606, where his life was saved by Pocahontas; became titular head of colony, 1608; interested in New England fisheries from 1609, and mapped out coast; captured by pirates, 1615.

[*Life*, by E. K. Chatterton (1927).]

Smith, JOSEPH (1805–44), founder of Mormon religion; *b.* Sharon, Vermont; in 1830 pub. *Book of Mormon*, which he claimed to have received by divine revelation; founded the Church of Jesus Christ of Latter Day Saints; assassinated, 1844.

Smith, SYDNEY (1771–1845), Eng. clergyman, author, and wit; *b.* Woodford, Essex; settled in Edinburgh, 1797; founded, along with Jeffrey and Brougham, the *Edinburgh Review* (1802). Removed to London, 1803; prebend of Bristol Cathedral, 1827, and canon of St. Paul's, 1831. As a man of letters his wit was unique and his style brilliant. His works include *Six Sermons Preached at Charlotte Chapel, Edinburgh* (1800), and *Letters on the Catholics, by Peter Plymley* (1807–8), a plea for Catholic emancipation.

[*Memoir and Letters* (1855); *Life*, by G. W. E. Russell ('Eng. Men of Letters,' 1905).]

Smith, WILLIAM (1769–1839), Eng. geologist; *b.* Churchill, Oxfordshire; known as 'the father of Eng. geology'; took up surveying and land draining; was engineer for Somerset Coal Canal, 1794; prepared valuable geological maps of England; awarded Wollaston medal by Geological Soc., London, 1831.

[*Memoirs* (ed. Phillips, 1844).]

Smith, WILLIAM ROBERTSON (1846–94), Scot. theologian; *b.* Keig, Aberdeenshire; entered Free Church ministry, and in 1870 became prof. of Oriental Languages and O.T. at the Free Church Coll., Aberdeen; certain of his articles on Biblical criticism so offended the Church authorities that he lost his chair, 1881. In 1882 he became ed. of the *Encyclopædia Britannica*; appointed prof. of Arabic at Cambridge, 1883.

Smith, SIR WILLIAM SIDNEY (1764–1840), Brit. sailor; *b.* London; served in Fr. wars; imprisoned in Paris, 1796–8; entered navy, 1777, and most famous exploit was his defence of Acre when it was besieged by Napoleon, 1799; admiral, 1841.

Smith - Dorrien, SIR HORACE LOCKWOOD (1858–1930), Brit. soldier; *b.* in Hertfordshire; entered army, 1876; served in Zulu War, 1879; raised and commanded mounted infantry in Egyptian War, 1882, and served in Sudan campaigns, 1885–6; gained distinction in the Boer War, 1899–1901; was commander-in-chief at Aldershot, 1907–12, and of the Southern Command, 1912–14. On outbreak of Great War commanded 2nd Army Corps, 1914–15, and made masterly retreat from Mons; was appointed to E. Africa, 1915, but his health broke down. He served as governor of Gibraltar, 1918–23. Pub.

Memories of Forty-eight Years' Service (1925).

Smoll'ett, TOBIAS GEORGE (1721–71), Brit. novelist and man of letters; *b.* Dalquhurn, Dumbartonshire; of good family and education; apprenticed to a doctor; went to London, 1739, with tragedy, *The Regicide*, which was unsuccessful; sailed as surgeon's mate on warship to W. Indies, 1740. Took to novel-writing and literary work. Best-known works are *Roderick Random* (1748), *Peregrine Pickle* (1751), and his masterpiece, *Humphrey Clinker* (1771), all of which are 'picaresque' romances, full of humour and observation. He was a caustic but not ungenerous satirist, with great narrative faculty.

[*Works* (ed. by Henley and Seccombe, 1899–1902), and *Life and Letters*, by L. Melville (1926).]

Smuts, JAN CHRISTIAAN (1870–), S. African statesman and soldier; *b.* near Riebeck West, Cape Province; educated at Cape Univ. and Cambridge, where he had a brilliant career; practised law at Cape Town; took active part in Boer War, being in command of republican forces in Cape Colony, 1901. In 1907, after the establishment of responsible government in S. Africa, he became colonial secretary in the Transvaal. At the outbreak of the Great War was minister of finance and defence in the Union of S. Africa. He took part in the conquest of Ger. S.W. Africa, and in 1916 became commander-in-chief in Ger. E. Africa, which office he vacated, 1917, to come to England as representative for S. Africa in the Imperial War Cabinet. He attended the Peace Conference, 1919. Returning to S. Africa, he was prime minister of the Union, 1919–24; minister of justice and deputy prime minister in coalition government, 1933. He has pub. *Holism and Evolution* (1926), and *Africa and Some World Problems* (1930).

Smyth, DAME ETHEL MARY (1858–), Brit. composer; *b.* London; studied music at Leipzig and quickly established herself as the leading woman composer of her time; her first opera, *Der Wald*, was produced, 1901, followed by *The Wreckers* (1909), and *The Boatswain's Mate* (1915), etc.; received D.B.E., 1922; and is author of volumes of reminiscences.

Snor'ri Stur'luson (1179–1241), Icelandic historian; *b.* near Breidafiord; was made supreme magistrate of Iceland, 1215. Compiled his *Edda* (1222); author of *Stories of the Kings of Norway* (*Heimskringla*) (trans. into English 1893–1905); assassinated at Reykjaholt by order of Hakon, King of Norway.

Snow'den, PHILIP, 1ST VISCOUNT (1864–), Brit. statesman; *b.* Cowling, Yorkshire; entered Civil Service, 1886; crippled by an accident, 1891, he took to lecturing and journalism; chairman of Independent Labour Party, 1903–6 and 1917–19; M.P. for Blackburn, 1906–18, for Colne Valley, 1922–31; chancellor of Exchequer, 1924 and 1929–31; on his advice commission was appointed to consider the question of national economy, the publication of whose report led to formation of National Government, 1931; after the General Election, 1931, took office as lord privy seal with seat in House of Lords; his Free Trade principles made him resign office, 1932; has been member of various royal commissions, and has written *Socialism and the Drink Question, The Living Wage, Labour and the New World.*

Sobieski, JOHN. See JOHN III.

Socinus (*sō-sī'nus*), two Ital. Prot. theologians, called SOZZINI. (1) LÆLIUS (1525–62), *b.* Siena;

threatened by the Inquisition, settled at Zurich and became leader of Swiss and Ger. reformers. (2) His nephew FAUSTUS (1539–1604), *b.* Siena; became the leader of new Unitarian movement, called after him *Socinian.*

Socrates (*sok'ra-tēz*) (*c.* 470–399 B.C.), Gr. philosopher; *b.* Athens; took little part in public affairs, but spent his time among friends and acquaintances discussing and searching after knowledge. He neither wrote nor professed to teach, but only to be a learner conscious of his ignorance, yet able, through question and answer, to bring forth, from his friends' minds, truths lying there unknown to them. Whilst his dialectical subtlety was unusual, his friends were still more impressed by his force of character and by his belief that a divine voice within him checked him from acting wrongly. In 399 B.C. he was accused of impiety and of corrupting the youth of the city. Found guilty by a small majority, he was condemned to death; he carried out the sentence by drinking hemlock.

The exact nature of his philosophical position is disputed. His chief concern was with man and human conduct. The usual view is that, as against contemporary scepticism, he maintained the possibility of finding a firm basis for morality in knowledge, going so far as to say that no one who knows what is right will act wrongly. It was this conviction of the paramount importance of real knowledge for good practice that inspired Socrates' untiring search for moral truth.

[*Socrates and the Socratic Schools*, by Zeller (1877); *Varia Socratica*, by A. E. Taylor (1911); and *Greek Philosophy*, by J. Burnet (1914).]

Sod'dy, FREDERICK (1877–), Brit. scientist; *b.* Eastbourne; studied under Rutherford and Ramsay, and specialized in researches in radioactivity; lecturer on physical chemistry and radioactivity, Glasgow Univ., 1904–14; professor of chemistry, 1914–19, and at Oxford since 1919; Nobel prizeman for chemistry, 1921; works include *Radioactivity* (1904), *The Interpretation of Radium* (1909 and 1920), *Science and Life* (1920); and works on economics.

Sol'omon, second son of David and Bathsheba, and third king of Israel (*c.* 970–930 B.C.); displayed administrative talent; strengthened military position of Jerusalem; built the temple, and made treaties with neighbouring powers, thus securing peace and giving scope to commerce. He was renowned for his wisdom and wealth. He is the reputed author of Proverbs, Ecclesiastes, Song of Solomon, and several apocryphal works. See 1 Kings 1–12.

Solomon, SOLOMON JOSEPH (1860–1927), Eng. painter; *b.* London; travelled in France, Italy, Spain, and Morocco; R.A., 1906; paintings include *Cassandra* (1886), *Samson* (1887), *Judgment of Paris* (1890), *Birth of Love* (1895). Also pub. *Strategic Camouflage* (1920).

So'lon (*fl.* 6th cent. B.C.), Athenian statesman and one of Seven Sages of Greece; of noble family, but reduced by poverty to trade; wrote poems; proposed internal reforms, and was elected archon (*c.* 594) to carry them out; was real founder of Athenian democracy.

Sophocles (*sof'ō-klēz*) (495–406 B.C.), Gr. poet; *b.* Colonus, Attica; famous for personal beauty, amiable character, and political qualities, as well as poetic genius; elected one of chief officers of Athenian state, 440 B.C. Author of over a hundred works, mostly dramas, and is said to have vanquished Æschylus in tragedy competition, 468 B.C. His tragedy is more human than that of his older rival, and he introduced a third performer, thus making the actors, not the chorus, the chief element in drama. Unlike Euripides, he had a firm faith in Gr. religion, and his work shows the typical restraint of Gr. art. Extant plays are *Antigone, Ajax, Electra, Œdipus Tyrannus, Œdipus Coloneus, Philoctetes,* and *Trachiniæ.*

Soult (*soolt*), NICOLAS JEAN-DE-DIEU, DUKE OF DALMATIA (1769–1851), Fr. soldier; *b.* in Tarn department; devoted favourite of Napoleon; led decisive charge at Austerlitz; as general in Span. army conquered Portugal; commander-in-chief in Spain, 1809–13; though repeatedly beaten, his campaigns showed great genius; rallied to Napoleon in Hundred Days, though he deserted his cause after Waterloo; held various political posts in Fr. Government, 1830–47; made marshal-general of France, 1847.

Sousa (*sooz'ä*), JOHN PHILIP (1854–1932), U.S.A. bandmaster and composer; *b.* Washington; conductor of U.S.A. Marine Corps band, 1880–92, and toured the world with his own band. His numerous marches include *The Washington Post, Semper Fidelis,* and *Stars and Stripes for Ever.*

Southey (*sowth'i* or *suth'i*), ROBERT (1774–1843), Eng. poet and man of letters; *b.* Bristol; lived at Keswick, where he became one of Coleridge's closest friends, and was included among the 'Lake Poets'; appointed poet laureate, 1813. Poems, including *Thalaba* (1801), *The Curse of Kehama* (1810), and *The Vision of Judgment* (1821), show careful craftsmanship, but lack spontaneous inspiration; he is remembered rather for his clever ballads, and for his prose, which includes *Life of Nelson* (1813), and *Lives* of Bunyan, Wesley, Cowper, etc.

[*Life*, by Dowden ('Eng. Men of Letters,' 1879).]

Spee, MAXIMILIAN VON (1861–1914), Ger. admiral; *b.* Copenhagen; was in command of the Ger. Far Eastern Squadron in the Pacific at the outbreak of the Great War; won a victory over Rear-admiral Sir Christopher Cradock off Coronel, Nov. 1, 1914, but was himself defeated and his squadron destroyed at the battle of the Falkland Islands, Dec. 8, 1914.

Speke, JOHN HANNING (1827–64), Eng. explorer; *b.* Jordans, Somersetshire; explored Tanganyika; discovered Victoria Nyanza and came to the conclusion that it must be the source of the Nile. In 1860 he made a second expedition, and from the lake followed the course of the Nile for a considerable distance. His works include *Journal of the Discovery of the Source of the Nile.*

Spencer, HERBERT (1820–1903), Eng. philosopher; *b.* Derby; sub-ed. of *Economist*, 1848–53; first studies were principally on social and political questions. His philosophy is based on evolution. His originality consists in the unique manner in which he has combined the two processes, induction and deduction, in his endeavour to include all sciences in one comprehensive system. His works, which are very voluminous, include *First Principles* (1862), *Principles of Biology* (1864–7), *Principles of Psychology* (1870–2), *Principles of Sociology* (1877–96), *Principles of Ethics* (1892), *Education* (1905).

[*Autobiography* (2 vols. 1904); *Lives*, by W. H. Hudson and J. A. Thomson.]

Spender, JOHN ALFRED (1862–), Eng. journalist; *b.* Bath; ed. *Westminster Gazette*, 1896–1922; author of *The Life of Sir*

H. Campbell Bannerman (1923), *The Changing East* (1926), *Life, Journalism, and Politics* (1927), and part author of *Life of Lord Oxford and Asquith.*

Spenser, EDMUND (1552–99), Eng. poet; *b.* London; educated Merchant Taylors' School and Pembroke Coll., Cambridge; became known to Sir Philip Sidney, and pub. his *Shepheard's Calendar* (1579), which at once gained him literary fame. In 1580 he received an appointment in Ireland, followed in 1586 by a grant of land near Cork. In that year he pub. *Astrophel*, an elegy on Sidney, and in 1590, at Raleigh's instance, came to court and issued the first part of his greatest work, the long allegorical poem, the *Faerie Queene*, with a dedication to Queen Elizabeth. Returning to Ireland, he wrote *Colin Clout's Come Home Againe.* He married Elizabeth Boyle in 1594, in whose honour he wrote the magnificent *Epithalamion.* Once more in England, he pub. in 1596 the second part of the *Faerie Queene*, and the *Prothalamion*, written to celebrate a marriage in Earl of Worcester's family. In 1598 he was appointed Sheriff of Cork, but after having his castle burnt and one of his children killed by rebels, he returned to London and died there, according to tradition, in poverty and disappointment. His poetry is remarkable for grace and melody and a sumptuous imagination, and he has enriched Eng. literature with a stanza, called after him the *Spenserian* stanza. For the influence he has exercised upon succeeding poets he has been well named 'The Poet's Poet.'

[*Poems*, ed. by J. C. Smith and E. de Sélincourt (1909–10), Globe ed. (1889); *Life*, by R. W. Church ('Eng. Men of Letters,' 1879).]

Spinoza (*spin-ōz'a*), BARUCH or BENEDICT (1632–77), Dutch philosopher; *b.* Amsterdam, of Jewish parents; educated in Heb. faith, but expelled as heretic; supported himself by polishing lenses while occupying leisure in philosophical studies; chief works, *Principles of the Philosophy of Descartes* (1663), *Tractatus Theologico-Politicus* (1670), *De Intellectus Emendatione, Ethica* (posthumous). The leading idea of his philosophy is that in becoming conscious of the unity of all things in God, we rise above the bondage of the passions and desires which belong to our finitude.

[*Lives*, by M. Lucas, ed. and trans. by A. Wolf (1927); by A. Wolf (1910); *Spinoza, His Life and Philosophy*, by F. Pollock (1911); *Spinoza*, by J. Caird (1901); *The Philosophy of Spinoza*, by R. McKeon (1928).]

Spohr (*spōr*), LUDWIG (1784–1859), Ger. composer and violinist; *b.* Brunswick; musical director successively at Gotha, 1805, Vienna, 1812, Frankfurt-on-Main, 1817–19, and Cassel, 1822–57; visited London, 1820. His works comprise compositions in nearly every branch of music, and include operas, as *Faust* and *Jessonda*; oratorios, as *Die letzten Dinge*; nine grand symphonies, violin concertos, etc. They exhibit mastery of technique and steady excellence rather than brilliance or genius. Also wrote a complete and invaluable *Violinschule.*

[*Autobiography* (Eng. ed. 1865); *Life*, by Schletterer (1881).]

Sprengel (*spreng'el*), HERMANN JOHANN PHILIPP (1834–1906), Ger. chemist and physicist; *b.* near Hanover; came to England, 1859. His name is connected with the Sprengel pump and Sprengel tube for determination of specific gravity.

Spur'geon, CHARLES HADDON (1834–92), Eng. Baptist divine; *b.* Kelvedon, Essex; as popular preacher drew enormous crowds by virtue of his eloquence and humour; first minister at the Tabernacle, London, from 1861; founded and ed. religious magazine, *The Sword and the Trowel*, and pub. his sermons weekly. He founded an undenominational orphanage at Stockwell, 1867.

[*Autobiography* (1897–1900); *Lives*, by Ray (1905) and Fullerton (1920).]

Squire, SIR JOHN COLLINGS (1884–), Eng. man of letters; *b.* Plymouth; founder and ed. of *The London Mercury*, 1919; editor of a new 'English Men of Letters' series; collected poems in *Poems in One Volume* (1926); produced *Collected Parodies* (1921); other works include reviews and anthologies, *Socialism and Art* (1907), *The Grub Street Nights Entertainments* (1924), etc.

Stacpoole, HENRY DE VERE, Brit. author, of Irish family; has travelled extensively. Works include novels: *The Blue Lagoon* (1908), *The Reef of Stars* (1916), *The Beach of Dreams* (1919), *Coblin Market* (1927), *Pacific Gold* (1931); poetry: *The Drums of War* (1910), *The North Sea and other Poems* (1915), etc.

Staël (*stäl*), MADAME DE, more correctly STAËL-HOLSTEIN, ANNE LOUISE GERMAINE, BARONNE DE (1766–1817), Fr. novelist and miscellaneous writer; *b.* Paris; daughter of financier Necker; married to Baron de Staël-Holstein, Swed. ambassador, 1786, and began to write her *Lettres sur J. J. Rousseau* (1788); welcomed Fr. Revolution, but was forced later to leave Paris; betook herself to Coppet on Lake Geneva. Her writings include essays on literary and political subjects, and two novels, *Delphine* (1802) and *Corinne* (1807), which are supposed to be autobiographical, also *De l'Allemagne* (1813), an account of German people and literature. Her *Dix Années d'Exil* (1821) and *Considérations sur la Révolution Française* (1818) were pub. posthumously.

Stalin ('steely'), IOSSIF VISSARIONOVICH DJUGUSHVILI (1879–), Russ. politician; *b.* in Transcaucasia; on expulsion from school became political organizer; suffered exile several times for his activities; Lenin's chief assistant, 1917; ed. Bolshevist journal *Pravda*; on death of Lenin assumed secretaryship of Central Communist Committee, and by 1928 his power in Soviet government was supreme; author of *Leninism* (Eng. trans. 1928).

Stambolisky, ALEXANDRE (1879–1923), Bulgarian statesman and journalist; *b.* Slavovitsa; as leader of Peasant party entered Parliament in 1908; opposed Bulgaria's entry into Great War as ally of Germany; prime minister, 1919 and 1920; signed Treaty of Peace at Neuilly-sur-Seine, 1920; brought about agreement between Bulgaria and Jugo-Slavia, 1922; assassinated, 1923.

Stamp, SIR JOSIAH CHARLES (1880–), Brit. economist; *b.* London; assistant secretary to Inland Revenue Board, 1916; left Civil Service, 1919, and became director of Nobel Industries, Ltd., and since 1925 chairman of the London, Midland, and Scottish Railway; has sat on many royal commissions, and is author of many books, including *Wealth and Taxable Capacity* (1922), *The Christian Ethic as an Economic Factor* (1926), and *Taxation during the War* (1932).

Stanford, SIR CHARLES VILLIERS (1852–1924), Brit. musical composer and conductor; *b.* Dublin; organist of Trinity Coll., Cambridge, 1872–92; prof. of composition and orchestral playing in the Royal Coll. of Music, 1883, and prof. of music at Cambridge, 1887; musical publications include symphonies, chamber music, part-songs, etc.; he is author of

Studies and Memories (1908), *Musical Composition* (1911), and *Pages from an Unwritten Diary* (1914).

Stan'hope, CHARLES, 3RD EARL (1753–1816), English scientist; *b.* London; F.R.S., 1772; experimented with the application of steam to ships; made great improvements in the art of printing, and constructed calculating machine; in politics, at first an ally of the younger Pitt, he disapproved of the war with the colonies, and welcomed the Fr. Revolution; was a consistent advocate of all kinds of reform.

Stanhope, PHILIP HENRY, 5TH EARL (1805–75), Eng. historian; *b.* Walmer; entered Parliament, 1830, and held minor government appointments, but is best remembered as the author of *History of the War of Succession in Spain, The History of England from the Peace of Utrecht to the Peace of Versailles, The History of England, comprising the Reign of Queen Anne to the Peace of Utrecht,* and *Life of the Right Hon. William Pitt.*

Stanley, ARTHUR PENRHYN (1815–81), Anglican divine; *b.* Alderley, Cheshire; appointed Dean of Westminster, 1863; was very liberal in his theological views, and aimed at a comprehensive Church; a great preacher, interested in philanthropic and social work; wrote numerous books, including *Life and Correspondence of Dr. Arnold* (1844).

[*Life and Letters,* by R. E. Prothero and G. G. Bradley (2 vols. 1893).]

Stan'ley, SIR HENRY MORTON (1840–1904), real name, JOHN ROWLANDS (ROLLANT), Brit. explorer of Africa; *b.* Denbigh; son of farmer; on father's death was sent, at age of seven, to workhouse; made his way to America, where he was adopted by Amer. merchant, whose name he assumed; enlisted in Confederate army; captured after battle of Shiloh, 1862; subsequently became journalist; went to Magdala with Brit. army as correspondent for *New York Herald*; commissioned to find Livingstone, 1869; he found him at Ujiji in 1871; returned, 1872; pub. *How I found Livingstone*; made second expedition, 1874–7, and followed out course of Congo; sent again to Africa by Leopold II. of Belgium, 1879, and established Congo Free State; undertook Brit. Emin Pasha relief expedition to East Equatorial region, 1887; recounted terrible sufferings in *In Darkest Africa* (1890); entered Parliament, 1895; knighted, 1899.

[*Autobiography* (ed. by his wife, 1909); *H. M. Stanley,* by Frank Hird (1935).]

Stead (*sted*), WILLIAM THOMAS (1849–1912), English journalist; *b.* Embleton, Northumberland; succeeded Morley as ed. of *Pall Mall Gazette,* 1883–9; initiated the 'new journalism' in sensational exposures of current abuses; founder and editor of *Review of Reviews* (1890); devoted to psychic research; introduced the 'interview' and pictorial illustrations; went down with the *Titanic.*

Steed, HENRY WICKHAM (1871–), Eng. journalist; *b.* Long Melford, Suffolk; proprietor and ed. of *Review of Reviews,* 1923–30; went as *Times* foreign correspondent to Berlin, Rome, and Vienna; in 1914 he became foreign ed., and in 1919 chief ed., of the *Times*; his works include *Hapsburg Monarchy* (1913), *L'Angleterre et la Guerre* (1915), *Through Thirty Years* (1924), *Journalism* (1928).

Steele, SIR RICHARD (1672–1729), Brit. essayist, dramatist, and man of letters; *b.* Dublin; educated Charterhouse and Oxford, where he formed lifelong friendship with Addison; joined army, but resigned to follow literature, 1706; already had pub. *The*

Christian Hero (1701), which won him favour with William III., and several comedies; appointed Gazetteer, 1707; ardent Whig M.P.; knighted by George I., 1715. Warm-hearted, and improvident by nature. His greatest title to fame is as pioneer of modern Eng. essay; established *Tatler* (1709), followed by *Spectator* (1711), *Guardian* (1713), etc., in which he was ably supported by Addison; comedies, including *The Funeral* (1701) and *The Conscious Lovers* (1722), are amusing, but inclined to sentimentality.

[*Works*, with *Memoir*, ed. by A. Dobson (1896) and G. A. Aitken (1898).]

Stef'ansson, VILHJALMUR (1879–), Can. explorer; *b.* in Manitoba, of Icelandic parents; took part in expeditions to Arctic regions, 1906–7, 1908–12; commanded Can. Government expedition, 1913–18; contributed valuable knowledge concerning that part of the world; author of *My Life with the Eskimo* (1913), *The Friendly Arctic* (1921), *Hunters of the Great North* (1922), and *The Standardization of Error* (1927).

Stein (*stīn*), SIR AUREL (1862–), British archæologist; *b.* Budapest; principal of Lahore Coll., 1888–99; appointed to Ind. Educational service, he conducted archæological explorations in Chinese Turkestan, 1900–1; explored in Central Asia, 1906–8, and again in Persia and Central Asia, 1913–18; superintendent Ind. Archæological Survey, 1910–29; works include *Chronicle of Kings of Kashmir* (1900), *Ruins of Desert Cathays* (1912), *Serindia* (5 vols. 1921), *The Thousand Buddhas* (1921).

Stein, HEINRICH FRIEDRICH KARL, BARON VON (1757–1831), Prussian statesman; *b.* near Nassau; one of the builders of modern Germany; head of department of trade and manufactures, 1804; formed general plan for union of Germany under hegemony of Prussia, but directed chief attention to military, administrative, and financial reform at home. He abolished some of the survivals of feudalism, promoted freedom of trade, and encouraged military reform. His energy and foresight alarmed Napoleon, who secured his dismissal; he then went to St. Petersburg and devoted himself to consolidating the league against Napoleon. After the Congress of Vienna he retired.

[*Life and Times*, by Sir J. Seely (1878).]

Steinmetz (*stīn'mets*), KARL FRIEDRICH VON (1796–1877), Prussian general; *b.* Eisenach; distinguished in war with Denmark, 1848; commanded an army against Austria, 1866, winning brilliant victories; commanded one of the Prussian armies in 1870; was defeated at Gravelotte and recalled; became gov.-gen. of Silesia and Posen; resigned in 1871; field-marshal, 1871.

Stendhal (*ston-dal'*) (1783–1842), pen-name of MARIE HENRI BEYLE, Fr. author; *b.* Grenoble; served in army during Napoleonic invasions of Italy and Russia; Fr. consul at Trieste, 1830–3, and at Civita Vecchia, 1833–41; works include *Le Rouge et le Noir* (1831), his greatest novel, *La Chartreuse de Parme* (1839), and *Shakespeare et Racine* (1822), a plea for Romanticism.

Stephen, one of the seven ordained by the Apostles to attend to the finances of the Church and distribute alms. He was accused of blasphemy and stoned to death. He was the first Christian martyr. (See Acts 6 and 7.)

Stephen (*c.* 1097–1154), King of England; son of Adela, William I.'s daughter, and Count of Blois; successfully claimed throne in opposition to Matilda,

Henry I.'s daughter, 1135; waged war against Matilda for several years; taken prisoner, 1141; on release, successfully besieged Oxford, 1142; Matilda gave up struggle, 1147; her son Henry was acknowledged as Stephen's heir, 1153.

Stephen, SIR LESLIE (1832–1904), Eng. biographer and critic; *b.* London; educated Cambridge; took orders, 1855, but resigned, 1875, on conscientious grounds; ed. *Cornhill*, 1871; ed. *Dictionary of National Biography*, 1882–91, to which he contributed some of the finest articles. His works, including *Hours in a Library*, *The History of English Thought in the Eighteenth Century*, *The Science of Ethics*, *The Agnostic's Apology*, and *The English Utilitarians*, show wide literary knowledge, a fine critical taste, and a clear, crisp style. His enthusiasm for Alpine climbing found expression in his *Playground of Europe*.

[*Life and Letters of Leslie Stephen*, by F. W. Maitland (1906).]

Stephens, JAMES (1882–), Irish poet; *b.* Dublin; won success with his *Crock of Gold* (1912), a collection of original fairy tales; other works include *Deirdre* (1923), *In the Land of Youth* (1924), *Strict Joy* (1931).

Stephenson. (1) GEORGE (1781–1848), Eng. engineer, 'the Father of Railways'; *b.* near Newcastle; built first locomotive when an engineer in Killingworth colliery, 1814; invented safety mine-lamp, 1815; chief engineer for construction of the Stockton and Darlington Railway, 1821, and of the Liverpool and Manchester Railway, where his 'Rocket' proved the fastest and most reliable locomotive, 1829.

[*Life of George Stephenson*, by S. Smiles (1858).]

(2) ROBERT (1803–59), Eng. engineer; *b.* Willington Quay; son of (1); was chief railway engineer of England, and built famous bridges at Newcastle, Montreal, and Menai Strait.

[*Lives of the Engineers*, by S. Smiles (ed. 1904), and *Life*, by Jeafferson (1864).]

Stern, DANIEL. See AGOULT, MARIE CATHERINE.

Sterne, LAURENCE (1713–68), Brit. novelist; *b.* Clonmel; educated Halifax School and Cambridge; took orders and obtained livings of Sutton and Stillington; rose to fame with first vol. of *Tristram Shandy* (1760). Eight other vols. followed at intervals; and in addition he issued collection of *Sermons* and *A Sentimental Journey* (1768). Sterne mingled genuine humour with clownish eccentricities, delicacy with gross indecency; his Uncle Toby, Corporal Trim, and Widow Wadman are immortal characters of fiction.

[*Works*, ed. G. Saintsbury (1894); *Lives*, by W. L. Cross and W. Sichel (1910).]

Stevenson, ROBERT (1772–1850), Scot. civil engineer; *b.* Glasgow; built several lighthouses, including the Bell Rock lighthouse, and improved the systems of lighting.

Stevenson, ROBERT LOUIS BALFOUR (1850–94), known as 'R.L.S.,' Brit. novelist, essayist, and poet; *b.* and educated in Edinburgh; grandson of Robert Stevenson, lighthouse engineer; travelled extensively, seeking health; settled finally at Samoa, where he died. As a novelist, he combined finished style with remarkable narrative faculty; his essays and poems display originality of thought and charm of style. His works include *An Inland Voyage* (1878), *Travels with a Donkey* (1879), *Virginibus Puerisque* (1881), *Men and Books* (1881), *New Arabian Nights* (1882), *Treasure Island* (1883), *A Child's Garden of Verses* (1885), *Prince Otto* (1885), *Dr. Jekyll and Mr. Hyde* (1886), *Kidnapped* (1887),

Underwoods (1887), *Black Arrow* (1888), *Ballads* (1889), *Master of Ballantrae* (1889), and *Catriona* (1893); also *St. Ives* and *Weir of Hermiston* (both unfinished; the former completed by Sir A. T. Quiller-Couch).

[*Lives*, by G. Balfour (1918; new ed. 1922), J. A. Steuart (1924).]

Stewart, CHARLES EDWARD. See under CHARLES EDWARD.

Stewart, DUGALD (1753–1828), Scot. philosopher; *b.* Edinburgh; prof. of moral philosophy at Edinburgh Univ., 1785–1820; brilliant lecturer; best work done in field of psychological observation. His works include *Elements of the Philosophy of the Human Mind* and *The Philosophy of the Active and Moral Powers.*

Stewart, HENRY BENEDICT MARIA CLEMENT, DUKE OF YORK, CARDINAL (1725–1807), younger brother of 'Bonnie Prince Charlie,' took holy orders, and received a cardinal's hat, 1747. To the Prince of Wales, afterwards George IV., he bequeathed the crown jewels which James II. carried with him to France in 1688.

Steyn (*stīn*), MARTINUS THEUNIS (1857–1916), S. African statesman; *b.* Winburg; last president of Orange Free State; elected, 1896; on outbreak of Boer War, 1899, threw in his lot with the Transvaal. He lived in retirement after the war, but took part in the National Convention which resulted in S. African Union.

Stilicho (*stil'i-kō*), FLAVIUS (*d.* 408), barbarian general of Rom. Empire; son of a Vandal; ruled empire during youth of Honorius; by military genius kept back Goths and Vandals, defeating Alaric. Suspected of treason and deserted by his army, he fled to Ravenna, where he was murdered.

Stirling, WILLIAM ALEXANDER, EARL OF (*c.* 1567–1640), Scot. statesman, dramatist, and poet; *b.* near Stirling; favourite at James I.'s court; friend of Drummond of Hawthornden; received vast grants of land in Nova Scotia and New Brunswick; king's secretary for Scotland. His works include several tragedies, a long poem *Doomsday* (1614, 1637), and *Aurora* (1604), a collection of songs and madrigals.

[*Poems* (ed. 1870); *Memorials*, by Rogers (1877).]

Stockmar, CHRISTIAN FRIEDRICH, BARON VON (1787–1863), Ger. statesman and physician; *b.* Coburg; physician to Prince Leopold of Coburg, whose elevation to throne of Belgium he helped to negotiate; a trusted friend of Prince Albert, he helped to arrange his marriage with Queen Victoria, with whom his counsels henceforth carried great weight.

Stokes (*stōks*), SIR GEORGE GABRIEL (1819–1903), Brit. mathematician; *b.* Sligo; senior wrangler, Cambridge, 1841; prof. of mathematics, Cambridge, 1849; president of Brit. Association, 1869, and of Royal Soc., 1885–8; received Rumford medal for investigations on light; wrote on mathematical and physical science.

Stoll, SIR OSWALD (1866–), Brit. theatre and cinema director; *b.* Melbourne, Australia; educated at Liverpool; chairman and managing director of several theatres; initiated War Seal Foundation; wrote *The People's Credit* (1916), *Freedom in Finance* (1918), and *Broadsheets on National Finance* (1920).

Stone, MARCUS (1840–1921), Brit. artist; R.A., 1887; winner of medals at various international exhibitions; painter of subjects of human interest and historical genre; works include *Rest, Edward II. and his Favourite, A Gambler's Wife,* and *The Peacemaker.*

Story, JOSEPH (1779–1845), U.S.A. lawyer and statesman;

b. Marblehead, Mass.; justice of Supreme Court of U.S.A., 1811–45; did valuable work in connection with admiralty law, equity jurisprudence, and patent law; Dane prof. of law at Harvard Univ., 1829–45; pub. works on legal subjects.

Story, William Wetmore (1819–95), U.S.A. sculptor, author, and poet; *b.* Salem, Mass.; educated at Harvard Univ. in law; went to Europe to study sculpture, and lived in Italy, forming friendships with Landor and the Brownings; his works in sculpture include *Cleopatra, Libyan Sibyl, Medea, Sappho*; amongst his writings are *Roba di Roma* (1862), *Nero* (1875), *Fiammetta* (1885), and vols. of poetry.

Stoth′ard, Thomas (1755–1834), Brit. designer, painter, and illustrator; *b.* London; paintings include his well-known *Canterbury Pilgrims* (1806); he illustrated Shakespeare, *Clarissa Harlowe, Tristram Shandy, Pilgrim's Progress*, and *Robinson Crusoe*.

[*Lives*, by Mrs. Bray (1851), by A. C. Copland (1906).]

Stow (*stō*), John (*c.* 1525–1605), Eng. chronicler and antiquary; *b.* London; pub. new ed. of Chaucer's works (1561), *Summary of English Chronicles* (1565), and *Annals of England* (1580); chief work is *Survey of London* (1598).

Stowe (*stō*), Harriet Elizabeth Beecher (1811–96), American novelist; *b.* Litchfield, Conn.; contributed to the anti-slavery paper, the *National Era*, her story *Uncle Tom's Cabin*, which was trans. into two dozen languages, and excited popular feeling against slavery. Also wrote *Dred, The Minister's Wooing*, etc.

[*Life*, by C. E. and L. B. Stowe (1911).]

Strabo (*strā′bō*) (*c.* 63 B.C.–A.D. 25), Gr. geographer; *b.* Amasia, Pontus; travelled widely between Armenia on the east, Italy on the west, the Euxine on the north, and Ethiopia on the south; his *Geography* is the most valuable work on the subject that has come down to us from ancient times; Eng. trans. by H L. Jones in Loeb Classical Library.

Strachey (*strā*-chi), Giles Lytton (1880–1932), Eng. author; his *Eminent Victorians* (1918) and *Queen Victoria* (1921) attracted considerable attention from their witty and caustic style; other works are *Books and Characters* (1922), *Pope* (1925), *Elizabeth and Essex* (1928), *Portraits in Miniature* (1931).

Strachey, John St. Loe (1860–1927), journalist; *b.* Sutton Court, Somerset; ed. and proprietor of *Spectator*, 1897–1925; works include *The Adventure of Living* (1922), *The River of Life* (1924).

Stradivari (*strä-dē-vä′rē*), Antonio (1644–1737), Ital. violin maker; *b.* Cremona; pupil of Amati; his violins are considered the most perfect in the world.

Straff′ord, Thomas Wentworth, Earl of (1593–1641), Brit. statesman; *b.* London; entered Parliament, 1614, and set himself against pretensions of the king and administration of Buckingham; imprisoned for refusing forced loan, 1627, and became leader of constitutional party; in crisis of struggle between king and people, chose to side with the king; created viscount, 1628; privy councillor, 1629; appointed lord-deputy (subsequently lord-lieutenant) of Ireland, 1632, and began to apply the system which he called 'thorough'; he restored order, 1633; returning to England, became king's chief adviser; created Earl of Strafford, 1640; attainted as traitor to the state by Long Parliament; Charles I., breaking his promise of protection, assented to his execution.

[*Life*, by H. D. Traill (1889).]

Strang, WILLIAM (1859–1921), Scot. painter and engraver; *b.* Dumbarton; studied at Slade School, London, 1875–81; R.A., 1921; illustrated *Kipling's Short Stories, Don Quixote*, and *Pilgrim's Progress*; also made portrait etchings of distinguished men, including Thomas Hardy and Rudyard Kipling.

Stratford-de-Redcliffe, STRATFORD CANNING, VISCOUNT (1786–1880), Brit. diplomatist; cousin of George Canning, who appointed him ambassador extraordinary to Turkey, 1825, to press the cause of Greece; ambassador at Constantinople, 1842–58, and won remarkable influence over Turk. mind; was largely responsible for Brit. aid to Turkey in Crimean War; created viscount, 1852.

[*Life*, by S. Lane-Poole (1888).]

Strathcona and Mount Royal, DONALD ALEXANDER SMITH, BARON (1820–1914), Can. politician; *b.* Forres, Scotland; became clerk in Hudson's Bay Co., 1838; chief commissioner and governor at Montreal, 1868–9; completion of Can. Pacific Railway largely attributable to him; high commissioner for Canada, 1896–1911; created baron, 1897.

Strauss (*strous*), DAVID FREDRICK (1808–74), Ger. theologian; *b.* Ludwigsburg, near Stuttgart; lecturer in philosophy, Tübingen, 1832; in 1835 he pub. his famous *Leben Jesu* (Eng. trans. *The Life of Christ*, by George Eliot, 1846), which aroused tremendous controversy; in 1864 pub. another ed. in which he took up an even more extreme position.

[*Lives*, by E. Zeller (1874), A. Hausrath (1876–8).]

Strauss, JOHANN (1804–49), Austrian composer; *b.* Vienna; conducted famous Strauss Orchestra, with which he visited the chief cities of Europe. His son, JOHANN (1825–99), the 'Waltz King,' conducted orchestra, 1849–63; he composed operettas (*e.g. Fledermaus*, 1874), and waltzes (*e.g. Blue Danube*).

Strauss, RICHARD (1864–), Ger. musical composer and conductor; *b.* Munich; court conductor at Berlin, 1898; was director, Vienna State Opera, 1919–24; works include orchestral symphonies, operas, etc., included in which are *Don Quixote* (1897), *Elektra* (1910), *Salome* (1905), *Der Rosenkavalier* (1911), *The Legend of Joseph* (1919), *Helen of Egypt* (1928).

Stravin'sky, IGOR FEDOROVICH (1882–), Russ. composer; *b.* near Leningrad; for its originality, vigour, and rhythmic variations, his music has been much criticized; works include *The Firebird* (1910), *Petrushka* (1912), *Le Sacre du Printemps* (1913), *L'Histoire du Soldat* (1917), *Œdipus Rex* (1927), *Symphonies de Psaumes* (1930).

Street, GEORGE EDMUND (1824–81), Eng. architect; *b.* Woodford, Essex; designed and restored many churches, including Christ Church, Dublin, also the Law Courts in London; an authority on mediæval architecture; author of *Brick and Marble Architecture of Northern Italy* (1855) and *Gothic Architecture in Spain* (1865).

[*Memoir*, by his son (1888).]

Stresemann (*strā'ze-man*), GUSTAV (1878–1929), German statesman and industrial organizer; after Revolution of 1918 became founder and president of People's Party; chancellor of the Republic, 1923; foreign minister, 1923–9; settled Ruhr dispute and brought about acceptance of Dawes plan in Germany; his foreign policy, directed towards peace, culminated in the Locarno Pact, which resulted in Germany's entry into the League of Nations; shared the Nobel Prize for Peace with Briand, 1926.

Strind'berg, JOHAN AUGUST (1849–1912), Swed. novelist and dramatist; *b.* Stockholm; his works are most voluminous, and, owing to his miserable boyhood and to unhappy marriage experiences, are marked by the deepest pessimism and hatred of women and marriage, but have nevertheless exerted a tremendous influence on the European novel and drama generally; most of them have been trans. into English, and include *The Red Room* (1879), *The Son of a Bondswoman* (1886), *A Fool's Defence* (1893), *To Damascus* (1898), *Crimes and Crimes* (1899), *The Dance of Death* (1901), *Alone* (1903), *A Blue Book* (1903).

[*August Strindberg: the Spirit of Revolt*, by L. Lind-af-Hageby (1913); *August Strindberg*, by V. J. McGill (1930).]

Stuart, ARABELLA (1575–1615), niece of Lord Darnley, and so first cousin to James I.; before the birth of his son, Henry, in 1594, she stood next in succession to the Eng. throne; in 1603 she was suddenly arrested, owing to a rumour that she intended to marry a foreigner, but made her peace with James; in July 1610, having secretly married William Seymour, she was imprisoned, but escaped, was recaptured, and confined in the Tower till death.

Stubbs, WILLIAM (1825–1901), Eng. bishop and historian; *b.* Knaresborough, Yorks; librarian to Archbishop of Canterbury at Lambeth, 1862; regius prof. of modern history, Oxford, 1866–84; Bishop of Chester, 1884, of Oxford, 1889; wrote standard *Constitutional History of England* and other important historical works.

Stur'dee, SIR FREDERICK CHARLES DOVETON (1859–1925), Brit. sailor; *b.* Charlton, Kent; entered the navy, 1871; captain, 1899; rear-admiral, 1908; rear-admiral of the 1st Battle Squadron, 1910; in command of 2nd Cruiser Squadron, 1912–13; during the Great War acted as chief of the War Staff, 1914–15; best remembered as commander-in-chief in the battle of the Falkland Islands, 1914; was divisional leader of the 4th Battle Squadron at the battle of Jutland, 1916; promoted admiral, 1917; commander-in-chief of the Nore, 1918–21.

Sturt, CHARLES (1795–1869), Brit. explorer; *b.* Bengal Presidency; went to Sydney, 1827; led several expeditions into the interior of Australia, returning from the last almost blinded; pub. *Journals* (1833), *Narrative of an Expedition into Central Australia* (1849).

Stuyvesant (*stiv'sant*), PETER (1592–1672), Dutch soldier; administrator of Dutch N. Amer. colonies, 1645; greatly furthered prosperity of New Amsterdam (now New York), which he had to surrender to British, 1664.

Suckling, SIR JOHN (1609–42), Eng. poet; *b.* Twickenham; in great favour at court on account of his wit and prodigality, but his attempt to enlist Fr. and Irish troops for a far-reaching plot in 1641 ruined his career. His fame rests on his ballads, such as 'Ballad upon a Wedding,' and his lyrics, for example, 'Why so pale and wan, fond lover?'

Sudermann (*zoo'der-man*), HERMANN (1857–1928), Ger. dramatist and novelist; *b.* Matziken, E. Prussia; began as journalist, then turned to novel writing, and eventually to the drama; his work in both kinds achieved immense popularity; novels include *Im Zwielicht* (1886), *Frau Sorge* (1887), *Geschwister* (1888), *Es War* (1894), *Das Hohe Lied* (1908), *Litanische Novellen* (1917), and *Purzelchen* (1928); dramas include *Die Ehre* (1880), *Heimat* or *Magda* (1892), *Sodoms Ende* (1891), *Es Lebe das Leben* (1912), *Stein Unter Den Steinen* (1915), and *Der Hasenfellhändler* (1925).

[*Autobiography* (Eng. trans. 1924).]

Sue (*soo*), EUGÈNE (JOSEPH MARIA) (1804–59), Fr. novelist; *b.* Paris; practised medicine for a time; pub. his first novel, 1840, and soon achieved success with stories of the mysterious and supernatural, and always with a touch of socialism of which he was a strong adherent; of this type are *Les Mystères de Paris* (1842), *Le Juif Errant* (1844–5), *Les Sept Péchés Capitaux* (1847–49), *Les Mystères du Peuple* (1848–9).

Sueto'nius, full name GAIUS SUETONIUS TRANQUILLUS (*c.* A.D. 75–160), Rom. historian; became private secretary to Emperor Hadrian; chiefly remembered for his *Lives of the Twelve Cæsars.*

Sul'la, LUCIUS CORNELIUS, 'FELIX' (138–78 B.C.), Rom. dictator; showed great military qualities in wars against Jugurtha, 107, Teutones and Cimbri, 104–101; consul, 88; he reduced Mithridates to submission, 87–84; found himself proscribed by Marian party in senate and retained army; defeated younger Marius at Præneste, 82; won battle of Colline Gate and entered Rome; as dictator carried out wide proscriptions and confiscations; made senate supreme.

Sullivan, SIR ARTHUR SEYMOUR (1842–1900), Eng. composer; *b.* London; studied in London and Leipzig; wrote overtures and incidental music for several of Shakespeare's plays; works for orchestra; popular songs, including 'The Lost Chord'; three oratorios and three cantatas, one of which, *The Golden Legend,* is frequently performed; and a grand opera, *Ivanhoe*; his name is, however, chiefly associated with the long series of comic operas, written mostly to libretti by Gilbert, of which *Patience, H.M.S. Pinafore, The Pirates of Penzance, The Mikado, The Gondoliers,* and *The Yeomen of the Guard* are the best known.

[*Lives,* by A. Lawrence (1899), H. Saxe-Wyndham (1926), and H. Sullivan and N. Flower (1928).]

Sully, JAMES (1842–1923), Eng. psychologist; *b.* Bridgwater; prof. of philosophy, Univ. Coll., London, 1892–1903; works include *Sensation and Intuition* (1874), *Pessimism* (1877), *Outlines of Psychology* (1884), *Studies of Childhood* (1895), *Children's Ways* (1897), *Essay on Laughter* (1902).

Sully-Prudhomme (*soo-lē' proo-dom'*), RENÉ FRANÇOIS ARMAND (1839–1907), Fr. poet; *b.* Paris; expounded nature, duty, and destiny of man. *Stances et Poèmes* (1866), *Les Epreuves* (1866), *Les Solitudes* (1869), *Les Destins* (1872), and *Le Bonheur* (1888) are his chief volumes of poems. He had great gift of melody and subtlety of thought.

Sun Yat-Sen (1867–1925), Chin. republican leader; graduated in medicine at Hong-kong, 1894; becoming associated with a revolutionary society, had to flee from China, and remained in exile, 1895–1911; during these years was recognized as leader of the Young China party; returning to China on outbreak of revolution, 1911, became provisional president of new republic, but resigned almost immediately in favour of Yuan Shih-Kai; in 1917 formed an independent republic in S. China; this involved him in fresh difficulties, and before he had time to adjust these he died.

[*Sun Yat-Sen, Memoirs of a Chinese Revolutionary* (1927); *Sun Yat-Sen and the Chinese Republic,* by P. Linebarger (1925).]

Suppé (*soo-pā'*) FRANZ VON (1820–95), Austrian musical composer; *b.* Spalato, Dalmatia; was musical director at Vienna; his works include light operas *Fatinitza* (1876) and *Boccaccio*

(1879), and an overture to *Dichter und Bauer.*

Sverdrup (*sver'droop*), Otto (1854–1930), Norweg. Arctic explorer; joined Nansen's Greenland expedition, 1888, and succeeded Nansen as leader of North Pole expedition in *Fram,* 1895; led second expedition, 1898–1901, and discovered islands near Greenland; started on another expedition, but recalled, 1914; returned his Ger. decorations because of Ger. cruelty at sea, 1917; rescued Russ. explorers in Kara Sea, 1920.

Swan, Annie S. (Mrs. Burnett Smith) (1860–), Scot. novelist; *b.* near Edinburgh; writer of popular novels, contributions to magazines, and children's books; novels include *Aldersyde* (1883), *Gates of Eden* (1886), *The Curse of Cowden* (1897), *Prairie Fires* (1913), *The Pendulum* (1928), *The Marching Feet* (1931).

[*Autobiography* (1934).]

Swan, Sir Joseph Wilson (1828–1914), Eng. inventor; *b.* Sunderland; invented the incandescent electric lamp and improved photographic methods; was awarded prizes for work in practical electricity and photography; knighted in 1904.

Swe'denborg, Emanuel (1688–1772), Swed. theologian and founder of sect bearing his name; *b.* Stockholm; studied at Uppsala, then in England and elsewhere; an able scientist, he anticipated many modern discoveries; became an intense mystic; devoted himself entirely to religious work after 1747. He claimed to have been called by the Lord to unfold the true teachings of the Divine word on all Christian doctrine. Swedenborg wrote numerous scientific works; his religious works include *Apocalypse Revealed, Apocalypse Explained, New Jerusalem, Heaven and Hell, The Last Judgment.* He did not intend to found a new denomination, but one, still existing, grew up after his death—Swedenborgians, or New Jerusalem Church.

[*Lives,* by W. White (1867–8), G. Trobridge (1907); *Compendium of the Theological Writings of Emanuel Swedenborg,* by S. Warren (1885).]

Swift, Jonathan (1667–1745), Brit. satirist, novelist, essayist, and pamphleteer; *b.* Dublin; appointed secretary to Sir William Temple, 1689; ordained in Ireland, 1694; returned to Temple, on whose death, 1699, Swift was appointed chaplain to lord-lieutenant of Ireland. During visits to London he met Addison, Steele, and other Whigs. In allegorical *Tale of a Tub*—pub. 1704, with *Battle of the Books* (written 1697), a brilliant mock-heroic prose epic on the quarrel of Ancients and Moderns — Swift satirizes the shams and excesses of the Churches. Leaving Whigs for Tories, 1710, he raked his former political friends in a series of powerful pamphlets, and received the Deanery of St. Patrick's, 1713, instead of the expected bishopric. On fall of Tories, 1714, Swift returned to Ireland, hopelessly embittered. Here he in all probability married 'Stella' (Esther Johnson), whom he had met at Temple's, and to whom his remarkable *Journal* was addressed. A disappointed admirer was Esther Vanhomrigh—the 'Vanessa' of his poem *Cadenus and Vanessa.* By *Drapier's Letters* (1724) he saved Ireland from 'Wood's halfpence' and became a national champion. *Gulliver's Travels,* his best-known work, appeared in 1726, anonymously. His last years were darkened by insanity.

[*Lives,* by Sir H. Craik (1882), L. Stephen ('Eng. Men of Letters,' 1882), J. C. Collins (1893), S. S. Smith (1910).]

Swinburne, Algernon Charles

(1837–1909), Eng. poet; *b.* London; educated at Eton and Oxford; in 1860 he pub. *The Queen Mother* and *Rosamund*, which attracted little attention; after travelling in Italy, he returned to London and lived in Chelsea with Rossetti, Meredith, and the pre-Raphaelites. In 1865 appeared his masterpiece, *Atalanta in Calydon*, which at once brought him recognition as a master of lyrical expression. This was followed by *Chastelard*, and in 1866 by *Poems and Ballads*, which, in spite of their lyrical power, aroused a storm of criticism on the score of immorality. He lived latterly with Theodore Watts-Dunton. Among his later works were *Songs of Italy* (1867), *Songs before Sunrise* (1871), *Erechtheus* (1876), *Poems and Ballads*, second series (1878), *Tristram of Lyonesse* (1882), *Locrine* (1887), *Astrophel* (1894), and *Duke of Gandia* (1908). He also wrote *Contemporaries of Shakespeare* (pub. 1919), and several essays (on Hugo, Byron, and Dickens). A poetic dramatist of great power, and a rhapsodist of emotional life, he is one of the greatest Brit. masters of metre.

[*Lives*, by H. Nicholson ('Eng. Men of Letters,' 1926), and S. C. Chew (1929).]

Swithin, St., Bishop of Winchester (*d.* 862); in favour with Egbert, king of the West Saxons, and his son, Ethelwulf; active as a builder of bridges and churches; his association with rain very likely signifies the attachment of some pagan festival to his day (July 15).

Sykes, Sir Mark (1879–1919), Eng. traveller and writer; *b.* London; made frequent journeys to the Near East; between 1905 and 1907, while honorary attaché at Constantinople, travelled throughout Asiatic Turkey; served in the S. African War (1899–1902), and during Great War was sent on special missions to Petrograd and the Caucasus, and to Aden, Basra, and Kut-el-Amara; devoted himself latterly to the scheme for establishing a Jewish Palestine; author of many works describing his travels.

Syme, James (1799–1870), Scot. surgeon; *b.* Edinburgh; established Minto House Hospital, where he put into practice his method of clinical lecturing; appointed, 1833, prof. of clinical surgery at Edinburgh Univ.; he was recognized as the leading surgeon in Scotland after Lister went to London, 1847; author of many surgical works; greatly promoted surgical and medical education.

Symonds, John Addington (1840–93), Eng. poet and critic; *b.* Bristol; fellow of Magdalen, Oxford; critical works, including *Studies of Greek Poets* (1873–6), *Life of Shelley* (1878), *Essays, Speculative and Suggestive* (1890), and *Walt Whitman* (1893), are of high value; his *magnum opus* was an exhaustive study of *The Renaissance in Italy* (1875–86).

[*Life*, by H. F. Brown (1895).]

Sy'mons, Arthur (1865–), Eng. man of letters; *b.* in Wales; earliest poems, *Days and Nights* (1889), *Silhouettes* (1892), and *London Nights* (1895); later works include studies in art and literature, a volume of *Confessions* (1930) and of *Wanderings* (1931).

Synge (*sing*), John Millington (1871–1909), Irish dramatist; *b.* Rathfarnham, near Dublin; pub. *The Aran Islands* (1907), a series of sketches of island life, and then, turning to the drama, produced *The Shadow of the Glen* (1903), *Riders to the Sea* (1904), *The Well of the Saints* (1905), *The Playboy of the Western World* (1907), and *Deirdre of the Sorrows* (1910); also wrote *Poems and Translations* (pub. in 1910).

T

Tacitus (*tas'i-tus*), PUBLIUS, or CAIUS CORNELIUS (*c.* A.D. 55–*c.* 120), Roman historian; son-in-law of Agricola; quæstor, 79; prætor, 88; consul, 97; intimate friend of younger Pliny; orator, but chiefly famed for literary work; writings, besides historical value, are prose masterpieces; *Life of Agricola* (*c.* 76), giving account of Britain, is a model biography; *Germania* (*c.* 98) is a political treatise; *Annals*, account of events 14–68, part lost; *Histories*, events 69–97, greater part destroyed. Style shows marked Virgilian influence.

Taft, WILLIAM HOWARD (1857–1930), president of U.S.A.; *b.* Cincinnati; called to bar, 1880; judge of Superior Court of Cincinnati, 1887; three years later solicitor-general of the U.S.A.; head of a civil commission to investigate the state of affairs in the Philippines, 1900; first civil governor of the Philippines, 1901; secretary of war, 1904. In 1909–13 president of the U.S.A.; appointed prof. of law in Yale Univ., 1913. As president was chiefly occupied in home affairs in furthering non-partisan measures, and in foreign affairs with the settlement of Atlantic Fisheries Arbitration, Mexican boundary dispute, and Bering Sea controversy; chief justice of U.S.A., 1921.

Tagore, SIR RABINDRANATH (1861–), Ind. author; *b.* Calcutta; founded a school in Bolpur, Bengal, 1901; travelled widely; trans. some of Bengali works into English; Nobel Prize for literature, 1913; knighted, 1915. Works, in Bengali, comprise poetry, novels, dramas, essays, etc.; English trans. include *Gitanjali* (1912), *Lover's Gift* (1918), *The Wreck* (1921), *Broken Ties* (1925), and *The Religion of Man* (1931); poetry characterized by idealistic tone and lyric beauty.

Taine (*tān*), HIPPOLYTE ADOLPHE (1828–93), Fr. historian, critic, and man of letters; *b.* in department Ardennes; in *Histoire de la Littérature Anglaise* (1864) expounded theory of scientific treatment of historical events; his *Origines de la France contemporaine* (unfinished, 1876–93) analyses minutely causes of Fr. Revolution; other works deal with æsthetics, literature, and history.

[*Life*, trans. by Mrs. R. L. Devonshire (1902–8).]

Tait, PETER GUTHRIE (1831–1901), Scot. physicist; *b.* Dalkeith; prof. of mathematics, Belfast, 1854, and of natural philosophy, Edinburgh, from 1860; works include *Properties of Matter* (1885), and, with Kelvin, *Treatise on Natural Philosophy* (1867).

[*Life and Scientific Work of P. G. Tait*, by C. G. Knott (1911).]

Talleyrand-Périgord (*tä-lē-ron' pā-rē-gōr'*), CHARLES MAURICE DE (1754–1838), Fr. statesman; *b.* Paris; Bishop of Autun, 1789; representative of diocese in States-General, 1789, as ardent democrat and reformer; helped to draft new constitution and advocated confiscation of Church property; resigned bishopric and was excommunicated, 1791; owing to failure of mission to England was proscribed, 1792; visited America; returned to France, 1795; foreign minister under Directory, 1799–1807; broke with Napoleon after Peace of Tilsit, 1807; brought back Louis XVIII., whose minister he became, 1814; supported Louis Philippe, 1830; always ready to sacrifice principle to expediency, but patriotic and an able diplomatist.

[*Talleyrand,* by J. McCabe (1906).]

Tamerlane. See TIMUR.

Tann'ahill, ROBERT (1774–1810), Scot. poet and weaver; *b.* Paisley; consumptive and disappointed, he ultimately drowned himself; songs include 'Gloomy Winter's noo awa'' and 'Jessie the Flower o' Dunblane.'

Tardieu (*tär-dyoo'*), ANDRÉ PIERRE GABRIEL AMÉDÉE (1876–), Fr. statesman; *b.* Paris; after working as journalist served in Great War; high commissioner to U.S.A., 1917–19; plenipotentiary at Peace Conference, 1918–19; minister of liberated regions, 1919–20 and 1926; a follower of Clemenceau, he opposed revisions of text of Versailles treaty; prime minister, 1929, 1930, 1932; author of works on Fr. politics.

Tar'kington, NEWTON BOOTH (1869–), Amer. author; *b.* Indianapolis; novels include *The Gentleman from Indiana* (1899), *Monsieur Beaucaire* (1900), *Penrod* (1914), and *The World does Move* (1929); plays include *Monsieur Beaucaire* (with E. G. Sutherland, 1902), *Springtime* (1909), *Maud and Bill* (1917), *Growing Pains* (1925).

Tas'man, ABEL JANSZOON (*c.* 1603–59), Dutch sailor and explorer; *b.* in Groningen; as commander of Van Diemen's expedition, 1642, discovered Tasmania (calling it Van Diemen's Land), New Zealand, Tonga, and Fiji Islands; made second voyage, discovering Gulf of Carpentaria; also made two important voyages of discovery in Pacific.

Tas'so, TORQUATO (1544–95), Ital. poet; *b.* Sorrento; forsook study of law for literature, and wrote *Rinaldo* (1562); courtier at Ferrara, 1565; diffidence prevented his publishing his masterpiece, *Gerusalemme Liberata* (completed 1574), although *Aminta* (1573), a simple pastoral drama, had won him fame; became subject to delusions, and passionate devotion to Leonora d'Este heightened his malady. Leaving Ferrara, he wandered from place to place; incarcerated in Ferrara as a lunatic, 1579–86; others edited his *Gerusalemme Liberata*; a master lyricist, but his genius blossomed young and lacked stability.

Tat'a, JAMSETJI NASARWANJI (1839–1904), Ind. Parsee merchant; *b.* in Baroda; developed cotton mills at Bombay and Nagpur; founded great iron works at Jamshedpur; endowed research institute at Bangalore.

Tate, SIR HENRY (1819–99), Eng. art collector; *b.* in Lancs; sugar refiner of Liverpool and London; donor of Tate Collection and picture gallery to Brit. nation.

Tate, NAHUM (1652–1715), Irish poetaster and dramatist; *b.* Dublin; succeeded Shadwell as poet laureate, 1692; works include *New Version of the Psalms* in conjunction with N. Brady (1696–8).

Tauchnitz (*touch'nits*), CHRISTIAN BERNHARD, FREIHERR VON (1816–95), Ger. printer and publisher; founded publishing house at Leipzig, 1837, which pub. collection of Brit. and Amer. authors, 1841–1934.

Tavernier (*tä-ver-nyā'*), JEAN BAPTISTE (1605–89), Fr. traveller; *b.* Paris; journeyed in S. Asia on six occasions between 1631 and 1668; ennobled by Louis XIV., 1669; pioneer of trade with India; works describe his travel.

Tay'lor, JEREMY (1613–67), Eng. clergyman and author; protégé of Archbishop Laud; imprisoned for political and religious views during Protectorate; Bishop of Down, Connor, and Dromore, and vice-chancellor of Dublin Univ., 1660;

chief works, *Holy Living* (1650), *Holy Dying* (1651); one of most poetic of Eng. prose writers.

Taylor, JOHN HENRY (1871–), Eng. professional golfer; *b.* in N. Devon; five times open champion, 1894, 1895, 1900, 1909, 1913; Fr. open champion, 1908, 1909; Ger. open champion, 1912.

Taylor, ZACHARY (1784–1850), president of U.S.A.; *b.* in Virginia; defended Fort Harrison against Indians, 1812; on the annexation of Texas marched, 1846, to the Rio Grande, Colorado, and gained victories over Mexicans; president, 1849; called by his men 'Old Rough-and-Ready.'

Tchaikovsky. See under TSCHAIKOVSKY.

Tchekov. See CHEKHOV.

Tchitcherin. See CHICHERIN.

Tecum'seh, TECUMTHE, or TECUMTHA (*c.* 1768–1813), SHAWNEE Ind. chief; organized Indians against Americans, who were driving Indians to north and west; defeated by Harrison at Tippecanoe, 1811; aided British, 1812; slain at battle of Thames, Canada.

Tel'ford, THOMAS (1757–1834), Scot. civil engineer; *b.* in Dumfriesshire; work includes Caledonian and Ellesmere Canals, Gota Canal in Sweden, a system of main roads in Scot. Highlands and N. Wales, Menai Bridge, and Clyde Bridge at Glasgow.

Tem'ple. (1) FREDERICK (1821–1902), Anglican divine; *b.* in Ionian Islands; headmaster of Rugby, 1858; ardent partisan of Gladstone; Bishop of Exeter, 1869, and of London, 1885; Archbishop of Canterbury, 1896; of forceful personality.

[*Memoirs of Archbishop Temple* (1906), ed. by Sandford.]

(2) WILLIAM (1881–), Eng. divine; son of (1); *b.* Exeter; headmaster, Repton School, 1910–14; Bishop of Manchester, 1921–9; Archbishop of York, 1929; works include *The Universality of Christ* (1921) and *Christianity and the State* (1928).

Temple, SIR WILLIAM (1628–99), Brit. statesman and writer; *b.* London; Irish M.P., 1660; envoy at Brussels, 1665; negotiated Triple Alliance between England, Holland, and Sweden to resist Fr. encroachments in Netherlands, 1668, nullified by Charles II.'s Treaty of Dover; ambassador at Hague, 1668; negotiated Treaty of Westminster, 1674, and marriage of William of Orange with Princess Mary, 1677; retired, 1681; essays, praised by Lamb, collected in *Miscellanea.*

Ten Brink, BERNARD (1841–92), Ger. philologist; *b.* Amsterdam; prof. of modern languages, Marburg, 1870, and Strasbourg, 1873; pub. studies of Chaucer from 1870, and *English Literature* (1877–93).

Tenniel (*ten-ēl'*), SIR JOHN (1820–1914), Eng. artist and cartoonist; *b.* London; on staff of *Punch,* 1851–1901; knighted, 1893; illustrated *Ingoldsby Legends, Alice in Wonderland, Through the Looking-Glass,* etc.

Tennyson (*ten'i-son*), ALFRED, LORD (1809–92), Eng. poet; *b.* Somersby, Lincs; went to Cambridge, 1828, but left in 1831 without graduating; formed here close friendship with Arthur Hallam. With his brother pub. *Poems by Two Brothers* (1827); later pub. two vols. of *Poems* (1830, 1833) which met with unfavourable criticism; third vol. (1842) brought him instant recognition; this contains some of his finest work, including 'Morte d'Arthur,' 'Ulysses,' 'Sir Galahad,' and 'Break, break, break.' Thenceforward his life was one of uninterrupted success; poet laureate, 1850; peerage, 1884. Works include *The Princess,* interspersed with charming lyrics (1847), *In Memoriam,* the record of the three years of sorrow, doubt, and hope that followed the death of his friend Arthur Hallam (1850), *Maud* (1855), *Idylls of the King* (1859, 1869, 1872), *Enoch Arden* (1864); *Harold* (1876) and *Becket* (1884), plays; *Demeter* (1889), *Death of Œnone* (1892). The variety of Tennyson made him a poet as popular as he was learned, and his mastery of the mystery of words and his perfection of style stamp his work as immortal.

[*Life* (1897), by his son.]

Ter′ence, PUBLIUS TERENTIUS AFER (*c.* 192–158 B.C.), Rom. comic poet; *b.* Carthage; brought to Rome as slave; kindly treated, and finally freed; author of six plays, *Andria, Hecyra, Heauton, Timoroumenos, Eunuchus, Phormio, Adelphæ*; plots drawn from Gr. comedy; his Latin is a model of purity.

Tere′sa, or THERESA, ST. (1515–82), Span. mystic; *b.* Avila; entered order of Carmelites, 1534; dedicated herself to reforming the order, and founded Descalzos ('Barefoots'), 1562. Canonized, 1622; proclaimed patron saint of Spain, 1814.

Terry. A family of Eng. actors. BENJAMIN TERRY (1818–92) and his wife did most of their work in old 'stock' companies. Two daughters, KATE (1844–1924) and ELLEN ALICIA (1848–1928), appeared on the stage when very young; Ellen married G. F. Watts, 1864, but marriage soon dissolved; married E. A. Wardell, actor, 1868, and retired from stage till 1874; the first real success of her brilliant career was as Portia at old Prince of Wales's Theatre, 1875; associated with Henry Irving at Lyceum, 1878–1902; on retirement of Irving, 1902, formed a company of her own; toured in America and married James Carew, 1907; G.B.E., 1925. Younger sisters, MARION (1856–1930) and FLORENCE (*d.* 1896), began careers in 1873 and 1870 respectively. FRED (1864–1933), youngest of family, first appeared at opening of Haymarket Theatre, London, 1880; married Julia Neilson, 1892. The third generation is represented by EDITH CRAIG and GORDON CRAIG, children of Ellen, and PHYLLIS NEILSON TERRY, daughter of Fred, who made her début in 1909.

Tertul′lian, QUINTUS SEPTIMUS FLORENS TERTULLIANUS (*c.* A.D. 155–222), Christian theologian; son of Rom. centurion; *b.* Carthage; presbyter in Carthaginian Church when about forty; Lat. Christianity has been said to start with him.

Tetrazzini (*tet-rä-tzē′nē*), LUISA (1871–), Ital. soprano; *b.* Florence; first appeared at Florence, 1895; Covent Garden, 1907; has toured in S. America, Russia, etc.; favourite operas, *Lucia di Lammermoor* and *La Sonnambula.*

Thack′eray, WILLIAM MAKEPEACE (1811–63), Brit. novelist and humorist; *b.* Calcutta; came to England at age of six; educ. at Charterhouse and Cambridge, where he became lifelong friend of Tennyson and Fitzgerald; abandoned law for journalism; studied painting in Paris; pub. *Paris Sketch Book* (1840), *Irish Sketch Book* (1843); with *Vanity Fair* (1848) attained celebrity as a novelist; *Pendennis* followed (1850), *Henry Esmond* (in 18th cent. style, 1852), *The Newcomes* (1855), *Virginians* (1858); combines humour and pathos with a streak of cynicism, due probably to his sensitive temperament; his style is cultured and craftsmanship masterly. Other works are *Hoggarty Diamond, Book of Snobs* (1848), *Barry Lyndon,* and an unfinished story, *Denis Duval*; lectures on *English Humorists of Eighteenth Century* (1851) and *The Four Georges* (1855); ed. *Cornhill Magazine* (1860–2), and was earlier a contributor to *Punch.*

[*Thackeray*, by C. Whibley (1903), by Merivale and Marzials (1891).]

Tha'les OF MILETUS (*c.* 640–546 B.C.), usually accounted the first Western philosopher; said to have predicted eclipse of the sun *c.* 585 B.C., and to have introduced Egyptian geometry into Greece; tried to solve problem of the substance of which the world is composed, and stated that all things are made of water.

Thayer (*thār*), ABBOTT HENDERSON (1849–1921), U.S.A. artist; *b.* Boston; studied in Paris; from study of protective colouring in animals became authority on camouflage in England during Great War.

Theal (*thēl*), GEORGE MCCALL (1837–1919), Brit. historian; *b.* in Canada; schoolmaster in Cape of Good Hope, 1858; colonial historiographer, 1891–1905; wrote *History of South Africa, 1486–1857* (1888–93); prepared many vols. of records of S. Africa.

Themistocles (*the-mis'tō-klēz*) (*c.* 515–449 B.C.), Athenian statesman and general; saviour of Greece from Persia, and founder of greatness of Athens as a sea-power; won naval victory of Salamis over Xerxes, 480, and restored Athens; ostracized, *c.* 476; governor of Magnesia under Artaxerxes, 464.

Theoc'ritus (3rd cent. B.C.), Gr. pastoral poet; probably *b.* Syracuse, Sicily; his poems in Doric dialect dealing with rustic, mythological, and topical subjects have served as a model for Virgil, Spenser, and Milton.

Thes'pis (*fl.* 6th cent. B.C.), real founder of drama; native of Icaria in Attica; devised idea of having actor to play part of Dionysus at festivals; said to have introduced tragic masks.

Thierry (*tē-er'-ē*), AUGUSTIN (1795–1856), Fr. historian; *b.* Blois; set example of research into sources of early Fr. history; blind for thirty years; wrote *L'Histoire de la Conquête de l'Angleterre par les Normands* (1825), *Récits des Temps Mérovingiens* (1840), *Essai sur l'Histoire du Tiers Etat* (1853).

Thiers (*tē-er'*), LOUIS ADOLPHE (1797–1877), Fr. historian and statesman; *b.* Marseilles; started journal, *National*, which provoked the revolution of July 1830; successively minister of interior, of commerce and public affairs, and of foreign affairs, 1832–6; unfavourable to revolution of 1848; opposed the Second Empire and was banished, 1851; re-entered chamber, 1863; opposed war, 1870; negotiated liberation of France from German occupation, 1871; president of republic, 1871–3; works include *Histoire de la Révolution Française* (1823), and *Histoire du Consulat et de l'Empire* (1845–62).

Thirl'wall, CONNOP (1797–1875), Eng. bishop and historian; *b.* London; author of *History of Greece* (1835–44); Bishop of St. David's, 1840; made many translations from Ger. authors.

Thomas, also known as Didymus, one of the twelve apostles; dismayed when Jesus announced His departure at Last Supper; refused to believe in resurrection till he had seen and touched Jesus.

Thomas (*tō-mä'*), ALBERT (1878–1932), Fr. Socialist; *b.* in department Seine; entered parliament, 1910; under-secretary for war, 1915; minister of munitions, 1916; appointed director International Labour Office of League of Nations, 1919.

Thomas, ARTHUR GORING (1850–92), Eng. musical composer; *b.* in Sussex; operas include *The Light of the Harem* (1879), *Esmeralda* (1883), *Nadeshda* (1885); choral ode, *The Sun Worshippers*; numerous songs and duets.

Thomas, JAMES HENRY (1875–), Brit. Labour leader; *b.* Newport, Mon; errand boy at age of nine; engine-driver on G.W.R.;

president, Amalgamated Soc. of Railway Servants, 1910, reorganized as National Union of Railwaymen; general secretary, 1918–24 and 1925–31; M.P. for Derby since 1910; privy councillor, 1917; president, International Federation of Trade Unions, 1920–4; secretary of state for Colonies, 1924, 1931, and since 1935; for Dominions, 1930–5.

Thomas à Kempis. See KEMPIS.

Thomas the Rhymer (THOMAS OF ERCILDOUNE) (*fl. c.* 1280), Scot. poet and seer; after death enjoyed a reputation rivalling that of Merlin.

[*Life*, by J. Geddie (1920).]

Thompson, ALICE. See MEYNELL, ALICE.

Thompson, FRANCIS (1859–1907), Eng. poet; *b.* Preston; began as medical student; befriended by the Meynells when in dire poverty; first vol. of *Poems* (1893), which includes 'The Hound of Heaven,' won admiration; other vols. are *Sister Songs* (1895), *New Poems* (1897), and a monograph on Shelley.

[*Life* (new ed. 1926), by E. Meynell.]

Thomson, SIR CHARLES WYVILLE (1830–82), Scot. naturalist and oceanographer; *b.* in W. Lothian; prof. of natural history at Aberdeen, 1850, at Cork, 1853, at Belfast, 1854, and at Edinburgh, 1870–9; head of scientific staff on voyage of *Challenger*, 1872–6; wrote *The Depths of the Sea* (1873) and *Voyage of the 'Challenger'* (1877).

Thomson, CHRISTOPHER BIRDWOOD, 1ST BARON (1875–1930), Brit. soldier; was on Supreme War Council, 1918; visited Ireland and Ruhr in interests of the Labour Party; air minister, 1924, peerage same year; killed in disaster to airship R101.

Thomson, JAMES (1700–48), Scot. poet; *b.* in Roxburghshire; tutor in London, 1725; held various appointments, including surveyorship of Leeward Islands; best-known work, *The Seasons* (1726–30), is pioneer of romantic revival in use of blank verse and nature descriptions; *Castle of Indolence* (1748) is his most finished work; dramas frigid and weak; *Masque of Alfred* contains song, 'Rule, Britannia.'

[*James Thomson* ('Eng. Men of Letters,' 1908), by G. C. Macaulay).]

Thomson, JAMES (1834–82), Scot. poet; *b.* in Renfrewshire; of pessimistic temperament; works include *The City of Dreadful Night and other Poems* (1880).

Thomson, SIR JOHN ARTHUR (1861–1934), Scot. biologist; *b.* in E. Lothian; prof. of natural history, Aberdeen Univ., 1899–1930; Gifford lecturer, St. Andrews, 1915; writings include *Outlines of Zoology* (8th ed. 1929), *Heredity* (5th ed. 1926), *The System of Animate Nature* (1920), *The Gospel of Evolution* (1925), *Biology for Everyman* (1934).

Thomson, JOSEPH (1858–95), Scot. explorer; *b.* in Dumfriesshire; geologist on Central African expedition for opening up route to north shore of Victoria Nyanza, 1878–80; explored Masailand, 1882–3; led expedition to Sokoto, 1885; made extensive additions to scientific knowledge of Africa.

Thomson, SIR JOSEPH JOHN (1856–), Brit. physicist; *b.* near Manchester; prof. of experimental physics, Cambridge, 1884–1918; master of Trinity Coll., Cambridge, since 1918; investigated problems connected with discharge of electricity through gases; Nobel Prize for physics, 1906; O.M., 1912; president of Royal Soc., 1916–20; writings include *Application of Dynamics to Physics and Chemistry* (1886), *Conduction of Electricity through Gases* (1903), *The Electron in Chemistry* (1923).

Thomson, William. See Kelvin.

Thoreau (*thō'rō*), Henry David (1817–62), U.S.A. writer; *b.* Concord, Mass.; educ. at Harvard; great poet-naturalist; recluse at Walden, 1845–7; works include *Walden* (1854), and *Excursions* (1863). One of the greatest nature writers of any country.

Thorn'dike, Dame Sybil (Mrs. Lewis Casson) (1885–), Eng. actress; *b.* Gainsborough; made reputation in repertory theatres and Old Vic. Theatre; notably successful in Shakespearian parts and in such plays as Bernard Shaw's *Saint Joan*; D.B.E., 1931.

Thorne, Will (1857–), Brit. Labour leader; *b.* Birmingham; commenced work at age of six; with others, founded National Union of General Workers, 1889, and general secretary ever since; mayor of West Ham, 1917–18; M.P. for West Ham since 1906; visited Russia, 1917; C.B.E., 1930; author of *My Life's Battles* (1925).

Thor'nycroft. (1) Sir John Isaac (1843–1928), Brit. naval architect and engineer; *b.* Rome; designed *Ariel*, forerunner of modern torpedo boat, 1863; founded shipbuilding works at Chiswick, 1866. (2) Sir William Hamo (1850–1925), Eng. sculptor, brother of (1); works, including *Artemis* (1880), statues of Gordon, Queen Victoria, and Gladstone, also King Edward Memorial at Karachi, and *The Kiss* (1916), show classical influences; R.A., 1888.

Thorwaldsen (*tor'valt-sen*), Bertel (1770–1844), Dan. sculptor; *b.* Copenhagen; worked chiefly in Rome; works include *Jason, Christ and Twelve Apostles, Lord Byron, Night and Morning* (bas-reliefs), and *Lion of Lucerne.*

Thring, Edward (1821–87), Eng. educationist; *b.* in Somerset; as headmaster of Uppingham from 1853 raised the school to high rank among public schools; writings include *The Theory and Practice of Teaching* (1883).

Thucydides (*thū-sid'id-ēz*) (*c.* 460–400 B.C.), Gr. historian; *b.* Athens; one of ten chief officials of Athens, 424; banished for twenty years on account of failure to relieve Amphipolis in Thrace; wrote history of Peloponnesian War down to 411; first historian to distinguish between myth and history; laid down rules of accuracy and impartiality; possessed great literary gifts, and a conception of political science which has never become antiquated.

Thuret (*too-rā'*), Gustave Adolphe (1817–75), Fr. botanist; *b.* Paris; travelled in Turkey, Syria, and Egypt; authority on cryptogams, especially algæ; writings include *Notes Algologiques* and *Etudes Phycologiques.*

Thur'low, Edward, 1st Baron (1731–1806), Eng. statesman; *b.* in Norfolk; made his name by speeches in Douglas peerage case, 1769; successively solicitor-general, attorney-general, lord chancellor of England; held Great Seal under three administrations.

Thurs'tan (*d.* 1140), Eng. Churchman; *b.* Bayeux; clerk in household of William Rufus; nominated Archbishop of York by Henry I., 1114; raised north England against Scots under David I., and gained battle of the Standard, 1138.

Thurs'ton, E. Temple (1879–1933), Eng. novelist and dramatist; his novels include *The City of Beautiful Nonsense* (1909); plays include *The Wandering Jew* (1920).

Tibe'rius (42 B.C.–A.D. 37), full name Tiberius Claudius Nero, second emperor of ancient Rome; quæstor, 23 B.C.; consul, 13; served in Armenia and Pannonia; was adopted by Augustus, A.D. 2; served in Bohemia, Dalmatia, Germany, and elsewhere; succeeded Augustus as emperor, 14; suppressed various risings in early part of reign and warred against Numidia and Parthia; later years marked by plots, suspicions, and murders; withdrew to Capreæ, 27, leaving conduct of affairs to Sejanus, whom he ultimately put to death for treason.

Tibul'lus, ALBIUS (*c.* 54–19 B.C.), Rom. elegiac poet; intimate with Virgil and Ovid; Quintilian gives him highest place among elegiac poets; lack of dramatic force redeemed by a vein of melancholy.

Tick'ell, THOMAS (1686–1740), Eng. poet; *b.* near Carlisle; friend of Addison, who gave him post of under-secretary of state, 1717; later, secretary to lord-justices of Ireland; poems include *Kensington Gardens.*

Til'lett, BENJAMIN (1860–), Brit. Labour leader; *b.* Bristol; founded London Dockers' Union; leader in dock strike, 1889; one of pioneer organizers of General Federation of Trade Unions; for many years alderman of London County Council; during Great War urged need for ample supply of munitions; M.P. for Salford, 1917–24 and 1929–31.

Til'lotson, JOHN (1630–94), Anglican divine; *b.* in Yorks; dean of Canterbury, 1672; archbishop, 1691; attempted to reform clerical abuses; renowned for his sermons.

Tilly, JOHANN TZERCLAES, COUNT OF (1559–1632), general; *b.* in Brabant; commanded army of Catholic League, 1618–32, during Thirty Years' War; only commander of genius on imperialist side till Wallenstein; behaved with great cruelty at sack of Magdeburg, 1631.

Timo'theus (*d. c.* 357 B.C.), Athenian general; defeated the Spartans, 375; secured Samos, Potidæa, and other towns for Athens; besieged Amphipolis; fined for failing to assist in engagement in Social War, 358; unable to pay fine; *d.* Chalcis.

Tim'othy, friend and companion of St. Paul; converted by Paul at Lystra; journeyed with Paul through Asia Minor, and followed him to Athens; sent on mission to Thessalonians and to Macedonia; joined Paul in his imprisonment at Rome; according to tradition, was Bishop of Ephesus until his martyrdom.

Timur (*tē-moor'*), or TAMERLANE (1336–1405), famous Eastern conqueror; *b.* near Samarqand; began military career *c.* 1358; after varied adventures became king at Samarqand, 1369; conquered most of Persia and Caucasia; successfully invaded India, 1398; captured Aleppo and Damascus; defeated Turks at Angora, 1402; died while marching to invade China.

Tintoret'to, properly JACOPO ROBUSTI (1518–94), Ital. painter; last great master of Venetian school; best pictures show superb colour work and mastery of chiaroscuro; works include decoration of Scuola di San Rocco, and *Last Judgment* in ducal palace, Venice.

[*Stones of Venice* (1863), by Ruskin; *Life* (1911), by E. M. Phillipps.]

Tippoo' Sa'hib (1753–99), the 'Tiger of Mysore'; succeeded his father Hyder Ali as sultan, 1782; hoped to expel British from India; invaded Travancore, 1789, but was defeated; intrigued with French, and was killed in capture of his capital, Seringapatam, by the British.

Tir'pitz, ALFRED VON (1849–1930), Ger. sailor; *b.* Küstrin; rear-admiral, 1895; secretary of state of imperial navy, 1897; built up Ger. fleet, with the barely concealed object of challenging Britain's supremacy; responsible for Germany's naval policy in Great War; advocated ruthless submarine war; retired, 1916; in *Memoirs* (1918) maintained that Germany had lost the war because she had not been ruthless enough; entered Reichstag as Ger. Nat. Deputy, 1921.

Tisch'endorf, LOBEGOTT FRIEDRICH KONSTANTIN VON (1815–74), Ger. Biblical critic; *b.* in Saxony; prof. at Leipzig Univ., 1845; travelled in Near East; issued twenty-four critical editions of N.T.; discoverer of Codex Sinaiticus at Mount Sinai.

Tissot (*tē-sō'*), JOSEPH JACQUES (JAMES) (1836–1902), Fr. painter; *b.* Nantes; painter of classic subjects, portraits, and *genre*; also studied etching; works include *Faust et Marguerite* (1861), *La Femme à Paris,* and 365 small water-colours illustrative of the *Life of Christ* (1894).

Tisza (*tē'sŏ*), STEPHEN, COUNT (1861–1918), Hungarian statesman; entered Hungarian Parliament, 1886, and quickly made his mark; most cherished aim was the Magyarizing of Hungary; premier, 1903; defeated, 1905, and retired from public life for some years; premier, 1912, and enjoyed unchallenged supremacy till 1917; joint-author of Austro-Hungarian Note to Serbia, 1914, which precipitated Great War. His resignation, 1917, was due to disagreement with Germany over the Polish question; assassinated, 1918. Fanatical and narrow, but fearless and honest; unpopularity largely due to resolute opposition to democratic reform.

Titian (*tish'yan*), properly TIZIANO VECELLIO (1477–1576), Venetian painter; one of greatest painters of all time; patrons included Doges of Venice, Pope Paul IV., also Charles V. and his son Philip II. of Spain; pictures include portraits, religious and mythological paintings, and allegorical works; all are painted in the grand style, and show highest skill in design and colouring; collections in nearly all European galleries; among his works are *Divine and Human Love, The Tribute Money, Bacchus and Ariadne, Venus Anadyomene, Presentation of the Virgin, Danae, Magdalene.*

[*The Early Work of Titian* (1897) and *The Later Work of Titian* (1898), by C. Phillips; *Titian* (1910), by C. Ricketts.]

Ti'tus, companion of St. Paul; a Gentile of Antioch, probably converted by the apostle himself; probably carried First and Second Epistles to the Corinthians to Corinth; organized local Church in Crete. According to tradition was Bishop of Crete till his death. (See Paul's Epistle to Titus.)

Titus, TITUS FLAVIUS SABINUS VESPASIANUS (A.D. 48–81), Rom. emperor; son of Vespasian; took Jerusalem, 70, and the arch of Titus in Rome was raised in commemoration; succeeded father, 79; famed for liberality.

Tocqueville (*tok-vēl'*), ALEXIS HENRI CHARLES MAURICE CLEREL, COMTE DE (1805–59), Fr. historian; *b.* in department Eure; sent by government to study penitentiary system in U.S.A.; wrote *La Démocratie en Amérique* (1835), a work of social philosophy, and *L'Ancien Régime et la Révolution* (1856).

Todleben (*tōt'lā-ben*), FRANZ EDUARD IVANOVICH, COUNT (1818–84), Russ. soldier; *b.* near Riga; erected fortifications of Sevastopol, which resisted 349 days during Crimean War; general, 1860; captured Plevna from Turks, 1877; commander-in-chief in Turk. War.

To'go, COUNT HEIHACHIRO (1847–1934), Jap. sailor; *b.* Kagoshima; studied at Naval Coll., Greenwich, 1873–4; commanded *Naniwa* in Chino-Jap. War of 1894–5; in Russo-Jap. War, 1904–5, commanded Jap. fleet, and destroyed Russ. fleet at Tsushima, 1905; Brit. Order of Merit, 1906; admiral of the fleet, 1912.

Tol'stoy, LEO NIKOLAYEVICH, COUNT (1828–1910), Russ. novelist and social reformer; *b.* in province Tula; entered army, 1851; served in Crimean War, during which he wrote *Childhood, Boyhood, and Youth*; *The Cossacks*; *Sebastopol*, etc.; retired from army, 1857; interested himself in the peasants, and settled among them, 1895, renouncing his property in copyright, land, and money; attitude towards Church that of socialistic iconoclast; excommunicated, 1901; works include two great novels, *War and Peace* (1863) and *Anna Karenina* (1871); also *My Confession* (1880), *Kreutzer Sonata* (1889), *Master and Man* (1895), and *Resurrection* (1900); attitude of mind altruistic and beneficent, but pessimistic and lacking in philosophic sanity; as a writer, intensely realistic and full of interest.

[*Life* (1910), by Aylmer Maude.]

Tone, THEOBALD WOLFE (1763–98), Irish lawyer and politician; *b.* Dublin; involved in political intrigue as secretary of Catholic committee; gave information about Ireland to France, and had to emigrate to America, 1795; sailed to France, 1796, and urged a Fr. invasion of Ireland; committed suicide in Irish prison while awaiting execution for treason.

Tooke, JOHN HORNE (1736–1812), Eng. politician and scholar; ordained, but gave up clerical work; M.P. for Old Sarum, 1801, but excluded from future Parliaments by Act which made clergymen ineligible; fined for political libels, but acquitted of high treason, 1794; author of *Diversions of Purley* (1786–1805), a philological work.

Toole, JOHN LAWRENCE (1830–1906), Eng. comedian; toured U.S.A., 1874–5, Australia, 1890; enjoyed great popularity, excelling in parts combining humour and pathos.

Top'lady, AUGUSTUS MONTAGUE (1740–78), Eng. hymn-writer; *b.* in Surrey; minister of Fr. Calvinist chapel, London, 1775; author of hymn 'Rock of Ages.'

Torquemada (*tōr-kā-mä'thä*), TOMAS DE (1420–98), first inquisitor-general of Spain; *b.* Valladolid; prior of Dominican monastery in Segovia for twenty-two years; reorganized Inquisition, and became head, 1481; favoured expulsion of Moors and Jews; notorious for cruelty and fanaticism.

Torricelli (*tor-ē-chel'ē*), EVANGELISTA (1608–47), Ital. mathematician and physicist; *b.* Faenza; Galileo's successor as prof. at Florence; first to measure atmospheric pressure by barometer, the vacuum in which is known as the Torricellian vacuum.

Tor'rington, GEORGE BYNG, VISCOUNT (1663–1733), Brit. naval officer; *b.* in Kent; instrumental in winning over fleet to Prince of Orange, 1688; served in battle off Beachy Head, 1690; in command at capture of Gibraltar, 1704; defeated Spaniards off Cape Passaro, 1718; first lord of Admiralty, 1727.

Toscanini (*tos-kä-nē'nē*), ARTURO (1867–), Ital. orchestral conductor; *b.* Parma; acted as conductor in various countries; conductor at Metropolitan Opera House, 1908–15, at La Scala, Milan, 1920–29; guest conductor at Bayreuth Festival, 1930–31; etc.

Tos'ti, SIR FRANCESCO PAOLO (1847–1916), Ital. musical composer; *b.* in Abruzzi; singing master to Queen of Italy, 1870; went to England, 1896, and later became teacher of singing to royal family; noted song-writer; among compositions is 'Good-bye.'

Toussaint L'Ouverture (*too-san' loo-ver-toor'*), PIERRE DOMINIQUE (*c.* 1746–1803), Negro revolutionary and liberator; *b.* Haiti; originally a slave; with whole body of Negroes joined Fr. republicans, 1794; later president of Haiti; forced by French to capitulate; died in captivity in France.

Tout, THOMAS FREDERICK (1855–1929), Eng. historian; *b.* London; prof. of history, Manchester, 1890–1925; fellow of Brit. Academy, 1911; works include *Edward the First* (1893), *The Empire and the Papacy* (1898), *History of England, 1216–1377* (1905), *Chapters in the Administrative History of Mediæval England* (5 vols. 1920–9).

To'vey, SIR DONALD FRANCIS (1875–), Brit. musician; *b.* Eton; organized first series of concerts of chamber music, London, Berlin, and Vienna; Reid prof. of music, Edinburgh Univ., since 1914; promoted musical art in Edinburgh by formation of Reid orchestra; publications include *Concerto for Pianoforte in A*, *Symphony in D*, and *The Bride of Dionysus* (opera, 1929); has written on musical analysis; is a brilliant pianist.

Townshend (*toun'zend*). (1) CHARLES, 2ND VISCOUNT (1674–1738), Brit. statesman; ambassador to States-General, 1709; appointed secretary of state for northern department by George I., 1714; introduced use of turnips and clover into England. (2) CHARLES (1725–67), Eng. statesman, grandson of (1); M.P. for Great Yarmouth, 1747–61; secretary for war, 1761; chancellor of Exchequer, 1766; taxed imports from America, which subsequently caused revolt of colonies. (3) SIR CHARLES VERE FERRERS (1861–1924), Brit. soldier, grand-nephew of (2); served in Egypt, 1884–5; commanded garrison of Chitral Fort during siege, 1895; served in Sudan expedition, 1898, and S. African War, 1899–1900; during Great War served in Mesopotamia; was besieged in Kut, Dec. 6 to April 27, 1916, when he surrendered and became a prisoner in Turk. hands; wrote *My Campaign in Mesopotamia* (1920).

Toyn'bee. (1) ARNOLD (1852–83), Eng. social reformer; *b.* London; tutor at Balliol Coll., Oxford; lectured to working-class audiences on economics and industrial questions; lectures pub. in *The Industrial Revolution* (1884); lived in Whitechapel, London, 1875; Toynbee Hall, Whitechapel, for the social improvement of E. London, was organized, 1884, in his memory. (2) ARNOLD JOSEPH (1889–), Eng. historian, nephew of (1); research prof. of international history, London Univ.; has written on Greek history and on modern international problems.

Traill, HENRY DUFF (1842–1900), Eng. man of letters; *b.* London; contributor to various periodicals, and first ed. of *Literature*; wrote *New Lucian* (1884), and lives of Coleridge, Sterne, William III., Shaftesbury, Strafford, Salisbury, Cromer, and Franklin; ed. *Social England*, 1892–6.

Tra'jan (A.D. 53–117), Rom. emperor; *b.* in Spain; emperor from 98; reign marked by many wars; first and second Dacian wars added Dacia to Rome; war on Parthia, 113, secured Armenia and Mesopotamia; during his absence in East, serious revolts took place in Cyprus, Africa, and Britain. A just and careful ruler, gaining name of 'Optimus.'

Tree, SIR HERBERT BEERBOHM (1853–1917), Eng. actor and theatrical manager; *b.* London; made a hit in *The Private Secretary*; as manager of Comedy, Haymarket, and Her Majesty's Theatres, produced in elaborate style many Shakespearian and other plays; founded Academy of Dramatic Art, 1904.

Treitschke (*trītsh'ke*), HEINRICH

GOTTHARD VON (1834–96), Ger. historian and political essayist; *b.* Dresden; prof. successively at Freiburg, Kiel, Heidelberg, and Berlin; violently anti-British, and greatly influenced Ger. opinion; chief work, *Deutsche Geschichte im 19 Jahrhundert* ('History of Germany in the Nineteenth Century').

Trench, RICHARD CHEVENIX (1807–86), Anglican divine; *b.* Dublin; Dean of Westminster, 1856; Archbishop of Dublin, 1864–84; wrote *Notes on the Parables*, *Notes on the Miracles*, and well-known works on philology, including *The Study of Words* (1851).

Trevel'yan. (1) SIR GEORGE OTTO (1838–1928), Eng. statesman and man of letters; *b.* in Leicestershire; nephew of Lord Macaulay; M.P., 1865–97; chief secretary for Ireland, 1882; chancellor of duchy of Lancaster, 1884–5; secretary for Scotland, 1886 and 1892–5; O.M., 1911; helped to bring about abolition of purchase in army and extension of household suffrage to the counties; writings include *Life and Letters of Lord Macaulay* (1876), *The Early History of Charles James Fox* (1880), *The American Revolution* (1909), *George III. and Charles Fox* (1912). (2) GEORGE MACAULAY (1876–), son of (1); prof. of modern history, Cambridge, since 1927; authority on Ital. history; works include a trilogy on *Garibaldi* (1907, 1909, and 1911), *History of England* (1926), and *England under Queen Anne* (2 vols. 1930 and 1932).

Tre'ves, SIR FREDERICK, 1ST BART. (1853–1923), Eng. surgeon and man of letters; *b.* Dorchester; prof., Royal Coll. of Surgeons, 1881–6; consulting surgeon to forces in S. Africa, 1900; operated on King Edward VII., 1902; lord rector, Aberdeen Univ., 1905–8; one of founders of Brit. Red Cross Soc.; publications include *Tale of a Field Hospital* (1900), *The Land that is Desolate* (1912), and *The Riviera of the Corniche Road* (1921).

Trev'ithick, RICHARD (1771–1833), Eng. engineer; *b.* in Cornwall; inventor of high-pressure steam engine; pioneer of locomotive engine; first applied iron to shipbuilding and used steam power for agricultural implements.

Trol'lope, ANTHONY (1815–82), Eng. novelist; *b.* London; post-office clerk, 1834; post-office surveyor in Ireland, 1841–67; made noted success with his 'Barchester' novels, beginning with *The Warden* (1855), and ending with *The Last Chronicle of Barset* (1867); excelled in portraying certain Eng. eccles. types.

Tromp. (1) MARTIN HARPERTSZOON (1597–1653), Dutch admiral; commanded against English at battles of Dover and Dungeness, 1652; and at Portland, N. Foreland, and Scheveningen, 1653. (2) CORNELIS (1629–91), son of above; *b.* Rotterdam; fought against England and France, 1673.

Trot'sky, LEV DAVIDOVICH (1877–), Russ. Soviet leader; *b.* near Zinovievsk; son of Jewish chemist; exiled to Siberia for political agitation, 1901; escaped, 1902, settled in London with Lenin, and returned to Russia, 1905; president of moderate revolutionary party, but associated with extremists under Lenin; arrested and sent to Siberia, but again escaped; in Paris at outbreak of Great War; expelled from France and Spain and went to U.S.A.; returned to Russia with Lenin to fan the revolution, 1917; people's commissar for foreign affairs, and later head of Red army; his downfall followed death of Lenin, 1924; exiled to Turkestan, 1928; banished, 1929.

Troubridge (*troo'brij*), SIR THOMAS (1758?–1807), Brit. rear-admiral; *b.* London; captured by

French, 1794; led Brit. fleet at Cape St. Vincent, and distinguished himself in Nelson's attack upon Santa Cruz; baronetcy, 1799; lost in wreck of *Blenheim.*

Tschaikovsky (*tchî-kof'ski*), PETER ILICH (1840–93), Russ. composer; *b.* in province Viatka; studied at St. Petersburg Conservatoire, where he became teacher of harmony, 1866–77; afterwards devoted himself entirely to composition; composed operas, as *Eugen Onegin* (1879); the *1812 Overture*; symphonies, as the *Pathétique*, which are regarded as amongst the greatest examples of symphonic music; and many other forms of composition.

[*Life*, by M. Tschaikovsky (Eng. trans. 1906).]

Tucker, CHARLOTTE MARIA (1821–93), pseudonym A.L.O.E. (*i.e.* A Lady of England), writer for children; *b.* Barnet. A voluminous writer; went as missionary to India, 1875, where she died.

Tup'per, MARTIN FARQUHAR (1810–89), Eng. author; *b.* London; works include *Proverbial Philosophy*, a series of didactic moralizings in blank verse.

Turenne (*tū-ren'*), HENRI DE LA TOUR D'AUVERGNE, VICOMTE DE (1611–75), Fr. general; *b.* Sedan; served in Thirty Years' War, later with rebels of the Fronde, 1650; restored to favour and defeated Condé and his Span. allies respectively at Arras, 1654, and battle of the Dunes, 1657; in Dutch War, 1672, won battle of Sinzheim, 1674; killed in engagement against Austrians. A great strategist; marshal of France, 1644.

Turgenev (*toor-gen'yef*), IVAN SERGEIEVICH (1818–83), Russian novelist with socialistic tendencies; *b.* Orel; master of the short story; works include *Rudin* (1856), *Fathers and Sons* (1861), *Smoke* (1867), and *Virgin Soil* (1876).

[*Turgenev, a Study* (1917), by E. Garnett.]

Turgot (*toor-gō'*), ANNE ROBERT JACQUES, BARON DE L'AULNE (1727–81), Fr. statesman and economist; *b.* Paris; as controller general of finances introduced many reforms, including free trade in grain, suppression of *corvées* (forced labour on roads), and abolition of *jurandes* (guild privileges); might have averted or postponed the Revolution, but his reforms were unpopular with nobles, Church, and merchants; dismissed, 1776; author of several works on economics.

Tur'ner, JOSEPH MALLORD WILLIAM (1775–1851), Eng. artist; *b.* London; as pupil of Royal Academy began exhibiting when only fifteen; R.A., 1803; prof. of perspective, 1808; travelled abroad and at home; as a man, unattractive and eccentric; as a landscape painter, ranks equal with Claude and Corot; knowledge of nature unrivalled; watercolours superb for delicacy and brilliant execution; main characteristic is an idealizing of things, together with a passion for expression through colour.

[*Modern Painters*, by Ruskin; *Life*, by Wyllie (1905).]

Tur'pin, DICK (1706–39), Eng. highwayman; *b.* in Essex; butcher's apprentice; joined gang of smugglers; the famous ride from London to York attributed to him was probably accomplished by another highwayman; hanged for horse-stealing at York.

Tussaud (*too-sō'*), MADAME MARIE (1760–1850), founder of famous waxwork exhibition, London; *b.* Berne; learned wax modelling in Paris; imprisoned during Fr. Revolution; settled in England, 1802.

Twain, MARK, pseudonym of SAMUEL LANGHORNE CLEMENS (1835–1910), Amer. author and humorist; *b.* in Missouri; after trying various occupations became pilot on the Mississippi, and later lecturer and newspaper editor; travelled widely, and had many vicissitudes of fortune; writings full of distinctive humour; works include *The Innocents Abroad*, *Tom Sawyer*, *Huckleberry Finn*, and *Pudd'nhead Wilson*.

[*Life* (1912), by A. B. Paine.]

Tweedsmuir, LORD. See BUCHAN, JOHN.

Tyler, JOHN (1790–1862), president of U.S.A.; *b.* in Virginia; vice-president, 1840; president, 1841; during his administration Texas was annexed; president of Peace Convention at Washington, 1861; sided with South in Civil War, and was member of Confederate Congress till death.

Tyler, WAT (*d.* 1381), Eng. rebel; with Jack Straw, led peasant revolt of 1381, and meeting Richard II. at Smithfield, demanded abolition of serfdom and free pardon for rebels; killed by lord mayor.

Ty'nan, KATHARINE (MRS. HINKSON) (1861–1931), Irish poet and novelist; *b.* Dublin; poems marked by freshness and delicacy; novels, full of poetic charm, include *A Daughter of Kings* (1905), *Wives* (1924), *The Infatuation of Peter* (1926).

Tyndale (*tin'dal*), WILLIAM (1492–1536), Eng. translator of the Bible and Prot. martyr; *b.* in Glos; printed his Eng. version of N.T. at Cologne, 1525, and Worms; owed much to Luther and Erasmus; his translation was opposed by eccles. authorities in England; his translation of the Pentateuch was pub. at Marburg, 1530; he was arrested, and during fifteen months' imprisonment translated as far as Books of Chronicles; burned at stake in Brussels.

Tyn'dall, JOHN (1820–93), Brit. physicist; *b.* in Ireland; prof. of natural philosophy in Royal Institution, London, 1853–67, succeeding Faraday as director, 1867–87; principal work was on heat, acoustics, and dust; popularizer of scientific truths.

Tyrcon'nel, RICHARD TALBOT, DUKE OF (1630–91), Irish soldier; supporter of Stewarts; fought against Cromwell; viceroy of Ireland, 1687; fought against William III., but fled after raising of siege of Limerick; returned to Ireland, 1690.

Tyr'rell, GEORGE (1861–1909), Irish theologian; *b.* Dublin; became R.C., 1879, and entered Soc. of Jesus, 1880; for his sympathy with modernism was expelled from order, and suspended, 1906.

Tyrtæus (*tir-tē'us*) (*fl.* *c.* 650 B.C.), Gr. elegiac poet; *b.* Athens; wrote elegiac and anapæstic poems of martial strain, and also one called *Eunomia*, or 'law-abidingness,' intended to allay political dissensions at Sparta.

Tyrwhitt (*tir'it*), SIR REGINALD YORKE (1870–), Brit. admiral; in charge of landing party at Nicaragua, 1894; during Great War took part in actions in Bight of Heligoland, 1914, Dogger Bank, 1915, and in operations at Zeebrugge and Ostend, 1918; commanding officer coast of Scotland, 1923–5; commander-in-chief, China station, 1927–9, and The Nore, 1930–3; admiral of the fleet, 1934.

Tytler (*tīt'ler*), WILLIAM (1711–92), Scot. historian and critic; works include defence of Mary Queen of Scots (1759) and *The Poetical Remains of James I. of Scotland* (1783).

Tze-hsi (*tsā-shē*) (1834–1908), dowager Empress of China, wife of Emperor Hsien-Feng; on death of her son, 1875, became regent for her nephew; arrested emperor's reforming advisers, and confined emperor; nominally resigned, 1889, but continued to influence emperor; encouraged Boxer insurrection; ordered expulsion of foreigners, 1900.

U

U'dall, Nicholas (1505–56), Eng. dramatist; *b.* in Hants; headmaster of Westminster School, 1555; author of *Ralph Roister Doister* (*c.* 1553), earliest known Eng. comedy.

Ugolino della Gherardesca (*oo-gō-lē'no del-a gā-rar-dās-ka*), Count (*d.* 1289), head of a Tuscan family; after several attempts became ruler of Pisa, and ruled as a tyrant till deposed by popular rising, 1288; he was starved to death in his tower. Was pilloried for his treachery in Dante's *Inferno*.

Uhland (*oo'länd*), Johann Ludwig (1787–1862), Ger. poet and politician; *b.* Tübingen; author of admirable lyrics and ballads.

Ulls'water, James William Lowther, 1st Viscount (1855–), Eng. politician; barrister, 1879; m.p., 1883; under-secretary for foreign affairs, 1891; as speaker of House of Commons effective and popular; viscount, 1921.

Und'set, Sigrid (1882–), Norweg. novelist; *b.* in Denmark; clerk, 1898–1909; her best works include *Jenny* (1912), *Kristin Lavransdatter* (1922), and *The Wild Orchid* (1931); Nobel Prize, 1928.

Ur'ban, the name of eight popes. Urban ii., pope 1088–99; *b.* near Reims; preached first crusade at Clermont, 1095; crusaders established him in Rome, 1097. Urban viii., pope 1623–44; *b.* Florence; strengthened temporal power of papacy; supported France in Thirty Years' War; condemned Galileo, 1633.

Ush'er (or Ussher), James (1581–1656), Anglican divine; *b.* Dublin; ordained, 1601; regius prof. of divinity, Dublin, 1607; Bishop of Meath, 1621; Archbishop of Armagh, 1625; visited England, 1640, where he remained permanently; formulated chronological scheme for Bible.

Uzzi'ah (*c.* 805–737 b.c.), son of Amaziah, King of Judah; at age of sixteen a vigorous and able monarch; fought against Philistines, Arabs, and Ammonites; died of leprosy. During his reign Isaiah began to prophesy.

V

Vacares'co, Helen (1866–), Romanian authoress and poetess; *b.* Bucharest; holds brilliant literary and social position in Paris; has retold myths of her country; Romanian delegate to League of Nations.

Vachell, Horace Annesley (1861–), Eng. novelist and playwright; his skilfully constructed novels include *John Charity* (1900), *The Hill* (1905), *Quinney's* (1914), *Fishpingle* (1917), *The Soul of Susan Yellam* (1918), *The Fourth Dimension* (1920), *A Woman in Exile* (1926), and *At the Sign of the Grid* (1931). Has written plays, and dramatized his novels.

Valera, Eamon de. See De Valera.

Vambéry (*väm'bā-rē*), Arminius (1832–1913), Hungarian traveller and Orientalist; had wonderful knowledge of Oriental and European languages; settled in Constantinople, 1852; travelled through Middle East, 1861–4; prof. of Oriental languages in univ. of Budapest; wrote autobiographical and philological works.

Vanbrugh (*van-broo'*). (1) IRENE (1872–), Eng. actress; *b.* Exeter; associated with leading actors from 1889; married Dion Boucicault (*d.* 1929); created many famous characters; toured Australia and New Zealand, 1923–25 and 1929–7. (2) VIOLET (1867–), Eng. actress; sister of (1); toured in America with the Kendals; played Shakespearian and other rôles; marriage with Arthur Bourchier, 1894, dissolved, 1918.

Vanbrugh, SIR JOHN (1664–1726), Eng. dramatist and architect; *b.* London; became soldier, went abroad, and imprisoned in Bastille as suspected spy, 1690; first play, *The Relapse* (1697); best work, *The Confederacy* (1705); knighted, 1714; plays marked by sparkling wit and originality, but marred by gross indecency, hence fierce attack by Jeremy Collier; was architect for Blenheim House and Castle Howard.

Vancou'ver, GEORGE (1758–98), British navigator; accompanied Cook on voyages of 1772–4 and 1776–9; surveyed west coast of N. America from 35° N. to 56° N., circumnavigating Vancouver I.

Van'derbilt, CORNELIUS (1794–1877), U.S.A. capitalist; *b.* in New York State; at sixteen was a ferryman between New York and Staten I.; successful boatbuilder and owner of steamships; engaged in railway ventures and president of New York Central Railway, 1867; left *c.* $100,000,000.

Vandervelde (*van-dĕ-vel'dĕ*), EMILE (1866–), Belgian Socialist statesman; *b.* near Brussels; entered Parliament, 1894; carried out social reforms as minister of justice, 1918–21; prof., univ. of Brussels, 1924; minister of foreign affairs, 1925–7.

Van Dyck (*dīk*), SIR ANTHONY (1599–1641), Flem. painter and etcher; *b.* Antwerp; studied under Rubens; travelled in Italy, 1621–6; chief court painter at Antwerp; painted for James I. and Charles I. in England; influence on Eng. school of painting great and lasting; in style more restrained and refined than Rubens; portraits, resembling those of Titian, include *Philip le Roy*, *James I.*, *Charles I.*, *Sir George Villiers*, and his wife, *Lady Mary Ruthven*; among religious paintings are *Crucifixion*, *St. Sebastian*, *The Mystic Marriage of Joseph*, and *The Elevation of the Cross*.

[*Life* (1906), by L. Cust.]

Van Dyke, HENRY (1852–1933), Amer. author and clergyman; *b.* in Penn.; prof. of Eng. literature in Princetown Univ., 1899–1923; works include *The Other Wise Man* (1896), *The White Bees and Other Poems* (1909), *The Lost Boy* (1914), *Half Told Tales* (1925), and *Gratitude* (1930).

Vane, SIR HENRY, the YOUNGER (1613–62), Eng. statesman; *b.* in Kent; governor of Massachusetts, 1636; returned to England, 1637; member of Short and Long Parliaments; promoted Solemn League and Covenant, 1643; executed by Charles II.

Van Eyck. See EYCK.

Van't Hoff, JACOBUS HENDRICUS (1852–1911), Dutch chemist; *b.* Rotterdam; investigated the oceanic salt deposits of Stassfurt; contributed to theory of solution.

Var'don, HARRY (1870–), Eng. golfer; *b.* in Jersey; trained as gardener; professional for various clubs, including Ganton; six times open champion, 1896, 1898, 1899, 1903, 1911, 1914; Amer. champion, 1900; Ger. champion, 1911.

Vasar'i, GIORGIO (1511–74), Ital.

art historian, architect, and painter; *b.* Arezzo; studied under Michelangelo and Andrea del Sarto; chiefly remembered for his *Vite de' più eccellenti Pittori, Scultori, e Architetti* (1550), which is basis of Ital. art history.

Vasco da Gama. See GAMA, VASCO DA.

Vauban (*vō-ban'*), SÉBASTIEN LE PRESTRE DE (1633–1707), Fr. soldier; *b.* in Burgundy; served under Condé in war of Fronde; taken prisoner by French; was persuaded by Mazarin to serve Fr. king; life passed chiefly in constructing and besieging fortresses; made Fr. school of fortification the first in Europe; works include *Traité de l'Attaque et de la Défense des Places* (1739), and *Traité des Sièges* (1747).

Vaughan, HENRY (1622–95), Welsh poet and mystic; *b.* in anc. territory of Silures, Wales, hence called himself the 'Silurist'; last of 'metaphysical' school; imaginative love of nature is his chief characteristic; works include *Poems* (1646), *Silex Scintillans* (1650), *Thalia Rediviva* (1678), and prose *Hermetical Physic* (1655).

Vaughan, HERBERT (1832–1903), R.C. divine; *b.* Gloucester; Archbishop of Westminster, 1892; cardinal, 1893; promoted erection of cathedral at Westminster.

Vaughan Williams. See WILLIAMS, R. VAUGHAN.

Vega (*vā'gä*), GARCILASO DE LA (1503–36), Span. poet and soldier; *b.* Toledo; favourite of Emperor Charles v.; mortally wounded in Provence; popularized the sonnet.

Vega Car'pio, LOPE FELIX DE (1562–1635), Span. dramatist and poet; *b.* Madrid; author of over 1,500 plays, which may be divided into contemporary, historical, and legendary; work valuable for the mine of ideas it provided for others.

Velazquez (*vā-läs'kāth*), DIEGO RODRIGUEZ DE SILVA Y (1599–1660), greatest of Span. painters; *b.* Seville; commissioned to paint Philip iv.'s portrait and became court painter and favourite; visited Italy, 1630 and 1649; representative in art of the dignified, aristocratic national types; superb colourist and admirable draughtsman; famous portraits include *Philip IV., Prince Don Balthasar Carlos, Queen Isabella of Bourbon, Charles I. of England* (then Prince of Wales), *Pope Innocent X.*; other paintings are religious, as *Christ on the Cross*, and mythological, as *The Forge of Vulcan* and the 'Rokeby' *Venus*.

[*Velasquez and Murillo* (1883), by C. B. Curtis; *Velasquez* (1914), by Davies.]

Venize'los, ELEUTHERIOS (1864–1936), Gr. statesman, maker of Greater Greece; *b.* in Crete; barrister; prime minister of Crete, 1909, and of Greece, 1911, after military *coup d'état* at Athens; founded Balkan League, 1912, and directed Gr. policy till 1915; directed insurrectionary movement at Salonika, 1916; represented Greece at Peace Conference, and by diplomatic skill won Thrace, Ægean Islands, and Smyrna for Greece. Defeated at general election on question of return of Constantine, 1920, and resigned; premier for a fortnight in 1924, resigning for health reasons; again premier, 1928–32; headed revolt, 1935, but had to flee into exile.

Ver'di, GIUSEPPE (1813–1901), Ital. composer; *b.* in Parma; known almost solely by his operas; achieved success with *Rigoletto* (1851), *Il Trovatore* (1853), and *La Traviata* (1855); *Aïda* produced at Cairo, 1871; career ended brilliantly with *Otello* (1887) and *Falstaff* (1893).

Verestchag'in (*vā-rest-chä'gēn*), VASSILI (1842–1904), Russ.

painter; *b.* in Novgorod; studied in Paris; served in wars with Turkey, 1877, and Japan, 1904; perished in *Petropavlovsk* outside Port Arthur; pictures on military subjects reveal Russ. fullness and crudeness of colouring; include *The Pyramid of Skulls* and *The Street of Plevna.*

Verhaeren (*fer-här'en*), EMILE (1855–1916), Belgian poet and dramatist; *b.* near Antwerp; style forceful and highly coloured; poetic works include *Les Flamandes* (1883), *Les Tendresses Premières* (1904), *La Belgique Sanglante* (1915); plays include *Le Cloître* (1900).

Verlaine (*ver-lān'*), PAUL (1844–96), Fr. lyrical poet; *b.* Metz; earliest volumes—*Poèmes Saturniens* (1866) and *Fêtes Galantes* (1869)—showed influence of Baudelaire; *Romances sans Paroles* (1874), *Jadis et Naguère* (1884), and *Bonheur* (1891), characterized by exquisite beauty of thought and rhythm.

Verne, JULES (1828–1905), Fr. novelist; *b.* Nantes; plot of each of his novels works round scientific or physiological fact; forecasted gramophone, cinematograph, airship, submarine, and television; best known, *Round the World in Eighty Days* and *Twenty Thousand Leagues under the Sea.*

Vernier (*ver-nyā'*), PIERRE (*c.* 1580–1637), Fr. scientist; *b.* near Besançon; inventor of the *vernier*, an instrument for accurately measuring small-scale divisions.

Ver'non, EDWARD (1684–1757), Eng. admiral; *b.* London; commanded expedition which captured Porto Bello, 1739; attacked Carta gena without success, 1740; dismissed the service, 1746, for publishing official letters.

Veronese (*vā-rō-nā'se*), PAOLO, cognomen of PAOLO CAGLIARI (1528–88), last great Venetian painter; *b.* Verona; settled in Venice, 1555; greatest work is decoration of church of San Sebastiano; superb colourist, but lacks dramatic intensity; pictures include *Marriage at Cana.*

Verrocchio (*vā-rok'ē-o*), ANDREA DEL, cognomen of ANDREA DE' CIONI (1435–88), Ital. goldsmith, sculptor, architect, and painter; *b.* Florence; executed works in bronze, including *Young David, Unbelief of St. Thomas, Bartolommeo Colleoni*; only extant canvas is *Baptism of Christ.*

Vespa'sian (TITUS FLAVIUS SABINUS VESPASIANUS) (A.D. 9–79), Rom. emperor; commanded legion in Britain, and subdued Isle of Wight, 43–44; consul, 51; governor of Africa, 63, of Judæa, 66; proclaimed emperor at Alexandria, 69; suppressed Batavians, Gauls, and Jews; restored peace to Rome; continued conquest of Britain; restored finances of state, and set example of personal simplicity and economy; built new temple of Jupiter on Capitol and temple of Peace; began Colosseum.

Vespucci (*ves-poo'che*), AMERIGO (1451–1512), Ital. navigator; *b.* Florence; fitted out Columbus's third expedition; explored Venezuelan coast, 1499; discovered All Saints' Bay in Brazil, 1503; pilot-major of Spain, 1508; America named after him.

Viaud, LOUIS MARIE JULIEN. See LOTI, PIERRE.

Vicente (*vē-sen'tā*), GIL (*c.* 1470–*c.* 1536), Port. dramatist; probably *b.* at Lisbon; works dating from 1502 include sacred pieces, comedies, and farces, many reaching a high level of excellence.

Vic'tor Amade'us II. (1666–1732), Duke of Savoy and first King of Sardinia; *b.* Turin; married Anne, niece of Louis XIV. of France; greater part of his reign spent in throwing off Fr. yoke; abdicated, 1730.

Victor Emman'uel II. (1820–78), first King of Italy; *b.* Turin;

King of Sardinia, 1849; joined England and France in sending troops to the Crimea, 1855; joined by Napoleon III. in war against Austria, 1859, and defeated Austrians; Tuscany, Parma, Modena, and Romagna joined Sardinia, 1860; in same year Garibaldi conquered Naples; Victor Emmanuel accepted sovereignty of S. Italy, and annexed majority of Papal States; proclaimed King of Italy by first Ital. Parliament at Turin, 1861; secured Venetia, 1866; made Rome capital of Italy, 1871.

Victor Emmanuel III. (1869–), King of Italy; *b.* Naples; succeeded on assassination of father, Humbert I., 1900; commanding general at Naples, 1897. On entry of Italy into Great War, 1915, assumed supreme command of Ital. forces; lived almost continuously among his troops. Refused to sign order proclaiming martial law throughout Italy, 1922, at *coup d'état* by Fascisti; signed treaty, 1929, recognizing independence of City of the Vatican.

Victo'ria (1819–1901), Queen of Great Britain and Ireland, Empress of India; daughter of Duke of Kent and niece of William IV.; succeeded, 1837; married, 1840, her cousin Albert (*d.* 1861), youngest son of Duke of Saxe-Coburg. She was prudently educated, and during her long reign was strictly impartial in party politics, while clearly recognizing that the crown was the central tie which bound the empire together; assumed title Empress of India, 1876; celebrated jubilee, 1887, and diamond jubilee, 1897. Her wisdom, knowledge of foreign politics, unselfishness, and uprightness were all remarkable traits of her long reign; the chief events of her reign include granting popular constitution to Canada, adoption of penny post, institution of Education Department, repeal of Corn Laws, Crimean War, Ind. Mutiny, disestablishment of Irish Church, Ballot Act passed, Berlin Conference, Zulu War, suzerainty in Egypt, Home Rule agitations in Ireland, S. African War, Australian Commonwealth Bill. Her reign was also a period of remarkable literary achievement.

[*Queen Victoria: a Biography* (1904), by Lee; *Queen Victoria* (1921), by Strachey.]

Vigée le Brun, MADAME. See LE BRUN.

Vignola Da. See BAROCCHIO.

Vigny (*vēn-yē'*), ALFRED VICTOR, COMTE DE (1797–1863), Fr. poet and author; *b.* in Indre-et-Loire; a leader of Romanticism, yet stoical, sometimes even pessimistic, in his philosophy; poetry shows uncommon range and delicacy; finest prose work is *Servitude et Grandeur Militaires*; novels include *Cinq-Mars*, the first Fr. historical romance.

Vil'lari, PASQUALE (1287–1917), Ital. historian and statesman; prof. of history, Florence, 1866; minister of public instruction, 1891–2; wrote *Savonarola and his Times*, *Machiavelli and his Times*, *First Two Centuries of Florentine History*, also *Meridional Letters* (1878), which brought about reforms in S. Italy.

Villars (*vē-yär'*), CLAUDE LOUIS HECTOR, DUC DE (1653–1734), marshal of France; *b.* Moulins; distinguished himself in Dutch wars; appointed to chief command, 1702, and won battle of Friedlingen; marshal, 1702; defeated at Malplaquet, 1709; his victory over Dutch Denain led to peace of Rastatt, 1714.

Villehardouin (*vēl-är-doo-an'*), GEOFFROI DE (*c.* 1160–*c.* 1213), Fr. historian; marshal of Champagne, 1191; negotiated with Venetians transport of crusaders to Holy Land; rescued crusading army from Bulgars at Adrianople; his

Conqueste de Constantinople narrates events of fourth crusade, 1197–1207.

Villeneuve (*vēl-noov'*), PIERRE CHARLES JEAN BAPTISTE SYLVESTRE DE (1763–1806), Fr. admiral; *b.* in Provence; commander of combined Fr. and Span. fleets, 1803; decoyed Nelson to W. Indies, but was afterwards defeated at Trafalgar; prisoner in Britain till 1806; returned to France and committed suicide.

Villiers, GEORGE. See BUCKINGHAM, 1ST and 2ND DUKES OF.

Villiers, G. W. F. See CLARENDON, 4TH EARL OF.

Villiers de l'Isle-Adam (*vē-yā' de lēl-ä-dan'*), AUGUSTE (1838–89), French poet and satirist; *b.* in Brittany; inaugurated symbolist movement, typified in great play *Axël*; other plays, *La Révolte*, *L'Eve Future*; wrote also clever and fantastic *Contes Cruels*.

Villon (*vē-yōn'*), FRANÇOIS (1431–*c.* 1485), Fr. poet; *b.* Paris; banished for killing priest in street brawl, 1455; pardoned and wrote *Le Petit Testament*; after period of imprisonment wrote *Le Grand Testament* (1462); banished for third time, 1463, and disappears from history; his writings display strong capacity of feeling, and a singularly mournful tone.

Vincent de Paul (*van-son' de pōl'*), ST. (1576–1660), Fr. priest; instituted Lazarist Soc. and the Sisterhood of Charity; worked among galley slaves; canonized, 1737; Soc. of St. Vincent de Paul was founded at Paris, 1833.

Vinci, LEONARDO DA. See LEONARDO DA VINCI.

Vinet (*vē-nā'*), ALEXANDRE RODOLPHE (1797–1847), Swiss critic and theologian; *b.* near Lausanne; advocated complete religious freedom, and founded Swiss Free Church, 1845; wrote *Etudes sur Pascal*, etc.

Vinograd'off, SIR PAUL (1854–1925), Russ. jurist; *b.* Kostroma; settled in England; prof. of jurisprudence, Oxford, from 1903; lectured in U.S.A. and Europe; knighted, 1917; author of *Villeinage in England*, *The Growth of the Manor*, *Self-Government in Russia* (1915), etc.

Virchow (*fĕr'chō*), RUDOLF (1821–1902), Ger. pathologist and politician; *b.* in Pomerania; prof. of pathological anatomy, Berlin, 1856; proved the cellular theory applicable in pathology as well as in physiology, and thus became father of modern pathology; renowned anthropologist; completely reformed health conditions of Berlin; vigorous opponent of Bismarck.

Vir'gil, PUBLIUS VERGILIUS MARO (70–19 B.C.), greatest of Rom. poets; *b.* near Mantua; when his father's farm was confiscated for military settlement, Virgil obtained its restitution from Octavianus; he became one of Mæcenas's circle of friends; withdrew from Rome to S. Italy in 37, made two journeys to Athens, and died shortly after returning to Italy with Augustus. His first important work was the *Eclogues* (42–37), ten pastoral pieces in hexameters; they are imitations of Theocritus; the *Georgics* (37–30) deal with art of husbandry from an idealistic point of view, and are among the most perfect of Rom. poems. His masterpiece is the *Æneid* (29–19), an epic in twelve books dealing with the fall of Troy and the wanderings of Æneas. This poem is the noblest monument of Rom. character and Rom. poetic genius.

[*Virgil and his Meaning to the World of To-day* (1923), by J. W. Mackail.]

Viscon'ti, GIAN GALEAZZO (*c.* 1347–1402), duke of Milan; encouraged arts; founded Milan cathedral; aspired to rule Italy; his daughter Valentine married, 1389, Louis, Duke of Orleans hence the claim of Louis XII. to Milan.

Vivian'i, René (1862–1925), Fr. independent Socialist statesman; *b.* in Algeria; studied for bar; deputy for Paris, 1893; minister of labour and public hygiene under Clemenceau, 1906, and under Briand, 1909–10; minister of public instruction, 1913; was prime minister on outbreak of Great War; minister of justice in coalition ministry of Briand, 1915–17; represented France at first meeting of League of Nations at Geneva, 1920, and at Washington Conference, 1921.

Vizetel'ly, Henry (1820–94), Eng. illustrated press pioneer; *b.* London; started *Pictorial Times,* 1843, *Illustrated Times,* 1855; Paris correspondent of *Illustrated London News,* 1865; fined, and on a second occasion imprisoned, for publishing translations of certain novels of Zola; works include *The Man with the Iron Mask* (1870) and *Glances Back through Seventy Years* (1893).

Vo'gler, George Joseph (1749–1814), 'Abt (Abbé) Vogler,' Ger. organist, composer, and teacher; *b.* in Bavaria; court chaplain, Mannheim; travelled widely; established music schools at Mannheim, Stockhold, and Darmstadt; invented orchestrion, hence Browning's poem 'Abt Vogler to the musical instruments of his invention.'

Vol'ta, Alessandro (1745–1827), Ital. physicist; *b.* Como; prof. of physics, Como, 1774, Pavia, 1779; Copley medallist, England, 1791; pensioned by Napoleon, 1801; director, philosophical faculty of Padua, 1815; a pioneer of electrical science; electric 'volt' named after him.

Voltaire (*vol-tār'*), François Marie Arouet de (1694–1778), Fr. poet and philosopher; *b.* Paris; imbibed deism from earliest teachers; imprisoned in Bastille, 1717, for literary attack on regent; wrote *Œdipe* and commenced *La Henriade*; assumed additional name 'de Voltaire,' 1718; after new imprisonment went to England, 1726, where he repub. *La Henriade* (1728), an epic poem on Henry of Navarre, and wrote *Brutus* (played 1730), and *Zaïre,* his masterpiece (1732); other noted plays are *Adélaïde du Guesclin* (1734), *Zulime* (1740), *Mahomet* (1741), *Mérope* (1743); his *Lettres Philosophiques* (1731), praising Eng. institutions at expense of Fr., was burned by the Parlement de Paris.

The tales *Zadig* (1747), *Micromégas* (1752), the famous *Candide* (1759), *L'Ingénu* (1767), *L'Homme aux Quarante Ecus* (1768), etc., are best of his writings for wit and style, but imprudently malicious. Voltaire entered Fr. Academy, 1746, and in 1750 accepted invitation to Berlin, where he pub. his best historical work, *Le Siècle de Louis XIV.* (1751); visit ended in quarrel with Frederick the Great. Other historical works are *History of Charles XII.* (1731), *History of Peter the Great* (1759), *Précis du Siècle de Louis XV.* (1768), *Histoire du Parlement de Paris* (1769), *Essay on the Manners and Spirit of Nations* (1769). Voltaire lived near Geneva, 1760–78. Now at height of his influence he exercised enormous power over European thought; built model village, established watchmaking industry, a church, and a theatre. Among his works is a long poem, *La Pucelle,* with a savour of iconoclasm and epigram; literary excellence of Voltaire (allowed by all) is that of wit and *esprit moqueur*; one of leaders of *Encyclopédistes* and father of free thought in France; returned to Paris, 1778; tremendous reception hastened his death; left vast *Correspondance* of first-rate kind.

[*Life,* by Lord Morley (1886), by Aldington (1925).]

Vor′onoff, Serge (1866–), Russ. physiologist; director of experimental surgery, Station Physiologique du Coll. de France; one of leading authorities on gland-grafting; experiments have aroused world-wide controversy; wrote *Rejuvenation by Grafting* (1925).

Voy′sey, Charles (1828–1912), founder of Theistic Church; *b.* London; ordained a clergyman of Church of England; deprived of his living, 1871, in consequence of certain publications adjudged heterodox; works include *Theism as a Science of Natural Theology and Natural Religion* (1895).

W

Waals, Johannes Diderik van der (1837–1923), Dutch scientist; *b.* Leyden; prof. of physics, Amsterdam Univ., 1877; conceived continuity of liquid and gaseous states; discovered law of binary mixtures; Nobel Prize for physics, 1910.

Wace (*wās*), Robert (*c.* 1100–*c.* 1175), Anglo-Norman chronicler; *b.* in Jersey; author of two chronicles in metre, *Roman de Brut* and *Roman de Rou.*

Wad′dington, William Henry (1826–94), Fr. diplomatist; *b.* St. Remi-sur-l'Avre, Eure et Loir, of English parents; naturalized Frenchman; travelled in East; studied and wrote on archæology; minister of public instruction, 1873, 1876–7, of foreign affairs, 1877–9; premier, 1879; ambassador to Great Britain, 1883–93; responsible in great part for friendly relations between Britain and France. His wife, Mary King Waddington (*d.* 1923), pub. interesting reminiscences.

Wade (*wād*), George (1673–1748), Brit. field-marshal; put down 1715 rebellion, and made military roads in Scot. Highlands; field-marshal commanding forces in Flanders against French, 1743; failed in Jacobite rising of 1745, and was succeeded by the Duke of Cumberland.

Wagner (*väg′ner*), Rudolf (1805–64), Ger. physiologist; *b.* Bayreuth; prof. of zoology and comparative anatomy at Erlangen, 1832, and Göttingen, 1840; important researches in anatomy and physiology, particularly in embryology; discovered germinal vesicle of human ovum.

Wagner, Wilhelm Richard (1813–83), Ger. composer; *b.* Leipzig; operatic conductor at Magdeburg, Königsberg, and Riga; first opera, *Rienzi,* refused in Paris, was accepted and performed at Dresden, 1842; followed by *The Flying Dutchman* (1843), *Tannhäuser, Lohengrin, Tristan and Isolde, The Mastersingers, Der Ring des Nibelungen* (including the four dramas—*The Rhinegold, Valkyrie, Siegfried, The Twilight of the Gods*), and *Parsifal,* his last and possibly his greatest work (1849–82). Owing to his revolutionary politics Wagner was exiled for some years; suffered great poverty till 1864, when Ludwig, King of Bavaria, provided him with home at Munich; later resided at Bayreuth, where his festival theatre was set up, 1876; married, 1870, Cosima, daughter of Liszt. Wagner created an entirely new form of opera in which the central aim was unity, and, to this end, he wrote all his own librettos; he also made a feature of the 'leading motive'—

a short, striking musical phrase associated with some character or incident, such as the 'Pilgrims' Chorus' in *Tannhäuser*. His work was highly original, and represented a complete departure from tradition.

He is universally regarded as one of the greatest of musicians, though his genius was exercised almost exclusively in opera; his productions have influenced nearly all subsequent compositions in every branch of music.

[*A Study of Wagner*, by Ernest Newman (1899); *My Life* (trans. 1911).]

Wain (*wān*), LOUIS WILLIAM (1860–), black-and-white artist and animal caricaturist; *b.* London; president National Cat Club, 1891–6; pub. *Louis Wain's Annual*, and numerous Cat and Kitten books.

Wakefield, EDWARD GIBBON (1796–1862), Brit. colonial statesman; *b.* London; emigrated to Australia, 1831, where he developed a plan of systematic colonization; forced British to annex New Zealand, where he settled, 1853.

[*Life*, by Garnett (1898).]

Walcott, CHARLES DOOLITTLE (1850–1927), U.S.A. palæontologist; *b.* New York Mills; director of U.S.A. geological survey, 1894–1907; secretary, Smithsonian Institution, 1907–27; discovered Cambrian fossils in Brit. Columbia. Author of numerous volumes on geology.

Walker, FREDERICK (1840–75), Eng. painter; *b.* London; designed woodcuts for books and magazines; worked in oils and water-colours. His *Harbour of Refuge* and *Vagrants* are in the Tate Gallery, London.

Walker, GEORGE (*c.* 1618–90), Irish clergyman; *b.* in Tyrone, of Eng. parents; educ. Glasgow; throughout the siege of Londonderry, 1689, upheld the resistance of the inhabitants. He became Bishop of Londonderry, but fell in the battle of the Boyne.

Wall'ace, ALFRED RUSSEL (1823–1913), Eng. naturalist; *b.* Usk, Monmouthshire; land surveyor and architect, 1838–44, but made botany, zoology, and geology his life's work; travelled on the Amazon, 1848–52, in the Malay Archipelago, 1854–62; made important discoveries regarding geographical distribution of animals; independently of Darwin, formulated theory of the survival of the fittest, and of natural selection; O.M., 1910; works include *Travels on the Amazon* (1853), *The Malay Archipelago* (1869), *The Geographical Distribution of Animals* (1876), and *My Life* (1905).

Wallace, EDGAR (1875–1932), Eng. novelist and playwright; early left a destitute orphan; worked in rubber factory, on a trawler, as a newsboy, etc.; soldier for six years; war correspondent in S. Africa, 1899–1900; captured reading public from 1907 with his 'thrillers,' of which he wrote about 150, in addition to several plays.

Wallace, LEWIS (LEW) (1827–1905), U.S.A. author and soldier; *b.* Brookville, Indiana; fought in Civil War; best known as author of *Ben Hur*.

Wallace, SIR RICHARD (1818–90), Eng. art collector; *b.* London; his kinsman, the fourth Marquess of Hertford, left him his art collection, which was bequeathed to nation by Wallace's widow, 1897; now in Hertford House, London (the Wallace Collection).

Wallace, SIR WILLIAM (*c.* 1270–1305), Scot. patriot and national hero, son of Malcolm Wallace of Elderslie, Renfrewshire; organized Scot. resistance to Edward I., 1297, and was for a time successful, gaining a signal victory at Stirling Bridge, 1297; defeated by Edward at Falkirk, 1298; taken prisoner by treachery in 1305; brought to London, and executed as traitor. His achievements have been specially celebrated by Henry the Minstrel (Blind Harry).

Wallace, William Vincent (1814–65), Brit. composer; *b.* Waterford; after leading a roving life in Australia and the East, settled in London, 1845; his opera *Maritana* (1845) is still popular.

Wallenstein (*val'en-stīn*), or Waldstein, Albrecht Wenzel Eusebius von, Duke of Friedland, etc. (1583–1634), Ger. general; *b.* in Bohemia; served in Rudolph ii.'s army in Hungary; supported Emperor Ferdinand in Thirty Years' War. Hated by the Ger. princes, Wallenstein was dismissed by the emperor, 1630, but recalled on Gustavus Adolphus's invasion of Germany; he was assassinated at Eger. He was the greatest leader in Thirty Years' War; a man of transcendent ability, but unscrupulous.

Wall'er, Edmund (1606–87), Eng. poet and Royalist politician; exiled on exposure of 'Waller's Plot' in favour of king, 1643; returned to public life after Restoration, 1660; popularizer of heroic couplet; verse lacks originality and passion; remembered chiefly for charming lyrics, such as 'Go, Lovely Rose.'

[*Life*, by Stockdale (1772).]

Wal'pole, Horace, 4th Earl of Orford (1717–97), Eng. author; *b.* London; son of Sir Robert Walpole. An ample fortune enabled him fully to indulge his social and antiquarian tastes, to purchase his villa at Strawberry Hill, near Twickenham, and set his printing-press there, the first book to be issued being Gray's *Odes*, with illustrations by Bentley; m.p. for twenty-seven years, but of little account as a politician. Among his works are *The Castle of Otranto* and *Memoirs* of reigns of George ii. and George iii. His correspondence has rendered his name famous, his letters being distinguished for their ease, playful wit, racy description, and lightness of touch. Taken with the *Memoirs*, they form important sources of information as to his period.

[*Horace Walpole*, by Austin Dobson (new ed. 1910).]

Walpole, Hugh Seymour (1884–), Eng. novelist; served with Russ. Red Cross in Great War, 1914–16; succeeds in creating 'atmosphere,' notably in *The Dark Forest* (1916) and *The Secret City* (1919), which deal with Russia, and in *The Captives* (1920); *The Golden Scarecrow* and *Jeremy* (1919) are clever sympathetic studies of children. Later writings include *Harmer John* (1926), *Wintersmoon* (1928), *Rogue Herries* (1930), and its sequels.

Walpole, Robert, 1st Earl of Orford (1676–1745), Brit. statesman; *b.* Houghton, Norfolk; m.p. for Castle Rising, 1701, for King's Linn, 1702–42; secretary for war, 1708; treasurer of the navy, 1710; charged with corruption and imprisoned, 1712; Townshend married his sister Dorothy, 1713, and Walpole became chancellor of Exchequer, 1715; on collapse of South Sea Co. was called to power, 1721; prime minister and held supreme power in parliament for twenty-one years. One of the greatest Brit. statesmen; sought to unite the nation under the new dynasty by keeping as free as possible from foreign alliances, and to make the nation prosperous; a man of gross pleasures and no intellectual tastes; gave a low tone to politics, and did not hesitate to stoop to corruption to secure party successes.

[*Life*, by Morley.]

Walsh, Maurice (1879–), Irish author; *b.* Ballydonohue, County Kerry; was Irish Free

State Civil servant; novels include *The Key Above the Door, While Rivers Run, The Small Dark Man*, etc.

Wal'singham, SIR FRANCIS (*c.* 1530–90), Eng. statesman; *b.* Chiselhurst; of Puritan party; ambassador to France, 1570; appointed one of Elizabeth's secretaries of state, 1573; employed in important negotiations with Netherlands, France, and Scotland, working, by means of army of spies, for alliance of England with Fr. Huguenots, and opposing Spain and Catholicism; chief agent in execution of Mary Queen of Scots.

Wal'ter, JOHN (1738–1812), Eng. publisher, son of a London coal merchant; founder of the *Daily Universal Register*, 1785, which he renamed the *Times*, 1788, and firmly established.

Wal'ton, IZAAK (1593–1683), Eng. author and angler; *b.* Stafford; after retiral from business as ironmonger spent most of his time visiting various country parsonages; among his friends were Michael Drayton, Ben Jonson, and Sir Henry Wotton; wrote several admirable biographies, but his masterpiece is *The Compleat Angler.*

Ward, SIR ADOLPHUS WILLIAM (1837–1924), Eng. scholar and man of letters; *b.* Hampstead; master of Peterhouse from 1900; president of Brit. Academy, 1911–13; knighted, 1913; one of editors of *Cambridge Modern History* and of *Cambridge History of English Literature*; wrote *Germany: 1815–90,* and other historical works.

Ward, ARTEMUS. See BROWNE, C. F.

Ward, EDWARD MATTHEW (1816–79), Eng. painter; *b.* London; R.A., 1855. Chief works are eight frescoes for House of Commons; *Doctor Johnson in Lord Chesterfield's Ante-room* (1845); *South Sea Bubble* (1847); *Marie Antoinette parting with the Dauphin* (1856); *Marie Antoinette listening to her Act of Accusation* (1859).

Ward, MRS. HUMPHRY, *née* MARY AUGUSTA ARNOLD (1851–1920), Eng. novelist; *b.* Hobart, Tasmania; granddaughter of Dr. Arnold of Rugby; married Thomas Humphry Ward of Oxford, 1872; *Robert Elsmere* (1888), her first novel, won immediate popularity; later works include *History of David Grieve* (1892), *The Marriage of William Ashe* (1905), etc.

Ward, WILFRID PHILIP (1856–1916), Eng. biographer; one of founders, and later secretary, of Synthetic Soc., Oxford; ed. the *Dublin Review*; best-known works are biographies of W. G. Ward (his father), Cardinal Wiseman, Aubrey de Vere, and Cardinal Newman.

War'ner, SUSAN (1819–85), U.S.A. authoress; *b.* New York; best-known novel is *The Wide, Wide World.*

War'ren, SIR CHARLES (1840–1927), Brit. general; engaged in excavation work, Palestine, 1867–70; commissioner for settlement of boundary between Orange Free State and Griqualand West, 1876–7; held commands in Kaffir War and in the Griqua rising, 1878; major-general commanding Bechuanaland Expedition, 1884–5; commissioner of Metropolitan Police, 1886–8; lieut.-general, 5th Division, S. African Field Force, 1899–1900.

Warren, SAMUEL (1807–77), Brit. novelist; *b.* Wales; called to bar, 1837; M.P. for Midhurst, 1856–9; some of his writings, especially *Ten Thousand a Year,* won considerable popularity.

War'ton, THOMAS (1728–90), Eng. poet; *b.* Basingstoke; entered Church; prof. of poetry, Oxford, 1757–67, of history, 1785; poet laureate, 1785; a pioneer of Romanticism. Most notable poem, *The Triumph of Isis.*

Warwick (*wor'ik*), EARL OF, title borne, since 12th cent., successively by families of name Newburgh, Beauchamp, Neville, Plantagenet, Dudley, Rich, Greville.

Warwick, RICHARD NEVILLE, EARL OF (1428–71), Eng. baron, called the 'king-maker'; distinguished himself at St. Albans under Duke of York, 1455; rewarded with governorship of Calais; again fought for Yorkists against great odds in 1459; joining forces with Edward, Earl of March, prevailed against Lancastrians, and Edward was proclaimed king, 1461; subsequently, having been slighted by Edward, he sided with Henry, and had him proclaimed Henry VI. and crowned, 1470; defeated and slain by Edward at Barnet.

[*Warwick*, by Oman (1891).]

Wash'ington, BOOKER TALIAFERRO (*c.* 1859–1915), U.S.A. Negro educationist and reformer; *b.* on Virginia plantation; educated at night schools and Hampton Industrial Institute; opened, 1881, Tuskegee Normal and Industrial Institute for education of Negroes; author of *Up from Slavery* (1901), *The Story of the Negro* (1909), etc.

Washington, GEORGE (1732–99), first president of U.S.A.; *b.* near Fredericksburg, Virginia; surveyor in early life; eventually first in command of Virginia forces against French, 1754; retired from active service, 1758; settled down as country gentleman at Mount Vernon; though deprecating revolt against Britain, supported resistance to Stamp Act, 1765; delegate to first Congress of Amer. colonies, 1774. After Lexington and Bunker's Hill, 1775, Washington became general of Amer. army, drove General Howe from Boston, 1776, but was defeated, 1777, and driven back in Pennsylvania. In 1778 compelled the British to retreat from Philadelphia. Washington forced Lord Cornwallis to capitulate at Yorktown, 1781; presided at convention, 1787, when constitution of U.S.A. was drawn up; president, 1789; issued proclamation of neutrality on outbreak of European War, 1793; retired from presidency after second term of office, 1796.

He was a man with an inflexible sense of justice, personal disinterestedness, and an indomitable will. He became identified in the minds of the people with the nation and still remains the 'Father of his Country.'

[*Life*, by Lodge (1889), Woodrow Wilson (1897), Harrison (1906).]

Wassermann (*vas'er-man*), AUGUST VON (1866–1925), Ger. doctor; *b.* Bamberg, Bavaria; director, Kaiser Wilhelm Institute, Berlin, 1913; discovered the Wassermann reaction in syphilis.

Waterhouse, ALFRED (1830–1905), Eng. architect; *b.* Liverpool; R.A., 1885; partially rebuilt Caius Coll., Cambridge; other works are Girton Coll., Cambridge; Eaton Hall; New Univ. Club; National Liberal Club; Natural History Museum, S. Kensington; Liverpool Infirmary, etc.

Wat'son, JOHN (1850–1907), Scot. minister and author; *b.* Manningtree, Essex; held pastorates of several Free churches; under name 'Ian Maclaren' wrote studies of Scot. life and character; best known, *Beside the Bonnie Brier Bush*; also wrote on religious subjects.

[*Life*, by Robertson Nicoll (1908).]

Watson, SIR WILLIAM (1858–1935), Eng. poet; *b.* Burley-in-Wharfedale, Yorkshire; began publication with *The Prince's Quest* (1880), followed, among other volumes, by *Wordsworth's Grave* (1890, which placed him among the greatest living poets),

Lacrimæ Musarum (1892), *Excursions in Criticism* (1893), *The Purple East* (1896), *For England* (1903), *The Muse in Exile* (1913), *Retrogression* (1916), *The Man Who Saw* (1917), *The Superhuman Antagonists* (1919), *Ireland Unfreed* (1920); knighted, 1917.

Watson-Gordon, SIR JOHN (1788–1864), Scottish portrait painter; younger contemporary of Raeburn; exhibited at Royal Scot. Academy from 1830: president, 1850, and knighted; R.A., 1851; among others, painted portraits of David Cox, Sir Walter Scott, Sir David Brewster, and De Quincey.

Watt, G. FIDDES (1873–), Scot. portrait painter; *b.* Aberdeen; R.S.A., 1924; portraits of Viscount Haldane, Rt. Hon. H. H. Asquith, Lord Loreburn, Archbishop of York, Earl Grey, Lord Balfour of Burleigh, Earl Minto, and other celebrities.

Watt, JAMES (1736–1819), Scot. engineer; *b.* Greenock; improver and generally reputed inventor of steam engine; mathematical instrument maker to Glasgow Univ., 1757; acted as civil engineer. The turning-point in his life came when he was sent a Newcomen fire (*i.e.* steam) engine to repair; it suggested to him the idea of a separate condenser, and his engine rapidly replaced Newcomen's. Watt went into partnership with Matthew Boulton, 1774, and carried on a successful business at the Soho Ironworks, Birmingham, retiring in 1800.

[*Boulton and Watt*, by Smiles (1865); *James Watt*, by Pemberton (1905).]

Watteau (*vä-tō'*), ANTOINE (1684–1721), Fr. painter; *b.* Valenciennes; went to Paris, 1702, and worked on decoration of Luxembourg Palace; gained entrance to Academy, 1717; became famous for his landscapes, with conventional shepherds and shepherdesses. His finest pictures are in the Louvre; in Wallace Collection, London; and in Berlin.

Watts, GEORGE FREDERICK (1817–1904), Brit. painter and sculptor; *b.* London; gained House of Lords prize, 1842, for fresco design *Caractacus in Rome* for new Houses of Parliament, and again, 1846, for *Alfred the Great* cartoon, and commissioned to paint *St. George and the Dragon* in Hall of Poets; his great works are symbolic; most notable of this group, *Faith, Hope, Charity, Love and Life, Love and Death, Love Triumphant*, trilogy of *Eve*; portraits include those of Gladstone, Browning, Tennyson, Swinburne, Garibaldi, etc.; sculptured works, *Hugo Lupus, Physical Energy, Bishop Lonsdale*, etc.; R.A., 1867; O.M., 1902; presented greater part of his work to the nation.

Watts, ISAAC (1674–1748), Eng. evangelical poet; *b.* Southampton; Independent minister, London; famed for his hymns—*e.g.* 'O God, our help in ages past.'

Watts-Dunton, WALTER THEODORE (1832–1914), Eng. critic, poet, and novelist; *b.* St. Ives, Huntingdon; for thirty years housemate with Swinburne; knowledge of gipsy life brought out in poem *The Coming of Love* (1897), and in romance *Aylwin* (1898); ed. G. Borrow's *Lavengro* and *Romany Rye*; pub. *Swinburne and Charles Dickens* (1913).

[*Life and Letters*, by Hake and Compton-Rickett (1916).]

Waugh (*wau*), ARTHUR (1866–), Brit. publisher and writer; educ. Sherbourne and Oxford; writer of many critical studies (Tennyson, Browning, Milton, etc.); chairman of Chapman and Hall, publishers. His sons ALEC and EVELYN are also writers.

Waugh, EDWIN (1817–90), Eng. poet; *b.* Rochdale; author of *Lancashire Songs*; prose works:

Factory Folk during the Cotton Famine, Besom Ben Stories, etc.

Waugh (*w*och), JOSEPH LAING (1868–1928), Scot. novelist; *b.* Thornhill, Dumfriesshire. Wrote *Robbie Doo* (1912), *Cracks wi' Robbie Doo, Betty Grier*, etc.

Waynflete (*wān'flēt*), WILLIAM (1395–1486), Eng. Churchman; *b.* Lincolnshire; headmaster of Winchester Coll., 1430; first provost of Eton Coll., 1440–7; Bishop of Winchester, 1447; founded Magdalen Coll., Oxford, 1458; lord chancellor under Henry VI., resigning 1460.

Webb, BEATRICE. See under WEBB, SIDNEY J.

Webb, MARY (1881–1927), Eng. authoress; *b.* Leighton Cressage, Shropshire; was not recognized as an author of note till after her death. Wrote *The Golden Arrow* (1916), *Gone to Earth* (1917), *The House in Dormer Forest* (1920), *Precious Bane* (1924), *Armour wherein he Trusted* (1926).

Webb, SIDNEY JAMES, 1ST BARON PASSFIELD (1859–), Eng. writer and authority on social questions; *b.* London; hon. prof. of public administration, Univ. of London; principal founder London School of Economics and Political Science; with wife, founded *The New Statesman*, 1913; M.P. (Labour) Seaham division, County Durham, 1922; served on various commissions and committees; president Board of Trade, Jan.–Nov. 1924; secretary of state for dominion affairs, 1929–30, and for the colonies, 1929–31; baron, 1929; author of *Socialism in England* (1890), *The Eight Hours Day* (1891; with Harold Cox), *Towards Social Democracy* (1916), etc.; and, with his wife, *The History of Trade Unionism* (1894), *Decay of Capitalist Civilization* (1923), *The Last Hundred Years* (1929), etc. His wife, BEATRICE POTTER (1858–), whom he married in 1892, is also an author and investigator of industrial conditions; member of Royal Commission on Poor Law and Unemployment, 1905–9, and joint ed. of Minority Report; also member of various other government committees; author of *The Co-operative Movement in Great Britain* (1891), etc.

Weber (*vā'ber*), KARL MARIA FRIEDRICH ERNST VON (1786–1826), Ger. composer and pianist; *b.* near Lübeck; founder of Ger. romantic opera; director of opera, Prague, 1813–16, Dresden, 1817; died in London. Leading dramatic works: *Der Freischütz* (1820), *Euryanthe* (1823), *Oberon* (1826), and music of play *Preciosa* (1820).

Web'ster, DANIEL (1782–1852), U.S.A. lawyer, statesman, and orator; *b.* in New Hampshire; delivered famous oration at Plymouth, 1820, on two hundredth anniversary of landing of the Pilgrim Fathers; entered Congress, 1822; secretary of state, 1841; negotiated Ashburton Treaty, 1842, settling boundary between Canada and Maine.

Webster, JOHN (?1580–?1625), Eng. dramatist, of obscure history; ranked second only to Shakespeare as a master of tragedy; chief works are: *The White Devil, The Duchess of Malfi, The Devil's Law Case.*

[*John Webster and the Elizabethan Drama*, by Rupert Brooke (1913).]

Webster, NOAH (1758–1843), U.S.A. lexicographer; *b.* West Hartford, Connecticut; pioneer of U.S.A. school textbooks; a founder of Amherst Coll.; fame rests on *Compendious Dictionary of the English Language.*

Wedgwood (*wej'wood*), JOSIAH (1730–95), Eng. potter; *b.* Burslem; began business in Burslem, Staffordshire, 1759; famed for cream-coloured 'Queen's Ware,' so called in honour of Queen Charlotte; inventor of black 'Basalt' ware, and of still more renowned 'Jasper' ware.

Weigall (*wī'gal*), ARTHUR EDWARD PEARSE BROME (1880–1934), Eng. Egyptologist and author; research work in Egypt, 1901–14; inspector-general of antiquities, Egyptian Government, 1905–14; works include *Life of Akhnaton, Pharaoh of Egypt* (1910), *Tutankhamen and other Essays* (1923), *The Way of the East* (1924), *The Grand Tour of Norman England* (1927).

Weingartner (*vīn-gart'ner*), PAUL FELIX (1863–), Austrian conductor; *b.* Zara. A pupil of Lizst, he conducted many German orchestras, including the Berlin Philharmonic. Since 1935 musical director of Vienna Opera. One of the most noted conductors of his day.

Weir (*wēr*), WILLIAM, 1ST BARON (1877–), Scot. steelmaster; *b.* Dumfriesshire; director of munitions in Scotland, 1915; director-general of Aircraft Production and secretary of state for Royal Air Force, 1918; peerage, 1918.

Weismann (*vīs'män*), AUGUST (1834–1914), Ger. biologist; *b.* Frankfurt-on-Main; prof. of zoology, Freiburg, 1866; researches devoted to problems of evolution; works include *Studies in the Theory of Descent* (1882), *Essays on Heredity* (1892), *The Germplasm* (1893), and *Evolution Theory* (1904).

Well'don, JAMES EDWARD COWELL (1854–), Eng. clergyman and scholar; *b.* Tonbridge; brilliant Cambridge Univ. career; headmaster of Dulwich, 1883, of Harrow, 1885–98; Bishop of Calcutta, 1898–1902; Canon of Westminster, 1902–6; Dean of Manchester, 1906–18; Dean of Durham, 1918–33; works include trans. of Aristotle, *Recollections and Reflections* (1915), *The English Church* (1926), *Time and Eternity* (1928).

Well'esley, RICHARD COLLEY, 1ST MARQUESS (1760–1842), Brit. statesman; *b.* Dublin; brother of Duke of Wellington; as gov.-gen. of India, 1797–1805, he firmly established Brit. rule and doubled the revenue of the E. India Co.

Wellhausen (*vel'hou-zen*), JULIUS (1844–1918), Ger. theologian and Oriental critic; *b.* Hameln, Westphalia; prof. of theology at Greifswald, 1872; resigned owing to heterodox beliefs, 1882; prof. of Oriental languages at Marburg, 1885, Göttingen, 1892; his Biblical criticism shows clear-headedness and caution; works include *Prolegomena zur Geschichte Israels* (1878; Eng. trans. 1885), *Das Arabische Reich und sein Sturz* (1902), etc.

Wel'lington, ARTHUR WELLESLEY, DUKE OF (1769–1852); *b.* Dublin; son of Lord Mornington; joined army under purchase system; at twenty-four he commanded 33rd Foot, still known as Duke of Wellington's regiment; first saw active service in Low Countries; afterwards went to India, and took part in the battles of Assaye and Argaum.

He returned in 1805, and was given command of expedition to expel French from Lisbon; defeated Marshal Junot at Vimeiro; ordered back to England, and replaced by Sir John Moore. After Moore's death, 1808, Wellington again commanded in the Peninsula, gaining many victories. He served as ambassador at Paris, 1814, until Napoleon reappeared at head of Fr. army. In 1815 Wellington commanded British forces, and aided by Blücher's army, completely defeated Napoleon at Waterloo, 18th June 1815.

Wellington's later career was associated with politics; opposed many domestic reforms which have since been carried out; member of the government, and prime minister, 1828. Was buried in St. Paul's Cathedral.

As a soldier, Wellington's talents are best seen in his conduct of the

Peninsular War. As a statesman he holds a high place for moderation, strong sense of duty, and perfect integrity.

[*Lives*, by Maxwell (2nd ed. 1900), Fortescue (1925).]

Wells, HERBERT GEORGE (1866–), Eng. novelist; *b.* Bromley, Kent; began life as teacher of science; started novel-writing with *The Time Machine* (1895), a semi-scientific type of romance, followed by long series of popular novels. The fruits of his study of Socialism appeared in such works as *Anticipations* (1901), *Mankind in the Making* (1903), *A Modern Utopia* (1905), *New Worlds for Old* (1908). Since 1909, when he pub. *Tono Bungay*, he has been engaged in writing a series of novels; a master of the short story, his writings of this kind have been collected in *The Country of the Blind* (1911). Amongst his other well-known works are *Kipps* (1905), *Ann Veronica* (1909), *History of Mr. Polly* (1910), *Marriage* (1912), *Bealby* (1915), *Mr. Britling sees it through* (1916), *The Soul of a Bishop* (1917), *Joan and Peter* (1918), *The Undying Fire* (1919), *Outline of History* (1920), *The World of William Clissold* (1926), *Mr. Blettsworthy on Rampole Island* (1928), *The Work, Wealth, and Happiness of Mankind* (1932), *Experiment in Autobiography* (1934).

Wemyss (*wēmz*), EARLDOM OF, honour held by Scot. family. Sir John Wemyss was created Baron Wemyss of Elcho, 1625. David, Lord Elcho, 1721–87, son of 4th Earl, was a Jacobite in '45 rising and was attainted. Francis Charteris, 10th Earl, 1818–1914, founded Volunteer movement.

Wennerberg (*ven'er-berg*), GUNNAR (1817–1901), Swed. poet and musician; *b.* Lidköping; composed *Gluntarne* (' The Boys '), thirty duets for students of Uppsala Univ.; *The Three*, his collected trios, appeared 1860; minister for education, 1870–5.

Wes'ley, CHARLES (1707–88), Eng. religious leader, brother of John Wesley; *b.* Epworth Rectory, Lincolnshire; educated at Oxford, where he was member of a religious society derisively called the 'Methodists'; wrote over 6,000 hymns, including 'Jesus, Lover of my soul,' and 'O for a thousand tongues to sing.'

Wesley, JOHN (1703–91), Eng. religious leader and founder of Wesleyan Methodism; *b.* Epworth Rectory, Lincs; ordained, 1725; became member of religious society known as Oxford 'Methodists'; visited Georgia, N. America, with his brother and preached to settlers and Indians there; came under influence of the Moravians, whom he visited in Saxony. In 1738 he passed through a great spiritual experience; began establishment of ' societies ' or churches, and drew up rules which are still in force; was excluded from Anglican pulpits; began to ordain clergy, and thus Wesleyan Methodist Church had its origin; engaged in open-air evangelistic effort, travelling thousands of miles each year; overtook much literary and philanthropic work. His preaching, zeal, and power of popular appeal were enormous. Wrote his *Journal*, and *Appeal to Men of Reason and Religion*.

[*Life*, by J. S. Simon (1927).]

Wesley, SAMUEL SEBASTIAN (1810–76), Eng. musical composer and organist, grandson of Charles Wesley; *b.* London; organist of Hereford Cathedral, 1832, of Gloucester, 1865; his compositions include the anthems 'The Wilderness,' 'O Lord, Thou art my God,' and 'Ascribe unto the Lord.'

West, BENJAMIN (1738–1820), Eng. artist; *b.* Springfield, Pennsylvania; after travelling on Continent, settled in England, where he secured patronage of George III.; revolutionized Eng. historical painting, as in his *Death of General Wolfe*; president of Royal Academy, 1792.

West'cott, BROOKE FOSS (1825–1901), Eng. churchman; *b.* near Birmingham; assistant master, Harrow, 1852–69; canon of Peterborough, 1869; prof. of divinity, Cambridge, 1870, of Westminster, 1883; Bishop of Durham, 1890; on committee for revision of N.T.; was first president of Christian Social Union; numerous theological works, including *The New Testament in the Original Greek* (with Dr. Hort, 1882).

West'inghouse, GEORGE (1846–1914), U.S.A. engineer; *b.* Central Bridge, New York; built dynamos for plant at Niagara Falls; invented automatic air-brake for railway rolling stock.

West'macott, SIR RICHARD (1775–1856), Eng. sculptor; *b.* London; prof. of sculpture, Royal Academy, 1827–56; statues include Pitt, Fox, Addison, in Westminster Abbey; Abercromby, Captain Cook, Collingwood, in St. Paul's; bronze Achilles, Hyde Park.

West'minster, DUKES OF, trace descent in male line to a Norman family; founder of Eng. Grosvenors, Gilbert le Grosvenor, came over with Conqueror.

Wet, CHRISTIAN DE. See DE WET.

Wettin (*vet'in*), HOUSE OF, Ger. dynastic family from which the reigning Saxon lines were descended. Wettin was surname of Prince Albert, consort of Queen Victoria, and up till 1917 of reigning royal family of U.K.

Weyman (*wī'man*), STANLEY JOHN (1855–1928), Eng. historical novelist; *b.* Ludlow, Shropshire; practised as barrister for eight years; wrote *The House of the Wolf*, *A Gentleman of France*, *Under the Red Robe*, *The Red Cockade*, *Count Hannibal*, *Chippinge*, *The Great House*, *The 'Lively Peggy*,' etc.

Whar'ton, EDITH (1862–), U.S.A. novelist; *b.* New York; reputation established by *The House of Mirth* (1905); works reflect life of cosmopolitan soc.; best known include *Tales of Men and Ghosts* (1910), *The Age of Innocence* (1920), *The Mother's Recompense* (1925), *Certain People* (1930).

Whately (*whāt'ly*), RICHARD (1787–1863), English theological writer; *b.* London; prof. of political economy at Oxford, 1829–31; Archbishop of Dublin, 1831; took prominent part in attempt to establish national and unsectarian system of education; author of *Christian Evidences* (1837) and many other theological works.

Wheat'stone, SIR CHARLES (1802–75), Eng. electrician; *b.* Gloucester; prof. of experimental philosophy, King's Coll., London, 1834; F.R.S., 1837; with W. F. Cooke, took out patent for first electric telegraph, 1837; pioneer experimenter with submarine cables; inventor of stereoscope and instruments for measuring electrical constants.

Whewell (*hū'el*), WILLIAM (1794–1866), Brit. philosopher and historian of science; *b.* Lancaster; master, Trinity Coll., Cambridge, 1841; took prominent part in univ. administration; many books on philosophy and science, including *History of the Inductive Sciences*.

Whistler, JAMES ABBOTT MCNEILL (1834–1903), painter and etcher; *b.* Lowell, U.S.A.; studied in Paris; first painting, *The White Girl*, exhibited at Salon des Refusés; settled in England, and in 1859 began to exhibit at Royal Academy; painted figure subjects and views, also many portraits, including those of his mother (Luxembourg, Paris), and Carlyle

(Glasgow); eminent as etcher, drypointer, and purely decorative artist; pioneer of mass-impressionism in Eng. art; style subtly but not powerfully original; attacked by Ruskin in *Fors Clavigera* (1877), and libel suit followed, in which Whistler was successful. See Whistler's *Gentle Art of Making Enemies* (1890).

White, CLAUDE GRAHAME-. See GRAHAME-WHITE.

White (*whit*), SIR GEORGE STUART (1835–1912), Brit. field-marshal; *b.* in Ireland; served in Ind. Mutiny, Afghan campaign, Nile expedition, and in Burma; won V.C., 1879; commander-in-chief of Ind. army, 1893–8; commanded Natal field force in S. African War, defending Ladysmith against Boers, 1899–1900; governor of Gibraltar, 1900–4; field-marshal, 1903; baronet, 1904; O.M., 1905.

White, GILBERT (1720–93), Eng. naturalist; *b.* Selborne, Hants; educated Oxford; settled at Selborne as curate, 1755; pub. *Natural History of Selborne* (1789); charming book by keen and kindly observer of nature.

White, WILLIAM HALE (1829–1913), known as 'Mark Rutherford,' Eng. novelist and journalist; *b.* Bedford; assistant-director of contracts, Admiralty, for some years; writings include *Autobiography of Mark Rutherford, Mark Rutherford's Deliverance, Revolution in Tanner's Lane, Catherine Furze, Pages from a Journal,* and *John Bunyan.*

White′field, GEORGE (1714–70), Eng. divine; *b.* Gloucester; one of early leaders of Methodism in England and America; his followers built for him the 'Tabernacle' in Moorfields, London; had great dramatic talent and eloquence as a preacher.

[*Life,* by Gledstone (2nd ed. 1900).]

White′ing, RICHARD (1840–1928), Eng. journalist and novelist; *b.* London; author of *The Island, No. 5 John Street* (1899), *My Harvest* (1915), and *Both Sides of the Curtain* (with Geneviève Ward, 1918).

Whit′ley, JOHN HENRY (1866–1935), Brit. politician; *b.* Halifax; M.P. for Halifax, 1900–28; held several minor offices; speaker of House of Commons, 1921–8; name associated with Whitley Councils for maintaining peace in industry; O.M., 1928; chairman of B.B.C. from 1930.

Whit′lock, BRAND (1869–1930), U.S.A. author and diplomatist; *b.* Urbana, Ohio; called to bar, 1894; minister (later ambassador) to Belgium, 1913–22; interested himself in the Cavell case and relief operations; works include *Life of Abraham Lincoln* (1908), *Belgium under German Occupation* (1919), *Uprooted* (1926), etc.

Whit′man, WALT (1819–92), U.S.A. poet; *b.* Long Island; ed. *Long Islander,* 1839, *Brooklyn Eagle,* 1846, and *Freeman* at Boston, 1851; pub. *Leaves of Grass* (1855), a collection of unrhymed and irregular verse of striking power; volunteer nurse in Civil War, 1862–5.

[*Life,* by Binns (1905).]

Whit′tier, JOHN GREENLEAF (1807–92), U.S.A. 'Quaker' poet and man of letters; *b.* near Haverhill, Massachusetts; became a journalist and strong Abolitionist agitator; his verse has a freshness, individuality, and sustained note of truth.

[*Life,* by Pickard (1899).]

Whit′worth, SIR JOSEPH (1803–87), Eng. engineer; *b.* Stockport; toolmaker, Manchester, 1833; noted experimenter in rifle and cannon manufacture; inventor of compressed steel casting.

Whymper (*whim′per*), EDWARD (1840–1911), Eng. mountaineer and explorer; *b.* London; ascended many peaks in the Alps for the first time, including the Matterhorn, 1865, when four of the party perished; visited Greenland, 1867 and 1872, the Andes, 1879–80, where he was the first to climb Chimborazo, and the Rockies, 1901; author of *Scrambles among the Alps* (1871), *Travels amongst the Great Andes of the Equator* (1892), etc.

Whyte, ALEXANDER (1837–1921), Scot. theologian; *b.* Kirriemuir; minister, Free St. George's, Edinburgh, 1873–1916; principal of New Coll., Edinburgh, 1909–18; works include *Bible Characters*; *Bunyan Characters*; *The Walk, Conversation, and Character of Jesus Christ, our Lord.*

Whyte, SIR ALEXANDER FREDERICK (1883–), political official; *b.* Edinburgh; son of above; M.P. for Perth, 1910–18; one of the founders of *The New Europe*; first president of India's new legislative assembly, 1920–25; political adviser to National Government of China, 1929–32; publications: *Asia in the Twentieth Century* (1926), *China and Foreign Powers* (1927).

Whyte-Melville, GEORGE JOHN (1821–78), Scot. novelist; *b.* Strathkinness, Fife; served in Crimean War; novels deal chiefly with field sports and country pursuits.

Wickham (*wik'am*), SIR HENRY (1846–1928), English explorer; planter in Brazil; collected seeds of rubber tree, brought them to Kew Gardens, and laid foundations of plantation rubber industry of the East; inspector of forests, India; pioneer planter in Central America, Australia, New Guinea, and Pacific Islands. Author of *Introduction, Plantation, and Cultivation of Pará Rubber*, and *Journey Through the Wilderness.*

Wieland (*vē'lant*), CHRISTOPH MARTIN (1733–1813), Ger. author; *b.* near Biberach, Württemberg; prof. of philosophy, Erfurt, 1769–72; works include *Don Sylvio von Rosalva* (1764, in prose), and *Oberon* (1780, in verse); translated twenty-two of Shakespeare's plays into Ger. prose.

Wien (*vēn*), WILHELM (1864–1928), Ger. scientist; *b.* Gaffken, E. Prussia; prof. of physics, Giessen, 1899, Würtzburg, 1900, Munich, 1920; valuable research worker in radiation; Noble Prize, 1911. Author of several scientific works.

Wiertz (*vērts*), ANTOINE JOSEPH (1806–65), Belgian painter, settled finally at Brussels, 1848, where the Musée Wiertz was built for him; works indicate grotesque and fantastic imagination.

Wiggin (*wig'in*), KATE DOUGLAS (MRS. RIGGS) (1857–1923), U.S.A. authoress; *b.* in Philadelphia; organized first free kindergartens for poor children on Pacific coast; numerous books include *Penelope's Experiences*, *Rebecca of Sunnybrook Farm.*

Wil'berforce, WILLIAM (1759–1833), Eng. philanthropist; *b.* Hull; M.P. for Hull when only twenty-one; supporter and friend of Pitt, but remained independent of party; in 1787 became leader of committee pledged to abolition of slavery, and ultimately succeeded in having Act abolishing slave trade in Brit. dominions passed in 1807.

Wilde (*wīld*), OSCAR O'FLAHERTIE WILLS (1854–1900), Irish author and dramatist; *b.* Dublin; went to Oxford and became the apostle of the æsthetic movement; works include *Dorian Gray*, a novel, and the plays, *Lady Windermere's Fan* (1892), *The Importance of being Earnest* (1895), *Salome* (1893) in French. Imprisoned (1895–7) for unnatural vice, he wrote after his release *A Ballad of Reading Gaol* and *De Profundis*. Wilde was a master of words; his plays scintillate with brilliant dialogue and epigram. Buried in Père Lachaise cemetery, Paris.

[*Oscar Wilde, his Life and Confessions,* by Harris (1920).]

Wild'er, THORNTON NIVEN (1897–), U.S.A. author; *b.* Madison, Wisconsin; worked as schoolmaster, 1920–5; works include *The Bridge of San Luis Rey, The Angel that troubled the Waters,* and *The Woman of Andros.*

Wilhelmina (*vil-hel-mē'na*) (WILHELMINA HELENA PAULINE MARIA) (1880–), Queen of Holland, daughter of William III. and Emma, a princess of Waldeck-Pyrmont; *b.* The Hague; succeeded to throne, 1890; assumed full sovereignty, 1898; married Henry, Duke of Mecklenburg-Schwerin, 1901, who died in 1934.

Wilkes (*wilks*), CHARLES (1798–1877), U.S.A. naval officer and explorer; *b.* New York; most important work was discovery of Wilkes Land in the Antarctic, 1838–40; author of volumes dealing with his expeditions.

Wilkes, JOHN (1727–97), Eng. politician; *b.* London; M.P. for Aylesbury, 1757; at first supported Pitt, but later attacked foreign policy of government; founded *North Briton,* 1762, which, being suppressed as seditious libel, led to his expulsion from House of Commons; M.P. for Middlesex, 1768, 1774–90; advocated parliamentary reform, and championed City in contests with Parliament and court; lord mayor, 1774; celebrated for wit and vigorous personality, but of dissolute character.

[*Life,* by H. Bleackley (1916).]

Wil'kie, SIR DAVID (1785–1841), Scot. painter and etcher; most distinguished of Brit. historical genre painters; *b.* Cults, Fife; studied art in Edinburgh and London; *Pitlessie Fair* (1804) was first important picture, followed by *Village Politicians, The Blind Fiddler, Rent Day, The Chelsea Pensioners, The Penny Wedding,* etc.; R.A., 1811; limner for Scotland, 1823; knighted, 1836. Wilkie visited Scott at Abbotsford, 1817, and painted *Sir Walter Scott and Family*; in later years tried more pretentious themes, such as *Princess Doria, Napoleon and Pius VII.,* but fame rests chiefly upon earlier work; buried at sea off Gibraltar.

Wil'kins, SIR (GEORGE) HUBERT (1888–), Australian explorer; *b.* Mt. Bryan East, S. Australia; accompanied Stefansson's Arctic expedition, 1913–17; navigated aeroplane, England to Australia flight, 1919; in command of Arctic and Antarctic expeditions, 1920–9; Arctic submarine expedition, 1931; author of *Flying the Arctic* (1928), *Undiscovered Australia* (1928), *Under the North Pole* (1931).

Will'cocks, SIR WILLIAM (1852–1932), Brit. engineer; *b.* India; official in Ind. public works, 1872–83; Egyptian public works, 1883–97; designed Aswan dam, 1898, and the irrigation of Mesopotamia, 1911. Author of *Egyptian Irrigation, The Irrigation of Mesopotamia, From the Garden of Eden to the Crossing of the Jordan.*

Will'ett, WILLIAM (1856–1915), originator of 'summer' time; *b.* Farnham, Surrey; master builder; conceived idea of saving daylight but did not live to see it carried into force.

William I., THE CONQUEROR (1027–87), King of England; natural son of Robert the Devil, Duke of Normandy, whom he succeeded, 1035. On Harold seizing Eng. throne, William invaded England, defeated and killed Harold at Hastings, 1066, and gradually forced all England to acknowledge his royal title; reduced York, 1069; put down Hereward's rebellion by successful siege of Ely, 1071; led successful expedition against Malcolm III. of Scotland, 1072; reduced Maine, 1073; quarrelled with his son Robert; compiled Domesday Book; reformed Church, checked power of the barons, established central authority; died at Rouen.

William II., Rufus (*c.* 1056–1100), King of England, son of William I.; succeeded, 1087; put down risings in Norfolk, Somerset, and rebellion led by Odo of Bayeux, 1087; invaded Normandy and acquired lands there, 1091; invaded Scotland; annexed Cumberland; defeated and killed Malcolm III. at Alnwick, 1093; tried to conquer Wales, but had to content himself with building castles on Welsh frontier; invaded Normandy, 1094; suppressed Eng. baronial rising, 1095; quarrelled with Anselm, Archbishop of Canterbury; killed while hunting in New Forest.

William III., of Orange (1650–1702), King of Great Britain and Ireland, son of William II. of Orange and Mary, daughter of Charles I. of England; *b.* The Hague; made Stadtholder, 1672; opposed Louis XIV. of France; defeated at St. Omer, 1677, at Mons, 1678; married Mary, daughter of James II. of England, 1677; was invited to deliver Britain from Stewarts, 1688, and landed at Torbay; after James's flight was proclaimed king, 1689; passed Acts of Toleration and Indemnity, 1690; won battle of the Boyne, 1690; victory off Cape la Hogue, 1692; under him England joined League of Augsburg; led expedition to Netherlands against French; lost Namur, 1692; defeated at Steinkirk, 1692; retook Namur, 1695; agreed to Peace of Ryswick, 1697. From 1697 to 1700 William was occupied with the Span. Succession question, but died before the outbreak of war.

William IV. (1765–1837), King of Great Britain and Ireland, third son of George III.; *b.* Buckingham Palace; entered navy; on death of Duke of York, 1827, became heir to throne; succeeded, 1830; reign marked by passing of Reform Bill, 1832, the emancipation of slaves, the settlement of the E. India Co., and the ascendancy of the middle classes.

William the Lion (1143–1214), King of Scotland; succeeded his brother, Malcolm IV., 1165; in order to recover the territory ceded to England, joined the rebellion of the Eng. barons; but his plans failed, and he was compelled to hold Scotland as a vassal. Richard I. released him from this burden. Built Arbroath Abbey, 1178.

William I. (1797–1888), King of Prussia and Ger. emperor; second son of Frederick William III.; *b.* Berlin; took part in campaigns, 1814–15, against Napoleon; regent, 1858; succeeded to throne, 1861; commanded in war against Austria, 1866, and at Gravelotte and Sedan, 1870; proclaimed Ger. Emperor at Versailles, 1871.

William II., of Hohenzollern (1859–), King of Prussia and Ger. emperor from 1888 to 1918, son of Emperor Frederick III. and Princess Victoria of Britain; grandson of Queen Victoria; *b.* Berlin; educated at Kassel and Bonn; married, 1881, Augusta Victoria (*d.* 1921), daughter of Duke of Augustenburg; in 1922 married Princess Hermine of Reuss. From day of accession he resolved to be his own chancellor, and in 1890 'dropped the pilot,' Bismarck; ambitious to extend the colonial possessions of Germany and to build powerful Ger. navy. At home the growth of the Social Democratic party caused him much anxiety. By temper and tradition he was a thorough autocrat, upholding the divine right of kings. His rhetorical speeches and messages involved him in many international incidents, more particularly with Great Britain over the 'Kruger telegram,' 1896, and the Tweedmouth correspondence, 1908. He urged the Tsar into the Russo-Jap. War, 1905. The most important event in his reign was the Great War, 1914–18, at the conclusion of which he was compelled to abdicate, Nov. 9, 1918, and escaped to Holland. Germany then became a republic.

William I. (1772–1844), King of the Netherlands; *b.* The Hague; son of William v., last Stadtholder of Dutch republic; commanded army against France, 1793–5; fought at Jena, where he was captured by French; accepted a command in Austrian army; proclaimed prince of Netherlands, 1813; king, 1814. The Treaty of Paris gave him sovereignty over S. Netherlands, the Congress of Vienna making him Grand-duke of Luxemburg. During his reign the kingdom of Belgium was constituted, 1831, although not recognized by William till 1839. In 1840 he abdicated.

William II. (1792–1849), King of the Netherlands, son of William I.; *b.* The Hague; took part with Brit. army in Peninsular War, and commanded Dutch army at Waterloo. On revolt of Belgians, 1830, acquiesced, in opposition to his father, in their independence, but two years later commanded army of the Netherlands against Belgium, till defeated by the French; king, 1840; accepted constitutional changes in direction of democracy, 1848.

William the Silent (1533–84), Prince of Orange; son of Count of Nassau; succeeded to principality of Orange, 1544; collected an army against Alva, 1568; became the leader of the Dutch against Spain; acknowledged as Stadtholder by Holland, Zealand, Friesland, and Utrecht, 1572; commander-in-chief and dictator, 1574; joined Reformed Church, but maintained open mind in religious matters; assassinated; real founder of Dutch republic; foremost statesman and diplomatist of his time.

William of Malmesbury (*c.* 1080–*c.* 1143), Eng. historian; monk of Malmesbury; best historian of his own time; author of *Gesta Regum* and *Historia novella*.

William of Wykeham (*wik'am*) (*c.* 1323–1404), Eng. churchman; *b.* Wickham, Hants; Bishop of Winchester, 1366; lord chancellor, 1367–72 and 1389–91; founder of Winchester Coll., and New Coll., Oxford.

Williams, RALPH VAUGHAN (1872–), Brit. composer; *b.* Down Ampney, Gloucestershire; specially interested in folk-songs; works include *London Symphony, Sea Symphony, Sancta Civitas,* and operas, *Hugh the Drover* and *Sir John in Love.*

Williamson, CHARLES NORRIS (*d.* 1920), Eng. journalist and novelist; *b.* Exeter; studied engineering, but later took to journalism; founded *Black and White,* 1891; author of *Life of Thomas Carlyle* (1881); married Alice Muriel Livingston, the novelist, with whom he collaborated in writing numerous novels and short stories, including *The Lightning Conductor* (1902), *The Motor Maid* (1909), and *The Dummy Hand* (1920).

Wills, WILLIAM GORMAN (1828–91), Irish dramatist; *b.* Kilmurry; settled in London, 1862; portrait painter, but more successful in drama; best known plays are *Charles I., Eugene Aram, Jane Shore,* and *Olivia*; ballads include *I'll sing thee songs of Araby.*

Wil'son, SIR HENRY HUGHES (1864–1922), British soldier; *b.* Edgeworthstown, Ireland; served in Burma, 1885–9, and in S. Africa, 1899–1901; commandant of the Staff Coll., 1907–10, and director of military operations at Army Headquarters, 1910–14. On outbreak of Great War he was assistant chief of general staff to Lord French, and later acted as liaison officer with Fr. higher command; went to Versailles as Brit. representative to Supreme War Council, 1917; chief of Imperial General Staff and general, 1918; advocated unity of command; baronet and field-marshal, 1919; M.P., North Down, 1922; assassinated, June 1922.

Wilson, JOHN (1785–1854), known as 'Christopher North,' Scot. man of letters; *b.* Paisley; prof. of moral philosophy, Edinburgh Univ., 1820–51; in 1817 became associated with *Blackwood's Magazine,* to which he contributed many essays, including *Noctes Ambrosianæ*; other works include *Lights and Shadows of Scottish Life.*

[*Life,* by Mrs. Gordon (1862).]

Wilson, RICHARD (1714–82), Eng. artist; *b.* Penegoes, Montgomery; pioneer of modern landscape painting; works include *Niobe, Mæcenas's Villa, The River Wye,* and *Lake Avernus.*

Wilson, THOMAS WOODROW (1856–1924), president of U.S.A.; *b.* Staunton, Virginia; studied law at Univ. of Virginia; practised at Atlanta, Georgia, 1882–3; associate prof. of history at Bryn Mawr, 1885–8; prof. of jurisprudence and politics at Princeton, 1889–1902; first non-clerical president of the univ., 1902–10; governor of New Jersey, 1910–12, and did much to purify politics in that state; president of the U.S.A., 1912.

When the Great War broke out President Wilson proclaimed U.S.A. neutrality. The sinking of *Lusitania,* on May 7, 1915, led to a protest by U.S.A., but trouble continued over submarine warfare, and Wilson advocated a stronger national defence. In 1916 he was re-elected president. Diplomatic relations with Germany were broken off on Feb. 3, 1917. On June 8, 1918, President Wilson made a speech before Congress, in which he laid down the celebrated 'fourteen points' which he considered should be the basis of peace with Germany. After the Armistice he visited England and Italy, and was a popular hero. By Jan. 25, 1919, the Peace Conference declared in favour of a League of Nations, and President Wilson became chairman of the Commission set up to draft a constitution. Opposition to the Peace Treaty conditions and to League of Nations was very strong in U.S.A., and the president determined to tour the country and bring before the people his appeal for ratification of the treaty. This effort caused a serious breakdown in health, and he demitted office, 1921. Awarded Nobel Peace Prize, 1920. Author of *International Ideals* (1919).

[*Woodrow Wilson and his Work,* by W. E. Dodd (1921).]

Wind'sor, HOUSE OF, name of royal family of U.K. since 1917; changed from Ger. name of Saxe-Coburg Gotha.

Winkelried (*ving'kel-rēt*), ARNOLD VON (*d.* 1386), Swiss patriot; at battle against the Austrians at Sempach, 1386, he is said to have rushed forward, grasped as many spears as he could, and thus made a way for his comrades over his dead body.

Wise'man, NICHOLAS PATRICK STEPHEN (1802–65), Eng. R.C. ecclesiastic; *b.* Seville, of Anglo-Irish parents; bishop, 1840; vicar-apostolic, 1849; Archbishop of Westminster and cardinal, 1850; won reputation as ecclesiastic and as lecturer on social and literary subjects.

Wish'art, GEORGE (*c.* 1513–46), Scot. martyr; accused of heresy, 1538; travelled on Continent; returned to Scotland, 1543; preached reformed doctrines at Perth, Edinburgh, etc.; burnt at St. Andrews by order of Cardinal Beaton.

Wis'ter, OWEN (1860–), U.S.A. writer; *b.* Philadelphia; lawyer for some time; among his works are *The Virginian, Red Men and White, Lin McLean, Lady Baltimore,* and essays on the Great War.

With'er, GEORGE (1588–1667), Eng. poet and satirist; *b.* Bentworth, Hampshire. For *Abuses Stript and Whipt* he was imprisoned; wrote delightful pastoral, *Shepherd's Hunting,* during his imprisonment. His finest poem is *Fair Virtue, or The Mistress of Philarete*; best remembered by his lyric, 'Shall I, wasting in despair?'

With'erspoon, JOHN (1723–94), Scot. minister and educator; *b.* Gifford; pastor at Beith and Paisley; emigrated to America; president of Princeton, 1768; only clergyman to sign Declaration of Independence.

Witt, JAN DE. See DE WITT.

Wodehouse (*wōd-house*), PELHAM GRENVILLE (1881–), Eng. humorous author; works include *The Inimitable Jeeves; Carry on, Jeeves; Leave it to Psmith; Meet Mr. Mulliner,* etc.

Wöhler (*ve'ler*), FRIEDRICH (1800–82), Ger. chemist; *b.* near Frankfurt; prof. of chemistry, Göttingen, 1836–82; discovered aluminium and beryllium, and produced synthetic urea; much research with Liebig.

Wolf (*vōlf*), HUGO (1860–1903), Austrian composer; *b.* Windischgraz, Styria; song-writer of exceptional power and style; fame chiefly rests on *Goethe Lieder, Eichendorf Lieder, Italienisches Liederbuch,* etc.

Wolfe (*wūlf*), CHARLES (1791–1823), Irish clergyman and poet; curate of Ballyclog and rector of Donoughmore; best remembered as author of 'The Burial of Sir John Moore' (1817).

Wolfe, JAMES (1727–59), Brit. soldier; *b.* Westerham, Kent; served in Rhine campaign, in the 'Forty-five,' and in the Flanders campaigns; fame rests on his victory and death on the Heights of Abraham in the Quebec expedition.

[*Life,* by W. T. Waugh (1929).]

Wollstonecraft, MARY. See GODWIN, MARY.

Wolseley (*woolz'li*), GARNET JOSEPH, 1ST VISCOUNT (1833–1913), Brit. soldier; *b.* County Dublin; entered army, 1852; served in Burmese War, 1852–3, Crimean War, Ind. Mutiny, and Chinese expedition of 1860; commanded Red River (Canada) expedition, 1870, and in Ashanti War, 1873–4; crushed revolt of Arabi Pasha at Tel-el-Kebir, 1882; in command of Sudan campaigns which attempted relief of General Gordon at Khartum, 1884–5; field-marshal, 1894; commander-in-chief, 1895–1900. Author of *The Soldier's Pocket-book for Field Service, Life of the Duke of Marlborough, The Story of a Soldier's Life.*

Wolsey (*wool'zi*), THOMAS (*c.* 1475–1530), Eng. churchman and statesman; *b.* Ipswich; fellow of Magdalen, 1497; chaplain to Henry VII.; almoner to Henry VIII. and early admitted to king's council; Archbishop of York, 1514, and chief statesman in England; cardinal, 1515, and appointed lord chancellor; showed zeal for reform and learning by his foundation of Cardinal (afterwards Christ Church) Coll., Oxford, and of a college at Ipswich; unable to assist Henry in divorcing Catherine of Aragon, he fell from royal favour; deprived of his chancellorship and forced to retire to his diocese of York. Summoned to London, he died on his way, at Leicester Abbey.

[*Cardinal Wolsey*, by Creighton (1888).]

Wood, MRS. HENRY (ELLEN PRICE) (1814–87), Eng. novelist; *b.* Worcester; first novel, *Danesbury House* (1860), was an immediate success; followed by *East Lynne* (1861), *Mrs. Halliburton's Troubles*, and *The Channings*.

Wood, SIR HENRY EVELYN (1838–1919), Brit. soldier; *b.* Cressing Vicarage, Essex; served with Naval Brigade in Crimean War; joined army and served throughout Ind. Mutiny, gaining the V.C.; in Ashanti, Kaffir, Zulu, and Transvaal Wars; sirdar of Egypt, 1882–5; field-marshal, 1903; wrote *Cavalry at Waterloo* (1896), *Achievements of Cavalry* (1900), and two autobiographical works, *From Midshipman to Field-Marshal* (1906) and *Winnowed Memories* (1917).

Wood, SIR HENRY JOSEPH (1869–), Eng. musician; *b.* London; has conducted opera companies as well as numerous important festivals; best known as conductor of Queen's Hall orchestra. Has pub. *The Gentle Art of Singing* (4 vols.).

Woodhead, SIR GERMAN SIMS (1855–1921), Eng. pathologist; *b.* near Huddersfield; member of Royal Commission on Tuberculosis, 1892–5; prof. of pathology at Cambridge Univ., 1899; president of Brit. Medical Temperance Association; works include *Practical Pathology* and *Bacteria and their Products*.

Woods, HENRY (1846–1921), Eng. artist; *b.* Warrington; member of original *Graphic* staff; R.A., 1893; settled in Venice, 1876.

Woods, MARGARET LOUISA, *née* BRADLEY (1856–), Eng. poet and novelist; *b.* Rugby; novels include *A Village Tragedy* (1887), *The Invader* (1907); *Collected Poems and Plays* (1913), *A Poet's Youth* (1923), *The Spanish Lady* (1927).

Words'worth, CHARLES (1806–92), Eng. ecclesiastic; *b.* London; nephew of the poet; educated at Oxford; brilliant classicist and famous athlete; Bishop of St. Andrews, 1852; works include *A Greek Grammar* and *Shakespeare's Historical Plays*.

Wordsworth, CHRISTOPHER (1807–85), Eng. writer and ecclesiastic; *b.* London; brother of above; headmaster of Harrow, 1836–44; Bishop of Lincoln, 1868; works include *Athens and Attica*, *Life of Wordsworth* (his uncle), and *The Greek New Testament*.

[*Life*, by Overton and E. Wordsworth (1888).]

Wordsworth, DOROTHY (1771–1855), Eng. writer; *b.* Cockermouth; only sister of the poet and his constant companion, sharing to a large extent his poetical labours; her own literary works consist of the *Journals* of her life at Alfoxden and Grasmere (ed. by Knight, 1897) and *Tour in Scotland* (also ed. by Knight, 1874).

[*Life*, by Edmund Lee (1886).]

Wordsworth, WILLIAM (1770–1850), Eng. poet; *b.* Cockermouth, Cumberland; visited France, 1790 and 1791–2. During this second visit, in spite of his revolutionary sympathies, he formed an attachment with Annette Vallon, of Royalist family, and their daughter is referred to in the sonnet 'It is a beauteous evening, calm and free'; returned to England, where he lived quietly at Alfoxden and Grasmere, 1799–1813, and at Rydal Mount, 1813–50. In 1793 his poems *An Evening Walk* and *Descriptive Sketches* attracted attention of Coleridge, who became his friend, and collaborated with him in *Lyrical Ballads* (1798; 2nd ed. 1800); other works include two vols. of miscellaneous poems, 1807, *The Excursion* (1814), and *The Prelude* (pub. posthumously). Chief of

Lake poets and one of leaders of romantic revival, he made Nature—and man as part of Nature—his great poetic theme. At its worst his poetry is dull and prosaic; at its best it is unsurpassed in expressing the elements of wonder and sublimity in man's nature.

[*Complete Works* (ed. Knight, 1896–7); *Life*, by Christopher Wordsworth (1851).]

Wot'ton, SIR HENRY (1568–1639), Eng. scholar, poet, and diplomatist; *b.* in Kent; knighted, 1603; ambassador at Venice, 1604–24; diplomatic envoy at Paris, 1612, The Hague, 1614, Vienna, 1620; provost of Eton Coll., 1624; his tracts, poems, letters, etc., were ed. by his friend Izaak Walton.

Wrangel (*vrang'el*), BARON PETER (1878–1928), Russian general; *b.* Leningrad; son of a Baltic baron; mining engineer in Siberia; served in Russo-Jap. War, 1904–5, and in Great War; after Russian revolution became leader of the anti-Bolshevist movement in the south; movement collapsed, Nov. 1920; Wrangel became engineer in Brussels, and died there.

Wray, JOHN. See RAY.

Wren, SIR CHRISTOPHER (1632–1723), Eng. architect; *b.* East Knoyle, Wiltshire; son of clergyman; interested in mathematics, astronomy, and chemistry; prof. of astronomy, Oxford, 1660; assistant surveyor of royal buildings, 1661; after fire of 1666, he was commissioned to rebuild St. Paul's Cathedral, and some fifty other London churches; other architectural works include Trinity Coll., Cambridge, and Temple Bar.

[*Life*, by Lena Milman (1908).]

Wren, PERCIVAL CHRISTOPHER (1873–), Eng. soldier and author; served in Brit., Fr., and Ind. armies, in Foreign Legion, and in Great War; Ind. Educational Service; novels include *Beau Geste*, *Beau Sabreur*, etc.

Wright, SIR ALMROTH EDWARD (1861–), Brit. physician and pathologist; *b.* in Yorkshire; prof. of pathology at London Univ., 1902; knighted, 1906; consultant physician in France, 1914–19; originator of theory of vaccines as curative agents in disease; author of *System of Anti-Typhoid Inoculation*, and other scientific works.

Wright, ORVILLE (1871–), U.S.A. aviator; *b.* Daytona, Ohio; first man, along with his brother, WILBUR WRIGHT (1867–1912), to fly with a heavier-than-air machine, 1903.

Wundt (*voont*), WILHELM MAX (1832–1920), Ger. psychologist; *b.* Neckarau, Baden; prof. of philosophy at Leipzig, 1875–1915; founder of 'laboratory school' in psychology; writings include *System of Philosophy* and *Principles of Physiological Psychology*.

Wurtz (*voorts*), CHARLES ADOLPHE (1817–84), Fr. chemist; *b.* near Strasbourg; first prof. of organic chemistry at the Sorbonne, 1875; discovered the amines, the compound ureas, aldol, etc.; author of numerous works on chemistry.

Wyatt (*wī'at*), SIR THOMAS (*c.* 1503–42), Eng. poet and diplomatist; *b.* near Maidstone, Kent; said to have been lover of Anne Boleyn; held various offices at court; employed diplomatically in France and Italy; knighted, 1536; introduced sonnet to England; poems were pub. in *Tottel's Miscellany* (1557; ed. Arber, 1870) and *Collected Poems* (ed. H. Nicolas, 1831).

Wycherley (*wich'er-li*), WILLIAM (1640–1716), Eng. dramatist; *b.* Clive, Shropshire; educated in France; *Love in a Wood* (1672) won him immediate fame in court circles; other plays are *The Dancing Master* (1673), *The Country Wife* (1675), and *The*

Plain Dealer (1677); marred by extreme licentiousness, but virile and humorous.

Wyclif (*wik'lif*), WYCLIFFE, or WICLIFFE, JOHN (*c.* 1320–84), Eng. religious reformer; said to have been born at Hipswell, near Richmond in Yorkshire; fellow and master of Balliol Coll., Oxford; rector of Lutterworth, 1374; attacked papal supremacy and sought to reform corruption of clergy; supported by nobles, John of Gaunt, and Prince of Wales; summoned to appear before council of bishops at St. Paul's, 1377, but council broke up in disorder; trans. Bible and organized body of poor priests. In 1379 he pub. *De Officii Regis*, declaring the king's jurisdiction to be above the Pope's, questioned the doctrine of transubstantiation; was attacked by eccles. authorities, his opinions condemned, and many of his followers persecuted, 1382, but he himself was unmolested; retired to Lutterworth; *d.* there. In England the Lollards carried on Wyclif's teaching; in Bohemia Huss was one of his disciples.

Wyntoun (*win'ton*), ANDREW OF (*c.* 1350–*c.* 1420), Scot. chronicler; canon of St. Andrews; wrote metrical history of Scotland called *Orygynale Cronykil of Scotland* in vernacular.

Wyss (*vēs*), JOHANN (1781–1830), Swiss author; *b.* Berne; prof. of philosophy, Berne, 1806; collector of Swiss folklore; author of Swiss national hymn; best known by *The Swiss Family Robinson.*

X

Xanthippe (*zan-thip'ē*), the wife of Socrates, the Gr. philosopher; traditionally notorious as a virago.

Xavier (*zav'i-er*), FRANCIS (1506–52), 'apostle of the Indies'; *b.* in Navarra, Spain; associated with Loyola in formation of Society of Jesus; missionary to Port. colonies in India; worked successfully among Europeans of Goa, and in Travancore, where he baptized 10,000 natives; gained adherents in Japan, 1549–51; died of fever in China; canonized, 1622. [*Life* (1917), by E. A. Stewart.]

Xenocrates (*ze-nok'ra-tēz*) (396–314 B.C.), of Chalcedon; Gr. philosopher, pupil of Plato; president of Academy, 339 B.C.; in ethics followed Plato; in theories as to number, Pythagoras.

Xenophanes (*ze-nof'a-nēz*) (*c.* 576–480 B.C.), of Colophon, Asia Minor; Gr. philosopher; founder of Eleatic philosophy; his poetry condemns the anthropomorphism of Homer and Hesiod; wrote elegiac poems and a work on nature in hexameters.

Xenophon (*zen'ō-fon*) (*c.* 430–355 B.C.), Greek prose writer; *b.* Athens; pupil of Socrates; joined expedition of Cyrus the Younger against Artaxerxes II., 401; formed friendship with Agesilaus, King of Sparta, 396; after break-up of Spartan ascendancy, 371, retired to Corinth; works, which deal with politics, ethics, and historical and technical subjects, include *Anabasis, Hellenica, Memorials of Socrates,* and *Hieron.*

Xerxes I. (*zerk'sēz*) (*c.* 519–465 B.C.), King of Persia from 485; led great expedition against Greece, 480, which was withstood at Thermopylæ by the immortal three hundred; his fleet was destroyed at Salamis, and he retired into Asia; murdered by officers of his court.

Y

Yamagat'a, ARITOMO, PRINCE (1838–1922), Jap. field-marshal and statesman; chief of staff during Civil War, 1877; commanded in China-Japan War, 1894–5; prime minister, 1889 and 1898; president of Privy Council, 1905; prince, 1907.

Yeats (*yātz*), WILLIAM BUTLER (1865–), Irish poet; *b.* near Dublin; superintendent of Irish Literary Theatre; writings marked by individuality of thought and vision, and subtlety and delicacy of expression; senator, Irish Free State, 1922–28; Nobel Prize for literature, 1924; works include *Wanderings of Oisin* (1889), *The Wild Swans of Coole* (1917), and *The Tower* (1927), in poetry; *Plays for an Irish Theatre* (1904 and 1912), in drama; and *Celtic Twilight* (1893), *Per Amica Silentia Lunæ* (1919), and *Four Years* (1922), in prose; *The Cat and the Moon* (play, 1931).

Yonge (*yung*), CHARLOTTE MARY (1823–1901), Eng. novelist; *b.* in Hants; most popular books, *The Heir of Redcliffe* (1853), *Heartease* (1854), *The Daisy Chain* (1856), and *Landmarks of History* (1852–57).

York, ARCHBISHOP OF. See TEMPLE, WILLIAM.

York, DUKE OF. See ALBERT FREDERICK ARTHUR GEORGE.

Young, ARTHUR (1741–1820), Eng. agricultural writer; *b.* in Suffolk; publications gave decided impulse to scientific study of agriculture, then almost unknown in England; works include famous *Travels in France* (1792).

Young, BRIGHAM (1801–77), U.S.A. Mormon leader; *b.* in Vermont; president of Mormon church, 1844; founded Salt Lake City, 1848; lost power when U.S.A. abolished polygamy, 1869.

Young, EDWARD (1683–1765), Eng. poet; *b.* near Winchester; his satires had considerable success; his *Night Thoughts* (1741–4) was his greatest poem.

Young, JAMES (1811–83), Scot. chemist; *b.* Glasgow; inventor of commercial method of preparing paraffin first from Boghead coal and later from bituminous shales in West Lothian; liberal supporter of Livingstone's expeditions.

Younghusband, SIR FRANCIS EDWARD (1863–), Brit. Ind. political officer and explorer; *b.* in India; travelled in Manchuria and Eastern Turkestan, 1886–7; political officer at Chitral, etc.; commissioner to Tibet, 1902–4; headed expedition to Lhasa, 1904; resident at Kashmir, 1906–9; wrote *The Heart of a Continent* (1896), *Kashmir* (1909), *The Epic of Everest* (1927), *Dawn in India* (1930), *The Living Universe* (1933), etc.

Ypres, EARL OF. See FRENCH.

Ysaye (*ē-sī'yĕ*), EUGÈNE (1858–1931), Belgian violinist; *b.* Liége; prof. of violin, Brussels, 1886; took refuge in Britain and U.S.A. during Great War; conductor of Cincinnati Orchestra from 1918; one of greatest of modern violinists.

Yuan' Shih-kai' (1859–1916), Chin. statesman; governor of Shantung, 1900; viceroy of Chihli, 1901; first president of Chin. republic, 1912; favoured re-establishment of monarchy.

Yves-Guyot (*ēv-gē-yō*) (1843–1928), Fr. journalist and publicist; *b.* in department Côtes-du-Nord; ed. of various periodicals and president of several economic societies; works (many trans. into English) include *La Science Economique* (1881; 6th ed. 1925), *La Guerre, ses Causes et ses Conséquences* (1916). *Les Problèmes de la Déflation* (1923) revealed wide knowledge of social and economic problems.

Z

Zagh'lul, SAAD (1860–1927), Egyptian politician; shared in Arabi revolt, 1882; minister of education, 1906, of justice, 1910; strongly nationalist and demanded Egyptian independence; deported, 1918 and 1921; prime minister, 1924.

Zaharoff, SIR BASIL (1850–), British banker and politician; *b.* Constantinople; built up large fortune; gave financial and other aid to Allied governments during Great War; endowed univ. chairs of aviation and literature in France and England.

Zaïmis, ALEXANDER (1855–), Gr. statesman; *b.* Athens; prime minister, 1897 and 1901; high commissioner for Crete, 1906; governor of National Bank, 1913; prime minister and foreign secretary, 1915; refused aid to Serbia under treaty of 1913 on ground that treaty was Balkan in character; premier in 1916 and 1917 for brief periods, and again in 1926–8; president of Greece since 1929.

Zam'enhof, LAZARUS LUDOVIC (1859–1917), Russ. oculist; inventor, 1887, of language Esperanto, for which decorated by Fr. and Span. governments.

Zang'will, ISRAEL (1864–1926), Eng. man of letters and Zionist lecturer; *b.* London; works include *Children of the Ghetto* (1892), *The Mantle of Elijah* (1900), and *The Voice of Jerusalem* (1920); plays include *Too Much Money* (1918) and *We Moderns* (1923).

Zechari'ah (*c.* 520 B.C.), one of the minor prophets; urged continuation of building the temple; foretold in form of vision the advent of a Messianic king. See Book of Zechariah.

Zeno'bia (3rd cent. A.D.), Queen of Palmyra; ruled alone after death of husband, Odenathus, 266 or 267; conquered Egypt; aimed at complete independence from Rome, but finally captured, 272, and taken to Rome; allowed to live near Tivoli; famed for beauty and physical as well as mental energy.

Zephani'ah (*c.* 626 B.C.), O.T. prophet and writer of the book bearing his name; probably a descendant of King Hezekiah.

Zep'pelin, FERDINAND, COUNT (1838–1917), Ger. aeronaut; *b.* Constance; served in Franco-Ger. War, 1870; retired, 1891; devoted time to practical study of aeronautics; for zeppelin airship of 1909 received Order of Black Eagle.

Zet'land, LAWRENCE JOHN LUMLEY DUNDAS, 2ND MARQUESS OF (1876–), Eng. traveller; Earl of Ronaldshay from 1892; travelled widely in Asia, 1898–1907; governor of Bengal, 1917–22; works include *A Wandering Student in the Far East* (1908), *The Life of Lord Curzon* (1928), and *Life of Lord Cromer* (1932).

Zeuxis (*zūk'sis*) (*fl.* 425–400 B.C.), Gr. painter; probably *b.* Heraclea, on Black Sea; none of his works survive, but many stories testify to his power; most famous picture, *Aphrodite*; others were *Helen*,

Infant Hercules Strangling the Serpents, and *Zeus Enthroned.*

Zim'mern, ALFRED (1879–), Eng. historian; *b.* in London; staff inspector, Board of Education, 1912–15; prof. of international politics, Univ. Coll. of Wales, 1919–21, and of international relations, Oxford Univ., since 1930; director, Geneva School of International Studies; works include *The Greek Commonwealth* (1911), *The Third British Empire* (1926), and *The Prospects of Democracy* (1929).

Zinoviev, GRIGORY EVSEYEVICH (1883–), Russ. politician; *b.* Zinovievsk (formerly Elisavetgrad); joined Lenin party, 1903; ed. of Bolshevist *Forward* and of *The Social Democrat*; imprisoned, 1908; lived abroad till 1917; president of Third International, 1919; expelled from Communist party, 1926, but readmitted, 1928.

Zog I, AHMED BEG ZOGU (1893–), King of Albania; minister of interior, 1920; president of republic, 1924; king, 1928.

Zo'la, EMILE EDOUARD CHARLES ANTOINE (1840–1902), Fr. novelist; *b.* Paris; first book, *Contes à Ninon* (1864); powerful but repulsive novel *Thérèse Raquin* (1867) strengthened his reputation, as did *Chronicles of the Rougon-Macquart Family*, a series depicting Fr. life and society and containing a study of heredity; *L'Assommoir* (1877) described awful consequences of craving for drink; *Rome*, a study of the papal court; *Paris*, study of the masses in Paris; the subject of population is dealt with in *Fécondité*; labour and its agencies in *Travail*; other novels are *La Terre, La Joie de Vivre*, and *Le Rêve*; wrote several plays; took part in successful rehabilitation of Captain Dreyfus. His remains were exhumed and re-interred with impressive ceremony in Panthéon in Paris, 1908.

Zorn, ANDERS LEONARD (1860–1920), Swed. artist; *b.* in Dalecarlia; famous both as painter of mass-impressionist school and as etcher; painted portraits of Swed. royal family, and executed statue of Gustavus Vasa.

Zoroas'ter (*fl. c.* 800 B.C.), a Pers. prophet, founder of Zoroastrianism; original form of his name is *Zarathustra*; his historicity has been doubted by scholars, but without adequate reason; preached a pure monotheism and an ideal morality; teaching is 'Perform good actions, and refrain from evil ones.'

Zwing'li, HULDREICH, or ULRICH (1484–1531), Swiss reformer; *b.* in canton St. Gall; pastor of Glarus, 1506; people's priest at Einsiedeln, 1516; declared that Scriptures were only safe rule in matters of faith; denied right of Pope to decide in religious questions; opposed sale of indulgences; pastor of cathedral church at Zurich, and supported Reformed doctrines; city council officially approved his doctrines, 1523; in 1531 fought in war declared by Papal cantons against Reformed cantons, Zurich and Bern; slain in defeat of the latter. He differed from Luther on the subject of the Lord's Supper; modern theology favours Zwinglian view that it is a commemorative meal.

[*Life* (1901), by Jackson.]

DICTIONARY OF MYTHOLOGY

Acas'tus, son of Pelias king of Iolcos; brother of Alcestis and father of Laodamia. He accompanied his cousin Jason on his quest for the Golden Fleece. On the return of the Argonauts from Colchis, Jason and Medea brought about the death of Pelias and were accordingly exiled from Iolcos by Acastus. At the funeral of Pelias, the wife of Acastus fell in love with Peleus, who scorned her. The angry queen sought to compass his death, but both she and Acastus were ultimately slain by Peleus.

Acha'tes, armour-bearer of Aeneas during the Trojan War, and his faithful companion in later wanderings.

Achill'es, son of Peleus king of the Myrmidons in Thessaly, and of the goddess Thetis, who dipped his body in the river Styx and so rendered him invulnerable, save in the heel by which she held him. He was the greatest of the Greek heroes who fought in the Trojan War. He quarrelled with Agamemnon on being compelled to surrender Briseis, and withdrew from fighting. Roused by the slaying of his great friend Patroclus by Hector, he re-entered the fray and slew Hector. He was killed before the Scaean Gate by Paris, who shot him in his defenceless heel with an arrow.

A'cis. See GALATEA.

Acris'ius. See DANAË.

Actae'on, son of Aristaeus; was transformed into a stag, and torn in pieces by his own dogs for intruding into the haunts of Artemis and watching her bathing with her nymphs.

Adme'tus, king of Pherae in Thessaly. When he was at the point of death his wife Alcestis saved him by offering to die in his stead. Hercules appeared as the funeral party was returning from her tomb and brought her back from the underworld.

Ado'nis, son of Cinyras, king in Cyprus. He was beloved by Aphrodite for his great beauty, but he rejected her. While hunting he met a boar that tore his thigh with its tusk so that he died. From his blood sprang the anemone. Adonis thereafter spent six months with Persephone in Hades, and six with Aphrodite on earth.

Adras'tus, king of Sicyon and Argos. Led the famous Seven against Thebes to assert the rights of Polynices, his son-in-law, to the throne. All perished save Adrastus. Ten years later he led the Epigoni, or descendants of the Seven, against Thebes and razed it to the ground.

Aeacus (*ē'a-kus*), son of Zeus and Aegina; king of the Myrmidons. Lost all his subjects through drought sent by Hera. He prayed not to be left alone, and presently his people were restored by a swarm of ants transformed into men. Renowned in life for justice and piety, after death he became a judge in Hades. Peleus, Telamon, and Achilles were among his descendants.

Aedon (*ă-ē'don*), wife of Zethus

king of Thebes. Envying her sister-in-law Niobe her six sons and six daughters, she resolved to kill Niobe's eldest son, but by mischance slew Itylus, her own child. She was changed by Zeus into a nightingale, whose plaintive notes express her grief.

Aegaeon (*ē-jē′on*). See BRIAREUS.

Aegeus (*ē′jūs*), king of Athens, son of Pandion, and father of Theseus. See THESEUS.

Aegir (*ā′jir*), in Norse mythology, god of the ocean depths, who raised or calmed storms at sea. He married Ran, his sister, who was greedy of gold. Seamen always carried some to satisfy her demands and earn her favours.

Aegis′thus, son of Thyestes. He murdered his uncle Atreus for depriving Thyestes of the throne, to which he now restored him and succeeded to it himself. He was the lover of Clytemnestra during the absence of Agamemnon at the Trojan War, and was finally slain by Orestes.

Aegyp′tus. See DANAUS.

Aene′as, son of Aphrodite and Anchises king of Dardanus, a town on Mount Ida near Troy. Took part in Trojan War, and on the night of Troy's capture carried his father on his shoulder and led his own little son Ascanius to a place of refuge on Ida, built a fleet there, and set sail for Italy. In Sicily Anchises died. From Sicily a storm drove his fleet to Carthage, where was enacted Dido's love tragedy. Thereafter he sailed to Latium, where he married Lavinia and succeeded her father Latinus. The gods carried off his body to heaven. He was traditionally believed to have laid the foundation of the Roman Empire as the ancestor of the Julian family.

Aeolus (*ē′olus*), son of Poseidon, and king over the winds.

Aesculap′ius, or ASCLEPIOS, the god of medicine, was the son of Apollo, and learned the healing art from Chiron.

Ae′son, father of Jason. On Jason's return with the Golden Fleece from Colchis, Medea, Jason's wife, rejuvenated her father-in-law with a decoction of herbs, and put to death Pelias, who had deprived Jason of the throne of Iolcos.

Agamem′non, grandson of Atreus king of Mycenae and Argos. After the murder of Atreus, Agamemnon and his brother Menelaus were expelled from Argos. While in exile in Sparta he and his brother married Clytemnestra and Helen, the daughters of Tyndareus king of Sparta, who helped Agamemnon to recover his grandfather's throne. When Helen was carried off by Paris, Agamemnon became leader of the Greeks in the Trojan War. At the end of the war he returned to Argos, where he was murdered in his bath by Clytemnestra and Aegisthus.

Agla′ia. See GRACES.

A′jax. (1) THE GREAT, son of Telamon king of Salamis. Was the greatest Greek warrior at Troy next to Achilles. On the death of Achilles his magnificent armour was given to Odysseus. Mad with rage and disappointment Ajax slaughtered the flocks and herds of the Greeks, thinking that they were his enemies, the sons of Atreus. On recovering sanity he stabbed himself. (2) THE LESS, son of Oileus king of the Locrians. Small of stature, but a skilled spearman and very swift. At Troy's capture he tore Cassandra from the Temple of Athena. On returning from Troy he was shipwrecked off Euboea and was drowned.

Alces′tis, daughter of Pelias. See ADMETUS.

Alcinous (*al-sin′ō-us*), grandson of Poseidon ; ruler of the Phaeacians on the island of Scheria, on which Odysseus was wrecked. Here the latter met Nausicaa, the king's daughter, who conducted him to her father's court. The islanders built him one of their famous ships, on which he reached Ithaca.

Alcme'ne, daughter of Electryon king of Mycenae. Betrothed to Amphitryon, she refused to marry him till he had avenged her brothers, slain by the Teleboans. In his absence she was visited by Zeus, disguised as Amphitryon. Next day the real Amphitryon returned. Alcmene in due time bore twin sons, Iphicles to Amphitryon, and Hercules to Zeus. On the death of Amphitryon she married Rhadamanthus, who trained Hercules in wisdom and virtue.

Alcyone (*al-sī'ō-ne*), or HALCYONE, daughter of Aeolus and wife of Ceyx. When her husband was drowned she flung herself into the sea and shared his fate. The two were transformed into kingfishers. When kingfishers (Greek *halcyones*) are sitting on their eggs the winds are hushed and the sea is at peace. Hence the phrase "halcyon days."

Am'azons, the name means the "breastless ones," and is applied to a warlike race of women in Asia Minor. See THESEUS, HERCULES, PENTHESILEA.

Am'mon, or AMEN, chief god of ancient Egyptians; by Greeks identified with Zeus; usually represented with ram's head.

Amphi'on, son of Zeus and Antiope, and twin-brother of Zethus. Husband of Niobe; his twelve children were all slain by Apollo and Artemis. He was one of the Epigoni who captured Thebes. The brothers fortified Thebes with walls and towers, Amphion's skill in playing the lyre causing the stones to move into place of their own accord.

Amphitri'te, a sea-nymph carried off by Poseidon from Naxos; became by him the mother of Triton.

Amphit'ryon. See ALCMENE.

Anchi'ses. See AENEAS.

Andro'geos, son of Minos, king of Crete, and Pasiphae. Won all the prizes at the games at Athens, but perished mysteriously. Aegeus king of Athens was held responsible. War broke out, in which Crete was victorious and compelled Athens to send every year to Crete seven noble sons and seven of her fairest daughters to be devoured by the Minotaur.

Andromache (*an-drom'a-ke*), wife of Hector. After the fall of Troy she became a slave to Pyrrhus, son of Achilles, and later married Helenus, Hector's brother, who had become a ruler in Epirus.

Androm'eda, daughter of Cepheus, king of Ethiopia, and Cassiopeia, who boasted that her daughter's beauty surpassed that of the Nereids. Poseidon, annoyed, sent a sea-monster to ravage the king's coasts, and only by the sacrifice of Andromeda would the ravages cease. Chained to a rock in the sea, she awaited death, but was rescued by Perseus. After her death she became a constellation in the heavens.

Antaeus (*an-tē'us*), a mighty Libyan giant, the son of Poseidon and Gaea (Earth). Wrestled invincibly with all strangers, but Hercules overcame him by lifting him from his Mother Earth, the source of his strength, and strangling him in mid-air.

Ante'nor, the wisest of the Elders of Troy. He advised the return of Helen to Menelaus, but got no support. After the war he founded the colony of Eneti, or Veneti, at the mouth of the river Po, in Italy.

Antigone (*an-tig'ō-ne*), daughter of Oedipus king of Thebes. One of the noblest women in Greek tragedy, heroic in her devotion to her blinded father and her brothers. Shared her father's exile at Colonus, then returned to Thebes only to see her brothers slay each other in single combat. Creon, Antigone's uncle, the new ruler of Thebes, forbade to Polynices, Antigone's brother, the ceremonial burial essential to his welfare in the next world. Antigone defied the ban and was walled up for her devotion. Haemon, the king's son, her lover, committed suicide by her side.

Antiope (*an-tī'o-pe*). See AMPHION.

Anu'bis, Egyptian deity; watcher of the dead; identified by the Greeks with Hermes; represented with jackal's head.

Aphrodite (*af-rō-di'te*), or VENUS, daughter of Zeus and Dione, but often represented as having sprung from the foam of the sea; the goddess of love and the loveliest of goddesses; conferred on women beauty and charm and the power to bewitch the wisest of men. She was the wife of Hephaestus, and was constantly accompanied by Hours and Graces, and by her little son Eros. She was the mother of Aeneas, and therefore supported the Trojans in the Trojan War. The chief seat of her worship was at Paphos, in the west of Cyprus.

Apol'lo, son of Zeus and Leto, and brother of Artemis. Was born on Delos, an island raised by Poseidon out of the Aegean Sea to receive Leto. Next to Zeus, Apollo is the noblest and mightiest of the gods of Olympus, and the true spiritual guide of the Greeks. He was the god of light, of healing, of music and poetry, of prophecy, and the punisher of the insolent. His oracle was situated at Delphi.

Arach'ne, a Lydian maiden, noted for her skill in weaving. She challenged Athene to compete with her, and produced so perfect a piece of work that Athene in jealousy tore the web to pieces. Arachne hanged herself, but Athene saved her life and turned her into a spider.

Ar'es, the god of war, son of Zeus and Hera; one of the greater Olympians. He was champion of the Trojans in the Trojan War. In later times the Latin Mars was identified with Ares.

Arethu'sa, a sea-nymph of the Mediterranean. Pestered by the attentions of the river-god Alpheus, in Elis, she was turned into a fountain in the island of Ortygia, off the coast of Sicily, at Syracuse. Thither, however, the god pursued her underneath the sea, and at last united his waters with the fountain.

Ar'gonauts, the name given to the fifty-four heroes who accompanied Jason in the *Argo* to Colchis in search of the Golden Fleece.

Ar'gus. (1) Son of Phrixos, and builder of the ship *Argo*. (2) The hundred-eyed son of Inachus, who was sent by Hera to guard Io from the advances of Zeus. Only two eyes went to sleep at a time, but Hermes, with his wand and pipes, charmed him completely to sleep and then slew him. The eyes of Argus were transferred to the peacock's tail.

Ariad'ne, daughter of Minos king of Crete. Assisted Theseus, in his contest with the Minotaur, and sailed from Crete with him. Abandoned by Theseus on the island of Naxos, Dionysus appeared and married her, and gave her as a wedding present a crown of seven stars, afterwards set among the constellations.

Ar'temis, or DIANA, the virgin goddess, daughter of Zeus and Leto; twin sister of Apollo; noted as a huntress; like Apollo she averted evil, alleviated suffering, and protected young life, especially in gentle, defenceless creatures.

Ascan'ius, or IULUS, son of Aeneas. Founded Alba Longa, and the Julian family of the Caesars at Rome claimed descent from him.

Asclep'ios. See AESCULAPIUS.

Astar'te, Phoenician goddess of love, identified with the Greek Aphrodite, the Assyrian Ashtoreth, and the Babylonian Ishtar.

Astrae'a, the star maiden, daughter of Astraeus. She lived in the Golden Age, and when the Iron Age came she left the earth and became the constellation Virgo. Men believed she would return as Astraea Redux, a title actually given to Queen Elizabeth.

Asty'anax, the son of Hector and Andromache.

Atalan'ta, a Boeotian (or in another legend an Arcadian) princess, a swift and beautiful huntress. Whenever a suitor appeared she proposed a foot-race and promised to wed him if he won, his life being forfeit if he lost. Hippomenes won the race by dropping three golden apples at intervals, which Atalanta stopped to pick up.

Ath'amas, king of Thebes. See HELLE and INO.

Athe'na (ATHENE, MINERVA, or PALLAS), goddess of wisdom; daughter of Zeus and Metis; sprang from the head of Zeus, when she was full grown, in full armour; always remained a virgin goddess. Hating Troy, she sided with the Greeks. As creator of the olive became the patron goddess of Athens, upholding law and order and all that promoted intellectual and moral progress. Invented the plough and yoke, and encouraged spinning and weaving.

Ath'or, or HATHOR, Egyptian goddess, daughter of Ra; her attributes were similar to those of Aphrodite.

Atlantides (*at-lan'ti-dēz*), daughters of Atlas. See HESPERIDES.

At'las, brother of Prometheus and Epimetheus, and grandfather of Hermes. Sided with the Giants in their revolt against Zeus and was condemned to shoulder the pillars which uphold the heavens. By Medusa's head Perseus turned him into the Atlas Mountains.

At'reus, king of Mycenae and Argos; son of Pelops and grandfather of Agamemnon and Menelaus, who were called the *Atrides.* He was murdered by Aegisthus.

At'ropos. See PARCAE.

Augeas (*au'jē-as*), king in Elis; an Argonaut. Hercules cleansed his foul stables, but slew him for refusing his reward.

Auro'ra, Latin goddess of the dawn.

Autol'ycus, son of Hermes, and the master thief of antiquity; he was outwitted by Sisyphus, who marked his cattle under their feet. Autolycus gave Sisyphus his daughter in marriage, who bore him Odysseus.

Baal ("lord"), the Semitic name for many local deities, each of whom was supposed to give fertility to his own region.

Bacchan'tes, or MAENADS, female devotees of Dionysus.

Bacchus (*bak'us*). See DIONYSUS.

Bal'der, the god of light and innocence, the son of Odin and Frigga. Everything in nature, except the mistletoe, took an oath not to harm him. Loki, hating Balder for his goodness, sharpened the mistletoe into an arrow and brought about Balder's death.

Bau'cis and Phile'mon, a Phrygian husband and wife in humble circumstances. For showing hospitality to Zeus and Hermes when travelling in disguise, their cottage was transformed into a temple. At their death they became a linden and an oak tree at the temple gate.

Bel, another form of Baal. See BAAL.

Beller'ophon, son of Glaucus king of Corinth, and grandson of Sisyphus. Mounted on his winged horse, Pegasus, he killed the Chimaera. Later attempted to fly to heaven, but Zeus sent a gadfly, whose sting caused Pegasus to rear; the rider was thrown, and for ever after was blind or lame.

Bello'na, Roman goddess of war; wife or sister of Mars.

Be'lus, mythical king of Egypt and founder of Babylon; son of Poseidon and Libya, and father of Aegyptus and Danaus.

Be'owulf, mythical Teutonic hero, who killed Grendel, a monster in human form who had been ravaging the court of Hrothgar, king of the Danes. He first succeeded in wounding Grendel, and later killed both him and his mother in their lair at the bottom of a mere. In his old age he slew a fiery dragon that had been laying waste his country, but was himself mortally wounded in the contest.

Brag'i, son of Odin; the Norse god of eloquence and poetry; patron of the scalds or court poets.

Brah'ma, Hindu deity, the creator of the Universe.

Briar'eus, or AEGAEON, a monster with fifty heads and a hundred hands, who aided Zeus in quelling the revolt of the Giants, and acted as their jailer in Tartarus.

Brise'is, a Trojan maiden captured by Achilles. Her cousin Chryseis, daughter of Chryses, priest of Apollo, was captured by Agamemnon, and Apollo sent a nine days' plague throughout the Greek host. To stay the plague Chryseis was restored, and Agamemnon took Briseis from Achilles, who thereupon sulked in his tent till the death of Patroclus.

Brunhil'da. See SIEGFRIED.

Cac'us, Giant living in the hill afterwards called the Aventine, Rome. Stole cattle belonging to Hercules, drawing them backward into his cave. Their mates lowed for the missing cattle and were answered from within the cave. Hercules tore open the cave and killed the Giant.

Cad'mus, son of Agenor king of Phoenicia, and brother of Europa. When sent to find his sister, who had been carried off by Zeus, he followed a cow whose wanderings carried him to Boeotia, where he founded Thebes. There he slew a dragon and sowed its teeth, whence sprang a race of warriors.

Calliope (*ka-lī'o-pe*), muse of epic poetry. See MUSES.

Callis'to, Arcadian nymph, companion of Artemis; beloved by Zeus, who changed her into a bear to protect her from Hera; slain by Artemis and placed among constellations as the Bear. Her son became Arcturus.

Calyp'so, daughter of Atlas; detained Odysseus on her isle, Ogygia, for seven years.

Cassan'dra, daughter of Priam and Hecuba; beloved by Apollo, who endowed her with the gift of prophecy, though none would believe her prophecies. At the fall of Troy she was carried off by Ajax, but was given as captive to Agamemnon, who took her to Mycenae, where she was murdered by Clytemnestra.

Cassiopeia (*ka-si-o-pī'a*), mother of Andromeda; placed after death among the stars.

Cas'tor and Pol'lux, twin sons of Zeus (hence called Dioscuri—the sons of Jupiter); took part in the quest of the Golden Fleece; Pollux in single combat slew Lynceus, while Castor was slain by Idas, the brother of Lynceus. Thereafter Castor and Pollux shared alternate days in Heaven and Hades, and formed the constellation Gemini. They were the patron deities of sailors and poets.

Cepheus (*se'fūs*), king of Ethiopia, husband of Cassiopeia; was placed among the stars at his death.

Cer'berus, the many-headed dog who guarded the entrance to Hades.

Ceres (*sē'rez*), Roman goddess of agriculture, corresponding to Greek Demeter; mother of Proserpina.

Cha'ron (*kā'ron*), son of Erebus and Styx; Pluto's ferryman; carried the souls of the dead across the rivers Acheron and Styx. His fee of an obol was placed in the mouth of every one who died.

Charybdis (*kar-ib'dis*). See SCYLLA AND CHARYBDIS.

Chimaera (*kim-e'ra*), fire-breathing monster in Lycia; devastated country until destroyed by Bellerophon; probably symbolized volcanic eruption.

Chiron (*kī'ron*), most famous of the centaurs; skilled in music, medicine, and prophecy; instructed most of the ancient heroes. Hercules unwittingly shot him with a poisoned arrow. He surrendered his immortality to Prometheus and became the constellation Sagittarius, the Archer.

Circe (*sir'sē*), daughter of Helios the sun-god; an enchantress, she was banished to the island of Aeaea, where she turned the followers of Odysseus into swine. Odysseus, who was proof against her spells, compelled her to restore his men.

Cli'o, Muse of History. See MUSES.

Clo'tho, one of the three Fates. See PARCAE.

Clytemnes'tra, daughter of Tyndareus king of Sparta, and sister of Helen of Troy. Married Agamemnon, but during his absence at Troy Aegisthus became her lover, and on his return from Troy they murdered him in his bath. Was killed by her son Orestes.

Cly'tie, sea-nymph beloved but abandoned by Helios; pining away in consequence, she was changed into a sunflower or the heliotrope.

Coryban'tes, priests of Cybele; their orgies were associated with her worship.

Cres'sida. See TROILUS.

Cron'os, youngest son of Uranus and Gaea; identified with the Roman god Saturnus; was originally a god of harvest; overthrew his father and was in turn overthrown by his son Zeus. See also RHEA and TITANS.

Cupid. See EROS.

Cyb'ele. See RHEA.

Cyclo'pes. (1) One-eyed race of giant shepherds, whose leader was Polyphemus. (2) Three Titans, each with a single eye, sons of Uranus; imprisoned in Tartarus by their father, but set free by Zeus; destroyed by Apollo for the slaying of Aesculapius. (3) Servants of Vulcan, with a workshop in Sicily, where they made the armour of the gods and heroes.

Dae'dalus, the "cunning craftsman"; built the famous labyrinth in Crete to house the Minotaur, and gave Ariadne the clue which guided Theseus. For this Minos imprisoned him, but he and his son Icarus escaped on wings fixed to their bodies by wax. Daedalus got safe to Italy, but Icarus soared too near the sun, the wax melted, and he fell into the Aegean, or Icarian Sea.

Da'gon, Philistine deity, worshipped at Gaza and Ashdod; represented as a fish with human face and hands.

Danaë (*dan'a-e*), daughter of Acrisius king of Argos; imprisoned in a brazen tower lest she should bear a son to murder her father, as had been prophesied. Zeus visited her in a shower of gold, and begat Perseus; mother and son escaped by sea to Polydectes king of Seriphus.

Danaus (*dan'a-us*), son of Belus king of Egypt, and brother of Aegyptus, in fear of whom he fled with his fifty daughters to Argos, where he became king. The fifty sons of Aegyptus pursued and married the daughters, who slew their husbands on the bridal night. Hypermnestra alone spared Lynceus; the other daughters were condemned to pour water into sieves for ever in Hades.

Daph'ne, nymph beloved by Apollo; changed into a laurel tree while he was pursuing her.

Dar'danus, son of Zeus and Electra; founded Dardania; gives name to Dardanelles; his grandson Tros founded Troy.

Deianira (*dā-ē-an-ē'ra*), wife of Hercules. Nessus the Centaur, shot by Hercules, told her that his blood would enable her to keep her husband's love. Seeing his attachment to Iole, she sent him a robe dipped in Nessus' blood, which killed him. In despair she committed suicide.

Deme'ter. See CERES.

Deuca'lion, prince of Thessaly. He and his wife Pyrrha alone survived the flood sent by Zeus because of man's wickedness. They repeopled the world by casting behind them the "bones of their mother," *i.e.* stones, which became men and women.

Dian'a. See ARTEMIS.

Di'do, sister of Pygmalion king of Tyre, who murdered her husband. She was the founder of Carthage. When Aeneas reached Carthage she fell in love with him, and on his departure perished on a funeral pyre she had built.

Diome'des, son of Tydeus, and king of Argos. Was one of the Epigoni. In Trojan War engaged Hector and Aeneas, and wounded even deities like Ares and Aphrodite. With Odysseus carried off the Palladium, the guarantee of Troy's safety. On returning home found his wife had been unfaithful, and quitted Argos for Italy.

Diony'sus, or BACCHUS, god of wine; son of Zeus and Semele. Driven mad by Hera he wandered through the world accompanied by Bacchantes. Visiting Naxos he married Ariadne. On his return to Greece compelled cities to acknowledge his divinity and to set up his festival, the Dionysia.

Dioscu'ri, sons of Zeus. See CASTOR AND POLLUX.

Dryads, wood nymphs. See NYMPHS.

Echo, a nymph who diverted the attention of Hera while Zeus sported with nymphs. Hera turned her into an echo, never allowed to speak first nor to be silent when spoken to. Narcissus repelled her proffered love and she pined till nothing but her voice was left.

Elec'tra, daughter of Agamemnon and Clytemnestra. After her father's murder she sent her brother Orestes to the care of King Strophius. On his return he married Electra to Pylades, son of Strophius.

Endym'ion, beautiful shepherd youth, put to sleep in a cave on Mount Latmos by Selene, so that she might embrace him for ever without his knowledge.

Eos (*ē'ōs*), or AURORA, goddess of dawn.

Epig'oni, *i.e.* the descendants, sons of the Seven Heroes who warred against Thebes. They themselves captured Thebes and razed it to the ground.

Epime'theus. See PANDORA.

Er'ato, the muse of love poetry. See MUSES.

Er'ebus, "darkness"; a god of Hades; son of Chaos, and the father of Sleep.

Erin'yes, EUMENIDES, or FURIES, three female divinities, Alecto, Megaera, and Tisiphone, who pursued and punished crime in this world and the next.

Er'is, goddess of discord, sister of Ares. Enraged at being excluded from the nuptials of Peleus and Thetis, she threw among the guests a golden apple inscribed "to the fairest," and thus aroused the rivalry of Hera, Athena, and Aphrodite, and indirectly the Trojan War.

Er'os, or CUPID, god of love, son of Aphrodite; a blind, beautiful boy, thoughtless and full of tricks and armed with bow and arrow.

Eteocles (*et-ē'-ō-klēz*), son of Oedipus; he and his brother Polynices agreed to rule over Thebes alternately for a year at a time; Eteocles broke the agreement, and Polynices formed the famous league of the Seven against Thebes. The brothers met in single combat and both were slain. See ANTIGONE.

Eumen'ides, "the well-meaning ones." See ERINYES.

Euphrosyne (*ū-froz'in-ā*). See GRACES.

Euro'pa, daughter of Agenor king of Phoenicia. Zeus in the form of a white bull carried her overseas to Crete, where she became the mother of Minos, Rhadamanthus, and Sarpedon.

Eurydice (*ū-rid'i-se*), wife of Orpheus; died from bite of serpent. Orpheus descended into underworld and charmed Pluto into allowing her to return on condition that he did not look behind until upper air was reached, which in over-anxiety he did, only to see her caught back into Hades.

Evan'der, son of Hermes; founded a settlement on the Tiber, at the foot of hill afterwards called the Palatine; was ally of Aeneas in his war with the Latins.

Fates. See PARCAE.

Fauns. See SATYRS.

Faun'us. See PAN.

Flo'ra, Roman goddess of spring and flowers; married Zephyrus.

Forset'i, son of Balder; god of light, truth, and justice, and the wisest, gentlest, and most eloquent of the Norse gods.

Frey, Norse god of peace and fruitfulness; dispensed rain and fertility. Married Gerda, daughter of the Frost Giant, and is associated with burning of the Yule Log.

Freyja (*frī'a*), sister of Frey; chief goddess after Frigga; the goddess of love.

Frig'ga, wife of Odin, and chief Norse goddess; goddess of marriage.

Furies. See ERINYES.

Gae'a, Earth goddess; first creature that sprang from Chaos; mother of Uranus, the Titans, Cyclopes, and Giants; worshipped as the All-Mother.

Galate'a. (1) Sea-nymph who loved Acis, a beautiful shepherd youth. Polyphemus crushed him beneath a rock, and Galatea changed him into a river on Mount Etna. (2) See PYGMALION.

Gane'sa, or GANA-PATI, Hindu deity, son of Siva; represented with elephant's head and four arms.

Gan'ymede, the beautiful son of Tros, carried off from Mount Ida by Zeus to be his cup-bearer. In the sky he is the constellation Aquarius.

Ger'yon, triple-bodied giant in Spain. His herd of red cattle was carried off by Hercules.

Giants, sons of Uranus and Gaea; rebelled against Zeus, and, piling Mount Pelion upon Ossa, stormed Heaven; but Zeus and the gods, aided by Hercules, overcame them, and many were buried under Etna.

Glau'cus. (1) Son of Sisyphus and father of Bellerophon; torn to pieces for despising Aphrodite. (2) Grandson of Bellerophon; fought for Trojans and was slain by Ajax.

Gorgons, three maidens, Medusa, Stheno, and Euryale, with hissing serpents instead of hair, and claws of brass; whoever looked on them was turned to stone. Medusa alone was mortal, and was slain by Perseus. Her blood became the winged horse Pegasus.

Graces, THE, three divinities, Aglaia, Thalia, and Euphrosyne (grace, beauty, and mirth), daughters of Zeus, and friends of the Muses.

Halcy'one. See ALCYONE.

He'be, goddess of youth; daughter of Zeus and Hera; cup-bearer to the gods before Ganymede; wife of Hercules.

Hecate (*hek'a-te*), either a moon or an earth goddess, was invoked in all sacrifices and solemn oaths; helped to find Persephone and then remained in Hades. As goddess of witchcraft taught sorcery to Medea.

Hec'tor, son of Priam king of Troy and Hecuba; husband of Andromache; leading Trojan warrior against the Greeks; killed Ajax and Patroclus, but was himself slain by Achilles.

Hec'uba, wife of Priam king of Troy; mother of Hector and Paris; at the fall of Troy was carried away as a slave by the Greeks.

Helen of Troy, daughter of Zeus and Leda; remarkable for her beauty; was carried off to Athens by Theseus, but was rescued by her brothers Castor and Pollux; married Menelaus, but was carried off by Paris, which led to the Trojan War. At the fall of Troy returned to Sparta, and was finally transported to Elysium without dying.

Hel'enus, son of Priam and Hecuba; famed for prophetic powers. After Trojan War went to Epirus, married Andromache, and welcomed Aeneas on his wanderings.

Heliades (*hel'ē-ă-dēz*) daughters of Helios. Bewailed the death of Phaeton so bitterly that the gods turned them into poplar trees and their tears into amber.

He'lios, the sun-god, later identified with Apollo.

Hel'le, daughter of Nephele and Athamas, who wished to marry Ino and in consequence desired to sacrifice Helle and her brother Phrixos to Zeus. Nephele escaped with them to Colchis upon the flying ram with the Golden Fleece. As they crossed the sea Helle fell off into the strait now known as the Hellespont.

Hephaes'tus. See VULCAN.

He'ra, or JUNO, wife of Zeus and queen of Heaven; the guardian goddess of marriage; denied the prize of beauty by Paris she conceived relentless hatred of the Trojans, and sided with the Greeks in the Trojan War.

Hercules (*her'kū-lēz*), or HER'ACLES, son of Zeus by Alcmene; the most famous hero of antiquity. While still in his cradle he strangled two serpents; kept his father's flocks on Mount Cithaeron, where he slew a lion, and thereafter wore its skin. Married Megara, but in fit of madness slew his children, and had to expiate his crime by performing for Eurystheus, king of Tiryns, the famous twelve labours:—to slay the Nemean lion; to destroy the hydra of Lerna; to capture the Arcadian stag; to slay the Erymanthian boar; to cleanse the Augean stables; to slay the Stymphalian birds; to capture the Cretan bull; to capture the savage mares of Diomedes; to seize the girdle of Hippolyte, queen of the Amazons; to capture the oxen of the giant Geryon; to obtain the golden apples of the Hesperides; and to bring up Cerberus from Hades. Later he served three years with Omphale queen of Lydia, rescued Alcestis from Hades, was an Argonaut, aided Zeus in suppressing the rebellion of the Giants. Was poisoned by the robe sent by Deianira, and ascended from his funeral pyre to Heaven, where he married Hebe.

Her′mes, or MERCURY, son of Zeus and Maia; messenger and herald of the gods, the god of eloquence, the god of roads, and the god of trade. Generally represented as a youth with wings on helmet, staff, and heels.

Hero and Leander, two lovers. Hero was priestess of Aphrodite at Sestos. Every night Leander swam the Hellespont from Abydos to Sestos. One stormy night the lamp which guided him was extinguished, and Leander was drowned. Hero, in despair, cast herself into the sea.

Hesperides (*hes-per′-id-ēz*), or ATLANTIDES, daughters of Hesperus or of Atlas; guarded the golden apples given by Gaea to Hera on her marriage with Zeus. The apples were carried off by Hercules, but later restored.

Hes′perus, or VESPER, son of Eos, identified with the evening star, and recognized as the same as Lucifer or the morning star.

Hippodami′a, wife of Pirithous king of the Lapithae, at whose wedding the famous fight took place between the Centaurs and the Lapithae.

Hippolyte (*hip-ol′-ĭ-te*), queen of the Amazons; slain by Hercules when he came to seize her girdle. Another legend says that she marched against Athens, but Theseus defeated and married her.

Hippol′ytus, son of Theseus and Hippolyte. His stepmother Phaedra, Ariadne's sister, conceived a passion for him and accused him falsely to his father. Theseus induced Poseidon to send a bull out of the sea, which scared the horses of Hippolytus and killed him. He was restored to life by Aesculapius.

Ho′rus, Egyptian sun-god, son of Osiris; identified by Greeks with Apollo; was the god of secrecy and mystery, and therefore was represented with his fingers on his lips.

Hyacinthus, beautiful Spartan youth, killed unintentionally by a quoit thrown by Apollo. From his blood sprang the flower of the same name.

Hyades (*hī′a-dēz*), the "rainy ones"; seven nymphs who brought up the infant Dionysus, and as a reward formed part of the constellation of Taurus. Their rising heralded wet weather.

Hygieia (*hī-ji-ē′a*), or HYGE′A, goddess of health; sister or wife of Aesculapius.

Hy′las, a beautiful youth, companion of Hercules on the Argo; the Naiads, enchanted by his beauty, drew him down into a river, and he was nevermore seen.

Hy′men, the god of marriage; the son of Apollo and one of the Muses.

Hype′rion, a Titan, son of Uranus and Gaea; father of Helios, Selene, and Eos.

Iap′etus, a Titan, father of Prometheus, Epimetheus, and Atlas; joined in a revolt against Zeus, and was imprisoned in Tartarus.

Ic′arus. See DAEDALUS.

I′das, most keen-sighted Greek warrior at Troy; brother of Lynceus; the devotion between them was proverbial; they had a notable contest with their cousins Castor and Pollux.

Idom′eneus, king of Crete, son of Deucalion; led the Cretans against Troy; caught by storm when returning, vowed to sacrifice to Poseidon the first thing he met on landing if he were saved; this was his son. He carried out his vow, Crete was stricken with plague, his subjects revolted, and he was exiled.

I′lia, daughter of Aeneas and Lavinia; mother of Romulus and Remus; known also as Rhea Silvia.

I'lus, son of Tros and grandfather of Priam; founder of Ilium or Troy.

I'no, daughter of Cadmus and wife of Athamas. When Hera drove Athamas mad for his desertion of Nephele he killed one of his sons by Ino. Thereupon she and her other son cast themselves into the sea and became the marine deities Leucothoe and Palaemon. See also HELLE.

I'o, daughter of Inachus, first king of Argo; beloved by Zeus, and changed into a heifer to protect her from Hera. Hera sent Argus to watch her, and on the death of Argus sent a gadfly which stung her to madness. She swam across the straits now called Bosporus. On the banks of the Nile she regained her natural form. She was identified with Isis.

Iphigeni'a, daughter of Agamemnon and Clytemnestra. When the Greek fleet was detained at Aulis by contrary winds Calchas, the seer, said that only by the sacrifice of Iphigenia could the host proceed to Troy, and she offered herself a willing victim. Artemis, however, substituted a hart upon the altar and carried her off to Tauris.

I'ris, messenger of the gods; personification of the rainbow.

I'sis, chief female divinity of Egypt; wife of Osiris; probably a corn goddess; has been identified with Demeter and Io.

It'ylus. See AEDON and TEREUS.

It'ys. See TEREUS.

Ixi'on, king of the Lapithae. In order to escape paying his father-in-law the gifts promised on his marriage he hurled him into a pit filled with fire. Zeus absolved him for his crime, but he attempted to win the affections of Hera, whereupon Zeus had him chained upon a wheel which revolved for ever in Hades.

Ja'nus, old Latin deity, represented with two faces looking opposite ways; was the god of beginnings. His temple doors were open in time of war and shut in time of peace.

Ja'son, son of Aeson king of Iolcos, who, deposed by his half-brother Pelias, sent Jason for safety to Chiron. When Jason came of age he demanded the throne. Pelias consented if Jason would bring the Golden Fleece from Colchis. The *Argo* was built, and all living Greek heroes joined the expedition. Medea, daughter of the king of Colchis, drugged the dragon, seized the Fleece, and all sailed for home. Reaching Iolcos Medea, by a ruse, caused Pelias's daughters to slay their father. Jason and Medea were banished and fled to Corinth, where Jason proposed to marry Glauce, daughter of king Creon. Medea destroyed Glauce and Creon with the gift of a poisoned bridal robe, slew her children by Jason, flew to Athens, where she became the wife of Aegeus, but finally returned to Colchis.

Jocas'ta, mother and wife of Oedipus. See OEDIPUS.

Juno. See HERA.

Jupiter, or JOVE, identified with the Greek Zeus, but with certain differences. He was the chief deity of the Roman religion and the protector of the Roman state.

Lachesis (*lak'e-sis*). See PARCAE.

Laertes (*lā-er'tēz*), king of Ithaca; father of Odysseus; was one of the Argonauts.

Laocoon (*la-ok'ō-on*), son of Priam and priest of Apollo at Troy. Tried to prevent the wooden horse being drawn within the walls. While sacrificing to Poseidon, two serpents out of the sea, sent by Athene, strangled him and his two sons.

Laodami'a, daughter of Acastus and wife of Protesilaus, the first Greek to leap ashore at Troy and perish, slain by Hector. She obtained consent of the gods to converse with her husband for three hours, and when the time was expired she accompanied him to Hades.

Lap'ithae, a mythical race in Thessaly, ruled by Ixion, whose son Pirithous married Hippodamia. At the wedding banquet a Centaur started a fight with the Lapithae in which the Centaurs were defeated. The fight is represented in a frieze on the Parthenon.

Lar'es, the spirits of dead ancestors in Roman religion; they watched over the household and the state, and were worshipped at the hearth fire daily.

Lati'nus, king of Latium and father of Lavinia, whom he gave in marriage to Aeneas.

Leander. See HERO AND LEANDER.

Le'da, wife of Tyndareus king of Sparta; mother, either by her husband or by Zeus, who visited her in the form of a swan, of Castor and Pollux, Helen of Troy, and Clytemnestra.

Le'to, daughter of a Titan; mother by Zeus of the twins Apollo and Artemis.

Lo'ki, in Norse mythology a fire god. At first simply a mischievous Puck, later more malevolent and an ally of the Giants; finally the Prince of Darkness, who brought about the death of Balder, and was banished from Asgard.

Lucifer (" the light bringer "). See HESPERUS.

Maen'ads. See BACCHANTES.

Ma'ia, daughter of Atlas and Pleione; the eldest and most beautiful of the Pleiades; was the mother of Hermes.

Mars, the Roman god of war. See ARES.

Mar'syas, a satyr who, having found a flute thrown away by Athena, discovered that it played of its own accord; challenged Apollo to a musical contest, and when the Muses decided in favour of Apollo was flayed alive by the victor.

Mede'a. See JASON.

Medu'sa. See GORGONS.

Melea'ger, son of Oeneus king of Calydon, and of Althea. In his infancy the Fates decreed that his life would only last as long as a firebrand then burning on the hearth. His mother, therefore, took up the firebrand and hid it. He sought the Golden Fleece with Jason, and later rallied the Argonauts to hunt the boar of Calydon. He presented to Atalanta the head and skin of the boar; his mother's brothers tried to rob Atalanta of them and Meleager slew them both. His mother to revenge her brothers took the fateful firebrand and flung it in the fire, and Meleager expired.

Melpomene (*mel-pom'-en-e*), the Muse of Tragedy. See MUSES.

Memnon, son of Tithonus and Eos; king of Ethiopia; went to Priam's aid at Troy and was slain by Achilles. Zeus made him immortal. His statue at Thebes, in Egypt, gives forth a musical sound when touched by the first rays of dawn, a supposed greeting to his mother.

Menela'us, king of Sparta; younger brother of Agamemnon and husband of Helen, whose abduction by Paris precipitated the Trojan War. In the war he engaged in single combat with Paris, who only escaped by the help of Aphrodite. After Troy's fall Helen was restored to him and he returned to Sparta.

Mentor, friend of Odysseus and faithful steward of his interests at Ithaca during his absence at Troy.

Mephistopheles (*mef-is-tof'el-ēz*) (" he who loves not light "), a Satanic being of the Middle Ages, to whom Faust sold his soul in return for a period of twenty-four years of pleasure. He represents all that is worst in man's intellectual nature, denying or jeering at the distinctions between good and evil.

Mercury. See HERMES.

Mi'das, king of Phrygia, was given by Dionysus the power of turning everything into gold, and as a result was faced with starvation. That the gift might be revoked he bathed in the river Pactolus, whose sands were golden ever after. Another legend gave him asses' ears, which his barber discovered. He told the secret to the reeds, which whispered it whenever the winds blew.

Miner'va, Roman goddess of wisdom. See ATHENA.

Mi'nos. (1) Son of Zeus and Europa; brother of Rhadamanthus; king of Crete; after death became a judge in Hades with his brother. (2) Grandson of above; father of Deucalion, Ariadne, Phaedra, and Androgeos. See ANDROGEOS and DAEDALUS.

Min'otaur, monster, half man and half bull, confined in the labyrinth at Crete by Minos, and slain by Theseus.

Mith'ras, Persian god of the sun and light; creator and saviour of man; represented in sculpture as slaying a bull. The cult of Mithras was introduced into Rome during the early Empire, and demanded a high moral standard from its followers.

Mnemosyne (*nem-oz'in-ē*) ("memory"), mother of the Muses.

Moir'ae, Greek word for the Fates. See PARCAE.

Mo'mus, the son of Night, and the spirit of mockery.

Mor'pheus, god of dreams; lived in Hades with his brothers Sleep and Death. Those dreams flitting out of his ivory gate are fair and false, those out of his horn gate are noble and true.

Muses, daughters of Zeus and Mnemosyne; haunted Mount Helicon and the Castalian fountain on Mount Parnassus; came from Pieria in Macedonia, hence often called Pierides. They were nine in number: Calliope, epic poetry; Clio, history; Euterpe, lyric poetry; Thalia, comedy; Melpomene, tragedy; Terpsichore, choral song and dance; Erato, love poetry; Polyhymnia or Polymnia, sacred poetry and rhetoric; Urania, astronomy.

Nai'ads. See NYMPHS.

Narcissus, a beautiful youth, punished for his vanity by Nemesis, who made him fall in love with his own image reflected in the water. He pined away and became the flower which bears his name.

Nausic'aa, the daughter of Alcinous, to whose court she brought Odysseus when he was cast ashore on the island of Scheria.

Nem'esis, Greek goddess, daughter of Erebus; she dealt out to mortals their due share of happiness and misery; afflicted those who enjoyed too many of fortune's gifts, and dogged the steps of the guilty and punished their crimes.

Neoptol'emus ("new warrior"), or PYRRHUS ("fair-haired"), son of Achilles; brought late to the war at Troy by Odysseus, because Troy could not be captured without him. Was one of the warriors enclosed in the Wooden Horse; slew Priam in a temple; and sacrificed Polyxena, Priam's daughter, at his father's tomb. Settled in Epirus after the fall of Troy.

Nephele (*nef'el-e*), wife of Athamas and mother of Phrixos and Helle. See HELLE.

Neptune, the Latin god of the sea. See POSEIDON.

Nereids (*nē'rē-idz*). See NYMPHS.

Ne'reus, marine deity; son of Pontus and Gaea; ruler of the Mediterranean, with his palace in the depths of the Aegean Sea; father of the Nereids.

Nessus, a Centaur who carried travellers across the river Evenus. When Hercules and his wife, Deianira, arrived at the river, Nessus carried Hercules across, returned for Deianira and attempted to carry her off. Hercules shot him with an arrow. See DEIANIRA.

Nestor, king of Pylos; lived to a great age and ruled over three generations of men; took part in the fight between Centaurs and Lapithae; in Jason's expedition; and was a valued counsellor to the Greeks in the Trojan War.

Nio'be, a daughter of Tantalus and wife of Amphion king of Thebes. Boasted that while Leto had only two children, she herself had six sons and six daughters. Apollo and Artemis shot her children for her presumption.

Njord, Norse god of agriculture and commerce, father of Frey and Freyja.

Norns, the Fates of Norse mythology, three sisters who wove the web of Fate and sang as they worked.

Nymphs, female divinities peopling all nature: Nereids, nymphs of the Mediterranean; Naiads, fresh-water nymphs; Oreads, nymphs of mountains and hills; Dryads, nymphs of trees, who lived and died with the trees they inhabited; Oceanides, nymphs of the great river Oceanus that girdled the earth.

O'din, or **Woden,** Norse king of the gods; wisest of the gods, ruler of heaven and earth, and god of war; by his wife Frigga he was the father of Balder; he was also the father of Thor, Vali, and Bragi.

Odys'seus, or ULYSSES, king of Ithaca; the son of Laertes; a great Greek hero at Troy, distinguished for prudence and eloquence; his long years of wandering after the Trojan War form the subject of the *Odyssey*; after twenty years' absence from home he returned to Ithaca and his faithful wife Penelope, and took vengeance on her suitors.

Oedipus (*ē'dip-us*) ("swell foot"), son of Laius, king of Thebes, and Jocasta; was exposed at birth with his feet bound and pierced, because of prophecy that he would kill his father; found by shepherds and adopted by king of Corinth. On reaching manhood journeyed to Thebes, unwittingly slaying his father on the way; delivered Thebes from the Sphinx, and thereby gained the throne of Thebes and the hand of Queen Jocasta, not knowing that she was his mother. Plague broke out in Thebes, Oedipus learned the truth, blinded himself, and went with his daughter Antigone into exile at Colonus. There he walked into the grove of the Furies and was nevermore seen.

Oenone (*ē-nō'-ne*), daughter of a river-god and wife of Paris, who deserted her when he carried off Helen; she committed suicide through remorse for refusing to nurse him when wounded. See PARIS.

Omphale (*om'fa-le*), queen of Libya, to whom Hercules was in bondage for three years, when he grew effeminate and wore women's clothes while she wore his lion's skin.

Oreads (*or'e-adz*). See NYMPHS.

Ores'tes, son of Agamemnon and Clytemnestra. After his father's murder was sent by his sister Electra to the care of his uncle Strophius, king of Phocis. Reaching manhood he returned to Argos and slew his mother and Aegisthus. He married Hermione, the only child of Menelaus and Helen.

Ori'on, a mighty hunter in Boeotia, of great strength and beauty; while hunting with Artemis he made love to her and she shot him for his presumption; later he was placed among the stars.

Orpheus (*or'fūs*), greatest Greek poet before Homer; son of Calliope and husband of Eurydice; accompanied Jason on his quest for the Golden Fleece. When he played his lyre he charmed both animate and inanimate objects. He was killed by Thracian women, who resented his fidelity to the memory of Eurydice. See EURYDICE.

Osi'ris, one of the chief Egyptian gods; husband of Isis and father of Horus. As ruler of Egypt, reclaimed the country from barbarism; was murdered by his brother Typhon, but restored to life by Isis and Horus, and thenceforth ruled over the empire of the dead.

Pai'an, name given to Apollo as the healer and deliverer.

Palae'mon. See INO.

Pallas. See ATHENA.

Pan (Latin *Faunus*), god of flocks and herds; patron of hunters and shepherds; son of Hermes. Invented the syrinx or Pan's Pipes. By his sudden appearances threw wayfarers into a "panic." Usually represented with a horned head and goat's feet.

Panace'a (the "all-healing"), daughter of Aesculapius.

Pandi'on. See TEREUS.

Pando'ra (the "all-gifted one"), a woman created by Zeus, moulded from clay and endowed with life, to punish mortals for the theft of fire from heaven by Prometheus. Zeus gave her a box containing every human ill; Epimetheus opened it, and its contents swarmed throughout the world, only Hope being left. Another version makes the box contain blessings, all of which escaped except Hope.

Par'cae, or MOIRAE, or FATES, three sister goddesses—Clotho, Lachesis, and Atropos—whose separate duties have been variously described; generally Clotho spins the thread of life, Lachesis measures it, and Atropos cuts it.

Paris, son of Priam and Hecuba; exposed by Priam as destined to bring doom on his country, but rescued and brought up by a shepherd, and later returned to Troy. Married Oenone; awarded the golden apple of Eris to Aphrodite, thus earning for Troy the hatred of Hera and Athena; visiting Sparta as guest of Menelaus he carried off Helen of Troy, causing the Trojan War. He shot Achilles in his defenceless heel, only to be shot in turn by Philoctetes, with one of the poisoned arrows of Hercules.

Patro'clus. See ACHILLES.

Pe'leus, son of Aeacus king of Aegina and of Endeis daughter of Chiron; was one of the Argonauts. Married the sea-nymph Thetis in spite of her changing herself into fire, water, beast, and fish; Peleus, aided by Chiron, held her fast till she submitted. Their first-born son was Achilles.

Pe'lias, son of Poseidon and Tyro; was exposed at birth by his mother, but was brought up by a shepherd. On attaining manhood he joined his mother, who had married Cretheus king of Iolcos. On the death of Cretheus Pelias usurped the throne from Aeson, the son of Cretheus and Tyro. To get rid of Jason, son of Aeson, he sent him on the quest for the Golden Fleece. On the return of Jason with Medea, Pelias was put to death.

Pel'ops, son of Tantalus king of Phrygia, who killed him and presented him as a dish to the gods. He was restored to life by Hermes. Expelled from Phrygia by Tros he came to Elis, whose king, destined to die when his daughter married, challenged all suitors to a chariot race. As his steeds were the fleetest in the world, he always overtook the suitors and stabbed them as he passed. Pelops got winged steeds from Poseidon and also bribed the royal charioteer to withdraw the lynch pins of the royal chariot. During the race the axle broke and the king was thrown out and killed. Pelops therefore won the race, married the king's daughter, and ascended the throne. The whole peninsula of south-west Greece was called Peloponnesus. Atreus was his son.

Pena'tes, Roman gods of hearth and home and also of the state. They were worshipped daily with the Lares in every household.

Penelope (*pen-el'o-pe*), wife of Odysseus. During her husband's twenty years' absence from home was beset by suitors. She invented excuses to put them off, in particular she refused to marry them until she had finished weaving a robe for Laertes, her father-in-law; at night she unravelled what she had woven during the day.

Penthesile'a, daughter of Ares; queen of the Amazons; came to aid the Trojans after Hector's death, but was killed by Achilles, who buried her on the banks of the Xanthus.

Persephone (*per-sef'on-e*), or PROSERPINA, daughter of Zeus and Demeter, was carried off by Pluto when gathering flowers in the vale of Enna; her mother, in her grief, forbade the earth to bring forth until Zeus interceded with Pluto, and Persephone was restored to her mother on condition that she should spend half the year with Pluto: an allegory of spring and autumn.

Per'seus, son of Zeus and Danaë. Polydectes king of Seriphus, wishing to marry Danaë, sent Perseus to fetch the head of the Medusa; with the aid of Hermes and Athena he accomplished this; on his way home rescued Andromeda and turned Atlas into a mountain; reaching Seriphus he turned Polydectes into stone, then returned to Argos. Accidentally killed his grandfather Acrisius with a quoit. Founded Mycenae, and was the ancestor of Hercules.

Phaed'ra. See HIPPOLYTUS.

Phaet'on, son of Helios; gained permission from his father to drive the sun chariot for one day. The horses reared up to heaven, then plunged so near the earth that it blackened the face of many of its inhabitants. Zeus smote him with his thunderbolt; he fell into a river, Eridanus, and was mourned by the Heliades.

Phile'mon. See BAUCIS AND PHILEMON.

Philocte'tes, armour-bearer and friend of Hercules, who bequeathed him his bow and poisoned arrows; during Trojan War he slew Paris.

Philome'la. See TEREUS.

Phoebus (*fē'bus*), name given to Apollo.

Phrix'os, son of Athamas and Nephele; brother of Helle. See HELLE.

Pierides (*pē-er'-id-ēz*). See MUSES.

Pirithous (*pī-rith'-o-us*), son of Ixion; king of the Lapithae in Thessaly; married Hippodamia, after whose death he resolved to carry off Persephone from Pluto, his friend Theseus accompanying him. Pluto chained them to a rock, where they remained till Hercules rescued Theseus. Pirithous remained imprisoned for ever.

Pleiades (*plī'ad-ēz*), the Seven Sisters, daughters of Atlas and Pleione; companions of Artemis. When pursued by Orion, Zeus changed hunters and hunted into stars.

Plu'to, god of the underworld (Hades), son of Cronos and Rhea, and brother of Zeus and Poseidon.

Plu'tus, god of riches. Zeus blinded him that he might distribute his gifts without regard to merit.

Pol'lux. See CASTOR AND POLLUX.

Polydec'tes. See DANAË and PERSEUS.

Polyhym'nia, or POLYM'NIA. See MUSES.

Polyni'ces, son of Oedipus, and brother of Eteocles and Antigone; married the daughter of Adrastus. See ADRASTUS, ETEOCLES, and ANTIGONE.

Polyphe'mus. See CYCLOPES.

Polyx'ena, daughter of Priam and Hecuba; beloved by Achilles, whose ghost appeared to the returning Greeks and demanded the sacrifice of Polyxena, that she might be his bride in Hades. This was carried out by his son Neoptolemus.

Posei'don, or NEPTUNE, god of the sea; brother of Zeus. Usually represented driving a sea-chariot and bearing a trident.

Pri'am, king of Troy; husband of Hecuba; father of fifty sons, including Hector, Aeneas, and Paris. On the capture of Troy he was slain by Neoptolemus.

Pria'pus, son of Dionysus and Aphrodite; the god who watched over the fruitfulness of fields and flocks.

Proc'ne. See TEREUS.

Procrus'tes, famous highwayman at Eleusis in Attica; he made all his guests lie on an iron bedstead, which he made them fit by lopping off their limbs or stretching them. He was slain by Theseus.

Prome'theus ("forethought"), a Titan; brother of Epimetheus and Atlas; sided with mortals in the strife between heaven and earth, and stole fire from heaven to give man mastery over Nature; as a punishment he was chained to a rock in the Caucasus, where an eagle preyed on his liver, which grew as fast as it was consumed. Finally Zeus relented; Hercules killed the eagle and set Prometheus free.

Proser'pina. See PERSEPHONE.

Pro'teus ("the old man of the sea") tended seals—the flocks of Poseidon; had prophetic powers, but hated to prophesy, and to escape an inquirer assumed various forms when caught. If the inquirer maintained his hold he resumed his true form and prophesied.

Psyche (*sī'-kē*), a maiden so beautiful that she aroused the jealousy of Venus, who sent Cupid to inspire her with love for the meanest of men; instead, Cupid fell in love with her himself, charging her not to inquire who he was. Psyche disobeying, the god left her, and Psyche sought for him everywhere. Venus relented, and Psyche and Cupid were reunited. The story is an allegory of the human soul purified by suffering.

Pygma'lion, king of Cyprus; fell so deeply in love with the ivory image of the maiden he had carved that he persuaded Aphrodite to breathe life into it; she became the maiden Galatea, whom he married.

Pyrrhus (*pir'us*). See NEOPTOLEMUS.

Quiri'nus. See ROMULUS AND REMUS.

Ra, Egyptian sun-god, with head of a hawk.

Rhadaman'thus, son of Zeus and Europa, brother of Minos; married Alcmene, after the death of Amphitryon. After death he became a judge in Hades.

Rhe'a, daughter of Uranus and Gaea, and the wife of Cronos; became the mighty mother of the gods—Zeus, Poseidon, Pluto, Hera, Demeter, etc. In Asia Minor she was known as Cybele.

Rhe'a Sil'via. See ROMULUS AND REMUS.

Rhe'sus, a Thracian king; supported Troy in Trojan War; if his horses drank of the river

Xanthus Troy could not be taken ; Odysseus and Diomedes therefore captured his horses and drove them to the Greek camp, and slew Rhesus.

Rom′ulus and Re′mus, twin sons of Mars and a vestal virgin, Rhea Silvia, daughter of Numitor, the exiled king of Alba Longa. At their birth they were thrown into the river Tiber, but were stranded and suckled by a wolf and brought up by a shepherd. They founded the city of Rome, and Romulus slew Remus for leaping over the unfinished wall. After a reign of thirty-seven years Mars translated Romulus to heaven, and he was worshipped by the Romans as Quirinus.

Satur′nus, Roman god of agriculture ; his reign was known as the Golden Age. See CRONOS.

Satyrs, or FAUNS, children of Pan ; always associated with the worship of Dionysus. They had pointed ears and small horns and goat's hoofs.

Scyl′la and Charyb′dis, two monsters who inhabited two opposite rocks in the strait of Messina ; they preyed on the sailors of passing ships, and those who escaped the one usually fell into the clutches of the other.

Sele′ne, the moon goddess.

Semele (*sem′e-le*), daughter of Cadmus king of Thebes ; beloved by Zeus, who at her entreaty appeared to her in all his majesty, and she was consumed by his lightning. Zeus saved her child Dionysus.

Semir′amis, wife of Ninus founder of Nineveh ; has been identified with Ashtoreth.

Sera′pis, the Egyptian god of healing.

Siegfried, or SIGURD, favourite Norse hero ; son of Sigmund king of the Netherlands ; killed the dragon that guarded the treasure of the Nibelungs, and, bathing in its blood, became invulnerable except between the shoulders, where a linden leaf had settled. Along with the treasure, he won a magic sword and a cloak of darkness. He went to the court of Burgundy and fell in love with the princess Kriemhilda. With the help of his cloak of darkness, won for Kriemhilda's brother Gunther the hand of Brunhilda queen of Iceland, and he himself married Kriemhilda. Hagen, Gunther's henchman, jealous of the fame of Siegfried, stabbed him in his one vulnerable spot at the end of a day's hunting. In another version of the legend Siegfried won the love of the Valkyrie Brunhilda by waking her from an enchanted sleep in a castle surrounded by a wall of fire. On leaving Brunhilda he was given a magic potion which made him forget her ; he married Kriemhilda, and Brunhilda herself caused his death.

Si′non, son of Sisyphus ; took part in the Trojan War, allowed himself to be captured by the Trojans, told them the Greeks had gone home weary of the siege, leaving a wooden horse, which he persuaded them to draw within the walls.

Sirens, sea-nymphs, with head and upper part of their body like a woman, and the wings and legs of a bird. By their sweet singing charmed mariners to their death. The Argonauts, by the finer singing of Orpheus, and Odysseus by the precautions he took, resisted their lure ; the sirens thereupon became rocks in the Bay of Naples.

Sis′yphus, son of Aeolus, and grandfather of Bellerophon. Full of lies and deceit he was thrown into Hades, and condemned for ever to roll up a steep hill a huge stone that always rolled back as it reached the summit.

Siva (*sē′va*), Hindu deity ; the Destroyer, who by destruction of life produces regeneration or transmigration.

Sphinx, a monster with the winged body of a lion and the bust and head of a woman. She propounded a riddle to the inhabitants of Thebes and killed all who were unable to answer. Oedipus solved it, and the Sphinx slew herself. The Egyptian sphinx has the body of a lion and the head of a man.

Tan'talus, son of Zeus; father of Pelops and Niobe; for various crimes was punished in Hades by being made to stand in water which receded whenever he tried to quench his thirst; bunches of fruit drew back when he stretched out his hand to grasp them.

Telem'achus, son of Odysseus and Penelope.

Te'reus, son of a king of the Thracians in Daulis; married Procne, daughter of Pandion king of Attica, and became the father of Itys (sometimes called Itylus). Falling in love with Procne's sister Philomela, he hid Procne, said she was dead, and married Philomela, whom he deprived of her tongue that she might not reveal the deception. She informed her sister by means of some words she wove into a robe. Thereupon Procne killed Itys, served up his flesh to Tereus, and fled with Philomela. Tereus pursued them, and they were changed into birds, the common version making Procne a swallow, Philomela a nightingale, and Tereus a hawk.

Terpsichore (*terp-sik'-ō-re*), the Muse of choral song and dance. See MUSES.

Teu'cer, first king of Troy.

Thalia (*thal-'īa*). See GRACES.

The'mis, daughter of Uranus and Gaea; married Zeus; personified the world as an established order based on divine justice.

Thersi'tes, the ugliest warrior and most talkative and insolent Greek at Troy.

The'seus, legendary hero of Attica; son of Aegeus; spent his childhood at Troezen, then made his way to Athens, killing Procrustes on the way. Destroyed the Marathonian Bull, and ended the paying of human tribute to Crete by slaying the Minotaur, with the aid of Ariadne. On the homeward voyage abandoned Ariadne on the island of Naxos, and arrived home with the rescued youths and maidens, but forgot to hoist white sails instead of black—the agreed signal of success — whereupon Aegeus threw himself into the sea, henceforth known as the Aegean. Theseus now conquered the Amazons and married Hippolyte their queen, who bore him Hippolytus. After her death he married Phaedra; was an Argonaut; went with Pirithous to Hades to rescue Persephone, and on his return was murdered by Lycomedes.

The'tis. See PELEUS.

Thor, Norse god, son of Odin; remarkable for size and strength; lord of thunder and lightning, his great weapon being the magic hammer, the thunderbolt.

Thoth, Egyptian god; patron of learning and intelligence; represented as an ape, or as an ibis with a human body.

Tire'sias, renowned soothsayer, blind from childhood; lived in Thebes; connected with many legendary events in the history of Greece; predicted the failure of the Seven against Thebes and the success of the Epigoni.

Titans. (1) The OLDER TITANS, sons and daughters of Uranus and Gaea; twelve in number; Uranus became afraid of them and threw them into Tartarus. Led by Cronos they revolted and deposed their father. (2) The YOUNGER TITANS, sons of Cronos and Rhea. With the aid of the Cyclopes and some of the Older Titans they rose against Cronos and the older dynasty, who were hurled into Tartarus. Cronos escaped to Italy. See SATURNUS.

Titho′nus, son of Laomedon king of Troy. Eos loved him and obtained for him the gift of immortality. She forgot to ask for eternal youth, so he shrank to a mere voice, and Eos changed him into a cicada. Their son was Memnon.

Tristan, or TRISTRAM, famous hero of mediaeval romance; the nephew of King Mark of Cornwall; lover of his uncle's wife Iseult or Isolde, and a knight at King Arthur's court; married Iseult of Brittany. The legend is a blending of elements from widely different sources—Celtic, Scandinavian, Classic, and French.

Triton, son of Poseidon and Amphitrite, and the trumpeter of the sea-gods.

Tro′ilus, youngest son of Priam and Hecuba, killed by Achilles. In mediaeval legend was in love with Cressida, daughter of Calchas. She proved faithless to him when she joined Calchas in the Greek camp. Her name is a synonym for inconstancy.

Tros, grandson of Dardanus; gave his name to the city and people of Troy.

Ty′deus, son of Oeneus king of Calydon, and father of Diomedes; was one of the Seven against Thebes. Was wounded in the hostilities; Athena appeared to heal his wound, but, sickened at his savagery, left him to die.

Tyndar′eus, son of Oebalus king of Sparta. See LEDA.

Ulys′ses. See ODYSSEUS.

Ura′nia, Muse of Astronomy. See MUSES.

U′ranus, first ruler of the universe, husband of Gaea, and father of the Older Titans.

Val′i, Norse god, son of Odin; attained full stature in a day, and stayed " neither to wash his face nor comb his hair," but hastened to Asgard, and there avenged the death of Balder.

Valkyries, or VALKYRS, in Norse mythology supernatural maidens of great beauty, who chose those slain heroes that were worthy to enter Valhalla, and handed them their drinking horns at their daily feast with Odin.

Venus, originally Latin goddess of Spring; later identified with Aphrodite.

Vesper. See HESPERUS.

Vesta, or HESTIA, goddess of hearth and home at Rome. In her temple in the Forum the Vestal Virgins kept the altar fire for ever burning.

Vishnu, Hindu deity; the Preserver; kind and gentle and sympathetic towards mankind.

Vulcan, or HEPHAESTUS, god of fire, son of Zeus and Hera; born lame, therefore hated by his parents, and twice thrown out of Olympus; rescued and tended by Thetis; married Aphrodite; forged the armour for Achilles. His servants, the Cyclopes, worked under Mount Etna and in Lipara.

Woden. See ODIN.

Zeph′yrus, son of Astraeus and Eos; the god of the west wind.

Zeus (*zūs*), king of gods and men; son of Cronos and Rhea; husband of Hera; identified with the Roman god Jupiter. Divided the government of the universe with his brothers Pluto and Poseidon, Zeus ruling the heavens from Mount Olympus. Was the father of Apollo, Ares, Hermes, Vulcan, Athena, Aphrodite, and Artemis, and many others.

PRINTED IN GREAT BRITAIN AT THE PRESS OF THE PUBLISHERS